NEW TESTAMENT INTRODUCTION

New Testament Introduction

by

DONALD GUTHRIE, B.D., M.Th., Ph.D.

Lecturer in New Testament Language and Literature,
and Registrar for Advanced Studies,
The London Bible College

INTER-VARSITY PRESS

BOX F, DOWNERS GROVE, ILLINOIS 60515

© *The Tyndale Press*

Originally published in three volumes:
The Gospels and Acts
First Edition March 1965
Reprinted 1966, 1968

The Pauline Epistles
First Edition February 1961
Reprinted 1963, 1964, 1966, 1968

Hebrews to Revelation
First Edition September 1962
Second Edition April 1964
Reprinted 1966

Third Edition (revised) in one
volume December 1970

ISBN 0-87784-953-6

InterVarsity Press is the book-publishing division of Inter-Varsity Christian Fellowship,
a student movement active on campus at hundreds of universities, colleges and
schools of nursing. For information about local and regional activities,
write IVCF, 233 Langdon St., Madison, WI 53703.

Distributed in Canada through InterVarsity Press, 1875 Leslie St., Unit 10,
Don Mills, Ontario M3B 2M5, Canada.

Printed in the United States of America

21	20	19	18	17	16	15	14	13	12	11	10
91	90	89	88	87	86	85	84	83	82	81	

CONTENTS

PREFACE

When the publishers proposed to produce a one-volume edition of my *New Testament Introduction*, I readily concurred in view of the obvious advantages of such a project. In carrying out the amalgamation it was decided to disturb the existing text of each of the three parts as little as possible. No change has been made in the order of the chapters. At the same time I considered it opportune to bring the *Introduction* up to date and this I have sought to do in two ways. A few additional passages have been inserted into the text. These include an enlargement of the section on form criticism, with a fuller treatment of redaction criticism, a revised section on the historicity of John and additional comments on the opponents of Paul at Corinth and Galatia.

At the end of each chapter further footnotes have been appended to provide relevant recent bibliographical information. In addition to various articles and books mentioned in these, other titles occur in the General Bibliography. The aim of this information is to provide for those wishing to pursue further studies in the New Testament field. Asterisks have been inserted at the relevant places in the text or existing footnotes as an aid to the relating of the additional footnotes to the text.

In preparing this work I have had the needs of theological students mainly in mind, but I hope that others may find the book a profitable introduction, not only to the New Testament itself, but to the great variety of views which it calls forth.

I am grateful to the publishers for the care with which the many problems arising from uniting the three volumes have been tackled. The original manuscripts were read by a number of friends and colleagues, who made helpful suggestions from which this *Introduction* has profited. I am particularly indebted to Ralph P. Martin, M.A., Ph.D., I. Howard Marshall, M.A., B.D., Ph.D., and Andrew F. Walls, M.A., B.Litt.

It is my hope that this revised edition will be as widely used and as warmly received as the individual volumes.

DONALD GUTHRIE.

ABBREVIATIONS

AB	Abingdon Bible Commentary.
ABR	Australian Biblical Review.
AbThANT	Abhandlungen zur Theologie des Alten und Neuen Testaments.
AJTh	American Journal of Theology.
ATR	Anglican Theological Review.
AV	Authorized Version (King James').
BC	Black's New Testament Commentary.
BJRL	Bulletin of the John Rylands Library.
CB	Century Bible.
CB, n.s.	Century Bible, new series.
CBC	Cambridge Bible Commentary.
CBQ	Catholic Biblical Quarterly.
CBS	Cambridge Bible for Schools and Colleges.
CGT	Cambridge Greek Testament.
CGT, n.s.	Cambridge Greek Testament, new series.
Clar B	Clarendon Bible.
CNT	Commentaire du Nouveau Testament.
CQR	Church Quarterly Review.
DSB	Daily Study Bible.
EB	Études Bibliques.
EC	Epworth Preacher's Commentary.
EGT	Expositor's Greek Testament.
Enc. Bib.	Encyclopaedia Biblica.
Eng. Tr.	English Translation.
EQ	Evangelical Quarterly.
ET	Expository Times.
ETL	Ephemerides Theologica Lovanienses.
EvTh	Evangelische Theologie.
Exp.	Expositor.
Exp. Bib.	Expositor's Bible.
HDB	Hastings' Dictionary of the Bible.
HE	Eusebius' Historia Ecclesia.
HTR	Harvard Theological Review.

HTS	Harvard Theological Studies.
IB	Interpreter's Bible.
ICC	International Critical Commentary.
ILNT	Introduction to the Literature of the New Testament.
INT	Introduction to the New Testament.
JBL	Journal of Biblical Literature.
JBR	Journal of Bible and Religion.
JPTh	Jahrbücher für protestantische Theologie.
JR	Journal of Religion.
JRS	Journal of Roman Studies.
JSemS	Journal of Semitic Studies.
JTS	Journal of Theological Studies.
KEK	Kritisch-exegetischer Kommentar.
LHB	Lietzmann's Handbuch zum Neuen Testament.
LNT	Literature of the New Testament.
LXX	Septuagint.
MC	Moffatt's New Testament Commentary.
NBD	New Bible Dictionary.
N Clar B	New Clarendon Bible.
NkZ	Neue kirkliche Zeitschrift.
NLC	New London Commentary.
Nov. Test.	Novum Testamentum (Journal).
NTD	Neue Testament Deutsch.
NTS	New Testament Studies.
PC	Peake's Commentary.
Pel C	Pelican Commentary.
RB	Revue Biblique.
rcvd.	Revised.
RGG	Die Religion in Geschichte und Gegenwart.
RHR	Revue de l'Histoire des Religions.
RSV	Revised Standard Version.
R ThPh	Revue de Théologie et de Philosophie.
RV	Revised Version.
SBA	Sitzungsberichte der Berliner Akademie der Wissenschaften, philosophisch-historische Klasse.
SJT	Scottish Journal of Theology.
SLA	Studies in Luke–Acts, edited by L. E. Keck and J. L. Martyn.
StTh	Studia Theologica.

TC	Torch Commentary.
ThBl	Theologische Blätter.
Theol.	Theology.
ThLZ	Theologische Literaturzeitung.
ThZ	Theologische Zeitschrift.
TNT	Tyndale New Testament Commentary.
TR	Theologische Rundschau.
TSK	Theologische Studien und Kritiken.
TU	Texte und Untersuchungen.
VC	Vigiliae Christianae.
VT	Vetus Testamentum (Journal).
WC	Westminster Commentary.
ZkT	Zeitschrift für katholische Theologie.
ZNTW	Zeitschrift für die neutestamentliche Wissenschaft.
ZTK	Zeitschrift für Theologie und Kirche.

CHAPTER ONE

THE GOSPELS

I. GENERAL INTRODUCTION

The four Gospels have always held a place of particular interest for Christian people. They are the main source of our knowledge of our Lord's life, for without them our data would be reduced to the barest outline. It is no wonder, therefore, that scholars have concentrated such interest upon them. Yet probably no writings are more baffling for the critical investigator. Most of the problems which have arisen in the course of the history of criticism are still the subject of debate, although the more radical theories have now been largely discounted. Before dealing with these problems it is best to form some estimate of the Gospels in the form in which they have been transmitted, for there can be no doubt that they have exercised a profound influence on Christian thought quite independently of any critical assessment of them. This approach differs from that of some modern schools of criticism which begin with certain presuppositions which affect the value of the extant Gospels. The tenets of such schools of thought will be fully examined in due time, but the present treatment is based on the assumption that it is the Gospels themselves and not their sources or origins which have moulded Christian history, and that the latter must be approached by means of the former.

II. THEIR LITERARY FORM

It is customary to think of the Gospels as accounts of the life of Christ, but it is at once apparent that they are not strict biographies. This is not merely because they concentrate upon a very small part of the life of Christ. It is rather because their dominant purpose is not solely a record of facts. Whereas they are historical in form, their purpose was something more than historical. It is not, in fact, an accident that they were called 'Gospels' at an early period in Christian history. They proclaimed good news (εὐαγγέλιοV), a message which was desperately needed.[1]

[1] Cf. F. F. Bruce's discussion of the true character of a gospel (*BJRL*, XLV, 1963, pp. 319–339). The use of the word εὐαγγέλιον of written records of the life and work of Jesus is testified by Justin Martyr (*Apol.* i. 66), but how long before Justin's time it was used is not known. Its basic meaning of 'good news' was used

But there were no parallels to the Gospel form which served as a pattern for the earliest writers. The literary genre arose out of the exigencies of the Gentile mission. The preachers had to stress the passion and resurrection, for these themes formed the kernel of their message. It is not surprising therefore that so much space is devoted to the narratives of these events in the written Gospels. Approximately one third of Mark's Gospel is taken up with them and the other Gospels contain proportionately only slightly less. This emphasis is in line with Paul's declaration that the tradition committed to him concerned the death and resurrection of Christ (1 Cor. xv. 3 ff.).

The accounts of our Lord's life, good deeds, miracles and teaching must have been regarded as secondary to this dominant interest, although at the same time essential to it. No mere writer of biography would ever have adopted such a perspective. The Evangelists, in short, were not literary men and were not setting out to be. They had no interest in conforming to any conventional pattern. They themselves had experienced a remarkable transformation as a result of the stupendous events they related. This at once marks out their records as set apart from other literary exercises and this fact must be constantly borne in mind when considering the critical problems of their origins. It cannot be claimed without reservation that these books should be set alongside other books on the assumption that precisely the same principles of criticism which are used in investigations of secular literary productions must necessarily be valid here also.[1] They may be so, but it is part of the problem of the literary investigation of the Gospels that no precise parallels exist by which to put this assumption to the test.[2] Such literary principles will therefore be regarded as guides rather than as criteria.

III. MOTIVES FOR THEIR PRODUCTION

The different purposes which prompted the production of the various Gospels will be dealt with when each Gospel is considered separately.

in both a secular and a sacred sense. The antecedents of the New Testament usage are to be found in the Old Testament, although it was paralleled in Emperor worship. Cf. the useful summary of the development of this word in A. Wikenhauser's *New Testament Introduction* (Eng. Tr. 1958), pp. 150–155.

[1] See p. 205 for further discussion of the uniqueness of the Gospels.

[2] The closest parallels which have been cited are Philostratus' *Life of Apollonius of Tyana* and Lucian's *False Prophet*. Cf. C. K. Barrett, *Luke the Historian in Recent Study* (1961), pp. 13–15.

But our present purpose is to deal with the general motives which led to the writing of Gospel accounts, since, as stated above, no previous patterns existed.

At first the oral apostolic testimony would possess such weight that an authenticated and consecutive Gospel in a written form may not have been conceived. There can be no denying that word of mouth carried more authority for the eastern mind than written documents, and for this reason it is generally supposed that written documents were regarded as a necessity only after the decease of the authorized eye-witnesses. In this case a period of some considerable time might well have elapsed before our earliest Gospels. The problem of the dating of the Gospels will be considered later, but it is necessary at this juncture to put in a word of caution against the too ready assumption that an extensive oral period is essential for the understanding of the origin of the Gospels. The rapid spread of Christianity may well have precipitated a need much earlier, for the apostles could not have been ubiquitous. Quite apart from the dating of the Gospels it is clear from Luke's preface that, at some undefined period before Luke himself wrote, others had produced written accounts. There is no knowing how early the earliest of these may have been and this uncertainty must condition our assessment of the view that at first no motive existed for the production of a written account.

It has often been asserted that delay was caused by the widespread belief in the imminence of the *parousia*, or return of Christ, which if taken seriously would clearly discourage any written records. What was the point if at any time the Lord might return? Records to perpetuate the story of the origin of the Church would appear relevant only when it was clear that the Church would have a continuing history. This is a reasonable conjecture and has much to commend it, but it is by no means certain that it is right. The New Testament Epistles antedate the Gospels in their canonical form. Moreover, our Lord made clear that before the *parousia* the nations must first hear the gospel. Is it then entirely unreasonable to suppose that some of the earliest preachers found use for written records? If conjecture is to be relied on, it might just as well be maintained that the production of written Gospels for propaganda purposes would have been regarded as an essential part in the Church's preparation for the *parousia*.

Other reasons which have been suggested for a delay in writing are the cost of materials and the difficulty of obtaining adequate data. The former of these cannot be lightly dismissed, for writing materials were expensive, but it is difficult to see how the problem was lessened at a later date. The view taken over the latter point will vary according to the view held regarding Gospel origins. If all the Evangelists had to go searching round for their material, some interval would probably be necessary, but this is not the only, nor is it the most reasonable, explanation of the Gospel origins, as will be seen when the Synoptic problem is dealt with later.

There were undoubtedly many motives which would have led to the production of the Gospels. The need for a historical record for catechetical purposes is at once obvious. Without minimizing the custom of oral instruction so highly esteemed among the Jews, it is questionable whether this procedure would have made so strong an appeal to Gentile converts. The Gentile mission, in fact, would have been greatly assisted by written documents for catechesis, and although the need may not have been at once recognized it must have dawned upon the missionary Church at an early stage. Closely linked with catechetical requirements would have been those of apologetics. The non-Christian world would naturally want to know what kind of person Jesus was, and the urgent need for an authoritative answer is easily recognizable. Whereas, again, an apostolic oral witness would at first suffice, the spreading work of the gospel would soon require more permanent accounts.

It has been suggested that a liturgical motive played a part in the production of some, at least, of the Gospels and those theories will be mentioned later on. Whatever decisions are reached regarding the part played by liturgical demands in prompting the production of written Gospels, it is highly probable that some account of the life, teaching, death and resurrection of Jesus would from earliest times need to be included in the forms of Christian worship. But although once again actual eyewitnesses would, at first, well supply the lack, in the Gentile regions where direct Palestinian eyewitnesses were not available the need for written records would require no time to develop.

Sufficient has been said to indicate a variety of reasons why Gospels were written. There were, on Luke's own showing, numerous attempts to meet the need, but only four of these have survived as authentic records and it will next be necessary to investigate briefly the approach of the early Church to these Gospels and its rejection of all others. The mass of apocryphal Gospels of later origin bears testimony both to the recurring fascination in filling in details which the canonical Gospels omit and to the vigilant discernment of the Christian Church in rejecting them as spurious. Some scholars have maintained that buried in the mass of fiction there may be preserved authentic sayings of the Lord.[1]

IV. THE PLACE OF THE GOSPELS IN THE NEW TESTAMENT

It is beyond the scope of our present study to investigate the growth of the Canon,[2] but a brief summary of the attitude of the early Church towards the Gospels is necessary in order to set the problems of introduction in their right perspective.

By the end of the second century it is clear from all the evidence available that our four Gospels were accepted, not only as authentic, but also as Scripture on a level with the Old Testament. Irenaeus has an illuminating passage in which he maintains that the fourfold character of the Gospel is analogous to the four quarters of the world, the four winds and the necessity for four pillars in an edifice.[3] While Irenaeus' method of reasoning may be questioned, his testimony to the exclusive use of our four Gospels is undeniable. Moreover, in the same passage he speaks of the author of each Gospel according to the traditional ascription. He goes on to adumbrate a doctrine of the inspiration of the Gospels. Admittedly Irenaeus is uncritical in his approach, but that is not to say that his testimony was not based on sound tradition. At least, it cannot be dismissed when discussing introductory questions.

Although Clement of Alexandria cites from other Gospels, as, for instance, from the *Gospel according to the Egyptians*, he carefully distinguishes them from the four canonical Gospels. Tertullian, on the other hand, exclusively cites only the four and argues strongly for the authority of those on the grounds that they were produced by apostles or by their immediate associates. None of these writers seems to have questioned the origin of these Gospels in the apostolic age, although

---

[1] Cf. J. Jeremias, *Unknown Sayings of Jesus* (1957).

[2] For a survey of the early approach to the Gospels, cf. A. H. McNeile, *INT*² (1953); A. Souter, *The Text and Canon of the New Testament*² (1954); Oxford Society, *The New Testament in the Apostolic Fathers* (1905); J. Knox, *Marcion and the New Testament* (1942); E. C. Blackman, *Marcion and his Influence* (1948); J. N. Sanders, *The Fourth Gospel in the Early Church* (1943); J. N. Birdsall, article 'Canon of the New Testament', *NBD*, pp. 194–199.

[3] For an English translation of Irenaeus' statement, cf. *A New Eusebius* (ed. J. Stevenson, 1957), p. 122.

their approach has been challenged by modern criticism. It may well be that these men were nearer the truth than is often allowed, a possibility which will be considered later.

Previous to AD 180 the evidence is less specific, but is nevertheless indicative of a high regard for the Gospels from the earliest times for which any data exist. Tatian's *Harmony* comprised extracts from our four Gospels[1] and is interesting as evidence of the perplexity which was then felt over the fourfold Gospel. In spite of its considerable influence in the Eastern Church, it was soon displaced by the separate Gospels, a fact which testifies to the respect with which the Synoptic Gospels were treated in spite of the large amount of common material contained in them. The Christians were less interested in a consecutive life of Christ compiled from authentic records than in the authentic records themselves. At a still earlier date Justin Martyr appears to have known and used all the Gospels, although in his case it is not possible to be certain, in view of the looseness of his citations. Of importance for our present study is his reference to the 'memoirs of the apostles' used in public services. These memoirs were elsewhere identified as 'Gospels' (εὐαγγέλια), and it is clear from this that the writings were authoritative because of their direct relationship to the apostolic recollections.

Both Clement of Rome and Ignatius made use of Gospel material, although more by way of allusion than by formal citation. All of the material, however, finds parallels in the canonical Gospels with the exception of one passage in Ignatius, which contains a Dominical saying from an extraneous source.[2] Nevertheless it has been disputed that these patristic writers were actually acquainted with the written Gospels. H. Köster,[3] for instance, speaks rather of pre-Synoptic traditions. On the other hand the *Epistle of Polycarp* contains parallels with the Gospels which reveal his undoubted acquaintance with them,[4] although in the

---

[1] Some scholars maintain that other material was also included in Tatian's *Diatessaron*. Indeed Victor of Capua called this work a *Diapente* (cf. G. Quispel, *VC*, 13, 1959, pp. 87–117; H. Montefiore and H. E. W. Turner, *Thomas and the Evangelists*, 1962, pp. 25–27) in which case it was evidently accepted that a non-canonical Gospel was drawn upon.

[2] Cf. A. Souter, *The Text and Canon of the New Testament*[2] (1954), p. 149.

[3] *Synoptische Überlieferung bei den apostolischen Vätern* (1957).

[4] Köster admits Polycarp's knowledge of Matthew and Luke, although he does not date this evidence as early as that of Ignatius, because he accepts P. N. Harrison's view that chapters i–xii of Polycarp's letter were written much later (*Polycarp's Two Epistles to the Philippians*, 1936).

case of all of these writers there has been dispute over their acquaintance with John's Gospel (see later comments, pp. 268 f.).

During the sub-apostolic period the testimony of Papias on the Gospels is highly significant, although somewhat enigmatic. As it will be considered in detail in the course of the discussions on various problems of introduction, it will be necessary here to do no more than point out that Papias says nothing which contradicts any of the patristic evidence so far cited. He made two statements about Matthew and Mark respectively, and these appear to be the earliest comments on the authorship of any of the Gospels. He believed that Mark was Peter's interpreter and that Matthew wrote in Hebrew, and although both statements have become a battleground of criticism (see pp. 33 ff., 69 f.) their evidence is of great importance because of their early date.

V. THE BEST METHOD OF APPROACHING THE GOSPELS

Before coming to the study of the separate Gospels, it may be helpful to point out some of the advantages of the method adopted in this Introduction. The first advantage is that it places the problems of sources and origins in their right perspective as subsidiary to the understanding and appreciation of the extant Gospels. However important these problems are in the study of the Gospels it is no gain to exalt them into a dominant position. The method adopted is not, however, without its difficulties, since some discussions on the separate Gospels are affected by conclusions reached regarding sources or the formation of traditions. In some cases these conclusions are anticipated, although the steps by which they are reached are postponed for later discussion. In these cases cross references will enable the reader to refer to subsequent discussions where necessary.

Another advantage is that the method chosen enables the study of each Gospel for its own sake, irrespective of the order in which it is supposed that they were actually produced. For this reason the canonical order has been retained. It will in fact be found that many important aspects of each Gospel may be discussed independently of the solution of the problem of their relationship.

Perhaps a brief reference here to the generally held theories of the origins of the first three Gospels may not, however, be amiss. The source-critical approach generally maintains that Mark was the earliest Gospel and that this was used by both Matthew and Luke, who in addition used another written source consisting mainly of sayings (Q), together with a quantity of special traditions (known respectively as M and L, irrespective of whether these were written or oral). The form-critical method of accounting for Gospel origins aims to push back the enquiry behind the sources and assumes as its guiding principle that the earliest traditions circulated as separate units, which were later edited into the sources proposed by source criticism and in this way became incorporated into our Gospels. Both source and form criticism are fully discussed in later chapters, but the work is so arranged that those who prefer to do so may study these before studying the individual Gospels.

The previous remarks have made no mention of the Gospel of John, since this is in a different category from the other three Gospels, and will be considered only after the Synoptic problem has been discussed.

CHAPTER TWO

MATTHEW'S GOSPEL

This Gospel, according to the citations found in early Christian writers, was used more than any of the other Gospels.[1] Some of the reasons for this will be seen when the purpose and structure are examined, for its adaptability to liturgical use will be especially brought out. The book has retained its appeal throughout Christian history and has exerted powerful influence, particularly through its presentation of the Sermon on the Mount.

I. CHARACTERISTICS

a. Conciseness

A feature of this Gospel as compared, for instance, with Mark is that its narratives are generally more concise. Such comparisons may be made in the account of the death of John the Baptist (Mt. xiv. 3–12; Mk. vi. 17–29) and in the incident of the healing of the epileptic child (Mt. xvii. 14–21; Mk. ix. 14–29). It may have been this feature, coupled with Matthew's general orderliness, which caused this Gospel to be so widely used for liturgical purposes in the early Church.

b. Messianic interest

It was natural for the early Christians to have an absorbing interest in the Old Testament predictions which were fulfilled in Jesus Christ, and Matthew's Gospel demonstrates this in a marked degree. There are many quotations from the Old Testament and these fall into two categories. The majority are cited from the LXX and are introduced by various formulae or else arise naturally out of the course of the narrative without special introduction. But Matthew also makes use of a group of citations from the Hebrew which are all introduced by variations of the formula—'that it might be fulfilled'. These sayings, which may have formed part of a previous collection (see later discussion on Matthew's *testimonia*, pp. 161 ff.), illustrate the deep conviction that

---

[1] Cf. E. Massaux, *Influence de l'Evangile de St. Matthieu sur la littérature chrétienne, avant St. Irenée* (1950).

there was an indisputable connection between Christianity and the Old Testament. They bear witness to a major part of the earliest creed of the Christian Church, i.e. Jesus is Messiah.[1] If it appears to modern readers that some of these 'fulfilments' are forced (e.g. Mt. ii. 15 = Ho. xi. 1), it should be remembered that for the earliest Christians who had inherited the Old Testament from Judaism and revered it as their sole Scriptures, its witness was unquestionably authoritative, and in such *testimonia* logical connection was not always looked for. In common with his Christian contemporaries Matthew in his approach to the Old Testament differed from that of the Rabbis in that he viewed it without being bound by a traditional method of interpretation. As a consequence many passages are treated as messianic which were not so treated by Jewish interpreters.[2]

c. Particularism and universalism

The Jewish interests of the author are seen in many other respects besides the appeal to the Old Testament. His Gospel often reflects the more restricted outlook of Jewish Christianity. Not one jot or tittle of the law will become invalid (v. 18 f.); the scribes and Pharisees occupy the seat of Moses and their instructions are to be observed (xxiii. 2 f.); Jesus enjoins the fulfilment of the commandments (xix. 17 ff., xxiii. 23); the Jewish temple tax is paid (xvii. 24 ff.); the disciples are expected to fast, keep the sabbath, and bring offerings as in the Jewish tradition (vi. 16 ff., xxiv. 20, v. 23 f.); Jesus Himself declares that He is sent only to the 'lost sheep of the house of Israel' (xv. 24); the genealogy of Jesus is traced from Abraham and is arranged in three groups of fourteen in rabbinic style (i. 1 ff.); and Jewish customs and phrases are included without elucidation (xv. 2, where the phrase 'tradition of the elders' occurs in the passage about handwashing scruples; xxiii. 5, where phylacteries are mentioned; and xxiii. 27, where allusion is made to whited sepulchres). In addition, the recurrent theme of Jesus as the Son of David and the triumphant entry into Jerusalem focus attention upon the Jewish Christian regard for Jesus as the Fulfiller of their national hopes.

But the significant thing about Matthew's Gospel is that universalism

[1] Cf. J. Knox, *The Early Church and the Coming Great Church* (1957), pp. 63 ff.
[2] Cf. B. F. Westcott's discussion of this in *Introduction to the Study of the Gospels*[7] (1888), pp. 159 ff. On Matthew's use of the Old Testament, cf. N. Hillyer, *EQ*, XXXVI (1964), pp. 12–26.*

appears alongside this particularism. If Christianity is seen as the ideal Israel it is also seen as the New Israel, unbounded by the restricted environment out of which it emerged. At the birth of Jesus homage is offered by Gentiles according to Matthew's account (ii. 1 ff.), and when the life of Jesus is in jeopardy it is a Gentile land, Egypt, which offers asylum and protection (ii. 13 ff.). At the conclusion of the Gospel Matthew records the great commission which extends to all nations (xxviii. 18 ff.). The severe attack on the Pharisees by Jesus in xxiii. 13 ff. was called forth by a wrong emphasis on the Jewish doctrine of righteousness by works. In the parable of the vineyard (xxi. 33 ff.) Jesus suggests that another nation will supplant the original husbandmen, who clearly represent the Jewish people. This enlargement by Christianity of the narrow limits of Judaism is not a peculiarity of Matthew's Gospel, originating in a dual outlook, but belongs to the very nature of Jesus Himself.[1]

d. Ecclesiastical elements

Matthew, alone of the Gospels, records any specific teaching about the Church. Here only does the word ἐκκλησία occur attributed to Jesus. The two passages where it is used are therefore of great importance. In xvi. 18, the basis of the Church is to be Peter and his confession, and to Peter are given the keys of the kingdom, with authority to bind or loose. In the other passage (xviii. 17 f.) similar authority appears to be vested in the Church as a whole. The Church is here set forth in its disciplinary capacity. But because no other Evangelist records the use

[1] H. J. Schoeps (*Theologie und Geschichte des Judenchristentums*, 1949, p. 47), although acknowledging Matthew's Jewish-Christian emphasis, maintains that there is little Judaizing tendency. To him, however, the Gospel represents emergent Catholicity rather than the universal outlook of Jesus Himself. Cf. J. Jeremias (*Jesus' Promise to the Nations*, 1958, p. 34), who brings out Matthew's strong emphasis on the missionary activity of Jesus among the Gentiles. Cf. also K. W. Clark ('The Gentile Bias of Matthew', *JBL*, LXVI, 1947, pp. 165–172), who uses these Gentile indications to imply that the author was a Gentile Christian rather than a Jewish Christian. Another scholar who maintains a Gentile destination and who stresses the universal element is P. Nepper-Christensen, *Das Matthäusevangelium—ein judenchristliches Evangelium?* (1958). Against the latter, cf. G. Bornkamm in *Tradition and Interpretation in Matthew* (Eng. Tr. 1963), p. 51. See p. 25 n.2 for others who regard the universal aim of this Gospel as dominant. G. Strecker (*Der Weg der Gerechtigkeit*, 1962, pp. 15–35), although admitting some earlier Jewish influences in the history of the Church to which the author belonged, regards him as belonging to the dominant Gentile section.

of the word ἐκκλησία by our Lord, many scholars[1] have disputed the originality of these sayings and suggest that they arose in the ecclesiastical environment of the early communities. Yet there is no strong ground for such an assumption.[2] There is on the other hand an absence of any other explanation of the universal acceptance of the term in the primitive Church.

Two other passages may be linked with these to show Matthew's ecclesiastical interests. xviii. 20 describes the simplest form of the local church, the gathering of two or three in the name of Christ with the promise of His presence. In the concluding commission two statements are made relevant to the future Church. Its work is to consist of teaching the nations and baptizing disciples in the triune Name (xxviii. 19). The believers are moreover to be taught to observe all that Jesus had commanded (xxviii. 20), and His own presence is assured to them to the end of the age.[3]

e. Eschatological interest

Because Matthew's apocalyptic section is much longer than that of Mark, it has been supposed that his Gospel reflects a period of deepening interest in apocalyptic. Thus Streeter[4] suggested that a revival of interest might have occurred as a result of the Nero Redivivus myth[5] which expected a return of Nero at the head of a Parthian invading army. But there is no need to postulate that Matthew's more lengthy treatment of our Lord's apocalyptic teaching was determined by external influences

---

[1] Cf. A. H. McNeile, *The Gospel according to St. Matthew* (1915), pp. 241 f., for details. For recent scholars who have adopted a similar view, cf. R. Bultmann, *The History of the Synoptic Tradition* (Eng. Tr. 1963), pp. 138–140; E. Schweizer, *Church Order in the New Testament* (Eng. Tr. 1961), pp. 2bf.; G. Bornkamm, *op. cit.*, pp. 44 f., who also cites H. von Campenhausen's opinion that the statement in Mt. xvi. 17 ff. is unthinkable in the mouth of Jesus (*Kirchliches Amt und geistliche Vollmacht*, 1953, pp. 140 f.).*

[2] Cf. V. Taylor, *The Gospels*[5] (1945), p. 81. Cf. also O. Cullmann, *Peter: Disciple, Apostle, and Martyr*[2] (1962), pp. 164 ff., for a discussion of Mt. xvi. 18; R. N. Flew, *Jesus and His Church* (1956), and A. Oepke, *St Th* (1948–50), pp. 110 ff.

[3] Quite apart from the ecclesiastical interests mentioned here, some scholars trace in Matthew's special emphases an echo of the ecclesiastical tensions in his own time (cf. C. W. F. Smith, *JBL*, LXXXII, 1963, pp. 149–168). But cf. C. H. Dodd's study of the similarity between Matthew's and Paul's approach to the idea of the Church and church order (*New Testament Studies*, 1953, pp. 57–62).

[4] *The Four Gospels* (1924), p. 523.

[5] Cf. R. H. Charles, *Commentary on the Revelation of St. John* (1920), II, pp. 76 ff.

in the later history of the Church. The words of Jesus cannot be divorced from eschatological interest, although there is considerable difference of opinion over the extent to which Matthew's recorded teaching (and similarly Mark's) is original to Jesus. In the absence of any positive evidence to the contrary, however, it is reasonable to conclude for the authenticity of these sayings.[1]

But Matthew does not confine his eschatological elements to the material in the great discourse of chapters xxiv, xxv, for they are apparent also in some of the parables which he alone records. The interpretation of the parable of the tares (xiii. 36 ff.) and the conclusions to both the parable of the ten virgins (xxv. 13) and the parable of the talents (xxv. 30), in all of which the end of the age is brought into sharp focus, are peculiar to Matthew.

II. PURPOSE, DESTINATION AND PLACE OF ORIGIN

It has already been shown that one of Matthew's main characteristics is the dominance, throughout his account, of Old Testament citations and allusions. This must obviously be a prime consideration in discussing the author's purpose. He writes his Gospel from a definite standpoint. He purposes to show that the major events in the life of Jesus took place in fulfilment of prophecy. In this he was not alone, for such a motive recurs frequently through the New Testament, although nowhere so clearly as in this Gospel. This feature alone would seem to indicate that the author was a Jew writing for Jews. The story begins with a genealogy intended to show our Lord's direct descent from Abraham and this gives a clear indication of what the author proposes to do. But it is significant that the book ends with a note of universalism in the sending of the disciples to preach the gospel throughout the world.[2] However Jewish many of Matthew's emphases are, his main target is to show Christianity as much more comprehensive than

---

[1] Cf. G. R. Beasley-Murray, *Jesus and the Future* (1954). Dodd (*op. cit.*, pp. 54–57) compares the eschatology in Matthew and Paul and considers that both reflect an early tradition.

[2] Many scholars regard this final commission as the real key to the understanding of Matthew's purpose. Cf. O. Michel, *Ev Th*, x (1950–51), p. 21; G. Schille, *NTS*, 4 (1957–58), p. 113; E. P. Blair, *Jesus in the Gospel of Matthew* (1960), pp. 44 ff. C. F. D. Moule (*The Birth of the New Testament*, 1962, p. 91 n.2) cites W. Trilling (*Das wahre Israel*, 1959) for the same opinion.

Judaism.[1] Here was Old Testament fulfilment in the widest possible sense.

In all probability there was an apologetic purpose behind this Gospel. It would have answered many questions about our Lord which may well have been raised against Him by calumnists. The infancy story, for instance, would answer any charge of illegitimacy against Jesus. The descent into Egypt and the subsequent return to Nazareth would account for the residence of Jesus in Nazareth rather than Bethlehem. The same might be said of the apologetic character of some of the details in the resurrection narrative which are peculiar to Matthew (e.g. the story of the bribing of the guard, which would refute any allegation that the disciples had stolen the body of Jesus). In view of this R. V. G. Tasker[2] calls this Gospel 'an early Christian apology'.

Naturally the author's purpose needs to be interpreted in the light of the construction of the Gospel, or more precisely of the historic occasion which prompted it. Because of this, comment must be made on two recent views of the composition of the Gospel which give a new slant to considerations of purpose. The first is the community idea put forth by G. D. Kilpatrick.[3] According to this writer, the Gospel is a revision of a lectionary which grew up in answer to the liturgical needs of some Christian community. Because he maintains the documentary theory as far as Mark and Q are concerned, Kilpatrick suggests that in this particular community these two documents would have been read during worship and that other written material would have been added. In this theory, the Gospel almost becomes a community product, although it is the work of one author officially commissioned to produce it. If Kilpatrick is right, the purpose of the Gospel was to put into more permanent form the liturgical material already in use. In other words the author was really an editor who fitted the existing writings into a united whole, suitable for liturgical use. Kilpatrick[4] deduces from the Gospel several lines of evidence which he thinks support his hypothesis. (1) Many stylistic changes from Mark increase lucidity, a valuable asset in liturgy. (2) Several unnecessary details are omitted from Mark.

[1] G. Hebert (*SJT*, 14, 1961, pp. 403–413) considers that the author wrote for 'the Great Church, the Church Catholic'. He suggests that it was written after the fall of Jerusalem to preserve for a predominantly Gentile Church the teaching which Jerusalem had preserved.

[2] In his article 'Matthew, Gospel of', *NBD*, p. 796.

[3] *The Origins of the Gospel according to St. Matthew* (1946).

[4] *Op. cit.*, pp. 72 ff.

(3) When additions occur they clarify the passages. (4) Antitheses and parallelisms are frequent. (5) Formulae are repeated after the main sections. (6) Phrasing is balanced and rounded, admirably suited for liturgical use. Whereas it may be granted that all these data can be used to support the hypothesis, it cannot be said that they demand the hypothesis to account for them. In other words, an alternative explanation is possible. Lucidity, conciseness, clarity, parallelisms, balanced language and similar characteristics are not the sole possessions of liturgies. They may be accounted for by the author's natural literary skill. At the same time it is highly probable that the possession of these qualities led to the widespread use of the Gospel for liturgical purposes in the developing Church.[1]

The other recent suggestion is that of K. Stendahl,[2] who has proposed that the Gospel originated from a Matthaean school, which was designed for teachers and Church leaders. According to this theory, the author, who is conceived of as a Christian Rabbi, produced the book in the form of 'a manual for teaching and administration within the church'. Such a purpose is distinguished by Stendahl from a catechetical purpose,[3] although he does not rule out the latter. He finds such teaching as Matthew xviii to be unsuitable for general catechetical instruction and to be clearly more appropriate for Church leaders. Stendahl illustrates his thesis of a Matthaean school by a study of the author's use of the Old Testament, on the assumption that the starting-point of instruction for teachers would have been the interpretation of the Old Testament from a Christian point of view.[4] A comparison with the Habakkuk commentary from Qumran shows certain similarities between the *pesher* method of quoting Scripture favoured by the Covenanters and Matthew's method, which according to Stendahl con-

[1] A view similar to Kilpatrick's has been advanced by P. Carrington (*The Primitive Christian Calendar*, 1952), who regarded Matthew as an enlarged lectionary based on Mark (see pp. 66 f. for a discussion of this theory for Mark).

[2] *The School of St. Matthew and its use of the Old Testament* (1954). The idea that Matthew's Gospel was a manual of instruction for Christian churches was earlier suggested by J. H. Ropes, *The Synoptic Gospels* (1934), pp. 112 ff. Stendahl is supported by G. Schille, *NTS*, 4 (1957–58), pp. 1–24, 101–114, although the latter conceives of the Gospel as intended for catechetical purposes.*

[3] For a catechetical purpose for Matthew, cf. the article of G. Schille, *NTS*, 4 (1958), pp. 101–114.

[4] Stendahl speaks of 'the rather elaborate School of Matthew with its ingenious interpretation of the Old Testament as the crown of its scholarship' (*op. cit.*, p. 34).

firms his opinion that behind Matthew's Gospel is an advanced study of Scripture.[1] This is certainly an interesting suggestion and there seems to be no intrinsic objection to it as far as the purpose of the Gospel is concerned. Yet it is strange that a Gospel which originated in such a learned school should become so popular in the second century.[2] At the same time it is not impossible, and some allowance must be made for it.

Perhaps more attention should be given, however, to the catechetical purpose of this Gospel. That there was a need for suitable material for catechetical instruction has already been mentioned.[3] The methods used in such instruction of new converts are, however, mainly a matter of conjecture. At least it may be said that Matthew's Gospel would well suit such a purpose, although this cannot establish that such a purpose is present. It may well be that the author exercised a ministry of teaching in his own church and would therefore be sensitive to the needs of his readers.*

There are various suggestions regarding the precise location of the readers of this Gospel, although the available data are wholly insufficient to produce certainty. The Jewish flavouring of the Gospel would suggest a church in which this emphasis would have some point, that is, a predominantly Jewish-Christian community. The traditional view is that the Gospel originated in Palestine and this has much to commend it. But B. H. Streeter[4] rejected this because he alleged that all the patristic evidence to this effect went back to Papias, who may not have been referring to the canonical Gospel at all, and because he maintained that the original language was Greek, which would not support a

---

[1] Cf. especially, ibid., pp. 35, 183–202.

[2] B. Gärtner (Studia Theologica, VIII, 1954, pp. 1–24) criticizes Stendahl's inferences from the Qumran evidence, and considers that the use of the Old Testament arose out of missionary preaching. C. F. D. Moule (op. cit., p. 91), who is favourably disposed towards Stendahl's view, suggests that the group which collected the Matthaean traditions were obliged to defend themselves against Jewish antagonists. G. Bornkamm (Tradition and Interpretation in Matthew (Eng. Tr. 1963), p. 51) finds Stendahl's idea of a school of scribes convincing, but is critical of other aspects of his thesis.

[3] See p. 16.

[4] The Four Gospels (1924), pp. 500 ff. It should be noted that the anti-Marcionite Prologue to Luke's Gospel states that Matthew was produced in Judaea. But it is questioned what value can be attached to this prologue (cf. E. Haenchen, Die Apostelgeschichte,[13] KEK, 1961, p. 8 n.3).

Palestinian origin.[1] Accordingly he suggested Antioch. Kilpatrick[2] is more general, preferring some church in Syria, probably in Phoenicia. Streeter would have rejected the latter on the grounds that an anonymous book, as he believed the original Matthew to have been, would need the backing of an influential church to secure a place in the New Testament Canon.[3] But the suggestions of both Antioch and Phoenicia are pure conjectures and it seems best in the circumstances to leave the question open. If the theory of an Aramaic original for this Gospel is accepted, a Jerusalem origin would have as much to commend it as any, especially as the early Church seems to have assumed this without question.[4]

III. STRUCTURE

This Gospel has sometimes been described as a stately structure and the description is not inappropriate. It has more of careful design than any other of the Gospels and this fact may account for its wider use in the early Church. It shows an author with an astonishingly orderly mind, as the following details will show.

a. The five great discourse sections

The most obvious feature of Matthew's structure is the alternation of large blocks of teaching material with the narrative sections. After an

[1] This basis of argument is rightly rejected by Michaelis, *Einleitung in das Neue Testament*[3] (1961), p. 40. J. Schniewind (*Das Evangelium nach Matthäus,*[9] *NTD*, 1960, pp. 2, 3) points out many internal indications of a Palestinian reader-circle, the most notable of which are the ways that Matthew takes for granted his readers' knowledge of Jewish customs, such as the allusion (left unexplained) to whited sepulchres (Mt. xxiii. 27), to the Jewish garment of Jesus (ix. 20) and to the practice of presenting gifts at the altar (v. 23 f.). While these allusions would not, of course, have been unintelligible to Jews elsewhere, they would have been most meaningful to Palestinian Jews whose scruples were stricter than those of the Dispersion.

[2] *Op. cit.*, pp. 124 ff. Cf. B. W. Bacon, *Studies in Matthew* (1930), pp. 3–23 and J. S. Kennard, *ATR*, xxxi (1949), pp. 243–246, for the choice of a Syrian community.

[3] *Op. cit.*, p. 501.

[4] Streeter asserted quite categorically that all the Fathers after Irenaeus had read his works and were simply repeating his statements regarding the Palestinian origin of this Gospel, and this, he thought, went back to Papias' dictum on τὰ λόγια (*op. cit.*, p. 500). But even if a tradition can be traced back to a single root, this is no justification for assuming that it must be suspect. It may, on the contrary, be an indication of the confidence which a series of writers placed in the tradition.

initial narrative section, which includes the infancy stories, the preparation for Jesus' ministry by John the Baptist and the first incidents of Jesus' preaching work, Matthew introduces the group of teaching known as the Sermon on the Mount (v–vii). It is not possible to discuss here whether our Lord spoke all this teaching on one occasion or whether the author himself has arranged the material into a discourse, but the former is certainly not improbable. At all events, Matthew saw the value of including the teaching in a continuous group and this is characteristic of his method.

Another narrative section follows, consisting mainly of a number of miracles, after which the second discourse section is inserted (x). This consists of the mission charge to the Twelve, again in a continuous discourse. The next descriptive sections deal with incidents which particularly illustrate growing opposition to Jesus and His method of dealing with controversies, which form a fitting introduction to the group of parables in xiii about the kingdom. Another narrative sequence follows in xiv–xvii, culminating in the transfiguration and the prediction of the passion, which prepares for another collection of sayings dealing with the Christian community (xviii). Now the scene of the ministry is set beyond Jordan, but rapidly moves towards Jerusalem, with our Lord's entry into the city and the subsequent series of controversies vividly described. Arising out of one of these controversies, Jesus pronounces a series of woes upon the scribes and Pharisees, which serve as a prelude to the great eschatological discourse (xxiii–xxv). The Gospel then closes with the passion and resurrection narratives.

This alternation of narrative and discourse is clearly not accidental.[1] A similar formula concludes all the five discourse sections, admirably serving the purpose of linking narrative and discourse in a natural sequence, as for instance in the first example (vii. 28), which leads into the statement that Jesus came down from the mountain with great crowds following Him. xi. 1 shows Jesus moving on and still addressing crowds (xi. 7), while after the kingdom parables of xiii, the formula shows Jesus proceeding to His own country and after xviii as moving on into Judaea. The concluding formula (xxvi. 1) shows our Lord anticipating the Passover and the subsequent arrest, and this is well suited to introduce the passion narrative. Each formula is therefore a

---

[1] K. Stendahl (*The School of St. Matthew and its use of the Old Testament* (1954), pp. 20 ff.) suggests that this structure is an example of the pattern—*kerygma* plus *didache* (according to Dodd's theory).

literary link which helps to give continuity to the whole and illustrates the author's skill.

It has been suggested that Matthew's fivefold scheme was patterned on the fivefold character of the books of the Law, the idea being that the author was attempting to provide a 'Pentateuch', as the new law for the community of the new Israel, that is, the Christian Church.[1] The suggestion is not without some merit, but is based wholly on speculation. There is no correlation between the five divisions of Matthew's Gospel and the corresponding five books of Moses. In fact the main point of contact is the number five, which forms too slender a basis for the theory. Admittedly, in the Sermon on the Mount there are many specific references to the superiority of Christ's teaching over the Mosaic Law, but this does not throw much light on Matthew's literary structure.* Although the parallelism between the Gospel and the Pentateuch cannot be entirely excluded, it would seem to be more probable that Matthew's fivefold arrangement bore no symbolic significance.[2]

The skilful planning of the book is clear in spite of the fact that the Evangelists did not belong to a literary group in the accepted sense of the word. They were men with a dominant purpose and what skill they possessed was, under the guidance of the Spirit of God, put to the fullest use.

b. Numerical groups

The author's methodical mind is also seen in the large number of times

[1] Kilpatrick (*The Origins of the Gospel according to St. Matthew*, 1946, p. 136) is quite certain that the fivefold division is modelled on the book of the Law. Cf. also B. W. Bacon, *op. cit.*, pp. 80–82; J. A. Findlay, *Exp.*, VIII, XX (1920), pp. 388–400. But against, cf. G. Barth in *Tradition and Interpretation in Matthew*, Bornkamm, Barth and Held (Eng. Tr. 1963), pp. 153–159, and P. Feine-J. Behm-W. G. Kümmel, *Einleitung*[12] (1963), p. 60 (=W. G. Kümmel, *INT*, Eng. Tr. 1965, p. 75). (In this volume, 'Feine-Behm' refers to the 11th edition of this work; 'Feine-Behm-Kümmel' to the completely revised 12th edition; 'W. G. Kümmel, *INT*, 1965' to the English edition. Kümmel often takes a different line from his predecessors.)*

[2] An interesting suggestion regarding Matthew's structure has been made by J. C. Fenton (*Studia Evangelica*, ed. K. Aland, W. Eltester and E. Klostermann, 1959, pp. 174–179), who finds evidence in this Gospel of the literary devices of *inclusio* and *chiasmus*, and thinks it may be possible to regard the whole book as a great *chiasmus*, chapters v–viii answering to xxii–xxv, x to xviii and xiii. 1–35 to xiii. 36–52. This sounds rather too artificial an arrangement to be convincing as an account of the disposition of Matthew's discourse material, but it may merit further investigation.

that he groups together similar sayings or events. His favourite number is three, although fives and sevens also occur.[1] Samples of 'three' groupings are the threefold division of the genealogy (i. 17), the three temptations (iv. 1–11), three illustrations of righteousness, three prohibitions, three commands (vi. 1–vii. 20), three groupings of three types of miracles—healings, power and restoration (viii. 1–ix. 34), and many instances of three parables, questions, prayers or denials. This need not imply that Matthew attached any symbolic importance to the number three, but it does vividly illustrate the way in which his mind worked, and for methodical arrangement marks him out from the other Gospel writers. It may be that Matthew generally cited three or more instances of a type of saying or event because he was influenced by the Mosaic principle that evidence is established by two or three witnesses. For him the multiplication of examples would be regarded as an authentication of the material incorporated.[2]

c. The grouping of material generally

Within both narrative and discourse Matthew aims to illustrate various aspects of the ministry of Jesus. Thus, while v–vii illustrates His teaching, viii–ix. 34 illustrates His work, and a similar combination is found throughout the Gospel. In xii. 1–45 are various illustrations of His controversies with the Pharisees, followed in xiii by illustrations of His parabolic teaching. Behind this conscious aim there is a discernible framework which compares with that used by both Mark and Luke. It speaks much for the author's skill that he welds the general scheme into the framework so well that the Gospel gives the impression of being a united whole. Once Matthew's literary procedure is grasped, it will be abundantly clear that he never conceived of his work as belonging to the category of biography, as at present understood. His literary structure is, rather, designed to give, as comprehensively as possible, the main facets of the life and character of Jesus. It is significant that it is in

---

[1] Note, for instance, his five discourse blocks and his groupings of fourteen in the genealogy, his seven parables in Mt. xiii and his seven woes in Mt. xxiii. On the genealogy G. H. Box suggested that the three groups of fourteen were governed by a numerical acrostic on the name 'David', which in Hebrew numerology totalled fourteen (*ZNTW*, 6, 1905, p. 85). But this idea seems rather far-fetched.

[2] It has been maintained by F. V. Filson (*JBL*, LXXV, 1956, pp. 227–231), that Matthew shows a tendency to break patterns contained in his sources and therefore it is assumed that topical arrangement took precedence for him over literary patterns, although some of the latter are admitted.

MATTHEW'S GOSPEL

and Luke in content and sequence. There was undoubtedly at an early
stage a relatively fixed structure for the relating of these solemn events.

IV. AUTHORSHIP

a. The title

The earliest description of this Gospel of which we have any evidence
attributes it to Matthew (KATA MATΘAION). This is testified by
strong tradition. It was indisputably acknowledged before the close of
the second century and there is no positive evidence that the book ever
circulated without this title. Indeed it may reasonably be claimed that
the title was affixed at least as early as AD 125.[1] It is, moreover, a fair
inference that the form of the title would have been understood as implying authorship. Nevertheless, the title cannot without hesitation be
regarded as a part of the original text. Indeed it is generally assumed
that no importance can be attached to it, since it was probably acquired
in the course of the early history of the document. There are no means
of reaching certainty about this. Some facts, however, are clear. The
author's name does not occur in the body of the text and this might
suggest that the original copy was anonymous. On the other hand the
absence of any parallel forms to our Gospels makes it difficult to be
certain whether this literary form lent itself to the personal identification of the author. Even Luke's preface, which uses the first person
singular, contains no hint of who is the writer. On the other hand the
apocryphal Gospels, which are clearly imitations of the canonical Gospels, are frequently attributed to an apostolic author in the body of the
text, evidently because an anonymous production was felt to be inadequate (cf. *The Gospel of Peter*).

b. Ancient tradition

But the title cannot be dismissed too lightly, for it has the support of
ancient tradition and this must be the starting-point of discussion regarding authorship. The main witnesses are as follows:[2]

First: *Papias* wrote, 'Matthew composed the Logia (τὰ λογία) in the
Hebrew tongue and everyone interpreted them as he was able.'[3] The

---

[1] Cf. J. H. Ropes, *The Synoptic Gospels* (1934), pp. 103 f.; N. B. Stonehouse,
Origins of the Synoptic Gospels (1963), p. 16; G. D. Kilpatrick, *op. cit.*, p. 4.
[2] For a full discussion of ancient tradition concerning Matthew and his Gospel,
cf. P. Nepper-Christensen, *Das Matthäusevangelium—ein judenchristliches Evangelium?* (1958), pp. 37–75. [3] Cited by Eusebius, *HE*, iii. 39. 16.

relevance of this statement for our present purpose will obviously depend on the meaning of the word λογία. Its usual meaning is an oracular utterance and it is used in this sense in the New Testament to describe the Old Testament (cf. Rom. iii. 2; Heb. v. 12).[1] It clearly cannot have such a meaning in Papias, but can it describe the Gospel? Certainly the teaching of Jesus could be compared with the oracular utterances of the Old Testament, but the Gospel contains much more than the sayings of Jesus and it becomes relevant to enquire whether Papias could possibly have meant to describe our Gospel by the term λογία.

(i) *The view that* λογία *meant the Gospel.* There are various reasons which support this interpretation of Papias' words.

1. It would be in harmony with the ancient superscription, κατὰ Ματθαῖον. If this title were in use at least as early as AD 125, it must have been known to Papias. If this were so, it would be strange indeed if he had spoken of Matthew as writing anything else and yet made no allusion to the Gospel circulating under his name. Unless the superscription were added after Papias' time, it is most natural to assume that Papias was taking for granted that his use of λογία would have been identified with κατὰ Ματθαῖον.[2]

2. Moreover, Papias' own usage would support this contention, for he apparently wrote a series of books entitled *Interpretations of the Lord's Logia* (κυριακῶν λογίων ἐξηγήσεις).[3] Since Papias uses the same word here as in the Matthew statement, it is reasonable to suppose that it is used in both cases in the same sense. This suggests that Papias expounded what Matthew (and others) wrote.[4] Whereas it is possible to

---

[1] T. W. Manson (*The Sayings of Jesus*, 1949, p. 18) maintained that λογία was used, not of Scripture as a whole, but only of God's word of guidance or encouragement to Israel contained within Scripture. He considered that it must be understood in this way in Papias and could not therefore refer to Matthew's Gospel.

[2] Kilpatrick (*op.cit.*, p. 4) suggests that the form of the notices in Papias favours the inference that he knew of a κατὰ Ματθαῖον and a κατὰ Μάρκον at least.*

[3] J. Quasten (*Patrology*, I, 1950, p. 82) translates the title of Papias' book as 'Explanations of the sayings of the Lord'. That sayings collections without narratives circulated is evident from such a book as the *Gospel of Thomas*, but this was, of course, a Gnostic production. For further comments on this, see pp. 152 f.

[4] This was admitted by B. W. Bacon, *The Gospel of Mark: its Composition and Date* (1925), p. 25, although he considered that Papias was wrong about Matthaean authorship.

deduce from his Matthew statement that he might have commented only on the sayings of Jesus, in which case λογία would not refer to the whole Gospel, yet such a supposition is not supported by Papias' parallel statements about Mark's Gospel, in which he not only mentions that Mark wrote down what he remembered of the words and deeds of the Lord, but implies that Mark did what Peter did not do, i.e. make a composition of Dominical oracles.[1] In that case λογία must be understood to include deeds as well as words. If this is Papias' meaning in reference to Mark it must also be so in reference to Matthew.

3. Another consideration which is not without some importance for this discussion is the fact that, whereas Papias feels it is necessary to cite his authority for his statement about Mark (i.e. the Elder), he does not do so in the case of Matthew.[2] Presumably this must mean that in Papias' time the origin of Matthew's Gospel was indisputable. An apostolic work would not require such authentication as a work by a non-apostolic author like Mark. Admittedly this argument would still obtain if λογία meant something other than the Gospel, but it is more credible if Papias is referring to a work which was generally recognized, as the Gospel is known to have been.

From these data it would seem to be a reasonable inference that Papias believed that what Matthew wrote was a Gospel.[3] And yet this has been challenged from various points of view and these objections must next be considered. The major problem is that Papias' statement would then conflict with the generally held theory regarding the origin of the Gospel, for it is generally denied that the apostle Matthew could have written it. The basis of this denial will be considered later, but for the present it should be noted that if this critical contention is correct it

---

[1] Papias uses the same expression—κυριακῶν λογίων—as is used in the title of his own book. Cf. J. Kürzinger's article in *NTS*, 10 (1963), p. 109. F. Godet (*Introduction to the New Testament: The Collection of the Four Gospels and the Gospel of St. Matthew*, 1899, p. 188) interpreted Papias' statement on Mark differently, maintaining that he is contrasting Matthew's λογία with Mark's account of both sayings *and* doings, and therefore interpreting λογία as referring to sayings only. Yet it is more probable that the contrast is over 'order' rather than content.

[2] Cf. Bacon, *op. cit.*, pp. 23 ff. For the full statement of Papias on Mark, see p. 70.

[3] It may be said that there are no philological grounds for arguing that λογία could not have meant the Gospel.

would clearly be necessary to suggest some other interpretation of Papias' statement.

(ii) *Alternative interpretations of Papias'* λογία. If λογία cannot on critical grounds refer to the Gospel, there are only two possible alternatives which have been suggested.

1. λογία refers to a sayings collection. Since the current solution to the Synoptic problem posits a sayings source Q used by both Matthew and Luke, it has seemed to many scholars a reasonable assumption that Papias knew of a tradition that Matthew wrote this source. Indeed, it is claimed that the basic meaning of λογία is far better fitted to describe an authoritative sayings collection than a Gospel.[1] Although this at first sight seems plausible it is not without considerable difficulties. It would appear to involve a confusion between λογία and λόγοι, as R. M. Grant[2] has pointed out, for it is not immediately apparent why they should be identified. Moreover there is no evidence that such a document existed in Papias' time, even if it had existed at an earlier time (see discussion on the Q source on pp. 143 ff.). It is difficult, if not impossible, to imagine an apostolic sayings collection surviving well into the second century and then vanishing without trace.[3] But it is not, of course, necessary to suppose that Papias knew the document to which he refers, in which case the λογία may have vanished long before Papias' time and the report of Matthew's authorship of it alone survived. But if so, what formed the basis of Papias' own expositions? If it was the Gospel, why did he use the same word λογία to describe it? There are too many difficulties in the way of interpreting λογία as Q to make it credible.

2. λογία refers to a *testimonia* collection. In view of the fact that λογ α is used in the New Testament to describe the Old Testament, and in view of the fact that Matthew's Gospel is thought by some scholars to have drawn from a collection of *testimonia*, at least for some of the Old Testament citations (see pp. 161 ff.), it has been suggested that Papias means that Matthew was the author of such a book of λογία.[4] There is less objection to this theory than to the last, although most of the

---

[1] Cf. V. H. Stanton, *The Gospels as Historical Documents* (1923), pp. 53 ff. Stanton could not conceive that by Papias' time any Gospel could have attained such esteem as to be called 'oracles'. Cf. also T. W. Manson, *op. cit.*, pp. 18, 19.

[2] *A Historical Introduction to the New Testament* (1963), p. 117.

[3] For T. W. Manson's answer to this objection, see comment on p. 156 n.1.

[4] Cf. the strong advocacy for this interpretation by B. P. W. S. Hunt, *Primitive Gospel Sources* (1951), pp. 182 ff.

criticisms would still apply.[1] There is no certain evidence of the existence of Christian *testimonia* books as early as this, and even if the
identification were conceded, it would be extremely difficult to imagine
how Matthew's name was transferred from such a document to a
Gospel in which it formed so small a part of the author's sources.

But if neither of these alternatives is valid, are there any other possibilities? It could, of course, be maintained that Matthew's λογία is some
unknown work which has now been hopelessly lost.[2] But this is highly
improbable in view of the existence of a Gospel circulating at the same
time under the name of Matthew. Or it could be maintained that Papias
was wrong, in which case his testimony can be ignored. If λογία means
the Gospel and yet it is supposed that Matthew was not the author of
the Gospel, there is little option but to regard Papias' statement as inaccurate, unless resort is made to some such theory as Kilpatrick's,[3] in which
the ascription to Matthew is regarded as pseudonymous, in which case
Papias may be regarded as a witness to the common assumption about
the authorship of the Gospel.

(iii) *The bearing of Matthew's language on the meaning of Papias' statement.*
If it is safe, therefore, to assume that Papias' λογία meant the Gospel, a
problem immediately arises concerning the further statement about
composition in the Hebrew tongue (dialect). Almost all scholars are
agreed that Matthew's Gospel was written in Greek, not in Hebrew or
Aramaic (as Papias probably meant). This either means that Papias
made a mistake or that our interpretation of λογία is incorrect. But
since there is a strong presumption against the latter, it seems better to
prefer the former. Yet how did the mistake arise? There are several
possible suggestions. It may have been an inference from the Jewish-
Christian characteristics of the Gospel, if it was assumed that a Gospel
designed for Palestinian Jewish Christians must have been in Aramaic.
On the other hand, the tradition may have arisen through confusion
over another book, like the *Gospel according to the Hebrews*, which was

---

[1] P. Parker (*The Gospel before Mark*, 1953, pp. 153 f.) raises three objections
against this interpretation: (1) The small quantity of *testimonia* peculiar to Matthew; (2) the omission of most of the *testimonia* used elsewhere in the New
Testament; (3) the context of Papias' statement in Eusebius, who is dealing with
Gospels not *testimonia*. Parker himself identifies the λογία with a pre-Mark,
pre-Matthew Gospel, which he calls K (see p. 146).

[2] Cf. F. C. Burkitt, *The Gospel History and its Transmission*[3] (1911), p. 127.

[3] *The Origins of the Gospel according to St. Matthew* (1946), pp. 138 ff.

mixed up in the tradition with a Hebrew Matthew. Or else a Semitic translation of Matthew's Greek Gospel was known at that time.[1] None of these is particularly convincing, and all lack corroborating evidence. But even if no adequate account of the rise of the tradition can be given, it clearly cannot be correct if the Gospel of Matthew is in mind. Yet this does raise a difficulty. If the statement about language is wrong, does this not reduce the value of the statement about authorship? If the former is an inference might not the latter be also? While it is not necessary to maintain that Papias was either all right or all wrong, this objection must be faced. Could it be that Papias' statement about language has been rightly understood? It has recently been maintained by J. Kürzinger[2] that the Hebrew dialect (διαλέκτος) must be understood in a literary rather than a linguistic sense, i.e. that Matthew arranged his material in a Jewish-Christian literary form, which would naturally be dominated by Old Testament characteristics. He claims justification for this interpretation from the use of the term in Greek rhetoric. Papias' statement then ceases to be a witness to the original language of Matthew's writing and becomes a statement comparing its literary purpose with that of Mark. In further support of this hypothesis Kürzinger understands Papias' words that each interpreted as he was able as a reference to Mark and Matthew and supposes that both these writers pursued a literary purpose in accordance with their ability. If Kürzinger is right, Papias' statement would stand and his testimony to Matthaean authorship would be strengthened. But it may be questioned whether this is a very natural way to interpret Papias' use of διαλέκτος.

If the more usual interpretation of διαλέκτος is preferred there would appear to be only one alternative to assuming that Papias was wrong, and that is to assume that Matthew was not only author of the Greek Gospel but also composed something in Hebrew (Aramaic) which he incorporated into the Gospel. This would be supported by M. Black's[3] contention for Aramaic sources behind the Gospel. But it may be wondered whether Papias' testimony on this is worth defending. In any case, his testimony must be considered in the light of later testimony.

Second: *Irenaeus* wrote: 'Now Matthew published also a book of the Gospel among the Hebrews in their own dialect, while Peter and Paul

[1] Cf. N. B. Stonehouse, *Origins of the Synoptic Gospels* (1963), pp. 90 ff.
[2] *NTS*, 10 (1963), pp. 108 ff.   [3] Cf. the section on Matthew's language, pp. 46 f.

were preaching the gospel in Rome and founding the Church.'[1] This testimony is clearly identical with Papias' statement only if λογία is interpreted as the Gospel. Since Irenaeus was acquainted with Papias' work it may reasonably be assumed that he is here giving his own interpretation of Papias' statement and that this was in agreement with the uniform tradition of the time, since Irenaeus mentions no dissentient voices.[2]

Third: *Pantaenus*, according to Eusebius,[3] found that the Gospel according to Matthew had preceded him to India and was preserved there in Hebrew letters, having been left there by Bartholomew. The veracity of this story must be doubted, but the fact remains that it bears testimony to a circulating tradition which is, at any rate, in harmony with the interpretation of Papias' λογία as Matthew's Gospel.

Fourth: *Origen*[4] similarly bears testimony to the fact that Matthew composed a Gospel in Hebrew letters.

This evidence points to an unbroken tradition that Matthew wrote his Gospel in Hebrew, and advocates of any hypothesis which disagrees with this must suggest an adequate explanation of so consistent a tradition. The usual explanation is that later Church Fathers were merely reiterating Papias' original mistake, or at least confusion, over what Matthew originally wrote in Aramaic. But since Irenaeus and Origen were both Greek-speaking and both presumably possessed Matthew's Gospel only in Greek, it is strange that neither of them considered the tradition of a Hebrew (or Aramaic) original to be at all suspicious.[5]

[1] *Adv. Haer.* iii. 1. 1, cited by Eusebius, *HE*, v. 8. 2. The translation cited is that of D. Theron's *Evidence of Tradition* (1957), p. 43.

[2] Since Irenaeus contains information not in the Papias tradition he may have been acquainted with other traditions besides that of Papias (cf. Nepper-Christensen, *Das Matthäusevangelium—ein judenchristliches Evangelium?* 1958, p. 56; J. Munck in *Neotestamentica et Patristica*, ed. W. C. van Unnik, 1962, p. 257). Kürzinger (*op. cit.*, pp. 110–115) interprets Irenaeus' statements in the same manner as he deals with Papias' (i.e. of Hebrew (Jewish) dialectic).

[3] *HE*, v. 10. Kürzinger considers that there is a confusion with the *Gospel to the Hebrews* in this tradition (*op. cit.*, p. 115). [4] *Apud* Eusebius, *HE*, vi. 25.

[5] J. Munck (*op. cit.*, pp. 249–260) attaches more importance to Origen's evidence than to that of Papias or Irenaeus, since there is evidence that Origen himself knew Hebrew and would therefore be a more competent judge. Munck discusses the possibility that Papias' statement may be an indication that several

This may be put down to their uncritical approach, but the possibility must always be allowed that there was some basis for the tradition,[1] as has been mentioned also in the case of Papias.[2]

Supposing, however, that in its views on authorship the tradition is incorrect, what are the current explanations of the rise of the tradition? Scholars who identify the λογία with a sayings collection or a Testimony Book consider an adequate solution is to suppose that Matthew's name was transferred at an early stage in the tradition from one of the sources of the Gospel to the Gospel as a whole.[3] The proposition sounds reasonable, but is it really valid? If an anonymous Gospel circulated for a while and was known to have incorporated an apostolic collection of teaching or testimonies, was it natural for it to be called later by the name of the compiler of the sayings? It would be difficult to find a parallel for such a process. It is much more probable that an anonymous Gospel would circulate without anyone having the slightest knowledge of the authorship of any of its sources. One presentation of this theory is to suppose that a tradition that Matthew wrote something was preserved in the same district and at the same time as the anonymous Gospel circulated, and that it was then assumed quite uncritically that Matthew must have written the Gospel. But this still leaves unidentified what Matthew actually wrote. A third possibility is that at the time of the publication it was known as Matthew's Gospel because one of the main sources was written by Matthew. This is perhaps more probable

Greek translations of Matthew's Gospel circulated in his time. W. C. Allen (*The Gospel according to St. Matthew*, ICC, 1907, p. lxxxi) suggested that everyone knew that Matthew had written something in Hebrew, and when his name was attached to the Gospel the statement about him writing in Hebrew was also attached.

[1] C. F. D. Moule (*The Birth of the New Testament*, 1962) admits that room must be found for this persistent tradition in any account of Matthew's origin. He favours a Semitic apostolic sayings collection (i.e. a Semitic Q). Feine-Behm (*Einleitung*,[11] p. 51) conclude from the linguistic evidence that the author must have been a Greek-speaking Jewish Christian who understood Hebrew. Cf. the section on the language of this Gospel (pp. 46 f.). J. Jeremias, because of the form of Dt. vi. 5 cited in Mt. xxii. 37, maintains that the author's mother-speech was Aramaic, but that his prayer-speech was Hebrew (*ZNTW*, 50, 1959, pp. 270–274).

[2] Cf. Kürzinger's discussion, *NTS*, 10 (1963), pp. 108 ff.

[3] W. C. Allen (*op. cit.*, pp. lxxx, lxxxi) contended that if Matthew wrote the sayings collection, it would be natural for his name to be added to a Gospel two fifths of which contained sayings, especially as an apostolic name would give sanction to it. Allen describes this as 'an irresistible tendency'.

than the other two suggestions, but is still without any clear parallels to support it, and is also faced with the difficulty of explaining away the complete disappearance of the source.

c. Objections to the tradition

Since the external evidence is so embarrassing for non-Matthaean authorship, may it not be better to assume that the traditional view is correct?[1] However, certain difficulties arise which are generally considered to make this impossible.

1. The most important obstacle to the acceptance of the tradition is the generally held assumption that Matthew used Mark as his basic source, and not only used Mark but incorporated nearly all of it into his Gospel. If this is a correct assumption it would mean that an apostolic author would have used a non-apostolic source, and this is considered improbable, indeed inconceivable. Reasons will be given later to show that Marcan priority has not gone completely unchallenged in recent times and if it is a false assumption the difficulty would, of course, disappear. But since Marcan priority may be regarded as probable in spite of its difficulties, does this at once rule out apostolic authorship for Matthew's Gospel? The view that it does would seem to proceed from a particular view of apostolicity, which considers that it would have detracted from Matthew's apostolic dignity if he had quoted a non-apostolic writer.[2] It is certainly surprising to find an eyewitness making use of a secondary source, even though it is allowed that Mark preserves Peter's reminiscences.[3] But though surprising, it is not impossible. It

---

[1] One explanation of Papias' words is that he refers to only part of what Matthew wrote and that his comments on the rest are not preserved (cf. T. Nicklin, *Gospel Gleanings*, 1950, pp. 51–56, who suggests that Matthew wrote an Oracles book (which was referred to by Papias), Q and later the extant Gospel in Greek). F. Godet (*Introduction to the New Testament: The Collection of the Four Gospels and the Gospel of St. Matthew*, 1899, pp. 217 ff.), who also considered that Matthew compiled the 'oracles', suggested that an anonymous collaborator of his translated these λογία into Greek and added the Matthaean narratives under Matthew's direction.

[2] A similar objection has been raised over Matthew's use of Q, a non-apostolic source according to many source theories (cf. Michaelis, *Einleitung in das Neue Testament*,[3] 1961, p. 32). But see pp. 143 ff. for discussion on the Q source.

[3] Vincent Taylor calls it 'improbable in the extreme that an apostle would have used as a source the work of one who was not an eyewitness of the ministry of Jesus' (*The Gospels*, p. 81). S. E. Johnson (*The Gospel according to St. Matthew*, IB, 1951, p. 242) rejects apostolic authorship on the grounds that Matthew is what he calls 'a compendium of church tradition artistically edited'.*

would be much more difficult to conceive if Matthew had incorporated Mark unaltered into his work, but he clearly has not done that, since no more than fifty per cent of Mark shows verbal agreement with Matthew (see p. 133). Moreover the ancient world's approach to literary borrowing was different from our modern approach, and the wholesale incorporation of another's work would not have been regarded as impermissible, especially in view of the fact that the Gospel traditions were common knowledge. Besides, the apostle Matthew, being himself an eyewitness of many of the events, would be in a position to recognize the authenticity of Mark.

2. Arising, however, from the latter consideration is the contention that Matthew could not have been written by an eyewitness since the book is much less vivid than Mark's, and this argument must be given full weight.[1] Yet it may be said that Matthew has had time to reflect upon the events that he records and gives more attention to their significance than to their vividness. But in the end this kind of consideration rarely leads to satisfactory conclusions in any direction.[2] A more important consideration is the view that an eyewitness would not have shown the tendencies found in this Gospel, especially ecclesiastical and legalistic, which assume a later editorial process. This would, of course, be a major obstacle to apostolic authorship if it were a valid objection. But its basis needs careful investigation. If Matthew's Gospel is more ecclesiastical than its sources, does this mean that the author's editorial purposes belong to a time when ecclesiastical concerns were more dominant in the Church? It does not immediately follow that this is so. Indeed, it appears to be based on the presupposition that the contemporary church situation created or at least deeply influenced the tradition. But it is equally possible to maintain that Matthew's editorial tendencies reflect a genuine early tradition, provided a more comprehensive picture of the teaching of Jesus is maintained.

3. Another objection of a different kind comes from Kilpatrick,[3] who, although he accepts the view that Papias meant the Gospel in the

[1] Cf. Michaelis, *Einleitung*, pp. 31 f.; also Feine-Behm, *Einleitung*[11], pp. 49 ff.

[2] The same may be said for the view that the peculiar material in the Gospel does not suggest the reminiscences of an apostle (cf. V. Taylor, *loc. cit.*). This assessment depends on the assumption that the special Matthew material is rather less historically reliable than the rest of Matthew (but see pp. 166 f. for a discussion of this).

[3] See pp. 26 f. for Kilpatrick's theory.

statement about the λογία, and therefore accepted its ascription to Matthew, explains away the tradition as a conscious community pseudonym, purposely affixed by the church which produced the Gospel in order to commend it. By this means Kilpatrick attempts in fact to explain away the tradition. But the idea of a community pseudonym is unparalleled. Even if the idea be conceded it would be necessary to explain how any one church managed to persuade all the other churches that the book was authentically Matthaean. Moreover, Kilpatrick himself admits that pseudonymity in an individual is a problem, but considers that for a community it is less so.[1] But this supposed double standard is not supported by the evidence, and from an ethical point of view is highly doubtful. Again, if Kilpatrick's theory that apostolic authorship would have guaranteed readier acceptance is correct, why was not the same procedure followed for Mark and Luke, which were accepted without such a device?

4. A somewhat different reinterpretation of the tradition is found in Stendahl's idea of a school of Matthew,[2] for in this case the identity of the author is lost in the school out of which the Gospel grew.[3] Since the school is said to have continued the tradition of Matthew's catechesis, the ascription of the subsequently written Gospel to Matthew would have seemed natural. But on this view the knowledge that Matthew's school and not Matthew himself produced the Gospel was forgotten long before Papias, a possible but not very probable eventuality. No parallels to such a happening are extant. Nevertheless if the previous objections to Matthaean authorship are considered to be strong enough to require an alternative, this group suggestion is more satisfactory than either a community pseudonym idea or the transference of Matthew's name from a source to the whole.

---

[1] *Op. cit.*, p. 139. [2] See pp. 27 f. for Stendahl's theory.

[3] *Op. cit.* Cf. P. Gaechter's view that Matthew was trained as a Rabbi, but later became a tax collector (*ZkT*, 75, 1933, pp. 480 ff.). This idea is an attempt to reconcile the clear indications of Matthew's profession in the Gospel text (Mt. ix. 9, x. 3) with certain rabbinical features noted in the Gospel. Stendahl, of course, does not have this problem, for he does not identify Matthew as the author and is free to postulate an unidentified Rabbi as author.*

E. P. Blair (*Jesus in the Gospel of Matthew*, 1960, pp. 138 ff.) regards the writer as belonging to the Hellenistic group of Christians represented by the approach of Stephen, but makes no further attempt to identify him, or to suggest why Matthew's name became attached to his work. He goes no further than to repeat the generally held hypothesis that Matthew may have written Q.

d. Incidental supports for the tradition

Supposing the tradition of Matthaean authorship to be correct, are there any incidental supporting evidences from within the Gospel itself? It must be admitted that the evidence is slight, but it may be worth mentioning. Whereas both Mark (ii. 14) and Luke (v. 27 f.) in describing the call of Matthew name him Levi, in Matthew's Gospel he is called Matthew (ix. 9). At the same time in the lists of the apostles in all the Gospels the name Matthew is used and not Levi. Could it be that for the author of this Gospel the name Matthew came to have greater significance than the name Levi, from the time of his dramatic call to follow Jesus? It is not impossible that this is a conscious personal touch.[1] Yet not all would agree with this interpretation, for it has been regarded as a device of pseudonymity,[2] but this idea is unlikely since the choice of Matthew rather than a more important apostle such as Peter would be hard to explain. Another feature is the agreement between the attention to detail essential to the tax-collector's profession and the methodical arrangement of this Gospel. It is, at least, not difficult to imagine that a former tax-collector produced it. It may be of some significance that in the dispute over paying tribute, which all the Synoptics record, it is Matthew alone who uses the more precise νόμισμα (state coin) instead of the common δηνάριον. But the variation may have nothing to do with a tax-collector's experience.

To sum up, it may be said that there is no conclusive reason for rejecting the strong external testimony regarding the authorship of Matthew, although some difficulties arise from source hypotheses. Most scholars, however, reject apostolic authorship. Yet if Matthew is not the author his identity is unknown. The idea that he was a Rabbi is purely speculative.[3]

[1] H. Alford (Greek Testament[6], 1868, I, p. 24) suggested that the author uses his apostolic name when referring to himself, in the same manner as Paul did. But Michaelis (Einleitung, pp. 33, 34) disputes that both names would be attached to one person, and considers that Matthew was later substituted for Levi in the tradition.

[2] Cf. G. D. Kilpatrick, The Origins of the Gospel according to St. Matthew (1946), p. 138. He suggests that ix. 9 and x. 3 were changed to Matthew when the title was affirmed in the original community which sanctioned the book.*

[3] In addition to those mentioned on p. 43 n.3 in support of this suggestion, cf. also E. von Dobschütz, ZNTW, 27 (1928), pp. 338–348, and B. W. Bacon, Studies in Matthew (1930), pp. 131 ff.

V. DATE

It is difficult to discuss the date of any of the Synoptic Gospels without reference to the Synoptic problem, but it is valuable to enquire what possible indications may be found apart from the solution to that problem. It must be admitted that the data available are very slight. It might be argued that certain strands of Matthaean tradition are of a secondary character (see pp. 166 f.), in which case an interval of time would be required to allow for such developments,[1] but this is a judgment which lacks positive proof and is controlled largely by certain presuppositions regarding the relative values of the sources used by the Evangelists.

Similar to this line of argument is the view that Matthew's special material shows ecclesiastical and explanatory interests[2] which point to a time beyond the primitive period. But again the force of this depends on the interpretation of, and the value attached to, the passages about the Church.[3] If it be assumed that our Lord did not foresee and could not have predicted the emergence of a Church, there would be force in the argument. But the character of Jesus would lead us to expect not only that He foresaw the future Church but even prepared for it.

This predictive power of Jesus is so generally denied by Synoptic investigators that it is no wonder that the dates of Mark, Matthew and Luke are all bound up together in the dating of Mark. The argument runs as follows:[4] First, since the predictive power of Christ is denied, it is assumed that Mark was produced only a few years before the fall of Jerusalem (cf. Mk. xiii. 14, and Mt. xxiv. 15). Secondly, Matthew used Mark and therefore must be dated after the fall of Jerusalem. Thirdly, both Ignatius and the *Didache* appear to have cited Matthew's Gospel and so the latter must have attained authority some time before the writings of the former. Fourthly, therefore the probable date of

---

[1] Cf. Streeter, *The Four Gospels* (1924), p. 524.

[2] Cf. V. Taylor, *The Gospels*, p. 82.

[3] It should not be forgotten in discussions of Matthew's ecclesiology that the doctrine in Matthew has certain affinities with Paul's doctrine, although differently expressed. Dodd (*New Testament Studies*, pp. 53–66) examines these points of contact and suggests that a common tradition lies behind them. In this case theological considerations are clearly unreliable indications of dating.

[4] For the generally held dating of Mark's Gospel, see the discussion on pp. 72 ff.

Matthew is AD 80–100. There is no general agreement on any more precise dating within this period.[1]

If, however, it be admitted that our Lord had power to predict the fall of Jerusalem, the main prop in the Marcan dating falls away and other data would need to be used in determining the dates of both Mark and Matthew.[2] But there is singularly little indication in either of them concerning their dates of origin and any suggestions must be largely guesswork. This is one of the problems which must therefore be left undetermined. Yet it affects our understanding of the Gospel as a whole very little, unless, of course, a purely tentative date, which can in no way be proved, is then appealed to as an indication of historical value, as has not infrequently been done. It is necessary to introduce a caution about this.

VI. LANGUAGE

There has been much discussion about the original language of the Gospels. No conclusive answer has yet been given to the question of the possible Aramaic forms from which our extant Gospels have been translated, although far less importance has been given to this than is perhaps justified by the evidence. As far as Matthew's Gospel is concerned, it has generally been held that its extant form shows no evidence of translation Greek. W. F. Howard[3] called it 'a correct if rather colourless Greek which avoids the vulgar forms without displaying a mastery of the literary syntax'. Many scholars are strongly influenced in their estimate of Matthew's language by the assumption that the author used the Greek Mark and could not, therefore, have composed in Aramaic.[4]

---

[1] Kilpatrick (op. cit., pp. 124 ff.) suggests a date at the end of the first century. F. V. Filson (The Gospel according to St. Matthew, 1960, p. 15) prefers a date in the eighties or nineties, but declines to be more specific. Streeter (op. cit., p. 524) was more precise in preferring AD 85, although he agreed it could not be mathematically demonstrated.

[2] The argument that external evidence supports the dating of Mark after Peter's death (see pp. 72 f.) would affect the dating of Matthew only on the usual assumption that Matthew used Mark. Michaelis (Einleitung, pp. 41, 42), who accepts Matthew's use of Mark, nevertheless suggests a date of AD 60–70 for this Gospel. For a dating a decade earlier, cf. M. Meinertz, Einleitung in das Neue Testament[5] (1950), pp. 176 ff.

[3] J. H. Moulton and W. F. Howard, A Grammar of New Testament Greek (1929), II, p. 29.

[4] Cf. Streeter's statement to this effect, op. cit., p. 500.

There has been increasing examination of the evidence from a philological point of view and the idea that our Greek Gospels may go back
to Aramaic originals or at least to Aramaic sources has gained some
support. The main scholars who have worked in this field are Burney,[1]
Torrey[2] and Matthew Black.[3] The two former, who favoured Aramaic
originals, drew their arguments mainly from evidence of mistransla-
tion, although Burney also gave attention to grammatical and syntactical considerations. Black, who maintains sources but not originals,
has developed this latter approach and has attempted to prove that
many grammatical peculiarities can best be explained on the assumption
of Aramaic influence. It is probable that increasing weight will be given
to evidence of this kind. For Matthew's Gospel it is basic to Vaganay's[4]
solution to the Synoptic problem (see discussion on pp. 138 f.),
which maintains an original Aramaic Matthew as the earliest Gospel,
from which the canonical Greek Synoptic Gospels have all been derived.

Black's conclusion regarding sources is that there is sufficient evidence
from the Gospels to point to a sayings source in Aramaic, but he does
not think that Matthew's narrative sections show such Aramaic influence as Mark's sections.[5] He admits, however, that Matthew shows
traces of what he calls a Jewish-Greek style.

Linguistic questions of this kind cannot be assessed in brief compass,
but sufficient has been said to indicate the complicated state of the problem. It may be assumed *a priori* that since our Lord taught in Aramaic
some Aramaic background would be found behind the teaching of
Jesus. But it will be seen that in Matthew's case the question is really
dominated by the Marcan hypothesis. It may perhaps be that this
hypothesis should come to grips more effectively with linguistic considerations (see later discussion on the Synoptic problem, pp. 133 ff.).

[1] *The Poetry of our Lord* (1925); *The Aramaic Origin of the Fourth Gospel* (1922).

[2] *The Four Gospels: A New Translation* (1933).

[3] *An Aramaic Approach to the Gospels and Acts* (1946).

[4] *Le Problème synoptique* (1954). This is somewhat akin to T. Zahn's view that our
Greek Matthew is a translation of an original Aramaic form of the Gospel,
influenced by the Greek Mark which had previously been produced from the
same Aramaic source (*INT*, 1909, II, pp. 601–617.)

[5] *Op. cit.*, pp. 206 ff.

CONTENTS

VII. NARRATIVE (xi. 1–xii. 50)

Jesus sets out to preach in Galilee (xi. 1). John the Baptist's enquiry (xi. 2–6). Jesus' testimony regarding John (xi. 7–15). His estimate of His own generation (xi. 16–19). Woes pronounced on Galilaean cities (xi. 20–24). Jesus' thanksgiving to God (xi. 25–27) and call to the weary (xi. 28–30). Sabbath in the cornfield (xii. 1–8). Healing in the synagogue (xii. 9–14). Healing of the multitude (xii. 15–21). Pharisaic criticism of Jesus, and His reply (xii. 22–37). Sign-seeking and the sign of Jonah (xii. 38–42). The return of an evil spirit (xii. 43–45). Jesus' real family (xii. 46–50).

VIII. THE THIRD DISCOURSE SECTION: THE KINGDOM PARABLES (xiii. 1–52)

The sower and the soils (xiii. 1–9). The reason for parables (xiii. 10–15), and the privileged position of the disciples (xiii. 16, 17). The first parable interpreted (xiii. 18–23). The tares (xiii. 24–30). The mustard seed and the leaven (xiii. 31–33). Old Testament support for the use of parables (xiii. 34, 35). The tares interpreted (xiii. 36–43). Hidden treasure, the valuable pearl and the dragnet (xiii. 44–51). The trained scribe of the kingdom (xiii. 52).

IX. NARRATIVE (xiii. 53–xvii. 27)

Jesus rejected at Nazareth (xiii. 53–58). The death of John the Baptist (xiv. 1–12). Miracles: five thousand fed; the walking on the water; healings at Gennesaret (xiv. 13–36). The tradition of the elders (xv. 1–20). More miracles: the Syro-Phoenician demoniac; healings of multitudes; four thousand fed (xv. 21–39). The Pharisees demand a sign (xvi. 1–4). Discourse on leaven (xvi. 5–12). Peter's confession at Caesarea Philippi (xvi. 13–20). First prediction of the passion (xvi. 21–23) and forecast of suffering for the disciples (xvi. 24–28). The transfiguration and the saying about Elijah (xvii. 1–13). The healing of an epileptic boy (xvii. 14–21). Second prediction of the passion (xvii. 22, 23). Discussion about the temple tax (xvii. 24–27).

X. THE FOURTH DISCOURSE SECTION: VARIOUS SAYINGS (xviii. 1–35)

An enquiry about greatness (xviii. 1–5). Responsibility for causing others to stumble (xviii. 6–10). Illustration of the lost sheep (xviii. 11–

14). Reproofs and reconciliation (xviii. 15–22). Parable of the unmerciful servant (xviii. 23–35).

XI. NARRATIVE: THE JUDAEAN PERIOD (xix. 1–xxii. 46)

Jesus goes to Perea (xix. 1, 2). Questions about marriage and divorce (xix. 3–12). Jesus blesses the little children (xix. 13–15). The rich young man comes to Jesus (xix. 16–22). Jesus' comment on riches and rewards (xix. 23–30). Parable of the labourers in the vineyard (xx. 1–16). The third prediction of the passion (xx. 17–19). Request by Zebedee's wife for places of honour for her sons (xx. 20–28). Healing of two blind men (xx. 29–34). Entry into Jerusalem (xxi. 1–11). Cleansing of the temple (xxi. 12–17). Cursing of the fig-tree (xxi. 18–22). Controversies in the temple court (xxi. 23–xxii. 46).

XII. THE FIFTH DISCOURSE SECTION: TEACHING ON ESCHATOLOGY (xxiii. 1–xxv. 46)

Pronouncement of woes against the Pharisees (xxiii. 1–36). Lament over Jerusalem (xxiii. 37–39). The apocalyptic discourse (xxiv. 1–xxv. 46).

XIII. THE PASSION AND RESURRECTION NARRATIVES (xxvi. 1–xxviii. 20)

The preparation (xxvi. 1–19). The betrayal predicted (xxvi. 20–25). The last supper (xxvi. 26–29). Peter's denial predicted (xxvi. 30–35). In Gethsemane (xxvi. 36–46). The arrest, trial and crucifixion (xxvi. 47–xxvii. 56). The burial (xxvii. 57–66). The resurrection, appearance to the eleven, and farewell commission (xxviii. 1–20).

ADDITIONAL NOTES

22. [2] For a more recent study of Matthew's use of the Old Testament, cf. R. H. Gundry, *The Use of the Old Testament in St. Matthew's Gospel, with special reference to the Messianic hope* (1967). Gundry finds LXX, Aramaic and Hebrew elements, which he regards as evidence of a Palestinian origin.

24. [1] Another view of Mt. xvi. 17–19 is that of K. L. Carroll (*Nov. Test.*, 6, 1963, pp. 268–276), who argues that the statement amounts to a declaration of independence on the part of the Antiochene church, of which Peter was claimed to have been bishop. But this view rests on supposition, for it is not known where Peter was bishop. The words do not sound like an apologia for Peter.

27. [2] Gundry (*op. cit.*) disagrees with Stendahl's deductions from Matthew's use of the Old Testament. Similarly G. Strecker (*Der Weg der Gerechtigkeit,*[2] 1966, p. 50) criticizes Stendahl's School idea because the *Einführungsformel* is Matthew's work and focuses on his creativity. Cf. J. Rohde (*Rediscovering the Teaching of the Evangelists,* 1968, pp. 92 ff.) for a survey of Strecker's position.

28. P. Bonnard (*L'Évangile selon Saint Matthieu,* 1963) sees Matthew's purpose as an interpretation of Jesus for his own times. The aim is therefore neither biographical nor didactic. As far as eschatology is concerned, 'Matthew' gives an ethical and catechetical re-interpretation. Bonnard sees the Gospel as an aid to the Church of *c.* AD 80–90 to understand the significance of the sufferings of Christ. It should be noted that no Gospel writer could have undertaken his task without taking into account the sufferings of Christ. All the Evangelists devote more space to this than to any other theme.

The place of the virgin birth in the purpose of Matthew is discussed by H. A. Guy (*ET,* LXXIX, 1968, p. 183), who traces the idea to the Second Adam concept. Once the tradition was established Matthew found an Old Testament passage to support it. On the other hand M. Krämer (*Biblica,* 45, 1964, pp. 1–50) denies that Matthew's purpose was to defend the virgin birth. He sees it as aimed to establish the Messiahship of Jesus.

A recent theory concerning the occasion of Matthew's Gospel connects it up with Jewish persecution of the Church. D. A. R. Hare (*The Theme of Jewish Persecution of Christians in the Gospel according to St. Matthew,* 1967) maintains that hostility between Jews and Christians had ceased by the time that Matthew wrote his Gospel. He thinks those texts which speak of persecution go back to already fulfilled predictions. According to Hare, Matthew shows the synagogue to be alien and therefore reflects a time when Jews and Christians were no longer in debate. Matthew does not conceive of the Church as a continuation of Israel. This view is criticized by R. P. Martin (*ET,* LXXX, 1969, p. 136) on the strength of other New Testament evidence, for instance Matthew xxiii. 39; Romans ix–xi and Ephesians. Similarly R. H. Gundry (*JBL,* LXXXVII, 1968, pp. 346 f.) points out that the view is preferable that Matthew wrote to influence Jews away from the synagogue. Cf. also the further comments of R. P. Martin in *EQ,* XL(1968), pp. 178–180.

Contrary to Hare's view of the absence of continuity between the Church and Israel, cf. W. Trilling (*Das wahre Israel,* 1959, pp. 84 ff.), who sees the Messiahship of Jesus as the common factor between the two. On the other hand R. Hummel (*Die Auseinandersetzung zwischen Kirche und Judentum im Matthäusevangelium,* 1963) sees the Torah as the common factor. Hummel's thesis is that the Church had a valid *halakah* which conflicted with Pharisaism and led to a break with it. (For a concise summary of the views of both Trilling and Hummel, cf. J. Rohde, *op. cit.,* pp. 74 ff., 99 ff.) P. Gaechter (*ZkT,* 87, 1965, pp. 337–339) criticizes Hummel's view on the grounds that nothing in Matthew's Gospel implies the destruction of Jerusalem, to which Hummel attaches importance. Moreover Gaechter questions whether the Torah, in the sense in which Hummel takes it, was valid for Christians as late as Hummel supposes.

31. W. D. Davies (*The Setting of the Sermon on the Mount*, 1964) considers that this sermon is a Christian Mishnaic counterpart to the formulations at Jamnia by the Jewish elders. Cf. J. M. Ford's view (*Biblica*, 48, 1967, pp. 623–628) that the sermon was a defence of Hillelite teaching against Shammaite teaching.

31. [1] For a recent supporter of the view that Matthew's discourses correspond to the five books of the Pentateuch, cf. R. H. Fuller, *INT* (1966), p. 117.

34. [2] For a comment on the Papias tradition, cf. C. S. Petrie, *NTS*, 14 (1967), pp. 15–32. He argues that Papias must have meant that what Matthew wrote was the Gospel. He supports the view that Papias was personally acquainted with the apostle John.

41. [3] On the problem whether Matthew, an apostle, would have used Mark, a non-apostolic source, cf. R. H. Gundry (*op. cit.*, p. 184), who wonders whether Matthew wished to preserve the unity of the apostolic tradition and for this reason used Mark's Gospel. W. Marxsen (*INT*, Eng. Tr. 1968, p. 153) rejects the view that the author was an eyewitness on the dubious grounds that since he used sources he could have made no use of his eyewitness experience.

43. [3] P. Bonnard (*op. cit.*) considers that the author was a Christian Jew, possibly a converted rabbi. In an article in *Studia Evangelica*, II (1964), pp. 91–99, C. F. D. Moule suggests that the author was a γραμματεύς (cf. Mt. xiii. 52) in a secula- sense. But he considers him to have been a Greek who shared a common profesr sion with his apostolic source. E. F. Harrison (*INT*, 1964, p. 167) declines to come to a confident decision regarding authorship.

44. [2] A recent writer, R. Pesch (*ZNTW*, 59, 1968, pp. 40–56), discusses the Levi-Matthew problem from the point of view that the Marcan reference (Mk. ii. 13, 14) and the Matthaean references (Mt. ix. 9 and x. 3) are redactional. In this case the identification of Levi and Matthew is also seen to be redactional and therefore unreliable. This identification did not take place until after the Gospel was attributed to Matthew. But there is no sure evidence that the passages con- cerned are redactional.

CHAPTER THREE

MARK'S GOSPEL

Until the period of modern criticism this Gospel was the most neg-lected of all. Ancient commentaries on it are very scarce and it clearly made little appeal. It was entirely overshadowed by the more stately Matthew, and since it was commonly regarded as no more than an abstract of Matthew this is not surprising. This opinion, however, was probably not the earliest view, since tradition closely linked it with Peter's preaching. It has come into its own through the modern opinion that it is the keystone of the Synoptic problem. Reasons for this opinion will be examined later (pp. 133 ff.), but for the present all that is necessary is to recognize the importance of this Gospel in modern discussions.

I. CHARACTERISTICS

a. A Gospel of action

A glance at the contents of this Gospel at once shows that for the writer movement is more fascinating than discourse. Where the teaching of Jesus is given it is nearly always in the setting of some narrative. The vividness of the style gives the impression of a quickly moving drama with the cross as its climax.

Examples of this characteristic might be multiplied, but the following will be sufficient to illustrate it. Mark describes the breaking up of the roof of the house to let down the palsied man (Mk. ii. 4); the sleeping Jesus with His head on a pillow in the stern of the boat in a furious storm (iv. 37, 38); the arrangement of the crowds in groups like an orderly vegetable patch on the green grass (vi. 39); the process by which Jesus healed the deaf and dumb man, i.e. by putting fingers into his ears and touching his tongue (vii. 33); the gradual restoration of sight to the blind man (viii. 23 ff.); and Peter sitting with the servants warming himself by the fire in the high priest's palace (xiv. 54). Such details as these are most naturally explained as being derived from eye-witnesses, although, as will be seen later, contrary opinions have been maintained.

Mark, with the minimum of preliminaries, goes straight to the narration of the ministry of Jesus and describes various phases of that ministry, paying particular attention to the increasing opposition of the Pharisees. A pivotal point in the unfolding drama is the disciple's affirmation of faith in Jesus at Caesarea Philippi, from which point the story moves steadily towards the passion.[1] Commenting on Mark's outline, Vincent Taylor writes, 'That there are many gaps in this outline, and that the arrangement is often topical, cannot be denied: but the outline itself, and the looseness with which it is drawn, suggest that it reflects good tradition.'[2]

Mark's is an essentially factual account of the life of Jesus. It tells the story in 'a strangely objective fashion'.[3] There is almost no emotional content and much less of Jesus' teaching than in the other Synoptists. What teaching there is is mostly in isolated sayings, many associated with brief narratives. Yet in spite of the considerable number of these, Mark's main interest appears to be more in the activity than in the teaching of Jesus. There are consequently fewer theological implications arising from Mark than from other Gospels, although here again contrary opinions exist over Mark's theological interests.[4]

b. A Gospel for Gentiles

There is an absence of those traces of Jewish-Christian colouring which have been noted in Matthew's Gospel. Where Matthew records Jesus' warning to His disciples to pray that their flight may not be in winter or on the sabbath, Mark mentions only winter (Mk. xiii. 18). In the story of the Syro-Phoenician woman there is no saying about Jesus' mission to the lost sheep of the house of Israel (vii. 24 ff.). There are no statements about the abiding validity of the law after the manner of Matthew's jot and tittle saying (Mt. v. 18). Indeed, there are no fundamental discussions about the law as in Matthew. Furthermore, the disciples are not in Mark forbidden to go on a mission among the Samaritans or Gentiles, and in the eschatological discourse Jesus specifies that all people must hear the gospel before the end comes (xiii.

---

[1] Cf. T. W. Manson's *The Teaching of Jesus* (1931).   [2] *The Gospels*, p. 54.
[3] Cf. T. H. Robinson, *St. Mark's Life of Jesus* (1922), p. 8.
[4] Several recent writers have placed emphasis on Mark's theologizing purpose, notably T. A. Burkill in several articles and in his book, *Mysterious Revelation: An examination of the Philosophy of Mark's Gospel* (1963). Cf. also W. Marxsen's *Der Evangelist Markus*[2] (1959), and E. Schweizer's article in *Neotestamentica et Patristica*, pp. 35-46.*

10).[1] It is clear that Mark has Gentile readers in mind in writing his Gospel.[2]

c. Mark's candour

There is no attempt to cast a halo around the disciples. In fact, the writer does not hesitate to narrate their lack of understanding on many occasions (iv. 13, vi. 52, viii. 17, 21, ix. 10, 32). The attitude of Jesus' relatives is described with similar frankness; they considered Him to be mad (iii. 21). Expressions of amazement on the part of Jesus' hearers are also included (i. 27, x. 24, 32), while Jesus' inability to work mighty deeds at Nazareth is directly attributed to the unbelief of the people (vi. 5, 6).

Mark is equally unreserved in his description of the human reactions of Jesus. The emotions of compassion, severity, anger, sorrow, tenderness and love are all in turn attributed to Him (i. 41, 43, iii. 5, viii. 12, 33, x. 14, 16, 21). There is no doubt that this is the Gospel of Jesus Christ, the Son of man, as well as the Gospel of Jesus Christ the Son of God (i. 1).

d. Mark's portrait of Jesus

There has been much discussion over the extent to which Mark has overlaid his portrait of Jesus with theological interpretation, although no agreement has been reached among scholars generally. But this does not mean that no clear picture can be drawn. Our purpose here is not to discuss the interpretative element, nor to consider the origins of the material, both of which will be dealt with later. Our task is but to indicate the view of our Lord which Mark in its present form contains.

(i) *Son of God.* Since the Gospel describes Jesus by means of this title in its opening words,[3] it must be assumed that it has some defining influence over the subsequent narrative, especially as the title occurs four times elsewhere in this Gospel. It is evident that this view of Christ is not developed in a doctrinal sense, but that it is worked out in His

---

[1] But cf. G. D. Kilpatrick's discussion of this verse in *Studies in the Gospels* (ed. D. E. Nineham, 1955), pp. 145 ff.

[2] For further arguments in support of this conclusion, see pp. 59 ff.

[3] Although many MSS omit the phrase τοῦ θεοῦ the weightiest evidence would appear to support its inclusion (cf. V. Taylor, *The Gospel according to St. Mark*, 1953, pp. 120 122, 152; S. E. Johnson, *The Gospel according to St. Mark*, BC, 1960, p. 32).

divine activity. His appeal to the multitudes is powerful. He possesses power over all types of illness and casts out evil spirits with irresistible authority. He stills storms with a word and thus shows His power over nature. When He dies, a pagan Roman centurion admits, 'Truly, this man was God's son' (xv. 39). Those who approach the Gospel with the presupposition that miracles do not happen naturally give no weight to this particular aspect of Mark's portrait. They see in it no more than the accretions of later hero-worship. The modern tendency in this direction will become clearer when certain form-critical hypotheses are discussed, but if any significance at all is to be attached to the Marcan story it is impossible to deny that the portrait it contains is of a more than human Person, although partially concealed.[1]

(ii) *Son of man.* Jesus' use of this title is especially noticeable in Mark's account, although it is frequent in the other Synoptics also. Whatever the precise significance of the title, which has been widely debated,[2] it seems clear that it contains an oblique reference to the true humanity of Jesus. Something has already been said about Mark's descriptions of the human reactions of Jesus, but this concept of our Lord's humanity is brought out in other ways. For instance, His need of prayer (i. 35, vi. 31) and His resolute steadfastness on His last journey to Jerusalem (x. 32) are both specifically mentioned. The Gospel abounds with references to the intermingling of Jesus with the common people, which

---

[1] Taylor (*op. cit.*, p. 120) considers that this title represents the most fundamental element in Mark's Christology.

[2] There has been much discussion over this term. Cf. G. Dalman, *The Words of Jesus* (1902), pp. 235–267; G. S. Duncan, *Jesus, Son of Man* (1948); R. Bultmann, *The History of the Synoptic Tradition* (translated by J. Marsh, 1963); W. L. Knox, *Sources of the Synoptic Gospels*, II (1957), pp. 140 ff.; S. Mowinckel, *He that Cometh* (1956), pp. 346 ff.; O. Cullmann, *Christology of the New Testament*[2] (1963), pp. 137–192; T. W. Manson, *BJRL*, XXXII (1950), pp. 171–193; J. W. Bowman, *ET*, LIX (1947–48), pp. 283–288; M. Black, *ET*, LX (1948–49), pp. 11–15, 32–36. Cf. also E. Sjöberg, *Der verborgene Menschensohn in den Evangelien* (1955); A. J. B. Higgins, in *New Testament Essays, Studies in Memory of T. W. Manson* (1959), pp. 119–135; H. E. Tödt, *Der Menschensohn in der synoptischen Überlieferung* (1959); E. Schweizer's article in *JBL*, LXXIX (1960), pp. 119–129.*
Many scholars have contended that Jesus identified the Son of man with the suffering Servant (cf. W. Manson, *Jesus the Messiah*, 1943). But this viewpoint has recently been challenged unsuccessfully by J. Knox, *The Death of Christ: The Cross in New Testament History* (1959) and M. D. Hooker, *Jesus and the Servant* (1958). Cf. the criticisms of the latter book by J. Jeremias, *JTS*, n.s., XI (1960), pp. 140–144.

strengthens the impression that He is a true representative of the people, a true Man among men.

But the title 'Son of man' must have more significance than this. A discussion of this subject belongs more to the sphere of biblical theology than to introduction, but it is not unimportant for the study of the latter. The problem whether or not Jesus intended to identify Himself with the Messiah when using this title may, for instance, affect the discussion on Mark's purpose. It may also affect the estimate of the historicity of Mark. Both these problems will be mentioned later, but for our present discussion it will be sufficient to observe that Mark presents a portrait of Jesus in which many times He urges silence upon people who have observed His works. It is at least clear that Jesus did not have as His purpose any public proclamation of His Messiahship. The most characteristic picture of the Lord in this Gospel lies elsewhere.

(iii) *The Redeemer*. In one of Mark's Son of man passages, Jesus declares that His purpose was to be a ransom for many (x. 45), and whereas this theme does not specifically recur in the Gospel, the great emphasis on the passion narrative shows the importance attached to it by the author. Mark devotes a greater proportion of space to the passion narrative than any of the other Gospels. Such an outlook is in full accord with the emphasis on the cross in primitive Christianity, as the early preaching and theology conclusively show (e.g. 1 Cor. xv. 3 ff.; Phil. ii. 5–11; 1 Pet. ii. 21 f.). Mark describes a Christ who had come to suffer.

II. PURPOSE AND READERS

In his opening sentence Mark makes clear that his intention is to write a 'Gospel', an account of the good news about Jesus Christ, the Son of God. This at once distinguishes the book from a biography[1] and explains the large proportion of space devoted to the last three weeks of the life of Jesus. The cross and resurrection were the central features of the Christian gospel. All the events and even the teaching which led up to the cross were preparatory. In this, of course, Mark's record is not unique. The same is true of all the Gospels. The movement of the narrative is dominated by the passion story, but in Mark's Gospel the

[1] Cf. A. E. J. Rawlinson's comments on this, *The Gospel according to St. Mark*[7] (1949), pp. xviii ff. He says of Mark, 'He is writing for Christians, to whom his main story, with the necessary clues for the clear understanding of the narrative, may be presumed to be familiar; and he writes in a religious, and not in a biographical interest' (p. xix).

action is heightened by the relative absence of blocks of teaching material.

This essentially evangelistic purpose should caution us against expecting too rigid a chronological framework. The purpose is to account for the historical events of the life of Jesus, who had no need to be introduced.[1] For Mark, birth-narratives and accounts of Jesus' early history were not relevant to his purpose. His narrative confronts us at once with Jesus Christ, the Son of God, as a historic fact,[2] and he assumes that his readers will know at once to whom he is referring.

Other motives undoubtedly played their part in formulating the author's purpose. It is probable that a catechetical design was in mind, especially as some at least of the material seems to have been arranged as an aid to memory.[3] A liturgical motive is less likely, for this Gospel does not seem to have been particularly adaptable for such a purpose. Its arrangement is far less symmetrical than Matthew's Gospel and its relative neglect by early writers would hardly have happened had it been widely used as a part of Christian liturgy. There was naturally an interest among the early Christians in the work of Jesus and it was part of Mark's purpose to satisfy this natural urge. It is remarkable that neither Mark nor any of the Evangelists has preserved any information about the personal appearance of our Lord, but no-one could miss the striking impression of His personality which Mark produces through his narrative.[4] Yet it was not part of his purpose to produce this im-

---

[1] All attempts to write an adequate life of Jesus must inevitably fail because the data are insufficient. All that can be achieved is an approximation.

[2] Some scholars have been influenced by the fact that, in Mark's Gospel, Jesus so often enjoins upon His disciples secrecy regarding His messianic claims, and have deduced from this that the author's purpose was to declare that Jesus was the Messiah and to explain why this was not generally known in Jesus' lifetime (cf. K. and S. Lake, *INT*, 1938, pp. 37, 38). For comments on Wrede's more radical deductions from the same data, see p. 189.*

[3] E.g. the arrangement of material into topical groups (cf. Mk. iv for a collection of parables and Mk. vi for mission instructions). Note also in Mark the arrangement according to keywords (cf. Mk. ix. 13–37). If, of course, these features are regarded as pre-Marcan, they furnish no indication of the author's purpose.

For a study of the catechetical purpose of Mark, cf. G. Schille's article in *NTS*, 4 (1957), pp. 1–24. He approaches the subject from a form-critical point of view. Even those who do not share Schille's presuppositions may grant the probability of some catechetical motive.

[4] J. Weiss (*The History of Primitive Christianity*, 1937, p. 701) refers to the unique and enigmatical greatness of the personality of Jesus.

pression. The impression itself was inescapable. Mark was no more than a channel for the tradition.

Some mention must be made of the theories of the author's purpose held by those who concentrate on the religious needs which the Gospel was intended to meet. They are connected with the form-historical method which sees in Mark an editor arranging units of material for a religious purpose; but no single motive, either theological or bio-graphical, suffices to explain the editorial process. D. E. Nineham[1] suggests several concerns which are evident in Mark's writing. (1) To show that Jesus as Messiah was innocent of Jewish charges and that His sufferings were part of God's purpose. (2) To explain why Jesus did not publicly declare Himself to be Messiah. (3) To explain why Christians have to suffer, i.e. because Jesus had to suffer. (4) To present the works of Jesus as a triumph over the forces of evil. Not all will agree with Nineham on his interpretation of these motives, but most would agree that they played some part in the writer's purpose. It is important, however, to draw a distinction between motives of selection and motives of creation. If, for instance, it is supposed that the messianic claim of Jesus was an invention of the community, the view of Mark's purpose would inevitably be affected. His aim would be to support the community tradition, and in pursuance of this aim he would create narratives which urged secrecy concerning Jesus' messianic claims, because otherwise the recollection that Jesus made no such claim would be inexplicable.[2] Reasons will be given later for questioning the validity of such form-critical presuppositions, but this example is quoted to demonstrate how ideas about an author's purpose must be affected by one's previous historical assessment of the material.*

The original destination of the Gospel is impossible to decide with any certainty. Yet there are some indications which point to Gentile readers and some evidence which supports the idea that these earliest readers were located in Rome. Evidence for Gentile readers may be summarized as follows:

1. Mark explains Palestinian customs. The Pharisaic custom of hand-washing and the general traditions regarding purification are explained in vii. 3, 4 and this would not have been necessary for a Jewish audience.[3]

[1] St. Mark (Pel C, 1963), pp. 30 ff.   [2] Cf. p. 58 n.2.

[3] Cf. Vincent Taylor, The Gospel according to St. Mark (1953), pp. 32, 335. H. G. Wood (Jesus in the Twentieth Century, 1960, pp. 25 ff.) suggests that the slight emphasis on John the Baptist indicates Gentile readers.

2. Some Aramaic expressions, which are retained in the text, are interpreted into Greek and this seems to be evidence that Mark's readers would not otherwise have understood them.[1]

3. If the author belongs to the same group as his readers, the many Latinisms in Mark may point to a Gentile environment, although this is not certain since there is evidence also of some Semitisms. If, of course, the readers were in a different place from the author, this evidence would be invalid and the same applies to the next consideration.

4. It is claimed that the author was unacquainted with Palestine, since he mentions Dalmanutha (viii. 10), which is otherwise unknown.[2] But the argument is tenuous, since it is not altogether impossible that this place-name is genuine in spite of the fact that no other record of it has been preserved. Again, Mark's location of the country of the Gerasenes as extending to the Sea of Galilee (v. 1), the description of Bethsaida as a village (viii. 26), the confused references to the Herodian family (vi. 17), the assumption that the appearance of Jesus before the high priest was a 'trial', and the reference to a wife's power to divorce her husband, which was against the Jewish law (x. 12), have all been claimed to point to a non-Palestinian origin.[3] But these alleged Palestinian discrepancies are open to challenge. There may not be precise information about the Gerasene country but, unless there are data which conflict with Mark's rather vague description, the possibility of his knowledge of the area must be admitted. Vagueness of description does not necessarily imply non-acquaintance. Mark's description of Bethsaida may be claimed to be technically correct, for there were few 'cities', in the Greek sense, in that area.[4] There may be some confusion about Herodias, who according to Luke was Philip's wife, which seems to conflict with Josephus, unless there were two Philips, Philip the Tetrarch, husband of Salome, and Herod Philip, former husband of Herodias. But the confusion, if it exists, is not enough to prove Mark's lack of acquaintance with Palestinian affairs, for a glance at Josephus is enough to show the complexity of the intrigues and inter-marriage in

---

[1] Cf. S. Johnson (*The Gospel according to St. Mark, BC*, 1960, pp. 15, 16), who points out that Mark's transliterations into Greek are at best approximations. He notes that a translation is even given for Abba (xiv. 36), but it may have been a customary practice to cite both the transliterated Aramaic and Greek, since Paul does the same (Rom. viii. 15; Gal. iv. 6).

[2] Cf. *ibid.*, p. 16.   [3] Cf. *ibid.*, p. 15.

[4] Cf. A. N. Sherwin-White, *Roman Society and Roman Law in the New Testament* (1963), pp. 127 ff.

the Herod family, and it cannot be supposed that these were necessarily common knowledge to all Palestinians. The supposed vagueness of Mark about the trial scene is equally open to challenge, for it is maintained by A. N. Sherwin-White[1] that Mark's description may be substantially correct. As to the question of a wife's power to divorce her husband, it is certain that in Josephus' time it was regarded as an offence against the Jewish law, as he mentions in the case of both Salome and Herodias.[2] But the statement in x. 12 cannot be regarded as an example of Mark's ignorance of Palestinian procedure unless that statement is Mark's own invention. As a saying of Jesus it consists of a pronouncement regarding adultery, not on the custom of a wife's divorcing her husband.[3] Our Lord was not confining His teaching to Jewish custom. It will be seen therefore that these data provide no certain evidence for place of origin or for destination.

Nevertheless there is some external evidence for the Roman origin of the Gospel and this must be taken in conjunction with the internal evidence.

1. The tradition preserved by Papias[4] that Mark was Peter's interpreter, and the latter's traditional martyrdom in Rome, would support a Roman origin.

2. The anti-Marcionite Prologue[5] is more specific and adds that after Peter's death Mark wrote the Gospel in Italy.

3. Irenaeus[6] also implies that Mark wrote after the deaths of Peter and Paul in Rome. On the other hand Clement of Alexandria states that Mark wrote while Peter was still preaching the gospel at Rome. If the traditions regarding the date appear to conflict, those regarding the place of origin nevertheless coincide.

4. The reference to Mark in 1 Peter v. 13 shows Mark's connection with Rome, if 'Babylon' is to be understood in this metaphorical sense.[7]

5. The earliest testimony to the use of the Gospel comes from *1 Clement* and *The Shepherd* of Hermas, both of which probably

---

[1] *Op. cit.*, pp. 24–47.

[2] *Antiquities*, xv. 7. 10, xviii. 5. 4.

[3] Cf. J. Murray, *Divorce* (1953), pp. 53 f.

[4] As quoted in Eusebius, *HE*, iii. 39. 15.

[5] For the Latin text of the fragment and an English translation, cf. Taylor, *op. cit.*, p. 3.

[6] *Adv. Haer.* iii. 1. 2.

[7] Cf. the discussion on pp. 801 ff.

show acquaintance with it,[1] and both of which are associated with Rome.

6. The references to sufferings and persecutions in Mark (viii. 34–38, x. 38 f., xiii. 9–13) have been claimed as allusions to Nero's persecutions and therefore cited as evidence of the author's connection with the Roman church.[2] But this line of evidence is inconclusive, since the references to persecution are very general and could refer to any persecution.

There would seem to be considerable justification for the view that Mark is a Roman Gospel designed for a Roman audience. There is in fact only one divergent tradition, that reported by Chrysostom,[3] that the Gospel was composed in Egypt, but this is most improbable in the absence of any corroborating evidence and in view of the strength of the Roman tradition. Some have suggested Antioch,[4] but the arguments for this are not particularly strong. If the Roman tradition is wrong, the place of origin and the identity of the original recipients are anyone's guess.[5] An incidental support for the Roman location of both author and readers has been suggested in the occurrence of the many Latinisms,[6] as previously mentioned, which would at least be intelligible in a Roman environment,[7] although not much weight should be attached to this argument since Latinisms were used in various Greek-speaking parts of the Empire.[8] In view of the lack of any supported alternative, this theory must be considered to be the most probable. It should, of course, be noted that most of the evidence cited concerns the author rather than his readers, and the possibility must be allowed for that the

---

[1] Cf. Johnson, op. cit., p. 16, for the evidence, which is not strong.

[2] Cf. V. Taylor, op. cit., p. 32.   [3] Prooem in Matt. (cf. Taylor, op. cit., p. 32).

[4] Cf. J. V. Bartlet, St. Mark (CB, 1922), pp. 36 f.

[5] W. C. Allen (The Gospel according to St. Mark, 1915, p. 6) suggested that the Gospel was first produced in Aramaic in Jerusalem and was later translated into Greek at Antioch. A Jerusalem origin was earlier suggested by J. Wellhausen, Einleitung in die drei ersten Evangelien[2] (1911), p. 78. A recent German writer, W. Marxsen (op. cit., p. 41), has suggested Galilee.*

[6] Mark uses only Roman monetary terms and not Greek terms, according to O. Roller, Münzen, Geld und Vermögensverhältnisse in den Evangelien (1929).

[7] Cf. Michaelis, Einleitung, p. 55. It should also be noted that the mention of Rufus, both in Mk. xv. 21 and in Rom. xvi. 13, has been thought to point to a Roman destination, since if Rufus were in Rome, there would be some point in Mark's incidental mention of him.

[8] Cf. S. Johnson, op. cit., p. 16. Cadbury (The Making of Luke-Acts, pp. 88, 89) is inclined to think that the Latinisms are against, rather than for, a Roman origin.

author wrote from Rome for readers who were elsewhere, but this seems unlikely.

III. STRUCTURE

It has already been pointed out that Mark was not intending to write a consecutive biography of Jesus. A problem therefore arises concerning what principle he adopted in the structure of his Gospel. Certain form critics[1] (see pp. 188 ff.) have adopted a somewhat sceptical attitude towards this problem, maintaining that no framework is discernible. This is no doubt a logical outcome of the dissection of the Gospel into 'forms' of different kinds, provided it be conceded that the author of the whole was no more than an editor of a mass of disparate sections. But the Gospel does not read like a hotchpotch of unconnected *pericopae* (sections), for although the connecting links are often vague the over-all movement of events is clear enough.[2]

After an introduction, the Galilaean ministry is illustrated in i. 14–vi. 13, followed by an account of Jesus' work outside Galilee (vi. 14–viii. 26), the journey to Jerusalem (viii. 27–x. 52) and the final ministry with its climax in the passion and resurrection of Jesus (xi. 1–xvi). This may be called the Synoptic framework since its main pattern is followed by all the Synoptic Gospels. There seems no weighty reason to deny that this framework existed in the oral tradition. In fact, C. H. Dodd[3] has argued that Mark's framework conforms to the pattern found in Acts, particularly in x. 37 f. in the speech of Peter in Cornelius' house. From this he deduces that the framework formed part of the Christian *kerygma*. It should be noted that the skeleton framework envisaged is assumed to have been longer than the summary of Acts x. 37 f., but nevertheless no more than a skeleton. As a result the major-

---

[1] This trend was begun by K. L. Schmidt, *Der Rahmen der Geschichte Jesu* (1919). The form-critical theories of Dibelius and Bultmann result in the same scepticism (see pp. 190 ff.).

[2] It is interesting to note that F. C. Grant (*The Earliest Gospel*, 1943), although he gives credence to the general approach of form criticism nevertheless supports Dodd (see next note) on a generalized Marcan structure, which he thinks was impressed on the pre-Marcan material (cf. *op. cit.*, pp. 38 ff.). Yet Grant is not sure about the basis of Dodd's argument, especially that drawn from the Acts speeches, both because he thinks that Luke may have here been influenced by Mark and because he is uncertain about the validity of the Acts speeches.

[3] In an article in *ET*, XLIII (1932), pp. 396–400, reproduced in his *New Testament Studies* (1953), pp. 1–11.

ity of Mark's material is considered to have existed either in isolated or grouped units, which have then been fitted into the general framework. In support of his contention, Dodd further suggests that when the brief connecting summaries found in Mark are extracted and placed end to end they form a continuous narrative. If, then, a framework was part of the earliest pronouncements about Jesus, we may maintain that this framework was based on fact. We need not commit ourselves, however, to maintaining that Mark has necessarily preserved the correct order in every detail.[1]

But Dodd's arguments have been challenged by D. E. Nineham,[2] whose criticisms will be enumerated because they are representative of the form-critical school of thought which sees the Marcan material as disconnected units. (1) He complains that the proposed framework is so brief that it would have afforded little help for the fitting in of the material. (2) He suggests that few units of tradition contained hints of time or place to enable them to be fitted in with certainty. (3) Some groups, for instance the group dealing with the theme of the approaching passion, may represent our Lord's sayings on a number of occasions and have been collected into a topical group in the Gospel. (4) The comparison with the Acts speeches is invalid, since Luke would not have introduced a different summary from what he had already reproduced in his Gospel (this argument assumes that Luke composed the speeches himself). (5) There would appear to be no relevance for the life and worship of the Church in an outline of the ministry, since the Church was not interested in that kind of thing. (6) Against Dodd's argument that where topical connection is lacking in the juxtaposition of unit-traditions the connection must be historical, Nineham raises two objections: first, units may be placed in contexts to which they do not appear to belong because there was nowhere else to put them, or

---

[1] In his book on *The Origin of the Gospel of Mark* (1954), H. A. Guy devotes a chapter to what he calls 'The Disorder of Mark's Gospel'. While not all of his examples are convincing, his evidence is sufficient to show that Mark's primary concern was not 'order' (see p. 70 n.2 for a discussion of Papias' statement about Mark's order). Guy's own explanation of the structure of the Gospel is that it grew out of the repetition of the material by Christian preachers, thus accounting for several 'asides'. This suggestion of oratorical 'asides', however, would transfer some of the Lord's sayings to the preachers without sufficient warrant. Cf. the view of C. H. Turner that Mark's Gospel contains many explanatory parentheses (*JTS*, xxvi, 1925, pp. 145 ff.).

[2] Cf. his article in *Studies in the Gospels*, pp. 223–239.

else they were attached to some other unit in the tradition; and, secondly, the supposed lack of topical order may be due to a lack of understanding and would therefore be unreal.

These objections to the idea of a historical framework in the tradition vary in their validity, but are worthy of careful consideration. They will have most weight for those who accept the view that the tradition circulated in units. In fact, Nineham seems to begin with a predisposition against a skeleton outline, so that his criticisms are not unexpected. Nevertheless, when allowance is made for this, it would appear that the case against a skeleton outline is rather stronger than that for it. But is there not a third possibility? If the passion narrative was preserved in a definite historical sequence, would not the same principle have been used for other narratives? Nineham anticipates this argument, but dismisses it because of the difference of the passion material from the rest, because of its close similarities in all four Gospels, and because of the absence in it of unit-narratives similar to those which are found elsewhere. But the evidence shows the possibility of the preservation of a historical sequence and shows, moreover, the Church's interest in such a sequence. There are no grounds, therefore, for maintaining that interest was lacking merely because such a sequence held no importance for the life and worship of the Church. Would not the form of the passion narrative have led people to expect some sequence in the remainder of the material? And would not catechetical instruction have fostered such an expectation? Since one third of Mark comprises the passion and resurrection narrative, is it not reasonable to suppose that the earlier material existed in some equally connected form?[1] The sequence would have been of importance only in so far as it contributed to the main purpose, i.e. to explain the passion and resurrection narratives.[2] It is difficult to conceive that Mark did not purpose to place the recorded events in some kind of chronological

---

[1] W. L. Knox's theory of a number of tracts behind Mark's Gospel should be noted here. In what he calls the Twelve Source, he suggests something of the same kind of outline as in Acts x. 37 (cf. his *Sources of the Synoptic Gospels*, I, 1953, p. 28). In an article on the Marcan Framework, H. Sawyerr (*SJT*, 14, 1961, pp. 279–294) disagrees with both Dodd and Nineham, and suggests that the key to Mark's structure is to be found in his presentation of Christ's conflict with evil. He finds this as a unifying thread through the material.

[2] C. E. B. Cranfield (*The Gospel according to St. Mark*, CGT, n.s., 1959, p. 14) rightly points out that all the other sections of Mark are dominated by these narratives.

order (however loosely), for the Gospel is full of notes of time and place.[1]

Granted the broad outline of the Marcan narrative, what further indications are there to explain the arrangement of material? Leaving aside for the moment the origin of this material, which will be dealt with in the section on Mark's sources, we must ask whether it is possible to examine the principles on which Mark acted. Vincent Taylor[2] finds what he calls 'complexes' which Mark has used in his compilation. These are small groups of narratives or sayings which belong together and which Taylor thinks were received by Mark in these groupings. Mark's method, according to this theory, was to leave intact any such complexes which he took over, adding little of his own comments and stringing them together somewhat loosely with simple connecting links.[3] In other words Mark was really editing. The complexes which Taylor isolates are classified into three groups—those shaped by the writer but based on existing tradition, those based on personal testimony (probably Petrine) and those containing topical arrangements of sayings and pronouncement stories[4] (see p. 207 for an explanation of these). It may be granted that Mark's work was largely that of an arranger, although some difference of opinion may exist regarding the form of the material used.[5] Personal testimony may account for more than Taylor allows (see pp. 139 ff. on Mark's sources), but his idea of pre-Marcan complexes is not improbable.

Another explanation of Mark's structure is that of P. Carrington[6] who has suggested that the Gospel was designed for liturgical use. The

[1] Cf. Swete, *The Gospel according to St. Mark*[3] (1927), p. lviii, for a list of these notes.

[2] *The Gospel according to St. Mark* (1953), pp. 90–104.

[3] *Ibid.*, pp. 112, 113. In his little book in the popular World Christian Books series, E. Lohse takes it for granted that even passages that appear connected are no real unities, but are the author's attempt to create a unity (*Mark's Witness to Jesus Christ*, 1955, pp. 28, 29).

[4] *Op. cit.*, pp. 102–104.

[5] T. Nicklin (*Gospel Gleanings*, pp. 9–17) attributes the grouping of the material by similarity of subject-matter to Mark himself, and disputes that the present order is chronological. According to this view, Mark like Matthew is governed by topical considerations.

[6] *The Primitive Christian Calendar* (1952). Cf. also his article in *ET*, LXVIII (1956), pp. 100–103 and his more recent commentary *According to Mark* (1960). Cf. the strong criticism of Carrington's position by W. D. Davies in *The Background of the New Testament and its Eschatology* (1956), pp. 124–152.

basis of the arrangement was a synagogue lectionary taken over by the Christian Church. The sequence of narrative was therefore dominated by the sequence of festivals in the Jewish calendar. But in order to maintain his hypothesis Carrington, who argues for a triadic structure but admits its complicated pattern, is obliged to coax the material in a way which is not always the most natural. At the same time this theory is a serious attempt to suggest a method by which the oral teaching was transmitted in an orderly way in the Christian Church. On the other hand this theory would require even the general framework to be a production designed to meet liturgical requirements, a not very convincing proposition[1] (but cf. the similar theory for the Fourth Gospel, pp. 282, 311). If Carrington is right the Evangelist would have to be regarded as possessing superb literary skill.

A different approach to the Marcan structure is made by A. Farrer,[2] who thinks that Mark was dominated by Old Testament typology and numerical schemes. His method of argument is at times tortuous and will hardly appeal to those with a more matter-of-fact approach. This would not surprise Farrer, for he admits that his interpretation of Mark's structure is alien to our modern scientific criticism, but nevertheless maintains that it may be true. The problem with this kind of numerical theory is its highly subjective nature. What appears convincing to Farrer may well seem non-existent to others. Nevertheless, his interpretations may be a fitting reminder that the approach of the Gospel authors is not necessarily easily intelligible to modern scholars. The fact that numerology has no significance for us does not justify us

[1] Michaelis (*Einleitung*, p. 53) considers that this theory involves a misunderstanding and an anachronism. Cf. also E. Percy's criticisms, *Die Botschaft Jesu* (1953), pp. 227 f., cited by Michaelis. At best the amount of extant data on early Christian liturgies is very small and is quite inadequate to explain the origin of Mark with any certainty (cf. T. W. Manson's comments, *JTS*, n.s., IV, 1953, p. 78). It is at least possible that the Gospel framework influenced the form of the liturgies, not *vice versa*. V. Taylor has pointed out that the value of Mark's outline, if based on a lectionary, is likely to be depreciated (*The Life and Ministry of Jesus*, 1954, p. 32). Another comment worth noting is that of R. P. Casey who questioned whether a Gentile readership such as Mark appears to have had in mind could have been expected to have any interest in a Jewish lectionary (*Theology*, LV, 1952, pp. 362–370).*

[2] *A Study in St. Mark* (1951) and *St. Matthew and St. Mark* (1953). In the latter book he changes his position somewhat and shows how Matthew sometimes breaks the numerical symbolism of Mark. Cf. the critique of Farrer's position in Helen Gardner's *The Limits of Literary Criticism* (1956).

in assuming that it had no meaning for primitive Christianity, especially in view of its undoubted occurrence in such a book as Revelation with its undisputed frequent sevenfold structures. At the same time a numerical basis for Mark's outline may raise the problem of its historicity (see pp. 83 ff.), for typology tends to obscure rather than clarify history;[1] but Farrer regards Mark as a theological structure and a lessening of its historical purpose therefore does not concern him. He sees the book as a theological interpretation of the history of Jesus.

An interesting suggestion has recently been made by W. Marxsen[2] to the effect that Mark composed his Gospel backwards. The earliest part of the tradition to be written down was therefore the passion story, out of which the rest grew. This is really a modification of what has already been pointed out, that for Mark the passion and resurrection story dominates the whole. It may with good reason be claimed that he had the climax in mind before he began to write.[3]

Whatever literary technique Mark used in producing his Gospel,[4] he achieved his obvious intention of presenting under the guidance of the Spirit of God a picture of the Son of God in action, moving towards

---

[1] Cf. V. Taylor, op. cit., pp. 29, 30.

[2] Der Evangelist Markus[2] (1959), pp. 18ff. Marxsen follows Schmidt's idea that the Marcan introduction indicates Mark's method of procedure throughout the Gospel.

[3] S. Johnson (The Gospel according to St. Mark, BC, 1960, p. 28) draws attention to Mark's frequent custom of including in the earlier part of the Gospel brief anticipations of what was to be dealt with more fully later, e.g. the call of the first disciples and the subsequent call of the Twelve. But there is no reason to suppose that these anticipations were Mark's own idea. Rather they occurred in the natural course of events. The whole life of Jesus moved on to an inevitable climax and Mark has fully grasped this fact.

F. C. Grant (The Earliest Gospel, 1943, pp. 70 ff.) suggests that the Gospel took shape in the author's mind in the following order: passion narrative, controversies, Petrine element, Q passages, little apocalypse, current oral tradition. Some of these supposed 'sources' or blocks of material are questionable, but few would doubt the controlling part played by the passion narratives in the author's mind.

[4] A suggestion has been made that parts of Mark's Gospel were based on the Greek device of chiasmus (according to the pattern—a b b a), cf. H. G. Wood, Jesus in the Twentieth Century (1960), pp. 44 ff. This is a suggestion which may be worthy of further examination.

Another feature which is evident in Mark's Gospel is the occasional insertion of one narrative inside another where some internal connection exists (J. Schniewind, Das Evangelium nach Markus,[8] NTD, 1958, p. 4, points to four examples, iii. 21–35, v. 22–43, vi. 7–33, xi. 11–25).

the cross. This was for him, as for all the Evangelists, the central theme of the Gospel.

IV. AUTHORSHIP

So strong is the early Christian testimony that Mark was the author of this Gospel that we need do little more than mention this attestation. Papias, Irenaeus, probably the Muratorian Canon, Clement of Alexandria, Origen and Jerome all refer to Mark's authorship of the Gospel. Moreover, all of them connect Mark with Peter in the production of the Gospel. Some modern criticism has challenged both of these traditional assumptions. Marcan authorship has been side-tracked by refusing to identify the Mark of the tradition with the John Mark of Acts, the companion of the apostle Paul. The Petrine witness behind the Gospel has been challenged as a result of form-critical work.

Is the Mark of the Gospel tradition the Mark of Acts? The main objections which have been raised against this identification are the non-Palestinian background of Mark's Gospel, which is said to be out of keeping with a one-time resident in Jerusalem, and the absence of any specific identification in the tradition until the time of Jerome.[1] But it has already been pointed out that the seeming indications of a non-Palestinian background may stem from our lack of data and if so the argument falls to the ground, or at least is seen to be insecurely based, while the argument from tradition is based on silence. It seems to have been assumed that Mark was John Mark.

With regard to Mark's connection with the apostle Peter, the questionings have arisen from theories which maintain that much if not all

---

[1] F. C. Grant (*op. cit.*, pp. 52 ff.) considers that Marcus was far too common a name in Rome for us to be certain that Barnabas' nephew was meant. He therefore considers that tradition mixed up the identities and that some Roman Mark, who knew Peter, was the author. Grant lets his imagination loose and visualizes a clerk in a Roman business house producing the Gospel in the evenings, much of the material coming from Peter. It is true that neither the Gospel itself nor Papias tells us which Mark was the author, but it is difficult to believe that the Roman community would have published a Gospel attributed to an unknown Christian named Mark, if it were known already that Barnabas' nephew with the same name had been a companion of both Paul and Peter. Grant queries whether Papias knew Luke-Acts and there is, of course, no means of ascertaining this, but if he did he must surely have meant John Mark in his comment on Mark's Gospel. For another recent writer who disputes the identifying of the Mark of the tradition with John Mark, cf. D. E. Nineham, *Saint Mark*, pp. 39, 40.

of Mark is composed of sections which have received their form in the life of the community. Only the more radical form critics would, however, deny all Petrine influence.[1] Many would hold that Mark was in possession of certain Petrine traditions and to this extent became Peter's interpreter. This proposition will become clearer when Mark's sources are discussed (see pp. 139 ff.), but no theory which does not adequately explain the strong tradition regarding Petrine testimony behind Mark can claim much support.[2]

[1] Cf. R. H. Lightfoot, *History and Interpretation in the Gospels* (1935), pp. 25 ff.

[2] The earliest form of this tradition is that of Papias, preserved by Eusebius, *HE*, iii. 39. 15: 'Mark indeed, since he was the interpreter (ἑρμηνευτής) of Peter, wrote accurately, but not in order (οὐ μέντοι τάξει), the things either said or done by the Lord as much as he remembered. For he neither heard the Lord nor followed Him, but afterwards, as I have said, [heard and followed] Peter, who fitted his discourses to the needs [of his hearers] but not as if making a narrative of the Lord's sayings (κυριακῶν λογίων); consequently, Mark, writing some things just as he remembered, erred in nothing; for he was careful of one thing—not to omit anything of the things he had heard or to falsify anything in them' (Eng. Tr. cited from D. Theron, *Evidence of Tradition*, p. 67). From this it will be seen that Mark's Gospel was thought to be directly related to Peter's preaching, that it was a record from memory, accurate in detail though not in order, and that Mark himself was not a hearer or a disciple of the Lord. Streeter (*The Four Gospels*, pp. 19, 20) regarded this as an apology for Mark in comparison with John. Swete (*The Gospel according to St. Mark*,[3] 1927, pp. lx, lxi) claimed that Papias' οὐ μέντοι τάξει (not in order) in this context means that Mark does not give his Gospel the kind of order belonging to an artificial treatise, and therefore that it should not be inferred from Papias' phrase that Mark had no thought for sequence. Similarly F. H. Colson (*JTS*, xiv, 1913, pp. 62 ff.) maintained that the 'order' implied was that of the rhetorical schools, but it is by no means certain that Papias is using the word in such a technical sense. For a detailed discussion of Papias' statement, with full bibliography, cf. H. A. Rigg's article, *Nov. Test.*, 1 (1956), pp. 161–183. He suggests an emendation to τάχει which then would mean that Mark did not write hurriedly. There is much to be said for Zahn's argument that the lack of order in Mark was due to the fact that he had to rely upon a witness, Peter, who was more concerned to adapt his teaching to his hearers' need (as Papias says) than to arrange it chronologically (*INT*, 1909, ii, p. 439).

There has been some dispute whether Papias' ἑρμηνευτής is to be rendered 'interpreter' or 'translator'. There is something to be said for the latter, since Papias may have used the corresponding verb ἑρμηνεύω in his Matthew statement in the sense of 'translating' (see pp. 33 ff.). Yet the former is the more probable, since Peter would almost certainly have been acquainted with Greek and it is not easy to see why he should have needed a translator. But cf. H. E. W. Turner's comments, *ET*, lxxi (1960), pp. 260–263.

Other patristic evidence for a connection between Mark and Peter is found in

'John Mark' is mentioned three times in the New Testament (Acts
xii. 12, 25, xv. 37) and 'Mark' several times (Acts xv. 39; Col. iv. 10;
2 Tim. iv. 11; Phm. 24; 1 Pet. v. 13). In the Colossian reference he is
identified as the nephew of Barnabas, which clearly equates him with
the John Mark of Acts. It is very probable that his mother was a person
of some substance since, according to Acts xii, her house was regarded
as a *rendezvous* for many members of the primitive Church (cf. xii. 12).
Mark accompanied Paul and Barnabas on part of the first missionary
journey, although he drew against him Paul's anger when he forsook
the party before the work was done. In spite of the fact that dissension
arose between Paul and Barnabas over him, a reconciliation must have
been effected later, since he was with Paul when the Epistles to the
Colossians and Philemon were written (Col. iv. 10; Phm. 24).[1] At a
still later date he is found in company with the apostle Peter (1 Pet. v.
13) and this association with both Peter and Paul is a most significant
feature about him. Only those who are influenced by the Tübingen
antithesis between Peter and Paul will consider a close connection with
both apostles to be improbable. It may justifiably be claimed that all
we know of Mark from the New Testament would predispose us to

Justin, *Dialogue*, 106. 3; Tertullian, *Adv. Marcion*, iv. 5; Clement of Alexandria
(Eusebius, *HE*, vi. 14. 6 f.).

It has been suggested that Papias' words refer not to Mark's Gospel but to Q,
which is then regarded as Mark's collection of Peter's catechetical instructions
(cf. J. N. Sanders, *The Foundations of the Christian Faith*, 1950, p. 53, who consequently regarded Mark's Gospel as anonymous, and the posthumous essay of
R. G. Heard, ed. C. F. D. Moule and A. M. G. Stephenson, in *NTS*, 2, 1956,
pp. 114-118). But this is not the most natural interpretation of Papias' words, as is
demonstrated from the subsequent strong tradition that he meant the Gospel.
D. E. Nineham (*JTS*, n.s, IX, 1958, pp. 20 ff.) follows Dibelius in interposing the
procedure of community tradition between Peter and Mark, which virtually
nullifies Papias' statement altogether.*

[1] Some earlier German scholars maintained that the Gospel of Mark was a
Pauline Gospel, and from this position it was inferred that Pauline theology had
influenced Marcan historicity (e.g. Volkmar, Holtzmann and Harnack). But this
position has been strongly challenged. Cf. M. Werner, *Der Einfluss paulinischer
Theologie im Mk-Ev* (1923; Beiheft *ZNTW*, 1). Cf. also the chapter on this subject in F. C. Grant's *The Earliest Gospel*, pp. 188-206. Both these writers tend to
go to the other extreme by making almost an antithesis between Marcan and
Pauline theology. Grant concludes that behind Mark there is 'common Gentile
Christianity' rather than Paulinism. If Mark truly represents primitive tradition
some alignment with Pauline theology is to be expected, in so far as Paul himself
received the basic elements of primitive tradition, as 1 Cor. xv. 3 shows.

consider him to be a likely candidate as author of a Gospel. At any rate there is nothing which renders this impossible.[1]

V. DATE

This Gospel is the only one of the Synoptics whose date can be discussed without reference to the Synoptic problem; at least, if the current hypothesis of the priority of Mark be accepted. If on the other hand the traditional view that Mark is an abstract from Matthew had proved correct, the date of Mark would clearly have depended on the decision regarding Matthew's date. It is advisable, in any case, to deal first with all the available evidence, irrespective of Mark's connection with the other Gospels. The external evidence will be considered first.

1. It has already been noted that the early tradition is conflicting, one tradition maintaining that Mark wrote subsequent to the death of Peter and another holding that it was during Peter's lifetime that Mark's Gospel was produced (reported by Irenaeus[2] and Clement of Alexandria[3] respectively). Since both of these traditions were early and were almost contemporaneous, there must have been uncertainty about the origin of Mark, unless one of the witnesses cited can be otherwise understood. An attempt has been made, in fact, to argue that Irenaeus does not conflict with Clement, since he was not giving chronological information regarding Mark's origin but simply stating the continuity of Mark's writing with Peter's preaching.[4] Although this is a possible interpretation of Irenaeus' words, it is not the most obvious, and the majority of scholars agree that Irenaeus meant to imply that Mark wrote after Peter's death. But if this is Irenaeus' meaning it is still

---

[1] W. G. Kümmel (*INT*, 1965, p. 70) considers that Marcan authorship is thoroughly possible, in spite of some difficulties. Kümmel cites four authors who have raised objections: Heard, Grant, Johnson, Beach. But the vast majority consider the author to be John Mark.

[2] *Adv. Haer.* iii. 1. 2: 'And after the death of these (Peter and Paul) Mark the disciple and interpreter (ἑρμηνευτής) of Peter, also handed down to us in writing the things preached by Peter.'

[3] According to Eusebius, *HE*, vi. 14. 6 f.: 'When Peter had preached the word publicly in Rome . . . those who were present . . . besought Mark, since he had followed him (i.e. Peter) for a long time and remembered the things that had been spoken, to write out the things that had been said; and when he had done this, he gave the Gospel to those who asked him. When Peter learned of it later, he neither obstructed nor commended' (cf. D. Theron's translation, *Evidence of Tradition*, p. 45).

[4] So Dom J. Chapman, *JTS*, VI (1905), pp. 563 ff.; A. Harnack, *The Date of Acts and the Synoptic Gospels* (1911), pp. 130 f., and W. C. Allen, *The Gospel according to St. Mark* (1915), p. 2.

necessary to decide between his statement and that of Clement. Most scholars prefer Irenaeus to Clement, but it should be observed that Irenaeus had just previously stated that Matthew was produced while Peter and Paul were still preaching, i.e. before Mark. In this case current criticism accepts one line of testimony from Irenaeus and rejects the other. It is at least a possibility that such an assessment of the evidence may be wrong. It is questionable, therefore, whether a date for Mark before Peter's death can be ruled out on the strength of Irenaeus' testimony. It is not in fact impossible to regard both Clement and Irenaeus as correct, if Mark began his Gospel before and completed it after Peter's death;[1] a suggestion which merits more consideration than it generally receives. Another possibility is that Irenaeus was not referring to Peter's death at all, but to his departure from the place where Mark was (the word ἔξοδος could clearly bear this meaning).[2] In this case it would also be possible to accept the statements of both Irenaeus and Clement, and this solution seems the more preferable.

2. The key item in the internal evidence concerns the reference in Mark xiii. 14 to the 'abomination of desolation', which was to be set up where it ought not to be, apparently an allusion to the Jerusalem temple. It is generally assumed that the event so obscurely mentioned was the siege and fall of Jerusalem in AD 70 and that Mark must have written in the period before the siege, when the political atmosphere was so tense that he or the editor of his sources here was able to foresee that the temple was likely to be defiled.[3] Some have supposed that the primary reference is to Caligula's attempt to place his own statue in the temple in AD 40, an attempt which failed because of the intervening assassination of the emperor.[4] C. C. Torrey[5] even dated Mark just after this

[1] Cf. H. A. Rigg, op. cit., p. 180 n.1.

[2] This interpretation was preferred by T. W. Manson in an essay reproduced in Studies in the Gospels and Epistles (1962), pp. 38–40.
Manson argues that a similar meaning attaches to the use of the word in the anti-Marcionite Prologue to Mark's Gospel. Cf. also F. F. Bruce, The Spreading Flame (1958), p. 139 n.1.

[3] Cf. V. Taylor, The Gospel according to St. Mark, p. 511.

[4] S. G. F. Brandon ('The Date of the Markan Gospel', NTS, 7, 1961, p. 133) takes the view that Mk. xiii. 14–22 forms a pericope containing a tradition of the temple's coming desecration which is intelligible against the background of Caligula's action, but he does not regard this as furnishing any indication of the date of the Gospel as a whole.

[5] Cf. The Four Gospels, pp. 261 f.; and for a review of Torrey's arguments, cf. Bacon, The Gospel of Mark, pp. 55–63.

event, but his views have not gained much support. These two methods of using this evidence to point to the date of Mark both depend on the assumption that Mark xiii. 14, although put on the lips of Jesus, was nevertheless prophecy either after the event or else in near anticipation of it. But if it be granted that our Lord had power to predict, Mark xiii. 14 ceases to be a crux of the chronological problem. The phrase used to describe the coming event is of such vagueness that it is even more reasonable to assume that it belongs to a time well before the actual events.[1] Who would deny to Jesus the power to foresee that the seething political situation would come some day to a head,[2] with the result that some act of desecration in the temple would take place? Or, as a further possibility, if the words of Mark xiii. 14 are interpreted of the coming antichrist[3] their relevance to the date problem would be obscured.

3. Other features of the Gospel which are claimed to support a date in the decade AD 60–70 are the references to suffering and persecution (see p. 62), and the interest of the author in Gentile freedom.[4] But neither of these helps much in specifying the date, since they are both too general to tie down to any specific period. For instance, when reference is made in Mark xiii. 8 to earthquakes and famines as being the 'beginning' of sufferings, there is no reason to suppose that this must refer to the beginning of the siege. Moreover, xiii. 10, which asserts that the gospel must be preached to all nations, can hardly be cited as evidence of a date AD 60–70, any more than of an earlier date,[5] since the Gentile mission was implicit in our Lord's plans for His Church.

In spite of the confidence of the majority of scholars that Mark must be dated AD 65–70, it is by no means impossible to maintain an earlier

---

[1] Brandon (op. cit., pp. 133, 134) regards the 'abomination' as an allusion to Titus, the emperor's son and heir, and the obscurity of the reference is because it was essential for security in Rome, especially at the time of the Flavian triumph, i.e. after AD 70, when, he believes, the Gospel was written.

[2] Cf. the further comments on this under the section dealing with the date of Luke (pp. 113 ff.).

[3] Cf. Streeter, The Four Gospels, pp. 492, 493; E. Lohmeyer, Das Evangelium des Markus (1937), p. 276; A. H. McNeile, The Gospel according to St. Matthew (1915), p. 348.

[4] Cf. V. Taylor, op. cit., p. 31. Brandon (op. cit., p. 137) confidently interprets xiii. 9 as a reference to martyrdom and refers it to the Neronian persecutions. But this goes beyond the text.

[5] This is one of the evidences cited by Taylor, op. cit., ad loc.

date. In fact, Harnack[1] maintained a date before AD 60 and Allen[2] a date before AD 50. Harnack's arguments were based on an early date for Acts (i.e. AD 63) which involved a slightly earlier date for Luke, and in his view a still earlier date for Mark. Allen's theory was influenced by his contention that the original Marcan Gospel was written in Aramaic, a hypothesis which would clearly require an early date. Harnack's dating is usually rejected because his dating for Acts is not accepted (see pp. 340 ff.).[3]

Some mention must be made of theories requiring a date later than the siege of Jerusalem. One advocate of such a date was B. W. Bacon,[4] who suggested a date subsequent to AD 75—the year in which a Cynic philosopher was beheaded for denouncing Titus' immoral conduct with Bernice, sister of Agrippa II—because he saw a parallel here with the murder of John the Baptist. But such an argument is not convincing and few scholars have followed Bacon in this.

A more closely reasoned approach is that of Brandon,[5] who argues mainly from the historical situation in which the Gospel was written. He suggests that the production of such a Gospel as Mark's must have had an effective cause, and he finds this in the situation in Rome a year or so after the Flavian triumphal procession celebrating the capture of Jerusalem. His general idea is that the Roman Christians would need a Gospel which dissociated Jesus from the Jerusalem Jews, because of the odium which attached to the Jews at that time. Brandon works out his theory with great ingenuity, accounting, as he thinks, for the eschatological discourse in Mark xiii and sundry other incidental characteristics in Mark's Gospel, such as the Roman centurion's recognition of Jesus' claims (whereas His own Jewish followers failed to accept them), the account of the rending of the temple veil, the attitude of Jesus towards tribute money to Rome and the omission to call Judas 'the Zealot'. But most of Brandon's reconstruction is conjectural and the evidence he quotes could well support an earlier date. The period after

[1] *Op. cit.*, p. 126.

[2] *Op. cit.*, pp. 5 f. M. Meinertz (*op. cit.*, p. 187) suggests a date between AD 50 and 60.

[3] Cf. J. Schniewind (*Das Evangelium nach Markus, NTD*[8], 1958, p. 7) for a less precise dating. He is content to assign Mark to the first decades of the Christian Church.

[4] *Op. cit.*, pp. 73 f.

[5] *Op. cit., passim.* Cf. also *idem, The Fall of Jerusalem and the Christian Church*[2] (1957), pp. 185 ff.

AD 70 was not the first time that odium had been attached to Jews in Roman minds. The edict of Claudius expelling Jews from Rome must have precipitated a sufficiently critical situation to provide an urge to make clear the relation of Christianity to Judaism. Moreover, Brandon's reconstruction is based on the presupposition that the author, after the fall of Jerusalem, would find it difficult to believe that Jesus had not predicted the event and thus a Dominical prediction to this effect was included.[1]

VI. TEXTUAL PROBLEMS

a. The Marcan ending

The concluding chapter of the Gospel presents a problem. The overwhelming majority of manuscripts contain the full twenty verses, and the earliest Christian writings which show acquaintance with Mark assume their genuineness. And yet there is some important evidence which suggests that the original ended at xvi. 8.

1. The two Alexandrian Uncial MSS, Vaticanus and Sinaiticus, end with ἐφοβοῦντο γάρ (xvi. 8).
2. The Sinaitic Old Syriac similarly omits the ending (i.e. xvi. 9–20).
3. Most of the Armenian MSS end at xvi. 8.
4. Some MSS contain two endings, verses 9–20 and another shorter ending (L Ψ 579 Sahidic, Ethiopic, Harklean Syriac and the earliest Bohairic versions).
5. In MS 'k' of the Old Latin the shorter ending stands alone.
6. One MS, Codex W, contains a third ending which comprises verses 9–20, plus an additional interpolation after verse 14.
7. Eusebius of Caesarea cites an apologist who appealed to 'inaccurate copies' of Mark as evidence against the genuineness of xvi. 9–20.
8. A late Armenian MS (10th century) contains a note between Mark xvi. 8 and the ending, stating 'Of the presbyter Aristion', but this note is too late to be of much value, although Swete was inclined to attach some importance to it.[2]

The following deductions may be made from this evidence: (1) the longer ending must have been attached to the Gospel at a very early

[1] *NTS*, 7 (1961), p. 135.
[2] Cf. F. C. Conybeare's advocacy of this view, *Exp.*, IV, viii (1893), pp. 241 ff.

period in its history; (2) the shorter ending is not well attested and must have been added in an attempt to fill a gap, a testimony to the circulation of Gospels ending at xvi. 8; (3) indeed, the most satisfactory explanation of all the textual evidence is that the original ended at xvi. 8 and that the three endings were different editorial attempts to deal with verse 8.

If these deductions are correct the mass of MSS containing the longer ending must have been due to the acceptance of this ending as the most preferable. But internal evidence combines with textual evidence to raise suspicions regarding this ending. There is a difference in Greek style between xvi. 9–20 and the rest of the Gospel,[1] and while this would not of itself rule out common authorship it is difficult to believe in common authorship in face of the combination of stylistic difficulties with textual suspicions.[2] Moreover, xvi. 9 does not well follow on from xvi. 1–8 since Mary Magdalene is described as one 'from whom he had cast out seven demons' in spite of the fact that she had already been mentioned in the first part. Again verses 9–20 seem to be composed from material drawn from the other three Gospels.[3] In short this ending wears the appearance of compilation distinct from the rest of the Gospel.

The question next arises whether the present form of xvi. 8 (ἐφοβοῦντο γάρ) could conceivably have been Mark's intended ending. Many scholars have answered in the affirmative on the basis of biblical and extra-biblical parallels[4] and yet there is no other example of a book

---

[1] Cf. Swete, *The Gospel according to St. Mark*[3] (1927), p. cx.

[2] G. Salmon (*INT*[6], 1892, pp. 150, 151) accepted the Marcan authorship of xvi. 9–20 on the grounds that if these verses must be attributed to an early author, Mark was as good as any. Cf. also the vigorous defence of the verses by J. W. Burgon, *The Last Twelve Verses of the Gospel according to St. Mark vindicated against recent objectors and established* (1871), and F. H. A. Scrivener, *A Plain Introduction to the Criticism of the New Testament*[4] (ed. E. Miller, 1894), II, pp. 337–344.

[3] There are no resurrection appearances in Mk. xvi. 9–20, which are not related in the other Gospels.

[4] Cf. J. M. Creed, *JTS*, xxxi (1930), pp. 175–180; R. R. Otley, *JTS*, xxvii (1926), pp. 407–409; E. Lohmeyer, *Das Evangelium des Markus* (1937), pp. 356–360; R. H. Lightfoot, *The Gospel Message of St. Mark* (1950), pp. 80–97, 106–116. The latter cites some biblical parallels and one from Justin, but he admits that the parallels are not exact (*ibid.*, p. 86). Cf. *idem, Locality and Doctrine in the Gospels* (1938), pp. 1–48. Lightfoot, who regarded xvi. 1–8 as a separate narrative unit, found little difficulty in the proposed ending.

ending like this.[1] It would moreover be strange to find a Gospel, a book of good news, ending on a note of fear. To meet this objection some have understood ἐφοβοῦντο as 'reverential awe' rather than fearful apprehension.[2] On the whole it seems improbable that Mark's resurrection account would have lacked any personal appearance of the risen Lord (in verses 1–8 only the fact of His resurrection is mentioned) The author of verses 9–20 clearly recognized this. But if xvi. 8 is not likely to have been the intentional ending, could it have been accidental? It is possible to conjecture that the scroll was damaged, but if so it must have happened to the original copy, or else to a very early copy.[3] There is no means of ascertaining the correctness or otherwise of this conjecture. It has further been suggested that something happened to Mark at this point, so that he never completed the task, a suggestion which is not impossible, but which in the nature of the case cannot be confirmed.[4] Yet another idea is that Mark intended a continuation volume similar to Acts (see p. 371) and would not therefore have regarded xvi. 8 as the virtual end of his story.[5] It would seem that the only course open is to admit that we do not know the original ending.[6]

---

[1] W. L. Knox (*HTR*, 35, 1942, pp. 13–23) argued that if Mk. xvi. 8 was the original ending the *pericope* would lack a sufficient rounding off, which in his view would be not only unparalleled but incredible. Cf. also V. Taylor, *The Gospels*, pp. 49 f.

[2] Cf. N. B. Stonehouse, *The Witness of Matthew and Mark to Christ* (1944), pp. 86–118. Cf. also Lightfoot, *op. cit.* J. B. Tyson (*JBL*, LXXX, 1961, pp. 261–268), who maintains that Mark considered that the disciples had too narrow an idea of Messiah, thinks that Mk. xvi. 8 would be appropriate if Mark wished to draw attention to the disciples' failure.

[3] Cf. Streeter, *op. cit.*, p. 338. He thought that this view was credible, but he strongly criticized the view that Mark's ending was intentionally suppressed (*ibid.*, pp. 341 f.). F. C. Burkitt, *AJTh*, 15 (1911), maintained the accidental damage theory, but this is criticized by Lightfoot, *Locality and Doctrine*, pp. 8 ff. Cf. also C. C. McCown, *HTR*, 34 (1941), pp. 239 f.

[4] Cf. Rawlinson, *The Gospel according to St. Mark*[7] (1949), p. 270.

[5] Many scholars have maintained that such a continuation was actually written and was used by Luke for the first part of Acts (Blass, Torrey and others). Cf. W. L. Clark, *Theology*, XXIX (1934), pp. 106, 107.

[6] A. Farrer (*St. Matthew and St. Mark*, 1954, pp. 144–159) makes an attempt to suggest the form which Mark's original ending probably took. His suggestion is that after xvi. 8 there originally stood a one-sentence conclusion which Matthew later expanded. Farrer's reasoning is influenced by his symbolical interpretation of Mark's structure. In this book he takes a different view from that which he expressed in his earlier books, *The Glass of Vision* (1948), pp. 136–146 and *A*

It remains to discuss the alternative endings. The shorter may be dismissed as obviously of late origin, but the longer ending would appear to possess greater antiquity. There is attestation of xvi. 9–20 as early as the time of Irenaeus[1] who regarded the verses as part of Mark. They must have been of considerably earlier origin than this. It is not impossible, therefore, to regard them as an early independent summary used for catechetical purposes, composed from the other Gospels (especially from Luke and John).[2] The abruptness of Mark xvi. 8 as an ending caused this summary to be attached to the Gospel not later than the mid-second century. While it cannot be regarded as part of Mark's Gospel, it nevertheless represents an authentic account of resurrection appearances.

b. The beginning

Problems have also arisen about the beginning of the Gospel, but these problems are connected with interpretation rather than textual criticism, although they have led to suggestions of textual corruption. Mark i. 1 begins with a statement which comprises a subject without a predicate. This is followed by an Old Testament citation (verses 2 and 3) which refers to John the Baptist, who is not mentioned until verse 4, and this contains no grammatical connection with what precedes. Various explanations have been offered.

1. The existing beginning may be treated as non-original on the assumption that a lost ending might have been accompanied by a lost beginning.[3] This would be a plausible suggestion if the original were in codex form, for then the outer sheet containing the first two and last two pages may have been lost. But the evidence for such an early use of codices is lacking, although it cannot be said to be impossible. A difficulty would arise over the consistent textual tradition for the beginning which shows no signs, as the ending does, of ever having been in question. We should almost be driven to suppose that the mutilation

---

Study in St. Mark (1951), pp. 172–181, in which he maintained that Mark intended to end at xvi. 8. Cf. the useful survey of theories concerning the Marcan ending by F. F. Bruce, in EQ, XVII (1945), pp. 169 ff.*

[1] Adv. Haer. iii. 10. 6.

[2] Cf. C. E. B. Cranfield, St. Mark, p. 472; F. F. Bruce, op. cit., p. 180.

[3] Cf. F. Spitta, ZNTW, 5 (1904), pp. 305–308; T. W. Manson, Studies in the Gospels and Epistles (1962), pp. 30–33.

of the first part of the text must have happened to the original copy.[1] It would seem better to adopt one of the following alternative interpretations, rather than resort to such a conjecture.

2. Verse 1 may be treated as a title, in which case the Gospel begins with the Old Testament citation. This would be unusual but not impossible.[2]

3. Verses 2 and 3 may be regarded as a parenthesis and the statement in verse 1 connected with John's preaching in verse 4, a solution which makes good sense, although it is not so convincing from the point of view of the Greek.[3]

VII. LANGUAGE

The Greek of Mark's Gospel is not of a literary type. It is rather the everyday spoken language, similar to that used in the Egyptian papyrus correspondence. There is an absence of the carefully chosen periods of the classical models. Indeed, Mark's favourite construction seems to be parataxis, that is the joining of clauses with a simple conjunction ($\varkappa\alpha\acute{\iota}$). It should not be assumed, however, that Mark had no concern at all for grammatical niceties, for on occasions he shows a careful use of tenses.[4]

The Latinisms of Mark, which have already been mentioned (see p. 60), are a marked characteristic of his style. It is highly unlikely, however, that they point to a Latin original as has been suggested.[5]

It should be noted that Mark's narratives are particularly striking for vividness, for fullness of detail, for use of numbers and other similar characteristics.[6] Whether these features of the Greek style are considered to be due to Mark or to his sources will be affected by the decision arrived at in the discussions on Mark's sources (see pp. 139 ff.).

Another matter of great interest is the possibility of an Aramaic

---

[1] T. W. Manson (*op. cit.*, p. 32) maintains that the loss must have been sustained at an early date since neither Matthew nor Luke appears to have known any other form of the Marcan text.

[2] In Hort's, Souter's and Nestlé's texts a full stop is inserted after verse 1, which must then be regarded as an introductory title. Cf. the discussion by V. Taylor, *St. Mark*, p. 152.

[3] Cf. C. H. Turner, in *A New Commentary on Holy Scripture*, III (1928), p. 50. Reprinted separately, *The Gospel according to St. Mark*, p. 11.

[4] Cf. Swete, *The Gospel according to St. Mark*[3] (1927), pp. xlix f.

[5] Cf. P. L. Couchard, 'Was the Gospel of Mark written in Latin?' (an article in the *Crozer Quarterly*, January 1928, cited by V. Taylor, *St. Mark*, p. 54).

[6] For a concise discussion of Mark's syntax, cf. Taylor, *op. cit.*, pp. 45–54.

original or of Aramaic sources. Most scholars are agreed that Mark's Greek has Semitic flavouring, but the extent of it and the inferences to be drawn from it are the subject of wide divergences of opinion. The more thoroughgoing hypothesis that Mark's Greek is a direct translation from the Aramaic has not found complete acceptance in spite of having some able advocates.[1] The more generally held opinion is that Mark's Greek is 'translation Greek'[2] because he reproduces an Aramaic κατήχησις. According to M. Black,[3] Aramaic influence in the Greek, particularly of the sayings material, points to an Aramaic sayings collection which was used by Mark in the production of his Gospel. The problems involved in this discussion are highly technical, and only Aramaic experts can decide them.[4] But the importance of the discussion must not for that reason be minimized, for it has a bearing upon the historicity of the Gospel. According to Vincent Taylor,[5] Mark's sympathies are Gentile, but his tradition is thoroughly Jewish Christian and this would appear to be a fair summary of Mark's position.

VIII. LOCALITY, HISTORICITY AND CHRONOLOGY

The importance of locality in Mark has been particularly emphasized by E. Lohmeyer,[6] who produced a theory that Galilee not Jerusalem was the first centre of early Christianity and that Mark's Gospel is a representative of this fact. He maintained that the ministry of Jesus in Galilee was not a failure, as is sometimes supposed, but a success. In-

[1] Strongly maintained by Torrey, *The Four Gospels* (1933). See pp. 46 f. for the note and bibliography on the Aramaic theory for Matthew.

[2] J. H. Moulton and W. F. Howard, *A Grammar of New Testament Greek*, II (1929), p. 481. Howard is in agreement with M. J. Lagrange, whose opinion he quotes.

[3] *An Aramaic Approach to the Gospels and Acts*, pp. 205 ff.

[4] F. C. Grant (*The Earliest Gospel*, pp. 89–124) examines Torrey's theory and comes to the conclusion that Torrey overstates his case, since many of the passages to which he appeals are in no need of retranslation, or are no clearer after retranslation, or when retranslated lack intrinsic probability. He admits some Aramaic influence, but he attributes this to oral tradition and not to a written document.

[5] *St. Mark*, p. 65.

[6] *Galiläa und Jerusalem* (1936). Cf. also *idem, Das Evangelium des Markus*[12] (1953). The theory is discussed by R. H. Lightfoot, *Locality and Doctrine in the Gospels*, pp. 124 ff., and by F. C. Grant, *The Earliest Gospel* (1943), pp. 125–147. Cf. also L. E. Elliott-Binns, *Galilean Christianity* (1956); M. Karnetski, *ZNTW*, 52 (1961), pp. 238 ff.; M. Black, *The Scrolls and Christian Origins* (1961), pp. 81 ff. T. A. Burkill has a critique of this theory in his *Mysterious Revelation* (1963), pp. 252–257.

deed, Galilee was considered to be *terra Christiana* in the primitive Church, having become so as a direct result of the ministry of Jesus. According to this theory a theological and especially eschatological emphasis arose in Galilee, distinct from that in Jerusalem. In the former area the Son of man Christology was dominant, but in the latter the messianic Christology. In the resurrection narratives, Mark xvi. 7 states that the risen Christ would precede His disciples into Galilee,[1] while the Lucan appearances are all centred in Jerusalem. This is interpreted by Lohmeyer as showing that Mark and Luke represent two different types of primitive Christianity with the former showing the more primitive form and the latter showing a shift of major locality from Galilee to Jerusalem. Indeed Lohmeyer even suggested two distinct Christological creeds, 'Jesus is Lord' for Galilee and 'Jesus is Christ' for Jerusalem. He not only appealed to the Marcan setting of all the main action and teaching of Jesus, apart from the passion narrative, as being Galilee-centred, but also showed a lingering on in the subsequent Church of the Galilaean type of Christianity in the sects of the Ebionites and of the Nazarenes. He thinks that this theory accounts for the choice of James, who was a Galilaean, as leader of the Jerusalem church.

There are, however, several indications that this antithesis between Galilee and Jerusalem is not supported by the facts.

1. The ministry of Jesus began with His baptism by John in the vicinity of Jerusalem, not in Galilee.

2. Several instances of hostility to Jesus occurred in Galilee. The series of controversies in Mark ii. 1 ff. may be cited as illustrating this, for there is no mention of the opposition coming from Jerusalem. Moreover, it was the people of His own country whose unbelief caused Him to point out that a prophet is not without honour except in his own country (vi. 4).

3. There is some evidence in this Gospel that Jesus met with favour among certain groups in Jerusalem. The hierarchy were afraid to act openly for fear of the people (cf. xi. 18, xii. 12, xiv. 2).

4. In the post-resurrection narrative, the prediction of an appearance of the risen Lord in Galilee (xvi. 7) may seem to contrast with Luke's record of Jerusalem appearances only, but the differences are rather complementary than contradictory. Both Matthew and John record

---

[1] Cf. C. F. Evans' article on this statement, *JTS*, n.s., v (1954), pp. 3ff.

appearances in both Galilee and Jerusalem, but Mark records none. At most the evidence shows that Mark has no interest in Jerusalem appearances, whereas Luke has no interest in Galilaean appearances. But it does not necessarily follow that each represents a different type of Christianity. It would be a different matter if in the various narratives of the same event Galilee was substituted for Jerusalem or *vice versa*. The theory of divergent Christologies is, moreover, not borne out by the evidence in Acts.

It would seem that the evidence[1] is insufficient to establish such opposition between Galilee and Jerusalem as both Lohmeyer and Lightfoot claim.

The problems of historicity naturally arise for all the Gospels, but they are particularly relevant for Mark if the presupposition that Mark was the written basis of the other Gospels is correct (see pp. 133 ff.). It is for this reason that recent discussions on historicity have focused most attention on this Gospel. It has been the main field of research of form criticism, and when that method of approach to the Gospels is later explained (see pp. 188 ff.), it will become more apparent that the problem has really resolved itself into an alternative, either of accepting the Gospel narratives as presenting the historical Jesus, or of treating these narratives as the products of Christian faith and therefore historically questionable. The problem cannot here receive the full discussion that it requires, but some indication must be given of the main trends of the debate in order to assess its significance for a true approach to Mark's Gospel.

1. The main interest of Mark was not biographical but evangelistic as already mentioned (pp. 57 ff.). But this must not blind our eyes to the historical element within it. A Gospel, designed as it was to proclaim salvation to needy people, must be historically based to be valid and only the most sceptical would assume that a 'Gospel' in the true sense of the word could ever have arisen without direct relationship to the historical events recorded.

2. The view that Mark is not biographical led to the further assumption that he was not chronological either. This, of course, is supported by Papias' comment, if it is correct to understand it in this way. The various connecting links which appear to give some sequence to the narrative are consequently regarded as editorial additions with no historical value. The contents must rather be treated as a collection of

---

[1] For further considerations, see Burkill, *op. cit.*

isolated units. If this hypothesis is correct, historicity could not be determined by examining the collection as a whole. Each unit would require separate assessment. Such a procedure would shift the historical responsibility to a large extent from the Evangelist on to the communities in which the units circulated. But to offset this type of theory it is necessary to recall what has already been demonstrated, that Mark includes blocks of incidents which certainly give the impression of a historical framework.[1]

3. The close connection between the historical narrative and the primitive *kerygma* must influence any assessment of the former. As already noted in the discussion on Mark's structure,[2] the contention that the early preaching was not lacking in some kind of historical framework must be regarded as valid, in spite of criticisms of this view.[3] Since the most whole-hearted form critics usually admit that the passion narrative preserves some historical sequence, this is an admission that the primitive Church was not entirely bereft of historical interest. Before we may reject the historicity of Mark's framework it is necessary to show that the early Christians would have preferred a collection of *disjecta membra* to a formal outline. D. E. Nineham may be right in asserting that there is no convincing evidence that the early Church agreed on a formal outline,[4] but neither is there any convincing evidence that they did not. If we must resort to conjecture in order to decide the issue, that which assumes a chronological framework in the body of the Gospel similar to that in the passion narratives is more likely to be correct.

The main advocates of the theory that we find in Mark practically

---

[1] The incorporation into Mark of certain blocks of incidents would not in itself prove that the whole of the Marcan sequence is historical, but it should urge considerable caution before any assumption to the contrary is made. An example of the type of hypothesis which maintains Mark's use of some sources which contained sequences, without being committed to the historicity of the whole, is that of W. L. Knox, *Sources of the Synoptic Gospels: I St. Mark* (1953). The caution of P. Gardner-Smith might be noted here. He maintained that the Gospel as a whole tells a sober story and was thought worthy of credence by the first-century Church. The *onus probandi* must therefore rest on those regarding it 'as no more than a collection of scattered and unreliable traditions' (*The Christ of the Gospels*, 1938, p. 36).

[2] For details see pp. 63 ff.

[3] In addition to D. E. Nineham's article in *Studies in the Gospels*, pp. 223 ff., cf. also C. F. Evans, *JTS*, n.s., VII (1956), pp. 25–41.

[4] *Op. cit.*, p. 229.

no reliable data for the historical life of Jesus are Bultmann and his associates in Germany,[1] R. H. Lightfoot and his school[2] in Britain and J. M. Robinson[3] in America. The approach of Bultmann and Lightfoot has been the most radical. If all the materials are community products they are not evidence for the history of Jesus, but what T. W. Manson[4] called 'psychological case-material concerning the early Christians'. They inform us only about the early Christian beliefs and we are left almost wholly in the dark about the life of Jesus. As Lightfoot puts it, the Gospels 'yield us little more than a whisper of his voice'.[5] More will be said about the general weakness of form criticism when that subject is discussed later (see pp. 208 ff.), but it must be noted here that such scepticism regarding the historicity of Mark is unavoidable if the principle that it is a collection of community *pericopae* be accepted. Because of this there has been a recent movement to salvage something from the wreckage. J. M. Robinson calls for a new quest for the historical Jesus,[6] although firmly repudiating the older view that Mark in its entirety is to be the basis of a historical account of Jesus' life. There are signs of a shift of emphasis in the Bultmann school of thought in the approach of both E. Käsemann[7] and G. Bornkamm.[8] The former has focused attention on the need to maintain some kind of connection between the message of Jesus and the proclamation of the Church, while the latter has produced a book on the historical Jesus based on the assumption that some such connection exists. Whereas Bultmann had attached no importance to the events in the life of Jesus but only to His words, his associates have shown a marked deviation from his position. As a result even Bultmann[9] himself has somewhat modified his former position.

[1] *The History of the Synoptic Tradition* (Eng. Tr. J. Marsh, 1963); idem, *Theology of the New Testament* (Eng. Tr. K. Grobel, 1952). See the discussion on form criticism, pp. 188 ff.

[2] *History and Interpretation in the Gospels* (1934).

[3] *The Problem of History in Mark* (1957).

[4] *Studies in the Gospels and Epistles*, p. 8.   [5] *Op. cit.*, p. 225.

[6] *A New Quest of the Historical Jesus* (1959). In this book he adopts a more thoroughgoing and theologically orientated approach.

[7] Cf. his essay in *ZTK*, 51 (1954), pp. 125–153, on the problem of the historical Jesus. Cf. also the similar approach of E. Fuchs, *ZTK*, 53 (1956), pp. 210–229.

[8] *Jesus of Nazareth* (Eng. Tr. 1960, from the German *Jesus von Nazareth*, 1956).

[9] Cf. *ZTK*, 54 (1957), pp. 244–254. Cf. also J. M. Robinson's discussion of Bultmann's shift of position (*A New Quest of the Historical Jesus*, pp. 19 ff.).

The course of the present debate illustrates a characteristic of thoroughgoing German criticism which is much less evident in British[1] and American scholarship. It is the principle of disputing everything until a query rests over all the traditionally established facts and then painfully struggling to remove at least some of the question-marks. In the case of the Gospels the validity of this procedure may be strongly challenged. The whole approach of Bultmann and his school is essentially negative; a more positive approach to the problem of Marcan historicity is to make an examination of the book itself,[2] assuming that its basis is historical until it can be proved otherwise. The theory of community invention cannot be regarded as providing such proof until evidence can be produced that the Gospel material could not have come into being in any other way—but this is an incredible suggestion.

CONTENTS

[1] For a recent British attempt to deal with the problem under discussion with an acknowledged indebtedness to the German form-critical school of thought, cf. G. Hebert's *The Christ of Faith and the Jesus of History* (1962). Cf. also the study of H. Zahrnt, *The Historical Jesus* (Eng. Tr. 1963) for a similar approach.*

[2] This was well recognized by T. W. Manson, *Studies*, pp. 3 ff.

III. THE GALILAEAN PERIOD:
FURTHER JOURNEYS IN GALILEE (vi. 1–ix. 50)

Jesus is rejected at Nazareth (vi. 1–6). The sending out of the Twelve (vi. 7–13). Herod's verdict on Jesus (vi. 14–16). The execution of John the Baptist (vi. 17–29). The Twelve return and attempt to avoid the crowds (vi. 30–32). Feeding of the five thousand (vi. 33–44). The walking on the water (vi. 45–52). Multitudes healed at Gennesaret (vi. 53–56). Jesus' attitude towards the tradition (vii. 1–23). Miracles (vii. 24–viii. 10): healing of the Syro-Phoenician woman's daughter and the deaf mute; feeding of the four thousand. Further controversy with the Pharisees (viii. 11–21). A blind man healed at Bethsaida (viii. 22–26). At Caesarea Philippi (viii. 27–ix. 29): Peter's confession; the first prediction of the passion; conditions of discipleship; the transfiguration; the coming of Elijah; the healing of the epileptic boy. Concluding events in Galilee (ix. 30–50): the second prediction of the passion; the dispute over greatness; Jesus advises tolerance towards a strange exorcist; sayings about offences towards others; about salt.

IV. THE JUDAEAN PERIOD (x. 1–xiii. 37)

The journey to Jerusalem (x. 1–52): Jesus' teaching on divorce; His attitude to children; encounter with the rich young man; sayings about riches and rewards; third prediction of the passion; request of Zebedee's sons for places of honour; healing of Bartimaeus. Entry into Jerusalem (xi. 1–10). Return to Bethany, and the cursing of the fig-tree (xi. 11–14). The cleansing of the temple (xi. 15–19). The withered fig-tree explained (xi. 20–26). Further controversies (xi. 27–xii. 44). The eschatological discourse (xiii. 1–37).

V. THE PASSION AND RESURRECTION NARRATIVES
(xiv. 1–xvi. 20)

The Jews' conspiracy against Jesus (xiv. 1, 2). The anointing of Jesus at Bethany (xiv. 3–9). Judas' plan to betray Jesus (xiv. 10, 11). Preparation for the Passover (xiv. 12–16). Prediction of the betrayal (xiv. 17–21). The last supper (xiv. 22–25). Peter's denial predicted (xiv. 26–31). In Gethsemane (xiv. 32–42). The arrest, trial and crucifixion (xiv. 43–xv. 41). The burial (xv. 42–47). The resurrection, and appearances of the risen Christ (xvi. 1–20).

ADDITIONAL NOTES

54. [4] See the discussion on Theological Composition, pp. 214 ff.

56. [2] Two further books on the title 'Son of man' should be noted. A. J. B. Higgins (*Jesus and the Son of Man*, 1964) agrees with Bultmann in accepting only the 'glory' sayings as genuine. He also maintains with Bultmann that Jesus did not equate Himself with the Son of man. But cf. the critique of Higgins' book by W. C. Robinson (*JBL*, LXXXIV, 1965, pp. 460 f.), who points out the paradox which his view contains. The other book is M. D. Hooker, *The Son of Man in Mark* (1967). This author rejects the methodology of both Higgins and Tödt and concentrates on the evidence from Mark alone. A more radical treatment of the Son of man sayings is found in P. Vielhauer (*ZTK*, 60, 1963, pp. 133–177), who denies the genuineness of all the sayings.

58. [2] The idea of the Messianic Secret has been the subject of a recent study by G. M. de Tilesse (*Le Secret Messianique dans l'Évangile de Marc*, 1968), who regards the Secret as the work of Mark the redactor. He considers that the content of the Secret was that Jesus must suffer to achieve His mission. A similar view has been expressed by C. Mauer (*NTS*, 14, 1968, pp. 515–526).

59. In a recent book on this Gospel, R. A. Harrisville (*The Miracle of Mark: A Study in the Gospel*, 1967) sees it as a sermon on the death of Christ of a similar kind to that found in Philippians ii. 5–11. He finds a theological purpose behind Mark similar to that proposed by J. Schreiber (*Theologie des Vertrauens: Eine redaktionsgeschichte Untersuchung des Markusevangeliums*, 1967), who regards Mark not as a naïve *Sammler* (collector) but as an astute theologian (cf. J. Rohde, *Rediscovering the Teaching of the Evangelists*, 1968, pp. 149 ff., for a summary of his views). In this he follows the lead of Marxsen (see p. 214 for further discussion of *Redaktionsgeschichte*). On the contrary R. P. Meye (*Jesus and the Twelve: Discipleship and Revelation in Mark's Gospel*, 1968) discusses Mark's purpose without reference to *Redaktionsgeschichte*. He sees that purpose to be didactic to supply a basis for the Twelve tradition. But see R. A. Edward's criticisms (*JBL*, LXXXVIII, 1969, pp. 361 f.).

E. Schweizer (*NTS*, 10, 1964, pp. 421–432) treats Mark's purpose rather differently. He maintains that (i) Mark wants to show that God's revelation happened in the historical life and death of Jesus, (ii) we need the Spirit's help to see the 'dimension' in which the events happened, and (iii) the life and death of Jesus show what the *kerygma* really means. These points need setting against the historical scepticism of Bultmann. They are an attempt to see some relevance in the Jesus of history as set out by Mark. Schweizer points out that because man is more than a computer, it is illogical for Bultmann to be satisfied with a mere 'that' (see the discussion on Form Criticism, pp. 188 ff.). In a recent article on 'A Gospel in Search of a Life-Setting' (*ET*, LXXX, 1969, pp. 361–364), R. P. Martin argues for a purpose for Mark which sets it over against the kind of opposition which Paul encountered in his *kerygma* with its emphasis on Christ's sufferings. His opponents had displaced the theology of the cross, and Mark's Gospel would set before such readers 'the paradox of Jesus' earthly life in which suffering and vindication form a two-beat rhythm'. Martin cites the similar view of S. Schulz (*Studia Evangelica*, II, 1964, p. 144), who considers that Mark re-interpreted the Jesus-traditions by means of an epiphany-Christological pattern of humiliation and exaltation. He also refers to U. Luz (*ZNTW*, 56, 1965, pp. 9–30).

Marxsen's view that Mark's purpose was to urge Jewish Christians to flee from Judaea to Galilee to await the *parousia* (see mention of this on p. 15) is highly improbable, because if the *parousia* were considered to be so imminent, Mark would hardly have had time to compose a Gospel to prepare his readers for it. Marxsen's view is criticized by J. Rohde (*op. cit.*, pp. 113 ff.) and H.-D. Knigge (*Interpretation*, 12, 1968, pp. 53–70).

62. [5] R. H. Fuller (*INT*, 1966, p. 107) regards Antioch as the most likely place of origin for Mark.

67. [1] No more convincing is the theory of J. Bowman (*The Gospel of Mark. The New Christian Jewish Passover Haggada*, 1965), which sees Mark as belonging to a Jewish liturgical genre.

70 f. [2] K. Niederwimmer (*ZNTW*, 58, 1967, pp. 172–188), in his discussion of the authorship of Mark, considers the evidence from Papias to be an apologetic fiction. He finds the geographical references and Jewish references to be evidence that the author of the Gospel could not have been John Mark. This is a case where internal considerations affect the evaluation of external evidence. But it is not clear why Papias should have wanted to create the fiction, nor why his fiction was accepted as truth by later patristic writers. The internal inconsistencies which seem convincing to Niederwimmer were not so apparent to them, not even the supposed geographical inaccuracies. Cf. also W. Marxsen's opinion that the Papias statement is 'historically worthless' (*INT*, pp. 142 f.).

78 f. [6] For a recent discussion of the Marcan ending, cf. K. Aland's essay, 'Bemerkungen zum Schluss des Markusevangeliums' (*Neotestamentica et Semitica*, edited by E. E. Ellis and M. Wilcox, 1969, pp. 157–180).

86. [1] For a survey of recent discussion on the problem of the historical Jesus, cf. W. G. Kümmel, *TR*, 31 (1966), pp. 289–315.

CHAPTER FOUR

LUKE'S GOSPEL

There is something especially attractive about this Gospel. It is full of superb stories and leaves the reader with a deep impression of the personality and teaching of Jesus. It is perhaps for this reason that for many it is their favourite Gospel. It has many characteristic features which distinguish it from the other Gospels, as will become clear from the following survey.

I. CHARACTERISTICS

a. Luke's comprehensive range

This Gospel commences with the annunciations of John the Baptist and of Jesus and includes the fullest infancy narratives. It ends with a reference to the ascension, which is absent from both Matthew and Mark. Its record is longer than its Synoptic counterparts and is especially detailed in its account of the last journey to Jerusalem. It is in fact the longest book in the New Testament.

b. Luke's universalism

There are several occasions when Luke brings out the wider implications of the gospel of Christ. (1) The angel's good-will message is directed to all men (ii. 14); (2) Simeon foretells that Jesus is to be a Light for the Gentiles (ii. 32); (3) when John the Baptist is described in the words of Isaiah as a voice crying in the wilderness, Luke continues the quotation to include the words 'all flesh shall see the salvation of God' (Is. xl. 3–5, cited in Lk. iii. 4–6); (4) the Samaritans are placed on a level with the Jews (ix. 54, x. 33, xvii. 16); (5) Luke records two illustrations which Jesus used from the Old Testament, centring on non-Israelites, the widow of Zarephath and Naaman the Syrian (iv. 25–27); (6) a significant addition appears in Luke's account of the parable of the great supper as compared with Matthew's, for he states that the servants were sent into the hedges to constrain more people to come to fill the banqueting hall (Matthew has 'highways'); (7) as in Matthew the great commission is directed to all nations (xxiv. 47).

90

c. Luke's interest in people

There are various ways in which Luke's interest in people manifests itself.

(i) *Focus on individuals.* Most of the parables peculiar to Luke centre attention on people, whereas Matthew's focus upon the kingdom. His portraits are incomparable. Such people as the priest Zacharias, the cousins Elizabeth and Mary, the sisters Mary and Martha, the extortionate tax-collector Zacchaeus, the mournful Cleopas and his companion, and many others spring to life through his descriptive skill. There is no doubt that Jesus' estimate of the individual greatly impressed Luke, who is obviously attracted to people himself.

(ii) *Interest in social outcasts.* In a greater measure than the other Synoptists Luke portrays our Lord's deep concern for the socially ostracized. He mentions the immoral woman in vii. 36 ff., the transformation of Zacchaeus (xix. 8 ff.), the repentance of the robber (xxiii. 39 ff.), and records three parables illustrative of the same gracious attitude—the prodigal son, the two debtors and the publican. The attitude of Jesus towards the Samaritans, nationally ostracized by the Jews, has already been referred to under the last section.

(iii) *Portrayal of women.* Luke mentions thirteen women[1] not mentioned elsewhere in the Gospels, including two who formed the subject of parables. Of particular interest is the inclusion of the story of the widow of Nain, the immoral woman, the women who supported Jesus with their gifts and those who lamented over Him on His way to the cross. Women figure prominently in both the birth and resurrection narratives (cf. xxiii. 49 (at the cross), xxiii. 55–xxiv. 11 (at the tomb)). Luke, as a Gentile, would know much of the degradation of women and would be concerned to emphasize all he had heard of the attitude of the Lord towards them.

(iv) *Interest in children.* Luke alone refers to the childhood of John the Baptist and of Jesus. On three occasions he specially mentions 'only children' (vii. 12, viii. 42, ix. 38). In the account of the children being brought to Jesus, Luke uses the word for 'infants' (βρέφη; xviii. 15), whereas both Matthew and Mark have a different word, παιδία (children).

(v) *Social relationships.* Luke records three instances of the Lord dining with Pharisees (vii. 36–50, xi. 37–44, xiv. 1–4). He mentions Jesus' social

[1] Cf. V. Taylor, *The Gospels*, p. 70.

intercourse at Bethany (x. 38–42), at Zacchaeus' house (xix. 1–10) and at Emmaus (xxiv. 13–32). He includes many of Jesus' homely illustrations, for instance, the belated traveller requiring refreshment (xi. 5–8), the lost coin (xv. 8–10), the merry-making at the prodigal's return (xv. 22 ff.) and the innkeeper tending the wounded man (x. 35).

(vi) *Poverty and wealth.* Many of Luke's special parables relate to money matters, e.g. the two debtors, the rich fool, the tower builder, the lost coin, the unjust steward, the rich man and Lazarus and the pounds. Those who are 'poor' and 'humble' are often the objects of the Saviour's mercy (vi. 20, 30, xiv. 11 ff.). The Pharisees are called 'lovers of money' (see xvi. 14). John the Baptist, in Luke's account of his ministry, warns tax-collectors against extortion and soldiers against discontent with their pay (iii. 13 ff.). At Nazareth, Jesus proclaims good tidings to the 'poor' (iv. 17–21). In the Magnificat the hungry are filled and the rich are sent away empty (i. 53). In the Sermon on the Plain the first woe is directed against the rich, who are said to have received their consolation (vi. 24), and the first beatitude is addressed to the poor, without the qualification ' in spirit' as found in Matthew (cf. Lk. vi. 20; Mt. v. 3), although the same sense may be intended.

d. Special emphases

There is more recorded in Luke of Jesus' teaching on the following topics than in the other Gospels.

(i) *Prayer.* Luke records nine prayers of Jesus, of which all but two are contained in no other Gospel. These prayers are associated with important events—at the baptism (iii. 21), after a day of miracles (v. 15, 16), before choosing the disciples (vi. 12), before the first prediction of the passion (ix. 18–22), at the transfiguration (ix. 29), on the return of the seventy (x. 17–21), before teaching the disciples how to pray (xi. 1), in Gethsemane (xxii. 39–46), on the cross (xxiii. 34, 46). Once He withdraws into a desert (v. 16) and once He spends a whole night in prayer (vi. 12). Two of Luke's special parables deal with prayer—the friend at midnight (xi. 5 ff.) and the unrighteous judge (xviii. 1–8) (cf. also the Pharisee and the publican (xviii. 9–14)). Luke alone relates that Jesus prayed for Peter (xxii. 31, 32), that He exhorted the disciples to pray in Gethsemane (xxii. 40), that He prayed for His enemies (xxiii. 34) and for Himself (xxii. 41). Jesus' love of quiet places is seen in iv. 42 (a lonely place), ix. 10 (apart to Bethsaida) and xxi. 37 (He went out at night and lodged on Mount Olivet).

(ii) *The Holy Spirit.* At the temptation Jesus is described as 'full of the Holy Spirit' and is led by the Spirit into the wilderness (iv. 1). He begins His ministry in the power of the Spirit (iv. 14). He rejoices in the Spirit when offering the prayer, 'Father, I thank thee', leading to the declaration of filial consciousness (x. 21, 22). The disciples are bidden to wait for the enduement of 'power from on high' (xxiv. 49), a clear allusion to the descent of the Holy Spirit at Pentecost.

(iii) *Joyfulness.* Luke uses words expressing joy or rejoicing many times (e.g. i. 14, 44, 47, x. 21), in addition to words expressing leaping for joy (vi. 23), laughter (vi. 21) and merriment (xv. 23, 32). In three of Luke's parables there is an element of rejoicing when the lost is found (xv), and also in the story of Zacchaeus. The Gospel begins and ends with rejoicing (cf. i. 47, xxiv. 52, 53). In Luke alone are the canticles recorded, Magnificat (i. 46–55), Benedictus (i. 68–79), Gloria in Excelsis (ii. 14) and Nunc Dimittis (ii. 29–32).

II. PURPOSE AND READERS

Where an author specifically states his own intention, that must always be given more weight than any scholarly conjectures. Fortunately Luke obliges us in his preface. He tells us he purposes 'to write an orderly account',[1] and while he may not mean by this a narrative in strict chronological order in every detail he is entitled to be taken seriously about his orderly intention. Moreover, he makes clear that his purpose is to be carried out after great care in ascertaining the facts.[2]

[1] The word καθεξῆς means 'successively' and would seem here to mean chronological and historical order (cf. J. M. Creed, *The Gospel according to St. Luke*, 1930, p. xi). H. J. Cadbury (*The Making of Luke-Acts*[2], 1958, p. 345) draws a distinction between a 'concordance between the order of events and the order of their narration' (which he thinks the words need not here imply) and 'a narrative orderly and continuous in itself' (which he prefers here).

[2] Luke's preface is illuminating in regard to his own approach to his task. He claims to have made a comprehensive and accurate survey over a considerable period, which throws a good deal of light on his seriousness of purpose. Moreover, Luke admits that others had previously attempted the same task, but his words imply that he found them unsatisfactory (cf. N. B. Stonehouse, *The Witness of Luke to Christ*, 1951, pp. 24–45, for a careful discussion of Luke's preface. Cf. also Cadbury's commentary on this section in *The Beginnings of Christianity*, II, 1922, pp. 489–510).

In short, Luke meant to write a historical account.[1]

Yet in considering this Gospel as history, an important distinction must be made between this writing and history pure and simple, either ancient or modern.[2] Because the history concerned a unique Person it would not be surprising to find no precise parallels to the form of the book. The Gospel as a literary form is in fact as unique as the Person around whom it grew. As a means of explaining the basic historic events on which the Christian faith is fashioned, it is ideal. In confirmation of this it should be noted that Luke, like his fellow Evangelists, placed the major emphasis on the passion and resurrection narratives. These were the main subjects of early Christian preaching, of which Theophilus had apparently already been informed (i. 4). But Luke aimed to describe the happenings which led up to the passion.

There have been recent attempts to claim that Luke's purpose was dominated by a theological motive.[3] In this kind of theory Luke is said to have had a different theological approach from his sources, and his own modifications are then regarded as evidence of his theology. No-one would deny that Luke's purpose is theological. But this is quite different from saying that the history has been conformed to the theology, an approach which had its origins in the Tübingen school of thought.[4] It is truer to say that Luke brings out the theological significance of the history. An interesting example of this is the prominence he gives to Jerusalem in his narrative,[5] although he does not include any

[1] H. Sahlin (*Der Messias und das Gottesvolk*, 1945, Acta Uppsala xii), who regards Luke-Acts as a whole, maintains that the author's intention was to produce a defence brief at Paul's trial and he supposed that the 'others' who had written were witnesses and minutes secretaries at the hearing of the case. But this view is criticized by Michaelis, *Einleitung*, p. 15.

[2] Any appeal to a historian such as Thucydides or any modern historian can have little relevance to Luke's work since the form of the latter's writing differs so fundamentally from theirs. See the comments on this in the section on Acts, pp. 359 ff.

[3] The most recent is H. Conzelmann, *The Theology of St. Luke* (1960), an Eng. Tr. of his *Die Mitte der Zeit*[2] (1960). Cf. E. Lohse, *Ev Th*, xiv (1954), pp. 256–275.

[4] The view of this school of thought was that the purpose of Luke's writings (particularly Acts) was to reconcile antagonistic Petrine and Pauline groups. The historical account was, therefore, considered to be dominated by this 'tendency'.

[5] Conzelmann (*op. cit.*, pp. 132 ff.) makes a special point of this when discussing Luke's eschatology. Cf. Michaelis's criticisms, *Einleitung*, pp. 67–69. A. Hastings, in his book *Prophet and Witness in Jerusalem. A Study of the Teaching of St. Luke* (1958), devotes a good deal of attention to the significance of Jerusalem. For a similar phenomenon in Acts, cf. J. Cambier, *NTS*, 8 (1962), pp. 249–257.

of the special Johannine Jerusalem material. Rather he depicts the dramatic progress of Jesus from Galilee to Jerusalem. The whole movement of events had meaning for him. Jesus was moving on towards Jerusalem in order to die. That was Luke's Gospel and that was his theology. It was also the centre of the theology of the whole primitive Church. And yet there is a sense in which Luke shows his own particular theological interests, in his choice and arrangement of his material. This is revealed not only in geographical details, but also in historical details (e.g. in the greater emphasis on the universal approach of Jesus).

It should be remembered in discussions of Luke's purpose that it is impossible to treat this Gospel apart from its sequel, the book of Acts. It may reasonably be supposed that any motives which become clearly apparent in Acts had their origin in the design of the Gospel, and if this supposition is correct it is at least possible that the double work had an apologetic purpose. Hence if part of Luke's purpose in Acts was to show that Christianity was not yet subversive (see pp. 350 ff.) and that as successor to the synagogue it was entitled to the same State protection,[1] it must be assumed that the account of our Lord was written with a similar motive. But not all are agreed about the apologetic purpose of Acts, and it is even less evident in the Gospel.[2] It may at least be said that the Gospel was intended to describe the beginnings of a process which reached beyond Jerusalem to the heart of imperial Rome itself. Yet there is a sense in which the Gospel is complete in itself,[3] for it provides the substance of the preaching which forms the basis of the Acts narrative.

Luke's preface also helps us in determining the readers. There is a dedication to one man, Theophilus, who is described as 'most excellent' (κράτιστε), an expression which looks like an indication of social rank.[4] Some have supposed that Theophilus is a coined name to represent any 'lover of God', but in view of the formal character of the preface and the conventional practice of ascribing treatises to notable people, it is

[1] Cf. the views of S. M. Gilmour, *The Gospel according to St. Luke* (IB, 1952), pp. 5-7.
[2] Appeal may be made to Lk. xxiii. 4, 14, 22, where three times Pilate pronounces Jesus not guilty.
[3] Cf. Creed, *op. cit.*, p. xi.
[4] That this was a title of honour and respect cannot be doubted. W. Manson (*The Gospel of Luke*, MC, 1930, pp. 2, 3) considered that the term pointed to the holder of some procuratorial or similar office within the empire.

much more natural to regard Theophilus as a real person.[1] He was clearly a Gentile and appears already to have had some catechetical instruction, if it is correct to interpret i. 4 in this manner.[2] This suggests that the Gospel was primarily designed for all people in a similar category.

There is abundant evidence to suggest a Gentile destination, and this has already been indicated in discussing one of Luke's main characteristics, his universalism.[3] The Gospel may therefore be said to be designed for all who in the non-Christian world were not averse to Christianity and were genuinely interested in having a historical account of its origins.

Are there any indications which enable us to define more precisely the first group of readers? The anti-Marcionite Prologue states that Luke was in Achaia when he wrote his Gospel, a view which Jerome[4] also expresses in one of his books, although in another he mentions Rome as the place of origin of Acts. Since the climax of Acts is seen in the arrival of Paul at Rome, the joint work (Luke-Acts) would have been very suitable for a Roman destination. In this case it may be conjectured that Theophilus was a Roman of noble birth.

III. STRUCTURE

Since Luke states so explicitly that he purposed to arrange his narrative in an orderly account, it is of great interest to examine his structure and

---

[1] Cf. Creed, *op. cit.*, p. 5.

[2] There is difference of opinion about the interpretation of κατηχήθης. It can certainly mean definite instruction in the Christian faith (cf. Creed, *op. cit.*, *ad loc.*), in which case Theophilus must have been a Christian. If, on the other hand, the word refers merely to information he has received, Theophilus may have been still an outsider, but interested in Christianity (so Manson, *op. cit.*, p. 3). Cadbury (*The Beginnings of Christianity*, II, pp. 508 ff.) maintained that the word could include hostile reports and that the book was written to counteract these (against this idea, cf. F. H. Colson, *JTS*, XXIV, 1923, p. 303). W. E. Bundy (*Jesus and the First Three Gospels*, 1955, p. 4) thinks that Luke's use of this title combined with his formality suggests that Theophilus was not a fellow-Christian.

[3] See p. 90. K. H. Rengstorf (*Das Evangelium nach Lukas*[8], 1958, p. 6) points out that in Luke there are few of our Lord's criticisms of the scribes and Pharisees, which would indicate a circle of readers not interested in the questions of first-century Judaism.

[4] In his commentary on Matthew he mentions parts of Achaia and Boeotia, but in *De Viris Illustribus* he maintained a Roman location. For Rome, cf. Michaelis, *Einleitung*, p. 78. Cf. also E. J. Goodspeed, *INT* (1937), p. 208.

to compare it with the other Synoptics. He uses the same general framework as Matthew and Mark, although he has many characteristic variations in his detailed structure.[1] His infancy narratives are much fuller than Matthew's and are of particular significance in the emphasis placed upon the birth of John the Baptist, to which Luke clearly attached considerable importance. This feature provides one of the main keys to Luke's structure. To him all the events are a part of a divine revelation, in a rather different sense from Matthew's viewpoint. He does not cite so specifically passages which show the fulfilment of prophecy. But to him the events themselves are significant, and John the Baptist figures prominently in the infancy stories because the public ministry of Jesus is so closely linked with John. The relevance of the birth of John for Luke lies in its miraculous character. It demonstrated that divine intervention which was operative in the history of Jesus. It is for the same reason that Luke, in giving his sixfold dating in iii. 1, connects it up with John's ministry and not with that of Jesus.

The Galilaean period of the ministry in Luke (iii. 1–ix. 50) is parallel in structure with Mark's and Matthew's, but the later period is differently arranged. Luke has what is commonly known as a travel narrative from ix. 51–xviii. 14, depicting the movement of Jesus from Galilee to Jerusalem. This is Luke's special modification of the Synoptic structure and will call for consideration later when the Synoptic problem is discussed. In this portion Luke not only includes much material which is peculiar to his Gospel, but arranges his material in such a way as to focus attention on Jerusalem as a preparation for the passion narratives. The Judaean period and passion narratives follow a pattern similar to that of the narratives in the other Synoptics, although again with some variations of detail.[2] The resurrection narratives, however, are mainly peculiar to Luke and here again one of the most striking features about

[1] A special feature of Luke's Gospel is the author's fondness for pairs, to which R. Morgenthaler (*Die lukanische Geschichtsschreibung als Zeugnis*, 1949) attaches considerable significance.

[2] H. Schürmann has made a very full study of the subject-matter of Lk. xxii. 7–38 (*Quellenkritische Untersuchung des lukanischen Abendmahlsberichtes*, 1953–57), in which he maintains that parts of this passage are Luke's editing of a non-Marcan source. Cf. V. Taylor's useful summary of Schürmann's views, *ET*, LXXIV (1962), pp. 77–81. Cf. J. Jeremias (*NTS*, 4, 1958, pp. 115–119), who also maintains that in the block Lk. xxii. 14 ff., Luke does not depend on Mark. For the view that Luke possibly did use Mk. xiv. 22–25, in disagreement with Jeremias, cf. H. F. D. Sparks, *NTS*, 3 (1957), pp. 219–223.

them is that the appearances of the risen Lord were all set in or near Jerusalem with no reference to any Galilaean appearances as in the other Gospels.[1]

To some scholars Luke's treatment of his material is evidence of his deliberate editorial work influenced by his theological approach.[2] The narrative ix. 51–xviii. 14 does not require a journey for its structure and this has led some to conclude that it must be historically secondary and therefore characteristically Lucan. But the journey motive may never really have been in Luke's mind. It looks as if he had collected much material which he knew belonged to the closing period of our Lord's life and he naturally fitted it in between the Galilaean and Judaean ministries. He gives little indication where the events happened, which is in striking contrast to the Acts, where place-names often occur without any events attached. It would be better to call this section simply 'From Galilee to Judaea' without using the word 'journey' which tends to suggest a detailed route.[3]

IV. AUTHORSHIP OF THE GOSPEL (AND ACTS)

a. The preface

The Gospel itself does not tell us anything specific about the identity of the author, but it does tell us about his methods. The preface to the Gospel accords with the literary customs of the period and it is the only example of a formal introduction in the New Testament. From it we

---

[1] Cf. A. R. C. Leaney (*NTS*, 2, 1955, pp. 110–114), who suggests that the narratives of Lk. xxiv and Jn. xx were both drawn from a common tradition. It is significant that John adds an 'appendix', including a Galilaean appearance. Cf. B. Lindars, *NTS*, 7 (1961), pp. 142–147, for comments on Leaney's view.

[2] This is particularly true of H. Conzelmann, *The Theology of St. Luke* (1960), p. 62. K. L. Schmidt (*Der Rahmen der Geschichte Jesu*, 1919, p. 269) did not consider that the section constituted the report of a journey, since Jesus never really makes any progress on His way to Jerusalem. Bultmann (*The History of the Synoptic Tradition*, pp. 25, 26) regards the journey through Samaria as Luke's own construction.*

[3] See further discussion of this section on pp. 169 f. A somewhat different approach to Luke's structure is maintained by those who consider that Luke prepared an earlier draft of his Gospel (Proto-Luke) which lacked all material paralleled in Mark. This latter material was inserted later. To discover Luke's structure, the focus must be fixed on Proto-Luke rather than Luke as a whole. But even if the Proto-Luke theory could be sustained (see pp. 175 ff. for a full discussion of the theory), it tells us more about Luke's editorial processes than about the structure of the Gospel.*

may make the following deductions. The author was clearly not an eyewitness, for he states that he had received information from others who were 'eyewitnesses and ministers of the word'. Moreover, he implies that he had access to earlier narratives which others had compiled, but which he seems to regard as unsatisfactory for his purpose. In addition he has himself made a thorough investigation of the facts as a result of which he claims to be able to write an orderly account. From these data, it may be inferred that the author was a cultured man in view of the style of the preface. He was also a careful writer who did not belong to the immediate circle of our Lord's followers.

For the identity of the author, reference will need to be made first to the external evidence, followed by an investigation of internal data. For this purpose it will be necessary to consider with the Gospel the authorship of the book of Acts also.

b. The testimony of tradition

The earliest witnesses to the authorship of the Gospel belong to the latter part of the second century AD, but the subsequent testimony is so fully in agreement with this that it may fairly be surmised that this tradition had already had a considerable history before its earliest witnesses. The Muratorian Canon, the anti-Marcionite Prologue to Luke, Irenaeus, Clement of Alexandria, Origen and Tertullian all specifically state that Luke was the author, not only of the Gospel, but also of the Acts of the Apostles. Moreover, at no time were any doubts raised regarding this attribution to Luke, and certainly no alternatives were mooted. The tradition could hardly be stronger, but some scholars attach little importance to it.

It is maintained by H. J. Cadbury,[1] for instance, that the earliest testimony, that of the Muratorian Canon, contains nothing that could not be inferred from the text of the New Testament itself and he, therefore, deduces that Lucan authorship was in all probability a guess based on the 'we-passages' of Acts (see pp. 367 ff.). He supports this supposition by an appeal to the uncritical approach of this Muratorian Fragment towards authorship generally, for instance, in the case of the Gospel of John (see discussion on p. 260). He is consequently not disposed to place much weight upon the tradition. It must, of course, be at once admitted that there is no certain evidence as to whether or

---

[1] Cf. his article on 'The Tradition' in Foakes Jackson-Lake's *The Beginnings of Christianity*, II, pp. 209–264. On the Muratorian Canon see *ibid.*, pp. 255 ff.

not the whole body of external testimony was based on solid know-ledge or on pure conjecture, but there is the strongest possible reason for favouring the former. It will not be denied that an initial conjecture may be repeated by successive witnesses until it becomes mistaken for fact, as the history of modern criticism abundantly illustrates, but Cad-bury's suggestion involves a remarkable and highly improbable pro-cess. Where various possibilities existed, what governed the choice of Luke? Cadbury,[1] with some hesitation, suggests a process of elimina-tion, but does not explain how it is that such a process led so inevitably to Luke. Why not Mark or Epaphras? In any case, why did not the second-century Church attribute both the third Gospel and Acts to an apostolic name rather than to the insignificant Luke? And how did the inference drawn from the books themselves gain such undisputed sway among the Church Fathers? These questions need more concrete answers than Cadbury gives before the tradition can so readily be set aside as relatively unimportant in discussions of authorship.

c. The internal testimony

It is against the background of the strong external evidence that the witness of the books themselves must be considered. Does it support the tradition or does it cast suspicions upon it? Various opinions have been expressed about these alternatives and it will be necessary to give some brief indication of the arguments advanced for each view, beginning with those in support of the tradition.

(i) *The unity of authorship of the third Gospel and Acts.* Since external testimony assumes common authorship of the Gospel and Acts, and since it may with good reason be maintained that the book of Acts was accepted into the New Testament Canon without hesitation because of its close association with the Gospel of Luke, it is of importance to investigate the grounds on which this association may be based. (1) Both books are dedicated to the same man, Theophilus; (2) Acts refers to the first treatise, which is most naturally understood as the Gospel; (3) the books contain strong similarities of language and style; (4) both contain common interests;[2] (5) Acts naturally follows on from

---

[1] *Ibid.*, p. 261.

[2] F. F. Bruce (*The Acts of the Apostles*[2], 1952, p. 2) gives the following examples: (1) Catholic sympathies; (2) interest in Gentiles; (3) prominence given to women; (4) similar apologetic tendencies; (5) resurrection appearances restricted to Judaea, and (6) Christ's appearance before Herod Antipas mentioned in both, but not elsewhere in the New Testament.

Luke's Gospel, although many scholars have found difficulties over the connecting links.[1] It may safely be concluded that the evidence is very strong for linking the two books as the work of one man, a conclusion which few modern scholars would dispute.[2] This is helpful in supporting Lucan authorship in so far as it confirms the traditional assumption and strengthens the opinion that the tradition of authorship was also correct.

(ii) *Evidence that the author was a companion of Paul.* That there are some passages in Acts where the first person plural is used instead of the third person (xvi. 10–17, xx. 5–15, xxi. 1–18 and xxvii. 1–xxviii. 16) is strongly suggestive that the author of these sections was an eyewitness and therefore a travelling companion of the apostle Paul. If this is a fair inference it considerably narrows down the possibilities of authorship. It would mean that the author (1) first joins Paul at Philippi; (2) reappears on Paul's return visit to Philippi; (3) accompanies the apostle on the journey towards Jerusalem and stays with Philip at Caesarea, and, (4) after Paul's two years' imprisonment at Caesarea, during which time there are no definite data regarding the author's whereabouts, accompanies Paul to Rome and experiences shipwreck with him. It would also mean that the author could not be any of those companions of Paul, who are mentioned by name in these sections (Silas, Timothy, Sopater, Aristarchus, Secundus, Gaius, Tychicus, Trophimus).

Such an interpretation of the we-sections is also suggested by the use of the first person singular in the introduction to both the books (Lk. i. 1–4; Acts i. 1),[3] and it is certainly most natural to suppose that the

---

[1] Cf. P. H. Menoud's article, 'Remarques sur les textes de l'ascension dans Luc-Actes', in *Neutestamentliche Studien für Rudolf Bultmann* (1954), pp. 148–156. Cf. also W. G. Kümmel, *TR*, 22 (1954), p. 196; A. N. Wilder, *JBL*, LXII (1943), pp. 307–318; H. Conzelmann, *The Theology of St. Luke* (1960), pp. 93, 94. All these incline towards an interpolation theory involving the end of Luke or the beginning of Acts. Against, cf. P. A. van Stempvoort, *NTS*, 5 (1958–59), pp. 30–42. Cf. also Kümmel's later comments in his *INT* (1965), pp. 109 ff.

[2] It was challenged by A. C. Clark, *The Acts of the Apostles* (1933), pp. 393 ff. Cf. the penetrating criticism of Clark's arguments in W. L. Knox's *The Acts of the Apostles* (1948), pp. 2–15.

[3] For a discussion of the bearing of the preface to Luke's Gospel on the significance of the we-sections, cf. W. G. Kümmel, *INT* (1965), p. 127; H. J. Cadbury, *NTS*, 3 (1957), pp. 128–131. The latter admits that Luke's παρηκολουθηκότι means that the author was an eyewitness of at least some of the events that he recorded. But Kümmel takes the opposite view.

author intended his readers to assume that he was himself present during the events recorded in these sections. Yet although this would seem to be natural it is by no means universally acknowledged, and other interpretations will be noted in later discussions (see pp. 367 ff.).

(iii) *Indirect evidence in support of Lucan authorship.* Since the account in Acts concludes with Paul imprisoned in Rome, it is highly probable that the author was one of those companions of Paul mentioned in the captivity Epistles, but not included in the we-sections (Mark, Jesus Justus, Epaphras, Demas, Luke and Epaphroditus). The force of this argument will naturally depend on the opinion held regarding the provenance of these Epistles,[1] but if the Roman tradition is correct there is strong probability that the author is among the above named. It would, on the other hand, not be altogether excluded if these Epistles were sent from Ephesus, although some difficulties would then arise since no we-section occurs during Paul's Ephesian ministry. However, since the probabilities that Colossians and Philemon were sent from Ephesus are slight, and an Ephesian origin of Philippians is by no means certain, the argument is at least worthy of consideration. Of those mentioned, Luke is as good as any, and since this is the traditional ascription there seems no reason to conjecture any other.

This suggestion is supported by several other more incidental considerations. In none of the Epistles written on the second and third journeys (Thessalonians, Galatians (?), Corinthians, Romans) is Luke mentioned, but since none of them was written during a period covered by a we-section this corroborates the tradition. Moreover, according to Colossians iv. 10, 14 and Philemon 24, Luke was in close touch with Mark and this may well account for the Marcan elements in the Gospel and the Marcan flavour of the first part of Acts, which has often been noted (see further discussion on sources, pp. 368 ff.). Further support has been suggested from the appropriateness of Paul's description of Luke as 'the beloved physician', not only because the author was clearly a man of some culture, but also because his vocabulary has been thought to be of a type which a physician might be expected to use. This was strongly stressed by W. K. Hobart[2] and was supported,

---

[1] Cf. the discussion on pp. 472 ff.
[2] *The Medical Language of St. Luke* (1882).

although rather more guardedly, by A. Harnack.[1] Yet although there are remarkable parallels between Luke's vocabulary and that of such medical writers as Hippocrates, Galen and Dioscorides, H. J. Cadbury[2] has pointed out that most of the examples cited could be paralleled in other educated Greek writers of that time. In short there was nothing distinctively medical about Luke's language. As a result of Cadbury's studies less emphasis is now placed on this evidence than at one time, yet his criticisms do not exclude the argument from being used to corroborate Lucan authorship,[3] although no-one would claim that it can prove it. There are some significant instances in which Luke describes illnesses and ailments with more medical precision than his fellow Synoptists. In Luke iv. 38 Peter's mother-in-law suffers from a 'great' fever, and in v. 12 a leper is said to be 'full of leprosy'. It should also be noted that in the case of the woman suffering from haemorrhage, Luke omits the comment that she had spent her savings on doctors and was not cured (cf. Mk. v. 26; Lk. viii. 43, RSV).[4]

Beyond the fact that he was a doctor and a companion of Paul (cf. Col. iv. 14; 2 Tim. iv. 11; Phm. 24), the New Testament tells us nothing more about him, although it implies that he was a Gentile, for in the list of greetings in Colossians iv Luke is distinguished from the men of the circumcision. Certain traditions connect him with the church at Antioch;[5] while the we-sections in Acts, which start at Philippi, might perhaps suggest that that was his home town. In fact, Ramsay[6] suggested that Luke was 'the man of Macedonia', whom Paul saw in his vision beckoning him across to Europe. It is an interesting conjecture but nothing more. It may be that Luke came into contact with Paul on his missionary journeys when the apostle was in need of medical attention. It may be that Paul was responsible for his hearing

---

[1] *Lukas der Arzt* (1906; Eng. Tr. *Luke the Physician*, 1907).

[2] *Style and Literary Method of Luke* (1920).

[3] Cf. the remarks of J. M. Creed, *The Gospel according to St. Luke* (1930), pp. xviii ff.

[4] K. H. Rengstorf (*Das Evangelium nach Lukas*[8], 1958, p. 12) claims rightly that neither Luke nor Acts contains anything against the view that Luke was the author. Cf. also J. M. Creed, *op. cit.*, pp. xviii ff.

[5] E.g. the anti-Marcionite Prologue. If the Western Text of Acts xi. 28 (in Codex Bezae) is correct, the first 'we-passage' occurred in Antioch. Cf. Eusebius, *HE*, iii. 4. 6.

[6] *St. Paul the Traveller and Roman Citizen* 1920), pp. 200–203; *Luke the Physician* (1908), pp. 35 ff.

about Christianity.[1] But nothing is certain,[2] except the debt of gratitude which the Christian Church owes to him for his exquisite account of the life and passion of his Lord and of the early developments in Christian history.

The traditional view of Lucan authorship, although widely held as the view which most satisfactorily explains all the data, is nevertheless not without its challengers. Cadbury,[3] for instance, considers that the tradition was no more than an inference from the New Testament data, but if so it was remarkably consistent and widespread, and in any case may have been a perfectly true inference.

Nevertheless in spite of the weight of external and internal evidence there has been strong opposition to this tradition. A detailed statement of the case against it was made by H. Windisch[4] in 1922, and his objections, together with others more recently made, will be considered next. Most of the arguments are concerned with problems arising from the book of Acts.

(i) *Historical discrepancies.* The view that Acts conflicts with the Pauline Epistles has been a favourite argument against Lucan authorship, for it has been maintained that no companion of Paul could have made the historical blunders with which the author of Acts is charged. Among the discrepancies often mentioned are the appearance of Ananias in the story of Paul's conversion, in supposed contradiction to the fact that Paul says in Galatians that no human agent had a share in his conversion;[5] the different account of Paul's Jerusalem visits as compared with Galatians; the different attitude of Paul towards the law seen in the circumcision of Timothy and in Paul's

---

[1] Cf. S. C. Carpenter, *Christianity according to St. Luke* (1919), pp. 11, 12.

[2] The obscurity of the data led to various suppositions concerning Luke. He was supposed to have been one of the seventy since he alone records the mission charge to this group (Lk. x). Or else the unnamed companion of Cleopas on the Emmaus road (Lk. xxiv. 13 f.). Or even the well-famed, but unnamed, brother mentioned by Paul in 2 Cor. viii. 18. All of these views secured patristic support (see Michaelis, *Einleitung*, p. 61, for details), but their conjectural character will be evident. The widespread tradition that Luke was a painter is interesting, but its origin is completely unknown.

[3] In his article in *The Beginnings of Christianity*, ii, pp. 250–264.

[4] In his article in *Beginnings*, ii, pp. 298–348.

[5] W. Prentice (*ZNTW*, 46, 1955, pp. 250–254) goes as far as to describe Luke's account as popular legend. But for a more favourable approach to Luke's historicity, cf. H. G. Wood's article on Paul's conversion, *NTS*, 1 (1955), pp. 276–282.

undertaking a Jewish vow (compared with his attitude towards circumcision in the Epistles); the problem of the Council decrees, and the improbability of Paul being prepared to accept any restrictions on Gentile Christians in view of his arguments to the Galatians; and the problem of the dispute between Peter and Paul at Antioch. The whole question of Luke's reliability as a historian will be dealt with later (see pp. 354 ff.), but it must be pointed out here that these discrepancies are more apparent than real and that, although not all the difficulties may be completely removed, because of insufficient data, alternative interpretations can render the force of this argument considerably less weighty. For instance, the alleged discrepancy over Paul's conversion may at once be dismissed since Acts makes abundantly clear the superhuman character of the event; the Jerusalem visits have been discussed elsewhere[1] and may be said to confirm the independence of both accounts without making Lucan authorship impossible; the Council decrees would not have imposed an impossible burden, indeed the word 'burden' is inapplicable, for the whole account is presented as a concession on the part of the Jerusalem church, not on the part of the apostle Paul. At least, it may be said that alleged discrepancies which are capable of an alternative explanation are an insecure basis for rejecting the tradition.[2]

(ii) *Different interpretations of the we-sections.* It is further maintained that the we-sections are capable of a different interpretation from that favoured by the upholders of the traditional authorship. The first person plural, in short, need not point to an author who was a companion of Paul, but may be either a literary convention or the relic of an earlier written source (a personal diary of some kind).

The idea of a literary convention is maintained by some authors who do not deny Lucan authorship, as for instance Dibelius,[3] who considers that the we-form is used by the author to indicate his presence in all the occurrences except the shipwreck narrative, where he suggests that it

---

[1] Cf. the comments on pp. 355 f. and the fuller discussion on pp. 458 ff.

[2] W. G. Kümmel (*INT*, 1965, p. 129) considers that the author shows himself to be too falsely informed to be a companion of Paul, Kümmel is particularly influenced by the references to the Jerusalem visits, the relation of Paul to the Jerusalem apostles and the Council decrees. But he gives no weight to alternative explanations of the difficulties.

[3] Cf. *Studies in the Acts of the Apostles*, pp. 104, 105, for the earlier we-forms, and for the shipwreck account, pp. 204–206.

incorporated an earlier secular account used by Luke (in this theory, Dibelius is following E. Norden).[1] The idea that Luke used the we-form to indicate that he was a companion of Paul is, therefore, in Dibelius' view, only partially true. Others assume that what has supposedly happened in the shipwreck account has happened in the other instances and the we-form may therefore be ignored for purposes of identifying the author. The most recent advocate of this type of theory is E. Haenchen,[2] to whom the 'we' is but a stylistic process to give force to the narrative and bears no historical significance. It should be noted that Haenchen on other grounds does not accept the Lucan authorship[3] and therefore is bound to suggest some alternative explanation of the we-passages.

The other possibility, which has been strongly advocated by a succession of scholars, is that the writer has used an earlier source written in the first person.[4] This source has been variously described as a diary or an itinerary (see the discussion of this idea on pp. 374 ff.). By means of such a theory some scholars have transferred the tradition of Lucan authorship from the whole book to this particular source.[5] But if this were so, two important considerations arise. Why did the author not indicate Luke's name, so as to add greater weight to his use of this eyewitness account? Or, if that were not his purpose in incorporating the source, why did he retain the first person plural? There are no satisfactory answers to these questions. The we-sections could hardly have been regarded by the uninitiated reader as an indication of an eyewitness written source without more indication of this fact. It would be more natural to suppose that he would assume that the author was himself present. Moreover, as Harnack[6] strongly maintained,

[1] *Agnostos Theos* (1913), pp. 313 f., 323 f.

[2] *Die Apostelgeschichte (KEK)*[13], (1961), pp. 428–431.

[3] Cf. especially his article, 'Tradition und Komposition in der Apostelgeschichte', *ZTK*, 52 (1955), pp. 205–225 and in his commentary *Die Apostelgeschichte*, pp. 99–103.

[4] Many of the earlier German critics maintained this view. J. Dupont, in his *Les Sources du Livre des Actes* (1960), pp. 76 ff., gives useful bibliographical information on this point. Not all advocates of a we-source have supposed that Luke was the author, for Timothy, Silas, Titus and even Epaphras have been proposed. Some have equated Titus with Silas as author. Yet in all these variations there is the underlying assumption that the author or redactor of the whole used someone else's personal memoirs.

[5] See especially the article by H. Windisch in *Beginnings*, II, pp. 342 ff.

[6] *Luke the Physician* (1907), pp. 1 ff.

the style and language of the we-passages agree so closely with the style and language of the rest of the book that it cannot be maintained that a separate source was used. In face of this evidence, the we-sections remain a stronger testimony to an author who was a companion of Paul than to any other.

(iii) *Theological difficulties.* The weightiest objection to Lucan authorship, or for that matter to authorship by any of Paul's companions, has been based on the theological differences between the Acts and the Pauline Epistles.[1] It is maintained by some that Luke's record of Paul's teaching differs so radically from Paul's own presentation that it can only be concluded that the author was unacquainted with Paul. The first theological discrepancy is Paul's solution of the problem of the law.[2] In the Acts, there is no hint of the theological tension which is reflected in Paul's Galatian letter, where law is seen as leading into bondage from which Christ has freed men. Circumcision is even supported by Paul in Acts (in the case of Timothy), although resisted by him in Galatians. Yet while it cannot be denied that the Lucan picture differs from Paul's, it cannot be asserted that the two pictures contradict one another. There is no ground for demanding that Luke must present Paul's theology in his historical book in precisely the same form as Paul presents it in his pastoral and didactic letters. The same applies to the speeches attributed to Paul in Acts, where it is maintained either that the author has composed the Pauline speeches without reference to Paul's Epistles and therefore with no attempt to make them conform to Pauline thought, or else that Luke has adapted some existing speechform, as in the case of the Areopagus speech in Athens (Acts xvii).[3] Although it is possible to hold that the Areopagus speech was Luke's own adaptation of material in order to give an example of what a sermon to cultured people ought to be, as Dibelius,[4] in fact, maintained, it is equally possible to maintain that the speech is a faithful representa-

---

[1] Cf. Haenchen's section 'Lukas und Paulus', *Die Apostelgeschichte* (*KEK*) pp. 99–103.

[2] Haenchen, *op. cit.*, pp. 99, 100.

[3] So E. Norden, *Agnostos Theos* (1913), pp. 3–83. Cf. also A. Loisy, *Les Actes des Apôtres* (1920), pp. 660–684, and more recently H. Hommel, *ZNTW*, 46 (1955), pp. 145–178; 48 (1957), pp. 193–200. Other recent studies on this speech are those of W. Nauck, *ZTK*, 53 (1956), pp. 11–52; W. Eltester, in *N. T. Studien für R. Bultmann* (1954), pp. 202–227.

[4] *Op. cit.*, pp. 26–77.

tion of Paul's own thought on the occasion.[1] Whatever conclusions are arrived at on this score, it is clear that no argument based upon them can prove conclusive in the question of authorship. The same may be said of Paul's speech at Pisidian Antioch (Acts xiii. 16 ff.).[2] It is hardly to be expected that during a mission address the apostle would present his teaching, either in form or content, in the same manner as when writing letters to those already committed to the Christian faith.[3] For instance, a theological presentation like the Epistle to the Romans would hardly have been suited to a primary preaching of the gospel. Objections based on the un-Pauline character of this Pisidian speech which do not take into account the historical situation can have little weight (see the discussion on the speeches on pp. 359 ff.)[4]

Closely linked with the problem based on alleged differences in theology is the difference between the Paul of Acts and the Paul of the Epistles. This will be discussed when the historicity of Acts is considered (see pp. 358 f.), but if the Acts portrait is out of harmony with Paul's own self-revelation it would obviously be difficult to maintain that the author was a personal companion of the apostle. Nevertheless, it will be shown that the differences are overdrawn and that there are no proved contradictions. Differences of emphasis must be admitted, but this has no bearing on Lucan authorship. It is not so unusual for a close

[1] Cf. A. Wikenhauser, *Die Apostelgeschichte und ihr Geschichtswert* (1921), pp. 390–394; N. B. Stonehouse, *Paul before the Areopagus* (1957), pp. 1–40. For an earlier treatment, cf. F. H. Chase, *The Credibility of the Book of the Acts of the Apostles* (1902), pp. 204–234. Cf. also the detailed study by B. Gärtner, *The Areopagus Speech and Natural Revelation* (Eng. Tr. by C. H. King, 1955), who concludes for the Pauline character of the speech although admitting Lucan influence in terminology and literary form (cf. pp. 248 ff.)

[2] H. Windisch (*op. cit.*, p. 337) categorically denied that this speech could be by a companion of Paul, for three reasons: (1) it borrows from Luke's Gospel; (2) it implies that Paul was not a witness of the resurrection (verse 30); and (3) it depends on Peter's Pentecost speech (verses 34–37). This reminiscence of Peter's speech is also noted by Dibelius (*op. cit.*, pp. 105, 119), but he does not draw the same conclusion as Windisch. He sees the Petrine echoes as Luke's work.

[3] The only Acts speech which bears any analogy to the situation behind the Pauline Epistles is Paul's address to the Ephesian elders at Miletus. And it is significant that this speech approximates most closely to Paul's Epistles in language and thought (cf. F. H. Chase, *op. cit.*, pp. 234–288).

[4] Scholars who regard the speeches of Acts as Luke's work will naturally allow little weight to this consideration. Cf. U. Wilckens, *Die Missionsreden der Apostelgeschichte*[2] (1963), who regards all the speeches in Acts ii-v, x and xiii as Lucan. On Paulinisms in Acts, cf. P. Vielhauer, *Ev Th*, x (1950), pp. 1–15.

companion to paint a portrait of a person which differs from that person's self-disclosures. There is certainly insufficient ground for the conclusion that the author of Acts is a man of the sub-apostolic age.[1] There is further no theological basis for denying that the author of Luke and Acts was a companion of Paul. If Luke shows independence of Paul,[2] there is no evidence of conflicting opinion between them.

(iv) *Literary parallels.* Another type of argument has recently been advanced against Lucan authorship based on a literary comparison between Acts and the works of Justin Martyr. This is the approach of J. C. O'Neill,[3] who maintains that the two authors held common theological positions and Luke-Acts must consequently be placed well into the second century, which at once rules out Lucan authorship.[4] But this theory gives insufficient attention to the alternative explanation of the parallels, i.e. that Justin learned his theology from Luke (see further discussion of this under the Date of Acts, p. 348).

d. Conclusion

There would appear to be far stronger grounds for retaining the tradition of Lucan authorship for both the Gospel and Acts than for rejecting it. This opinion is confirmed by the fact that advocates of Lucan authorship are not only in the majority, but are also drawn from widely differing schools of theological opinion.[5]

[1] Cf. Haenchen, *op. cit.*, pp. 100–103.

[2] Cf. Creed, *The Gospel according to St. Luke* (1930), p. xviii. As R. M. Grant (*A Historical Introduction to the New Testament*, 1963, p. 135) points out, any who assume that Luke must echo Paul neglect to give sufficient weight to the variety within the unity of the early Church. The idea of Pauline influence on Luke was firmly rejected by T. E. Bleiben (*JTS*, xlv, 1944, pp. 134–140) on the grounds that Luke and Paul hold different views regarding the passion.

[3] *The Theology of Acts* (1961), pp. 10 ff., 21.

[4] There is no doubt that O'Neill comes to the study of the parallels between Acts and Justin with a strong bias against an early date, and his judgments are coloured by this disinclination to accept the primitive character of Acts (cf. *op. cit.*, pp. 4 ff.).

[5] Among those maintaining authorship by Luke the physician may be cited F. F. Bruce, *The Acts of the Apostles*[2] (1952), pp. 1–6; C. S. C. Williams, *The Acts of the Apostles* (BC, 1957), pp. 1 ff.; W. Michaelis, *Einleitung*, pp. 61–64; Bo Reicke, *Glaube und Leben der Urgemeinde* (1957), pp. 6, 7; F. V. Filson, *Three Crucial Decades* (1963), p. 10; M. Dibelius, *Studies in the Acts of the Apostles* (Eng. Tr. 1956), p. 123; R. M. Grant, *A Historical Introduction to the New Testament* (1963), pp. 134, 135 (although he does not consider the identification of the author to be

V. DATE

In some ways the date of Luke is tied up with the date of Acts, but it is advisable to begin the discussion by marshalling the evidence for the Gospel alone.

a. External evidence

This evidence suggests that in the early part of the second century the Gospel was fully recognized, and it would be a fair inference from this that it was widely known before the end of the first century. It seems to be reflected in the *Didache*[1] and in works of the Gnostics, Basilides and Valentinus,[2] while Marcion[3] used a mutilated form of this Gospel and excluded all others. Justin[4] made much use of it in the mid-second century.

b. Arguments for a second-century date

Not all scholars, however, have agreed that, if Lucan authorship is rejected, the external evidence requires a first-century dating for the Gospel. Admittedly the earlier evidence (*Didache*, Basilides and Valentinus) is not strong numerically,[5] while Marcion's and Justin's evidence, although it has generally been regarded as conclusive, has been challenged by a few scholars. The former's use of Luke has been challenged by J. Knox[6] on the supposition that he used an earlier Gospel which was later used by the writer of the canonical Gospel. But there are several reasons why this theory must be rejected. There is no doubt

as important as discussions about the purpose). B. Gärtner, *The Areopagus Speech and Natural Revelation* (1955), assumes it. Cf. also W. L. Knox, *op. cit.*; R. R. Williams, *The Acts of the Apostles* (*TC*, 1953); E. M. Blaiklock, *The Acts of the Apostles* (*TNT*, 1959), and W. Grundmann, *Das Evangelium nach Lukas*, p. 39. W. G. Kümmel (*INT*, 1965, p. 131) cites the following recent scholars as rejecting Lucan authorship, Beyer, Conzelmann, Haenchen, Vielhauer, Klein, Evans and O'Neill, to whom should be added Kümmel himself. E. Trocmé, *Le 'Livre des Actes' et l'Histoire* (1957) refers throughout his book to 'l'auteur ad Theophilum'.*

[1] Cf. Creed, *op. cit.*, pp. xxv ff., for these parallels.

[2] Cf. *ibid.*, pp. xxvii, xxviii, for details.

[3] Cf. Tertullian, *Adv. Marc.* iv.

[4] Cf. Creed, *op. cit.*, p. xxvii. J. N. Geldenhuys (*Commentary on the Gospel of Luke*, 1950, p. 30) cites especially Justin's *Dialogue*, 78, 88, 100, 103, 105, 106.

[5] To this evidence may be added that of Polycarp (see note on p. 18 n.4 on Köster's opinion on this).

[6] *Marcion and the New Testament* (1942).

that the orthodox apologists maintained that Marcion's Gospel was based on the canonical Gospel of Luke. If this had been known by Marcion's supporters to be incorrect, they could at once have countered the orthodox arguments. It is difficult to believe that the defenders of the faith would have based their attack on so insecure a foundation as the antiquity and apostolicity of the four Gospels if Knox's theory is correct. Moreover, the customary trend in Gospel editing as far as it is known suggests that editors tended to omit certain material found in their sources, while at the same time adding other material. But Marcion included no material not in Luke, although he appears to have omitted considerable portions which are present in that Gospel. A perfectly satisfactory explanation may be found in Marcion's known propensity to abbreviate, although it is not always clear why he did so in some of his omissions from Luke. It is further to be noted that the reconstructed text of Marcion's Luke made by Harnack and used as a basis for Knox's linguistic and stylistic arguments is conjectural in character and cannot for that reason form a secure foundation for challenging the general assumption that Marcion used the Gospel of Luke. Knox himself is not unmindful of this factor, but believes that the reconstructed text may in general be relied upon. The effect of his theory on the date of Luke will at once be evident, for it means that in its final form Luke must be subsequent to Marcion's adoption of its earlier form as his Gospel.

Justin's use of Luke has been challenged by J. C. O'Neill,[1] on the ground that Justin used the same special source as Luke used.[2] This common source, according to O'Neill, may have been much earlier, but the Gospel itself was not produced much before Justin's time. He tentatively suggests a date between AD 115 and 130 for Luke-Acts.[3] The fundamental weakness of this position is that it assumes that Luke, in a period of from ten to twenty years, could have gained such authority in the Christian Church that Marcion could be sure of gaining support in his exclusive choice of this Gospel. Surely such a proposition is completely incredible and must at once be abandoned. The earlier evidence for the circulation of Matthew and Mark suggests that by

---

[1] *Op. cit.*, pp. 28 ff.

[2] In his review of O'Neill's book, H. F. D. Sparks rejects the idea that Justin did not know Luke, which is the real basis of O'Neill's dating of Luke-Acts (*JTS*, n.s., XIV, 1963, pp. 457 ff.).

[3] *Op. cit.*, p. 25.

Marcion's time these other Gospels had been widely used and it is incredible to suppose that Marcion could have ousted these Gospels with one produced only a few years before and yet regarded as basic for his *Apostolikon*.

A date about AD 100 has sometimes been supposed on the ground that Luke knew of and consulted Josephus' *Antiquities* (published about AD 94). Part of the evidence consists of items cited in Acts, which will be mentioned later (see pp. 347 f.), but for Luke's Gospel it has been maintained that Luke iii. 1, 2 shows dependence on Josephus. The argument assumes that when Luke referred to Lysanias as tetrarch of Abilene he obtained this information from Josephus. In one passage[1] the latter refers to Abila as a place which had previously been in the tetrarchy of Lysanias and in another passage[2] he describes it simply as Abila of Lysanias. On the other hand Josephus also mentions a Lysanias who was killed by Anthony (36 BC)[3] and if Luke, as is alleged, was thinking of this man his chronology was clearly wrong. But since this Lysanias had only a brief reign and the place was named after him, it is reasonable to suppose that one of his descendants of the same name may later have been appointed tetrarch. Unless it can be established that Josephus implies only one Lysanias, and that Luke could not have obtained his information elsewhere, there is no ground for maintaining that Luke was subsequent to Josephus. Indeed, Sir William Ramsay[4] cites an inscription from ancient Abilene which refers to a Lysanias who must have been tetrarch there some time between AD 14 and 29 and this would suit Luke's reference. The Josephus theory must be as strongly discounted as the last.

c. Arguments for a late first-century date

A date in the ninth decade of the first century is favoured by most scholars on the following grounds: (1) On the basis of the theory that Luke used Mark, it is naturally required that Luke should be later than Mark. This fixes the *terminus a quo* at about AD 68 (see discussion on pp. 72 ff.). (2) A comparison of Mark xiii. 14 with Luke xxi. 20 shows that for Mark's 'abomination of desolation' which was to be set up where it ought not, Luke records that Jerusalem will be surrounded by armies. It is usually assumed that Luke has deliberately altered Mark

---

[1] *Antiquities*, xx. 7. 1.   [2] *Antiquities*, xix. 5. 1.   [3] *Antiquities*, xv. 4. 1.
[4] *The Bearing of Recent Discoveries on the Trustworthiness of the New Testament* (1915), pp. 297 f.

because by the time of writing he knew precisely what had happened.[1] In other words this is a *vaticinium ex eventu*, and would require for Luke a date subsequent to AD 70. (3) The fact that Luke wrote after many others had made the attempt is supposed by some to require an interval subsequent to AD 70, since there is no evidence of 'many' Gospels being produced before AD 70.[2] (4) It is sometimes assumed that no great interval could have separated Luke's Gospel and Matthew's,[3] and since the latter is generally dated in the ninth decade, Luke's must be also.

It is surprising that on such inconclusive evidence as the above there should be such widespread acceptance of a date between AD 75 and 85, but the insecurity of the evidence will become clear when the following considerations are weighed. No doubt the preference for this date is due to the general feeling that none of the alternatives is more convincing. Whether Luke used Mark as a written source or not, no great interval need have separated them, for if he did use Mark he may well have gained access to it very soon after it was written. After all, they were both members of Paul's group of companions. Since it has been shown that Mark need not be dated as late as the period immediately prior to the siege of Jerusalem (see pp. 73 f.), it follows that on this score Luke may also be earlier.[4]

The argument from Luke xxi. 20 is not conclusive for the following reasons: (1) It assumes that Luke's statement could have been formulated only after the event, but if the argument is valid, why is Luke's description so vague?[5] Why does not Luke give some indication of the nature of the siege to identify it more closely? (2) Moreover, is it quite

[1] Creed (*The Gospel according to St. Luke*, 1930, p. xxii) considered this to be a conclusive deduction from Lk. xxi. 20, which made it impossible to date Luke before AD 70. He admitted that taken on its own Lk. xxi might be compatible with a date in the early sixties, but claimed that when Lk. xxi was compared with Mk. xiii this was impossible. But see a criticism of this below.

[2] Geldenhuys (*Commentary on the Gospel of Luke*, 1950, p. 33) mentions this view as a secondary argument for this dating.

[3] Cf. V. Taylor, *The Gospels*, p. 73. G. D. Kilpatrick (*Origins of the Gospel according to St. Matthew*, p. 7) considers that Matthew's and Luke's independent use of two common sources, Mark and Q, requires that they be dated sufficiently near to each to avoid the possibility of one losing his independence of the other.

[4] T. W. Manson (*Studies in the Gospels and Epistles*, pp. 28 ff.), who dated Mark about AD 60, allocated Luke-Acts to the period about AD 70, somewhat earlier than the more generally held theory.

[5] Cf. S. C. Carpenter, *Christianity according to St. Luke* (1919), p. 230.

certain that Luke's statement could not have been a genuine prophecy of Jesus? Much Gospel criticism is so dominated by rigid source hypotheses that it is assumed that the only possible explanation in a case like this is that one author has modified the other for some specific motive, either theological, historical or perhaps linguistic. But it is not impossible to suppose that Mark (and Matthew) used the more obscure 'abomination of desolation' and Luke the more precise 'Jerusalem surrounded by armies' because our Lord used both expressions.[1] To Matthew the phrase at once linked the Lord's prediction with the book of Daniel, where the phrase also occurs, and would, therefore, emphasize its significance as a fulfilment of Old Testament prophecy. To Luke, on the other hand, with Gentile readers specifically in mind, the explanation regarding the surrounding armies would fit in better with his purpose.[2] That this explanation of the words of the Lord was current before AD 70 seems proved by the fact that many Jerusalem Christians fled to Pella in obedience to their Master's words when the Roman armies began to invest Jerusalem.[3] Moreover, if Luke was interpreting Mark xiii after the event, why did not Matthew do the same, since his Gospel is generally dated contemporaneously? Furthermore, history has known other instances of accurate prediction several years before the event (e.g. Savonarola's prediction of the capture of Rome[4]) and there is every indication in our Lord's character and personality to suggest that prediction of this kind should be expected from Him. No great confidence can therefore be placed in the argument from Luke xxi. 20.

The third and fourth grounds cited above are no more than doubtful inferences. There are no indications in Luke's preface as to the date when the 'many' other attempts were made and there is nothing whatever to exclude a period well before AD 70 for such literary activity. As to the relation between Matthew and Luke, more will be said in

[1] Cf. F. Blass, *Philology of the Gospels* (1898), p. 46.
[2] J. N. Geldenhuys (*op. cit.*, p. 32), who regards Luke's readers as mainly Roman Christians, suggests that Luke would never have called the Roman army or a Roman leader 'the abomination'.
[3] Reported by Eusebius, *HE*, iii. 32.
[4] Mentioned by Blass, *op.cit.*, pp. 41 f. C. H. Dodd (*JRS*, xxxvii, 1947, pp. 47–54) contends that Luke's version is not coloured by the events of AD 66–70. It is coloured, in fact, by Old Testament references to the fall of Jerusalem in 586 BC. R. M. Grant (*A Historical Introduction to the New Testament*, 1963, p. 69) refers to Dodd's argument with some favour.

discussing the Synoptic problem (see pp. 143 ff.), but for the purpose of dating it must be noted that no confidence can be placed on relative dating of the Gospels until their literary relationships can be determined in a manner independent of pure conjecture.

d. Arguments for a date prior to AD 70

The remaining possibility is a date prior to AD 70, and those favouring this dating generally fix upon a date about AD 60–61.[1] The supporting arguments for this are closely tied up with the date of Acts, but if the latter may reasonably be dated about AD 63 (see pp. 340 ff. for the discussion of this) Luke must clearly be before that. Moreover, Luke had spent some time in Palestine while Paul was imprisoned at Caesarea. There is indeed a we-passage which suggests that Luke was with Paul when he visited Philip the Evangelist (see pp. 368 f.). It is a reasonable conjecture (although no more than a conjecture) that Luke collected up much of his own special material while at Caesarea, and it is an equally reasonable conjecture that he would have proceeded to write his Gospel soon after.[2] If these conjectures are correct they would support the date mentioned above.

Once the argument from Luke xxi. 20 is dismissed, there is really little tangible data to enable the date of the Gospel to be specifically fixed.

VI. LANGUAGE

Luke's Greek is remarkable for its adaptability. The preface is modelled on classical patterns, which gives some insight into his cultural background. But after writing i. 1–4, he drops the literary style for a type of Greek strongly flavoured with Semitisms, which he uses for the infancy narratives. Subsequent to this he generally uses what may be

---

[1] Harnack (*The Date of Acts and the Synoptic Gospels*, 1911, pp. 90 ff.) was a notable advocate for an early date for Luke on the strength of an early date for Acts.

[2] Those who accept Lucan authorship, but who date the Gospel about AD 80, must suppose that Luke was several years collecting his own information. It is difficult to believe that he would have made notes of the testimony he received before AD 60 and have done nothing about it for another twenty years. The Proto-Luke hypothesis (see pp. 175 ff.) does nothing to alleviate the difficulty, for under this theory the first draft of Luke must have been carried about for a similar period. Cf. Streeter (*The Four Gospels*, pp. 217–221) and V. Taylor (*Behind the Third Gospel*, 1926, pp. 202–215) who both regard Proto-Luke as having been written soon after Luke left Caesarea.

described as a good literary *Koiné* Greek,[1] although even here some Semitisms are found. Clearly Luke did not consider that the literary style of the preface was at all suitable for the narration of the life and teaching of Jesus. But in his choice of suitable literary styles he shows himself to be a considerable literary artist.

Particularly noticeable is the type of Septuagint Greek used for the infancy narratives which seems to have been strongly influenced by the style of the canticles which he includes in his narratives.[2] The strongly Hebraistic character of Luke's Greek in this section is admirably adapted to link the incarnation of Jesus with the Old Testament history and that may well be the effect that Luke wished to create. By his obvious familiarity with the Septuagint, which he often cites throughout the Gospel, Luke's Greek has become strongly coloured with Hebraisms. At the same time Luke's vocabulary is unusually rich and varied for a New Testament writer, for he uses several hundred words[3] which no other New Testament writer uses.

CONTENTS

I. THE PROLOGUE (i. 1–4)

II. THE INFANCY NARRATIVES (i. 5–ii. 52)

The foretelling of John the Baptist's birth (i. 5–25). The annunciation to Mary (i. 26–38). Mary visits Elizabeth (i. 39–56). John's birth (i. 57–80). Jesus' birth (ii. 1–20). The circumcision and presentation of Christ (ii. 21–40). Jesus in Jerusalem when twelve years old (ii. 41–52).

[1] That Luke was acquainted with good literary style is apparent in the main body of the Gospel, when he uses certain idioms which are relatively absent from the other New Testament writers, e.g. the optative, the articular infinitive, the use of the article in indirect questions, the use of πρίν with the subjunctive or optative (cf. Creed, *The Gospel according to St. Luke*, 1930, p. lxxxii, for details and examples).

[2] For a fuller discussion of the linguistic characteristics of the infancy narratives, see pp. 170 ff.

[3] Sir J. C. Hawkins (*Horae Synopticae*[2], 1909, pp. 201–207) gives a list of 261 words peculiar to this Gospel, 58 shared by Luke and Acts only, and 413 peculiar to Acts. R. Morgenthaler (*Statistik des Neutestamentlichen Wortschatzes*, 1958, p. 170) gives the numbers as 266, 60 and 415 respectively, excluding proper names.

III. THE PREPARATION FOR THE MINISTRY (iii. 1–iv. 13)

The mission of John the Baptist (iii. 1–20). The baptism of Jesus (iii. 21, 22). The genealogy of Jesus (iii. 23–38). The temptation (iv. 1–13).

IV. THE GALILAEAN MINISTRY (iv. 14–ix. 50)

a. The beginnings (iv. 14–44)

Jesus rejected at Nazareth (iv. 16–30); a miracle in the synagogue at Capernaum (iv. 31–37); Peter's mother-in-law healed (iv. 38, 39); other healings in the evening (iv. 40, 41); Jesus' withdrawal to a lonely place, followed by further preaching (iv. 42–44).

b. The call of the disciples (v. 1–vi. 16)

The miraculous draught of fishes, and Simon's call (v. 1–11); a leper and a paralytic healed (v. 12–26); the call of Levi (v. 27–32); an enquiry about fasting (v. 33–39); controversies over the sabbath (vi. 1–11); the appointment of the Twelve (vi. 12–16).

c. The Sermon on the Plain (vi. 17–49)

Introduction (vi. 17–19); Beatitudes (vi. 20–23); woes (vi. 24–26); other sayings (vi. 27–49).

d. At Capernaum and the surrounding district (vii. 1–viii. 56)

The healing of the centurion's slave (vii. 1–10); the raising of the widow's son at Nain (vii. 11–17); John the Baptist's enquiry about Jesus (vii. 18–23); Jesus' testimony about John (vii. 24–30); His estimate of His own generation (vii. 31–35); the anointing by the sinful woman (vii. 36–50); the women disciples of Jesus (viii. 1–3).

The parable of the sower and the soils, and its interpretation; the reason for parables, and their right use (viii. 4–18).

Jesus' true family relationships (viii. 19–21).

A series of miracles (viii. 22–56): the stilling of the storm, and healing of the Gerasene demoniac, the woman with the haemorrhage and Jairus' daughter.

e. Incidents centring on the Twelve (ix. 1–50)

Their mission (ix. 1–6); Herod's reaction to Jesus (ix. 7–9); the return of the Twelve and the feeding of the five thousand (ix. 10–17); Peter's confession at Caesarea Philippi (ix. 18–21); first prediction of the passion (ix. 22); conditions for discipleship (ix. 23–27); the transfiguration (ix. 28–36); healing of the epileptic boy (ix. 37–43); second prediction of the passion (ix. 44, 45); a dispute about greatness (ix. 46–48); Jesus' attitude towards the strange exorcist (ix. 49, 50).

V. FROM GALILEE TO JERUSALEM (ix. 51–xix. 27)

a. Jesus and the Samaritans (ix. 51–x. 37)

A Samaritan village unwilling to receive Jesus (ix. 51–56); tests for aspiring disciples (ix. 57–62); the mission of the seventy (x. 1–20); Jesus' thanksgiving and pronouncement of blessing on the disciples (x. 21–24); the lawyer's enquiries and the parable of the good Samaritan (x. 25–37).

b. On the value of meditation and prayer (x. 38–xi. 13)

Mary and Martha (x. 38–42); the Lord's prayer (xi. 1–4); the friend at midnight (xi. 5–13).

c. Jesus and the Pharisees (xi. 14–54)

The Beelzebub controversy (xi. 14–23); the return of the evil spirit (xi. 24–26); a blessing pronounced on Jesus' mother (xi. 27, 28); Jesus condemns His contemporaries for sign-seeking (xi. 29–32); sayings about light (xi. 33–36); criticism of the Pharisees and the lawyers (xi. 37–54).

d. Jesus' advice to His disciples (xii. 1–53)

Exhortations to fearless witness (xii. 1–12); parable of the rich fool (xii. 13–21); about anxiety (xii. 22–34); about watchfulness and responsibility (xii. 35–48); warnings about the repercussions of Jesus' mission on family life (xii. 49–53).

e. Various sayings and events (xii. 54–xix. 27)

On interpreting signs (xii. 54–56); on settling legal disputes (xii. 57–59); examples of catastrophes cited to press the need for repentance (xiii. 1–9); the crippled woman healed, and consequent sabbath controversy (xiii. 10–17); parables of the mustard seed and the leaven (xiii. 18–21); sayings about the coming kingdom (xiii. 22–30); Jesus leaves Galilee (xiii. 31–33); lament over Jerusalem (xiii. 34, 35).

Jesus dines out (xiv. 1–24): sabbath healing of a man with dropsy (xiv. 1–6); saying about choosing the lowest places (xiv. 7–14); parable of the great supper (xiv. 15–24).

Sayings on discipleship (xiv. 25–35): cost of discipleship (xiv. 25–33); saying about savourless salt (xiv. 34, 35).

The parables of the lost sheep, lost coin, prodigal son and unjust steward (xv. 1–xvi. 13). Warnings against Pharisaic hypocrisy (xvi. 14–18). Dives and Lazarus (xvi. 19–31). Teaching about offences, forgiveness, faith and rewards (xvii. 1–10).

The healing of ten lepers (xvii. 11–19). Teaching about the end of the age (xvii. 20–37). Parables of the unjust judge, and the Pharisee and the tax-collector (xviii. 1–14). Young children blessed (xviii. 15–17). The rich young man (xviii. 18–30). The third prediction of the passion (xviii. 31–34). Events in Jericho (xviii. 35–xix. 27): a blind man healed; Zacchaeus entertains Jesus; the parable of the pounds.

VI. IN JERUSALEM (xix. 28–xxi. 38)

The entry (xix. 28–38). Prediction of destruction of Jerusalem (xix. 39–44). Cleansing of, and daily teaching in, the temple (xix. 45–48). Jesus' authority challenged (xx. 1–8). The parable of the wicked husbandmen (xx. 9–19) and questions on tribute, the resurrection and the son of David (xx. 20–44). Warnings and commendations (xx. 45–xxi. 4). The eschatological discourse (xxi. 5–36). Summary of the Jerusalem ministry (xxi. 37, 38).

VII. THE PASSION AND RESURRECTION NARRATIVES (xxii. 1–xxiv. 53)

The preparation (xxii. 1–13). The institution of the last supper (xxii. 14–20). The betrayal predicted (xxii. 21–23). The disciples' dispute over greatness (xxii. 24–30). Peter's denial predicted (xxii. 31–34). The incident of the two swords (xxii. 35–38). In Gethsemane (xxii. 39–46). The arrest, trial and crucifixion (xxii. 47–xxiii. 49). The burial (xxiii. 50–56). The resurrection, the appearances on the Emmaus road and in Jerusalem (xxiv. 1–49). The ascension (xxiv. 50–53).

ADDITIONAL NOTES

98. [2] Conzelmann's theory of Luke's structure is subjected to criticism by Ws C. Robinson, Jnr, in *Der Weg des Herrn* (1964). Robinson maintains that Luke.'

main thesis consists of a journey theme, but not tied to specific places as it is in Conzelmann's view (cf. J. Rohde, *Rediscovering the Teaching of the Evangelists*, 1968, pp. 236 ff.). Cf. also the criticism by E. E. Ellis to the effect that Conzelmann's view is inconsistent, since Luke himself leaves a number of episodes unaltered which nevertheless are incompatible with Conzelmann's view of his theological purpose (*The Gospel of Luke*, CB, n.s., 1966, p. 147). Ellis himself prefers a thematic interpretation of this central section in Luke. Another recent writer who sees theological influences on Luke is S. E. Johnson (*JBL*, LXXXVII, 1968, pp. 136–150), who examines the Davidic-royal motif in the Gospels and concludes that Luke's traditions concerning the descent of Jesus are Judaean, while Matthew's traditions are Galilaean.

98. [3] In his recent commentary, E. E. Ellis (see previous note) proposes an elaborate sixfold thematic structure for Luke. He neatly fits the whole Gospel into a series of sections each containing six sub-sections. But it leaves one wondering whether Luke had so detailed a numerical arrangement in his mind when writing his book. It is, however, an interesting attempt to break away from the more conventional method of analysing Luke.

According to C. H. Talbert (*NTS*, 14, 1968, pp. 259–271), Luke's structure reflects his theological purpose. Talbert concentrates on the beginning and ending, the baptism and the ascension. Gnostics interpreted the latter in a spiritual sense and the former as the point of descent of the spiritual redeemer. From this Talbert concludes that Luke presents an answer to the type of Docetism expounded by Cerinthus. Such a theory would clearly demand a date about the turn of the century, since there is no clear evidence of Docetism earlier. But, although it may be said that Luke's presentation would have been useful for anti-Docetic purposes, this is not the same as saying that Luke designed his Gospel for such purposes. On the other hand Gnostic Docetism may well have had roots earlier in the first century.

109 f. [5] W. Marxsen (*INT*, pp. 171 f.) declines to consider the possibility of Lucan authorship on the grounds that both Luke and Acts reflect Church life around the end of the first century.

CHAPTER FIVE

THE SYNOPTIC PROBLEM

I. THE NATURE OF THE PROBLEM

Arising out of a detailed study of the three Synoptic Gospels is the important question of their relationship to each other, and this is affected by the following main considerations.

a. Similarity of arrangement

All these Gospels are based on the same general historical structure. They begin with the baptism and temptation of Jesus; they deal in varying detail with the public ministry in Galilee; they all portray Peter's confession at Caesarea Philippi as the turning-point in the ministry; they all describe the last journey to Jerusalem, the trial, the crucifixion and resurrection. Moreover, there is a high proportion of the Gospel material common to all three Gospels.[1]

b. Similarity of style and wording

In many sections of the Gospels not only is there similarity of contents but also of vocabulary. Examples of such close verbal agreements may be seen in the following incidents—the healing of the leper (Mt. viii. 1 ff.; Mk. i. 40 ff.; Lk. v. 12 ff.), the question of Jesus' authority (Mt. xxi. 23 ff.; Mk. xi. 27 ff.; Lk. xx. 1 ff.), portions of the eschatological discourse (Mt. xxiv. 4 ff., 15 ff.; Mk. xiii. 5 ff., 14 ff.; Lk. xxi. 8 ff., 20 ff.), and the request of Joseph of Arimathaea for the body of Jesus (Mt. xxvii. 58; Mk. xv. 43; Lk. xxiii. 52).[2]

c. Similarities in two Gospels only

(1) There are some cases where sections recorded in all three Gospels agree more closely in style and wording in two as compared with the

---

[1] For further details, cf. p. 133.

[2] These parallels are best studied in a synopsis of the Gospels in the Greek text. The most convenient is that of A. Huck, *Synopsis of the First Three Gospels*[9] (ed. H. Lietzmann, English edition by F. L. Cross, 1949).*

Cf. B. de Solages, *A Greek Synopsis of the Gospels* (1959), for a mathematical comparison. For an English Harmony, cf. J. M. Thomson, *The Synoptic Gospels* (1910) and H. F. D. Sparks, *A Synopsis of the Gospels* (1964).

third, and this phenomenon is not without some significance in determining their origins and relationships. (2) But the more important data under this heading relate to Matthew and Luke, which contain a considerable amount of material common to both but omitted from Mark. Most of this material comprises the teaching of Jesus, with very little narrative and no part of the passion story. As with the material common to all three, the similarity in this Matthew–Luke material often extends to the wording (cf. Mt. iii. 7–10; Lk. iii. 7–9, relating to the preaching of John the Baptist; Mt. vi. 24; Lk. xvi. 13, on serving two masters; Mt. xi. 4 ff.; Lk. vii. 22 ff., containing Jesus' answer to John the Baptist's question; Mt. xxiii. 37–39; Lk. xiii. 34, 35, recording Jesus' lament over Jerusalem).

d. Divergences

The problem would be less difficult to solve were it not for the considerable differences both in arrangement and vocabulary over many points of detail. Some sections of common material have little verbal similarity, while others are placed in different historical settings. The healing of the centurion's servant, for instance (Mt. viii. 5 ff.; Lk. vii. 1 ff.), is not only placed in a different order in the two Gospels, but differs widely in its narration. The passion narratives of the three Gospels, while conforming fairly closely to a similar sequence, nevertheless contain many differences of detail and wording.

In addition to the difference just mentioned, each of the three Synoptics has certain sections peculiar to it. This is particularly so in the cases of Matthew and Luke. The birth narratives of the first and third Gospels are quite different and bear very little relationship to each other, while Luke has a long section, commonly known as the 'travel' narrative (ix. 51–xviii. 14), which largely comprises his own material. Matthew records such stories as Peter's walking on the water and the coin in the fish's mouth, which neither of the others contains. Matthew's Sermon on the Mount is related only loosely to Luke's Sermon on the Plain, which is much shorter, although some of the omitted material occurs elsewhere in Luke in scattered contexts. Other details will be given later, when source theories are discussed.

Whereas the three Synoptics often agree in sections common to them all, Matthew and Mark often agree against Luke, and Luke and Mark against Matthew, and sometimes, though more rarely, Matthew and Luke against Mark.

These are the basic details which constitute the problem. A brief historical summary will now be given of the various solutions which have been proposed.

II. A BRIEF HISTORICAL SURVEY OF SOLUTIONS

Little attention was given to this problem until the eighteenth century, although its existence had been obvious from earliest times. The widespread influence of Tatian's *Diatessaron* is sufficient evidence of the desire for the removal of the difficulties by means of harmonization. Even when the separate Gospels displaced Tatian's harmony in the Eastern Church and were indisputably established in the West, the difficulties were resolved by harmonization without any attempt being made to settle the problem of origins or relationship. Indeed, these questions were not seriously considered until they were forced to the forefront by the upsurge of rationalism in the eighteenth century.[1]

a. The original Gospel hypothesis

The first solution suggested was that of G. E. Lessing,[2] who postulated that our Gospels were different translations or abstracts from an old Aramaic *Gospel of the Nazarenes*, which Jerome mentions as still being current among the sect of the Nazarenes in the fourth century. This was further elaborated in a complicated and rather artificial manner by J. G. Eichhorn,[3] who not only proposed that nine different Gospels issued from the original Aramaic (which he considered to have been an apostolic rough draft for use in the instruction of teachers) but that the Synoptics were the concluding phenomena of this literary process.*

b. The fragment theory

The unsatisfactory character of Eichhorn's solution led F. Schleiermacher[4] to produce a different, though no more satisfactory, suggestion. He postulated that the apostles wrote down records of the words of Jesus as they were known to witnesses. These were later required

---

[1] It is interesting to note that John Calvin, who wrote a commentary on *A Harmonie upon the three Evangelistes, Matthewe, Marke and Luke* (Eng. Tr. by E. Paget, 1584), chose this form for convenience and not because he was seriously concerned about the Synoptic problem.

[2] *Neue Hypothese über die Evangelisten als bloss menschliche Geschichtsschreiber* (1778).

[3] *Historische-kritische Einleitung in das Neue Testament* (1812).

[4] *A critical Essay on the Gospel of St. Luke* (Eng. Tr. 1825).

for use beyond the borders of Palestine and various collections were made. One teacher might have collected miracle-stories, another sayings, a third passion narratives, and so on. Luke's Prologue was appealed to in support of this hypothesis, and the collected records were then held to have been used in the production of the canonical Gospels. The major weaknesses of this hypothesis are the absence of any traces of such early records and the inability of the theory to account for the remarkable similarities in the Synoptic Gospels, not only in vocabulary but in the sequence of events. Its importance, however, cannot be lightly dismissed since it has much in common with certain types of form criticism. It may also be said to have set the stage for the appearance of various other fragment hypotheses in attempted solutions of other New Testament problems.[1]

c. The oral theory

In view of the lack of sufficient data on the state of Gospel traditions prior to our written Gospels, it is natural to investigate the possibility that similarities and divergences arose in the course of a period of oral transmission. Even if the theory can claim no notable recent supporters, it merits careful consideration because it has at least some affinity with form criticism.

In the era during which the first indications of the urge towards a scientific study of the New Testament arose, the idea that oral tradition lay at the base of the Synoptic material was mooted by G. Herder.[2] Soon after this, in 1818, J. K. L. Gieseler,[3] produced what might be called the prototype of the oral theory, maintaining that the apostolic preaching would form itself into similar oral traditions which would then form a kind of basic oral Gospel. This oral Gospel was preserved in the original Aramaic, but the needs of the Gentile mission would give rise to the demand for a Greek translation. This basic Aramaic and the Greek translation later became the main source for the three Evangelists, being used differently according to the different approach of each writer. Thus Matthew produced a genuine Palestinian Gospel,

---

[1] The theory of W. L. Knox that various 'tracts' lay behind Mark is similar to Schleiermacher's theory. Cf. his *Sources of the Synoptic Gospels: I St. Mark* (1953).

[2] *Von der Regel der Zustimmung unserer Evangelien* (1797), reproduced in *Werke zur Religion und Theologie*, 12 (1810).

[3] *Historisch-kritischer Versuch über die Entstehung und die frühesten Schicksale der schriftlichen Evangelien* (1818).

Mark a modified Palestinian and Luke a Pauline Gospel. The literary differences between them were conditioned by the respective authors' training and ability. There are some similarities between this and later oral theories, but one significant difference should be noted. Gieseler disputed the possibility of any systematic learning by heart, on which Westcott, for instance, placed such stress.

Westcott's presentation of the oral theory may be regarded as its classic formulation,[1] which for a time secured many adherents, particularly among those who rejected the German source theories dominant in his day. The main idea of his theory may be briefly summarized as follows.

1. Since the Jews would not commit to writing their mass of oral traditions, it is improbable that the first Christian leaders would have entertained doing so.[2] The literary traditions of the Jews, with their great emphasis on oral transmission as the main educative medium, would encourage the Church to prefer oral rather than written teaching. This would mean a considerable period during which the traditions would be floating in an oral form.

2. Since the apostolic circle was primarily composed of preachers and not writers, literary enterprises would not at once have occurred to them.[3] Here Westcott assumed that, on the one hand, the work of preaching would occupy the apostles to such an extent that literary methods of propaganda would be ruled out, and, on the other hand, that these men by education and culture would have been unfitted for the task, even if its possibilities had been recognized. Nevertheless, he maintained that this disinclination towards an immediate reduction of the Gospel material to writing was later invaluable since 'the very form of the Gospels was only determined by the experience of teaching'.[4]

3. Since the Gospels arose out of the recurring needs of the community, the most attention would naturally be given to those narratives which were most used in the apostolic preaching, and this would admirably account for the space devoted to the passion and resurrection narratives.[5] Such a feature accords with the testimony of the Acts and the Epistles.

4. Westcott claimed that the testimony of the Apostolic Fathers, in so far as they bear any witness to the origin of the Gospels, supports an

[1] B. F. Westcott, *An Introduction to the Study of the Gospels*[7] (1888, first published in 1851).
[2] *Ibid.*, p. 167.   [3] *Ibid.*, pp. 168 ff.   [4] *Ibid.*, p. 170.   [5] *Ibid.*, pp. 174 ff.

oral theory.[1] Papias, for instance, expressed a definite preference for oral testimony himself and may be reflecting a much earlier tendency. Moreover the same writer implies that Mark wrote down some of the things he had heard Peter narrate.

5. Assuming that Mark's Gospel, by reason of its 'vivid simplicity', was the 'most direct representation of the Evangelic tradition', which was the common foundation on which the others were reared, Westcott[2] regarded Matthew's and Luke's Gospels as types of recension of the simple narrative. Matthew preserves the Hebraic form of the tradition while Luke presents the Greek form.[3]

Subsequent to Westcott's formulation of the theory, two other writers introduced significant modifications. G. Wetzel[4] evolved the theory that one apostle (Matthew) was specially assigned to oral instruction. As a result of constant repetition of the instruction the tradition would acquire fixation. The hearers would pass on the tradition in the form taught and would often make notes to aid their memories. Such notes would later have been used to compile the accounts to which Luke makes reference in his preface, and the use of such notes by the writers of the Synoptic Gospels would, in Wetzel's view, account for the similarities and differences in their accounts.

A different modification of the theory was proposed by A. Wright.[5] In his opinion Peter, in Jerusalem, gave Aramaic oral instruction, while Mark acted as his interpreter for Greek-speaking people. Those so instructed became catechists to other churches.[6] At the same time in Jerusalem another collection of material arose, which Wright called by the name Logia. In order to account for the common structure of the narratives, he further postulated that the order became fixed as an aid to the memory.[7] He also suggested that the oral Gospel may have been divided into weekly church lessons,[8] an idea which may find some

---

[1] Ibid., pp. 184 ff.   [2] Ibid., pp. 209 f.

[3] Westcott (op. cit., pp. 192 f.) maintained that the oral Gospel originally existed in both Aramaic and Greek.

[4] Die synoptischen Evangelien (1883).

[5] Synopsis of the Gospels in Greek (1896); The Composition of the Four Gospels (1890); Some New Testament Problems (1898); St. Luke in Greek (1900).

[6] Wright insisted that some form of definite catechizing which involved committing the teaching to memory was essential for any soundly based oral theory (cf. his Synopsis, p. xiv).

[7] Ibid., p. xvii.

[8] St. Luke in Greek, p. xi.

support from recent suggestions which have been made about the relation between the Gospels and Jewish lectionaries.[1]

But the majority of scholars have discounted the oral theory and their main objections will need to be mentioned.

1. The first difficulty concerns the narrative sequence. Most scholars find it hard to believe that both the precise order of events and in many cases the precise words could have been orally preserved in the forms in which they are recorded in the canonical Gospels. Westcott had maintained that 'the whole period was one in essence, undivided by years or festivals and the record would be marked not so much by divisions of time as by groups of events'.[2] But it is generally felt that this does not adequately account for the variations as well as the similarities occurring in the Gospels. It must not, however, be overlooked that there is little material available for deciding this issue conclusively, and the fact that careful memory work was certainly widely known among the Jews should make the investigator cautious about too much dogmatism regarding it.[3]

2. In view of the fact that both Matthew and Luke always return to Mark's order after deviation from it, it is considered much more reasonable to suppose that they worked from a written rather than from an oral tradition. This is a more weighty objection than the last, for it may be maintained that the Evangelists would not revert to their original sequence so readily after a break if they were relying on memory alone. But again a caution is necessary, since the dominant sequence might have become deeply imprinted through constant repetition, and have reasserted itself almost subconsciously without the intervention of a written reminder. Yet this is pure conjecture and all that can safely be said is that it is possible.[4] It is not surprising that those

[1] Cf. especially the work of A. Farrer and P. Carrington on Mark and A. Guilding on John. For comments on these theories see pp. 66 ff., 311 f.

[2] *Op. cit.*, p. 208.

[3] B. Gerhardsson (*Memory and Manuscript*, 1961) gives a thorough and illuminating study of the methods of oral transmission in rabbinic Judaism and suggests that similar methods would have been adopted among Christians. See pp. 222 ff. for further discussion of Gerhardsson's ideas.

[4] Westcott accounted for the phenomenon by maintaining that Mark's account was the earliest and therefore 'represents most closely the original form' from which the Gospel started (*op. cit.*, p. 211). In this case the dominance of Mark's order would not be surprising. The real crux seems to be whether an extensive Gospel framework could have been transmitted by oral methods. Form criticism is against the possibility, but it cannot be said to be entirely out of the ques-

committed to source criticism rejected the oral solution on this score.

3. A more perplexing difficulty for the oral theory is the omission from Mark of the mass of teaching material incorporated by Matthew and Luke in different ways. If, as Westcott maintained, Mark's Gospel was the first to be produced, why was so little of the teaching incorporated in it? This is by no means an unanswerable objection to the oral theory, for on any theory which assumes Marcan priority the difficulty exists. The postulation of a sayings source 'Q' (see pp. 143 ff.) does little to remove this difficulty unless it can be shown that Mark knew of the existence of Q, but this is open to question. Also, it is not entirely improbable that Mark, if he were the first to produce a written Gospel, preferred narrative material to discourse material and for that reason left the latter for others to reduce to writing. In other words, his omission of the discourse material would be damaging to the oral theory only in so far as it is assumed that he must have reduced to writing at least some samples of all the material in the oral tradition. But this condition is not so evident if his purpose was to highlight the narrative, which he has certainly done with considerable vividness.

The above reasons are nevertheless considered by most scholars to be sufficient to dispense with the oral hypothesis in favour of a source solution. But the shift of emphasis in recent times from the minutiae of source analysis to form criticism has once again brought the oral phase of Gospel transmission into focus and the relationship between the oral theory and form criticism therefore warrants some comment.

As form criticism is fully discussed later, all that is here intended is to give some indication of its points of contact and contrast with the oral theory. These may be summarized as follows.

1. Both emphasize the importance of the pre-literary period of the tradition. It is significant that after a century of source criticism which led, in its extreme forms, to too great a bondage to written origins, the critical pendulum has swung towards the oral tradition, although with a vital difference.

2. Whereas the oral theory denies the use of written sources by the Gospel writers, form criticism generally accepts the documentary framework but pushes the investigation behind those sources. In this

tion in view of the contemporary Jewish procedure in the transmission of rabbinic traditions, although these are mainly didactic. Modern criticism tends to place too much emphasis on editorial practices which were alien to the first-century outlook. It is a danger that must constantly be borne in mind.

way form criticism allows an additional factor (intermediary sources) which the oral theory saw no need to postulate. Nevertheless it must be admitted that focus upon the pre-literary stage cannot fail in some degree to lessen complete confidence in the adequacy of the source hypotheses. This will become clearer later, but if different literary forms could arise from the oral tradition it is perhaps not unreasonable to suggest that each Evangelist may have drawn material from such oral forms, especially if he had had any hand in the shaping of the forms through catechetical instruction. But this latter possibility is generally ruled out by both source and form critics.

3. The oral theory contrasts with the form-critical approach in leaving the oral tradition in a somewhat nebulous state, whereas the latter attempts to classify the various materials into precise literary categories and then proceeds to investigate their *Sitz im Leben* (the life-situation in which they arose). On the face of it the latter method has the appearance of being more scientific and, in so far as it confines itself to classification of literary forms, this may well be justified. Yet it may be said from the side of the less precise oral theory that scientific investigation cannot be based on insufficient data, and no-one can deny that the data available for pre-literary study are not particularly weighty.

d. The mutual dependence hypothesis

Another eighteenth-century proposal which has been subject to many variations is the idea of literary dependence one upon another. J. J. Griesbach,[1] following the suggestion of Augustine, considered Mark as an epitomizer of Matthew, while even Luke was considered to be earlier than Mark. Mark i. 32 became a celebrated illustration of this process, since it appears to conflate the accounts of the other Synoptic Gospels. But this theory, although embraced by the Tübingen school of critics, has been discounted because it fails to do justice to the literary characteristics of Mark.[2] The theory that Mark was basic, followed by

[1] *Commentatio qua Marci evangelium totum e Matthaei et Lucae commentariis decerptum esse demonstratur* (1789).

[2] H. G. Jameson (*The Origin of the Synoptic Gospels*, 1922) maintained a theory similar to Griesbach's but he considered that Matthew was basic to Mark and that both Matthew and Mark were used by Luke. It should be noted that the order Matthew–Mark–Luke appears to have been assumed in the second century *milieu* to which the anti-Marcionite Prologue to Luke belonged. Another modification is that of W. Lockton (*Church Quarterly Review*, July, 1922), who suggested that Luke was basic to Mark and that both these were used by Matthew.

Matthew and Luke in that order, was propounded by C. Lachmann.[1] Although not now acceptable in the form originally suggested, it undoubtedly prepared the way for the source hypothesis, which we shall consider next.[2]

e. The documentary hypothesis

The basic form of this theory is that the similarities and divergences can be accounted for by the postulation of two written sources, one of which was the canonical Mark or an earlier written form of it, and the other a common source used by Matthew and Luke in different ways. This latter source was named Q, probably after the German *Quelle* (source). The Mark-Q theory may be regarded as the basic element in modern source criticism of the Synoptic Gospels. But many of the variations between Matthew and Luke are difficult to account for adequately under this theory and this has led to a number of proposed modifications. In many hypotheses Q became not a single source but a multiplication of sources,[3] and this understandably tended to weaken confidence in the hypothesis.

Owing to the cosmopolitan characteristics of the so-called Q-document under the two document theory, B. H. Streeter[4] posited a four source hypothesis which has won wide support and will merit detailed examination. For the purpose of the present survey, it may be said that Streeter's solution supplied two new developments in the study of the Synoptic problem. In the first place, he strictly limited the source Q to that material which was used by both Matthew and Luke but not Mark, and two other sources were proposed for Matthew's (M) and Luke's (L) special sayings material. This meant that Matthew used Mark, Q and M as his main sources, and Luke used Mark, Q and L. In the second place Streeter called attention to the need for noting the locality from which the different earlier sources originated. Mark was the Roman Gospel, Q was probably based on Antioch, M represented

---

[1] 'De ordine narrationum in evangeliis synopticis', *TSK*, 8 (1835), pp. 570 ff.

[2] The view that Luke used Matthew was held by E. Simons, *Hat der dritte Evangelist den kanonischen Matthäus benutzt?* (1880; cited by Stanton, *The Gospels as Historical Documents*, II, p. 30). Most recently this has been advocated by A. Farrer in *Studies in the Gospels* (ed. D. E. Nineham, 1955), pp. 55 ff.*

[3] See the later discussion on Q on pp. 143 ff.

[4] *The Four Gospels* (1924).

a Jerusalem sayings-document and L represented the Caesarean tradition, probably oral in character.[1] These proposals were admittedly conjectural, but Streeter considered that the association of sources with important centres guaranteed their authority, but when the Gospels became accepted the preservation of these earlier sources, with the exception of Mark, was rendered unnecessary. While there have been many modifications of this type of four document theory and a decided lessening of emphasis upon a multiplication of written sources due largely to the influence of form criticism, it is still widely regarded, at least among British scholars, as the most workable hypothesis of Gospel origins.[2]

f. The form-historical method

In reaction to the multiplicity of written sources which had been postulated and the minute attention which had been devoted to source analysis, a movement sprang up to investigate more closely the manner in which these sources had themselves been codified from the oral tradition. This movement, called in Germany *Die formgeschichtliche Methode* but generally known in England as form criticism, had as its aim not only to classify the material into 'forms' of tradition, but also to attempt to discover the historical situation (*Sitz im Leben*) in which they grew. This type of approach will require detailed examination in a separate chapter, for it has had considerable influence in recent New Testament criticism. Its chief advocates have been M. Dibelius, R. Bultmann, M. Albertz in Germany, B. S. Easton, W. E. Bundy and F. C. Grant in America, and E. B. Redlich, R. H. Lightfoot, V. Taylor and D. E. Nineham in this country.[3]

III. THE FOUR SOURCE THEORY

It has already been shown that the four source theory is really a modification of the two source theory. Still fundamental to it is the assumption that the basic sources of Matthew and Luke were Mark and Q.

[1] Vincent Taylor, who accepts much of Streeter's theory, in his recent *The Life and Ministry of Jesus* (1954), p. 14, maintains only Mark, Q and M as written sources and this approach is representative of a wide circle of scholars committed to the four source theory.

[2] Cf. F. C. Grant, *The Gospels, their origin and growth* (1957), pp. 50, 51, who holds to a multiple source theory, which is essentially based on Streeter's proposals.

[3] See pp. 188 ff. for a full discussion of form criticism.

In other words it preserves what has become a basic principle of Synoptic criticism, i.e. that the similarities observable in the Synoptic Gospels can be accounted for only on the basis of literary dependence. The king-pin of the whole hypothesis is Marcan priority, which has become an almost undisputed canon of criticism. The reasons for this are discussed in the next section, but it should be noted that however strong these reasons appear to be, the inferences drawn from them can never be finally conclusive. It may be the best explanation of the phenomena, but it cannot be proved because the data available for tracing the processes of early Christian transmission are too limited.

As far as Q is concerned its postulation is much more hypothetical, and this is clear from Streeter's plea that it should be limited to the material common to Matthew and Luke, but excluded from Mark. As will be seen later the delineation and even the very existence of Q has been much discussed, particularly in recent years, and Streeter's conception of it cannot be regarded as unchallengeable. Nevertheless the assumption that it is basic to Synoptic criticism is still generally dominant. Modern criticism finds it difficult to conceive that the common teaching material in Matthew and Luke could have come about in any other way than by their respective authors both using an earlier source. But the New Testament investigator must guard against the fallacious assumption that what is inconceivable to him must be false. It may have happened in a manner alien to twentieth-century experience of the transmission of ideas. Q may after all be no more than the creation of modern imagination. As to Streeter's other sources, M and L, the postulation of these was just as logical as the postulation of various recensions of Q, but little more so. The theory is more realistic in allowing that L may be oral tradition rather than a written source, but this concession to oral transmission is made only because this material exists in a single tradition instead of a double or triple tradition.[1]

Our next task will be to examine the evidence for the four source hypothesis.

---

[1] Although this concession to oral tradition is made for L, it is maintained that it was probably reduced to writing before Luke left Caesarea. This assumption has led H. Montefiore to question whether the L hypothesis, in the form in which it is generally held, is tenable since the document would not have survived the shipwreck in which Luke was involved (Acts xxvii; cf. his article, 'Does "L" hold water?', *JTS*, n.s., XII, 1961, pp. 59, 60). He thinks L cannot represent pure Caesarean tradition.

IV. THE MARCAN SOURCE

a. Reasons for its priority

Augustine's opinion that Mark was an abstract of Matthew was generally held until the early part of the nineteenth century, but with the exception of certain recent Roman Catholic scholars this opinion is now almost wholly discounted. The reasons for this change of outlook may be summarized as follows.

(i) *The proportion of Mark reproduced.* Almost the whole of Mark is paralleled in Matthew (about 90 per cent). There are, in fact, only seven short passages which do not appear. About half of Mark also appears in Luke. In Matthew and Luke combined all but four paragraphs of Mark are paralleled.[1] In just over half of the common material which Matthew and Luke respectively share with Mark, there is more or less verbal agreement.

(ii) *The primary order of Mark.* In the main the three Gospels keep to the same general outline, but where they diverge in matters of detail it is more rare for Matthew and Luke to agree against Mark, than for Mark to be in the majority.[2] In the case of Matthew the transpositions may generally be accounted for satisfactorily by the editor's desire to group his material into series.

(iii) *The literary characteristics.* There are a number of ways in which Mark's language and style appear to give a more primitive account.[3] First, Mark's amplifications of details and even of whole sections are made more concise in Matthew and Luke. For Mark's details, absent from Matthew and Luke, compare the following examples—'when the sun did set' (i. 32; Mt. viii. 16), the 'green' grass (vi. 39; Mt. xiv. 19; Lk. ix. 14), the 'three hundred pence' (xiv. 5; Mt. xxvi. 9). An example of the shortening of a whole narrative may be seen in the account of the healing of the multitudes (iii. 7–12; Mt. xii. 15, 16; Lk. vi. 17–19). Secondly, Mark's style is polished by Matthew and Luke. His vivid historic presents (151 times) are rarely paralleled in Matthew (21 times)

---

[1] Cf. H. B. Swete, *Mark,* p. lxiii.

[2] Cf. W. G. Kümmel's tabulated comparisons (*INT,* 1965, pp. 46, 47). These comparisons show how Mark's order is dominant in both Matthew and Luke.

[3] W. C. Allen (*The Gospel according to St. Matthew,* pp. xix ff.) gives a very useful list of instances where he considers Matthew has changed Mark's language. Cf. also V. H. Stanton, *The Gospels as Historical Documents* (1923), pp. 51–53.

and only once in Luke, in passages common to all three. It should be noted, however, that Matthew uses historic presents 72 times in his non-Marcan material and this must be taken into account in assessing this evidence for priority. In many cases grammatical improvements are observed when Matthew and Luke are compared with the parallel passage in Mark, e.g. redundant negatives, unusual words and difficult constructions are removed. Thirdly, some weight has also been placed on Mark's inclusion of eight Aramaic words of Jesus as compared with one in Matthew and none in Luke. It is contended that Aramaic words would be more readily omitted from, rather than added to, an existing source.

(iv) *The greater historical candour.* Because Mark often records evidences of Jesus' human emotions (see p. 55 for details) where Matthew and Luke in parallel passages either omit or modify, it is supposed that he must represent an earlier tradition. The modifications are regarded as signs of increasing reverence. Of a similar character are those passages in which the other Synoptics appear to tone down statements which in Mark might be thought to give Jesus' limitations too great a prominence. A well-known case of such modification is found in Mark vi. 5; Matthew xiii. 58, where Mark states that Jesus could not do any mighty work in Nazareth, whereas Matthew has 'not many' and Luke omits the episode altogether. But it should be noted that Mark refers to a few sick people who were healed, which somewhat lessens the alleged modification. In the account of the cursing of the fig-tree the withering is more protracted in Mark than in Matthew (Mk. xi. 12 ff.; Mt. xxi. 18 ff.), while the words in Mark which might suggest that Jesus expected to find figs on the tree but was disappointed are lacking in Matthew, although the idea is implied. Although it is quite intelligible to explain these as reverential modifications, it is not impossible to give a different explanation. It may be a case of different emphases in parallel traditions, in which event it would cease to be evidence of later modifications of Mark. All that can safely be said is that if literary dependence is accepted it is more reasonable to suppose that Mark has been modified by Matthew and Luke than *vice versa*.

The greater candour of Mark is also said to be reflected in the portrayal of the disciples. The implied rebuke of Mark iv. 13 because of the disciples' failure to understand the parable of the sower is absent from both Matthew and Luke (Mt. xiii. 18; Lk. viii. 11). In the account of the stilling of the storm Mark records Jesus' question, 'How is it that you have no faith?' but Luke has 'Where is your faith?' and Matthew uses the word 'of small faith' (ὀλιγόπιστοι) (Mk. iv. 40; Mt. viii. 26; Lk. viii. 25). In the same incident Mark's 'Carest thou not that we perish?' appears in both Matthew and Luke as a statement, 'we perish'.

(v) *The least explicit account.* In the narrative of Peter's confession at Caesarea Philippi Mark has only 'Thou art the Christ', but both Matthew and Luke add further descriptions (Mk. viii. 29; Mt. xvi. 16; Lk. ix. 20). In referring to Herod, Mark calls him a king but the other two use the more precise 'tetrarch' (Mk. vi. 14; Mt. xiv. 1; Lk. ix. 7). On the occasion of the third prediction of the passion, Mark's 'kill' appears in Matthew as 'crucify', although Luke has the same as Mark (Mk. x. 34; Mt. xx. 19; Lk. xviii. 33).

These differences in Matthew and Luke when compared with Mark are considered by the majority of scholars[1] to be of sufficient weight to establish the priority of Mark. The contrary hypothesis that Mark is dependent on either one or both of the others raises more problems. Even if the Marcan hypothesis is not without its own problems, it is generally maintained to be most probable on the grounds that the theory which solves a greater number of the difficulties is more likely to be correct. Another subsidiary consideration in favour of the Marcan hypothesis is the claim that the most vivid Gospel is more likely to be prior, since vividness is not likely to have been impressed upon an existing source.

b. Problems arising from the theory of Marcan priority

(i) The first problem arises from the agreements of Matthew and Luke against Mark.[2] These agreements were at one time made the basis of a theory that an earlier source of Mark's Gospel existed (Ur-Markus) from which both Matthew and Luke copied their records. But these

[1] Cf. the full discussion in Streeter's *The Four Gospels*, pp. 151–168, and the concise summary in V. Taylor, *The Gospels*, pp. 44 ff.; cf. also W. G. Kümmel, *INT* (1965), pp. 46 ff.*

[2] E. A. Abbott's *Corrections of Mark* (1901) contains a full list of the coincidences of Matthew and Luke against Mark. Cf. also J. C. Hawkins, *Horae Synopticae*, pp. 174 ff.; F. C. Burkitt, *The Gospel History and its Transmission*[3] (1911), pp. 42–58; L. Vaganay, *Le Problème synoptique* (1954), pp. 319 ff.*

agreements have been variously assessed by different scholars. Streeter[1] claimed that they could mostly be eliminated by means of textual criticism, being explained as scribal corruptions. But others who have not been impressed by Streeter's solution have maintained that Matthew and Luke have independently corrected Mark and that their agreements are due to the 'naturalness' of these editorial corrections.[2] Another suggestion is that at these points Q may have overlapped Mark and that Matthew and Luke preferred the Q version to Mark, while yet another is that Matthew and Luke knew Mark in an Aramaic and a Greek form and that they corrected the Greek by means of the Aramaic.[3] The conjectural character of most of these reasons will be readily apparent and will lead cautious minds to recognize that the Marcan hypothesis is still not without its difficulties.[4] At the same time it must be recognized that the agreements under discussion form only a small percentage of the common material.[5]

(ii) The second problem concerns the great omission, the name given to that section in the middle of Mark (vi. 45–viii. 26) which Luke entirely omits. So striking is this omission that some satisfactory reason is demanded, and four types of solution have been proposed.

1. That an editor has added it to the original Mark after Luke had used Mark as the basis for his Gospel. This requires the acceptance of the Ur-Markus hypothesis already mentioned, but there seems to be no adequate motive for a later editor inserting this section if it did not exist in the original copy. In any case Matthew has used much of this material, which makes the above explanation more difficult, for it

---

[1] *The Four Gospels*, pp. 293–331. W. Sanday (*Oxford Studies*, p. 21) suggested that Matthew and Luke used a different recension of Mark from that from which the extant MSS are descended. Quite recently a similar theory has been advanced by J. P. Brown (*JBL*, LXXVIII, 1959, pp. 215–227), who maintains that the Caesarean text is the best witness to the recension of Mark which was used by Matthew and Luke.

[2] K. and S. Lake (*An Introduction to the New Testament*, 1938, pp. 6, 7), who regard textual corruption as responsible for only a few of the agreements, explain the rest as natural editorial corrections by Matthew and Luke. C. H. Turner (*JTS*, x, 1909, pp. 175 ff.) considered our knowledge of the original text of the Gospels to be insufficient to enable the textual critical argument to be used with certainty.

[3] Cf. the theory of C. C. Torrey, *The Four Gospels: A New Translation*, 1933.

[4] Cf. W. Sanday, in *Oxford Studies in the Synoptic Problem* (1911), p. 20.

[5] Cf. N. B. Stonehouse, *Origins of the Synoptic Gospels* (1963), p. 63.

would necessitate the assumption that Matthew used the edited form of Mark and not Ur-Markus.

2. That Luke accidentally omitted this section by passing from the feeding of the crowds in Mark vi. 42–44 to the similar incident in viii. 19–21. Sanday[1] pointed out that ancient writers had much greater difficulties in composing documents than modern writers especially when using other written sources, since it was no easy process to verify material from cumbrous rolls. A mistake of this kind is therefore by no means improbable.*

3. That Luke deliberately omitted the section. This may have been either because it did not suit his purpose or because he preferred his alternative source and limits of space prevented him from making use of all his material. Hawkins[2] suggested that the solution might lie in a combination of accident and intention if Luke first accidentally omitted it and later realized that its inclusion would add nothing to his narrative. But Vincent Taylor,[3] who advocates an original draft of Luke (see the discussion on Proto-Luke, pp. 175 ff.), thinks that this section is not the kind that Luke would have selected when expanding his original draft by means of Mark.[4]

4. That Luke used a mutilated copy of Mark. This view, put forward by Streeter,[5] postulates that Luke's copy contained only the commencement of the section, and that he had to patch together the mutilated portions. Streeter admitted that this was merely a tentative suggestion and it has not commended itself to other scholars.[6]

[1] Op. cit., pp. 16, 17.   [2] Op. cit., p. 74.   [3] Op. cit., p. 48.

[4] Many scholars have considered that Luke's omission of this material may have been due to his desire to avoid 'doublets'. W. Bussmann (Synoptische Studien, I, 1925, pp. 1–66) gives detailed attention to these so-called 'doublets'. But W. Grundmann (Das Evangelium nach Lukas, p. 8) rightly points out that Luke does in fact include many examples of duplicated material (e.g. the double mission passages and the double apocalyptic sections). It is reasonable to conclude therefore that this duplicated material was included because Luke assumed that both accounts were relevant.

[5] Op. cit., pp. 176 ff.

[6] A modification of this view is that of T. Nicklin (Gospel Gleanings, 1950, pp. 3 ff.) who maintains that Mk. vi. 47–viii. 27a occupied twelve pages (three complete sheets) of Mark's original and that these pages formed the middle portion of a quire which would readily account for their being detached. In this theory there are two assumptions: one that the Gospel was originally written in codex form, which although not altogether improbable lacks proof, and the other that Luke's copy of Mark was the only copy to suffer mutilation in this way and that Luke did not suspect it.

There seems to be no need, in order to maintain the theory of Marcan priority and the use of it in the production of Luke's Gospel, to postulate any other reason than Luke's individual choice. Only those not satisfied with anything less than a minute analysis of the author's mind will feel confident when pushing the enquiry further. Those who challenge the literary dependence altogether will not, of course, regard the problem as a relevant one.

c. Alternatives to Marcan priority

The foregoing considerations have been regarded by the great majority of scholars as sufficient to establish the theory. In fact, it is generally treated as the one assured result of criticism. It is certainly the foundation-stone of most Synoptic literary criticism. Hypotheses regarding Matthew's and Luke's Gospels almost invariably proceed from the assumption that both have used Mark as a source.

There have been, nevertheless, some recent attempts to solve the Synoptic problem apart from the Marcan hypothesis. The most thoroughgoing of these attempts is that of B. C. Butler[1] who maintains the priority of Matthew over against Mark. By postulating such a theory, Butler also dispenses with Q, and much of the force of his arguments against Marcan priority depends on the inadmissibility of appealing to Q as an explanation of cases where Matthew appears to be the more original. The records of the preaching of John the Baptist may be quoted as an example. But since most source critics maintain the Q hypothesis, Butler's arguments are generally regarded as unconvincing. Although he has found few supporters for his contentions, he has drawn attention to difficulties in the Marcan hypothesis which would be obviated if Matthew were the first Gospel. Other Roman Catholic writers have maintained a modified form of Matthaean priority, suggesting the use by Mark of an earlier and shorter edition of Matthew as the basic Gospel. This view has been maintained by L. Vaganay,[2] who claims to be able to account for the various phenomena more adequately by postulating two main sources from which the

---

[1] *The Originality of Matthew* (1951). Cf. the criticisms of H. G. Wood (*ET*, LXV, 1953–54, pp. 17–19), who maintained that the order and arrangement of incidents in Matthew and Mark exclude Butler's view. Another careful critique of Butler may be found in G. M. Styler's 'Excursus on the Priority of Mark' in C. F. D. Moule's *The Birth of the New Testament*, pp. 223–232.

[2] *Op. cit.* See further comment on pp. 145 f.

three Synoptic Gospels were derived, a Greek translation of an original Aramaic Matthew and a sayings source used in Greek by Matthew and Luke. If this is correct neither Matthew nor Luke need have used Mark as a basic source, although Vaganay supposed that Luke did in fact use Mark. A rather similar theory has been maintained by L. Cerfaux[1] in that he too postulates a Proto-Matthew, and at the same time retains the current view that our present Greek Matthew and Luke depend on Mark.

Dissatisfaction with the Marcan hypothesis has also led to a modification of it by the postulation of various sources of which Matthew had access to only a part.[2] This is really a revised version of the earlier Ur-Markus theory, but is rather more thoroughgoing in its scope. None of these challenges to the established theory of Marcan priority has received much support, and yet they are significant reminders that the theory may not be as assured as it has been alleged to be.[3] All that can be said is that the theory may be regarded as the most probable basic source hypothesis yet proposed.

d. Sources of the Marcan source

Generally speaking source criticism has been content to treat Mark as a basic source without enquiring too specifically into its origins. One exception to this attitude has been the suggestion first proposed by T. Colani[4] in 1864 that Mark has incorporated a previously existing Jewish Christian apocalypse (Mk. xiii). There has been considerable support for this theory, so much so that it has come to be regarded almost as a fact of Synoptic criticism.[5] The main basis for the theory is the

---

[1] Cf. *Recueil Lucien Cerfaux*, I (1954), pp. 399–469.

[2] Cf. D. F. Robinson's suggestion that Matthew used a shorter form of Mark, which was later enlarged from additional sources (*JBL*, LXVI, 1947, pp. 153 ff.). He based his suggestions on a comparative study of the arrangement of the common material in Matthew and Mark.

[3] In his recent article on the alleged Matthaean errata, N. Walker (*NTS*, 9, 1963, pp. 391–394) suggests that a study of the passages which are supposed to show Matthew's inaccuracies not only shows that such allegations are unjustified but casts doubt on Marcan priority. He speaks of Mark reducing Matthew.

[4] *Jésus Christ et les croyances messianiques de son temps*[2] (1864).

[5] Cf. Moffatt, *ILNT*, p. 209; Stanton, *The Gospels as Historical Documents* 1923), pp. 115–121; Streeter, *The Four Gospels*, pp. 491–494; Rawlinson, *The Gospel according to St. Mark*, pp. 177–182, 187 ff.; T. W. Manson, *The Teaching of Jesus* (1931), pp. 260–263; V. Taylor, *The Gospels*, p. 50; *idem*, *The Gospel*

alleged inconsistencies within the passage as it stands, inconsistencies with the teaching of Jesus elsewhere and incongruities between the passage and its immediate context. But the hypothesis has not gone without its challengers. G. R. Beasley-Murray[1] has traced the development of the theory from its origins and has pointed out the insecurity of its foundations. His work may pave the way for a more traditional approach to the acceptance of the fact that Jesus Himself used apocalyptic language. It may be shown also that the alleged inconsistencies are capable of intelligible interpretations without recourse to this theory. In spite of the fact that many still regard some earlier source as practically certain, there are signs that the theory may be loosening its grip. C. E. B. Cranfield[2] concludes his investigation of Mark xiii. 5–37 with the opinion that it gives substantially our Lord's teaching.

Some attention has been paid to the special sources of Mark's passion narrative. It has recently been maintained that Mark has used two main sources for his account, one of which was non-Semitic, containing a straightforward narrative, and the other a strongly Semitic collection of self-contained narratives.[3] The two sources were, of course, parallel but independent[4] and Mark has merged the two together in his account. The basis of this theory is mainly linguistic and stylistic and depends on the general source-critical presupposition that similarities in language denote a similar source, and dissimilarities indicate dissimilar sources. Provided this principle of criticism is accepted there is some support for the two source theory for Mark's passion narrative. It is not impossible, in fact, on this basis to suppose that Mark has here drawn from different strata of the tradition. Taylor suggests that Mark found a passion narrative at Rome and expanded it by means of Petrine tradi-

---

according to St. Mark, ad loc. E. Klostermann (*Das Markusevangelium*[4], 1950, pp. 131, 132) accepts with very little discussion or comment the view that Mk. xiii consists of a Jewish apocalyptic document with Christian editorial additions.*

[1] *Jesus and the Future* (1954). Cf. idem, *A Commentary on Mark Thirteen* (1957). For a criticism of this author's arguments, cf. S. G. F. Brandon, *The Fall of Jerusalem and the Christian Church*, Note III, pp. 270 ff., and H. Conzelmann, *ZNTW*, 50 (1959), pp. 210–221.

[2] *The Gospel according to St. Mark* (*CGT*, n.s., 1959), p. 390. Cf. also his articles in *SJT*, 6 (1953), pp. 189–196, 287–303, 7 (1954), pp. 284–303.

[3] Cf. V. Taylor, *The Gospel according to St. Mark*, pp. 653–664. Cf. also his articles in *NTS*, 4 (1958), pp. 215 ff.

[4] Cf. the further study of S. Temple, *NTS*, 7 (1960), pp. 77–85.

tion. But the main weakness of Taylor's linguistic analysis is its complicated character. His A source is divided into eighteen sections in
order to be combined with seventeen sections of the B source, many of
which sections are exceedingly brief.[1] It would seem better to
speak of an editorial process rather than a source, at least for his B
material. It must also be noted that this analysis is based mainly on the
presence or absence of Semitisms (A mainly lacking them), but it is
difficult to be sure of the Semitic character of all the evidence Taylor
cites.*

Although the earlier Ur-Markus theory[2] is now out of favour, there
are some recent theories which are closely akin to it. One such complicated theory[3] proposes an original form of the Gospel (Mk. I)
which existed in Aramaic and was used by a later editor with the help
of another source to become eventually our Gospel of Mark. This is
not likely to win support, but there are other less radical propositions
which are based on the groupings of pre-Marcan material.[4] But although groupings within the oral tradition are highly probable, it
cannot be excluded that Mark himself was the collector and arranger.
It makes little difference who grouped the material provided its origin
can be traced in some way (as in the Papias tradition) to an apostolic,
and therefore authoritative, source.

There have been different opinions about Mark's use of Q (see next
section), but the discussion has not been profitable.[5] Reasons will be
given for regarding Q as no more than a convenient symbol for the
material common to Matthew and Luke and lacking from Mark, in
which case Mark's use of Q cannot arise. Even if a specific written

[1] Taylor (*St. Mark*, p. 658) gives the following list for source A, the rest being
attributed to B: xiv. I, 2, 10, 11 (12–16), 17–21, 26–31, 43–46 (53, 55–64), xv. I,
3–5, 15, 21–24, 26, 29 f., 34–37, 39, 42–46 (xvi. 1–8).

[2] Cf. E. Wendling, *Ur-Marcus* (1905). Cf. also J. Jeremias (*ZNTW*, 35, 1936,
pp. 280–282), who revives a kind of Ur-Markus theory based on textual criticism.

[3] So E. Hirsch, whose theory is summarized by Michaelis (*Einleitung*, p. 49),
who cites from Hirsch's *Frühgeschichte des Ev: I. Das Werden des Mk-Ev²* (1951).
Cf. also W. Eltester's critique, *ZNTW*, 44 (1952–53), pp. 265 ff.

[4] See p. 66 for comments on V. Taylor's theory of Marcan complexes. Cf.
W. L. Knox's *Sources of the Synoptic Gospels: I St Mark* (1953). Cf. also J. Jere-
mias, *The Eucharistic Words of Jesus* (1955), pp. 132 ff., for the suggestion of a pre-
Marcan form of the account of the last supper.*

[5] B. H. Throckmorton (*JBL*, LXVII, 1948, pp. 319–329) rightly pointed out the
futility of discussing Mark's use of Q until the latter has been more clearly
defined.

document existed which was wider than the common material of Matthew and Luke, there is no means of identifying any of this additional material in Mark. Where similarities between Mark and Q exist it is much more credible to postulate an oral basis for this common material.[1]

If the tradition is correct that the apostle Peter is behind this Gospel, we possess most valuable information about the author's sources. We need not, of course, assume that all Mark's information came *via* Peter, but there is nothing to exclude the idea that much of it did.[2] If Mark was the young man who fled from the garden, it may be that he was personally acquainted with some of the events of passion week. This is no more than a conjecture. Some scholars have found difficulty in this interpretation because of their acceptance of the Johannine chronology, the assumption being that the young man must surely have known the precise day of those momentous happenings. If the chronology of John and of the Synoptists can be reconciled (see discussion on pp. 293 ff.), or if Mark's chronology is preferred to John's, this difficulty would not arise.

Some attempt has been made to isolate parts of the Gospel which may be traced to Peter. C. H. Turner appealed to a number of passages in which Mark's third person plural could quite easily be changed into the first person plural and these passages, he maintained, could be assumed to be Petrine eyewitness reminiscences.[3] T. W. Manson took the process further and included many of the passages adjacent to Turner's pass-

---

[1] For an advocacy of Mark's use of Q, cf. F. C. Grant, *The Gospels, their origin and growth* (1957), pp. 108, 109. S. Johnson (*The Gospel according to St. Matthew, IB*, 1951, p. 237) seems favourable to the view that Mark may have heard Q read and have remembered some sayings from it.

[2] F. C. Burkitt (*The Earliest Sources for the Life of Jesus*, 1922, pp. 77 ff.) accepted a general Petrine source, but considered that some portions were independent of such a source (as for instance the incident of the demoniac and the swine). Burkitt, however, did not favour the view that the general plan of the work was traceable to Peter (*ibid.*, p. 93). In support of the Petrine tradition, cf. H. E. W. Turner, *ET*, LXXI (1960), pp. 260–263. Against the tradition, cf. D. E. Nineham (*Saint Mark*, Pelican Gospel Commentaries, 1963, p. 27), who argues that since *some* Marcan material is non-Petrine (because he considers it to be community products), therefore it is logical to suppose that *none* of the material is Petrine because *all* could be understood as community products.

[3] Cf. C. H. Turner, in *A New Commentary on Holy Scripture*, III, p. 54. His passages are i. 21, 29, v. 1, 38, vi. 53, 54, viii. 22, ix. 14, 30, 33, x. 32, 46, xi. 1, 12, 15, 20, 27, xiv. 18, 22, 26, 32.

ages, because there were clear connections between them.[1] In this way a considerable proportion of the Marcan material may be traceable to Peter. Of the remaining material it has been suggested that much of this consisted of well-defined blocks, which may indicate some already arranged pre-Marcan material. It must also not be lost sight of that if the tradition of Marcan authorship is correct, he would have been in touch with a large number of eyewitnesses in his Jerusalem days and this must have contributed much to the composition of his Gospel.

V. THE SOURCE Q

a. Reasons for alleging its existence

Because of the large amount of non-Marcan material which is found in both Matthew and Luke it has been presumed by many scholars that these Evangelists must both have used a common source. This follows from the rejection of any possibility that one used the other or that both could have drawn so much common material, often closely related verbally, from oral tradition. The common source Q, if it existed, would have contained mainly the teaching of Jesus with only a few narrative sections. It is this feature that has led to the use of the description 'Logia', after the allusion in the report of Papias that Matthew wrote such *logia*.

Once New Testament scholarship was committed to the pursuit of written documents behind the Gospels, the postulation of Q as a written source was considered most reasonable and in fact almost inevitable. The data upon which this hypothesis was founded are as follows.

1. The large amount of common material in Matthew and Luke only (up to 250 verses), much of it possessing a considerable measure of verbal agreement, was felt to be impossible on any theory but a common written source.[2]

---

[1] *Studies in the Gospels and Epistles*, p. 42. Manson's list is as follows: Mk. i. 16–39, ii. 1–14, iii. 13–19, iv. 35–v. 43, vi. 7–13, 50–56, viii. 14–ix. 48, x. 32–52, xi. 1–33, xiii. 3,4, 32–37, xiv. 17–50, 53, 54, 66–72. This totals almost half the Gospel.

[2] For a rejection of the oral hypothesis as an adequate account of this phenomenon, cf. J. C. Hawkins' study in *Oxford Studies in the Synoptic Problem* (1911), pp. 98 ff.

2. The order in which both Matthew and Luke have used their common material is roughly similar. Yet the variations in order are not inconsiderable and the question naturally arises whether Matthew or Luke is closer to the original order of Q. There are differing opinions on this matter. Those who prefer Matthew's order claim that his literary method would not lead him to treat his sources with the same artistic freedom as Luke may have done.[1] But this seems to be contradicted by Matthew's acknowledged habit of conflating his sources. Luke, inclined generally to incorporate his sources in 'blocks', would probably see less reason than Matthew for changing the order.[2] While a common order, therefore, must be regarded with some reserve, most advocates of the Q hypothesis consider it to be strong enough to suggest the use of a common source.

3. The existence of so-called doublets in Matthew and Luke is also claimed to support the Q hypothesis. These are sayings which occur twice, in which one comes from Mark and the other, because of some variations, apparently does not and this requires the postulation of another source which contained some parallel traditions.[3]

4. Another consideration is that sometimes the agreements in Matthew and Luke reach to unusual words and phrases and also to grammatical peculiarities.[4]

The conclusion of Vincent Taylor is that 'these considerations justify us in believing that a written source lay before Matthew and Luke, containing sayings of Jesus'.[5] But not all scholars have been so certain that Q was a single source. W. Bussmann,[6] for example, split it

[1] C. F. Burney (*The Poetry of our Lord*, 1925, pp. 87 f.) suggested that Matthew more often preserves the poetical pattern.

[2] B. H. Streeter (*The Four Gospels*, p. 275) maintained that Luke's order was plainly more original because of Matthew's disposition towards topical arrangement and the inappropriateness of certain sayings in their Matthaean context. Against this view, cf. A. Farrer, *Studies in the Gospels* (ed. D. E. Nineham, 1955), pp. 62 ff. E. Nestlé (*ZNTW*, 1, 1900, pp. 252 ff.) suggested that the original collection of sayings may have been arranged in five books, as Papias so arranged his expositions and as was common among the Jews after the pattern of the Pentateuch.

[3] Cf. Hawkins, *Horae Synopticae*[2] (1909), pp. 80 ff.

[4] Cf. Hawkins, *Oxford Studies*, p. 99.

[5] *The Gospels*, p. 22. B. de Solages, *A Greek Synopsis of the Gospels* (1959), claims to reach the same conclusion by mathematical demonstration.

[6] *Synoptische Studien*, II (1929).

into two sources, an Aramaic source R and a Greek source T. The latter was used with a large measure of agreement by Matthew and Luke, but the former with considerable variations. This hypothesis, however, has not commended itself.[1] W. L. Knox[2] suggested that some of the Q material originally existed in the form of tracts, the whole falling into two sections which roughly corresponded with Bussmann's sources. The single source idea has been further weakened by the tendency to regard Q as the stratum of common material used by Matthew and Luke without specifying whether it was one source or many.[3]

Owing to the problems of the Q sources (see below), Vaganay[4] has dispensed with Q altogether, but has substituted for it another source (Sg) which he thinks more adequately accounts for the double tradition. This source differs from Q both in its character and extent. It consists mainly of sayings of the kind Luke includes in his 'travel' document (ix. 51–xviii. 14), mostly common to Matthew but with many verses which Matthew and Luke individually include. This source, like Vaganay's Proto-Matthew, is supposed to have existed in the form of five books. It was not homogeneous either in vocabulary or style. This theory was prompted by Vaganay's assumption that the earliest writing was an Aramaic Proto-Matthew, which necessitated the postulation of another source which lay behind the canonical Gospels. Both these earlier sources, he thinks, were used by the Evangelists in a Greek form. But Vaganay's Sg source is no more certain in its

---

[1] Cf. the criticism of T. W. Manson, *The Sayings of Jesus* (1949), p. 20. An Aramaic Q has been suggested quite apart from Bussmann's theory of dual sources (cf. P. Bussby, *ET*, LXV, 1954, pp. 272–275). M. Black (*An Aramaic Approach to the Gospels and Acts*, 1954, pp. 270 ff.) criticizes Bussmann's theory, but considers that Q was originally in Aramaic. He nevertheless feels that the presence of non-translation Greek in the Q material shows that we cannot speak without qualification of a translation from Aramaic. He further suggests that Matthew's Q is a Greek literary composition, while Luke's Q, although it shows evidence of having been edited to remove Jewish materials for the benefit of Gentile readers, is nevertheless the more primitive translation from Aramaic. On the strength of the postulation of this Aramaic source, Black believes that in a limited number of cases the presence of some Synoptic variants can be explained. But his list of thirteen examples shows a drastic reduction from Bussmann's list of more than one hundred.

[2] *Sources of the Synoptic Gospels*, II (1957), pp. 3 ff., 45–47.

[3] E.g. C. K. Barrett, 'Q: A re-examination', *ET*, LIV (1943), pp. 320–323.

[4] *Le Problème synoptique* (1954).

content than the Q source which it displaces, for it must unavoidably be a matter of the proposer's own selection.[1]

Another recent hypothesis is that of P. Parker,[2] who calls the original document K (virtually a Proto-Matthew) and admits a second source Q, which nevertheless differs from former proposals regarding the Q source. His main idea is that Matthew and Mark used K, but that Luke knew it only through Mark. But he thinks that both Matthew and Luke used Q.[3]

b. The contents of Q

There is considerable difference of opinion among scholars who postulate a Q source as to the precise details of contents,[4] but there is general agreement about the major sections. The following outline gives the main features which are assumed to have belonged to Q, although many scholars would add other passages where verbal agreement is more slight or where only one of the Evangelists has used the material. These latter details must necessarily be speculative.

(i) The preparation
John's preaching of repentance (Lk. iii. 7–9; Mt. iii. 7–10).
The temptation of Jesus (Lk. iv. 1–13; Mt. iv. 1–11).

(ii) Sayings (Sermon on the Mount)
Beatitudes (Lk. vi. 20–23; Mt. v. 3, 4, 6, 11, 12).
Love to one's enemies (Lk. vi. 27–36; Mt. v. 39–42, 44–48, vii. 12).
On judging (Lk. vi. 37–42; Mt. vii. 1–5, x. 24, 25, xv. 14).
Hearers and doers of the Word (Lk. vi. 47–49; Mt. vii. 24–27).

---

[1] X. Léon-Dufour points out this weakness in his article on 'Le fait synoptique', *Introduction à la Bible* (ed. A. Robert-A. Feuillet), II (1959), p. 291. For a concise résumé and critique of Vaganay's theory, cf. A. Wikenhauser, *New Testament Introduction*, pp. 235–239.　　　　[2] *The Gospel before Mark* (1953).

[3] For yet another theory, cf. A. M. Perry's suggestion that Luke used a Jewish-Christian source, which he called N, in Lk. xi. 33–xii. 46, which consisted mainly of Q materials (*JBL*, LXIX, 1950, pp. 181–194). The many modifications and complications of the Q theory raise doubts regarding its validity, as J. H. Ropes (*The Synoptic Gospels*, 1934, p. 93) noted long before the theory met its more serious challengers. Cf. also P. Gardner-Smith (*The Christ of the Gospels*, 1938, p. 39), who thought that some of the common material of Matthew and Luke differed so much as to be best explained on the basis of oral teaching.*

[4] Cf. J. Moffatt (*ILNT*[3], 1918, pp. 197 ff.), who gives sixteen reconstructions of Q.

(iii) *Narratives*
The centurion's servant (Lk. vii. 1–10; Mt. vii. 28a, viii. 5–10, 13).
The Baptist's question (Lk. vii. 18–20; Mt. xi. 2, 3).
The Lord's answer (Lk. vii. 22–35; Mt. xi. 4–19).

(iv) *On discipleship*
Its cost (Lk. ix. 57–60; Mt. viii. 19–22).
The mission charge (Lk. x. 2–12; Mt. ix. 37, 38, x. 9–15).
Woes on recalcitrant Galilaean cities (Lk. x. 13–15; Mt. xi. 20–24).

(v) *Various sayings*
The pattern prayer (Lk. xi. 2–4; Mt. vi. 9–13).
On answers to prayer (Lk. xi. 9–13; Mt. vii. 7–11).
About the Beelzebub controversy (Lk. xi. 14–22; Mt. xii. 12–32).
About unclean spirits (Lk. xi. 24–26; Mt. xii. 43–45).
The sign of the prophet Jonah (Lk. xi. 29–32; Mt. xii. 38–42).
About light (Lk. xi. 33–36; Mt. v. 15, vi. 22, 23).

(vi) *Discourse*
Warnings against the Pharisees (Lk. xi. 37–xii. 1; Mt. xxiii. 1–36).

(vii) *Further sayings*
About fearless confession (Lk. xii. 2–12; Mt. x. 19, 26–33).
On cares about earthly things (Lk. xii. 22–34; Mt. vi. 19–21, 25–33).
On faithfulness (Lk. xii. 39–46; Mt. xxiv. 43–51).
On signs for this age (Lk. xii. 51–56; Mt. x. 34–36, xvi. 2, 3).
On agreeing with one's adversaries (Lk. xii. 57–59; Mt. v. 25, 26).

(viii) *Parables*
The mustard seed and the leaven (Lk. xiii. 18–21; Mt. xiii. 31–33).

(ix) *Other sayings*
Condemnation of Israel (Lk. xiii. 23–30; Mt. vii. 13, 14, viii. 11, 12, xxv. 10–12).
Lament over Jerusalem (Lk. xiii. 34, 35; Mt. xxiii. 37–39).
Cost of discipleship (Lk. xiv. 26–35; Mt. x. 37, 38, v. 13).
On serving two masters (Lk. xvi. 13; Mt. vi. 24).
On law and divorce (Lk. xvi. 16–18; Mt. xi. 12, 13, v. 18, 32).
On offences, forgiveness and faith (Lk. xvii. 1–6; Mt. xviii. 6, 7, 15, 21, 22).
The day of the Son of man (Lk. xvii. 22–27, 33–37; Mt. xxiv. 26–28, 37–39).

Although this list would be regarded as tentative by most advocates of the two basic source theory, there are many modifications proposed by different scholars. Nevertheless these modifications do not materially alter the essential character of the document. The most important question is whether or not it included any passion narratives, although most source critics tend to deny this.

It will be seen that the above reconstruction of Q presents a document with little apparent cohesion and with an extraordinary paucity of narrative material. The inclusion of the healing of the centurion's servant is certainly mystifying. Moreover there appears to be a preponderance of isolated sayings with no evident framework to hold them together.

The order given is that in which the material is used by Luke, following the generally accepted opinion that his order is more original than Matthew's.[1] But if Luke's order is that of the original certain problems arise. It would be clear that the compiler of Q had little conception of chronological or topical arrangement and that his primary purpose was the preservation of the teaching of Jesus without much regard for sequence. It would also appear that he had no reason to record the passion narratives. It is not easy to believe that an original document existed in this form, but the difficulties are certainly lessened if the theory of various tracts comprising Q material is maintained. Yet, as mentioned previously, a multiplication of Q sources goes far to weaken the whole hypothesis. It may be more reasonable to maintain that part only of the Q source has been preserved by Matthew and Luke between them, on the analogy of the use of Mark by both these Evangelists. Since it is possible to reconstruct with certainty the whole of Mark from Matthew and Luke[2] it may reasonably be expected that the same will apply to Q.

[1] V. Taylor (*JTS*, n.s., IV, 1953, pp. 27–31) has defended the Lucan order by maintaining that the difficulties in this hypothesis vanish if the parallel Matthaean material is arranged in six columns, corresponding to the five great discourses and an additional column for the rest. In each column occur many sequences in the same order as Luke, which is then claimed as evidence of a common documentary source, since the theory that one used the other is unacceptable to Taylor. Commenting on the data given in the above article, O. E. Evans (*ET*, LXXII, 1960–61, pp. 295–299) regards the Q hypothesis as the only reasonable explanation. In an article in *New Testament Essays* (ed. A. J. B. Higgins, 1959), pp. 246–269, V. Taylor has further developed the argument of the previously mentioned article, and again firmly asserts that Luke has followed the order of Q with great fidelity.

[2] F. C. Burkitt (*The Gospel History and its Transmission*, p. 17) considered the attempt to reconstruct Mark from Matthew and Luke to be futile, and argued that the same applies to the contents of Q. K. and S. Lake (*INT*, pp. 12, 13) speak of such attempts as miserable failures.

The different ways in which the Q material was used by Matthew and Luke are striking, particularly the highly selective method employed by Matthew. It is also noticeable that in the outline given above only one section of considerable length runs parallel in order in Matthew and Luke, i.e. the sayings from the Sermon on the Mount, which according to Hawkins[1] formed the basic structure on which the teaching of Jesus was moulded. But it is here that it is most noticeable that according to the generally held source theory Matthew has not only grouped this material into topics but has drawn other material into his discourse section from other contexts in Q and from his own special sources.

There have been different explanations of the fact that in some Q passages there are close agreements while in others there are wide divergences. V. Taylor[2] lists four proposals: (1) editorial modifications;[3] (2) different recensions;[4] (3) parallel versions;[5] and (4) composite theories of Q.[6] He considers that the choice must rest between (3) and (4), and in common with most source critics he prefers (3), in which, according to Streeter, Q and M overlapped. In these cases Luke

---

[1] In *Oxford Studies*, p. 121. W. L. Knox (*Sources of the Synoptic Gospels*, II, 1957, pp. 7 ff.) strongly maintained the greater originality of Luke's version of the Sermon on the Mount. W. Grundmann ('Die Bergpredigt nach der Lukasfassung', *Studia Evangelica*, pp. 180–189) finds an earlier theology in Luke's version as compared with Matthew's, but this view assumes that the theology of each author has affected his reconstruction of the Sermon. Yet the notion that Matthew's theology differs from Luke's is not the only possible explanation. The view that Jesus repeated this sermon material on many occasions with varying emphases cannot be dismissed without consideration. If Luke's and Matthew's versions relate to different events, the evidence of this material for the order of Q is at once nullified.

J. Schniewind (*Das Evangelium nach Matthäus*, p. 4) makes much of the differences between Matthew's and Luke's Sermon on the Mount material (and other discourse material) as a reason for rejecting the hypothesis that Luke used Matthew, a factor which counts strongly with many scholars.

[2] Cf. his article on 'The Elusive Q', in *ET*, XLVI (1934), pp. 68 ff.

[3] Cf. A. Harnack's *The Sayings of Jesus* (1908), pp. 1 ff.

[4] Cf. C. S. Patten (*Sources of the Synoptic Gospels*, 1915), who argued for an Aramaic document behind Q, which was translated into two Greek recensions. G. Bornkamm, who maintains a two recension theory, is content to explain this by the continuing influence of oral tradition, a significant concession (*Jesus of Nazareth*, 1960, p. 217).

[5] As proposed by Streeter in his four source theory.

[6] As Bussmann; see pp. 144 f. for details.

followed Q and Matthew M. But the existence of these variations emphasizes the fact that Q is not without its problems.

If a written source is felt necessary, the idea of different recensions must result in a weakening of the evidence, since the main prop of the theory is that too much verbal similarity exists for anything but a written basis to be envisaged. This merely pushes the problem one stage further back. If Luke used Q1 and Matthew used Q2, it is then necessary to postulate an Ur-Q from which both recensions developed, unless Q2 is an edited form of Q1. This latter proposition has recently been strongly maintained by J. P. Brown[1] who regards Matthew's source Q as an ecclesiastically revised form of Luke's Q material. It is difficult to see how this recension theory avoids the problems which are alleged to belong to any theory that Luke used Matthew or *vice versa*.

c. Problems of the Q source

Mention has already been made of the existence of passages where Matthew and Luke agree against Mark, and this was cited as a difficulty in the theory of Marcan priority. But the evidence could be regarded as a support for the theory that Luke used Matthew (or *vice versa*), in which case the reason for Q's existence vanishes.[2] Nevertheless it is generally felt to be difficult to hold such a theory because Luke's change of order of the sayings in Matthew would become incomprehensible. But the change of order may have been occasioned by Luke's greater desire to preserve the historical framework of the sayings as compared with Matthew's topical arrangement, although under this theory it would be necessary to assume that Luke had access to other

[1] Cf. *NTS*, 8 (1961–62), pp. 27–42. In a further article in *NTS*, 10 (1963), Brown examines the Synoptic parallels in the Epistles and suggests that most of the sayings echoed in the Epistles are derived from Q. The Epistles, according to him, have modified the original sayings of Jesus into something more useful for their immediate situation, and Matthew's Q approximates to this. But all Brown has really succeeded in doing is to demonstrate the flexible character which any theory of Q must have to be tenable at all.

[2] W. C. Allen (*St. Matthew*, pp. xlvii ff.) admitted this as a possibility more credible than the Q source. It has recently been strongly proposed by Austin Farrer in his article in *Studies in the Gospels* (ed. D. E. Nineham), p. 62. R. M. Wilson, in *Studia Evangelica*, pp. 254–257, is critical of Farrer's methods of disposing of Streeter's arguments. E. L. Bradby (*ET*, LXVIII, 1956–57, pp. 315–318) has argued from some passages common to the three Synoptics that Luke is closer to Mark than to Matthew, which suggests to him Luke's ignorance of Matthew and therefore in his opinion supports the Q hypothesis. But does it?*

information about the framework. Indeed, the basis of the difficulty over the order of Luke's Q material is the assumption that Luke's order is more natural than Matthew's. Or to put it in another way, a topical arrangement, being less natural, must be secondary and therefore Matthew cannot be basic to Luke. Clearly the original order of Q is of paramount importance. Once admit the originality of Matthew's arrangement and the *raison d'être* for Q's existence is virtually at an end. Another solution would be to regard the Q material as oral rather than written,[1] but in this case also the existence of Q as a self-contained entity becomes more difficult to maintain, and indeed hardly remains necessary.

But the classical source structure with Mark and Q as its foundation-stones strongly excludes the idea of Luke's use of Matthew on yet other grounds. We need not take seriously the argument that Luke would not have omitted so much of Matthew had he known it,[2] for Luke was clearly writing for a specific purpose and must surely be allowed the liberty of leaving out from his source anything he wished. Another argument is that some of Luke's sayings look more primitive in form than the parallel sayings in Matthew,[3] but the weakness in the argument is the difficulty in defining primitiveness. Indeed, it may equally well be maintained that on the whole Matthew looks more primitive than Luke, as for instance in its Jewish-Christian emphases. A further consideration arises from Luke's use of Mark. It can be demonstrated that he used Mark in roughly the same order as the material appears in that Gospel. If he used Matthew it is maintained that with this source he followed a quite different method. But it is not clear why he should not have adapted his method to his purpose. The amount of data available for determining Luke's literary methods is too slight to carry

[1] Cf. J. Jeremias, *ZNTW*, 29 (1930), pp. 147–149. R. H. Fuller (*The New Testament in Current Study*, 1962, p. 74) approves of E. Fascher's description of the Q material as 'a layer of tradition'.

[2] Cf. A. Wikenhauser, *New Testament Introduction*, p. 251.

[3] It is generally maintained that Matthew's topical arrangement of the discourses shows a more developed stage in the transmission of the tradition than Luke's more isolated sayings (cf. Schniewind, *Das Evangelium nach Matthäus*, p. 5). This view assumes that our Lord never delivered connected discourses of the type found, for instance, in Mt. v–vii, but this assumption may be challenged. As pointed out elsewhere (see pp. 211, 224) there is no logical reason why Jesus should not have repeated the same material on different occasions and in different contexts.

conviction.[1] Moreover, under the hypothesis being reviewed Luke would have incorporated more of Matthew than of Mark, if the passion narratives are disregarded. The concluding consideration is that whereas Matthew places some of his common sayings material in Marcan contexts, Luke places them in non-Marcan contexts. But the argument could be used in two ways. It could mean that both have used Q but have chosen different contexts for it, or that Luke has used Matthew and has rearranged the material. Is it certain that the former is more credible than the latter? It needs to be demonstrable if it is to serve as a support for the Q hypothesis.

Another consideration which presents a problem for the Q theory is the lack of any contemporary literature parallel to the type of document which Q is supposed to be.[2] It was clearly not a Gospel, for it lacked the most essential feature of the Gospel-form, the passion narrative. A document consisting mainly of teaching is not, of course, impossible to conceive, as the Gnostic *Gospel of Thomas* shows.[3]

The teaching of Jesus would naturally have been of surpassing interest to the early Christians as it was to the Gnostics, and it may at first seem that the analogous form of the Gnostic *Thomas* and the proposed Q source is a strong argument in favour of the latter. But is the analogy sufficiently close? If, as seems most likely, the *Gospel of Thomas* consists mainly of extracts from our written Gospels, it becomes at once distinguished from Q which *ex hypothesi* clearly had no such origin. This means that the form of *Thomas* was dictated by a principle of selection, which did not obtain in the same way for Q. The Gnostic compiler of the former has no interest in the historical context and for this reason excludes all narrative material.[4] But Q not only contains a few narrative sections, but lacks the dogmatic purpose of *Thomas*.

---

[1] This has been recognized by the advocates of the Proto-Luke hypothesis in which it is denied that Luke based his structure on Mark. Cf. V. Taylor, *op. cit.*, p. 37, and *idem, Behind the Third Gospel*. See pp. 175 ff. for a further discussion of Proto-Luke.

[2] Farrer (*Studies in the Gospels*, pp. 58 ff.) makes a strong point of this.

[3] It should be noted, however, that the extant evidence belongs to a later period than the formative period of the Synoptic Gospels. Cf. R. M. Wilson, *HTR*, 53 (1960), pp. 231–250; H. Montefiore and H. E. W. Turner, *Thomas and the Evangelists* (1962).

[4] H. E. W. Turner (*op. cit.*, p. 114) says of Thomas, 'The principle of selection is itself evidence of intention and gives no indication that the compiler assigned any real place to history in his economy of salvation.'

The most that the evidence demonstrates is that a sayings collection was not considered incongruous in Gnostic circles and may not therefore have been regarded as unsuitable among the orthodox Christians.[1] At the same time, the existence of a document like Q during the first century AD must be considered to be unparalleled. The uniqueness of Q would not, of course, be damaging to the hypothesis, if there were such convincing grounds for it that a new type of literature could be confidently assumed. But it is otherwise with Q. It is hypothetical, unsupported by any external evidence—a precarious basis for a unique document.

Some scholars who admit difficulties in supposing that Luke used Matthew dispense with Q by maintaining that he used an Aramaic Proto-Matthew, as for instance in the theory of Vaganay already mentioned. But, increasingly, many who still retain the Q hypothesis in name are disinclined to regard it any more definitely than as a convenient symbol of Matthaean-Lucan common material.[2]

d. The probable purpose of Q

It is essential for the proposers of Q to suggest an adequate motive for its production and this is usually done by appealing to the catechetical demands of the early Church. It is not difficult to imagine the usefulness of a collection of the sayings of Jesus in the primitive communities. The majority of those assigned to Q deal with practical questions of Christian discipleship. Thus Q, if it existed, would have formed a kind

[1] W. G. Kümmel (*INT*, 1965, p. 58) does not regard this Gnostic Gospel as belonging to the same kind (*Gattung*) as Q.

[2] This has been trenchantly emphasized by Stewart Petrie in an article in which he maintains that Q is what you make it (*Nov. Test.*, 3, 1959, pp. 28–33). He suggestively points out that so varied have been the hypotheses concerning Q that the value of the theory may be questioned. Another who has called for a greater precision among scholars in the use of the symbol Q is T. R. Rosché (*JBL*, LXXIX, 1960, pp. 210–220). He draws attention to the fact that both Matthew and Luke, where they parallel Marcan sayings material, reproduce it with a high percentage of verbal agreement, although not quite so high in the narrative portions. The agreement reached also to the order of the contents. But these two factors are absent from Matthew's and Luke's alleged use of Q sayings material, where differences of order are clear enough. Unless it can be shown that the authors of Matthew and Luke differed widely when using sources, the source Q becomes suspect. There is much that is suggestive in Rosché's article. R. M. Grant (*A Historical Introduction to the New Testament*, 1963, p. 116) regards Q as no more than a symbol of material which was partly written and partly oral.

of primitive manual of discipline, backed by the authority of the Lord Himself. It would presumably have helped in the solving of many problems which became living issues as Christianity spread into Gentile lands.[1] There are passages in Q, for instance, which deal with John the Baptist, his preaching of repentance, his question to Jesus about His messianic office and Jesus' own testimony to John. It is conceivable that this material would have been useful in dealing with the problem of the relationship of John's disciples to the Christian Church. Similarly the passages giving our Lord's teaching about taxes would have had an obviously practical application in settling Christian obligation towards the State.

While these probable purposes may be admitted, they could, of course, have been met in other ways. Teaching on these important questions may have been part of the process of oral catechesis rather than incorporated in a written document. On the other hand, the finished Gospels would have performed the same purpose, and this leads to the enquiry whether the Q source, if substantiated, could possess any greater value than Matthew's and Luke's Gospels.

e. The value of the Q hypothesis

The most obvious value may be said to be for Christian evidences, since, if true, Q would push the written records nearer to the time of Jesus. Vincent Taylor[2] suggests the following particular values which can be attached to it. (1) It is the most valuable source of the teaching of Jesus, although it should be noted that other teaching was recorded elsewhere. (2) It gives insight into the character of Jesus. Many sayings are autobiographical in character, illuminating the inner consciousness of Jesus (cf. Mt. xi. 27; Lk. x. 22). There are abundant references to nature, showing a real appreciation of it. Many of the sayings are in poetic form.[3] There are allusions to the healing ministry, to lack of mighty works done and to unrecorded visits to Jerusalem culminating in the lament. (3) It shows our Lord's interest in common life, particularly in the countryside. So much so that J. M. C. Crum[4] maintained that Q must have had a country origin.

---

[1] Cf. R. V. G. Tasker, *The Nature and Purpose of the Gospels* (1944), p. 23. Streeter, in *Oxford Studies*, pp. 209 ff., and F. B. Clogg, *INT*³ (1948), p. 190, considered that Q was intended to supplement oral tradition.

[2] *The Gospels*, pp. 24 ff.

[3] Cf. C. F. Burney, *The Poetry of our Lord* (1925), pp. 87 ff.

[4] Cf. J. M. C. Crum, *The Original Jerusalem Gospel* (1927), pp. 49–63.

Although Vincent Taylor himself warns against over-emphasizing the value of Q, there is a tendency among many source critics to attach higher value to this hypothetical source than to the two canonical Gospels which incorporate the material. But it must never be overlooked that these Gospels were accorded a status which was never attained by the source Q, or, if it was, this was not of sufficient weight to prevent it from being entirely superseded. If the Gospels are dated much later than Q (i.e. twenty-five to thirty years, as is generally maintained), then the advocates of the latter can reasonably claim to have pushed back the evidence to a significantly earlier time. But if the dating of the Gospels is considerably brought forward it is more difficult to attach any significant value to Q.[1]

f. Date and place of origin

Because of its hypothetical character it is clearly not possible to specify with any exactness either the date or provenance of Q. Streeter[2] suggested (and T. W. Manson[3] concurred) that it was written about AD 50, probably at Antioch. This is, of course, a guess, and since there are no data to lead to greater certainty it is probably as good a guess as any. In any case it is generally admitted that it could not have been much later than AD 60.[4]

g. The authorship of Q

It is difficult enough to establish authorship of some of the extant New Testament writings, but it is doubly difficult to discuss the author of a hypothetical source. The suggestions which have been made have been mainly influenced by the statement of Papias, recorded by Eusebius (see pp. 33 ff. for a discussion of the statement). Traditionally it was assumed that Papias was asserting that Matthew wrote his Gospel

---

[1] R. M. Grant (*op. cit.*, p. 116) warns against treating Q as a written source in any way comparable to Mark. An important suggestion has recently been made by H. Schürmann, in *Der historische Jesus und der kerygmatische Christus* (ed. H. Ristow and K. Matthiae, 1962, pp. 342–370), who believes that some of the Q materials were not only collected in the time of Jesus but were also used by the disciples. If the suggestion is valid, it would support the authenticity of these sayings materials in the Gospels.

[2] *The Four Gospels*, p. 150.

[3] *The Sayings of Jesus* (1949), p. 20.

[4] W. G. Kümmel (*INT*, 1965, p. 56) says vaguely that it is improbable that Q was later than AD 50–70.

(τὰ λογία) in the Hebrew dialect, but with the postulation of a source Q
it was only natural that Papias' λογία would be identified with this
source. If this identification is correct it would be very early evidence
not only for the authorship of Q, but for its very existence. If, then, it be
supposed that Matthew did not write his Gospel and if it be further
supposed that the writer of that Gospel used Q, it would clearly be a
useful explanation of the attachment of Matthew's name to the whole
Gospel if he were known to have been the author of one of its sources.
But apart from Papias' ambiguous statement there is no other hint in
early Christian history that anyone ever suspected that Matthew wrote
only a portion of the Gospel attributed to him. Moreover, some explanation would need to be given of the complete disappearance of an apostolic source such as Q in favour of two presumably non-apostolic
Gospels.[1] If Papias meant our canonical Gospel and not Q, the quest
for the author of the hypothetical Q must be regarded as hopeless.
He must remain one of the early Christian unknowns, perhaps even
the greatest. It may be that this is a further reason, although by no
means conclusive, for questioning the validity of the hypothesis of
a written source Q.

h. Conclusion

It will be apparent from the preceding discussion that there is no unanimity about the Q source. It would be fair to say, however, that the
great majority of scholars still regard it, in spite of its inherent difficulties, as the most reasonable explanation of the origin of the double
tradition (Mt./Lk.). Between this full source theory and the other
extreme of supposing that both authors have drawn material from oral
tradition lie various other possibilities. Luke's use of Matthew cannot
be pronounced impossible, although it is not without special difficulties of its own. It is perhaps preferable to suppose that early catechetical
instruction included much of the teaching of Jesus and this would be

---

[1] Cf. Kilpatrick, *The Origins of the Gospel according to St. Matthew* (1946), p. 4.
T. W. Manson (*op. cit.*, pp. 19, 20) explains the disappearance on the following
grounds: the primitive Church was not interested in archives, especially in view
of the end-expectation, and an Aramaic document (as he held Q to be) would
have held interest for few at the turn of the century. Moreover, Manson tries to
find an analogy in the disappearance of Shakespeare's autographs. But none of
these reasons really explains the disappearance of an *apostolic* source of such importance, which must have been treasured from more than mere interest in archaic things.

imparted according to a fixed pattern. Hence the Q material may well have existed in an oral form of a sufficiently fixed character to account for both the verbal similarities and differences. Alternatively it may be conjectured that part of the sayings material was reduced to writing in the form of brief notes and that these were used by Matthew and Luke and supplemented by other oral traditions. One advantage of both these proposals is that they obviate the need for differentiating too sharply between Q and the special material of Matthew and Luke. In a field of study in which there is so much which must be considered conjectural, it would be foolish to be dogmatic. The symbol Q may still be used as a convenient description of the common material, while each investigator must be left to make clear whether he is thinking of written or oral material or a mixture of both.

VI. SOURCES PECULIAR TO MATTHEW

According to the four source hypothesis Matthew used in addition to Mark and Q other sources of information either unknown to or unused by the other Evangelists.[1] It is this unique material which gives the Gospel its distinctive characteristics and which has also been determinative in discussions of the historical value of the Gospel as a whole.* The material may conveniently be studied under the following subdivisions: (a) sayings collection;[2] (b) testimonia; (c) birth narratives; (d) other narratives.

a. Sayings collection (M)

Streeter's postulated M source[3] for Matthew consisted of a certain amount of sayings material which could not readily be assigned to Q because of the lack of any close parallels between Matthew and Luke. This M source, he thought, was based on Jerusalem, largely because of

[1] It should be noted that continental scholars have been less inclined than British scholars to follow Streeter's M hypothesis. A recent writer, G. Strecker (Der Weg der Gerechtigkeit, 1962, pp. 12, 13), considers it to be basically unnecessary so long as Q material is not tied too rigidly to the double tradition of Matthew and Luke. Strecker does not accept Streeter's distinction between a Judaistic M and a Hellenistic-Christian Q.
[2] W. C. Allen (Oxford Studies, pp. 233–286) argued for a Book of Sayings used by the First Gospel, but far more comprehensive than Streeter's M source, because he did not admit Matthew's use of Q.
[3] The Four Gospels, pp. 254 ff.

its predominantly Jewish tone. The following suggestions may be noted about this material.

(i) *Reasons for the postulation of this source.* (1) In view of the similarity of subject-matter in Matthew and Luke, combined with many instances of dissimilarity of verbal forms, it is suggested that a source which overlapped the Q source in these cases would account for both. In other words these sections cannot with confidence be assigned to Q and must therefore have been derived from another parallel source which Matthew alone has used. (2) This theory is said by some scholars to be supported by Matthew's method of conflating his Marcan source with Q, thus providing an assumption that he did the same thing with M and Q. Vincent Taylor[1] cites Matthew iv. 11, x. 9–15, xii. 22–32, xiii. 31, 32 as illustrations of this process. (3) If Matthew conflates M and Q, Luke, in accordance with his usual practice of using one source at a time, is thought to have preferred Q. It is then suggested that this would account for the differences as well as the principles of selection used by the two Evangelists.[2] (4) Various data are thought to distinguish the M sayings from the Q sayings, such as evidence from structure and stereotyped explanations.[3]

Whether these reasons are sufficient for the postulation of a special M source will appear differently to different minds, depending largely on the presuppositions with which the problem is approached. For instance, if the priority of Matthew to Luke can be maintained, much of the justification for M vanishes, at least in the form in which Streeter proposed it. It would then be more difficult to distinguish Matthew's unique sayings from those of the double tradition (i.e. Q). Indeed, there would be no motive for doing so. Consequently those who would dispense with Q generally also dispense with M, at least as a written source,[4] although the symbol may still be used to denote the material peculiar to Matthew. It is moreover difficult to decide to what extent the interplay of oral tradition and written sources may have produced

---

[1] *The Gospels*, p. 30. In the parallel passages Mt. iv. 11; Lk. iv. 13, ὁ διάβολος is the only word in common.

[2] Hawkins (*Oxford Studies*, pp. 29–59) strongly maintained that Luke did not use Mark in his 'travel' narrative (ix. 51–xviii. 14) but alternates Q with his own special material. Such a phenomenon does not occur in Matthew. Cf. on this point the discussions of the Proto-Luke theory, pp. 175 ff.

[3] See G. D. Kilpatrick's discussion of this material, *The Origins of the Gospel according to St. Matthew* (1946), pp. 8 ff.

[4] As for instance in A. Farrer's theory (see p. 150 n.2).

the parallel traditions, with their similarities and differences, which the Q and M hypothesis is intended to explain.[1] At best the M source, in any of its proposed forms, lacks much connection of thought[2] and it is not easy therefore to conceive how it was originally compiled.

(ii) *The main characteristics of the source.* The Jewish character of Matthew's Gospel has already been indicated (see pp. 21 ff.), but it is necessary here to point out that some of this Jewish emphasis appears in passages which are paralleled in Luke, although mostly it occurs in the material peculiar to Matthew. An example of the former may be seen in the statement about the Law and the Prophets (Mt. v. 17–19; Lk. xvi. 17). Matthew has, 'Think not that I have come to abolish the law and the prophets; I have come not to abolish them but to fulfil them. For truly, I say to you, till heaven and earth pass away, not an iota, not a dot, will pass from the law until all is accomplished. Whoever then relaxes one of the least of these commandments and teaches men so, shall be called least in the kingdom of heaven; but he who does them and teaches them shall be called great in the kingdom of heaven' (RSV). Luke much more briefly and in a quite different context has, 'But it is easier for heaven and earth to pass away, than for one dot of the law to become void' (RSV). In a later context Luke has, 'Heaven and earth will pass away, but my words will not pass away' (xxi. 33, RSV; cf. Mt. xxiv. 35; Mk. xiii. 31). It will be seen that what is explicit in Matthew is nevertheless implicit in Luke, although by treating it less emphatically Luke would have had in mind his predominantly Gentile readership.

Examples of Judaistic emphasis in Matthew's own material may be seen in isolated sayings in Q contexts, such as the passage about the lost sheep of the house of Israel (x. 6), and in Matthew's sayings collection, such as the statement about things old and new at the close of the parable section (xiii. 52) and the later parables of the wedding garment, the virgins, and the sheep and the goats (xxii, xxv). The sayings about Moses' seat (xxiii. 2) and the twelve thrones of Israel (xix. 28) come under the same category.

If M existed as a source its most dominant feature was, therefore, its Jewish flavouring.

(iii) *The probable contents of the source.* Since the existence of M is even

---

[1] H. E. W. Turner (*Jesus, Master and Lord*[2], 1954, pp. 51, 52) is very doubtful whether the lack of homogeneity in this material warrants the postulation of a written source. He prefers to regard it as due to editorial modifications and oral tradition.

[2] Kilpatrick, *op. cit.*, p. 36, admits this.

more hypothetical than Q, and is admitted to be so even by its own advocates, it is impossible to define its original contents.[1] Any suggestions will amount to little more than that it was a collection of the sayings material peculiar to Matthew. As in the case of Q, however, it cannot be assumed that all the material which originally belonged to M has been preserved in Matthew's Gospel. The following contents list must, even from the source-critical point of view, be regarded as highly tentative.

1. A discourse containing material which was mainly anti-Pharisaical and which was incorporated in Matthew's Sermon on the Mount. McNeile[2] suggested that two sermons originally existed in written form, the Lucan form and this Matthaean discourse.[3] Matthew is then supposed to have conflated the two.

2. A similar anti-Pharisaic discourse, incorporated in Matthew xxiii, which is also thought to have been conflated.

3. Parts of the mission charge absent from Q, or in other words absent from Luke.

4. A collection of parables, comprising the tares, hidden treasure, merchant, dragnet (Mt. xiii), the debtor (Mt. xviii. 23–35), the labourers (xx. 1–16), the two sons (xxi. 28–32), wedding garment (xxii. 11–14), virgins (xxv. 1–13) and the sheep and the goats (xxv. 31–33). Streeter also added three parables with parallels in Luke, the lost sheep (xviii. 10–14), marriage feast (xxii. 1–10) and talents (xxv. 14–30).

In addition to these main features many other isolated sayings are assigned to Matthew's special source (e.g. xii. 11, 12, xiii. 52).

(iv) *The value of M.* Advocates of the four source theory have usually claimed to be able to pronounce on the comparative value of the various sources. These are arranged in descending order of importance and it is only natural that Mark and Q have been accorded first place and all other source material tends to be regarded as correspondingly less original. It is no surprise, therefore, that traces of what are presumed

---

[1] E. B. Redlich (*The Student's Introduction to the Synoptic Gospels*, 1936, pp. 203–218) attempted a reconstruction of M but, as S. Johnson (*The Gospel according to St. Matthew*, IB, 1951, p. 238) pointed out, if this is correct, the author of Matthew's Gospel must have used a scissors and paste method. The Gospel as a whole does not give such an impression.

[2] *St. Matthew*, p. 86.

[3] W. E. Bundy (*Jesus and the First Three Gospels*, 1955, pp. 93, 94) regards Matthew's Sermon as primarily an early Christian tract. He holds, however, that the original source of this Sermon was identical with the source of Luke's because of its similar beginning and ending and its seven common discourse units.

to be later Jewish-Christian influences are found in the source M, especially in view of its distinctively Jewish tone, together with other influences such as the teaching of John the Baptist.[1] But this method of assessment depends for its validity on the acceptance of the view that Mark and Q are sufficient criteria for measuring primitive documents. But this virtually means that all material which differs from these tends to be regarded with preliminary suspicion. This tendency in its developed form leads to suspicion being cast on any facts or sayings which are not witnessed to by more than one author.

Vincent Taylor,[2] in claiming justification for the existence of M, at least as a body of oral tradition if not as a written source, maintains that it does justice to the Judaic character of the tradition. But if this Jewish colouring was due to Matthew's own selection it would be more adequately explained. The author or 'editor' of the Gospel must be allowed more personal initiative than many source critics are prepared to assign to him. Those who regard M as a symbol for a body of oral tradition are, of course, not so open to this criticism, and for this reason there is a preference among many scholars for using the term 'strata' rather than written 'sources'.[3]

(v) *Date and place of origin.* Any scholar who attempts to define either the date or place of origin of M knows only too well that he has no data to rely upon other than his own speculations. Streeter[4] suggested a date about AD 65 and located it in Jerusalem. The date must clearly be arbitrary, although it must have preceded the publication of the Gospel, and is naturally dated after Mark and Q. The location may be indicated by its Jewish characteristics, although Jerusalem was not the only place where Jewish influences were strong. The matter is of slight importance in the study of Gospel origins, because of its wholly conjectural character.

b. The book of testimonies

The many citations from the Old Testament in Matthew's Gospel fall into two distinct groups. The majority reproduce more or less precisely

---

[1] T. W. Manson (*The Sayings of Jesus*, p. 25) regards M with some suspicion, owing to these two influences.   [2] *The Gospels*, p. 32.

[3] Cf. V. Taylor, *op. cit.*, p. 34. Bornkamm (*Jesus of Nazareth*, 1960, p. 216), like most German scholars, rejects the idea of a special Matthew source (and a special Luke source) because of the widely varied character of the material.

[4] *The Four Gospels*, pp. 500–524.

the text of the LXX, or at least a Greek translation of the Hebrew text.[1] A small group of citations, twelve in number, is apparently derived direct from the Hebrew text. This latter group is exclusive to Matthew with the exception of one quotation which occurs also in Mark and Luke (i.e. the passage about the voice crying in the wilderness applied to John the Baptist—Mt. iii. 3; Mk. i. 2, 3; Lk. iii. 4–6). The others are: the virgin passage (i. 23), the ruler from Bethlehem (ii. 6), the call out of Egypt (ii. 15), the voice in Ramah applied to the incident of the slaughter of the innocents (ii. 18), the Nazarene statement (ii. 23), the people in darkness see a great light (iv. 15, 16), 'He took our infirmities' applied to the healing ministry (viii. 17), the Servant passage illustrating the non-belligerent attitude of Jesus (xii. 18–21), the statement about parables (xiii. 35), the king riding upon an ass (xxi. 5), and the thirty pieces of silver (xxvii. 9).

Since each of these citations is introduced by a similar formula ('that it might be fulfilled which was spoken through . . .') it has been suggested that an independent collection of Old Testament citations existed distinct from those used elsewhere in the Gospel. F. C. Burkitt[2] and J. Rendel Harris[3] argued that this type of collection was in existence in the contemporary Jewish world.[4] These scholars postulated an Aramaic collection of testimonies as the source of Matthew's citations. In some cases (e.g. i. 23) the citation differs from both the LXX and Hebrew texts and may perhaps be explained by Aramaic influence, in which case it would be support for an Aramaic original. McNeile[5] suggested on the contrary that this source may have been translated into Greek before Matthew used it.

The idea of a collection of *testimonia* is supported by what is known of early Christian interest in the Old Testament witness to Christ. It

---

[1] Cf. W. G. Kümmel (*INT*, 1965, p. 78) for the view that some of Matthew's citations could be from another translation of the Hebrew text rather than from the LXX.

[2] *The Gospel History and its Transmission*³ (1911), p. 127.

[3] *Testimonies*, I (1916). Cf. also D. Plooij's monograph *Studies in the Testimony Book* (1932).

[4] It should be noted that some support may be found for this contention in the Qumran *testimonia* document (4 Q Test), in which three sections consist wholly of biblical quotations of messianic expectations and the fourth is from the apocryphal *Psalms of Joshua*. For a translation of the complete text cf. A. Dupont-Sommer, *The Essene Writings from Qumran* (1961), pp. 315 ff.

[5] *INT*, p. 85.

is not, therefore, intrinsically improbable that such Christian collections existed. Yet certain features of this hypothesis cannot be substantiated.

1. Both Burkitt and Harris maintained, on the basis of Papias' reference to Matthew's λογία, that Matthew was the author of such a book of *testimonia*, but this is improbable because Papias uses the word in relation to Jesus but not, it would seem, of Old Testament proof-texts.[1]

2. The theory moreover lacks primitive Christian parallels, although it is known that similar *testimonia* existed in the time of Tertullian and Cyprian. Moreover, these later testimony books do not follow Matthew's model in sequence or in language.[2]

3. Some at least of these proof-texts would certainly have been unintelligible if they had existed in isolation from any context, although the possibility that a tradition of interpretation may have accompanied such a list cannot be ruled out. Christian interest in Old Testament *testimonia* is more likely to have been centred in important passages than in proof-texts, as C. H. Dodd[3] has pointed out.

4. Insufficient attention has been given by the advocates of the theory to the connection which the citations have with their Matthaean contexts. Are they perhaps proof-texts which suggested themselves to the mind of the author in the course of his compilation? Some of them may be more reasonably accounted for in this manner, as for instance the citing of Hosea xi. 1 ('out of Egypt have I called my son') to demonstrate that the descent into Egypt was a divinely foreshadowed event.[4] However strange the exegesis may appear to modern standards it is reasonable to suppose that the writer recalled the Hosea passage as he meditated on the event itself. The alternative would appear to be that the author selected his events to illustrate the *testimonia*, but this is less likely.[5]

---

[1] See comments on pp. 33 ff.

[2] Cf. J. A. Findlay, *The First Gospel and the Book of Testimonies* (1933), pp. 57–71.

[3] *According to the Scriptures* (1952).

[4] Cf. N. Walker (*NTS*, 9, 1963, p. 393) who suggests that Matthew's intention was to find Old Testament texts to fit the events of the story, not *vice versa*. For a full examination of Matthew's use of these passages from the point of view that they reveal Matthew's theologizing purpose, cf. G. Strecker, *Der Weg der Gerechtigkeit* (1962), pp. 49–85.

[5] S. V. McCasland (*JBL*, LXXX, 1961, pp. 143–148) charges Matthew with twisting the Scriptures. His views are answered by Walker.

W. L. Knox[1] maintained that the *testimonia* did not all belong to one source. The first five of those unique in Matthew occur in the birth narratives and were part of that source (see next section). Of the remaining six, four formed part of another source consisting of *testimonia* and the remaining two were added from yet another source, possibly oral.[2] But such a multiplication of *testimonia* sources makes the whole hypothesis less credible.[3] Even if all the relevant passages were originally in a testimony source there are hardly sufficient to have formed a book, and to split them still further would require the postulation of testimony fly-sheets, which is possible but improbable.

The idea of a Matthaean school, which has already been mentioned in the discussion over the purpose of the Gospel,[4] has been mainly based on Matthew's use of the Old Testament. Exegesis of selected *testimonia* would have been a major method in New Testament apologetics,[5] and to this extent Matthew's concentration upon proof-texts is not surprising. But the school idea is not the most probable explanation of the origin of these *testimonia* texts which are cited by Matthew, although it may explain the author's interest in exegesis. If Matthew belonged to a group which, like the men of Qumran, were devoted to such exegesis, it is easy to see how many of the texts would spring naturally to his mind when he was writing his narrative.[6] But why did he use a special formula for one group of citations and not for the rest? It would seem that this was specifically used to draw attention to the fulfilment of prophecies which were being interpreted in a messianic way by Christian apologists.

c. Matthew's birth narratives

Although these will be dealt with under a separate sub-heading, they are sometimes regarded as part of the larger cycle of narratives peculiar

---

[1] *Sources of the Synoptic Gospels*, II, pp. 121 ff.

[2] G. D. Kilpatrick, *The Origins of the Gospel according to St. Matthew* (1946), p. 46. Cf. also p. 66, where Kilpatrick expresses his doubts about the existence of a testimony book.

[3] Cf. A. M. Hunter, *Paul and his Predecessors*[2] (1961), pp. 58 ff.

[4] Cf. pp. 27 f. for comments on K. Stendahl's book, *The School of Matthew and its use of the Old Testament* (1954).

[5] B. Lindars' book on *New Testament Apologetic* (1961) makes a great deal of this.

[6] Lindars (*op. cit.*, p. 265) suggests that the school's stock of quotations which were used orally in catechetical work would have been known to Matthew.

to Matthew.[1] It is useful, however, to consider these narratives separately.

1. Matthew's birth narratives are quite different from Luke's and clearly came from a different source. The interest in Joseph's part of the story is significant when compared with Luke's greater interest in Mary.

2. There is an absorbing interest in the Old Testament to such an extent that Knox maintained that 'each story is woven round a *testimonium* from the Old Testament'.[2] This goes too far, but there is no doubt that the primitive Church was particularly concerned to demonstrate the Old Testament predictions of Christ's advent, and this concern would have affected the form in which the tradition was preserved. It is equally possible, however, that the author himself was the first to reduce these particular traditions to writing and has himself introduced the relevant *testimonia* as suggested in the last section.

3. It has been further proposed that these stories arose from a Christianizing of the story of Moses and Israel,[3] forming a kind of commentary on them. But although Old Testament interest is undeniable, this is very different from maintaining that the Old Testament formed the motif for the formation of the stories. It is reasonable to suppose that a close check would have been kept on such compilations.

4. It has often been maintained that Matthew's birth narratives cannot be considered historical, but that they arose at a later period prompted by dogmatic concern to embellish the coming of Jesus. Yet such a view springs all too often more from a dislike of the supernatural and a disbelief in the virgin birth than from a historical appraisal of the data.[4]

---

[1] Cf. Streeter, *The Four Gospels*, pp. 266, 502 f.

[2] *Op. cit.*, p. 121.

[3] Cf. A. H. McNeile, *St. Matthew*, p. 23; W. C. Allen, *St. Matthew*, p. 18. A rather different, although allied, theory is that of C. H. Cave (*NTS*, 9, 1963, pp. 382–390) who develops the view of D. Daube (*The New Testament and Rabbinic Judaism*, 1955, pp. 158 ff.) that the background of the Matthaean birth narratives is to be found in the Passover Midrash and the synagogue lections.

[4] It should be noted that Matthew does not actually describe the birth of Jesus. His name and its significance is more important in Matthew's narrative than the event itself. Cf. K. Stendahl's study, 'Quis et unde?' in *Judentum, Urchristentum, Kirche* (ed. W. Eltester, 1960), pp. 94–105. He rightly points out that Matthew's narrative not only shows the author's knowledge of the virgin birth, but also the slanders which it had occasioned.

d. *Matthew's other narratives*

The main narratives which are found in no other source are: (1) the hesitation of John the Baptist at the baptism of Jesus (iii. 14 f.); (2) the account of Peter walking on the water (xiv. 28–31); (3) the coin in the fish's mouth (xvii. 24–27); (4) several stories in the passion narratives, such as Judas' bargain with the priests (xxvi. 14–16), Pilate's hand-washing (xxvii. 24 f.), the earthquake and the resurrection of certain saints (xxvii. 51–53), and, in the concluding section, the reference to the watch, the angel rolling away the stone and the bribing of the guard (xxvii. 62–xxviii. 15). Kilpatrick[1] divides the material into three sections, Petrine stories (xiv. 28–31, xvi. 17–19, xvii. 24–27, xviii. 15–22), passion and resurrection stories (xxvi. 52–54, xxvii. 3–10, 19, 24 f., 51–53, 62–66, xxviii. 2–4, 9–20) and miscellaneous narratives (iii. 14 f., iv. 23, ix. 35, xv. 22–24, xvii. 6 f., xxi. 10 f., 14–16).

Many scholars have found some homogeneity in these sections and have suggested a common source with the birth narratives. The characteristic features which are said to unite this material are: (1) stylistic features; (2) references to angels and prophecy; (3) an emphasis upon the miraculous, and (4) a dogmatic purpose to support primitive tradition.[2] Not much value can be attached to the first point since there are few distinctive features to mark these narratives as stylistically different from the rest of the Gospel, but the other three points, if valid, may certainly suggest a common origin for these narratives. Interest in angels, however, is not confined to this special source, except the expression 'angel of the Lord'. Moreover, both Mark and Luke contain references to angels and this must therefore be considered to be a common feature in the primitive tradition. Admittedly the prophetic element is more dominant in Matthew than in the other Synoptic Gospels, which is no doubt mainly due to the purpose of the Gospel. It is probably true that the miraculous element is more emphasized in Matthew's narratives than elsewhere, but Matthew's treatment seems highly restrained when compared with the supernatural embellishments of apocryphal Gospels. It is mis-

[1] *Op. cit.*, p. 37. Sometimes the symbol N has been used to denote the source of Matthew's special narratives, but Kilpatrick rejects this because he regards the material as derived from oral tradition.

[2] Cf. V. Taylor, *The Gospels*, p. 65.

leading, therefore, to describe Matthew's special material as 'apocryphal'.[1]

Peter's attempt to walk on the water is no more improbable than Jesus' own action as far as the physical aspect of it is concerned, and the latter event is not confined to Matthew's record. Indeed the sequel rather suggests a quite different motive from embellishment, for Peter cannot be said to come out of the story particularly enhanced. Vincent Taylor[2] finds dogmatic purpose in John's hesitation, in the story of the coin in the fish's mouth and in the account of the resurrection guard, all of which are supposed to answer difficulties currently felt. The second, for example, is claimed to offer a solution to the problem whether or not Christians should pay taxes.[3] But though this suggestion *may* explain the origin of these stories, the narratives themselves do not necessarily *require* such an explanation. If they had historical validity, which is denied by many scholars, they would still be answers to the same problems. It is often assumed that the difficulties created the narratives to solve them, but it is surely more reasonable to suppose that the problems themselves were a dominant factor in the processes of selection and preservation of already existing material.

Vincent Taylor's conclusion that this cycle of tradition is the least valuable of the Gospel traditions is prompted by his low estimate of the influences described above. If this assessment is correct, the conclusion must be allowed. Yet reasons have been given which suggest the advisability of great caution in assessing historical value by this means.

VII. SOURCES PECULIAR TO LUKE

The amount of material not found elsewhere which has been incorporated in Luke is even greater than that in Matthew. Streeter suggested that this special Lucan material L was based on Caesarea. It is not generally supposed that it existed in a written form and the symbol

[1] F. C. Grant (*The Gospels, their origin and growth*, p. 147) unhesitatingly describes this material as 'apocryphal'. Cf. also A. J. B. Higgins (*The Reliability of the Gospels*, 1952, pp. 22 ff.) who makes a comparison with the type of development found in the *Gospel of Peter*. But there is an obvious difference between this material in the canonical and apocryphal Gospels.

[2] *Op. cit.*, p. 65.

[3] Both G. Bornkamm and G. Barth regard this story as evidence that at the time when Matthew's Gospel was issued the congregation represented by Matthew still regarded itself as a part of Judaism, liable for the temple tax (*Tradition and Interpretation in Matthew*, pp. 19 f., 90).

L may therefore be regarded as representative of the oral tradition,[1] probably collected by Luke while he was at Caesarea.

a. General contents

Within this L material there are fourteen parables: the two debtors (Lk. vii. 41–43), the good Samaritan (x. 29–37), the friend at midnight (xi. 5–8), the rich fool (xii. 13–21), the fig-tree (xiii. 6–9), the tower builder (xiv. 28–30), the rash king (xiv. 31–33), the lost coin (xv. 8–10), the prodigal son (xv. 11–32), the dishonest steward (xvi. 1–9), the rich man and Lazarus (xvi. 19–31), the servant's duty (xvii. 7–10), the unjust judge (xviii. 1–8), the Pharisee and the tax collector (xviii. 9–14). If the parable of the pounds (xix. 11–27) is considered separate from the parable of the talents this too must be added, but many scholars think them to be variants of the same parable. The differences are, however, sufficient to justify treating them separately.

In addition to these parables there are also a number of isolated sayings such as the dispute about the inheritance (xii. 13–15), statements on the disaster which overtook the Galilaeans at Siloam (xiii. 1–5) and sayings about humility (xiv. 7–14) and hypocrisy (xvi. 14, 15).

A large amount of narrative material is also peculiar to this L-stratum, and this may be summarized as follows:

(i) *During the Galilaean period*
The rejection at Nazareth (iv. 16–30).
The miraculous draught of fishes (v. 1–11).
The widow's son at Nain (vii. 11–17).
The sinful woman (vii. 36–50).
The ministering women (viii. 1–3).

(ii) *In the 'travel' narrative*
The Samaritan villages (ix. 51–56).
The mission of the seventy (x. 1–16).
Mary and Martha (x. 38–42).
The woman who declared the blessedness of Christ's mother (xi. 27, 28).
The woman with the spirit of infirmity (xiii. 10–17).
The man with the dropsy (xiv. 1–6).

---

[1] Some scholars have sought evidence for pre-Lucan structural forms. Cf. W. R. Farmer's discussion of the parallel groupings of materials in Lk. xiii. 1–9 and xv. 1–32 and their comparison with the Greek rhetorical form of *chreia*, with concise introduction, two brief parables and a third parable to illustrate the point of the former (*NTS*, 8, 1962, pp. 301–316).

The ten lepers (xvii. 11–19).

Zacchaeus (xix. 1–10).

(iii) *The passion narratives*

Differences in the account of the institution of the last supper (xxii. 15–30).

The sweat of blood (xxii. 40–46).

The arrest (xxii. 47–53).

The triple trial (xxii. 54–xxiii. 16).

The weeping women (xxiii. 26–31).

The penitent thief at the cross (xxiii. 39–43).

(iv) *The resurrection narratives*

The women at the tomb (xxiv. 1–12).

The Emmaus walk (xxiv. 13–35).

The appearance at Jerusalem (xxiv. 36–49).

The departure of Jesus (xxiv. 50–53).

This list must be regarded as tentative,[1] as some of the accounts overlap narratives in the other Gospels (e.g. xxiv. 1–12), but there are significant differences which have been thought sufficient to suggest a different source.

It is noteworthy that most of Luke's special parables and sayings material occurs in his 'travel' narrative, together with many of his special narratives. This will have a bearing on our consideration of the Proto-Luke hypothesis (see pp. 175 ff.). From the material detailed above certain characteristic features of Luke's special source may be noted. (1) The parables are not, as so often in Matthew, called kingdom parables, although, according to Jeremias, they are equally full of the secret of the kingdom. Interest in people is particularly evident. (2) The narratives contain a number of miracles, some of them very striking, but they are not generally classed by source critics in the same category as those of Matthew's special source. (3) There is a marked interest in women.

It has already been noted that the description of Luke ix. 51–xviii. 14 as a 'travel' narrative is not altogether apt (see p. 98). It certainly fills in the gap between the Galilaean and Judaean ministries left by the other Synoptics, but there are in fact very few references to a journey.

---

[1] The list given follows V. Taylor's list (*The Gospels*, pp. 32 f.), but Streeter allowed more material in L (*The Four Gospels*, pp. 198). McNeile-Williams (*INT*, pp. 87 ff.) adhere to Streeter's list.

At its commencement Jesus is in Galilee with His face set towards Jerusalem (ix. 51) and just after its ending He is near Jerusalem (xix. 28), but the progress of any journey in the body of the section is vague.[1] This has led to the view that Luke has himself filled the gap mainly with a mixture of his own special material and Q with little attention to geographical detail.[2] Indeed it is maintained that xiii. 31–33 is inconsistent with ix. 51 since it implies that Jesus is only just about to leave Galilee.[3] But Galilee is not mentioned, only Herod's territory (which included a part of Perea), and the alleged inconsistency would vanish if Jesus was then in Perea. Again xvii. 11, which states that Jesus journeyed to Jerusalem between Samaria and Galilee, is considered to be geographically difficult. It would certainly be strange if xiii. 31–33 had earlier placed Jesus in Perea. The explanation may be that xvii. 11 is reminiscent of an earlier incident, but if so Luke's attention to the journey sequence was overshadowed by his greater interest in the character of the contents. It has been suggested[4] that the dominating feature of the material as Luke has arranged it is an alternation between instruction and discussion, designed especially for the training of preachers and missionaries. It has also been proposed that in this material is a higher proportion of polemical matter than elsewhere.[5]

b. Luke's nativity narratives

There is much discussion over Luke's infancy stories. It is generally supposed that he possessed a special source for this material, in which

[1] Jerusalem itself is mentioned only at xiii. 22, 33 and xvii. 11, while the movements of Jesus and His disciples are elsewhere described in very general terms.

[2] Cf. H. Conzelmann, *The Theology of St. Luke* (1960), pp. 60 ff., for the view that in parts Luke's topography is unreliable, since geographical elements are introduced for a theological purpose.

[3] Cf. Bo Reicke's article in *Studia Evangelica*, p. 214. He cites J. Schneider's article in *Synoptische Studien für A. Wikenhauser* (1935), pp. 215 ff., for this view, and from it deduces that chapter xiv marks a new part of the narrative distinct from the opening section.

[4] Cf. Bo Reicke, *op. cit.*, pp. 206–216.

[5] Cf. Manson, *The Sayings of Jesus*, p. 28. Yet another, but less likely, explanation is the typological theory suggested by C. F. Evans, who wonders whether there are parallels between Luke's central section and Dt. i–xxvi. The idea that Luke presents a kind of Christian 'Deuteronomy' requires more convincing evidence than Evans is able to give (cf. his article, 'The Central Section of St. Luke's Gospel', in *Studies in the Gospels*, ed. D. E. Nineham, 1955, pp. 37–53). He attempts to establish a coincidence of order in the parallel material, but many of his parallels are very strained.

case it may have been distinct from the general L material. If L consisted of oral tradition it is easier to believe that such oral tradition included the nativity narratives than that a written source included them. This is due to the marked linguistic differences between Luke i and ii and the rest of the special Lucan material. The special characteristics of these stories may be briefly summarized as follows.

1. Their language and style are distinctive. After his literary preface (i. 1–4), Luke's style in the next section (i. 5–ii. 52) drops into what W. L. Knox[1] calls 'an orgy of Hebraic Greek with occasional improvements'. McNeile[2] called the language 'translation Greek'. Whatever its description the Greek of this part of Luke differs markedly from the Greek before and after, for from iii. 1 ff. the style lacks the strong Hebraic features of the infancy stories and may generally be regarded as literary *Koiné* Greek. This linguistic peculiarity clearly requires some explanation.

2. Their contents are also unusual. It is remarkable that it is in this section alone that Luke includes canticles and these are written in a form which appears to be modelled on the more poetic portions of the LXX. They are all saturated with Old Testament allusions.

3. They are independent of Matthew's stories.[3] Luke's interest centres on Nazareth rather than on Judaea, on Mary more than on Joseph, on the relationship between John the Baptist and Jesus, and on the childhood of Jesus.

Various explanations of the origin of these narratives have been proposed, but it is not possible to give more than the briefest mention of them here.

(i) *The theory of a Hebrew source.* The idea that Luke has used an older Hebrew source has often been proposed. It was strongly maintained by C. C. Torrey[4] and was regarded by McNeile[5] as a 'certain' conclusion. More recently it has been advocated from various points of view, one suggestion being that it originated in a John the Baptist sect,[6] while yet another basis for this contention has been the occurrence

---

[1] *Sources of the Synoptic Gospels*, II, p. 40.   [2] *INT*, p. 88.

[3] For an attempt to show that Luke's narrative was composed with Matthew's infancy stories in view, cf. P. J. Thompson, *Studia Evangelica* (1959), pp. 217–222, but his arguments are not convincing.

[4] *The Four Gospels*, p. 266.   [5] *INT*, p. 88.

[6] Cf. P. Vielhauer, *ZTK*, 49 (1952), pp. 255 ff.; P. Winter, *Nov. Test.*, I (1956), pp. 184–199. Cf. also H. Sahlin, *Der Messias und das Gottesvolk* (1945), cited by Feine–Behm, *Einleitung*, p. 45.

in these narratives of features similar to the word-plays which were so characteristic in Hebrew literature, since this is apparent only if an underlying Hebrew text is presupposed.[1] P. Winter[2] has an involved theory for the origin of Luke's material, including the suggestion that the Magnificat and part of the Benedictus were originally Maccabean battle hymns, while part of the narrative sections (Lk. i. 5–80, ii. 1–21) was from a 'baptist' document and another part was associated with James the Just (ii. 22–39, 41–51a). It is, however, highly doubtful whether Luke would have so radically adapted a John the Baptist source as this theory supposes, in view of his tendency to retain his sources with as little alteration as possible.[3]

Even if an original Hebrew source were admitted there would still remain the question of whether Luke himself translated it into Greek or already possessed a Greek translation of it.[4] It makes little difference to the general theory, however, whether Luke or someone else translated the Hebrew, as long as it is recognized that he retained much evidence of Semitisms.

(ii) *The theory of an Aramaic source.* This was favoured by certain older scholars,[5] but it is not now in such wide favour.[6] McNeile[7] remarked that the absence of distinctive Aramaisms in this section would involve for this theory the notion that the Aramaic was rendered into Greek,

[1] Cf. R. Laurentin's articles in *Biblica*, 37 (1956), pp. 435 ff.; 38 (1957), pp. 1 ff. He has fully treated the whole subject in his *Structure et Théologie de Luc I–II* (1957). In the first article mentioned, Laurentin gives a useful summary of arguments for a Hebrew source (pp. 454–456).

[2] Winter has discussed these chapters in a number of articles (*NTS*, 1, 1955, pp. 111 ff.; *ZNTW*, 45, 1954, pp. 145–179; 46, 1955, pp. 261–263; 47, 1956, pp. 217–242; *HTR*, 48, 1955, pp. 213 ff.; *BJRL*, xxxvii, 1954, p. 328). His general position is concisely summarized by R. McL. Wilson in his article in *Studia Evangelica*, pp. 242–248. Winter speaks of a Baptist document, of temple *pericopae* and of a Nazarene adaptation. As a basis for his Baptist document, Winter appeals to Pseudo-Philo's *Liber Antiquitatum Biblicarum* (cf. *Nov. Test.*, 1956, 1, pp. 186 ff.).

[3] Cf. Wilson's criticisms, *op. cit.*, p. 248. Cf. also P. Benoit, *NTS*, 3 (1957), pp. 169–194.

[4] W. L. Knox suggested that Luke tried to reduce his source to tolerable Greek, but abandoned the attempt (*op. cit.*, p. 41).

[5] Cf. A. Plummer, *St. Luke* (ICC, 1896), p. xxvi; C. A. Briggs, *The Messiah of the Gospels* (1895); F. Spitta, *ZNTW*, 7 (1906), p. 294.

[6] But cf. Feine-Behm, *op. cit.*, p. 45. However, the influence of the LXX on Luke's treatment of his source is admitted.

[7] *Op. cit.*, p. 89.

modelled after the LXX, but with a skilful avoidance of Aramaisms. This he thought to be improbable.

(iii) *The theory of Luke's free composition.* A widely advocated hypothesis is that these narratives are Luke's own work. Howard,[1] for instance, considered that Luke was so steeped in the diction of the LXX and especially of the Psalter that this might well account for the Hebraisms. Harnack[2] went further and suggested that the Hebraisms were intentional, but this suggestion was dismissed by Torrey[3] because it would involve 'a grotesque performance' on Luke's part for which there was no apparent motive. But if Luke intentionally composed his infancy stories in imitation of the LXX, why did he do it? It has been suggested with some plausibility that Luke's intention was to show the close connection between the birth events and the Old Testament.[4] In this case he would have followed Old Testament (LXX) models and the presence of Hebraisms would at once be accounted for, unless of course there was enough evidence to show that the Hebrew text and not the LXX could best account for his style. In the latter event a Hebrew original would be more probable, but the evidence is not sufficient to dispose of the LXX as the main influence on Luke's Greek.[5] If he did base his language on LXX models the result bears eloquent testimony to his literary artistry.[6]

There are various forms in which the hypothesis of Luke's combining oral traditional material with Old Testament models can be presented.[7] It can be maintained that Luke selected biblical material to combine with and illustrate the oral traditions in his possession.[8] Or it can be suggested that the oral tradition was itself strongly influenced by biblical models because the canticles, if any authenticity is to be attached to

[1] In Moulton and Howard, *Grammar of New Testament Greek*, II, p. 483. Cf. also N. Turner's article, *NTS*, 2 (1956), pp. 100 ff.

[2] *Luke the Physician* (1907), pp. 96–105, 190–218.

[3] Cf. his article in C. H. *Toy Studies*, pp. 286 ff., cited by Howard, *op. cit.*, p. 482.

[4] Cf. W. L. Knox, *op. cit.*, p. 39.

[5] Cf. P. Benoit's article in *NTS*, 3 (1957), pp. 169 ff. It may be, as R. McL. Wilson suggests, that Luke used a Hebrew source but was naturally influenced by his strong liking for LXX Greek (*op. cit.*, pp. 252, 253).

[6] Cf. V. Taylor, *The Gospels*, p. 63.

[7] The idea that Luke's work in these narratives consisted largely of accommodating two sources has recently been suggested by A. R. C. Leaney (*NTS*, 8, 1962, pp. 158–166), who does not, however, discuss their probable language.

[8] So P. Benoit, *op. cit.*

them, must by their very character have influenced the form of the narrative. Another, but very radical, view is that Luke ignored oral tradition altogether and composed his infancy stories as pious fictions after the manner of the rabbinic Haggadists.[1] Of these views, the second would seem the most probable, particularly if Luke had personal acquaintance with Mary the mother of our Lord, which is not at all improbable. The first is conceivable, but makes much greater demands on Luke's artistry. The third must be dismissed, for it is inconceivable that these priceless stories had no basis in fact, nor is it credible that they are the products of the author's imagination playing upon Old Testament typologies.*

(iv) *The historical value of these narratives.* The assessment of historical worth is inevitably affected by views regarding the origin of the material. If the whole is a fiction there is no point in discussing historicity. But if sources, either written or oral, were used the value of Luke's record will depend on their reliability. Many scholars have impugned Luke's historicity on the grounds that he made an error over the enrolment under Quirinius (Lk. ii. 3), but the evidence from archaeology has helped to restore more confidence in Luke's veracity.[2] Nevertheless there have been theories of pagan influences[3] which have seriously called in question Luke's historicity. Yet, as Taylor has pointed out, the narratives are as a whole free from mythological colouring and are Jewish Christian in theology and spirit.[4] It is of course necessary

---

[1] Cf. M. D. Goulder and M. L. Sanderson, *JTS*, n.s., VIII (1957), pp. 12 ff.

[2] Cf. the discussion on this point in E. Stauffer, *Jesus and His Story* (1960), pp. 27 ff. The theory is here advanced that Quirinius was appointed Governor of the East and that he held this office from 12 BC to AD 16, together with the office of Governor of Judaea from AD 6. Unfortunately, Stauffer cites no specific supporting evidence, although if his theory is true it would remove all the difficulties. A. N. Sherwin-White (*Roman Society and Roman Law in the New Testament*, 1963, pp. 162–171) has a note about Quirinius in which he maintains the accuracy of Luke's dating of the census in AD 6 but considers Matthew to be incorrect.*

[3] Cf. J. M. Creed, *The Gospel according to St. Luke* (1930), pp. 30–32. Cf. also the study of M. Dibelius from a form-critical point of view, *Jungfrauensohn und Krippenkind* (1932).

[4] *Op. cit.*, p. 64. Yet H. K. Luce (*St. Luke*, CGT, 1949, p. 84) calls these stories 'the imaginative poetry of devotion rather than the sober prose of history', but their poetic form need not imply non-historicity. Cf. G. H. Box (*ZNTW*, 6, 1905, pp. 80–101), against the view that Luke (or Matthew) shows the influence of heathen ideas. Cf. J. G. Machen, *The Virgin Birth* (1930), for a full discussion of

here to be clear what is meant by Jewish Christian. It must be understood in the broadest sense, in a manner which would be true of our Lord Himself, for these narratives transcend all narrowness and contain more than one indication of His universal mission (cf. Simeon's song, Lk. ii. 29–32).

Those who connect up one of the sources with the Baptist sect tend to see these narratives as an attempt to link the movement of John the Baptist with Jewish Christianity.[1] But this seems most improbable in view of the smallness of the Baptist's group of adherents.[2] Luke's purpose as a whole is much larger than this. Quite apart from the birth narratives he shows an impressive sense of John's importance in the scheme of things, marking the commencement of his ministry with an elaborate dating (iii. 1). This dating suggests that the preceding narratives were not originally attached (see next section on the Proto-Luke hypothesis). But it cannot be entirely ruled out that Luke intentionally regarded the birth narratives as a kind of prelude to the formal announcement of the commencement of the public ministry of Jesus.

c. The Proto-Luke hypothesis

The theory that Luke put together a draft of his Gospel before he became acquainted with Mark and later inserted some Marcan material before publishing the Gospel was first seriously proposed by Streeter.[3] Many other scholars had, however, prepared the way by various studies which focused attention on the difficulties in the established hypothesis that Luke's Gospel was built on a Marcan framework.[4] Streeter found a staunch ally in Vincent Taylor, whose admirable presentation of the theory has done much to commend it to many scholars. He proposes that Luke came into possession of a copy of Q

Lk. i and ii. On the subject of the virgin birth, cf. also D. Edwards (*The Virgin Birth in History and Faith*, 1941), who adopts a similar line to Machen, and T. Boslooper (*The Virgin Birth*, 1962), who regards the nativity narratives as mythological and opposes the literal historical interpretation.

[1] Cf. H. L. MacNeill, *JBL*, LXV (1946), pp. 123–130. W. L. Knox (*Sources of the Synoptic Gospels*, II, p. 41) partly favours the idea.

[2] The precise origin and extent of the Baptist sect is not known, but it is doubtful whether it was widespread (see p. 280 n.3).

[3] Cf. *The Four Gospels*, pp. 199 ff.

[4] V. Taylor (*Behind the Third Gospel*, 1926, pp. 2 ff.) traces the development of the idea in the works of Feine, Weiss (B. and J.), Burkitt, Stanton, Hawkins Bartlet, Sanday and Perry.

and while at Caesarea collected information (L) which he then combined with Q. This combination was called Proto-Luke, but it was not
suggested that this was any more than a rough draft. It was not a published Gospel. According to Vincent Taylor it 'was not, and could not,
be published until Luke was able to expand it by drawing upon Mark'.[1]
It is important for this to be borne in mind when assessing the value of
the hypothesis.

(i) *The grounds for the hypothesis*. The basis cannot be better presented
than by using Vincent Taylor's own summary.[2]

1. The passion narrative. By a careful comparison of Luke's narrative of the passion with Mark's, Taylor comes to the conclusion that
Luke's version is not a recasting of Mark, but is based on an independent
narrative.[3] It is claimed that the Marcan material has been added, because when it is extracted the residue is a continuous narrative. This
view is further supported by the numerous occasions when Luke
changes the Marcan order in this section.[4] Hence the Proto-Luke theory
is claimed to account satisfactorily for this phenomenon.[5]

2. The eschatological discourse. Luke xxi shows the same characteristics as the passion narrative and this has led to the suggestion that part
at least (verses 20-34) 'rests on a non-Markan source supplemented by
Markan insertions'.[6] Vincent Taylor did not include this in Proto-

---

[1] *ET*, LXVII (1955), p. 15.   [2] Cf. *ibid.*, p. 12.

[3] R. Bultmann thought it most probable that Luke used an older redaction
of the passion narrative used by Mark, a view which focuses attention upon the
differences between the two narratives (cf. *The History of the Synoptic Tradition*,
pp. 262 ff.). In his recent book on *Historical Tradition in the Fourth Gospel* (1963),
p. 52, C. H. Dodd regards any theory that Luke is editing Mark's passion narrative
as having no plausibility. G. B. Caird (*Saint Luke*, *The Pelican Gospel Commentaries*, 1963, p. 25) maintains that in these narratives verbal similarity amounts
to only 20 per cent, compared with 53 per cent elsewhere when Luke uses Mark.

[4] Cf. J. C. Hawkins in *Oxford Studies*, pp. 80–84, who mentions twelve instances between Lk. xxii. 14 and xxiv. 11.

[5] There has been much recent discussion over Luke's passion narrative, but
agreement has not been reached over Luke's relation to Mark. Cf. S. I. Buse's
articles in *NTS*, 1 (1954), pp. 29–41; 7 (1960), pp. 65–76. Cf. also P. Borgen,
NTS, 5 (1959), pp. 249 ff.; C. E. Osty, *Recherches de Science religieuse*, XXXIX
(1951). Buse's suggestion is that behind Luke's narrative is a passion source which
was known to Luke before he knew Mark, and if this is established it would lend
support to the Proto-Luke hypothesis. Cf. also S. Temple's study, *NTS*, 7 (1960),
pp. 77–85. An earlier advocate for an independent source for Luke's passion
narrative was A. M. Perry, *ET*, XLVI (1935), pp. 256–260.

[6] V. Taylor, *ET*, LXVII (1955), p. 16.

Luke, but considered that its structure illustrated the literary processes behind the Gospel.

3. The main narrative section. In those parts which deal with the public ministry and the travel narrative, the Marcan material exists in blocks alternating with blocks of non-Marcan material. When the Marcan material is extracted the remainder possesses 'a relative continuity'. On the contrary, the Marcan sections are claimed to be 'topical panels' lacking any connection between them.

4. The treatment of Q. It is claimed that Luke's use of Q shows a tendency to expansion by the addition of the L material. In other words the Q material is always combined with the L material and never inserted into the Marcan material. It is then presumed that Q and L must have been combined together before the insertion of the Marcan material. If this claim could be substantiated it would be a strong argument for the hypothesis. It is certainly evident that Luke has left his Marcan material in blocks and it has accordingly been supposed that the only satisfactory explanation of this is that the rest of the material was already fused.[1]

5. The omission of Marcan material. Altogether about half of Mark's Gospel is paralleled in Luke. The omitted material according to this theory may be explained by supposing that Luke preferred a parallel tradition or else had no need for the material in his expansion of QL.[2] The strength of this factor must be gauged by the fact that a similar explanation could apply without recourse to the Proto-Luke theory.

6. The use of Marcan material. The Proto-Luke draft had deficiencies regarding Galilaean material, nature miracles and kingdom parables. Luke therefore supplied this lack from Marcan material.

[1] Cf. G. B. Caird, op. cit., p. 26. Caird argues that the only alternative is to suppose that Luke had so high an opinion of Mark that he determined to keep it distinct, which he rightly dismisses as less satisfactory. But he does not take into account the possibility that Luke may have decided on a scheme which involved the alternation of non-Marcan and Marcan material. Cf. R. M. Grant's scheme of Luke's use of Mark, A Historical Introduction to the New Testament (1963), p. 136. Caird apparently does not consider this to be a possible procedure.

[2] Where sayings are duplicated and one comes from Mark and the other from another source (of which there are eleven instances in Luke), the author had overlapping sources. (Cf. Caird, op. cit., p. 24.) The overlapping of Mark and Q is also said to be supported by several occasions where Luke diverges from Mark's order (Caird, op. cit., pp. 24, 25).

Vincent Taylor calls Mark a 'quarry' from which stone is obtained to enlarge an existing building.[1] The difficulty with this line of argument is that the deficiencies are laid bare only because the 'quarried stone' has already been removed.[2] It may quite well have been part of the original design.

7. Luke's literary method. The elaborate dating in iii. 1 certainly looks like a beginning, and if this is so it would support the contention that Proto-Luke began at this point. This is also supported by the position of the genealogy, which unlike that of Matthew appears after the birth narratives, and indeed after the first mention of the ministry of Jesus. This is undoubtedly one of the strongest arguments in favour of Proto-Luke.[3] To this may be added the indication of Luke's method which may be inferred from his preface and his use of the we-sections of Acts, both of which are claimed to show that the manner in which Luke treats his sources is in full accord with the Proto-Luke hypothesis.[4]

Certain other considerations have been brought forward in support of the theory. Luke refers to Jesus as Lord on fourteen occasions, whereas Mark and Matthew never do, which supports the contention that this feature is editorial. Similarly a different word is used for the exponents of the Jewish law in passages derived from Mark (γραμματευς) as compared with those derived from Q (νομικος). Both these features are said to be intelligible if Luke composed the Gospel in two stages.

[1] *Op. cit.*, p. 39.

[2] R. M. Grant (*op. cit.*, p. 118) considers that the Proto-Luke theory carries no more conviction than any theory which is based on an analysis of the remainder of a book after a portion has been removed.

[3] M. Goguel (*HTR*, 26, 1933, p. 12) maintained that Luke's position for the genealogy between the baptism and the temptation 'suggests that he found it as a separate piece, not as part of a general account'. But Goguel did not support the Proto-Luke hypothesis.

[4] Goguel disputed the validity of this point on the grounds that literary analysis in Acts is uncertain (yet see pp. 363 ff. for discussion of this) and on the further grounds that Acts is not a fair subject for comparison since no parallel existed as a model as in the case of the Gospels (*op. cit.*, pp. 8, 9 n.). In a recent book A. Q. Morton and G. H. C. Macgregor (*The Structure of Luke and Acts*, 1964) have claimed to show by statistical methods that Luke and Acts are closely parallel in literary structure, which is in turn controlled by what they call the 'physical structure', i.e. the need to arrange the material to fit in with a predetermined number of a specified size of papyrus. In their opinion this lends support to the Proto-Luke hypothesis. Yet mathematical considerations cannot prove the theory although they may have some bearing on Luke's method once the theory has been adopted on other grounds.

Another consideration is the echo of the phrase from the mission charge to the seventy (Lk. x. 4) in a reminder by Jesus to the Twelve (Lk. xxii. 35), which is felt to be best explained by supposing that at the time of composing xxii. 35, Luke did not possess the mission charge to the Twelve (ix. 3), which expresses the phrase in a different way.[1] Such an argument would naturally have force only if it were accepted that in Luke xxii the author had no dependable tradition on which to rely.

The above-mentioned arguments are considered by the advocates of the hypothesis to constitute a sound basis, provided the evidence is considered cumulatively. Nevertheless there have been many criticisms levelled against the theory, often against single issues, admittedly, but this is unavoidable. It is important, however, when considering these to keep in mind the contribution which the issue being discussed makes to the cumulative whole, to keep the matter in true perspective.

(ii) *Criticisms of the hypothesis.* 1. The non-Marcan character of the passion narratives has been challenged, particularly by G. D. Kilpatrick,[2] who maintains that the Evangelist has so modified the Marcan material that the basis for a continuous non-Marcan passion narrative vanishes. His arguments are based mainly on linguistic considerations, but Vincent Taylor has replied that such considerations afford 'too slender a ground for the total rejection of a Lukan passion narrative'.[3]

The narrative runs from xxii. 14 to xxiv. 11 and is preceded, in Vincent Taylor's reconstruction, by xix. 47, 48, which describes the daily teaching of Jesus in the temple and the determination of the chief priests to destroy Him. But it is difficult to imagine, even in a rough draft, that Luke would have proposed so abrupt a transference of thought as to make the immediate sequel of this plot the scene in the upper room with the passover meal about to begin. The Marcan section, Luke xx. 1–8, in which the previously mentioned plot begins to be implemented, links so naturally with the context that it is difficult to believe that it was missing from Luke's original draft. The dramatic suspense of the repeated mention of the plot in xxii. 1 ff. would entirely vanish if the Marcan sections were withdrawn, and without them Luke's passion narratives would be robbed of some of their signifi-

---

[1] All these considerations are listed by Caird, *op. cit.*, p. 26.

[2] *JTS*, XLIII (1942), pp. 34–36; n.s., 1 (1950), pp. 56–60. Kilpatrick thinks that there are suggestions that Luke has modified Mark in order to portray the trial of Jesus as a miscarriage of justice.

[3] *ET*, LXVII (1955), p. 15.

cance.[1] The question resolves itself into which it seems more reasonable
to suppose: that the non–Proto-Luke elements (xx–xxii. 13) were
added as an explanatory suture between xix. 48 and xxii. 14; or that
Luke originally planned his material in such a way as to show the
development of the final plot as the background against which he sets
the institution of the Lord's supper. It is admittedly not easy to decide,
but the latter seems to accord best with the historical and literary sense
of Luke.[2] Some scholars find linguistic justification for maintaining
that even in the Marcan part of Luke there is evidence that Luke has
used his own source for part of the narrative and has enriched it from
Marcan material.[3] Although such a theory could fit into the Proto-
Luke hypothesis, it does not require it, for Luke might have drawn
from his two sources at the time of the composition of the whole
book.

The appeal to Luke's twelve changes in the Marcan order as pointed
out by Hawkins is differently used by him and Taylor. The former
considered that these possibly occurred in oral rather than written
transmission, and he therefore contended that Luke did not use Mark
in this section. Although Taylor accepts a similar position, he uses it to
support his Proto-Luke hypothesis by claiming that elsewhere when
the order is the same as Mark's the sections may be regarded as insertions. In other words Luke used oral tradition for most of the passion
narratives, but imposed upon it certain snippets of written material
culled from Mark. But in this case it would be simpler to suppose that
the Marcan 'insertions' were also preserved in oral tradition.

2. Little need be said about the eschatological discourse (which if it

---

[1] V. Taylor tries to lessen this difficulty by postulating that the section xxii.
1–13 (Marcan) replaced Proto-Luke's original introduction to the passion narratives (*Behind the Third Gospel*, pp. 177–181).

[2] S. M. Gilmour contends that Taylor has underrated the Marcan material
in the passion narrative (*JBL*, LXVII, 1948, pp. 143–152). Cf. the same writer's
arguments against Proto-Luke in *The Gospel according to St. Luke* (IB, 1952),
pp. 16–18. Gilmour thinks that the difficulty of the 'gap' would disappear if
Proto-Luke is abandoned (*JBL*, LXVII, p. 147). Cf. also J. M. Creed's contentions
along the same line (*St. Luke*, p. lviii). For the view that Luke re-wrote Mark's
passion narratives, see Creed's articles, *ET*, XLVI (1934), pp. 101 ff., 378 f. and cf.
also A. Barr's article, *ET*, LV (1944), pp. 227–231. For Taylor's reply to Creed,
ET, XLVI (1934), pp. 236 ff.

[3] Cf. F. Rehkopf's examination of two passages in Lk. xxii, *Die lukanische
Sonderquelle* (1959), and H. Schürmann's studies on the same chapter, *Quellenkritische Untersuchung des lukanischen Abendmahlsberichtes* (1953–57).

is an independent narrative would support the Proto-Luke theory), apart from the fact that it is not universally agreed that Luke xxi was from an entirely independent source.

3. There have been criticisms of the continuity of the narrative in the Proto-Lucan sections. Creed called it an 'amorphous collection'[1] and this description is not without some weight. An analysis of Proto-Luke[2] shows that it contains 706 verses, of which no fewer than 556 are concerned with the concluding journey to Jerusalem and the passion narratives. It is, of course, possible that such a lop-sided arrangement existed in Luke's original draft,[3] but it is difficult to believe that he was so limited in his description of the early ministry merely because he did not know Mark, whereas he had succeeded in collecting a particularly varied body of tradition for the later ministry. A major difficulty is caused by the assumption that the Marcan material existed *only* in the form of Mark's Gospel, but it may be questioned whether this makes sufficient allowance for the possibility of some oral transmission of this material.

4. The occurrence in Luke iii. 1–iv. 30 of some phrases identical with Mark is admitted by Vincent Taylor,[4] but he does not attach much importance to it. C. S. Petrie[5] further pointed out that half the section from Luke iii. 1 to ix. 50 is Marcan, but Taylor does not consider this is sufficient to disprove his own theory that this Marcan material was an addition to the original draft.[6] Questions of this kind are notoriously difficult to decide on any objective basis. An alterna-

---

[1] *Op. cit.*, p. lviii n. Bundy (*Jesus and the First Three Gospels*, pp. 328, 329), considers that this section of Luke contains a 'formless mass of matter'.

[2] Based on the details given by V. Taylor, *The Gospels*, p. 41. The following will serve as a brief résumé:

The opening portion of the ministry: Lk. iii. 1–iv. 30, v. 1–11, vi. 12–viii. 3.
The 'travel' narrative: ix. 51–xviii. 14.
Judaean events: xix. 1–28, 37–44, 47, 48.
Passion narratives: xxii. 14–xxiv.

An analysis of the number of verses shows 170 in the first section, 334 in the 'travel' section and 202 in the rest.

[3] The lack of clear sequence in the material in this 'travel' narrative may possibly be explained by the absence of chronological or geographical data in Luke's sources (cf. Michaelis, *Einleitung*, p. 67). If this is a true supposition it may account for Luke's grouping of this material between the Galilaean and Judaean work of Jesus.

[4] *Loc. cit.*   [5] *ET*, LIV (1943), pp. 172–177.

[6] Cf. his reply to Petrie in *ET*, LIV (1943), pp. 219–222.

tive explanation of these Marcan sections is that they formed part of Q.[1]

5. Another difficulty is the awkward gap in the section viii. 3–ix. 51, when the Marcan material is removed. An attempt by Vincent Taylor to find non-Marcan traces in this section in order to postulate their probable inclusion in Proto-Luke is not self-evidently convincing.

In assessing the *pros* and *cons* of this theory it must be admitted that many of the supporting arguments contain considerable weaknesses when submitted to detailed analysis. Yet in fairness to the advocates of the theory the evidence must also be considered in its cumulative effect. However, although the hypothesis *may* explain certain features in the literary construction of Luke, it cannot be said that these features *demand* the hypothesis.

If Conzelmann's theory of Luke's free editing of Mark is correct, the Proto-Luke theory would at once be ruled out. But it must not be imagined that the only alternative to the acceptance of the theory is to postulate a wholesale rewriting of sources from Luke's own theological standpoint, for if more allowance is made for Luke's own industry in the collection of authentic information a two-stage production of his Gospel becomes equally unnecessary. Supposing that Luke had at his disposal Mark, the Q material and the L material, the fact that he prefers to use his material in blocks and prefers to combine Q with L material does not necessarily mean that he must have done this before incorporating the Marcan material. But the Proto-Luke hypothesis would have little point if it merely consisted of a suggestion regarding the manner in which Luke went to work. This leads to the enquiry as to its positive value.

(iii) *The value of the hypothesis.* It is a relevant question whether the theory, if proved, would have any value. There are four main claims in this direction: (1) the existence of an authority comparable to Mark (Streeter stressed the importance of this); (2) a corroboration of the Johannine tradition; (3) a basis for the traditional ideas characteristic of Paul; (4) a confirmation of the early character of the Lucan portraiture of Jesus. The first of these features has validity only within the framework of a rigid source criticism, which not only makes Mark early but the canonical Luke late. The second loses its value if the Johannine tradition is shown to be early, as is being increasingly recognized. The

---

[1] This is substantially Caird's solution, *Saint Luke*, p. 24.

third point is by no means clear, since Paul's close association with Luke would equally well account for any similarity of emphasis which may be observed in their writings. The final point is singularly incon-clusive since the Lucan portraiture of Jesus is no clearer in Proto-Luke than in the Gospel, and if the latter is early the postulation of an earlier draft does not seem to be required. Since these values all depend on the assumption that Proto-Luke is rightly dated about AD 60–65,[1] they become less weighty if the canonical Luke is placed much earlier than is generally proposed under the four source theory. In proportion as the interval between Proto-Luke and the Gospel becomes less, so the value of the hypothesis necessarily weakens.

Nevertheless there are a number of scholars who would maintain that, however early Luke might be, Proto-Luke is a valuable witness to an earlier fixation of the tradition. But it is still questionable how Proto-Luke could be regarded as a fixation of the tradition until it was published, which does not appear to have happened until it was expanded into Luke's Gospel.

The theory of Streeter and Vincent Taylor has been given at some length because it has exerted most influence, but there have been other types of Proto-Luke theories. H. Sahlin's theory,[2] although called by the same name, is a very different proposition, in that he supposes that Luke i. 5–Acts xv. 35 was written in Aramaic by one author. This Proto-Luke was later translated and supplemented (Lk. i. 1–4; Acts xv. 36 ff.) by Luke, who is to be distinguished from the author of Proto-Luke, said to have been a Jewish Christian of Syria. Another theory is that of E. Schweizer,[3] who suggests an original source consisting of Wonder-stories (W) and an additional Hebraistic source for Luke's special narratives, these two sources being combined into one by Luke's predecessor, whom he calls H. Still later, Luke edits this com-bination with the aid of Mark. It will be seen that Schweizer's theory bears closer resemblance to Streeter's than Sahlin's does, although it differs from Streeter's theory in that Schweizer does not regard Luke as author of his Proto-Luke.

---

[1] Cf. V. Taylor, *op. cit.*, p. 40.

[2] *Der Messias und das Gottesvolk* (1945) and *Studien zum dritten Kapitel des Lukasevangeliums* (1949).

[3] E. Schweizer, *ThZ*, IV (1949), pp. 469–471; V (1949), pp. 228–231. For a summary of Sahlin's and Schweizer's views, cf. Michaelis, *Einleitung*, pp. 71–74; W. Grundmann, *Das Evangelium nach Lukas*, p. 16.

VIII. CONCLUSION

This survey of the various source theories has shown that the Synoptic problem still remains, and it will therefore be necessary to discuss possible avenues along which further investigations may be made. Before doing this, a survey of form-critical studies will be made in order to discern whether these studies have in any way modified the generally maintained source hypotheses.

ADDITIONAL NOTES

121. [2] Another useful Harmony which may be mentioned is that by E. D. Burton and E. J. Goodspeed, *A Harmony of the Synoptic Gospels in Greek* (1922). For a different kind of tool for Synoptic studies, reference may be made to W. R. Farmer's *Synopticon* (1969), which prints the texts of the three Gospels consecutively, indicating their agreements by means of different coloured print. This follows the same method, but with a different arrangement, as W. Rushbrooke's *Synopticon* (1880), which placed similar passages parallel to illustrate the currently-held source theory.

123. *The original Gospel hypothesis.* Although this earliest theory is now abandoned, S. Porúbčan (*Nov. Test.*, 7, 1964, pp. 81–118) has proposed a theory of an original common Gospel which accorded with the apostolic preaching. He reaches this suggestion through an examination of the common material in the Synoptics.

130. [2] *The mutual dependence hypothesis.* Variations of this type of theory are still being proposed. Those who dispute the Marcan priority normally propose some modified form of this theory (e.g. B. C. Butler, see p. 138), but even within the Marcan hypothesis, the view that either Matthew or Luke were dependent on the other is not without some support. A variation of the view that Matthew used both Mark and Luke is proposed by H. P. West (*NTS*, 14, 1967, pp. 75–95), who suggests that Matthew used in addition to Mark a primitive form of Luke. He admits the hypothetical character of this proposal but considers it to be as probable as the hypothetical Q. West maintains that Matthew frequently follows primitive-Luke's modifications of Mark. For the reverse view that Luke used Matthew, cf. U. Wilckens (*Nov. Test.*, 8, 1966, pp. 48–57) and A. W. Argyle (*JBL*, LXXXIII, 1964, pp. 390–396). Another view is advanced by R. L. Lindsey (*A Hebrew Translation of the Gospel of Mark*, 1969), who maintains that Matthew used Mark, but that Mark used Luke plus another source which he calls Proto-Narrative. Cf. his earlier article in *Nov. Test.*, 6 (1963), pp. 239–263.

135. [1] Attention has been drawn to the fallacy in Lachmann's argument on lack of agreement as a basis for establishing Marcan priority. Cf. N. H. Palmer (*NTS*, 13, 1967, pp. 368–378) and W. R. Farmer (*NTS*, 14, 1968, pp. 441–443).

135. [2] R. T. Simpson (*NTS*, 12, 1966, pp. 273–284), as a result of an examination of Matthew's and Luke's agreements against Mark, has suggested that Luke used Matthew as one of his sources, but regarded it as of secondary importance. He sometimes rewrote it. In this way Simpson regards Luke as an author rather than an editor in his approach to his sources. Cf. the work of A. W. Argyle (*ET*, LXXIII, 1961, pp. 19–22 and *Theol.*, LXVII, 1964, pp. 156 f.) on the agreements between Matthew and Luke and the Q hypothesis. In his commentary, *The Gospel according to Matthew* (*CBC*, 1963, p. 14), Argyle regards the Q hypothesis as far from proved.

137. In connection with Luke's omission of the section Mark vi. 45–viii. 6 and the suggestion that he might have passed from one feeding miracle to the other similar miracle, it must be noted that many scholars regard these accounts as doublets. But recently J. Knackstadt (*NTS*, 10, 1964, pp. 309–335) has strongly argued for two feeding miracles, thus supporting both Mark's and Matthew's accounts. Luke's reason for omitting the second may not be because he regarded it as a doublet, but because his additional material obliged him to be selective.

139 f. [5] In a recent study of Mark xiii, L. Hartmann (*Prophecy Interpreted. The Formation of Some Jewish Apocalyptic Texts and of the Eschatological Discourse Mark 13 par.*, Eng. Tr. by N. Tomkinson and T. Gray, 1966) appeals to the Old Testament background of the discourse, especially the book of Daniel, but also 2 Ch. xv. 6; Is. xix. 2 and Gn. xix. 17. Hartmann is arguing for a Midrash basis for Mark xiii. But this view of the origin of the discourse is opposed by J. Lambrecht (*Biblica*, 49, 1968, pp. 254–270) on the grounds that Hartmann does not give sufficient weight to Mark's editorial activity. This is the main emphasis in Lambrecht's own book, *Die Redaktion des Markus-Apokalypse* (1967). For other critiques of Hartmann's theory, cf. T. Holz (*ThLZ*, 92, 1967, cols. 910–912) and M. D. Hooker (*JTS*, n.s., XIX, 1968, pp. 263–265).

141. Mark's passion narrative. In considering Mk. xiv. 1–25, F. W. Dinkler (*JBL*, LXXXV, 1966, pp. 467–472) argues that Psalm xl provides the ingredients out of which this passage is narrated. The main idea is the poor sufferer seen against the background of his ultimate triumph.

141. [4] The idea of an earlier edition of Mark continues to find some advocates. S. Sandmel (*JBR*, 31, 1963, pp. 294–300) suggests that our present Mark has been rewritten. According to him the date of the crucifixion in Ur-Markus was the same as in John, but he regards both as theological rather than as historical. It is interesting to find a Jewish author supporting the Ur-Markus theory, which most scholars have not favoured.

Although not specifically connected with this theory, reference may be to T. F. Glasson's view that both Matthew and Luke used a Western text of Mark (*JBL*, LXXXV, 1966, pp. 231–233).

A kind of Proto-Mark theory is advanced by E. Trocmé, *La Formation de l'Évangile selon Marc* (1963). He suggests that the original edition consisted of Mark i–xiii, which he thinks was written by Philip the evangelist and produced at Caesarea *c.* AD 50. The passion narrative of the Jerusalem Church was then added later. But it may be questioned whether on literary grounds Mark can be so divided.

146. [3] A more recent proposal which dispenses with Q is W. R. Farmer's theory as propounded in his book, *The Synoptic Problem. A Critical Analysis* (1964). He not only sees no need for Q but also rejects the theory of Marcan priority. He maintains that Luke depends on Matthew, and Mark on both. In criticism of the theory F. W. Beare (*JBL*, LXXXIV, 1965, pp. 295–297) asks why Mark was ever written if Matthew and Luke were already known, and this must be admitted as a major difficulty. Nevertheless the appearance of this book is a salutary reminder that the last word has not yet been said about Marcan priority. H. Meynell (*Theol.*, LXX, 1967, pp. 386–397) has compared Farmer's theory with P. Parker's in their respective treatment of nine selected problems and prefers Parker's treatment to Farmer's. He admits the latter has a pull over Parker in dealing with order. Meynell suggests that the order of the original Mark was rearranged to tally with Matthew and Luke (where these agreed), when they had become known.

150. [2] The Q hypothesis has found a supporter in F. G. Downing (*NTS*, 11, 1965, pp. 169–181), who criticizes A. Farrer's arguments for Matthew's use of Luke. He finds support for the form of the Q document in the Gospel of Thomas. But see p. 152 n. 4. More recently E. P. Sanders (*NTS*, 15, 1969, pp. 249–261) has examined the argument from order in the relationship between Matthew and Luke and has concluded that the evidence does not support the view that Matthew and Luke wrote independently of each other. He thinks it likely that Luke used Matthew. See also N. Turner (*ET*, LXXX, 1969, pp. 324–328) for comments on Q in recent thought.

157. Matthew's reliability as a historian continues to come under fire. F. W. Beare (*JBL*, LXXXVII, 1968, pp. 125–135) considers that Matthew is not reliable as a historical source. His main reason appears to be that no account of the story of Jesus could escape interaction with other events which would be transferred to it. This approach is thoroughly in line with form critical assumptions, but leaves too much to the critic's own reconstructions.

174. There have been several recent studies of Luke's nativity narratives. P. S. Minear (*SLA*, 1966, pp. 111–130) has rightly argued that the unity of these narratives with the Gospel as a whole must be examined. In this he opposes Conzelmann's exclusion of them from his theological interpretation of the Gospel. W. B. Tatum (*NTS*, 13, 1967, pp. 184–195) takes a similar line. He regards the narratives as an essential part of Luke's salvation-history. They show the end of the 'epoch of Israel' and the beginning of the 'epoch of the Church'. The Semitic colouring is basic to this understanding of the narratives.

Another who approaches Luke's nativity narratives in a similar way to that used by Conzelmann in the rest of the Gospel is H. H. Oliver (*NTS*, 10, 1963, pp. 202–226). He sees Luke's theological purpose in these narratives, which show the superiority of the Middle of Time period (the period of Jesus) over the Time of Israel (as represented by John the baptist). In Oliver's view the narratives need not be factual, but could be regarded as a device to introduce Luke's purpose. In this article there is a valuable survey of approaches to Luke's nativity narratives.

On the question whether Luke has used a John the baptist source for the narratives, cf. S. Benko (*JBL*, LXXXVI, 1967, pp. 263–275), who answers in the affirmative. He maintains that Luke's interest in the 'how' of the incarnation did not develop until after his first draft was completed. Attention is given to Luke's Old Testament sources by D. Jones (*JTS*, n.s., XIX, 1968, pp. 19–50), who finds in Luke's canticles a more sophisticated type of psalmody than that found at Qumran. He finds a unity in Luke's three canticles, seen in the fact that all show Old Testament allusions rather than quotations, all regard salvation as the fulfilment of Scripture and all refer to someone secondary to the person of the Messiah.

174. [2] G. Ogg (*ET*, LXXIX, 1968, pp. 231–236) discusses the various solutions to the Quirinius problem, but concludes that there is no satisfactory solution.

CHAPTER SIX

FORM CRITICISM AND ITS DEVELOPMENTS

The most significant development in Gospel criticism in the twentieth century has been the rise of form criticism (in Germany, its home of origin, it is generally known as *Formgeschichte* (form history)). To appreciate its significance it is necessary to survey its historical setting and to study the reasons for its rise.

I. REASONS FOR THE RISE OF FORM CRITICISM

Many influences converged to produce this movement, and the main ones may fairly easily be discerned.

1. The first is the weakness of source criticism. Although form criticism is not an alternative for, but a supplement to, source criticism, it owed much of its origin to certain basic weaknesses in current source-critical speculations. Source criticism claimed to be a literary discipline and accordingly confined itself to the documents to hand. In the case of Matthew and Luke, the basic assumptions, as has been shown, centred around the use of Mark and Q. But source criticism could not push the study behind these documents. The most it could do was to suggest an earlier form of Mark (Ur-Markus) which proved unsatisfactory, or a multiplication of Q's which increasingly weakened the whole structure of the hypothesis. The form critic, however, proposed to study the origins of both Mark and Q and this appeared to be a laudable objective. The fact that the source critic could produce no documentary theory of Mark's origin offered a *carte blanche* to the form critic to suggest methods by which the original tradition was fixed.

The source critic had left a gap of some twenty to thirty years after the death of Jesus before any written documents had appeared and it was only natural that some attempt should be made to fill in the deficiency. However speculative the attempt, it must be made, and form criticism is the result. In some respects form criticism was traversing the same tracks as the earlier oral tradition theory, although there was little recognition of this fact, for the methods employed were very different, as indeed were the results.

The very fact that our historical data for the first thirty years of

Christian history are so limited means that form critics inevitably had to draw a good deal on imagination, although not all of them were conscious of doing so. Indeed, the attempt to classify the Gospel material into various literary forms was considered to be wholly scientific in scope and in fact a continuation of the best traditions of source criticism. But the large measure of conjecture will become apparent when the various types of theory are outlined.

2. Secondly, form criticism resulted from the challenge to the historicity of the Marcan account of Jesus. The way was prepared by W. Wrede's[1] theory that the framework of Mark's Gospel was the author's own creation in the interests of what he called 'the Messianic Secret'. He maintained that Jesus did not reveal His Messiahship until the resurrection, which meant that Mark's account of Peter's confession was not historical. The author of Mark, according to this view, has imposed his own framework on what were previously independently circulating units. In spite of the fact that Wrede's theory was strongly criticized,[2] it undoubtedly exerted a powerful influence on early form critics who turned their attention to the units of tradition and assumed as a valid presupposition that the framework of the Gospel narrative was suspect and the context of stories and sayings consequently of little importance.

Akin to Wrede's view was that of Wellhausen,[3] who claimed that the primitive tradition was overlaid with editorial additions which were influenced by contemporary Christian theology. This theory gave impetus to those form-critical theories which attribute much of the shaping of the material, and even its origin, to the Christian community (see discussion below).

A later writer, K. L. Schmidt,[4] examined the framework of Mark more thoroughly and concluded that the Gospel is chronologically and also geographically unreliable. No biographical reconstruction of the life of Jesus is now possible, on this theory.

Such challenges to the historicity of Mark drew attention to the need for a careful sifting of the evidence for the reliability of Mark's material, and this need the form critics claimed to meet. Nevertheless some of the theories proposed actually undermined still further the historical

---

[1] *Das Messiasgeheimnis in den Evangelien* (1901; reprinted Göttingen, 1963).*

[2] Cf. J. Weiss, *Das älteste Evangelium* (1903); A. E. J. Rawlinson, *The Gospel according to St. Mark*[7] (1949), pp. 258–262.

[3] *Das Evangelium Marci* (1903).

[4] *Der Rahmen der Geschichte Jesu* (1919).

veracity of the Gospel narratives as a whole (see comments on Bult-mann's theories below).[1]

3. Another factor which helped to promote form criticism was the desire to modernize the Gospels. The assumption that much of the material in the canonical Gospels was couched in first-century concep-tions of the world of nature and of men which are quite outdated by modern scientific knowledge gave birth to the movement for restating the Gospel in concepts acceptable to twentieth-century thought. This naturally focused attention upon the original literary forms and led, among some form critics, to the quest for the essence of the Gospel apart from these 'forms' (e.g. miracle stories). In other words, interest in the forms was mainly in order to reinterpret them, and to recast in modern dress the material which could be salvaged from them. This was the approach of Bultmann, in particular, whose purpose was governed by his philosophical presuppositions. The movement to which it led, known as 'demythologization',[2] is the attempt to interpret the Gospels stripped of all elements which form analysis have shown to belong to the first-century environment of the early Church. Not sur-prisingly the movement reached its climax in historical scepticism.[3] It would be wrong however to suppose that all form criticism was motivated by such apologetic considerations.

4. A further reason for form criticism was the urge to place the literary materials in the Gospels in their historical situation, i.e. the *Sitz im Leben*, or life-situation. This historical quest appealed strongly to the modern tendency to emphasize the background of the Gospels. It was a legitimate quest, but it contained within it a hidden snare. It was inclined to assume without adequate proof that the material owed its present shape to the practical needs of the community. A good deal of

[1] That the views of Wrede and Wellhausen exercised a powerful influence on Bultmann is clear from his own works; cf. 'The Study of the Synoptic Gospels' in *Form Criticism* (two essays by R. Bultmann and K. Kundsin, 1962), pp. 22 ff. Cf. also *idem, The History of the Synoptic Tradition*, pp. 1 ff. A useful brief critique of Bultmann's position and an assessment of the influence of the work of Wrede and others upon him can be found in H. G. Wood's *Jesus in the Twentieth Century* (1960), pp. 78 ff. Cf. also T. W. Manson's essay in *The Background of the New Testament and its Eschatology* (ed. Davies and Daube), pp. 211–221.

[2] For a discussion of this movement, cf. I. Henderson, *Myth in the New Testa-ment* (1952); P. E. Hughes, *Scripture and Myth* (1956); D. M. Baillie, *God was in Christ*[2] (1955), pp. 211–227.

[3] Bultmann himself denies that complete scepticism is the result, although he admits 'considerable uncertainty' (cf. his essay in *Form Criticism*. p. 60).

the life-situations proposed for isolated units of tradition is purely speculative. This important factor must not be lost sight of when assessing the rise and achievements of form criticism. What began with a perfectly legitimate historical motive has tended to develop along un-historical lines.[1]

This latter tendency arises very largely from the basic assumption of most form criticism that the *Sitz im Leben* must be found in the post-Easter period and could not have existed in the pre-Easter period. Such an assumption excludes any possibility of a continuation between the two periods, and leads to the inevitable concentration of attention on the Christ of faith rather than the Jesus of history. But, as has recently been argued by H. Schürmann,[2] form-critical enquiries need not and should not be confined to the post-Easter *Sitz im Leben*. The recognition of this fact puts the *Sitz im Leben* motive on a firmer footing.

II. VARIOUS TYPES OF THEORY

Before a general critique of form criticism is given, a summary of the main theories, arranged according to their chief advocates, will be made. Only the broadest outline will be possible, but with sufficient illustrations in detail to make the outline intelligible. Particular criticisms of individual theories will also be added.

a. The missionary preaching theory

M. Dibelius[3] began by assuming that traditions in the early Church were conditioned by missionary needs. This meant that he proceeded

[1] E. Fascher (*Die formgeschichtliche Methode*, 1924), in his survey and criticism of various form-critical theories (those of Dibelius, Bultmann, Albertz and Bertram), points out that all the theories under review postulate at times a different *Sitz im Leben* for the same form, which shows that form and history are distinct and that the latter cannot be safely inferred from the former (cf. especially pp. 212 ff.). It is significant that all the scholars mentioned were desirous of making such an inference.

[2] Cf. his essay in *Der historische Jesus und der kerygmatische Christus* (ed. H. Ristow and K. Matthiae, 1962), pp. 342–370. Schürmann maintains that since Jesus sent out His disciples to preach during His own ministry, this would have provided a *Sitz im Leben* for many of the sayings preserved in the Gospels, since the disciples would have needed teaching materials themselves and would also have required instruction for the undertaking of the task.

[3] *From Tradition to Gospel* (translated by B. Lee Woolf[2], 1934, from *Die Form-geschichte des Evangeliums*, first published in 1919). Cf. also *idem, A Fresh Approach to the New Testament and Early Christian Literature* (1936), pp. 27 ff., for further comments on his classification, and his article in *TR*, n.f., I (1929), pp. 185–216, for an assessment of form-critical trends up to that date.

from what he conceived to have been the early Christian method to an analysis of the text of the Gospels. According to him the traditions existed first of all in sermons and the earliest forms were therefore imposed by the demands of the *kerygma*, to be added to later by more developed forms adaptable to other practical needs.

(i) *Paradigms*. These were short narratives which ended with a saying and which were designed mainly to bring out the importance of the saying. Examples of these are the healing of the sick of the palsy and the incident of the ears of corn.

(ii) *Novellen or tales*. These were narratives which aimed to show Jesus as a wonder-worker. According to Dibelius these are differentiated from the former by having no saying attached to them and by having a more secular tone. Moreover, while the paradigms were used by preachers, *Novellen* were created by story-tellers. Examples are the cleansing of the leper and the stilling of the storm.

(iii) *Sayings*. For the purpose of catechesis there would be collections of sayings, distinct from those in the paradigms because unattached to any narratives.

(iv) *Legends*. The name is unfortunate for it at once suggests something unhistorical. Under it Dibelius classed narratives relating extraordinary things about holy people. As an example, the infancy stories may be mentioned.

(v) *Myths*. Under this classification, Dibelius included the baptism, temptation and transfiguration, in each of which he found an interaction between what he called mythological persons.

Because of the varied character of the forms thus classified, Dibelius supposed that there were at least three different types of Christian workers involved—preachers, teachers and narrators. But the distinction seems to have been created by Dibelius' analysis rather than being vouched for by independent historical testimony. In fact, it is difficult to conceive of any certain method of defining the difference between the various functions, while there is no evidence at all for a class of people wholly devoted to telling stories about Jesus without preaching the gospel.[1]

[1] It should be noted that many scholars who do not accept Dibelius' categories nevertheless maintain that mission work exerted a formative influence on the tradition. In a study of a portion of Luke's special material, W. R. Farmer (*NTS*, 8, 1962, pp. 301–316), suggests that a certain Greek rhetorical form (*Chreia*) is

b. The Christian imagination theory

Appearing about the same time as Dibelius' theory and somewhat akin to it was R. Bultmann's exposition of form criticism.[1] But his approach was both more radical and more influential than that of Dibelius. Indeed so widespread has been the impact of Bultmann on Gospel studies that his presentation must be considered in greater detail.

(i) In order to appreciate Bultmann's opinions, some attention must be given to his particular background.[2] He was reared in the Liberal school of thought which focused on the quest of the historical Jesus as the most important task for Christian faith. This is the position for which A. Harnack and H. J. Holtzmann[3] may be regarded as major representatives. Bultmann studied under Harnack and the latter's opinions naturally formed an important part of his background in his formative years. His own reaction against the historical Jesus of the Liberal school in favour of a more dynamic Christ of faith was the result of his disillusionment with the Liberal Jesus. He recognized that if faith depended on the quest for the historical Jesus, it became dependent on historical research, with all its uncertainties.

Bultmann's disillusionment led him to seek an approach to the Gospels which would emancipate him from the need for historical demonstration. Only so could the simplest, in his opinion, ever come to faith. He was further prompted to this non-historical approach by his commitment to existential philosophy. Deeply influenced by Heidegger, Bultmann maintained that the most important element in

discernible in the introductory material to some of Luke's parables, and this leads him to suppose that Christian preachers and teachers often conformed to this contemporary method of presenting material. Cf. M. Dibelius, *From Tradition to Gospel* (1934), pp. 152 ff., for a similar line of argument. Farmer does not hold that the preachers created the material, but only that they selected the form in which to present it, and there is clearly less objection to this view than to that of Dibelius. It is by no means evident, however, that the 'form' could not have been part of our Lord's own presentation.

[1] *The History of the Synoptic Tradition*. For a more concise statement of Bultmann's position, cf. his essay in *Form Criticism* (Eng. Tr.[2] 1962) combined with the essay of K. Kundsin. For a summary and critique of his position cf. E. B. Redlich, *Form Criticism* (1939), pp. 30 ff., R. H. Fuller, *The New Testament in Current Study* (1962), pp. 9 ff., and W. Barclay, *The First Three Gospels* (1966), pp. 43 ff.

[2] Cf. J. D. Smart, *The Divided Mind of Modern Theology* (1967), pp. 31 ff.

[3] Cf. A. Harnack, *What is Christianity?* (1901); H. J. Holtzmann, *Die synoptischen Evangelien* (1863).

Christian faith was an existential encounter with Christ, by which he meant a confrontation with Christ which demanded a decision whether to accept or reject. If existential encounter was all important, historical proof was clearly irrelevant. It is essential to note that Bultmann's non-historical approach to the Gospel materials was part of his pre-suppositions. In short, historical enquiry itself becomes little more than an academic exercise.

One other factor has dominated the approach of Bultmann to form criticism and that is his continued allegiance to the History of Religion School of thought (*religionsgeschichtliche Schule*)[1] which was a powerful movement in the early part of the twentieth century. According to this School the earliest Jewish traditions were translated into new forms suitable for the Gentile world, making full use of Gentile categories of thought. Although the main thrust of this School was in the interpretation of the Epistles, it could not fail to affect the approach to the Gospels. It at once suggested that the investigator should look for the interpretative elements. A clear-cut distinction between Judaic and Hellenistic Christianity must inevitably affect one's approach to history. It should be noted, however, that the grounds of this *religionsgeschichtlich* theory have been undermined through an acknowledgment of the lateness of the evidence on which it was based and through the increasing evidence from Jewish sources (such as Qumran) that the supposed gap between Jewish and Gentile Christianity has been considerably overdrawn.

(ii) Bultmann's approach to the Gospel material is therefore dominated by various influences which dispose him to treat history as irrelevant. The sharp distinction between the historical Jesus and the Christ of faith arose, according to him, through the Easter event. Those who had come to have an encounter with the Christ of faith could no longer look at the Jesus of history except in the light of their new experience.[2] They could no longer be impartial observers. But this would apply to

---

[1] The main representatives of this school were R. Reitzenstein, *Die hellenistischen Mysterienreligionen* (1927) and W. Bousset, *Kyrios Christos*[3] (1926).

[2] Bultmann continually appeals to the *kerygma* as evidence of the Christ of faith. By this term he draws attention to the dynamic activity of preaching, but it should be noted that some scholars use the term in a different sense, i.e. of its content (as for instance C. H. Dodd). Cf. J. P. M. Sweet's discussion, *ET*, 76 (1965), pp. 143–147.

all the Evangelists. They must have written from the standpoint of faith. Hence was born what the Germans call *Gemeindetheologie*. The Gospel records become sources of early Christian theology rather than historical data for the life of Jesus.[1] Bultmann makes so much appeal to the community that his species of form criticism may not unjustly be called a theory of community creativeness. It will be noticed that Bultmann has here combined two aspects. All would agree that the traditions were preserved by those who had come to faith and that the Gospel writers were writing to encourage faith in others. But Bultmann has gone much further when he claims that the 'community' created most of the material.

(iii) Some indication of the details in Bultmann's theory will illustrate the extent to which he attributes traditions to community origin. His classification of material resembles that of Dibelius. Instead of paradigms, Bultmann speaks of apophthegms, but he means practically the same. The main distinction is the extent to which material under this classification is attributed to the community. Dibelius is content to suggest that frequently an additional saying was attributed to Jesus in order to apply His teaching to the needs of the community. For Dibelius,[2] the additional explanatory statement was not arbitrarily invented by the community, but considered to be a loyal interpretation of the teaching of Jesus. But Bultmann goes much further in holding that the community invented the whole incident.

[1] This negative approach to history is shared by all who have adopted the Bultmann position. It is basic to D. E. Nineham's interpretation of Mark in his *Pelican Commentary* (1963). Wherever possible Nineham intentionally avoids considering the historicity of events precisely because they cannot be proved. But Bultmann's non-historical approach raises a difficulty since it creates the need for some other source of faith if there is no possibility of basing it on the historical Jesus. He has denied the dilemma, but Nineham takes refuge in the Church (cf. his article in *The Church's Use of the Bible*, 1963, pp. 159 ff.). J. Knox has proposed a similar solution in his book *The Church and the Reality of Christ* (1964). But neither Nineham nor Knox has recognized the inconsistency of appealing to the testimony of the Church when they have already denied the historical accounts, which they regard as products of the Church. Cf. the criticisms of this point of view by A. T. Hanson, *Vindications* (edited A. T. Hanson, 1966), pp. 74 ff. But cf. also Nineham's defence of his position in *Christian History and Interpretation* (edited W. R. Farmer, C. F. D. Moule, R. R. Niebuhr, 1967), pp. 199–222.
[2] Cf. *From Tradition to Gospel* (1934), pp. 64 ff.

Instead of Dibelius' *Novellen*, Bultmann prefers *miracle stories*. Not all the miracles are included in this group, which is restricted to those in which no specific teaching material is included. Both Dibelius and Bultmann reject the miraculous and therefore the historicity of the Gospel account of miracles. This is not so much on the basis of 'form' as on philosophical and theological grounds. Yet some explanation is necessary of how these stories arose. Various suggestions are made. It may have happened as a result of a dramatization of a saying of Jesus, as in the case of the healing of the blind man which illustrates the saying that Jesus is the light of the world. Or the withering of the fig tree could be a development from the parable of the barren fig tree. Or some Old Testament miracle may have suggested a parallel New Testament miracle. Or else some alien miracle story from another source has been transferred to Jesus. In all these suggested explanations, the development of the miracle story is directly attributable to the creation of the community. Bultmann cites many supposed parallels from pagan sources which relate wonder stories[1] and supposes that these justify his conclusion that many of the miracle stories in the Gospels are of the same type and must therefore be regarded as legendary. Yet the parallels cited are vastly different in content. Unlike the pagan parallels, there is an absence in the Gospel narratives of magical incantations and the like which at once puts them into a different category.[2]

Bultmann, like Dibelius, chooses the term *legend* for one of his classification of forms. Both men regard this group as influenced by the current practice of ascribing to holy men extraordinary happenings. As with the other groups, Bultmann sees here again the creation of the community, whose interest in the many people other than Jesus mentioned in the narrative would lead them to create legends concerning them.

In close association with legend is the classification of *myth*. Indeed Bultmann places these myths under legends. It is necessary at once to know in what sense he uses the term. His own definition will be valuable: 'Mythology is the use of imagery to express the otherworldly in terms of this world, and the divine in terms of human life, and the

---

[1] For instance, a story of a Finnish fairy tale in which a girl fed an army on three barley corns (*The History of the Synoptic Tradition*, p. 236) is considered as a parallel to the feeding of the five thousand.

[2] Cf. E. B. Redlich, *Form Criticism* (1939), p. 127.

other side in terms of this side' (*Kerygma and Myth*, p. 10). The descending dove and the heavenly voice at the baptism of Jesus come under this category. Although myth in this sense may not necessarily refer to something unhistorical, Bultmann would not give historical credence to any of these narratives. To him they contain elements which are unintelligible today.

It is in the sayings of Jesus that Bultmann shows his most characteristic approach.[1] He divides them into several groups—Wisdom words, 'I' words, Prophetic and Apocalyptic Sayings, Law words and rules and parables.

Under the first group, Bultmann analyses wisdom sayings in general and particularly the Old Testament wisdom literature and observes parallels with many of the sayings of Jesus. He suggests that three possibilities exist. (a) Jesus may have used existing secular wisdom sayings and proverbs and adapted them to His own needs. (b) He may have created His own sayings and (c) the Church may have used secular wisdom sayings and attributed them to Jesus. Bultmann places much of this class of sayings material in the Gospels under the third classification.[2] But he does admit a few sayings where he is prepared to see characteristic teaching of Jesus. His criteria for genuineness are those sayings where the sense of eschatology is strong (e.g. Mk. iii. 24–27, where the strong man is overcome), those which involve a summons to repentance (e.g. Lk. ix. 62), those involving 'reversal' (such as Mk. x. 31) and those requiring some change in people (Mk. x. 15). It must be noted that Bultmann's judgment is not based on 'form', but on his own preference. It is almost entirely subjective.

The 'I' sayings of Jesus are sayings in which He makes a special claim or specific demand. In the majority of these sayings Bultmann sees something which the community has produced to meet its own situations. Wherever sayings imply some theological view of Jesus (as, e.g., Mt. x. 32, 33; Lk. xii. 8, 9) these are community products. When they predict the death or resurrection of Jesus (as Mt. xvii. 12) they are

---

[1] Cf. his full discussion, *op. cit.*, pp. 69–179.

[2] Examples of such non-authentic sayings singled out by Bultmann are Mk. viii. 36, 37; Mt. v. 14, 42; x. 24; xii. 30; Lk. xvi. 10. In commenting on the Golden Rule (Mt. vii. 12; Lk. vi. 31), Bultmann draws no distinction between the positive form in the teaching of Jesus and the negative form in Rabbinical usage. To him the expression reflects naïve egoism.

sayings created after the event. Those which involve doing things 'in the Name' (e.g. Mt. vii. 22) reflect an ecclesiastical situation. There are other sayings said to be by the Risen Lord transferred to the earthly Jesus (as, e.g., Mt. xviii 20) and others relating to persecution which reflect back from the subsequent history of the Church. Yet other sayings presuppose an assessment of the life of Jesus as a whole and must have come from a later situation (e.g. Mk. x. 45; Mt. xi. 19). To summarize Bultmann's approach in this section, it may be said that anything which could conceivably have been a community product could not have been original to Jesus.

Those which Bultmann classes as Prophetic and Apocalyptic sayings fare no better. He sees much material which is attributed to Jesus after the event, such as the predictions of persecutions for His followers (e.g. Mt. v. 10, 11; Lk. vi. 22, 23; Mt. x. 17–22). Those which foretell the fall of Jerusalem, which have long been regarded by scholars as readings back, are treated in the same way. In some instances Jewish material has been attributed to Jesus (as, e.g., the apocalyptic passages in Mk. xiii, the sheep and goats parable in Mt. xxv. 31–46 and the lament over Jerusalem in Lk. xiii. 34, 35). In other cases Bultmann sees late Hellenistic formulations (as in Lk. xxi. 34–36). His argument regarding these sayings is that the Church made no distinction between sayings of Jesus and pronouncements of Christian prophets and therefore was not aware of what was the community product and what was a genuine saying.[1] But John xiv. 26 is to the point here, which mentions the special promise that the Spirit would remind the disciples of what Jesus had personally said.

Many of the Law words and rules are easily assigned by Bultmann to the community since they recall a situation in which the church has become an organized institution. This group of sayings are community sayings in that they are community summaries of the principles of Jesus. Examples may be found in Mark ii. 27, 28 (on the attitude to the Sabbath), Mark x. 11, 12 (on divorce), Matthew vi. 1–18 (on alms, prayer, fasting) and Mark vii. 6–8 (on the oral law). Further, some sayings reflect a period of controversies, which are seen as controversies of the Church period rather than the time of Jesus (e.g. Mt. v. 17–20, concerning the Law; Mt. xvi. 18, 19, concerning Peter's position; Mt. xviii. 15–17, concerning Christian relationships; Mt. xviii. 19, 20,

[1] *Form Criticism* (1934), pp. 56 ff.

concerning community prayer; Mt. x. 5–16, concerning the missionary task).

Nevertheless some of the Law sayings which disagree with the Jewish attitude are conceded to be probably genuine.

Among the parables Bultmann finds more that is authentic, because most of them force a man to come to a decision. They do not make a man's mind up for him.

It will be seen, therefore, that as a result of Bultmann's theories, little authentic material remains. He accepts only about forty sayings as genuine and the mere event (the 'thatness') of the life and death of Jesus on the cross.[1] All the rest of the Gospel material is either the creation or adaptation of the community. Such a result will seem shattering to those who require some historical basis for their faith, but for Bultmann this presents no problem, since he begins by denying the necessity of any connection between history and faith.

What he does not explain is how the community imagination developed. It needs some convincing parallels to make credible the idea that the vast majority of Christian traditions were formed by the community and then implicitly believed by them to be historically true. In cases where Bultmann admits genuine material (mostly in the sayings of Jesus) he attributes their context to the creation of later tradition, especially to the Evangelists themselves.[2] He attempts to salvage something by admitting that even sayings which may have originated in the community may show in them the spirit of Jesus.[3]

---

[1] Although Bultmann considers that the function of the Gospels is to proclaim the *Dass* (Thatness) of Jesus, he has repudiated the suggestion that this means that nothing can be known of the historical Jesus (cf. the recent comments on his position in C. E. Braaten and R. A. Harrisville, *The Historical Jesus and the Kerygmatic Christ*, 1964, pp. 22 f.). But Bultmann's position remains one of historical scepticism. Cf. also J. M. Robinson's discussion of Bultmann's slight shift of position from his earlier work (*A New Quest for the Historical Jesus*, 1959, pp. 19 ff.), with special reference to Bultmann's article in *ZTK*, 54 (1957), pp. 244–254.

[2] Cf., e.g., his *Form Criticism*, p. 55.

[3] *Ibid.*, p. 58. F. C. Grant, in *N. T. Studien für R. Bultmann* (1954), pp. 137–143, in an attempt to maintain some authenticity for the sayings of Jesus within the framework of Bultmann's general approach, includes in his notion of authenticity both 'historical authenticity' and 'veracious representation'—a highly dubious distinction, for under the latter category he could then include material which was regarded by him as non-historical!

He considers that his method can be scientifically demonstrated, for instance, where material exists in the triple tradition. Here he assumes that variations must be due to editorial processes and this forms the basis of his stripping procedure. In the end his criterion is what he conceives must have happened in the transmission of Christian tradition and not what is known to have happened. His theory takes insufficient account of the presence of responsible eyewitnesses who might at least be expected to have exerted some restraining influence on the creative ingenuity of the Christian community as a whole.[1] Moreover, no importance is attached to the fact that communities lean on their leaders,[2] and in the case of the early Church these would have been apostolic men who would have been too close in time to the dominating influence of Jesus to have given free rein to their imagination. It is quite unconvincing to attribute such key narratives as the resurrection and the institution of the Lord's supper to the 'cultic motive' behind Christian imagination.[3] It is inconceivable that these narratives grew up because Christians wished to establish a historical basis for their faith. Such a reconstruction of early traditions is wholly inadequate to explain the growth and development of the early Church.[4] It might

---

[1] Cf. V. Taylor, *Formation of the Gospel Tradition* (1935), pp. 41–43, 107. He maintains that if this theory is correct all the disciples must have been translated to heaven after the resurrection. H. E. W. Turner (*Jesus, Master and Lord*, p. 81) points out that the Christian preacher always faced the risk of an eyewitness being in his audience to challenge him. Acts i. 21, 22; Lk. i. 2 and the whole conception of the apostolate show the importance of eyewitness testimony. Cf. also P. Benoit, *RB*, LIII (1946), pp. 504, 505. See pp. 208 f. for a criticism of D. E. Nineham's dismissal of eyewitnesses.

[2] W. Manson, in his brief but incisive comments on the presuppositions of form criticism in his *Jesus the Messiah* (1943), pp. 24 ff., places emphasis upon this. He draws attention to the fact that the tradition of Peter's influence behind Mark is contrary to the community hypothesis of Mark's origin and cannot be discredited as easily as most form critics suppose. Moreover, why did the communities from which the authors of Matthew and Luke drew their traditions not create enough material to render it unnecessary for both authors to use Mark, supposed to be the product of another community? Thus Manson suggests that if Matthew was connected with Antioch, 'the rich communal tradition' of that church would lead us to expect much greater independence of Mark.

[3] Bultmann, *op. cit.*, pp. 66 f.

[4] Turner (*op. cit.*, p. 84) rightly draws attention to the urgent need for advocates of this type of theory to account for the origin of the community. Moreover, if the communities 'created' the Gospel material to lend support to their own doctrinal bent or to help to solve ecclesiastical problems, why is there no reflection

have happened in the case of one or two individuals, but could not have commended itself to whole communities, still less to groups of communities, with any degree of unanimity. The quest for the *Sitz im Leben* along this track would lead to a *Sitz im Leben* which seems to be far removed from real life.

Moreover, this type of form criticism is based on a definite presupposition regarding the earliest Christian period. It first is assumed that all the Synoptic Gospel records are community products and it then follows automatically that they become witnesses to the actual life and teaching of the Church rather than to the life and teaching of Jesus. Thus Kundsin[1] can reconstruct the main steps of sub-apostolic development from the Synoptic material itself, dividing it into three stages, the Son of man approach, the ecstatic spiritual approach and the ecclesiastical approach.[2] The supporters of each of these groups are represented as attributing to Jesus statements which uphold their own particular point of view.[3] But the superstructure so ingeniously worked out collapses if the presupposition is proved to be invalid. And this is where the Bultmann school of form criticism has conspicuously failed. It is not enough to conceive what might have happened. No theory can have a solid foundation on such a basis. It amounts to taking traditionally attested sayings of Jesus and asserting without warrant, apart from the proposer's imagination, that these cannot be 'uncoloured' tradition. But what Bultmann and his followers cannot explain is how the original Jesus became so 'coloured' or adapted to their own point of view by the later Christian community.[4] Is it not much more credible

of spiritual gifts, circumcision and the Gentile problem, all of which were pressing issues in primitive Church history? P. Benoit (*op. cit.*, pp. 505, 506) points out that Christians did not survive opposition and persecution by the inventions of an anonymous crowd.

[1] 'Primitive Christianity in the light of Gospel research', in *Form Criticism*, pp. 79 ff.

[2] Cf. especially *ibid.*, pp. 96 ff.

[3] To illustrate, Kundsin speaks of Luke retouching the picture of Jesus' life in view of the Hellenistic conception of the Spirit (*op. cit.*, p. 127), and of Matthew tracing back the Church idea to Jesus (p. 143). This kind of approach is fundamental to his whole interpretation of the Gospels.

[4] H. E. W. Turner, in his *Historicity and the Gospels* (1963), has some acute comments on Bultmann's approach to history. He particularly challenges the validity of Bultmann's appeal to a distinction between *Geschichte* and *Historie*. The latter term is reserved for events which can be scientifically proved, the former for what has arisen from faith. This means for Bultmann that little relevant

202 NEW TESTAMENT INTRODUCTION

to believe that the Christian community was 'coloured' by the authentic teaching of Jesus?

c. The New Quest

The historical scepticism of Bultmann led to a position so evidently unsatisfactory that even among his closest followers there has been a reaction. It is generally referred to as the 'New Quest of the Historical Jesus' after the title of a book by one of its advocates, J. M. Robinson.[1] Some reference has already been made to this New Quest (pp. 85, 86), but fuller discussion is needed here in the context of form criticism generally. A distinction must at once be drawn between the New Quest and the older Liberal Quest, which all form critics have rejected.[2] The New Quest does not admit of the possibility of ever regaining complete knowledge of the historical Jesus in the sense of biographical or psychological details, but seeks rather to fill out the content of the *kerygma* with some knowledge of Jesus apart from the mere 'thatness'. If no more than thatness were required, the 'Christ-event' of which Bultmann speaks would have no more relevance than a Mary-event or even a Mohammed-event.[3] Yet in spite of much emphasis on the need for a New Quest, the advocates have shown no agreement regarding the historical content, as the following brief survey of four major advocates will show.

It was E. Käsemann[4] who first launched the movement. With Bultmann, he denies the possibility of a chronological or psychological

data about the historical Jesus remains. Turner (*op. cit.*, pp. 61 ff.) rightly points out that those who wrote early Christian records could not detach themselves from the history they wrote. To this extent all Christian history must in a measure be 'coloured' by the standpoint of the writer, but this does not make it unhistorical, as Bultmann seems to take for granted.

[1] Robinson's *A New Quest for the Historical Jesus* (1959) shows a shift of position from his earlier book, *The Problem of History in Mark* (1957). The later book, therefore, more nearly represents his present position.

[2] Whereas Robinson has been anxious to dissociate himself from the old Quest, many of his critics have not been so sure that he has succeeded. Cf. P. Meyer, *Nov. Test.*, 4 (1960), p. 133, and A. van Harvey and S. M. Ogden, in Braaten and Harrisville, *op. cit.*, pp. 222 ff. The latter writers complain that Robinson's *existentiell* selfhood is no different from the Old Quest's 'inner life' of Jesus.

[3] Cf. the acute criticisms of R. P. C. Hanson in *Vindications* (edited A. T. Hanson, 1966), p. 69.

[4] *Essays on New Testament Themes* (1964), which includes many of Käsemann's earlier essays, including his well-known essay on 'The Problem of the Historical Jesus' first published in *ZTK*, 51 (1954), pp. 125–153.

reconstruction of the life of Jesus, but he cannot escape from the dilemma that the historian sees pieces of tradition in the Gospels which he recognizes as authentic. If he denies these he not only ceases to be a historian, but is in real danger of the charge of Docetism, the heresy which rejected the relevance of the historic Jesus for faith. Käsemann finds his cue in the preaching of Jesus. The following quotation will show in what respect. 'Our investigation has led to the conclusion that we must look for the distinctive element in the earthly Jesus in his preaching and interpret both his other activities and his destiny in the light of this preaching.'[1] The distinctive elements are seen in the super-cession of the Mosaic Law, the freedom in dealing with ritual require-ments, such as the Sabbath, His authority in dealing with demons, His awareness of God's will for human life and use of such authoritative formulae as Amen, and His relation to John the Baptist, the latter merely announcing the kingdom, whereas Jesus inaugurated it.[2]

G. Bornkamm's contribution[3] concentrates more on the acts of Jesus than Käsemann had done. He shows more concern for Jesus' dealing with people and even with His attitude towards them. In this latter respect he shows a significant departure from Bultmann's position, however tentatively he puts forward his views. At least Bornkamm is feeling after some continuity between the Christ of faith and the Jesus of history.

Another Bultmannian scholar who has advanced New Quest views is E. Fuchs,[4] who has gone even further in attempting to establish a connection between the Church's proclamation and the historical events. Fuchs concentrates on the social concern of Jesus, His attitude

---

[1] *Op. cit.*, p. 44.

[2] D. P. Fuller, *Easter Faith and History* (1965), p. 118, in commenting on Käse-mann's position, notes his concession that the historical method had something to say relevant to faith, but considers that faith still plays the decisive role in Käse-mann's thought.

[3] *Jesus von Nazareth* (1956), which appeared in an English translation as *Jesus of Nazareth* in 1960. Fuller (*op. cit.*, p. 123) points out that Bornkamm differs in his treatment from Käsemann and Fuchs in not singling out separate passages which were then claimed to be unique, but considered that 'the immediate present' of Jesus pervaded the Gospels. Fuller notes that in this Bornkamm approximates to the position of P. Althaus, *Das sogenannte Kerygma und der historische Jesus* (1958), p. 40, who appeals to the 'intuition' of historians.

[4] *Studies of the Historical Jesus* (1964). Fuchs' earliest article in favour of the New Quest was in *ZTK*, 54 (1957), pp. 244–254.

towards the wayward and social outcasts. Moreover he considers that the death of John the Baptist had some significance for Jesus as He approached His own death. This latter point introduces a historical-psychological interpretation which has been regarded by Bultmann as a relapse.[1]

The New Quest has found disciples outside Germany, the most notable of whom is J. M. Robinson,[2] who has staunchly maintained the need for some historical quest and has concentrated his appeal on what he at first called the understanding of self-hood by Jesus, but what he has since changed to the understanding of existence, because his former position was criticized for being indistinguishable from the 'inner life' quest of the older Liberal school.[3]

In Robinson's approach the real dilemma comes most clearly into focus. The New Quest is in reaction against Bultmann's conclusions, but is nevertheless still strongly tied to his presuppositions. Faith must not depend on history and yet cannot satisfactorily be wholly independent of it. Form criticism has not produced an adequate solution in either its earlier or its later Bultmannian forms, but it has focused acutely on the problem of continuity between the historical Jesus and the Church's kerygma.[4]

The following comments may be made by way of criticism of this New Quest. It does not come to grips any better than Dibelius and Bultmann with the interest of the Evangelists in the human Jesus. The Gospels do not read as if the historical material is a product of the community. Moreover, it is difficult to conceive of an original kerygma

[1] Cf. Braaten and Harrisville, op. cit., pp. 32 f. Bultmann sets his face firmly against any psychological approach to the personality of Jesus. Commenting on Bultmann's reaction to Fuchs, R. P. Martin, in Jesus of Nazareth: Saviour and Lord (edited C. Henry, 1966), p. 34, remarks, 'Bultmann had conceded some elements of Fuchs' construction of Jesus' attitude to sinners and consciousness of His mission, but had shied away from any biographical-psychological interpretation, especially of Jesus' understanding of His death.'

[2] A New Quest for the Historical Jesus (1959). R. P. Martin (op. cit., p. 35) points out that a major thesis in Robinson's approach is the modern attitude to historiography, which sees history as an existential undertaking on the part of the historian.

[3] Cf. R. H. Fuller, ATR, 47 (1965), pp. 119 f.

[4] In a recent book, J. Reumann, Jesus in the Church's Gospels (1969), attempts a New Quest study of Jesus. He rejects a literal historical approach, but sees some history in the Gospels. The problem of historicity is a long way from being satisfactorily solved. The New Quest is a witness to the existence of the problem.

which did not present a Jesus who had lived and taught in specific ways.[1] Another criticism which may be levelled against the New Quest is that its advocates have not managed to avoid the danger of Docetism.[2] As long as the New Questers cling to a Christ-event rather than to a fully historical person, the danger is real. Form criticism in all its more thoroughgoing forms presents Christianity as a movement of the same abstract type as Gnosticism. It opens the door, in fact, to any aberration which its creators like to introduce since it is not sufficiently tied to history. The New Quest is as committed as Bultmann to the dictates of an existential approach, as if this were the only norm whereby to judge the Gospel material. But it seems to have been overlooked that some authentic material may have other purposes than existential challenge.[3] Not all true history is bent on making the reader reach a decision. There is no doubt, moreover, that the New Questers have not succeeded in avoiding the scepticism of Bultmann. The authenticity of material is made to depend too much on the opinion of the New Questers and the amount of variation among them has been sufficiently illustrated above to show the precarious nature of this criterion. The fact is, the approach is almost entirely negative, non-authenticity being assumed until authenticity can be justified. It should further be noted that the assumption that every saying that met the needs of the community must be the product of the community is methodologically open to challenge, both because it contains an inherent improbability and because it ignores the probability that

---

[1] The failure of the New Questers as well as the earlier form critics to come to grips with history is well brought out by three essays in *Vindications*: R. P. C. Hanson, 'The Enterprise of Emancipating Christian Belief from History' (pp. 29–73); A. Hanson, 'The Quandary of Historical Scepticism' (pp. 74–102) and A. R. C. Leaney, 'Historicity in the Gospels' (pp. 103–134). Cf. also F. F. Bruce's study, 'History and the Gospel' in *Jesus of Nazareth: Saviour and Lord* (pp. 89–107).

[2] R. P. Martin (*op. cit.*, p. 40) mentions among those who have pointed out the danger of Docetism, E. Lohmeyer (cited by W. G. Kümmel, *Das Neue Testament, Geschichte der Erforschung seiner Probleme*, 1958, p. 65), N. A. Dahl (*Kerygma and Dogma*, 1955, p. 129), H. Zahrnt (*The Historical Jesus*, 1963, p. 89), and G. Miegge (*Gospel and Myth in the Thought of Rudolph Bultmann*, 1960, p. 128).

[3] C. Tennant, *ET*, 75 (1963), p. 95, has stressed that the only options are to regard the records as substantially genuine or else to accept the impossibility of knowing anything about the historical Jesus. Most scholars, faced with this alternative, would incline to the former rather than to the latter. Cf. W. Neil, *ET*, 75 (1964), pp. 260–263, who maintains there is ample evidence for historicity.

many sayings of Jesus had a dual purpose, for His own contemporaries and for the later Church.[1]

d. The theory of purely literary analysis

Several form critics have recognized the largely subjective character of the views already mentioned and prefer to limit the movement to a study of literary forms, without claiming that such study can conclusively give the relative ages of the forms (as Dibelius believed) or their historical value. One of the leading representatives of this approach was B. S. Easton,[2] who, although he did not exclude all legendary elements and did not regard all the material as historical, nevertheless claimed that the study of forms is no guide to historical reliability.[3] Although he is much more reserved in his conclusions than Dibelius or Bultmann, Easton allows for apologetic and ecclesiastical influences having affected the tradition. For instance, in the case of Luke xi. 42b, Matthew xxiii. 23b, he considers the statement about tithing mint, anise and cummin to be impossible in Jesus' mouth.[4] At the same time his examination of the different forms is more literary and less dogmatic than the views of those mentioned above.

In contrast to the scepticism of Bultmann, Easton compares the teaching of the various forms with what is known to have been the teaching of the early Church, a sure safeguard against the unrestrained imagination. His conclusion is that 'where beliefs of the Synoptic period can be distinguished with certainty from the teachings of Jesus, we find the former most scantily supported by sayings placed in his mouth'.[5] This shows a rather more realistic approach to the sayings than Bultmann's, although it is disputable with what certainty, if any, the beliefs of the period when the Synoptic Gospels were produced can be distinguished from the teachings of our Lord.

[1] This is brought out by R. E. Brown in his article in *CBQ*, 26 (1964), pp. 1–30. For another Roman Catholic criticism of the Bultmannians and post-Bultmannians, cf. P. J. Cahill, *CBQ*, 26 (1964), pp. 153–178. For a full survey of approaches to the historical Jesus since 1950, cf. W. G. Kümmel, *TR*, 31 (1966), pp. 15–46, 289–315.

[2] *The Gospel before the Gospels* (1928), pp. 80, 81.

[3] F. C. Grant (*The Earliest Gospel*, 1943, p. 41) maintains that it is an impossible position to suppose that form criticism has nothing to do with the historicity of the events, but only with the tradition's outward form. But surely Easton is nearer the truth when he claims that 'forms' give no indication of historicity. Both truth and error can be expressed in the same literary form.

[4] *Ibid.*, p. 107.   [5] *Ibid.*, p. 109.

e. Theories of limited value

Two English writers on form criticism may be cited as representing a view of its value in much more restricted terms. Vincent Taylor[1] takes the view that much of form criticism is open to question, particularly those theories which take no account of the influence of eyewitnesses during the formative period of the tradition. And yet he does not class all form criticism as valueless. He himself examines the forms under the following categories—passion narratives, pronouncement stories, sayings and parables, miracle stories and stories about Jesus. His pronouncement stories roughly correspond with Dibelius' paradigms and Bultmann's apophthegms, but he strongly rejects the historical scepticism of the latter. Moreover, in discussing the miracle stories he admits that form criticism cannot solve the problem of the miracles. It cannot reject them as worthless. It can only place them in the best position for the historical critic to decide. Such temperate claims have done much to rescue form criticism from the vagaries of mere speculation and to set it in its place, subsidiary to historical criticism.

Basil Redlich[2] has taken up a similar position and before considering the apophthegm stories (as he prefers to call the pronouncement stories of Taylor), the miracle stories, sayings and parables and the passion narrative, together with material which he classes as 'formless stories', he gives a concise critique of the assumptions of form criticism. Some of his points will be mentioned in the next section, but the reserve with which he approaches the subject will be seen from the fact that he categorically claims that a mass of stories in the Gospels are beyond the province of form criticism (hence his classification of 'formless stories'). Redlich rightly rejected such classifications as legends and myths, favoured by Dibelius and Bultmann, because they are dictated not by literary form but by content. After a careful examination of these, he concludes, 'The Form-less stories, even those called myths, bear their witness to the reality of the Cross and of the Personality of Jesus.'[3]

Another scholar who has claimed certain historical values for form criticism and who does not support the German sceptical schools of thought is C. H. Dodd,[4] who regards the form-critical method as

---

[1] *Formation of the Gospel Tradition* (1935), pp. 41 ff.

[2] *Form Criticism* (1939), pp. 34 ff.   [3] *Ibid.*, p. 196.

[4] Cf. his *History and the Gospel* (1938), pp. 86–110. In his article on 'The Appearances of the Risen Christ', in *Studies in the Gospels* (ed. D. E. Nineham, 1955), pp. 9–35, Dodd applies the form-critical method to the resurrection narratives.

valuable for demonstrating the substantial historicity of some, at least, of the traditions. His method of procedure is to select certain themes and then to show that these themes recur in different strains of the tradition such as aphorisms, parables, poetical sayings, dialogues and various story forms. He has contended that such analysis enables comparisons to be made between the various types of tradition, by which means he claims to be able more easily to check on the historicity of the material. While he admits that such a method of approach shows the influence of the interpretative element in Gospel tradition, yet he maintains that the Gospels represent a substantially true memory of the facts. The difference between this approach and Bultmann's will be readily apparent.

III. GENERAL CRITICISMS OF FORM CRITICISM

It will now be valuable to summarize the most important criticisms of form criticism in order to get the whole movement into perspective and to assess its value. According to Redlich[1] there are six assumptions made by the thoroughgoing form critics:

1. That before the written Gospels there was a period of oral tradition.

2. That during this period, narratives and sayings (except the passion narrative) circulated as separate self-contained units.

3. That the Gospel material can be classified according to literary form.

4. That the vital factors which produced and preserved these forms are to be found in the practical interests of the Christian community.

5. That the traditions have no chronological or geographical value.

6. That the original form of the traditions may be recovered by studying the laws of the tradition.

Very few of these assumptions can be considered valid, at least in the form in which form critics generally accept them. Even the first must be qualified by the recognition of eyewitnesses who would have exercised some constraining influence on the tradition. But it is a basic assumption of form criticism that eyewitness testimony had no influence upon the development of community products. This has recently been vigorously maintained by D. E. Nineham,[2] who considers

[1] *Op. cit.*, pp. 34 ff.
[2] *JTS*, n.s., IX (1958), pp. 13–25, 243–252; XI (1960), pp. 253–264.

the community argument to be *a posteriori* and the eyewitness point of view to be *a priori*. This is because he regards the Gospels as no more than collections of 'units', and from this deduces that eyewitnesses could have had nothing to do with the preservation of the material. But in rejecting the *a priori* view in favour of the *a posteriori* he comes very near to arguing in a circle. Since he accepts as the basic article of form criticism the virtual exclusion of eyewitness influence he is bound to explain away all eyewitness traces. The fallacy of his method is clearly seen when, in order to dispute Petrine recollections behind Mark, he enquires why Mark did not make more use of these (if he had access to them) in preference to community traditions.[1] As a concluding justification for the form-critical approach he appeals to the fact that the modern approach to history puts less value on eyewitness attestation than on later assessment. But it is difficult to suppose, for instance, that a Christian some thirty or forty years after the incident of, let us say, the coin and the tribute problem, would have been in a better position to assess its validity than an eyewitness who not only saw the coin and heard the conversation, but was himself under obligation to pay tribute. This method of making the alleged absence of eyewitness attestation into a virtue must be rejected.

The idea of detached units may be true of some of the material, but the Gospels themselves bear testimony to many connected sequences (e.g. Mk. i. 21–39, ii. 1–iii. 6). If the passion narrative existed in continuous form, as is generally conceded, why not other narratives? The fallacy of supposing that the Christian community was wholly responsible for the origin of the different forms has already been exposed when criticizing Bultmann. As far as the sayings material is concerned it may just as well be assumed that the originator of the forms was our Lord Himself. Moreover, to maintain that the traditional materials have no chronological or geographical value is a value judgment which is not borne out by the evidence of the New Testament as a whole. The resemblance of the general outline of Mark's Gospel to the summary of Peter's proclamation in Cornelius' house (Acts x. 38 f.) has been shown to point to some sequence. Moreover, the tradition that behind Mark may be traced the reminiscences of Peter has too much to commend it to be lightly dismissed (see pp. 142 f.) and it is impossible to suppose that an eyewitness would be entirely bereft of

[1] *JTS*, IX, p. 22.*

chronological or geographical sense.[1] Again, since the events contained in the Gospels present a reasonably intelligible sequence and location, it is unreasonable to deny this impression or to attribute it to later influences without the strongest possible justification; but this would seem to be lacking.[2] The idea of laws of the traditions is misleading, for it suggests a rigidity which is not only most unlikely, but definitely unsupported by other evidence. When dealing with human minds, through whom the tradition was passed on, it is difficult to speak of laws. Moreover, if the proposed laws are deduced from a wide range of folk material stretching over centuries it could not be assumed that oral traditions must always conform to these.[3] There are too many unpredictable factors. Moreover, the controlling influence of the Holy Spirit over the tradition finds no place in this conception.*

The limits of form criticism

But in spite of the very considerable modifications which need to be made to the assumptions just considered, is there not some ground for maintaining that the Gospels material can be classified according to literary form? The form critics would, of course, reply in the affirmative although, as already mentioned, with various emphases. The obvious danger of classifying the material according to content rather than literary form is well illustrated in the hypotheses of Dibelius and Bultmann, but such procedure ceases to be form criticism, in the strict sense of the word.

Any assessment of form criticism must take into account the following limits.

[1] Form critics would not, of course, admit the validity of this argument since eyewitness testimony is *ex hypothesi* excluded.

[2] Conzelmann's carefully reasoned arguments that Luke's geographical allusions are dictated by his theological purpose, if valid, would supply such justification, but his arguments are too often dominated by his form-critical method to be convincing. To cite one example, in discussing the passage Lk. vi. 1–vii. 50, he sees the references to some places (mountain, lake) as symbolic or where specific, as in vi. 17, as being more significant for omissions (Galilee, Idumaea, Peraea) than inclusions (*The Theology of St. Luke*, pp. 44 ff.). Yet he gives no serious consideration to the references to Capernaum and Nain in this passage. It is difficult to escape the impression that much of the symbolism is Conzelmann's rather than Luke's. But these arguments warrant a fuller and more detailed critique than is possible here.

[3] C. H. Dodd, in his *Historical Tradition in the Fourth Gospel* (1963), p. 6, cautions against such an assumption.*

1. Only materials with recognized forms may be included and classification according to contents must be excluded.

2. It must be remembered that Christ the Teacher was greater than the Christian community which He founded and it must be expected that He left His stamp on the form as well as the content of the oral tradition of His teaching.

3. Variations in the tradition may not be assumed on that account to be unhistorical, since Jesus may Himself have repeated some of His teachings on different occasions and in different forms.

4. No form-critical hypotheses are justified which ignore the presence of eyewitnesses during the oral period.

5. Form criticism cannot assume that a study of non-Christian forms such as legends and myths must supply sufficient parallels without regard to the uniqueness of content of the Gospel material.

6. The uniqueness of the material is because of the uniqueness of the Person in whom it is centred and for whom the early Christians were prepared to suffer even death. Any form criticism which loses sight of this becomes at once divorced from reality. The Christians would not have been prepared to die in order to defend the products of their own imaginations.

When all the limitations are taken into account the scope of a true form-critical approach will be seen to be severely restricted. Yet with such restrictions it may well be asked whether such a movement can really make any effective contribution to Gospel criticism. Some indication of the claims made for it by the more moderate form critics may consequently be given.

IV. THE VALUE OF FORM CRITICISM

1. It has been claimed to be an indispensable adjunct to source criticism because it draws attention to problems with which the latter does not and cannot deal. In so far as it focuses attention on certain pressing problems, which would not otherwise have been brought to notice, such a claim is justified.

2. It has been said that form criticism plunges us into the twilight period of the Christian Church and directly connects up the formation of the oral tradition with the life of the early communities. Inasmuch as source criticism had tended to obscure this fact, form criticism has performed a useful service. But it should be noted that to account for the Synoptic problem, the advocates of the theory of oral tradition

had earlier called attention to the many-sided aspects of early Christian traditions, although they did not tackle the problem from quite the same point of view nor in the same detail.

3. It has been suggested that form criticism has pointed to the possibility of collections of the *ipsissima verba* of our Lord. This claim is obviously not true for so radical a form critic as Bultmann, except in a severely restricted sense. But there is a greater tendency among less radical critics to recognize that much care would have been exercised by the primitive communities in the transmission of the words of the Lord.

4. The idea that the Gospels contain insertions added by the Christian community has been claimed as a fruitful product of form-critical research. In other words an analysis of literary form is said to reveal extraneous material. But the source critics had always claimed to make similar discoveries and this can hardly be regarded, therefore, as a form-critical achievement, if achievement it is. And where there is the possibility of accepting the documents as they stand, as preserving reliable tradition, this must be preferable to the speculations of form-critics.[1]

5. Some value must be attached to the failure of much form criticism, for the quest for Gospel origins has at least been stimulated, even if it has not achieved much success. It should mean that more reserve will be exercised by all Gospel critics before asserting that any assured results have been secured.[2] If this is a negative value it is nevertheless a factor which it is hoped will exert increasing influence on future Gospel criticism.

6. The important question remaining is whether form criticism has contributed anything valuable to the interpretation of the Gospels, and if so to what extent. This question will naturally be answered in different ways according to the weight attached to the preceding values. If,

---

[1] In referring to what they call the 'most solid and undoubtedly permanent achievement' of form criticism, K. and S. Lake (*INT*, p. 20) paradoxically state this to be the bringing of more imagination into the question. But when investigators have to rely on imagination the results can never be solid and permanent. Had the movement brought to bear less imagination and more historical data its achievements would have been considerably greater.

[2] When discussing the methods of Gospel criticism, V. Taylor admits that none of the current methods—statistical, literary and stylistic or form-critical—can lead to absolute certainty, but he pleads for what he calls 'moral certainty' (*ET*, LXXI, 1959, pp. 68–72).

for instance, the form of the interpretation of the parable of the sower be considered secondary, it may be claimed that the true interpretation of the parable may be independent of that preserved in the tradition.[1] But if it be considered that a parabolic interpretation may require a different form from the parable itself, form criticism would contribute nothing. Perhaps the most significant way in which Gospel interpretation has been affected is in the lessening of dependence on parallel sources. Source criticism has all too often tended to assume that double or triple traditions (as in most of Mark and in Q) are more reliable than single traditions (as in M and L materials), but since form criticism concentrates on units of material this tendency has diminished. Another factor which has come to the fore is the ability more readily to explain gaps in the material. It can no longer be assumed that absence of any major theme in parts of the tradition means that it was unknown in the area where that tradition was preserved. The paucity of references to the Holy Spirit in Mark and Matthew may be a case in point, for the traditions, according to form criticism, were formulated under the influence of the needs of the community. It could be argued that in a society under the conscious guidance of the Spirit there would be no need for catechetical instruction regarding His activity, and hence material about the Spirit would tend to be less repeated. Whether or not this is a valid approach may be worth considering.[2]

What gains there have been have not been spectacular and form criticism can hardly be said to have advanced very far the cause of Gospel understanding. But we should be grateful for any movement which assists in freeing criticism from excessive confidence in and multiplication of sources, which in the nature of the case must remain hypothetical, and form criticism has certainly done that. In spite of its

[1] J. Jeremias, *The Parables of Jesus*[2] (Eng. Tr. 1963), claims by form-critical methods to have cleared away several alterations which have occurred in the transmission of the parables, and therefore to have made possible a more adequate exegesis. Such alterations he attributes to translation, to embellishments, to change of audience, to new situations to which the parables were applied, to the fusing of parables and to the influence of their present contexts. But although much of his evidence may be otherwise explained, his treatment at least provides a warning against both a moralizing and an allegorizing interpretation. For a critique of modern approaches to the parables, cf. I. H. Marshall, *Eschatology and the Parables* (1963).

[2] For an advocacy of this, cf. V. Taylor, *The Holy Spirit* (1937), pp. 53–55, and for a criticism, cf. C. K. Barrett, *The Holy Spirit and the Gospel Tradition* (1947), pp. 140 ff.

extravagances, it has begun a new era in the approach to the Synoptic problem, an era in which oral tradition is justly receiving attention.

V. THEORIES OF THEOLOGICAL COMPOSITION

After the preceding examination of the contribution of form criticism to the understanding of the Gospels, it is now necessary to outline a more recent approach which has arisen out of the form-critical school itself. The form critics had concentrated their attention on the mass of disconnected units in which it was claimed that the Gospel material first circulated and were content to regard the Evangelists as arrangers rather than as authors. The tendency developed of failing to recognize the Gospels as wholes.[1] This has been a serious fault of form critics generally and of Bultmann in particular, in spite of the latter's attempt to deny this.[2] It was pointed out in the earliest stages of the development of the form-critical movement, but little heed was given to the criticism.[3]

But the emphasis within form criticism on *Gemeindetheologie*[4] was bound to lead sooner or later to the shifting of the focus to the theology of the Evangelists themselves. This movement has become known as *Redaktionsgeschichte* or composition-history. It began with H. Conzelmann[5] in Luke and W. Marxsen[6] in Mark. It will be better to begin with Marxsen, because he enunciates clearly the distinctiveness of this new approach. Marxsen distinguishes between three *Sitze im Leben*. The first is the *Sitz im Leben* in the life of Jesus Himself and has to do with the relationship between the written records and the actual events. The second has to do with the *Sitz im Leben* of the early Church and is illuminated by form-critical attempts to differentiate community

---

[1] This is admitted by E. Haenchen, *Der Weg Jesu* (1966), p. 23.

[2] *Form Criticism*, p. 4.

[3] Cf. E. von Dobschütz, *ZNTW*, 27 (1928), pp. 193 f.

[4] E. F. Harrison has provided a valuable critique of this movement in his article 'Gemeindetheologie: the Bane of Gospel Criticism', *Jesus of Nazareth: Saviour and Lord*, pp. 157 ff. Cf. also the remark of O. Piper (*JBL*, 78, 1959, p. 123), that it is time to demythologize the myth of a creative collectivity called *die Gemeinde*.

[5] *The Theology of St. Luke* (Eng.Tr. 1960). See J. Rohde's summary, *Rediscovering the Teaching of the Evangelists* (1968), pp. 154 ff.

[6] *Mark the Evangelist* (Eng. Tr. 1969). Cf. Rohde, *op. cit.*, pp. 113 ff. for an assessment. Cf. also Marxsen's *INT*, pp. 163–166 on the effect of his approach on exegesis.

theology from the words and acts of Jesus. The third has to do with the authors and strives to delineate the theology of the Evangelists as distinguished from the community theology. Marxsen used the term *Redaktionsgeschichte* of this third pursuit. By definition, therefore, he treated it as a further development from form criticism and not as part of the latter. Nevertheless, he recognized that stage three could not be reached except *via* stage two. All advocates of *Redaktionsgeschichte* have admitted this, for all have been advocates of form criticism.

Nevertheless, not all have agreed with Marxsen. Many would treat his second and third stage as one,[1] although differing from form critics of the older schools in placing more emphasis on the theological editing than on the units of tradition. This would be substantially the position of Conzelmann.[2] Whether or not Marxsen is correct in drawing a sharp distinction between form criticism and *Redaktion* criticism,[3] it is clear that the newer movement has gone considerably beyond form criticism in its emphasis on the theology of the individual Gospels. The Evangelists, in this movement, have once more become individuals rather than nonentities. This much must be considered gain, although there are some aspects of this movement which are more open to criticism.[4]

In his treatment of Mark, Marxsen views the whole book as a sermon written to warn the Church in Judaea to flee to Galilee to await the *parousia*. Whatever improbabilities attach to this view of Mark, such as the unlikelihood of the Gospel being addressed to Jews and the further unlikelihood that Mark regarded the *parousia* as so imminent (in view of Mk. xiii. 10), Marxsen has rightly seen the need to treat the Gospel as a whole. It is not surprising with his form-critical background that he is more interested in Mark's theology than his history.

A similar tendency may be seen in Conzelmann's approach to Luke.[5]

---

[1] Cf. E. Haenchen, *op. cit.*, pp. 20 f. In other respects Haenchen's treatment of Mark is from the same point of view as Marxsen's.

[2] *Op. cit.*, p. 12.

[3] Cf. R. H. Stein's discussion in *JBL*, 87 (1969), pp. 45–56, in which he strongly resists the classification of *Redaktionsgeschichte* under form criticism. He supports Marxsen's contentions.

[4] G. Strecker (*Der Weg der Gerechtigkeit*, 1962, p. 10) refuses to support the movement to individualize the Evangelists. He regards them as collectors (*Sämmler*).

[5] Although Strecker does not support the individualizing of the Evangelists as Conzelmann does, he agrees with his time-scheme, cf. *Ev Th*, 26 (1966), pp. 57–74.

He sees a special scheme behind this Gospel. According to him Luke has a three-stage conception of time, the time of Israel (the era of the prophets), the middle of time (the era of the earthly Jesus) and the time of the Church. Luke's Gospel is concerned with the middle of time. According to Conzelmann,[1] the period of Jesus was unique in the sense of being free from the activity of Satan, and in this respect distinct from the Church age. But Luke himself does not seem to support Conzelmann's view of him, for he stresses the activity of evil in the ministry of Jesus as well as the continuity of the mission of Jesus with the mission of the Church.[2] Conzelmann also sees theological significance in Luke's references of a chronological and particularly geographical nature. This tendency is not, of course, new, for E. Lohmeyer[3] and R. H. Lightfoot[4] had done the same thing in Mark. It is worth noting that this tendency to see meaning in chronology and geography is directly complementary to K. L. Schmidt's[5] denial of the genuineness of either in Mark.

A collection of three essays by G. Bornkamm, G. Barth and H. J. Held[6] has approached the Gospel of Matthew from the same point of view. One illustration of their method will suffice. In considering the incident of the stilling of the storm, Bornkamm finds a large amount

For a discussion of the redaction of Luke, cf. R. A. Edwards, *JR*, 49 (1969), pp. 392–405.

[1] Cf. *op. cit.*, pp. 36, 170, 195. For a comment on Conzelmann's scheme, cf. D. P. Fuller, *Easter Faith and History*, pp. 242 f.

[2] Conzelmann's view here is criticized by E. E. Ellis, *The Gospel of Luke* (*CB*, n.s., 1966), pp. 15, 16, who points out the activity of Satan in the pre-resurrection mission. Others have recently focused attention on the theologizing activity of Luke. Cf. C. H. Talbert, *NTS*, 14 (1968), pp. 259–271, who finds Luke's purpose reflected in his structure. He thinks that as Gnostics interpreted both the baptism and the ascension in a Docetic sense, so Luke has provided an answer to this kind of unorthodox theology. Cf. also O. Betz's discussion of Luke's *kerygma* in *Interpretation*, 22 (1968), pp. 131–146. H. H. Oliver has concentrated on Luke's infancy narratives, but takes a line similar to Conzelmann's treatment of the rest of Luke (*NTS*, 10, 1963, pp. 202–206). The study by H. Flender, *St. Luke: Theologian of Redemptive History* (1967), although from a different point of view from Conzelmann, is nevertheless a study based on redaction theory. Cf. Rohde's summary of Flender's position, *op. cit.*, pp. 229 ff. and J. C. O'Neill's unfavourable review of this book in *JTS*, 19 (1968), pp. 269, 270.

[3] See p. 81 n. 6.

[4] See p. 85 n. 2.

[5] See p. 63 n. 1.

[6] *Tradition and Interpretation in Matthew* (1963). Cf. Rohde, *op. cit.*, pp. 47 ff.

of interpretation and concludes that the incident is intended to show the danger and glory of discipleship.[1] This type of *Redaktionsgeschichte* makes no attempt to consider the historical nature of the narrative, for this is assumed at the outset to be impossible. The Evangelists were using the material as a vehicle for the expression of their theology. A similar approach is made to Matthew by P. Bonnard[2] and to the book of Acts by E. Haenchen.[3]

Some comments are necessary on this new movement which may help to place it in its true perspective.

1. *Its form-critical basis.* Even if Marxsen's arguments are followed, the essential contribution of form criticism to its development is admitted by all its advocates, which means that the same weaknesses which apply to form criticism generally apply to *Redaktionsgeschichte*.

2. *Its individualism.* This has undoubtedly been its strongest point, in that it has brought back a personal element into Gospel criticism. Yet it should be noted that this is not an entirely new emphasis. The older types of Synoptic theory, both in the oral form and in the mutual dependence form, had not overlooked the important part played by the authors of the Gospels. Moreover, W. Wrede, whose book on the Messianic Secret did a great deal to spark off form criticism, laid great emphasis on the theological editing of Mark.[4] *Redaktionsgeschichte*, however, must be seen against the background of the anonymity which was the keynote of form criticism. The idea of the circulation of a vast mass of isolated units had obscured the personal contribution of the Evangelists. In this respect the new movement provides a welcome reaction.[5]

[1] *Op. cit.*, p. 57.
[2] *L'Évangile selon Saint Matthieu* (1963). This author has been criticized by C. Masson (*RThPh*, 97, 1964, pp. 155–158) for not examining the historical problem but assuming non-historicity. Bonnard is satisfied with Matthew's account of the Saviour. Cf. also the reviews of E. Best, *SJT*, 18 (1965), pp. 358–361 and C. W. F. Smith, *JBL*, 84 (1965), pp. 80–84.
[3] *Die Apostelgeschichte*, 1961.
[4] See additional note on Mark's Gospel in respect of p. 58 n. 2 (on p. 88).
[5] J. Schreiber, *Theologie des Vertrauens: Eine redaktionsgeschichte Untersuchung des Markusevangeliums* (1967), treats the author of Mark's Gospel, not as a naïve *Sammler*, but as an astute theologian. He explores Mark's historiography and eschatology. Similarly E. Schweizer, *Das Evangelium nach Markus* (NTD, 11 1967), stresses Mark's theological contribution. Cf. also his article in *NTS*, 10 (1964), pp. 421–432. L. E. Keck (*NTS*, 12, 1966, pp. 352–370) pleads for an approach to Mark's theology via the whole plan of the Gospel.

3. *Its relation to source criticism.* When emphases shift in New Testament criticism, it is important not to lose sight of essential connections with older movements. It must be emphasized that, as form criticism lies at the basis of redaction criticism, so source criticism is basic to both. The focus on the Evangelists as authors in their own right cannot fail to introduce a more personal element into source criticism.

4. *Dangers inherent in Redaktionsgeschichte.* Whereas form criticism has tended to overstress the part of the community in the transmission of traditions, the newer movement will be exposed to the opposite danger unless the theology of the writer is seen as representative of the theology of his church. It cannot be supposed that Gospels which received the approbation not only of the church in which they arose, but also of other churches, could have arisen as a result of an individual theology. Care must therefore be taken in studying the theological bent of the Evangelists not to emphasize their individuality to such an extent that the variety of Christian experience is stressed to the detriment of its unity. Luke, for instance, may have different theological emphases than Mark, but both were presenting the same Lord and Saviour, as the later patristic writers unanimously recognized.

5. *The necessity of examining its presuppositions.* Because of its close connection with form criticism, *Redaktionsgeschichte* too often assumes in general the non-historical character of the events, which predisposes it to see theological motives where others would not. Advocates of this kind of approach are entitled to their own opinion, but they are not entitled to assume that their theological interpretations are the only possible approach. To illustrate the point: Conzelmann's theological deductions from geographical data need careful scrutiny before it is assumed that Luke could not have intended his references to be considered factually.

It cannot be claimed that *Redaktionsgeschichte* helps the investigator to get any nearer to the events related. Indeed, Conzelmann sides with Bultmann in rejecting such a quest. The newer discipline is therefore an attempt to shift the emphasis from community to personal theology, but in doing this is pushing the focus of attention even further away from the original events.[1]

To sum up, it may be legitimate to enquire the extent to which a

---

[1] J. Rohde (*op. cit.*, pp. 256–258) argues for the reverse when comparing the form critic Bultmann with the redaction critic Bornkamm, but he admits that redaction criticism excludes the problem of historicity from its considerations.

Redaktionsgeschichte is possible divorced from form-critical pre-suppositions. If a more historical approach to Gospel material is adopted, is any theory of theological editing possible? In other words, can a theologian write history? Provided some definition of history is accepted which leaves room for interpretation, there seems no reason why a different type of *Redaktionsgeschichte* should not be conceived. Indeed, appeal may be made to John's Gospel with its specifically stated theological purpose, where the historicity of the events is defensible (see discussion on pp. 323ff.). All the Evangelists were men who saw events as vehicles of truth regarding Jesus Christ, but there is no reason to suppose that the events were created in a theological interest.

ADDITIONAL NOTES

189. [1] It is significant that interest has revived in Wrede's theory, particularly because of its kinship with the approach of the *Redaktionsgeschichte* school. To Wrede the 'secret' was attributable to Mark's own theology. Cf. G. M. de Tilesse, *Le Secret Messianique dans l'Évangile de Marc* (1968) and C. Mauer, *NTS*, 14 (1968), pp. 515–526. See additional footnotes to Mark. W. Barclay (*The First Three Gospels*, 1966, pp. 184 ff.) gives a useful brief survey of Wrede's position.

209. [1] R. P. C. Hanson (*Vindications*, 1966, p. 38) has expressed the vicious circle into which form critics fall in the following way: '1. The materials of the Gospels have been radically altered and re-handled in order to speak appropriately to the *Sitz im Leben* of the Church which re-handled them. 2. The *Sitz im Leben* of the Church which was the criterion by which materials of the Gospels were re-handled can be reconstructed—from the materials in the Gospels.'

210. On the subject of the place of the Holy Spirit in the tradition, E. F. Harrison (*Jesus of Nazareth: Saviour and Lord*, 1966, p. 163) points out that it may not be accidental that Bultmann has no real doctrine of the Spirit.

210. [3] For a criticism of the appeal to 'laws of traditions', cf. R. P. C. Hanson (*op. cit.*, pp. 42 ff.). E. P. Sanders, in his book *The Tendencies of the Synoptic Tradition* (1969), comes to the conclusion that the tendencies to change in the tradition are not sufficiently consistent to be called laws.

CHAPTER SEVEN

TOWARDS A SOLUTION

It would be foolish to affirm that the last word has yet been said about the Synoptic problem. The variety of theories, together with the evident inadequacies of each, is a sufficient incentive to continue the quest, although there may be a feeling that the impossible is being attempted. Even confident critics are generally wary of adopting an attitude of finality in respect of proposed hypotheses. The following comments may be regarded as no more than an assessment of the present position and an attempt to indicate possible avenues which may yet need to be more fully explored.

I. GUIDING PRINCIPLES

a. The need to account for external testimony

One of the most difficult problems to settle in Gospel criticism is the place of tradition. Some schools of criticism play down external evidence as a datum for scientific criticism on the grounds that the witnesses were not scientific in their approach and cannot be relied upon to preserve authentic traditions. On the other extreme is that school of thought which almost regards ancient testimony as sacrosanct and therefore unquestionably true. Neither of these approaches is satisfactory. The former is guilty of over-modernization in assuming that only testimony presented in accordance with modern scientific formulae can be valid. In spite of the fact that the early Christians were men of their own age, a largely non-critical and non-scientific age, it does not follow that they were credulous over matters vitally affecting their faith when they knew that at any time they might be called upon to defend their position. As to the view which regards tradition as being as important as internal evidence, this is indefensible since some traditions are manifestly inaccurate. No-one would take too seriously, for example, the part that Andrew is supposed to have played in the production of John's Gospel according to the Muratorian Canon (see p. 260). Clearly traditions must be carefully weighed.

Where there is a strongly attested ancient tradition, it is a fair approach to suppose that this tradition is probably correct, until it can be proved wrong. In other words, where tradition and internal considerations conflict, the interpretation of the latter must be beyond challenge before it may be confidently assumed that the traditional view must be wrong. Where the internal testimony clearly and indisputably contradicts the tradition, the latter must certainly be rejected. To cite a case in which internal considerations are by no means unanimous against the tradition, reference may be made to the relationship between Peter and Mark's Gospel.

Although it is possible to make out a case for disputing any connection between the two, as certain form critics have done, yet probability is strongly in support of some connection, since there is a known association of Peter with Mark. In other words, the general agreement of all the extant early traditions on this matter establishes a strong probability that it is based on fact, which requires more than a mere possibility to dislodge. Suggestions as to how something *could* have happened may be very far removed from what actually *did* happen. Where tradition asserts the latter with reasonable unanimity and clarity, criticism must prove first that this could *not* have happened, before producing any evidence in support of an alternative. In other words, possibilities cannot oust probabilities.

Another factor in assessing the value of traditions regarding authorship and kindred factors of Gospel criticism is the need for furnishing some adequate account of the origin of a rejected tradition. Too often scholars have resorted to the 'guesswork' method. If a tradition does not accord with modern theories about any Gospel, the ancient witness is supposed to be propagating his own guess. It is not, of course, impossible that some traditions had their origin in this way. But this kind of thing is very difficult to track down. For instance, did Papias guess at the Hebrew origin of Matthew's Gospel, or is he merely reflecting an earlier tradition? If the latter, which seems highly probable, where did the guess enter the stream of tradition? The fact that no-one can answer this question does not necessarily mean that the 'guess' could not have happened, but it does mean that considerable reserve should be exercised over such a theory. Probability is against the Christians of the first century being left to their unguided imaginations to decide the not unimportant issue of the origins of their treasured literature about Jesus Christ.

In considering any possible solution to the Synoptic problem, therefore, due attention must be paid to ancient traditions. The task will be to disentangle what is true from what is false. It may be assumed as a starting-point that most of the well-attested traditions were based, at least partially, on fact. After eliminating any which are clearly and conclusively wrong, the rest must be regarded as part of the data on the basis of which a solution is proposed.

b. The place of personal reminiscence in theories of development

It has already been pointed out that the most important service rendered by form criticism has been to concentrate interest once more on the oral period and there can be no question but that any real advance in solving the Synoptic problem must be located in this period. Is it possible, however, to define more closely what is meant by the oral period? Vagueness over this issue may well lead to confusion over the whole solution proposed. The existence of such an oral period immediately subsequent to the events recorded in the Gospels is undeniable. But the terminus of this period is much less easy to fix, for it depends on the dating of the Gospels and on the view held regarding intermediate written sources. It is generally assumed that the oral period stretched over about thirty years, i.e. across the life-span of the first generation of Christians. But it should be noted that this need not exclude the parallel development of written sources. It would seem reasonable to suppose, without fixing too rigidly a thirty-year oral period, that for a time oral teaching was the main means of communicating the Christian traditions, but that it was supplemented by some literary productions. Although few data are available for this primitive period, there are certain lines of investigation which throw some light upon it.

The starting-point may be found in a closer examination of the Jewish oral tradition and its methods of transmission. The careful study of B. Gerhardsson[1] and the earlier suggestions of H. Riesenfeld[2] have provided an impetus in this direction. Gerhardsson's main contention is that rabbinical teachers not only taught traditional material, but taught it in set forms and vocabulary which the pupils were expected to learn by heart. There were various mnemonic devices to help them in this task. Since the earliest Christian preachers were Jews, Gerhardsson

[1] *Memory and Manuscript* (1961).
[2] In his article, 'The Gospel Tradition and its Beginnings', in *Studia Evangelica* (1959), pp. 43–65.

envisages that they would have followed the rabbinical practice. He also supposes that our Lord instructed His disciples in the same manner. From this it follows that a basic oral tradition would be formulated which could be transmitted through catechesis. But there are some basic assumptions in Gerhardsson's theory which require careful consideration.

To begin with, it needs to be demonstrated that our Lord's teaching was similar in kind to that of the Rabbis, if similar teaching methods are supposed. But this has been challenged. For instance, E. Fuchs[1] has claimed that the early Christian speech was creative and therefore novel. A. N. Wilder[2] takes this up as a basis for criticising Gerhardston, maintaining that the Gospel material was too novel for convensional methods of transmission. Moreover the novelty of Jesus' speech-forms is linked with the novelty of His mode of life, which differed so radically from that of the conventional Rabbi. He established no catechetical school and His method of instruction must, therefore, have differed from the regular memorization methods of the Jewish teachers. Moreover, W. D. Davies[3] draws attention to the vital difference between Judaism and Christianity in its centre of gravity. In the former it was the Torah, in the latter it was Jesus Christ Himself. This shift of emphasis makes it more dubious to assume that Jesus taught His disciples in a manner similar to the Rabbis.[4]

Yet if Gerhardsson's propositions need modification they are invaluable in drawing attention to various factors in the background of

---

[1] 'Die Sprache im Neuen Testament', in *Das Problem der Sprache in Theologie und Kirche* (ed. W. Schneemelcher, 1959), pp. 21–55.

[2] 'Form-history and the oldest tradition', in *Neotestamentica et Patristica* (ed. W. C. van Unnik, 1962), pp. 3–13.

[3] 'The Gospel Tradition' in *Neotestamentica et Patristica*, pp. 14–34.*

[4] Morton Smith (*JBL*, LXXXII, 1963, pp. 169–176) strongly criticizes Gerhardsson for misrepresenting both the rabbinic and Christian tradition. He maintains that no evidence exists for the memory techniques of Judaism before AD 70 and further complains that Gerhardsson pays no attention to other Jewish groups outside Pharisaism. He claims that those parts of the Mishnah dealing with daily life (as distinct from historical tractates) were created by the second-century Rabbis. There are, moreover, marked differences between rabbinic and New Testament material and this must clearly be taken into account, although it need not altogether, as Morton Smith claims, refute Gerhardsson's hypothesis. It is possible that different types of material required different memory techniques, but evidence on this subject during the first century is too scanty for any fixed opinion to be formed about it.

early Christian tradition. Memorization was a cardinal principle in religious education and it is impossible to suppose that no use was made of it in Christian catechesis. Even if our Lord was not a conventional Rabbi, which very clearly He was not, it does not automatically follow that He would have refused to use any memory techniques. The probability that He repeated His teaching material many times would in itself account for some of the differences in the Synoptic records. But if the Jewish educative procedure had had any influence upon our Lord and upon the apostolic circle, it would also go far to explain many of the similarities, particularly in language.

Another important consideration arises from the thesis of J. W. Doeve[1] that the Gospel material was taught, rabbinic fashion, as a commentary upon various Old Testament passages. The preoccupation of the early Christian preachers with Old Testament *testimonia* strongly supports this point of view, which had been adumbrated by Rendel Harris,[2] advocated by Stather Hunt[3] and modified by C. H. Dodd.[4] It would be claiming too much to maintain that a theory of Old Testament exegesis accounts for the majority of the material incorporated in the Gospels. But it was undoubtedly a contributory factor in recalling to the minds of eyewitnesses events which they recognized as being in fulfilment of Old Testament prophecy. Because of the conviction that there was a continuity between the Old and New, the early Christians sought out the incidents which emphasized fulfilment. This was not merely for apologetic purposes, but primarily for theological reasons. The Old Testament Scriptures took on a new meaning because of the close connection between event and fulfilment. Recognition of this fact enables the student of Gospel origins to postulate regulative influences in the oral period. The tradition was partially controlled by means of Scripture, but there were other constraining influences.

The words of Jesus would be regarded as sacred and committed to memory because of their intrinsic worth and because of the regard in which the Christians held their Lord. This surpassed any rabbinical

---

[1] 'Le Rôle de la Tradition orale dans la composition des Evangiles synoptiques', in *La Formation des Evangiles* (ed. J. Heuschen, 1957), pp. 70–84. Cf. also *idem*, *Jewish Hermeneutics in the Synoptic Gospels and Acts* (1954), pp. 177 ff.
[2] *Testimonies*, I (1916).   [3] *Primitive Gospel Sources* (1951).
[4] *According to the Scriptures* (1952).

teacher–pupil relationship.[1] They recognized His divine nature which invested His words with such authority that every effort would be made to retain as far as possible the very words in which He taught. This accounts for the significant fact that fewer deviations occur in parallel accounts of His sayings than in the narratives of His doings. When it is remembered that Jesus was acknowledged as Lord, it is difficult to conceive that the primitive communities would have 'created' in His honour Gospel material which could be placed on a level with His own authentic teaching. This would appear to make the Christians as great or greater than Christ Himself, a presupposition which is impossible. Oral tradition for this reason could never run riot. Moreover, as men of the Spirit the Gospel writers were sensitive to the quality of the tradition,[2] a fact to which the more extreme form critics have paid no attention.

Another factor which needs serious consideration in any tentative solution of the Synoptic problem is the possibility of the use of written notes as aids to memory. Gerhardsson[3] produces some evidence which suggests that such notes were used in Jewish oral tradition and it seems quite natural to suppose that Christian tradition would not have neglected to use aids of this kind. Admittedly this is conjectural, but it is based on some probability. If this happened the tradition may have reached a stage of partial fixation long before the written Gospels were produced.[4] The conjectural character of this suggestion will render it improbable for some, but there is no evidence which makes it impossible. Eyewitnesses may well have considered it worth while to jot down reminiscences, especially of the sayings of Jesus, and these jottings would have proved invaluable when the Gospels came to be written. It is not impossible that some of Luke's predecessors may have used written notes. It may be so, but there is no means of being certain about this.

The real problem is to determine the degree in which oral tradition

[1] For a presentation of Jesus as Teacher, cf. W. A. Curtis' book *Jesus Christ the Teacher* (1943). He brings out the parallels between the teaching methods of Jesus and the methods of the Rabbis, but also shows the superiority of Jesus.

[2] For further discussion on this, see pp. 231 ff.

[3] *Memory and Manuscript* (1961), pp. 157 ff.

[4] Gerhardsson (*op. cit.*, p. 335) considers that the Evangelists 'worked on a basis of a fixed, distinct tradition from, and about, Jesus—a tradition which was partly memorized and partly written down in notebooks and private scrolls, but invariably isolated from the teachings of other doctrinal authorities'.

could account for the similarities in the Synoptic Gospels. It is almost an axiom of New Testament criticism that, at most, oral tradition could account for differences but not similarities.[1] But where can the justification for this point of view be found? It assumes that divergences must occur in oral transmission. But whereas full allowance must be made for such divergences, a study of the place of memory in ancient catechesis, especially Jewish, as outlined above, shows that a far greater measure of agreement might be achieved in oral tradition than is generally conceded. In fact the proportion of similarity was very much greater than the divergence and it is to be expected that the degree of accuracy was certainly no less, probably very much more than this, in Christian tradition.

In the final analysis, however, it is not the methods of transmission which are the determining factors in the Synoptic problem, but the proximity of the writers to the sources of those traditions. This leads to our next important consideration. Were the writers authors in the fullest sense of the word, or were they no more than editors or arrangers of a conglomerate of existing traditions, whether floating or fixed, oral or written?

c. The distinction between authorship and editorship in New Testament criticism

It would not be realistic to attempt to draw too fine a distinction between authorship and editorship, and yet some differentiation is essential if a true picture of the Synoptic literature is to be sketched. Theories which suppose a direct eyewitness account to be behind any of the Gospels (as for instance Mark's reliance on Peter's personal testimony) are here faced with no difficulty. In such cases it is proper to speak of an author rather than an editor. But is this to be regarded as an indication of what might be expected as a norm? There is strong corroborating evidence that this is so.

Luke's preface is invaluable for ascertaining the method used by

---

[1] Artificial methods of testing the processes of oral tradition such as the classroom experiments of Vincent Taylor, reported in his *Formation of the Gospel Tradition* (1935), pp. 202–209, must be rejected. To be valid the experiment would need to be conducted among students whose mental processes were thoroughly conditioned by oral transmission methods. The method was severely criticized by K. Grobel (*Formgeschichte und synoptische Quellenanalyse*, 1937, p. 111) who called it absurd because an academic atmosphere could not reproduce the right conditions for ancient oral transmission.

Gospel writers, although some reserve is necessary before concluding that all the Gospel writers necessarily followed a similar course. Compilation of written narratives was evidently common in Luke's time. It is equally evident that these writings were based on reports of eyewitnesses and ministers of the word. There seems to be little room here for the idea of an editor in the narrower sense of an arranger of tractates of disconnected narratives and sayings. Each writer would choose from eyewitness accounts material that was most relevant to his own particular purpose. But it is impossible to say what measure of agreement would have been achieved by Luke's many predecessors. It is at least a reasonable assumption that had these attempts remained extant they would have shown the same phenomena of similarities and divergences as are visible in our Synoptic Gospels. In other words, if two authors recorded the same incident from the same eyewitness (or group of eyewitnesses) a large measure of agreement would be expected, even in the verbal expressions of the narrative.

Luke seems to suggest that he is writing an independent account, for although he mentions the earlier attempts he does not say that he used them. In fact, as mentioned in discussing Luke's Gospel, he claims quite specifically to have made a thorough investigation himself on the same basis of reliable personal sources as his predecessors. Yet according to the generally assumed theory of Lucan origin, this search for authentic material on Luke's part was confined largely to his own peculiar material (L). There is, of course, no need to exclude from Luke's statement the use of written sources. It may be that among the predecessors to whom Luke refers was Mark, perhaps even Matthew. But the fact remains that Luke puts most emphasis upon his own careful investigations.

One question of great importance in this discussion is the meaning of ὑπηρέται τοῦ λόγου in Luke's preface. Did these 'ministers of the word' have any special function as tradition-bearers? Since Luke specifically states that these, together with eyewitnesses, delivered (παρέδοσαν) the material to him and to others, it is highly probable that this special function was not only recognized but was officially controlled. Such a factor can be regarded as only hypothetical, but it has strong probability on its side. It has been noted in connection with the position of elders, but has been allowed little part in considerations of the Synoptic problem. Form criticism has tended to over-emphasize the part played by the community, without giving sufficient attention to the possible part played by official 'tradition-bearers'. If the probability of these be admitted it is not difficult to imagine that the tradition would have been handed on in set forms which met with the approval of the apostolic circle. It is far more difficult to imagine that the transmission of the traditions of the life and teaching of our Lord would have been left to chance, to be hammered out in the experience of the early Church. Were no discussions held among the early Christian leaders to decide on the best method of spreading the news, and would not the content of the teaching have been of vital concern to them?

There is much to be said for the view that the 'eyewitnesses' and 'ministers of the word' in Luke i were the same group and that this group consisted mainly of apostles or apostolic men. If this is correct it means that the tradition was apostolically authenticated in its basic form, and would have become modified only if the apostles had re-laxed their careful surveillance, which they would surely not have done while they were capable of exerting any influence over it.

d. The value of simplification

In view of the variety of complicated source theories it is relevant to ask whether the Synoptic problem cannot be solved in a simpler manner. There is a tendency in scholastic circles to eschew simple solutions, but these may often be nearer the truth than proposals in-volving multiple sources. For instance, an appeal to an eyewitness account in discussing the origin of a Gospel narrative is clearly a simpler proposition than an appeal to underlying units of tradition preserved in the course of catechetical instruction in the community. The former introduces less 'unknowns' and is therefore definitely preferable. But is it an over-simplification?

It has already been shown that the older presentation of the oral theory was criticized because it was thought to leave unanswered too many phenomena in the Synoptic Gospels (see pp. 127 ff.). But the same charge may be made against source criticism and form criticism. The simple two source theory had become a conglomerate of many sources before it developed into a more specific four source theory, which in turn has never been quite convincing. Indeed most scholars would admit that no thoroughgoing source theory has yet been pro-duced which answers all the major problems in these Gospels. It is even more noticeable that form criticism has been obliged to resort to many questionable propositions in an endeavour to account for the variety of forms observed—and thus the initial urge towards greater simplicity becomes lost. At the same time it would be idle to expect a simple answer to a very complex problem. It may reasonably be assumed, however, that the simplest answer with the fewest 'unknowns' is probably nearer the truth than more complicated theories.

II. IMPORTANT FACTORS IN THE SEARCH FOR A SOLUTION

Owing to lack of sufficient data the Synoptic problem must very largely remain unsolved. Yet this does not mean that there can be no certainty anywhere in this field, for there are some propositions which, in spite of the variety of Gospel hypotheses, remain valid, and it is as well for these to be asserted even if the details of Gospel origins continue in a state of uncertainty.

1. The written Gospels were accepted at a very early period as authoritative. Their authority was inherent and not imposed upon them from without. Their claims to authenticity must, therefore, have been beyond dispute. By the first half of the second century they were so widely esteemed that heretical groups such as the Gnostics had taken them over and had even considered it worth while to produce commentaries upon them. But was there a period before the end of the first century when they were not regarded as authoritative? Since this is the twilight period of Christian development as far as our information is concerned, it is impossible to be dogmatic, but probability is against the notion of non-authoritative initial circulation. For if this had been the case, it would involve the assumption that at some stage in its primitive history each Gospel acquired an authority which it did not previously possess, and while this is not intrinsically impossible it is difficult to imagine how such a process could so soon have led to unanimity. It may be questioned, however, why the attempts of Luke's predecessors, who must have written at an early stage in Christian history, were not similarly accorded an authoritative position. The only possible answer to this question seems to be that these previous attempts evidently did not possess an inherent authority, however authentic their contents may have been. If Mark was included among Luke's predecessors, it would mean that the distinction between Mark and the rest was so obvious that no-one confused the issue. This may, of course, have been brought about by the known connection of Mark with Peter. But it is unprofitable to speculate further. All that is known for certain is that the Gospels now extant were alone regarded as

authoritative and that there is no evidence (except in the case of the Fourth Gospel among the small group known as the Alogi, see pp. 270 f.) that their authority was ever challenged.

2. The Gospels concern a unique Person and must therefore themselves be in some measure unique. Comparative studies in Jewish and Hellenistic oral and literary procedures may throw much valuable light upon the background of the Gospels but they cannot produce exact parallels, for the Gospels are essentially Christocentric and there are no parallels to this. The very uniqueness of Christ demands the possibility that the records of His life and teaching will possess unique characteristics. Some differences must therefore be anticipated between Synoptic criticism and general literary methods.[1] It is reasonable to suppose that the originality of our Lord's teaching and the originality of the influence of His actions upon His followers produced a unique situation for the germination of unique records of His life and teaching.[2] Had this not been so the Synoptic problem would never have arisen, for there must have been a unique regard for the records for three so similar and yet divergent records to have been retained with equal authority. Recognition of this uniqueness will promote caution in appealing too readily to non-Christian parallels. Too often Gospel criticism has begun from some point outside the phenomena of the Gospels themselves and the latter have been forced into a mould that they were never meant to fill. One of the major contributory factors in Bultmann's scepticism is a failure to recognize the literary uniqueness of the Gospels.

3. Arising directly out of the previous consideration is the fact that

[1] Many scholars maintain as a fundamental presupposition that the Gospels must be regarded on the same footing as any other books (cf. V. Taylor, *The Gospels*, p. 11; T. Henshaw, *New Testament Literature*, 1952, p. 63). But this presupposition may be strongly challenged on the grounds of the uniqueness of the subject-matter of the Gospels. At the same time their unique theme does not exempt them from all critical examination. It does mean, however, that what is valid for other writings may not necessarily be valid for these.

[2] H. G. Wood (*Jesus in the Twentieth Century*, 1960, p. 80), in emphasizing the uniqueness of the Gospels, drew attention to the lack of any exact parallels. Cf. also H. E. W. Turner, *Jesus, Master and Lord*[2] (1954), pp. 29 ff. There is no doubt that where this fact has been recognized, it has restrained the critic from many speculations based on doubtful parallels. Whatever may have been the custom in contemporary literary practice, it cannot be accepted *a priori* that a similar process must have taken place in the development of such unique documents as the Gospels.

the Gospel material formed the basis of Christian preaching and teaching and was not the consequence of those Christian activities. The *Sitz im Leben* school of thought has tended to reverse this procedure. But the early missionaries must have possessed certain Christian traditions which were agreed upon and which they were able to impart to others. Indeed few scholars would deny this, although there are wide differences over the extent of the authentic traditions. It is not enough to claim that each preacher and teacher exercised a charismatic ministry and that catechetical material was spontaneously passed on. This was undoubtedly true in the application of the Christian message, but is it necessary to suppose that every one who proclaimed the facts of Christ's life and teaching relied wholly on independent charismatic prompting? Our Lord promised such prompting when His disciples were confronted with magisterial inquisitors, but this cannot be regarded as a normal procedure whenever and in whatever circumstances the disciples might be placed. Nor can it have any direct relation to the transmission of the authentic Gospel material.

It seems most natural to assume that the Christian traditions were transmitted because they were believed to be authentic and were most probably regarded as authentic in the form in which they were transmitted. This means that the 'forms' were essential parts of the tradition and were not, as some form-critics have maintained, the productions of the community. Whatever part the community played in the process of transmission, it is inconceivable that the community created either the sayings of Jesus or the narratives about Him. The Christian communities were groups of people who had 'received' Christian traditions, and had believed them to be true and on the basis of them had made personal committal of themselves to Christ.[1] No other explanation can make early Christian development intelligible. The future of form criticism will largely depend on the degree to which this fact is recognized.

4. The final consideration is the impossibility of explaining the origins of the Gospels apart from the activity of the Holy Spirit. This consideration rarely finds a place in discussions on the Synoptic pro-

---

[1] S. H. Hooke (*Alpha and Omega*, 1961, p. 137) points out that behind all textual criticism, source criticism and form criticism lies the fact that the Gospels were the products of minds dedicated to making known the pattern of redemption. He agrees with Austin Farrer's strictures against theories which make the authors 'colourless disciples'.

blem, because it is thought to belong to dogmatics rather than to historical criticism. But in this case no divorce can be allowed, for the operation of the Spirit in Gospel origins is a vital factor, indeed *the* vital factor, in the historical situation. The clear promise of Jesus that the Spirit would teach the disciples all things and bring to their remembrance all that He had said to them (Jn. xiv. 26) cannot be dismissed simply because it does not fit into the normal categories of literary criticism. Whatever view is adopted regarding John's Gospel, it cannot be denied that this is testimony that the immediate disciples of Jesus were to receive special help of the Spirit in recalling what Jesus had said and that this help was directly promised by Jesus Himself. The only alternative would be to suppose that the Johannine account was an attempt to justify the self-claims of the disciples, but this would make unintelligible the teaching about the Spirit found elsewhere in the New Testament.

In the light of our Lord's promise certain propositions may be made which have a direct bearing on the Synoptic problem. It may first be asserted that the Holy Spirit controlled the traditions. However transmission was made during the preliterary period, it cannot be supposed that the Holy Spirit would leave this to chance procedures. The tradition-bearers were men of the Spirit, sensitive to the promptings of the Spirit and anxious to maintain the honour of Christ in accordance with the purpose of the Spirit (Jn. xv. 26, xvi. 13, 14). The Gospel writers come under the same category. Literary and historical criticism may throw light on the external circumstances and conditions of the oral period, but cannot pronounce upon the psychological and spiritual factors which led to the preservation of the Gospel traditions during this period.

The next proposition affects the selective processes of the separate authors. If the Spirit aided memory it is inconceivable that He did not also control selection. There were clearly more traditions than could be incorporated, as John xx. 30, xxi. 25 show. There was need therefore for the authors to select, whether from eyewitness oral accounts or written sources or perhaps their own personal observations. In this they would have submitted themselves as fully to the guidance of the Spirit as in the collection of the data. This view need not exclude the personal contribution of each. Matthew's Gospel, for example, was clearly written by a man whose mind was deeply impressed by the royal dignity of Jesus and by His fulfilment of Old Testament prophecy.

This was one of the controlling principles in his selection and arrangement of material. Yet it was mediated to him through the Spirit. The different emphases of the four Evangelists resulting in different methods of presentation may be more adequately explained by the controlling influence of the same Spirit than by the natural theological bent of the individual authors. Whatever the psychological motives which prompted each author to write, the evident spiritual power and general harmony of their presentations is unaccountable apart from the acceptance of a more than normal intuition. Whereas such a conception does not rule out the source hypotheses for Gospel origins, it is one of the fundamental weaknesses of all thoroughgoing source criticism that little room is left for the dynamic operation of the Spirit of God in the final writers of the canonical Gospels. It invariably leads to too mechanical and rigid an interpretation of the psychology of Gospel authorship. It tends to tie down the authors so closely to their sources that it becomes a matter of great importance to postulate why they modify them as they do. Yet very often no satisfactory answers can be given and the barrenness of much thoroughgoing source criticism bears witness to a lack of fluidity in the fundamental premises. A more moderate approach to source criticism, in which the author is allowed more freedom to draw where necessary from oral traditions, is more in keeping with the New Testament conception of the early Christians as men of the Spirit.

It is furthermore difficult to envisage a Spirit-controlled development of unitary literary forms as posited by form criticism, for it is a tacit assumption of that method that various church conditions have been the dominant factors in the shaping of the material. It would be nearer the truth to maintain that the Gospel material was found to be ideally suited to the needs of the communities because of the sovereign direction of the Spirit in the selection of the material. Or, on the other hand, the Spirit may have used the interaction between the oral tradition and the Church's needs as the controlling factor. It is unimportant so long as it is recognized that the Gospels were the result, not of editorial ingenuity in creating a continuous narrative out of a mass of disconnected units, but of a purposive selective process in keeping with the Spirit's control. The Gospel writers were men of the Spirit whose purpose was to produce documents which would be spiritually useful in the ministry of the Church, and any theory of origins must accord with this fact.

III. A TENTATIVE THEORY OF ORIGINS

In the light of the considerations just enumerated, a tentative hypothesis may be proposed, taking into account all that may be regarded as solid contributions of New Testament scholarship.

Stage 1. The apostolic preachers gave most prominence to the passion material, but they could not present this narrative in isolation. Hence Peter in his preaching gave connected accounts of the events of Jesus (cf. his discourse recorded in Acts x. 39 ff.) and this may well have been the standard pattern.

Stage 2. At the same time catechetical instruction was being given to the new converts and this would most certainly have required some careful arrangements. The major content of the catechesis would most probably have been the sayings of Jesus, especially chosen under the guidance of the Spirit to meet the needs of the communities. Such catechesis may have been entirely in oral form, or entirely written (Q?), or a mixture of both. The latter suggestion has much to commend it and, if valid, may lead us to suppose that certain tracts were officially produced to assist the catechetical teachers. The methods used by the early Church in this process are unfortunately impossible to ascertain. It is possible that this early catechesis was closely connected with Matthew and that it existed in its earliest form in Aramaic.

Stage 3. Mark, who had had close contact with Peter and had many times heard Peter preach, reduced the content of Peter's preaching to writing. The result was a Gospel with more action than discourse. It is not impossible to suppose that Mark made notes in the course of his association with Peter and later used these when writing his Gospel. If the external tradition is correct, Mark and Peter were together at Rome and after Peter's departure Mark wrote down his recollections.

Stage 4. After the production of Mark's Gospel, probably at Rome, Matthew may have come into possession of a copy of it and have been led to expand it by the addition of a considerable amount of teaching material from the catechesis and other material, some of which was drawn from personal reminiscences. Much of the sayings material was preserved in discourses and these were utilized by Matthew to dovetail the teaching material into Mark's framework.

Stage 5. Luke, who was personally acquainted with Mark, conceived a plan to write a careful account of the course of events from the beginning (i.e. from the advent of Jesus). He studied all the material he could lay his hands upon and all the reports given to him orally by eye-witnesses. He appears to have had a copy of Mark, although he may not have come into possession of this until after making an initial draft consisting of teaching material plus much narrative material (if some form of Proto-Luke theory is valid). The bulk of the teaching material was transmitted to him through catechesis, picked up mainly when Luke was at Caesarea, where he probably stayed for some time. He may have had access to some written tracts. He may even have had a copy of Matthew. It is impossible to be certain. But if he did use Matthew he supplemented Matthew from the oral tradition which by this time was well fixed. The catechesis to which Luke had access tended to preserve shorter discourses of Jesus than those preserved in Matthew. This may account for the differences between the arrangement of the sayings material in Matthew and Luke. On the whole it would seem easier to account for the peculiarities of each if Luke did not use Matthew as a source, but if both drew independently from the catechesis material.

Stage 6. It is probable that at first the tendency was for churches to use one only of the three Gospels as authoritative, because all would not necessarily circulate in the same areas. How long an interval elapsed before all three became widely known cannot now be ascertained, but the interchange which took place over Paul's Epistles would lead us to expect a similar process over the Gospels. Ease of communication in the ancient world would greatly facilitate this. But why were all three preserved? Variations of emphasis and content were evidently no barrier to the eventual acceptance of the three. Were the early Christians unaware of the problems, or did they consider that these were insignificant when set over against the immeasurable advantage of having a multiple witness to the life and teaching of Jesus? Here again it must not be forgotten that they were men of the Spirit who would recognize at once those literary productions which were authentically Spirit-directed, in which case the variations in the narratives would themselves be regarded as a part of the revelatory character of the records.

Through these various stages the Synoptic Gospels may have reached the forms in which we now know them. But the tentative character of these suggestions must not be lost sight of, for in the ultimate analysis our data are insufficient to lead to definite conclusions. We are dealing at best with probabilities. We cannot be certain, but we can affirm the powerful influence that these Gospels exerted at an early stage in their history. If the last word has not yet been said about their origins, their importance throughout Christian history cannot be disputed.

ADDITIONAL NOTE

223. [3] W. D. Davies has added an appendix to his book *The Setting of the Sermon on the Mount* (1964), in which he criticizes Gerhardsson (Appendix XV). The latter has defended himself against his various critics in *Tradition and Transmission in Early Christianity* (1964). Although it is generally thought that Gerhardsson has claimed too much, there is no doubt that his studies have been valuable in focusing attention on Jewish methods of oral transmission. Cf. also W. D. Davies' remarks in his article 'Reflexions on Tradition: The Aboth revisited', in *Christian History and Interpretation* (edited W. R. Farmer, C. F. D. Moule and R. R. Niebuhr, 1967, pp. 127–159); E. P. Sanders, *The Tendencies of the Synoptic Tradition* (1969), pp. 26 ff.

CHAPTER EIGHT

JOHN'S GOSPEL

It is obvious to the most casual reader that John has features which are strikingly different from the Synoptic Gospels. The problems which this creates will be considered later, but for the present it will be valuable to mention some of the dominating characteristics of this Gospel.

I. CHARACTERISTICS

a. The place of the Old Testament

So much emphasis has been placed on Hellenistic influences on John's Gospel (see later discussion, pp. 277 f., 321 f.) that the part played by Old Testament ideas has not always been fully realized. There is much which bears on Jewish history. The Gospel shows that Jesus was a part of that history, and that the Jews, in rejecting Christ, were rejecting One who belonged to them (cf. Jn. i. 11). When He came to the temple He claimed a rightful authority over it (Jn. ii. 16). The Jewish leader Nicodemus recognized Jesus' authority as a teacher (iii. 2), while Jesus classed Himself among the Jews as possessing the secret of salvation (iv. 22).

It is against this background that our Lord's own appeal to Scripture in this Gospel must be measured. He charged His hearers with searching Scripture and yet not recognizing that it testified to Him (v. 39). Moreover, He maintained that those who believed Moses would believe Him (v. 45 f.), implying that there was a clear continuity between them. The Old Testament colouring in the bread discourse is unmistakable, with its allusions to the manna in the wilderness (vi). When referring to the coming of the Spirit (vii. 38), Jesus appeals again to Scripture, even though the precise passage in mind cannot be identified with certainty. Old Testament shepherd-imagery lay behind the discourse on the shepherd and sheep in chapter x. As in Matthew the entry into Jerusalem on an ass is viewed as a fulfilment of Old Testament prophecy (xii. 14), while the unbelief of the Jews is illustrated from Isaiah (xii. 38, 39). John alone records that at the crucifixion Jesus' legs were not broken, as a fulfilment of Scripture, and in this case the inviolability of Scripture is particularly stressed (xix. 36).

In addition, Jesus several times refers to Old Testament figures, particularly Abraham. Appeal to Abrahamic descent forms the theme of the dialogue in chapter viii, reaching its climax in the claim that Abraham saw Christ's day (viii. 56). Nothing could express more clearly that there was a direct continuity between the Old and the New. Another link with the patriarchal age is found in the vision of Jacob cited by Jesus to Nathanael as being fulfilled in the Son of man (i. 50, 51). Jesus, speaking to Nicodemus, makes a comparison between a typical act of Moses and its counterpart in the Son of man, thus expressing His death in Old Testament terminology (iii. 14, 15). Jesus, moreover, claims the support of Moses in His approach to the sabbath (vii. 22). The prophet Isaiah is said to have seen the glory of Christ (xii. 41). The same prophet predicted the forerunner (i. 23), a fact mentioned in all the Gospels.

It is significant that Jesus appealed to the Scriptures on occasions when dealing with opponents, as in x. 34 where He brings out an interpretation which is regarded as authoritative. It will be seen, therefore, that both our Lord's use of the Old Testament and the Evangelist's own comments assume that all Scripture points to Christ. He is the fulfilment of the Old, and this fact must guide us in interpreting the concepts of the Gospel.

b. Teaching on the Spirit

There is more of our Lord's teaching about the Spirit in this Gospel than in any other.

In the Nicodemus discourse, the work of the Spirit in regeneration is clearly brought out (Jn. iii). A distinction is made between natural and spiritual birth which focuses attention on one of the major antitheses of this Gospel. Our Lord's teaching is frequently misunderstood because its spiritual character has not been apprehended. It is as impossible to predict the operation of the Spirit as that of the wind (Jn. iii. 8), which leads Jesus to point out that heavenly things need a different method of apprehension from earthly things. The mission of Jesus must be spiritually interpreted.

In harmony with this is our Lord's insistence on the spiritual nature of God (iv. 24), which requires therefore a spiritual method of worship. This was a definite advance on the limited conception of Judaism which itself had nobler notions than its pagan contemporaries. The Spirit of God was promised after the glorification of Jesus (vii. 39), when He would come as streams of refreshing water on those who believe in Christ.

It is in the farewell discourses (xiv–xvi) that the fullest exposition of the Spirit's work is found. His names, Paraclete and Spirit of truth, reveal His character, the former meaning Counsellor or Advocate or Comforter.[1] xiv. 16, 17 shows Him as representative of Christ indwelling the believer. In xiv. 26, Jesus assures the disciples that the Holy Spirit will teach all things, recalling to their minds what Jesus had said. He will be a witness to Christ, which is to be His main function (xv. 26, xvi. 14). He it is who will convince the world of sin, righteousness and judgment (xvi. 8–11), and who will guide His own people into all the truth (xvi. 13). It is evident that on the eve of His death Jesus' thoughts were much concentrated on the Spirit's work, but John's Gospel alone focuses attention upon this.

c. Prevalence of great themes

Unlike the teaching in the Synoptic Gospels the teaching in John tends to present abstract themes such as light, life, love, truth, abiding, which recur at intervals throughout the book. Some of these occur first in the Prologue (i. 1–18), which may be regarded as introductory to the whole, giving some indication of the type of themes to be presented in the following discourses. For instance i. 4 states that in Him was life and the life was the light of men. This verse combines two themes which find several later echoes. Christ came to give eternal life (iii. 15, 16, 36, vi. 47, 54, xvii. 2). Indeed, He describes Himself as the 'bread of life' (vi. 35), offers water which wells up to eternal life (iv. 14), declares His purpose is to confer abundant life on others (x. 10), to mention only a few of the references to life in this Gospel. It is not surprising to find the theme often recurring, in view of the Evangelist's expressly stated purpose in xx. 31, i.e. that his readers might believe and have life. Similarly the idea of light recurs in viii. 12 where another of Jesus' great 'I am' statements is found, reiterated again in ix. 5 and illustrated in the subsequent healing of the blind man. But there are many other echoes of the light theme (see, for example, iii. 19 ff., v. 35, xi. 9, xii. 46).

The theme of love is no less dominant, although most pronounced in the farewell discourses. The Father's love of the Son is often stressed

[1] Cf. S. Mowinckel, *ZNTW*, 32 (1933), pp. 97–130, for a full discussion of this.

(cf. iii. 35, v. 20, x. 17), as is also His love towards men (iii. 16, xiv. 23, xvi. 27). In fact the whole mission of Jesus has its basis in the love of God. In the concluding chapter love forms the key to Peter's reconciliation. While the theme occurs in the Synoptics it is nowhere so clearly expressed as here.

It is unnecessary to cite further instances to illustrate the characteristic recurrence of these abstract themes.

d. The comparative lack of movement

It has often been noted that John's record tends to be static, although this is largely due to the amount of discourse material. The proportion of narrative to discourse is much less in this Gospel than in the Synoptic Gospels. Nevertheless movement is not entirely absent. In i. 19–ii. 11 a whole week's events seem to be in mind, and several journeys are mentioned (e.g. ii. 12, iii. 22, iv. 3 f., 43 f., v. 1, vi. 1, vii. 1, x. 40). At the same time the Evangelist is not primarily interested in movements, nor for that matter in events, at least, not for their own sake. He concentrated on their significance. Thus in chapter iii Nicodemus fades out, and in the bread discourse the audience seems to alternate between the disciples and the hostile Jews. This characteristic of John's Gospel emphasizes the weakness of attempting to regard the book as in any sense biographical. The same is true, of course, of the Synoptics, but not to the same extent as here. This absorbing interest in discourse material has, in fact, given a particular colouring to the Gospel as a whole. It is reflective in mood.

e. The portrait of Jesus

Since the problems raised by the Johannine portrait of Jesus will be discussed later, it will be necessary here only to give an account of the positive emphasis made by John. The title Son of man is more sparingly found than in the Synoptics, although where it does occur it is significant (cf. for instance, i. 51, iii. 13, 14). More often the title Son of God is used, or else the unqualified 'Son'. There is much stress on the filial relationship of Jesus to God and its significance for His relationship to believers.

Nevertheless, the humanity of Jesus is not lacking and is in fact brought out with almost greater clarity than in the Synoptics. The wedding at Cana shows Jesus in an essentially domestic scene and in fact in a domestic capacity. At the well at Sychar He is seen as tired and thirsty. At the grave of Lazarus He is deeply moved and then weeps. In the upper room He washes the disciples' feet, and on the cross He thirsts.

More of the inner consciousness of Jesus is revealed in this Gospel than in the others and this reaches its climax in xvii where He prays aloud. It is this special characteristic of the portrait which is deeply impressive and which makes the reader realize that the Person of Christ is beyond comprehension in its depth.

It is easier to trace the messianic idea in this Gospel. Right at its commencement Christ's messianic office is recognized by some of His disciples (i. 41). Moreover, at an early stage it is also recognized by the Samaritan woman following a direct claim to this effect by Jesus Himself. This differs from the Synoptic Gospels and has been considered a contradiction (see later discussion). But John clearly brings out our Lord's willingness to admit His messianic office to a Samaritan, although He may well have hesitated to do so to the Jews because of their erroneous ideas about the function of the coming Messiah. It is significant that in John alone is it recorded that the multitude which Jesus had fed desired to make Him king (vi. 15), but Jesus at once thwarted this intention.

Perhaps the most characteristic feature in John's Gospel regarding the Person of Christ is the Logos doctrine which serves as an introduction to this Gospel. Whatever the background of the Prologue (see later discussion), it is evident that the Jesus to be presented in the body of the Gospel is first portrayed not only as pre-existent but as possessing the nature of God Himself.

II. AUTHORSHIP

The problem of the authorship of this Gospel has been so widely and so thoroughly discussed that it is not easy to express with any conciseness all the ramifications of the different hypotheses which have been proposed.[1] Moreover it is difficult to approach the problem without preconceptions. In the following summary the evidence from within the Gospel will be considered first, as it is recognized that this may be an important factor in examining the external evidence.

[1] The recent literature on this and kindred Johannine critical problems is summarized by E. Haenchen (TR, n.f., 23, 1955, pp. 295–335), who discusses the position since 1929.

a. Personal allusions in the Gospel

Nowhere in the Gospel does the author state his name, and yet he has not left his work without any traces of his own hand. These must be carefully considered and assessed in the light of the author's obvious desire to obscure his own identity as much as possible.

(i) *Self-indications in the Gospel.* In the Prologue of the Gospel the author states 'We beheld his glory' (i. 14), and it is natural to suppose that this is an indication of eyewitnesses among whom the author is himself included. This interpretation is confirmed by 1 John i. 1–4 where the first person plural performs a similar function. Some have interpreted the 'we' of the Epistle as referring to Christians generally,[1] but the statement in the Gospel would lose much of its point unless understood as an eyewitness claim. The author is not merely asserting that the Word became flesh in a general sense, but that in a particular sense the Word dwelt among us (ἐν ἡμῖν). While it is no doubt possible to regard ἐν ἡμῖν as referring to humanity in general, the subsequent verb (ἐθεασάμεθα) must clearly be restricted to Christians. Moreover the New Testament use of this verb suggests that the 'seeing' is physical and not spiritual sight,[2] in spite of the fact that many have interpreted it in the latter sense.[3]

Whatever conclusion is reached regarding the meaning of the word 'glory', which is here said to be the content of what was seen, it seems most reasonable to suppose that the author intended his readers to

---

[1] See the discussion of this interpretation on pp. 865 f. It is maintained by C. H. Dodd, *The Johannine Epistles* (1946), p. 12.

[2] Cf. the discussion of J. H. Bernard, *Gospel according to St. John*, 1 (1928), pp. 19 ff.

[3] C. K. Barrett (*The Gospel according to St. John*, 1956, p. 138) states categorically that it is not an eyewitness but the apostolic Church which speaks in Jn. i. 14, but his reason for excluding apostolic witnesses is that he had already concluded that the author was not an apostle (cf. p. 119). Whereas it is not impossible to interpret Jn. i. 14 in this way, it involves an assumption—i.e. that the author speaks on behalf of the apostolic Church. It would have had considerably more point, however, if the spokesman had been an eyewitness. W. G. Kümmel (*INT*, 1965, p. 164) agrees with Barrett here. Bultmann (*Das Evangelium des Johannes*,[11] 1950, pp. 45 f.) steers between the bare alternative of an historical or spiritual interpretation, although he interprets i. 14 in the light of i. 16 as the 'sight' of faith. He admits that such 'sight' must be connected, however, with the event (ὁ λόγος σὰρξ ἐγένετο) as well as its consequences (δόξα).

understand that the facts of the Gospel could be authenticated by visual witnesses and that some at least had been seen by himself.

Another passage which bears directly on the question of authorship is xix. 35 where the words occur, 'He who saw it has borne witness— his testimony is true, and he (ἐκεῖνος) knows that he tells the truth' (RSV). The immediate context is the piercing of our Lord's side and the initial reference must be to this. But since in the next verse the plural ταῦτα is used, the reference may be intended to indicate the whole content of our Lord's ministry of which this special phenomenon accompanying His death was the climax (cf. the use of ταῦτα in xxi. 24, which is discussed below). The problem here is whether the writer is referring to himself or to someone else bearing witness. If he does not intend his readers to understand himself as an eyewitness, the statement must have been added to make clear that the source of the narrative was an eyewitness. The ἐκεῖνος is somewhat ambiguous, for this could refer to the witness distinct from the author, the witness identified with the author, or to God as the witness's Authenticator. The third suggestion is least probable since the context contains no hint that ἐκεῖνος is to be understood as referring to God. The other two suggestions are equally possible, although some scholars maintain that it is less natural for the author to use ἐκεῖνος of himself than for another to use it of him and they consequently prefer the first interpretation. On the other hand the elusive character of the statement is more probable if the witness is the author than if he is another person, for in that case the testimony would have been more weighty if the author had named his source. But the matter cannot be pressed. It is sufficient to note that the author may be making a reference to himself as an eyewitness, although this is perhaps not conclusive.

The remaining passage is xxi. 24, 25, although this is more problematic because of the dispute whether these words are the author's own work or are editorial. At the same time there is no evidence that this statement was not an original part of the Gospel and it must therefore be regarded as a valuable witness on the matter of authorship. Verse 24 states, 'This is the disciple who is bearing witness to these things, and who has written these things; and we know that his testimony is true' (RSV). It is most natural to interpret the οὗτος of the subject of the preceding statement, i.e. the beloved disciple who leaned on Jesus' breast (verse 20). If this is correct the statement appears to assert that this disciple was not only the witness but also the author. Some have avoided this conclusion by stressing that the witnessing is mentioned before the writing and was, therefore, considered to be of greater importance and may indicate that the author of the appendix was not sure about the authorship.[1] But the order of verbs is perfectly natural to express the idea of a writing based on personal testimony, since the testimony existed before the writing. It may be possible to maintain that the 'writing' could have been done through another as no doubt happened when, as John records, Pilate 'wrote' the superscription over the cross (xix. 19–22). But this is a strained interpretation, for since μαρτυρῶν can be understood only of personal witness it is most natural to suppose that γράψας should be taken in the same way. If, then, this verse claims that the beloved disciple was the author,[2] what has led to so many alternative interpretations? The fact is that advocates of theories of authorship which deny an eyewitness author treat the clear testimony of this verse as a redactional device. C. K. Barrett[3] considers that those who published the Gospel modelled this statement on xix. 35 and claimed for it by this means the authority of the beloved disciple.[4] Although Barrett considers that this was done in all good faith, it is an unsatisfactory method of dealing with internal evidence. By such a method any embarrassing evidence can be disposed of. Unless there are convincing grounds for maintaining a contrary opinion (and they are yet to be produced) the words of verse 24 must be taken with full seriousness as an indication of an author who claims to be an eyewitness.[5]

[1] A view mentioned by Redlich (*Form Criticism*, 1939, p. 43).

[2] C. H. Dodd (*Historical Tradition in the Fourth Gospel*, p. 12, and *JTS*, n.s., IV, 1953, pp. 212, 213) understands ταῦτα in xxi. 24 as a reference to the preceding *pericope*, or at most to the whole appendix only, and he therefore disputes this verse as evidence for the authorship of the whole Gospel.

[3] *Op. cit.*, p. 489.

[4] Cf. also A. Harnack (*Die Chronologie der altchristlichen Literatur bis Eusebius.* 1897, pp. 678 ff.), who maintained that this Gospel was attributed to John the apostle by a legend purposely set on foot. But cf. W. Sanday's criticisms, *The Criticism of the Fourth Gospel* (1905), pp. 63 ff.

[5] It should be noted that if these verses are regarded as an appendage made by someone belonging to the apostle's own circle they would still be a very early testimony to apostolic authorship (cf. Meinertz, *Einleitung*, p. 232, on Jn. xxi. 25; Tasker, *The Gospel according to St. John*, TNT, 1960, pp. 13 f.).

In addition to the specific statements made in the Gospel it is necessary to take account of the general impression of the whole. As A. C. Headlam (*The Fourth Gospel as History*, 1948, p. 44) pointed out, the Gospel demands as its author one who had a close intimacy with Jesus. Cf. also Sir F. Kenyon, *The Bible and Modern Scholarship* (1948), pp. 24, 25.

(ii) *The problem of the 'beloved disciple'*. The expression 'the disciple whom Jesus loved' has just been considered in the context of the Appendix (xxi) where it was shown that xxi. 24 seems intended to identify this disciple as the author of the Gospel. His name is not given, but he was among the group mentioned in xxi. 2, comprising Peter, Thomas, Nathanael, the sons of Zebedee and two others. The 'beloved disciple' who is unnamed must be among the last four. Other details concerning him, recorded in chapter xxi, are firstly, that he leaned on Jesus' breast at the last supper and asked about the betrayer, and secondly, that he appears to have had close association with Peter. Both facts are closely linked in xiii. 23, 24, the first occasion on which this disciple is so described. The echo of xiii. 23 f. in xxi shows how vividly the writer recalls the incident, which is most intelligible if the writer was himself that beloved disciple.[1]

It is significant that when earlier in chapter xxi 'the beloved disciple' is introduced he addresses himself to Simon Peter (verse 7) and announces the presence of the Lord. He was evidently in close contact with Peter. These two are found in each other's company by Mary Magdalene when she rushes to tell them of the disappearance of the body of Jesus (xx. 2). Moreover, the writer mentions that the beloved disciple when he saw the empty tomb believed (xx. 8), which is again highly intelligible if the author were that disciple, who would not easily forget the precise moment when faith took possession of him. Such a detail might, of course, have been passed on by the beloved disciple to the author, but the narrative is so natural that the former interpretation is preferable.

The remaining reference to the beloved disciple is in the account of the crucifixion, where Jesus commends His mother to the care of this disciple, who at once took her to his own home (xix. 26). This is the only occasion when he is mentioned apart from Peter.

It is reasonable to suppose, therefore, that the beloved disciple was an associate of Peter and that there was a particular reason for his being introduced in this oblique way in the passion narratives and not in the earlier part of the Gospel. The obvious choice in fulfilment of the former of these conditions is John, son of Zebedee. He and Peter belonged to the inner circle of disciples and were present, together with

[1] Michaelis (*Einleitung*, pp. 98 f.) argues firmly for the identification of the beloved disciple with John the son of Zebedee, particularly on the strength of the evidence of xxi. 2.

James, on three occasions when the others were absent (cf. Mk. v. 37, ix. 2, xiv. 33). Moreover, Peter and John were selected by Jesus to prepare the Passover for Himself and His disciples (Lk. xxii. 8). They were still closely associated together after the resurrection, as Acts iii. 1, 11, iv. 13 show. They are mentioned together again in Acts viii. 14 as delegates sent from Jerusalem to Samaria. The same association is found in Paul's reference to the 'pillar apostles', James, Cephas and John (Gal. ii. 9). All this evidence suggests a strong probability that the 'beloved disciple' was intended to describe the son of Zebedee.[1] This supposition is strengthened by the fact that nowhere in the Gospel is the apostle John mentioned by name, although he is mentioned twenty times (including parallels) in the Synoptic Gospels. Moreover, John the Baptist is described as 'John' without further qualification, which strongly suggests that the writer intended the apostle John to be understood under another title. It cannot be denied that absence of specific reference to him creates a definite predisposition towards Johannine authorship and any alternative views must reckon with this peculiarity and provide an adequate explanation.

Yet some consideration must be given to the delayed appearance of the 'beloved disciple' in the Gospel narrative. Why does he not appear until the events in the upper room? When Matthew's references to John are examined it is found that John comes into the story only in the narrative of his call, in the names of the Twelve and in the transfiguration account. In Mark he is also mentioned as being in the house when Peter's mother-in-law was healed (i. 29), as being taken with Peter and James into Jairus' house (v. 37), as reporting to Jesus his well-intentioned but officious action in forbidding an exorcist who was casting out demons in Jesus' name (ix. 38), as requesting the place of honour in the kingdom with James (x. 35 ff.), as being among the small group of disciples who asked for a sign (xiii. 3 f.), and as being with Jesus in the Garden of Gethsemane (xiv. 32 f.). On the whole Mark's picture does not flatter John. Nor in fact does Luke's, for he has only two references not in the other Synoptics, his part in the preparation of the Passover

---

[1] It is significant that this identification was assumed without question by patristic writers, who regarded the apostle John as the author of the Gospel (cf. M. F. Wiles, *The Spiritual Gospel*, 1960, pp. 9 f.). This writer notes that Origen and Chrysostom regarded the description 'the beloved disciple' as furnishing the key to the purpose of the Gospel. The author's own exalted position tallies with the exalted character of the Gospel.

(Matthew refers vaguely to 'disciples', Mark to 'two of the disciples', but Luke alone names them), and his desire with James to call down heavenly fire on an unreceptive Samaritan village. Supposing John to have been the beloved disciple and the writer of the Gospel, which of these Synoptic incidents would we have expected him to relate? Those which illustrated his fiery nature? Since the stories of his weakness were no doubt already well known and his triumph over these weaknesses was abundantly manifest in his life, he would reserve his personal appearances in his own story of Jesus for those hours during which he had learned in a special measure to draw closer to the heart and mind of Jesus than others had done.

But a problem arises at this juncture. Is it conceivable that any man would have described himself as 'the disciple whom Jesus loved'? Some scholars are so convinced that such a process is highly improbable that they feel obliged, in spite of the strength of the evidence just quoted, either to find some other identification for the beloved disciple, or to draw a distinction between that disciple and the writer of the Gospel.[1]

The difficulty must be admitted, but is it entirely improbable for John to have called himself the disciple ὃν ἠγάπα ὁ Ἰησοῦς?[2] If the phrase means any preferential love on Jesus' part towards this disciple it would certainly be difficult to conceive. Yet John, as his First Epistle shows,[3] had grasped something of the significance of God's love in Christ and the phrase may have sprung out of his wonder that Jesus should fasten His love upon him. It must not be overlooked that it would be almost as difficult for someone else to single out one of the

[1] R. H. Strachan (*The Fourth Evangelist, Dramatist or Historian?*, 1925), who fully accepted the identification of the beloved disciple as John, son of Zebedee, considered that the Evangelist was one of John's closest disciples who had imbibed so much of his leader's spiritual experience that it had become his own. According to this theory the Evangelist called upon his dramatic imagination for the eyewitness touches, in which case these touches would give no support to apostolic authorship. Even the Evangelist's picture of the beloved disciple was considered to be idealized (cf. *op. cit.*, pp. 49 ff., 73 ff.). Yet the unpretentious manner in which the beloved disciple is introduced does not at once suggest any desire for dramatic effect. If this is dramatic skill, it is so superbly executed as to be almost completely unselfconscious.

[2] The phrase is identical in xiii. 23, xix. 26, xxi. 7, 20, but in xx. 2 the verb ἐφίλει is substituted for ἠγάπα.

[3] The verb ἀγαπάω occurs twenty-one times in 1 John alone, more times than any other New Testament book except John's Gospel.

disciples as the special object of Jesus' love as for the beloved disciple himself. It might, of course, be that this was the familiar description of the aged apostle in Asia, in which case the original readers would at once identify him and would not misunderstand the motives for its use. Far from being an evidence of arrogance, as is so often suggested, it may perhaps be regarded as a sign of modesty. John will not mention his name but will rather draw attention to what he owes to the love of Jesus.

Nevertheless, those who deny the identity of the beloved disciple with the apostle John claim to avoid this difficulty by suggesting a different identity. The rich young ruler has been suggested because Mark x. 21 states that Jesus, looking upon him, loved him. But since we do not even know whether this man became a believer the suggestion is precarious. Another suggestion is Nathanael, but this, in the nature of the case, is conjectural since we know so little about him and in any case he is named in John xxi in such a way as to suggest that he is distinct from the beloved disciple. A more widely held theory is that the disciple was Lazarus and there is rather more to be said for this.[1] He first appears after Lazarus is introduced into the narrative in chapters xi and xii. Moreover in xi. 3 Lazarus is described by his sisters as 'he whom you love' (RSV; ὃν φιλεῖς). The suggestion is interesting, but was Lazarus in the upper room, and would he especially have reclined on Jesus' breast? It is highly improbable. The Synoptic Gospels, at any rate, make it clear that only the apostles were with Jesus on the Passover night. But if the possibility be admitted it would still be necessary to explain why Lazarus is mentioned by name in xi and xii and then by a descriptive phrase in xiii ff., a difficulty which is obviated if the beloved disciple remains anonymous throughout.

Yet another interpretation of the beloved disciple is to regard him as an ideal figure.[2] His anonymity is then interpreted as indicating that

[1] For a recent advocacy of this view, cf. J. N. Sanders' article 'Who was the disciple whom Jesus loved?' in *Studies in the Fourth Gospel* (ed. F. L. Cross, 1957), pp. 72–82. Cf. also F. V. Filson's article in *JBL*, LXVIII (1949), pp. 83–88, and his exposition of the same view in his article on John in *Current Issues in New Testament Interpretation* (ed. W. Klassen and G. F. Snyder, 1962), pp. 111–123, in which he argues that this view best fits into the theme of life, which is so dominant in the Gospel. Another suggestion, Matthias, is proposed by E. L. Titus, *JBL*, LXIX (1950), pp. 323–328, based on the symbolism of Judas as a type of the Jews being replaced by a man who was a representative Christian, but the connection of Acts i with John's Gospel is not at all apparent.*

[2] Cf. A. Correll's *Consummatum Est* (1958), pp. 204 ff.

the Gospel is not the work of a single individual but of the Church. The presentation of the life and teaching of Jesus becomes in this view the Church's own testimony to itself and to its Lord.[1] But this is a most unsatisfactory interpretation because it involves treating the beloved disciple as unhistorical in spite of the contrary impression in the narrative, and because it assumes that any community could create such an idealization to represent its collective experience of Jesus. Yet the almost incidental allusions to the beloved disciple in the Gospel do not read like symbolic allusions. It is a fair principle of criticism that if a figure can reasonably be regarded as historical it should not be turned into a symbol which can mean anything the interpreter cares to read into it. It may further be questioned whether any of the allusions to the beloved disciple would make any sense in the context if considered as no more than fictitious idealizations.

It would seem at least a reasonable conclusion to maintain that there are no irrefutable historical grounds for rejecting the identification of the beloved disciple as John the son of Zebedee.[2]

b. Palestinian background

The preceding discussion has shown that the writer intended his readers to recognize that the events were related from first-hand witnesses, and the next consideration is whether there are indirect confirmations of this from the way in which he refers to Palestinian affairs. Is he thoroughly acquainted with them or does he introduce improbabilities or inaccuracies? If the latter, an eyewitness behind the Gospel would clearly be excluded.

(i) *Knowledge of Jewish customs.* Several times in the course of the Gospel the writer displays accurate and detailed knowledge of Jewish

[1] E. F. Scott (*The Fourth Gospel, its Purpose and Theology*, 1906, p. 144) suggested that the beloved disciple was 'the prototype of the future Church'. R. M. Grant (*HTR*, 35, 1942, p. 116) regards him as symbolic and non-historical. On this, cf. also H. Lietzmann, *The Beginnings of the Christian Church* (Eng. Tr. 1937), p. 311. E. Käsemann (*Exegetische Versüche und Besinnungen*, 1, 1960, p. 180) suggests that he was the ideal bearer of apostolic testimony. R. Bultmann (*Das Evangelium des Johannes*, pp. 369 f.) regards him as an ideal figure representative of Gentile Christianity, and finds significance in his close association with Peter, the representative of Jewish Christianity (xiii. 21–30, xx. 2–10).

[2] Another proposed solution of the beloved disciple problem is to treat all the allusions as interpolations (cf. A. Kragerud, *Der Lieblingsjünger im Joh.*, 1959, cited by W. G. Kümmel, *INT*, 1965, p. 168, who mentions some proposers of this view).

life in the period before the fall of Jerusalem. He knows about Jewish ritual scruples, as is plain from ii. 6 (purification rites), vii. 37, viii. 12 (libation and illumination ritual at the Feast of Tabernacles), and xviii. 28, xix. 31–42 (pollution regulations regarding the Passover). He mentions several Jewish feasts (e.g. Passover, Tabernacles, Dedication). He is acquainted with specific Jewish doctrines, as for instance the inferiority of women (iv. 27), the laws concerning the sabbath (v. 10, vii. 21–23, ix. 14 ff.), and ideas of hereditary sin (ix. 2).[1]

(ii) *Knowledge of Jewish history*. The author possessed detailed knowledge about the time taken to build the temple up to the time of Jesus' cleansing of it, and as far as can be ascertained his knowledge appears to be accurate. He is aware, moreover, of the political attitudes of the Jewish people seen especially in their enmity against the Samaritans (iv. 9). He knows of the Palestinian contempt for the Jews of the Dispersion (vii. 35). He is acquainted with the history of the hierarchy, mentioning both Annas and Caiaphas as high priests and yet describing Caiaphas as *the* high priest in that fateful year (xi. 49, xviii. 13 ff.).

(iii) *Knowledge of Palestinian geography*. The writer has clearly had some first-hand acquaintance with Jerusalem, for he knows the Hebrew name of a pool near the Sheep Gate and knows that it had five porches. This detail is strikingly confirmed by recent excavations near the temple revealing a pool with five porticos with inscriptions suggesting the healing properties of the water.[2] He similarly knows the Hebrew name (*Gabbatha*) of a paved area outside the Praetorium, another detail confirmed by archaeological discovery near the tower of Antonia, which overlooked the temple area. Since this pavement stood on a

[1] Some scholars discount the strength of this evidence by maintaining that it shows only a general knowledge of Judaism and need not point to an author who was a native of Palestine. C. K. Barrett, for instance, takes the view that any material connected with Jesus would be expected to show traces of Palestinian origin (*The Gospel according to St. John*, 1956, p. 104), but this really evades the issue. It may as confidently be said that such traces would be expected in an apostolic work, and if there are other internal considerations which point in the same direction it is unsatisfactory to claim that a non-Palestinian Jew *could* have possessed such knowledge. The more relevant enquiry is whether a Palestinian Jew *must* have had more detailed knowledge, but this surely cannot be answered in the affirmative.

[2] Cf. J. Jeremias, *Die Wiederentdeckung von Bethesda* (1949) and W. F. Howard, *Commentary on John* (IB, 1952), pp. 539 f. Cf. also R. D. Potter's article on the Johannine topography in *Studia Evangelica*, pp. 329–337.*

rocky ledge, the Hebrew name, which means 'ridge', would be descriptive of its position.[1] He also knows about the pool of Siloam (ix. 7) and the brook Kidron (xviii. 1).

On numerous occasions topographical details are given in this Gospel, sometimes in narratives where the Synoptic parallels lack them.[2] There is mention of two Bethanys (i. 28, RV, RSV, xii. 1), of Aenon near to Salim (iii. 23),[3] of Cana in Galilee (ii. 1, iv. 46, xxi. 2), of Tiberias as an alternative name for the Sea of Galilee (vi. 1, xxi. 1), of Sychar near Shechem (iv. 5), Mt. Gerizim near a well (iv. 21), and of Ephraim near the wilderness (xi. 54).[4]

It seems impossible to deny that the author was either himself a

[1] Cf. A. J. B. Higgins, *The Historicity of the Fourth Gospel* (1960), pp. 81, 82.

[2] E.g. Philip, Andrew and Peter are all said to come from Bethsaida (or Bethzatha).

[3] Archaeologists have recently claimed to have identified this place as the modern *Ainun* (cf. W. F. Albright, 'Recent Discoveries in Palestine and the Gospel of St. John', *The Background of the New Testament and its Eschatology*, ed. W. D. Davies and D. Daube, 1956, pp. 158–160).

[4] Barrett's approach to this topographical evidence is that John's special knowledge refers to the south rather than the north of Palestine, which does not suggest a close dependence on John, son of Zebedee (*op. cit.*, p. 102). But this cannot be taken seriously since the bulk of the Gospel deals with our Lord's ministry in the south, which gives no indication at all of the author's place of origin. It is possible, for instance, for a Scotsman to give accurate topographical descriptions of an English scene without it being assumed that he could not have been a Scotsman. More serious, and yet equally unsupportable, is Barrett's observation that tradition tends to add names of places, with the inference, presumably, that the Johannine topographical details may be traditional accretions. An examination of the allusions to the Gospels in the Apostolic Fathers and in the apocryphal literature does not support this view of tradition. Rather the reverse seems to be true. Names of persons and places tend to give way to much vaguer or more muddled allusions. In the *Protevangelium of James*, for instance, names from the canonical Gospels are used, but mostly in a different context (e.g. Simeon becomes high priest). In the *Acts of Paul* no fewer than fifty-six persons are named, but there is no instance of a person mentioned anonymously in the canonical Acts reappearing in the apocryphal *Acts* with an identity attached. Topographical details in the latter are extraordinarily vague compared with the canonical book. For a study of the topographical details in John's Gospel which are claimed to possess special significance, cf. K. Kundsin's *Topologische Überlieferungsstücke im Joh.* (1925). Bultmann (*The History of the Synoptic Tradition*, pp. 67 f.) argues that with the development of the tradition there was a tendency to add more precise details, including the addition of names to previously anonymous speakers. This tendency may be found in later apocryphal literature, but Bultmann cites no first-century parallels.

native of Palestine or else in very close touch with someone who was.[1] The former alternative seems the more likely since in many cases there appears to be no reason for the inclusion of topographical details if personal reminiscence is not responsible.

c. Details which suggest an eyewitness

Any such emphasis on detail, however, inevitably raises the question of John's historical accuracy. For if the Gospel is no more than an imaginative writing-up of narrative and discourse based on a genuine core of tradition, or if, as some maintain, it is pure fiction, there is clearly little value in appealing to those touches which serve to point to an eyewitness.[2] The general question of historicity will be discussed later, but for our present purpose it must be noted that it is highly improbable that some of the details should have been created as pure fiction. What purpose would be served by the mention of six waterpots at Cana (ii. 6), of the twenty-five or thirty stadia as the distance rowed by the disciples across the Sea of Galilee (vi. 19), or of the number of fish caught, and the distance the boat was from the land, on the occasion of the post-resurrection appearance of Jesus to His disciples (xxi. 8, 11)? It is not convincing to regard these details as possessing symbolical rather than historical significance, unless there is clear indication that they were intended so to be understood. C. K. Barrett,[3] for instance, on ii. 6 admits the possibility of a symbolic interpretation, but agrees that such a suggestion is not entirely satisfactory, although he favours an allegorical treatment of xxi. 11, representing the full total of the catholic Church. Those for whom this method of approach appears fanciful may prefer to regard the 153 fish as the vivid recollection of an eyewitness. Had the author intended an allegorical meaning, surely he would have given some hint of it?[4]

---

[1] C. H. Dodd (*Historical Tradition in the Fourth Gospel*, pp. 243 ff.) gives some attention to topographical details but regards these as evidence that the author has used an earlier tradition which he believed to be trustworthy.

[2] In a recent article S. Temple (*JBL*, LXXX, 1961, pp. 220–232) argues for an eyewitness core for the Gospel into which other material has been worked. In this case the eyewitness details would help to authenticate the tradition, but would be valueless as an indication of authorship.

[3] *Op. cit., ad loc.*

[4] Barrett (*op. cit.*, p. 104) explains the occurrence of such details as resulting from the author's sources or his desire to give verisimilitude to his work. But it is debatable whether John used sources (see pp. 303 ff.), and the appeal to the verisi-

Other small details, such as the following, leave the reader with the impression that the writer was personally present at the events: the barley loaves (vi. 9), the odour-filled house (xii. 3), Peter's beckoning action (xiii. 24), the reaction of the soldiers at the arrest of Jesus (xviii. 6), the weight of spices used in the embalming (xix. 39). In addition there are occasions when the writer purports to have remarkable knowledge of the reactions of the disciples (e.g. ii. 11 f., iv. 27, vi. 19, xii. 16, xiii. 22 f.) and of the Lord Himself (cf. ii. 11, 24, vi. 15, 61, xiii. 1).

More significant still is the number of times that John gives names to people mentioned anonymously in the parallel Synoptic records.[1] Thus Philip and Andrew are named in the narrative of the feeding of the multitude (vi. 7 f.), the Mary who anoints Jesus is shown to be the sister of Lazarus (xii. 3), the name of the high priest's servant whose ear Peter struck with his sword is given (xviii. 10). In addition, some are introduced into the narrative without parallels in the Synoptics, the most notable being Nathanael, Nicodemus and Lazarus. The least that can be deduced from these details is that the writer has based his narratives on good tradition;[2] the most, that the writer recalled the names of these people because he was personally acquainted with them. This latter suggestion seems no less probable than the former.

d. Comparisons with the Synoptic Gospels

This is not the place for a general discussion of Johannine-Synoptic relationships, which will be considered elsewhere. The present intention is simply to enquire whether the Synoptic Gospels throw any light on the authorship of the Fourth Gospel. It would at first seem highly unlikely, and yet certain approaches to the Fourth Gospel are so decidedly conditioned by its relationship to the Synoptic Gospels that

---

militude motive is invalid unless it can be shown that the author is the type of person who both psychologically and spiritually might be expected to resort to this method. But the Fourth Gospel does not suggest such a man. The problem arises, What amount of detail is a mark of genuineness in a work? Too much vagueness on the one hand, and too much detail on the other, have each at times been claimed to exclude an eyewitness author, so that such an author has a slender chance of his work being accepted as genuine.

[1] See earlier footnote, p. 251 n.4.
[2] Cf. A. J. B. Higgins, *The Historicity of the Fourth Gospel* (1960), p. 57.

no discussion of authorship would be complete without drawing attention to this matter.

(i) *Treatment of similar material.* The crucial problem is whether or not John's Gospel was dependent on the Synoptic Gospels. Many scholars consider that the author used both Mark and Luke (see later discussion) and if this opinion is correct it raises the problem whether an apostle would have used writings by non-apostles. It is widely assumed that no apostolic eyewitness would have depended on second-hand accounts, and full consideration must be given to this assumption (cf. the discussion on Matthew's Gospel, p. 41). But are its basic premises correct? To begin with it may be disputed whether John has used either of these Gospels, since the small amount of detail in which they run parallel is so slight that it may well be accounted for by oral tradition. If this be so the problem has no relevance for the solution of the authorship question of this Gospel. But even if it be admitted that it reflects both Mark and Luke, it is not entirely apparent why this could not have happened in any apostolic writing. Few scholars would dispute that the Fourth Gospel presupposes that the readers are acquainted with the Synoptic tradition. To cite one example, the apostles are abruptly introduced as 'the twelve' without further definition, and it is clearly assumed that the readers will know who they were. The scanty inclusion of snippits from Mark and Luke (if this is what the author did) could not be construed as too undignified for an apostle. Indeed, it may have been designed to jog the readers' memory of what they already knew.

(ii) *Introduction of unique material.* It is this material which leads at once to the heart of the Johannine problem. Criticism has tended to be dominated by the deviations and innovations of John as compared with the Synoptic Gospels and to have assumed that the latter must be regarded as a historical yardstick against which the former must be measured. The consequence has been that many scholars have dismissed the Fourth Gospel as unhistorical, and with such an assumption apostolic authorship was unthinkable, and the possibility of an eyewitness source ruled out. Differences in the account of John the Baptist, the cleansing of the temple, the chronology of our Lord's ministry, the presentation of miracles and the method of our Lord's teaching, to name the most prominent, were all reckoned to prove John's non-historicity. Such evidence was considered quite sufficient to set aside all the previously stated evidence which suggests an eyewitness, and therefore authentic, account. As will be noted later, critical opinions regarding John's historicity are showing a marked inclination to assign more historical value to this Gospel and this trend, if it continues, will make the objection now being considered less weighty.

It may, in fact, be maintained with considerable credibility that John's innovations are more an evidence for than against apostolic authorship. If the three Synoptics were already in circulation and were accepted as authentic accounts, it would need an author of no mean authority to introduce a Gospel differing from them so greatly in form and substance as does the Fourth Gospel. The only intelligible hypothesis is that an apostle was directly responsible for it, either as author or as main witness. If it has already been decided on other grounds that no apostle had anything to do with it, the production and reception of the Gospel remains an enigma. The best that can be supposed is that the churches generally assumed that an apostle was author (see discussion below on the external history of the Gospel). More details of alternative suggestions will be given when dealing with various hypotheses regarding authorship, but it should be noted here that uniqueness of material cannot be regarded as conflicting with the Gospel's own eyewitness claims and impressions. This is not to ignore the very real character of the Johannine problem, but merely to point out that it has little bearing on authorship except for those who altogether deny the historicity of the book.

e. Hellenistic thought

The extent of the Hellenistic background will be considered later, but those who find strong affinities in this Gospel with the higher religious concepts of the contemporary Hellenistic world[1] find difficulty in attributing such a Gospel to a Galilaean Jewish fisherman. If the background assumption is correct the difficulty must be conceded. But the extent of the difficulty will depend on several factors. The assessment of the author's indebtedness to Hellenism has been variously estimated, but the school of thought which could find almost nothing else but Hellenism would naturally find it impossible to ascribe the Gospel either to the apostle John or to any Palestinian Jew.[2] But this school of

---

[1] Cf. the approach of C. H. Dodd, *The Interpretation of the Fourth Gospel* (1953).

[2] F. C. Grant (*The Gospels, their origin and growth*, 1957, p. 175) is a strong representative of this position.

thought has lost considerable ground in recent years and most scholars would be prepared to grant, at most, only a measure of Hellenistic influence, and some would agree to very little, if any. The real problem is whether the apostle John would have been acquainted with Hellenistic thought. Hellenistic influence was certainly widespread in Palestine,[1] and the possibility of a Palestinian work showing such influence must be conceded. But if John is regarded as an uneducated Galilaean peasant, it may be argued that one would not normally expect such a man to produce such a Gospel.

But it is by no means certain that John was as uneducated as some have supposed. Zebedee appears to have been in a position to hire servants and it is not impossible that John and James may have been better educated than their fellow apostles. Admittedly this cannot be proved, but neither can it be disproved, at least unless Acts iv. 13 (ἀγράμματοι and ἰδιῶται) is assumed to disprove it. But a not improbable interpretation is that these terms were used contemptuously of those unschooled in rabbinic lore.

This whole matter of Hellenism and the author problem in John further depends on the degree to which the major thought-concepts are allowed to Jesus or are considered to be interpretations by the author. If, of course, our Lord is given credit for expressing His message in a form which could be adaptable to the universal mission, the existence of concepts which would be appreciated by Gentiles is no surprise in an apostolic writing. Nevertheless some consider it improbable that Jesus was in touch with such thought-forms. The Qumran discoveries have at least opened up the probability that the Johannine type of thought, from a literary point of view, was more widespread than is often supposed.[2]

[1] Cf. Barrett, *The Gospel according to St. John* (1956), p. 32; W. D. Davies, *Paul and Rabbinic Judaism* (1948), pp. 1–16; S. Liebermann, *Hellenism in Jewish Palestine* (1950).

[2] F. C. Grant (*op. cit.*) protests that the small amount of parallels with the Qumran literature do not compare with what he calls 'the vast array of parallels' with the Hellenistic literature. Yet the Qumran parallels are, at least, more contemporary with our Lord's time than much of the Hellenistic literature cited in support (as, for instance, in the Hermetic tracts). A. M. Hunter views the Qumran parallels as much more favourable to a Palestinian and probably apostolic authorship, especially when this is linked with linguistic considerations (Aramaicized Greek) and accurate Palestinian topography (*ET*, LXXI, 1959–60, pp. 164–167). On the other hand C. H. Dodd finds the main difficulty for apostolic authorship in the combination of rabbinic and Hellenistic motives at a deep level (*Historical Tradition in the Fourth Gospel*, p. 16).

f. Other considerations

It has sometimes been maintained as evidence against authorship by a Palestinian Jew that the writer always uses the description 'Jews' of those opposed to our Lord, in a manner which suggests that he is dissociated from the Jewish people and must therefore be a Gentile.[1] Too much stress cannot, however, be placed on this usage, for it may be an indication that the readers were Gentile, but not the author. If this were so we should expect the term used to be that with which Gentiles were most familiar.[2] It is probable that the term 'Jew' is used more especially in contradistinction from 'Christians', rather than from 'Gentiles', in the same sense in which it occurs in Revelation iii. 9. That the use of the term 'Jew' need not indicate a non-Jewish author is shown by Paul's usage in 1 Corinthians x. 32. It may in fact be maintained that only a Christian Jew would have felt as strongly as this author does the bitter hostility of his own people against his Lord and Master,[3] and the feeling would have been all the deeper had the author witnessed it with his own eyes.

Another factor is the author's alleged acquaintance with rabbinic methods of argument, which is then thought to be improbable in a working Galilaean fisherman. Would he have had opportunity to acquaint himself with current themes of discussion and become steeped in the Torah?[4] At first it may seem that this would not have been possible. But the force of the argument depends upon a certain view of John's position. Since it is possible to maintain that Zebedee was a master fisherman in a fair way of business, in view of the references to his hired servants, it follows that John may not have been so unac-

---

[1] For a critique of this view, cf. H. R. Reynolds, *HDB*, III (1899), p. 702. R. M. Grant (*A Historical Introduction to the New Testament*, 1963, p. 155) points out that the Qumran sectaries criticized the 'orthodox' Jews. Bultmann (*Das Evangelium des Johannes (KEK)*[13], p. 59) discusses the fact that the Jews are sometimes differentiated from ὁ ὄχλος. He considers that Ἰουδαῖοι is therefore used to denote the Jews in their essential characteristics, represented by the authorities. The speech-usage tells us nothing about the origin of the Evangelist (whether Jewish or not).

[2] Cf. A. P. Peabody, in E. Abbott, A. P. Peabody and J. B. Lightfoot, *The Fourth Gospel* (1892), p. 112.

[3] Cf. V. Taylor (*The Gospels*, p. 98) who, while admitting a polemic against unbelieving Jews, nevertheless denies any racial hatred and in fact suggests that only a Jew could feel as this author does.

[4] Cf. Dodd, *op. cit.*, p. 15.

quainted with Jewish rhetoric. Moreover, if John is the disciple known to the high priest (xviii. 15) he may not have been out of touch with rabbinical methods of discussion. Moreover, it is not impossible to suppose that our Lord Himself had some acquaintance with contemporary Jewish trends and fashioned some of His teaching accordingly.

g. External evidence

It is always difficult to assess the evidence of the second-century Church Fathers on the New Testament books, for a critic's estimate will be invariably influenced by his general presuppositions. Thus some will place more emphasis than others on negative evidence, rather than positive, and others will be inclined to give credence only to the first of a sequence of witnesses, dismissing the rest as mere echoes of the first and therefore weakening the whole cumulative testimony. Although a completely unprejudiced approach is probably not possible, an attempt will be made here to give a brief survey of the facts.

(i) *Evidence for the apostolic authorship of the Gospel.* There is no writer who names the author of the Gospel until Irenaeus, who not only makes clear that the author was John the Lord's disciple but also that he published the Gospel at Ephesus and remained in that city until Trajan's time.[1] Moreover, Eusebius reports that Irenaeus' authority was Polycarp, who was claimed to have learned the truth from the apostles.[2] It is in this context that the story is reported of John's encounter with Cerinthus at Ephesus. Another reference to Polycarp is found in Irenaeus' letter to Florinus, in which he reminds his boyhood friend of their early acquaintance with Polycarp and of the latter's reminiscences of his conversations with John and others who had seen the Lord.[3] There can be no doubt, therefore, that Irenaeus accepted John the apostle as author of the Gospel and believed it to have been published at Ephesus on the basis of Polycarp's testimony.

A similar witness is found in Polycrates, who was bishop of Ephesus (AD 189–198) and who wrote in a letter to Victor of Rome that John, who had been a witness and a teacher, now sleeps at Ephesus. Nevertheless in this case nothing is said about him publishing a Gospel.

The evidence of Irenaeus has been subjected to searching criticism

---

[1] Cf. *Adv. Haer.* ii. 22. 5, iii. 3. 4 cited in Eusebius, *HE*, iii. 23. 3 f. Cf. also *Adv. Haer.* iii. 1. 1 cited in Eusebius *HE*, v. 8. 4

[2] *HE*, iv. 14. 3–8.   [3] Eusebius, *HE*, v. 20. 4–8.

and many scholars have not been disposed to grant its validity. Their reluctance to do so springs mainly from the fact that Irenaeus' evidence conflicts with their critical conclusions. If on other grounds it is concluded that John could not have written the Gospel, then clearly Irenaeus must be wrong. Once we suspect that his tradition is inaccurate, it would not be difficult to suggest a plausible reason for the rise of the inaccurate tradition. Irenaeus' memory from boyhood times plays tricks with him, for the John of Polycarp's acquaintance was not John the apostle but another John. It was a case of mistaken identity.[1]

Now this theory is neat and sounds plausible, but is it valid? It supposes that Irenaeus had no other source of information than Polycarp, a supposition which is highly improbable. He frequently refers to an anonymous Presbyter (who was not a direct hearer of the apostles, according to Harnack), who is generally supposed to have been his predecessor at Vienne and Lyons, Pothinus, a man born well before the end of the first century (he died in AD 177 when over ninety years old.)[2] Moreover, Irenaeus was in close touch with Rome. Would he have held to a tradition which was not confirmed by the traditions of other important churches, especially in view of the fact that he had himself lived previously in the East?[3]

[1] J. N. Sanders (*The Fourth Gospel in the Early Church*, 1943, pp. 38, 39) went further and suggested that it was the pride of the Ephesian Christians which raised their John to the apostolate, and their anxiety for apostolic support in the Quartodeciman controversy which attributed to him the Fourth Gospel. But Sanders seems to have overlooked the futility of the Ephesian Christians attributing the Gospel to the apostle John unless their protagonists in the controversy acknowledged his authorship.

B. W. Bacon (*ZNTW*, 26, 1927, pp. 187–202; 31, 1932, pp. 132–150) attributed Irenaeus' testimony with regard to an Ephesian John not only to inaccuracy but to deliberate intention. He accepted an elder John but placed him in Jerusalem.

[2] H. P. V. Nunn (*The Fourth Gospel*, 1946, p. 19) pointed out that Irenaeus had seen some of his friends tortured to death for the sake of their beliefs and suggested that this must have affected the care with which he would accept Gospels which claimed to support those beliefs.

[3] James Drummond (*An Inquiry into the Character and Authorship of the Fourth Gospel*, 1903, p. 348) remarked, 'Critics speak of Irenaeus as though he had fallen out of the moon, paid two or three visits to Polycarp's lecture-room, and never known anyone else . . . he must have had numerous links with the early part of the century.' W. Bauer, on the other hand, suggested that suspicions arise over Irenaeus' evidence, because according to Eusebius' report Irenaeus stated that Papias was a disciple of John (*Das Johannesevangelium*[2], 1925, p. 235). But even if this be granted as an inaccuracy, it need not impugn the whole of Irenaeus'

Our confidence in Irenaeus' testimony is supported by the recognition that all subsequent to him assume the apostolic authorship of the Gospel without question (Tertullian, Clement of Alexandria, Origen). If they were merely repeating Irenaeus' opinion, they must have considered that opinion of sufficient value to repeat without suspicion. In addition there is the important evidence of the Muratorian Canon, contemporary with the time of Irenaeus, which describes the origin of the Gospel as proceeding from John after a vision given to Andrew that John should write and his associates should revise. In spite of the fact that this statement must be received with reserve, in view of what is generally thought to be the improbability of Andrew surviving until the late date to which the Gospel is assigned[1] (although it should be noted that there is no independent evidence of Andrew's later history), there is no reason to dispute that the general connection of John with the production of the Gospel was commonly accepted at that time in Rome. Another line of evidence which may be cited, but whose value is difficult to assess, is the anti-Marcionite Prologue. The text is corrupt, but it witnesses to the apostolic authorship (although it suggests that he dictated the Gospel) and states that it was produced in Asia. Both these witnesses, however, suggest that others were associated with John in the actual production of the Gospel, and this must be borne in mind in deciding its origin.

It may be assumed with certainty that the tradition of Johannine authorship was considerably older than the time of Irenaeus, but why, it may be asked, does not Polycarp mention John in his letter to the Philippian church? He mentions Paul by name, but not John, whom he is supposed to have known. But this presents no difficulty unless more weight is to be attached to the argument from silence than it will reasonably bear. There was obvious point in Polycarp mentioning Paul in writing to a Pauline church, but there is no compelling reason why he must have mentioned John. One thing is clear and this is that Polycarp cannot be cited as evidence against the existence of the Gospel, or against the apostolic authorship. His silence may seem strange, but Polycarp's mind must not be assessed by comparison with what the

testimony. It is strange that Bauer is inclined to accept the witness of a much later and less reliable witness such as Philip of Side regarding John's early martyrdom. Cf. also C. K. Barrett (*The Gospel according to St. John*, 1956, pp. 86, 87), who equally distrusts Irenaeus' evidence.

[1] Cf. J. H. Bernard, *St. John*, I (*ICC*, 1928), p. lvi.

modern scholar would have done. Common sense suggests that arguments from silence could produce very misleading results,[1] and yet the criticism of the Fourth Gospel has suffered more from such methods than any other part of the New Testament. This will be further illustrated when the early use and authority of the Gospel is considered (see below).

(ii) *Evidence for John's early martyrdom and the tradition of Ephesian residence.* The preceding evidence has been considered in some detail because a misunderstanding of it has exercised a deep influence on Johannine criticism, but the evidence for John's early martyrdom may be dealt with more summarily in view of its slightness. It may be summarized as follows:

1. The martyrdom is deduced from Mark x. 39. Since both James and John are promised that they will drink the same cup as our Lord, it is claimed that John must have suffered the same fate as James. It is supposed that if this had not happened Mark would have altered his text.

2. Two late writers, an epitomist of Philip of Side (fifth century)[2] and George Hamartolus (ninth century)[3] report statements purported to have been made by Papias to the effect that John as well as James was killed by the Jews. In the case of Hamartolus the statement is followed by a citation of Mark x. 39.

3. A Syrian martyrology of AD 411[4] commemorates John and James on the same day (27 December) and describes them as 'apostles in Jerusalem'.

4. The Carthaginian Calendar (c. AD 505),[5] which has a similar entry for 27 December, links John the Baptist with James, but many scholars regard this as an error for John the apostle and claim this as evidence for his early death.

5. A homily of Aphraates (21)[6] states that apart from Stephen,

---

[1] W. Sanday (*The Criticism of the Fourth Gospel*, 1905, pp. 32 ff.) has some trenchant criticisms of this method of argument, approvingly citing Drummond's exposures. The latter writer has a telling example from Theophilus of Antioch, who does not mention the names of any Gospel writers except John and does not even mention the name of Christ (*op. cit.*, pp. 157 f.). He could not have been ignorant of these facts, but for some reason chose not to mention them.

[2] Cf. C. de Boor, *TU*, v, ii (1888), p. 170.   [3] *Chronicle*, iii. 134. 1.

[4] Cf. H. Lietzmann, *Die drei ältesten Martyrologien* (Kleine Texte, 2), 1911, pp. 7 f.

[5] Cf. Lietzmann, *op. cit.*, pp. 5 f.

[6] Cited by Feine-Behm, *Einleitung*, p. 105.

Peter and Paul there were only two martyr apostles, John and James.

The cumulative effect of this evidence is very small, while the individual links in the chain become even weaker on examination.[1]

Mark x. 39 is capable of other interpretations than as a prediction of martyrdom; and the *vaticinium ex eventu* approach to exegesis is open to grave suspicion since it supposes that all the Gospel writers were editors who took upon themselves the responsibility of adjusting their material to their own understanding of the events and had no intention of recording what was actually said. The deduction of martyrdom from this passage, which amounts to no more than a prediction of suffering, necessitates presuppositions regarding John's early death.

The evidence of Philip's epitomist and of George Hamartolus cannot be taken seriously since neither of them was noted for accuracy as a historian. Moreover, as C. K. Barrett[2] points out, both Irenaeus and Eusebius knew of Papias' writings but neither refers to this statement about John's martyrdom. It is further questionable whether Papias would have used the late Greek title 'The Theologian' for John, as Philip's report says that he did, while George himself clearly did not take the Papias report seriously, since he also speaks of the apostle John's peaceful end.

The rest of the evidence may be dismissed, for in all probability the martyrologies and Aphraates are confusing John the apostle with John the Baptist. The notion of John's early martyrdom may therefore be regarded as purely legendary. Galatians ii. 9, which must be dated after James' martyrdom in AD 44, shows John as one of the pillar-apostles, while Acts xii. 2, which records James' death, contains no hint of John's. In addition to appealing to evidence of such flimsy character, the advocates of the theory are obliged to juggle with these conflicting considerations and the best that can be done is to suppose that John Mark was one of the 'pillar-apostles' and to suggest that later tradition caused an omission from Acts xii. 2, both without any supporting evidence.

But is the Ephesian residence of John equally legendary? Some scholars consider that it is, but largely on negative grounds. There is no mention of John's connection with Ephesus in the New Testament,

---

[1] C. K. Barrett (*op. cit.*, p. 87), who admits that an early martyrdom of John would solve some problems, pointedly remarks that we cannot martyr the apostle for our critical convenience.*

[2] *Op. cit., ad loc.*

unless the exile of the John of the Apocalypse be claimed as evidence of an Asiatic sphere, since Patmos is off the Ephesian coast. But this will carry weight only for those who regard John the apostle as author of the Apocalypse,[1] which many consider disputable. Moreover, it is thought strange that the author of Acts allowed Paul to address the Ephesian elders without referring to John, if by the time Acts was written John was resident in Ephesus. This is another *vaticinium ex eventu* approach, which would be entirely invalidated if Acts was published before John took up residence in Asia, which is not at all impossible. There is perhaps more point in the argument from Ignatius' omission of any reference to the apostle in his address to the Ephesian church, especially as this was so soon after John's reputed residence there. Barrett[2] places much weight on this consideration, disputing that it is a common argument from silence. The argument certainly supposes that Ignatius *must* have referred to John had he had any connection with Ephesus, but it is difficult to see on what conclusive grounds this view can be maintained. Ignatius does refer to several members of the church by name, including the bishop Onesimus, but he seems more concerned about securing the church's present devotion and loyalty to Onesimus than about its previous history—which is understandable since he wrote this on his way to martyrdom!

The same kind of argument from silence is made from the omission of any reference to John's place of residence in the writings of Polycarp, Papias or Justin.[3] The fact that Irenaeus is the first specific witness for Ephesus (apart from the legendary *Acts of John*) need not mean that his source of knowledge was unreliable. It need mean no more than our ignorance of the transmission of the tradition. Nevertheless, Irenaeus may be wrong and John may have had no connection with Ephesus at all. But if so, there is no knowing what happened to him after he withdrew from Jerusalem, nor where he was when the Fourth Gospel was produced. There is no other more reputable tradition.[4]

[1] Cf. pp. 934 ff.

[2] *The Gospel according to St. John* (1956), p. 87.

[3] Justin is an indirect witness, however, since he states that 'A certain man among us, by name John, one of the apostles of Christ, prophesied in a revelation which was made to him' (*Dialogue*, 81). The dialogue, according to Eusebius, took place at Ephesus.

[4] T. W. Manson (*Studies in the Gospels and Epistles*, 1962, pp. 118 ff.) was dubious about the Ephesus tradition, but suggested that the Fourth Gospel shows traces of an earlier Antiochene provenance. But there is no external evidence for this, and

h. Various propositions regarding authorship

There have been three main types of theory regarding authorship, but within each there have been many variations and the main proposals will now be summarized.

(i) *The apostle John.* This, as has been seen, is the traditional view, which has much support for it in the internal evidence. Indeed, it may be said that there is no evidence which conclusively disproves it, in spite of much opposition to it. This view would, on the whole, seem to account for more facts than any other, even if it is not without its difficulties.

A modification of the view is that John the apostle was the witness and some other was the author. A parallel to this solution may be found in the traditional relationship between Peter and Mark in the production of the Second Gospel.[1] There is no fundamental objection to this approach, but it does involve a rather broad interpretation of the γράψας of John xxi. 24, in the sense of writing by means of another. There are nevertheless other New Testament parallels for this. It would not be out of keeping with the external evidence provided the apostle himself was assigned the main responsibility in the production of the Gospel. Under this theory the assistant or amanuensis would remain anonymous and the apostle would take the credit for the Gospel. In this respect it would differ from the Peter-Mark relationship and would suggest that John had more of a personal hand in the writing than Peter had in the case of Mark's Gospel.

A further modification, which seems less likely, is that a disciple of John wrote down the memoirs of the apostle after his death. According to this theory, the substance of the Gospel is John's but not the writing.

(ii) *John of Jerusalem.* The existence of a John of Jerusalem who had entrée into the high priest's house was first proposed by H. Delff.[2] In his view the John of the tradition was this Jerusalem John who later

---

Manson's evidence is mainly inferential. Cf. K. Aland's comments on the place of origin of the Gospel, *ZNTW*, 46 (1955), pp. 114-116; he argues for Asia Minor on the grounds of the use of John by the Montanists. Some scholars prefer Syria as the place of provenance of the Gospel, but most of these dispute Johannine authorship (cf. those mentioned by W. G. Kümmel, *INT*, 1965, p. 175).

[1] A view recently adopted by R. V. G. Tasker, *The Gospel according to St. John* (*TNT*, 1960), p. 11. Cf. also V. Taylor, *The Gospels*, p. 106.*

[2] *Die Geschichte des Rabbi Jesus von Nazareth* (1889).

became influential among the Asiatic churches. He was trained in rabbinism and was present at the last supper. Yet apart from the advantage in this theory of the association of a personal eyewitness with the production of the Gospel, it has little to be said for it. Moreover, no external evidence of any kind exists for such a person.[1]

(iii) *Non-Johannine theories.* Several hypotheses have been suggested which simply ignore the name of John altogether. The logic of this general position is that if the internal considerations are believed to make apostolic authorship impossible, the external evidence must clearly be wrong. If it is, there is no reason to retain the name John at all. All that needs to be done is to suggest some theory for the rise of the tradition. Later apostolic ascription is the obvious answer. Thus J. N. Sanders[2] connected this ascription with the need for apostolic support in the Quartodeciman dispute, a view considerably weakened by the fact that John's Gospel would have been of little value in that dispute in any case, and by the futility of claiming any work as apostolic unless it was generally accepted as such.

Others have advocated a more direct theory of pseudonymity, in which all the eyewitness details are regarded as a skilful device to create the impression of apostolic authorship. But if so, why did the author not mention John's name, which would have been so much more effective and more in harmony with general pseudepigraphical practice? Moreover, such a theory demands some explanation as to how the work ever became generally accepted, but this provides an insuperable difficulty. Unless the Gospel were at once assumed to be genuinely apostolic it would have had increasing difficulty in creating that impression as time went on. There are no known cases of works recognized as pseudonymous ever later losing their pseudonymous ascription. If the writer designed to make his book seem truly apostolic he must have succeded in a manner wholly without parallel among the pseudepigrapha.

There has been some support for the view that this Gospel must be attributed to a group rather than to a single witness. It becomes in that

---

[1] Another unlikely candidate for authorship whose name was John is Mark, as proposed by P. Parker (*JBL*, LXXIX, 1960, pp. 97-110). But in his earlier article (*JBL*, LXXV, 1956, pp. 303-314), Parker argues for a second edition of the Gospel issued fairly late and it is difficult to see how this can be reconciled with his Mark suggestion.*

[2] *The Fourth Gospel in the Early Church* (1943), pp. 38, 39.

case the product of a school. A parallel to this has already been seen in Stendahl's theory for the production of Matthew (see pp. 27 f.). There may be something to be said for this type of theory but when it comes to authorship it must be a question of a single individual, although the epilogue would lend support to the view that others were associated with him.

Some comments on various redactional theories will be made later, but it should be noted here that advocates of such theories naturally think more of a redactor than of an author. Such editorial theories may appear to have a considerable advantage in that any material not in harmony with what is thought to have been the mind of the original writer may be readily transferred to the redactor and its evidential value at once nullified. But the validity of this type of criticism must be seriously challenged.*

(iv) *'John the Elder'*. A famous statement of Papias has given rise to a widespread conviction among many scholars that there was another John who had associations with Ephesus and had some connection with the production of the Fourth Gospel. This has led to what might be called the confusion theory for interpreting the external evidence. John the Elder became mixed up in the tradition with John the apostle. By this method Irenaeus' evidence is easily discounted by assuming that he was really referring to John the Elder. But before such a theory can claim credence the existence of this elder must be established beyond dispute. The evidence is as follows.

Papias is quoted by Eusebius[1] as stating in his *Dominican Expositions*, 'And again, if anyone came who had been a follower of the Elders, I used to enquire about the sayings of the Elders—what Andrew, or Peter, or Philip, or Thomas, or James, or John, or Matthew, or any other of the Lord's disciples, said (εἶπεν) and what Aristion and the Elder John, the Disciples of the Lord, say (λέγουσιν). For I did not think that I could get so much profit from the contents of books as from the utterances of a living and abiding voice.' The problem is one of interpretation, for Papias' words are not unambiguous. It is possible, for instance, to construe this statement, as C. K. Barrett[2] does, as indicating a chain of three groups between the time of our Lord and Papias; the apostles, the elders and other disciples. If this interpretation is correct it at once disposes of Irenaeus' assumption that Papias was a

---

[1] *He*, iii. 39.4.   [2] *The Gospel according to St. John* (1956), pp. 88 ff.

hearer of the apostle John and a companion of Polycarp. But this interpretation is open to challenge. The crucial question is what Papias means by the elders—are they to be distinguished from or identified with the Lord's disciples who are named? Barrett is convinced that the 'sayings of the elders' consisted of reports of what the named disciples (i.e. apostles) had already said, and that Papias only heard these elders' recollections through the medium of their followers. But if Papias is describing the apostles as 'elders' an entirely different interpretation results, for now it is from followers of the apostles that Papias sought his information, and this would be much closer to the evidence from Irenaeus. It is admittedly strange that Papias uses the word 'elders' (πρεσβύτεροι) if he meant to describe the apostles, but it is equally strange that he calls one of the elders a disciple of the Lord (i.e. the Elder John) and that one of the Lord's disciples is not even graced with this title. All would agree that Papias has expressed himself badly, but on the theory that he intends to distinguish between John the apostle and a John the Elder there are more difficulties than are generally realized. The main snag is Papias' description of both Aristion and John as οἱ τοῦ κυρίου μαθηταί which would appear to mean personal followers of the Lord and therefore indicate more than a synonym for 'Christians'. Aristion is not mentioned in the New Testament, but that need not, of course, exclude the possibility that he was a disciple of the Lord who survived until towards the end of the century. It must surely be admitted that it becomes slightly more conceivable if at least one of them (the Elder John) can be identified with one otherwise known. Moreover, under the theory being discussed, if personal disciples of the Lord were still testifying at the time of Papias' enquiries, why did not Papias enquire about the sayings of the Lord rather than the sayings of the elders? There seems no satisfactory answer.[1]

It is difficult under the three-link construction to understand Papias' description of the end result as 'A living and abiding voice'. But if by this he means the direct testimony of personal disciples of the Lord, his words become more intelligible. Moreover, he is clearly acquainted with books, among which must surely be included the Synoptic Gospels, at least Matthew and Mark, on whose authorship he comments

---

[1] B. W. Bacon (ZNTW, 26, 1927, pp. 197, 198) admitted the difficulty of the Greek phrase, but disposed of it by textual emendation, based on the Syriac. But textual emendations of this kind are never a satisfactory method of dealing with difficulties of interpretation.

elsewhere. But it is significant that Papias places the non-literary apostles before the literary ones, suggesting that he may have paid more attention to the oral teaching of the former because their testimony had not been reduced to writing. It seems that on the whole a more intelligible understanding of Papias' words is obtained if it be assumed that the two Johns are to be identified and that Papias is distinguishing between what John had said in the past and what at the time of his enquiry he was still saying. At the same time the possibility that there may have been two Johns cannot be excluded. It is supported by Eusebius' interpretation of Papias' words,[1] but since he wished to attribute the Apocalypse to a different John from the author of the Gospel his interpretation may not have been impartial. There is, in any case, no other historical evidence for the existence of this shadowy figure, unless it be the introduction to 2 and 3 John where the author introduces himself as the 'elder'.

One concluding comment is necessary. If it be granted that an Elder John did exist, Papias gives no information regarding his domicile, nor does he give any hint of his literary prowess. In fact, even if this elder's feet can be firmly planted in history on Papias' ambiguous evidence, there is no reason to believe that his pen could have produced the Fourth Gospel. The only tenuous connection is that he happened to possess a name identical with that to which the Fourth Gospel was traditionally ascribed, which facilitates the appeal to a 'confusion theory'. But if the later Christian Church thus mixed up apostles and elders might not Papias have done the same, which might well destroy the *raison d'être* for John the Elder's existence?[2]

On the assumption that John the Elder was a real historical figure many scholars have adopted the view that John the apostle was the witness and John the Elder was the author. This solution is something of a compromise, but it involves the assumption that two Johns belonged to the same circle and that the Gospel was their joint effort, a possible but not very probable proposition.

(v) *Evidence for the early use and authority of the Gospel.* It has already been shown that by the time of Irenaeus the Gospel was accepted as

---

[1] *HE*, iii. 39. 6. Eusebius also cites Dionysius' hearsay comment about there being two tombs bearing the name of John in Ephesus (*HE*, vii. 25. 16).*

[2] It is not without strong reason that B. W. Bacon concluded that the Elder at Ephesus theory was 'a higher critical mare's nest'. (*Hibbert Journal.* 1931, p. 321.)

apostolic. It remains to enquire into its history before this date, but the investigator is here hampered by lack of information.[1] It was possibly known to Ignatius, although it is difficult to be certain. The language and theological ideas in several places show kinship with the Gospel which would support the opinion that Ignatius knew the Gospel. Polycarp nowhere cites it, although he appears to cite from the First Epistle. One or two passages in the *Epistle of Barnabas* could reflect knowledge of the Gospel, and the same applies to the *Shepherd of Hermas*, but literary dependence is difficult to establish.[2]

There is difference of opinion about Justin's knowledge of the Fourth Gospel. Certainly the theological ideas of Justin would seem to find roots in the Gospel and in one or two places it is highly probable that Justin directly cites it. Bernard's[3] conclusion was that 'Justin, then, used the Fourth Gospel a little before 150 AD and at one point (*Apol.* 61) quotes it as authoritative for a saying of Jesus'. J. N. Sanders[4] admitted that Justin used the Gospel, but thought that he did not regard it as Scripture or as apostolic. Barrett[5] is rather more cautious, denying that the evidence proves that Justin knew the Gospel, but agreeing that it gives some plausibility to that hypothesis. Much more telling evidence for Justin's knowledge of the Fourth Gospel is the fact that his pupil Tatian used it in his *Diatessaron* on an equal footing with the Synoptics.[6] It should also be noted that the first writer to produce a commentary on this Gospel was the Gnostic Heracleon. Indeed, this

[1] The paucity of positive evidence has led some scholars to maintain that the Gospel must be dated only a short time before the earliest definite traces of acquaintance. Thus P. W. Schmiedel (*Enc. Bib.*, 1914, col. 2550) placed it not earlier than AD 170. But this principle of criticism was proved false by the discovery of earlier papyrus fragments.

[2] Cf. J. H. Bernard (*op. cit.*, pp. lxxiff.) for the detailed evidence for these Apostolic Fathers. F. M. Braun (*NTS*, 4, 1958, pp. 119–124), suggests that the author of the *Epistle of Barnabas* had heard echoes of the Johannine preaching. On the relation of Clement of Rome to John's Gospel, cf. M. E. Boismard (*RB*, LV, 1948, pp. 376–387). He thinks Clement shows evidence of Johannine impressions but not citations.

[3] *Op. cit.*, p. lxxvi.

[4] *The Fourth Gospel in the Early Church* (1943), p. 31.

[5] *The Gospel according to St. John* (1956), p. 94.

[6] The force of this evidence is often disregarded. H. P. V. Nunn (*The Fourth Gospel*, 1946, p. 17), who considered that the *Diatessaron* evidence was an insuperable obstacle to those who would argue that Justin was unacquainted with the Fourth Gospel, is strongly critical of Sanders for ignoring it altogether.

Gospel seems to have enjoyed wide usage among the Gnostics. It is possible that this led to Irenaeus' use of the Gospel to demonstrate its essentially non-Gnostic character.[1]

In addition to the patristic evidence there are two fragments of papyrus which contain either the text of the Gospel itself (as the Rylands Papyrus 457)[2] or reminiscences of it (as the Egerton Papyrus 2),[3] both dated at least in the first half of the second century, possibly as early as about AD 130. Although these are no evidence for authorship, they do show that the Gospel circulated at an early date.[4]

Another line of evidence which is claimed to have a bearing on authorship is the alleged opposition to the Fourth Gospel in the second century. Appeal is made to the Alogi who are mentioned by Epiphanius[5] as having rejected the Gospel and as actually ascribing it to Cerinthus. Whether these Alogi represent a group or only one man, Gaius of Rome (as has been argued),[6] is not certain, but it is reasonably clear that their opinions were not widely held. In all probability they rejected the Gospel merely because they did not like its Logos doctrine. This Gaius, mentioned by Eusebius,[7] was anti-Montanist and might also have felt that the teaching on the Holy Spirit in John favoured Montanism. In addition, the publication by Hippolytus of a *Defence of the Gospel according to St. John and the Apocalypse* points to a prevalent opposition towards the Gospel, at least in Rome. Irenaeus also refers to people who rejected the Gospel. Now all these allusions may refer to one man, Gaius, with his immediate followers, and if so the opposition need not be taken seriously. Some scholars give more weight to this opposition by appealing to the evidence of the Muratorian Canon, which is said to go to some lengths in establishing the Gospel. This opposition is considered by J. N. Sanders[8] as evidence

---

[1] Cf. W. von Loewenich, *Das Johannesverständnis im zweiten Jahrhundert* (1932).

[2] Cf. C. H. Roberts, *An Unpublished Fragment of the Fourth Gospel* (1935).

[3] Cf. C. H. Dodd, *BJRL*, xx (1936), pp. 56–92 (reproduced in his *New Testament Studies*, pp. 12–52).

[4] T. W. Manson maintained, in view of this evidence, that if Justin did not quote the Gospel it was not because no copies were available (*Studies in the Gospels and Epistles*, 1962, p. 112).

[5] ii. 31.

[6] Cf. the discussion of V. H. Stanton (*The Gospels as Historical Documents*, 1923, p. 239) who criticizes Rendel Harris' advocacy of the theory that Gaius was associated with the Alogi.

[7] *HE*, iii. 28.   [8] *Op. cit.*, p. 38.

that the Gospel had to *fight* for recognition, which he then thought was inconceivable if it were the work of an apostle. But the evidence cited is inadequate as a proof that the Gospel gained its place only after a struggle. Had the opposition come from the general membership of some influential church the position might have been different. But it is inadvisable to place too much weight on the opinions of a small group such as Gaius and his companions.

III. PURPOSE

As with every other aspect of the Gospel, this problem has been fully discussed, but with widely differing conclusions. In this case, however, the author himself furnishes his readers with so specific a statement of his purpose that this must form the starting-place for any discussion. Yet it has not always done so. Many scholars are more intrigued with John's beginning than with his conclusion, as a result of which John xx. 31 is passed by with less than just attention, and theories of purpose are proposed which are entirely out of harmony with this statement.

a. The author's own statement

John says, 'these are written that you may believe that Jesus is the Christ, the Son of God, and that believing you may have life in his name' (Jn. xx. 31, RSV). It is clear from this statement that the primary aim was to encourage faith.[1] That must mean that the work was designed as an evangelistic instrument.[2]

It was, in fact, essentially a 'Gospel'. But John does not leave the readers in any doubt as to what the *content* of their faith was to be. It was not merely a general faith but a particular view of Jesus which John sought to inculcate, a view of Him under two distinct, yet closely

[1] Three important MSS, Sinaiticus, Vaticanus and Koredethi read the present tense instead of the aorist (πιστεύσητε). This reading would mean that the Gospel would confirm existing faith. Cf. Barrett, *op. cit.*, p. 479. C. H. Dodd (*The Interpretation of the Fourth Gospel*, p. 9) suggests that quite apart from the grammatical consideration the whole presentation of the Gospel supports an evangelistic aim.

[2] This purpose has been compared with the purpose of a dramatist who selects his material with an eye to persuading his public (cf. C. M. Connick, *JBL*, LXVII, 1948, pp. 159–169). C. F. D. Moule (*The Birth of the New Testament*, 1962, p. 94) points out that John's purpose is extremely individualistic and answers the question, What must *I* do to be saved? (Cf. also the same author's article in E. Stauffer's *Festschrift, Donum Gratulatorium*, 1962, pp. 171–190 (also published in *Nov. Test.*, 5, Fasc. 2–3), on the Individualism of the Fourth Gospel.)

connected ascriptions—the Christ and the Son of God. The former is more than a title, as W. C. van Unnik[1] has convincingly shown. It must mean 'the anointed One', i.e. 'the Anointed King', an ascription which could have its fullest relevance only to Jewish people, since the concept was not familiar to the Gentile world. A right understanding of this must have a profound bearing on discussions of the author's purpose. Whatever parallels with current Hellenistic thought are found, the author does not appear to have had a predominant Hellenistic circle of readers in mind when pursuing his purpose. But the other description is generally emphasized by those preferring a Hellenizing purpose, because it is thought that 'Son of God' is capable, as 'Christ' is not, of a Hellenistic interpretation.[2] Yet John's own combination of the two ascriptions must be maintained.

The author's preceding statement that Jesus did many signs not included in the book, but which were attested by eyewitnesses, gives further insight into his purpose. He was clearly selective, for he was acquainted with a mass of traditions which it was beyond the scope of his book to include (cf. xxi. 25). He apparently chose out only those 'signs' which would serve his immediate purpose, which should put us on our guard about placing too much emphasis on John's omissions. He was a writer with one dominant purpose and it must be expected that his handling of his material will support this purpose.

It is significant that only in this Gospel is the title 'Messiah' preserved in its transliterated form. The earliest encounter of Jesus with the disciples leads them to use this title to describe Him (i. 41), and it is evident that John intends his readers to understand this in a thoroughly Jewish sense (cf. i. 45, 49). The portrait of Jesus in John is therefore messianic at its commencement. At the other end of the ministry this theme is still dominant, for the messianic character of the entry into Jerusalem can hardly be disputed (xii. 12–19). Similarly our Lord admits His Kingship before Pilate (xviii. 33–37). He is also condemned and crucified as King of the Jews (xix. 3, 12–15, 19, 20), and it is not without point that John alone records Pilate's rejection of the chief priests' request for the wording over the cross to be modified. In the account of the feeding of the multitude, John alone tells us that the

[1] 'The purpose of St. John's Gospel', *Studia Evangelica* (1959), pp. 382–411.
[2] Cf. E. F. Scott, *The Fourth Gospel, its Purpose and Theology*[2] (1908), pp.182 ff.; G. H. C. Macgregor, *The Gospel of John* (MC, 1928), p. 367. R. Bultmann, in his *Theology of the New Testament*, does not discuss the implication of Jn. xx. 31.

people sought to make Jesus King but that Jesus withdrew Himself (vi. 15), no doubt because their conception of messianic Kingship differed radically from His.

A particular application of the view that John wrote not only for unbelievers but for Jews is seen in the theory of K. Bornhäuser[1] that the Gospel was intended as a missionary document for Israel. He considered that only Israelites would have fully comprehended this Gospel. The omission of the Christian ordinances from John's Gospel would also be in harmony with this view, since these ordinances could not be appreciated by unbelievers.[2]

b. An ancient account of John's purpose

One of the earliest attempts to analyse the author's aim was made by Clement of Alexandria and since his comments have had an influence on modern assessments of the Gospel, it is as well to give his statement in full. 'Last of all John perceiving that the bodily (or external) facts had been set forth in the (other) Gospels, at the instance of his disciples and with the inspiration of the Spirit composed a spiritual Gospel.'[3] This at once raises the problem of the relationship of John to the Synoptists, as far as it affects John's purpose. Two facts seem to be involved in Clement's evidence, first that John followed the Synoptists and was fully acquainted with the contents of their Gospels and, second, that John's Gospel was of a more spiritual character than the others, although here it is clearly necessary to define what Clement meant by 'spiritual'. Sanday[4] defined it as 'one that sought to bring out the divine side of its subject'. In other words, Clement believed that John's Gospel was supplementary to the Synoptic Gospels and was different in kind from them.[5] Moreover, he says that he received this tradition from the 'early presbyters', which shows that it represents an ancient and probably widely held viewpoint. Because of this it merits serious attention. Whether John actually used any of the Synoptic material or whether he drew what parallels there are from oral tradition is still a debated point,

---

[1] *Das Johannesevangelium eine Missionsschrift für Israel* (1928).

[2] Cf. *ibid.*, pp. 158–167.

[3] *Hypotyposes*, cited in Eusebius, *HE*, vi. 14. 7.

[4] *The Criticism of the Fourth Gospel* (1905), p. 71.

[5] A different explanation of Clement's statement is given by R. M. Grant (*JBL*, LXIX, 1950, pp. 305–322), who considers that by 'spiritual' he meant 'gnostic' and that he conceived John's purpose to have been the presentation of the secret teaching of Jesus. But such a use of 'gnostic' is likely to be misleading.

but there is much to be said for the latter (see later discussion of this problem). Nevertheless, if the evidence is insufficient to prove literary dependence on the Synoptists, there are enough indications to show that the author assumed that his readers would be acquainted with the contents of the other Gospels. Only under such a hypothesis can his choice of material be intelligently understood. Thus the omission of several significant Synoptic narratives occasions no surprise, neither does the abrupt introduction of material which presupposes knowledge of Synoptic tradition.

At the same time the large amount of didactic material in John's Gospel is well characterized as 'spiritual', for not only does John pay much attention to the Lord's teaching on the Holy Spirit, but the various discourses bring out the inner meaning of His teaching and even of some of His miracles. Some caution, however, is necessary lest the spiritual character of John's Gospel be emphasized to such an extent that the Synoptics are supposed to be wholly unspiritual.

c. The theory that John aimed to supersede the Synoptic Gospels

This view, advocated by H. Windisch,[1] has not found much support for the obvious reason that, taken alone, the Gospel would give an incomplete and inadequate account of the ministry of Jesus. It needs the Synoptics to make it intelligible and it is therefore inconceivable that any writer should imagine that this Gospel would have ousted any of the Synoptic Gospels, which were presumably well established by this time. This theory may therefore be dismissed without further discussion.[2]

d. The theory that the Gospel was a polemic against unbelieving Jews

The rather hostile manner in which the author refers to the Jews is claimed to support this theory. Indeed, the Jews throughout the Gospel seem to be opposed to Jesus, and although this attitude of hostility is plainly present in the Synoptic Gospels, in these latter the main offenders are the scribes and Pharisees and sometimes the Sadducees, as

[1] *Johannes und die Synoptiker* (1926), pp. 87 f. The theory was approved by Walter Bauer in an article surveying Johannine research in *TR*, n.f., 1 (1929), pp. 135–160.

[2] W. F. Howard (*The Fourth Gospel in Recent Criticism*[2], 1955, ed. C. K. Barrett, p. 135) justly considers the theory too artificial, although he considers that John sometimes corrects the Synoptic Gospels (he cites, for example, the timing of the anointing at Bethany and the dating of the last supper).

compared with the Johannine principle of referring to the nation as a whole.[1] It has already been noted that some have considered this as evidence enough that the author could not have been a Jew, but it has also been said that only a Jew could feel as deeply as John the bitter hostility of his own people toward Jesus.[2] Thus while there may be some truth in the theory that this anti-Jewish polemic formed part of the aim of the Gospel, it could have been only a subsidiary part.[3]

e. The view that John was combating Gnosticism

This approach is naturally closely tied to a near second-century dating for the Gospel (or even later), when the movements generally classed as Gnosticism were flourishing. The particular form of Gnosticism which John is claimed to be combating is Docetism, which maintained that Christ could never have been contaminated by the world which was essentially evil. This meant that Christ did not really become flesh. It may have seemed as if He did, but any contact with matter would have defiled Him. Hence, He could not suffer. It was not He who was nailed to the cross. His purpose was revelatory not redemptive. It is not difficult to see that the Fourth Gospel would have been a very useful instrument in combating this kind of error, for much stress is laid on the truly human character of the incarnation and passion. Our Lord is depicted as being weary and thirsty (iv. 6, 7), as weeping at Lazarus' grave (xi. 35), as admitting a real thirst on the cross (xix. 28),

[1] G. H. C. Macgregor(*JBL*, LXIX, 1950, pp. 150–159) maintained that the Gospel reflects the conflict between Judaism and apostolic Christianity. The references to the Jews are therefore a 'reading back'.

[2] Cf. p. 257 n.3. Cf. also Lord Charnwood, *According to St. John* (1925).

[3] V. Taylor (*The Gospels*, p. 98) suggests that the writer may have had in mind the antagonism to which his readers were exposed from Jewish opponents, but it is not clear in what way this Gospel would have been especially designed to help them. They might have derived encouragement from our Lord's attitude in face of Jewish opposition, but the same encouragement is available for all who are meeting hostility, whether from Jews or not. Nevertheless, if on other grounds Jewish-Christian readers are indicated, the suggestion might have some weight. R. M. Grant (*JBL*, LXIX, 1950, pp. 305–322) maintains that John's purpose was to reinterpret the career of Jesus by attacking Judaism. J. A. T. Robinson (*NTS*, 6, 1960, pp. 117–131) takes a different view, maintaining that the Gospel belongs to Hellenistic Judaism. It is not therefore a polemic against non-Christian Jews, but is an appeal to Diaspora Judaism not to refuse the Christ. C. F. D. Moule (*The Birth of the New Testament*, pp. 94, 95) sees John's purpose as a retelling of genuine Dominical tradition (as in Jn. ix) in the light of prevailing Jewish conflicts.*

as possessing a real body out of which could flow blood and water (xix. 34). The anti-Docetism of John is even more evident in the First Epistle, and especially in the Second. Yet even if the Evangelist's representation effectively refutes the Docetic error, this need not mean that this was integral to the author's purpose. It is going too far to claim with R. H. Strachan[1] that a polemic against this error was one of the main purposes of the Gospel, but this is not to say that the author did not bear in mind the rising influence of Gnostic thought.

F. C. Grant[2] supposes that the author belonged to a circle devoted to early Christian Gnostic mysticism, as if he was rewriting the life of Christ using the language of contemporary Gnostic mysticism. However, Grant admits that the wonder is that this Gospel contains so few 'Gnostic or quasi-Gnostic elements'. A somewhat similar view was held by E. F. Scott,[3] who found a double reaction to Gnosticism in this Gospel, for, coupled with a studied avoidance of Gnostic terms such as γνῶσις, σοφία and πίστις, to exclude any possible confusion between the author's presentation and that of the heretical systems, he maintains that there is some sympathy with the doctrines of Gnosticism. He finds this in the writer's emphasis on the ideal value of the life of Christ, on the Gnostic antithesis between the lower and higher worlds, and on the importance of the act of 'knowing' in the religious life. He suggests that this double approach was possible because the relationship between Gnosticism and Christianity was as yet loosely defined. He posits, in fact, an age for the production of the Gospel between the first opposition to Gnosticism (as in Paul's Epistle to the Colossians) and the later all-out struggle to uproot it. But it must remain a problem for Scott's proposition that a church possessing the Colossian Epistle could have found sympathy for a movement whose beginnings Paul and the writer of the Epistle to the Hebrews had so strongly opposed. Another theory is that of Bultmann,[4] who understands the Gospel as a presentation of Christianity in terms of the Gnostic redeemer myth, but this is much more radical in character. He points out certain similarities between the Gospel and Gnostic mythological ideas and makes much of the view

[1] *The Fourth Gospel*[3] (1941), pp. 44 f.

[2] *The Gospels, their origin and growth*, pp. 163 ff.

[3] *The Fourth Gospel*, pp. 86–103.

[4] His commentary is presented from this point of view. Cf. also *Theology of the New Testament*, II (1955). Bultmann's basic theory for this Gospel was strongly criticized by E. Percy, *Untersuchungen über den Ursprung der johanneischen Theologie* (1939).

that Christ is essentially the Revealer. This interpretation of the purpose of the Gospel is dominated by Bultmann's general philosophical approach to Christianity and it is not surprising, therefore, that he himself finds some sympathy with certain aspects of Gnosticism which he finds echoed in this Gospel.*

f. The theory that John was presenting a Hellenized Christianity

This is a view that has long been popular with the comparative religions school of thought. The Gospel is regarded as addressed to the contemporary Greek non-Christian world to persuade them to adopt Christianity, and to do this the life of Christ is expressed in religious terms which would be readily intelligible to them. This opinion finds its classic expression in the work of C. H. Dodd.[1] By marshalling an impressive array of parallels with the Hermetic literature, Philo of Alexandria, and Gnosticism (he considers Mandaism, but does not favour this as background for the Gospel), Dodd claims that the Gospel shows particular affinities with Philo and the *Hermetica*, and transforms ideas which are held in common with these contemporary religious movements (see discussion on the background of the Gospel, pp. 319 ff.). The existence of parallels in thought might not in itself throw any light on the purpose of the Gospel, especially as in all cases there are vital differences between the Johannine use of parallel terms and the use in contemporary movements. The use of Logos is a case in point, for John and Philo are poles apart in their fundamental conceptions. All this Dodd, of course, admits. The real crux is whether he is right in maintaining that the Gospel must be interpreted against a Hellenistic background.[2] There is less inclination than formerly to

[1] *The Interpretation of the Fourth Gospel* (1953). Cf. p. 9.

[2] It should be noted that whereas Dodd puts the main emphasis upon Hellenistic parallels he does not neglect Semitic parallels. Indeed he regards the Gospel as the best example among the literature of this period of the interpenetration of Greek and Semitic thought (cf. his book, *The Authority of the Bible*, 1938, p. 200). Moreover, he considers rabbinism as a parallel milieu with Hellenism in the interpretation of the Gospel (cf. *The Interpretation of the Fourth Gospel*, pp. 3 ff.). In his most recent book, *Historical Tradition in the Fourth Gospel*, Dodd argues for a considerable core of Palestinian tradition although he still maintains the Hellenistic flavouring. S. G. F. Brandon (*The Fall of Jerusalem and the Christian Church*[2], 1957) holds much the same viewpoint but from very different presuppositions, for he advocates that John shows the co-mingling of Jerusalemite Christianity with Paul and Hellenic Christianity, which in his view were previously strongly antagonistic (cf. also H. C. Snape, *HTR*, 47, 1954, pp. 1-14).

place such stress on Hellenistic influences on New Testament literature, but the Fourth Gospel is perhaps the strongest fortress of that view. It has received some recent knocks through the Dead Sea discoveries,[1] since certain parallels in the Qumran literature with the Johannine literature suggest that some of the terms which were previously confidently regarded as of Greek origin were in fact found in a Jewish milieu just prior to and contemporary with the rise of Christianity. Nevertheless, there have been some scholars who have declined to regard the Qumran evidence as damaging to a Hellenistic origin.[2] F. C. Grant, for example, points out that there are far more parallels in Hellenistic religious literature than in the Qumran literature and therefore on grounds of quantity the Hellenists defeat the Essenes. Another champion for the older view, H. M. Teeple[3] takes a different line, and maintains that there are many features in the Scrolls absent from John, many also in John absent from the Scrolls, and many partial parallels where similar terms are used in different ways. All this, according to him, shows that the origin of the Fourth Gospel cannot be found in the kind of milieu at Qumran. To back up this opinion he then shows that almost all the parallels claimed between John and the Scrolls can be more closely illustrated by comparison between the Scrolls and the Old Testament and/or the Apocrypha and pseudepigrapha. Moreover, he asserts that other New Testament books, which cannot claim a Palestinian origin, show as many parallels with the Scrolls as John. In fact, Teeple maintains that where John's parallels differ from Qumran thought they differ towards Hellenism and away from primitive Jewish thought.[4] Such careful comparisons as this author has made will be valuable in putting scholars on their guard against claiming too much from Qumran, but there are some presuppositions in Teeple's method of approach which considerably

---

[1] Particularly by W. F. Albright in his essay on 'Recent Discoveries in Palestine and the Gospel of St. John', in *The Background of the New Testament and its Eschatology* (ed. W. D. Davies and D. Daube, 1956), pp. 153–171. Cf. also F. M. Cross, Jr. (*The Ancient Library of Qumran and Modern Biblical Studies*,[2] 1961, pp. 206 ff., who maintains that the evidence shows that John preserved primitive and authentic Jerusalem tradition, and J. A. T. Robinson's article, 'The New Look on the Fourth Gospel', in *Studia Evangelica*, pp. 338–350.

[2] For instance F. C. Grant, *op. cit.*, p. 175. Cf. also M. Burrows, *More Light on the Dead Sea Scrolls* (1958), p. 129.

[3] 'Qumran and the Origin of the Fourth Gospel', *Nov. Test.*, 4 (1960), pp. 6–25.

[4] *Ibid.*, p. 24.*

weaken the force of his conclusions. He takes it for granted, for instance, that in this Gospel we are dealing with the author's background of thought and not Christ's. Those more disposed to place greater confidence in the teaching of the Lord as being sufficiently comprehensive to appeal to men of all backgrounds will be less inclined to see the force of Teeple's arguments. Moreover, to argue from what is present in Qumran sources but absent from John misses the whole point of the uniqueness of Christianity. No-one who appeals to the Dead Sea Scrolls to support a Jewish milieu for John would ever imagine that John (or more precisely Jesus) would take over the tenets of Qumran lock, stock and barrel, as Teeple's argument supposes. The question of interdependence between John and Qumran is really irrelevant in the search for origins, since all that needs to be claimed is that the Scrolls show the currency of certain concepts, such as light and truth, which many earlier scholars considered to be essentially Greek. It may be true that John is more Hellenistic than the Scrolls, but this may be due to the breadth of our Lord's own mind rather than to the Hellenism of a Gentile mind imposed upon His teaching.

In spite of all the amassing of Hellenistic parallels, it is still possible for the Gospel to be read intelligibly against an essentially Jewish background and since this fits in with the author's own claims, it should not be jettisoned in favour of a view which virtually makes the Evangelist a greater genius than Christ Himself. This is not to deny that some interpretation of our Lord's teaching was necessary, but it is a plea to regard with strong suspicion any theory which finds it necessary to treat a whole Gospel as interpretation without paying attention to the historic facts. More will be said on this subject when the Evangelist's sources are discussed, but the general view under consideration must be regarded with the utmost reserve. It is tenable in a satisfying form only in so far as it derives its impulse from the genuine teaching of Jesus.

g. The suggestion that John was correcting a Baptist cult

It is known that in Ephesus there were groups of followers of John the Baptist who were imperfectly instructed in the tenets of Christianity (cf. Acts xix. 1–7). This kind of movement may well have been more widespread and it is an attractive hypothesis that this Gospel may have been partially designed to counteract an allegiance to John the Baptist which should have been given to Christ. The author goes to some lengths to demonstrate that Jesus was superior to John. Indeed,

John's sole function is to witness to Christ. In fact, he states categorically that he himself must decrease while Christ must increase (iii. 30).
Moreover, Jesus Himself, while admitting John's greatness, shows that
He has greater testimony than John's (v. 33 f.). All this must be granted,[1]
but would not the Synoptic Gospels perform the same function with
their inclusion of John's definite statement that Christ was mightier
than he (cf. Mt. iii. 11; Mk. i. 7; Lk. iii. 16)? Admittedly the Fourth
Gospel omits the narrative of the baptism of Jesus, but in the three
Synoptic accounts John makes a clear distinction between his own baptism and that of Jesus.[2] Nevertheless, the existence of such a sect may
have influenced the author in his choice of material in the opening
portions of his Gospel.[3]

h. The idea that John pursued an ecclesiastical polemic

This is less evident, but has been seriously maintained by those who find
in this Gospel sacramental teaching.[4] It is maintained that the omission
of the Lord's supper was to offset a wrong approach to it in some of
the churches of the writer's acquaintance. In its place he gives teaching
regarding the inner meaning of the institution (vi).[5] It is further thought
that the teaching of the new birth was to bring out the spiritual significance of the rite of baptism (cf. iii. 5).[6]

[1] For advocates of this view, cf. W. Baldensperger (*Die Prolog des vierten
Evangeliums*, 1898), who found traces of this anti-Baptist polemic throughout the
Gospel. Cf. Howard, *The Fourth Gospel in Recent Criticism*[2] (1955), ed. C. K.
Barrett, pp. 57, 58, for comments on Baldensperger's view. This view was
favoured by Strachan, *The Fourth Gospel*[3] (1941), pp. 109, 110 and W. Bauer,
Das Johannesevangelium[2] (1925), pp. 14 ff. The latter cites Mandaean literature
in honour of John.

[2] For a discussion of the Synoptic and Johannine references to John the Baptist,
cf. J. A. T. Robinson's article on 'Elijah, John and Jesus', *NTS*, 4 (1958), pp. 263–
281.

[3] Robinson (*op. cit.*, p. 279 n.2) questions the alleged existence of this sect and
suggests the need for a thorough re-examination.

[4] For a full treatment of this view, cf. W. F. Howard, *Christianity according to
St. John* (1943), pp. 143–150. Howard considered that over against all the pagan
interpretations of the sacraments 'there stood the witness of the life of the Church
and its sacramental tendency' (cf. p. 149).

[5] J. Jeremias (*The Eucharistic Words of Jesus*, Eng. Tr. 1955, pp. 72–87) takes
a quite different line and maintains that the author consciously omitted the
account to avoid disclosing the sacred formula to the heathen (i.e. as part of the
Church's *disciplina arcani*).

[6] Some scholars have claimed many other veiled allusions to the sacraments in
John's Gospel. O. Cullmann, for instance, finds such allusions in i. 29, 36, in the

Certainly this Gospel would correct any wrong sacramental tendencies, if such there were, when it was written, but it is rather precarious to infer this kind of sacramentalism from John's omission to mention the ordinances. Nonetheless, there are ecclesiastical interests in this Gospel which should not be overlooked. The allegories of the sheepfold and of the vine both contribute to the teaching of this Gospel about the Church, as does the high-priestly prayer of chapter xvii.

i. The view that John aimed to correct the Church's eschatology

It has been proposed (e.g. by C. K. Barrett)[1] that owing to the extended delay in the *parousia* it was necessary to provide an interpretation of primitive apocalyptic hopes. This, it is suggested, was provided by John. Such a theory might gain some apparent support from the kind of eschatological teaching contained in the Gospel. There is an absence of the apocalyptic kind of teaching found in the Synoptic Gospels. Instead there is what C. H. Dodd[2] calls 'realized eschatology'. The idea of an imminent return has receded and it is, therefore, proposed that John presents an eschatology which is a present reality rather than just a future hope. Yet the weakness of this general viewpoint is that too strong an antithesis is drawn between futuristic and realized eschatology. The latter is not the creation of the Church to explain away an unexpected delay. The two aspects are directly traceable to the teaching of Christ. Moreover, allusions to futuristic eschatology are found in John (cf. v. 25–29) alongside the 'realized' type of escha-

---

feeding of the multitude, in the allegory of the vine, in the miracle at Cana, in the feet-washing, in the blood and water from Christ's wounds, among others (cf. *Early Christian Worship*, Eng. Tr. 1953, pp. 37 ff.). For others tending towards the same direction, cf. C. K. Barrett, *The Gospel according to St. John* (1956), pp 69-71, and W. Bauer, *op. cit.*, pp. 95 ff. See Sir F. C. Hoskyns and F. N. Davey's *The Fourth Gospel*[2] (1947), pp. 363 f., on the early lectionaries' interpretation of the miracles of the healing of the paralytic and of the blind man as baptismal miracles. Some admit the presence of sacramental allusions but consider these to be editorial (cf. E. Lohse, 'Wort und Sakrament in Johannesevangelium', *NTS*, 7, 1961, pp. 110–125, who attributes xix. 34b, iii. 5 and vi. 51b–58 to the editor of the Gospel; cf. J. Jeremias, *ZNTW*, 44, 1952–53, pp. 256, 257, and the critique of his article by G. Bornkamm, *ZNTW*, 47, 1956, pp. 161–169, and cf. also W. Michaelis, *Die Sakramente im Joh.*, 1946).

[1] *Op. cit.*, pp. 115, 116.
[2] *The Apostolic Preaching and its Developments*[2] (1944), pp. 65 ff.

tology. An adequate exegesis demands that both should be retained.[1]

j. The suggestion that John aimed to preserve a tradition suitable for liturgical use

If the theory that behind this Gospel lies a Jewish triennial lectionary is correct (see pp. 311 f.), it may follow that the author was aiming to present the discourses and narratives in a form which would appeal to Jewish Christians who were well familiar with the lectionary. Such a scheme, if the theory is correct, would provide sermon material suitable for the different Jewish festivals.[2]

Another suggestion of a somewhat similar character is that John's Gospel incorporates various prose-hymns which were intended to be sung chorally in the Church's worship.[3] These hymns which had been developed as a result of long meditation on Christ and His teaching have been incorporated, according to this theory, with an eye on the liturgical needs of the Church.

While in both these theories it is not impossible that the Gospel readily found adaptation for liturgical needs, it is not easy to believe that this was part of the original purpose. If the style shows affinities with poetic methods, for instance, there is no immediate justification for maintaining that material in hymnic form was editorially attributed to Jesus. It could equally well be true that Jesus Himself used poetic forms[4] and that this is the explanation of the inclusion of such material. At most, a liturgical purpose cannot be considered as more than subsidiary.

IV. DATE

As is so often the case with New Testament books, the dating of this Gospel is not possible with any precision. Various suggestions have been

---

[1] For a recent study of John's eschatology cf. L. van Hartingsveld's *Die Eschatologie des Johannesevangeliums* (1962).*

[2] Cf. A. Guilding, *The Fourth Gospel and Jewish Worship* (1960), p. 57.*

[3] Cf. W. H. Raney, *The Relation of the Fourth Gospel to the Christian Cultus* (1933). The passages which this writer isolates as showing the characteristics of hymnic structures are i. 1–18, iii. 14–21, 31–36, x. 1–18 and the discourses in xiv–xvi and the prayer of xvii. These, he thinks, were intended to be chanted by a choir. Other passages (v. 19–47, vi. 32–58, viii. 12–20, 21–30, 31–58, x. 25–38, xii. 20–36, 44–50, xiii. 12–30, 31b–35) consisting of narratives were probably intoned by a reader.

[4] Cf. C. F. Burney, *The Poetry of our Lord* (1925).

proposed, ranging from before the fall of Jerusalem to as late as the last quarter of the second century. The more extreme theories have been rejected and the majority of scholars are inclined to accept a date somewhere between AD 90 and 110. The following are the main considerations which enter into the question of date.

a. The external evidence for the early use of the Gospel

Various early evidences for the circulation of the Gospel during the first half of the second century have already been mentioned. The earliest certain evidence is that of the Rylands Papyrus 457, which is recognized by Sir F. Kenyon[1] as an early second-century manuscript. Whether this papyrus was used by orthodox Christians or by Gnostics,[2] it is proof of the existence of the Gospel at that early date. The discovery of this fragment, together with the Egerton Papyrus 2, has effectively silenced the earlier radical dating of the Gospel late in the second century.[3]

The question of whether Ignatius knew this Gospel has already been

---

[1] *The Text of the Greek Bible*[2] (1949), p. 75.

[2] Cf. C. K. Barrett, *op. cit.*, p. 106.

[3] Although there is still some debate regarding the relation of Egerton Papyrus 2 to John's Gospel, there are good grounds for maintaining its use of John's Gospel (cf. C. H. Dodd, *Historical Tradition in the Fourth Gospel*, p. 328 n.2, who admits borrowing in at least fragment 1 of the papyrus. Cf. also C. K. Barrett's comment, *op. cit.*, p. 92). Baur and the Tübingen school had dated John in the last quarter of the second century by virtually ignoring altogether the external evidence. Subsequently various scholars dated the Gospel about AD 135, as for instance P. Schmiedel (art. 'John, Son of Zebedee', in *Encyclopaedia Biblica*, 1914, col. 2551), who placed it in the period after Bar-Cochba's rebellion in AD 135, which was assumed to be alluded to in Jn. v. 43. This position was at first supported by E. Meyer (*Ursprung und Anfänge des Christentums*, I, 1921, pp. 310–340) but abandoned in Vol. III of the same work published two years later (p. 650). The idea is now regarded as 'a curiosity of criticism' (to cite Vincent Taylor, *The Gospels*, p. 84 n.2). So is the suggestion of H. Delafosse (*Le Quatrième Evangile*, 1925) that the Gospel was Marcionite (*c.* AD 135) and was later worked over by an orthodox writer (*c.* AD 170). (Cf. Howard's comment, *The Fourth Gospel in Recent Criticism*, p. 89.)

A more recent theory of a later editing of John's Gospel about AD 135 has been advanced by P. N. Harrison (*Polycarp's Two Epistles to the Philippians*, 1936, pp. 255–266, 302–310) on the grounds that the earlier part of Polycarp's epistle shows no knowledge of John, and since he dates this part *c.* AD 135, the Gospel, he considers, must be placed after this. But this is an argument based on silence and is too precarious to be regarded as an adequate basis for dating.

raised (p. 269), but many scholars deny that he did.[1] Some, however, consider that he quoted it rather loosely, and used its terminology in a new sense.[2] If it could be shown with any certainty that Ignatius knew the Gospel it would establish a *terminus ad quem* of AD 110 for the Gospel, and would furnish a strong ground for claiming a date some while earlier than this.[3] However, since this Ignatius evidence is disputed, other grounds for an early date will need to be considered.

b. The historical situation

This has already been discussed in the section on Purpose and there is no necessity to repeat the details here. Most of those who see some allusions to Gnosticism in this Gospel are nevertheless agreed that there is no evidence of developed Gnosticism here.[4] It is, therefore, assumed that the Gospel must have arisen before the period of the more highly organized Gnostic sects. If Docetism is sometimes in mind this would suggest a period when this tendency was exerting an influence, and it is known to have done this at the turn of the century, especially in Asia. There is rather more definite allusion to Docetic views in 1 John than in the Gospel,[5] and if both works were published at roughly the same time the evidence of 1 John would need to be taken into account in dating the Gospel. But the date of the Epistle cannot be conclusively

---

[1] E.g. J. N. Sanders (*The Fourth Gospel in the Early Church*, 1943, pp. 12 ff.) admitted that a common theological tradition lies behind both writers, but was not prepared to agree that Ignatius knew the Gospel.

[2] Cf. C. Maurer, *Ignatius von Antiochien und das Johannesevangelium* (1949) Cf. also the discussion of F.-M. Braun, *Jean le Théologien* (1959), pp. 262–282.

[3] Even some scholars who do not admit the Ignatius evidence suggest a date round about AD 100–110, as for instance Sanders, *op. cit.*, p. 45, and C. H. Dodd, *BJRL*, xx (1936), pp. 56–92 (reproduced in his *New Testament Studies*, pp. 12–52). In his latest book, *Historical Tradition in the Fourth Gospel*, p. 424, Dodd considers a date about AD 100, and rather before than after, to be reasonable.

[4] For instance, J. Réville, *Le Quatrième Evangile, son Origine et sa Valeur historique* (1901), and A. Loisy, *Le Quatrième Evangile, deuxième édition refondue: Les Epîtres dites de Jean* (1921), both dated the Gospel before AD 125 on these grounds. Cf. also E. F. Scott (*The Fourth Gospel, its Purpose and Theology*[2], 1908, p. 103), who expresses the opinion that John wrote during the 'period of truce' before the great conflict with Gnosticism began.

[5] E. R. Goodenough (*JBL*, LXIV, 1945, pp. 164, 165) argues that 1 John does not deal with Docetism and need not be dated late. For a discussion on the date of the Epistle, see pp. 883f.

determined, and even if it could it is not indisputable that the Gospel must have been contemporary.

c. Relationship to the Synoptic Gospels

It goes without saying that if John used the Synoptics, or even if he was acquainted with them but did not use them, his Gospel must be dated later than the latest Synoptic Gospel. Those who date Matthew c. AD 80–85 are therefore unable to date John before about AD 90–95. On the other hand John shows no certain signs of acquaintance with Matthew. Moreover, a similar late dating for Luke is open to challenge, and if an early date for Luke is maintained (see p. 115) the *terminus a quo* for John would be more difficult to fix. And it would be still less conclusive if the view is held that John did not use the Synoptic Gospels. On the whole the relation to the Synoptics supplies little ground for the dating of this Gospel. Nevertheless, the general assumption that John is later than the other Gospels,[1] and the testimony of Clement of Alexandria in confirmation of this, have exerted considerable influence in dating the Gospel just before the turn of the century.

d. The effect on dating of decisions regarding authorship

If John the apostle was author of the Gospel, it could not have been published later than AD 100 at the outside limit, and hardly as late as this. The testimony of Irenaeus that John lived until Trajan's reign could place the Gospel during the last decades of the first century. Similar restrictions on dating would be imposed if John the Elder were author, if Papias' description of him as 'a disciple of the Lord' is taken seriously. Naturally, if no eyewitness had anything to do with the production of the book, there is no means of arriving at the *terminus a quo*, as is evident from the wide variety of opinions (and their wide chronological range) held by the earlier Johannine critics.

e. A theory for a dating before AD 70

Not many scholars have ventured to date the Gospel as early as pre-AD 70 and yet there are considerations in support of such a theory which have not received the attention which they deserve. V. Burch[2]

[1] R. M. Grant, in his recent book, *A Historical Introduction to the New Testament* (1963), p. 155, disputes that on literary or historical grounds it can be proved that John is either earlier or later than the Synoptic Gospels. This is a significant breakaway from the general assumption.*

[2] *The Structure and Message of St. John's Gospel* (1928).

in his book on this Gospel, proposed an author and an editor and maintained that John's original contents and structure must be dated near to the date of the crucifixion and its final editing before AD 70.[1] This is an astonishing theory, which if true would make the core of John's Gospel the earliest material in the New Testament. It depends for its validity on Burch's treatment of the structure of the Gospel, and not all would accept this in its entirety. Nevertheless, it is likely that, if John was the author, he wrote some of this Gospel long before the book was published. Indeed, there is something to be said for the view that John made notes of our Lord's discourses shortly after hearing them. Most scholars reject such a notion as highly improbable, but a careful examination of the discourses lends it more support than is generally recognized. They are recorded in such a way as to give the impression that the writer is reporting what he has actually heard.[2] They must either represent very early tradition or else be an example of superb artistry.

Several scholars who feel that the external evidence excludes an early date for publication draw a distinction between the Johannine catechesis and the actual production of the Gospel, the former being early, the latter late.[3] There is no fundamental objection to this hypothesis, especially if John did not use the Synoptics. Moreover, doctrinal considerations, which have for so long been regarded as pointing to a time of full development for Johannine theology, have more recently tended to support an earlier rather than a later date, as for instance affinities with Qumran[4] and arguments for an early ecclesiasticism.[5]

Various forms of this theory of an early origin for John have been proposed. Some, for example, suggest that at an early date the writer

[1] *Ibid.*, pp. 225 ff.

[2] A recent writer, H. E. Edwards (*The disciple who wrote these things*, 1953), has devoted his attention to a study of this aspect.

[3] In addition to Burch mentioned above, reference may be made to C. Spicq's *L'Epître aux Hébreux* (1952), pp. 109–138, in which he discusses the author of Hebrews' relation to the Johannine catechesis and concludes that the former knew and was influenced by the latter. Cf. also C. H. Dodd's arguments for a distinction between Johannine tradition before AD 70 and the later publication of the Gospel (*Historical Tradition in the Fourth Gospel*).

[4] See earlier discussion, pp. 277 ff. Recently both A. M. Hunter (*ET*, LXXI, 1959–60, pp. 164–167) and C. L. Mitton (*ET*, LXXIII, 1961–62, pp. 19–22) have been favourable to an earlier date for John than AD 100. Hunter suggests AD 80 or even a decade earlier.

[5] Cf. E. R. Goodenough, *JBL*, LXIV (1945), pp. 145–182 (especially pp. 166 ff.)

recorded the *ipsissima verba* of John the teacher, and this personal oral instruction was formulated well before AD 70.[1] Others suggest that the Johannine Gospel depends on a Johannine catechesis which was independent of the Synoptic traditions and was worked up into its present state by a later editor.[2] Whatever be the merits of these varied hypotheses, they are significant because they all assume a much greater historical veracity for the material than the alternative hypotheses do. This is in line with the increasing tendency to give more credence than formerly to the Johannine traditions. This will be touched upon when dealing with historicity, but it is clear that the earlier the date that can be attached to the Johannine material the greater will its claim to reliability tend to be.

V. RELATION TO THE SYNOPTIC GOSPELS

Many of the crucial problems concerning John's Gospel arise from its relationship to the Synoptic Gospels. If John's Gospel existed on its own it would undoubtedly raise many problems in its own right, and the same would be true of the Synoptics apart from John. Whatever view of their relationship is held, it cannot be denied that each is necessary to make the other intelligible.[3] In so far as John's Gospel is generally regarded as being subsequent to the others (see discussion on dating), there is special significance in observing that John answers many of the problems raised by the others, a factor which will become clearer as we proceed.

[1] This is the opinion of H. E. Edwards, who connects up the production of the Gospel with the flight of the Christians to Pella (*op. cit.*, pp. 129, 130). C. C. Tarelli ('Clement of Rome and the Fourth Gospel', *JTS*, XLVIII, 1947, pp. 208, 209) reckoned that John was *published* before AD 70. Cf. P. Gardner-Smith's opinion that John may be as old as Mark (*St. John and the Synoptic Gospels*, 1938, pp. 93 ff.). R. M. Grant (*op. cit.*, pp. 159 f.) dates this Gospel just after AD 70 on the grounds that the author was aiming to present Christian faith to bewildered Jewish sectarians, and if these were connected with the Dead Sea Community the period may have been soon after AD 68 when it was destroyed.

[2] Zahn (*INT*, III, 1909, p. 347) cites H. H. Wendt (*Lehre Jesus*, I, 1886, pp. 215–342) as maintaining this view.

[3] H. S. Holland, in his book *The Fourth Gospel* (1923), bases his main argument for the character of John's Gospel on the observation that the Synoptic Gospels leave unsolved many problems to which John provides the answer. In other words the Synoptic Gospels required another Gospel to be written to make them intelligible.

a. Comparison of the Gospel material

Whereas the differences are at once apparent, the similarities between
John and the Synoptic Gospels are not so obvious. Yet it is as well to
approach the differences by means of the similarities.

(i) *Similarities*. All the records include narratives and comments about
John the Baptist, the call of the disciples, the feeding of the five thous-
and, the sea trip of the disciples, the confession of Peter, the entry to
Jerusalem, the last meal and various sections of the passion narrative.[1]
In addition there are common narratives about the cleansing of the
temple and an anointing of Jesus, but both placed in a different setting.
These similarities may also be supplemented by a number of isolated
words of Jesus and others.[2] Yet the whole of this common material
contains very little verbal agreement. There are a few other allusions
which are hardly sufficiently close to be called similarities, such as the
placing of resurrection appearances by both Luke and John in Jerusalem, the possible connection between the feet-washing incident in
John and the words of Luke xxii. 27, and the parallel fishing episodes of
John xxi. 1 ff. and Luke v. 1 ff.

In common with the Synoptists John records samples of both healing
and nature miracles of our Lord, although he treats them differently.
Moreover, although John concentrates on the Jerusalem ministry, he
records some Galilaean material in common with the Synoptists. But
when this has been said we come to the end of the similarities. The
differences are much more numerous.

(ii) *Differences*. It will be valuable to classify these differences in order to
clarify this very complicated problem. The first class of difference is due
to material in the Synoptic Gospels which John does not record. It is
necessary here only to state the main omissions,[3] although there are
very many more of a minor character. John does not record the virgin
birth, the baptism, temptation or transfiguration of Jesus, the cure of
any demoniacs or lepers, the parables, the institution of the Lord's
supper, the agony in the garden, the cry of dereliction or the ascension.
This is a considerable list and demands some explanation. If we may
assume that the readers were acquainted with the Synoptic Gospels a

---

[1] These are the most important parallels (cf. Feine-Behm, *Einleitung*, p. 111).
[2] For details, cf. C. K. Barrett, *The Gospel according to St. John* (1956), pp. 34 ff.
[3] These are conveniently and concisely discussed by E. B. Redlich, *An Introduction to the Fourth Gospel* (1939), pp. 56 ff.

ready answer may be that the author has presupposed this and has seen no reason to repeat material that was already widely known. Yet many scholars feel that this explanation is inadequate and suggest that theological reasons prompted the omissions. Any theory which involves intentional suppressions must be regarded as highly improbable, for these are hardly intelligible if the readers were already acquainted with the Synoptic Gospels.[1] The theory of C. K. Barrett,[2] however, has perhaps more to be said for it, although it is not without considerable difficulties. He maintains that John has taken many of these events which are detachable from their Synoptic contexts, has stripped them of their 'historical individuality' and has built them into the 'theological framework of his gospel'. In this way he attempts to explain John's omission of the virgin birth. But this type of theory presupposes that neither John nor the Synoptists has preserved true history, which prejudges the whole matter. It would be nearer the truth to say that any omissions by John were dictated by his assuming his readers' acquaintance with the events, and by his specific purpose, which certainly took into account theological considerations, as xx. 31 shows. In this case John vi is not to be regarded as a substitute for the institution of the Lord's supper,[3] but as a complement to the Synoptic accounts, describing the Lord's preparation of the minds of His disciples for the significance of the ordinance.[4]

A second category of differences consists of the additional material in John's Gospel. This comprises a large proportion of the whole and includes certain incidents of considerable importance. The main material consists of the early Judaean ministry including the miracle at Cana, the encounters of Jesus with Nicodemus and the Samaritan woman, the healing of the cripple and the blind man in Jerusalem, the raising of Lazarus, the washing of the disciples' feet, the farewell discourses and

[1] Redlich (*op. cit.*, p. 57) rightly points out that such an intention would have defeated the author's main object in inculcating belief in Jesus Christ.

[2] *Op. cit.*, p. 42.

[3] Most scholars agree that Jn. vi is the Johannine account of the institution of the Eucharist. Cf. A. Correll, *Consummatum Est* (1958), pp. 63 ff., for a brief statement of various views. He maintains that John omitted the narrative of the institution because he considered that the Eucharist was impossible before Jesus' death. See pp. 280 f. for a different view.

[4] For this interpretation of Jn. vi, cf. B. F. Westcott, *The Gospel according to St. John* (1887), p. 113. Also A. Plummer, *The Gospel according to St. John* (1900), pp. 152–154.

parts of the passion narrative. John's Prologue (i. 1–18) is also unique. All this singular material requires as much explanation as do the Johannine omissions of Synoptic material. Why is so much new material introduced? If John is designed to supplement the Synoptic Gospels the answer will be ready to hand. But the problem has been raised whether John's unique material has the same authentic character as the Synoptic Gospels. Further comments will be made later regarding John's historicity, but special mention is required here of the problem of Lazarus, in view of its close connection with the Lord's arrest. In the Synoptics the arrest is precipitated by the cleansing of the temple, whereas in John that event is related much earlier, and the raising of Lazarus seems to take its place.[1] Yet to regard this as a discrepancy on John's part is to misunderstand the whole situation. The Lazarus event certainly stirred up the hatred of the chief priests and Pharisees, and spurred them on to seek the Lord's arrest, but they needed a more concrete charge to present to a Roman court than one based on a miracle.[2] The cleansing of the temple seemed to them to provide a sufficient cause to institute proceedings against Jesus. The contradiction is therefore only apparent.[3] As for the other events, most of them have similar parallels in the Synoptics. The multiplication of wine at Cana, for instance, is of the same type as the multiplication of the bread and fish by the Sea of Galilee.

A third category is the difference in presentation. There is less narrative and more discourse, and the introduction is more philosophical than that of the Synoptics. The Johannine portrait of Jesus differs from that of the others in presenting Him almost in the role of a Jewish Rabbi, using rabbinical methods of argument and lacking the more popular approach so prominent in the others. It may well be asked whether the two pictures are not incompatible. The discourses present

---

[1] As the reason for the Synoptists' omission of the Lazarus incident, it has sometimes been suggested that Lazarus may still have been alive when they were produced, in which case no mention would have been m.... of him then for reasons of discretion. But it is more probable that an explanation is to be found in the respective authors' purposes. J. N. Sanders (*NTS*, 1, 1954, p. 34) did not consider the silence of the Synoptists to be insuperable since other raisings are reported.

[2] Cf. E. B. Redlich (*op. cit.*, pp. 60 ff.), who argued that the raising of Lazarus was the *occasion* but not the *cause* of our Lord's arrest.

[3] Cf. A. J. B. Higgins, *The Historicity of the Fourth Gospel* (1960), p. 48.

a problem which must be faced. It has often been argued that the absence of Synoptic-type parables in John and of Johannine-type discourses in the Synoptics presents a contradiction. But this has been partially due to a misunderstanding. It is not true to say that John's account is altogether lacking in parabolic teaching. While the precise forms of the Synoptic parables may not be so clearly evident, there are passages in John in which sayings approximating to the Synoptic forms are discernible. C. H. Dodd,[1] for instance, has isolated seven such passages which he calls Johannine parabolic forms. Moreover the allegorical style of John x and xv is not so far removed from the parabolic style of the Synoptics. It is not difficult to regard one as a development from the other. In addition, John contains a considerable number of aphoristic sayings which are comparable to the type found in the other Gospels.[2]

The connected discourses present a more difficult problem since the Synoptic Christ does not engage in the same type of discourse as the Johannine Christ, and many scholars therefore regard the two presentations of Christ the Teacher as incompatible. The only recourse in this event is to treat the Johannine discourses as no more than a literary creation of the author himself or else as having been already reduced to this form in his sources. Owing to its somewhat homiletical character, C. K. Barrett[3] suggested that much of the discourse material was originally delivered in the form of sermons by the Evangelist. Some have posited a discourse source, while others have attributed the form of teaching to the author's own skill. All these theories are prompted by the dissimilarity with the Synoptic teaching material. But can the difficulty not be explained in a way which renders it unnecessary to suppose that Jesus could not have taught in the manner which John describes?

One consideration which may explain some of the phenomena is that almost all the discourses in John were delivered to the more educated people, mostly in Jerusalem, whereas the Synoptic audiences were more often the common people of Galilee. That a difference of audience would cause any skilled teacher to adapt his

[1] *Historical Tradition in the Fourth Gospel*, pp. 366–387.*

[2] This was pointed out by J. Drummond (*An Inquiry into the Character and Authorship of the Fourth Gospel*, 1903, pp. 17 ff.), whose detailed list is conveniently summarized by Howard, *The Fourth Gospel in Recent Criticism*, p. 306.

[3] *The Gospel according to St. John* (1956), pp. 17, 20, 113 ff.

method can hardly be questioned.[1] But there are some passages for which this explanation would not seem to be valid, notably John vi, in which a discourse on the bread is delivered in Galilee in the same form and style as those in Jerusalem. But even here it should be noted that the discourse as a whole was not delivered in the open air but in the synagogue (vi. 59), and it is significant that the protagonists in the discussion are specifically described as Jews (vi. 41, 52), a term used characteristically by John of those who were particularly hostile to Jesus and who were representative of Judaism. It is, of course, true that John vi begins with a description of the feeding of the multitudes and leads on to the discussion about the heavenly bread, but it is evident that the discussion must have been restricted to a small number of people. It is quite clear that Jesus is not addressing the multitudes, and there is no reason therefore to suppose that He could not have addressed His audience on this occasion in the manner which John records. If the Synoptic presentation is the sole authentic tradition of Jesus the Teacher, the Johannine discourses must be admitted as a serious problem. But if Jesus could not have taught as the Johannine Christ taught, where did the idea arise that He did? It is inconceivable that such an unfamiliar picture could have received authentication if there were not already some basis for it in the tradition. Barrett's theory might seem in part to meet the difficulty if the Evangelist's sermons had conditioned his readers to expect Jesus to teach in the manner in which they had been accustomed to hear His teaching presented. But this theory could not account for the dialogue type of discourse, although it might apply to the farewell discourses (xiv–xvii), but even here the setting in the upper room restricts the applicability of the teaching, and makes it difficult to imagine that it could have been delivered from sermon material.

The difference between the Synoptic and Johannine teaching material must not be minimized, but is it not possible to find a solution in the versatility of Jesus as a teacher,[2] rather than in the acceptance of one

---

[1] Cf. Meinertz, *Einleitung*, p. 233.

[2] Even a Jewish scholar such as I. Abrahams (*Studies in Pharisaism and the Gospels*, I, 1917, p. 12) considered that John's discourses enshrine a genuine aspect of Jesus' teaching omitted from the Synoptics. Cf. also F. C. Burkitt, *The Gospel History and its Transmission*, pp. 239 ff.; Drummond, *op. cit.*, pp. 35 ff. W. H. Raney (*The Relation of the Fourth Gospel to the Christian Cultus*, 1933, pp. 71 ff.) maintains that most of the long discourse materials in John were Christian prose-hymns and if this theory is correct it would furnish an explanation of the different forms of our Lord's teaching in John and the Synoptics. He draws a distinction between

picture as authentic and the rejection of the other? Those who adopt the latter course (and the majority of scholars tend to do so) must frankly face the implications that they may be presupposing as the originator of the Johannine discourses one who was greater than Jesus Himself. If the great Johannine discourses are in no way related to the *ipsissima verba* of Jesus[1] they must have been the production of a greater reflective genius. But it is reasonable to suppose that the genius of Jesus' teaching method was capable of the Johannine discourses as well as of the Synoptic parables and aphorisms. This being so, the particular contribution of the author lay in a greater and more sympathetic understanding of this method of teaching than is found in the other Gospel writers.

The fourth category of differences consists of historical and chronological problems. The most notable differences are in the dating of the cleansing of the temple, the duration of the ministry, and the dating of the last supper. The first difficulty may be obviated by postulating two cleansings,[2] although this suggestion is usually dismissed, almost without consideration, as highly improbable.[3] On the other hand it cannot be argued conclusively that a double cleansing was impossible. If it happened once it could in theory happen twice, if similar conditions were repeated. It would not be the first time that such a double act of reformation proved necessary. The view that the temple police would not have allowed it to happen twice is not altogether convincing, for during the passion week the Lord's enemies were on the watch for Him in any case, but seem to have been powerless to stop Him. When they ultimately arrested Him they had to do it secretly for fear of the people. The whole act was done with such moral authority that it may

what he calls the continuous prose-hymns of John and the isolated poetic statements in the Synoptics. (Cf. his critique of C. F. Burney's evidence, *ibid.*, pp. 69, 70.) But a teacher capable of one would be equally capable of the other. Another theory particularly relating to the dialogue form in John's Gospel is that of C. H. Dodd(*BJRL*, xxxvii, 1954–55, pp. 54–67), who finds in them traces of the influence of current Hellenistic religious and philosophical models. According to him the Evangelist must be viewed as a literary craftsman who was himself responsible for the peculiarities of the Johannine discourses.

[1] Cf. R. H. Strachan's discussion, *The Fourth Gospel*[3] (1941), pp. 15–26.

[2] For a recent advocacy of a double cleansing, cf. R. V. G. Tasker, *The Gospel according to St. John* (1960), p. 61.

[3] The approach of C. K. Barrett is typical (cf. *op. cit.*, p. 163). He accepts John's dependence on Mark, which makes a double cleansing lacking in *literary* support.

even be questioned whether Jesus could have gone near the temple without doing it. Nevertheless, if there was one cleansing only, it needs to be decided whether the Synoptic or the Johannine timing of it is correct, and to suggest a reason for the variation between them. The majority of scholars maintain the Synoptic positioning of the incident because it leads naturally to the arrest and it is then supposed that John placed it early for symbolic reasons.[1] It is not conceivable that John was correcting the Synoptic narratives at this point, for his own passion story presupposes some such event to account for the arrest.[2] This consideration has led one scholar[3] to maintain a rearrangement of John with ii. 13b–25 placed after the raising of Lazarus, a reshuffling which would certainly resolve the difficulty if it could be substantiated.

The seeming variation in the duration of the ministry poses less of a problem than is often imagined. It is generally supposed that the Synoptists require only one year, whereas John requires almost three. But the chronological indications in the Synoptics are too vague to settle the question of the duration and there are in fact many incidental details which suggest a much longer period than one year.[4] Moreover, there are some obvious gaps in the Synoptic narratives, particularly in relation to the Judaean ministry. It is not impossible to regard both Synoptic and Johannine accounts as complementary in this matter. The one point of chronology in the midst of the ministry, common to all the Gospels, is the feeding of the five thousand, which John dates just before a Jewish Passover (Jn. vi. 4).[5] This dating is confirmed by the incidental comment of Mark that the grass was green (Mk. vi. 39),

[1] Cf. Higgins, *The Historicity of the Fourth Gospel* (1960), p. 44. Barrett (*op. cit.*, p. 163) attributes the change of position to theological rather than chronological motives. Cf. also J. H. Bernard (*St. John*, I, pp. 86 ff.) in support of the Synoptic dating. But C. J. Cadoux (*JTS*, xx, 1919, pp. 311 ff.) preferred the Johannine setting. T. W. Manson ('The Cleansing of the Temple', *BJRL*, xxxiii, 1951, pp. 271 ff.) dates the cleansing in Mark about six months before the passion narrative proper begins.

[2] See previous discussion on the Lazarus incident, p. 290.

[3] T. Cottam, *The Fourth Gospel Rearranged* (1952), pp. 47 ff.

[4] E. B. Redlich (*An Introduction to the Fourth Gospel*, 1939, pp. 68 ff.) sets these out concisely.

[5] If the theory is allowed that chapters v and vi should be reversed (see discussion on pp. 313 ff.), this will affect the duration of the ministry in John. Cf. E. F. Sutcliffe's advocacy of a two-year ministry, based on such a dislocation, *A Two Year Public Ministry* (1938), especially pp. 84 ff.

which shows that the season was April.[1] There was moreover another harvest season before this (i.e. one year earlier) when the disciples plucked the ears of corn (Mt. xii. 1; Mk. ii. 23; Lk. vi. 1). Another year must have elapsed after the feeding of the five thousand before the final Passover season at which Jesus was crucified. In addition John mentions another earlier Passover (ii. 13) during the early Judaean ministry. The major difference, therefore, is one of impression rather than of fact, owing mainly to the omission of the Judaean ministry from the Synoptics and their lack of data concerning the Jewish festivals.

The date of the last supper is a well-known crux, in which the Synoptic and Johannine records appear to differ in their account of its relation to the Jewish Passover. The former seem to identify the two, whereas John states clearly that the last supper was partaken before the Passover (xiii. 1). The whole problem is difficult and cannot be disposed of in the short space available in an introductory study. Yet the nature of the problem must be indicated and its suggested solutions briefly noted. The main factors may be summarized as follows:

1. The Synoptic Gospels are definite that the Sanhedrin determined not to arrest Jesus on the feast day (Mk. xiv. 2), which must mean that their plan was to arrest Him *before* the Passover. Now this is what John's narrative specifically implies.

2. Nevertheless Mark xiv. 12 makes equally clear that the place for the Passover was prepared on the same day as the sacrificing of the Passover lambs, which would seem to date the last meal on the same evening as the Passover.

3. Some details of the narrative relate to matters such as the carrying of arms, the buying of linen clothes and spices, and the hurried meeting of the Sanhedrin,[2] which would have been prohibited on a feast day. When the soldiers hurriedly remove the body of Jesus it is because of the scruples of the Jews regarding their holy days, which suggests that the crucifixion did not take place on a festival day. It is sometimes also claimed that the detail about Simon Cyrene returning from the country might indicate that he was returning home from work. This method of argument may, however, be questioned and the evidence cannot be pressed.[3]

---

[1] Cf. Higgins, *op. cit.*, pp. 30, 31.

[2] Cf. V. Taylor, *The Gospel according to St. Mark*, p. 666.

[3] A. J. B. Higgins (*The Lord's Supper in the New Testament*, 1952, pp. 17 ff.), who favours the Synoptic account in preference to the Johannine, minimizes

4. When Paul speaks of Christ our Passover (1 Cor. v. 7) he may have had in mind an actual tradition that Jesus was crucified at the same time as the Passover lambs were being slain, which would agree with John's account.

A variety of solutions has been proposed. Those who dispute the authenticity of the Fourth Gospel narrative as a whole take up the view that John is wrong and the Synoptics are right.[1] With the recent greater inclination to give more credence to the historicity of John's Gospel, the tendency to accept its testimony regarding the supper has gathered weight. In this case John's Gospel is regarded as a correction of the Synoptic dating. These two opposing points of view are based on the principle of either/or. Yet the last word has not been said, for a third possibility is a both/and solution, in which both John and the Synoptics may possibly be right. It is difficult to maintain that John was correcting the Synoptics on this matter unless some adequate explanation is forthcoming of the strength of the contrary tradition. It is better, therefore, if at all possible, to search for a solution which maintains the validity of both. Recently such a solution has been proposed by Mlle A. Jaubert.[2]

It is not possible to discuss all the details, but the general idea is that there were two calendars which fixed the Passover by different methods; in one it always fell on the same day of the week (i.e. Wednesday), and in the other it was adjustable in accordance with lunar calculations. The evidence for the former, which is the more unusual, is found in the Book of Jubilees. Since this calendar is now believed to

---

the strength of the objections listed above. Cf. the same author's article on 'The Origins of the Eucharist', NTS, 1 (1954–55), pp. 200–209. Higgins' own view is that John has antedated the chronology for theological reasons. The objections are even more strongly challenged by J. Jeremias, The Eucharistic Words of Jesus (1955), pp. 49–57.

[1] The negative criticism of the nineteenth century, which strongly called in question the Johannine historicity, inevitably left in its wake a bias against the veracity of any element of Johannine testimony. For a résumé of the earlier critical approach to John, cf. H. W. Watkins' Bampton Lectures, Modern Criticism considered in its relation to the Fourth Gospel (1890). For an account of the gradual change of attitude in the twentieth century, cf. W. F. Howard's The Fourth Gospel in Recent Criticism, pp. 128 ff., pp. 164 ff.

[2] 'La date de la dernière Cène', RHR, 146 (1954), pp. 140–173; La Date de la Cène (1957); 'Jésus et le calendrier de Qumrân', NTS, 7 (1960), pp. 1–30.

have been used in the Qumran community,[1] there is the possibility
that at the time of the passion of our Lord the Essenes were observing
the Passover before the Pharisaic observance in Jerusalem. If this is a
valid inference it is further possible that the Synoptic accounts might
be understood against the background of this calendar, whereas the
Johannine narrative might be related to the Jerusalem calendar. There
is some evidence that special regulations applied to Galilee[2] and it may
be that the same calendar as in the Book of Jubilees was observed there,
in which case it would be easy to see why Jesus and His disciples would
have kept the Passover before the official feast in Jerusalem. M. Black,
in fact, even wonders whether the Passover observed by our Lord was
regarded in Jerusalem as illegal.[3] No solution to the problem is wholly
without difficulties,[4] but this theory of divergent calendars seems to
point the way to a possible answer.[5]

Another idea closely akin to this, but which does not bring in the
Essenes, is to suppose that John reflects Sadducean custom in his Passover chronology, whereas the Synoptic narratives reflect the Pharisaic.[6]

[1] This was pointed out by D. Barthélemy, *VT*, 3 (1953), pp. 250–264, and is
supported by J. T. Milik, *Ten Years of Discovery in the Wilderness of Judaea* (1959),
pp. 107–113. Cf. also J. Morgenstern, *VT*, 5 (1955), pp. 34–76. On the significance
of the Qumran evidence on this question, cf. J. Blinzler, *ZNTW*, 49 (1958), pp.
238–251; J. Jeremias, *JTS*, n.s., x (1959), pp. 131–133.

[2] M. Black (*The Scrolls and Christian Origins*, 1961, p. 200) cites the Babylonian
Talmud, *Pes.* iv. 5 ff. Cf. the discussion by B. Gärtner, *John 6 and the Jewish
Passover* (1959).

[3] *Op. cit.*, p. 201. Cf. also E. Stauffer, *Jesus and His Story*, pp. 94, 95, who maintains that Jesus, accused of heresy, would not be allowed to partake of an official
Passover meal.

[4] A. J. B. Higgins (*The Historicity of the Fourth Gospel*, pp. 61, 62) is critical of
Mlle Jaubert's theory on two main grounds. First, the occurrence in the same week
of the Essene Passover and the Jerusalem Passover could happen only every thirty
years, and he thinks this coincidence is therefore suppositional, in addition to the
fact that no evidence remains that Jesus observed the Essene calendar. Secondly,
the evidence cited by Mlle Jaubert of an early Christian practice of celebrating the
last supper on a Tuesday evening, Higgins regards as worthless because it arose
out of an arbitrary fixing of Christian feast days. Another critic whose opinion
cannot be ignored is J. Jeremias, who considers that the author is more persuasive
than convincing (*JTS*, x, 1959, pp. 131 ff.).

[5] In his article on 'The Date and Significance of the Last Supper', *SJT*, 14 (1961),
pp. 256–269, A. Gilmore prefers an open verdict, but is not unsympathetic towards Mlle Jaubert's views.*

[6] This proposal is discussed by R. P. Martin in the *Theological Students' Fellowship Bulletin*, 29 (1961), pp. 4–8.

According to the former custom the 'Omer' was offered on the day following the sabbath after the Passover (i.e. Nisan 16), whereas the Pharisees interpreted Leviticus xxiii. 11 as meaning the day following the Passover (i.e. Nisan 15). Some scholars have claimed that John belonged to the Sadducean party[1] and that this accounts for his narrative reflecting the Sadducean tradition. It may well be, therefore, that the last meal was not the regular Passover meal, but came to be interpreted in that way.

It will be seen, therefore, that the historical and chronological differences may well be capable of an interpretation which does not involve contradictions or corrections, and this will clearly affect any theory of relationship.

b. Explanation of the relationship

Windisch[2] pointed out that there are four possible explanations. John may be either supplementary to, independent of, interpretative of, or a substitute for, the Synoptists. The first of these has most to be said for it and is most generally accepted. It is supported by several considerations. The large amount of material in John, which is absent from the Synoptics, would be well accounted for if John were filling in the gaps. Moreover, John often avoids unnecessary duplication, so that it would seem he assumes his readers will be acquainted with the Synoptic records. Since the Gospel as a whole, with its concentration upon the ministry in Judaea and Jerusalem and its greater quantity of discourse material, was evidently conceived on a different pattern from that of the Synoptics, it is reasonable to suppose that it was composed with the others in mind. It should be noted that this view is tenable even if it be maintained that John did not use the Synoptic Gospels as a source. But it does, of course, presuppose some knowledge of the content of those Gospels by both the author and his readers.

The second possibility, that of independence,[3] is difficult to maintain

---

[1] Cf. E. Stauffer, *New Testament Theology* (1955), pp. 40 f.; F. C. Burkitt, *The Gospel History and its Transmission* (1906), pp. 248 ff.

[2] *Johannes und die Synoptiker* (1926).

[3] In his recent article comparing the Johannine and Synoptic passion narratives, P. Borgen (*NTS*, 5, 1959, pp. 246–259) maintains that John follows a tradition independent of the Synoptics, although that tradition had become fused with Synoptic tradition before coming into the hands of the Evangelist. Yet as Higgins (*op. cit.*, p. 21) points out, it is strange that the Synoptics show no evidence of fusion with the Johannine tradition.

in view of the factors mentioned above. It is extremely difficult, for instance, to see why John should omit all direct reference to the ordinances if he were ignorant of the other Gospels. Furthermore it is difficult to conceive of any historical situation at a relatively late date in which the Synoptic Gospels were unknown. It is significant that this problem has led some advocates of the independence theory to postulate an early date for John.[1]

The third possibility, that of interpretation, has many advocates. It has been particularly favoured by the Hellenistic school of Johannine scholars,[2] who treat the whole Gospel as an interpretation of Jesus and His teaching especially designed for Gentile readers. Although this school of thought is not now as strong as it was, it still appears to many scholars as the best solution of the Johannine problem.[3] It is built, nevertheless, on an assumption, i.e. that the content of the Gospel is not intended to give an objective historical account. If this assumption should prove incorrect, the main support for the theory collapses with it. Moreover, if John were seriously attempting to 'interpret' the other Gospels, it is difficult to see why he includes so few parallels to them. There are, therefore, some major problems attached to this view. At the same time, there is clearly some element of interpretation, as, for example, in the Prologue.

The fourth suggestion, held by Windisch himself, is that John aimed to replace the Synoptics. But this has already been pointed out as highly improbable. There is, in fact, no evidence which leads us to suppose

[1] Cf. E. R. Goodenough, *JBL*, LXIV (1945), pp. 145–182; cf. also H. E. Edwards, *The disciple who wrote these things* (1953). J. A. T. Robinson ('The Place of the Fourth Gospel', in *The Roads Converge*, ed. P. Gardner-Smith, 1963, pp. 49–74) argues that the Johannine tradition is pre-AD 70. *N.B.* R. Gyllenberg maintained that the beginning of the Johannine tradition was as old as that of the Synoptists (*Neutestamentliche Studien für R. Bultmann*, ed. W. Eltester, 1954, pp. 144–147). He deduces this from a form-critical point of view.

[2] Cf. E. F. Scott, *The Fourth Gospel, its Purpose and Theology*[2] (1908), pp. 53 ff. J. Grill (*Untersuchungen über die Entstehung des vierten Evangeliums*, I, 1902, II, 1923) is one of the more extreme advocates of Hellenizing influences. But for a more moderate view see also C. H. Dodd, *The Interpretation of the Fourth Gospel*. R. Bultmann in *Eucharistion*, II (1923), pp. 1–26; *idem*, *ZNTW*, 24 (1925), pp. 100–146, and W. Bauer, *Das Johannesevangelium*[2] (1925), both make much of Mandaean parallels. Cf. also B. W. Bacon's *The Gospel of the Hellenists* (1933).

[3] R. H. Lightfoot (*St. John's Gospel: a Commentary*, 1956, pp. 33 ff.) held to John's interpretative purpose, although he was much more moderate in his approach to John's historicity than Bultmann and Bauer.

that John ever supplanted any of the other Gospels in any section of the Church. In fact, as has already been shown, the earliest Gospel to attain widespread distribution was Matthew's Gospel, not John's, and it would be necessary to suppose, on Windisch's theory, that the author was entirely unsuccessful in his quest.

VI. STRUCTURE

There are several problems which arise from a study of the Johannine structure: its comparison with the Synoptic structure, the question of literary sources and editorial processes, and the unity of the Gospel. There has been discussion of all or most of these problems through the whole period of critical enquiry. As a reaction to the sceptical attitude of the more destructive school of critics, many of the source-critical theories were attempts to salvage something of value from the Fourth Gospel while jettisoning the other material. It is small wonder that a large number of divergent theories resulted.[1]

a. The unity of the Gospel

It is of first importance to discover whether or not the book as it has been transmitted was the work of one author or of more than one, for it is useless to discuss the structure until this matter has been settled. Some would treat the Prologue (i. 1–18) as apart from the rest.[2] Others maintain the separateness of chapter xxi.[3] Many theories of disparate material in the body of the Gospel have also circulated.[4] Since there are so many divergences in the different theories it is impossible to give details. In fact, what is more important is to give some indication of the principles on which such theories have been variously based.

One idea which has led to theories of different sources used in the structure of John is that the discourse sections must be separated from

---

[1] A convenient summary of these may be found in Howard, *The Fourth Gospel in Recent Criticism*, pp. 297 ff.

[2] See pp. 309 f.

[3] L. Vaganay, *RB*, XLV (1936), pp. 512 ff.; M. E. Boismard, *RB*, LIV (1947), pp. 473–501. The latter suggests as author of this chapter a disciple of John who has been influenced by his oral teaching, thus accounting for the similarities and differences which he detects in this chapter compared with the rest. For a recent defence of chapter xxi, cf. Cassian, *NTS*, 3 (1957), pp. 133–136.

[4] See p. 301.

the narrative portions.[1] But the narrative portions so often merge almost imperceptibly into the discourse material (as for example in Jn. iii) that it is impossible to draw any clear line of demarcation between them. One source consisting entirely or even mainly of Johannine discourse material is most improbable, since in most cases the narrative sections are the setting for the discourses which follow.

Another criterion which some scholars have used is that of alleged discrepancies and contradictions, which are reckoned to point to different strata. Many of the older liberal critics[2] argued along this line, but the alleged 'discrepancies' and 'contradictions' were not impossible to obviate by some other quite satisfactory interpretation. In other words, this process was largely governed by the presuppositions with which individual critics approached the Gospel.

A third method of approach is to suppose an author and a redactor and to attempt to discern what portions of the book might be attributed to the latter. There is a large conjectural element here also, for it is often impossible to differentiate between the various types of style which are alleged to be present. One such theory was that of B. W. Bacon,[3] who attributed chapter xxi to the redactor, together with various other portions which were connected in some way with the Appendix (he includes, for instance, the account of Peter's denial). But Bacon's analysis was dominated by his theory regarding the purpose of the redactor, i.e. to harmonize the Asiatic and Roman traditions. Another theory is Bultmann's,[4] which postulates an ecclesiastical redactor, who has added some passages and phrases to bring the Gospel into line with the Synoptic tradition and ecclesiastical theology (sacra-

[1] As, for example, by H. H. Wendt (cited by Howard, *op. cit.*, p. 96). E. Renan (*Vie de Jésus*, 1863) questioned the discourses rather than the narratives, which he preferred to those of the Synoptics (cf. p. xxx). Recently a similar view has been advocated by E. Schweizer, *Ego Eimi* (1939), p. 106 (cited by Barrett, *op. cit.*, p. 8).

[2] For a review of older theories, cf. H. W. Watkins, *Modern Criticism considered in its relation to the Fourth Gospel* (1890), pp. 169 ff.

[3] *The Fourth Gospel in Research and Debate*[2] (1918), pp. 481 ff.*

[4] Cf. *RGG*, III[3] (1959), pp. 842 ff. R. H. Strachan (*The Fourth Evangelist, Dramatist or Historian?*, 1925, pp. 84 ff.) maintained a theory that the ideal plan of the Gospel was governed by symbolic considerations and that a redactor superimposed some chronological sequence to bring it into line with what he conceived a Gospel should be. But the extent of symbolism may be questioned, and in any case it is a matter of opinion whether or not one author may be responsible for these two different plans, assuming that two plans can positively be deciphered.

ments and eschatology). But the same conjectural basis is evident here.[1]

A rather more reliable criterion, although fraught with considerable dangers, is that of literary and stylistic comparisons. If there were passages which differed in a marked way from the style of the main portions of the Gospel, this might be some indication of the use of separate sources, or of the hand of a redactor, but stylistic changes within the Gospel are hard to substantiate, even in chapter xxi. The general impression of unity is, in fact, borne out by stylistic considerations. The Johannine grammatical peculiarities are fairly evenly distributed throughout the Gospel.[2] On the whole, therefore, it may be said that stylistic criteria favour the unity of the Gospel.

Yet another method of discrimination has quite recently been used—that of statistics. It has been maintained that by statistical investigation an original form of the Gospel can be differentiated from the existing enlarged copy. The pioneers in this field are G. H. C. Macgregor and A. Q. Morton,[3] the latter claiming to supply statistical justification of the theories of the former. Certain passages are observed to have longer paragraphs than others, and these are regarded as belonging to a hand different from that responsible for the remainder of the Gospel. Statistical methods are also used to support theories of widespread textual dislocations. But, as Morton himself admits,[4] paragraph study is not a conclusive guide. It can only assist in source analysis. Thus Macgregor claims that the J_2 panels (as these writers call the additional material) are introduced at exactly equal intervals, thus giving an indication of the almost mathematical bent of the editor's mind. He further claims that the evidence shows that there are numerous derangements in the text which he suspects are due to the processes of conflating J_1 and J_2.[5] By means of comparisons between the length of paragraphs, sentences and even words in each of these parts, Morton concludes

[1] Cf. also the theory of E. Hirsch (*Studien zum vierten Evangelium*, 1936), who proposed an original form of the Gospel which was written by an unknown Antiochian and was later adapted for the general use of the Asiatic churches. But cf. the criticisms of E. Ruckstuhl, *Die literarische Einheit des Johannesevangeliums* (1951), pp. 13 ff. Both Hirsch and Bultmann base their theories on style-critical methods (cf. Hirsch's discussion on style criticism, *ZNTW*, 43, 1950–51, pp. 129–143), but in general it is difficult to free style criticism from the investigator's personal inclinations. For Bultmann's sources theory for this Gospel, see p. 306.

[2] Cf. Howard, *op. cit.*, p. 107.   [3] *The Structure of the Fourth Gospel* (1961).
[4] *Ibid.*, p. 47.   [5] *Ibid.*, p. 56.

that there are real and substantial differences.[1] It is not at once obvious that the method used is justifiable, for no confirming parallels are cited to support the assumption that differences in length (in word, or sentence or paragraph) are indicative of difference of authorship. Until such confirmation is forthcoming, to maintain that it is illogical to argue for the unity of the material is unconvincing.

A critical study of the style of John's Gospel has in fact convinced E. Schweizer[2] of its essential unity. He finds similar characteristics in all its parts and concludes that no theory but uniform authorship is adequate to explain these stylistic facts.

Various theories based on the idea of partition and redaction have been advanced. It is not possible to give more than a general impression of these—details can be sought elsewhere.[3] Some of these theories assume a basic document which has been subjected to various later modifications. Either the basic document has been supplemented from the Synoptic Gospels and the combined material furnished with editorial comments, or the latter process alone has been used extensively. Other hypotheses presuppose that the basic document did not materially differ from the finished product, except in the case of a few small editorial comments. The main problem with all these theories is the lack of agreement between different exponents about the extent and delineation of the redactional material, which at least suggests that the method of determination is ultimately unsatisfactory. Moreover, since it is possible to make an intelligible interpretation of the Gospel without recourse to theories of interpolation or redaction, it would seem reasonable to require an indisputable basis for such theories before they can lay claim to credibility. No such claim could fairly be made for any of those theories so far produced, and in the absence of this the unity of the Gospel may legitimately be maintained.

b. *The problem of literary sources*

The major question is whether or not the author has used any of the Synoptic Gospels. Since both tradition and literary analysis suggest

---

[1] *Ibid.*, pp. 86–92.*

[2] *Ego Eimi* (1939). For a full discussion of Schweizer's viewpoint, cf. E. Ruckstuhl, *op. cit.*, pp. 180 ff.

[3] Cf. Howard's useful summary, *The Fourth Gospel in Recent Criticism*, pp. 297 ff.

304 NEW TESTAMENT INTRODUCTION

that John's Gospel came after the Synoptics, there is at once a likelihood that the author was aware of their existence. But does this
involve his use of Mark as a source? Two opposing answers have
been given.

The view that John has used Mark is widely held and is based on the
following considerations. Portions of John's Gospel are claimed to be
so closely paralleled in Mark as to require a theory of literary dependence. The most notable passages are the anointing at Bethany (Jn. xii.
1–8; Mk. xiv. 3–9), the cure of the impotent man at Bethesda (Jn. v. 8;
Mk. ii. 9), and the feeding of the five thousand (Jn. vi. 1–21; Mk. vi.
30–52), which are all said to reveal verbal similarities. With regard to
the first, J. H. Bernard[1] claimed that these similarities are too close to
be explained by a common oral tradition. However, when the total
number of verbal agreements is reckoned up they amount to a very
small proportion of the common material, and would hardly justify
the definite rejection of the possibility of a common source. This is
particularly so if eyewitness reminiscences lie behind both accounts.
Bernard referred to a number of other traces, largely of incidental
character, of John having used Mark.

C. K. Barrett,[2] who strongly maintains John's use of Mark,
places emphasis upon the fact that several narrative portions which
show some verbal contact follow the same sequence in John as
they do in Mark. This factor must clearly be given full weight,
but the support for the theory would be much stronger if the verbal agreements were more substantial. Nevertheless, this approach
to the relationship between John and Mark is supported by many
scholars.[3]

In addition there are claims that John has used Luke, of which the
most weighty instances usually cited are the anointing (cf. Lk. vii.
38), the prediction of the denial (Jn. xiii. 38; Lk. xxii. 34), the reference to the unused tomb (Jn. xix. 41; Lk. xxiii. 53) and details in the

---

[1] *St. John*, I, pp. xcvi, xcvii.

[2] *The Gospel according to St. John* (1956), pp. 34, 35. He cites a list of ten narrative sections occurring in the same order in John and Mark.

[3] For details, cf. W. G. Kümmel, *INT* (1965), p. 144. Cf. E. K. Lee, *NTS*, 3
(1956), pp. 50–58. In the passion narratives there are many incidental similarities
between Mark and John, but there are also many differences of language and
detail. S. I. Buse (*NTS*, 4, 1958, pp. 215–219) has suggested that the Fourth
Evangelist was acquainted not with Mark but with one his passion sources
(Vincent Taylor's B source).*

resurrection accounts[1] (cf. Jn. xx. 12, Lk. xxiv. 4; Jn. xx. 6, 7, 19, 20, Lk. xxiv. 12, 36). Again this evidence is sparse in quantity and could demonstrate literary dependence only if it were altogether unlikely that the data could have been obtained from another source.[2] There has been little support for the view that John shows literary dependence on Matthew.[3]

The contrary view that John did not use the Synoptic Gospels at all has been championed by P. Gardner-Smith,[4] who not only complained about the paucity of evidence for literary dependence but also its inconclusive nature. According to him the parallels are capable of being explained without recourse to the theory that John used the Synoptics as sources. Moreover, Gardner-Smith pointed out that the differences in the common material are more significant than the similarities. As a result of this careful study there has been less inclination to assume John's use of either Mark or Luke.[5]

[1] Cf. B. Lindars' examination of the sources of John's resurrection narratives (*NTS*, 7, 1961, pp. 142–147). He considers that these narratives cannot be traced to any one of the Synoptic Gospels, but rather depend on the traditions behind them. For a recent examination of all the relevant material and an advocacy of John's use of Luke's Gospel, cf. J. A. Bailey, *The Traditions common to the Gospels of Luke and John* (1963). This author supposes, nevertheless, that many traditions came to both Luke and John independently, sometimes written, sometimes oral.

[2] A different view of the relation between Luke and John is advocated by M. E. Boismard (*RB*, LXIX, 1962, pp. 185–211), who suggests an editing of John by Luke, at least in Jn. iv. 46b–53 and xx. 24–29. On the anointing cf. the article of K. Weiss (*ZNTW*, 46, 1955, pp. 241–245), who argues that the Western Text in Lk. vii. 46 was original and that John had misunderstood Luke's version of the anointing. Another view is that John combined Mk. xiv. 3 ff. (= Mt. xxvi. 6 ff.) with Lk. vii. 36 ff. (cf. W. G. Kümmel, *INT*, 1965, p. 145). W. Grundmann (*Das Evangelium nach Lukas*, pp. 17–22) denies literary dependence between Luke and John, but prefers to think of a common tradition.

[3] Cf. H. F. D. Sparks (*JTS*, n.s., III, 1952, pp. 58–61). But Gardner-Smith criticizes this point of view (*JTS*, n.s., IV, 1953, pp. 31–35).

[4] *St. John and the Synoptic Gospels* (1938). Cf., for similar views, F. C. Grant, *JBL*, LVI (1937), pp. 290–307. At an earlier date J. Schniewind (*Die Parallelperikopen bei Lukas und Johannes*, 1914) had strongly maintained that John did not use Luke. Bultmann thinks that John was independent of Luke, but used Mark, Q and L (*ThLZ*, 80, 1955, cols. 521–526). P. Parker (*NTS*, 9, 1963, pp. 317–336) suggests that Luke and John must have been associated in mission work.

[5] Cf. C. H. Dodd's article in *NTS*, 2 (1955), pp. 75, 76, on the Johannine *Herrnworte*, and his *Historical Tradition in the Fourth Gospel*. He argues for an independent tradition. For further recent discussions see S. Mendner, *ZNTW*, 47 (1956), pp. 93–112; J. N. Sanders, *NTS*, I (1954–55), pp. 29 ff.; D. M. Smith,

It should be noted that not all the arguments used by Gardner-Smith can be considered valid, for he argues that several of the parallels between John and the Synoptic Gospels cannot be due to literary dependence, because if they were it would mean that John would be flatly contradicting his source Mark. But the argument would not apply if such contradiction is not first of all assumed.[1] In other words the basis of some, at least, of Gardner-Smith's hypothesis is the irreconcilability of John and the Synoptics. Nevertheless, if this basis be rejected, it may still be reasonably maintained that the similarities and differences in the Gospels are more likely to have arisen during the oral period or through the different sources of evidence available (e.g. from eyewitness accounts[2]) than from the use of written sources.

Whatever conclusions are reached about this matter, it can safely be said that John did not use Mark as a framework. It is in fact John's distinctive framework which has distinguished his Gospel most notably from the Synoptics.

A complicated theory of John's literary sources is held by R. Bultmann,[3] who suggests two main sources, a revelation discourses source (*Offenbarungsreden*) and a signs source. In addition, the author possibly had a third source for the passion narrative which Bultmann believes was independent of the Synoptic Gospels. He arrives at his sources by an examination of stylistic phenomena and rhythmic patterns, as a result of which he claims to be able to distinguish not only the separate sources but also the redactional elements. The revelation discourses were based on Gnostic materials and originally existed in Aramaic. In spite of the great learning with which the theory has been presented it has not commended itself to many scholars. Bultmann's pupil, H.

Jnr., *JBL*, LXXXII, 1963, pp. 58–64 (who disputes dependence) and E. D. Freed, *JBL*, LXXX (1961), pp. 329–338 (who maintains it). It has been argued that the common belief that John was the end-product of primitive Christian development was responsible for the literary dependence theory (cf. E. R. Goodenough, *JBL*, LXIV, 1945, pp. 145–182).

On the other hand, a recent article by C. Goodwin (*JBL*, LXXIII, 1954, pp. 61–75) has argued from John's use of the Old Testament that it may be expected that he would use his sources with even greater freedom. He thinks this might mean that he may have used the other Synoptics when verbal parallels are slight.

[1] Examples may be found in P. Gardner-Smith, *op. cit.*, pp. 8, 16, 23, 48.

[2] Michaelis (*Einleitung*, p. 106) considers that the author relied on eyewitness sources.

[3] Cf. his *Das Evangelium des Johannes* and his article in *RGG*, III[3] (1959), pp. 842 ff.*

Becker,[1] developed the idea of the Gnostic origin of the revelation discourses, but other pupils of Bultmann have been more sceptical of this proposition.[2]

Stylistic phenomena are not a reliable indication of Johannine sources as E. Ruckstuhl[3] has cogently pointed out in his criticism of Bultmann's theory. He maintains that the stylistic features that Bultmann used as criteria for distinguishing between his two major sources occur in both. In fact, Ruckstuhl claims that style criticism must lead to the denial of written sources altogether. Although not all Bultmann's critics would go as far as this, most agree that the stylistic unity of John's Gospel is a difficulty for his theory. B. Noack,[4] however, argues for oral traditions behind the Gospel, maintaining that a purely narrative document like Bultmann's signs source is without precedent. He maintains further that the Evangelist's citations of the Old Testament appear to be from memory, and this would lead to the assumption that it was not his habit to cite sources meticulously. A major weakness in Bultmann's method is in his dealing with the editorial comments of the Evangelist. When these betray stylistic peculiarities similar to those of the sources, he resorts to the theory that here the editor is affected by the style of his sources, but this brings the whole method under suspicion.[5] Moreover, to maintain his rhythm criterion Bultmann is obliged to conjecture an Aramaic origin of the discourses which then leaves him free to attribute all non-rhythmic features to a prosaic redactor. But this method of dealing with difficulties is unconvincing.[6] E. Käsemann[7] has criticized Bultmann on other grounds, particularly disagreeing with the idea of a Gnostic source being used by a Christian Evangelist. In fact, by challenging Bultmann's theological interpretation, Käsemann questions the necessity for his source theory.

[1] *Die Reden des Johannesevangeliums und der Stil der gnostischen Offenbarungsreden* (1956).

[2] Cf., for instance, Käsemann: see below.

[3] *Die literarische Einheit des Johannesevangeliums* (1951), pp. 20–179. On the unity of the Gospel, W. Grossouw (*Nov. Test.*, 1, 1956, pp. 35–46) points out that in spite of his literary theories, Bultmann treats the Gospel as a unity in his *Theologie* (except for sacramental theology and eschatology).

[4] *Zur johanneischen Tradition, Beiträge zur Kritik an der literarkritischen Analyse des vierten Evangeliums* (1954), pp. 9–42.

[5] Cf. Noack, *op. cit.*, pp. 31 ff.

[6] Cf. R. H. Fuller's criticism, *The New Testament in Current Study* (1962), p. 113.

[7] Cf. his article, 'Neutestamentliche Fragen von heute', *ZTK*, 54 (1957), pp. 15 f.

A modified theory of Johannine origins has been put forward by W. Wilkens[1] who suggests that the author as it were made his own sources, and has written his Gospel in three stages or editions. In this way he attempts to account for the differences as well as the stylistic unity. However, the attempt to distinguish the stages must inevitably be difficult and to a large extent conjectural. It is unlikely for this reason that any general agreement will be reached along such lines. Another scholar who concentrates on the earlier stages of the Johannine material is S. Schulz[2] who, although claiming to find some Gnostic reinterpretations of originally Jewish elements, and therefore showing some points of contact with Bultmann's position, nevertheless rejects the idea of written sources.[3]

More recently C. H. Dodd has investigated the possibility of isolating what he calls the pre-canonical tradition behind this Gospel, which he considers must have existed in an oral form.[4] This he suggests is much closer to the Synoptic tradition than the rest of the Gospel, but is nevertheless independent of the Synoptic Gospels. He has summarized the contents of this traditional material in the following way.[5] (1) A full account of the work of John the Baptist, particularly as a reformer within Judaism; (2) testimonies of John the Baptist to Jesus (although Dodd does not date this element in the tradition so early); (3) an account of the early ministry of Jesus and the relationship between Jesus and John during this period; (4) an account of Jesus the Healer, although this was little used by the Evangelist; (5) a considerable amount of topographical information; (6) probably a fuller account of the Gali-

---

[1] *Die Entstehungsgeschichte des vierten Evangeliums* (1958).

[2] *Untersuchungen zur Menschensohnchristologie im Johannesevangelium, zugleich ein Beitrag zur Methodengeschichte der Auslegung des 4 Evangeliums* (1957). The same author has a second book *Komposition und Herkunft der johanneischen Reden* (1960).

[3] For another advocacy of written sources approached from a different point of view from that of Bultmann, cf. C. Broome (*JBL*, LXIII, 1944, pp. 107–121) who maintained John's use of written sources, but supposed that only the shorter *logia* sources were reproduced *verbatim*, the longer passages being more freely edited. Several recent articles have dealt with source criticism in John. Cf. H. M. Teeple's article on Methodology (*JBL*, LXXXI, 1962, pp. 279–286); D. M. Smith's article in *NTS*, 10 (1964), pp. 336–351, mainly on Bultmann and his critics; J. M. Robinson, *JBL*, LXXVIII (1959), pp. 242 ff.; C. K. Barrett, *ThLZ*, 84 (1959), cols. 828 f.; E. Haenchen, *ZTK*, 56 (1959), pp. 15–54.

[4] His book, *Historical Tradition in the Fourth Gospel* (1963), is wholly devoted to this investigation.*

[5] A useful summary is given, *ibid.*, pp. 429, 430.

laean ministry than the author has used; (7) a detailed passion narrative; (8) a body of traditional teaching material, including sayings, parables and dialogues. Dodd's investigations, which are carried out in a detailed and penetrating manner, are significant for various reasons. Having rejected the theory of literary dependence on the Synoptic Gospels, he has made a serious attempt to explain the presence in John of Synoptic-like material and in doing so has shown this material to be much more extensive than has often been supposed. It follows from this that, if Dodd is correct, much of the Johannine tradition rests on oral material which circulated before the production of the Synoptic Gospels and was contemporaneous with the oral sources of the latter. Such a conclusion could not fail to contribute towards a greater appreciation of the validity of the Johannine tradition and would help to combat any theory which erected insuperable barriers between John and the Synoptics.

c. The Johannine framework

The Gospel has a distinctive introduction which is unparalleled in the Synoptic Gospels. This Prologue is most significant because of its theological character and because of the importance it attaches to the manifestation of John the Baptist. Our present purpose is to consider how far the Prologue was intended to be an integral part of the Gospel. Again this has led to a variety of answers.

It has been supposed that the Prologue must be regarded as detached from the rest of the Gospel, as if the author introduced Christ's incarnation in Hellenistic terminology to capture the attention of his contemporaries.[1] Another view is that the author has incorporated a hymn on the Logos and has sought to integrate this with his purpose for the Gospel as a whole.[2] Both of these views assume that the interpretation of the Prologue furnishes the key to the understanding of the author's purpose. But it is possible to conceive that the author's main aim in the Prologue was to lead into his historical account of the life and teaching

[1] W. Baldensperger, *Der Prolog des vierten Evangeliums* (1898), cited by Howard, *The Fourth Gospel in Recent Criticism*, p. 57. It should be noted that Baldensperger did not regard the references to John the Baptist as intrusions into the Logos material, but as an essential part of the author's purpose. For a contrary view, cf. P. Gaechter, *ZkT*, 78 (1936), pp. 99–111.*

[2] Cf. C. Cryer, *ET*, xxxii (1921), pp. 440 ff.; J. H. Bernard, *St. John*, i, p. xxx. W. G. Kümmel (*INT*, 1965, p. 153) cites E. Käsemann and R. Schnackenburg as recent advocates for a pre-Johannine Christian hymn behind the Prologue.

of Jesus. This latter view is proposed by C. H. Dodd,[1] who regards the Logos doctrine as appropriate for leading 'a public nurtured in the higher religion of Hellenism' to 'the central purport of the Gospel, through which he (i.e. the writer) may lead them to the historical actuality of its story'. Some scholars firmly reject the view that the Prologue is Hellenistic and maintain on the contrary a Jewish origin. Both Rendel Harris[2] and C. F. Burney[3] argued strongly for this position. It is reasonable, therefore, to regard the Prologue as an integral part of the author's purpose in introducing his historical account.[4]

It is when the main body of the Gospel material is examined that it is difficult to discover the author's method of arrangement. The structure seems to be very loose. Dodd[5] connects i. 19–51 with the Prologue and considers the theme of the passage to be testimony, which leads up to what he calls the book of signs (ii–xii). This book consists of seven episodes and a conclusion. Each episode consists of both narrative and discourse related to a dominant theme.[6] There are many variations in the pattern on which the different episodes are constructed, but Dodd maintains that the episodes are so arranged as to be linked together. He has affixed titles to his episodes in the following manner: the new beginning (ii. 1–iv. 42); the life-giving Word (iv. 46–v. 47); Bread of life (vi); light and life: manifestation and rejection (vii–viii); judgment by the light (ix. 1–x. 21, x. 22–39); the victory of life over death (xi. 1–53); life through death: the meaning of the cross (xii. 1–36). This book of signs is then followed by the book of the passion (xiii–xxi). Such a scheme is a serious attempt to do justice to the structure of the book and draws particular attention to the Johannine emphasis on 'signs'.* Other scholars have been content with a much looser understanding of the structure. J. H. Bernard,[7] for instance, divides the main portion of the Gospel into two parts, the first embracing the ministry in Galilee, Jerusalem and Samaria (Jn. i. 19–iv, vi), and the second

---

[1] *The Interpretation of the Fourth Gospel* (1953), p. 296.

[2] *The Origin of the Prologue of St. John's Gospel* (1917).

[3] *The Aramaic Origin of the Fourth Gospel* (1922). The same conclusion was arrived at by D. Plooij, *Studies in the Testimony Book* (1932), p. 27. Cf. also T. W. Manson, *On Paul and John* (1963), p. 148, and M. Black, *An Aramaic Approach to the Gospels and Acts*[2] (1954), pp. 207–209.

[4] J. A. T. Robinson maintains that the original Gospel opened with a historical account of John the Baptist and that this was later superimposed with the Logos material (*NTS*, 9, 1963, pp. 120–129).

[5] *Op. cit.*, pp. 292 ff.   [6] *Ibid.*, p. 384.   [7] *Op. cit.*, pp. xxx ff.

dealing only with the ministry in Jerusalem (v, vii–xii. 50), but he makes no attempt to systematize the material within these sections. Similarly C. K. Barrett[1] finds the material in the section i. 19–xii very disparate, but he does find a discernible movement of thought which links together the various units.

Bultmann[2] divides the book into two main parts: the revelation of the glory before the world (ii–xii) and the revelation of the glory before the Church (xiii–xx). In the first part he finds four main sections: the encounter with the Revealer (ii. 23–iv. 42); the revelation as decision (iv. 43–vi. 59, vii. 15–24, viii. 13–20); the Revealer in conflict with the world (most of vii–x); the secret victory of the Revealer over the world (x. 40–xii. 33, viii. 30–40, vi. 60–71). In the second part is contained the farewell of the Revealer (xiii–xvii) and the passion and Easter narratives (xviii–xx). It will be seen that Bultmann achieves some unity of theme by means of rearrangement. Moreover, his dominant idea of a Revealer is influenced by his philosophical and theological position. Nevertheless, his two major divisions are suggestive.[3]

Some have attempted to find in John a sevenfold structure pervading the whole,[4] but this seems to be artificial in character. Others have proposed a kind of Jewish liturgical structure based on the feasts.[5] But it is difficult to believe that this framework formed the main basis for the Johannine structure. Another hypothesis somewhat akin to this is the view that behind the Gospel is to be discerned a Jewish lectionary and that the structure of the Gospel has been determined by this lectionary, with the result that the materials were arranged to form a commentary on the Old Testament passages set in the calendar.[6] This is an interesting theory, although it is again difficult to imagine that the finished product grew up in this way. If it did, the author

[1] The Gospel according to St. John (1956), pp. 11 ff.
[2] Das Evangelium des Johannes, cf. pp. 5–7.
[3] This is followed by I. H. Marshall (NBD, p. 645), although without Bultmann's rearrangement or presuppositions.
[4] Cf. E. Lohmeyer's view, ZNTW, 27 (1928), pp. 11–36. A. Feuillet cites J. Rabenech, Einführung in die Evangelien (1921), for a similar theory (Robert-Feuillet's Introduction, II, p. 623).
[5] Cf. D. Mollat in the Jerusalem Bible (cited in Robert-Feuillet, op. cit., p. 623).
[6] Cf. A. Guilding, The Fourth Gospel and Jewish Worship (1960). For a brief critique of this theory, cf. J. R. Porter's article 'The Pentateuch and the Triennial Lectionary Cycle: An Examination of a Recent Theory', in Promise and Fulfilment, Essays presented to S. H. Hooke (ed. F. F. Bruce, 1963), pp. 163–174. Also L. Morris, The New Testament and the Jewish Lectionaries (1964).

certainly used considerable skill in imposing an essential unity on the material. At the same time there are many interesting parallels and the idea that John's Gospel was arranged with a view to providing a Christian lectionary over a period of three and a half years is intriguing. It is not easy, however, to see that any validity can in this case be placed on John's historical sequence.[1]

Mention must also be made of theories which propose a typological motive as an element in the Johannine structure. Several writers[2] have found typological parallels between various Old Testament passages and Johannine material, notably from the book of Exodus. But even where the parallels are confined to Exodus different schemes have been proposed and the question naturally arises whether any importance can be attached to theories of this sort. For instance, a theory[3] which sees parallels between the Mosaic miracles of Exodus ii. 23–xii. 51 and the Johannine signs presents a fascinating prospect, but stretches credulity when detailed comparisons are made. It is hard enough to believe that the author himself had such parallels in mind and almost inconceivable that any of his original readers would have suspected it.*

VII. THEORIES OF DISLOCATION

In spite of the fact that this Gospel gives a general impression of unity, some scholars consider that there is evidence of dislocation. In some cases the connecting links which join adjacent sections are very loose and have therefore given rise to the hypothesis that the original text has suffered some mechanical disarrangements in course of transmission. The suggestion is not entirely impossible, especially if the autograph was in codex form, although there is no certain evidence to show whether codices were used quite as early as this.[4] The major objection

---

[1] A. Guilding maintains that the author is more interested in lectionary time than in historical time. This, she thinks, accounts for the different chronology of the cleansing of the temple (cf. *op. cit.*, pp. 4, 186 ff.).

The view that this Gospel was designed for liturgical use was maintained by A. Schlatter, *The Church in the New Testament Period* (1955), p. 300.

[2] Cf. H. Sahlin, *Zur Typologie des Johannesevangeliums* (1950); J. J. Enz, *JBL*, LXXVI (1957), pp. 208–215; B. P. W. S. Hunt, *Some Johannine Problems* (1958); T. F. Glasson, *Moses in the Fourth Gospel* (1963).

[3] Cf. R. H. Smith, *JBL*, LXXXI (1962), pp. 329–342.

[4] On the development of the codex form of manuscript, cf. Sir F. Kenyon's *The Story of the Bible* (1936), pp. 27 ff. More recently C. H. Roberts has published an important article on 'The Codex' (*The Proceedings of the British Academy*, XXXII, 1954), in which he shows that during the second century the codex seems

to this kind of hypothesis is the great number of different theories proposed, which considerably lessens the credibility of the idea as a whole.[1] It is possible to give only the main passages involved, but these will give sufficient indication of the type of data on which the theories are based.

1. iii. 22–30. It is suggested that this passage would fit better if placed between ii. 12 and ii. 13, on the grounds that in its present position it interrupts the Nicodemus discourse.[2]

2. v and vi. These chapters are thought to be better if transposed, as in chapters iv and vi Jesus is in Galilee, whereas in chapter v He is in Jerusalem.

3. vii. 15–24 is regarded as a continuation of the controversy at the close of chapter v, and it is claimed that when this passage is brought forward, vii. 25 ff. follows naturally on vii. 1–14.

4. x. 19–29 is similarly thought to continue the earlier controversy of chapter ix, hence x. 30 ff. would then follow x. 1–18. It is claimed that x. 1–18 would follow naturally after x. 19–29.

5. xiii–xvi. A rearrangement of these chapters so that xv and xvi precede xiv is thought necessary in view of xiv. 31 which appears to be the conclusion of the discourses.

6. xviii. 13–24 is said to contain confusion in its account of the trial. Some rearrangement is supported by the Sinaitic Syriac text of the Gospel, which has the following order, xviii. 12, 13, 24, 14, 15, 19–23, 16–18, 25 f.[3]

to have been used more widely for Christian purposes than for secular purposes which suggests that this form may have originated among the Christians at a very early date. It is not inconceivable, therefore, that the original, or else a very early copy of John, may have been in such a form.

[1] Moffatt gives several suggestions (*ILNT*, p. 554). Bernard provides a very full discussion of these proposed dislocations and favours all those cited and more beside (*St. John*, I, pp. xvi ff.). Other exponents who may be mentioned are J. M. Thomson, *Exp.*, VIII, ix (1915), pp. 421 ff.; Warburton Lewis, *Disarrangements in the Fourth Gospel* (1910); G. H. C. Macgregor, *The Gospel of John* (MC, 1928); F. R. Hoare, *The Original Order and Chapters of St. John's Gospel* (1944); T. Cottam, *The Fourth Gospel Rearranged* (1952).

[2] A different approach to the Nicodemus incident is that of S. Mendner (*JBL*, LXXVII, 1958, pp. 293–323) who thinks that portions of chapter iii belonged originally after vii. 51 and were dislocated after AD 135.

[3] For a theory based on the changes of order in the Syriac but differing slightly in detail by placing verse 15 after and not before verses 19–23, cf. W. R. Church, *JBL*, LXIX (1950), pp. 375–383.

Although some of these suggested rearrangements may possibly improve the connection of thought, there are some important considerations against such theories generally.

1. Amended arrangements can be justified only if the existing arrangement is incapable of intelligent interpretation and that can hardly be said of many, if any, of the above proposals. Indeed, it may be suggested that in some cases the rearrangements cause more dislocation to the connection of thought than the original alleged dislocations.[1]

2. Only for the last rearrangement suggested above can any textual evidence be produced. This must inevitably lessen the credibility of the hypotheses, even if it does not actually rule them out. It is possible to suppose that the dislocations happened in the original copy or else in a very early copy before the existing textual evidence arose. It is difficult however to maintain that disarrangements happened in an original autograph without the writer or his closest associates noticing.[2] It has further been noted in support of this kind of dislocation theory that Tatian placed the cleansing of the temple and the Nicodemus episode after vii. 31 in his *Diatessaron*, but this can hardly be taken as evidence for the order of the original text of John.[3]

3. The suggested rearrangements rest on the assumption that the author was meticulous about chronological and topographical order, but there is little evidence that he was. For instance, he often uses the vague μετὰ τοῦτο (or ταῦτα), by which he implies no more than a

---

[1] C. K. Barrett (*The Gospel according to St. John*, 1956, p. 183) strongly maintains the unity of chapter iii as it stands. In his opinion iii. 31–36 carries on the sense of iii. 22–30, in which case there is no need to reverse them. Bernard (*op. cit.*, p. xxiv) admits that to place this section before the cleansing of the temple and the 'signs' at Jerusalem would be unnatural, but he treats this section as a dislocation by placing it after iii. 36, a view supported by C. J. Cadoux, *JTS*, xx (1919), p. 317. This is rather less difficult and shows a better connection with chapter iv.

[2] Cf. Barrett, *op. cit.*, pp. 19, 20. It is little more convincing to maintain, as W. H. Raney does (*The Relation of the Fourth Gospel to the Christian Cultus*, 1933, pp. 75 ff.), that some of these dislocated sections consist of prose-hymns which were written on detachable hymn-sheets for choral purposes and which became deranged when replaced. It would be more reasonable to suppose with T. Cottam (*op. cit.*, pp. 77 ff.) that the author left his work in draft form on separate papyrus sheets and that after his death someone prepared them for publication and in doing so deranged the order.

[3] Cf. E. B. Redlich, *An Introduction to the Fourth Gospel* (1939), p. 104.

general idea of sequence. At the same time it would be a mistake to suppose that John was entirely disinterested in chronology, for both at the beginning and the end of the Gospel he includes a sequence of days, and in several incidents he mentions the hours when events happened. The point is that what appears disjointed to the modern scholar may not have appeared so to John.[1]

4. It is claimed by Barrett[2] that John's theological thought does not always move in straight lines, by which he means that he changes his point of view in course of dealing with the same subject, thus enlarging the whole theme. Whereas this may be true of some of the discourses, in which case the method of exposition could be that of Jesus and not John, it should be noted that the suggested dislocations affect narratives more than discourses (except in the case of the rearrangement of whole chapters). Nevertheless, the whole Gospel as it stands contains a fair impression of continuity which may well represent John's original conception.[3]

5. The *pericope adulterae* (vii. 53–viii. 11), which not only looks out of keeping with its immediate context but is treated as such in some strata of the textual tradition,* is sometimes claimed as justification for the theory that other sections may be displaced. This would be further strengthened by the consideration sometimes brought forward that some, at least, of the rearranged sections mentioned above are similar in length to this *pericope*, while others are in multiples of it.[4] This line of argument, if true, cannot be lightly dismissed, but its validity needs to be tested and its credibility carefully weighed. The suggestion that vii. 53–viii. 11 can be used as a standard of measurement is highly dubious, for comparison with the number of lines for this passage and those mentioned above shows that this passage contains

---

[1] J. Moffatt (*ILNT*, p. 552) admitted the danger of making the assumption that John's mind was as logical or chronological as his critics', but he nevertheless favoured widespread dislocations, although he attributed these to copyists or later editors.

[2] *Op. cit.* p. 20.

[3] See discussion on the unity of the Gospel, pp. 300 ff.

[4] First suggested by F. Spitta, *Zur Geschichte und Literatur des Urchristentums* (1893) I, p. 157. Cf. Warburton Lewis (*Disarrangements in the Fourth Gospel*, 1910 p. 15), who argued that xv and xvi were exactly six times the length of vii. 15–24, and the similar methods of A. C. Clark, *The Primitive Text of the Gospels and the Acts* (1914), pp. vi, 68 ff.; idem, *JTS*, xvi (1915), pp. 225 ff.; H. S. Cronin, *JTS*, xiii (1912), pp. 563–571.

more lines (16½ of Souter's text) than, for instance, vii. 15–24 (14½ lines) or iii. 22–30 (14 lines). On the other hand, Bernard works out the number of letters in each of six of his suggested dislocations and makes them all come very approximately to multiples of 750 letters, which he supposes was an average per leaf of papyrus. Unfortunately Bernard does not include in his calculations his two most impressive dislocations, chapters vi and xiv, but nevertheless his evidence is suggestive. It is known from Oxyrhynchus Papyrus P⁵, which preserves the outermost leaf but one of John's Gospel, that an equivalent of about fourteen lines of Souter's text would have occupied each page, which would confirm Bernard's estimate of about 750 letters *per page*. But in considering dislocations it is necessary to take into account more than *one* page. In fact, in a codex book *four* pages (*recto* and *verso* on a folded sheet) would be involved, as P⁵ demonstrates.[1] But the above dislocations could not be made to fit neatly into such a scheme. It might be more conceivable if smaller quires were used (i.e. of 8 to 12 leaves, of which there are some early examples), but the problem still arises of more than one page being involved for each dislocation.[2]

On the whole there appear to be too many doubtful assumptions in this type of theory to make it convincing, and since the text is at least intelligible as it stands it is preferable to leave it as it is.

VIII. LANGUAGE AND STYLE

The author of this Gospel writes in a form of Greek which is stamped with his own individuality. The range of his vocabulary is severely limited and yet the effect that he produces is dignified and compelling. He is given to repetition of words and phrases, which nevertheless is

---

[1] If, of course, the *verso* was not used only two pages of the codex would be involved. Cf. the argument of W. G. Wilson (*JTS*, L, 1949, pp. 59, 60) that none of the dislocations suggested would fit exactly into multiples of two full pages. He thought that disarrangement of pages in a codex was therefore improbable. It could not have happened on a scroll, since the papyri sheets were joined before, not after, they were written on.

[2] Taking the P⁵ fragment as a model of a sheet of the whole codex, it would be difficult, for instance, to make the chapter iii dislocation correspond with the chapter xviii dislocation, and unless they did the error could not have arisen through mechanical misplacement. At most, the theory would require that a scribe placed some of these sections accidentally on the *verso* instead of the *recto* side. But again it is difficult to conceive that this would have happened, and then entirely escaped detection.

never monotonous. He does not contrive to achieve elegance of expression by classical standards, but what he does achieve is a simple
impressiveness of presentation. In spite of his simple style, his Greek
never becomes inaccurate. C. K. Barrett[1] says, 'It is neither bad Greek
nor (according to classical standards) good Greek.' W. F. Howard[2]
considered that the author 'was a man who, while cultured to the last
degree, wrote Greek after the fashion of men of quite elementary attainment'. The same writer thought that the linguistic evidence indicated
that Greek was not the author's mother tongue.[3] This will have
some bearing on the question of the original language of the Gospel
mentioned below.

It is worth noting that many of the theological words found frequently in John occur much less often in the Synoptic Gospels (e.g.
such words as love, truth, life, light, witness, abide). Similarly, in the
reverse direction, many of the expressions used frequently in the
Synoptics are little used, or do not occur at all, in John (e.g. kingdom,
people (λαός), call, pray or prayer).[4]

Perhaps the most characteristic feature of John's style is the widespread use of καί, instead of subordinating clauses, in joining sentences
(*parataxis*). It is this feature more than any other which creates such an
impression of simplicity in the Greek. The author is clearly more in-
tent on imparting a message than on stylistic niceties.[5]

The presence of poetic forms in this Gospel has not escaped the
notice of scholars. For instance, Rendel Harris[6] noted such a
form in John vii. 37, 38, while C. F. Burney[7] devoted careful attention to poetic forms in John and found the same phenomenon
in the teaching of Jesus in this Gospel as in the Synoptics. He found
evidence of such poetic forms as synonymous-, antithetic-, synthetic-

---

[1] *Op. cit.*, p. 5.

[2] J. H. Moulton and W. F. Howard, *A Grammar of New Testament Greek*, II,
p. 33.

[3] *Ibid.*, pp. 31, 32.

[4] For a list of the occurrences of these and other words in John and the Synoptics, see Barrett, *The Gospel according to St. John* (1956), pp. 5, 6.

[5] For a study of characteristic Johannine words or constructions which are
rare in, or absent from, the rest of the New Testament, cf. E. Schweizer's study
Ego Eimi (1939); J. Jeremias' article on 'Johanneischer Literarkritik', *Theologische
Blätter* (1941), pp. 33–46, and E. Ruckstuhl, *Die literarische Einheit des Johannesevangeliums* (1951), pp. 180 ff.

[6] *Exp.*, VIII, XX (1920), p. 196.   [7] *The Poetry of our Lord* (1925).

and step-parallelism. This and other features influenced Burney in his theory of an Aramaic origin for this Gospel, which will be considered next.

The attempts to prove an Aramaic original for any of the Gospels cannot be said to have succeeded, although interest in this subject remains unabated. The two most thoroughgoing advocates of the Aramaic origin of John are C. F. Burney[1] and C. C. Torrey,[2] but most scholars agree that their evidence for an Aramaic written source from which our Greek Gospel was translated is improbable. W. F. Howard[3] criticized Burney's arguments on the ground that he did not distinguish between Aramaic constructions found in the Gospel and not found in the contemporary colloquial Greek from those which were common to both. When the latter are eliminated the evidence looks far less impressive. If, of course, specific mistranslations are traceable this would be far stronger support for the theory. But Matthew Black,[4] who advocates Semitic influence on the writers of the Gospels, admits only a very few mistranslations. Even in these cases, it is not agreed that this is the only possible explanation for the Greek text.[5]

It would seem a fair conclusion that the author was not unacquainted with Semitic idioms, although he does not allow glaring Semitisms to intrude into his Greek. If the author were the apostle John some Semitic influence would naturally be expected. The main problem would then be whether a Galilaean such as John would have been able to avoid giving more evidence than he has of Aramaic influence. The answer is bound to be affected by other considerations, since no conclusive linguistic criterion exists. Barrett,[6] who does not regard the apostle as author, contents himself with suggesting that the writer treads 'the boundary between the Hellenic and the Semitic'.

---

[1] *The Aramaic Origin of the Fourth Gospel* (1922).

[2] *The Four Gospels* (1933). 'The Aramaic Origin of the Gospel of St. John', *HTR*, 16 (1923), pp. 305–344.   [3] *Op. cit.*, pp. 483 ff.

[4] *An Aramaic Approach to the Gospels and Acts* (1946), pp. 207, 208.

[5] M. Burrows (*JBL*, XLIX, 1930, pp. 95–139) was favourable to the view that an Aramaic original was translated into Greek by a redactor, a view not unfavourably considered by G. H. C. Macgregor, *The Gospel of John* (*MC*, 1928), p. lxvi. Burrow's article supported in the main the position of Burney and Torrey, although critical of details.

[6] *Op. cit.*, p. 11.

IX. THE BACKGROUND OF THE GOSPEL

In all New Testament books the background is important, and in none is it more so than this Gospel. The exegesis of the whole book has been considerably influenced by different opinions regarding the milieu of both writer and readers. It will be possible to give only the barest outline of the main elements which have been claimed to contribute to this milieu, and to indicate the probability or improbability of each.

a. Primitive Christianity

This Gospel cannot be regarded in isolation from early Christian history. It was produced within the context of that history and cannot be interpreted apart from the background of primitive theology. This goes without saying if the author was either an eyewitness or someone in touch with an eyewitness. We have already dealt with the impact of the Synoptic tradition, which from a literary point of view is not extensive. But how does the Johannine presentation of Christ relate to the Synoptic description? It would be a fair answer to state that there is no conflict between the two presentations, although the Johannine account is clearly different in emphasis. If the early character of the Johannine material is admitted, it may be that this material must be regarded as contemporary with primitive Christianity. In other words it represents a parallel genuine tradition. At all events, a close connection of this Gospel with the primitive tradition must be maintained.[1]

b. Paulinism

It has been claimed by some that the author of this Gospel was a Paulinist.[2] This type of theory assumes that Johannine theology is one stage further developed than Paul's teaching, just as the latter is a development of Jesus' teaching. Indeed it has been supposed that the Epistle to the Hebrews[3] falls between Paul and John in the line of development, and this would push John to the end position in Christian theology. Yet it is probably nearer the true position to maintain that Christian theology did not develop by this method, but that several co-lateral streams, of which Paul, Hebrews and John represent con-

[1] Cf. C. H. Dodd's conclusion in his *Historical Tradition in the Fourth Gospel*, pp. 423 ff.

[2] Cf. E. F. Scott (*The Fourth Gospel, its Purpose and Theology*[2], 1908, p. 46), who considers that John is everywhere indebted to Paul.

[3] Cf. R. H. Strachan, *The Historic Jesus in the New Testament* (1931).

temporary manifestations, developed at an early stage. Dodd[1] has urged caution in the use of Paul to interpret John. At the same time the two cannot be separated. Both present a vital aspect of Christian theology.

c. Judaism

It would be surprising if there were no points of contact between John and contemporary Judaism, though in assessing the evidence the investigator must carefully distinguish between influences derived from Old Testament sources and those belonging to rabbinism.[2] The main problem confronting the study of the latter is that much of the evidence comes from a later period, although it is confidently maintained that our extant sources preserve material contemporary with John, if not with Jesus. Many parallels may be cited which might at least show that Judaism may have contributed to the setting of the Gospel. Since Jesus was a Jew it would be extraordinary if this had not happened, but the points of difference between the teaching of Jesus as John reports it and the teaching of the Rabbis are more striking than the similarities. One scholar, H. Odeberg,[3] has suggested that this Gospel has sometimes a greater affinity with Jewish mysticism than with rabbinism, but again the wide differences between such mysticism and the Gospel cannot be overstressed.

Some comment must here be made on the relation of John to Essenism. Some of the features of the Qumran literature find echoes in John and, although some scholars have made exaggerated claims for the connection of John's Gospel with the Qumran type of approach, there can be no doubt that these recently discovered MSS have influenced the general approach to John's Gospel. It is no longer convincing to maintain that the Gospel is wholly Hellenistic in view of the fact that many of the abstract concepts which were characteristic of Greek thought are also found in the Qumran literature, e.g. light and truth. There is also a similar love of antitheses such as light versus darkness,

---

[1] Op. cit., p. 5.

[2] Cf. ibid., pp. 74–94, for a discussion of rabbinic Judaism as a background to John. Cf. also A. Schlatter, Der Evangelist Johannes[2] (1930) and the relevant sections in Strack-Billerbeck's Kommentar for studies in the Jewish background of this Gospel.*

[3] The Fourth Gospel interpreted in its Relation to Contemporaneous Religious Currents (1929). Cf. W. F. Howard's brief comments in The Fourth Gospel in Recent Criticism, pp. 158, 159.

truth against error. Moreover, there are some remarkable parallels in language. R. E. Brown[1] considers that the author was acquainted with the Qumran thought and expression, although the evidence is not enough to suggest knowledge of the sectarian literature. O. Cullmann[2] has rightly pointed out that the differences are more significant than the similarities, particularly in relation to the Person of Christ.

d. Hermetic literature

It is only comparatively recently that attention has been turned to the Johannine parallels with the *Hermetica*, which was a body of philosophical and religious tractates attributed in Egypt to Hermes Trismegistus. The extant remains are very late, but these writings are believed to have originated in the second and third centuries AD. C. H. Dodd,[3] who has made a special study of this literature, considers that John shows a kinship with the *Hermetica*, but that there is no evidence of literary borrowing. Once again, when this connection of John with the kind of thought represented by the *Hermetica* is examined, it must at once be admitted that John's characteristic features are very different from the Hermetic literature. Dodd himself makes wide use of the *Hermetica* to illustrate the background of thought of the Gospel, but it may be questioned whether this kind of background was in the author's mind to the extent that he supposes. In fact there is closer linguistic affinity between John and the Septuagint than between John and the *Hermetica*.[4]

e. Philonism

The Alexandrian Philo may be cited as representative of Hellenistic Judaism, in which he was by far the most influential figure. The main point of contact between John and Philo relates to the Prologue, it being supposed that the Logos idea must be interpreted in the light of Philo's treatment. Such a viewpoint has recently lessened in influence

[1] Cf. his article in *The Scrolls and the New Testament* (ed. K. Stendahl), pp. 183–207. Cf. *idem*, in *Neotestamentica et Patristica*, pp. 111–122. Cf. also the works of F. C. Grant, M. Burrows and H. M. Teeple mentioned on p. 278 n.2, 3 and cf. F. M. Braun, *RB*, LXII (1955), pp. 5–44.

[2] Cf. his article in *The Scrolls and the New Testament*, p. 22.

[3] Cf. *The Bible and the Greeks* (1935), and his *The Interpretation of the Fourth Gospel*, pp. 10–53.

[4] Cf. the study by G. D. Kilpatrick on 'The Religious Background of the Fourth Gospel' in *Studies in the Fourth Gospel* (ed. F. L. Cross, 1957), pp. 36–44.

following the greater inclination to find the roots of the Logos idea in Hebraic thought. Nevertheless, since Philo was so influential in Hellenistic Judaism during the period of early Christian history, his mode of teaching cannot be ignored in outlining the background of the Gospel. In both Philo and John certain symbolism is used, as for instance the description of God as Light, as a Fountain and as a Shepherd.[1] As in the case of all the other elements in the non-Christian background the differences are more striking than the similarities. Whereas the differences belong to the essentials, the similarities are peripheral. The Logos of Philo becomes radically transformed in John's account. It becomes incarnate in Christ, an idea quite alien to Philo.

f. Other possible background features

Gnosticism sometimes speaks in language similar to John's, particularly in respect of dualistic conceptions and ideas of redemption. But it is important to note that recent studies have stressed the necessity of drawing a distinction between developed Gnosticism and the early Gnostic stage.[2] It is only the latter which could have any relevance to the Johannine literature, but the difficulties of determining the content of this incipient movement are not inconsiderable.[3] Most of the extant literature belongs to the later stage. Nevertheless, it is at least probable that John's Gospel was produced at a time when Gnostic ideas were becoming more dominant in pagan and Christian circles in Asia.[4] At the same time there is no evidence in the Gospels that the

[1] For details, cf. Dodd, *op. cit.*, pp. 54 ff. Parallels in thought do not, of course, involve literary dependence (cf. R. M. Wilson, *Nov. Test.*, 1, 1956, pp. 225 ff.).

[2] Cf. R. McL. Wilson's study, *The Gnostic Problem* (1958).

[3] Bultmann, in his *Das Evangelium des Johannes* (KEK[13], 1953), is the most thoroughgoing commentator appealing to a Gnostic milieu for John's Gospel. Cf. also the work of H. Becker (*Die Reden des Johannesevangeliums und der Stil der gnostischen Offenbarungsreden*, 1956), who carries Bultmann's suggestions still further and actually attempts to reconstruct the Greek Gnostic source which he supposes John used. Cf. the review of this book by K. Grayston (*NTS*, 5, 1959, pp. 82–84), who shows the fallacy of Becker's method in using for his parallels materials which are much later than John's Gospel. The Gospel is, in fact, the middle term between the Wisdom Literature and Gnosticism.

[4] Cf. the recent articles of C. K. Barrett and J. Munck in *Current Issues in New Testament Interpretation* (ed. W. Klassen and G. F. Snyder, 1962), pp. 210–233, 234–238. The former speaks of a pre-Johannine Gnosticism whose language John appears to use, while the latter criticizes Bultmann's theory for John on the grounds that he has not critically evaluated the Gnostic material and has too readily assumed that this was a unity.

author is consciously selecting or adapting his material to meet this particular threat, unless it was the beginnings of Docetism.[1] It is of interest that the later Gnostics seem to have been particularly attracted to this Gospel,[2] but they did not derive their characteristic emphases from this source.

Mandaism is another movement which has been appealed to as a part of the Johannine background. But this idea cannot be substantiated. The data on Mandaism are too late to provide any certain idea of a pre-Christian cult as Reitzenstein[3] maintained. The Mandaean literature may therefore be disregarded as a contribution to the Johannine background. If there are parallels it is certain that the Fourth Gospel has contributed to the thought-forms of the later Mandaean movement and not *vice versa*. The appeal to Mandaean parallels has been made by both Bultmann[4] and Bauer,[5] but has found little favour among other scholars.[6]

X. HISTORICITY

Because of the unique character of John's Gospel more discussion has ranged around its historicity than over that of the Synoptic Gospels. In the section dealing with its relation to the Synoptics some indications were given of the various explanations of this relationship, and it was noted that in some hypotheses the unhistorical character of John was taken for granted. The problems of historicity are too wide to be dealt with here, but the main schools of thought will be indicated, to give a general idea of the issues involved.

[1] Already discussed under Purpose, pp. 275 ff.

[2] For a detailed treatment, cf. W. von Loewenich, *Das Johannesverständnis im zweiten Jahrhundert*, Beiheft *ZNTW*, 13 (1932).

[3] *Das iranische Erlösungsmysterium* (1921)—cited by Dodd, *The Interpretation of the Fourth Gospel*, p. 128.

[4] 'Der religionsgeschichtliche Hintergrund des Prologs zum Johannes-Evangelium', *Eucharistion*, II (1923), pp. 1–26, and *ZNTW*, 24 (1925), pp. 100–146.

[5] *Das Johannesevangelium* (*LHB*[2], 1925).

[6] C. H. Dodd (*op. cit.*, pp. 115–130) rejects the evidence as too late to be significant. Cf. W. G. Kümmel, *Das Neue Testament* (1958), pp. 449 ff. S. Schulz (*Komposition und Herkunft der johanneischen Reden*, 1960) considers that the background of some of the units of tradition in this Gospel (he concentrates on the Prologue and the ἐγώ εἰμί sayings) is mainly to be found in Jewish sectarianism and Mandaean Gnosticism. Cf. also his earlier book *Untersuchungen zur Menschensohnchristologie* (1957).*

Ever since the attack of D. Strauss[1] on the authenticity of John's Gospel in the first half of the nineteenth century, there has been the tendency among some schools of thought to exclude this Gospel from any consideration of the historical Jesus.[2] It was set over against the Synoptic Gospels and the assumption was made that any discrepancies which could be detected were always to the disadvantage of the Johannine account. All attempts at harmonization were considered taboo, while the possibility that John could be more correct than the Synoptics was not even considered.

Few would deny that the Johannine account is primarily theological. The recent discipline of redaction criticism in the Synoptic Gospels (see pp. 214 ff.), with its stress on the theological interests of the Evangelists, has brought these Gospels nearer to John in this respect. But in both John and the Synoptics the problem of the extent to which an author's theological purpose affects the historicity of his account is a live issue. When it is once admitted that history includes interpretation, it will be seen that history and theology need not be mutually exclusive. John has made no attempt to present a sequence of bare historical facts. He is concerned that what he relates has a dogmatic purpose. He relates incidents, not for their own sake, but to lead his readers to faith. He specifically handles his material in a theological way. His description of the miracles as 'signs' is a case in point.[3]

There would appear to be no grounds for disputing the influence of theology in this Gospel. But the question remains concerning the extent to which the Johannine account can contribute anything to the historical account of Jesus. What value has it as a source? It is in answer to this problem that fundamental differences arise among different schools of thought. Strauss's theory that myth rather than history was the basis of the Gospels has been exploded. But many scholars treat what purports to be historical as symbolic, which virtually dispenses with it as history altogether. An earlier representative of this approach was P. Schmiedel.[4] An example of his treatment may be seen in the

[1] D. Strauss, *Life of Jesus* (1835).
[2] Cf., for instance, G. Ebeling, *The Nature of Faith* (Eng. Tr. 1961), p. 50, for a modern example of this tendency.
[3] Cf. the writer's study on the importance of the Johannine signs, *Vox Evangelica*, V, 1967, pp. 72–83. Cf. also P. Riga, *Interpretation*, 17 (1963), pp. 402–424, M. Inch, *EQ*, XLII (1970), pp. 35–43.
[4] Art. 'Gospels', *Encylopaedia Biblica* (1914), col. 1796.

fact that he regarded the six water-pots at Cana as representing the six week-days (the Law), which prepared for the Sabbath (the gospel wedding feast). This kind of treatment, if valid, would be possible even if the incident had never happened, since the main point is the symbolism. Not all who favour an element of symbolism would share a sceptical approach to history.[1] Some see a symbolic purpose in the history, without necessarily endorsing the non-historicity of all the events. It is probable, for instance, that the repeated occurrence of the 'hour' in John's Gospel has a symbolic aspect, without the statements being called in question.[2] The balance between symbolism and historicity is nevertheless heavily weighted on the side of the view that symbolism involves non-historicity.

Another approach which is parallel, but which has a stronger pull towards historicity, is the view that John presents an 'interpreted' history.[3] The basic material is acknowledged to be genuine, but is claimed to have been seriously adapted to the author's own interpretation. According to this view history and interpretation merge into one another. The result is not pure history, although the bare facts of the history are the essential basis of much of the interpretation. Thus the cleansing of the Temple may be regarded as a historical event, but the Johannine setting of it claimed to be due to the author's own theological understanding of the narratives. There may be much to be said for this view, provided it is made clear that a true sense of 'history' is being understood. C. K. Barrett, who advocates this view, describes the Gospel as 'impressionistic rather than photographically accurate in detail'.[4] In other words, as long as the observer does not look too closely, he will gain a good general idea of the person of Jesus. But the problem here is one of methodology. How is a decision to be made between an 'impression' and an accurate detail? Estimates would vary with different scholars. Did Jesus, for instance, discourse with His disciples in the upper room? Or is the author giving an impression of what Jesus would have said had the discourse been authentic? It is still possible to

---

[1] Cf., for instance, C. K. Barrett on Jn. ii. 1–12 (*The Gospel according to St. John*, pp. 156–162). C. H. Dodd seems to place more emphasis on a symbolic type of interpretation (*op. cit.*, pp. 84, 138), although he does not regard the Gospel generally as unhistorical.

[2] Cf. J. E. Bruns (*NTS*, 13, 1967, 285–290), who considers that all John's references to time except i. 39 can be treated symbolically.

[3] Cf. C. K. Barrett, *op. cit.*, p. 117.   [4] *Ibid.*, p. 118.

hold the latter view and regard the event itself as authentic, i.e. the fact that Jesus ate a last meal with His disciples on the night of the betrayal. But is it not more natural to regard both event and discourse as authentic?

A recent writer J. L. Martyn,[1] in discussing the history and theology of this Gospel, regards the history as 'read-back' history. The Evangelist, according to this view, has modified the tradition to express his own purpose. Throughout the Gospel there is a dual presentation. On the one hand the material is addressed to the circumstances of the readers, and on the other hand it is related to the circumstances surrounding the event in the life of Jesus. Thus John ix can refer both to a blind man in the time of Jesus and also to a Christian convert. Part of the narrative relates to the first and part to the second. This whole presentation revolves around Martyn's thesis regarding the occasion of the Gospel and serves as an illustration of the influence of presuppositions on one's view of history. He claims that the separation of Jews from Gentiles reflected in this Gospel was occasioned by a decision of the Jewish elders at Jamnia on the procedure regarding heretics. Martyn sees the Pharisees of John xii. 42 as those who delivered or else enforced the new 'benediction'. The Jewish *gerousia*, according to this theory, would consider Christian missionaries as beguilers. The Gospel, as interpreted history, is therefore addressed to readers who have been forced to make clear their separation from the synagogue. Although the main thesis proposed is not likely to prove generally acceptable, Martyn has attempted to come to grips with the historical problem. But in propounding his solution, he has made the real events subservient to the theological purpose.[2]

With the increasing movement for reassessing the historicity of John,[3] it must be considered whether there is no other approach to history. There have always been those who have played down the

---

[1] *History and Theology in the Fourth Gospel* (1968).

[2] T. A. Burkill (*JBL*, LXXXVII, 1968, pp. 439–442) commends Martyn's book as a redactional history of John. But A. M. Ward (*ET*, LXXXI, 1969, pp. 68–72) calls Martyn's method 'uncontrolled Form Criticism'.

[3] Cf. T. W. Manson's article 'The Life of Jesus: Some Tendencies in Present-day Research' in *The Background of the New Testament and its Eschatology* (ed. W. D. Davies and D. Daube, 1956), p. 219 n. 2. Cf. also J. A. T. Robinson's article 'The New Look on the Fourth Gospel' in *Studia Evangelica* II (1964), pp. 338–350.

interpretative element, although they have granted the theological purpose of the Gospel.[1] The question arises whether the author was the kind of man who would have modified the facts to further his theological purpose, whether in fact he allowed the theology to dominate the history or vice versa. Some light is shed on the problem if it is approached through John's own statement of his purpose. An intention to lead people to faith in Jesus as Messiah and as Son of God is hardly likely to be furthered by an account of Jesus which was not closely related to the historical facts. Indeed it may be reasoned that John wants his readers to believe in Jesus in a certain way because this was the kind of person that the historical events show. His description of Jesus as Messiah and Son of God is not historical but theological, but this is not to say that Jesus was not a historical person, nor that John does not set out to portray Him as such. The incidental references to the timing of events, the precise geographical notes and the over-all impression of Jesus in this Gospel lead to an assumption that it is intended as a historical account.[2] There can be little doubt that the Evangelist has access to genuine tradition, whether or not he was himself an eyewitness. It seems reasonable to suppose that his account should be regarded as historical unless there is some clear and conclusive evidence to the contrary. But it is doubtful whether such conclusive evidence is forthcoming, although this must be a matter of opinion. If the view is held that the post-Easter Church was incapable of thinking back to the historical Jesus, as many form critics insist, all thoughts of John's historicity must be abandoned.[3] But this historical scepticism is being increasingly challenged.[4]

One aspect of John's historicity which is worth noting is the emphasis on truth and witness in his Gospel.[5] Both ideas occur many more

[1] Cf. A. C. Headlam, *The Fourth Gospel as History* (1948), pp. 11–31.

[2] Cf. L. Morris, 'The Fourth Gospel and History' in *Jesus of Nazareth; Saviour and Lord* (ed. C. Henry), pp. 125 ff.

[3] See p. 324 n. 2 above.

[4] Cf. L. Morris, *op. cit.*, p. 132. O. Cullmann (*NTS*, 11, 1965, pp. 111–122) appeals to the Johannine insistence on the precise hours at which events took place, the linking of the work of the Church to the work of Jesus (e.g. John iv, missionary work, and John vi, worship), the appeal to the Old Testament as evidence of the author's conviction in the continuity of the historical sequence, and the eschatological teaching. All these, he thinks, point to a salvation history in John.

[5] Cf. L. Morris, *op. cit.*, pp. 129 f.

times in John than in the Synoptics and may be said to be characteristic
of the Gospel. It is, of course, possible to draw a distinction between
historical and theological truth, but in this case it is unconvincing. It is
hardly probable that an author who wished to present Jesus as the
perfect fulfilment of truth and who included a self-testimony of Jesus
to this effect, would have considered it legitimate to manipulate the
tradition to serve his own purposes. His Gospel does not give the
impression in its narrative portions of being other than a historical
account. It must be conceded that any view which treats it as historical
runs into some difficulties over its relationship to the Synoptics. But
this seems preferable to the attempt to solve the problem by resorting
to a theory of non-historicity and thereby creating other problems.

In those parts of the Gospel where parallels exist with the Synoptic
Gospels, it may be claimed that the former are consistent with the
latter. For those who are disposed to grant historicity to Mark's Gospel,
this raises a presumption in favour of John's Gospel. A. J. B. Higgins,[1]
for instance, has drawn attention to the incidental confirmation of this
view in the personal names used in the Johannine account, especially
when these are compared with the Synoptic usage. If to this line of
argument is added the corroborative evidence from Qumran of the
Palestinian colouring of some of the Johannine material,[2] a more literal
approach to the historicity will not appear to be unreasonable.

CONTENTS

I. THE PROLOGUE (i. 1–18)

The main theme is the incarnation of the Word.

The Word and the created order (i. 1–5). The Word as God's revelation of Himself (i. 6–18).

II. INTRODUCTORY EVENTS (i. 19–ii. 12)

The incarnate Word is introduced in typically Jewish scenes, covering
one complete week.

The witness of John the Baptist (i. 19–34). The call of the first
disciples (i. 35–51). The marriage at Cana—*Sign 1* (ii. 1–12).

---

[1] *The Historicity of the Fourth Gospel*, pp. 53 ff.
[2] See pp. 278 ff. Cf. also L. Morris, *The Dead Sea Scrolls and St. John's Gospel* (1960).

III. THE PUBLIC MINISTRY (ii. 13–xii. 50)

a. Encounters (ii. 13–iv. 45)

This section gives some examples of the impact of Jesus on various groups.

The cleansing of the temple (ii. 13–22). The discussion with Nicodemus and the subsequent witnesses to the claims of Jesus (iii. 1–36). The dialogue with the Samaritan woman and its sequel (iv. 1–42). Warm reception by the Galilaeans (iv. 43–45).

b. Healings (iv. 46–v. 9)

The nobleman's son—*Sign 2* (iv. 46–54). The man at the pool of Bethesda—*Sign 3* (v. 1–9). Dispute over healing on the sabbath, and subsequent discourse (v. 10–47).

c. Further signs (vi. 1–vii. 1)

The feeding of the multitude—*Sign 4* (vi. 1–14). Jesus walking on the lake—*Sign 5* (vi. 15–21). Discourse on the bread of life (vi. 22–vii. 1).

d. Jesus at the Feast of Tabernacles (vii. 2–viii. 59)

Disputes about the Messiah, and official moves to arrest Jesus (vii. 2–52). The adulteress (vii. 53–viii. 11). Disputes over Jesus' claim to be the Light of the world, over His departure, over Abrahamic descent generally and Jesus' relation to Abraham in particular (viii. 12–59).

e. The healing of the man born blind (ix. 1–41)

The miracle—*Sign 6* (ix. 1–7). The reaction of neighbours, Pharisees and parents (ix. 8–23). The man's developing faith (ix. 24–41).

f. Discourse on the Shepherd (x. 1–42)

Jesus claims to be the good Shepherd and rouses conflicting reactions (x. 1–30). Growing hostility leads to Jesus' withdrawal beyond Jordan (x. 31–42).

g. The death and resurrection of Lazarus (xi. 1–46)

The report of his death (xi. 1–16). Discussion about resurrection and life (xi. 17–37). The miracle—*Sign 7* (xi. 38–44). The reaction of the authorities (xi. 45–57).

h. Further developments in and around Jerusalem (xii. 1–50)

The anointing at Bethany (xii. 1–8). The plot to kill Lazarus (xii. 9–11). The entry into Jerusalem (xii. 12–19). The quest of some Greeks for Jesus, and His statements to them (xii. 20–26). Divine attestation to Jesus, and His explanation of His approaching death (xii. 27–36a). The withdrawal of Jesus (xii. 36b–50).

IV. THE PASSION AND RESURRECTION NARRATIVES
(xiii. 1–xxi. 25)

a. The last supper (xiii. 1–xvii. 26)

The symbolic action of feet-washing and its meaning (xiii. 1–20). The betrayal predicted and Judas' hasty departure (xiii. 21–30). The glorification of Jesus, the establishment of a new commandment and the prediction of Peter's denial (xiii. 31–38).

The farewell discourses (xiv. 1–xvi. 33). Promises for the future (xiv. 1–4). Christ as Revealer (xiv. 5–15). Teaching about the Spirit (xiv. 16–26). The gift of peace (xiv. 27–31). The vine analogy (xv. 1–17). Statements about the believer's relation to the world (xv. 18–27). Warnings about persecutions (xvi. 1–4). Further teaching about the Spirit (xvi. 5–15). Jesus speaks of His death but expresses confidence in His ultimate victory (xvi. 16–33).

The prayer of consecration (xvii. 1–26): a prayer for the glorification of the Son and for the encouragement of believers.

b. The passion of Jesus (xviii. 1–xix. 42)

The arrest (xviii. 1–12). The examination before Annas and Caiaphas, and the denial of Peter (xviii. 13–27). Jesus before Pilate (xviii. 28–xix. 16). The crucifixion (xix. 17–37). The burial (xix. 38–42).

c. The resurrection narratives (xx. 1–xxi. 25).

The appearances in Jerusalem (xx. 1–31). The appearances in Galilee (xxi. 1–23). The final certification of the record (xxi. 24, 25).

ADDITIONAL NOTES

248. [1] J. N. Sanders followed up his suggestion that Lazarus was the beloved disciple with an article in *NTS*, 9 (1962), pp. 75–85, in which he maintained that the attribution of the Gospel to John began as a heretical opinion. The same author has maintained his Lazarus idea in his posthumously published commentary, *The Gospel according to St. John* (1968), edited by B. A. Mastin. F. V. Filson has followed up the view expressed in his articles in his commentary, *The Gospel according to St. John* (1963), pp. 244 f. Cf. E. F. Harrison (*INT*, p. 213) for the view that the use of the expression 'Beloved disciple' did not imply lack of love for the other disciples.

250. [2] On John's topology, cf. W. F. Albright, *The Archaeology of Palestine* (1949), pp. 244 ff.; C. H. Dodd, *Historical Tradition in the Fourth Gospel* (1963), pp. 244 f.; R. E. Brown, *The Gospel according to John i–xii* (1966), pp. xlii f.

262. [1] Cf. also L. Morris, *Studies in the Fourth Gospel* (1969), pp. 280 ff.

264. [1] A recent support for the apostolic authorship of this Gospel has come from E. K. Lee (*CQR*, 167, 1966, pp. 292–302), who argues that the Qumran evidence has made such a suggestion more probable than twenty years previously. Cf. also N. E. Johnson (*CQR*, 167, 1966, pp. 278–291), who considers that John of Zebedee wrote the passion narrative but someone else later worked this up into a Gospel.

265. [1] A further support for P. Parker's idea that the beloved disciple was John Mark is found in L. Johnson's article (*ET*, LXXVII, 1966, pp. 157–168), but this view was opposed by D. G. Rogers (*ET*, LXXVII, 1966, p. 214).

266. In his recent commentary on John's Gospel, R. Schnackenburg (*Das Johannesevangelium* I, 1965) maintains apostolic authorship, but emphasizes that there are redactional elements in the final form of the book. John, in his view, supplied the data, but a school of writers was responsible for the production of the Johannine literature. In this sense therefore the apostle John was 'author', but not 'evangelist'. This seems rather a loose way of speaking of authorship. It would be better to refer to the author as 'witness'. This Roman Catholic view may be compared with another advanced by R. E. Brown (*The Gospel according to John i–xii*, 1966), who proposes a five-stage theory for the origin of the Gospel, of which John the apostle was probably involved only in stage one. The apostolic authorship in this case becomes rather remote.

268. [1] In a recent comment on the Papias statement, C. S. Petrie (*NTS*, 14, 1967, pp. 15–32) maintains that Eusebius did not mean John the Elder, but the already mentioned Elder John, i.e. the apostle.

275. [3] On the question whether John's Gospel is an anti-Jewish polemic, cf. J. W. Bowker (*NTS*, 11, 1965, pp. 398–408), who comes out against this view. He considers that 'Jews' in this Gospel are often distinguished from 'Pharisees'. The latter are consistently hostile to Jesus. Bowker contends that John is presenting some of the issues by which the new Israel came to be distinct from the old. He sees various viewpoints in John's presentation of Jesus: in relation to His antecedents (i. 1–ii. 11), in relation to Judaism in general (ii. 12–iv. 54), in relation to Judaism in the matter of specific questions (v–viii) and in the relation between Judaism and the community derived from Jesus (ix–xii).

Another theory that touches on the Jewish approach is the view that behind the Gospel is Samaritan influence. Cf. E. D. Freed, *CBQ*, 30 (1968), pp. 580–587. Cf. also the appendix of A. Spiro in J. Munck's *The Acts of the Apostles* (1967), in which he argues for Stephen's Samaritan background.

277. The Gnostic background of John's Gospel finds an advocate in E. Käsemann (*The Testament of Jesus*, 1968), who takes his cue for understanding the Gospel from Jn. xvii. Käsemann does not treat either the deeds or speeches as historical. He makes a charge of naïve Docetism against the author of the Gospel, whom he sees as a man affected by gnosticizing tendencies. The book was admitted into the Canon by mistake. Käsemann's gnosticizing charge is based on his own interpretation of Jn. i. 14 and on his claim to find in John's Gospel a sectarian type of piety. But both G. Bornkamm (*EvTh*, xxviii, 1968, pp. 8–25) and G. Delling (*ThLZ*, 93, 1968, cols. 38–40) object to Käsemann's theory of naïve Docetism. Bornkamm considers that the focus of the farewell discourses is not on Christ as a figure of glory, as Käsemann maintains, but on the death of Christ.

J. P. Martin (*SJT*, 17, 1964, pp. 332–343) also makes reference to Gnosticism in discussing history and eschatology in Jn. xi. 1–44. He sees the Lazarus account as an answer not only to the problem of the delay of the *parousia*, but also to the problem of death. The latter problem would be accentuated by Gnostic indifference to death. It is not impossible that John may have been influenced in his choice of material by his knowledge of incipient Gnosticism, but this does not mean that such Gnostic tendencies provide the *Sitz im Leben* for parts of the Gospel material.

278. [4] Against the theory of dominant Hellenistic influences may be cited the view of A. J. B. Higgins (*BJRL*, xlix, 1967, pp. 363–386), that those sections of John which show Aramaizing tendencies are nearest in style to the Qumran texts. He suggests that this fact increases the probability of genuine sayings material in John.

282. [1] The eschatology of John continues to be discussed. A defence of the traditional view is found in D. E. Holwerda, *The Holy Spirit and Eschatology in the Gospel of John. A Critique of Rudolph Bultmann's Present Eschatology* (1959). Bultmann (*ThLZ*, 87, 1962, cols. 5–8) complained that Holwerda had misunderstood his use of the term 'existential'. But many would agree with Holwerda that Bultmann relies too much on subjectivism. Cf. R. E. Brown, *The Gospel according to John i–xii* (1966), pp. xxiv–xxxix, 219–221, for details of redactional theories to remove the futuristic eschatology. For Bultmann's view, cf. D. M. Smith, Jnr, *The Composition and Order of the Fourth Gospel* (1965), pp. 134 ff., 217 ff.

282. [2] Although A. Guilding's hypothesis has aroused considerable interest, it has not escaped criticism. L. Morris (*The New Testament and the Jewish Lection-*

aries, 1964) argues that there is inadequate evidence for Jewish lectionaries in the first century, a point of view supported by P. Wernberg-Møller(*JSemS*, 10, 1965, pp. 286–288). Cf. also M. Barth (*JR*, 42, 1962, pp. 65 f.). E. Haenchen objects to Guilding's thesis on different grounds (*ThLZ*, 86, 1961, cols. 670–672). He rejects the view that John presents synagogue discourses.

285. [1] An advocate of an early date for John is W. Gericke (*ThLZ*, 90, 1965, cols. 807–820), who argues that John was written before either Matthew or Luke. He suggests a date about AD 68, which would make it contemporary with Mark. One of the evidences to which he appeals is Jn. v. 43 ('another shall come in his own name') which he interprets as relating to Nero.

291. [1] Cf. also C. H. Dodd's article, 'The portrait of Jesus in John and the Synoptics', in *Christian History and Interpretation* (1967), pp. 183–198.

297. [5] The problem of the date of the crucifixion in John and in the Synoptics is discussed by M. H. Shepherd (*JBL*, LXXX, 1961, pp. 123–132). He suggests that the Synoptics follow the Diaspora reckoning in which the Passover was on a fixed day of the week, whereas John follows a reckoning which determined the day according to the new moon. Shepherd denies, therefore, that John is correcting the Synoptics. On the problems of the passion chronology, cf. E. Ruckstuhl, *The Chronology of the Last Days of Jesus* (1965).

301. [3] E. D. Freed (*ZNTW*, 55, 1964, pp. 167–197) has examined the variations in thought between Jn. i–xx and Jn. xxi and the Johannine Epistles. Although Freed raises the question about different authors to account for the variations, he does not consider that these variations could have come from different sources.

Another theory involving a part of the Gospel as distinct from the rest is C. Dekker's view (*NTS*, 13, 1966, pp. 66–80) that Jn. vi is a non-Jewish source added by a non-Jewish redactor to a work by a Jewish author. Dekker argues his case on the basis of the use of the term 'Jews' in Jn. vi and the rest of the Gospel. Having excised chapter vi, he is able to condense the Johannine ministry into one year. But the evidence is not sufficiently broadly based to make this thesis convincing.

303. [1] The statistical calculations of G. H. C. Macgregor and A. Q. Morton have been subjected to criticism by E. Haenchen (*ThLZ*, 87, 1962, cols. 487–498) on the grounds that the Beatty and Bodmer papyri do not support the idea of a normal page. Haenchen rightly points out the failure of Macgregor and Morton to suggest any reason why the J2 panels should have been inserted at exactly regular intervals.

304. [3] As a contribution to the debate whether John used the Synoptic Gospels, F. E. Williams (*JBL*, LXXXVI, 1967, pp. 311–319) has made a study of two specific passages, Jn. ii. 1–11 and Jn. i. 19–23. He inclines to think on the strength of his examination that John used the Synoptics as a source. Clearly this debate is not yet resolved.

306. [3] Bultmann's theory of sources has come under fire from D. M. Smith, Jnr, *The Composition and Order of the Fourth Gospel. Bultmann's Literary Theory* (1965). To facilitate a proper examination of Bultmann's sources, Smith sets them out in Greek. He admits that Bultmann has focused on some of the difficulties, but complains that he does not provide an adequate answer. In view of the arguments for unity advanced by Schweizer and Ruckstuhl, Smith considers Bultmann's theory to be suspect. He points out John's loose use of the Old Testament, but denies that he used the Synoptics. H. M. Teeple (*JBL*, LXXXIV, 1965, pp. 305–308) criticizes Smith's methodology here since John might have used the Synoptics as loosely as he used the Old Testament. Teeple also queries Smith's assertion that John did not finish his Gospel.

308. [4] C. H. Dodd's book has come under criticism by G. Strecker (*Gnomon*, 36, 1964, pp. 773–778), who disputes a pre-Johannine tradition before AD 70. Strecker regards vi. 15 as redactional and therefore of no value in indicating an early date for this material. Nevertheless the evidence that Dodd educes is more favourable to an early pre-Johannine tradition than Strecker allows.

309. [1] In discussing the provenance of the Prologue, J. Jeremias (*ZNTW*, 59, 1968, pp. 82–85) rejects a Gnostic source, but considers that the absolute use of Logos in Jn. i. 1, 14 points to a Christian pre-history in Hellenistic Jewish Christianity. The term, he thinks, was employed to designate the returning Lord.

310. For a discussion of the signs, see the writer's article, 'The Importance of Signs in the Fourth Gospel', in *Vox Evangelica*, V (1967), pp. 72–83.

312. A recent hypothesis for the Johannine framework is that it is based on a geographical symbolism. W. A. Meeks (*JBL*, LXXXV, 1966, pp. 159–169) argues for a deliberate dialectic between Jerusalem, representing the theme of judgment and rejection, and Galilee and Samaria, representing acceptance and discipleship. Meeks does not accept Lohmeyer's Galilee thesis (see pp. 81 f.), but he claims that Lohmeyer's insight regarding a distinctive Galilaean type of Christianity is valid.

Another writer who bases his approach to John on a symbolic approach is M. Weise, *Kerygma und Dogma*, 12 (1966), pp. 48–62. His theory is that John's structure should be understood by reference to the opening and concluding weeks of the ministry. The opening week centres on the incarnation, which Weise sees as the epiphany of the Redeemer, whereas the closing week presents a paschal lamb theology which in fact dominates the Gospel. There is no doubt that these two weeks of activity play an important part in the author's design.

For a treatment of the Moses motif, cf. W. A. Meeks, *The Prophet-King. Moses Traditions in the Johannine Christology* (1967).

315. The textual evidence concerning the *pericope adulterae* (Jn. vii. 53–viii. 11) may be summarized as follows. (a) It occurs in none of the early Uncials except D. Some leave a space, but others do not. (b) Many cursives omit. One group, Family 13, places it after Lk. xxi. 38. (c) Many versions omit, including the Syriac and Egyptian and some MSS of the Old Latin. (d) All Greek commentators before the time of Euthymius Zygadenus (AD 1118) omit, and the latter admits that the most accurate copies do not contain it. (e) Among those MSS which do contain it the position varies—some have it before Jn. viii. 12, some at the end of John and some after Lk. xxi. 38. (f) Origen and Chrysostom do not mention it, which suggests that it was absent from their MSS. (g) Many internal features, such as style and vocabulary, suggest a non-Johannine origin. (h) On the other hand evidence of its genuineness is found in many Western authorities, including D. (i) Its prevalence in the later MSS led to its inclusion in the Textus Receptus. (j) Jerome states that it was in many Greek and Latin MSS, which must mean that the Greek MSS have not survived. (k) Ambrose and Augustine both use it, but Augustine admits that some have doubts about it. (l) The narrative is cited in the Apostolic Constitutions as a lesson in leniency.

From this survey of the evidence, two general observations may be made. The strongest evidence is clearly for its exclusion from John's Gospel, and yet the evidence in support of its genuineness is by no means inconsiderable. If genuine it might have been added originally to the Four Gospels, which would account for its attachment to John, in the Eastern order. On the other hand, it is generally supposed that this is a gloss which became incorporated into the Johannine MS, though why it was placed after vii. 52 has not been satisfactorily explained.

The passage has received detailed examination from U. Becker, *Jesus und die Ehebrecherin—Untersuchungen zur Text und Überlieferungsgeschichte von Jn. 7:53–8:11* (1963). He favours the view that the *pericope* was inserted into the Gospel against the wishes of the Church. Nevertheless Becker maintains that the incident must have originated in the life of Jesus, because of the contents of the passage.

320. [2] Increasing interest is being shown in the Old Testament background of this Gospel. F.-M. Braun (*Jean le Théologien. Les grandes traditions d'Israël et l'accord des Écritures selon le Quatrième Évangile, EB,* 1964) has made a detailed examination of this. Cf. also O. Böcher (*ThLZ,* 90, 1965, col. 223), who maintains that the Johannine writings are rooted more in the Old Testament and Apocalyptic Judaism than in Hellenism.

323. [6] Schulz's theory has been criticized by E. Haenchen (*ThLZ,* 87, 1962, col. 209) on the ground that Schulz's view that the Johannine discourses were produced by a fellowship from Baptist, apocalyptic, early Mandaen and Gnostic groups would subordinate the Evangelist to the fellowship. M. E. Boismard (*RB,* LXIX, 1962, pp. 421–424) comments that if such a fellowship existed it must have been dominated by one personality. Boismard denies Gnostic influence behind the Prologue.

CHAPTER NINE

THE ACTS OF THE APOSTLES

I. CHARACTERISTICS

The importance of this book cannot be exaggerated and it is no wonder that it has frequently been the focus of attention during the period of historical criticism (i.e. since 1800). Its importance must, however, be deduced first of all from the nature of its contents and only secondarily from the part it has played in critical discussions. Its main features may be summarized as follows.[1]

a. Its place in the New Testament

It is not without some significance that in the present canonical order Acts has been placed between the Gospels and Epistles, although it did not occupy this position in all the ancient canonical lists. It serves admirably as a link between the records of Jesus and the apostolic correspondence. In many ways the Epistles are not fully intelligible until they are read against the background of the book of Acts. The book shows effectively the main trends in the development of Christianity and presents in effect samples of the continuing work of Jesus. It therefore makes a vital contribution to the discussion of the relationship between the teaching of Jesus and the apostolic doctrine. As will be shown later, the value of its contribution has been variously estimated according to the view taken of its historicity, but the fact remains that it is the only extant historical account of the primitive Christian period outside the Epistles, from a Christian point of view.

b. Its view of history

The many references to the Holy Spirit in this book are a sufficient indication that the writer regards the development of Christian history as due to a superhuman control. He does not gloss over the difficulties which the Christian mission encountered, but he purposes to show that God was directing each movement of the history. As Christian influence spreads from Jerusalem to Rome there is no impression given

---

[1] For a brief survey of recent literature on Acts, see the writer's article in *Vox Evangelica* (ed. R. P. Martin), II (1963), pp. 33–49. Also E. Grässer, *TR*, n.f., 26 (1960), pp. 93–167, and W. C. Kümmel, *TR*, 22 (1954), pp. 194 ff.

that this progress is due ultimately to human achievement, not even to the dynamic and indefatigable labours of an apostle Paul. God was hedging His people round, preventing undesirable developments here and prompting to sustained evangelistic efforts there. In short, God was as active in the early Christian communities and in the messengers of the gospel as He had been in the movements and teachings of Jesus.

c. Its portrait of primitive communities

In spite of the fact that the author gives glimpses into church life during the first generation, there is no consecutive attempt to describe the conditions within the various churches, nor to give much information about early church orders or methods of worship. All that can justly be said is that Acts gives a valuable general impression of primitive church life. It is necessary to supplement its data with other material from the Epistles and even then there is much more that we could wish to know. The author of Acts has, however, clearly portrayed the spiritual and moral characteristics of the early Christians. The impression of unity is inescapable, in spite of the existence of differences of opinion. The account of the Council of Jerusalem in Acts xv shows the importance which not only the leaders but the rank and file members attached to presenting a united front. The early experiment in communal living, in spite of its ultimate cessation, bears eloquent testimony to the strong desire for unity. Even here the Acts presents in vivid contrast the failure of Ananias and Sapphira to enter into the true spirit of the other believers. The severe condemnation of their moral lapse is recorded in order to make clear the moral aspect of primitive community life. One of the most characteristic features of the book, however, is the element of joyfulness among these early Christians,[1] and this is a striking example of the continuation of a theme which had been notably stressed in the Gospel of Luke. Without the book of Acts our knowledge of the spiritual outlook of those believers would be immeasurably the poorer.

d. Its record of primitive theology

In a book which consists so largely of narratives and concentrates upon the missionary movements it is surprising to find so much indication of primitive doctrine. This is naturally mainly contained in the numer-

[1] Cf. P. G. S. Hopwood, *The Religious Experience of the Primitive Church* (1936).

ous speeches which present samples of the apostolic preaching. The primitive character of this doctrine may be seen from a comparison with the evidence of the primitive *kerygma* as found in various parts of the Epistles. Those passages which are said to be traceable to the apostolic proclamation as distinct from the apostolic teaching (*didache*) bear close resemblance to the content of the early speeches in Acts. C. H. Dodd,[1] in his notable work on this subject, finds several passages in Romans, 1 Corinthians, Galatians and Thessalonians which compare with passages in the speeches of Acts ii, iii, iv, v, x and xiii. In this case the book of Acts is a valuable source-book for the study of primitive theology. Not all have followed Dodd in his clear-cut dissection between *kerygma* and *didache*, and it would probably be wiser to assume that they were contemporary developments which often in fact overlapped.[2] At the same time the book does not narrate the genesis of early creeds, and what information it gives is wholly of an incidental and informal kind. The titles ascribed to our Lord are a valuable guide to primitive Christology. Jesus is both Lord and Christ, God's Servant and His Son, Prince of Life and Saviour, the Righteous One and Lord of all. This presents a rich if embryonic Christology,[3] but it would be misleading to suppose that there were not other aspects which the Acts speeches do not happen to mention. In other words, the book of Acts presents us with samples of early Christian mission preaching but gives no samples of didactic addresses to believers, unless Paul's speech to the Ephesian elders at Miletus comes under this category (but it contains little didactic material). The importance of the book of Acts is in its preservation of the main doctrinal themes presented in apostolic preaching, even if there is no evidence of an attempt to develop a systematized theology.

e. Its focus on Peter and Paul

It is one of the most striking features about Acts that it says so little about the other apostles and so much about Peter and Paul. This is

---

[1] *The Apostolic Preaching and its Developments.*

[2] Cf. the detailed discussion of this in R. H. Mounce's book, *The Essential Nature of New Testament Preaching* (1960), pp. 40 f., 60 ff. It should be noted that it cannot be supposed that the *kerygma*, if recoverable, represents a stock outline used by the early preachers, for a study of Acts speeches disposes of this idea. It is rather a convenient survey of primitive Christology, cf. W. Baird, *JBL*, LXXVI (1957), pp. 181-191.

[3] Cf. S. S. Smalley, *ET*, LXXIII (1961-62), pp. 35 ff.

obviously intentional, but it is not easy to find a reason. It may have been because the author was acquainted with these two more than the others. Or it may have been that the chief apostle to the Gentiles was matched with the chief apostle to the Circumcision. There are some striking parallels in the two parts of the record, which have suggested to some that one part was written in imitation of the other. The effect of this phenomenon on criticism will be noted later, but for the present it is the facts which concern us.

In chapters i–xii the narrative moves from Jerusalem to Antioch and in this section it is Peter who occupies the limelight. He takes the lead both before and after Pentecost. Although accompanied by John when they met the impotent man, it was Peter who commanded him in Christ's name to walk. It was he who twice led the defence before the Sanhedrin, and when deception was discovered within the Church it was he who voiced the condemnation against Ananias and Sapphira. His shadow was the means used to heal many sick people. Moreover, when he and John were sent from Jerusalem to Samaria, it was Peter who dealt with Simon the sorcerer. Dorcas was raised from the dead and the paralysed Aeneas was healed through his agency. And Cornelius was directed to send specifically for Simon Peter, who later found it necessary to explain his action before the Jerusalem church. The first part then ends with Peter's miraculous deliverance from prison.

Several of these features reoccur in the story of Paul. Both heal cripples (iii. 2–8, xiv. 8–12), both heal by strange means, Peter through his shadow, Paul with his clothes (v. 15, xix. 12), both have encounters with sorcerers (viii. 18, xiii. 6), both are concerned in restoration scenes (ix. 36, xx. 9), and both are miraculously released from prison (xii. 7, xvi. 26). The parallels are striking and draw attention to the fact that Paul was as much an apostle as Peter.

The personality of Paul is strongly portrayed. He is introduced dramatically at Stephen's death, and his ravages against the Church are faithfully mentioned. Many little details in the subsequent narrative bring him to life. The intensity of his gaze (xiii. 9, xiv. 9, xxiii. 1), the beckoning of his hand (xiii. 16, xxvi. 1), his kneeling at Miletus (xx. 36–38) and his rending of his clothes at Lystra (xiv. 14). The narrative at the end of Acts (from xx onwards) centres almost wholly on Paul and shows him moving on towards Rome inevitably but with courageous determination.

II. DATE

In a historical book such as Acts, which constitutes the main document on primitive Christianity, the date of production is clearly of considerable importance. As so often in problems of dating New Testament books, the prior decision regarding authorship will naturally affect the presuppositions with which the subject is approached. Moreover, in this case, the decision already reached regarding the date of the third Gospel will clearly have an influence on the date of Acts, since this book must be dated subsequent to Luke. Our present approach will be first to treat the subject of date in the light of the traditional position concerning authorship, and then to discuss alternatives. If, of course, the conclusions regarding date demand a period too late to make the traditional authorship possible, it would require a fresh consideration of the latter problem.

There are three main proposals: first, before AD 64, secondly AD 70-85 and thirdly a second-century date. They will be considered in this order.

a. Arguments for a date before AD 64

(i) *The absence of reference to important events which happened between AD 60 and 70.* The fall of Jerusalem is nowhere referred to and, although it is not decisive that Luke must have hinted at it if it had already occurred,[1] there is a strong presumption in favour of this opinion. It would have been difficult for him to avoid some allusion to it, although it must be recognized that the destiny of Jerusalem would not have appeared so tragic to the Christian Church as a whole as it would to the Jewish people. At the same time it is not without significance that Luke in his Gospel centres more attention on Jerusalem than do his fellow Synoptists.[2]

---

[1] E. M. Blaiklock (*The Acts of the Apostles*, 1959, p. 16) expresses a caution about placing too much weight upon this kind of evidence. 'Luke, an accomplished historian and a disciplined writer, need not have coloured his narrative of doings in Jerusalem by references to later events irrelevant to his theme.'*

[2] Luke's so-called 'travel-narrative' (Lk. ix. 51–xviii. 14) has as its focal point the movement of Jesus towards Jerusalem, and the same interest in the holy city is seen in the author's choice of resurrection narratives, all of which are centred in Jerusalem.

Another event of importance was the persecution of the Church under the Emperor Nero.[1] This precipitated so great a crisis that it is difficult to imagine that the earliest Christian historian could have ignored it so completely if he wrote after the event. Although the geographical area affected was confined to Italy, it is still astonishing that Luke makes no mention of it in ending his story at Rome. The only other possibilities would be to suppose that Acts was written after such an interval that the grim details of the horror had faded from the author's mind, or else that he was unaware of it. It might just conceivably be agreed that the author would have no cause to mention it, in which case it could be discounted as a factor affecting dating, but probability is on the side of a date before it.

A further event of less widespread importance, but one which might well have interested Luke, was the martyrdom of James, the Lord's brother. In fact Luke mentions two early martyrs: James, son of Zebedee, and Stephen. Moreover, the description of James' position as president of the Jerusalem church and the care with which Luke describes his relationships with Paul show that the author regarded him as a key figure in primitive Christian history.

Yet all these three suggestions are arguments from silence and must be used with reserve.

(ii) *The absence of reference to the death of Paul.* The abrupt ending of Acts has for long been an enigma. The author leaves his readers with a description of Paul, a prisoner at Rome, but enjoying considerable liberty to preach and teach. Yet there is no indication about what happened to Paul after this. The reason for the abrupt ending is subject to various interpretations and these must be carefully examined in considering its effect upon the dating.

1. The author records all he knew. If, at the time of writing, Paul was still in his own hired house awaiting further developments, the abruptness is at once explained. There was nothing else to report.[2]

---

[1] Cf. R. B. Rackham, *The Acts of the Apostles*[14] (1951), pp. li f.

[2] Ancient support for such a view may be found in the comment in the Muratorian Canon, which states that Luke recorded those events which fell under his notice ('conprendit quae sub praesentia eius singula gerebantur'), but adds, somewhat apologetically, 'sicuti et semota passione Petri euidenter declarat, et profectione Pauli ab urbe ad Hispaniam proficiscentis'. But it is strange that this Canon makes no reference to the martyrdom of Paul. It should be noted that the ending of Acts may not have seemed so unsatisfactory to Luke as it does to many.

2. The author did not wish to mention the outcome of the trial. It is suggested that he knew of Paul's death, but that it was no part of his purpose to close with this.[1] Such a procedure would, in fact, draw too much attention to the man, whereas Luke's purpose was to describe rather the progress of the gospel. It has even been suggested that to conclude with Paul's death would hint at a parallel with the conclusion of the Gospel with its climax in the passion story and that it was to avoid this that Luke omits all reference to it.[2] But this latter motive would not be applicable if the Gospel and Acts were conceived as a continuous narrative, and in any case the author regarded the passion of Jesus as the beginning and not the end of the real work of Jesus in the world.[3] It is not sufficient, on the other hand, to propose a theory of the author's intention without supplying an adequate motive for the intention, and it may be questioned whether this condition has been fulfilled.

3. The author intended to write a third volume. On the analogy of the connection between the Gospel and Acts it has been proposed that Luke had in mind another volume which would have related the subsequent history of Paul and his associates, and this has had the support of some notable scholars.[4] It would, of course, get over the difficulty of the abrupt end of Acts, but such a desirable end is achieved only by the postulation of an entirely hypothetical volume which has left no trace in Christian history. The theory admittedly does not demand that

F. J. Foakes Jackson (*The Acts of the Apostles*, 1931, p. 236) even described the ending as 'highly artistic'. It certainly brings out, even at the end, the triumphant note in the ministry of Paul, an emphasis to which R. R. Williams (*The Acts of the Apostles*, 1953, pp. 24–33) calls attention in his analysis of the structure of the book as a whole. Cf. also J. A. Bengel, *Gnomon of the New Testament* (Eng. Tr. 1858), II, pp. 731, 732.

[1] This is the position adopted by E. Trocmé, *Le 'Livre des Actes' et l'Histoire* (1957), p. 36.*

[2] A. Jülicher in his *Einleitung*[7] (1931, ed. E. Fascher), p. 433, considers that there is no mention of the martyrdom of either Peter or Paul because there was no resurrection narrative corresponding to the passion story in the Gospels.

[3] J. C. O'Neill (*The Theology of Acts in its Historical Setting*, 1961, pp. 56 f.) finds significance in the fact that Luke does not end with Paul's martyrdom, although he regards Acts xx as a clear prophecy of it. According to him, Luke considered the place of the end of his history (Rome) to be more important than Paul's death. A similar emphasis on a place (Jerusalem) is found at the end of the Gospel.

[4] For instance F. Spitta, *Die Apostelgeschichte* (1891), pp. 318, 319; Sir W. M. Ramsay, *St. Paul the Traveller and Roman Citizen* (1920), pp. 27 ff.; T. Zahn, *NkZ*, 28 (1917), pp. 373–395; W. L. Knox, *The Acts of the Apostles* (1948), p. 59 n.1.

the proposed volume should have left any trace, for it does not demand that Luke actually wrote the third instalment.[1] It would suffice that the author intended to write it. But the Acts does not give the impression that it was written as part of a continuing series. The gospel has reached Rome and this forms a natural climax to the history of the primitive period. There is something to be said for the objection that it is difficult to imagine what a third volume would have contained in order to have reached the same spiritual stature as the two former volumes.[2] Moreover the great amount of space devoted to Paul's trials is unintelligible as an introduction to a further narrative of the same kind. In other words, it is easier to assume that Paul's trial was still in progress than that the author has in this way drawn his second book to a close in anticipating a third volume. While the suggestion cannot be ruled out, it cannot be said to be very convincing.

The silence of Acts regarding the death of Paul may, therefore, be said to raise a presumption in favour of an early date. But one objection to this conclusion needs to be noted. In Acts xx. 25 ('I know that ye all . . . shall see my face no more') some scholars find clear evidence that the author knew that martyrdom crowned Paul's Roman imprisonment.[3] But if this passage preserves the genuine tradition of Paul's address to the Ephesian elders, it is capable of being interpreted as a presentiment on Paul's part without necessitating the presumption that it must have been fulfilled. After all, Paul's plans, according to Romans, were to turn westwards towards Spain and he evidently at that time had no intention of revisiting Ephesus.[4] The Pastoral Epistles presuppose that he did,[5] but scholars who dispute an early date for Acts almost invariably regard the Pastorals as non-Pauline and for them this line of argument would naturally lack validity.

(iii) *The primitive character of the subject-matter.* It is significant that the

---

[1] Cf. E. M. Blaiklock, *op. cit.*, p. 195.

[2] Cf. the criticisms to this effect by Trocmé, *op. cit.*, p. 36.

[3] O'Neill (*op. cit.*, p. 56) goes so far as to maintain that the author included an allusion to Paul's martyrdom in Acts xx so that it might overshadow the latter part of the story without actually concluding with an account of the event itself. M. Dibelius (*Studies in the Acts of the Apostles*, 1956, p. 158 n. 46) thinks it certain that Acts xx. 25 presupposes that Paul has already been put to death.

[4] F. F. Bruce (*The Acts of the Apostles*², Greek Text, 1952, pp. 11, 12) denies that Acts xx. 25 shows the author's knowledge of Paul's martyrdom, and regards the statement as descriptive only of Paul's expectation.

[5] Cf. pp. 589 ff., 596 ff. for a discussion of the evidence.

major interests of the author of Acts are those prevalent in the earliest period of Church history, but which were not so relevant in later times. The Jewish-Gentile controversy is dominant and all other evidence apart from Acts suggests that this was a vital issue only in the period before the fall of Jerusalem. Even by the time of Paul's later letters it had ceased to be a burning issue. Moreover, the question of Gentile inclusion was taken for granted when once the universal character of the Christian Church had been established. Again, the preoccupation with food requirements in the report of the decisions of the Jerusalem Council points to an early stage of Christian development. Before the fall of Jerusalem all these factors were of vital significance.

(iv) *The primitive nature of the theology.* Supporting evidence of a more incidental character, but nevertheless highly significant, is found in the theological language. The whole book gives the impression of primitiveness. Such titles for Jesus as 'the Christ', 'the Servant of God', 'the Son of man', reflect primitive tradition. Equally primitive are the description of Christians as 'disciples', the use of λαός for the Jewish nation, and the reference to Sunday as the first day of the week.[1] Either the author writes early enough to be in direct, living touch with actual eyewitnesses, or he possesses such remarkable historical skill that he is able to reproduce with clear fidelity the primitive climate of thought. The former alternative is the more credible.

(v) *The attitude of the State towards the Church.* Luke is at pains to demonstrate the impartiality of the imperial officials regarding Christianity. In no case is it the Roman officials who persecute the Church. The local government at Ephesus is represented as distinctly helpful towards Paul and his companions, while the cause of persecution against the Church is in every case the intrigues of the Jews. This is precisely what might be expected before Nero's persecution in AD 64,[2] but

---

[1] Cf. the discussion of F. F. Bruce, *op. cit.*, pp. 12, 13; O'Neill, who on other grounds dates Acts late, denies the primitive meaning of the use of Χριστός and κύριος in Acts, although admitting that they are used in a purely primitive way (*op. cit.*, p. 119). The same goes for ὁ παῖς τοῦ θεοῦ (*ibid.*, pp. 133 ff.) which quickly dropped out of Christian vocabulary. But on O'Neill's presuppositions no other assessment is really possible, for primitive traces in a so-called late document must be considered insertions designed to create the impression of primitiveness.

[2] This is strongly maintained by Rackham, *The Acts of the Apostles*[14] (1951), p. lii.

subsequent to that date the imperial officials would be more suspicious of Christianity and less inclined to treat it under the general concession to Judaism as a *religio licita*. The concluding word in Acts (ἀκωλύτως) is significant in this respect, for it forms a fitting climax to Luke's design to show the unhindered progress of the gospel.[1]

(vi) *The relation of Acts to the Pauline Epistles.* It is universally admitted that the author of Acts shows little or no acquaintance with Paul's Epistles and it may reasonably be claimed as a consequence that Acts must have been published before the collection of the *Corpus Paulinum*, or at least before this collection had had much general circulation. There are differences of opinion as to when the collection was made, but this circumstance favours as early a date as possible for Acts.[2] Those who consider that the collection was actually prompted by the publication of Acts assume a period, subsequent to Paul's death, during which he was neglected, and this automatically excludes an early date for Acts, but the whole theory is open to serious challenge.[3]

b. Arguments for a date between AD 70 and 85

The major reason for preferring this to the earlier date is the author's use of Mark. It has already been shown that the dating of Luke generally takes as its starting-point the date of Mark as AD 60–65 and assumes that Luke has adjusted the vague reference in Mark xiii to 'the abomination of desolation', to the more specific 'compassed with armies' through his knowledge of the details of the siege. In other words, Luke is supposed to have written after AD 70. In that case Acts

---

[1] Cf. F. Stagg, *The Book of Acts. The Early Struggle for an unhindered Gospel* (1955). E. Haenchen (*Die Apostelgeschichte*, p. 656) discusses the possibility that ἀκωλύτως may have been an attempt to conciliate the Roman authorities even in spite of the Neronian persecutions, but this is less probable than the alternative view that places the statement in a milieu before these persecutions.

[2] This factor will clearly be assessed differently by different scholars. G. H. C. Macgregor (*The Acts of the Apostles*, IB, 1954, p. 11), who dated Acts AD 80–85, nevertheless considered that the absence of use of Paul's letters not only favoured an early date, but favoured Lucan authorship, and this view is widely shared. But if the collection of Paul's letters is dated earlier than this (cf. pp. 653 ff.), it would require an earlier date for Acts, unless it could be maintained that Luke had no interest in Paul as a letter-writer.

[3] For a discussion of the theory see pp. 647 ff.

NEW TESTAMENT INTRODUCTION

would clearly need to be dated later still.[1] Reasons have already been given why this widely accepted dating of Luke may be challenged, and if the Gospel is dated as early as AD 60 (see discussion on p. 115) this would suggest an early date for Acts and would be in keeping with the argument already given for a date before AD 64. It is a doubtful method of dating early books to use a particular interpretation of the one available datum and then to build a superstructure of other books upon it. It will be clear that if a predictive element in the ministry of Jesus is allowed the whole basis of this generally held dating collapses.

It should nevertheless be noted that not all who accept the traditional authorship of Luke date the book before the fall of Jerusalem. If Luke is the author and it is deemed necessary to date the Gospel after AD 70, the upper limit for the dating of Acts is restricted only by the probability of Luke's life-span, which is very difficult to estimate. It would certainly not be impossible for Luke to have written Acts any time up to about AD 85 but it could hardly have been much later. A date between AD 70 and 85 is, therefore, preferred by the majority of scholars.

E. J. Goodspeed[2] produced a list of additional reasons for a date as late as AD 90 for Luke-Acts, which were mainly inferences from the contents. Late features, according to him, can be seen in certain literary characteristics, in the infancy interest, in the resurrection interest, in the doctrine of the Spirit, primitive miracles, cessation of the Jewish controversy, interest in psalmody, church organization, primitive glossalalia, the inferences from xx. 25, 38 that Paul is dead, Paul's heroic stature, the emergence of the sects, lack of acquaintance with Paul's letters and the historical background of a successful Gentile mission. Quite apart from the questionable character of some of Goodspeed's inferences (e.g. that Paul is dead from Acts xx. 25, 38), it is by no means clear that any of the points he mentions requires a date any later than the early sixties. In any case he accepts the Lucan authorship and supposes that the author collected his material long before his book was actually published.

---

[1] It may be of interest to note that one or two scholars have maintained that Acts was published before Luke. C. S. C. Williams (*ET*, LXIV, 1952–53, pp. 283 ff.) argues that Acts followed Proto-Luke in production but preceded the publication of the Gospel, while H. G. Russell (*HTR*, 48, 1955, pp. 167–174) suggests that Acts influenced the production of the Gospel.*

[2] *Introduction to the New Testament* (1937), pp. 191 ff.*

c. Arguments for a second-century date

Earlier critics of the Tübingen school popularized a second-century dating for Acts because their reconstruction of the history demanded it. The reconciliation tendency of the author to patch up the Petrine-Pauline clash required a considerable time interval to develop. But the subjective character of this kind of criticism has assured its doom and the dismissal of the historical reconstruction of this school of thought has caused a general disinclination towards a second-century dating. But there are still some arguments which are advanced in support of this dating.

(i) *The relation of Acts to Josephus.* The fact that both Acts (in the speech of Gamaliel, v. 36) and Josephus refer to a rising under a Jew named Theudas has given rise to the theory that the author of Acts consulted Josephus' *Antiquities*[1] while writing his history. If this deduction is correct Acts must be dated after AD 94.[2] An alleged contradiction between Josephus and the Gospel has already been cited in discussing the dating of Luke (see p. 112), and a similar contradiction is suggested here. Acts places the rising of Theudas before the rising of Judas the Galilaean, but the latter happened in the time of Augustus, while Josephus dates the former at a period subsequent to Gamaliel's speech. There are two possible explanations. Either one of these reports must be wrong, or else the Theudas mentioned by Luke was not the Theudas mentioned by Josephus. Most scholars prefer the former alternative and generally presume that the historian in error must be Luke. But the author of Acts almost certainly did not consult Josephus, for had he done so he would surely not have made so obvious a blunder. Moreover, it is no more self-evident that Acts must be wrong and Josephus correct than *vice versa*.[3] It is, of course, possible that two rebellions were instigated by men named Theudas, since this was a

---

[1] *Antiquities*, xx. 5 (Whiston's edition).

[2] This theory was maintained by F. C. Burkitt (*The Gospel History and its Transmission*[3], 1911, pp. 105–110), following the arguments of Krenkel's *Josephus und Lucas* (1894). It has had considerable influence. Its traces are even found among some who maintain Lucan authorship. R. R. Williams, in his Torch Commentary on Acts, suggests that Luke may have had no exact report of Gamaliel's speech and that the error crept in through careless editing of the text with the aid of Josephus' works (*op. cit.*, pp. 64, 65).

[3] F. F. Bruce (*The Acts of the Apostles*[2], 1952, p. 25) comments, 'There is nothing here to suggest literary dependence; as for discrepancies, Luke is as likely to be right as Josephus.'

fairly common name, but such a theory is none too convincing without corroborating evidence.

(ii) *The relation of Acts to second-century writers*. Some scholars have gone much farther than Josephus and have found affinities between Acts and the second-century Church Fathers. It has recently been maintained that Justin shared the same theological outlook as Acts although he makes no literary use of the book.[1] But theological affinities are a precarious method of assessing dating, for the theory that Acts and Justin's works were both produced about the same time is certainly not the only explanation of the relationship, nor is it even the most reasonable, for it raises far more problems than it solves.[2] It may be assumed that Acts was linked with the third Gospel almost from its inception, in which case it would be inconceivable for Marcion to have been acquainted with Luke and not Acts. But it would have been equally improbable for Marcion to have chosen as his one Gospel a book which was clearly not of ancient standing. All the evidence points to an arbitrary rejection of Acts by Marcion on the same grounds as those on which he rejected the remaining Gospels.[3]

A second-century dating of Acts which gained such favour among earlier critics is not likely to be reinstituted by any argument based on theological affinities, in view of the strong traditional testimony against such a theory. Moreover, it is difficult to imagine that the strong impression Acts gives of recording factual details, particularly in the latter part dealing with Paul's activities, is the work of a second-century writer.[4] It is far less credible to regard the book as the product of a writer's historical imagination than it is to regard it as the record of one who was in close proximity to the events he relates—which would be the case with a first-century dating.

---

[1] Cf. J. C. O'Neill, *The Theology of Acts*, pp. 10 ff. In an appendix, O'Neill claims to establish that Justin did not know Luke's Gospel either (pp. 28–53). But H. F. D. Sparks(*JTS*, n.s., xiv, 1963, pp. 462–466) strongly criticizes his method.*

[2] Cf. W. G. Kümmel, *INT* (1965), pp. 132 f.

[3] O'Neill gets over the difficulty by maintaining that Marcion's copy of Luke was a form of the canonical Gospel corrected against what he supposed were older sources (*op. cit.*, pp. 19 ff.). O'Neill's conclusion is that Luke-Acts need not have been issued until about ten years before Marcion's Canon (i.e. *c.* AD 130). Contrast the view expressed by H. J. Cadbury and the editors in Jackson-Lake's *Beginnings of Christianity*, II, p. 358, that it is extremely unlikely that Luke would ever have been canonized had it not been generally known before the time of Marcion.*

[4] Cf. Sparks, *op. cit.*, p. 461.

III. PURPOSE

Since the book of Acts is a continuation of the third Gospel, it is reasonable to suppose that the purpose which is there clearly stated in the preface will obtain for this part of the work as well. It has been shown (see pp. 93 ff.) that Luke's primary purpose was historical and this must be considered as the major aim of Acts, whatever subsidiary motives may have contributed towards its production.

a. A narrative of history

Leaving aside for the present the much-debated question of the historical value of Acts, we may assume that Luke intended his work to be regarded as historical, but not in the sense of a dry chronicle of events. The author, by reason of the wide range of his subject, has been forced to be selective. There is much that we would like to know of which Luke says nothing. The history before the narrative of Paul's life and work is somewhat scrappy and gives the impression that the author's purpose is to get to Paul as soon as possible. Even when dealing with Paul he omits certain features, for example Paul's visit to Arabia after his conversion and the journeys of Timothy and Erastus between Macedonia, Athens and Corinth.[1] The author clearly had a different approach towards his historical record than have modern historians because, quite apart from the assumption that ancient historians had little conception of exact scientific writing, Luke was more than a historian. He was in a real way a part of the history itself. He was describing events which had made a deep impression upon his mind. He could not detach himself, even had he wanted to, from the thrill of the divine happenings which he had heard about or had seen with his own eyes.

There is an implication in Luke's preface that others before him had felt the urge to commit to writing the events which lay behind the early Christian movement, and it may be that Luke considered unsatisfactory such attempts as he had seen. This latter presupposition is not, however, conclusively demanded by the evidence.[2] It could be that the author possessed a dominant urge to produce a record of the facts irrespective of the work of his predecessors.

[1] See p. 569. W. G. Kümmel (*INT*, 1965, p. 113) appeals to the omissions in Acts as evidence that Acts is not a historical work.
[2] Cf. H. J. Cadbury, *The Making of Luke-Acts* (1927), p. 303.

b. A Gospel of the Spirit

Since Luke-Acts must be considered as a whole, and since the first part possesses the character of a Gospel, the second part must be viewed in the light of this fact.[1] For the author the important thing is the recognition of a divine activity behind the events, hence his great emphasis on the work of the Holy Spirit.[2] The Church comes into being through the baptism of the Spirit (ii. 38). Fullness of the Spirit was the evidence of true Christianity (ii. 4, vi. 3, viii. 17, x. 44, xix. 6). It was the Spirit who directed the mission work of the primitive Church, seen for instance in the action of the Antiochene church (xiii. 2) and in the prohibitions which prevented Paul and his party from entering Bithynia (xvi. 7). It is not inappropriate that this book has been called the Acts of the Holy Spirit and it is significant that several times the record of events is described as the continued activity of Jesus. In His name the lame man is healed (iii. 6, iv. 10), in His name the apostles preached (v. 40). Both Stephen and Saul see a heavenly vision of Jesus (vii. 55, ix. 5). This is but an illustration of what Luke says in his preface that in his former book he wrote what Jesus *began* to do and teach (Acts i. 1), which shows that his present purpose is to describe the continuation of that work.[3]

c. An apology

The two former propositions would not explain the particular selection of material which Luke has made and consequently many scholars have proposed an apologetic purpose. There is much to be said for this,

---

[1] This has recently been stressed by Trocmé (*Le 'Livre des Actes' et l'Histoire*, 1957, pp. 42 ff.), who maintains that the new form of historical narrative was preserved only because it was attached to an already acknowledged Gospel form.

[2] In his article on 'The Construction and Purpose of the Acts of the Apostles' (*StTh*, 12, 1958, p. 55) A. Ehrhardt claims, 'For the whole purpose of the Book of Acts . . . is no less than to be the Gospel of the Holy Spirit.' This approach was stressed by many older exegetes, but it is good to find some modern authors who are prepared to find in this the key to the understanding of Luke's purpose.

[3] As Rackham (*The Acts of the Apostles*[14], 1951, p. xxxviii) states, 'These twenty-eight chapters are but *the beginning* (i. 1, xi. 15): we are still living under the dispensation of the Spirit.' By this he explains the lack of a conclusion. Cf. W. C. van Unnik's view that Acts was designed to be a confirmation of the Gospel for those who had had no personal acquaintance with Christ in the flesh (*Nov. Test.*, 4, 1960, pp. 26–59).

although not all the forms in which the theory is presented are accept-able. The earlier Tübingen critics saw Acts as a compromise between Petrinism and Paulinism, in which case the author was dominated by a very definite 'tendency'. But this kind of criticism is now discounted.[1] The apologetic purpose is seen in two directions: the approach to the Jews and the approach to the Roman authorities.

The author appears to go out of his way to show the close connec-tion between Christianity and its antecedents in Judaism. The Christ-ians, and particularly Paul himself, still observe Jewish ceremonial requirements: Timothy is circumcised and Paul takes a vow, while James, both at the Council of Jerusalem and on the occasion of his later meeting with Paul, draws attention to the relationship between Jewish practices and Christian procedure. The appeal to the Old Testament as predicting events which were happening in the Christian Church would influence Jewish readers in the direction of a favourable view of the Church. But it is in its approach to official relationships with the Roman Empire that Acts becomes most clearly apologetic. In every case the author brings out the impartiality of the Roman officials. The attitude of Gallio may be viewed as typical. He cared for none of the religious questions which formed the basis of Jewish charges against Paul. The fact is that he would not have understood them. Another proconsul, Sergius Paulus, is seen to be most favourable towards the gospel. The city secretary at Ephesus was conciliatory, and the Asiarchs (probably here officials appointed to maintain order at religious festi-vals) are seen as helpful to Paul. Is all this an attempt to exonerate Rome from implication in the constant harassing of the Christian Church? Throughout it is the Jews who are the instigators, and throughout the Roman authorities do not take their charges seriously. Both Agrippa and Festus agreed that Paul might have been freed if he had not appealed to Caesar (xxvi. 32).[2]

It is an attractive idea that the author wished to show that Christian-ity was politically harmless in order that the authorities might be pre-

[1] The idea of the Tübingen critics that Gnosticism is the key to the understand-ing of Acts is not altogether rejected, for C. K. Barrett regards Acts as an apology addressed to the Church showing Paul's anti-Gnostic orthodoxy (*Luke the His-torian in Recent Study*, 1961, p. 63).

[2] It should be noted that Festus had the power to acquit Paul in spite of the appeal, but it would have been politically inexpedient for him to have done so. Cf. Sherwin-White, *Roman Society and Roman Law in the New Testament* (1963), p. 65.

pared to extend to it the same toleration as they gave to Judaism.[1] Yet it must not be supposed that Luke takes up a position of compromise in order to persuade the authorities to regard Christianity under the umbrella of Judaism. Had such been his purpose he would surely have omitted to mention the constant hostility of the Jews towards Christian mission preaching. To throw all the onus for the disturbance on to the Jews would be a strange way of convincing anybody that Christianity was still to be regarded as a branch of Judaism, quite apart from the obvious dangers of such a compromise for the subsequent history of the Church.*

d. A defence brief for Paul's trial

This suggestion is closely linked to the apologetic motive, but is tied to a particular occasion.[2] The idea is that Paul's trial is still in progress and Luke has prepared for Theophilus a full explanation of the rise and character of Christianity for the purpose of correcting misunderstandings. It is assumed under this view that Theophilus was a person of high rank who would have influence with the emperor. Streeter[3] suggested that he was Flavius Clemens. But the identity of Theophilus is mere conjecture and it is purely hypothetical that such a book as Acts would have allayed the suspicions of so infamous a character as Nero.[4] Moreover, Luke's preface suggests that Theophilus had already been instructed in the Christian faith and it would appear to have been at least part of Luke's purpose to instruct him more fully.[5] Although

[1] M. Schneckenberger (*Ueber den Zweck der Apostelgeschichte*, 1841, pp. 244 ff.) first argued for this view (cited by Trocmé, *op. cit.*, p. 52). For a modern presentation, cf. B. S. Easton's essay on 'The Purpose of Acts' in *Early Christianity* (ed. F. C. Grant, 1954), pp. 41 ff.*

In his book *Roman Hellenism and the New Testament* (1962), pp. 172–178, F. C. Grant maintains that the term *religio licita* was not used until the third century of the Christian era. He considers that in Roman eyes *religio* was so bound up with the State that a rival *religio* would have been regarded as intolerable. All that Christianity could hope for would be toleration, not recognition.

[2] Cf. D. Plooij, *Exp.*, VIII, viii (1914), pp. 511–523; VIII, xiii (1917), pp. 108–124; A. Wikenhauser, *Die Apostelgeschichte und ihr Geschichtswert* (1921), pp. 30–34; H. Sahlin, *Der Messias und das Gottesvolk* (1945, *Acta Seminarii Neotestamentici Upsaliensis*, XII, pp. 30–56. The latter regards part of Acts as part of Proto-Luke which has been later edited as a defence for Paul (cf. Michaelis' criticisms, *Einleitung*, p. 137).*

[3] *The Four Gospels*, pp. 533 ff.

[4] C. K. Barrett (*op. cit.*, p. 63) calls such an idea 'absurd'.

[5] H. J. Cadbury (*op. cit.*, p. 315) prefers to understand Luke's preface as indicating Luke's intention to correct a misunderstanding of Christianity.

this theory cannot be disproved, it lacks strong historical probability.[1]

e. A theological document

Many scholars have placed the emphasis on Luke's theological interests.
The movement of Christianity from Jerusalem to Rome had more than
geographical interest[2] for the author. It had theological significance. It
revealed the triumph of Christianity in a hostile world.[3] Thus the
arrival of Paul in Rome was a fitting conclusion to the history.

Some scholars have taken this point of view much further and have
seen in Luke a historian who is wholly dominated by a theological
purpose. His narrative is treated not so much as a record of facts as an
interpretation. Thus Dibelius[4] maintained, 'The whole work aims not
so much at letting the readers know what really happened as at helping
them to understand what all this means, the invasion of the world of
hellenistic culture by the Christian Church.' In similar vein J. C.
O'Neill[5] considers that both Jerusalem and Rome have for the author
tremendous theological importance. Haenchen[6] maintains a similar
theory, but sees Acts as an edifying piece of literature, in which the
author uses literary means to make the events memorable to his readers,
and for this purpose uses what material he possesses with considerable
freedom.* While it is probable that not enough weight has been attached to theological motives, the approach of these scholars impinges

---

[1] W. G. Kümmel (*INT*, 1965, p. 113) dismisses this view as false because an
early date for Acts is unacceptable. But if that obstacle is removed and Acts is
dated early (as argued above, pp. 340 ff.) this objection is invalid. A great obstacle
to the theory is the absence from Acts of any reference to the trial in Rome.

[2] Several scholars have maintained that Luke's main purpose was geographical,
to record the planting of the gospel in the imperial city. (Cf. E. Jacquier, *Les
Actes des Apôtres*[2], 1926, p. cii; T. Zahn, *Die Apostelgeschichte*, 1919–21, pp. 14,
15.) This view is criticized by Trocmé (*op. cit.*, pp. 83 ff.) on the grounds that
Christianity had reached Rome before Paul, and in any case there was no need
to demonstrate by this means the triumph of universalism since this is clear from
Acts xv.*

[3] This is well brought out in the analysis of the book by R. R. Williams under
the caption, 'Nothing can stop the Gospel' (*The Acts of the Apostles*, 1953, pp.
24–33).

[4] *Studies in the Acts of the Apostles* (1956), p. 133.

[5] *The Theology of Acts*, pp. 58 ff.   [6] Cf. *Die Apostelgeschichte*, pp. 93–99 *

on the historicity of Acts, and this raises a problem which will merit further consideration.

IV. HISTORICITY

IV. HISTORICITY

This book has been a constant battleground for critical scholars obsessed with the problem of Luke's veracity. The era has now passed when the historicity of Acts can with any plausibility be wholly discredited, but nevertheless many scholars find difficulty in some of Luke's details. A brief indication of these difficulties will be given in the following discussion.

a. Luke's political knowledge

Sir William Ramsay has done much to reinstate Luke as a serious historian and this is largely due to archaeological researches. The author of Acts was acquainted with all the different political arrangements in those provinces which enter into the narration of Paul's missionary journeys. This is a remarkable testimony to Luke's accurate knowledge in view of the several changes in administration of parts of the empire effected during the period covered by his history. The following details will give some indication of the extent of this knowledge. At the time when Paul was in Cyprus a proconsul was in charge, and although there had been many changes within a brief period Luke used the correct title when describing Sergius Paulus. Philippi is accurately described as a Roman colony, whose officials are called στρατηγοί, apparently representing the senior magistrates according to the Roman pattern of *duoviri iuri dicundo*.[1] At Thessalonica the unusual *politarchs*, for which no parallels were known to exist in imperial organization, are now vouched for by inscriptions. At Malta the ruler is correctly styled the πρῶτος or chief man, while at Ephesus there are correct references to the local government organization, with Asiarchs[2] controlling

---

[1] Cf. A. N. Sherwin-White, *Roman Society and Roman Law in the New Testament* (1963), pp. 92, 93. This author rejects the older view that στρατηγοί represents the Latin *praetores*, on the grounds that this term was already becoming archaic by 63 BC.

[2] Sherwin-White points out that this title was used of presidents (and perhaps ex-presidents) of the Council of Asia, but was also used of administrators of the imperial cult, or of the city deputies who formed the Council (*ibid.*, p. 90). In some provinces the corresponding title (e.g. Lyciarch, Pontarch, Bithyniarch) was restricted to one holder, the president. Luke's use of the plural, therefore, shows specific knowledge of the different set-up in Asia.

religious affairs, the Secretary (or Chief Clerk)[1] wielding considerable influence, and the proconsular authorities being regarded as the final court of appeal.

In addition to these, Luke shows detailed knowledge of the rights and privileges of Roman citizens. Especially is this evident in the reluctance of the apostle Paul to invoke his privileges, for not only was it true that in the New Testament period provincials who possessed Roman citizenship claimed also citizenship of their own cities, but it was also difficult for wandering peoples to prove their Roman citizenship by appeal to the official registers in their own home areas. It would not always have been to Paul's advantage to invoke his privileges, although in the case of his appeal to Caesar it was clearly to escape from the hostility of the Jews. In Luke's various references to Roman legal procedures, he shows himself to be well informed. In fact, there is no instance where Luke has introduced an anachronism, which is a striking testimony to the general reliability of his narrative.[2] Moreover, the description of the Gentile world which forms the background of Paul's mission perfectly fits into what is known of city life in the Graeco-Roman world. Nevertheless many other considerations have been held to dispute this conclusion.

b. *The relationship with Paul's Epistles*

This problem has been the subject of a mass of literature and it will be impossible to give more than the main features which have caused difficulties in the minds of many scholars.

(i) *Paul and the church of Jerusalem.* The fact that in Acts Paul appears to visit Jerusalem three times (ix. 20 ff., xi. 30, xv. 2), compared with the two occasions (Gal. i. 16 ff., ii) which Paul himself mentions for the same period (if Galatians is dated *after* the Council of Jerusalem), has led to the assumption that Luke is incorrect. But the validity of this

---

[1] The official title was Clerk of the People. He was the chief administrative official of the city and there is evidence for such an official in Ephesus and other Asiatic cities during the New Testament period. There was a lesser official called the Clerk of the Council, but the Acts story, which describes the γραμματεύς as addressing the people, is clearly referring to the more important office (cf. Sherwin-White, *op. cit.*, pp. 86, 87).

[2] On the whole subject of Luke's reliability in this respect, cf. Sherwin-White *op. cit.*, *passim*. It is well demonstrated that the dramatic date of the Acts narrative belongs to the Julio-Claudian period of Roman administration, which strikingly supports the contention that the author had access to first-hand information,

assumption depends on far too many dubious propositions. It requires us to suppose that Paul is stating *all* the occasions when he visited Jerusalem, whereas he may well be citing only the occasions when he had personal contact with the apostles, and this would appear to exclude xi. 30. Nevertheless, some scholars have proposed to treat the visits of xi. 30 and xv as duplicate accounts of the same event, which would, of course, impugn the accuracy of Luke's information.[1] But it is highly improbable that the author would have become muddle-headed over such an important and significant event as this.[2] Moreover, such a theory is not demanded by the evidence.[3]

(ii) *Paul and the Jewish law.* The Acts twice describes Paul as supporting Jewish ritual observances, once when recommending the circumcision of Timothy and again when he submitted to James' suggestion regarding the vow and its accompanying shaving of the head. Such deference to Jewish scruples is, however, reckoned by some to be alien to the attitude of Paul in his Epistles, where he not only resists the perpetuation of circumcision, but also proclaims Christian freedom from bondage to the law. Is this a real contradiction or is it merely apparent? When Paul's own dictum (in 1 Corinthians) that the strong must be prepared to consider the effect of their actions on the weak is taken into account, his own willingness to take a Jewish vow is not inexplicable. It was not a matter which had a vital effect on his Christian position. His attitude towards circumcision was rather different. In the Epistles Paul makes clear his decided opposition to circumcision being regarded as a *sine qua non* for Gentile believers, but there is no reason to suppose that Paul intended to oppose circumcision as a Jewish practice (cf. Rom. ii. 25). The circumcision of Timothy, whose mother was Jewish, would merely regularize his racial affinities, but the circumcision of a Gentile

[1] Cf. A. C. McGiffert, *A History of Christianity in the Apostolic Age* (1897), p. 171; K. Lake in *The Beginnings of Christianity*, v, pp. 195 ff. More recently E. Hirsch, *ZNTW*, 29 (1930), pp. 63–76; J. R. Porter, *JTS*, XLVIII (1947), pp. 169 ff.

[2] H. Windisch, although inclined to regard Acts xi and xv as duplicate accounts, nevertheless admitted that it 'is strange that "Luke" was ignorant of these matters; nevertheless it is not impossible that he might have given an incorrect version of the matter' (*The Beginnings of Christianity*, II, p. 319).

[3] For a full discussion of this problem see pp. 458 ff. In view of the difficulties of the traditional view, J. N. Sanders speculated about a new reconstruction of the course of events in which he maintained two Jerusalem visits before AD 44, and suggested that Paul was not present at the Council (*NTS*, 2, 1955, pp. 133–143).*

Christian, with no Jewish background whatever, would give the impression that circumcision was an essential part of Christianity, which would then have been constituted a sect of Judaism. There is no essential contradiction over this question. It has sometimes been supposed on the strength of Galatians ii. 3 that Paul had at the Council of Jerusalem opposed the demand that Titus should be circumcised.[1] But since Titus was a Greek he was in a different position from Timothy.

(iii) *Paul and the Council decrees.* According to the Acts, certain decrees were proposed and agreed to by Paul which involved the enforcement of certain ritual prohibitions on the Gentile converts. The generally accepted text contains four such prohibitions: idolatrous pollutions, unchastity, things strangled and blood (Acts xv. 20). The last two relate to dietary regulations. The 'Western' text omits the third taboo and the list in that case becomes a moral catechism, assuming 'blood' to be an equivalent for murder. But it seems quite unnecessary to urge Gentile Christians to abstain from murder. The common text makes more sense, although it would appear to enjoin a Jewish food law on Gentile converts and would raise a difficulty as to whether Paul would ever have agreed to that. Moreover, in Galatians ii, Paul not only does not mention the decrees, but expressly says that no obligations were laid upon him but to remember the poor (verses 6, 10). While this at first sight looks like a discrepancy, there are considerations which should cause us to think carefully before reaching this conclusion. Paul, in Galatians, is referring to his own position, not that of all the Gentile converts. He is speaking in self-defence.

It is significant that the decrees were addressed only to the Gentiles in the churches of Antioch, Syria and Cilicia (Acts xv. 23). At the same time, Acts xvi. 4 states clearly that Paul delivered the decrees to the South Galatian churches, which suggests that he regarded them as generally applicable. In any case there are no strong reasons for supposing that Paul *must* quote them in Galatians, since he may have preferred direct arguments to support his claims. Furthermore if Galatians was written before the Council of Jerusalem the decrees were not by then agreed upon.

The incident at Antioch in which Paul resisted Peter's action is thought to be strange following the agreements at the Council, and consequently the veracity of the Acts account is called in question.[2]

<hr>

[1] Cf. H. Windisch, *op. cit.*, p. 320. [2] *Ibid.*, p. 326.

But this discrepancy is more apparent than real, for Paul makes it clear that Peter had acted inconsistently, and this cannot be said to be impossible although it is certainly unexpected. But it is equally strange that Paul should charge Barnabas with insincerity. The difficulty is, of course, lessened if the dissimulation occurred before the Council, although Peter's earlier Caesarean experience should have prepared him to resist the pressure of the Jewish rigorists.

(iv) *Luke's portrait of Paul.* When considering the question of authorship it was pointed out that a comparison between the Paul presented in Acts and the Paul who reveals himself in his letters has led some scholars to find discrepancies. E. Haenchen[1] places emphasis on three differences.

1. Acts presents Paul as a wonder-worker who can heal through communicating his power through a handkerchief, or who can raise the dead Eutychus, or can shake off a deadly serpent unharmed. But the apostle makes reference to working wonders in 2 Corinthians xii. 12, which Haenchen does not regard as very exceptional, since in any case Paul did not base the evidence for his apostleship on such external factors. There is a difficulty here only if it is assumed that Luke records the miraculous as an evidence of Paul's apostleship, but he nowhere says this, and the interpretation may be challenged.

2. Whereas in Acts Paul is portrayed as a convincing speaker to a variety of different audiences, whether to Jews or Greeks, government officials or philosophers, in the Epistles Paul himself disclaims any rhetorical power and even includes his opponents' estimate of him as of no account as a speaker (cf. 2 Cor. x. 10). Haenchen sees this contradiction as having arisen from a later assumption that Paul the great missionary must have been Paul the great speaker, although in fact it was not so. But it is noteworthy that Acts nowhere describes Paul in such terms as Apollos is described ('an eloquent man', Acts xviii. 24), although on Haenchen's theory this might well have been expected. Moreover, on many of the occasions in Acts his so-called eloquence was far from persuasive, for it frequently resulted in open hostility and on at least one occasion in ridicule. It is very doubtful, therefore, whether much weight should be attached to this supposed discrepancy.

3. Although in the Epistles Paul strongly affirms his equality with the Jerusalem apostles, Acts gives no hint that Paul had any need to do

[1] *Die Apostelgeschichte*, pp. 100 ff.*

this. His apostolic status seems to have been assumed at an early point in the narrative. But it is precisely because it is assumed, that the supposed discrepancy loses weight. Luke portrays Paul's apostolic mission to the Gentiles as a continuation of the earlier activities of Peter and others in Judaea and Samaria. To him apostolic status was incidental to his main purpose in describing the spread of the gospel. Paul's own battle for equality of status had as its setting the internal conditions of the primitive churches, but Acts says very little about these.

None of these problems requires the conclusion that Luke's history is unreliable, for a reasonable solution is possible in each case. An additional consideration which is not unfavourable to Luke's reliability is the primitiveness of the conditions in the early Church reflected in his account.[1] Whatever value is placed on alleged parallels between Acts and the Qumran literature,[2] they draw attention to some points of contact and may suggest a similar general milieu. It should be noted that the differences[3] between Qumran and the primitive Christian community are greater than the similarities, which again emphasizes Luke's knowledge of the distinctive Christian features of the Jewish-Christian community.[4]

c. The speeches in Acts

The assessment of the Acts speeches forms an important factor in determining the historicity of the book, and some indication must therefore be given of the various ways of approaching the author's method. Peter, Stephen and Paul are the main orators and to these are attributed various types of speeches. F. F. Bruce[5] has divided these speeches into

---

[1] Bo Reicke, in his *Glaube und Leben der Urgemeinde* (1957), maintains the genuinely early character of the traditions incorporated into Acts i-vii.*

[2] Cf. S. E. Johnson's suggestions in *The Scrolls and the New Testament* (ed. K. Stendahl, 1958), pp. 129 ff. He found parallels in the reception of the Spirit as pledge of eternal life, the idea of communal life and of religious poverty, the organization into a Council of twelve, the distinction between the members and the leaders, the common meal and the method of biblical citation and interpretation.*

[3] For example, the absence from Acts of a novitiate, of probation, or of classification of members into trades, or of communal works.

[4] O. Cullmann considers that the Hellenists of Acts vi were connected with the kind of Judaism represented by the Qumran texts (*JBL*, LXXIV, 1955, pp. 213-226, reproduced in Stendahl's collection, *op. cit.*, pp. 18 ff.). But against this, cf. P. Winter, *ThLZ*, 82 (1957), col. 835.

[5] *The Speeches in the Acts of the Apostles* (1944), p. 5.

four groups: evangelistic, deliberative, apologetic and hortatory. The form of each is determined by its respective occasion and purpose. But the major question regarding them all is whether they reproduce the content of the words spoken or whether they are inventions of Luke in order to represent what he considered would have been said. To answer this question it will be necessary to consider various propositions.

(i) *The approach of ancient historiography.* The classical statement on this is that of Thucydides, who carefully described his method. He admitted that he could not always recall the speeches word for word, so that he had formed the habit of making the speakers speak in a way which seemed to him to be demanded by the occasion, though he concluded, 'of course adhering as closely as possible to the general sense of what was actually said'.[1] It is often supposed that this means that Thucydides invented most of his speeches, although occasionally conforming them to actual reports.[2] Yet Thucydides seems to be arguing for the substantial historicity of his speeches, for otherwise he would not have been at such pains to stress that some of the speeches he had himself heard, while others he received from various sources. Basically truth lies behind the record. Thucydides' successors did not maintain his high notion of the historian's task and many of them produced historical works in the manner of dramatic or rhetorical exercises. But to which of these categories does Luke belong? M. Dibelius was quite emphatic that Luke invented his speeches and supported this contention by an appeal to their general similarities, irrespective of the identity of the speakers. But this conclusion has been as strongly challenged by others, notably Foakes Jackson,[3] Sir William Ramsay[4] and B. Gärtner.[5]

[1] *History of the Peloponnesian War*, i. 22. 1.

[2] For a discussion of Thucydides' statement, cf. H. Patzer, *Das Problem der Geschichtsschreibung des Thukydides und die thukydideische Frage* (1937), pp. 44 ff.; A. W. Gomme, *A Historical Commentary on Thucydides* (1945), I, pp. 140, 141; M. Dibelius, *Studies in the Acts of the Apostles* (1956), pp. 140 ff.; B. Gärtner, *The Areopagus Speech and Natural Revelation* (1955), pp. 13 f. Gomme thinks that Thucydides put the speeches in his own style, but this does not mean that the content was his own. The fact that different interpretations can be put on Thucydides' words should lead to some caution in building too much upon them. It cannot be cited as the main evidence in support of a literary process of inventiveness.*

[3] *The Acts of the Apostles* (1931), p. xvi.

[4] *St. Paul the Traveller and Roman Citizen* (1920), p. 27.

[5] *Op. cit.*, pp. 26 ff.

Gärtner rightly pleads for greater emphasis upon the Jewish historical tradition to counterbalance the Greek tradition in the background of Luke's writings. In other words it is by no means obvious that Luke's historical method must be interpreted on the basis of Greek principles, if indeed there were principles which can in any sense be regarded as generally adopted among Greek historians.[1]

(ii) *The approach of Luke in his Gospel.* Although no canonical parallels exist by which the Acts speeches may be gauged, the method used in the Gospel can be compared with the other Synoptic accounts and a comparative estimate of Luke's reliability can be formed. It has already been seen that Luke exercised great care over his choice of sources and that he has faithfully reproduced his material (see comments on Luke's preface, p. 227). Especially is this seen in his treatment of the discourse material in Luke xxi, if it is established that he used Mark xiii. Although there are minor changes, there is no evidence that Luke has invented material not found in his sources.[2] Indeed, the Gospel as a whole shows no evidence of such a tendency, and in view of this it is a fair assumption that he would not have resorted to it in the continuation in Acts.

(iii) *The primitive character of the theology of the speeches.* It has been emphasized, particularly by C. H. Dodd,[3] that the early speeches of Acts contain the primitive *kerygma*. They are, therefore, a true representation of an early pre-Pauline theology and this can only reasonably be accounted for on the assumption that Luke incorporates a genuine tradition in his speeches. Those who dispute Luke's historicity, however, claim that the theology is of a later type.[4] Yet if Luke was the author the theology cannot be very developed, particularly if the book of Acts was published before the death of Paul (see discussion above, pp. 340 ff.).

[1] R. M. Grant (*A Historical Introduction to the New Testament*, 1963, p. 141), in urging caution against regarding Thucydides as the only model of ancient historians, remarks that Polybius (second century BC) was severely critical of speech invention and regarded the historian's task as recording what was actually said.

[2] Cf. F. C. Burkitt's opinion in his article on 'Luke's use of Mark' in *The Beginnings of Christianity* (ed. Foakes Jackson and Lake), II, pp. 106 ff.

[3] *The Apostolic Preaching and its Developments*[2] (1944), pp. 7 ff.

[4] Thus J. C. O'Neill (*The Theology of Acts*, 1961) maintains that Luke is dominated by the theology of the first half of the second century (see especially pp. 166 ff.).

exact words

(iv) *The relation of the content of the speeches to the ipsissima verba.* Even if the tradition which is incorporated in the speeches is substantially historically correct, does this mean that Luke has preserved the precise words which were spoken? The majority of those who would maintain the reliability of Luke's record would not be prepared to maintain that he has preserved the *ipsissima verba*.[1] The content is historically true, but the words are Luke's own. The same kind of approach has already been met in dealing with the Fourth Gospel, but it has yet to be proved that the words could not bear any relationship to what was actually spoken. Each speech is so exactly adapted to its historical situation[2] that it would have been an example of consummate art on Luke's part to provide so perfectly suitable a framework for the words. It is not true, as some have maintained, that all the Acts speakers speak alike,[3] for the various types of speeches are admirably suited to their respective audiences,[4] the *Areopagitica* in Acts xvii. 22 ff. furnishing a conspicuous example.[5] There seems to be no substantial reason for rejecting the view that Luke has preserved personal reminiscences, either his own or those of others, of the speeches that he has chosen to incorporate into his own history. Recent emphasis on form criticism has led some to deny even the possibility of this, since no *Sitz im Leben* can be envisaged in which the speeches could have been preserved for twenty to thirty years.[6] But it is not altogether impossible that some written transcripts

[1] Cf. the recent approach of B. Gärtner (*The Areopagus Speech and Natural Revelation*, p. 33) who attributes the 'outer form' of the speeches to Luke, although considering that Luke gives reliable specimens of the apostolic message.

[2] Foakes Jackson (*The Acts of the Apostles*, p. xvi), for instance, considered that the speeches were 'wonderfully varied as to their character, and as a rule admirably suited to the occasion on which they were delivered'.

[3] So M. Dibelius, *A Fresh Approach to the New Testament and Early Christian Literature* (1936), p. 262. In a recent study, E. Schweizer (*ThZ*, XIII, 1957, pp. 1–11) claims that a basic pattern lies behind all the Acts speeches and that it is necessary to combine the individual speeches to obtain a total picture. J. T. Townsend (*ATR*, XLII, 1960, pp. 150 ff.) also considers that the speeches must be treated as a whole, which, if true, would lessen the connection of each speech with its specific situation. *

[4] Cf. F. F. Bruce, *The Acts of the Apostles*[2] (1952), pp. 18 ff.; F. J. Foakes Jackson, *op. cit.*, p. xiv. For a study of the particular emphasis in Stephen's speech, cf. M. Simon, *St. Stephen and the Hellenists in the Primitive Church* (1958); A. F. J. Klijn, *NTS*, 4 (1958), pp. 25–31.

[5] N. B. Stonehouse, *Paul before the Areopagus and other New Testament Studies* (1957), pp. 1–40. For authors adopting a contrary opinion, cf. p. 101 n.3. *

[6] Cf. C. F. Evans, *JTS*, n.s., VII (1956), pp. 25 ff.

may have existed.[1] It may have been Luke's intention to give samples of different kinds of mission preaching, and if this were so the samples would lose in weight if they were Luke's own compositions. On the other hand, the manner in which they are introduced gives the impression that they are an integral part of the narrative.[2]

V. SOURCES

It was inevitable that source criticism, which had found so fruitful a field for its conjectures in the Synoptic Gospels, should turn its attention to the book of Acts. It had strong grounds for doing so, since the reliability of a historical work depends on the reliability of its sources. But the desirability of isolating sources did not guarantee that such a quest was possible. Certainly criticism left no stone unturned in the attempt, as the great number of widely differing hypotheses amply testifies. But their very diversity suggests a basic weakness of approach and it will be profitable, before outlining the various types of theories, to discuss first the factors which affect the different critics' approach to the whole subject. Lack of agreement on sources springs generally from a basic difference in presuppositions regarding a number of closely related problems.

a. Factors affecting the source criticism of Acts

(i) *Unity of authorship*. Is the book a unity or not? If the answer is in the affirmative, the question of sources can be approached from only two possible points of view. Either the unity of the book stems from the mind of one author who has not only left the imprint of his own mind upon the book, but has also himself been the main collector of the materials; or it stems from the mind of an author who has imposed upon separate materials his own unifying influence in both content and style. Those who maintain unity of authorship, therefore, tend to classify themselves in one of two categories: those who deny sources altogether or those who adopt an author–editor hypothesis as distinct from a compiler hypothesis.

---

[1] E. M. Blaiklock (*The Acts of the Apostles*, 1959, p. 17) suggested that Paul's speeches existed in manuscript form. Against this view, cf. W. G. Kümmel, *INT* (1965), p. 118.

[2] For the substantial historicity of the early speeches in Acts, cf. L. Goppelt's study, *Die apostolische und nachapostolische Zeit* (1962), pp. 24 f.*

Those who deny the unity of the book will naturally advocate some kind of source theory to account for the supposed differences which have led them to deny the unity. In these cases the source hypotheses become strictly a corollary of previously formed opinions regarding the unity. The sources need not, of course, be written, but they must have left their mark on the author, who in turn must be regarded either as none too skilful in his use of information which has come to him, or else as having left his work unfinished. Since it has already been shown, however, that there are strong grounds for maintaining the unity of the book, these latter theories have a considerable initial disadvantage.

(ii) *The identity of the author.* In the previous discussion on authorship it was shown that a reasonable case may be made out for the view that the author was a companion of Paul and that the traditional ascription to Luke was in all probability correct. Those scholars who do not accept this identification fall into two groups: some admit that behind at least part of the book there is the personal witness of one or more of Paul's travelling companions (Luke, Silas, Timothy), while others deny altogether that any eyewitness accounts are behind it. Clearly there will be far fewer problems for those who accept Lucan authorship than for those who do not, since it may reasonably be maintained that Luke would have had access to a number of eyewitnesses for those parts of the story where he was not personally present. This is particularly evident for the major section of the book dealing with Paul's experiences. But acceptance of Lucan authorship does not, of course, eliminate the possibility of the use of written sources and this must be borne in mind.

On the other hand, those who adopt an anonymous authorship for Acts have less to guide them in their proposals regarding sources, and may very well depend too much on their own guesses. Theories proceeding from such presuppositions obviously demand most careful scrutiny before any weight is attached to them. This is particularly evident in the case of theories depending on a late date (e.g. second century), for these must necessarily place less credence on the author's sources of information than other theories.

(iii) *The interpretation of Luke's preface.* This has already been discussed in the chapter on Luke's Gospel (see p. 98) and it is a fair inference that the principles which apply to the Gospel will apply equally to Acts.

Yet there is a distinction which is not unimportant in the discussion of sources. Whereas in the case of the Gospel other parallel accounts are known, which at least opens up the possibility that Luke was acquainted with them, in the case of Acts no similar record exists. This means that more stress must be placed on the author's own researches. Cadbury,[1] in fact, maintains that Luke is perhaps intending to include himself in the category of eyewitnesses. While this cannot, of course, be applied to the Gospel, the preface clearly does not exclude the possibility that Luke was a witness of some of the events related in Acts. If this is a true interpretation it will clearly have a bearing on the problem of sources. But some scholars have interpreted the preface to mean that the generation of eyewitnesses is now passed.[2] Yet since the author expressly claims to have followed carefully the events he records, it is most intelligible to suppose that he belongs to the same period. It is also most intelligible to suppose that he uses the first person when he wishes to indicate his own presence at the events he records (see discussion on the we-sections, pp. 101 f.).

(iv) *Criteria used for distinguishing sources.* As is apparent in the criticism of the Gospels, different criteria seem to have been employed at different periods and the success or failure of the criticism is made or marred by the validity of the supporting evidence used. In the Acts, a *linguistic* criterion has been used for various purposes. Some have traced an Aramaic origin for the first part of Acts or at least for portions of this first part; others have claimed a different Greek style for certain parts (e.g. the we-sections); while still others have as strongly maintained the linguistic unity of the whole. In face of these different conclusions from the same criterion it is obviously impossible to place much weight upon it. It is at best a precarious method of locating sources.

Another is the *historical* criterion, which proves almost as unsatisfactory. If two of the same type of event are recorded in any book and there happen to be certain similarities in the records, it is at once assumed by some scholars that they are duplicates and that, therefore, one is less historical than the other. A notable example is Harnack's opinion that the account of the gift of the Holy Spirit in Acts ii is less authentic than that in Acts iv, which led him to attribute them to

---

[1] *Exp.*, VIII, xxiv (1924), pp. 411–416. Cf. also *Beginnings*, v, pp. 497, 498. See also p. 101 n.3.

[2] Cf. A. Loisy (*Evangile selon Luc*, 1924, p. 75) and all who date Acts in the second century.

different sources. But since these accounts may more intelligibly be understood as complementary than as being duplicates, Harnack's basis of criticism is considerably weakened. No satisfactory approach is possible unless it is assumed as a first principle that the account must be treated as it stands unless in this case it is unintelligible. Appeal to doublets, contradictions and the like has littered the history of criticism with far too many hypotheses which are indefensible on sound principles of criticism.

No more successful has been the *theological* criterion whereby different strata have also been distinguished, as for instance the use of the expression Servant (or Son) of God in the first part of Acts in contradistinction from its context. Or again, the differences in content of the Pauline speeches and the Pauline Epistles have been claimed to indicate an author out of touch with Pauline theology. But such principles of criticism are based on a confusion between an author, his sources and his mental environment. As a companion of Paul was not obliged to reflect Pauline thought in imitation of Paul's Epistles, so the theological content of his narrative is an unreliable guide to his probable sources.

(v) *The influence of form criticism.* It is not surprising that the form-historical method which has had such an effect on the criticism of the Synoptic Gospels should equally be applied to the problem of the Acts sources and should similarly have had the effect of drawing attention away from source criticism. But classification of forms is more limited in Acts and has been confined mostly to itineraries and speeches. Its most notable advocate has been Dibelius[1] (see below), whose influence is apparent in much recent criticism. The method has had a notable

---

[1] Cf. his series of essays, *Studies in the Acts of the Apostles* (1956). In his first essay, 'Style Criticism of the Book of Acts', pp. 1–25, Dibelius examines the various narrative materials, classifying them into legend, tale or anecdote. While he claims by this to be assessing only the story-teller's method, yet in actual fact he is also assessing the authenticity of the material. Innumerable details are regarded as the author's own composition, which in itself indicates Dibelius' historical assessment of the value of the material. The story about the eunuch and the conversion of Cornelius are both, for instance, classed as legends, which have been influenced in their narration by the author's literary purpose. In some cases the original form of the story was actually non-Christian, examples of which are found in the account of the sons of Sceva (xix. 14–16) and in the story of the death of Herod (xii. 20–23). These examples will suffice to show the way in which form criticism deals with historical material.

effect in concentrating interest on the historical situation rather than on the fruitless attempt to establish a multiplicity of written sources. Although it has sometimes led to 'historical' verdicts which are far from historical, its positive effect has been in lessening dependence on source criticism. Its greatest weakness has been to assume that the early Christians were not interested in their own earlier history, with the consequence that Luke's data have become suspect. But this assumption is sufficiently disposed of by appeal to the historical situation underlying Paul's Epistles.[1]

(vi) *The explanation of the we-sections.* In any conjectures which might be proposed to account for the origin of Luke's information, the passages where the author uses the first person (the we-sections) are the natural starting-point. These passages[2] are introduced without explanation into narratives in the third person. There have been various theories to explain this phenomenon.

1. The most obvious reason for the first person is that the author wishes to indicate that in these passages he was himself present among the travelling companions of Paul. This interpretation would mean that the author merely changes from the third to the first person, almost unconsciously, because he is at these points producing a first-hand account. It may be called a literary device to differentiate between primary and secondary sources of information. This view is supported by the uniformity of style and language with the rest of the book and the use of the first person singular in i. 1.

2. Somewhat akin to the foregoing is the view that the we-sections form the whole or part of the author's own personal diary or travel jottings which contained information regarding places visited, people contacted and notable events witnessed. In that case he would have quoted the relevant portions, retaining the first person as in the original entry. That this view is less natural than the former is evident from the

---

[1] J. Jervell (*StTh*, 16, 1962, pp. 25–41) criticizes the position adopted by both Dibelius and Haenchen by drawing attention to occasions when Paul refers to the knowledge of other churches among various Christian groups (e.g. Rom. i. 8; 2 Cor. iii. 1–3; 1 Thes. i. 8; 2 Cor. viii. 1). Jervell maintains that this formed a part of God's Word to unbelievers. At least it shows that in Paul's time efforts were made to spread news from church to church of the 'faith' of various groups of believers.

[2] For details, see p. 101. There is no need, of course, to limit the we-sections too narrowly to those passages where the first person actually occurs (cf. Michaelis, *Einleitung*, p. 133).

fact that it presupposes an extraordinarily mechanical use of his own 'diary' on the part of the author, a process which is out of character with his literary method, not only in the rest of Acts but also in the Gospel. On the other hand certain parallels might be cited to illustrate this procedure from other ancient writers. Yet the fact remains that it is difficult to believe that any author would incorporate jottings, in all their stylistic peculiarities, which in their original form were probably never intended to be published without adaptation.

3. Another view is that the author has used someone else's diary or travel notes and has consequently retained the first person when he has incorporated this material. But it is even less natural to suppose that another author would have retained the 'we' form, particularly without giving any indication of the identity of the person speaking. If the author of the personal diary is the author of the whole, this procedure is at least intelligible in spite of its difficulties. But if he is a different man it is not easy to see any reason for his method.

4. The only other possibility is to suppose that the first person is no indication of an eyewitness, but is introduced intentionally by the author to give the impression of verisimilitude to his record. In this view it would be a purely fictional device.[1] But this raises far more problems than it solves, for it would be difficult to account for the relatively little use made of such a device. Why is it limited to the concluding part of the book if it rests on no historical basis? Moreover a greater impression of verisimilitude would surely have been created by a fiction writer if a name had been indicated in connection with the we-sections, after the manner in which apocryphal writings generally make indisputably clear which apostle is speaking when the first person is used.

Any source theories which proceed from these we-sections must reckon with the probabilities and the difficulties of these various interpretations. These general remarks will enable the following theories to be considered in their right perspective and will be a useful guide in assessing them.

b. Various types of theories

(i) *Personal information.* Those who maintain that Luke is the author of Acts have ready to hand a most likely hypothesis regarding the origin

---

[1] Cf. Haenchen, *Die Apostelgeschichte*, pp. 76–78.

of his information, at least for the major part of the book.[1] Since *ex hypothesi* the author was among Paul's travelling companions, he would have immediate access to all the necessary information recorded in ix. 1–31, xi. 25–30, xii. 25–xxviii. 31. For the rest of the book the source of information can only be conjectured, but there are some reasonable suggestions which may very well be right. It is certain that Luke knew Mark, for both were with Paul when he wrote his Colossian Epistle (Col. iv. 10, 14), and from him he may have received much useful information regarding the early days of the Church in Jerusalem. As there is in Acts xii. 12 mention of a prayer-meeting at the house of Mark's mother, it is justifiable to suppose that his home was a regular *rendezvous* not only for the Christians generally but also for the apostles. There could have been few happenings before the Council at Jerusalem (Acts xv) of which Mark had no first-hand knowledge.

If, as some suppose, Luke's home was at Antioch he would, moreover, have had access to a group of eyewitnesses who could have told him much about the history of Antiochene Christianity, and it is significant that Luke says a great deal about happenings at Antioch, so much so that some scholars have suggested a special Antiochene written source (see below). Then there were Philip and his daughters at Caesarea, who entertained Luke with Paul (according to Acts xxi. 8) and from whom he could have obtained much information regarding the events recorded in Acts vi. 1–viii. 3, for Philip was associated with Stephen in administration and ministry. About the same time Luke lodged with a Cypriot named Mnason who is described as an early[2] disciple (Acts xxi. 16). In addition to all these there was Mark's uncle Barnabas who was well known at Antioch, and if Luke was a native there, would be well known to him, but in any case Paul would have been able to tell Luke about Barnabas' part in early Christian history. By direct contact with all these Christians named above, with the rest of Paul's close circle of friends, such as Silas, Titus, Timothy,

---

[1] Among those who have strongly favoured this theory may be mentioned F. H. Chase, *The Credibility of the Book of the Acts of the Apostles* (1902), pp. 19 ff.; R. B. Rackham, *The Acts of the Apostles* (1901), pp. xli ff.; F. F. Bruce, *The Acts of the Apostles* (Greek Text)[2] (1952), pp. 21 ff. J. V. Bartlet (*The Acts*, CB, 1901, p. 22) mentions that after several years' careful study of Acts he abandoned the idea of written sources and resorted to the theory that Luke made notes from eyewitnesses.

[2] The word ἀρχαῖος means 'original', suggesting that Mnason was one of the earliest disciples.

Tychicus, and with a great number of unnamed eyewitnesses,[1] Luke could have obtained all the data he needed for his history.

In spite of the reasonable character of these conjectures many scholars have rejected them in favour of written sources. Those who reject the Lucan authorship of the whole book have no alternative, if they are to maintain any basic historical material in the narrative. Yet there is no need to exclude personal reminiscences from theories of written sources, if these are granted to be based on authentic material. On the other hand, some of the advocates of the following theories admit Lucan authorship, but are not satisfied with a purely oral theory of sources.

(ii) *A combination of written and oral sources.* Since the subject-matter of the book of Acts divides naturally into two parts, focused respectively on the two great personalities of Peter and Paul, it is not surprising that theories have been proposed which combine a written source for the first part with an oral or personal source for the second.[2] B. Weiss[3] noted that the first part was more Hebraistic than the second part and therefore proposed that this first part was derived from a Jewish-Christian history of the primitive Church up to the Council of Jerusalem. This idea of an original Hebrew or Aramaic source has received an impetus through the work of C. C. Torrey,[4] who considered that

---

[1] A recent Roman Catholic writer, A. Hastings (*Prophet and Witness in Jerusalem*, 1958, pp. 26 ff.), suggests that among these eyewitnesses were Simeon of Cyrene (whom he identifies with Simeon the Black in Acts xiii. 1) and Joanna, the wife of Chuza, Herod's steward, from whom he suggests that Luke may have obtained information about Herod (some of which is not recorded in the other Synoptic Gospels). W. Michaelis (*Einleitung*, pp. 131 f.) suggested that some of the eyewitnesses may have made written notes, or even that some churches may have preserved written notes of their past history. This would approximate to some of the theories of written sources considered below. It is not altogether improbable that Luke had access to the original letter (or copy) mentioned in Acts xv. 23 ff.

[2] E. Barnikol ('Das Fehlen der Taufe in den Quellenschriften der Apostelgeschichte und in den Urgemeinden der Hebräer und Hellenisten', in *Wissenschaftliche Zeitscrift der Martin-Luther-Universität Halle-Wittenberg*, VI, 4, 1957, pp. 593–610) holds that Luke uses two sources, a Peter-Philip source and a we-source, but that he adapted both to his own views, especially on baptism.

[3] *Manual Introduction to the New Testament* (Eng. Tr.), II, 1888, pp. 332 ff.

[4] *The Composition and Date of Acts* (Harvard Theological Studies, I, 1916). Cf. also *idem, Documents of the Primitive Church* (1941), pp. 112–148; *ZNTW*, 44 (1952–53), pp. 205–223. This view is supported by W. J. Wilson, *HTR*, II

many of the difficulties in Acts i–xv are solved if they are regarded as mistranslations of Semitisms. This view has been contested,[1] although it has gained some support in a modified form.[2]

Closely linked with this type of theory is the view that the first part of Acts was originally a continuation of Mark's Gospel written by Mark but taken over and adapted by Luke.[3] Or else that Luke was in possession of the Gospel when writing Acts and either consciously or unconsciously assimilated the apostles' actions to those of Jesus.[4] The main difficulty of any theory which rests on the supposition of greater Aramaic influence in one part than in another is the general stylistic and linguistic unity of the whole. If, of course, Luke fashioned his sources and conformed them to his own style, the phenomenon may be admissible. At the same time M. Black does not think the Aramaisms are sufficient to prove an Aramaic source,[5] although he admits the possibility in the speeches of Peter and Stephen.

(iii) *A combination of duplicate sources.* The main advocate for the theory that in the first part of Acts two parallel sources were used was A.

(1918), pp. 74–99, 322–335 and more recently and more tentatively by M. Black, *An Aramaic Approach to the Gospels and Acts* (1946), p. 207. Cf. also G. Kittel, *Die Probleme des palästinnischen Spätjudentums und das Urchristentum* (1926), pp. 56–58.

[1] Cf. the criticisms and modifications of F. J. Foakes Jackson, *HTR*, 10 (1917), pp. 325–361; F. C. Burkitt, *JTS*, xx (1919), pp. 320–329; H. J. Cadbury, *AJTh*, 34 (1920), pp. 436–450 and E. J. Goodspeed, *JBL*, xxxix (1920), pp. 83–101. It has been pointed out by H. F. D. Sparks that the influence of the LXX on Luke should be set against the Semitisms (*JTS*, xliv, 1943, pp. 129–138; *idem*, n.s., I, 1950, pp. 16–28; *idem*, Bulletin of *Studiorum Novi Testamenti Societas*, II, 1951, pp. 33–42). Cf. also A. W. Argyle, *JTS*, n.s., iv (1953), pp. 213 f.

[2] W. L. Knox (*Some Hellenistic Elements in Primitive Christianity*, 1944, p. 7; *idem*, *The Acts of the Apostles*, 1948, pp. 18 f.) restricted the possible Aramaic source to i. 2–v. 16. J. de Zwaan (*The Beginnings of Christianity*, II, pp. 44 ff.) similarly with the addition of ix. 31–xi. 18. C. H. Dodd (*The Apostolic Preaching and its Developments*[2], 1944, p. 20) agrees with these modifications.

[3] Cf. L. Dieu, *RB*, xxix (1920), pp. 555–569; xxx (1921), pp. 86–96. Cf. also F. C. Burkitt, *Christian Beginnings* (1924), p. 83. A. E. Haefner has recently revived this type of theory and has professed to find a bridge between Mk. xvi. 8 and Acts iii. 1 ff. (which he considers a continuation of Mark, cf. Harnack's views) in Acts i. 13, 14 (*JBL*, lxxvii, 1958, pp. 67–71). But his arguments are highly conjectural.

[4] So C. S. C. Williams, *ET*, lxiv (1952–53), pp. 283 f.; *idem*, *The Acts of the Apostles* (1957), pp. 12, 13.

[5] *Op. cit.*, p. 207. Some of Luke's oral traditions may, of course, have been transmitted to him in an Aramaic form (cf. Michaelis, *Einleitung*, p. 133).

Harnack.[1] The following is a summary of his proposals, A and B standing for the two distinct sources: i, ii (B), iii. 1–v. 16 (A), v. 17–42 (B), vi. 1–viii. 4 (a Jerusalem-Antiochene source), viii. 5–40 (A), ix. 1–30 (Paul's conversion source), ix. 31–xi. 18 (A), xi. 19–30 (a Jerusalem-Antiochene source), xii. 1–23 (A), xii. 25–xv. 35 (a Jerusalem-Antiochene source). The basis of Harnack's differentiation between these sources was mainly on supposed differences of narratives, inaccuracies and even contradictions. Thus he found much material in his B source which he thought was a doublet from his A source (e.g. the accounts of the outpouring of the Spirit in Acts ii and iv) and he therefore concluded that the B material was historically useless. Most of the A source was derived from good Jerusalem tradition, although some parts seem connected with Caesarea (e.g. viii. 8–40, ix. 29–xi. 18 and xii. 1–24).

Harnack's theory, with various modifications, has had a wide vogue among scholars who have shared his presuppositions,[2] but with the recent diminution of attention paid to minute problems of sources, and a lessening also of inclination to attribute every apparent difference to a different written source, its influence has definitely waned. Its basis has been strongly criticized by J. Jeremias[3] on the grounds that the doublets are capable of an alternative explanation, which is true of most cases of alleged duplicate narratives in biblical criticism. Accord-

[1] *Die Apostelgeschichte* (1908), pp. 131–188. This type of theory was first proposed by F. Spitta, *Die Apostelgeschichte, ihre Quellen und deren geschichtlicher Wert* (1891).

[2] Cf. F. J. Foakes Jackson and K. Lake, *The Beginnings of Christianity*, II (1922), pp. 137–157. Cf. also M. Goguel, *Introduction au Nouveau Testament*, III (1922), pp. 172 ff. More recently, H. W. Beyer (*Die Apostelgeschichte*[9], 1959, pp. 15 ff. and pp. 28 ff.) still shows the influence of Harnack's theory, and it forms the basis of A. Q. Morton and G. H. C. Macgregor's mathematical hypothesis of the structure of the Acts. Cf. *The Structure of Luke and Acts* (1964), pp. 34 ff. Cf. J. Dupont (*Les Sources du Livre des Actes*, 1960, pp. 40 ff.) for information on Harnack's influence.

[3] *ZNTW*, 36 (1937), pp. 205–221. With regard to the two accounts of the apostles' appearance before the Sanhedrin in Acts iv. 5–22, v. 21b–41, Jeremias suggests that the first was for legal warning which was necessary before legal action could be taken. The idea was hinted at by K. Bornhäuser, *Studien zur Apostelgeschichte* (1934), p. 58, and has since been favoured by W. G. Kümmel (*TR*, 14, 1942, p. 169), but has been rejected by Bo Reicke, *Glaube und Leben der Urgemeinde* (1957), pp. 108–110, and E. Haenchen, *Die Apostelgeschichte*, pp. 209 ff., on the ground that the warning would have been given privately before two witnesses.

ing to Jeremias the accounts are complementary and not repetitive. It is a sound principle of criticism, which has been too little observed, that where an explanation based on the text as it stands is possible, that is to be preferred to conjectures based on alleged contradictions. By this canon Harnack's theory must be considered unjustified.

(iv) *A combination of complementary sources.* Not all who believe that more than one source lies behind the first part of Acts adhere to Harnack's theory, either in its contents or in its principles of criticism. Setting aside the idea of duplicate sources, some scholars have nevertheless found several sources which have been amalgamated to form the first part of the book. The main theories of this type to be noted are those of L. Cerfaux and E. Trocmé. The former[1] conceives of a basic descriptive document comprising ii. 41–v. 40, to which are added several other groups of tradition, some Galilaean, some Caesarean and one described as a 'Hellenistic dossier'; some are written, some oral.[2]

Trocmé[3] expounds a theory very similar, with chapters iii–v regarded as based on a homogeneous document, which Luke has adapted and expanded. In addition, other documents were used, one for the geographical material in chapter ii, another for the discourses, another, a Hellenistic source, for vi. 1–7 and so on. Luke, according to this theory, had at his disposal a number of sources, many of them small traditional fragments, which he has welded into a whole. Once again the multiplication of written sources tends to lessen the credibility of the theories.[4] Nevertheless, if such theories as these are true, they can only enhance our admiration for the literary skill of Luke in editing them into such an apparent unity.

(v) *The Antiochene source theory.* Most of the theories already considered have in different ways acknowledged indebtedness to Antioch as a source of information regarding the primitive Church. But some

[1] *ETL*, 13 (1936), pp. 667–691 (reproduced in *Recueil Lucien Cerfaux*, 1954, pp. 63–91).

[2] In his later work Cerfaux himself is far less confident about the possibility of fixing the limits of written sources other than the we-sections. Cf. *ETL*, 16 (1939), pp. 5–31, reproduced in *Recueil Lucien Cerfaux*, Tome II (1954), pp. 125–156; *idem*, in Robert-Feuillet's *Introduction* (1959), pp. 349 ff.

[3] *Le 'Livre des Actes' et L'Histoire*, pp. 154–214.

[4] P. Benoit (*Biblica*, XL, 1959, pp. 778–792) speaks of a criss-crossing of Palestinian, Pauline and Antiochene traditions, but the difficulties of unravelling these with any certainty will at once be apparent.

scholars have made an Antiochene written source the main feature of their theories. Many have advocated it,[1] but there is no necessity to mention more than the two most recent advocates. J. Jeremias[2] begins with Acts vi. 1 and decides that certain portions are superimposed. When these are eliminated what is left is an Antiochene source comprising vi. 1–viii. 4, ix. 1–30, xi. 19–30, xii. 25–xiv. 28, xv. 35 ff. But the case for a homogeneous source is not given a convincing basis by a rather arbitrary elimination of all heterogeneous elements. Moreover, it is difficult to believe that a source began at vi. 1 without some indication of the previous history of the Jerusalem church.[3] One of the very doubtful consequences of Jeremias' theory is the placing of the apostolic Council before the first missionary journey.

R. Bultmann[4] acknowledges indebtedness to both Harnack and Jeremias but differs from both in the constitution of his Antiochene source, supposing that the source is prolonged into chapter xvi, perhaps to xxviii, but is partial only in xiii and xiv. At the same time he seems to envisage two documents, both of which were connected with the Antiochene church and were, perhaps, found in its archives. This theory presupposes that the Antiochene church had composed a kind of chronicle of their earlier history, a not impossible procedure in spite of Haenchen's[5] objection that the Christians would not have thought of writing for a future generation.

(vi) *The 'itinerary' theory*. Largely owing to the influence of form criticism there has arisen a school of thought which does not consider it possible to locate sources for the first part of Acts. In this part the attention is focused on small units in which the tradition circulated before becoming fixed in the Acts narrative. Interest in sources is

---

[1] E.g. H. H. Wendt, *ZNTW*, 24 (1925), pp. 293–305. He had expressed the idea in his *Die Apostelgeschichte*[8] (1899) before Harnack's work appeared. Cf. also J. Weiss, 'Das Judenchristentum in der Apostelgeschichte und das sogennante Apostelkonzil', *TSK*, 66 (1893), pp. 480–540. For an English advocate, compare J. A. Findlay, *The Acts of the Apostles*[2] (1936), pp. 50 f.

[2] *ZNTW*, 36 (1937), pp. 205–221.

[3] W. Grundmann saw this difficulty and suggested that the source must have begun with such an account (*ZNTW*, 38, 1939, pp. 45–73). But in this case, Luke must have used an inferior substitute in his account of the earlier history, which is improbable.

[4] 'Zur Frage nach den Quellen der Apostelgeschichte' in *New Testament Essays: Studies in Memory of T. W. Manson* (ed. A. J. B. Higgins, 1959), pp. 68–80.

[5] *Op. cit.*, pp. 75, 76.

therefore concentrated on the second part particularly (xiii. 4–xiv. 28, xvi. 1–xxi. 26), where Paul's journeys are then traced to an 'itinerary source'. This is the position of Dibelius.[1] The idea of an itinerary source is not new, since the 'we-sections' would naturally suggest this possibility, particularly if the author of Acts is not considered to be a companion of Paul. But Dibelius does not tie his source to the we-passages, and explains the latter as a simple device by which Luke indicates his presence with Paul. In this way Dibelius' view seems somewhat akin to the first theory mentioned, that of personal information, but the fundamental difference is that Dibelius does not consider the occurrence of the 'we' to be an indication of the source of Luke's account. It is important to him, nevertheless, to isolate the source, and he does this by maintaining that some non-edificatory material has been used and that certain incoherences are apparent, both of which, he thinks, point to a source rather than to personal reminiscences or local traditions.[2] In an attempt to explain the usefulness of an 'itinerary document', Dibelius suggests that it might have served a useful purpose if the same journey had to be repeated.[3] But the unconvincing character of this suggestion gives the measure of the difficulty of finding an adequate motive, for it is inconceivable that Paul would have needed an 'itinerary' to remind him where he had been, especially in the case of places where he had established churches.

It will be seen that the only justification for this theory is the claim that it accounts for a series of insignificant details and supposed discrepancies. But if Luke is the author, as Dibelius himself strongly held,[4] it is difficult to see what advantage is gained by attributing these to Luke's editorial processes rather than to his personal recollections. At least, the discrepancies are a matter of interpretation[5] and may be

---

[1] Dibelius expressed his opinions in a number of essays from 1923 to 1947 and these were conveniently collected in his *Aufsätze zur Apostelgeschichte* (1951), Eng. Tr. by Mary Ling, *Studies in the Acts of the Apostles* (1956). The references are to the English edition (cf. pp. 104 ff.). Cf. also Dibelius' article in *TR*, n.f., 3 (1931), pp. 233–241 on the form-historical problem in the Acts of the Apostles.

[2] Cf. the reasons stated and the conclusions drawn in his latest essay, *Studies in the Acts of the Apostles*, pp. 196 ff.

[3] *Ibid.*, p. 199.   [4] Cf., for example, *ibid.*, pp. 135 ff.

[5] To consider one instance cited by Dibelius, Acts xiv. 8–18 is said to be an insertion, because verses 6 and 7 have already mentioned the apostle at Lystra and Derbe, whereas verse 8 returns to an incident at Lystra (*ibid.*, p. 198). But verses 6, 7 give a general summary of the whole work in Lycaonia. Could not Luke have paused then to cite the most striking incidents during this part of the

otherwise explained, and the mention of insignificant details is of the very warp and woof of personal narrative.[1]

(vii) *The fiction theory*. In varying degrees many hypotheses have attributed the whole or part of Acts to the literary ingenuity of a fiction writer. It has already been remarked that the we-sections are supposed by some scholars to be a fictitious device. But the idea that the whole itinerary is a fiction is not without recent advocates. The most notable is G. Schille,[2] who conceives that the sections which give information regarding Paul's journeys, consisting of four geographical blocks (xiii–xiv, xvi–xviii, xix–xx and xxi ff.), are simply a literary fiction. The narratives are, moreover, said to be strewn with errors which prove that the author had no source at his disposal. Schille concedes that Luke may have possessed some traditions, but the itinerary imposed upon them is his own composition. In fact, in disposing of Dibelius' itinerary theory, Schille seems to land himself in scepticism regarding the historicity of Acts, for he suggests that the itinerary in Acts is more in line with the missionary policy reflected in the *Didache* than with that of the apostolic age, not recognizing that the *Didache*, with its advice to stay only a day or so at one place, does not deal with the problem of the longer time needed for the establishment of churches.

(viii) *The theories of successive redactions*. In common with other New Testament books, Acts has been subjected to a series of redactional hypotheses. Many of those already mentioned depend on redactional processes, but a type of theory not so far included is that of H. Sahlin[3] which conceives of the process of publication for Luke-Acts in three stages: (1) a Jewish-Christian writing comprising Luke i. 5–Acts xv. 41,

journey, which happened at Lystra? Another example is the omission of any reference to the earthquake at Philippi after the conversion of the gaoler in Acts xvi. 35 ff., but the account is obviously much abridged and the earthquake motive would not have added anything to the story of Paul's release.

[1] A. D. Nock (*Gnomon*, xxv, 1953, pp. 597 ff.), while adhering in general to an 'itinerary' hypothesis, has criticized Dibelius on the grounds that the passages without edificatory purpose are inserted for literary reasons to give the reader time to relax from the main action of the narrative.

[2] *ThLZ*, 84 (1959), cols. 165–174. For a criticism of Schille's views, cf. J. Dupont, *Les Sources du Livre des Actes* (1960), p. 149. Cf. also E. Haenchen, *op. cit.*, pp. 14*, 15*.

[3] *Der Messias und das Gottesvolk. Studien zur proto-lukanischen Theologie*, pp. 11–18. Cf. also P. H. Menoud, 'Remarques sur les textes de l'ascension dans Luc-Actes', *Neutestamentliche Studien für R. Bultmann* (1954), pp. 148–156.

part Hebrew and part Aramaic; (2) a Greek revision and adaptation of this for Paul's trial, perhaps by Luke himself; (3) a later editorial process which divided it into two by the addition of a conclusion to Luke and an introduction to Acts. That there may have been stages in the preparation of the manuscript cannot be denied, but any theory based on redactional processes is bound to be very largely conjectural. In this case, the difficulty of conceiving a scroll of sufficient length to accommodate Luke-Acts is against the theory. It is more natural to suppose that the whole work was originally in two parts on separate scrolls of similar length.[1]

From this brief survey two facts stand out. Attempts to isolate the sources which Luke has used have not been successful, and it is questionable whether any further progress in this direction is likely to be made. This means that the idea of assuming Luke's personal knowledge of the events, either from his own observations or from direct eyewitnesses, is as credible as any, and much more credible than most, of the alternative suggestions.

VI. THE TEXT

One of the most interesting problems in textual criticism concerns the original form of the book of Acts. A discussion of the problem lies beyond the scope of this Introduction[2] and no more than the briefest explanation can be included here. The 'Western'[3] Text of Acts differs so considerably from the other early texts that it has posed the question of whether there were in fact two editions. It was F. Blass[4] who suggested that Luke himself prepared two editions, but his views on this have not won much support.[5] A. C. Clark[6] was pre-

---

[1] Cf. W. G. Kümmel, *INT* (1965), p. 110.

[2] For a useful survey of literature on this subject, cf. E. Trocmé, *Le 'Livre des Actes' et l'Histoire*, pp. 20–37. Cf. also C. S. C. Williams' study, *Alterations to the Text of the Synoptic Gospels and Acts,* 1951, pp. 54–82.

[3] The chief witness for this text is a fifth-century MS, Codex Bezae (D).

[4] Fr. Blass, 'Die Textüberlieferung in der Apostelgeschichte', *TSK*, 67 (1894), pp. 86–119. Zahn argued for the same view in *Die Urausgabe der Apostelgeschichte des Lukas* (1916), pp. 1–10.

[5] Haenchen suggests a common author is highly improbable since the two texts often contradict one another (*Die Apostelgeschichte*, p. 48). F. Kenyon's criticism (*The Text of the Greek Bible*², 1949, pp. 232, 233) mainly concerns the difficulty of finding an adequate motive for many of the alterations.

[6] *The Primitive Text of the Gospels and Acts* (1914). Idem, *The Acts of the Apostles* (1933), pp. xlix ff., 374–376.

pared to argue that the 'Western Text' is more original than the generally accepted text, which he considered to be an edited form. But this idea has gained even less support.[1] The opposite view, that the 'Western Text' forms a deviation from the original text, is much more probable.

A mediating proposal, which amounts to a modification of Blass's theory, is that Luke made several drafts in the successive processes of revision and that some of the earlier drafts may have been circulated and may have formed the basis of the 'Western Text', while the more authoritative form of text became the basis of the 'Alexandrian' and other types of texts.[2] It is possible that the author himself never quite finished the work of editing.

The opinion of such an authority as Sir Frederick Kenyon[3] is that, unless future discoveries supply further data which enable the critic to reach a solution to the problem of the text, 'the problem must be solved according to the intrinsic probabilities of the methods of insertion or excision'. Since the 'Western Text' of Acts is longer than the Alexandrian Text, Kenyon feels that probability is against the insertions of the former, and this is where the matter must perhaps rest for the present.

Attempts to explain the history of the 'Western Text' by an appeal to the processes of translation from an Aramaic document have been made, notably by C. C. Torrey[4] who maintained that an Aramaic version of the original Greek text was produced with the special intention of commending Luke-Acts to Jewish readers. Torrey held that many of the modifications in the Western Text may be explained as insertions to make the text more acceptable to such readers.[5]

VII. LANGUAGE

In the sections dealing with sources and with textual tradition mention was made of the theory of an Aramaic source used for the early part of Acts. C. C. Torrey's theory (see pp. 370 f.) has not won general support. It has been criticized on the grounds that many of Torrey's

---

[1] Cf. Kenyon's criticisms, op. cit., pp. 234 ff. J. H. Ropes, The Beginnings of Christianity (1926), III, pp. ccxv–ccxlvi, maintained that the 'Western Text' was a later edited text.

[2] Cf. R. B. Rackham, op. cit., p. xxvi.   [3] Op. cit., p. 236.
[4] Documents of the Primitive Church (1941), pp. 112–148.   [5] Ibid., pp. 127 ff.

Aramaisms can be shown to be Septuagintalisms.[1] There can be no doubt that Luke was very well acquainted with the Septuagint, but apart from this the *Koiné* Greek tended to be charged with Semitisms in the eastern district.[2]

One of the peculiarities of Luke to which attention has recently been drawn is his tendency towards certain rhythmic qualities of language, particularly to a love for doubling. R. Morgenthaler[3] has compiled a mass of impressive lists of instances in which Luke has doubled isolated words, full sentences, and whole sections, while this doubling even affects the conception of the entire work. It is built up on the principle of pairs. There is no doubt that Morgenthaler has overdone his examples, for which he has been criticized,[4] but when due allowance has been made for his too confident claims enough evidence still remains to demonstrate without question Luke's love of doubling. This is part of his artistic equipment.

Luke's style is good but not particularly literary. It is rather of a good conversational type. It would have been readily understood by any readers of general intelligence. It was, therefore, admirably adapted to his purpose.

[1] Cf. H. F. D. Sparks, 'The Semitisms of Acts', *JTS*, n.s., I (1950), pp. 16–28. Also E. Jacquier (*Les Actes des Apôtres*[2], 1926, p. cxvii), who called Luke's language 'sacred prose'.*

[2] Cf. the comments on this by L. Cerfaux, 'Les Actes des Apôtres' in Robert-Feuillet's *Introduction*, II, p. 372.

[3] *Die lukanische Geschichtsschreibung als Zeugnis* (1949). This work is in two volumes, of which the first deals with the form and the second with the content of Luke-Acts. The idea of Luke's rhythmic style was earlier suggested by A. Loisy, *Les Actes des Apôtres* (1925), p. 302.

[4] Cf. the comments of W. G. Kümmel in *TR*, n.f., 22 (1954), pp. 197 ff. Others who have criticized the theory are E. Käsemann, *Verkündigung und Forschungen* (1950–51), pp. 219 ff.; H. Conzelmann, *ThZ*, IX (1953), pp. 304 ff., and C. K. Barrett, *Luke the Historian in Recent Study* (1961), pp. 36 ff. But Trocmé (*op. cit.*, p. 17) considers that Morgenthaler's theory is worthy of consideration.

CONTENTS

Iconium, Lystra, Derbe—and return to Antioch (xiv. 1–28). The Jerusalem Council (xv. 1–29). The letter delivered to the church at Antioch; plans for a return visit to the churches established on the first journey, and disagreement over Mark (xv. 30–41).

VII. THE SECOND MISSIONARY JOURNEY (xvi. 1–xviii. 23)

Timothy joins Paul on the return visit to Lystra (xvi. 1–5). Fresh horizons: work in Europe—the call to Macedonia and journey to Philippi (xvi. 6–12). Work in Philippi (xvi. 13–40). Work in Thessalonica and Berea (xvii. 1–14). Paul at Athens (xvii. 15–34). Work in Corinth (xviii. 1–17). A brief visit to Palestine and Antioch (xviii. 18–23).

VIII. THE THIRD MISSIONARY JOURNEY (xviii. 24–xx. 6)

Extensive work in Ephesus (xviii. 24–xix. 20). Second visit planned to Macedonia and Greece (xix. 21, 22). The riot at Ephesus and Paul's departure (xix. 23–xx. 1). Further work in Macedonia and Greece (xx. 2–6).

IX. JOURNEY TO JERUSALEM (xx. 7–xxi. 17)

At Troas: the incident over Eutychus (xx. 7–12). Paul's journey to Miletus, and his address to the Ephesian elders there (xx. 13–38). Brief visit to Tyre (xxi. 1–6). Events at Caesarea: Agabus' prophecy (xxi. 7–14). Arrival at Jerusalem (xxi. 15–17).

X. PAUL IN JERUSALEM (xxi. 18–xxiii. 35)

Events leading to his arrest and appearance before the Sanhedrin (xxi. 18–xxii. 29). Paul before the Sanhedrin (xxii. 30–xxiii. 10). Paul sent to Felix by Lysias (xxiii. 11–35).

XI. PAUL BEFORE FELIX, FESTUS AND AGRIPPA AT CAESAREA (xxiv. 1–xxvi. 32)

Accusation and defence before Felix (xxiv. 1–27). Investigation by Festus (xxv. 1–12). Hearing before Agrippa (xxv. 13–xxvi. 32).

XII. THE JOURNEY TO ROME (xxvii. 1–xxviii. 31)

The account of the voyage and the shipwreck (xxvii. 1–44). Hospitality at Malta, where Paul escapes death from a viper and performs many healings (xxviii. 1–10). Paul arrives in Rome and remains under house arrest, preaching and teaching (xxviii. 11–31).

ADDITIONAL NOTES

340. ¹ The view that the author of Acts has not mentioned the fall of Jerusalem because it had not yet happened is supported by P. Parker (*JBL*, LXXXIV, 1965, pp. 52–58), who argues for an early date for Acts on the strength of it.

342. ¹ R. P. C. Hanson (*NTS*, 12, 1966, pp. 211–230) claims that the author of Acts did not mention the death of Paul because everyone knew of it. It is interesting to compare the use of the argument from silence in this view with that of Parker mentioned in the previous note. On the whole Parker's logic seems to be better than Hanson's, for it might reasonably be argued that if the readers knew of Paul's death they would surely also have known of many of the events which Acts records. Why then did he narrate them?

346. ¹ The most recent writer to maintain that Acts was published before Luke is P. Parker (*op. cit.*), who rejects the view that the 'former treatise' in Acts i. 1 is Luke. He suggests in fact that it was Proto-Luke. This enables him to date Acts much earlier than the final edition of Luke. Indeed, Parker maintains that an early date for Acts explains the author's non-acquaintance with Mark at the time of writing.

346. ² Among the reasons for a late date advanced by Goodspeed is one that has come under criticism from J. Knox. Goodspeed made a strong point of the failure of Acts to mention the Pauline Epistles and concluded that they had not been collected. But Knox (*SLA*, 1966, pp. 279–287) rejects this argument and then proceeds to date Acts as late as AD 125. In reviewing H. Conzelmann's *Die Apostelgeschichte* (1963), R. P. C. Hanson (*JTS*, n.s., xv, 1964, pp. 371–375) criticizes the former's dating of Acts late in the first century, because of the lack of mention of Gnosticism.

348. ¹ The view of J. C. O'Neill has secured some support from H. Conzelmann (*SLA*, 1966, pp. 298–316) in his examination of Luke's place in the development of early Christianity. But Conzelmann is not convinced that Justin did not know Luke. He claims that Acts belongs to a time when the Church is at home in the world, which, he thinks, reflects a later age than Paul's, whose position he represents from Phil. iii. 20.

348. ³ J. Knox (*op. cit.*) has argued that Luke presents a different portrait of Paul in reaction against Marcion's use of Luke and Paul. But it is not self-evident why Marcion should not be the one who was concocting a different portrait from the one generally accepted in orthodox circles.

352. According to D. P. Fuller, *Easter Faith and History* (1965), p. 223, Luke's purpose was 'to show that the Gentile mission was the fulfilment of the Christ event as brought to a climax in the resurrection and ascension'.

352. ¹ Easton's view of the purpose of Acts is criticized by D. P. Fuller (*op. cit.*, pp. 203 f.) on two grounds. The theme of continuity with Judaism would presuppose that the readers had a good knowledge of the Old Testament, but Fuller thinks this would be difficult for a pagan Roman official (assuming Theophilus to be a pagan). Moreover, the Acts portrays many instances of clashes, which do not support Easton's viewpoint. It is only fair to note that Easton proposed a second purpose—to provide a source of comfort for suffering Christians by showing how Christians had already triumphed.

352. [2] The defence-brief theory has been espoused by J. Munck, *The Acts of the Apostles* (1967).

353. Several scholars have maintained that Luke considered that the Gentile mission depended on Jewish rejection (e.g. Haenchen, Conzelmann, Wilckens, O'Neill). But J. Jervell (*StTh*, 19, 1965, pp. 68–96) rejects this view, arguing that it was Jewish acceptance which opened the door for the Gentile mission. The latter view seems more in accord with the evidence of the Pauline Epistles and places less stress on Luke's theologizing purpose.

353. [2] E. Trocmé (*Le 'Livre des Actes' et l'Histoire*, 1957) proposed a theory that Luke-Acts was intended to deal with a clash between the Alexandrine and Pauline churches. The former were Judaizing. The Pauline churches needed a book to show their superiority over the rival groups, and such a provision is found in Acts. The focus on Paul alone as the representative of the mission of the Twelve was designed to show how the Jerusalem church and the Gentile mission had achieved unity. But Fuller (*op. cit.*, pp. 204–206) criticizes this view because had this been Luke's purpose he would have made it more obvious that Paul had been commissioned by the Jerusalem apostles.

353. [6] Haenchen follows the same line as adopted in his commentary in a more recent essay in *SLA* (1966, pp. 258–278), in which he maintains that Luke used his materials to express his theology. He recognizes that this raises the question of the value of the book of Acts as source material for the history of early Christianity. His view is that Acts contains some historical tradition mixed up with legendary material (for instance, the shaking off of the chains of prisoners by means of an earthquake). But the distinction between true tradition and legend is bound to depend, as it does for Haenchen, on presuppositions regarding the nature of legend.

356. [3] Another method of dealing with the relationship between Acts and Galatians is adopted by P. Parker (*JBL*, LXXXVI, 1967, pp. 175–182), who maintains that the statement in Acts ix. 26 is inaccurate. But this is a solution which is unlikely to commend itself to those who attach a high value to Luke's historical knowledge. The conversion of Saul of Tarsus was of such importance that he relates it three times and it is difficult to believe he would commit such a *faux pas* regarding Saul's relationship with the Jerusalem church.

358. [1] E. R. Goodenough (*SLA*, 1966, pp. 51–59) also claims that Acts creates a fictional Paul. In fact, Goodenough argues that the book was written in the early sixties of the first century to assure Theophilus that Paul was a very great man who preached and lived for what the author of Acts, like the author of the Epistle to the Hebrews, considered 'the childish milk of the gospel'. Goodenough asserts that no-one in the Galatian or Corinthian churches would have recognized the Paul of Acts. But such a statement takes no account of the many undesigned coincidences between Acts and the Pauline Epistles and assumes that a dichotomy between them is preferable to any attempt to regard them as presenting different facets of the same person.

359. [1] Some attention has been given to the function of typology in Acts, especially by M. D. Goulder, *Type and History in Acts* (1964). He regards Acts as typological history, in which the life of Jesus provided the types. In this he has been influenced by the approach of Austin Farrer to the Gospels.

359. [2] A further study of the relationship between the Qumran Community and the Christian Church is found in B. Gärtner's *The Temple and the Community in Qumran and the New Testament* (1965). He argues for a Jewish rather than a Hellenistic basis. J. A. Fitzmeyer (*SLA*, 1966, pp. 233–257) thinks that although Qumran sheds light on the Palestinian matrix of early Christianity, the evidence does not support the view that Christianity arose from an Essene group.

360. [2] Sir F. Adcock (*Thucydides and his History*, 1963) doubts whether Thucydides would have considered himself free to compose speeches without restraint (pp. 27–42). Cf. the comments of T. F. Glasson (*ET*, LXXVI, 1965, p. 165), who draws attention to Thucydides' statement that he adhered as closely as possible to what the speaker said. It is worth noting, as P. Schubert (*JBL*, LXXXVII, 1968, pp. 1–16) has pointed out, that Luke's speeches differ from those of Thucydides in that they are an essential part of the story. He notes that the speeches in Luke occupy 75 per cent of the whole, whereas those in Thucydides occupy only 25 per cent. It would appear from this that they are more a literary device in Thucydides than in Luke, since the narrative in Acts is dependent upon them. Cf. also J. H. Crehan's study of Luke's purpose in the light of Thucydides as his model (*Studia Evangelica* II, 1964, pp. 354–368).

362. [3] Schweizer's article in *ThZ*, XIII (1957) has now appeared in English in *SLA*, 1966, pp. 208–216. In discussing the historiography of Acts, P. Vielhauer (*SLA*, 1966, pp. 33–50) concludes that the author does not stand within the earliest Christianity. But he concedes that the Christology is pre-Pauline, although the natural theology, law and eschatology is post-Pauline. It is because of this that he maintains that the author stands in the nascent catholic church. He further considers that Acts presents no specifically Pauline idea.

C. F. D. Moule (*SLA*, 1966, pp. 159–185) concludes that the Christology of Acts is not uniform. Where he discerns evidence of Luke's own mentality, he finds a different Christology from that of Paul or John and suggests that it approximates to that of the 'average Christian'.

362. [5] In the same volume Conzelmann concentrates on the Areopagus speech and considers it to be the author's own work (*SLA*, 1966, pp. 217–230). He sees both a Jewish and Greek component in the speech.

363. [2] A. W. Mosley (*NTS*, 12, 1965, pp. 10–26) has contributed a valuable survey of what ancient historians thought about their own task. He shows that many held a high ideal of accuracy. It cannot, therefore, be assumed that New Testament writers had no concern for historical accuracy, when judged by contemporary standards.

J. W. Bowker (*NTS*, 14, 1967, pp. 96–111) considers that some of the Acts speeches may have originated in a synagogue context. He finds signs of *proem homily* in Acts xiii. 14 f. He suggests that in this case the *sedev* reading was Dt. iv. 25, 26, the *haphtarah* (prophets) was 2 Sa. vii. 6–16 and the *proem text* 1 Sa. xiii. 14. Bowker suggests that the form belongs to a time when the *proem homily* was almost but not quite fixed. He concludes that part of Luke's material belongs to such a context.

379. [1] For the most recent linguistic examination of Acts, cf. M. Wilcox, *The Semitisms of Acts* (1965).

CHAPTER TEN

PAUL, THE MAN BEHIND THE LETTERS

The study of the letters of Paul is not a mere literary exercise, for it is not primarily as great literature that they hold their fascination for the modern mind. They are the result of a momentous experience and have become the basis of similar experience for multitudes of others. They are not theological treatises, although innumerable such treatises have been based upon them. They cannot be studied in isolation from the historical situation which occasioned them, and yet such study is no more than a prelude to their deeper appreciation. It is valuable before treating Paul's letters to a critical examination to have some picture of the personality behind them and for this purpose the following brief sketch of his salient characteristics is appended.

a. His sense of divine vocation

The key to the personality of the apostle lies in his soul-stirring experience on the Damascus road. Constantly shining through his writings is the wonder of that divine encounter.[1] He knows he is called of God (Rom. i. 1–6). He has received a revelation not from men but from Jesus Christ (Gal. i. 12). He is commissioned as a minister of the gospel. He is a man with a compulsion upon him (1 Cor. ix. 16). He is no time-server, but God's man doing God's work. He has experienced grace and finds no rest unless he is channelling that grace to others. All his Jewish training[2] and his zeal for the law of his fathers became his servant in this greater enterprise.

In spite of attempts to describe Paul's experience in psychological terms,[3] there is something mysterious and miraculous about it which

[1] Cf. the note by H. W. Beyer, *Der Brief an die Galater* (*NTD*, 1955), p. 12, on Paul's conversion as a source of his theology, and H. A. A. Kennedy, *The Theology of the Epistles* (1919), pp. 50–96.

[2] Cf. the recent study by Earle Ellis on *Paul's Use of the Old Testament* (1957); cf. also W. D. Davies, *Paul and Rabbinic Judaism* (1948) and W. D. Stacey, *The Pauline View of Man* (1956).

[3] Cf. W. Wrede, *Paulus* (1907) and the criticisms of J. Weiss, *Jesus and Paul* (Eng. Tr. 1909). For a concise survey of the various opinions about Paul's conversion and its influence upon his theology, see H. N. Ridderbos, *Paul and Jesus* (1958), pp. 43 ff. Ridderbos gives a useful critique of Bultmann's approach to Paul.

defies analysis. That he had not known Jesus in the flesh seems probable from 2 Corinthians v. 16. In any case it was not the human Jesus who captivated his heart, but the human Jesus in His glorious risen form. In this he was no different from the other apostles. The teachings of Paul are in fact rooted in his awareness of a direct continuity between the risen Lord and the Christian Church.*

b. His authority

One of the most striking features of Paul's letters is the remarkable authority which he assumes in addressing Christian churches, even in some cases where he is unknown personally to the members. There are admittedly traces of a rebellious attitude towards this authoritative approach, as for instance in Corinth and Galatia, but the very challenge to his authority only calls forth more vehement spiritual commands and exhortations. Was the man too overbearing? Had he the right to assume the reins? Had he too high an opinion of his own importance? It is a strange paradox that this immediate impression is not gained by a reading through of his letters. He seems to command with a perfect naturalness, as if he can do no other. It is an authority based on his sense of divine vocation, in the belief that an appointment of God carries with it its own stamp of authenticity. It is his deep conviction that he writes the commands of God that makes his letters so compelling not only for the recipients for whom they were intended, but also for all who treasure the same spiritual heritage.[1]

Arising out of his authoritative approach comes the question whether Paul was conscious of the inspiration of his writings. At times he distinguishes between his own opinions and what he knows to be the Lord's commands (cf. 1 Cor. vii. 6, 10, 12; 2 Cor. xi. 17). Was he at these times so uncertain of himself that any self-awareness of the inspiration of his writings cannot be admitted?[2] It is not easy to analyse

[1] Cf. 2 Cor. vii. 15, x. 6; Phil. ii. 12; 2 Thes. iii. 4; Phm. 21.

[2] For such a view, cf. C. A. A. Scott, St Paul the Man and the Teacher (1936), pp. 67–71, who also appeals in support to Paul's readiness to correct himself (1 Cor. i. 14–16), his inconsistency (no examples cited), his mistakes (e.g. he cannot believe that God cares for oxen), and his failure to recognize slavery as against God's will. But these supposed evidences of Paul's unawareness of his own inspiration are mainly due to Scott's interpretation of the data and need not carry the implications he puts upon them. Paul's desire to be scrupulously accurate, even in details such as 1 Cor. i. 16, shows his consciousness of the importance of his words, while his attitude to slavery may be otherwise explained (see p. 640).

the consciousness of any author writing under the inspiration of God, but it is clear that Paul generally acknowledged the authoritative character of his own writings. The occasions when he seems to dissociate his own opinions from the commands of the Lord are rare, and even where they occur seem to be concerned with issues over which he knew that no general agreement existed among Christians (e.g. the marriage question). These few occasions rather strengthen than lessen the general impression that Paul gives that on all other occasions he knows he speaks with the authority of the Lord.

c. His love for his converts

If he must command and exhort, correct and rebuke, it is only because of a deep affection for the people of God. The most striking example of this love is his moving attitude towards the Philippian Christians, but it is by no means absent even towards those whose actions caused him the greatest distress. His somewhat turbulent relationships with the Corinthian Christians are softened by glimpses of the apostle's real longing for their welfare and rejoicing over their concern for him (cf. 2 Cor. vii. 7). Nor can we forget that it was in writing to this same church that Paul penned his exquisite hymn on charity (1 Cor. xiii) and we cannot suppose that its challenging tenets had made no mark upon the life and character of the writer. This man of authority was also a man of love. He was, moreover, a man capable of drawing out love, even the love of those inclined to be hostile to him.

d. His convictions

With extraordinary God-given insight Paul guided his people in matters of doctrine and practice. The principles he deduced are still valid because of his power to arrive at universal applications to particular problems. But more than that, he grasped the major issues of that formative period with such tenacious conviction that could admit of no doubt. Whether he was dealing with the great Jewish-Gentile controversy in which he saw the conflict so clearly as Christ versus Judaism, or with local disturbances over the Lord's Supper, or was urging contributions to the collection scheme for the poor believers of Judaea as a means of assisting the solidarity of the Church, he is clear as to the spiritual basis of his opinions. And this is never more true than when he is expounding such great truths as justification, salvation by grace, the redemptive work of Christ, the ministry of the Spirit or the cosmic significance of the Church. His thoughts move with a certainty which springs from personal conviction and a deep experience of God.

e. His versatility

The apostle set before himself the goal to be all things to all men and this principle had an important effect on his approach to the many human problems with which he had to deal. He could well adapt himself to his circumstances, but this did not mean that he adapted his principles to suit his situation. To be all things to all men meant for Paul a genuine desire to see the other person's point of view. This may account for his method of dealing with several of the problems of the Corinthian church, for his aim was partly apologetic to minimize the gulf between himself and the Corinthians.[1] At times he seems almost to side with those whose practices he is opposing.[2] In any case Paul's delicate handling of so many different situations and problems reveals a dexterity of mind and an astonishing power of adaptation which has seldom been surpassed. Here is a man who can deal with equal masterliness with all sorts and conditions of men.

f. His language and style

The opinion, found within the pages of the New Testament itself (2 Pet. iii. 16), that in Paul's letters are things hard to be understood has met with the assent of most, if not all, who have come to study them. Part of the difficulty arises from the concepts, but part also from the language. His language was not governed by Hellenistic culture, as we might have expected, but by the needs of the readers. He inclines away from the literary Greek towards the vernacular.[3] Yet his writings are not a good example of the *Koinē* (common) style. He is too individualistic, too given to frequent diversions of thought and too apt to express himself in broken syntax. In a sense the style is as adaptable as the man. It can be rhetorical as in the doctrinal parts of Romans and Galatians, lyrical as in 1 Corinthians xiii and xv. 42, 43 or matter of

[1] Cf. the article by H. Chadwick, 'All things to all men', *NTS*, 1 (1954–55), pp. 261–275.

[2] As in the case of the ascetic approach to marriage if J. Weiss (*Der ersten Korintherbrief*, 1910, p. 169) is right in his suggestion that Paul is dealing with those denying the compatibility of the marriage state. Cf. Chadwick's comments, *op. cit.*

[3] Cf. Moulton and Howard, *A Grammar of New Testament Greek*, II (1920), p. 9.

fact as in the ethical instructions of many letters (especially Rom xii. 1 ff.).[1]

As a letter writer Paul conforms to the contemporary pattern as far as the literary form is concerned. He uses the accepted structure of greeting, thanksgiving and prayer, main subject-matter and exordium as in contemporary private letters and yet goes beyond the purpose of private letters in that he writes for communities and to that extent approximates to the current epistolary practice.[2] His letters do not strictly conform to either class, but rather to a mixture of both. The needs of the communities and the letter-writing skill of the apostle seem to have created a new literary medium admirably suited for the edification of the Church.

g. His physical powers of endurance

This brief survey would be incomplete without mention of the amazing physique of the missionary who according to his own admission had passed through constant hazards for the sake of the gospel. Imprisonments, beatings, stoning, shipwrecks, hazards from many sources, both natural and human, lack of food and scantiness of clothing seem to have been his normal experience. He must have had robust health in spite of the occasional allusions in his letters which suggest the reverse. The thorn in the flesh (2 Cor. xii. 7) may have been a physical malady,[3] the sympathy of some Christians towards his eyesight (Gal. iv. 15) may suggest some ophthalmic defect, while Paul cites his opponents' description of him as contemptible in bodily appearance. Yet these hints cannot blind us to the fact that Paul's physique must have been unusually tough to have survived so long the rigours of his missionary journeys. It cannot be too strongly emphasized that the writer of these priceless Christian letters is no arm-chair theologian but a missionary-hearted apostle who encountered and survived more than his fair share of the punishing rigours of life. The letters themselves must be set against such a background if they are to be rightly appreciated. All too

---

[1] Cf. M. Dibelius–W. G. Kümmel, *Paul* (1953), pp. 99 ff. J. Stalker, *The Life of St. Paul* (n.d.), pp. 93, 94, makes an interesting comparison of Paul's style with the rugged and somewhat incoherent style of Cromwell's *Letters and Speeches*.

[2] Cf. A. Deissmann, *Light from the Ancient East* (1923), pp. 233 ff., who classes Paul's Epistles as real letters, not literary epistles. Cf. also P. Wendland, *Die urchristlichen Literaturformen* (*LHB*, I. 3, 1912), pp. 343 ff.

[3] See R. V. G. Tasker's full note on the thorn in the flesh, *The Second Epistle of Paul to the Corinthians* (1958), pp. 173–177.

often academic difficulties have arisen because of a failure to form a true picture of Paul the man.[1]

h. His spiritual experiences

There were crises in Paul's inner life which affected his literary productions. This is clear from a study of 2 Corinthians. C. H. Dodd[2] has suggested that this Epistle represents a turning-point in Paul's experience, and this may well be true especially of his eschatology. In the same Epistle an account is given by Paul of certain ecstatic experiences which are described as having happened in the third heaven (2 Cor. xii). There is an air of mystery about all this for Paul claims to have heard unspeakable words. Whatever he means it is clear that the subject of the visions was a man of intense religious feeling and perception.

Although a critical introduction must necessarily focus attention on the literary and historical problems associated with the letters, yet it cannot be done without constant reference to the personality of the writer. But here a danger enters, for criticism has sometimes arbitrarily evaluated 'what we know of Paul' and then used this as a yard-stick for measuring non-Pauline characteristics and traits. The sound and logical method is to form our opinion of Paul from all sources traditionally attributed to him and to modify that picture only when the assured results of critical inquiry demand it.*

[1] Cf. J. S. Stewart, *A Man in Christ* (1935), chapter 1.
[2] *New Testament Studies* (1953), pp. 67 ff.

ADDITIONAL NOTES

387. The relationship between the theology of Paul and the teaching of Jesus is a major theological problem. For a recent survey of this debate, cf. V. P. Furnish, *BJRL*, xlvii (1965), pp. 342–381.

391. For recent studies of Paul and his letters, cf. D. J. Selby, *Towards an Understanding of St. Paul* (1962); K. Zimmermann, *Der Apostel Paulus. Ein Lebensbild* (1962); F. W. Beare, *St. Paul and his Letters* (1962); B. Rigaux, *Saint Paul et ses lettres* (1962); N. Hugedé, *Saint Paul et la Culture grecque* (1966); W. C. van Unnik, *Tarsus or Jerusalem, The City of Paul's Youth* (1962). Cf. also F. W. Beare's article, 'St. Paul as Spiritual Director', *Studia Evangelica*, II (1964), pp. 303–314.

An important book on the relationship between Paul and James is W. Schmithals' *Paulus und Jakobus* (1963) (Eng. tr. *Paul and James*, 1965). This author's main contention is that everywhere Paul was opposed by Gnostic Jewish Christians or judaizing Gentile Christians. James supported Paul against these. Cf. H. J. Schoeps' review, *JBL*, LXXXIV (1965), pp. 176 ff.; cf. also J. J. Scott, *JBL*, LXXXV (1966), pp. 262 f.; U. Wilckens, *ThLZ*, 90 (1965), cols. 598–601. Wilckens cannot accept that there were no Jewish Christian Judaizers among the opponents of Paul. Schmithals' Gnostic theories have been advanced in various other works which will be mentioned in connection with the relevant Epistles.

For a study of Paul's legality-liberty dialectic, cf. R. N. Longenecker, *Paul, Apostle of Liberty* (1964). For a Jewish presentation of Paul, cf. H. J. Schoeps, *Paulus, Die Theologie des Apostels im Lichte der Jüdischen Religionsgeschichte* (1959) (Eng. tr. *Paul*, 1961). Cf. also various criticisms of it such as C. K. Barrett, *JTS*, n.s., XII (1961), pp. 324–327; O. Michel, *ThLZ*, 86 (1961), cols. 196–198. For as tudy of Paul's relationship to Apocalyptic Judaism, cf. D. B. Bronson, *JBL*, LXXXIII (1964), pp. 287–292.

For two studies of Paul's mission, cf. J. Knox, *JBL*, LXXXIII (1964), pp. 1–11; W. Grundmann, *Nov. Test.*, 4 (1960), pp. 267–291.

CHAPTER ELEVEN

THE EPISTLE TO THE ROMANS

I. THE CHURCH IN ROME

At an early stage in his missionary labours Paul recognized the importance of strategic centres for the propagation of the gospel, and Rome, the metropolis of the world, was an obvious choice. Although he did not himself found the church he cherished it as part of his field as apostle to the Gentiles and clearly set great store upon it. But before discussing the apostle's own relations with the Roman church it is relevant to enquire into its origin and composition.

a. The origin of the church

On this subject we know virtually nothing for certain but there are some indications which help us to suggest a possible reconstruction. Paul had never visited the church at the time of writing the Epistle and it seems by that time to have become fairly well established. The data available may be tabulated as follows.

1. It is almost certain that no apostle founded it. Paul claims, in Romans xv. 20, that he did not build on another man's foundation, and yet he seems to regard the Roman church as within the sphere of his own commission. The claim that Peter founded it is brought under serious suspicion by the fact that Peter was still in Jerusalem at the time of the Council (c. AD 50) whereas it is almost certain that a church existed in Rome prior to this.[1] Suetonius records that Claudius banished Jews from Rome in AD 49 because there had been rioting at the instigation of one called Chrestus. While this may not be a reference to Christ, there is a strong possibility that Christians were somehow mixed up in this matter.

2. There is no reference in this Epistle to Peter and it is difficult to imagine that Paul could have written as he did if Peter had in fact

---

[1] This is admitted by the Roman Catholic scholar A. Wikenhauser, *New Testament Introduction* (1958), p. 399. Cf. the discussion of O. Cullmann, *Peter, Apostle and Martyr* (1953), pp. 70–152. On the recent excavations of Peter's tomb in Rome, see J. Toynbee and J. W. Perkins, *The Shrine of St. Peter* (1958).

founded the church. This inference is supported by the further suggestion that Acts xviii. 2, 3 implies that Priscilla and Aquila, who came from Rome, were already Christians when they arrived at Corinth and became companions of Paul. If so the church existed before AD 49, since Priscilla and Aquila were banished under the edict of Claudius. But this date is before Peter moved from Jerusalem.[1]

3. There is mention in Acts ii. 10 of visiting Jews and proselytes from Rome who were among the crowds and may well have been among the converted on the day of Pentecost. Could these have been the founders of the church? Sanday and Headlam dismiss this suggestion because in their opinion it would have taken more than what these people brought away with them at Pentecost to lay the foundations of a church.[2] But is this a valid assumption? These converts would have been well grounded in the Old Testament Scriptures and it is surely not impossible for the work already begun in them to be brought to fruition without apostolic intervention. To maintain that a church of believers could not have come into being without apostolic agency is not only unhistorical[3] but denies the illuminating power of the Holy Spirit. Their knowledge of the life and teaching of Jesus would be continually increasing as Christian travellers brought back with them accounts of apostolic preaching and teaching. In this way the Roman church must have heard a good deal about the work and ministry of the apostle Paul before he wrote to them, and there is a fair presumption that they had heard from other sources about the primitive Christian tradition.[4]

4. Early external evidence connects the names of both Peter and Paul with Rome. Clement of Rome[5] suggests that they were both martyred there, while by the time of Tertullian the tradition of a double martyrdom was generally accepted. There is strong possibility that this tradition is correct, but it tells us nothing about the origin of the church at Rome.[6]

[1] Cf. W. Michaelis, *Einleitung in das Neue Testament*[2] (1954), pp. 154 f.

[2] Cf. *The Epistle to the Romans (ICC*, 1895), p. xxviii.

[3] Cf. B. Weiss, *Manual Introduction to the New Testament* (1887), p. 295.

[4] Hort, *Prolegomena to St. Paul's Epistles to the Romans and Ephesians* (1895), pp. 15–18, thought that the type of Christianity at Rome prior to Paul's personal contact with them was nevertheless Pauline.

[5] *Ad Cor.* v. 4.

[6] Cullmann, *op. cit.*, pp. 70–152, discusses the external evidence for Peter's residence in Rome very thoroughly.

b. The composition of the church

Of greater importance than its origin is the question whether the church was Jewish Christian, Gentile Christian, or a mixture of both, for the answer to this question affects the understanding of the historical situation to which the apostle addressed himself.

(i) *Mainly Jewish Christian.* The Tübingen school of criticism considered that chapters ix–xi were the main portion of the Epistle, but this opinion largely passed with the general discarding of their presuppositions.[1] Recently, however, William Manson[2] resuscitated the notion that the major portion of the church was Jewish on the grounds that the argument throughout the Epistle is more applicable to Jews than to Gentiles (note the reference to Abraham as our father and the constant appeal to the Old Testament Scriptures).

(ii) *Mainly Gentile Christian.*[3] In Romans i. 5 ff. Paul includes the readers among the Gentiles to whom he has been particularly commissioned, while in i. 12–14 he compares them with the 'other Gentiles'. When in vi. 19 Paul states that the readers had yielded their members 'servants to uncleanness' it might seem to support a Gentile group rather than a Jewish group. Moreover in xi. 13 the apostle says, 'I speak to you Gentiles' and it cannot easily be maintained that a minority is here being addressed in view of xi. 28–31, where the readers are said to have obtained mercy through Jewish unbelief. The reference to Abraham as 'our father' (iv. 1) need not indicate a Jewish church in view of I Corinthians x. 1 where 'our fathers' is used in a letter sent to a definitely Gentile church.

(iii) *A mixed community.* This is the view advocated by Sanday and Headlam,[4] who nevertheless considered that it was the Gentile element which gave it its colour. Dodd[5] agrees on the fact of mixed membership but thinks that the Jewish influence was probably stronger than it

---

[1] Renan, *Saint Paul* (n.d.) (p. 254), thought that, together with Judaeo-Christians, Ebionites formed the main content of the church. Proselytes and converted pagans were in the minority.

[2] *Epistle to the Hebrews* (1951), pp. 172–184; and *New Testament Essays, Studies in Memory of T. W. Manson* (1959), pp. 150 f.

[3] Cf. J. Munck, *Paul and the Salvation of Mankind* (1959), p. 200, who regards all Paul's churches as Gentile Christian because of the negligible number of Jewish Christians.

[4] *Op. cit.*, p. xxxiii; cf. also Hort, *op. cit.*, pp. 19–33 *

[5] *Romans* (MC, 1932), p. xxviii.

would have been in a church of which Paul was the founder. The former of these views seems the more probable in view of the evidence given under section (ii) above, and because in xv. 16 the apostle particularly appeals to his commission among the Gentiles, which would clearly have less weight if directed mainly to Jews. From the evidence of *I Clement* vi. 1 and Tacitus (*Annals*, xv, 44) it would seem that the church was of a considerable size by the time of the Neronian persecutions.

II. OCCASION AND DATE

These questions are affected by decisions about the integrity of chapters xv and xvi (see discussion below); but assuming these belonged to the original Epistle they supply clear data for fixing the occasion which gave rise to the composition of the whole.[1]

1. Paul had been intending to visit the church but had been prevented (xv. 21 f., i. 13). His purpose was to preach the gospel among them and to impart some spiritual gift (i. 11, 15).

2. He has just completed his collection for the poverty-stricken believers at Jerusalem (xv. 22 ff.), after having preached the gospel throughout the district from Jerusalem to Illyricum. His face is set towards Jerusalem and this would identify the occasion with Acts xx. 1 ff., and date the Epistle in the year after Paul left Ephesus on the third missionary journey. It may therefore be confidently concluded that Paul was in Greece at the time of writing.

3. This conclusion is confirmed by the commendation of Phoebe (xvi. 1, 2) who belonged to the church at Cenchreae, the port of Corinth;[2] the greeting of Gaius (xvi. 23), Paul's host at the time, who may possibly be identified with the Corinthian whom Paul mentions in 1 Corinthians i. 14; the greeting of Erastus, who held the important post of city treasurer (xvi. 23) and who may possibly be identified with the man of the same name (who was left at Corinth) as mentioned in 2 Timothy iv. 20 (although this identification cannot be proved); and

[1] If chapter xvi is not original to the Epistle there is very little indication of the place of writing. T. M. Taylor (*JBL*, 67, 1948, pp. 281–295) suggested Philippi as Paul was then prepared for his Jerusalem journey.

[2] Cf. W. Michaelis, *Einleitung*[2] (1954), pp. 165–166, for the view that the Cenchreae of Rom. xvi. 1 was near Troas and that the Epistle to the Romans was written in Philippi (cf. also his article in *ZNTW*, 25, 1926, pp. 144–154). But most scholars prefer the identification with the better known Corinthian Cenchreae.

the mention of Timothy and Sopater (or Sosipater) as sending greetings, since these were Paul's companions when he left Greece on his last journey to Jerusalem.

4. Paul's future missionary plans are directed towards work in Spain (xv. 24, 28) and he hopes to gain the goodwill and support of the Roman Christians for this venture.

If the unity of the Epistle is maintained the date may be fixed approximately without much difficulty. Working from the time of Gallio's appointment to the proconsular office at Corinth, it is possible to calculate that Paul's departure from Corinth on his third missionary journey *en route* for Jerusalem took place either in AD 57 or 58 (see pp. 566, 662 f. for a discussion of the alternative dates for Gallio's proconsulate). C. H. Dodd[1] favours a year later because it fits better the termination of Paul's Roman imprisonment (Acts xxviii. 30) as AD 64, about the time Nero's persecutions broke out. But those who, unlike Professor Dodd, adhere to the second Roman imprisonment hypothesis favour a date just before the outbreak of persecution for the termination of the first imprisonment (i.e. AD 63) and a date some three or four years later for Paul's martyrdom. Any date for this Epistle between 57 and 59 would fall within the quinquennium of Nero when law and order was established throughout the provinces, and this would agree with Paul's exhortations to the readers to respect the 'authorities' (see Rom. xiii. 1).[2]

III. PURPOSE

The purpose of the Epistle arises naturally out of the occasion, but is not as easy to define with any precision. Paul's immediate purpose is to create interest in his Spanish mission, but that would not seem to account adequately for the theological character of the letter. Various explanations have been given.

---

[1] *Romans* (MC, 1932), p. xxvi.

[2] If chapter xvi is regarded as an Ephesian letter (see the discussion below) it cannot with such cogent reasons be assigned to Corinth as the place of dispatch. It may, therefore, under this hypothesis be dated earlier in Paul's Asian ministry. Duncan (*ET*, LXVIII, 6, March 1956, p. 165), who inclines to the view that Romans is earlier than Colossians and Ephesians, which according to him belong to the Ephesian ministry, assigns this Epistle to the middle of the Asian ministry.*

a. The purpose was polemical

F. C. Baur[1] and his school maintained that the main target at which Paul was aiming was Jewish Christianity. But this contention has found little favour.

b. The purpose was conciliatory

Some who have maintained the church to be Jewish Christian considered that Paul was attempting to vindicate his Gentile commission and to reconcile Jewish and Gentile elements.[2] But this too is based on the presuppositions of the Tübingen school. Others have maintained a conciliatory purpose even if the Gentile element was in the majority, but Paul's exposition clearly goes far beyond this.

c. The purpose was doctrinal

This is the traditional explanation which sees in the Epistle a *full* statement of Paul's doctrinal position. This really means that it was more a treatise than a letter and bore little reference to the historical situation out of which it arose. But this view is not entirely satisfactory for the following reasons. (1) There are some important truths which the apostle does not here enlarge upon, such as cosmic reconciliation and developed eschatology. (2) The section ix–xi cannot be accounted for without some reference to a historical situation. (3) The personal allusions and especially the section i. 7–15, which show the letter to have been written specially to the Roman community, are an integral part of the letter and must be taken into account when discussing its purpose.

d. The purpose was to sum up Paul's present experience

The apostle had reached a turning-point in his missionary career in that his face was turned towards Jerusalem and Rome and he could not be certain what the outcome would be. He therefore casts his mind back and gathers up almost unconsciously the fruits of his past work.[3]

---

[1] Cf. F. C. Baur, *Paul, the Apostle of Jesus Christ* (1876), I, pp. 308 ff.

[2] So Mangold; cf. B. Weiss, *op. cit.*, p. 301.

[3] Cf. Sanday and Headlam, *op. cit.*, p. xlii; G. G. Findlay, *The Epistles of Paul* (1892), p. 137, called the Epistle a formal manifesto. Cf. T. W. Manson, *BJRL*, xxxi (1948), p. 140: Goguel suggestively speaks of the Epistle as a balance sheet of Paul's ideas, *The Birth of Christianity* (1953), pp. 316 ff.

His mind had been dwelling on many great themes and he now proceeds to write down his conclusions. He may well have chosen to send the results of his meditations to the church at Rome because he foresaw its strategic importance for the future.[1] Or he may have had in mind these maturing thoughts and the occasion to commit them to writing arose with the need to write to the Roman church about his coming visit.[2] Another factor in the apostle's desire to commit these thoughts to some more permanent form may have been the general incapacity of even his own disciples to understand and appreciate them.

e. The purpose was to meet the immediate needs of the readers

Although undoubtedly much weight must be given to the last proposition, full account must be taken of the situation of the readers. Much primitive doctrine is taken for granted.[3] The apostle has probably received a fairly comprehensive report of the state of the church from Aquila and Priscilla and others of his associates and converts who had had contact with the church. He seems to have been aware of certain intellectual problems which were of some concern to the Christians and sets out to answer them. The main problem appears to have arisen from the need to frame what McNeile calls 'a comprehensive apologia for the principle of a universal religion as set over against Jewish nationalism'.[4] For this reason Paul deals with the fundamental Christian principle of 'righteousness' as contrasted with the Jewish approach, and then discusses the problem of Israel's failure and her relationship to the universal Christian Church.[5]

---

[1] J. Denney, in *Expositor's Greek Testament* II (1900), p. 569, suggests that in writing to the Romans Paul would naturally have made his communication catholic and comprehensive in proportion to his realization of the coming importance of their church. J. Munck, *op. cit.*, p. 196, following T. W. Manson's suggestion, regards the Epistle as a prepared manifesto based on material from Paul's debates over the relation of Judaism and Christianity.

[2] A. Wikenhauser, *op. cit.*, p. 407, suggests Paul may have wondered whether what the Romans had heard about his gospel was true, in view of the possible intrigues of Judaizers.

[3] Cf. Rom. vi. 17.*   [4] *St. Paul* (1932), p. 190.

[5] F. J. Leenhardt, *L'Épître de Paul aux Romains* (1957), pp. 10–15, maintains that the central idea of the Epistle is the problem of the Church and that justification by faith cannot be considered in isolation from the Church. He admits, however, that it is paradoxical that the Epistle does not mention the word ἐκκλησία (except in chapter xvi, which he detaches from the main Epistle).*

There may have been other practical difficulties which are reflected in the apostle's ethical injunctions in chapters xii–xv. The unexpected warning in xvi. 17–19 suggests that the apostle had also heard of some who were making trouble, but the fact that this reference occupies so insignificant a place in the Epistle shows that he either lacked detailed information about them or else knew that they had so far caused no difficulties. In the latter case he merely wished to warn the church that the best procedure is to avoid those who teach any other doctrine than the teaching they had already received and that Paul was now expounding to them.

IV. STRUCTURE AND INTEGRITY

The last two chapters of the Epistle have given rise to a great deal of discussion based on two separate lines of evidence. The first concerns the contents of chapter xvi, which according to some scholars is not original to this Epistle; and the second concerns the textual history, which suggests that there was more than one recension involving the circulation of a shorter edition of our existing Epistle. These problems will be separately considered although they bear some relation to each other.

a. The problem of chapter sixteen

There are several reasons which have prompted the hypothesis that this chapter was the whole or part of an Epistle sent not to Rome but to Ephesus.

1. Paul had never visited Rome and yet sends greetings to a large number of people in the church. This is considered unlikely. But it would be quite reasonable if these greetings were sent to Ephesus, where he had worked for about three years. Moreover, none of those mentioned in this chapter is mentioned in any of the later Epistles which are generally thought to have been sent from Rome, i.e. the Captivity Epistles (this point would of course have no relevance if the Ephesian hypothesis held good, see pp. 472 ff.).

2. Priscilla and Aquila and the church in their house are mentioned in 1 Corinthians xvi. 19, written shortly before the Roman Epistle, but at that time they were residing at Ephesus. By the time Paul writes to Rome after an interval of not more than two years at the most, probably much less, they had not only transferred their household to Rome but

had established another Christian centre there. The unlikelihood of this is said to be further accentuated by the fact that when 2 Timothy iv. 19 was written they were once more at Ephesus.

3. Epaenetus (see xvi. 5) is called the 'firstfruits of Asia unto Christ'. This is said to be a suitable description if he were then in Ephesus but would have little point if he were in Rome.[1]

4. Phoebe is commended in xvi. 1, 2 and it is maintained that Paul would have been more likely to send such commendation to a church he knew well than to a church he had never visited.

5. The tone of the warnings in xvi. 17–19 is thought to be alien to the tone of the rest of the Epistle, in which the apostle's chief concerns about disunity centre in Jewish-Gentile relationships (cf. xv. 1–13). The warnings in xvi. 17–19, however, appear to be against a form of antinomianism which is known to have thrived at Ephesus.

6. Chapter xv ends with what might have been the conclusion of a letter, which would support the contention that the final chapter was appended later during the transmission of the Epistle.

These reasons have appeared to some scholars conclusive for the hypothesis that the chapter was originally sent to Ephesus but became attached to the Epistle to the Romans when the letters of Paul were collected into a corpus.[2] But the grounds for the hypothesis are less conclusive than they appear as the following counter-considerations show.

1. There would be no parallel if this long series of greetings were sent to a church such as Ephesus which Paul knew well, for the only other occasion when he appended many personal greetings was when writing to Colossae which he had never visited. It was apparently against his policy to single out any individuals in churches that he knew well since he considered all the Christians to be his friends. But in a church like Rome, where he was not personally known, it would serve as a useful commendation that so many of the Christians there were his former acquaintances. That the apostle does not refer to any of those mentioned in chapter xvi in any other letter need occasion no surprise for the great majority of them were clearly not his intimate circle of

[1] Cf. McNeile–Williams, *INT* (1953), p. 155.

[2] Cf. the discussion in J. Moffatt, *Introduction to the Literature of the New Testament*[2] (1912), pp. 134 139. For a more recent discussion of the view that chapter xvi was sent to Ephesus, cf. T. M. Taylor, *JBL*, 67 (1948), pp. 281–295.

fellow-workers and in all probability had had no connection with those churches to which he wrote later.

2. Not only were there at that time extraordinary travel facilities to and from the imperial capital which would make it not so improbable as it seems at first that so many of Paul's acquaintances had migrated to Rome,[1] but the position of Aquila and Priscilla may possibly be explained in the same way. The fact that both at Rome and Ephesus they had a church in their house suggests that they may have been well-to-do. In fact, Dodd[2] has argued with much plausibility that they might have had a business establishment in both cities at once. On the edict of Claudius they were obliged to leave, but this does not necessarily mean that they had to close down their business. The appointment of a non-Jewish manager would have been enough.

3. There seems to be no particular reason why the first convert in Asia must have remained there, and so the reference to Epaenetus contributes nothing of value to the discussion. If he had gone to Rome there would have been good reason for Paul's greeting to him, for he would warmly remember the encouragement this first convert gave him. The description 'firstfruits' would naturally be associated in Paul's mind with this Christian.[3]

4. In the case of the commendation of Phoebe, it is by no means cogent reasoning to claim that this was more probable when Paul was writing to a church where he was known. It would be so only if the writer were some obscure person of whom the church in question had no knowledge. But in this case if Paul has no authority to commend anyone to a church where he is unknown he would equally have no authority to write to them as he has done in chapters i–xv.

5. The objection raised over the schismatics is no more convincing. True there is no record of any such problems confronting the Roman church except in Romans xvi, whereas Acts xx. 19, 29 f. predicts a situation at Ephesus which closely resembles that described in the Romans passage. But this is no proof that the words could have had no

---

[1] Cf. *Cambridge Ancient History*, vol. x (1927), pp. 387, 421 f.

[2] Cf. *Romans* (*MC*), p. xxi. Dodd cites evidence from early inscriptions which might support the connection of Aquila and Priscilla with Rome (*op. cit., ad loc.*).

[3] Montgomery Hitchcock, *A Study of Romans XVI*, a reprint from *The Church Quarterly Review* (January 1936), p. 193, cites an interesting parallel from Cicero to support his contention that this reference to Epaenetus does not indicate an Ephesian destination.

relevance to Rome, unless of course the idea is considered to be out of keeping with the character of the church reflected in the earlier part of the Epistle. In any case the difficulty would be removed altogether if the trouble-makers were as yet no more than a threat. It may on the other hand be objected that Paul's words of warning would lose a good deal of their point if the people in mind were as yet unknown to the readers.[1] They could hardly then mark and turn away from them (Rom. xvi. 17). Moreover, as Dodd[2] suggests, it may be that in the earlier part of the Epistle Paul has been scrupulously correct, but at the close he takes the pen from his amanuensis and adds a pastoral appeal about these teachers. This might account for the sudden change of tone, for he had bitter memories of the struggles he had had with similar false teachers in other churches.

6. Although xv. 33 could be the ending of an epistle it is without precedent among Paul's Epistles.

Quite apart from the inconclusive nature of the evidence brought in support of an Ephesian destination, the proposal that chapter xvi was originally a commendatory letter for Phoebe[3] is pointedly criticized by Lietzmann[4] who calls it a monstrosity in any age prior to the advent of the picture postcard. Two alternative suggestions which have been made have not much more to commend them. If Romans xvi is but a fragment of a lost letter to Ephesus the hypothesis becomes even more hypothetical, for some reasonable explanation must be given for the

---

[1] Cf. Moffatt, *ILNT*, p. 137.*

[2] *Romans, op. cit.*, pp. xxiii ff., 242.

[3] E. J. Goodspeed (*New Chapters in New Testament Study*, 1937, pp. 25, 26) calls chapter xvi an 'epistole systatike' (a letter of introduction), for which he claims many papyrological parallels exist.*

[4] Cited by C. H. Dodd, *op. cit.*, p. xix. Sir F. Kenyon also found difficulty in imagining how a commendatory letter, without beginning or ending, could ever have been attached to Romans: *Chester Beatty Biblical Papyri, Fasc. III, Supplement* (1936), p. xviii. This objection would, of course, be lessened if xvi. 1, 2 formed a postscript for the Roman Epistle and xvi. 3–24 formed a fragment of another Epistle to Ephesus (cf. W. Michaelis, *Einleitung*, p. 159). In this case it would be necessary to assume that Phoebe was the messenger who took the Roman Epistle (cf. Feine–Behm, *Einleitung in das Neue Testament*[11] (1956), pp. 146 ff.; Hort, *op. cit.*, pp. 51–53). Goodspeed, however, criticized Dodd on the ground that the list of names in chapter xvi represented a list of suitable people in Ephesus who would offer Phoebe hospitality (*HTR*, 44, 1951, pp. 55–57). He is forced to regard the loss of the opening salutation as 'natural enough', but this is not a satisfactory solution since it involves a purely subjective assessment.

strange preservation of the greetings and the loss of the Epistle. Common sense would suggest the reverse. The other theory is that Paul enclosed the Roman letter with the commendatory letter for Phoebe and sent them both to Ephesus. But he did not resort to this method when he wished the Colossians to read the letter sent to the Laodiceans, although it must be admitted that in this latter case the close proximity of the churches would make such interchange reasonably easy compared with Rome and Ephesus.

Further corroboration of a Roman destination for chapter xvi has been sought in the names found in Paul's greetings which correspond to those found in Roman inscriptions. The list of correspondences is impressive,[1] but it has been criticized on the grounds that many of the names were very common in the Roman world and are found in provincial inscriptions as well as in Rome itself.[2] This evidence would be of value only if some link could be shown between the names and Roman Christianity. This can reasonably be supported only in the cases of Rufus, Narcissus, Aristobulus, Amplias and Nereus which may inferentially be associated both with the church (as in Rom. xvi) and with the imperial city.

Since there is one name only which is known to have been connected with Ephesus and which lacks any supporting connection with Rome (i.e. Epaenetus) and since the remaining evidence may be explained at least as adequately of a Roman destination, Harnack's[3] conclusion that this Ephesian destination theory is a 'badly supported hypothesis' is fully justified. There is no MS support for the contention that the Epistle ever circulated without the concluding chapter, in spite of the complicated textual history affecting the ending of the Epistle. The Chester Beatty papyrus, the only early MS which places the doxology at the end of chapter xv, ends with chapter xvi, and cannot easily be used in support. Moreover the theory of an Ephesian destination for chapter xvi does nothing to solve the textual problems of the last two chapters, but on the contrary introduces further confusion.

---

[1] See J. B. Lightfoot, *Philippians* (1898), pp. 171 ff., and Sanday and Headlam, *op. cit.*, p. xciv, for details.

[2] Cf. H. Lietzmann, *An die Römer*⁴ (1933), p. 73; and K. Lake, *The Earlier Epistles of Paul* (1911), pp. 324–335.

[3] *Die Briefsammlung des Apostels Paulus* (1926), pp. 13 ff. Cf. A. M. Hunter, *Romans* (1955), p. 129, who ends his discussion on the destination of Rom. xvi by considering it wiser to prefer tradition to speculation.*

b. The recensions of the Epistle

The problems raised by the textual history of the Epistle must now be briefly stated and discussed.

(i) *The references to Rome*. The words ἐν ʻΡώμῃ (in Rome) (i. 7, 15) are entirely lacking in one bi-lingual MS Gg while the reference in verse 7 is also omitted in one minuscule (1908*mg*) and in the text used by Origen who understood the remaining words to mean 'those who are really saints'.

(ii) *The doxology* (xvi. 25–27). Its appearance in various positions constitutes the biggest problem of the textual history.

1. The best MSS, both Alexandrian and Western, place it at the end of chapter xvi (אBCD, Latin, Peshitta Syriac, Boharic and Ethiopic versions).[1]

2. Many less important MSS place it at the end of chapter xiv. Among the more weighty of these are Codex L, many minuscules, some codices used by Origen (according to the Latin translation) and the Harklean Syriac.

3. A few late authorities place it after both chapter xiv and chapter xvi (the Codices A and P, minuscules 5 and 33).

4. The Chester Beatty papyrus (P46) places it after chapter xv.

5. The Graeco-Latin MS Gg, supported by Marcion, omits it altogether. In Gg, however, a space is left.[2]

(iii) *The benediction* ('The grace of our Lord Jesus Christ be with you all').[3] This is placed in various positions in chapter xvi as follows:

1. At the end of verse 20 by the best Alexandrian MSS and some others (אABC, *al.*) together with the Vulgate.

2. At verse 24 in some good Western authorities only (D, G, and other uncials, Old Latin, Harklean Syriac). As some of these omit the doxology, the benediction then forms the conclusion of the Epistle (F, L, G).

3. After verse 27 in a few late authorities (Codex P, 33, 436, the Syriac Peshitta, Armenian version and Ambrosiaster).

---

[1] Origen in his Greek texts knew the doxology in this position.

[2] This omission looks like a scribe's attempt to solve the problem, and little weight can be attached to it.

[3] The 'all' is omitted in position 1, and 'Amen' is added in positions 2 and 3; while in 2 ὑμῶν becomes ἡμῶν.

(iv) *Chapters xv and xvi.* There is some evidence that Marcion's text did not contain these chapters.

1. In Rufinus' Latin version of Origen's works Origen states that Marcion removed (*abstulit*) the doxology and cut out (*dissecuit*) chapters xv and xvi. There is some doubt whether he himself excised the text or whether he found an already existing shorter recension.[1]

2. Tertullian when referring to Marcion's treatment of xiv. 10 refers to it as 'in clausula' (i.e. at the end of the Epistle).

3. Tertullian, Irenaeus and Cyprian make no quotations from chapters xv and xvi. This has little evidential value as the same might be said of 1 Corinthians xvi.

4. The chapter headings which occur in several MSS of the Latin Vulgate suggest that the Epistle was circulating without chapters xv and xvi. The evidence of Codex Amiatinus and Codex Fuldensis is particularly important, as the headings in the former can be traced to a text earlier than Jerome.

To sum up this mass of textual evidence, it would seem certain that a shorter recension of the Epistle was in circulation at one time in its textual history. That this recension was also very early is at least probable. But to account for all the variations is by no means an easy matter and a number of explanations have been suggested, and these will need to be briefly considered.

Nevertheless, before the various solutions are mentioned some attention must be given to the integrity of the doxology itself since this will clearly bear on the textual problem. Some scholars have pointed out that the style and language differ from the remainder of the Epistle and approximate more closely to Ephesians and the Pastoral Epistles.[2] If the Pauline authorship of these latter is disputed[3] a problem may arise over the doxology. But in any case historical criticism has found it

---

[1] McNeile–Williams, *INT*, p. 156, states that *dissecuit* 'may mean either the same as *abstulit*, or "separated off", i.e. treated as not belonging to the epistle'. Cf. P. Corssen, *ZNTW*, 10, 1909, pp. 13 f.*

[2] G. Zuntz, *The Text of the Epistles* (1953), p. 227, and T. W. Manson, *BJRL*, XXXI (1948), pp. 224–240, regard the doxology as Marcionite but later adapted for orthodox use. C. K. Barrett inclines to the same view after emphatically disputing its Pauline origin, *The Epistle to the Romans* (1958), pp. 11, 12. The reference to the prophetic writings is so clearly contrary to Marcion that it is suggested that this wording is an attempt to counteract the Marcionite character of the remainder (cf. C. K. Barrett, *op. cit.*, p. 287).*

[3] See the discussions on pp. 589 ff.

notoriously difficult to establish any conclusive tests of style.[1] Objection has been made to the expression 'the mystery which hath been kept in silence through times eternal, but now is manifested' (Rom. xvi. 25, 26, RV), because it is not in keeping with Paul's teaching elsewhere. Moffatt,[2] for instance, considered it went beyond Colossians i. 26 and was hardly in agreement with Romans i. 2, iii. 21. But there is nothing in this use of the word which is opposed to Paul's theology. Corssen[3] suggested that the doxology was the work of a Marcionite and others have suggested that the collector of the Pauline Corpus placed the Epistle at the end of the collection and composed the doxology to round it off.[4] Appeal is made to the position of Romans as the last of the church Epistles in the Muratorian Canon, but the value of this evidence is lessened by the fact that Philemon and the Pastoral Epistles are placed in the same list after Romans, which shows that the latter Epistle did not then stand at the end of the Pauline Corpus.

The opinion of Hort, followed by Sanday and Headlam, seems more in harmony with the facts. The doxology is claimed to be a résumé of the main subject-matter of the Epistle,[5] a procedure which would be quite in accordance with Paul's mind. If this opinion is correct it must

[1] This is not to deny the possibility of using literary criteria in stylistic questions but it is doubted whether the validity of the method can be maintained in the case of so small a section as the Roman doxology. Karl Barth, following Corssen, Lietzmann and Harnack, rejects the Pauline character of the doxology on stylistic grounds, although he seems to have been mainly influenced by differences from the parallel passage in Eph. iii. 20 (*The Epistle to the Romans* (Eng. Tr. 1933 from 6th German edition by E. C. Hoskyns), pp. 522, 523).   [2] *ILNT*, p. 135.

[3] For Corssen's view, cf. *ZNTW* (1909), pp. 32 f. C. K. Barrett favours this suggestion (*Romans*, pp. 11, 12). So also K. Barth, *op. cit.*, p. 523.

[4] So J. Weiss, *History of Primitive Christianity*, 11, p. 284, cited by McNeile-Williams, *INT*, p. 155. R. Scott (*The Pauline Epistles*, 1909, p. 246) considered the doxology was almost certainly Luke's, but this was based mainly on linguistic and stylistic similarities to the Pastorals which he also attributed to Luke. W. Michaelis (*Einleitung*, pp. 163, 164) does not regard the doxology as belonging to chapter xvi. 3–24 which he considers to be a fragment of an Ephesian letter, but he does not dispute its Pauline authorship. He agrees with Feine–Behm that the two fragments were probably attached to the Epistle (at the conclusion of the collection) by the collector of the Pauline Corpus. K. and S. Lake, *Introduction to the New Testament* (1938), p. 98, dispute its Pauline authorship but consider it to be the work of the collector or a Catholic redactor.

[5] Cf. Sanday and Headlam, *Romans* (1895), pp. xcv, xcvi; cf. Hort, *op. cit.*, pp. 56 ff. This is also maintained by A. Nygren, *Commentary on Romans* (Eng. Tr. 1952), p. 457.

of course mean that chapter xvi was an integral part of the original Epistle. But not all the theories regarding the ending admit this. Indeed the major themes such as justification, grace, righteousness, sin, flesh, find no place in the doxology and throw doubts on this theory. Nevertheless, even if it does not gather up the themes of the Epistle, it does form a fitting conclusion to the Epistle.[1]

c. Suggested solutions to the textual history

(i) *Theories that maintain that the longer recension is original.* These commence with the decided advantage of having the best MSS supporting them, and the problem is therefore to account for the existence of the shorter recension and the various positions of the doxology and benediction. Three different theories have been proposed.

1. That the longer Epistle was shortened by Paul. J. B. Lightfoot[2] contended that the original was the longer recension minus the doxology. This was later turned by Paul himself into a circular letter which necessitated the elimination of the last two chapters and the references to Rome. The doxology was then added after xiv. 23 because Paul did not consider this a suitable ending. During later textual transmission the doxology was transferred from the shorter to the longer recension.

The major criticism of this theory is that it leaves unexplained the unnatural break at xiv. 23. The argument is continued until xv. 13 and it is difficult to believe that the apostle would ever have cut this part of the discussion, especially as he found it necessary on this hypothesis to compose a doxology to sum up the main themes of the Epistle.

2. That the longer Epistle was shortened by the church. This view was firmly advocated by Hort,[3] who suggested that for lectionary pur-

---

[1] Cf. the careful discussion of F. R. M. Hitchcock, *A Study of Romans XVI* (1936), p. 202. Barth finds it impossible to conceive of Paul adding a 'solemn liturgical conclusion' after xvi. 24 (*op. cit.*, p. 523), but this is no more than a subjective opinion with which many scholars would not agree. It may, in any case, be doubted whether 'liturgical' is an exact description, unless it be used in the sense in which all doxologies share a liturgical character. No canon of criticism can be made out excluding the possibility that Paul would so conclude. Yet Barth is not drawn to the theory of a separate Ephesian destination of chapter xvi on the grounds that the whole Epistle would be incomplete if not addressed to particular men with human names (*op. cit.*, p. 536).

[2] *Biblical Essays* (1893), pp. 287 ff.

[3] *Prolegomena to St. Paul's Epistles to the Romans and Ephesians* (1895); E. F. Scott, *The Literature of the New Testament* (1932), propounded a similar view but, unlike Hort, considered a later hand added the doxology.

poses the church omitted the concluding section of the Epistle (i.e. chapters xv and xvi) because of their lack of much edifying material. The noble doxology, however, was in a different category and was consequently retained at the end of chapter xiv. The omission of allusions to Rome was a transcriptional error, while the omission of the doxology was due to Marcion or was omitted from an earlier text which Marcion used. The omission may in fact have arisen purely by accident.

But this suggestion is faced with the same difficulty as the last over the arbitrary division at xiv. 23, although the problem is here lessened by attributing the unnatural break to some ecclesiastical editor.[1] Why it should ever have been made there is a mystery to which the only answer seems to be what Dodd[2] calls 'the illimitable stupidity of editors'. Yet that is hardly an adequate explanation.

3. That the longer Epistle was shortened by Marcion. This view claims to have strong support from both external and internal evidence.[3] Marcion is the only positive evidence for the excision of the last two chapters, although as mentioned above there is dispute whether he made the excision himself or found it in his existing text.[4] But Origen's word *dissecuit* describing Marcion's treatment of the text most naturally means that Marcion himself cut off the latter chapters. In view of Marcion's whole approach to the canon, we may assume that he would not have hesitated to excise what did not suit him. Since parts of chapter xv were contrary to Marcion's tenets it seems the most reasonable solution that he himself made the mutilation. This is further borne out by the omission of the doxology in Marcion's text.

The sections to which Marcion would have objected are verse 8, which describes Christ as a 'minister of the circumcision', i.e. a minister

---

[1] This difficulty would be lessened if on the evidence of P46 it is assumed that from the original Epistle a 'liturgical' version consisting of chapters i–xv was prepared for ecclesiastical use with the doxology added.

[2] *Op. cit.*, p. xvi.

[3] This is held in two different forms: (a) assuming the doxology to be included in the original (as Sanday and Headlam); (b) assuming the original ended at xvi. 23 (as Lietzmann, *op. cit.*, pp. 130 f.).

[4] Otto Michel, *Der Brief an die Römer*[10] (1955), p. 350, mentions the suggestion that the two concluding chapters dropped out and a solemn conclusion became necessary after xiv. 23. It would, as Michel points out, seem to be more necessary there than after xvi. 23. Barth also considers it to be a liturgical conclusion to xiv. 23 (*op. cit.*, pp. 522, 523).

to the circumcised, and verse 4 which declares that 'whatsoever things were written aforetime were written for our learning'. Both of these statements would have cut right across Marcion's rejection of the Old Testament and his strong dislike of Judaism. There are also four citations from the Old Testament in verses 9–12 which would possibly have contributed to Marcion's dislike of these verses. If he took exception to xv. 1–13 he would have had little interest in retaining the remainder of the Epistle and would have no scruples about omitting it. His omission of the doxology may similarly be accounted for because of its reference to the value of the prophetic writings. Those who dismiss this theory[1] generally base their objections on the grounds that Marcion received an already mutilated text, but the evidence for this, as we have seen, turns on the precise meaning of one Latin word and this is hardly sufficient to overthrow a hypothesis which has such strong historical probability. If Marcion's edition was due to his own shortening process, the position of the doxology after xv. 33 in P46 may be due to a later interaction between the shorter and longer editions.[2]

(ii) *Theories that maintain that a shorter recension is original.* There are three different solutions which have been proposed on the basis of a shorter recension.

1. That the original Epistle consisted of chapters i–xv, later expanded by part of an epistle to Ephesus. Moffatt[3] suggested rather tentatively that the original Epistle ended at xv. 33, that xvi. 1–23 was added when the Pauline letters were collected at Ephesus, and that the doxology was then added by an editor to provide a climax to the whole collection. The omission of 'in Rome' in i. 7 and the change of position of the doxology to the end of xiv were due to liturgical procedure. The speculative character of this view is demonstrated by the fact that no definite evidence exists for the independent circulation of chapters i–xv, unless P46 can be said to support this theory. The position of the doxology after chapter xv is certainly suggestive, especially as this MS is the oldest text of the Pauline letters. Yet even in this text chapter xvi is added and there is no means of knowing whether the Epistle ever

---

[1] Cf. A. H. McNeile, *St. Paul*, p. 186.

[2] H. Lietzmann (*op. cit.*, pp. 130 f.) considers that the peculiar positions of the doxology were due to different expansions of Marcion's shorter recension after the doxology had been added to supply a satisfactory conclusion.

[3] *ILNT*, pp. 139–142. This view is supported by Goodspeed, *INT* (1937), p. 85, and F. J. Leenhardt, *L'Epître de Saint Paul aux Romains* (1957), pp. 16–18.

circulated without it in this form.[1] Moffatt's own theory is in fact built on the hypothesis that chapter xvi was sent to Ephesus and not to Rome and that the doxology is not original.[2] If either of these is disputed the theory falls to the ground.

2. That the original (i–xiv) was a circular, later expanded by Paul himself. This was expounded by Lake,[3] who considered that the circular was designed for mixed churches which he had not visited and was written at the same time as Galatians.[4] He later had occasion to write to Rome and adapted the circular by the addition of the specific reference to Rome and chapters xv and xvi as a covering letter. Lake attempted to explain the fact that xv. 1–13 continues the argument of chapter xiv by suggesting that Aquila had told him that such a continuation would be desirable. Burkitt[5] suggested with little more probability that xv. 1–13 was a mere weld or adaptation to join the existing Epistle with the additional material which Paul wished to add.

Apart from the lack of an adequate explanation for the addition of xv. 1–13, the theory cannot account for the personal allusions in i. 7–15. It is quite inconceivable that these words belonged originally to a general circular, and there is no textual evidence that the Epistle ever circulated without them. This consideration seems fatal to the theory. Another objection to this theory is that it offers no explanation of Marcion's activities.[6]

[1] Sir F. Kenyon, *The Story of the Bible* (1936), p. 122, hesitated to accept this theory in the absence of other support.

[2] J. Knox, *Romans (IB)*, p. 368, who adopts a similar view, tentatively suggests that after the corpus of Paul's letters was collected, one chapter (i.e. xv) was removed in one edition (or manuscript) and in another edition a chapter (xvi) was added. Chapters i–xvi became the sole survivor. But this solution is highly mechanical, and Knox can suggest no adequate reason for the removal of chapter xv from the original form.

[3] *The Earlier Epistles of Paul*, p. 362. In their *Introduction to the New Testament* (p. 108) K. and S. Lake suggest that only the shorter recension was sent to 'some other church', apparently dropping the general letter idea.

[4] Renan's earlier solution has some affinity with Lake's but was much more complicated, involving four letters to the churches of Rome, Macedonia, Thessalonica and Ephesus respectively, each comprising chapters i–xi plus certain parts of chapters xii–xvi according to the church addressed (*Saint Paul*, pp. xxvii–xxx). It was strongly criticized by Lightfoot (cf. *Biblical Essays*, pp. 287 ff.).

[5] *Christian Beginnings* (1924), pp. 126, 127.

[6] W. Manson, in *New Testament Essays, Studies in memory of T. W. Manson* (1959), pp. 150 ff., on the basis that Marcion shortened the text, maintained he must have worked on the longer recension.

3. That the original Epistle consisted of chapters i–xv, expanded by Paul himself. This is substantially the view advocated by T. W. Manson,[1] who maintained that i–xv was sent to Rome; that i–xvi was at the same time sent to Ephesus; that Marcion was responsible for shortening the first letter, and his edition influenced the Western textual tradition. The Alexandrian tradition was based on the letter to Ephesus, but the Chester Beatty papyrus (P46) shows a tradition stemming from the letter to Rome with its doxology at the end of chapter xv. The fact that P46 also included chapter xvi means, however, that it has been influenced by the Alexandrian tradition.[2]

Although this rather complicated theory seems to provide a solution to many of the textual variations, it is based on an original form of the letter to the church at Rome (i.e. i–xv) for which no direct evidence is forthcoming. Moreover, the problem of the personal data in chapter i still remains, since these would have no relevance if sent to Ephesus.

A modification of this type of theory is that proposed by Montgomery Hitchcock,[3] who maintained that Romans xvi was not a part of the Roman Epistle but consisted of a letter of recommendation for Phoebe on the occasion of her being involved in a legal case referred to the Roman courts. Its destination was, therefore, Rome, but it was dispatched some years later than the Roman Epistle. When the Pauline Canon was constituted it was added to the earlier Epistle. This theory gives an account of the differences between chapters i–xv and xvi, and yet furnishes a more reasonable explanation of the ultimate linking of the two. But if both shared a common destination it is difficult to see what is gained by separating them by an interval of time. The evidence for the doxology placed at the end of chapter xv would seem strange

[1] BJRL, xxxi (1948), pp. 237–240. Cf. also the similar suggestion of R. Heard, INT (1950), pp. 195, 196.

[2] K. E. Kirk, The Epistle to the Romans (Clar. B, 1937), pp. 12–22, has much the same theory, but thinks the spurious doxology added to the original copy accounts for all the variations in the tradition. Thus three forms developed: (a) i–xvi. 23 (as in G); (b) i–xvi. 25 (as in ℵ BCD); and (c) i–xv, xvi. 25–27, xvi. 1–23 (as in P46). But it should be noted that the peculiar position of the doxology in P46 may have arisen through a scribal error.

C. S. C. Williams, ET, LXI (1949–50), pp. 125 f., supports Manson's theory but shows that the text of P46 is based on the Western form of Rom. i–xv and not the later form i–xvi (found in the Alexandrian tradition), although it was certainly influenced by the later form. Cf. J. Munck's discussion, op. cit., pp. 197 ff.

[3] Op. cit., pp. 187 ff.

under this theory for the change in the position of the doxology must *ex hypothesi* have taken place after the two letters were joined, which is highly improbable.

It is not easy to decide which of these theories provides the best solution, but on the whole that which traces the recensions of the Epistle to Marcion is perhaps least open to objection.

d. Theories of interpolation and redaction

In addition to the problems arising from chapter xvi and, to a lesser extent, xv, there have been other theories which have questioned the integrity of the text. One such theory concerns the passage xiii. 1–7, in which is discussed the attitude to be adopted towards the State. It has been maintained[1] that the passage interrupts the context and can be treated as an independent unit. Moreover, in the preceding passage (xii) and the succeeding passage, Paul seems to show reminiscences of the teaching of Jesus in the Synoptic Gospels, but not so in xiii. 1–7. It is the contents of this passage which are seen to be non-Pauline, mainly on eschatological grounds. Paul believed in an imminent *parousia*, but xiii. 1–7 suggests a continuing world. Moreover, the 'authorities' in Paul are usually demonic, but not in this passage. Paul's world-view is said to involve the basic evil of this world, and yet he speaks of its rulers here as ministers of God. Many commentators have noted the difficulties, but have maintained the Pauline origin of the passage. C. H. Dodd[2], for instance, takes the view that Paul had come to see the empire as 'a providential instrument'. But J. Kallas[3] considers that the only satisfactory solution is to treat it as an interpolation alien to Paul's thought. But this is not as convincing as it first appears, for the fact that Paul uses the term 'authorities' in a different sense shows that he is not contradicting his view that the spiritual powers are evil. The whole question of Paul's view of the *parousia* is also more complex than Kallas supposes.[4] Digressions in Paul's letters are, moreover, not unknown.

Another theory of a non-Pauline fragment concerns Romans iii. 25,

[1] Cf. J. Kallas, *NTS*, 11 (1965), pp. 365–374. For a monograph on this passage see C. D. Morrison, *The Powers that Be* (1960). Cf. also C. E . B. Cranfield, *NTS*, 6 (1960), p. 241, and E. Barnikol, 'Römer 13', *Studien zum Neuen Testament und zur Patristik (für E. Klostermann)* (1961), pp. 65–133.

[2] *The Epistle to the Romans*, p. 202.

[3] *Op. cit.*, p. 374.   [4] See p. 571.

26, which C. H. Talbert[1] considers to be untypical of Paul. This is based on use of terms unique in Paul's Epistles, on the supposed liturgical style, on non-Pauline theology and on the inappropriateness of the passage in the context. But this method of redaction-criticism could jeopardize the genuineness of many other Pauline statements if it be admitted as a valid principle of criticism that any idea which occurs only once is suspect. Talbert admits the difficulty of the lack of textual evidence for the interpolation, but curiously appeals to the similar lack of such evidence in other theories of interpolation in Paul's Epistles (in Corinthians and Philippians).

A compilation theory is advanced by J. Kinoshita,[2] who sees our present Epistle as an editing of two original epistles. One was a manual for a mixed community (ii. 1–5; ii. 17–iii. 20; iii. 27–iv. 25; v. 12–vii. 25; ix. 1–xi. 36; xiv. 1–xv. 3; xv. 4–13). The remainder was specifically addressed to Gentiles. But the Epistle does not read like a combination of two such letters, and it is more reasonable to suppose that a double purpose was in view throughout.

CONTENTS

I. INTRODUCTION (i. 1–15)

a. Greeting (i. 1–7)

This is more formal than in most of Paul's letters and brings out more clearly the commission to preach the gospel which had been entrusted to him by God. By this means he summarizes the content of the gospel and the divine origin of his apostleship.

b. Paul's relation to the Roman church (i. 8–15)

He has heard good reports of them and expresses his desire to visit them that he and they may be mutually encouraged. Above all he desires to preach the gospel at Rome, and the main part of the Epistle is an exposition of that gospel.

---

[1] C. H. Talbert, *JBL*, LXXXV (1966), pp. 287–296. The kind of interpolation criticism proposed by this writer has support from R. Bultmann's earlier article on glosses in Romans (*ThLZ*, 72, 1947, cols. 197–202).

[2] *Nov. Test.*, 7 (1965), pp. 258–277.

II. DOCTRINAL EXPOSITION (i. 16-viii. 39)

a. Statement of the theme (i. 16, 17)

Paul summarizes his gospel as righteousness obtained by faith. It concerns the true method of man's acceptance with God.

b. Evidence of the need for righteousness (i. 18-iii. 20)

Paul begins by demonstrating that all sections of mankind are under condemnation before God. First, the Gentiles are notorious for vice and idolatry, which are indisputable evidence of their rebellion against the Creator (i. 18-32). But then the Jews are in no better condition, for although they are not chargeable with idolatry they are nevertheless addicted to self-righteousness. Whether man disobeys the voice of conscience (as the Gentiles) or the voice of special revelation (as the Jew), the disobedience involves guilt. Circumcision cannot gloss over this fact. But does this mean that the Jew has no advantage? Paul admits the privileges of the Jews in that they were entrusted with the revelation, but he denies that such privileges carry any immunity from guilt for Jewish offenders (ii. 1-iii. 8). The conclusion reached is that none, neither Gentile nor Jew, is righteous and this is supported by an appeal to Scripture, to the very revelation entrusted to the Jews. Their own oracles condemn them (iii. 9-20).

c. The divine method of meeting the need (iii. 21-v. 21)

Having shown that the need is universal Paul next considers God's answer.

1. Righteousness can be attained only by faith in God, who has provided a propitiatory sacrifice in Christ, on the basis of which pardon is freely granted and man is justified. This passage contains the doctrinal key to the whole Epistle (iii. 21-26).

2. There are therefore no grounds of boasting on the part of the Jew since this righteousness by faith is equally open to Gentiles (iii. 27-31).

3. The case of Abraham is cited because of a possible Jewish objection that Abraham's justification was really by works, but Paul shows that the righteousness reckoned to him was essentially on the basis of his trust in God. Nor could anyone claim that Abraham's covenant came through circumcision, for the promise was given before he was circumcised. Paul enlarges upon the circumstances in which Abraham be-

lieved God to make abundantly clear that it was not Abraham's achievements (in which every Jew gloried) but his faith that was the ground of his justification (chapter iv).

4. Paul next mentions the blessings attending justification. The righteous in Christ experience peace, joy, perseverance, hope, all because of the indwelling Spirit, through whom they become aware of the greatness of God's love in providing a means of reconciliation through the death of Christ (v. 1–11).

5. The efficacy of God's free gift to mankind is then illustrated by a comparison between Adam and Christ. The universality of sin through the former is outmatched by the abundance of grace through the latter (v. 12–21).

d. The application of righteousness to individual life (vi. 1–viii. 39)

If it is faith rather than works that counts, how does justification affect conduct? This is the question that Paul next answers.

1. By means of the symbolism of baptism Paul shows that the believer, through union with Christ, dies to sin and rises to a resurrection life. This means a new approach to sin. It cannot be indulged in view of the abundance of grace, for it no longer has dominion over the believer (vi. 1–14). This is borne out by experience, for those who have been freed from the slavery of sin have in fact become slaves of God, committing themselves to His service (vi. 15–23).

2. By an illustration from the marriage laws, Paul proceeds to show that the old bond to the law is dissolved, leaving the believer free for a new union, that is to Christ Himself in a life of loving service (vii. 1–6).

3. But the question arises whether the law might not assist in the subduing of the sinful nature, and Paul answers this with an emphatic negative by citing his experience under the law. It resulted only in inner conflict, from which Christ alone could deliver (vii. 7–25).

4. The Christian is in fact called to a new kind of life energized by the Spirit who wars against the flesh. The law of the Spirit sets free from the guilt and the power of sin and gives liberation even to the body· (viii. 1–13).

5. This new life conveys a new status, that of sons, by means of the process of adoption. Such a thought leads to the climax that we are joint-heirs with Christ (viii. 14–17).

6. God's redemptive action is so great and comprehensive that it envelops the material creation, whose yearning is cited to illustrate

the greatness of the contrast between present sufferings and future glory (viii. 18–25).

7. Life in the Spirit is not, however, confined to future hope. It provides present help through the Spirit's intercession (viii. 26, 27) and through the security and blessings which abound to those who love God (viii. 28–39). So ends Paul's doctrinal exposition on a triumphant note.

III. AN HISTORICAL PROBLEM (ix. 1–xi. 36)

Paul introduces the important question of Israel's rejection of the gospel at this juncture possibly because he is impressed by the contrast between Israel's blindness and the blessedness of the Christian position he has just expounded. This cannot be considered an interlude for it must have been a burning question in Paul's mind and is well prepared for by the earlier discussion. He sums up this present section in ix. 6—the word of God has not failed, however perplexing the historic facts might be.

a. The fact of Israel's rejection (ix. 1–5)

In spite of its many privileges, Israel's attitude fills the apostle with intense sorrow.

b. The justice of Israel's rejection (ix. 6–29)

God's choice was not indiscriminate nor all-inclusive. Only some of Abraham's seed were chosen and this demonstrates the sovereignty of God's choice. But there is no possibility of injustice with God, for man cannot pronounce on the rightness or wrongness of divine actions. There is undoubtedly a mystery here but the creature must recognize his fundamental difference from the Creator (illustrated by the potter's power over the clay). This whole section is designed to demonstrate the sovereign freedom of God.

c. The real cause of Israel's rejection (ix. 30–x. 21)

Paul next shows that God is absolved from the responsibility for Israel's rejection. They themselves are at fault because they sought a righteousness through self-effort. This kind of righteousness is contrasted with that received by faith, which is open to all who call upon the name of the Lord. Jews, therefore, have an equal opportunity with Gentiles and cannot charge God with rejecting them. Nor is it a question of the Jews not having heard, for in that case they might have had an excuse. But the scriptures bear abundant witness to the opportunities they have rejected.

d. The partial character of the rejection and hopes of restoration (xi. 1–36)

In spite of the previous adverse statements there are mitigating circumstances for the rejection has never been total. There has always been a remnant chosen by grace and it is with this remnant that the hope of the future lies. In any case the fall of Israel has prompted the conversion of the Gentiles, through whose agency they will themselves be restored. This is illustrated by the olive-tree allegory. But there is no place for Gentile boasting for God intends the full restoration of Israel. Such thoughts as these call forth in the apostle's mind an expression of amazement at the inscrutable wisdom of God.

IV. PRACTICAL EXHORTATIONS (xii. 1–xv. 13)

In this section of the Epistle, Paul shows the application of the principle of righteousness to practical duties.

a. General duties (xii. 1–21)

Christians are to learn the duty of dedicated lives (xii. 1, 2), to develop a sober estimate of themselves (xii. 3–8) and to cultivate a regard for the claims of others and live peacefully as far as possible with all (xii. 9–21).

b. Civic and social duties (xiii. 1–14)

The Christian's attitude towards the State must be one of loyalty and orderliness (xiii. 1–7), while his duty towards his neighbour must be conditioned by the law of love (xiii. 8–10). Right conduct is particularly important in view of the approaching day of the Lord (xiii. 11–14).

c. A special problem (xiv. 1–xv. 13)

The problem of what foods are permissible for a Christian is singled out because of its special relevance to the contemporary situation, although Paul's enunciation of the principle of toleration (let the strong bear with the failings of the weak) has a universal application. Personal convictions are secondary to the spiritual welfare of the kingdom of God since full glory to God can be maintained only where there is harmony.

V. CONCLUSION (xv. 14–xvi. 27)

The apostle gives an explanation of the motives which led to the writing of the Epistle and then gives a general outline of his plans. He hopes to visit the readers, but only for a while since his real objective is mission work in Spain. He appears to have some misgivings about his Jerusalem visit for he makes a special plea for their supporting prayers.

After a list of greetings unparalleled for length in any other Pauline Epistle (xvi. 1–16), the apostle gives a parting warning against false teachers who cause dissensions (xvi. 17–19), adds a few personal greetings from his companions, during which he allows his amanuensis Tertius to express his own (xvi. 21–23), and then concludes with a benediction and a magnificent doxology (xvi. 24–27).

ADDITIONAL NOTES

395. [4] W. G. Kümmel (*INT*, 1965, p. 219), in favouring a mixed congregation, rightly points out that Rom. ix–xi would be incomprehensible if no Jewish Christians were involved.

397. [2] In a recent article J. R. Richards (*NTS*, 13, 1966, pp. 211–230) argues that Rom. i–xv preceded the writing of 1 Corinthians and was written from Ephesus. He bases this view on a comparison of the two Epistles, in which he examines common words and expressions and also doctrinal parallels and concludes that 1 Corinthians is best understood if placed after Romans. This clearly affects the date of Romans, since it affects the generally accepted understanding of Paul's movements. Richards argues that Paul suddenly changed his plans after writing Romans and delayed longer at Ephesus than he originally intended. The cause of the sudden change was the death of Claudius (whom he understands as ὁ κατέχων, 2 Thes. ii. 7). According to this theory 1 Corinthians was issued almost immediately after Romans.

399. [3] Cf. K. H. Rengstorf, 'Paulus und die älteste römische Christenheit' (*Studia Evangelica*, II, 1964, pp. 447–464).

399. [5] E. Schweizer has advanced the view that Romans, because it presents God's relationship to His own people, shows the Gentile mission in relation to the Old Testament *Heilsgeschichte* (*Ev Th*, XXII, 1962, pp. 105–107). A similar view is supported by M. Baillet (*RB*, LXVIII, 1961, pp. 199 ff.) by appealing to the evidence from Qumran. The apostle clearly writes against an Old Testament background and his purpose must be related to this.

There is much to be said for the view that the major focal point of the Epistle is ix–xi rather than i–viii (cf. B. Noack, *StTh*, 19, 1965, pp. 155–166; S. Neill, *The Interpretation of the New Testament*, 1964, pp. 183 f.). It is easier to relate ix–xi to a specific historical situation than i–viii. The problem of Israel's position in a Church which had become predominantly Gentile was a real one. According to J. Knox (*JBL*, LXXXIII, 1964, pp. 1–11), Paul did not believe that he had to preach to all nations before the *parousia* (as J. Munck suggested). It is important to recognize that Paul did not see the Roman church as a missionary sphere, but as a base for further missionary operations (cf. G. Schrenk, 'Der Römerbrief als Missions-dokument', *Studien zu Paulus, AbThANT*, 26, 1954, pp. 81 ff.). This occasion must be borne in mind in discussions of the purpose. Cf. N. Krieger, *Nov.Test.*, 3 (1959), pp. 146–148.

E. Trocmé (*NTS*, 7, 1961, pp. 148–153) points out that Romans deals with a situation which must have occurred whenever a new church was founded in an area where Jewish Christians formed part of the Church. The type of argumentation in this Epistle would help to convince new believers that the new community was as capable as Judaism in sustaining them in their new moral life. For various theories of the polemical purpose in Romans, cf. W. G. Kümmel, *INT* (1965), p. 221. Kümmel considers that all that can be said with certainty is that Paul opposes Jewish teaching of salvation and antinomian charges against his message. A. Roosen (*Studia Evangelica*, II, 1964, pp. 465–471) argues that Romans is essentially a proclamation of the gospel, accompanied by a letter in the form of an appendix.

G. Bornkamm (*ABR*, 11, 1963, pp. 2–14) considers this Epistle to be Paul's last will and testament, since he regards Philemon and Philippians as earlier than Romans, and Colossians, Ephesians and the Pastoral Epistles as non-Pauline.

403. [1] For an attempt to identify these false teachers as Gnostics, cf. W. Schmithals, *StTh*, 12 (1958), pp. 51 ff. This writer is a strong contender for the theory of Gnostic influence in several Pauline churches (cf. his theory for Corinthians, pp. 422 f.; Galatians, p. 467; Philippians, p. 543).

403. [3] W. G. Kümmel (*INT*, 1965, p. 225) rejects Goodspeed's theory.

404. [3] Cf. Kümmel (*op. cit.*, pp. 224 ff.) for the view that Rom. xvi is integral to the Epistle.

406. [1] For a more detailed yet concise survey of the textual evidence for the last two chapters of Romans, cf. F. F. Bruce, *The Epistle of Paul to the Romans* (*TNT*, 1963), pp. 25–31. For an older monograph on the subject, cf. R. Schumacher, *Die beiden letzten Kapitel des Römerbriefs* (1929).

406. [2] For literature on the doxology, cf. J. Dupont, *Revue Bénédictine*, 58 (1948), pp. 1 ff.

CHAPTER TWELVE

THE CORINTHIAN EPISTLES

I. THE CHURCH IN CORINTH

The city of Corinth was set in a peculiarly advantageous situation. Not only did the main land route between East and West pass through it, but several sea routes converged upon its two harbours. It consequently became very prosperous and was honoured by being chosen the capital of the province of Achaia and the seat of the Roman proconsul. Although surpassed in culture by Athens, it was nevertheless proud of its political status and mental acuteness. It was never famed for its contribution to the arts or philosophy, but it became infamous for vice and particularly licentiousness. Its name, in fact, became a by-word for profligacy. This was not helped by the fact that Corinth was the centre for worship of the goddess Aphrodite, whose worship is known, at least in earlier times, to have been of a very immoral kind. Its population was cosmopolitan, comprising Romans, Greeks, Orientals and Jews. It was thus a strategic centre for the gospel.

The establishment of the church is related in Acts xviii. Paul came to Corinth on his second missionary journey, after a not too successful visit to Athens. He made his home with two exiled Jews from Rome, Aquila and Priscilla, and began his evangelistic work in the synagogue. After a short time, owing to the opposition of the Jews, he turned to the Gentiles, making use of the house of Titius Justus and this resulted in many believing. There were therefore both Jews and Gentiles in the Corinthian church. Paul appears to have worked there for a year and a half (Acts xviii. 11), and during this period was brought before the proconsul Gallio, who refused to take action against him. This virtually secured him from further attack from the Jews during his stay in the province. On leaving Corinth Paul proceeded via Ephesus to Antioch. The many problems which surround his subsequent relations with the Corinthian church will form the subject of our next inquiry, but we can at least be certain that he had no communications with them until the period of his three years' mission work in Ephesus during his third missionary journey.

In such an atmosphere of moral laxity and intellectual pride the

421

Corinthian church was bound to be troubled with many problems arising from the impact of Christianity on its pagan environment.[1] This background can in many places be traced in the Corinthian correspondence. Many of the Christians were as yet undisciplined extremists and needed strong handling. None of the apostle's churches seems to have given him such grave cause for concern as this, for these Christians were setting a poor example to their pagan neighbours. They also did not take too kindly to the apostle's authority, no doubt because of a false estimate of their own importance. The letters preserved for us (1 and 2 Corinthians) are invaluable for the light they throw, not only on the practical problems of a primitive community but also on the personality of the great apostle.

II. PAUL'S OPPONENTS AT CORINTH

In order to understand the background of Paul's relationship with the Corinthians, it is necessary to ascertain as far as possible the identity of those who were opposed to the apostle at Corinth. Any information on this subject will clearly be invaluable in reconstructing the occasion of each of his Epistles to this church. The older view of F. C. Baur,[2] that the opponents were representatives of Jewish Christianity, was based on his presupposition of a fundamental clash between the Jewish and Gentile sections of the church. Although Baur's presuppositions have been rejected, there have been others more recently who have maintained that the opponents were Jewish.[3]

It is the contention of W. Schmithals[4] that the opponents of Paul were Jewish Christian Gnostics. This writer sees Gnosticism in many New Testament churches,[5] but this is on the basis that Gnosis is pre-Pauline and pre-Christian, a view which confuses Gnostic reflections with developed Gnosticism. R. M. Wilson[6] has argued that parallels

[1] Cf. W. R. Halliday, *The Pagan Background of Early Christianity* (1925), and E. M. Blaiklock's monograph, *The Christian in Pagan Society*[2] (1956).

[2] Cf. *Tübinger Zeitschrift für Theologie*, 4 (1831), pp. 61 ff., cited in W. G. Kümmel, *Das Neue Testament* (1958), pp. 158 ff.

[3] Cf. E. Bammel, *ThZ*, XI (1955), p. 412. Cf. D. W. Oostendorp, *Another Jesus: A Gospel of Jewish Christian Superiority in II Corinthians* (1967).

[4] *Die Gnosis in Korinth. Eine Untersuchung zu den Korintherbriefen* (1956).

[5] Cf. his views on Romans (p. 420), Galatians (p. 467), Philippians (p. 543).

[6] Cf. his *Gnosis and the New Testament* (1968), pp. 51 ff. Cf. also his criticism of Schmithals, *SJT*, 15 (1962), pp. 324–327. H. J. Schoeps (*Paul*, p. 78) dismisses Schmithals' idea in a brief footnote.

in terminology and thought between New Testament books and developed Gnosticism are not sufficient to conclude for a first-century Gnosticism. He pleads for a distinction between Gnosis and Gnosticism. It is certain, therefore, that there can be no question of thoroughgoing Gnosticism, although some of the characteristics of the opponents were similar to those found in later Gnosticism. This criticism also goes for U. Wilckens[1] who argues that certain expressions used by Paul in the Corinthian letters have infiltrated from Gnosticism, in which case Pauline Christianity would be indebted to it. But again the evidence will not support such a hypothesis. It is not necessary, for instance, to suppose that because both Paul and the Gnostics speak of Wisdom (Sophia) that the former is indebted to the latter.[2]

Not all scholars treat the opponents contested in 1 Corinthians as the same as those behind 2 Corinthians.[3] The view that the opponents in 2 Corinthians were Jewish Christians with Hellenistic propaganda techniques has recently been proposed,[4] but if this were so their syncretism would not allow the description of them as Gnostics. A more likely view is that the opponents were not prepared to accept the full gospel preached by Paul. They may have believed in Christ crucified, but not Christ risen. They may also have added some kind of ecstatic experiences which would nullify Paul's gospel.[5] W. G. Kümmel[6] sees in the opponents behind 2 Corinthians, not Judaizers but Palestinians who were claiming superiority over Paul in respect of contact with the earthly Jesus, their Jewish descent, spiritual gifts and letters of com-

[1] *Weisheit und Torheit* (1959).

[2] Cf. K. Prümm's criticisms of Wilckens' theory, *ZKT*, 87 (1965), pp. 399–442; 88 (1966), pp. 1–50. C. K. Barrett (*BJRL*, XLVI, 1964, pp. 269–297) calls the theory an oversimplification. Cf. also N. A. Dahl ('Paul and the Church at Corinth in 1 Cor. i. 10–iv. 21', *Christian History and Interpretation*, 1967, pp. 313–335), who sees no need to appeal to Gnosticism in discussing Paul's opponents.

[3] Cf. C. K. Barrett, *op. cit.*

[4] Cf. D. Georgi, *Die Gegner des Paulus im 2 Korintherbrief* (1964).

[5] Cf. W. Bieder (*ThZ*, XVII, 1961, pp. 319–333), who suggests also some element of spiritism, hence Paul's reference to servants of Satan (2 Cor. xi. 14f.). W. G. Kümmel (*INT*, 1965, p. 202) considers that Paul sees basically one opposing front, i.e. the Gnostic, but is against the view that all questions dealt with in the Corinthian Epistles are influenced by Gnostic presuppositions.

[6] W. G. Kümmel, *INT* (1965), p. 209. Cf. G. Friedrich, *Festschrift O. Michel* (1963), pp. 181–215, for the view that the opponents were *Ekstatiker*. C. K. Barrett (*op. cit.*, pp. 1–12) connects the opposition specifically with Peter.

mendation. Their opposition to Paul may then have been strengthened by Gnostic elements. Kümmel's suggestion, apart from the last point, illuminates many features of this Epistle.

If the source of opposition to Paul at Corinth cannot be precisely determined, it is undeniable that he had to deal with various groups of Christians with tendencies which were leading to an inadequate view of Christianity. Among these may be noted such groups as libertines, who had misunderstood Christian freedom, ascetics who had adopted too rigid an approach to Christian behaviour, and ecstatics who were allowing their spiritual experiences to lead to disorderliness. Not all these may be described as opponents to Paul, but he saw that their policies would result in a contradiction of his gospel.

III. PAUL'S RELATIONSHIP WITH THE CORINTHIANS

It is difficult to be certain of the apostle's relationship with this church during and subsequent to his work at Ephesus, as many problems have to be considered. But the most widely held hypothesis will first be outlined to form a basis for the subsequent discussions.

(1.) Paul wrote a letter, known now as the 'previous letter', in which he warned the Corinthians not to associate with immoral persons (1 Cor. v. 9), but this appears to have been misunderstood (1 Cor. v. 10, 11).

(2.) At the same time as hearing of their misunderstanding of his previous letter Paul heard reports of certain disorders in the Corinthian church from the household of Chloe. He possibly then received a delegation from the church in the persons of Stephanas, Fortunatus and Achaicus who brought a number of questions which needed answering. As a result he sent 1 Corinthians.

(3.) Timothy, who was apparently not sent with this letter but who had proceeded to Macedonia with Erastus (Acts xix. 22), may never have reached Corinth, for he is not mentioned in the body of 2 Corinthians but is linked with Paul in the salutation.

(4.) Paul probably heard other adverse reports and decided to pay a visit which was a painful experience, and from which he was obliged to withdraw in haste (known as the 'painful visit').

(5.) On his return he sent a letter 'out of much affliction and anguish of heart' (2 Cor. ii. 4) in an attempt to rectify the matter. This letter, which was probably carried by Titus, is known as the 'sorrowful letter'.

6. Paul had in the meantime left Ephesus and was awaiting the arrival of Titus at Troas with news of the reception of the 'sorrowful letter'. He failed to meet him there, but after he had moved to Macedonia Titus arrived with good news of the Corinthian situation.

7. Paul wrote 2 Corinthians to express his relief at the success of his severe letter and Titus' mission.

8. He later spent the winter at Corinth prior to proceeding by way of Macedonia to Jerusalem with the collection for the poverty-stricken Christians.

If this reconstruction is correct it means that the apostle paid three visits and wrote at least four letters to the Corinthian church. But there are several problems in interpreting the data and these must next be considered.

a. The 'previous letter'

It has been cogently argued by many scholars that the section 2 Corinthians vi. 14–vii. 1 breaks the connection of thought and should therefore be regarded as an interpolated fragment from another genuine epistle. Since it deals with the problem of the believer's relationship with the unbeliever and since in 1 Corinthians v. 9 the apostle writes, 'I wrote to you in my letter not to be mixed up with fornicators', it is an attractive hypothesis that the 2 Corinthians passage is in mind. Moreover, 1 Corinthians v. 10, 11 shows clearly that Paul's letter has been misunderstood, and it is at least conceivable that some might understand from 2 Corinthians vi. 14–vii. 1 that Paul is advising believers to have nothing to do with unbelievers.

It must further be admitted that 2 Corinthians vi. 13 ('be ye also enlarged') shows an excellent connection with vii. 2 ('Open your hearts to us'), which supports the idea that vi. 14–vii. 1 is an interruption in the sequence of thought. Yet before concluding that the section is an interpolation the investigator must be satisfied that this is not another example of the apostle's tendency to digress. The change from vi. 13 to vi. 14 is unquestionably abrupt and different in tone from the preceding section. Such unexpected digression would be unpardonable in a treatise but is not altogether improbable in a letter. If the Epistle was composed at several sittings, it might well be that Paul paused for a while after vi. 13, and upon resuming the letter dwells on the problems of the Christian's relationship with unbelievers before continuing where he had left off.

This explanation is at least more probable than attempting to find a connection with the preceding context. It has been suggested[1] that vi. 14 ff. gives a specific explanation of what Paul means by the words of verse 1, 'We entreat also that ye receive not the grace of God in vain', but the connection is not self-apparent. If on the other hand the section is regarded as a part of the 'previous letter', the problem arises why it was ever inserted in its present position. It is difficult to believe that anyone would intentionally place it after vi. 13 in view of the absence of any clear connection of thought in the context and the only recourse is to suppose it to have got there accidentally.[2] But a theory of interpolation into the middle of an epistle without any supporting MS evidence is not without considerable difficulties. Nevertheless the scantiness of our present knowledge of the processes of preservation of the Pauline Epistles allows for the possibility of such an hypothesis. It can neither be conclusively proved, nor emphatically denied.*

Assuming that the 'previous letter' is probably now lost, the gist of its contents may nevertheless be inferred from 1 Corinthians v. 9–13. The apostle had evidently issued a warning to the Corinthians to maintain a clear line of demarcation between their heathen neighbours and themselves. Their city was renowned for immorality and the problem of the Christian's attitude towards his pagan environment was particularly acute. It would seem that Paul had urged them not to associate with immoral men and they had misunderstood him to mean that Christians should have no dealings at all with non-Christians. In 1 Corinthians v. 11 the apostle clarifies the position by showing that association with immoral Christians was in his mind. It is probable that the strong injunction of 1 Corinthians v. 13 ('Drive out the wicked person from among you') was not stated in the 'previous letter', but Paul has since seen reason to be more specific and in fact more severe in his advice.

b. 1 Corinthians

This is the most business-like of all Paul's Epistles. He has a number of subjects with which he intends to deal and he sets about them in a most orderly manner. He has two main sources of information about the Corinthian situation and it is most likely that he sets about his task in

---

[1] Cf. A. Plummer, 2 Corinthians (ICC, 1915), ad loc.
[2] Cf. R. P. C. Hanson's opinion, 2 Corinthians (1954), pp. 21–22. See p. 437 n.1.

the order in which he had been informed about the various problems. At the commencement of the letter he deals with the contentions about which he has heard from the household of Chloe (1 Cor. i. 11). It is only at the conclusion of the Epistle that he mentions the delegation of Stephanas, Fortunatus and Achaicus (xvi. 17). It is a fair assumption that Paul began the letter on the receipt of reports from Chloe's household not only about the contentions but also about the case of incest and the Christian appeal to heathen law-courts, all of which Paul deals with in the first six chapters of the Epistle. It may well be, although it cannot be regarded as certain, that he had not at that time received the letter written to him by the Corinthians, which was probably brought by the three delegates. At all events Paul deals with such practical issues as marriage, meats offered to idols, disorders in public worship, spiritual gifts and the resurrection. It is not certain whether the problem of the resurrection was raised by the Corinthians themselves or was brought to Paul's notice by someone else, but the other themes appear to be Paul's answers to their queries (in each case he introduces a fresh subject with the characteristic 'now concerning . . .'). In 1 Corinthians iv. 17–21 Paul refers to the movements of Timothy and tells the Corinthians that he will remind them of what Paul has already taught them. He also makes clear that he hopes to visit them shortly. This is reiterated in chapter xvi. It is also evident that the apostle at the time of writing has the collection scheme for the saints at Jerusalem much upon his mind and hopes to stir up the support of the Corinthians by this letter (xvi. 1–4).

c. The 'painful visit'

There are three possible views regarding this visit: (i) that it did not happen at all, (ii) that it happened before 1 Corinthians was written, or (iii) that it happened after 1 Corinthians, as outlined in the scheme above. These three alternatives will be briefly considered.

(i) *That it did not happen.* This view depends on a particular interpretation of the main evidence from 2 Corinthians on which the theory of a 'painful visit' is based. The data are found in 2 Corinthians xii. 14 ('Behold, the third time I am ready to come to you') and xiii. 1, 2 ('This is the third time I am coming to you . . . I have said beforehand . . . as when I was present the second time', RV). These statements would seem to imply that two visits preceded the sending of 2 Corinthians (which means there was at least one not recorded in the Acts), but those who deny this unrecorded visit take 2 Corinthians xii. 14 and xiii. 1, 2 to refer not to visits but to intentions, as if Paul really meant, 'This is the third time I am on the point of coming to you'.[1] But this is unlikely (1) because it is not the most natural interpretation of the words,[2] and (2) because in 2 Corinthians ii Paul defends himself against the charge of fickleness, and this charge would hardly be lessened if the readers knew that he had three times been on the point of coming to them.[3]

Relevant to this discussion is the meaning of 2 Corinthians ii. 1 ('But I determined this for myself, that I would not come again to you with sorrow', RV). It is generally supposed that 'again' implies that Paul had already once visited them with sorrow. But those who deny the visit less probably connect the word 'again' with 'come', and understand Paul to mean that when he does come again he does not wish it to be with sorrow. The most probable conclusion, therefore, is that Paul paid a painful visit to Corinth before writing 2 Corinthians. But the question remains, When?

(ii) *That it happened before* 1 *Corinthians.* This is most improbable because of the silence of 1 Corinthians concerning it,[4] for it can hardly be supposed that Paul passed over his sorrowful memories when writing 1 Corinthians only to revive them when 2 Corinthians was written. There is, further, no adequate purpose for such a visit. Had he made it he

---

[1] Or else it is assumed that the first visit was actual and the second intended but not carried out (see J. H. Kennedy's criticism of this, *The Second and Third Epistles of St. Paul to the Corinthians*, 1900, pp. 6 ff.). Kennedy can see no purpose in Paul's introduction of a supposed visit into the argument of xiii. 1 ff. and xii. 14 ff. J. Sickenberger, *Die beiden Briefe des hl. Paulus an die Kor. und Röm.*[4] (1932), pp. 158, 163, takes the view that Paul changed his plans for the second visit owing to the prevailing circumstances (cf. Meinertz's criticism, *Einleitung in das Neue Testament* (1950, p. 102 n.)).

[2] Most of the older commentators considered that the grammar suggests intentions rather than visits on the strength of the ἑτοίμως of 2 Cor. xii. 14. But this is difficult in view of the 'second time' mentioned in xiii. 2 which cannot be construed to mean an intended visit, but must on this hypothesis be regarded as a hypothetical visit (i.e. 'as though I were present the second time').

[3] F. C. Baur, *The Apostle of Jesus Christ*[2] (1876), pp. 302 ff., took the view that the whole Epistle was designed to defend Paul against this charge of changeableness and therefore he refers to his threefold intention not as a sign of unreliability but rather the reverse. There were three witnesses of his resolution. But few modern scholars are convinced by this line of reasoning.

[4] Feine–Behm, *Einleitung*[11] (1956, p. 158), point out that in 1 Cor. there is an absence of that tension which the 'sorrowful visit' presupposes. There is no question whether Paul's apostolic authority would be heeded.*

would not have needed to write the 'previous note' about immoral persons (1 Cor. v. 9).

(iii) *That it happened subsequent to* 1 *Corinthians.* This is the view held by the majority of recent scholars, who regard it as the prelude to the 'sorrowful letter'. There is some difference of opinion over the time and place of its dispatch. Some regard it as having taken place from Ephesus just before the riot, while others think it occurred as a break in Paul's journey to Macedonia, and still others from Macedonia itself. The first seems the most probable although it is impossible to dogmatize. It is a question of importance only in the attempt to reconstruct the timing of events between 1 and 2 Corinthians (it affects, for instance, Duncan's Ephesian reconstruction).[1]

d. The 'sorrowful letter'

In the tentative reconstruction given above it was assumed that there were three letters preceding 2 Corinthians, but this view was not the traditional explanation of 2 Corinthians ii. 4. Before the postulation of an intervening letter it was always assumed that the sorrowful letter was 1 Corinthians.

(i) *Could the 'sorrowful letter' be* 1 *Corinthians?* It is generally thought to be highly improbable that the terms 'much affliction', 'anguish of heart' and 'many tears' could have described Paul's state of mind when writing 1 Corinthians. The language suggests a time of intense emotional strain which does not appear very evident in that Epistle. Certain parts of it no doubt caused him some pain to write, as for instance the passages dealing with moral disorders and lawsuits (1 Cor. v–vi), although his words are relatively restrained. If 1 Corinthians is in mind, the apostle must be giving a kind of flashback to his subjective reactions when writing that Epistle, although at the time he had so carefully veiled them. Furthermore, 2 Corinthians vii. 8 makes clear that the letter under review not only made the readers sorry but made the apostle regret ever sending it. It is difficult to believe that he had any

[1] Duncan suggests that on reaching Troas Paul spent considerable time there, as he had previously had insufficient opportunity to evangelize the district (cf. 2 Cor. ii. 12). From there he paid a fleeting visit to Corinth. But this involves a period of eighteen months between 1 and 2 Corinthians (see discussion on date, pp. 64 ff.), which is not the most natural understanding of Acts xx. 1 (*St. Paul's Ephesian Ministry* (1929), pp. 219 ff.). T. W. Manson suggested that Paul's route was Corinth (the 'painful visit'), Macedonia, the Troad, Macedonia (*BJRL,* XXVI, 1942, pp. 327 ff.).

such regrets over the sending of 1 Corinthians, although it cannot be pronounced entirely impossible since our data are not enough to lead to certainty. Some have maintained that a statement like 1 Corinthians v. 5 in which the offender is to be delivered to Satan would be quite enough to cause him regret, especially if he has now learned of the offender's repentance and of his excessive sorrow as a result of the punishment meted out to him. Now this presupposes that the offenders of 1 Corinthians v and 2 Corinthians ii are the same person, but modern scholars generally reject this identification on the grounds that the offender of 2 Corinthians ii seems to have committed a personal offence against the apostle (cf. verses 5 and 10). Nevertheless there is always the bare possibility that it is the same offender who is in mind in both Epistles, especially as this identification seems to have been assumed without question by Christian interpreters until comparatively recent times.[1]

(ii) *Is the 'sorrowful letter' partially preserved in 2 Corinthians x–xiii?* If we assume that the modern view is correct that 1 Corinthians is distinct from the 'sorrowful letter', are we to regard the latter as lost? Many scholars[2] believe that it has been partially preserved in 2 Corinthians x–xiii and the grounds for this theory must now be assessed.

1. The change of tone. In the former part of the Epistle (chapters i–ix) the apostle writes with considerable relief over what he has heard of the change of attitude on the part of the Corinthians. There is an absence of hostility, and friendly relations seem to have been restored. But the latter chapters are written in remonstrance and self-defence. It is therefore claimed that these two sections are incongruous, a claim, incidentally, first made as early as the eighteenth century by Semler, who considered chapters x–xiii to represent a later Epistle. It was not until a century later that Hausrath[3] proposed the view that x–xiii preceded i–ix, but this view has since been gathering momentum. Its best advocate among English scholars has been J. H. Kennedy.[4]

---

[1] A. Plummer (2 *Corinthians*, p. xxviii) cites among others Alford, Bernard, Denney, Meyer, B. Weiss and Zahn as supporting this identification.

[2] Cf. Plummer, *op. cit.*, p. xxviii, for authorities supporting this theory up to 1915. Since then cf. especially R. H. Strachan, *The Second Epistle to the Corinthians* (1935).*

[3] *Der Vier-Capitelbrief des Paulus an die Korinther* (1870).

[4] J. H. Kennedy, *The Second and Third Epistles to the Corinthians* (1900), claimed not only that a marked change of tone but also a distinct break in syntax separated the two parts, cf. pp. 94 ff.

The problem arises whether the apostle, having already expressed his happiness over the success of an earlier and severer letter and having during the course of these expressions of relief given some hint of the regret he experienced after writing the severer letter, would have closed his further Epistle with such unparalleled invective in self-defence as is found in 2 Corinthians x–xiii. Many scholars consider it to be improbable, but the contrast between the two sections must not be over-stressed.[1] There are in the former section various hints of still prevalent opposition to the apostle's teaching and authority. In i. 17 ff. he argues strongly in self-defence, while in ii. 6 he speaks of the offender being punished by the majority, implying the existence of a minority who probably did not agree with Paul's authoritative pronouncement in the case. There are many who are still mishandling the Word of God (ii. 17, iv. 2–5), and there are those who are priding themselves on their position (v. 12) and who consider the apostle to be beside himself (v. 13). These data are enough to show that chapters i–ix do not represent the Corinthians as being wholly on Paul's side. His relief was occasioned by the response of the majority, which was undoubtedly a big forward step, but he must still deal with the dangerous minority.

This hypothesis that the former section of the Epistle with its conciliatory attitude was designed for the majority and the latter section with its heated self-defence was designed for the minority has, however, been strongly criticized. It has been argued that there is no hint that Paul is making such a transition, so how could the readers be expected to differentiate? The apostle's words would have conveyed to them an altogether unexpected invective after his earlier attempts to conciliate. Would this not have aggravated their antagonism towards him?[2] In view of this it is thought to be psychologically impossible to regard the two sections as belonging to the same letter. Yet these objections make insufficient allowance for two factors. The Corinthian Christians who had taken to heart Paul's earlier reproofs would be in no doubt as to the

[1] Cf. R. A. Knox, *A New Testament Commentary for English Readers*, vol. II (1954), p. 175, suggests that chapters vii–ix are in greater contrast to the rest of the Epistle than x–xiii are to i–ix. Most of the Epistle in his view reflects disappointment and only the central part real confidence. R. V. G. Tasker, *2 Corinthians* (1958), pp. 32 f., suggests that the severity of x–xiii is modified by a playful strain that lessens the apparent sharpness.
[2] Cf. Moffatt, *ILNT*, pp. 119 ff. Peake, *Critical Introduction to the New Testament* (1909), pp. 36, 37, finds this an insuperable difficulty.

application of the various sections of the Epistle. They themselves would have to deal with the minority and would welcome a strong assertion of the apostle's authority. The ending of the Epistle, which could not possibly apply to the loyal section, would supply that section with much needed support in its own loyal stand.[1] The other factor is the inconclusive character of any appeal to psychological probability in this case, for it is not unknown for the apostle to reserve strong words of condemnation until the end. He does the same in the Philippian letter, where the change of tone in chapter iii has also led to theories of the composite character of the Epistle without due regard for the apostle's psychological make-up. He would naturally warmly commend the loyal section before bringing in criticisms of his continuous opponents.[2] It would have been a blunder of the first magnitude to have reversed the order.

Another view of the change of tone is that Paul received more disquieting news after the first section was completed.[3] This may have happened but no indication of any source of information other than Titus is given in the latter section. Nor can Lietzmann's suggestion[4] that

---

[1] It cannot be supposed that this treatment is unwisely isolating a minority (cf. T. Henshaw, *New Testament Literature*, p. 244), for whenever minorities need reproving they are bound to be brought into prominence. On the other hand, the stronger tones of chapters x–xiii may have been intended for all of them, lest even those who had come round to the apostle's point of view should again dispute his authority (cf. R. V. G. Tasker, *2 Corinthians*, 1958, p. 32). It should be noted that x. 2 seems to make clear that the subsequent passage is intended for 'some' who are distinguished from the community as a whole (cf. also verse 12).

[2] R. Heard (*INT*, p. 192) draws attention to the fact that in some of Paul's other letters there is an evident determination not to close without vindicating his personal authority against his opponents (e.g. 1 Cor. iv. 14–21; Gal. vi. 12–17; 2 Thes. iii. 6–15; 2 Tim. iv. 14–18).

[3] Munck, *op. cit.*, pp. 171 f., who holds that x–xiii is later than i–ix but who nevertheless admits that the interval between them must have been so short that they may after all be parts of one letter, thinks that i–vii looks back to a time before the arrival of the Jewish 'apostles' mentioned in x–xiii, of whose arrival at Corinth he has only recently heard. Yet the real opponents in x–xiii are not these Jewish apostles but the Corinthians themselves. Munck's view that x–xiii was later is not new, however, for it was previously suggested by Drescher, Krenkel and Weber (cf. Plummer's criticism, *op. cit.*, pp. xxviii, xxix).

[4] *Die Briefe des Apostels Paulus an die Korinther*[4] (1933), *ad loc.*; cf. Moffatt's criticism (*ILNT*, p. 123). The idea that the break between ix. 15 and x. 1 indicates a dictation-pause is supported by E. Stange, 'Diktierpausen in den Paulusbriefen', *ZNTW* (1917–18), pp. 109–117.

a sleepless night would have been enough to bring about the change be taken too seriously, for while we know Paul to have been a man of moods we have no warrant for supposing that he allowed his feelings so to run away with him that he turned his irritability into such devastating invective. It is preferable on psychological grounds to suppose that the apostle intended from the start to reserve his strongest words until the end. Or it may even be that he was suddenly possessed with misgivings about the genuineness of their change of attitude and decided to end on a firmer note.

2. The references to the apostle's visit. There are three pairs of passages which are reckoned to support the contention that chapters x–xiii preceded chapters i–ix.[1] They are quoted in parallel columns to facilitate comparison.

'Being in readiness to avenge all disobedience, when your obedience shall be fulfilled.' (x. 6, RV)	'For to this end also did I write, that I might know the proof of you, whether ye are obedient in all things.' (ii. 9, RV)
'If I come again, I will not spare.' (xiii. 2, RV)	'To spare you I forbare to come unto Corinth.' (i. 23, RV)
'For this cause I write these things while absent, that I may not when present deal sharply.' (xiii. 10, RV)	'And I wrote this very thing, lest, when I came, I should have sorrow.' (ii. 3, RV)

It is evident that the references in the latter part of the Epistle are all forward looking, whereas those in the earlier section are all in the past. If the chronological order of these parts is reversed both groups of references could allude to the same visit. There is much to be said for this line of argument, but it cannot be considered conclusive, for the three pairs of references are capable of an alternative interpretation. In comparing xiii. 2 with i. 23 it should be noted that in i. 23 Paul is concluding his explanation of his altered plans following upon his

---

[1] J. H. Kennedy, *op. cit.*, p. 135, placed greatest weight on this line of evidence in dispensing with the traditional view of the unity of 2 Corinthians. Cf. also K. Lake, *The Earlier Epistles of St. Paul*[2] (1927), pp. 159 ff.*

'painful visit', while xiii. 2 refers to his intended severity towards those who are still recalcitrant and might with good reason anticipate the visit he intends paying from Macedonia. A comparison of ii. 3 and xiii. 10 would certainly support the suggested hypothesis since ii. 3 ff. refers to the previous 'sorrowful letter', while xiii. 10 is still present. But since in both parts of the Epistle Paul speaks of a visit still future, and therefore subsequent to the 'painful visit', it is as reasonable to suppose that ii. 3 refers to a letter now lost and xiii. 10 to the present letter (i.e. 2 Corinthians). Under this latter alternative Paul is merely repeating his wish to come peaceably. There is also no obvious reason for placing x. 6 before ii. 9 since the context of the latter does not suggest that their obedience is now complete. If, however, in ii. 9 the apostle is saying that in his former letter he was seeking proof of their obedience, it is reasonable to assume that the answer he received was not fully satisfactory and that he still looks forward to its completion in x. 6.[1]

Another problem arises from the apostle's geographical position. In x. 16 Paul expresses his intention to preach the gospel 'in lands beyond' the Corinthians' own district, which is thought to be more intelligible if Paul was at the time of writing at Ephesus and was looking westwards (as he was when he sent the 'sorrowful letter') than if he was in Macedonia as he clearly was when writing chapters i–ix (cf. ii. 13, vii. 5, ix. 2). There is force in this argument, but unless we are to be overliteral in our interpretation of Paul's words it cannot overturn the unity of the Epistle. It may, however, corroborate if other evidence is strong enough to support the contention that x–xiii were written before i–ix and were written from Ephesus.[2]

3. The different attitude towards self-commendation. It is alleged that in iii. 1 ('Are we beginning again to commend ourselves?' RV) the apostle deprecates self-commendation, whereas in chapters x–xiii he

[1] Cf. A. Menzies' discussion on the whole of 2 Corinthians as dealing with the promised visit (*The Second Epistle of the Apostle Paul to the Corinthians*, 1912, pp. xxxvii–xlii).

[2] Another consideration which cannot be said to support this hypothesis is the incongruity of xii. 14 and xiii. 1 (where a 'third visit' is mentioned) when placed before i. 15 where Paul explains why he did not pay a 'second visit' (cf. W. M. Ramsay, *Expositor*, VI, iii, p. 240). Of rather more weight is J. H. Kennedy's suggestion that if chapters x–xiii are detached from 2 Corinthians the collection section (viii, ix) would then close the Epistle and this would compare favourably with the reference at the close of 1 Corinthians (*op. cit.*, p. 136). But there is no obvious reason why the same procedure must be followed in both Epistles.

is at great pains to commend himself.[1] In v. 12 the apostle definitely asserts, 'We do not again commend ourselves to you'. Since in both of these references from the earlier section of the Epistle the word 'again' (πάλιν) is used, it is an attractive suggestion that Paul is thinking of the wording of x–xiii sent at an earlier date. But iii. 1 is clearly an allusion to the practice of some of these Corinthian opponents of Paul to arm themselves with letters of commendation, a practice which Paul himself strongly deprecates. Indeed he sees no need for it since the Corinthians themselves are his commendation. The same thought is present in v. 12. But in chapters x–xiii he addresses those who still oppose him and dispute his credentials. For these a different approach is clearly necessary.

It will be seen that although these reasons for allocating chapters x–xiii to an earlier period in Paul's relationship with the Corinthians may support the hypothesis they do not demand it. There are two other considerations, however, which increase its improbability.

Firstly, if it is true an explanation is necessary for the mention in xii. 18 of Titus' previous visit.[2] This could not have been the occasion when Titus conveyed the 'sorrowful letter', for it must have happened before chapters x–xiii were written. Various attempts have been made to treat the aorists in this verse as epistolary, but the question, 'Did Titus take advantage of you?' cannot very intelligently be understood in this way. It is more natural to suppose that the allusion is to the earlier visit when Titus took the 'sorrowful letter'.[3] He seems to have returned to report the changed conditions to Paul and was sent back with 2 Corinthians. If this reconstruction is correct it is difficult to see how x–xiii could be part of the 'sorrowful letter'.

Secondly, it seems likely from ii. 1 ff. that the reason for the 'sorrow-

---

[1] R. H. Strachan, *The Second Epistle to the Corinthians* (1935), p. xx, expresses this contradiction forcibly—'If the last four chapters were written on the same occasion as the rest of the Epistle, Paul has completely violated his assurance of iii. 1–3'.

[2] A. Menzies, *op. cit., ad loc.*, considers this statement could not have come before viii. 6 where the delegates, including Titus, are introduced. R. V. G. Tasker (*op. cit.*, p. 35) regards this as a convincing argument for the unity of the Epistle.*

[3] L. P. Pherigo, 'Paul and the Corinthian Church' (*JBL*, 68, 1949, pp. 341–350), gets over the difficulty by dissociating 2 Cor. x–xiii from the 'sorrowful letter', although still maintaining the partition theory. He suggests, in fact, a considerable interval between the two parts with the second part belonging to the period of Paul's release from his Roman imprisonment.

ful letter' was the wrongdoing of some individual and yet there is no mention of such a matter in chapters x–xiii. If these chapters formed a part of the 'sorrowful letter' the only recourse is to suppose that some reference was made to this person in a part of the letter which is now lost, either through accidental severance from the rest or deliberate suppression while the offender was still living. But this is rather a precarious assumption which should be resorted to only if all other attempts at a solution are unsuccessful. It would seem better to assume that the whole of the 'sorrowful letter' is now lost than to assume that its most important part is no longer extant.[1] In fact, the lack of any clear similarity between ii. 3 ff. and x–xiii is a vital missing link in the hypothesis under consideration. Moreover if x–xiii preceded i–ix there would surely be some reference in i–ix to the opponents dealt with in x–xiii but no certain evidence can be produced for this.[2]

In conclusion it should be pointed out that the absence of MS evidence for this hypothesis places some discount upon it, although it could possibly be maintained that at a very early date the two letters x–xiii and i–ix, existing as fragments, were combined to form one letter. In attempting to explain the inverted order J. H. Kennedy[3] suggested that the editor of the letters placed them in this order because chapter x assumes a visit while chapter ix predicts one. Moffatt was more candid. He remarked, 'Here, as elsewhere in ancient literature, the reasons for such editorial handling elude the modern critic.'[4] But the modern critic is himself responsible for the hypothesis of editorial handling and his difficulties in supplying reasons are readily understandable. It may be that the difficulties are themselves reasons for suspecting the theory. In any event hypotheses which require such a baffling editorial method must be at a greater disadvantage than those which do not require it. The present hypothesis involves the partial preservation of two genuine Epistles, from which the end of one and the beginning of the other were missing.[5] It must have been extremely fortunate that the two depleted fragments happened to join together or were skilfully

---

[1] Cf. M. Dibelius–W. G. Kümmel, *Paul* (1953), p. 95; J. Munck, *Paul and the Salvation of Mankind* (1959), p. 170.

[2] Cf. Munck, *op. cit.*, p. 171.

[3] *The Second and Third Epistles to the Corinthians*, pp. 79 ff.

[4] *ILNT*, p. 122.*

[5] R. V. G. Tasker, *op. cit.*, pp. 32, 33, questions whether the subject-matter of x–xiii reads like a 'painful letter'. It reveals rather an apostle giving a firm but gentle warning.

manipulated to make a single Epistle with at least the appearance of a whole, enough at any rate to elude suspicion until the eighteenth century.[1]

(iii) *Is the 'sorrowful letter' now lost?* If the identification of the 'sorrowful letter' with 1 Corinthians is rejected and the grounds for assuming that part of it is preserved in 2 Corinthians x–xiii are deemed insufficient, the only alternative is to assume that the Epistle is now lost. There were undoubtedly other letters of Paul which have been lost (as for instance the letter to Laodicea, Col. iv. 16) and there is no reason to think that all Paul's correspondence with the Corinthians, in whole or in part, has been preserved. This view is faced with fewer difficulties than the others, although it leaves us without any data for reconstructing the subject-matter of the letter. It may be presumed that since it apparently dealt with some personal opponent of the apostle it did not contain matter of sufficient general interest to be preserved.

(iv) *The purpose of the 'sorrowful letter'.* The decision regarding the purpose of this will be affected by the view taken about the identification of the severe letter with 2 Corinthians x–xiii. If the identification is accepted the letter must have had at least two purposes. It must have dealt with the problem of the offender mentioned in 2 Corin-

---

[1] It is not certain at what date the text of the Epistles was written in codex form, but in all probability this occurred in the first century, cf. C. H. Roberts' article on 'The Codex' in *The Proceedings of the British Academy*, xxxii (1954). As in the case of legal books, the codex form with its table of contents would have safeguarded the manuscript from scribal interpolation more certainly than the roll. On the other hand, the beginning and end of a scroll would be less vulnerable. J. H. Kennedy, *op. cit.*, pp. 153 ff., conjectured that Clement's messengers, who were sent to Corinth with his letter, were shown two mutilated letters and the suggestion was made that they should be joined and then published as a whole. Presumably a new copy would be made incorporating both fragments. R. H. Strachan, *The Second Epistle to the Corinthians*, pp. xx–xxii, contents himself with the theory of scribal editing to the extent of the appropriate trimming of the beginning and ending of fragments to make them fit. R. Hanson, 2 *Corinthians* (1954, pp. 21, 22), suggests that the three parts of 2 Corinthians were rolled up in a bundle and when found were edited in the form in which we now have them, with the tiny fragment vi. 14–vii. 1 included in the body of i–ix where it happened to be found. But such an insertion could hardly have been made in a continuous scroll, while x–xiii must have been attached at the end rather than the beginning because of the greeting of i. 1. In other words, in one case the editor uses common sense and in the other he does not. It seems more reasonable to suppose the unity of the Epistle.

thians ii. 5 ff. and it must have been particularly designed to substantiate the apostle's authority, as the strong invective of 2 Corinthians
x–xiii makes clear. Paul's position had been challenged. He had been
taunted for not accepting maintenance, as if this was sure proof that he
was not entitled to it and was therefore no true apostle. His rivals had
moreover apparently claimed superior merits. These charges drew out
from the apostle a vigorous presentation of his own achievements,
including a record of the special revelations which he had been privileged to receive. Some have thought that the vigorous defence may
have been connected with the individual offender previously mentioned,
who may well have been the main cause of the trouble. But of this we
cannot be certain. It is a fairly safe guess that the instigator or instigators
were members of the Judaizing party.

If the identification of the sorrowful letter with 2 Corinthians x–xiii
is rejected, its contents can be inferred only from the scanty reference in
2 Corinthians ii. 1 ff. and from the historical situation in which it is
assumed to have been sent. If it was a sequence to the painful visit of the
apostle it must have been designed to put right certain matters which
had caused him considerable perplexity and had occasioned his speedy
withdrawal from the church. In all probability he had been openly
insulted before the whole church by some person who challenged his
authority, since 2 Corinthians ii. 10 is most naturally understood as
referring to Paul himself. The Corinthians generally must have been so
much in sympathy with the challenger that the apostle had no alternative but to leave hurriedly. The 'sorrowful letter' must then have
been written by the indignant apostle and sent by the hand of Titus
with the difficult commission to smooth out the revolt. This reconstruction is, of course, tenable only if a preceding 'painful visit' by Paul
subsequent to 1 Corinthians is admitted.

e. 2 Corinthians

The main motive of this letter appears to be to express relief at the
good news that Titus brought to Paul about the improved attitude of
the Corinthians towards the apostle. This is particularly clear from
chapter vii. But there are certain explanations which Paul found it
necessary to mention. His supposed change of plans had called forth a
charge of fickleness and this had to be refuted. The church had to be
encouraged to exercise sympathy towards the repentant offender. The
apostle had to point out the true character of the Christian ministry in

order to make his own position indisputably clear. All these are dealt with in the first part of the Epistle (i–vii). Paul then devoted considerable space to the collection scheme and it may be inferred that the readers had not fulfilled their earlier promises to assist in this scheme. He therefore wrote specifically to spur them into action in order that their contributions might be to hand when Paul arrived on his visit. In all probability Titus needed the apostle's moral backing in his attempts to implement the scheme among them.

The probable purpose of the concluding part of the Epistle (x–xiii) has already been dealt with under the 'sorrowful letter', and the historical situation envisaged there would still be applicable, though in a more restricted sense, if these chapters belong to 2 Corinthians. The opponents of Paul, now a minority element, called forth a strong self-vindication and a vehement condemnation (x, xi). In concluding his impassioned outburst the apostle expressed the hope that he would not need to use severity against these people on his next visit (xii, xiii).

IV. METHOD OF COMPILATION

There have been various attempts to divide up these Epistles in order to demonstrate the method of compilation. Among the more recent partition theories have been those of J. Weiss, Héring, Goguel and Dean. Weiss[1] proposed three parts for 1 Corinthians, dealing with the subject-matter from different points of view and representing three stages in the development of Paul's relations with the Corinthians. 'A': concerning idolatry, fornication, the unveiling of women and common meals; 'B.1': concerning marriage, idol meat, Paul's renunciation, spiritual gifts and resurrection; and 'B.2': concerning parties, the incestuous person and lawsuits. But this involves the editor in too great a mixing up of the parts to make the theory tenable. J. Héring's[2] analysis is not quite so complicated, for he is satisfied with two parts. Part 'A' comprises i–viii, x. 23–xi. 1, xvi. 1–4, 10–14, and part 'B' the remaining sections. M. Goguel[3] on the other hand takes 1

[1] *History of Primitive Christianity* (Eng. Tr. 1937), i, pp. 340 f.

[2] *La première Epître de St. Paul aux Corinthiens.* Letter 'A' was sent after Paul had received information from the house of Chloe and the Corinthians' own enquiry and letter 'B' following later disturbing reports.

[3] *Introduction au Nouveau Testament*, IV, 2, pp. 74–86. E. B. Allo, 2 *Corinthians* (1937), pp. liv–lvi, gives a convenient summary of the compilation theories of Hagge (1876), Lisco (1896), Völter (1905), Clemen (1894 and 1907), Halmel (1894–1909), J. Weiss (1917), Loisy (1922), Couchard (1923), Windisch (1924) and

and 2 Corinthians together and finds six different sections. None of these compilation theories allows sufficient scope for the extraordinary psychological variations in the apostle. Many of the supposed contradictions which form the main basis for these theories are the result of what Moffatt once called 'prosaic exegesis'. J. Héring, for instance, contrasts the rigorist attitude towards pagan sacrifices in x. 1–22 and the liberal approach to the weak brethren in viii and x. 23–xi. 1. The assumption is that the apostle could not have adapted his attitude to the subject in hand and so vary his approach at the same time in the same Epistle; but such an assumption is entirely unrealistic.

J. T. Dean[1] finds in 2 Corinthians parts of four letters but his theory is not more convincing.[2] He finds (1) the letter of defence (x–xii, ii. 14–vi. 13, vii. 2–4, xiii. 1–10); (2) the letter of reconciliation (i–ii. 13, vii. 5–viii. 24, xiii. 11–14); (3) another letter (chapter ix); (4) a fragment of the 'previous letter' (vi. 14–vii. 1). But could not Paul combine defence and reconciliation in one letter? And need we separate chapter ix from chapter viii for no other reason than the different impression of urgency they may respectively create upon our minds? Such subjective bases will commend themselves differently to different minds, but for those who on other grounds regard the Epistle as a unity they will not seem convincing.[3]

Ramsay's[4] view that neither 1 nor 2 Corinthians was composed at a

Goguel (1926) and it is significant that there is little agreement among them. More recently D. W. Riddle and H. Hutson, *New Testament Life and Literature* (1946), regard 1 Cor. ix as apart from the rest of 1 Corinthians and take it as a fragment of a letter sent between 1 Corinthians and 2 Cor. x–xiii (pp. 132–135).

[1] *St. Paul and Corinth* (1947), pp. 40 ff.

[2] Moffatt (*ILNT*[3], 1918, p. 128) at an earlier date had strongly rejected the idea of incongruity between viii. 24 and ix. 1. He considered the unity of the situation in chapters viii and ix to be too well marked to be separated. On the isolation of ii. 14–vii. 4, which C. L. Mitton (*The Formation of the Pauline Corpus of Letters*, 1955, p. 26) regards as almost certain on the grounds that vii. 5 resumes the urgent narrative, the same kind of comment may be made. The whole passage (ii. 14–vii. 4) is integral to Paul's argument, the stress on the glory of the ministry for the time being captivating the apostle's attention. Cf. R. V. G. Tasker's comment on Mitton's contention (*op. cit.*, p. 29). J. Héring, *La deuxième Epître de St. Paul aux Corinthiens* (1958), pp. 12, 13, who finds the theory that x–xiii is the 'sorrowful letter' strongly plausible, also regards chapter ix as a separate letter taken by Titus to Corinth at a date previous to chapters i–viii.

[3] Cf. T. W. Manson's study of the connection of 2 Cor. ii. 14–17 with its context, *Studia Paulina* (1953), pp. 155–162 (edited by van Unnik).*

[4] *Expositor*, VI, iii.

single sitting but that there are many indications of intervals or pauses in the course of composition is worthy of more careful consideration. In I Corinthians he found evidence of an interval in the following positions—after chapters iv, vi, viii, x and xii. He claimed that chapters i–iv come to a distinct climax and are in the same emotional tone throughout. Paul mentions Timothy's mission and his own intention soon to visit Corinth, but the next section is pervaded with what Ramsay called a 'feeling of horror', opening with a statement of astonishment—'It is actually reported that . . .' After the severer tones of chapters v and vi, the apostle returns to calmer discussions in chapters vii and viii, and Ramsay suggested that some intervals, probably quite short, separated the writing of these different sections. This kind of hypothesis is, of course, impossible to prove or disprove, but it has at least historical probability and may account for some of the observable phenomena in the two Epistles. It may, for example, account for the double reference to the Lord's Supper in chapters x and xi, and it may furnish the most reasonable explanation of the abrupt changes in tone already noticed in 2 Corinthians.

V. THE DATES OF THE EPISTLES

Because of the complicated character of the historical background it is not possible to be quite certain about the dating of these letters, especially 2 Corinthians. The most widely held dating of the first Epistle is in the spring of AD 57, although some have proposed an earlier dating. Harnack, for instance, proposed 53, Turner 55 and Ramsay 56. The more important consideration for the Corinthian correspondence is the interval separating 1 and 2 Corinthians. This depends very largely on the meaning of the phrase 'a year ago' (ἀπὸ πέρυσι) in 2 Corinthians viii. 10, ix. 2. This appears to be the time when the collection was commenced at Corinth, organized by Titus (viii. 6). But does this mean that at least a year must have elapsed between 1 and 2 Corinthians? In 1 Corinthians xvi. 1 ff. the collection scheme is referred to in such a way that it is generally supposed that it had not until that time been introduced, although the manner in which it is introduced suggests that Paul is answering a question concerning it.[1] But if the apostle is introducing a new subject, it must mean that the interval between the two

---

[1] L. P. Pherigo (JBL, 68, 1949, p. 343) has made the interesting suggestion that an earlier intimation of the collection scheme was included in the previous letter mentioned in 1 Cor. v. 9 and there seems to be nothing against this view.

Epistles is described by the phrase ἀπὸ πέρυσι. Now this phrase need not indicate a period extending over one year, for the most that is definitely required is that a new year had commenced since the inception of the scheme.[1] The Macedonian New Year began on 21 September and the civil reckoning of the Jews coincided within a few days. If Paul had written in October he might easily have referred to the preceding Easter as 'last year', and 2 Corinthians would then be placed in the autumn of the same year as 1 Corinthians, separated by about seven months. Certain other considerations confirm the probability of this suggestion.

It is clear that Paul wrote 1 Corinthians some time before Pentecost, as he stated in 1 Corinthians xvi. 8 that he intended to stay in Ephesus until Pentecost. The most natural interpretation of the evidence from Acts xx suggests that the following Pentecost Paul arrived at Jerusalem or at least shortly afterwards (Acts xx. 16). Moreover, according to Acts xx. 1–6 Paul spent some time in Macedonia after leaving Ephesus and then moved on to Greece for three months before returning to Macedonia on his way to Jerusalem. This means that most if not all of his stay in Greece was in the wintertime, since it was the Paschal season while he was at Philippi (Acts xx. 6). He must have arrived at Corinth, therefore, about the preceding December or January. If then 2 Corinthians was sent in the October, this would mean a period of only a few weeks before Paul arrived, which fits well the anticipations of a visit which pervade the letter.

Some scholars have rejected this reconstruction. Duncan,[2] for instance, maintains that two winters intervened the period of Acts xx. 1–3. The main basis of his contention is that too many journeys and too much work must be crowded into this period to make seven months its probable duration. But a good deal of the work and journeys that Duncan has in mind is the result of his own conjectures. He maintains, for example, that Paul had spent so little time in Macedonia on his previous visit that he must later have devoted more time there than the traditional interpretation given above would allow. But this is mere conjecture, for the apostle clearly apportioned his time according to the needs of the particular churches under his care and his references to the Philippians are of such a nature as to cause him little concern. Duncan also postulates during the same period further evangelistic activity of

---

[1] Cf. W. Michaelis, *Einleitung*, p. 181.
[2] *St. Paul's Ephesian Ministry* (1929), pp. 218 ff.

Paul in Troas and a mission of Titus to Dalmatia. But it is more obvious that all this additional activity could not possibly fit into the accepted chronology than that the activity itself is supported by the evidence.

J. H. Kennedy[1] also extended the interval between the Epistles by an additional year by suggesting that 1 Corinthians was dispatched before the Pentecost preceding Paul's departure from Ephesus. While this is not impossible the details of Paul's plans in 1 Corinthians xvi. 3–6 coincide so well with Acts xx. 1–3 that to separate them by an interval of a year during which Paul was engaged in continued work in Ephesus seems highly improbable. The winter referred to in 1 Corinthians xvi. 6 is most naturally the next winter subsequent to the time of writing.

The shorter period would just leave sufficient time for an additional visit and an additional letter to be interposed between 1 and 2 Corinthians, although if Titus took all three letters (which is by no means certain) it would admittedly not leave him much breathing space.[2] It is possible that Paul was obliged to leave Ephesus earlier than he anticipated owing to the riot (Acts xix. 23–41), and if this conjecture is correct it would leave more time for his subsequent movements in Macedonia.

CONTENTS OF 1 CORINTHIANS

I. GREETING AND THANKSGIVING (i. 1–9)

The letter is sent in the names of Paul and Sosthenes to the Corinthian believers and all others who call on the name of Christ. The thanksgiving is specially focused on the spiritual endowments of this church and concludes with an assurance that God will keep them to the end. This serves as a preface to his subsequent censures.

II. DISORDERS REPORTED TO PAUL (i. 10–vi. 20)

a. The spirit of divisiveness (i. 10–iv. 21)

There were factions in the church which ranged under the names of Paul, Apollos and Cephas and which were rooted in a false affection towards philosophical speculation. Paul's first concern is to refute mere reliance on wisdom by contrasting it with the folly of the cross, which

---

[1] *The Second and Third Epistles of St. Paul to the Corinthians* (1900).
[2] Cf. A. Robertson, *HDB*, vol. I, p. 495.

formed the centre of Paul's preaching (i. 17–ii. 16). In the next section he discusses the true nature of the Christian ministry, using illustrations from husbandry and building, and he concludes that any boasting in men is utterly vain (iii). But Paul is sensitive to criticisms of his own methods and demonstrates his own position in contrast with them ('We are fools for Christ's sake, but ye are wise', iv. 10). Yet he does not intend to shame them but to act as their spiritual father. For this purpose he is sending Timothy and hopes soon to visit them himself. On this visit he hopes he will not need to come with a rod (iv. 21).

b. The problems of moral lapses (v. 1–13 and vi. 12–20)

1. The case of incest is a serious one. The offender should be removed and delivered to Satan for remedial action, since moral sin, like foul leaven, must be purged from the church (v. 1–8).

2. Paul's 'previous letter' about association with immoral people has been misunderstood and he proceeds to clarify the matter and to re-affirm the necessity to excommunicate any professing Christian guilty of immorality (v. 9–13).

3. Moral judgments, however, require discernment, and distinction must be made between matters such as food, which are questions of expediency, and immoral acts, which are sins against the Holy Spirit (vi. 12–20).

c. Appeals to heathen law-courts (vi. 1–11)

As this comes in the middle of the section on moral offences it may have some connection with the case of incest. Paul shows the fallacy of those destined to judge the world submitting themselves in cases of dispute to unbelievers. They ought to be able to deal with such cases themselves.

III. PROBLEMS RAISED BY THE CORINTHIANS (vii. 1–xv. 58)

a. Marriage (vii. 1–40)

The apostle explains what he conceived to be the Christian approach to marriage, carefully distinguishing the Lord's command from his own opinion, which was conditioned by his own times and circumstances.

b. Meats sacrificed to idols (viii. 1–xi. 1)

The Corinthians were faced with the problem whether it was lawful for a Christian to eat meat already sacrificed to idols. Paul's answer is

(1) that concern for the conscience of the weaker Christian should be the ruling principle (chapter viii); (2) that his own inclination is towards freedom, although he would not insist on his rights, as was clear from his attitude towards material maintenance, but would rather exercise a rigid self-control like an athlete (chapter ix); (3) that the Corinthians must certainly avoid idolatrous feasts, the dangers of which may be illustrated from the history of Israel, while such feasts are completely incompatible with the sacredness of the Lord's Supper (x. 1–xi. 1). To the dictum 'All things are lawful', the theme-song of Christian freedom, Paul adds the rider 'but all things do not edify', the theme-song of Christian self-control.

c. Disorders in public worship (xi. 2–34)

There were two problems here, one concerning the demeanour and dress of women and the other concerning the Lord's Supper. In the former case Paul urges Christian women to respect the social customs of their time, in spite of their new-found freedom. In the latter case he makes clear that each believer is held responsible to examine himself lest he dishonours the Lord's table with his presence. It is a sacred not a secular feast, although it incorporated a communal meal.

d. Spiritual gifts (xii. 1–xiv. 40)

Paul first describes the variety of these gifts and then by means of the illustration of the body shows them all to be necessary to the larger whole (chapter xii). But love is more important than all these gifts, even greater than faith and hope (chapter xiii). Yet the apostle does not disparage the use of these gifts but declares that prophecy, a gift that edifies, is much superior to tongues, a gift that does not (xiv. 1–25). Orderliness above all things is essential in the church, whether it concerns the use of gifts or the ministry of women (xiv. 26–40).

e. Resurrection (xv. 1–58)

The main problem on this subject was whether or not the resurrection was a vital doctrine of Christianity, for some were professing not to believe it. Paul deals with this in four ways. (1) He shows that to deny the believer's resurrection is virtually to deny Christ's, which would in fact involve a denial of the Christian faith (xv. 1–19); (2) he asserts, on the basis of Christ's resurrection, that the believer may have the assurance of the final subjection of all things to Him, and of his own ultimate resurrection (xv. 20–34); (3) he answers the question, 'What kind of body will the dead receive?' by appealing to the principle of resurrection running throughout the natural world, that is, that the higher forms of life come forth from the death of the lower (xv. 35–50); and (4) he concludes with a statement that the resurrection will take place at the *parousia*, and on the strength of this he exhorts the Corinthians at the present time to be steadfast in God's work (xv. 51–58).

IV. CONCLUSION (xvi. 1–24)

Paul tells the Corinthians how to organize the collection, sets out his own plans of travel for the immediate future, urges them to receive Timothy when he comes, mentions the delegates from the Corinthian church and expresses greetings to the Christians and an anathema on those who do not love the Lord. He concludes with an assurance of his love.

CONTENTS OF 2 CORINTHIANS

I. GREETING AND THANKSGIVING (i. 1–11)

After the usual greeting in which Timothy's name is linked with his own, Paul expresses his thankfulness for all the comfort he had received throughout his recent afflictions and the readers are urged to share in his ministry by their prayers.

II. THE APOSTLE'S MINISTRY (i. 12–vii. 16)

a. His plans (i. 12–ii. 17)

He seems to have been charged with fickleness on the grounds that he had changed his plans, but he defends himself by showing that the change was due to the Corinthians themselves (i. 15–ii. 1). His relationship with them had been severely strained, but the delay in his coming had allowed time for the repentance of the man who had caused particular offence and who now needed sympathy, which the readers are urged to give (ii. 2–17).

b. The character of the ministry (iii. 1–vii. 16)

The apostle next dwells upon the credentials for preaching the gospel, having been prompted to do so because his own had been challenged.

1. The ministry is in the service of a new covenant (chapter iii). This makes it superior to the old and since the old was so glorious that Moses, its chief minister, had to veil his face, how much more glorious is the ministry of the new. This glory is, moreover, guaranteed by the lordship of the Spirit.

2. The ministry imposes tremendous responsibilities (iv. 1–15). Although it is of divine origin, its ministers are compared to earthen vessels. Yet the life of Jesus is manifested in these.

3. The ministry must be carried out in the light of the judgment seat of Christ (iv. 16–vi. 2). It involves both hope, focusing on an eternal weight of glory, and fear, resulting in the persuasion of men. The minister of Christ is an ambassador of reconciliation between man and God.

4. Paul's own ministry has involved much hardship and suffering (vi. 3–13). Yet his heart is enlarged towards them and he exhorts them to enlarge their hearts towards him.

5. A digression occurs (vi. 14–vii. 1) in which the readers are urged to cleanse themselves from all uncleanness since righteousness and iniquity can have no fellowship together.

6. An account then follows of Titus' meeting with Paul in Macedonia and the apostle expresses the peculiar joy with which the tidings brought by Titus were received (vii. 2–16). He is greatly comforted on hearing of their grief unto repentance.

III. THE COLLECTION SCHEME (viii. 1–ix. 15)

The Corinthians had already shown themselves willing to share in the collection scheme for the poor at Jerusalem, but their resolve had apparently not been implemented and Paul explains what he expects of them. He uses the poverty of Christ and the extraordinary liberality of the Macedonians to spur them on to greater effort. The section closes with a homily on Christian giving.

IV. PAUL'S VINDICATION OF HIS APOSTLESHIP (x. 1–xiii. 10)

1. In the first part of this section the apostle is concerned to defend himself against those who were questioning his credentials. He seems to be dealing mainly with personal enemies. They may disparage his appearance but he tenaciously resists any attempt to detract from his authority. Being the first to preach the gosepl to them, he claims the right to boast of his authority over them (chapter x).

2. He next denounces his opponents and answers the misrepre-

sentations they have brought against him. His apostleship is not in the least inferior, but on the contrary impressive, for he challenges anyone to produce a comparable list of sufferings for Christ as he can boast. Moreover, he can boast of having received some inexpressible revelations. These credentials are more than adequate to establish his authority (xi. 1–xii. 13).

3. He proposes soon to visit Corinth, but he anticipates the visit with some misgivings, although he hopes he will not have to use severity against those who are still disputing his authority (xii. 14–xiii. 10).

v. conclusion (xiii. 11–14)

These closing words are calmer, though even here Paul makes a parting appeal to them to mend their ways, but the final blessing is similar to those familiar from his other letters.

ADDITIONAL NOTES

426. *The 'previous letter'.* A quite different reconstruction of the letter mentioned in 1 Cor. v. 9 is made by J. C. Hurd, Jnr, *The Origin of 1 Corinthians* (1965). He considers that this letter referred to those subjects dealt with in 1 Cor. vii–xvi, in which Paul answers their objections to this 'previous letter'. The previous letter had in fact represented a change of opinion from his earlier preaching to conform his position to the apostolic decrees of Acts xv. Our 1 Corinthians would then represent a mediating position. But no mention is made of the apostolic decrees and insufficient time seems available for such changes in Paul's position. Cf. the review of Hurd's position by L. W. Barnard, *CQR*, 166 (1965), pp. 516 f., and C. K. Barrett's comments, *The First Epistle to the Corinthians* (1968), pp. 6–8.

J. A. Fitzmeyer (*CBQ*, 23, 1961, pp. 271–280) regards 2 Corinthians vi. 14–vii. 1 as a Qumran passage which has been reworked and inserted into 2 Corinthians. It is, therefore, in his view non-Pauline. He finds Qumran contacts in dualism, opposition to idols, the concept of the temple of God, separation from impurity and the manner of grouping of Old Testament texts. Another scholar, J. Gnilka, in an article '2 Cor. 6: 14–7: 1 in the Light of the Qumran texts and the Testaments of the Twelve Patriarchs', in *Paul and Qumran* (edited J. Murphy-O'Connor, 1968, pp. 48–68), also regards it as non-Pauline. He sees it as a Christian exhortation in the Essene tradition. His reason for considering the section to be later is the use of πιστός in vi. 15. Cf. also K. G. Kuhn (*RB*, 61, 1954, p. 203), who considers that Paul has Christianized an Essene text.

Another suggestion regarding the 'previous letter' is that proposed by N. A. Dahl, 'Der Epheserbrief und der verlorene erste Brief des Paulus an die Korinther', in *Abraham unser Vater* (*Festschrift O. Michel*, edited O. Betz, M. Hengel, P. Schmidt, 1963), pp. 65–77, who connects it with Ephesians v. 5–11.

428. [4] The reference in W. G. Kümmel is *INT* (1965), p. 207.

430. [2] For a spirited criticism of the view that 2 Cor. x–xiii formed part of the 'severe' letter, cf. A. M. G. Stephenson's article in *The Authorship and Integrity of the New Testament* (SPCK Collections 4, 1965), pp. 82–97. For the contrary opinion, cf. G. Bornkamm, *ibid.*, pp. 73–81 (reprinted from *NTS*, 8, 1962, pp. 258–264).

R. Batey (*JBL*, LXXXIV, 1965, pp. 139–146) also objects to the placing of 2 Cor. x–xiii before 2 Cor. i–ix. He proposes the following reconstruction of Paul's relationship to the Corinthians. 1. First visit AD 50–51; 2. In Asia from Summer 52 to Fall 54, when the 'previous letter' and 1 Corinthians were written; 3. The 'severe' letter sent with Titus, but no painful visit by Paul; 4. Good news received and Titus sent with 2 Cor. i–ix (Nov. 54); 5. Winter in Corinth; 6. Retreat to Macedonia where 2 Cor. x–xiii was written (Spring 55); 7. Paul left for Jerusalem without a third visit to Corinth. C. K. Barrett (*Neotestamentica et Semitica*, edited E. E. Ellis and M. Wilcox, 1969, pp. 1–14) has a similar theory for 2 Cor. x–xiii, written after i–ix, following bad news from Titus.

433. [1] Against the pairing of passages between 2 Cor. x–xiii and 2 Cor. i–ix, cf. R. Batey, *op. cit.*, who maintains that the latter could as easily be paired with passages in 1 Corinthians.

435. [2] W. H. Bates (*NTS*, 12, 1965, pp. 56–69), who does not regard 2 Cor. x–xiii as separate from the rest of the Epistle, lays particular stress on the Titus passage. Bates regards x–xiii as a recapitulation of i–ix, maintaining that the mood of both parts is one of strife rather than peace. P. E. Hughes, *Paul's Second Epistle to the Corinthians* (1962), pp. xxi ff., strongly supports unity.

436. [4] Cf. Kümmel, *INT*, pp. 203 f., on the difficulties confronting compilation theories. Reference is made to W. Michaelis' article 'Teilungshypothesen bei Paulusbriefen' (*ThZ*, XIV, 1958, pp. 321 ff.).

440. [3] Bornkamm (*op. cit.*) sees several letters in 2 Corinthians, treating ii. 14–vii. 4, viii, ix, x–xiii as separate letters from the rest. He makes the attempt to explain the strange procedure of the compiler, by appealing to a formal rule of placing warnings at the end. This stamped the apostle as a protector of his congregation, which Bornkamm sees as a later tendency towards idealization. Against Bornkamm cf. W. G. Kümmel, *INT* (1965), p. 214; R. H. Fuller, *INT* (1966), pp. 48 f. Cf. J. Harrison (*ET*, LXXVII, 1966, pp. 285 f.), who suggests that 1 Cor. i. 1–iv. 21 forms a unity with 2 Cor. x–xiii. Cf. also A. Q. Morton (*ET*, LXXVIII, 1967, p. 119), who on the basis of sentence lengths finds dislocations in 1 and 2 Corinthians.

CHAPTER THIRTEEN

THE EPISTLE TO THE GALATIANS

I. DESTINATION OF THE EPISTLE

From the Epistle itself it is clear that the readers were called Galatians (iii. 1) and were grouped in what is described as 'the churches of Galatia' (i. 2). But there has been a great deal of discussion over the identification of these Galatians. Traditional opinion was never in any doubt. The geographical district of Galatia lay in the northern part of the Roman province of Galatia, and it was assumed by all commentators until the nineteenth century that Paul established churches in this northern district and that this Epistle was written to a group of communities there. Such evangelistic activity must have taken place on the second missionary journey after Paul had been forbidden by the Spirit to preach the gospel in Asia (Acts xvi. 6). If this is a true account of the founding of these Galatian churches the Epistle could not have been sent until Paul was on his third missionary journey. The main arguments in support of this theory are as follows.[1]

a. The North Galatian theory

(i) *The popular use of the term 'Galatians'.* The area of North Galatia was originally populated by Phrygians but became overrun by Gauls, who by the end of the third century BC had established themselves in three cities in the central mountainous districts, Ancyra, Tavium and Pessinus. These Gauls gave their name to the district they inhabited, hence the term 'Galatians'.[2]

(ii) *The normal practice of Luke.* He uses Pamphylia (Acts xiii. 13), Pisidia (Acts xiii. 14) and Lycaonia (Acts xiv. 6), all of which are geographical locations, and it is therefore thought reasonable to conclude that when in Acts xvi. 6 he speaks of Paul and his companions going

---

[1] The ablest presentations of this theory are found in J. B. Lightfoot's *Epistle to the Galatians*[10] (1900), pp. 1–35, and in J. Moffatt, *ILNT* (1912), pp. 90 ff. See also P. W. Schmiedel, *Enc. Bib.* (1901), II, pp. 1596 ff.; M. Goguel, *Introduction*, IV, 2, pp. 157 ff.; A. Oepke, pp. 4 ff.; and H. Schlier, pp. 5 f. in their commentaries.

[2] Cf. J. B. Lightfoot, *op. cit.*, pp. 1–9, for a concise history of the settlement of these Gauls in the district.

through the region of Phrygia and Galatia he means these terms also to be understood in a geographical sense. In that case, North Galatia would be indicated.

(iii) *Luke's description of South Galatian towns.* When referring to Antioch, Luke adds the words 'of Pisidia' (Acts xiii. 14), while Lystra and Derbe are described as cities of Lycaonia (xiv. 6), which shows that the geographical district was used for purposes of identification in preference to the Roman provincial title, which would here have been 'Galatia'. The province of that name stretched over a much larger area than the geographical district and included the geographical districts of Lycaonia, Pisidia and part of Phrygia, but Luke does not appear to have used the provincial title for the entire district.

(iv) *The meaning of Acts xvi. 6.* The upholders of the North Galatian view have laid great stress upon the fact that these words can only mean that Paul and his companions went through Phrygia and the district of Galatia. It is maintained that two districts, not one, are indicated, which means that the latter term could not be the provincial title since this included a part of the former mentioned district of Phrygia.

(v) *The meaning of Acts xviii. 23.* This passage describes Paul's missionary activities after spending time at Antioch prior to the commencement of his third journey. Lightfoot maintained that these words must be understood in the same way as the similar words of xvi. 6, in which case Paul must have visited the northern geographical district during the early part of this journey. If this interpretation of these two passages is correct it must mean that the Acts records two visits of the apostle to the northern region, with the strong assumption that he founded churches there.

(vi) *The characteristics of the inhabitants.* Lightfoot[1] attached much importance to the consideration that the characteristics of the readers as reflected in the Epistle correspond closely to the characteristics of the Gallic peoples. They are described as being inclined towards drunkenness, niggardliness, strife, vainglory, anger, impulsiveness, and fickleness. According to Lightfoot the Gauls were well known for fickleness, and he therefore concluded that the readers were in all probability descendants of the original Gauls who settled in the district of northern Galatia. There is no doubt that Lightfoot has here inferred too much from the evidence, for the characteristics are so generally human that

[1] *Op. cit.,* pp. 13 ff.

they cannot safely be attached to any one racial group. Moreover the Gallic section of the communities constituted only a part of the whole and no account is taken of the Phrygic and other peoples, including Roman, who were intermingled with the Gauls.

(vii) *Paul's movements after leaving Iconium (Acts xvi. 6 ff.).* Moffatt[1] argues that Luke's wording 'went through' (διῆλθον), taken in conjunction with the use of the same word in xviii. 23, means not merely 'transit across' but 'transit with preaching activity'. This understanding of the word would support the view that Paul established churches in the northern district. Another consideration is the meaning of the participle κωλυθέντες ('having been forbidden'). This restriction by the Spirit on activity in the province of Asia when Paul was already in Lycaonia left him no alternative but to go north. Moffatt quotes approvingly the comment of Chase that the South Galatian theory 'is shipwrecked on the rock of Greek grammar'.[2] It should be noted that the tense of the participle implies that after being prevented from speaking the word in Asia Paul and his companions proceeded through Phrygia and Galatia.

These reasons in support of the traditional view have seemed sufficient to some scholars to conclude that Paul was writing to the northern area. But this opinion is now very widely disputed in favour of the South Galatian theory.

b. The South Galatian theory

Since the nineteenth century many scholars have advocated this view, but it was Sir William Ramsay[3] who popularized it and gave it its most cogent expression. The main points which have led to a widespread abandonment of the traditional view are as follows.

(i) *A different interpretation of Acts xvi. 6 and xviii. 23.* According to Ramsay Acts xvi. 6 refers to the Phrygic-Galatic region, by which he meant that part of the Roman province of Galatia which was inhabited by Phrygians and was known geographically as Phrygia. This involves treating 'Phrygian' (Φρυγίαν) as an adjective, a usage which Moffatt strongly disputed. The parallel description in Acts xviii. 23 was taken

---

[1] *ILNT*, p. 95. [2] *Op. cit.*, p. 93.

[3] Cf. *Historical Commentary on Galatians* (1899) and *The Church in the Roman Empire*[3] (1894), pp. 74 ff. It is held by Burton (*ICC*), Duncan (*MC*), Goodspeed (*INT*), Michaelis (*Einleitung*) and the majority of recent scholars.

to mean districts in the province of Galatia and the part of Phrygia in the adjoining province of Asia. By understanding these two passages in this way Ramsay maintained that Acts contains no reference to Paul visiting North Galatia. But not all those who support the South Galatian theory have followed Ramsay in this interpretation. Lake regarded these phrases as descriptive of a region whose people were partly Phrygian-speaking and partly Galatian-speaking. This latter view avoids the objection that no division of Galatia was known with the title Phrygian Galatian[1].

(ii) *Lack of information in Acts about the North Galatian churches.* Even if Acts does contain passing references to Pauline activity in the North Galatian area, it is strange that so little is said about churches where such an important controversy arose as is reflected in the Galatian Epistle. It is maintained that it is far more probable that the churches in mind are those to which Luke devoted considerable attention in the earlier stages of Paul's missionary activity. Moffatt[2] admitted the plausibility of this but countered it by pointing out that Luke by-passes several aspects of Paul's work (e.g. Syria, Dalmatia and some details of Paul's relationship with the Corinthians) and therefore little significance can be attached to his omission of detail regarding Paul's North Galatian work. Nevertheless it is greatly to the favour of the southern theory that Luke does specifically mention churches in the southern district but is silent about churches in the northern area.

(iii) *The isolation of the North Galatian district.* According to the Epistle Paul first visited the readers during a convalescence following a physical illness (Gal. iv. 13), but this would be highly improbable in the northern area, which was not only off the beaten track but necessitated a journey over difficult country. The cities of Pessinus, Tavium and Ancyra were all on the central plateau and were not the sort of places to be visited at a time of bodily weakness. Moffatt[3] thought that Tavium as a military base would probably have been directly linked with Pisidian Antioch and if so would be no more difficult than the road from

[1] Cf. *The Beginnings of Christianity*, vol. v, pp. 224 ff. and K. and S. Lake, *INT*, pp. 127 ff. Lake placed the district described in Acts xvi. 6 on the road from Iconium to Troas.

[2] *ILNT*, p. 97.

[3] *ILNT*, p. 97. It has been questioned whether Acts xiii and xiv can be understood against a background of physical weakness (cf. Feine–Behm, *Einleitung*, p. 135), but the same difficulty obtains for Acts xvi. 6.

Perga to Antioch. But the lesser distance involved would favour Ramsay's opinion that convalescence was more likely in the south than in the north.

(iv) *Paul's use of provincial titles*. It was Paul's habit when describing churches founded by him to use the titles of the provinces in which they were situated, as for example Achaia, Asia and Macedonia.[1] It is most probable therefore that his use of 'Galatians' must be taken in the same way. Even if Luke used geographical locations there is no reason to suppose that Paul must have done the same. But Moffatt appealed to Galatians i. 21 as evidence that he did, for there the geographical regions of Syria and Cilicia, which together formed one Roman province, are mentioned as the sphere of Paul's activity after his early visit to Jerusalem.[2] But there is a distinction here, for Paul is describing his own movements not the location of churches. It seems probable that he followed Luke's practice when tracing itineraries, but considered it more appropriate to group his churches under their respective provincial areas.

(v) *The appropriateness of the name Galatians for the southern area*. Ramsay[3] maintained that it is difficult to think of any other name which could have applied all-inclusively to the various peoples of the southern district. He argued that the name of the province would be used to

---

[1] It is significant that Philippi and Thessalonica were in the province of Macedonia but were in the geographical district whose indigenous people were Thracian. Cf. W. F. Adeney, *Galatians* (*CB*), 1903, p. 60.

[2] Because Paul does not suggest that the Galatians know anything about this period M. Dibelius considers this speaks against the South Galatian theory (*A Fresh Approach to the New Testament*, 1937, p. 158). But his reasoning here rests on the unreliability of Acts xiii. 14, which makes no room for this Syria and Cilicia visit on the first missionary journey. For a different reason Wikenhauser (*New Testament Introduction*, p. 376) takes Syria and Cilicia as regions, maintaining that Paul's references to Judea are always regional and not provincial (cf. Rom. xv. 31; 2 Cor. i. 16; Gal. i. 22; 1 Thes. ii. 14).

[3] *Historical Commentary on Galatians* (1899), p. 319. Mommsen (*ZNTW*, 1901, p. 86) disagreed with the view that 'Galatians' as a title could be understood in any sense larger than its normal ethnical significance. But Goodspeed (*INT*, p. 35) rightly points to Paul's use of 'Macedonian' for both Thessalonians and Philippians (2 Cor. ix. 2, 4). In Acts xx. 4 Tychicus is called an Asian. Feine–Behm, *Einleitung*, p. 142, maintain that the use of the term would have offended the national feelings of the southerners. Contemporary writers (Strabo, Pliny, Tacitus, Plutarch and others) clearly distinguished the Asiatics from their near neighbours and Feine–Behm argue that Paul would have done the same.*

describe all the inhabitants of that province without implying any ethnical significance. Moreover, the southern peoples would have been proud of a title which carried with it the implication of Roman citizenship.

(vi) *A different interpretation of the participle in Acts xvi. 6.* The sweeping claim that Greek grammar wrecks the southern theory cannot be maintained as Askwith[1] effectively proved by citing other examples from Acts to show that the participle would more naturally refer to a prohibition subsequent to the journey through Phrygia and Galatia. In any case the South Galatian theory does not hang upon the meaning of this participle, but on the indisputable fact that there were churches in South Galatia. Indeed, the meaning of this participle is much more crucial to the northern theory than to the southern.

(vii) *The mention of Barnabas.* Three times in Galatians ii Barnabas is mentioned (verses 1, 9, 13), and it is maintained by advocates of the southern theory that this is more natural if he were known to the readers, which could be so only if the churches in mind are the southern churches. It was only on the first journey that he accompanied Paul. But this argument is weakened by the similar mention of Barnabas in 1 Corinthians ix. 6, where his practice of refusing support is assumed to be well known and yet according to Acts he was not with Paul on the Corinthian mission. It may be that the Galatians had heard of Barnabas and that reference to him would therefore be meaningful. Yet it must be admitted that these references would have a great deal more force if he were personally known to the readers as would be the case on the southern theory. When Paul says that 'even Barnabas' (ii. 13) was carried away by the insincerity of Peter and other Jews, he seems to imply that this was unexpected in view of what was known of Barnabas' character.

(viii) *The collection delegation contained no representative from North Galatia.* The reference to Paul's companions in Acts xx. 4 ff. includes Gaius from Derbe (if that is the correct reading)[2] and Timothy from Lystra, both from South Galatia, but no-one is mentioned from the northern district. That the churches of Galatia participated in the scheme

---

[1] *The Epistle to the Galatians: an essay on its destination and date* (1899), pp. 7 ff.

[2] Or, if the Western text is to be followed here, from Doberus in Macedonia. This would agree with the description in Acts xix. 29 of Gaius and Aristarchus as men of Macedonia.

is clear from 1 Corinthians xvi. 1, and it is therefore most reasonable to suppose that these churches were represented at least by Timothy, if not by Gaius also. Admittedly no mention is made of any delegates from Corinth or Philippi and this might seem to offset this argument.[1] It must further be borne in mind that Acts xx. 4 ff. does not describe Paul's companions as collection delegates, and although this is an attractive suggestion and is probably correct, it cannot be regarded as certain.

(ix) *Incidental details in the Epistle.* The reference in Galatians iv. 14 to the 'messenger of God' might possibly be an indirect allusion to Acts xiv. 12 (the incident at Lystra) and the phrase 'marks of the Lord Jesus' (Gal. vi. 17) might connect up with the stoning (Acts xiv. 19), in which case the southern churches must be the recipients of the letter. In addition Galatians ii. 5 would seem to imply that Paul's struggles at Jerusalem over circumcision were subsequent to the establishment of the Galatian churches, for Paul adds that he would not yield for a moment 'that the truth of the gospel might continue with you', which seems clearly to mean that the gospel had already been preached among them. But if so, the southern churches must be in view since the Jerusalem controversy was prior to Paul's alleged journeys into the northern area. The force of this evidence cannot be disposed of by taking the 'you' quite generally as denoting Gentiles as distinct from Jews (so Moffatt), since Paul in this passage goes into considerable detail in describing a specific situation.

(x) *The activity of Judaizing Christians.* The Epistle leaves us in no doubt that the troublers of the church were Jewish Christians who wished to impose Jewish ritual requirements on the Gentile members. The hypothesis which makes such activity more probable must be more favoured and this would seem to add weight to the southern theory, since it is more readily conceivable that Judaizers had dogged Paul's steps to the regions of Pisidian Antioch than that they had trailed him across the more obscure districts of the north. In any case, Acts makes abundantly clear that such Judaizers had been at work in the southern district and that their activity was the immediate cause of the council at Jerusalem.

---

[1] It could, of course, be maintained that Titus, although not mentioned in Acts, represented the Corinthian church (1 Cor. xvi. 3; 2 Cor. viii. 16 ff.) and that Luke was delegate from Philippi (a 'we' passage commences at xx. 5 when Paul is at Philippi).

Most modern scholars lean to the South Galatian theory although few would deny that the traditional theory carries considerable weight. So strong an advocate of the southern theory as Duncan admits that if the destination could be discussed as an isolated question the fairest answer would be *non liquet*.[1] But what tips the balance for him in favour of the southern theory is the more satisfactory exegesis of the Epistle which it provides and his own strong preference for an early date which automatically rules out the northern theory. Some scholars have attempted to steer a middle course by suggesting that Paul was addressing himself both to the southern churches and to some communities in part of the geographical district of Galatia.[2] But even if this view could be maintained it would mean that the main people addressed were those of the south among whom Paul had done the most work.

II. DATE

The date of the Epistle depends on the decision regarding its destination. The North Galatian theory necessitates a date late enough to allow for Paul's visit to the northern area. Now it is often supposed that Galatians iv. 13 ('I preached the gospel to you at the first'—τὸ πρότερον) implies that two visits had been paid by Paul before the writing of the Epistle, and on the northern theory this would mean that the second visit would need to be identified with Acts xviii. 23. At some subsequent date, probably while he was at Ephesus, Paul must have written the letter. Yet τὸ πρότερον could be understood to mean 'originally', after its more common *Koinē* meaning, and two visits would not then be implied.[3]

a. Dates according to the North Galatian theory

1. The first proposed date is early in the Ephesian ministry. Mainly on the strength of the word ταχέως (quickly) in Galatians i. 6, it has been maintained that the letter must have rapidly followed Paul's visit. But this reasoning is not conclusive since the word ταχέως seems more naturally to refer to the conversion of the Galatians, rather than to Paul's work among them, in which case it has a relative significance.

[1] *Galatians (MC)*, p. xx.
[2] Cf. Zahn, *INT* (Eng. Tr. 1909), vol. i, pp. 193 ff. Meinertz, *Einleitung*, p. 89, n. 2, cites also Mynster (*Einleitung in den Brief an der Galater*, 1825, pp. 49 ff.), Cornely and Jacquier as maintaining this view.
[3] Cf. Lake, *Earlier Epistles*, p. 266.

2. An alternative date is shortly after Paul left Ephesus. Lightfoot[1] strongly maintained that this Epistle preceded Romans because the latter showed a more matured approach to the same problems. He further argued that Galatians must have followed 1 and 2 Corinthians because no indication of the Jewish controversy occurs in the latter.[2] He therefore regarded the Epistle as sent from Corinth (i.e. towards the end of the third missionary journey).

b. Dates according to the South Galatian theory

There are two main alternatives under this theory depending on the identification of Paul's second visit implied in Galatians iv. 13.

1. If the second visit is the one mentioned in Acts xvi. 6, the Epistle must have been written after the Council of Jerusalem (probably a year or two after).

2. If on the other hand the second visit is identified with that mentioned in Acts xiv. 21 when Paul and Barnabas revisited the southern Galatian churches on their return journey to Antioch, the date may be before the Council and consequently about AD 49.

3. A similar early dating is equally possible if Galatians iv. 13 implies only one earlier visit. Which of these alternatives is correct can be decided only by a careful consideration of the Jerusalem visits of Paul mentioned in both Acts and Galatians.

c. The Jerusalem visits

(i) *The view that Galatians ii. 1–10 is the Council visit of Acts xv.* This is the traditional view and is supported by the alleged similarities between the two visits. In both Acts and Galatians Paul and Barnabas consult the Jerusalem church, and in both cases they have to overcome strong opposition. These similarities have, however, been challenged by many scholars who adhere to the South Galatian theory and their objections must be carefully weighed. It should be observed that those who maintain that the readers were North Galatians have no option but to accept the identification of Acts xv with Galatians ii. There are, however, certain objections to this identification.

1. There is some doubt as to the meaning of 'again' in Galatians ii. 1. In Galatians i and ii Paul is setting out historical facts and it is most

---

[1] *Galatians*, pp. 48, 49.
[2] E. J. Goodspeed uses the same argument for rejecting a dating before the Council of Jerusalem (*INT*, p. 11).*

reasonable to suppose, therefore, that when he says in Galatians ii. 1 that he went up 'again' to Jerusalem he means that this visit is the second he has made. But the Acts mentions two visits of the apostle before the Council visit, the first in ix. 26 ff. immediately following his conversion and the second in xi. 30 when with Barnabas he took the relief fund from Antioch to Jerusalem. It is contended, therefore, that the most natural interpretation of the 'again' in Galatians ii. 1 is that the famine relief visit is in mind.

To avoid this difficulty arising from Galatians ii some have resorted to the expedient of declaring Acts xi. 30 unhistorical, but with no other justification than the difficulty imposed by their particular interpretation of Paul's 'again'. A more reasonable suggestion is that Paul passed over the visit of Acts xi. 30 because he saw only the elders on this occasion, whereas in Galatians his argument revolves around his relationship to the apostles. Duncan thinks it is questionable whether the mention of 'elders' is intended to exclude the apostles,[1] but in any case he suggests that Paul would surely have mentioned this intervening visit. Yet it is not particularly obvious why he should do so, especially in recalling events after several years and with an immediate aim of focusing attention on official relationships rather than movements to and from Jerusalem.

Some scholars (e.g. McGiffert[2] and Kirsopp Lake[3]) suggested that Acts xi. 30 and xv relate to the same visit but were derived from different sources and therefore present the material differently. But such a theory plays havoc with the historicity of Acts without any adequate justification and can contribute nothing of value to the present discussion.[4]

2. In addition there are certain differences between Galatians ii and Acts xv. Whereas Acts xv records a formal discussion between Paul and Barnabas on the one hand and the assembled church on the other, Galatians ii gives the impression of a private interview with the leaders alone. Yet it is not impossible that at a public conference of the whole

[1] See p. 463 for a criticism of this view.
[2] *A History of Christianity in the Apostolic Age* (1897), p. 171.
[3] *The Beginnings of Christianity*, I, vol. v, pp. 195 ff. He thought Luke confused a Jerusalem and an Antiochene source of the tradition of the apostolic conference.
[4] Cf. also E. Hirsch, 'Petrus und Paulus', *ZNTW* (1930), pp. 65 ff.; J. R. Porter, 'The Apostolic Decree and Paul's Second Visit to Jerusalem', *JTS* (1947), pp. 169 ff. To solve the problem of the relationship of Galatians to Acts by denying the reliability of the latter was first mooted by F. C. Baur, *op. cit.*, pp. 105 ff.*

church there would have been some private discussions preparatory or subsequent to the general assembly, and if so Paul may have had greater cause to mention these talks since they clearly indicated his relationship with the Jerusalem leaders.[1]

A more important difference is the omission from Galatians of any reference to the decrees which according to Acts xv were agreed upon at the time of the Council. On the contrary, Galatians ii. 6 states that the leaders did not insist on any addition, and this would seem to exclude the possibility of any decrees having been issued on this occasion. Moreover, it would have been surprising if Paul had made no reference to the Council decision if the Council visit is equated with Galatians ii.[2] Defendants of the later dating claim that the apostle was not the kind of man to appeal to authoritarian decrees in solving the Jewish-Gentile controversy with which the Epistle deals, and this claim is not without considerable cogency in view of his sturdy independence. To him the enunciation of theological principles was of much greater value than ecclesiastical pronouncements.

3. A further objection concerns the dispute between Peter and Paul. Paul's rebuke of Peter over the question of Jewish-Gentile fellowship at

---

[1] Paul's description of these leaders as those reputed to be 'pillars' (Gal. ii. 9) seems to emphasize their authority. But cf. C. K. Barrett's article 'Paul and the "pillar" Apostles' in *Studia Paulina* (1953), pp. 1–19, in which he suggests their status as 'pillars' was eschatological and not ecclesiastical. Baur, *op. cit.*, pp. 117 ff., found great difficulty in believing that Paul would mention the private talks and omit all reference to the great conference and there is substance in his criticism on this point despite the unacceptable character of his solution.*

[2] The problem here would be considerably lessened if it is maintained that the original decrees were intended only for Syria and Cilicia and were not general instructions for all Pauline churches. Codex D includes Acts xvi. 4 at the end of Acts xv. 41, as well as in the usual place. A. S. Geyser (*Studia Paulina*, 1953), pp. 136–138, suggests Acts xv. 41 was the original position and that Paul did not take the decrees beyond the districts mentioned there. This is possible, but the MS evidence in support is slight and a more natural explanation is to suppose that the words were brought forward to xv. 41 because of their appropriateness in view of the specific address of the apostolic letter (xv. 23). Some scholars obviate the difficulty by regarding the Acts' Council account as no more than a freely composed dramatized version of an historical event (cf. D. T. Rowlingson, 'The Jerusalem Conference and Jesus' Nazareth Visit', *JBL*, June 1952, pp. 69 ff.). E. Hirsch (*ZNTW*, 1930, pp. 65 ff.) denied Paul's presence at the Council. F. C. Burkitt, *Christian Beginnings*, p. 123, pointed out that Paul did not hesitate on occasions to issue his own decrees and there is therefore no reason to suppose that he would not have been prepared to endorse the Council decrees.*

meals is less likely after than before the Council where that question was discussed and settled. Some scholars (e.g. Moffatt) have denied that the Council decisions 'regulated the social intercourse' of Jewish and Gentile Christians, but it is difficult to see how discussions could have proceeded far without problems of this kind being aired, especially after three years' mission work.

But there is a problem about the chronology of Galatians ii. Does ii. 11 ff. precede in time the events of ii. 1–10, or did the events occur in the order in which Paul records them? If the latter alternative is correct it would imply that the Council decisions needed time to be worked out in practice, even by apostles like Peter and Barnabas. But Peter's act in separating himself from the Gentiles cuts right across his support for Paul's policy at the Council, and would be a glaring case of inconsistency. It may of course be claimed that such changeableness would fit in well with Peter's changeable nature which would lessen to some extent the surprising character of this inconsistency. But the fact remains that the difficulty would be removed if the dispute between Peter and Paul occurred before any formal decision on the matter had been reached. It is moreover difficult to imagine that the question of receiving Gentiles into the fellowship could have been discussed without the related question of Jewish-Gentile relationships within the fellowship.[1]

In order to get over the difficulty of Peter's culpable inconsistency and at the same time to preserve the identification of Galatians ii. 1–10 with Acts xv some have maintained that in Galatians ii. 11 ff. Paul is recalling an incident which happened before the events of verses 1–10,[2] but this suggestion gains no support from the opening words of verse 11 which seem to place the following statements in direct historical sequence with verses 1–10. The sole remaining alternative is to deny the identification of Galatians ii and Acts xv.

(ii) *The view that Galatians ii. 1–10 is the visit of Acts xi. 30.* This theory, which has received widespread support in recent times, is claimed to avoid all the difficulties mentioned above. It means that Galatians ii. 1 may be interpreted literally of the second visit of the apostle to Jerusalem. It also obviates any problem over the omission of the Council decrees from the Epistle. It further lessens considerably the charge of inconsistency against Peter if the Antioch incident preceded the Council.

[1] Cf. G. Duncan, *Galatians* (MC), pp. xxvi ff.
[2] Cf. C. H. Turner, 'Chronology of the New Testament', *HDB*, vol. 1, p. 424.

Under this hypothesis the following reconstruction is suggested.[1]

1. About a year after Paul and Barnabas began work at Antioch (Acts xi. 26) the church decided to send them to Jerusalem with a relief fund for the Judaean churches after hearing about the conditions from some itinerant prophets. During this visit Paul and Barnabas had opportunity to inform the leaders at Jerusalem about developments in the work among the Gentiles.

2. As Titus was with them the question of Jewish-Gentile fellowship was brought into sharp focus, but Titus was not compelled to be circumcised (Gal. ii. 3).

3. The Jerusalem apostles acknowledged Paul's credentials as apostle to the uncircumcision (Gal. ii. 7 ff.), but laid him under obligation to remember the poor. This was the very thing he had already done, as Galatians ii. 10 makes clear. Such a request on the part of the Jerusalem apostles would have been perfectly natural on the occasion of his relief visit, but no such obligation is mentioned in connection with the Council of Acts xv.

4. On their return to Antioch they encouraged Jewish and Gentile Christians to have fellowship together. Acts xi. 19 ff. certainly suggests that at an early stage there were Gentiles in the church, but no crisis seems to have arisen until the arrival of emissaries from Jerusalem (Gal. ii. 12). Just previously Peter had visited the church and had joined in fellowship with the Christians, Gentiles as well as Jews. Following the remonstrance of James' men, first Peter then Barnabas withdrew, but this position seemed so intolerable to Paul that he challenged and rebuked Peter before the whole church.

5. Immediately following this incident the Antioch church commended Paul and Barnabas to their missionary work, which was destined to raise the same problems in a more acute form. Without doubt the Jerusalem leaders soon heard of the success of Paul's mission among the Gentiles and the Jewish-Gentile question reached a crisis for the Judaean Christians. They were quite prepared to acknowledge Paul's work among the Gentiles and were quite willing to concede that Gentiles could become Christians, but they could not tolerate the abolition of all distinction between Jew and Gentile. If Gentiles wished to have fellowship with Jewish Christians they must conform to Jewish scruples. They must be circumcised and must respect Jewish ritual

---

[1] Cf. Duncan, *Galatians*, pp. xxvi ff. Cf. also C. W. Emmet, *Galatians* (1912), pp. xiv ff.; K. Lake, *The Earlier Epistles of St. Paul*, pp. 279 ff.

requirements at meal times. The Jewish leaders consequentlydispatched representatives to the Galatian churches and to the sponsoring church at Antioch (Gal. i. 7; Acts xv. 1).

6. The Antioch church, following the lead of Paul and Barnabas, recognized the necessity of discussing this burning question at top level, and sent Paul, Barnabas and others unnamed in Acts as delegates to the Jerusalem church, as a result of which a conference was convened Acts xv).

7. If this reconstruction is correct the Epistle was written before the Council was convened, but it is not possible to be any more specific than that. It may have been sent before Paul arrived back in Antioch from his first journey, but this would hardly allow enough time for the serious situation to develop as reflected in the Epistle. It is more probable that he wrote after a skirmish with the Judaizers who were probably trying to influence the Judaean church. The letter may have been written on Paul's way to Jerusalem for the Council. In any case it would be dated AD 49–50, and in that event would become the earliest of Paul's extant Epistles.

This hypothesis is not without certain difficulties of its own.[1] The apostles are not mentioned in Acts xi. 30, where Barnabas and Saul are said to deliver the contributions to 'the elders'. It cannot easily be argued that 'elders' is here a general term inclusive of apostles, for in the account of the Jerusalem Council in Acts xv and xvi. 4 the apostles are mentioned with the elders in a way which clearly differentiates the two classes. It is also not easy to fit Titus into the visit of Acts xi. 30, since Paul and Barnabas are alone mentioned as delegates to the Judaean church. It is more intelligible when linked with Acts xv. 2 where in addition to Paul and Barnabas 'some of the others' are mentioned, among whom it is

---

[1] A recent commentator, H. N. Ridderbos, *Galatians* (1954), pp. 31–35, regards the difficulties as insurmountable and accordingly rejects the identification of Acts xi with Gal. ii. Cf. also J. A. Allan, *Galatians* (1951), pp. 23–26, who rejects it because of the absence of the Gentile-Jewish controversy from the Thessalonian correspondence and the similarities in thought between Galatians and Romans.

T. W. Manson, 'St. Paul in Ephesus: (2) The Problem of the Epistle to the Galatians', *BJRL*, 24 (1940), pp. 59–80, also disagrees with this identification, but proposes another Jerusalem visit unrecorded in Acts which took place prior to the first missionary journey. The Jerusalem Council therefore followed the incident at Antioch and the problem of Jewish-Gentile meals was dealt with before the circumcision issue was raised. But this theory does not take Acts xv at its face value but supposes it may be composite.*

highly probable that Titus was included. Moreover, the placing of Peter's dissimulation before the Council involves a curious omission on the part of the 'men from James' (Gal. ii. 12) to raise the crucial question of circumcision although they were greatly disturbed about Gentile fellowship. This is all the more strange in the light of James' own words in the letter recorded in Acts xv. 24, where the trouble-makers are described as 'from us' although they have received no instructions from the Jerusalem apostolate (i.e. about circumcision). It seems unlikely that the problem of fellowship would arise before and independent of the Jewish-Christian demand for Gentile circumcision.

Another difficulty in the reconstruction arises from Paul's account in Galatians ii. 7 ff. of the way in which he and Barnabas were confirmed in their work among the Gentiles. This was agreed upon when the apostles saw that Paul had been entrusted with the gospel for the un-circumcised (Gal. ii. 7) and when they perceived the grace granted to him (verse 9). But how could this have happened before the first missionary journey? This is the more emphasized by verse 2 where Paul states categorically that he laid before the leaders ('those of repute') the gospel which he preached among the Gentiles. If the above reconstruction is valid Paul must have done preaching work among the Gentiles before the first missionary journey, on which the Acts record is silent, unless his ministry at Antioch is intended. When all these data are taken into consideration there would seem to be no clear conclusion either way, but an early date has perhaps fewer difficulties than a later.

Not all those who advocate the South Galatian theory follow Duncan in dating the Epistle before the Council. Some place it at the end of the second or before or during the third missionary journey, and this latter dating approximates to the dating of the North Galatian theory.[1] Doctrinal affinities are sometimes used to determine the question. As J. B. Lightfoot[2], for instance, contended on doctrinal grounds that it must have preceded Romans and it must have come after 2 Corinthians, so the same line of argument has led many South Galatian advocates to maintain a late date. One objection to the dating of the Epistle before the Council of Jerusalem which has been suggested is the difference between the eschatology of this Epistle and the Thessalonian corres-

[1] E. de W. Burton (*Galatians*, ICC, 1921), p. xlvii, sets out four possibilities and cautiously suggests that Ephesus, during the third journey, is the most probable place of dispatch, whether the Epistle was written to North or South Galatia.
[2] *Commentary on Galatians*, pp. 43 ff.; see above, p. 458.

pondence, which would then be dated rather later.[1] But the Thessalonian correspondence need not be regarded as a more primitive stage in Paul's development[2] and in any case arguments from development have too large a subjective element to be of much value in determining dates.

III. OCCASION AND PURPOSE

The reconstruction of the occasion under the South Galatian theory has already been given and little more needs to be added. Paul saw clearly that the issues raised by the subversive activities of the Judaizers had wider implications than were realized by the dominant Jewish Christian element, and the rapidity with which the Galatians had departed from the freedom of the gospel served as a goad to the apostle. He wrote without formal greeting or thanksgiving, deeply moved by the state of affairs which had developed. In addressing a specific and urgent situation the apostle set out what was destined to become the charter of Christian liberty through the subsequent history of the Church.[3]

According to the North Galatian theory a rather different situation is presupposed, for the churches had, in all probability, received the decrees from the Council of Jerusalem (Acts xvi. 4), but they had apparently allowed the Judaizing Christians to rob them of the benefits. The same reconstruction is required under the South Galatian theory if the Epistle is dated after the Council.

Whatever the dating it is clear that part of the tactics of the Judaizers

---

[1] Whereas in 1 and 2 Thessalonians there is a sense of imminence in Paul's allusions to the *parousia*, no such tension is found in Galatians. Yet this is no inherent reason why all these Epistles could not belong to the same period, unless it could be shown that eschatology so dominated Paul's mind at this time that he could not write without mentioning it. Moreover, some case could be made out for an eschatological background in Galatians consistent with that of 1 and 2 Thessalonians (cf. Bicknell, *First and Second Epistles to the Thessalonians*, 1932, pp. xxxv–xxxvii). (Cf. Gal. i. 1–5, v. 5.)

[2] Cf. Duncan, *Galatians*, p. xxxi. Duncan goes so far as to claim that certain features of the theology of Galatians point towards an early date, e.g. the absence of the use of 'body of Christ' to describe the Church and the absence of the word 'mystery'. These can, at best, be only confirmatory.

[3] There is no need to suppose that the apostle had given no previous thought to the problems dealt with in the Epistle. There is a maturity of approach and a thorough grasp of the implications which could not have happened without previous reflection (cf. C. W. Emmet, *op. cit.*, pp. xxi–xxii).

was to discredit the apostle, for he deals at length with the criticisms levelled against him before coming to the main burden of the letter.

IV. THE SOURCE OF OPPOSITION IN THE GALATIAN CHURCHES

The traditional view that the trouble-makers were over-zealous Jewish Christians who were convinced that the sanctity of the law must be maintained and circumcision imposed has not been generally challenged. Whatever opinion has been held about the destination of the Epistle, scholars have on the whole recognized that Jewish Christians were the source of the trouble.[1] But there have been two dissentient theories.

Kirsopp Lake[2] denied that there was a rival Jewish Christian mission, but suggested that the purpose that Paul had in mind was to protect Gentile converts from the attempts of local Jews seeking to win them over to the synagogue. Duncan[3] admits that this might be a possible explanation if no other source of information existed about Paul's pursuers. But since Acts xv shows a vigorous Jewish Christian movement based on Judaea and spreading at least as far as Antioch, it is more reasonable to suppose that the Gentile churches were not exempt from their activities. Duncan thinks that such Jewish Christian movements would have had the support of local Jews.

In addition to this Jewish opposition, J. H. Ropes[4] has suggested that there was a group of Gentile 'perfectionists' among the trouble-makers. They believed themselves to be superior to the law and to recognized principles of morality. The words of Galatians vi. 1, 'you who are spiritual', are thought to be an allusion to this party, whose erroneous approach drew from the apostle strong warnings about the true nature

---

[1] Cf. the discussion of Bo Reicke, 'Der geschichtliche Hintergrund des Apostelkonzils und der Antiochia-Episode, Gal. ii. 1–14', in *Studia Paulina* (1953), pp. 172 ff. He points out that owing perhaps to famine conditions in Jerusalem in AD 47–48, probably accentuated by the occurrence of a sabbatical year, the Jerusalem church may have been more favourable towards Gentile Christianity at the time of the Council than at a later date (cf. pp. 181 f.). But even apart from any official attitude, there is the definite implication of Acts xv. 24 that certain Jewish Christian groups were pursuing a rigid policy without authorization from the Jerusalem leaders.

[2] *Beginnings of Christianity*, v, p. 215.   [3] *Galatians*, p. xxxiii.

[4] 'The Singular Problem of the Epistle to the Galatians', *Harvard Theological Studies*, 14 (1929). Cf. J. M. Creed's refutation in *JTS*, xxxi (1930), pp, 421 ff. This view had been advocated earlier by W. Lütgert, *Gesetz und Geist* (1919).

THE EPISTLE TO THE GALATIANS

of freedom. It is further maintained that Paul's description of Christians as Abraham's offspring was designed to combat attempts to sever Christians from all contact with Judaism. But this theory has little to commend it. As Duncan rightly points out, it makes Paul the Judaizer, and this is unthinkable. There is also no support in the Epistle for the existence of two parties radically opposed.

The recent theory of J. Munck,[1] that not only was this a Gentile church but that the opponents were themselves Gentile 'Judaizers', is not likely to command widespread support, because it is far more probable that the trouble-makers are Jewish. The argument of the Epistle supports this. But other theories must be mentioned which see the opponents as Jews, but Jews influenced by Gentile tendencies. One such theory considers that the opposition comes from Jewish syncretists, whose whole approach was a search for illumination through legalism.[2] Another sees Gnostic influence. This view, advocated by W. Schmithals,[3] is based on some dubious suppositions. It supposes, for instance, that the trouble-makers needed to be informed by Paul that submission to circumcision involved a commitment to keep the whole law. Gnostic circumcision did not carry with it such a commitment. But Galatians v. 3, to which Schmithals appeals, can be better understood as a reminder rather than as a first intimation. There are no doubt some expressions in the Epistle, which can be fitted into a Gnostic mould (such as iv. 8 ff.), but these can be equally well understood in relation to the Jewish Law. Indeed, it cannot be denied that the trouble-makers were insisting on a close observance of the Law, and this does not easily fit into Schmithals' Gnostic theory. The main objection is that there is no evidence in this Epistle that circumcision was regarded as a means of securing release from the flesh,[4] which would have been expected of Gnostic opponents. The further problem arises that we know so little about first-century Gnostic ideas.[5]

---

[1] *Paul and the Salvation of Mankind*, (1959), pp. 87 ff.

[2] Cf. F. C. Crownfield, *JBL*, LXIV (1945), pp. 491–500.

[3] *ZNTW*, 47 (1956), pp. 25–67. Cf. K. Wegenast, *Das Verständnis der Tradition bei Paulus und in den Deuteropaulinen* (1962), for a similar view.

[4] Cf. W. G. Kümmel, *INT* (1965), p. 195. R. H. Fuller (*INT*, 1966, p. 29) criticizes Schmithals' view on the grounds that Paul's arguments are only partially relevant against Gnosticism.

[5] Cf. R. M. Wilson, *The Gnostic Problem* (1958), *Gnosis and the New Testament* (1968).

We may presume therefore that Jewish Christians from Jerusalem were the source of opposition. It is significant to note that on more than one occasion Paul speaks of one person troubling them (iii. 1, v. 7, 10), which suggests that the group probably had a powerful leader, but need not imply that the opposition came only from a single individual. In dealing with the attacks of the group Paul would naturally address himself at times more particularly to the ringleader.

V. AUTHENTICITY

Of all Paul's Epistles Galatians has always been among the least challenged. It so evidently has the stamp of authenticity upon it that only the most radical critics have raised doubts, as for instance the sceptical Dutch school at the end of the eighteenth century. It is surprising, therefore, to find a recent writer challenging authenticity. F. R. McGuire[1] argues that, since Galatians ii depends on Acts xv, although it contradicts the Council decrees, it could not have been written by Paul. But it should be noted that when selecting the genuine Paul, some pattern must first be chosen. A critic like A. Q. Morton,[2] who challenges all but five of Paul's Epistles, selects this Epistle as a norm for measuring authenticity in the other Epistles. Most who reject Morton's methods would nevertheless not quarrel with him over his high regard for Galatians.

CONTENTS

I. GREETING (i. 1–5)

This opening is more self-consciously apologetic than Paul's usual style. He asserts even in the first words his divinely received apostleship.

II. ANATHEMA AGAINST THE DEFECTORS (i. 6–10)

In place of the usual thanksgiving, which is entirely lacking, Paul denounces the perverters of the gospel who are, in fact, preaching another gospel.

[1] *Hibbert Journal*, 66 (1967–68), pp. 52–57.
[2] *Christianity and the Computer* (1964), pp. 24 ff. (in conjunction with J. McLeman).

III. PAUL'S PERSONAL ARGUMENT (i. 11–ii. 21)

In refuting his opponents he appeals to his own history.

1. His teaching was not received from man but from God, and his apostleship is therefore divinely sanctioned (i. 11, 12).

2. He had been zealous for the traditions of the fathers, but God had called him to be a preacher among the Gentiles (i. 13–17).

3. He mentions two occasions when he had had meetings with the Jerusalem apostles, who had on the second occasion extended to him the right hand of fellowship in agreement with his work among the Gentiles. On both occasions his apostleship was unquestioned (i. 18–ii. 10).

4. There was even an occasion at Antioch when he was obliged to withstand one of the 'pillar' apostles to his face because of his inconsistency (ii. 11–14). This was an active demonstration of his apostolic authority.

5. He saw clearly that the real issue was a choice between Christ and the law (ii. 15–21). With this consideration his personal apologia gives place to a dogmatic argument against the Judaizers.

IV. PAUL'S DOGMATIC ARGUMENT (iii. 1–iv. 31)

The gist of Paul's argument is to show that Judaistic Christianity or Christianity according to the law is inferior to the doctrine of faith.

1. The Galatians had not become Christians by the law but by the Spirit. To retrogress to the law could only be evidence of bewitched minds (iii. 1–5).

2. The blessing which Abraham received was by faith not by law (iii. 6–9).

3. The law could in fact do no more than impose a curse, but Christ had removed this by becoming a curse for us (iii. 10–14).

4. In case anyone should object to his appeal to the promise to Abraham on the ground that it was antecedent to law and therefore invalid, Paul shows that God's covenant of promise could never be made void by the law, for it possessed a divine validity (iii. 15–18).

5. This does not imply that the law has no function, but that its function is limited to preparing the way for Christ (iii. 19–29).

6. This means that tutelage under the law must cease when the infinitely superior state of responsible sonship is reached. Whereas law makes slaves, faith makes sons and heirs (iv. 1–7).

7. The doctrinal argument has ended, but Paul now makes a personal appeal, pointing out first the poverty and barrenness of mere ritualism for those who have come to know God (illustrated in the observance of certain days and festivals, iv. 8–11), and then describing the close and affectionate relationship which previously existed between himself and his readers but which has now given place to perplexity over them (iv. 12–20).

8. He further supports his doctrinal argument by means of a scriptural allegory (Sarah and Hagar) to contrast the freedom of Christianity with legal bondage (iv. 21–31).

V. ETHICAL EXHORTATIONS (v. 1–vi. 10)

On the basis of the previous arguments Paul proceeds to expound the true character of Christian freedom.

1. It excludes circumcision, and therefore Judaism (v. 1–6).

2. Those then who were leading the readers astray by putting obstacles before them are strongly comdemned (v. 7–12).

3. But liberty must not be confused with libertinism, which will not happen if love is allowed to rule (v. 13–15).

4. The superiority of the freedom of the Spirit as compared with the freedom of the flesh is forcefully demonstrated by a comparison of their results. The spiritually minded will live by the Spirit (v. 16–26).

5. Spiritual freedom will lead to an attitude of sympathy for the burdened (vi. 1–5), and of liberality, especially to the household of faith, in view of the fact that we shall reap in due season what we sow now (vi. 6–10).

VI. CONCLUSION (vi. 11–18)

This is written with Paul's own hand and in it he summarizes and presses home the main purpose of the letter. He contrasts the Judaizers' insincere motives with his own, i.e. to glory only in the cross of Christ (vi. 11–15). The benediction follows without any personal greetings and with a somewhat impatient request that he should not be further annoyed (vi. 16–18).

ADDITIONAL NOTES

450. [1] W. Marxsen (*INT*, 1968, p. 46) rejects the South Galatian theory as improbable.

454. [3] Cf. W. G. Kümmel, *INT* (1965), p. 193.

458. [2] Kümmel (*op. cit.*, pp. 193–197) strongly supports a dating of Galatians after the Council of Jerusalem and about the same time as Romans and 2 Corinthians. Cf. C. H. Buck (*JBL*, LXX, 1951, pp. 113 ff.) for the theory of a close connection between Galatians and 2 Corinthians.

459. [4] P. Parker (*JBL*, LXXXVI, 1967, pp. 175–182) discusses the relationship between Galatians and Acts, arguing that Gal. ii and Acts xv both refer to Paul's second visit to Jerusalem. He concludes that Acts ix. 26 must, therefore, be a mistake by Luke. But this view is rejected by F. F. Bruce (*BJRL*, LI, 1969, p. 301).

460. [1] The relationship of Paul to the Jerusalem apostles is the subject of D. M. Hay's examination of Paul's attitude to authority (*JBL*, LXXXVIII, 1969, pp. 36–44). He sees Paul as the kind of man who did not consider the apostolic office as authoritative and who, if the Jerusalem apostles had not agreed with him, would have rejected their authority. Cf. J. T. Sanders' view that Paul sometimes uses personal past events as historic rather than as historical for theological purposes (*JBL*, LXXXV, 1966, pp. 335–343). This virtually means that facts were being subjugated to theology, which in the Galatians' church situation would have been a highly unlikely procedure for Paul (cf. F. F. Bruce, *op. cit.*, p. 296). Bruce identifies Acts ix. 30 with Gal. ii. 1–10, treating verses 4 and 5 as a parenthesis. On Gal. ii. 6–9, cf. G. Klein, *ZTK*, 57 (1960), pp. 275–295.

460. [2] Cf. C. H. Talbert (*Nov. Test.*, 9, 1967, pp. 26–40) for the view that Galatians was published after Acts xv. But he holds that Gal. i. 18 relates to Acts ix and Gal. ii. 1 to Acts xi–xii.

463. [1] One problem which arises from an early dating concerns the fitting of Paul's chronological references in Galatians (i. 18, ii. 1) into the general scheme of the chronology of his life. If the Council visit was AD 49 (see p. 458), fourteen years earlier would bring his conversion to AD 35 (or AD 32, if the three years was additional). But if Gal. ii = Acts xi, the conversion would be pushed earlier, yet it could hardly have happened before about AD 33, if the crucifixion is dated at AD 29. See my *Galatians* (CB, n.s., 1969), pp. 35 f. In his recent book on *The Chronology of the Life of Paul* (1968), pp. 72 ff., G. Ogg contends for the date for the Council as AD 48, which would make an early date for Galatians even more difficult. E. F. Harrison (*INT*, 1964, p. 262) points out the chronological difficulty of fitting Acts xi in with Gal. ii, because of the close connection of the famine mentioned there with Herod's death (AD 44). Taking either 14 or 17 years earlier would place Paul's conversion too early.

CHAPTER FOURTEEN

THE CAPTIVITY EPISTLES

The Epistles to the Ephesians, Colossians, Philippians and Philemon are generally known as 'Captivity Epistles' because in all of them Paul writes as a prisoner. But the problem is to allocate them to the right imprisonment. Of those mentioned in Acts, Philippi must clearly be ruled out, leaving the choice between Caesarea and Rome.[1] The respective claims of these have been dealt with in the introductions to the various Epistles, and our present purpose is to discuss a third alternative, Ephesus. Although no mention is made of this in Acts many scholars have suggested that Paul may have been imprisoned there and if so the possibility of assigning the Captivity Epistles (wholly or partly) to Ephesus must be carefully considered.

The evidence may be summed up as follows.[2]

1. In 2 Corinthians xi. 23 Paul speaks of being 'in prisons far more frequently' (i.e. than other servants of Christ) and yet up to the time of the dispatch of this letter Paul had suffered only the Philippian imprisonment, according to Acts.

2. In 1 Corinthians xv. 32 the occurrence of the word ἐθηριομάχησα ('I fought with wild beasts') has been interpreted literally as suggesting that Paul had faced the possibility of being thrown into the arena at Ephesus.

3. In 2 Corinthians i. 8 Paul mentions some severe trial (θλίψις) which he had passed through in Asia. of such severity that he despaired even of life itself.

4. The occasion on which Priscilla and Aquila risked their lives for Paul's sake (Rom. xvi. 3, 4) is most likely to have been at Ephesus. It is certainly a reference to some happening preceding the writing of Romans, or at least of chapter xvi if that was a separate note.[3]

[1] For a recent view that Acts xxviii. 30, 31 is displaced from a position after xxiv. 26 and therefore refers to the extensive imprisonment at Caesarea and not Rome, see L. Johnson, 'The Pauline Letters from Caesarea', *ET*, LXVIII (1956–57), pp. 24–26. But see the criticism of this on p. 478 n. 2.

[2] This summary is based mainly on Duncan's *St. Paul's Ephesian Ministry* (1929), pp. 66 ff. Cf. also W. Michaelis, *Einleitung*, pp. 207 ff.

[3] See pp. 400 ff.

5. Clement of Rome mentions seven imprisonments of Paul (*Ad Cor.* v. 6).

6. Several traces have been preserved of a tradition that Paul had an encounter with a lion. Duncan cites the *Acts of Titus*, Hippolytus' commentary on Daniel, the fourteenth-century historian Nicephorus Callisti and the *Acts of Paul* (mid-second century), the latter specifically identifying the incident as happening at Ephesus.

7. In Ephesus a building is shown which is known as Paul's prison.

8. The Marcionite Prologue to Colossians states that it was written from Ephesus.

Duncan admits that this evidence is not of itself convincing without the support of the indirect evidence of the Epistles themselves. This evidence is discussed in the introductions to each Epistle,[1] but such internal evidence is support for an Ephesian imprisonment only if there is adequate basis for assuming such an imprisonment. Our present purpose is to test the validity of the evidence mentioned above.

The statement of Paul's many imprisonments shows clearly that many events of a critical nature are not recorded in Acts and this at least prepares the way for the assignment of an imprisonment to Ephesus. But there are many other places where Paul might well have been imprisoned, particularly in those districts where Jewish opposition incited the people to take action against him. Luke is more likely to have been less well informed about the earlier period than about the Ephesian ministry (but see discussion below on the silence of Acts).

The understanding of ἐθηριομάχησα in 1 Corinthians xv. 32 in a literal sense is criticized by Dodd[2] on the following grounds.

1. In the same context Paul says 'I die daily' and yet at the time of writing he is a free man. The 'dying' can only be understood in a metaphorical sense.

2. For a Roman citizen to be condemned to the lions was very rare and would never have been officially contemplated on so slender a charge as temple robbery (as Duncan[3] suggests). In any case Paul's statement is purely hypothetical and does not necessitate his being

---

[1] See pp. 531 ff. for Philippians; pp. 555 ff. for Colossians (with Philemon).

[2] *New Testament Studies* (1953), pp. 100 ff.

[3] *St. Paul's Ephesian Ministry*, pp. 116 ff. F. J. Badcock (*The Pauline Epistles and the Epistle to the Hebrews*, 1937, p. 68) makes the same suggestion and further proposes that Paul escaped from this serious situation after the murder of the proconsul Silanus, who according to Badcock's suggestion had been responsible for Paul's arrest.

actually thrown into the arena. The Ephesian hypothesis supposes at least that it was a possibility, which Dodd considers very doubtful. The metaphorical interpretation seems preferable in view of Paul's prophecy in his address to the Ephesian elders that 'fierce wolves will come in among you' (Acts xx. 29), which no-one has suggested should be taken literally.[1] Paul's argument is that if the resurrection is not a reality he might as well join the materialists in their philosophy of 'let us eat and drink, for to-morrow we die' instead of opposing them.

The affliction ($\theta\lambda\tilde{\iota}\psi\iota\varsigma$) in 2 Corinthians i. 8, which appears to have had a threatening character, for ·Paul felt as if he had received the sentence of death, would certainly be illuminated if he had been imprisoned and action had been taken against him which threatened capital punishment; but is the theory required by the data? Paul describes himself and perhaps others with him (he uses the plural 'we') as 'utterly, unbearably crushed' (RSV) and he writes of his deliverance from some 'deadly peril' (verse 10, RSV). While these statements could refer to an imprisonment they could equally relate to a serious illness[2] or a serious spiritual crisis.[3] This in any case must have happened after the conflict of 1 Corinthians xv. 32, for Paul writes as if he is informing them of something they did not know. Indeed Duncan places this after Paul's 'sorrowful visit' to Corinth and considers that it took place not in Ephesus but somewhere in the province of Asia, probably Laodicea. But the separation of these two imprisonments weakens the relative evidence for each.

Whether the statement that Priscilla and Aquila 'risked their necks' for Paul may be regarded as support for an Ephesian imprisonment is doubtful, although it cannot be said to be an impossibility. We know that they were at Ephesus (Acts xviii. 19) but we hear nothing of them after Paul's arrival there (Acts xix. 1), and since they are apparently in Rome[4] when Paul writes to that church it is reasonable to suppose that they moved on from Ephesus before Paul arrived there. They may have

[1] The same Greek word is used by Ignatius (*Ad Rom.* v. 1) in a clearly metaphorical sense (i.e. of the detachment of soldiers) (cf. Arndt and Gingrich, *A Greek-English Lexicon of the New Testament*, 1957, p. 361).*

[2] Cf. E. B. Allo, *St. Paul, Seconde Epître aux Corinthiens* (1937), pp. 15 ff.; M. Goguel, *Introduction*, vol. IV, p. 132; cf. also H. Clavier, 'La Santé de l'apôtre Paul', *Studia Paulina*, pp. 66–82.

[3] Goodspeed, *INT*, p. 105, suggests it may refer to agony of mind over the Corinthians' hostility.

[4] Duncan regards Rom. xvi as part of the Roman letter (*ET*, April 1935, p. 298 n.).

risked their necks for Paul's sake when they were not actually with Paul, but this is not the most natural understanding of the words. We conclude, therefore, that the internal evidence does not require an Ephesian imprisonment, although it does point to some crisis in which Paul was involved.

The external evidence is more precarious. Clement's statement may be no more than an inference from 2 Corinthians xi. 23, although the specific number seven looks like a piece of authentic tradition.[1] If the statement is a valid piece of historical evidence it may certainly be used in confirmation of possible imprisonments unrecorded in Acts, but it does not prove that any such imprisonment happened at Ephesus. The lion episode is not well supported for the two apocryphal *Acts* cannot safely be appealed to as evidence for authentic traditions. The *Acts of Titus* probably borrows from the *Acts of Paul*,[2] and the latter wears too boldly the appearance of fiction to provide much confidence in its historical data. It may of course preserve traces of a genuine event, but the setting in which it is found in this spurious work is not particularly helpful to the Ephesian imprisonment theory. The governor is called Hieronymus, but this provides no point of contact with the history of the period. The whole incident has every appearance of being legendary not only in the manner in which it is related but also in the basic ideas of the story. As far as it is possible to surmise it would seem that the Ephesus incident is developed from a combination of 1 Corinthians xv. 32 and Acts xix. 23 ff., with the author's own imagination supplying the other details.[3] His placing of the Ephesus incident is not certain because of the incomplete character of the text, but in all probability he thought of it as after Paul's release from his first Roman imprisonment.

Not much importance can be attached to the traditional prison of Paul in Ephesus for nothing is known of its history or origin,[4] and its description is probably an ingenious guess based on the apocryphal stories mentioned above. The Colossian Prologue is curious when com-

---

[1] J. Schmid, *Zeit und Ort der paulinischen Gefangenschaftsbriefe* (1931), p. 65 n., notes the suggestion of E. Zeller that Clement's seven is comprised of the Roman and Caesarean imprisonments plus the fivefold stripes of 2 Cor. xi. 24 (cf. also Mommsen, *ZNTW*, 1901, p. 89).

[2] Cf. M. R. James, *The Apocryphal New Testament* (1924), pp. 271 f., 291.

[3] Cf. Leon Vouaux's examination of the author's methods in *Les Actes de Paul et ses lettres apocryphes* (1913), pp. 112 ff.

[4] Cf. M. Jones, *Philippians, WC* (1912), p. xxxiii.

pared with those attached to the letters to the Philippians and to Philemon, which are both stated to be from Rome. Duncan inquires
whether the latter two may not be guesswork and the former an independent tradition. It is impossible to say which is right, but since
Colossians and Philemon belong so closely together it is difficult to see
why in one case a true tradition is preserved and not in the other.[1] The
same position admittedly obtains for Rome as well as Ephesus, but the
former has the almost unchallenged support of other tradition.

When the evidence is carefully sifted it cannot be said to point very
strongly to an Ephesian imprisonment, and there is still the silence of
Acts to consider. Paul appears to have worked at Ephesus for about
three years (Acts xx. 31) and he states specifically that during this time
he did not cease admonishing them night or day. While these words
need not be understood literally in every detail, they suggest an unbroken period of mission work among the people of Ephesus. This does
not, of course, rule out the possibility of one or more imprisonments but
it does constitute a difficulty for the hypothesis. A still greater difficulty
is the total omission of any such imprisonment in the Acts account of
Paul's Ephesian ministry.[2] That there was opposition is clear enough
from the riot, but on that occasion Paul was not present, for the Asiarchs, who were officials entrusted with the task of maintaining order
in religious affairs and who were well disposed towards Paul, persuaded
him not to go to the assistance of his two companions Gaius and Aristarchus. There is no hint of any arrest and the best that Duncan can
suggest is that the Asiarchs took Paul into protective custody. But they
would hardly have 'begged' Paul to come into custody (cf. Acts xix.
31), and even if they had done so such custody would not square with
the kind of imprisonment reflected in the Captivity Epistles.[3]

---

[1] P. Corssen, ZNTW (1909), pp. 37 ff., considered the imprisonment was the
well-known one mentioned at the end of Acts and suggested that Paul was taken
to Ephesus on his way from Caesarea to Rome and wrote the Epistle while detained there. But this theory has little to commend it.

[2] Deissmann, Anatolian Studies presented to Sir W. Ramsay, p. 124 n., assumed
that the omission was due partly to Luke's lack of close knowledge of the Ephesian
period and partly to the fact that it did not fall within his programme.

[3] Duncan assigned Col. and Phm. to this riot-imprisonment (op. cit., pp. 140 ff.).
He has since modified this by assigning them to a second Ephesian imprisonment
more than a year before (NTS, 3 (1957), pp. 211 ff.; 5 (1958), pp. 43 ff.). The
difference between the imprisonments is a considerable difficulty for the Ephesian
hypothesis (cf. Meinertz, Einleitung, p. 122).

It is impossible, without ignoring the plain meaning of Acts xx. 1, to fit in an imprisonment at Ephesus subsequent to the riot. Nor is it convincing to suggest an imprisonment at Laodicea before Paul proceeded to Macedonia, for the Lycus valley would not lie on the route from Ephesus to Macedonia. The Acts historian was sufficiently well informed to state not only Paul's route but also the precise time spent in Greece (three months) and it is not easy to suppose that he would have omitted all reference to the Lycus valley if Paul had visited there after leaving Ephesus.

There is rather less objection to the earlier imprisonment postulated by Duncan, during which he thinks Philippians was written, for the silence of Acts cannot in this case be considered conclusive against it in view of other data which the author is known to have omitted (cf. the list in 2 Corinthians xi. 21 ff.). The major problem is to discover a motive for the omission of what must have been an important crisis, if due weight is to be given to Paul's words in Philippians i. It must have been of brief duration and must have ended in Paul's acquittal, but if so it is difficult to see why Luke did not include it as a striking example of Roman justice, as in the case of Gallio. Duncan[1] attempts to explain the silence of Acts on the assumption that Junius Silanus was proconsul at the time, and since he was murdered on the orders of Agrippina and his name was therefore out of favour at the court it would have been impolitic to have mentioned him. Dodd[2] points out that this reasoning has force only if Acts was written for the defence of Paul.[3] It may in that case be a possible explanation of Luke's omission. The account of the Ephesian ministry in Acts is so sketchy that it is not impossible to make room for unrecorded crises, but if there were imprisonments it is perplexing not to know why Luke preferred the riot account to the earlier imprisonment with its more serious implications for the apostle. On the other hand some weight must be given to the fact that Luke was not at Ephesus during Paul's ministry there and was not therefore reporting at first hand. The riot account would suit his purpose of illustrating the fair-mindedness of Roman officials, and he has clearly received a vivid

[1] *Op. cit.*, pp. 100 ff.

[2] *New Testament Studies*, pp. 102, 103.

[3] Most scholars prefer a later dating, but among those maintaining a date about AD 63 are F. F. Bruce, *The Acts of the Apostles* (1951); R. B. Rackham, *The Acts of the Apostles*[4] (1908). C. S. C. Williams, *The Acts of the Apostles* (1957), p. 15, admits the strength of the case for an early date but mentions the possibility that publication was delayed for some years.

report of this. To mention other imprisonments, even if he had known them, may not have served any useful purpose.

Our conclusion is that the evidence is not strong enough to demonstrate an Ephesian imprisonment, although such an imprisonment is not impossible.[1] Whether any or all of the Captivity Epistles belong to such a postulated imprisonment is a separate question and will be considered in the introductions to Philippians, Colossians and Philemon.[2]

[1] Cf. the brief evaluation of the evidence by D. T. Rowlingson (*ATR*, xxxii, 1950, pp. 1–7), 'Paul's Ephesian Imprisonment', in which he admits most of the evidence to be neutral but concludes in favour of an Ephesian imprisonment because of two 'straws' which he considers to be non-neutral, i.e. (a) Paul's intention to visit the Lycus valley and (b) his intention to send Timothy. The former of these is dealt with in the introduction to Colossians (see pp. 555 f.) and the latter in the introduction to Philippians (see pp. 532 f.).

[2] It will be convenient to mention here the hypothesis of L. Johnson ('The Pauline Letters from Caesarea', *ET*, lxviii, 1956–57, pp. 24 ff.) that all the Captivity Epistles and 2 Timothy were sent from Caesarea on the ground that Acts xxviii. 30, 31 does not belong after Acts xxviii. 29 but after Acts xxiv. 26. He arrives at this through stichometrical calculation that Acts should contain, as Luke, ninety columns and that our present ending is incomplete and merely patched up. This method of textual emendation is of doubtful validity, especially when it is used to dispose of the reference to Rome in 2 Tim. i. 17. It is true that this reconstruction would avoid some of the objections to a Caesarean place of dispatch for the Captivity Epistles as mentioned in the introduction to Colossians and Philippians, since it would mean that Paul enjoyed partial liberty during his two-year imprisonment there. But the absence at present of supporting evidence for this textual change must render it suspicious

ADDITIONAL NOTE

474. [1] R. E. Osborne (*JBL*, lxxxv, 1966, pp. 225–230) considers that ἐθηριομάχησα (1 Cor. xv. 32) may be paralleled to the Habakkuk scroll's use of $w^e habb^e h\bar{e}m\^ot$ for the 'simple' in Judah who keep the law. The same may be applicable to Paul's opponents. Another writer, A. J. Malherbe (*JBL*, lxxxvii, 1968, pp. 71–80), argues from Greek rather than Hebrew parallels. According to parallel usages in the diatribe ἐθηριομάχησα would be taken metaphorically. The argument in the passage is that the beasts were heretics, who had no eschatology to govern their morality.

CHAPTER FIFTEEN

THE EPISTLE TO THE EPHESIANS

To many this is one of Paul's most moving Epistles and yet to others it is only a reproduction of Pauline themes by another mind. Much controversy has surrounded and still surrounds the question of authenticity and the evidence for and against will need to be examined in some detail.

I. AUTHENTICITY

a. The traditional view

Since this Epistle had been regarded as a genuine Epistle of Paul until nineteenth-century criticism attacked it, it will be advisable first of all to enumerate the positive grounds upon which this traditional view was based.

(i) *Its self-claims.* In the opening address, which is identical with those of 2 Corinthians and Colossians, the writer not only claims to be Paul, but claims also the authority of apostleship by the will of God. This is as characteristic of Paul as is the greeting with its combination of grace and peace (i. 2). But this is not all, for the name recurs in the body of the Epistle (iii. 1) in the same manner as in 2 Corinthians x. 1, Galatians v. 2, Colossians i. 23, 1 Thessalonians ii. 18 and Philemon 9 (cf. also 1 Cor. xvi. 21, Col. iv. 18, 2 Thes. iii. 17 and Phm. 19 where it occurs at the close of the letters).

The whole Epistle and particularly the section from iii. 1 ff. abounds with statements in the first person and it is instructive to note the picture that the author gives of himself. He has personally heard of the readers' faith and of their love towards other Christians (i. 15); he expresses his personal thanks to God for them (i. 16); describes himself as a 'prisoner of Jesus Christ' (iii. 1, iv. 1); points out that he is writing about a mystery personally revealed to him (iii. 3 ff.); appeals to his own divine appointment to the ministry (iii. 7); exhorts the readers not to lose heart over his present sufferings (iii. 13); assumes an attitude of humble intercession for them (iii. 14 ff.); affirms the readers' present need of a new way of living and of thinking against a background of Gentile ignorance and licentiousness (iv. 17 ff.); gives his own interpretation of the 'mystery' (v. 32); appeals for prayer on his own behalf as a chained ambassador that he might have boldness to speak (vi. 19, 20); and concludes with a personal salutation (vi. 21, 22). From these persistent witnesses to the author-reader relationship the personality of Paul may be sufficiently discerned. Indeed it seems in agreement with what is seen of him from his other Epistles. A different interpretation of this evidence will be considered later, but it is difficult not to see in it a personal knowledge on the author's part of the present circumstances of the readers.

(ii) *Its external attestation*. This Epistle appears to have been in wide circulation by the middle of the second century among both orthodox Christians and heretics. It was included in the earliest formal Canon, that of Marcion (*c.* AD 140), though under the name of 'Laodiceans'. Its Pauline origin was therefore at this time undisputed, since Marcion acknowledged only the apostle Paul as his authority. In the Muratorian Canon (*c.* AD 180) it was included under the Epistles of Paul. It forms part of the Pauline Epistles in the earliest evidence for the Latin and Syriac versions. It was used by the Ophites, Valentinians and Basilideans.[1] There are reminiscences of its language in the writings of Clement of Rome, Ignatius, Polycarp, Hermas and possibly the Didache. The explanation of these reminiscences cannot be a similar milieu of thought, for these sub-apostolic writers reflect a more developed state of church life and thought. Most scholars are therefore agreed that Ephesians must have preceded the Epistle of Clement of Rome to the Corinthians (AD 95).

(iii) *Its Pauline structure*. Leaving aside stylistic considerations which will be dealt with later (pp. 482 ff., 491 ff.) it may here be pointed out that there are distinct affinities with Paul's other Epistles in the literary type to which they all belong. We find the characteristically Pauline sequence of opening greeting, thanksgiving, doctrinal exposition, ethical exhortations, concluding salutations and benediction. While this generally conforms to the contemporary literary epistolary pattern, it is treated in a distinctively Pauline manner compared with the non-Pauline New Testament Epistles (and incidentally with the spurious 3 Corinthians). In particular, the basing of moral appeal on theological argument can not only be paralleled in Paul's other Epistles but was in fact an integral part of the apostle's approach to practical problems.

---

[1] Cf. Westcott, *On the Canon of the New Testament*, pp. 314, 323, 338.

(iv) *Its language and literary affinities.* There are many words common to the Epistle and to the other Pauline Epistles which do not occur elsewhere in the New Testament. The vocabulary is, in fact, nearer to that of the earlier Pauline Epistles than its sister Epistle, Colossians. There are the characteristic paradoxical antitheses (cf. vi. 15, 20), free citations from the Old Testament (iv. 8–11, cf. Rom. x. 6–8) and adaption of Old Testament language (i. 22, ii. 13, 17, iv. 25, v. 2, vi. 1–3, cf. 1 Cor. iii. 9).

The literary connection with the other Pauline Epistles and the other New Testament Epistles will be discussed later, but the striking similarities between Ephesians and Colossians call for some comment here as the close connection between the Epistles has undoubtedly played some part in the traditional approach. If Colossians is a genuine Epistle of Paul, and few modern scholars doubt that it is (see pp. 551 ff.), its close connection with Ephesians and the patristic assumption that both Epistles were genuine raise a strong presumption in favour of Ephesians. In fact the attestation is stronger for Ephesians than for Colossians.

(v) *Its theological affinities.* While there are some new emphases in the Epistle (as for instance in the doctrine of the Church), the background of Pauline theology is unmistakable. There is the characteristic conception of God as not only glorious (i. 17) and powerful (i. 19 ff.) but also merciful (ii. 4 ff.), the same consciousness of mystic wonder that the believer is 'in Christ' (i. 3, 10, 11, *al.*), the same appreciation of the reconciliatory value of the cross (ii. 13 ff.), the same grasp of the ministry of the Holy Spirit (ii. 18, iii. 5, iv. 1 ff., 30, v. 18) and the same humble awareness of the predestinating counsel of God (i. 5 ff.). In fact this Epistle has often not inappropriately been called the crown of Paulinism.[1]

(vi) *Its historical data.* Because of the almost entire absence of any historical clues in this Epistle it may seem an unlikely quest to educe historical data in support of the tradition, but this line of approach

---

[1] So J. Armitage Robinson, *The Epistle to the Ephesians*[2] (1904), p. vii. W. Barclay, *Galatians and Ephesians*, DSB (1958), pp. 79, 80, cites this against a pseudonymous theory because imitation always produces secondary material. The theological quality of this Epistle is certainly not inferior to the theological quality of Paul's greatest Epistles. Cf. also E. F. Scott, *The Literature of the New Testament* (1932), p. 180, who considered that, if not by Paul, Ephesians must have been written by his equal.

rests rather on negative than positive evidence. The silence regarding the fall of Jerusalem is rather remarkable in view of the argument about the destruction of the dividing wall between Jew and Gentile (ii. 14 ff.),[1] while the absence of reference to the persecution of the readers may indicate a date during the early period of the Church's history, i.e. the apostolic period. Moreover, the absence of developed ecclesiastical organization fits an early date better than a later. Historical considerations, as far as they can be ascertained, give the impression of an early setting in agreement with a genuine Epistle of Paul.

(vii) *Conclusion.* This brief introductory survey of the traditional position has enabled us to see the strong external background and primary internal impressions of authenticity given by the Epistle itself. It is against this background that the objections raised by certain schools of criticism must be stated and examined. The arguments against will first be given in order to present as completely as possible the cumulative grounds for dispensing with this Epistle as a genuine work of Paul. The burden of proof must in any case lie with the challengers since the Epistle not only claims to be Pauline but has also been regarded as such by the Christian Church. As Mitton, who himself denies Pauline authorship, admits, 'Pauline authorship can rightly be assumed until it is disproved'.[2] This means that those maintaining Pauline authorship will need only to bring adequate counter-arguments against the arguments of the challengers. This is naturally a defensive approach, but it cannot in the nature of the case be otherwise.

b. The case against Pauline authorship

These objections may be conveniently grouped under four main heads, linguistic and stylistic, literary, historical and doctrinal, and they will be considered in that order.

(i) *Linguistic and stylistic arguments.*[3] First it may be noted that there are a number of words which do not occur elsewhere in the New Testament and others which are New Testament words but are absent from the other generally accepted Pauline Epistles. Some of these are said to be significant. For instance, whereas Paul refers to the devil by

[1] See pp. 502 f. for further discussion on this point. Cf. also the comments of R. D. Shaw, *The Pauline Epistles*[4] (1913), p. 369.

[2] *The Epistle to the Ephesians* (1951), p. 7.

[3] For the corresponding arguments in support of Pauline authorship, see pp. 491 ff.

various titles in his other letters he does not use διάβολος as he does in Ephesians (it is used in the Pastoral Epistles, but since their authenticity is also widely disputed they are excluded in the present argument). The phrase 'in the heavenlies', which occurs many times in Ephesians, does not occur elsewhere in Paul. The prepositions ἐν and κατά occur with unusual frequency for Paul, while there is an unparalleled number of genitival formations.[1]

Goodspeed[2] thinks that the novel element in the vocabulary shows a close relationship with works like Luke-Acts, 1 Clement, 1 Peter and Hebrews, which he considers were all written towards the close of the first century. On this basis he regards the linguistic data as pointing to a time later than the apostle Paul.

The style is certainly different from the other nine undisputed Pauline Epistles and this has seemed to some to weigh against Pauline authorship. Goodspeed calls it 'reverberating and liturgical, not at all the direct, rapid Pauline give-and-take'.[3] Mitton remarks that 'we are uncomfortably aware in Ephesians of a somewhat artificial eloquence, which Paul elsewhere seemed deliberately to avoid (cf. 1 Cor. i. 17, ii. 4, 13)'.[4] There are also many redundant expressions, such as τὴν βουλὴν τοῦ θελήματος (i. 11) and τοῦ κράτους τῆς ἰσχύος (i. 19), which have appeared to some scholars as evidence of non-Pauline practice. Many who have admitted these difficulties over the style have not, however, considered the difficulties sufficiently weighty to overthrow authenticity.

It has further been maintained by Goodspeed that the review of blessings in the opening part of the Epistle is not Pauline because his usual method was to take up a theme and dwell upon it, whereas in Ephesians the themes 'fairly tumble over one another'. He thinks this would be natural if the Epistle was the work of a Paulinist who wrote to introduce the collected works of Paul.

(ii) *Literary arguments*.[5] The most important consideration is the relationship between Ephesians and Colossians. It is maintained that over a quarter of the words in Ephesians are borrowed from Colossians,

[1] M. Goguel, *Introduction*, IV, ii, 433 n., cites fifteen examples of what he terms this 'construction pléonastique'.
[2] *Key to Ephesians* (1956), p. vi.
[3] *Key to Ephesians*, p. vii.
[4] *The Epistle to the Ephesians*, p. 11.
[5] For the arguments for Pauline authorship, see pp. 492 ff.

484 NEW TESTAMENT INTRODUCTION

while more than a third of the words in Colossians reappear in Ephesians. There is no parallel to this in any other of Paul's Epistles, and the phenomenon demands an explanation. The view that both Epistles were written by the same author on different occasions is rejected in favour of the theory that the author of Ephesians was so familiar with Colossians that his mind moved in accordance with the development of argument in that Epistle and at times brought together passages which were separated in the earlier Epistle. Yet because the exact similarities with Colossians are not as great as would be expected under this hypothesis, it has been considered doubtful that the author knew Colossians off by heart.[1] There is, in fact, only one passage of any length which can be verbally paralleled in the two Epistles, and that concerns Tychicus. Nevertheless the alleged use of Colossians by the author is considered by Dibelius[2] to be decisive against Pauline authorship.

It is not the mere use of Colossians, however, which generally weighs heaviest against Pauline authorship in the minds of its opponents. It is rather the frequency of parallel words and terminology used in a completely different sense. Some scholars, for example, cannot imagine a man like Paul refusing original terms to express new ideas and borrowing instead phrases from Colossians to express something quite different.[3] The problem is whether it is psychologically possible for a man with such fluency as Paul to repeat words and phrases, but with a different meaning. Opponents of Pauline authorship answer in the negative. To illustrate this latter point, one or two examples may be cited. The description of Christ as Head of the Church in Ephesians iv. 15, 16 is claimed to be borrowed from Colossians ii. 19, but there it is applied

---

[1] Cf. Mitton, op. cit., pp. 57, 58.

[2] Kolosser-Epheser und Philemonbriefe[2] (1927), p. 63. Not all scholars who dispute the authenticity of the Epistle are agreed on the complete priority of Colossians. Holtzmann, for instance, found some cases in which he felt bound to conclude for the priority of Ephesians, which led to his improbable theory of interpolations into the genuine Epistle to the Colossians by the author of Ephesians (Kritik der Epheser und Kolosserbriefe, 1892, pp. 46–55). G. Salmon (Introduction to the New Testament, 1892, p. 391) in criticism of Holtzmann rightly pointed out that the data appealed to would naturally lead to the conclusion that conscious imitation on either side cannot be the explanation. C. H. Dodd (Colossians, AB, 1929, p. 1224) agrees that it is not always clear on which side the borrowing lies. See p. 552 n. 3 for details of the views of P. N. Harrison and C. Masson, who both follow Holtzmann's main contentions.

[3] Cf. D. E. Nineham in Studies in Ephesians, edited by F. L. Cross (1956), pp. 27 ff. See also J. A. Allan, Ephesians (1951), pp. 14–23.

to the cosmic powers.[1] Whereas the word 'mystery' in Colossians is applied to Christ, in Ephesians it is used of the unifying of Jew and Gentile. In Colossians the word οἰκονομία (stewardship) is used to describe an entrusted task (i. 25), but in Ephesians it refers to the planned economy of God (iii. 2). This sort of thing is said to be characteristic of Ephesians.

Mitton[2] draws attention to many occasions in Ephesians where two passages from Colossians have been conflated into one passage (e.g. Col. i. 14, 20 and Eph. i. 7; Col. i. 9, 4 and Eph. i. 15, 16; Col. ii. 13, iii. 6 and Eph. ii. 1–5). He claims that some similarity of wording in the Colossians passages serves as a link to combine them in Ephesians. This evidence is alleged to show not only that the author was not the author of Colossians but that he was citing the latter from memory.

So far we have mentioned only the literary relation between Ephesians and Colossians, but some scholars place equal emphasis upon its literary dependence on the other eight 'genuine' letters of Paul. Goodspeed,[3] for instance, maintains that the author of Ephesians knew well all the other letters, but his familiarity with them was not that of Paul but of an admiring disciple. Largely on the basis of this supposition Goodspeed argues that Ephesians must have been written after the collection of the other letters. The manner in which the author has incorporated material from these other letters seems to Mitton to differ considerably from that of Paul, so much so that the phenomena of Ephesians are thought to betray the hand of an imitator. An attempt is made to prove this by comparing Ephesians with Philippians, which has far fewer parallels with the other Paulines. Mitton[4] claims that Philippians is a fair standard to which to appeal because it belongs to the same period as Ephesians purports to belong to and can be claimed as typical of Paul's writings. When these Epistles are compared, not only does Ephesians show a much greater proportion of Pauline parallels but also a greater tendency to draw from some of the more striking passages in the other Epistles, which is reckoned by Mitton[5] to be a test by which an imitator may be distinguished from Paul. The basis of this

[1] Cf. Dibelius, op. cit., p. 64. See also C. L. Mitton, Ephesians, pp. 61, 84.

[2] Op. cit., pp. 65–67.

[3] Key to Ephesians, p. vii; the evidence is tabulated in his Introduction to the New Testament (1937), p. 213. Cf. also A. E. Barnett, Paul becomes a Literary Influence (1941), pp. 1–40.

[4] Cf. op. cit., p. 108.   [5] Op. cit., pp. 108 ff.

test is the assumption that only an imitator would be inclined to reproduce certain passages which had made a deeper impression on his mind than others. Another test proposed by the same scholar is the use of 'striking and memorable' phrases from the other Pauline Epistles, which he considers to be an indication of an imitator. This second test also shows a difference between Ephesians and Philippians, which therefore suggests, if the test is valid, that the former must be non-Pauline.

The literary parallels between Ephesians and other New Testament books also present a problem and are particularly important because of their use in the attempt to fix a date for the Epistle. There are many parallels between the Epistle and 1 Peter although it is difficult to determine the direction of literary dependence, if such dependence seems probable. Those who assume that Ephesians has borrowed from 1 Peter do not place themselves in so vulnerable a position as those who make the reverse assumption. Among the latter is Mitton,[1] who makes the significant admission that if 1 Peter belonged to Peter's lifetime, it would be almost conclusive that Ephesians belonged to Paul's own time, and must therefore have been written by him. But he does not accept the Petrine authorship of 1 Peter and can therefore adhere to a date for both far later than the lifetime of Paul. There are similarly more parallels between Ephesians and the Acts than is the case for any other Pauline Epistle, and this has produced various explanations. If the author of Acts used Ephesians it would be difficult if not impossible to deny the Pauline authorship of the latter. But the opponents of Pauline authorship invariably deny that the author of Acts was acquainted with Ephesians, in which case the only options are either to hold that Ephesians was written under the influence of Acts or else that both were written within the same decade and were the products of the same spiritual atmosphere. In neither case would Pauline authorship be possible. Goodspeed conjectures that the author of Ephesians thinks of Paul in the condition in which the Acts left him, i.e. 'a prisoner for the Greek mission'.[2]

One of the reasons why some scholars think that Ephesians could not have been published until after Luke-Acts is the absence of any trace of Ephesians in Matthew and Mark. Goodspeed suggests that the appearance of Luke-Acts supplied the impetus for the collection of the Pauline letters. On the other hand there are similarities between Ephesians and

---

[1] *Op. cit.*, p. 177.   [2] *Key to Ephesians*, p. vi.*

John which are claimed to support the theory that the Epistle belongs to the period separating the Synoptic Gospels from John.[1]

Another important literary problem is the form of the letter. It differs from the other Paulines in the absence of any concrete situation to which Paul is addressing himself. Moffatt[2] regarded it as a homily rather than a letter, while many scholars have strongly criticized the encyclical explanation of its peculiar form.[3]

The references to Paul in the letter are said to be forced. For instance, the words 'I am the least of all saints' (iii. 8) sound in Mitton's opinion 'calmly deliberate, even self-conscious and a little theatrical'.[4] In iii. 2 Paul writes rather awkwardly, 'If you have heard' of God's steward-ship granted to me. Again in iii. 4 Paul appears to be commending his own insight into the mystery of Christ in such a way as to constitute a difficulty in the minds of some. He is said to be too complacent and to 'protest too much' for the genuine Paul.[5] Because of this it is supposed that the writer's admiration for Paul constitutes a real difficulty for the defenders of Pauline authorship. It is maintained that Paul did not overstress his own activity in such sweeping terms as we find here.[6]

(iii) *Historical arguments.*[7] There is such strong external attestation for the early recognition of Ephesians as Pauline that the objectors to authenticity are hard put to it to explain it away. The usual line of attack against this damaging external evidence is to maintain that pseudepigraphy was very common at that time, even among Christians. In support of this, appeal is made to those parts of the New Testament which some scholars regard as pseudepigraphical, e.g. 2 Peter, Jude, James, Apocalypse, 1 Peter and the Pastoral Epistles. If pseudepigraphy was as common a Christian practice as this, so the argument proceeds, the Christian Church would have had no hesitancy in accepting it, even if they had known it to be non-Pauline. Early attestation to its circulation and use may if necessary be set aside if it clashes with a hypothesis which offers a reasonable explanation of the internal data. Thus if internal evidence is assumed to be against Pauline authorship it is considered to take precedence over external attestation.[8]

[1] Cf. W. Lock, *HDB*, vol. I, p. 716.   [2] *ILNT*, pp. 373 ff.
[3] See later discussion, pp. 510 f. Cf. Dibelius, *KEP*, pp. 43 f.   [4] *Op. cit.*, p. 15.
[5] Cf. Mitton, *op. cit.*, p. 15, and Nineham, *Studies in Ephesians* (edited by F. L. Cross), p. 35.   [6] Cf. Nineham, *op. cit.*, p. 35.
[7] For the arguments for Pauline authorship, see pp. 502 ff.
[8] See the discussion on Epistolary Pseudepigraphy, Appendix C, pp. 671 ff., for a consideration of the validity of this approach.

One of the strongest historical factors alleged to weigh heavily against Pauline authorship is the state of the Jewish-Gentile controversy. It seems already settled, whereas in Paul's other Epistles the conflict still appears to be active. The basic assumption of scholars maintaining this position is that the controversy could not have been settled in Paul's lifetime.[1]

Goodspeed[2] further maintains that the breaking down of the barrier separating Jew and Gentile, although figurative, is more natural after AD 70 when the destruction of the temple had effectively eliminated the barrier. Closely akin to this view is the contention that the Church has now become Greek with no room for Jewish Christianity. Ephesians ii. 2, 11 is said to prove that all the readers were once heathen, while ii. 3 suggests that the author identifies himself in this respect with the readers and must therefore have been a Gentile and could not have been Paul.

(iv) *Doctrinal arguments*.[3] Arguments based on doctrinal differences are notoriously vulnerable as most challengers of Pauline authorship admit. But the plea is made that the evidence, though weak taken point by point, is nevertheless much weightier when considered cumulatively. The main points may be grouped as follows.

1. Differences have been noticed in Paul's teaching on the doctrine of the Church. In this Epistle the Church is universal and not local as it often is in Paul's other Epistles. Paul admittedly uses the word in both senses, but Goodspeed[4] stresses the fact that the local is more frequent in the Pauline Epistles than the universal. He further maintains that the writer is more of an ecclesiastic. 'He finds in the church a great spiritual fellowship, built upon the apostles and prophets'.[5] As in the book of Revelation the Church is the Bride of Christ.

Those who deny Pauline authorship place much stress on the unusual authority which appears to be vested in the apostles and prophets. Ephesians ii. 20 is a particular stumbling-block, for the apostles and prophets are said to be the foundation of the Church, a statement which seems at variance with 1 Corinthians iii. 11, where Christ is described as the only foundation.

The reference in iii. 5 to the 'holy apostles and prophets in the Spirit'

---

[1] Cf. Mitton, *op. cit.*, p. 16.   [2] *Key to Ephesians*, p. vii.
[3] For the arguments for Pauline authorship, see pp. 503 ff.
[4] *Key to Ephesians*, p. v.   [5] *Op. cit.*, p. vii.

is said to belong to a later date than Paul when the apostles were becoming increasingly venerated. Objection is made to the use of the word 'holy' because it suggests a greater deference to the apostles than could have existed in Paul's time. In fact, Goodspeed[1] claims that it belongs to the latter part of the first century and bases his contention on similar phraseology in Luke i. 70, Revelation xviii. 20, xxi. 14, and a similar attitude in Matthew, all of which books he dates late.

2. Further differences are claimed to appear in Paul's Christology in this Epistle. Certain acts which are attributed to God in the other Epistles are attributed to Christ in this. Two instances are specially singled out: firstly Ephesians ii. 16, where reconciliation is described as the work of Christ, as compared with Colossians i. 20, ii. 13–14; and secondly Ephesians iv. 11, where Christ is said to appoint officials in the Church, as compared with 1 Corinthians xii. 28.

It is claimed that nowhere else in the Pauline Epistles does Paul speak of Christ's descent into Hades and this is considered a difficult concept to fit into his theology (Eph. iv. 9). It is on the other hand supposed to be akin to the doctrine of ascension in Luke's Gospel.

Another criticism is based on the use of the formula 'In Christ'. Although occurring in this Epistle frequently it is claimed to lack the deeper meanings of Paul's usage. Whereas Paul used it for a personal identification with Christ and for the idea of corporate personality, Ephesians uses it predominantly in an instrumental sense.[2]

The small attention given to the death of Christ has also raised doubts about the authenticity of the Epistle. The writer is alleged to be more concerned about the exaltation of Christ than His death. In the main section on the redemptive activity of God (Eph. i. 15–ii. 10) the death is not mentioned although the resurrection twice comes into view. Moreover, the primary aim of the work of Christ is said to be the unification of the Jew and Gentile (ii. 13–18).

3. Finally, differences are claimed in Paul's social teaching here. As contrasted with Paul's attitude towards marriage in 1 Corinthians vii the writer of Ephesians is alleged to have a much more exalted view. To him the institution is worthy enough to illustrate the relationship between Christ and His Church. The weight of this objection will nevertheless appeal differently to different scholars, for many consider

---

[1] *INT*, p. 232. Cf. Mitton, *op. cit.*, p. 19.

[2] Cf. J. A. Allan, 'The "In Christ" Formula in Ephesians', *NTS*, vol. 5 (October 1958), pp. 54–62.

that Paul's earlier attitude to marriage was conditioned by his belief in the imminence of the *parousia*.

According to Goodspeed[1] a different approach towards children is discernible when Ephesians is compared with Colossians. In the former Epistle believers are to bring up their children 'in the discipline and instruction of the Lord' (vi. 4, RSV), while in Colossians iii. 21 they are urged not to provoke them and nothing more is said about training them. Goodspeed interprets this to mean that Ephesians urges a more long-term policy of religious education.

Another alleged difference is the way in which the writer refers to circumcision. In Ephesians he is said to have treated it with contempt, whereas in Paul's other Epistles it receives greater reverence, although the apostle is clear enough that it should not be enforced upon Gentiles.*

c. The case for Pauline authorship

The main arguments against authenticity have been stated as a whole without challenging any separate points in order to give the evidence the most favourable opportunity to make a cumulative impression. But the evidence must now be examined point by point to test its validity. Defenders of Pauline authorship have sometimes been accused of resorting to a method of 'divide and conquer', as if any analytical criticism of the cumulative evidence is quite unfair. But any hypothesis built on no more than an over-all effect which fears the scrutiny of analytical treatment does not deserve to survive.

Any statement of the case for Pauline authorship must commence with the external evidence. Mitton[2] concedes that this is the 'strongest bulwark in the defence of Pauline authorship', while Nineham[3] goes further and frankly admits that 'as far as external evidence goes Ephesians is unassailable'.

In view of the unfavourable character of external attestation for any theory that denies Pauline authorship, the advocates of authenticity may reasonably demand that internal arguments brought against the tradition should be of such a conclusive character as to provide no other option than the rejection of the tradition. Furthermore, if the tradition is rejected some adequate explanation must be given for the unanimity of the inaccurate tradition. Our next inquiry must therefore be to discover whether these opposing arguments are in fact conclusive.

[1] *Key to Ephesians*, p. vii.   [2] *Op. cit.*, p. 160.
[3] *Studies in Ephesians*, p. 22.

(i) *Linguistic and stylistic arguments*.[1] To deduce non-Pauline authorship from the fact that Ephesians contains a large number of non-Pauline words is an argument which must be used with very great reserve.[2] It is not unusual for Paul to use new words when dealing with new subject-matter, and this objection could carry weight only if it could be shown that Paul could not have used the new words in question. But this cannot be substantiated.

The claim that different words are used in Ephesians to express ideas which occur in other Pauline Epistles presents a weightier problem, but even here it cannot be said to suggest non-Pauline authorship unless it is conclusive that Paul would not have used the changed expressions. There is, for instance, no reason why Paul should not have used the phrase 'in the heavenlies', nor why he could not have introduced different grammatical constructions.

The comparison of the vocabulary with so-called later first-century books will be an obstacle only to those who are confident of the late dating of these books. Of the books mentioned by Goodspeed only I Clement can be dated with any certainty at the close of the century,[3] and since it is generally admitted that Clement knew and used Ephesians this line of attack may safely be discounted.

The style may be different from Paul's usual manner of writing, more reflective, moving in a more carefully considered way, lacking the somewhat turbulent approach of Galatians or the Corinthian Epistles and less logically argued than the Epistle to the Romans; but does this justify the conclusion that Paul could not have written it?[4] It is of course open to anyone to express the opinion that Paul could not have written Ephesians on stylistic grounds, but the evidence does not

[1] Cf. pp. 482 ff.

[2] It should also be noted that Colossians has a vocabulary showing fewer affinities with Paul than that of Ephesians and yet many scholars who reject the latter retain the former. On the difficulty of settling the authenticity of Ephesians on stylistic grounds, cf. the cautious discussion of H. J. Cadbury, 'The Dilemma of Ephesians', *NTS* (January 1959), pp. 91–102.

[3] Some writers have preferred an earlier date; cf. L. E. Elliott-Binns, *The Beginnings of Western Christendom* (1948), pp. 101, 224 ff. He favours the opinion of Edmundson for a date about AD 70.

[4] Meinertz, *Einleitung*, p. 130, considers the more clumsy expressions are not surprising in the work of an imprisoned, reflecting apostle. Not enough weight is given by opponents of Pauline authorship to the effect of changed circumstances on Paul's vocabulary, nor, for that matter, to change of mood (cf. G. G. Findlay, *The Epistles of Paul the Apostle*, 1892, p. 180).

demand this view. It may, in fact, be regarded as evidence of Paul's versatility. In any case it should be noted that the stylistic peculiarities occur mostly in the first part of the Epistle where statements of doctrine are presented in reflective mood and where controversy is absent.[1] This absence of controversy must have had an effect upon Paul's mind and it is most natural to suppose that his style would reflect his own reactions. Clogg[2] is surely right in maintaining that the style found in Ephesians fits Paul in contemplative mood.

A more important question is whether an imitator would have consciously produced a work with such a style as this,[3] so close to Paul and yet different, so breathing the same atmosphere and yet expressing it in another way. Is Goodspeed justified in maintaining that Ephesians i is not Pauline because the author does not stay to dwell upon the various themes he mentions? Surely an author is at liberty to choose which method he will adopt without running the risk of being denied his own writing if he is thoughtless enough to choose a method he has not previously used! But even if it be conceded that this change of method may be an indication of, or an indirect support for, non-Pauline authorship, it is by no means self-evident that the review of blessings in chapter i is natural if the author was a Paulinist writing to introduce Paul's collected works. It is improbable psychology to suggest that an imitator making a conscious effort to recall the great Pauline themes would have made them 'tumble over one another'[4] in the manner found here. The natural result would have been a more stilted summary. If, then, Ephesians is the work of an imitator, the author must have been an extraordinary literary artist.

(ii) *Literary arguments*.[5] The close relation between Ephesians and Colossians appears to be capable of opposing explanations. Advocates of non-Pauline authorship find it difficult to conceive that one mind could have produced two works possessing so remarkable a degree of

---

[1] E. Percy (*Die Probleme der Kolosser- und Epheserbriefe*, 1946, pp. 179–252) has made a thorough study of the language and style of Ephesians and finds many striking agreements between Ephesians and the acknowledged letters of Paul, which speak strongly for a common author.*

[2] F. B. Clogg, *INT*, p. 96.

[3] Cf. E. F. Scott, *The Epistles of Paul to the Colossians, to Philemon and to the Ephesians* (*MC*, 1930), p. 119.

[4] To use Goodspeed's expression, *Key to Ephesians*, p. vii.

[5] Cf. pp. 483 ff.

similarity in theme and phraseology and yet differing in so many other respects, whereas advocates of Pauline authorship are equally emphatic that two minds could not have produced two such works with so much subtle interdependence blended with independence. This close relationship is, in fact, exactly what might be reasonably expected if Paul had produced the two Epistles within a short period of time and had applied in a general way in the second (i.e. Ephesians) the great themes of the first, divorced from their specific situation.[1] Mitton[2] agrees that an imitator producing Ephesians would have kept closer to Colossians if he had had his model before his eyes, and he is therefore driven to suppose that the imitator knew it so well that he could easily recall its themes and phraseology. This means that the two Epistles in his judgment are not similar enough for both to be attributed to Paul, nor are they similar enough for one to be the work of an imitator copying Paul. Yet what critical criterion can pronounce with any confidence that they are sufficiently dissimilar for one of them to be the work of an imitator writing generally from memory?[3] If this hypothesis were valid we should hardly expect to find the only passage with any extended verbal parallels with Colossians to be the concluding reference to Tychicus. It is difficult to see why any Paulinist should have committed this passage to memory with so great a degree of verbal accuracy and have seen any purpose in reproducing it in a letter purporting to introduce

---

[1] Cf. E. F. Scott, *op. cit.*, pp. 121 ff.; C. L. Mitton agrees that if Paul were the author of Ephesians it must have been written immediately after Colossians, but this he rejects because it does not allow time for differences in doctrine and use of words (cf. *op. cit.*, pp. 254, 255). J. Coutts, 'The Relationship of Ephesians and Colossians', *NTS*, vol. 4 (1957–58), pp. 201–207, suggests from an examination of selected passages that Colossians is dependent on Ephesians. In an earlier article Coutts mentioned the possibility of Ephesians being a baptismal Encyclical, *NTS*, vol. 3 (1956–57), pp. 115–127. But the majority of scholars assume the priority of Colossians.*

[2] *Op. cit.*, pp. 78, 79.

[3] A. B. Cook, in an article on 'Unconscious Iteration, with special reference to Classical Literature', *Classical Review*, XVI (1902), p. 264, maintained that it is often impossible to differentiate between conscious and unconscious iteration in two works of one author. It must surely be impossible in two. An alternative theory is that the Tychicus passage is not original, neither are the following passages (i. 1, iii. 1–13, iv. 1, vi. 20); they were added to an original homily, perhaps delivered by Tychicus, to turn it into a Pauline Epistle (cf. Goguel, *Introd.*, IV, ii, 473, 474). Cf. also W. L. Knox, *St. Paul and the Church of the Gentiles* (1939), p. 203, for another suggestion associating Tychicus with the writing of Ephesians.

the Pauline Corpus of letters as Goodspeed suggests. The proposal of Mitton[1] that it may have been introduced in honour of Tychicus who may still have been alive seems utterly pointless since the same words already existed in Colossians. This shows the extent of the difficulty for the non-Pauline theory. Indeed it may fairly be claimed that this passage is a great stumbling-block to the opponents of authenticity. The best explanation of the repetition is to suppose that Paul directed his amanuensis to use the same words in referring to Tychicus as in the Colossian letter.[2]

Advocates of the imitator-hypothesis are, in fact, using an argument which can be used against them, for it may reasonably be supposed that a conscious imitator would have endeavoured to keep as close as possible to his model. But the spiritual and intellectual power of Ephesians,[3] together with its freedom from a slavish reproduction of Colossians, is extremely improbable in an imitator, even if the memory-hypothesis be allowed. But this hypothesis looks like an attempt to stave off a difficult problem. It is even more difficult to explain why a Paulinist writing towards the end of the first century should have picked on Colossians to form the basis of his summary of Pauline teaching.[4] The theory that Colossians was for a long time the only Pauline Epistle known to the author might at first sight appear a reasonable explanation of the phenomenon, but the force of it depends entirely on the further theory of the late collection of Paul's letters, for which the evidence is too scanty to enable us to reach anything but the most tentative conclusions.[5] Clement of Rome certainly knew of more than one of Paul's Epistles and it seems most probable that they were more generally known than this theory allows. To make the hypothesis

---

[1] *Op. cit.*, p. 268.

[2] Cf. F. F. Bruce (*Colossians*, 1957), p. 301. Mitton agrees that if both Epistles were dispatched at the same time the repetition of the Tychicus passage would be entirely natural (*op. cit.*, p. 77). Surely F. Godet (*INT*, 1899), p. 490, was right in considering it would have been an act of 'unheard-of impudence' for a later writer some years after Paul's death to have reproduced this passage.

[3] Cf. C. H. Dodd, *Colossians*, AB (1929), pp. 122, 124, 125, who considers the thought of this Epistle to be the 'crown of Paulinism'. But against this view see Jülicher–Fascher, *Einleitung*[7] (1931), p. 139.

[4] Von Dobschütz, *Christian Life in the Primitive Church* (1904, p. 176), suggested that the author of Ephesians was a profound thinker excited by the thoughts of Colossians.

[5] Cf. the survey of evidence collected by Mitton in *The Formation of the Pauline Corpus of Letters* (1955). See pp. 648 ff. for a further discussion of this evidence.

sound at all probable it is necessary to suppose that the Paulinist was cut off in some obscure Christian centre while his mind was becoming saturated with Colossians. But this is rather a desperate alternative to the traditional view.

We must next consider the objection based on the use of words said to have been borrowed from Colossians and then used in a quite different sense. No one would dispute that a writer may on occasion use words in different senses, but the difficulty seems to arise from the necessity to suppose a very short interval between the two Epistles. This is a difficulty only if two conditions are first fulfilled. The differences in usage must be shown to be incompatible in one mind at one period of time, and they must further be inconceivable in the works of the writer to whom they are attributed. But the examples cited by the opponents of authenticity fulfil neither of these conditions. The alleged difference between Ephesians iv. 15, 16 and Colossians ii. 19 in their description of Christ's Headship cannot seriously be maintained in view of the fact that both Epistles specifically identify 'the body' as the Church (Col. i. 18; Eph. v. 23). That the further thought of Christ as Head of the universe, if this can be maintained, is not explicit in Ephesians is no basis for denying its Pauline authorship, for it is not incompatible with the more restricted application, as Colossians shows.[1] There would seem to be more validity in the objection based on the word 'mystery', but it cannot be said that Paul would never have described the unification of mankind as 'the mystery of his will' (Eph. i. 9), nor is it particularly apparent that he could not at the same time have used the same word to describe the Indwelling Christ (Col. i. 27). Indeed, when Paul uses the word in the Roman doxology (Rom. xvi. 25, 26)[2] he is marvelling that the mystery is 'made known to all nations', a thought closely akin to that in Ephesians. Again the different uses of οἰκονομία are not inconceivable in one mind. These variations of meaning will naturally assume a greater significance for those already persuaded of non-Pauline authorship than for supporters of authenti-

[1] Cf. C. F. D. Moule, *Epistle to the Colossians*, p. 6. Cf. also *ET*, LX (1948–49), p. 224, where the author expresses doubt about any difference between the use of σῶμα (body) in Col. ii. 19 and Eph. iv. 16. F. F. Bruce (*Colossians*, p. 251) definitely rejects Dibelius' interpretation of the 'body' in Col. ii. 19 as the cosmic powers and sees no difference, therefore, in the two passages under consideration. (Cf. also the discussion of O. Cullmann, *Christ and Time*, 1951, p. 187; and E. Best, *One Body in Christ*, 1955, p. 123.)

[2] See pp. 406 ff. for a discussion of the authenticity of this doxology.

city. A fair conclusion would be that the evidence does not demand the rejection of Pauline authorship.

The examples of conflation already quoted, in which two passages in Colossians are found combined in one passage in Ephesians, are not as impressive as Mitton claims, for this kind of thing would be perfectly natural for Paul writing Ephesians shortly after Colossians with the thoughts and phraseology of the latter much in his mind. It can hardly be expected that Paul himself would have linked together certain phrases in exactly the same way in both Epistles. It is extremely difficult, if not impossible, to imagine why an imitator should have resorted to conflation. Mitton's[1] own explanation that the imitator is quoting from memory certain phrases but does not recall their exact relationship in Colossians is really making a virtue out of necessity.[2] There is no other more probable solution that the advocate of non-Pauline authorship can bring if he denies that the imitator was writing with Colossians before him. But it would be interesting to know why he does not consult Colossians as this must have been included in the Pauline Corpus, which *ex hypothesi* he is proposing to introduce. But no satisfactory explanation of this strange behaviour has yet been given. It is clearly more reasonable to suppose that Paul did not consult his own Epistle than that an admirer of his, who had possessed a copy of Paul's Colossian Epistle and who set out to produce a résumé of his master's doctrine, would have discarded the immeasurable advantage of consulting it.

It is the claim that Ephesians shows dependence on all the other Pauline Epistles (excluding the Pastorals) that has provided the basis for the hypothesis that it was intended to introduce the collection of these Epistles. In fact, if it can be shown that Ephesians does not depend in a literary way on the other Epistles the introduction theory would fall to pieces. Both Goodspeed[3] and Mitton[4] have set out clearly by means of parallel columns the passages from the other Pauline Epistles which show similarity with Ephesians. The number of parallels looks very impressive, but the evidence is of course capable of more than one

[1] Cf. *Ephesians*, pp. 55–81.
[2] E. Percy (*op. cit.*, p. 422 n.) in criticizing the similar theory of E. J. Goodspeed thinks it too naïve to warrant serious consideration.
[3] Cf. *The Key to Ephesians*, in which the parallels are set out in the English texts.
[4] In Appendix I of his book, *The Epistle to the Ephesians*, pp. 279–315, using the Greek texts.

explanation.[1] The existence of parallels is not in itself sufficient to establish dependence. And this leads to the real crux of the problem. According to Mitton's analysis there are three types of parallels.

1. Isolated parallels are those where the verbal similarity extends to no more than a word or two. Goodspeed includes a great quantity of these but Mitton rightly rejects the majority of them.[2] He includes some in his statistical calculations, but his main emphasis is on the two other classes of parallels.

2. Sustained parallels are passages from other Pauline Epistles from which a number of phrases are reproduced in one or more contexts in Ephesians. For instance, many phrases in Romans i. 21–24 can be paralleled in Ephesians iv. 17–19. Mitton cites more than twenty examples of this kind of thing.[3]

3. Conflated parallels[4] are those in which two passages from different parts of Paul's other Epistles have been combined in Ephesians. It is impossible in a small compass to examine adequately the evidence on which these two latter classifications of parallels are based. It is sufficient to state that the parallels show a rather uneven degree of similarity, yet on the whole they do demonstrate the closeness of the language of Ephesians with the other Pauline Epistles. What needs more careful examination is the validity of Mitton's claims that in both of these latter categories the evidence favours more the work of an imitator than of Paul.

The most natural conclusion from the abundance of parallel passages is that the same mind is reflected in Ephesians as in the other Pauline Epistles.[5] In fact it has for long been assumed as a critical presupposition that the absence rather than the presence of such parallels is an indication of non-Pauline authorship in the investigation of certain other Epistles, notably the Pastorals. But Mitton claims to have discovered evidence which disproves this kind of presupposition. Taking Philippians as a representative Pauline Epistle, he claims that in this Epistle there is considerably less evidence of either sustained parallels or con-

[1] E. Percy, after thoroughly examining the ideas of Ephesians, has remarked that the author was so well versed in Pauline thought that if he were not Paul he stands unique in the whole period of sub-Pauline Christian literature before the time of Luther (op. cit., p. 356).

[2] Op. cit., p. 101.   [3] Op. cit., pp. 120 ff.   [4] Cf. Mitton, op. cit., pp. 138 ff.

[5] H. J. Cadbury, NTS (January 1959), p. 100, considers the parallels are insufficient to suggest a borrower. He admits further in the case of the similarity with Colossians that there is no reason why Paul should not be the borrower.

flated parallels with the other Pauline Epistles.[1] Assuming that in the case of Philippians this conclusion is correct, does this justify the further deduction that Ephesians cannot on this score be attributed to Paul? The assumption here is that what Paul does in Philippians he must do in all other writings. But the basis of this assumption is not obvious. To use Philippians alone in the comparison involves an over-simplification of a very complicated process. The difference in occasion, specific in Philippians, very general in Ephesians, must have had some bearing on the writer's mental processes. Indeed the only thing which these Epistles have in common is that both were written when Paul was a prisoner. Philippians as a sample Epistle is much too small to be con-vincing. It consists of about one-sixteenth of the eight Epistles which Mitton accepts. Surely a wider basis is required before his suppositions can be assumed to be correct? Whether the subject to be studied is literary parallelism or linguistic dissimilarities as a basis for settling dis-puted points of authorship, the sample chosen must be clearly recog-nized as both representative and quantitatively adequate.[2] But the choice of Philippians does not fulfil either of these conditions.

[1] Cf. op. cit., pp. 107–110, 322–332. The Philippian parallels are not presented with the same thoroughness as for Ephesians, and some clear parallels have been omitted. It is curious for instance that τοῖς οὖσιν ἐν is underlined in Ephesians but not in Philippians. Mitton (p. 110) does admit that further parallels might have been found as a result of intensive study, but he does not recognize that this admission might affect the validity of his comparisons. It is interesting to note that when F. C. Baur denied the authenticity of Philippians he made a note of ten specifically Pauline expressions which the author had drawn from Paul and yet Mitton has noticed only four of these (cf. Baur, Paul, II, p. 79). Some of these ought certainly to come under the category of 'striking phrases' on which Mitton places such stress as being fewer in Philippians than in Ephesians (e.g. cf. Phil. ii. 30; 1 Cor. xvi. 10; 2 Cor. ix. 12). It seems highly probable that a thorough in-vestigation would put a different complexion on Mitton's claims.

[2] This principle is clearly brought out in the matter of statistical linguistics by G. U. Yule, The Statistical Study of Literary Vocabulary (1944), p. 281, who not only suggested that samples of not less than 10,000 words should be used but also that samples must be similar in length and subject-matter. Comparisons of un-equal samples lead to fallacies. Moreover, the wider the area covered by the samples the less is the risk of false deduction. In the literary examination of Paul's Epistles another factor must be carefully considered. The chronology of the letters will affect the possibility of dependence, for the earlier cannot reflect dependence on the later. Mitton chooses Philippians mainly on the basis that it comes from the same period as Ephesians when regarded as a Pauline Epistle op. cit., p. 108). He admits, however, that a completely satisfactory test would require an examination of all the Epistles (op. cit., p. 107).

It would be convenient here to comment on Mitton's two tests for discriminating between a writer and his imitator. An imitator, he thinks, would tend to concentrate coincidences with other Pauline Epistles in groups associated with passages which had particularly impressed his mind, whereas Paul would scatter them evenly. Unfortunately, no adequate evidence is given to substantiate the validity of this test apart from the appeal to Philippians mentioned above. But the test is not self-evident, for any writer might equally well concentrate his allusions to his earlier writings into certain groups if he happened to be writing on a similar subject and his former thoughts on the same subject automatically sprang to mind. Deep impressions made on the subconscious mind may easily be reproduced with sufficient stimulus, and there seems no reason for confining this to imitators and denying it to original authors.[1]

The second test maintains that an imitator would reproduce 'striking and memorable phrases' whereas an authentic writer would not.[2] But this again wears the appearance of an over-simplification. The impact of words on human minds is always complex and it cannot be assumed that all readers must necessarily react in the same way. If a reader sets out to reproduce Paul, the degree of reproduction of striking phrases will vary according to his familiarity with the genuine Epistles, his own particular interests, his purpose in imitating Paul, and most important of all the retentiveness or otherwise of his own mind. The same variety of factors would, of course, apply to a writer's reproduction of ideas from his own earlier writings. But no test can take into account all these different factors. It is by no means apparent that different imitators setting to work on Paul's Epistles would all tend to reproduce striking and memorable phrases, nor is it evident that Paul would never do so himself.[3]

[1] For examples of unconscious repetitions occurring in writings of one author cited from a wide range of classical and other authors cf. A. B. Cook's article on 'Unconscious Iteration', *Classical Review*, XVI (1902), pp. 146–158, 256–267. Cook, for example, compared two works of Euripides, the *Troades* and the *Hecuba*, separated by about ten years and yet containing many instances of words and phrases repeated, and concluded that the author slipped 'naturally and without conscious effort into the wording of his previous description' (p. 153). Cf. also E. Laughton's article, 'Subconscious Repetition and Textual Criticism', *Classical Philology*, XLV (1950), pp. 73–83.

[2] Cf. Mitton, *op. cit.*, p. 113.

[3] Mitton attempts to support the validity of his test by an appeal to the spurious Epistle to the Laodiceans, which he describes as 'an unskilful collection of

The question of the relation between Ephesians and the non-Pauline books of the New Testament is of special importance in Goodspeed's theory since it bolsters his claim for a late date for the collection of Paul's letters. But the evidence from literary allusions or their absence is generally unreliable since there are rarely any concrete grounds for determining the all-important question of priority. In dealing with Ephesians and 1 Peter this consideration is crucial. If 1 Peter has borrowed

sayings from genuinely Pauline Epistles' (*op. cit.*, p. 116). Most of these are from Philippians and many of them are claimed to fall into the category of 'striking and memorable phrases'. But this evidence is of little weight for the following reasons. Firstly, the imitator has clearly planned the structure of his spurious epistle on the structure of Philippians, taking sayings from all four chapters in the same order as his model. It is a reasonable assumption that he wrote with a copy of Philippians before him, in which case his work is not parallel to Ephesians; secondly, if he had the original before him the reproduction of 'striking and memorable phrases' would not be very remarkable. The force of the test obtains only if the imitator writes from memory.

Moreover, the phenomenon does not occur very obviously in the equally spurious 3 Corinthians. It is strange that Mitton does not apply his tests to the Pastoral Epistles, which he regards as non-Pauline except for a few genuine notes, for *ex hypothesi* the tests should show similar results if both they and Ephesians are claimed to be by imitators. But an examination of Harrison's lists of Pauline parallels, *The Problem of the Pastorals* (1921), pp. 167-175, and his underlined texts do not bear out this expectation. As compared with Mitton's figures of 29.1% of the text of Ephesians furnishing parallels with eight Pauline Epistles (*op. cit.*, p. 104), the Pastorals all show lower percentages (1 Timothy 27.7%, 2 Timothy 22.7% and Titus 20.9%) of parallels with ten Epistles. When adjustments are made to compensate for this larger area from which parallels are drawn, Ephesians has 32.7% (Mitton, *op. cit.*, p. 109), 1 Timothy 23.7%, 2 Timothy 19.4% and Titus 17.9%, while Philippians has 15.2%. If Mitton still insists on the imitator-theory for both Ephesians and the Pastorals there must be something faulty about the deductions he draws from the parallels. Another point is the absence of sustained parallels in the Pastorals to compare with those Mitton finds in Ephesians. The 'striking-phrase' test is also perplexing, for Harrison collects a group of stereotyped phrases in the Pastorals (*op. cit.*, p. 166), presumably as evidence of non-Pauline authorship, whereas Mitton says it is the stock phrase rather than the striking one which reappears in Philippians and this he finds in line with Pauline authorship. These tests seem to have too great a subjective element to commend themselves, at least in their present form. Mitton's assumption may possibly be correct for conscious literary works, such as those of the Greek classical period, when definite avoidance of verbal repetitions was a virtue and when any iteration that had crept in must be considered subconscious; but the apostle Paul was governed by wholly different motives from those dominating the ancient rhetoricians and literary artists (cf. A. B. Cook, *Classical Review*, XVI (1902), p. 256, for the view that forcible expressions in writers of merit are too intense to remain subconscious).

from Ephesians[1] (as Mitton agrees) the date of Ephesians is affected by the date of 1 Peter, which is in turn affected by its authorship. It will inevitably follow, therefore, that those disputing Pauline authorship of Ephesians have little option but to reject Petrine authorship of 1 Peter. But this is not an undisputed opinion since many scholars find strong arguments in support of Petrine authorship. There is no doubt that if the early date for Ephesians is established its Pauline authorship cannot be disputed.

The non-reflection of the Pauline Epistles in the Synoptic Gospels is no evidence of a late date for Ephesians unless there is some good reason why the Evangelists should have cited them. But such a reason is inconceivable. It was the life and teaching of Jesus, not Paul, that they were describing. The parallels with Acts are even more inconclusive and at most could be used only as corroborative evidence of an hypothesis already proved on other grounds. Such suggested parallels are therefore entirely neutral and depend on a preconceived approach (either for or against authenticity) to give them any positive value. There tends to be too great a subjective element in the assessing of these literary priorities.

It remains to consider the problem of literary form. Ephesians certainly differs from the other Pauline Epistles in the absence of a specific situation and Moffatt[2] may be near the truth in classing it as a homily rather than a letter, but this does not in itself support non-Pauline authorship unless it could be shown that Paul could not have written a letter in such a form. But this latter condition cannot be fulfilled, and although the circular letter theory has been strongly criticized (see below) it does at least provide as probable a situation for the production of the Epistle as any other theory, if not considerably more so. In that case the occasion determined the form.[3]

The personal references in Ephesians iii and the lack of the usual Pauline salutations may readily be regarded as non-Pauline once non-apostolicity has been accepted. But until nineteenth-century criticism spotted them, no one regarded these references as forced, as if the writer was protesting too much his own identity. It is purely a matter

---

[1] Ernst Percy (*Die Probleme der Kolosser– und Epheserbriefe*, 1946, pp. 433–440) admits many striking similarities in thought but does not think literary dependence can be certainly established. If it existed, priority would rest with Ephesians.

[2] *ILNT*, pp. 373 ff.

[3] See the later discussion on the circular letter theory (pp. 510 f.).

of opinion whether it is theatrical for Paul to call himself 'the least of all saints'. When due allowance is made for the overwhelming sense of God's grace of which Paul was particularly conscious nothing seems more natural than this self-depreciation. It is not otherwise with iii. 2 and iii. 4 where self-commendation is alleged to be unPauline, for the apostle is certainly not evaluating himself, but the immense effectiveness of the grace of God entrusted to him. What 'knowledge' (iii. 4) he has is no ground for boasting, for he expressly traces its origin to divine 'revelation' (iii. 3) in complete harmony with his other Epistles. It is difficult to see how an imitator whose 'admiration and regard for Paul are so emphasized in Ephesians' could in the same passage have made Paul call himself 'the least of all saints', which is surely the last thing an ardent admirer of the great apostle would have done. If it is a little theatrical for Paul to have used these words, it is inconceivably overdramatic for a zealous Paulinist.

(iii) *Historical arguments.*[1] The overwhelming testimony of tradition in favour of Pauline authorship has already been considered and its embarrassment to advocates of non-Pauline authorship noted. But the supposed internal problems merit some comment. The history of the Jewish-Gentile controversy is not easy to trace with any certainty and no deductions can fairly be made from its presence or absence from any Pauline writing. The st ate of the controversy must have varied from church to church. Yet the position in Ephesians shows a remarkable affinity with that dealt with in Romans, especially Romans xi. 17–24. In both Paul sets out the unification of Jew and Gentile through Christ.[2]

Goodspeed's argument from the destruction of the temple is open to dispute. In fact, the evidence can more reasonably be made to do service for Pauline authorship. For instance, C. A. A. Scott[3] asks the following three cogent questions on this matter. (1) Is it likely that anyone would address Gentiles in these terms (i.e. using the figure of the

---

[1] Cf. pp. 487 ff.

[2] Much modern criticism is still unconsciously influenced by the Tübingen type of criticism with its arbitrary reconstruction of early Christian history. The words of G. Salmon (*INT*) in rejecting this earlier trend of criticism are worth pondering still, 'it shows inability to grasp the historic situation if a man expects Paul's letters at this date (i.e. at the time of the Roman imprisonment) to exhibit him still employed in controversial defence of the position of his Gentile converts, or if he is surprised to find Paul taking for granted that the barrier between Jew and Gentile had been thrown down' (pp. 393, 394).

[3] *Footnotes to St. Paul* (1935), pp. 173, 174.

'barrier') after AD 70 when Jerusalem was in ruins? (2) Is it likely that before AD 70 anyone but Paul with his keen perceptions of Israel's privileges would have done this? (3) Is it likely that even Paul would have done so if he were describing an ideal and not a realized unification of Jew and Gentile? He concludes that if these questions are answered negatively, as he maintains they must be, doubts regarding Pauline authorship must be otherwise explained. It may further be argued that if the author were writing after the fall of the temple it would have given him an admirable symbolic illustration to press home his point, and the omission to use it militates against the view that Ephesians was later than AD 70. It must however be admitted that no later New Testament writers show any interest in the historic event. To the primitive Church the elimination of the spiritual barrier was of far greater importance than the destruction of the material edifice. To sum up, it cannot be claimed that anything in the treatment of this theme in Ephesians is unPauline.

The appeal to ii. 3 as evidence that the author was a Gentile and therefore not Paul depends on a false assumption.[1] It may be true that an orthodox Jew would never have admitted that he was among the 'children of wrath' having his manner of life 'in the lusts of the flesh', but a Christian Jew, who had become an apostle to Gentiles and whose aim was to be all things to all men, would surely not have hesitated to identify himself in this way with his Gentile readers. It would have been bordering on the pedantic if he had not been prepared to do so. Moreover, since in the same chapter (verse 11) Paul addresses himself to 'you Gentiles' (ὑμεῖς τὰ ἔθνη) it is clear that in verse 3 he is speaking universally and it is doubtful whether he would regard the statement about 'passions', 'desires' and 'children of wrath' as inapplicable to Jews, however strongly the Jews themselves may have repudiated the idea. For Paul both Jew and Gentile were in a condition of desperate need of God's mercy (verse 4).

(iv) *Doctrinal arguments*.[2] The special plea for cumulative consideration of this evidence rather than analytical approach amounts to an admission of its weakness. The fact is that the advocate of non-Pauline

[1] C. F. D. Moule, *ET*, IX (1948–49), pp. 224–225, who criticizes Mitton and Goodspeed on the ground of putting too much emphasis on differences between Ephesians and Colossians, nevertheless concedes that Goodspeed's theory would remove the difficulty of chapter ii.

[2] Cf. pp. 488 ff.

authorship is bound to search in all quarters for every scrap of evidence which might lend support to his theory, and when he becomes conscious of the insubstantial character of the evidences he has gathered he finds it necessary to plead that these must not be treated as isolated scraps but as fragments of a united whole. Such an approach will seem more impressive to those already disposed to dispute Pauline authorship than those convinced on other grounds of its authenticity. Mitton,[1] in conceding that the separate units may be satisfactorily answered but that the cumulative effect is considerable in supporting non-Pauline authorship, is virtually pleading that the weakness of his evidence should be ignored but his conclusions accepted. A chain is as strong as its weakest link and it is impossible to assess the strength of the chain as a whole until its separate links have been tested, always provided they are regarded separately as links in a whole. The main objections will be considered from this point of view.

The treatment of the doctrine of the Church is more developed than in Paul's other writings, but Goodspeed's contention that the writer of Ephesians is more 'of an ecclesiastic than Paul' must be strongly contested.* An ecclesiastic would have laboured his comments on the Christian ministry far more than this writer has done. There is a wide gap between Ephesians and Clement's letter to the Corinthians on this subject, yet according to Goodspeed's theory both belong to the same period of Church development. When compared with Clement's views of the ministry, Ephesians is essentially Pauline. The problem is the writer's attitude towards the apostles and prophets, but the difficulty may be due to faulty exegesis rather than to the intrinsic meaning of the text. Ephesians ii. 20 could mean that the foundation of the Church is the same as the foundation of the apostles, i.e. Christ, and there would then be no disagreement with 1 Corinthians iii. 11.[2] The alternative and most generally accepted interpretation that the apostles were themselves the foundation may present a different point of view from 1 Corinthians iii. 11, but it would not be out of harmony with the authority which Paul so frequently claims for apostles, himself included.[3] He clearly

[1] Cf. op. cit., pp. 16, 17.

[2] E. K. Simpson, The Epistle to the Ephesians (1958), p. 66, understands it in the sense that the foundation is the apostolic testimony to Christ.

[3] S. Hanson, The Unity of the Church in the New Testament: Colossians and Ephesians (1946), p. 131, regards the apostles as the foundation in their position as witnesses and ministers of Christ, and in this sense he thinks it makes little difference whether Christ or His apostles are so described.

considered his own position and that of the other apostles as different in status from the communities in general, and he expected their authority to be unquestionably recognized. That Paul considered himself among the authorized bearers of the Christian revelation is evident from such passages as Galatians i. 8, 11, 1 Corinthians iv. 17.

Greater difficulty is generally found in the description of the apostles and prophets as 'holy' (ἅγιοι) in Ephesians iii. 5, as if this indicates a time when greater reverence was accorded to them than would have been likely in the apostolic age. But, as T. K. Abbott[1] pointed out, the objectors are really boggling over a modern connotation of the word 'holy' and not over its essential New Testament use to denote those set apart for a special sacred purpose. If Paul could use the word as a synonym for believers it can hardly be considered incongruous when applied to the apostles.[2] In Colossians i. 26 it is the 'holy ones' (οἱ ἅγιοι) who are the recipients of the mystery once hidden but now revealed, whereas in Ephesians iii. 5 the recipients are more closely defined as apostles and prophets, but since the same descriptive term is used it cannot be considered more inappropriate in the one case than in the other. Opponents of Pauline authorship may be justified in claiming that the description 'holy' seems stranger on the lips of Paul than on the lips of one of his admirers, but there are difficulties in the latter view because of the conjunction of apostles with prophets, a combination which fits better the primitive Christian period than that at the close of the century. To sum up, it may reasonably be asserted that there is nothing inconsistent with Paul in the references to the Church in this Epistle.

The Christology of Ephesians may similarly be shown to be in harmony with Pauline doctrine, although certain differences in expression may be found. Mere differences in doctrine cannot, as Hort[3] noted, be regarded as evidence of dissimilarity of authorship unless real want of harmony is proved. In his other letters Paul was not consistent in attributing certain acts to God and others to Christ (cf. 1 Cor. viii. 6), and to expect such consistency in Ephesians would be unreasonable. The

---

[1] *Ephesians and Colossians* (*ICC*, 1899), pp. xvi, 82.

[2] W. Lock, 'Ephesians' in *HDB*, vol. I, p. 717, considered that the word 'holy' refers to the special consecration of the prophets and apostles in contrast to the sons of men.

[3] Cf. F. J. A. Hort, *Prolegomena to St. Paul's Epistles to the Romans and Ephesians* (1895), p. 123.

distinction assumed in the objection is too subtle to carry weight. The problem raised over the descent of Christ into Hades is no more substantial, in spite of the absence of any specific teaching to this effect in Paul's other letters. Goodspeed's argument that this doctrine is virtually excluded by Romans x. 6, 7 cannot seriously be maintained, for in this passage Paul is asserting the inability of human effort to bring Christ up from the abyss, but the statement says nothing about the reality or otherwise of Christ's descent,[1] and is certainly not inconsistent with Ephesians iv. 9.[2] The objection based on the absence of the characteristic Pauline use of the formula 'In Christ' cannot be sustained, for many of the occurrences in Ephesians can be paralleled in other Pauline Epistles. For instance, ii. 13 seems a clear case of a deep Pauline meaning.[3]

Of greater significance is the objection based on the writer's approach to the work of Christ. But it would be inaccurate to maintain that the presentation of the work of Christ differed in any essential manner from Paul's teaching elsewhere. He relates it here more specifically to the unification of Jew and Gentile, but there is nothing in Paul's other letters to suggest that he would not have agreed with this. Nor can it be said that in Ephesians this unification is presented as the primary aim of the work of Christ. If this feature is reckoned to be a difficulty for Pauline authorship it would be a far greater one for a Paulinist. Indeed, it would be quite inexplicable for such a man who was setting out to give a summary of Paul's teaching to include as a sample of that teaching on redemption one of the subsidiary results of the death of Christ. It may not be a prominent emphasis in Paul to relate the purpose of the cross to the universal appeal of the gospel,[4] but it would have been inexcusable in a Paulinist to omit the great themes so apparent elsewhere in Paul's letters.

---

[1] Sanday and Headlam, *Romans, ad loc.*, do not regard the doctrine as excluded by Paul's statement, but consider it to be referred to in 'indefinite and untechnical language'.

[2] F. Godet, *INT* (1899), I, p. 484, appealed to Rom. xiv. 9 as inferring the idea of a descent into hell.

[3] J. A. Allan, *op. cit., NTS* (1958), p. 58, admits that in this and other passages it is possible to give the deeper Pauline meaning, although he claims it is equally possible to attach the instrumental meaning. In deciding which, the author's predisposition towards non-Pauline authorship naturally prefers the latter. But advocates of authenticity may equally well prefer the former.

[4] Yet cf. Rom. iii. 21 ff., xi. 11 ff., Gal. iii, iv, where the thought is at least adumbrated.

Little importance can be attached to the social teaching of the Epistle as compared with Paul's other letters, for no more than a quite natural variation of emphasis due to the writer's different reaction to changed circumstances is discernible. Paul's use of the marriage metaphor for illuminating the relationship between Christ and His Church is not excluded by his own personal approach to matrimony. Even a confirmed bachelor need not be entirely insensible to the appropriateness of such a figure of speech. It is also difficult to take very seriously Goodspeed's idea that Colossians differs from Ephesians in its approach to the behaviour of children. It is unconvincing to maintain that Paul would not have urged fathers to bring up children 'in the nurture and admonition of the Lord', and scarcely less so to claim that this represents 'a long-term policy of religious education'. When Paul was dwelling upon the theme of Christian responsibilities in the home, it was not unnatural for him to exhort fathers to take care over the training of their children.

There are so many weak links in this doctrinal attack on the Pauline authorship of Ephesians that no amount of cumulative consideration can redeem it. The only possible conclusion to which a detailed examination can lead us is that there is nothing incompatible with the doctrinal teaching of the apostle.*

d. Conclusion to the discussion of Pauline authorship

When all the objections are carefully considered it will be seen that the weight of evidence is inadequate to overthrow the overwhelming external attestation to Pauline authorship, and the Epistle's own claims. The fact that the writer plainly calls himself Paul has not been greatly stressed in the preceding discussion in order not to prejudice judgment. But in spite of the fact that pseudonymity is regarded by many modern scholars to have been an established practice among the early Christians,[1] the advocates of the traditional view are entitled to emphasize the self-testimony of the Epistle as support for their position until some satisfactory explanation is found which accounts for the universal acceptance of the Epistle at its face value. To maintain that the Paulinist out of his sheer love for Paul and through his own self-effacement composed the letter, attributed it to Paul and found an astonishing and immediate readiness on the part of the Church to recognize it as such is consider-

[1] See Appendix C on Epistolary Pseudepigraphy, pp. 671 ff., against this view.

ably less credible than the simple alternative of regarding it as Paul's own work.[1]

II. DESTINATION

Although tradition has handed down this Epistle as a letter sent to the Ephesian church, modern criticism, backed by uncertainty regarding the text of Ephesians i. 1, has strongly disputed this opinion. The words ἐν Ἐφέσῳ ('in Ephesus') are omitted from the oldest Greek codices of the Pauline Epistles (P[46], ℵ B). They were also omitted from some old codices known to Basil. It may further be inferred that the words were omitted from Marcion's text since he seems to have considered that the Epistle was addressed to the Laodiceans, not the Ephesians. On the other hand Epiphanius[2] infers that Marcion possessed parts only of Laodiceans and this being so the commencement of the Epistle may have been wanting.[3] In all probability, therefore, Marcion's attribution of the Epistle to the Laodiceans was no more than an ingenious guess.[4]

On the strength of this evidence, particularly from the generally reliable Alexandrian tradition, most modern scholars conclude that the original reading omitted the words. There are various suggestions to account for the lack of any specific address, but before discussing these it is relevant to discuss what explanations, if any, can be given for the omission of the words 'in Ephesus' if they were in fact original. Such

[1] Another view which has been proposed is that Paul commissioned an amanuensis to produce Ephesians on the basis of Colossians. But this is no more convincing for the following reasons: (a) he would hardly have had access to all the Pauline Epistles with which Ephesians has contacts; (b) his work would not have reflected the same kind of literary relationship with Colossians—it would surely have been closer in phraseology; (c) he would hardly have enlarged upon the ethical sections as the author of Ephesians has done; (d) this hypothesis does not explain the author's references to himself in the Epistle; (e) it is difficult to find an adequate motive for the apostle to adopt so unusual a procedure (cf. E. Percy, *op. cit.*, pp. 421, 422). Some scholars regard the verdict over Pauline authorship as open. Jülicher–Fascher, for instance, while inclining to think an apostolic disciple to be more intelligible as author, yet admit that the whole question remains problematic (*Einleitung in das Neue Testament*[7], 1931, p. 142).*

[2] i. 3. 12, vol. I, p. 375, as cited by Alford, *Greek New Testament* (1871), vol. III, p. 16. J. Eadie, *Commentary on Ephesians*[3] (1883), p. xxviii, records Epiphanius' opinion that Marcion placed as the seventh epistle of Paul ΠΡΟΣ ΕΦΕΣΙΟΥ.Σ

[3] Cf. Feine–Behm, *op. cit.*, p. 195.

[4] On the other hand Tertullian writes as if Marcion professed to have tampered with the title after most diligent inquiry ('quasi et in isto diligentissimus explorator'), *Adv. Marc.* v. 17.

an inquiry is necessary because all the versions without exception include the words, and since some of these are of great antiquity there is at least a possibility that they have preserved a purer text than the Greek MSS. Moreover, the title ΠΡΟΣ ΕΦΕΣΙΟΥΣ ('To the Ephesians') attached to all the Greek MSS reflects the tradition current at the time in spite of the doubt about the reading of i. 1. Irenaeus[1] cites Ephesians v. 30 as being in the Epistle to the Ephesians, and Clement[2] of Alexandria cites words from Ephesians v. 21–25 in the same way. Moreover, Tertullian is in no doubt that the Epistle was sent to Ephesus when he criticizes Marcion for having a strong desire to change the title.[3] There is no doubt therefore that these early Fathers regarded the Epistle as addressed to the Ephesian church whatever the reading of the first verse in their texts.

Assuming the possibility that the Epistle was addressed specifically to the Ephesian church, it would be necessary to suggest that at some stage in the use of the Epistle, particularly in Egypt, the words 'in Ephesus' were omitted for liturgical purposes.[4] There may seem to be some slight support for this supposition in the parallel case of the omission of 'in Rome' (ἐν 'Ρώμῃ) in a few MSS[5] of Romans i. 7, especially as this Epistle is nearer in form to Romans than to any other of Paul's Epistles. But the evidence is quite inadequate to establish any general practice of turning specific letters into general treatises in this way.

The reading 'in Ephesus' which is suspect on textual grounds becomes more so in the light of internal evidence. The writer does not appear to know the readers personally (i. 15, iii. 2, iv. 21). All these references suggest that the readers had only heard of Paul, but this could not be said of the Ephesian church. The first (i. 15) could perhaps refer to what Paul had heard of them since leaving Ephesus, and the other two references may be no more than rhetorical hypothetical statements. But when these considerations are added to the fact that no term of endearment or reference to beloved or faithful brethren is found and only an indirect concluding benediction is given, it would seem highly improbable that the Ephesian church was specifically in mind. Some

---

[1] *Adv. Haer.* v. 2. 36.   [2] *Strom.* iv. 65. Cf. also *Paed.* iv. 65.

[3] *Adv. Marc.* v. 11, 17. See previous note above.

[4] For a full discussion of the various hypotheses regarding the original reading of i. 1, cf. N. A. Dahl, 'Addresse und Proemium des Epheserbriefes', *ThZ*, VII (1951), pp. 241–264.*

[5] For the evidence see p. 405

other explanation must be sought. The various proposed explanations of the destination of the Epistle are examined below.

a. The Epistle was sent to Laodicea

This hypothesis follows the evidence from Marcion's Canon but it is open to criticism on various grounds. It probably arose from the desire to locate the Epistle referred to in Colossians iv. 16.[1] Many ancients and not a few moderns have found it difficult to conceive that any of Paul's letters could be lost; hence the many hypotheses attempting to track them down. But in the present case the fact that Paul urges the Colossians to read the letter from Laodicea and to send theirs to Laodicea creates a difficulty,[2] for the similarity between the two letters is so striking (if the former is identified with Ephesians) that it is questionable whether there would be any point in exchanging them. On the other hand the different approach in each could have proved edifying to both. The major obstacle is the absence of any MS evidence replacing 'Ephesus' with 'Laodicea'.[3]

b. The Epistle was a circular letter

It is widely held that Ephesians, designed as a circular, was written at the same time as Colossians and Philemon and was probably taken to various churches in the province of Asia by Tychicus. Some forms of this theory assume that a blank was left in the original copies and Tychicus was requested to fill in the name as he visited each church. The following objections have been raised against this circular-letter theory.[4]

[1] Cf. Harnack's view that the address 'to the Laodiceans' was later omitted because the church had received a bad name (cf. Rev. iii. 14 ff.), SBA (1910), pp. 701 ff.

[2] Cf. J. N. Sanders, Studies in Ephesians, edited by F. L. Cross (1956), p. 14.*

[3] Since Col. iv. 16 bears testimony to the fact that Paul wrote to the Laodiceans at the same period as he wrote Colossians it may be that Laodicea was one of the places which received our 'Ephesians', and to this extent Marcion may be reflecting a true tradition. Yet because Colossians must have been written before Ephesians, it would then be necessary to suppose either that Col. iv. 16 was added as a postscript after the completion of our 'Ephesians' or else that Paul is referring to a letter he still intends to write. McNeile (St. Paul), p. 216, who conjectures that our Epistle is the one sent to the Laodiceans, accounts for the blank by suggesting that the Laodiceans sent a copy of the letter with their own address omitted.

[4] For a concise summary of objections, cf. D. E. Nineham, Studies in Ephesians (edited by F. L. Cross), p. 25.

1. If it was designed for a group of churches in the Lycus valley, why did not Paul include some greetings of a general kind as he did in writing to the Colossians?

2. If separate copies were prepared for each church, why did the scribe not fill in the appropriate name? The other Pauline letter which was designed for a group of churches, i.e. Galatians, did not treat the situation in this way.

3. The theory of a blank would be more intelligible if the ἐν had not also been omitted.

4. The MS evidence does not support the theory since no MS has survived with another name than Ephesus. It would be strange if the only copy that originally survived was one which was not used and therefore still left blank in the address. The possibilities of its preservation in this case would be remote.[1]

It may be admitted that these objections are strong enough to cast suspicion on the blank-address theory, but they do not dispose of the circular theory as an explanation of the Epistle. If the original text did not possess the words 'in Ephesus' it may be taken as addressed in a very general way 'to the saints who are also faithful in Christ Jesus', which would well fit a general circular theory. It would then be suitable for the Christian communities of Asia and other provinces, especially where Paul was not personally known.[2] It may be assumed that as Tychicus was the bearer of the circular or circulars, there would be no particular need for a specific address as no definite situation is reflected in the Epistle.[3]

c. The Epistle was Paul's spiritual testament

Those who maintain this view generally place it at the end of the Roman imprisonment and deny the second imprisonment hypothesis. It is then

---

[1] If an unaddressed circular had been preserved at Ephesus it might have been kept for a time and later assumed to have been addressed to that church, hence the textual addition. Cf. G. Zuntz, *The Text of the Epistles* (1953), p. 228 n., who cites other evidence for circulars in the ancient world.

[2] Cf. the discussion of W. Michaelis, *Einleitung*, pp. 195 ff.

[3] J. P. Wilson (*ET*, LX, 1948-49, pp. 225, 226) makes the interesting suggestion that the original reading was τοῖς οὖσιν ἐνὶ καὶ πιστοῖς ἐν Χριστῷ Ἰησοῦ ('to the saints who are *one* and faithful'), which would well fit the theme of unity in the Epistle. He appeals to the use of ἐνί in Col. iii. 15. But his emendation cannot be said to read naturally. On the analogy of Paul's usage (e.g. Rom. i. 7, 15) ἐν with a place name would be expected.

viewed as the apostle's parting message to the church as a whole.[1] It is certainly not impossible that Paul speaks to the Ephesians as a type of the universal Church, for there is no denying that Paul is more reflective in this Epistle than in any other and he may well be intending to give a summary of his doctrine. To maintain this view it is not necessary, however, to regard Ephesians as Paul's latest Epistle, for the need for such a statement of doctrine for the Asiatic churches must have been present over a long period. But the greatest obstacle to this theory is the fact that the Epistle does not appear to be addressed to the universal Church but to particular people, although the personal references are admittedly rather vague.

d. The Epistle was an introduction to the Pauline Corpus

This theory suggested by Goodspeed and John Knox has been taken over by Mitton with some minor modifications.[2] The devoted Paulinist who is said to have written Ephesians feared that the readers, unfamiliar as they were *ex hypothesi* with the Pauline Epistles, needed a summary of the teaching contained in them. This introductory treatise became known as 'To the Ephesians' because the collected letters were first made known to the Ephesian church.

This theory is open to several criticisms.

1. There is no trace of Ephesians ever standing at the head of the Pauline Corpus. If, as both Goodspeed[3] and Mitton[4] maintain, the Epistle was composed and the collection published about AD 90 we should expect to find some trace of this position in the lists of the second century, but such evidence is lacking.[5]

2. The Tychicus passage in Ephesians vi. 21, 22, which is in verbatim

---

[1] This is the view of J. N. Sanders, *Studies in Ephesians* (1956), p. 16.

[2] Goodspeed in his various works on Ephesians, John Knox in his *Philemon among the Letters of Paul* (1935), and Mitton in his *Epistle to the Ephesians*. Cf. also W. L. Knox, *St. Paul and the Church of the Gentiles* (1939), p. 184; K. and S. Lake, *An Introduction to the New Testament* (1938), p. 142; S. G. F. Brandon, *The Fall of Jerusalem*[2] (1957), pp. 213 ff. The last writer, however, rejects Goodspeed's theory that Acts promoted the collection of the Corpus, which is the mainstay of the theory.

[3] *INT* (1937), pp. 230 ff.; *Key to Ephesians* (1956), p. xiii.

[4] Cf. *op. cit.*, pp. 160 ff.

[5] Cf. Mitton's summary of attempts to prove that Marcion dislocated the original order by exchanging Galatians with Ephesians (i.e. Laodiceans in Marcion's Canon), *The Formation of the Pauline Corpus*, pp. 61 ff. He follows the arguments of J. Knox's *Marcion and the New Testament* (1942).

agreement with Colossians iv. 7, 8, is a real problem for Goodspeed's theory. There is no adequate occasion for adding so personal and direct a reference to Tychicus when the other parts of the Epistle are allegedly so impersonal. It would have been obvious to the observant reader that these words, so curious in an introductory letter, were borrowed without modification from Colossians. A natural course for a Pauline imitator would have been to omit all reference to Paul's companions, unless of course his purpose was to stamp his work with the appearance of genuineness. But if the Tychicus passage was included to add verisimilitude to an imitation it could hardly have been done more clumsily than by an isolated but wholesale borrowing from an existing Epistle. The letter would certainly not become more realistic by the statement that Tychicus would tell the readers everything (vi. 21). The suggestion of J. N. Sanders[1] that this passage is an interpolation probably by Marcion to lend colour to his theory that it was sent to Laodicea and hence comparable with Colossians is not more convincing. It assumes without adequate evidence that Marcion could have made such an interpolation in so convincing a manner that all subsequent copies of the text were influenced by it, or else were directly descended from Marcion's interpolated copy.[2]

3. The theory depends on the presupposition that Paul's letters suffered a period of neglect (see further discussion on pp. 647 ff.) and that interest was revived on the publication of Acts, but this puts too much weight on the influence of literature.[3] The failure of other writers of the same period to which Goodspeed assigns Ephesians to grasp the main characteristic ideas of Paul's Epistles does not lead us to suppose that Ephesians could have been produced solely by literary influences.

4. The major difficulty is the literary problem. As an introduction to the whole Pauline Corpus it is inconceivable that the writer would have given such preponderance to Colossians.[4] It certainly cannot be adequately explained as accidental (as Goodspeed's theory seems to imply). Moreover, the claim that it reflects all the other Epistles is only

[1] *Studies in Ephesians* (edited by F. L. Cross), p. 15. It should be noted that Marcion was more noted for excision than interpolation.

[2] M. Dibelius' explanation of the Tychicus passage is equally unconvincing. He assumed that Ephesians was composed at a later date to replace the Laodicean letter mentioned in Col. iv. 16 and that it then became naturalized as an Epistle to the Ephesians on the strength of the Tychicus passage (*A Fresh Approach*, p. 170).

[3] Cf. F. W. Beare, *Ephesians* (IB), p. 603.

[4] See previous discussion, p. 495.

partially true[1] and it would for that reason be a very strange introduction to them.

e. The Epistle was intended as a philosophy of religion for the whole Christian world

Another theory based on non-Pauline authorship is the view that a personal acquaintance of the apostle produced it as an attempt to formulate a kind of religious philosophy of history from the teaching of Paul, using Colossians extensively as his framework because in that Epistle Paul came closest to the doctrine he wished to express.[2] Under this theory the title 'To the Ephesians' was a scribal addition which is therefore of no significance. But as with the last-mentioned theory, no satisfactory account of the insertion of the Tychicus passage can be given, nor is the scribal addition of the title easy to imagine if the address in i. 1 was intelligible without it and was taken to indicate a general letter. It must have had some close connection with Ephesus for such a title to stick to it so firmly in the tradition. The best that can be suggested under this theory is that the Ephesian church sponsored it,[3] but there is no other evidence that any important church ever sponsored a pseudonymous Epistle.

f. The Epistle was a general safeguard against the spread of the Colossian heresy

This is usually held in conjunction with the circular-letter theory, it being supposed that Paul envisaged that the problems that had actually beset the Colossian church might well seep into other churches in the same district, and a general letter was therefore sent to all the churches in the vicinity. The Tychicus passage would be quite naturally explained as a reference to the bearer of the Epistle. He would be acting as Paul's representative to many groups of Gentile Christians whom Paul had never visited. But on his way he would pass through Ephesus and may well have left there a copy of the Epistle while he himself proceeded up the Lycus valley to the other Christian communities.[4]*

[1] See previous discussion, pp. 496 ff.

[2] Cf. Beare, *op. cit.*, pp. 601 ff.   [3] Cf. Beare, *op. cit.*, p. 605.

[4] W. Michaelis suggests that the circular returned to Ephesus, from which he believes it was sent, and this would account for the addition of the Ephesian destination by a later Christian (*op. cit.*, p. 194). A. Wikenhauser, *New Testament Introduction*, p. 426, accounts for the Ephesian destination on the ground that copies of the circular were made at Ephesus.

III. PURPOSE

It is difficult to determine with any certainty the occasion and purpose of a letter of whose destination there is so much doubt. But if we assume some kind of circular-letter theory we are able to suggest a probable purpose from the circumstances of the writer rather than of the readers. Since Paul was in prison he has clearly had time to reflect and this would well account for the more contemplative mood of the Epistle, together with the absence of any tension connected with a specific situation with which he was dealing. His mind dwells on the theme of Christ and the Church, resulting in an exalted Christology and a high appraisal of the privileges of believers in Christ.[1]

The close connection between this Epistle and Colossians has a direct bearing on its purpose. The same themes are dealt with although in a modified way. It seems probable that the apostle, with the positive doctrine of the Colossian letter still in his mind, wrote it down again in a general way without the specific background of the heresy. Something of the same process may well have taken place in the case of the Galatian and Roman letters.

IV. DATE

Since Paul is a prisoner (Eph. iii. 1, iv. 1), and since its close association with Colossians presupposes the same imprisonment as when that Epistle was sent, the traditional allocation of this Epistle to the first Roman imprisonment seems most probably correct.[2] Those who deny Pauline authorship generally date the letter about AD 90,[3] the date when

[1] J. Armitage Robinson, *Epistle of the Ephesians*[2] (1904), summed up the purpose as a non-controversial exposition of the unity of mankind in Christ and God's purpose through the Church. H. Rendtorff, 'Der Brief an die Epheser' in *Die kleineren Briefe des Apostels Paulus (NTD)*, 1955, p. 56, takes the view that Paul dwelt on the thoughts expressed in Colossians in his own meditations and prayers and then committed them soon after to a writing lacking any specific address. The Epistle, therefore, may be regarded as a meditation on great Christian themes.*

[2] See pp. 557 f. for a discussion of the dating of Colossians. If the Ephesian hypothesis of the origin of Ephesians is maintained a much earlier date is necessary. W. Michaelis (*op. cit.*, p. 199), for instance, dates it in the winter of 54–55 (the date to which he assigns the close of the Ephesian ministry), having concluded a similar date for Colossians and Philemon.

[3] Some, e.g. H. F. D. Sparks, *The Formation of the New Testament* (1952), p. 72, date it earlier, c. AD 75–80. For a discussion of Goodspeed's dating of the formation of the Corpus, see pp. 647 ff.

the Pauline Corpus is alleged to have been collected. Since Clement of Rome cites the Epistle it must on any theory be dated earlier than AD 95.

CONTENTS

I. GREETING (i. 1, 2)

The apostle associates no one else with him in this address.

II. DOXOLOGY (i. 3–14)

It is not Paul's usual style to enter directly into a statement of general thanksgiving for all the spiritual blessings received in Christ, but this opening section sets the tone of reflective worship evident throughout the whole of the first half of the Epistle. The salient features of this extended doxology are (1) the sovereign choice of God (verses 3–6); (2) the manifestation of His wisdom in the provision of redemption through the blood of Christ (verses 7–10); and (3) the assurance, through the Holy Spirit, of the predestined inheritance of believers (verses 11–14).

III. THANKSGIVING AND PRAYER FOR THE READERS (i. 15–23)

Paul has heard of their faith and love and is thankful for this, but his main prayer is that they should have wisdom to comprehend the greatness of the revelation in Christ, especially the power of His resurrection and His exalted position as Head of the Church.

IV. DOCTRINAL SECTION (ii. 1–iii. 21)

This has in essence already begun in the doxology and prayer, but the burden of the next section is a more detailed exposition of two important themes.

a. The greatness of Christian salvation (ii. 1–22)

The apostle expounds the theme by appealing to experience both in a personal and corporate sense.

(i) *Personally* (ii. 1–10). The readers have been quickened into a higher life in Christ through the gracious act of God. They are reminded of what they were (dead in trespasses and sins) and of what they now are (God's workmanship created in Christ Jesus for good works).

(ii) *Corporately* (ii. 11–22). Recollection of what they were reminds Paul of another glorious fact of experience, i.e. that Gentiles have become fellow citizens with Jews, which leads him to dwell upon the doctrinal basis of their unity in Christ. The readers were 'once afar off' and were 'strangers and sojourners', but Christ has abolished the dividing wall and has made peace through His cross. The result is a single structure in which all the members, Jew and Gentile, are inter-knit into a holy temple in the Lord.

b. The greatness of the ministry of the Church (iii. 1–21)

Paul continues to reason from experience, appealing from his own vocation to that of the Church as a whole.

(i) *Paul's own commission* (iii. 1–9). The mystery was communicated by revelation and therefore has upon it the divine authentication. The incorporation of Gentiles as fellow-heirs was an essential part of the gospel, and Paul reiterates his call to preach this gospel in spite of his own unworthiness.

(ii) *The Church's vocation* (iii. 10–12). God's eternal purpose has been to use His Church to make known this wisdom of the oneness of all men in Christ.

(iii) *Paul's prayer for his readers* (iii. 13–21). Their great need is for inner strength and loving steadfastness, which would lead to a greater comprehension of the love of Christ. This thought leads to another doxology to God for His abundant power in His Church.

V. THE PRACTICAL SECTION (iv. 1–vi. 17)
The apostle now turns to the Church's duties.

a. Exhortations to unity (iv. 1–6)
The unity of the Spirit must be maintained and Paul therefore describes various aspects of this unity, culminating in the thought of God gathering up all things in Himself.

b. A description of the diversity of gifts (iv. 7–13)
Unity is not achieved by uniformity. The ascension of Christ has resulted in the bestowal of a multiplicity of gifts which find expression in

differing functions, all of which are intended for the edification of the Church.

c. Practical means of maintaining unity (iv. 14–16)

Instability of doctrine is an evidence of an immaturity incapable of discerning the cunning of wily men. But spiritual growth is achieved through speaking the truth in love, i.e. in contrast to the craftiness of the deceivers. This growth takes place through the close connection between Christ, the Head, and the members, each making his own appropriate contribution.

d. The old life and the new (iv. 17–32)

Paul may have feared that the preceding statements sounded rather idealistic, for his mind at once goes back to the heathen background of his readers, in the light of which he makes certain specific recommendations. (i) They must make a clean break with the old environment, which is characterized by spiritual callousness and moral uncleanness (iv. 17–22). (ii) They must put on the new nature as they renew their minds, and this involves accepting new standards of righteousness and holiness (iv. 23, 24). (iii) They must exercise special watchfulness over certain sins which would destroy the unity of the Spirit, especially falsehood, anger, dishonesty and harmful speech, all of which grieve Him. Such undesirable attitudes must give place to kindness and a forgiving spirit (iv. 25–32).

e. Warnings against the works of darkness (v. 1–14)

Paul is still dwelling on the old nature and finds it necessary to warn against several specific tendencies. Christians must be noted for purity of life and conversation in contrast to the frivolity and immorality of those upon whom God's wrath will descend. They must not only refrain from associating with such people but must expose their darkness.

f. Exhortations on the wise use of time (v. 15–21)

The believers must take care to walk wisely and to understand the Lord's will for them. Drunkenness is singled out as a thing to be avoided in striking contrast to the fulness of the Spirit, which manifests itself in the corporate activity of worship and public thanksgiving. Those who have learned to reverence Christ will learn to respect other believers.

g. Christian homelife (v. 22–vi. 9)

(i) *Wives and husbands* (v. 22–33). The Christian approach to the marriage relationship is based on the analogy of the relationship of Christ to His Church. In this section the purely practical issues become an opportunity for an exposition of Paul's doctrine of the Church. (1) It is the body of Christ, who is its Saviour; (2) it is the special object of His love; (3) it is made clean through His self-offering and will be presented to God without blemish, and (4) it is nourished by Christ. The relationship between Christ and His Church becomes, in fact, the pattern for Christian homelife.

(ii) *Children and parents* (vi. 1–4). Children are told to obey and fathers are to exercise restraint and helpful discipline.

(iii) *Slaves and masters* (vi. 5–9). Paul's attitude towards slavery is to transform it from within by urging slaves to regard their service as service to Christ and to leave to Him all thought of recompense. Masters must avoid threatening and partiality in view of their own responsibility to their heavenly Master.

h. Christian warfare (vi. 10–17)

The final exhortation is for Christians to arm for the fight since they are engaged in unceasing conflict with the powers of darkness. The armour although entirely spiritual is nevertheless effective, for the victory is assured.

VI. CONCLUSION (vi. 18–24)

In addition to requesting prayer for himself that he may have all boldness to preach, the apostle urges the readers to pray continually for all saints. There follows a warm commendation of Tychicus in the same terms as in the Colossian letter. In the closing benediction Paul covets for his readers peace, love and grace.

ADDITIONAL NOTES

486. [2] In his recent essay in *SLA* (1966), pp. 288–297, E. Käsemann sees both Ephesians and Acts as showing kinship with the hymnic-liturgical tradition, which in his opinion makes them both later than Paul.

490. H. Conzelmann, in his editing of Ephesians and Colossians in *NTD*, 8 (1962), replacing the work of H. Rendtorff, regards both these Epistles as by a

disciple of the apostle. Pauline authorship of Ephesians is also rejected by G. Johnston in his *CB*, n.s. (1967) commentary. Cf. also W. Marxsen (*INT*, 1968, pp.
187 ff.), who, having rejected the authenticity of Colossians, does the same with
Ephesians. But authenticity is maintained by F. F. Bruce, *The Epistle to the Ephesians*
(1962); F. Foulkes, *The Epistle of Paul to the Ephesians* (*TNT*, 1963); H. Schlier,
Der Brief an die Epheser[5] (1965), pp. 22 ff.; A. F. J. Klijn, *INT* (1967), pp. 103 f.

492. [1] For a comparison between Ephesians and the Qumran Literature, see
K. G. Kuhn, *NTS*, 7 (1961), pp. 334–346 (reprinted in *Paul and Qumran*, edited
J. Murphy-O'Connor, 1968, pp. 115–131). This author considers that the style,
particularly the long sentences, is characteristic of Qumran literature. The
parenetic sections, except v. 22–vi. 9, show close connection with Qumran. But
Kuhn makes no deductions from this which affect authorship.

493. [1] For further support for Coutts' baptismal theory for Ephesians, cf. R. A.
Wilson, *Studia Evangelica*, II (1964), pp. 676–680.

504. F. F. Bruce (*BJRL*, XLIX, 1967, pp. 312 ff.) discusses Paul's doctrine of the
Church and concedes that Ephesians shows a more developed doctrine than 1
Corinthians. Indeed, he admits some elements of *Frühkatholizismus*, but disputes
that this involves the denial of its Pauline character.

507. In a study of some of the great themes of the Epistle, L. Cerfaux (*Littérature et Théologie Pauliniennes*, 1960, pp. 60–71) argues that the homogeneity
between Ephesians and the great Pauline Epistles favours the authenticity of the
former. Cf. also P. Benoit, *Exégèse et Théologie*, II (1961), pp. 53 ff. (an article
originally published in *RB*, XLVI, 1937, pp. 342 ff., 506 ff.). Note that W. Marxsen
(*INT*, 1968, p. 196) admits the use of Pauline ideas, but considers that the author
goes beyond Paul.

508. [1] The theory that Luke may have been the author of Ephesians is tentatively suggested by R. P. Martin, *ET*, LXXIX (1968), pp. 296–302. He comes to
this conclusion as a result of a study of Luke-Acts in comparison with this Epistle.

509. [4] On Eph. i. 1, R. Batey (*JBL*, LXXXII, 1963, p. 101) has suggested that a
scribe might have confused Ἀσίας for οὖσαις. Cf. M. Santer's suggestion (*NTS*,
15, 1969, pp. 247 f.) that Eph. i. 1 originally read καὶ πιστοῖς before τοῖς οὖσιν
(omitting ἐν Ἐφέσῳ). This phrase was accidentally omitted and later inserted by
another scribe in the wrong place. ἐν Ἐφέσῳ was added later by analogy with
Paul's other letters. This seems a rather complicated process, but is worth consideration.

510. [2] P. N. Harrison ('The Author of Ephesians', *Studia Evangelica*, II, 1964
pp. 595–604) makes the unlikely suggestion that Onesimus wrote Ephesians to
compensate for the loss of the original letter to Laodicea.

514. Some see a background of syncretistic Gnosticism behind this Epistle, but
only in so far as Ephesians combats such a movement. Cf. P. Pokorny (*ZNTW*,
53, 1962, pp. 160–194), who points out the marked differences between the Gnostic
Urmensch and Christ. Cf. *idem.*, *Der Epheserbrief und die Gnosis* (1965). H. Schlier

(*Der Brief an die Epheser*,[5] 1965) explains certain of Paul's ideas by appealing to Jewish-Greek Gnosticism.

Liturgical theory for Ephesians. J. C. Kirby (*Ephesians, Baptism and Pentecost*, 1968), who does not accept the authenticity of this Epistle, suggests that it consists of two parts, one based on a liturgy and the other consisting of a Pentecost discourse. The former has similarities with the Qumran covenant-renewing service. But the theory is not convincing, because it does not do justice to the essential unity of the Epistle, nor can it adequately account for the compilation into a pseudonymous Pauline epistle. For theories of part of Ephesians as a baptismal liturgy, cf. W. Nauck, *Ev Th*, XIII (1953), pp. 362 ff. and G. Schille, *ThLZ*, 80 (1955), col. 183.

515. [1] H. Chadwick sees the aim of the Epistle as a provision of a basis of unity between the Pauline and non-Pauline churches (*ZNTW*, 51, 1960, pp. 143–153). M. Barth (*Interpreter*, 17, 1963, pp. 3–24) thinks that Ephesians shows that Gentile Christians must learn to respect what God does for Israel.

CHAPTER SIXTEEN

THE EPISTLE TO THE PHILIPPIANS

I. THE PHILIPPIAN CHURCH

An account of the origin of this church, the first in Europe, is recorded with particular vividness in Acts xvi, where three examples of the power of Christianity in Philippi are selected. They are (1) the devout proselyte, Lydia, a trader in purple cloth from Asia, who serves as a representative of those well-prepared to receive the gospel (xvi.11–15); (2) the soothsaying girl whose spirit of divination was exorcized by Paul, and who illustrates the triumph of Christ over the powers of darkness (xvi. 16–18); and (3) the gaoler, shaken into a realization of his own need by an earthquake, who shows the power of the gospel to transform entire families, for both he and his household were baptized (xvi. 27–34). Whether the girl became a Christian we are not definitely told, but the others no doubt formed the nucleus of the Philippian church.

Other members of the church who are mentioned in the Epistle are Epaphroditus, Euodia, Syntyche and Clement,[1] all names which point to a predominantly Gentile church, which is an impression confirmed by certain indications in the Epistle. In Philippians iii. 3 ff. Paul speaks of the 'true circumcision' in a manner which suggests the readers were not circumcised Jews. In his list of desirable qualities in iv. 8 ff. he includes terms current in the contemporary Gentile world, which may suggest that he was using words with which his readers, if Gentiles, would be most familiar.

All that is known of the organization of this church is what Paul states in the opening salutation. Although the Epistle is significantly addressed to 'the saints in Christ Jesus who are at Philippi', Paul links with this description the more specific reference to 'bishops and deacons', who nevertheless appear to be almost in the background. They are probably mentioned only because they were responsible for the organizing of the collection for Paul's work, to acknowledge which was one of the reasons for the Epistle. Their specific mention here shows

[1] Some would also include Syzygus, taking the Greek word σύζυγος in Phil. iv. 3 as a proper name.

indisputably that two distinct orders of officials were in existence at an early stage in the history of the Church. Those who dispute that such a state of organization could have existed in Paul's lifetime are hard put to it to explain away the present reference. B. S. Easton,[1] for instance, sees in the terms used not distinct orders of rule-elders but general descriptions of functions as the 'governments' and 'helps' of 1 Corinthians xii. 28. It seems impossible, however, to draw such a distinction, and since Acts xiv. 23 reports that Paul and Barnabas appointed elders in every church established on their missionary journey it seems most reasonable to suppose that Paul had something to do with the organization of the Philippian church.[2]

These Christians maintained strong links with the apostle, who in all probability visited them about five years later on leaving his work in Ephesus, for Acts xx. 1, 2 states that Paul went on his way to Macedonia and gave the people much encouragement, and it is certain this tour would have included the Philippian church. He had, moreover, previously sent Timothy and Erastus to Macedonia to prepare the way for his visit and it would appear that they were still there when he himself arrived. But during this period of Paul's absence from them the Philippians had shown warm affection for him by sending sustenance for his work at Thessalonica (Phil. iv. 15) and had apparently sent other gifts ater (2 Cor. xi. 9). After spending a further three months in Greece Paul again visits Philippi and spends Easter there on his way to Jerusalem with the collection for the poor saints.

This church was situated in a historic city founded by the father of Alexander the Great and named after him. After the rout of Mark Antony's forces by Octavian at the battle of Actium in 31 BC, it was established as a military colony with special privileges of citizenship.

---

[1] Cf. *The Pastoral Epistles* (1948), pp. 224 ff. Easton regards Acts xiv. 23 and xx. 17 as an anachronism (p. 226), but admits a Palestinian elder-system. He seems to regard the Gentile elder-office as a development from the Jewish pattern, but too late to belong to apostolic times on the ground that charismatic ministry alone was recognized among Gentile churches. But see the present writer's *The Pastoral Epistles* (1957), pp. 26 ff., and W. Michaelis, *Pastoralbriefe und Gefangenschaftsbriefe* (1930). Riddle and Hutson, *New Testament Life and Literature* (1946), p. 123, regard the salutation as an editorial addition, an easy way out of the difficulty but without any other support than the assumption that bishops were unknown as early as this.

[2] For a thorough examination of the terms 'bishops and deacons' in Phil. i. 1 cf. W. Michaelis, *Pastoralbriefe und Gefangenschaftsbriefe* (1930), pp. 5 ff. Michaelis considers both terms to be descriptive of functionaries, not merely functions.

This fact may account for the terminology used in Philippians i. 27, iii. 20, where Paul speaks of a heavenly citizenship. The Acts story contains many hints of the Philippians' pride in their privileges (cf. xvi. 20, 21 and the terms used for their officials—*praetors* and *lictors*—xvi. 20, 35).

II. OCCASION

In Philippians iv. 18 Paul refers to the gifts sent to him from the readers by the hand of Epaphroditus. Although he expresses thankfulness for their generosity at the conclusion of the Epistle it need not be assumed that this is the first acknowledgment of the gifts that Paul has made. He would hardly have left so important a matter to the end had this been the case.[1] But if an earlier acknowledgment had been sent, the occasion of the present letter could not have been the arrival of the gifts.

The position of Epaphroditus deserves special consideration in this connection. It would appear from Philippians ii. 25 that the Philippians had themselves sent Epaphroditus for the special purpose of ministering to Paul's needs. During his service with Paul he suffered a serious illness which proved almost fatal (ii. 27), and the apostle recognized the goodness of God in sparing him. But the Philippians had heard that Epaphroditus had been ill and a report of their concern for him had reached the sick man. Paul sensed the longing of Epaphroditus to return home and decided to send him back. This decision furnished an occasion, probably the main one, for the present letter.[2]

It has been suggested[3] that the Philippians may have been critical of the apostle for retaining the services of Epaphroditus too long and that this criticism prompted his decision to send him back. It is a less likely suggestion that the Philippians had not taken seriously the reports of Epaphroditus' illness and needed to be told of its serious character, although it is significant that he twice mentions the almost fatal sequel and further describes Epaphroditus as 'risking his life to complete your

---

[1] Some expositors have found an acknowledgment of the gifts in i. 3, understanding Paul to be speaking of 'all your remembrance of me'. See R. P. Martin, *The Epistle of Paul to the Philippians* (1959), pp. 59, 60, and P. Schubert, *Form and Function of the Pauline Thanksgivings* (ZNTW, 20), pp. 71–82. Schubert reached his conclusion after careful structural comparison of this thanksgiving with other Pauline thanksgivings.*

[2] Cf. E. F. Scott, *Philippians* (IB), xi (1955), p. 10.

[3] Cf. Feine–Behm, *Einleitung*[11] (1956), p. 179.*

service to me' (Phil. ii. 30, RSV). But do these allusions contain an implicit criticism of Epaphroditus which Paul finds it necessary to answer? Was there some feeling that Epaphroditus had not completed his task, or that Paul was not appreciative of his services? If that were so, Paul's words in Philippians ii. 25–30 would certainly rectify any wrong impressions that the Philippians may have formed. This suggestion may possibly be supported by Paul's exhortation to the readers to receive Epaphroditus 'with all joy and hold such in honour' (ii. 29).

If, then, the return of Epaphroditus provided the main reason for the Epistle, what was the purpose of the concluding reference to the gifts? J. H. Michael[1] has pointed out that Paul must have written at least one other Epistle to this church and suggests that the manner in which Paul refers to the subject in the present Epistle is too indirect to be a first acknowledgment. He[2] also detects a note of gentle rebuke in the apostle's words, suggesting that the Philippians had misrepresented what he had previously written. They may have thought that he was unappreciative of their generosity and so he goes out of his way to trace their liberality towards him from the very first days since the founding of the church in Philippi. He praises their service to him as superior to all other churches in such a way as to suggest a certain self-consciousness about the whole subject. This is further accentuated by his paradoxical assertions of independence (cf. iv. 17: 'Not because I desire a gift: but I desire fruit that may abound to your account'). He has learned in whatever state he is to be content (iv. 11). Perhaps the Philippians had misunderstood some previous statement to the same effect as indicating that Paul had no need of their gifts. J. H. Michael, in fact, thinks that the present passage in Philippians is an enlargement of what the apostle had said earlier in order to make clear that his seeming independence in no way conflicted with his real appreciation of their gifts.[3] There is much to be said for this reconstruction, but the data available do not require it. It may be that the apostle when nearing the end of his letter is dwelling on his own present circumstances and is much encouraged by his recollection of the Philippians' recent resumption of material assistance. Having written iv. 10–13, he may possibly have feared that the readers would misunderstand the words as imply-

---

[1] 'The First and Second Epistles to the Philippians', *ET*, xxxiv (1922), pp. 106–109.

[2] *Philippians* (*MC*), p. 210. Cf. T. Zahn, *Introduction* (1909), I, pp. 525–527.

[3] Cf. R. P. Martin, *Philippians* (1959), pp. 174, 179, who disputes this hypothesi-

ing censure, and consequently concludes (iv. 14–20) with a reiteration of his appreciation of their help.

Other reasons for the present letter may be found in (1) the intimation of Timothy's approaching visit; (2) the apostle's own intention, if possible, to visit them in the near future, and (3) the emphasis in the Epistle on unity, which suggests there was a tendency towards divisiveness or at least strained relationships (cf. iv. 2, where two women are urged to reach agreement in the Lord). The purpose of chapter iii will be discussed later, but Paul is here warning against Judaizers in a way that suggests an anticipated threat which has not as yet actually arrived.

III. AUTHENTICITY

It is hardly necessary to discuss the question of the Epistle's genuineness (except the hymn in chapter ii, for which see pp. 539 f.) as the great majority of scholars regard it as indisputable. A few, however, have adhered to interpolation theories. Yet most of those who cannot accept the unity of the existing Epistle (see discussion below) nevertheless regard the separate parts as truly Pauline, so strong are the marks of authenticity impressed upon the Epistle itself. This internal evidence is strongly supported by external evidence, which contains no hint of doubt that the Epistle in its entirety was Paul's own work.

IV. THE PLACE AND DATE OF DISPATCH

Since Paul is clearly a prisoner (Phil. i. 7, 13, 16)[1] the main problem is to identify the imprisonment. The traditional opinion has always been Rome, but this has been challenged by two other theories, the Caesarean and the Ephesian.

a. Caesarea

This hypothesis will be considered first because its claims are far less strong than either of the other theories, and because it possesses few modern advocates.[2] In fact all the reasons that were at one time ad-

[1] T. W. Manson attempted to maintain that these references need not indicate that Paul is *now* a prisoner, but his arguments are not convincing (cf. *BJRL*, 23, 1939, pp. 182 ff.). He considered the references in the Epistle were to Paul's experience before Gallio. In this way he maintained the Ephesian origin of Philippians without the necessity to maintain an Ephesian imprisonment.

[2] Surprisingly E. H. Lohmeyer, *Der Brief an die Philipper* (1930), supports this view.*

vanced to support the Caesarean theory are now used with far more probability to support the Ephesian.

1. It has been contended that Paul's imprisonment appears to have been recent and therefore of short duration, but the Epistle supplies no definite information regarding either the duration of the imprisonment or its recentness in relation to the apostle's last visit to Philippi (cf. Phil. i. 30, iv. 10).

2. The polemic against Jewish teachers in chapter iii has been claimed as evidence that this Epistle belonged to the period of the Jewish-Gentile controversy and must therefore be dated with Paul's earlier Epistles, which contain certain similarities of expression with Philippians (cf. Phil. iii. 2 with 2 Cor. xi. 13 and Gal. v. 12; Phil. iii. 3 with Gal. vi. 13; Phil. iii. 18 with Gal. vi. 12 and 1 Cor. i. 23; and Phil. iii. 19 with 2 Cor. iv. 3, Rom. xvi. 18, Gal. vi. 12, 14, and 2 Cor. iv. 2).

3. The praetorium mentioned in Philippians i. 13 could be understood in the sense of Acts xxiii. 35 as Herod's palace, in which case the occupants would be sufficiently limited for all to learn the reason for Paul's arrest. Yet the reference to the praetorium in Philippians i. 13 is most naturally understood in a personal sense, i.e. of the guard itself and not of the palace housing them (although this latter sense is the older usage). Paul links the guard with all 'the rest' which must be understood in a personal sense.

4. The Philippian Epistle makes it clear that Paul's imprisonment had caused many to become courageous in preaching the gospel (i. 14), but this presupposes a place possessing a church of some size. Yet Caesarea does not easily fit this requirement.

b. Rome

The tradition which allocates this Epistle to Rome as the place of dispatch has much stronger basis.

1. It is suggested by the most natural understanding of both 'praetorium' (i. 13) and 'Caesar's household' (iv. 22). If the former means the Praetorian Guard whose headquarters were in Rome or more probably the Imperial Guard,[1] the latter would suggest the slaves and freedmen attached to the Emperor's residence in the same city, among whom there were some who had responded to the claims of the gospel.[2]

2. The apostle's trial seems to have been in process and he is awaiting with some sense of imminence the pronouncement of a judgment

[1] Cf. Ramsay, *St. Paul the Traveller* (1920), p. 357.   [2] But see pp. 534 f.

which could issue in life or death. If this is a correct assumption it could apply only to a trial from which no appeal could be made. This could clearly not apply to the Caesarean imprisonment during which Paul appealed to Caesar. Indeed it is difficult to believe that any provincial court could have produced in Paul the sense of approaching finality of decision which the Philippian letter implies (cf. i. 19 ff.).

3. The courage of 'many' to preach the gospel would be readily understandable in a place like Rome where a considerable church already existed, and this gives it decided advantages over Caesarea.[1]

4. The personal circumstances of the apostle fit easily into the conditions of the Roman imprisonment, for he has enough freedom to carry on correspondence with his various churches, to receive his companions and to arrange for their missions. This would well accord with Acts xxviii. 16, 30, 31.

5. Paul clearly has strong hopes of being released in order to visit Philippi in the near future,[2] but at Caesarea his face was turned westwards, and his intentions were furthered by his appeal to Caesar.

6. There is some early traditional support for this Roman hypothesis from the Marcionite Prologue attached to this Epistle, which states that it was sent from Rome. This is particularly interesting in view of the corresponding Prologue to the Colossian Epistle which mentions Ephesus for that Epistle, although Philemon like Philippians is stated to have been sent from Rome (see pp. 473, 476 for further discussion of this evidence).

Although the evidence has traditionally been considered strong enough to establish the Roman hypothesis, and although it seems definitely preferable to the Caesarean, several objections have recently been raised against it. The major objection is the difficulty, if not the improbability, of fitting in so many communications and journeys between Rome and Philippi—a considerable distance requiring about a month's travel to traverse—into a comparatively short space of time. It is generally agreed that the period under review was one of remarkable facility for travel, but it is questioned whether such journeys as the theory demands can be paralleled. These journeys may be summarized as follows:

1. The Philippians had received news of Paul.
2. Epaphroditus arrives in Rome with the gift.

[1] Cf. Moffatt, *ILNT*, p. 169.
[2] On the question of Paul's release, see pp. 534, 596 ff.

3. He falls ill, presumably after some period of active ministering to Paul's needs, and a report of his illness reaches Philippi (iv. 18, ii. 26). The Philippians may have at this point received Paul's acknowledgment of the gift.

4. Paul receives word from Philippi of their distress over Epaphroditus (ii. 26).

5. Epaphroditus takes the Epistle to Philippi (ii. 25).

6. Timothy is soon to visit Philippi and is to report back to Paul (ii. 19).[1]

This appears on the surface a formidable list of journeyings which raises suspicions about the possibility of ascribing the writing of the Epistle to Rome. But some modifications of the apparent difficulties may be necessary. There is nothing in the Epistle which requires that the readers had heard details of Paul's Roman imprisonment before sending the gift. All that Paul says on this subject is that it was kind of them to share his trouble (iv. 14), but he had had trouble enough long before reaching Rome. It is not an impossible suggestion that Epaphroditus was on his way to convey the gift before Paul's arrival in the imperial city, especially in view of the latter's unexpected delay through wintering in Malta.[2] When Paul arrives in Rome the brethren who went to meet him at the Forum of Appius and The Three Taverns (Acts xxviii. 15) seem to have heard previously about his coming. Is it possible that Epaphroditus had arrived first and had informed them about

---

[1] Cf. G. S. Duncan, *St. Paul's Ephesian Ministry* (1929), p. 80. Cf. also A. Deissmann's article in *Anatolian Studies* (1923), 'Zur ephesinischen Gefangenschaft des Apostels Paulus', pp. 121–127. Deissmann would include another journey, previous to the first mentioned above, i.e. the journey of Timothy, on the ground that Acts xxvii. 2 excludes Timothy from accompanying Paul on the voyage. But we have no certain knowledge of Timothy's movements at the time. He might equally well have been in Rome before Paul or have arrived at the same time as or subsequent to Epaphroditus.

[2] Cf. Schmid, *Zeit und Ort der paulinischen Gefangenschaftbriefe* (1931), pp. 78–90. Goodspeed (*INT*, p. 106) lays stress upon the fact that at Ephesus Paul was surrounded by many Ephesian friends and would hardly need the ministry of Epaphroditus. But at Rome his service would be more welcome. Bishop Lightfoot (*Philippians*, pp. 36 ff.) took a view similar to Schmid, although he suggested Aristarchus left Paul at Myra during the voyage to Rome and proceeded to his native Macedonia where he informed the Philippians of the developments of Paul's case, causing them to organize a gift collection which Epaphroditus conveyed to Paul. In this case he may well have arrived at the same time as or even prior to Paul's own arrival.

his coming? But this is mere conjecture. All that can be said is that the evidence does not demand a journey from Rome to Philippi with news of Paul's imprisonment before the dispatch of the gift.

There is no means of determining the period of Epaphroditus' ministry to Paul nor of the duration of his illness. This may have been brief although severe. If there were an earlier acknowledgment of the gift than our present Epistle it is probable that at the same time he informed the Philippians of Epaphroditus' illness and may also have mentioned his own present sufferings. The apostle mentions in ii. 26 the distress of the Philippians over Epaphroditus which would seem to require some reply from Philippi to Rome, and this would also be necessary on the hypothesis already mentioned that in iv. 10 ff. he is correcting a misunderstanding of a former letter.*

After this double journey the Epistle is written and Epaphroditus returns. So far there is no insuperable objection to the Roman hypothesis, for these events need not have occupied more than a year.[1] But the real problem arises over the future journeys involved. Paul writes as if a verdict is imminent which might involve the death sentence, and yet he expects to send Timothy soon and to receive him back again with news of the Philippians that he might be cheered as a result (ii. 19). This certainly seems strange, but although Paul is uncertain of the outcome of his trial he obviously has strong hopes that he will be released (i. 25), in which case his proposals regarding Timothy become intelligible. Dodd's[2] opinion that the two years of the Acts house-imprisonment would be ample for all the journeys required seems a reasonable conclusion, but many scholars find this difficulty the deciding factor in rejecting the Roman hypothesis.[3]

Another objection centres round Paul's own intention of visiting Philippi. When he appealed to Caesar, he seems to have turned his back on the scenes of his former activity and was looking towards the West. He had made it quite clear in Romans xv. 22 ff. that he had no further plans for work in the eastern regions but was intending to visit

---

[1] Bishop Lightfoot (*Philippians*, p. 38 n.) considered a month was a fair allowance for a journey from Rome to Philippi via Brundisium. He quotes from numerous Roman writers in support of his contention and there seems to be no valid ground for disputing this estimate. In this case considerably less than a year would suffice.

[2] *New Testament Studies*, p. 97.

[3] So A. Deissmann, article, *op. cit.*, in *Anatolian Studies* (1923), pp. 121–127.

Spain. If we are to regard Paul's plans as inexorable,[1] this in itself would rule out the Roman hypothesis for Philippians. But it is not inconceivable that after a two-year imprisonment in Rome he may have had cause to revise his plans, especially if in the meantime he had received disturbing reports from his eastern churches. That he dropped his Spanish plans seems to be suggested by the Pastorals' personalia (see pp. 597 ff.), and if so no difficulty would arise from his intention to revisit Philippi as soon as he was released (the same applies to Colossae, see p. 556).

c. Ephesus

Assuming the possibility of an Ephesian imprisonment is it possible to allot Philippians to such a period? An increasing number of recent scholars[2] believe that it is. Indeed there is a much greater inclination to attribute Philippians than the other Captivity Epistles to Ephesus. The grounds for this theory will now be considered.

(i) *The problem of the gifts.* Duncan maintains that as the Philippian church had made more than one contribution towards Paul's work in the early stages it is incredible that an interval of about ten years should elapse before another contribution is made. Philippians iv. 10, it is argued, cannot span so great an interval during which the Philippians had no opportunity to send a contribution. If the letter was sent from Ephesus the interval involved would be much shorter and the gift would arrive at the peak of the stress and strain of the Ephesian ministry, which would provide an appropriate setting for it. But two considerations lessen the weight of this argument. Paul does not in fact state that the readers had had no opportunity to assist him since contributing to his support at Thessalonica. What he does say is that they had shared his troubles 'in the beginning of the gospel' (Phil. iv. 15),

---

[1] G. S. Duncan, *ET* (April 1935), p. 296, argues that Paul's plans were made under divine guidance and would not easily be altered. But he appears to have changed his plans for visiting Corinth, presumably also under divine guidance (see 1 Cor. xvi and 2 Cor. i).

[2] Duncan (*ET*, LXVII, 6, March 1956) cites the following as supporting the hypothesis—McNeile, Kirsopp Lake, Clogg, Bruce, Michael, Dibelius, Bonnard, Benoit, Feine–Behm, Albertz and especially W. Michaelis in his many books on this subject. Not all these scholars, it should be noted, commit themselves unreservedly to the theory but they do all admit the possibility of its truth. The opinion of A. Wikenhauser (*New Testament Introduction*, 1958, p. 436) that it is not possible to decide the issue with certainty is typical of that of many scholars.*

which must mean from the time that the gospel was preached to them, as no other church had. We are not bound from this passage to infer that no opportunity had occurred over the space of ten years for them to send a contribution, which is admittedly difficult to imagine.

The second consideration concerns the collection scheme. Dodd[1] has drawn attention to the fact that Paul was particularly concerned about this scheme during his Ephesian ministry, and it would therefore hardly be a suitable time for him to have accepted a gift for himself for fear of being charged with covetousness. Since the Philippians had contributed generously towards the collection scheme they may not have been in a position to make additional contributions towards Paul's work, and this may be the explanation of Philippians iv. 10. Now that the collection scheme has been completed they have revived their concern for Paul's needs. It may even be that Paul himself suggested the suspension of contributions for himself in favour of the relief scheme which he passionately believed would be an invaluable demonstration of Gentile-Jewish unity.

(ii) *The proposed visits.* The difficulties raised by the Roman hypothesis discussed above would completely disappear if Paul is writing from Ephesus, for we know from Acts xx. 1 that Paul actually did visit Macedonia immediately after leaving Ephesus. No change of plans would be involved. In fact, the intended visit of Timothy mentioned in Philippians ii. 19 would fit in perfectly with Acts xix. 22 which records the sending of Timothy and Erastus to Macedonia. This looks like a strong argument, perhaps the strongest argument in support of the Ephesian hypothesis. Further support for this could be found in the references to Timothy's proposed visit to Corinth in 1 Corinthians iv. 17, xvi. 10, which would be an extension of the Macedonian visit. Although the chronological sequence of events in Acts xix is not precisely defined it would seem that Timothy's mission to Macedonia occurred but a short time before the riot (Acts xix. 22 states that Paul himself stayed in Asia for a while). All these data would certainly dovetail into the Ephesian hypothesis, but there is one consideration which suggests the need for caution. If Philippians ii. 19 implies that Paul expects Timothy to return to him while he is still in prison, in

---

[1] *New Testament Studies*, p. 98. Cf. the criticism of the Ephesian hypothesis by M. Jones, *Philippians* (1912), p. xxxiv, on the ground that no mention is made of the collection scheme in Philippians in spite of Paul's preoccupation with it during the Ephesian ministry.

order that he might be cheered by news of the Philippians' welfare (as Duncan[1] maintains in criticism of the Roman imprisonment), it is difficult to fit into the description of Acts xix. 22. It would mean (1) that the Ephesian imprisonment was of sufficient length to allow for a return journey; (2) that the imprisonment must be placed between Acts xix. 21 and xix. 23; and (3) that the mission of Timothy and Erastus must have been completed within this period. But Philippians ii. 20, 21 would appear to exclude all Paul's companions except Timothy. Why is there, then, no mention of Erastus if he accompanied him? It is moreover difficult to believe that the author of Acts was unaware of Paul's imprisonment at the time of the sending of these two companions. In fact, Acts xix. 22 f. makes clear (1) that there were others with Paul ministering to him at the time when Timothy and Erastus were sent and (2) that Paul stayed in Asia for a season, but no indication is given that he spent part of his time in prison. To equate Philippians ii. 19 with Acts xix. 22, although in many ways an attractive suggestion, is not therefore without considerable difficulties.

(iii) *The frequency of communication between Paul and Philippi.* If Paul is writing from Ephesus the distance to be covered in the numerous journeys would be considerably less, and this is a point in favour of the Ephesian hypothesis. But its weight depends largely on whether the journeys between Philippi and Rome are considered impossible. As long as the distances could reasonably be encompassed in the time available it is immaterial whether those distances were short or long.[2]

(iv) *Literary associations.* When the literary style and language of Philippians is compared with the earlier Epistles (Corinthians, Romans and Galatians) on the one hand and Colossians and Ephesians on the other, there are stronger affinities with the earlier than with the later group.[3] It is deduced from this that Philippians cannot belong to the same imprisonment as Colossians and Ephesians, but belongs to the period during which the Corinthian correspondence was written, i.e. about the

---

[1] *St. Paul's Ephesian Ministry*, p. 81.

[2] A. Deissmann, in *Anatolian Studies, op. cit.*, pp. 126 ff., found the evidence of these journeys a major difficulty if Paul was in Rome, but if in Ephesus he estimated all the journeys could be accomplished in 10 to 11 weeks.

[3] Cf. Feine-Behm, *Einleitung*, p. 183, for details. The opinion is there expressed that Ephesians and Colossians could not belong to the same imprisonment as Philippians.

time of the Ephesian ministry.[1] Yet deductions from literary affinities must be treated with considerable caution.

(v) *The Jewish controversy.* From the Epistle there are pointers that the Jewish controversy was not yet over (cf. chapter iii and the possible allusion in i. 30) and this would be more true of the Ephesian than the Roman period.[2] But in spite of this the warnings against Judaizers in Philippians iii cannot be regarded as completely inappropriate at a later date, for there were no doubt isolated pockets of resistance for some time after the major issues were settled.[3] Paul's manner of dealing with the question in Philippians is in any case in striking contrast to his doctrinal onslaught in the earlier letters. At the same time Philippians iii would suit well the Ephesian period.

(vi) *The trial.* The references to Paul's imprisonment in this Epistle (i. 7, 12 f., 16, ii. 17) do not fit in with the accusations in Acts xxi. 28, xxv. 7 ff., xxviii. 17 ff., and must therefore allude to a different imprisonment.[4] Paul is not as in Acts under house-restraint, but according to Duncan[5] is being subjected to much more serious conditions. But there seems little weight in this line of argument for Paul gives no indication of the precise charges brought against him. He simply describes all his sufferings as in the cause of the gospel.

(vii) *The praetorium and Caesar's household.* Inscriptions bear testimony that a detachment of the Praetorian Guard was at one time stationed at Ephesus and it is therefore considered not improbable that such a detachment was present during Paul's ministry at Ephesus. In that event the reference in Philippians i. 13 would be just as applicable to Ephesus as it is to Rome.[6] Similarly, imperial slaves and freedmen were sent

---

[1] Certain similarities exist between Philippians and Thessalonians (e.g. absence of the title 'apostle' from the greeting and the rarity of Old Testament citations). Cf. Goguel, *Introduc. au Nouv. Test.* IV, i, 417 n.

[2] Goguel, *op. cit.*, IV, i, pp. 380 ff., discussing the identity of the people against whom Paul is severely warning in iii. 2 ff., maintained that they were not Jewish Christians within the church, but adversaries from without. He concluded that this situation could belong only to the period of Paul's Ephesian captivity.

[3] If the passage has no connection with Judaizers this point would lose weight (cf. M. Jones, *Philippians*, p. xxxiv).

[4] Cf. Feine–Behm, *op. cit.*, p. 183.*

[5] *St. Paul's Ephesian Ministry*, p. 159.

[6] F. C. Synge, *Philippians and Colossians* (1951), p. 13, argues that Phil. i. 13 is definitely more favourable to Ephesus than to Rome because an unimportant

throughout the Empire to watch the Emperor's interests and there appears to have been a House of Caesar at Ephesus from the time of Augustus.[1] 'The saints in Caesar's household' (iv. 22) may in that case have been a group of Christian civil servants at Ephesus. There can be no objection to this interpretation, but it is rather an accommodation than a natural inference from the evidence. If on other grounds it is desirable to attribute Philippians to the Ephesian period, Philippians i. 13 and iv. 22 would not constitute an insuperable barrier.

(viii) *The position of Luke.* The omission of any mention of Luke in the Philippian Epistle points to a time when he was not present with Paul. But this condition is fulfilled by the period of the Ephesian ministry, which falls outside the 'we' sections in Acts and which may reasonably be taken to indicate Luke's absence (he appears again at Philippi in the following year, Acts xx. 1-6).[2]

The cumulative effect of this evidence is undoubtedly strong but it falls short of proof. If the Roman hypothesis were proved untenable the Ephesian would probably be unchallenged as an alternative theory. But the grounds for disputing the Roman theory are far from conclusive, and in view of this uncertainty and the fact that the Acts' silence about an Ephesian imprisonment must be a certain embarrassment to the Ephesian theory, it seems better to give the preference to Rome as the place of dispatch. In that case it would probably have to be dated to-

---

civilian prisoner like Paul would not have been committed to the important military guard. But, according to Acts xxviii. 30, Paul seems to have received favourable treatment at Rome and it cannot be presumed that he could not have come into contact with the Praetorian Guard. The further observation of Synge that Paul's contacts with Caesar's household would be easy in a provincial governor's house but not at Rome is no more conclusive, for no restriction seems to have been placed on him regarding visitors at Rome, and among these it is natural to suppose that Christians of Caesar's household probably formed the greater part.

[1] Cf. Feine–Behm, *op. cit.,* p. 184.

[2] In Duncan's presentation of the theory Colossians and Philemon are also placed in the Ephesian period, which means that Luke paid a visit to Paul during his second imprisonment there. Duncan suggests that this may have been a private visit, hence no 'we' passage (the force of this is not clear) and yet the account of the riot is so detailed as to suggest an eye-witness (*ET*, April 1935, p. 296). J. B. Lightfoot, in defence of his theory that this Epistle should be placed early in the Roman imprisonment, suggested that, at the time of Paul's writing, Luke had temporarily either returned to his home or else was engaged on a mission (*Philippians*, pp. 35, 36).

wards the end of the two-year imprisonment mentioned in Acts xxviii. 30.[1]

V. UNITY OF THE EPISTLE

Some scholars have advocated theories of material interpolated into the main body of Philippians. In general, advocates of such theories have not disputed the Pauline authorship of the material but have questioned the relevance of its present position (except in the case of the hymn which is considered separately). The major problem concerns chapter iii, and arises from the following observations.

1. The opening part of verse 1 appears to prepare for the conclusion of the letter ('Finally, my brethren, rejoice in the Lord'), but in the latter half of the verse the tone becomes unexpectedly more severe and in verse 2 becomes definitely harsh.

2. This sudden change is said to be out of harmony with the warm affection displayed in chapters i, ii and iv.

3. Paul's assertion of his own authority in verses 4 ff. is not prepared for by the earlier tone of the Epistle and would seem to be quite unfitted for the occasion.

4. The apostle appears to be attacking two different tendencies: the circumcision party, whom he calls 'dogs' and 'concision'; and the libertines, whose 'god is their belly' (iii. 19).

Because of the unexpected character of these data it has been suggested that the whole or part of chapter iii is an interpolated fragment from another letter of Paul's to the same church. There are three main proposals, among a score of minor deviations, for determining the extent of the interpolated material; either iii. 1b–iv. 3 (as Lake) or iii. 1b–19 (as Michael) or iii. 2–iv. 1 (as Beare).[2] Some difference of opinion exists about the precise point of commencement, as the words 'to write the same things' could refer either to what precedes[3] or to what follows. Similar differences exist regarding the ending. Michael,[4] for instance,

---

[1] Lightfoot preferred an earlier dating in view of the literary affinity with the great evangelical Epistles. He placed it first among the Roman Captivity Epistles (*Philippians*, pp. 30 ff.). If the Ephesian hypothesis is maintained the date must be towards the end of Paul's ministry there, since Paul is anticipating on his release that he will leave his Asiatic field of labour.

[2] Cf. K. Lake, *Exp.*, VIII, vii (June 1914), pp. 481 ff.; J. H. Michael, *MC*, p. xi; F. W. Beare, *Epistle to the Philippians* (1959), p. 5; D. W. Riddle and H. Hutson, *New Testament Life and Literature* (1946), pp. 123, 124, prefer iii. 2–16.

[3] So Bishop Lightfoot, *op. cit., ad loc.*   [4] *Philippians*, p. xii.

contends that verse 20 follows well from verse 1a if the conjunction in verse 20 is taken as 'for'[1] instead of 'but', and the sequence would then run, 'Rejoice in the Lord for we are a colony of heaven'. This is no doubt ingenious, but it must always detract from the convincing status of any theory when its advocates cannot agree on essential details. Moreover, no interpolation theory is justified unless there is lacking an alternative explanation which maintains satisfactorily the unity of the whole.

J. B. Lightfoot's suggestion that Paul was interrupted in his writing and before resuming heard about the Judaizers troubling the church, although it has been criticized as 'mechanical',[2] may well be an approximation to the true situation. It is highly probable that Paul was often interrupted in the course of his letter-writing and it may well be that his mind had in the interval been dwelling on Judaistic activities elsewhere[3] and he cannot refrain from warning the Philippians strongly against them. His words in iii. 2—'Beware of dogs, beware of evil workers, beware of the concision'—do not wear the appearance of being premeditated. They are rather the outburst of a man who suddenly has a burden upon his mind which he must express, however abruptly. His sudden attitude of self-defence in iii. 4 ff., which has already been noted as bearing striking affinity with 2 Corinthians xi. 21 ff. and which has in fact been used as evidence for an early date, may be no more than a natural recollection in Paul's mind, conjured up by its association with his earlier contests with Judaizers. The development of ideas in chapter iii is certainly in accord with Paul's style, especially the manner in which its somewhat turbulent opening leads gradually to a calmer conclusion.[4]

If anything, the charge of 'mechanical' must rather be levelled against

[1] This reading is by no means certain since it lacks the support of the Greek uncials, although contained in early versions and patristic evidence. Even if this reading is adopted it is not necessary to regard its connection with the previous section as improbable.

[2] Cf. McNeile-Williams, *INT*, p. 179.

[3] Michael (*Philippians*, p. xi) objects that it is highly unlikely that the sudden change was caused by an occurrence in Paul's own vicinity.

[4] Cf. H. N. Bate, *A Guide to the Epistles of Paul*[2] (1933), pp. 169 ff. In fact the sudden change of tone at the beginning is paralleled by other changes, though of a more gradual kind as Paul regains his earlier happy equilibrium (cf. Meinertz, *Einleitung*, p. 135). M. Dibelius (*A Fresh Approach*, op. cit., pp. 166, 167) rightly points out that the style fits in well with the idea of private speech.

the interpolation theory, for no very satisfactory explanation of the presence of the fragment in the canonical Philippians has yet been suggested. The best that can be proposed is that a MS sheet has been accidentally displaced, thus accounting for the incongruity of its presence in the Epistle. But this must have happened in a very early copy which became the archetype of all other copies, a not very probable suggestion. Even if the possibility be admitted it is difficult to believe that any scribe who found a fragment consisting only of iii. 1b–19 (or iv. 1 or iv. 3) would have placed it in its present context unless he had a completely blank mind for any connection of thought. Abruptness and even seeming incongruity may not improbably be ascribed to the author, but cannot with as much plausibility be attributed to another mind seeking a possible place for a loose fragment. The appeal to the plural in Polycarp's reference to Paul's 'letters to the Philippians' as a reference to more than one Epistle, of which iii. 1b ff. is a fragment, is even less convincing, for the plural may be used of a single letter or may be used to include other Macedonian Epistles (i.e. Thessalonians[1]). It is, of course, certain that Paul wrote other letters besides those in the canon, but to regard Philippians iii. 1b ff. as part of an otherwise lost letter involves an extraordinary combination of circumstances. The portion of letter preserved is oddly enough a part containing strong invective, but according to this theory it was apparently known to have been sent to the Philippians and for that reason became quite accidentally though inappropriately embedded in the Philippian Epistle, and all this without anyone detecting it! The improbabilities of this theory far outweigh the by no means insuperable difficulties of accounting for Paul's change of tone.

Some scholars have also had misgivings about ii. 19–24 because of the difficulty of reconstructing a situation in which Paul delays the sending of Timothy until he sees how the issue of his imprisonment will be decided and yet expects to be cheered by news of the Philippians' welfare on Timothy's return (see discussion above, p. 530). Michael,[2] for instance, wonders whether the passage is a fragment belonging to another situation in which the imprisonment is over a less serious issue than that reflected in Philippians. But if Paul is writing

---

[1] Polycarp, *Ad Phil.* xi. 3, appears to be a citation from 2 Thes. i. 4, used as if the Philippians were addressed in that Epistle. This would support the suggestion that in Polycarp's collection the Macedonian Epistles were united.

[2] *MC*, p. 112.

with a strong conviction that he will be released the difficulty disappears and the suggested interpolation becomes unnecessary.

A more recent partition theory is that of F. W. Beare[1] who finds two separate letters and an interpolation combined in our present Epistle. iv. 10–20 is a letter of thanks; i. 1–iii. 1, iv. 2–9, 21–23 a letter sent with Epaphroditus; and iii. 2–iv. 1 an interpolation into the second. This solution is promoted by the difficulty of imagining that Paul had never acknowledged the gift before writing the main portion of the Epistle. But the explanations given above provide an alternative and render this partition theory unnecessary. Moreover, as with all such theories, it is difficult to see how the final editor combined the passages into the form in which they have been preserved. *

In the next section mention will be made of the theory that the hymn in ii. 6–11 is an interpolation, but this is not widely held.

VI. THE COMPILATION OF PHILIPPIANS ii. 6–11

Many scholars hold that the section ii. 6–11 is a hymn composed independently of the rest of the Epistle. The theory has appeared in various forms which may be classified under the following types. (1) Those which regard Paul as the author;[2] (2) those which consider that Paul is citing an existing Christian hymn; and (3) those which regard the hymn as non-Pauline and therefore as a later interpolation. If the first solution is correct there are no difficulties and the only question which arises is whether Paul composed it at the same time as the Epistle or prior to it. Since the section fits so perfectly into the context of the Epistle there seems no reason why the former explanation cannot be correct, although the latter is more generally held.[3]

But the Pauline authorship of the hymn is disputed by some scholars on stylistic and doctrinal grounds and for this reason the second solution has commended itself. This has two forms, one regarding it as a pre-Pauline hymn and the other as a hymn contemporaneous with Paul. The former is based on alleged pre-Pauline Christology,

[1] Op. cit., pp. 4, 5.
[2] Cf. the Tyndale monograph by R. P. Martin, An Early Christian Confession: Philippians ii. 5–11 in Recent Interpretation (1960). Cf. also J. M. Furness, ET, LXX (May 1959), pp. 240–243. L. Cerfaux, Le Christ dans la Théologie de S. Paul (1954), pp. 283, 284, regards the hymn as not only Pauline but as forming an answer to the specific needs of the Philippians dealt with in the same context.
[3] For a concise account of various views on this passage cf. V. Taylor, The Person of Christ (1958), pp. 62 ff.

while the latter is based on the influence of the pagan hero-hymns on the author. F. W. Beare,[1] an advocate of the latter view, considers the hymn to be a compilation of a Gentile contemporary of Paul who puts into poetic form his praise to Christ in a way similar to his pre-Christian pagan practice of lauding divine heroes.

The remaining theory mentioned above, i.e. the interpolation theory, does not warrant serious attention since it is entirely lacking in manuscript support and no satisfactory situation can be proposed which facilitated the interpolation of so large a section subsequent to publication, while previous to publication there would be no conceivable motive.

There have been various analyses of the hymn, of which the best known is Lohmeyer's,[2] which treats it as consisting of two strophes, each with three verses (ii. 6–8, 9–11). Jeremias[3] suggests three strophes (ii. 6, 7a; 7b, 8; 9–11), in which the pre-existent, the earthly and the exalted Christ are successively described, and on the strength of this suggests that the document testifies to the primitive yet developed doctrine of the three phases of Christ's existence.*

CONTENTS

I. GREETING (i. 1, 2)

Timothy is linked with Paul in his greeting to the church and its officers.

II. THANKSGIVING (i. 3–8)

Paul rejoices in their partnership with him in the work of the gospel and shows by his gratitude his deep affection towards them.

III. PRAYER (i. 9–11)

His prayer is that their love may increase and that knowledge may be added.

[1] *The Epistle to the Philippians* (1959), pp. 1, 2.
[2] Cf. 'Kyrios Jesus', *Sitzungsber. d. Heidelberger Akad. d. Wiss. Phil.-hist. Klase*, 1927-28, Nr. 4, and his commentary *Der Brief an der Philipper* (1930), p. 91 n.1.
[3] Cf. Article 'Zur Gedankenführung in den paulinischen Briefen', in *Studia Paulina* (1953).

IV. PAUL'S PRESENT CIRCUMSTANCES (i. 12–26)

As a result of his imprisonment the majority of the local Christians have become bold to preach the gospel, not always with the right motives, but Paul nevertheless rejoices in the more widespread preaching of the gospel (i. 12–18). His own position is uncertain and this causes a division of opinion on his part between a desire to be with Christ and a desire to remain. He is confident of release for the sake of his assistance to them (i. 19–26).

V. EXHORTATIONS (i. 27–ii. 18)

The apostle draws attention to the need for a number of qualities.

a. Steadfastness (i. 27–30)

The Philippians must live worthily, especially by showing steadfastness both in unity of spirit and suffering for Christ's sake.

b. Unity (ii. 1, 2)

The unity mentioned in the last section is so important that it is repeated with particular emphasis (same love, in full accord, of one mind).

c. Humility (ii. 3–11)

The mind of Jesus is the norm for Christian humility and this is illustrated by a classic Christological passage which merges exhortation with doctrine. Since Christ humbled Himself, every Christian should do likewise.

d. Obedience and purity (ii. 12–18)

They were to work out their own salvation, to refrain from grumbling and to live lives of such purity that Paul would not be ashamed of them in the day of Christ.

VI. TIMOTHY AND EPAPHRODITUS (ii. 19–30)

The former is warmly commended for his loyalty to Paul, who hopes soon to send him to Philippi when he knows how things would go with him. Epaphroditus is being sent with the Epistle and Paul records gratitude for his ministry, but his illness has prompted Paul to send him back. On his return he is to be duly honoured for his readiness to hazard his life for Paul's sake.

VII. WARNINGS AGAINST FALSE TEACHERS (iii. 1–iv. 1)

1. Paul warns against Judaizers, calling them sarcastically 'the muti-lators'. He appeals to his own renunciation of Judaism in spite of the exceptional privileges he enjoyed. Now he counts everything loss for Christ's sake and his greatest desire is to know Him better. He is still straining forward towards greater things (iii. 1–16).

2. He then warns against those given over to profligacy, who wor-ship their belly. Such people are strikingly contrasted with the true citizens of heaven who are awaiting the return of Christ (iii. 17–iv. 1).

VIII. FURTHER EXHORTATIONS (iv. 2–9)

Again Paul brings in the theme of unity, this time in a specific case of two ladies, Euodia and Syntyche, who were apparently disagreeing. Again the theme of rejoicing is underlined and a trustful attitude of prayer is assured to lead to a peace which surpasses understanding. Since the mind plays so important a part in human actions, there must be a pursuit of the noblest thoughts if this peace is to be fully enjoyed.

IX. ACKNOWLEDGMENT OF THE GIFTS (iv. 10–20)

The Philippians' revival of their concern for the apostle's material welfare has caused him much joy, although he has learned the secret of contentment in all circumstances. He recalls their earlier generosity and describes their present contributions as a fragrant offering to God.

X. CONCLUDING SALUTATION (iv. 21–23)

Greetings are exchanged and those of Caesar's household are specially mentioned as sending greetings. The usual benediction closes the letter.

ADDITIONAL NOTES

524. [1] It is possible to understand Phil. i. 3–5 of fellowship in the gospel, and O. Glombitza (*Nov. Test.*, 7, 1964, pp. 135–141) has interpreted iv. 10–20 in the same way. No doubt Paul regarded any material gifts as an evidence of the more far-reaching spiritual participation.

524. [3] W. G. Kümmel (*INT*, 1965, p. 228) considers that Paul refers to the illness of Epaphroditus to increase their esteem for him.

526. [2] Cf. also the view of L. Johnson referred to on p. 478 n. 2.

530. For a study of Epaphroditus' illness in relation to the sending of this Epistle, cf. C. O. Buchanan, *EQ*, XXXVI (1964), pp. 157 ff.

531. [2] For more recent advocates of an Ephesian origin, cf. G. Friedrich, *NTD*, 8[9] (1962); G. Bornkamm, 'Der Philipperbrief als paulinische Briefsammlung', *Neotestamentica et Patristica, Freundesgabe O. Cullmann* (1962), pp. 192 ff.; A. F. J. Klijn, *INT* (1967), p. 112; R. H. Fuller, *INT* (1966), pp. 31 ff. But against, cf. G. Johnston (*CB*, n.s., 1967). K. Grayston (*CBC*, 1967) arrives at no decision.

534. [4] Cf. W. G. Kümmel, *INT* (1965), p. 233.

539. Several studies on the unity of the Epistle must be added to those mentioned in the text. W. Schmithals (*ZTK*, 54, 1957, pp. 299–305) regards the present letter as consisting of three sections: iv. 10–23; i. 1–iii. 1 and iv. 4–7; iii. 2–iv. 8, 9, and maintains that in the third the opponents were Gnostic libertines. B. D. Rahtjen (*NTS*, 6, 1960, pp. 167–173) has a similar theory with slight adjustments (iv. 10–20; i. 1–ii. 30 and iv. 21–23; iii. 1–iv. 9). He considers the third to have been written during the Neronic persecutions. A four letter theory is that of G. Bornkamm (*op. cit.*), who proposes i. 1–iii. 1; iv. 4–7, 21–23; iii. 2–iv. 3; iv. 10–20 and suggests that the editor who compiled the Corinthian letters compiled these. The diversity of these proposals (cf. also their differences from Beare's scheme, p. 539) raises suspicions about their validity. It will be noted that all these scholars isolate the letter of thanks (iv. 10 ff.) and the whole of chapter iii from the rest.

There have, however, been some defenders of the view that chapter iii belongs to the rest of the Epistle. T. E. Pollard (*NTS*, 13, 1966, pp. 57–66) argues from parallels of thought and terminology that a continuity exists between Phil. ii and Phil. iii. On this basis he rejects the interpolation theory. Cf. also B. S. Mackay, *NTS*, 7 (1960), pp. 161–169; G. Delling, *RGG*[3] (1961), pp. 333–336. According to V. P. Furnish (*NTS*, 10, 1963, pp. 80–88), Paul intended to end his letter at iii. 1a, but adds a postscript which proceeds to the end of the Epistle. What he writes in this could have been conveyed orally by Timothy and Epaphroditus. But Paul fears this might be his last letter.

A. F. J. Klijn regards Philippians iii as a unity (*Nov. Test.*, 7, 1965, pp. 278–284) and considers that Paul was comparing his own position with Jewish missionaries whose concept of perfection differed from his. This view is similar to that of H. Köster (*NTS*, 8, 1962, pp. 317–332), who calls the opponents Jewish-Christian apostles, who held a perfectionist doctrine. He regards this as typical of an early type of Christian Gnosticism, but uses the term too loosely (see R. M. Wilson's view on this, *Gnosis and the New Testament*, pp. 31 ff.). In his recent commentary, J. Gnilka, *Der Philipperbrief* (1968), regards iii. 1b–iv. 1, 8, 9 as separate from the rest.

540. Among recent studies on Phil. ii. 6–11 should be noted the following. The major work is R. P. Martin's *Carmen Christi: Philippians ii. 5–11 in Recent Interpretation and in the Setting of Early Christian Worship* (1967). In this book Martin has shifted his position and now regards the hymn as pre-Pauline. He considers that Paul has used it to stress Christ's Lordship (as Käsemann holds). He also thinks the hymn was arranged in six couplets to be sung antiphonally, but to do this he is obliged to omit two phrases from the Greek. In criticism of this, cf. J. Bligh, *Biblica*, 49 (1968), pp. 127–129. For comments on the interpretation of the passage in Martin's book, cf. R. H. Fuller, *CBQ*, 30 (1968), pp. 274 f. and J. Murphy-

O'Connor, *RB*, LXXV (1968), pp. 113–116. For a discussion of the biblical sources of the passages, cf. A. Feuillet, *RB*, LXXII (1965), pp. 352–380. Cf. also J. M. Furness, *ET*, LXXIX (1968), pp. 178–182.

Another scholar who sees the passage as a pre-Pauline Christian hymn is G. Strecker (*ZNTW*, 55, 1964, pp. 63–78), who proposes a rather different strophe arrangement from Lohmeyer and Jeremias. Strecker finds another pre-Pauline hymn in iii. 20, 21 which, he thinks, illuminates the soteriology of Phil. ii (see also his article in *ThLZ*, 89, 1964, cols 521 f.). The importance of the form of the hymn for its interpretation is brought out by C. H. Talbert (*JBL*, LXXXVI, 1967, pp. 141–153). Talbert is criticized, however, by J. A. Sanders (*JBL*, LXXXVIII, 1969, pp. 279–290), who although inclining to the Anthropos-myth view of its background, considers that Paul alone helps us to understand its context and significance.

CHAPTER SEVENTEEN

THE EPISTLE TO THE COLOSSIANS

I. ORIGIN OF THE CHURCH

The city of Colossae lay in the valley of the Lycus, a tributary of the Meander, in a district of mountainous beauty about one hundred miles inland from Ephesus. It was overshadowed in importance by the neighbouring cities of Laodicea and Hierapolis, in both of which Christian churches had been established (Col. iv. 13). The Christian community at Colossae had never been visited by Paul, for he says in i. 4, 'since we heard of your faith in Christ Jesus' and in ii. 1 he states explicitly, 'For I would that ye knew what great conflict I have for you, and for them at Laodicea, and for as many as have not seen my face in the flesh'. It appears that Epaphras had acquainted Paul with the Colossians' 'love in the Spirit' (i. 8).

From the references to Epaphras it would seem reasonable to suppose that the church originated as a result of his ministry. In i. 7 Paul says, 'As you also learned of Epaphras our dear fellowservant, who is for you a faithful minister of Christ', which suggests that he was responsible for the instruction of these Christians. In iv. 12, 13 he is described as 'one of you', i.e. he was a Colossian, and Paul testifies to his great zeal for his own people and for the neighbouring Christians in the Lycus valley. Although no definite statement is made to this effect there is strong probability that Epaphras was converted to Christianity as a result of Paul's ministry at Ephesus (cf. Acts xix. 10). Such a supposition would supply an admirable reason why Epaphras sought out the apostle during his present imprisonment. He may have had previous contact with Paul over the affairs of the church and in any case seems to have regarded it as falling under Paul's missionary jurisdiction. The apostle assumes a position of authority when he writes, in spite of the lack of personal contact with them. He has no doubt that the church has been well instructed in the Christian faith (ii. 6) and has every confidence in Epaphras whom he describes as a 'faithful minister of Christ' (i. 7).

II. OCCASION

One of the reasons for Epaphras' journey to Rome and his willingness to share for a time the apostle Paul's imprisonment (in Phm. 23 he is described as a 'fellow-prisoner') was his desire to acquaint Paul with the progress of the gospel in the Lycus valley and so encourage the great apostle's heart. But the main reason was undoubtedly to solicit advice about a dangerous heresy which had arisen in Colossae and was threatening the security of the church. Probably Epaphras could not cope with the specious arguments and assumed humility of the leader of the false teachers and needed the greater wisdom of the apostle. In the meantime it is possible that Archippus had been left in charge of the work at Colossae, since he is mentioned both in Colossians iv. 17 as one who had received a ministry in the Lord, and in Philemon 2 as a 'fellow-soldier' of Paul.[1]

III. THE HERESY

It is never easy to reconstruct the precise tenets of a heresy when the only data available are indirect allusions in the course of a positive statement of doctrine intended to counteract it. Yet such is the situation in the Colossian Epistle. It is impossible to determine whether or not this heresy had any coherent form, and we must content ourselves with extracting those particular emphases with which Paul deals and which he immediately recognized as constituting a definite danger to the Christian Church.*

a. Its Christology

It is clear enough that the false teaching was in some way detracting from the Person of Christ, for Paul lays great stress upon His pre-eminence (i. 15–19). This was a tendency which became fully developed in the Gnosticism[2] of the second century.*

---

[1] W. Bieder, *Colossians* (1943), pp. 302 ff. (cited by Moule, *Colossians and Philemon*, 1957, p. 15), suggests that a rift had occurred between Epaphras and the Colossian church and that Archippus had taken over. Cf. J. Knox's view that Archippus was the owner of Onesimus and that Philemon was successor to Epaphras in the Lycus valley. See pp. 635 ff. and cf. Moule's discussion, *op. cit.*, p. 15.

[2] In discussions on New Testament heresies it is important to define as precisely as possible the meaning attached to the word Gnosticism. Without excluding the possibility of much earlier roots, the term itself is restricted to the somewhat amorphous systems of the second century which Irenaeus and Hippolytus are concerned to combat (cf. R. M. Wilson, *The Gnostic Problem*, 1958, pp. 64–68). Earlier tendencies towards Gnosticism of this systematic type are labelled 'pre-Gnostic' or 'incipient Gnosticism'. It is better, therefore, not to speak of a pre-Christian Jewish Gnosticism (although its existence is not improbable) since, as

b. Its philosophic character

The apostle specifically warns against 'philosophy and vain deceit' (ii. 8), which suggests a tendency on the part of some of the Colossians to be attracted by it. It cannot be determined with any certainty in what sense Paul uses the word 'philosophy', but it is generally supposed to point to Hellenistic elements. It is possible that the use of the terms πλήρωμα ('fulness') i. 19, γνῶσις ('knowledge') ii. 3, and ἀφειδία σώματος ('neglect of the body') ii. 23 may also be drawn from the same general background. All these terms were in use in second-century Gnosticism.*

c. Its Jewish environment

Many such features are reflected in the Epistle. The most conclusive is the reference to circumcision (ii. 11, iii. 11), which Paul finds it necessary to put into its true Christian perspective. The warning against human 'tradition' (ii. 8) would be an apt reference to the familiar Jewish tendency to superimpose the traditions of the elders upon the ancient law, but it could also be understood of Gentile tradition in view of its close association here with philosophy.[1] The ritual tendencies found in ii. 16, where the readers are urged not to allow anyone to judge them in respect of meat or drink, or feasts or new moons or sabbaths, are predominantly, if not exclusively, Jewish.[2]

Wilson points out (p. 261), such a Gnosticism would be more a 'tendency of accommodation' than a system. In its widest sense, Gnosticism was an atmosphere breathed in by many other systems than those which affected the Christian Church, including most contemporary thought, Hermetica, philosophy and mysteries. But such a wide use of the term can lead only to confusion in New Testament studies. Cf. also R. P. Casey, 'Gnosis, Gnosticism and the New Testament', in *The Background of the New Testament and its Eschatology*, edited by Davies and Daube (1956), pp. 52–80. Casey concludes that 'The New Testament requires no explanation, either as a whole or in any of its parts, in terms of an hypothetical primitive Gnosticism' (p. 80).

[1] F. F. Bruce (*Colossians, NLC*, 1958, p. 231 n.) agrees it might be Jewish or Gentile. C. F. D. Moule (*Colossians and Philemon*, p. 90) inclines to see here the tenets of Palestinian Judaism, but he cites 1 Pet. i. 18 as possibly a reference to pagan traditions.

[2] E. F. Scott, *Varieties of New Testament Religion* (1946), pp. 145, 146, does not appear to give enough weight to these Jewish indications when he describes the heresy as 'essentially pagan', although a strong pagan influence was undoubtedly present.

d. Its angel worship

In Jewish thought angels performed a mediatorial function in relation to the law although there is no evidence at this stage of any tendency to worship them.[1] It is at least possible that some teacher with a Jewish background may have developed the mediatorial agencies into objects of worship. Such a process is not difficult to imagine, although it would have been strongly resisted by orthodox Jews with their tenacious monotheism.*

e. The elements of the world

These elements or *stoicheia* may be understood in two ways, either as (1) elementary spirits or (2) elementary teaching. Although there is no earlier warrant for the former meaning many commentators consider it to be the more probable in the context of the Colossian Epistle. In this case it would be a reference to the powerful spirit-world which was at that time widely believed to control the affairs of the natural world. If it means 'elementary teaching' it would presumably describe a purely materialistic doctrine concerned only with this world.[2]

f. Exclusivism

It is possible that there was a tendency towards exclusivism among the false teachers since Paul seems to be at pains to express the all-inclusiveness of Christianity (cf. Col. i. 20, 28, iii. 11). It is significant that in i. 28 Paul states his aim to be to present every man as *perfect*, since 'perfection' was regarded in most Gnostic circles as the privilege of the few.

From this somewhat fragmentary evidence it may safely be deduced

---

[1] A belief in an angelic hierarchy is particularly marked in the Books of Enoch and the Testaments of the XII Patriarchs. It was the direct result of Jewish transcendental theology, which demanded an efficient mediatorial system to bridge the ever-widening gap between man and God. For the view that angelology was the predominating feature in the Colossian heresy cf. Maurice Jones, *The Epistle of St. Paul to the Colossians* (1923), pp. 27–47.

[2] C. F. D. Moule, *op. cit.*, p. 92, understands it in this sense. E. Percy, *op. cit.*, p. 167, prefers the alternative meaning. F. F. Bruce finds good sense in both meanings (*Colossians*, pp. 231, 232). For a full discussion of the meaning of this term, cf. E. de W. Burton, *Galatians* (*ICC*, 1921), pp. 510–518, who maintains that the only meaning which is relevant to all three occurrences of the word in the New Testament (Gal. iv. 3, Col. ii. 8, 20) is one which refers to rudimentary religious teachings of the world of men.

that the heresy was of a syncretistic Jewish–Gnosticizing type.[1] Such a combination of ideas would have found ready acceptance in Asia with its flourishing cults and its considerable Jewish population.[2] In Colossae in particular the worship of the heathen goddess Cybele was deeply rooted and showed a tendency towards love of extravagances among the people. Oriental speculation would easily spread along the trade routes of the Lycus valley and be hungrily absorbed by the populace.

In his famous discussion of the Colossian heresy, Bishop Lightfoot[3] identified it with a form of Essenism which while fundamentally Jewish nevertheless contained many extraneous features, some of which at least were similar to those prevalent among the Colossians. It advocated a rigid observance of the Jewish law together with severe asceticism. There may also have been some form of sun-worship linked with an esoteric doctrine of angels. Since Lightfoot's day much more is known of the Essenes through the discovery of the Qumran Library and although no evidence has come to light supporting angel worship, the tenets of the sect show a similar phenomenon of a Jewish basis intermixed with extraneous elements.[4] This evidence testifies to the existence of such mixtures of ideas in one part at least of contemporary nonconformist Judaism in the first century of our era.[5] It may easily have spread from Palestine to the receptive province of Asia Minor, although there is no definite evidence that it did.[6]

---

[1] All the Gnostic systems were syncretistic, blending all types of thought from highest philosophy to lowest magic (cf. Wilson, op. cit., p. 69), but the Colossian heresy gives no indications of those elaborations which were characteristic of second-century thought.*

[2] R. D. Shaw, The Pauline Epistles[4] (1924), p. 283.

[3] Colossians[2] (1900), pp. 71–111.

[4] Cf. Millar Burrows, The Dead Sea Scrolls (1955), pp. 246–272; K. G. Kuhn, 'Die Sektenschrift und die iranische Religion', ZTK (1952), pp. 296–316. Many features common to the Colossian heresy and the Qumran Sect are mentioned by W. D. Davies, 'Paul on Flesh and Spirit' in The Scrolls and the New Testament (1958), pp. 166–168. Wilson, op. cit., p. 74, calls the scrolls pre-Gnostic, not Gnostic proper.

[5] Cf. A. Lukyn Williams' detailed discussion of later angel-worship among the Jews, JTS, x (1909), pp. 413–438.

[6] L. B. Radford, Colossians and Philemon (WC, 1931), pp. 57–77, regarded the Jewish influences in this heresy at Colossae as no more than a contributory factor. He suggested Phrygian influences such as the moon cult, the cults of Attis, Sabazius and Cybele, Egyptian theosophy and perhaps Mithraism (p. 75). But the Colossian heresy probably had a far simpler background than this.

Even if Lightfoot's theory is not accepted[1] it seems undeniable that the heresy in question is closer to Essenism than to developed second-century Gnosticism. There is an absence of reference to elaborate systems of intermediaries which dominated the later systems and this would be incredible if the author had before his mind developed Gnosticism. Such omission would not of course be a problem if Marcionism was in mind, but this is highly improbable. (See later section on the authenticity of the Epistle.) Moreover, in Marcionism there was an antithesis against anything Jewish,[2] but in the Colossian heresy the reverse is true.[3] There is certainly no trace of the peculiar doctrines of Cerinthianism, with its distinction between the human Jesus and the divine Christ. At most the connections with Gnosticism are of the vaguest kind and point to an incipient Gnosticism which had not as yet been formulated into a fixed system.[4]

IV. PURPOSE

We may certainly conclude that the threat from this false teaching was of such a character that an immediate corrective was imperative and

[1] F. F. Bruce (*Colossians*), p. 167 n., is of the opinion that it could be accepted only if the term 'Essenism' is abnormally stretched.

[2] This is not to deny that many Gnostic ideas may have been introduced through the channel of Hellenistic Judaism, at least through its more lax adherents. R. M. Wilson, *The Gnostic Problem* (1958), p. 182, calls it a bridge across the gulf between the Graeco-Oriental and Jewish-Christian worlds of thought. The two main anti-semitic tendencies characteristic of Gnosticism were depreciation of the God of the Old Testament and repudiation of the Jewish law. It was only in Marcionism, however, that these tendencies were so thoroughgoing as to lead to the attempt to expurgate everything Jewish.

[3] Cullmann, 'The Significance of the Qumran Texts for Research into the Beginnings of Christianity', *JBL* (1955), pp. 213 ff., finds the Jewish character of the teaching behind the Colossian heresy (and that reflected in the Pastoral Epistles) suggestive of a pre-Christian Jewish Gnosticism.

[4] This conclusion is supported by E. Percy's suggestion that the heresy was a form of Jewish Christianity with a strong mixture of later Greek speculation and ascetic piety but with no direct contact with Gnosticism (see his discussion, *op. cit.*, pp. 137–178). Cf. G. Salmon's argument that no reliable evidence exists that Gnosticism began in the second century, but rather that the early haeresiologists trace its origin to Simon Magus, i.e. in apostolic times (*INT*, pp. 385 ff.). Some scholars have disputed the reliability of this early evidence from the Fathers, maintaining that Gnostics tended to trace their teachings to the earliest possible sources. Cf. Wilson, *op. cit.*, pp. 97 ff., for a full discussion of early Gnostic sects, and G. Quispel, *Gnosis als Weltreligion* (1951), for the evidence of the Nag Hammadi Library on the early history of Gnosticism.

that this was the real purpose of this letter. Paul has two main problems to settle, one doctrinal, concerning the Person of Christ, the other practical, respecting the life of the Christian.

The Epistle contains a high Christology. Christ is pre-eminent over all other creatures and over creation itself. In fact, all things were not only created by Him but for Him. He is seen at the centre of the universe, sovereign over all principalities and powers, over all agencies, that is to say, which might challenge His authority. Not only so, He is the Image of God and the Possessor of the fulness (*plēroma*) of God, and these statements could not fail to exalt Him to an equality with God. He is further described as the Head of the Church, which is conceived of as His body. The Christological passage (Col. i. 15–19)* in which all these ideas are expressed is followed immediately by a statement regarding Christ's redemptive work (i. 20 ff.) and this work is supported by the further statement in ii. 14 that in the cross Christ triumphed over all His enemies. Clearly Paul's purpose is to demonstrate the immeasurable superiority of Christ, as contrasted with the inadequate presentation of Him being advocated by the Colossian false teachers.

In his refutation of the practical error Paul strongly attacks the ascetic tendencies on the ground that they are merely human ordinances. The Christian is rather to hold to the Head (ii. 19). He is risen with Christ (ii. 12, iii. 1 ff.) and should therefore live the risen life. It requires self-mortification (iii. 5), but Paul recognizes the clear distinction between this and rigid asceticism. The Christian is called upon to 'put on' the new man (iii. 10) as well as to 'put off' the old; positive action is linked with prohibition, in contrast with rigid asceticism which always tends to overstress the negative to the neglect of the positive.

V. AUTHENTICITY

Although the great majority of scholars accept the genuineness of this Epistle, there are still some who do not, and the problems must consequently be briefly stated. Even before the Tübingen school of F. C. Baur and his associates disputed the Epistle, Mayerhoff[1] found in it un-Pauline thoughts, evidences of disputation with the second-century Cerinthus and a dependence on Ephesians. The main plank of Baur and his school was the alleged evidence that the heresy combated in the Epistle was second-century Gnosticism, in which case Pauline author-

---

[1] *Der Brief an die Kolosser* (1838), cited in Feine–Behm, *Einleitung*, p. 190.

ship was sufficiently disproved. In attempting to salvage something from the results of this radical criticism, H. J. Holtzmann[1] resorted to the theory of interpolations made by the author of Ephesians into an original shorter but genuine Epistle to the Colossians. Others (e.g. von Soden[2]) modified Holtzmann's theory by reducing the amount of interpolations, but all such partition theories are doomed to failure because of the manifest unity of our canonical Epistle. Jülicher rightly pointed out that the suspicion that there are interpolations in this Epistle would never have arisen had it not been for the presence of the Epistle to the Ephesians.[3]

The question of authenticity is decided on two issues, one literary, the other doctrinal. As C. F. D. Moule[4] expresses it, 'a decision turns largely on whether or not one can imagine the type of error implied by Colossians having appeared already in St. Paul's lifetime, and can conceive of St. Paul dealing with it in this way and in these words'.

---

[1] *Kritik der Epheser- u. Kolosserbriefe* (1872). See F. F. Bruce, *Colossians*, p. 172 n., for details.

[2] *JPTh*, 11 (1885), pp. 320 ff., 497 ff., 672 ff.

[3] Cf. *INT* (Eng. Tr. 1903), pp. 137, 138; and Jülicher–Fascher, *Einleitung*[7] (1931), p. 134. Cf. also W. Sanday's refutation of Holtzmann's theory in *Smith's Dictionary of the Bible*, Article 'Colossians'. More recently C. Masson (*L'Épître de Saint Paul aux Colossiens*, 1950), *CNT*, x (see F. F. Bruce, *Colossians*, p. 172 n.) and P. N. Harrison, 'Onesimus and Philemon' in *ATR*, vol. xxxii (October 1950), pp. 268–294, have maintained theories of partial Pauline authorship. Dr. Harrison's theory is closely akin to Holtzmann's but he restricts the non-genuine material to i. 15–25, ii. 4, 8–23, in which he maintains all the non-Pauline characteristics occur. He also differs from Holtzmann in placing the original Colossians during the period of Paul's Ephesian ministry. The interpolations were added forty to fifty years later. Such a view is not only speculative but is entirely unnecessary on a more probable theory of Pauline development and a more accurate appraisal of the incipient character of Gnosticism. Masson takes over Holtzmann's theory without detailed discussion but claims it to be the most satisfactory explanation of the relation between Colossians and Ephesians (*op. cit.*, p. 86).*

The theory of F. C. Synge, *Philippians and Colossians*, 1951, pp. 51–57, that Ephesians is genuine but Colossians is not is an echo of Mayerhoff's original contention, but few scholars would agree that Colossians was produced by an imitator of Ephesians plus certain personalia culled from Philemon. It is much more credible that the authenticity of Philemon carries with it the genuineness of Colossians (see discussion on p. 554). Synge seems to regard Colossians as inferior to Ephesians as a work of art, but his judgments on this score are necessarily highly subjective.

[4] *Colossians and Philemon*, p. 13.

Among the literary features which have sometimes been regarded as non-Pauline are:

1. A number of unusual genitival combinations as, for instance, 'the reward of the inheritance' (iii. 24), 'putting off the body of . . . flesh' (ii. 11), 'the increase of God' (ii. 19) and 'the hope of glory' (i. 27).

2. The style is more laboured, with many more subsidiary clauses than in Paul's earlier letters, and there are an unusual number of substantives with the preposition ἐν (see, for example, Col. i. 9–23 where thirteen instances occur, and Col. ii. 9–15 where nine occur).

3. Many new words are used, while many well-known Pauline ideas are missing.

But these difficulties are not great. Stylistic differences are generally attributable to changing circumstances or subject-matter.[1] The strongest peculiarities, as E. Percy[2] observes, are found in those sections which deal with the false teaching, which is most natural in view of the fact that such teaching is not dealt with in any earlier letters. The same author suggests that the style shows a greater use of what may be called a liturgical hymn style, similar to that found in the prayers and thanksgivings of the other Epistles. No doubt Paul's circumstances of imprisonment also contributed towards changes of style. Certain differences are indisputable but there seem to be quite inadequate grounds for claiming that Paul could not have written in the style of this Epistle.[3]

The doctrinal problem turns on the presence of Gnostic ideas. It has already been shown that the false teaching is at most allied to an incipient Gnosticism, which is by no means improbable in Paul's lifetime. Only a criticism which insists that fully developed Gnosticism is in mind will feel bound on the basis of doctrine to attribute the letter to a second-century origin (as the earlier critics did).[4] Not all Pauline con-

---

[1] On Paul's many different styles and their relationship to a missionary's subject-matter cf. Dibelius–Kümmel, *Paul* (1953), p. 99.

[2] *Op. cit.*, p. 66.

[3] E. Percy (*op. cit.*, p. 66) goes further and maintains that the speech and style of Colossians is more strongly for than against Pauline authorship.

[4] Too much early criticism proceeded on the unreal assumption that similar language implied identical meaning. Consequently if similar terms were found in New Testament writings and Gnostic heresies, the New Testament content was assumed to be identical with the Gnostic and those parts containing it removed to the second century. But the most important question, whether the respective authors intended them to be used in a similar sense, was by-passed (cf. Wilson, *op. cit.*, p. 175).

cepts find a place in the Epistle, but it is quite unnatural to insist that a writer must express all his beliefs in every letter he writes. The new ideas are not out of harmony with Paul's earlier thoughts, but are rather developments from them. The Christology of Colossians may be compared, for instance, with the germ ideas in 1 Corinthians viii. 6 and 2 Corinthians iv. 4.We may safely conclude that the apostle could have expressed all the doctrinal ideas of the Colossian Epistle.[1]

The strongest arguments in support of its authenticity are the indisputable nature of the external evidence and the inseparable connection of the Epistle with Philemon. There is no shred of evidence that the Pauline authorship of the whole or any part of this Epistle was ever disputed until the nineteenth century. It formed part of the Pauline Corpus as far back as can be traced, and evidence of such a character cannot lightly be swept aside. This strong external attestation is further supported by the close link between the Epistle and Philemon, whose authenticity has been challenged by only the most extreme negative critics.[2] The reasons for maintaining this link may be stated as follows.

1. Both contain Timothy's name with Paul's in the opening greeting (Col. i. 1; Phm. 1).

2. Greetings are sent in both letters from Aristarchus, Mark, Epaphras, Luke and Demas, who are all clearly with Paul at the time (Col. iv. 10–14; Phm. 23, 24).

3. In Philemon 2 Archippus is called a 'fellowsoldier', and in Colossians iv. 17 he is directed to fulfil his ministry.

4. Onesimus, the slave concerning whom the letter to Philemon is written, is mentioned in Colossians iv. 9 as being sent with Tychicus and is described as 'one of you'.

In the light of these data it is impossible to imagine that the two Epistles were sent at different times, and since the authenticity of Philemon is generally unquestioned it carries with it the certainty that Colossians is a genuine work of Paul. The most that disputants of

---

[1] Quite apart from alignment with incipient Gnosticism, the theological background of the Epistle is so thoroughly and characteristically Pauline that to attribute the Epistle to an author other than Paul becomes highly improbable (cf. Percy, *op. cit.*, p. 136).*

[2] A critic like Renan, who had some difficulties over Colossians, nevertheless recognized that its connection with Philemon must be in favour of its authenticity (*Saint Paul*, n.d., pp. ix, x).

authenticity may reasonably claim is that the Epistle is but partially genuine, but this raises more difficulties than it solves.[1]

VI. PLACE AND DATE OF DISPATCH

Until comparatively recently there has been little doubt that at the time of writing this Epistle Paul was in Rome. There was at an early stage in Christian history a dissentient opinion that the Epistle was written from Ephesus (cf. the Marcionite Prologue to this Epistle), but this tradition seems to have had a short life. The corresponding Prologue to Philemon, incidentally, claimed that that Epistle was written from Rome, in spite of the close connection between the two Epistles as mentioned above. The recent Ephesian imprisonment hypothesis, which has already been discussed (see pp. 472 ff.), challenges the Roman hypothesis much more strongly than the Caesarean[2] hypothesis has been able to do. The latter is improbable for two reasons. (1) A runaway slave would surely not have fled to Caesarea to escape detection and would still more certainly not have found access to the apostle. We know that at Rome Paul was under house-arrest and was therefore allowed visitors, apparently without restriction, but the same privileged conditions do not appear to have obtained in Caesarea.[3] (2) The apostle clearly expects to be released in the near future since he requests Philemon to prepare him a lodging (Phm. 22), but this request would hardly have been made at Caesarea where Paul knew that his only hope was to appeal to Caesar, and where his face was definitely turned westward as the Epistle to the Romans shows (Rom. i. 10 ff., xv. 19 ff.).

The Ephesian hypothesis, assuming that it could be proved that Paul

[1] W. Michaelis, *Einleitung*, p. 199, maintains that the authenticity of this Epistle is still the best solution.

[2] This hypothesis is maintained by Lohmeyer, Dibelius, Goguel and de Zwaan among others (cf. Feine–Behm, *Einleitung*, p. 192).*

[3] Paul's prayer request for an open door to preach and the activities of his mission-helpers would not suit the circumstances of Acts xxiii. 35 and xxiv. 27 (cf. Feine–Behm, *op. cit.*, p. 192). The same applies to the Ephesian imprisonment unless the circumstances of Acts xix. 8 ff. had deteriorated when this Epistle was written. In the former case the imprisonment seems to have been too rigid to allow the possibility of preaching work, while in the latter case the door seems open enough already. The request would fit better the partial restrictions of the Roman imprisonment. E. Percy, *op. cit.*, p. 473, in rejecting the hypothesis of the Ephesian imprisonment in explanation of the place of origin of this Epistle and Ephesians, maintains that we should expect Paul's companions to have suffered the same fate if Paul was imprisoned in Ephesus on account of his Christian work.

was imprisoned there, would still not conclusively account for the facts. It would still be questionable, perhaps even more so, whether a runaway slave would have fled to Ephesus, a distance of no more than a hundred miles, and would have expected to escape detection there.[1] On this point the Roman hypothesis seems preferable in spite of the much greater distances involved. Indeed, as C. H. Dodd cogently remarks, 'If we are to *surmise*, then it is as likely that the fugitive slave, his pockets lined at his master's expense, made for Rome, *because* it was distant, as that he went to Ephesus because it was near.'[2]

Due weight must be given to the fact that if Paul was at Ephesus his request for a lodging at Colossae immediately following his release becomes reasonable. On the Roman hypothesis such a request would conflict with his previously expressed intention to visit Spain. But there is no necessity to suppose that at the time of writing Colossians Paul was still contemplating a westwards mission, for he may well have abandoned it. If on the second Roman imprisonment hypothesis Paul did journey to Spain, it would make the Roman origin of the Colossian letter less probable than the Ephesian. But we have no means of verifying Paul's movements at the close of his ministry.

In further support of the Ephesian hypothesis, C. R. Bowen[3] maintained that the Epistle suggests that the Colossian church was recently founded. But this claim is difficult to substantiate, for the origin of the Colossian church is obscure. Epaphras certainly seems to have been the founder, and it is a reasonable suggestion that he was himself one of the converts of Paul's Ephesian ministry. But the evidence does not demand this hypothesis. It may have been later on that Epaphras returned to Colossae and established the church. In any case, some interval would seem necessary to allow for the development of the false teaching although this admittedly need not have been of great duration. Heresy may rapidly attack a newly-formed church as readily as an established one, perhaps even more so, and would have been more threatening at an early stage in the church's history.

The Roman hypothesis, however, has certain positive considerations

[1] F. J. Badcock suggests some friend may have hidden him there (*The Pauline Epistles and the Epistle to the Hebrews*, 1937, p. 65). In any case he would have to pass through Ephesus *en route* for Rome. But he would hardly have stayed there long enough to be of service to Paul in prison.

[2] *New Testament Studies*, p. 95. Goodspeed (*INT*, p. 105) wisely points out the folly of judging runaways by the standards of stay-at-homes.

[3] *JBL*, XLIII (1924), pp. 189 ff.

in its favour. It is built on a known imprisonment of such a character as to allow all the events reflected in Colossians and Philemon to happen. The presence of Luke with Paul is supported by the Acts record, whereas the Ephesian ministry of Paul does not occur in a 'we' section and it may reasonably be doubted whether Luke was with Paul during this period. The description of Aristarchus and Epaphras as Paul's 'fellow-prisoners' suggests to Duncan[1] that an Ephesian imprisonment is in mind because Aristarchus was arrested there (cf. Acts xix. 29). But this passage in Acts does not specifically mention an official arrest, but only the seizure of Aristarchus by mob-violence. On the other hand it would seem from Acts xxvii. 2 that he accompanied Paul to Rome and may well have shared to some extent in his privations. This evidence from Acts seems more in support of a Roman than an Ephesian imprisonment. Of the other companions of Paul mentioned in Colossians and Philemon there is no other evidence to connect any of them (except Timothy) either with Ephesus or Rome and even if all of them were Asiatics this is no reason for preferring Ephesus to Rome. As Dodd[2] has pointed out, such an argument misconceives the mobility of the persons belonging to Paul's personal staff, like Luke and Timothy, or his delegates like Tychicus.

Arguments based on development of thought are too difficult to establish to bear much weight, but there would seem to be some force in the contention that the doctrinal outlook of Colossians belongs rather to a later than to an earlier period, and this would furnish corroborating evidence for a Roman origin.[3] The Ephesian hypothesis cannot be ruled out as impossible, but the traditional view has the balance of probability.

The dating of the Epistle will obviously depend on the conclusion

[1] St. Paul's Ephesian Ministry (1929), pp. 148 ff.
[2] New Testament Studies, p. 93.
[3] Duncan, op. cit., pp. 115 ff., argues that the theological position reflected in Colossians and the other Captivity Epistles might well have been reached during the period of the Ephesian ministry. But E. Percy (op. cit., pp. 467 ff.) and F. F. Bruce (Colossians, p. 165) conclude that the presentation of Colossians (and Ephesians) is more developed than 1 Corinthians and Romans and therefore favours Rome rather than Ephesus as the place of origin. A. Wikenhauser makes the point that Ephesians (which he dates during the same period as Colossians) presupposes Romans and cannot have preceded it (New Testament Introduction, p. 419). But against the notion of doctrinal development in Paul's theology cf. Dibelius–Kümmel, Paul (1953), pp. 59, 60.

reached regarding its place of origin. According to the Roman theory the most likely and generally accepted placing is in the middle or latter half of Paul's first Roman imprisonment. Such a dating would allow time for the news of Paul's imprisonment to spread to such scattered communities as those in the Lycus valley and for Epaphras to seek out Paul in Rome. Those advocating the Ephesian hypothesis are obliged to place it at the close of the Ephesian ministry. Because of the difficulties in assigning both Philippians and Colossians to the same imprisonment, Duncan[1] postulates a second imprisonment towards the end of the period to accommodate this Epistle and Philemon. But the necessity to multiply Ephesian imprisonments weakens rather than strengthens the whole hypothesis.

VII. THE LETTER FROM LAODICEA

Much speculation has surrounded Paul's request in Colossians iv. 16 that the Colossian letter should be passed on to Laodicea in exchange for one from them. Some early Fathers (Theodore of Mopsuestia and Theodoret) imagined that a letter written by the Laodiceans to Paul was in mind, but the more natural understanding of the words is to take them as a reference to a letter from Paul to the Laodiceans, possibly written at the same time as Colossians. Paul is hardly likely to have urged an exchange of a letter from him to one church with a letter to him from another.

Various attempts have been made to identify this Epistle.

1. In the Medieval Church a letter was current under the title of 'the letter to the Laodiceans', but this may safely be rejected as spurious because of its absence from all Greek mss and because of its late appearance even in Latin mss. It is a not very clever attempt to produce an Epistle which would solve the problem of Colossians iv. 16.[2]

2. Some have maintained that the Epistle is our present Epistle to the Ephesians, and this has the support of Marcion's Canon. But this was probably a mere guess on his part (see pp. 510 f. for further discussion of this view).[3]

---

[1] Op. cit., pp. 140 ff.

[2] Cf. B. F. Westcott, On the Canon of the New Testament (1875), pp. 572 ff.; J. B. Lightfoot, Colossians (1900), pp. 272 ff.; A. Souter, The Text and Canon of the New Testament (1913), p. 193 (revised edition 1954, p. 152).

[3] Among those who have adhered to this view are Mill, J. B. Lightfoot, Harnack, Knabenbauer. Cf. B. W. Bacon, Expositor, VIII, xvii (1919), pp. 19 ff.; F. F. Bruce, Colossians, p. 310 n.

3. J. Knox has suggested that the letter is to be identified with our letter to Philemon, but this conjecture has little to commend it beyond its ingenuity (see pp. 636 ff. for discussion of the theory).

4. The most likely solution seems to be that the Epistle in question is now lost.[1]

CONTENTS

I. GREETING (i. 1, 2)

Paul associates Timothy with him in addressing the Christians at Colossae.

II. THANKSGIVING (i. 3–8)

The reception of the gospel at Colossae, as a result of the faithful ministry of Epaphras, provided a real basis for thankfulness.

III. PRAYER (i. 9–12)

Paul prays that they might have knowledge of God's will to live worthily and might be strengthened with God's power to endure joyfully, knowing that they have gained a share in the believers' inheritance.

IV. DOCTRINAL SECTION: AN EXPOSITION OF THE DOCTRINE OF CHRIST (i. 13–ii. 23)

a. A positive statement (i. 13–ii. 7)

Before dealing with the false teaching which was affecting the church at Colossae, Paul presents his doctrine positively and makes the following assertions about Christ.

1. Through Him comes deliverance and redemption for sinners (i. 13, 14).

2. He is described as 'the image of the invisible God' (i. 15).

---

[1] Cf. J. Moffatt, *ILNT* (1912), p. 160; C. H. Dodd, *Colossians* (AB, 1929), p. 1262. P. N. Harrison, *ATR* (1950), p. 284, who holds that this letter together with Colossians (in its original state) and Philemon was sent about AD 56 from Ephesus, suggests that the Laodicean letter may have perished in the great earthquake of AD 60 of which Tacitus writes. *

3. He is the Source and Upholder of the material creation (i. 16, 17).

4. He is Head of the Church, the spiritual creation, and by virtue of the indwelling fulness of the Godhead He has become the Reconciler of all things to Himself (i. 18–20).

5. What He has done for the universe He has done for the Colossian Christians. They have been reconciled through Christ in order to be presented without fault to God. Paul's own ministry consists, in fact, in proclaiming this gospel of hope. It involves suffering for Christ's sake, but he would nevertheless toil with all his energy to preach this open mystery of the indwelling Christ (i. 21–29).

6. The readers, together with the Laodiceans and all others who have not seen Paul's face but who possess knowledge of this mystery, are exhorted to be firmly established in the faith (ii. 1–7).

b. A polemical statement (ii. 8–23)

There are those who are not true to the faith and the apostle next comes to grips with the specific dangers of these false teachers.

1. Speculative philosophy is to be avoided, for it obscures the doctrine of Christ's fulness (ii. 8–10), the true character of His spiritual circumcision and His triumph over the powers of darkness (ii. 11–15).

2. Ritual observances are similarly to be shunned, particularly food laws and festivals, which at best are but a shadow of what has become real in Christ (ii. 16, 17).

3. Worship of angels could only be derogatory to the sole headship of Christ in His Church (ii. 18, 19).

4. Rigid asceticism must also be strongly denounced as being no more than a human device which was in any case powerless to check self-indulgence (ii. 20–23).

V. PRACTICAL SECTION (iii. 1–iv. 6)

There is throughout this section a close relationship between doctrine and practice. The exhortations are in harmony with the exalted Christology of the preceding statements.

a. The doctrinal basis of Christian living (iii. 1–4)

Since the believer's life is hidden with Christ in God, the aspirations of his mind must be focused on higher things in harmony with his Lord.

b. The old life and the new (iii. 5–17)

Following from the Christian's union with Christ there are implications which must at once be worked out in practice. (1) There must be a putting off of the old life, with its evil passions (iii. 5–9) and (2) a putting on of the new, which sets Christlikeness as its pattern and its goal, and which has universal application irrespective of race or class. Paul describes in detail how this new life manifests itself in Christian graces, especially love, peace and thankfulness, in corporate edification through the Word of God and in mutual worship with its keynote of praise (iii. 10–17).

c. Christian homelife (iii. 18–iv. 1)

The general injunctions of the previous section narrow to the particular duties in this.

(i) *Wives and husbands* (iii. 18, 19). There must here be an attitude of mutual respect.

(ii) *Children and parents* (iii. 20, 21). There should be obedience on the part of children and restraint on the part of parents.

(iii) *Slaves and masters* (iii. 22–iv. 1). The former are reminded that they are servants of Christ and must therefore conduct themselves towards their earthly masters as if they were serving the Lord, while the latter are urged to treat their slaves with justice, remembering their heavenly Master.

d. General Christian behaviour (iv. 2–6)

Prayerfulness, thankfulness, soberness and graciousness are enjoined, with special reference to their effect on outsiders.

VI. CONCLUSION (iv. 7–18)

a. Commendation of Tychicus and Onesimus (iv. 7–9)

Both are warmly described as faithful and beloved and both are being sent, presumably with this Epistle.

b. Greetings from Paul's companions (iv. 10–14)

Aristarchus, Mark, Jesus Justus, Epaphras, Luke and Demas are mentioned, with a special word of testimony for Epaphras.

c. Messages to Laodicea and Archippus (iv. 15–17)

Directions are given regarding an exchange of letters between Laodicea and Colossae, and Archippus is urged to fulfil his ministry.

d. Paul's own greeting (iv. 18)

He concludes in his own hand with a touching request that they should remember his bonds.

ADDITIONAL NOTES

546. *The heresy.* For a general discussion of this, cf. G. Bornkamm, *Das ende des Gesetzes*[2] (1958), pp. 139 ff. (= *ThLZ*, 73, 1948, cols. 11 ff.).

546. *Its Christology.* F. O. Francis (*StTh*, 16, 1962, pp. 109–134) denies that the Colossian errorists did not accept the pre-eminence of Christ. He thinks on the contrary that what they lacked was perception of the reconciliation and fullness which was theirs in Christ. Francis suggests that the major obstacle was a failure to apply this to themselves. This consideration may be worth pursuing.

547. For the view that behind the presentation of Christ in Colossians is the Greek conception of Cosmos, cf. R. S. Barbour, *SJT*, 20 (1967), pp. 257–271. The Gnostic solution to the problem of man's relation to the Cosmos was a God-man. But Paul presents Christ as ruler of the Cosmos, who by means of His death and resurrection has gained the victory on earth.

548. F. O. Francis (*op. cit.*) does not consider that Col. ii. 18 relates to worship of angels, but to worship of God. F. F. Bruce (*BJRL*, XLVIII, 1966, pp. 268–285) mentions a Nag Hammadi text which shows that some Jewish sects believed that God created the world through angels. A. F. J. Klijn (*INT*, 1967, p. 115) suggests an angel-cult in which planets and angels were not kept strictly distinct.

549. [1] G. Bornkamm (*op. cit.*, p. 150) has no doubt that behind the Colossian heresy there is a Jewish Gnosis influenced by Iranian ideas. His use of Gnosis rather than Gnosticism is supported by R. M. Wilson, *Gnosis and the New Testament*, pp. 31 ff., especially pp. 55 ff. Yet Bornkamm tends to connect too closely the concept of Gnosis and Gnosticism. As Wilson remarks, 'a considerable leap of faith is involved in the assumption that these pre-Christian ideas already carried with them the full implications of the alleged Gnostic Redeemer-myth' (p. 57). Cf. E. Haenchen, *RGG*, II[3], col. 1654; H. M. Schenke, *ZTK*, 61 (1964), pp. 391–403. W. G. Kümmel (*INT*, 1965, p. 240) favours some kind of Jewish Gnosis.

551. There have been several recent studies of Col. i. 15–20. R. P. Martin (*EQ*, XXXVI, 1964, pp. 195–205) considers that it is an early Christian non-Pauline hymn in honour of Christ which was borrowed by Paul. But N. Kehl (*Der Christushymnus im Kolosserbrief*, 1967) considers on stylistic grounds that the author of the hymn was the author of the whole Epistle (cf. G. Schille's criticism, *ThLZ*, 93, 1968, cols. 667 f.). For another stylistic analysis, cf. E. Bammel, *ZNTW*, 52

(1961), pp. 88–95. From the use of σῶμα in this hymn, E. Lohse (*NTS*, 11, 1965, pp. 203–216) expounds his doctrine of the Church in this Epistle.

552. [3] For a critique of Masson's theory, cf. W. G. Kümmel, *INT* (1965), p. 244. In a recent article, E. Lohse (*NTS*, 15, 1969, pp. 211–220) admits that several features in this Epistle reflect the same approach as Pauline theology, but he considers the author was perhaps a member of a Pauline school tradition. Emphasis falls on parallels between Colossians and Romans.

E. P. Sanders (*JBL*, LXXXV, 1966, pp. 28–45) claims that a test for the authenticity of Colossians is whether it shows dependence on genuine Pauline Epistles. The method adopted is to assume that Paul would not have quoted himself. As a result of his examination of Colossians and Philippians he finds evidence of conflation in the former, but not in the latter. He wonders whether there might not be some support for Holtzmann's theory because he finds his evidence clearer in Col. i and ii than elsewhere. Another recent advocate of a non-Pauline author is H. Conzelmann, *NTD*[8] (1962). Cf. also W. Marxsen, *INT* (1968), pp. 177 ff., who classes Colossians among the Pseudo-Pauline Epistles.

554. [1] Cf. G. Bornkamm's argument against authenticity based on the different use of 'hope', in 'Die Hoffnung im Kolosserbrief', *Studien zum NT und zur Patristik (Festschrift für E. Klostermann,* 1962), pp. 56–64.

555. [2] Cf. W. G. Kümmel, *INT* (1965), p. 245.

559. [1] Cf. C. P. Anderson (*JBL*, LXXXV, 1966, pp. 436–440), who considers that the letter from Laodicea was not written by Paul. The author may have been Epaphras who may not have been able to return because he was a fellow-prisoner. But there does not seem to be sufficient reason to doubt that Paul was author of this letter.

CHAPTER EIGHTEEN

THE THESSALONIAN EPISTLES

PAUL'S MISSION IN THESSALONICA

The city of Thessalonica was important not only because it was the capital of Macedonia but also because it stood on the Via Egnatia, the Roman highway to the East. It possessed its own system of government with magistrates called politarchs, and included within it a colony of Jews as is evident from the synagogue there (Acts xvii. 1).

It was on Paul's second missionary journey that he visited the place in company with Silas and Timothy. They had just left Philippi where Paul and Silas had been imprisoned. Their mission was an immediate success and many believed. Among these were apparently a certain number of Jews (Acts xvii. 4), a great many devout Greeks or God-fearers and not a few of the principal women. But from 1 Thessalonians i. 9 we may surmise that the majority were idol-worshippers won from heathenism. No doubt the stable core of the young church were the God-fearers, who were particularly open to the reception of the gospel. They had a real dissatisfaction with pagan morality and had turned their attentions to the purer ethical teaching of the Jews. They had, moreover, been attracted to the lofty conception of Jewish monotheism as contrasted with the puerility of idol-worship. Yet they had found themselves dissatisfied with the narrow nationalism and ritual requirements of Judaism, and the advent of Christianity supplied their demand for an adequate and even greater conception of God than that which Judaism provided, a nobler ethic centred in the remarkable personal example of Jesus, and a universal outlook which came as a breath of liberation after the tightness of Jewish exclusivism. It is not surprising therefore that at Thessalonica so great a company of these serious-minded proselytes embraced the message.

But this very section on the fringe of Judaism was cherished by the synagogue authorities and very soon their defection from Judaism to the new faith of Christianity stirred up the jealousy and opposition of the Jews. Their plan of action was to use mob-violence. A street-corner gang was goaded to attack Jason's house where Paul and his companions were staying. The visitors were out but mob-violence knows no

564

discrimination and Jason and some fellow Christians were dragged out and brought before the magistrates as disturbers of the peace. Jason appears to have been bound over on the charge of adhering to another king than Caesar and then released. The magistrates' decision probably means that he was ordered to keep the peace, but it need not have involved him in any undertaking to secure the withdrawal of Paul from the city. The fact that Paul, in writing to the Christians, indicates that he had every intention of returning to the city would be against such a suggestion. Nevertheless, the Christians apparently thought it was expedient for Jason's sake to send Paul and his companions away.

Subsequently Paul went to Berea, where he once more met with opposition from Thessalonian Jews and was forced to move on. He came to Athens and then moved on to Corinth. While at Athens, Paul had sent Timothy to Thessalonica to ascertain the condition of the church and on his return to Paul at Corinth the first letter was written.

THE FIRST EPISTLE

I. PURPOSE

Undoubtedly it was the specific news received through Timothy that not only prompted the letter but dictated its contents.[1] (1) First, Paul had to express his general satisfaction over the progress of the community and he reflects his joy throughout the Epistle. (2) He finds it necessary to answer certain charges of self-seeking and cowardice which have been brought against him, apparently by his Jewish opponents (ii.

---

[1] Some scholars have claimed that there was a letter from the Thessalonians in addition to Timothy's oral report which Paul answers in our canonical first Epistle: cf. B. W. Bacon (*INT*, 1900, p. 73); J. E. Frame (*1 and 2 Thessalonians*, 1912, p. 9). J. Moffatt considered the theory tenable but the evidence elusive (*ILNT*, p. 67). B. Rigaux (*Les Épîtres aux Thessaloniciens*, pp. 55–57) maintains Paul is not responding to a letter but to a situation. C. E. Faw, 'On the writing of First Thessalonians', *JBL*, LXXI (1952), pp. 217–225, suggested improbably that chapters iv and v are particularly devoted to a point-by-point answer to the Thessalonians' own queries, whereas echoes of Timothy's oral report and the Thessalonians' letter are found in chapters i–iii, but the details are indistinguishable. Cf. L. Morris, *The First and Second Epistles to the Thessalonians* (NLC, 1959), p. 39 n., or a criticism of Faw's view.

1-12). (3) He encourages the Christians to persevere even in face of Jewish opposition and persecution (ii. 14 ff.). (4) He points out the superiority of Christian morality over pagan (iv. 4 ff.), probably to safeguard them from pagan attempts to make new converts to Christianity revert to their old standards. (5) He writes to correct a misunderstanding about the *parousia*. Some of the Christians were worried over loved ones who had died, while others were resorting to idleness, believing that the return of the Lord was imminent. (6) He also urges his readers to respect their leaders (v. 12), which may suggest that some tension, if not insubordination, existed in the church.[1] (7) He may also have had in mind the need to give some gentle hint about ecstatic manifestations (v. 19, 20). The whole letter is essentially practical, containing a message directly geared to the contemporary problems of the primitive Christian community.*

II. DATE

The date of this Epistle may be fixed with a fair degree of precision since it falls within Paul's period at Corinth, which provides us with one of the most certain contacts with secular chronology in the proconsulate of Gallio. According to an inscription at Delphi, Gallio was proconsul during the twelfth year of Claudius' tribunicial power and after his twenty-sixth proclamation as Emperor. This must have been before August 52, when the twenty-seventh proclamation had already been made. As proconsuls normally took office in midsummer, it is generally supposed that midsummer of 52 must be the date of the commencement of Gallio's office. But some prefer the previous year, to allow an adequate time for the proconsul to refer some questions to the Emperor, as the inscription mentions that he did.[2]

It is not possible to say exactly when Paul appeared before Gallio, but Acts xviii. 12–18 suggests that this happened shortly after Gallio assumed office and probably towards the end of Paul's eighteen months in the city. It is most probable that 1 Thessalonians was written shortly after Paul's arrival in Corinth and it may therefore be dated in the

[1] K. Lake, *Earlier Epistles of St. Paul* (1927), p. 89, thought iii. 12, v. 11, 15 implied some disunity in the church, but the exhortations to unity are of too general a nature to be certain (cf. Goguel, *INT*, IV, i, 291).

[2] Goodspeed, *INT* (1937), dates Gallio's year of office from June 51 to June 52 and accepts AD 50 as the date of writing of 1 Thessalonians. So also Michaelis, *Einleitung*, p. 152.

early part of 51 (or 50 if the earlier dating of Gallio's assumption of office is preferred[1]).

III. AUTHENTICITY

The genuineness of this Epistle has been challenged only by the most radical criticism. Both the Tübingen and Dutch schools denied it to Paul, but few modern scholars find any adequate grounds for maintaining the same opinion.[2] External evidence for authenticity is strong. It is included in Marcion's collection of Paul's works (c. 140); it is mentioned in the Muratorian Canon (c. 180), is quoted by name by Irenaeus, is acknowledged as genuinely Pauline by the time of Clement of Alexandria and Tertullian and is included in both Old Latin and Old Syriac Versions.[3]

The internal evidence is equally strong for Pauline authorship. The church organization is clearly early, for the only officials mentioned are 'those who are over you' (v. 12). The language and style are certainly Pauline, while the subject-matter would be inconceivable after Paul's death. No one would have thought of representing the apostle as expecting to be alive at the *parousia* when it was known that he was already dead.[4] The imminence of the *parousia* is in itself a strong argument in favour of authenticity since it reflects a primitive period in

---

[1] Cf. Leon Morris, *1 and 2 Thessalonians* (*TNT*, 1956), p. 15, for detailed discussion.*

[2] F. C. Baur and his school denied authenticity mainly on three grounds: (a) differences in vocabulary and style from the four great Epistles; (b) absence of Old Testament citations; (c) absence of the predominant Pauline ideas. But the different circumstances in which the Epistle was sent are a sufficient reason for the deviations (cf. Goguel's discussion, *Introduction*, IV, i, 304 ff. See also the account of Baur's arguments in B. Rigaux, *Aux Thessaloniciens*, pp. 120–123). At the beginning of the twentieth century, R. Scott (*The Pauline Epistles*, 1909), pp. 215–233, maintained non-Pauline authorship of both Epistles but suggested that both consisted of two parts, one of which was written by Timothy and the other by Silas. But Scott's theory won little support (cf. the criticism of J. E. Frame, *1 and 2 Thessalonians*, ICC, 1912, p. 39).

[3] There are also some reasons to suppose that Ignatius, *Ad Rom.* ii. 1, cites 1 Thes. ii. 4 and that Polycarp cites 2 Thessalonians (cf. E. H. Askwith's careful discussion of this evidence, *An Introduction to the Thessalonian Epistles* (1902), pp. 40–52. Cf. also A. E. Barnett, *Paul becomes a Literary Influence* (1941), pp. 160, 178–180).

[4] Strongly stressed by von Dobschütz (Meyer x[7]), 1919. Cf. also Wikenhauser, *op. cit.*, p. 366, and Askwith, *op. cit.*, p. 74

church development. Even if these obstacles to a forgery theory were not considered insuperable, it would be wrecked by the fact that no adequate motive for such a production has ever been suggested.[1] Some have further maintained that the existence of 2 Thessalonians is itself a strong support for the authenticity of 1 Thessalonians.[2]*

In spite of the strong character of the evidence for genuineness, it has sometimes been maintained that there are historical discrepancies between this Epistle and the Acts.

a. The period of Paul's mission

In Acts xvii. 2 Paul is stated to have spent three sabbaths at Thessalonica whereas the way in which Paul himself describes his relationship with the Thessalonians (1 Thes. ii. 7–11) has suggested to some scholars a longer stay, especially as Paul refers to labouring with his own hands to support himself. In addition Paul mentions in writing to the Philippians that they sent gifts, probably more than once, to Paul while he was at Thessalonica. This alleged discrepancy has been answered in two ways. Ramsay[3] suggested that the Acts recorded only the synagogue preaching and that the three-week period covered only the period of Paul's Jewish mission. Subsequent to this Paul is alleged to have spent further time among the Gentiles and the period of his stay in the city is extended to six months. But the Acts record does not give this impression even if it does not definitely exclude it. Perhaps the better solution is to suppose that the short period mentioned by the Acts was the whole of his period of work there, cut short by Jewish opposition. This brief period would allow enough time for Paul to work with his own hands and would certainly give opportunity for spiritual counsel of the kind hinted at in the Epistle. The gifts from Philippi are admittedly a difficulty on this view, but only if such gifts were sent more than once.[4] The data are not enough to establish a discrepancy between the Epistle and the Acts.

---

[1] Cf. W. Neil, Thessalonians (MC, 1950), p. xviii; Askwith, op. cit., p. 75, considers the personal element in the Epistle to be the strongest internal corroboration of genuineness.

[2] Cf. W. Lock, HDB, IV, p. 745.

[3] St. Paul the Traveller and Roman Citizen (1920), p. 228.

[4] Cf. L. Morris, Thessalonians (TNT), p. 17, who thinks Phil. iv. 16 need not mean that Paul received help more than once from the Philippians. Cf. also Morris' article in Novum Testamentum, I (1956), pp. 205–208.

b. The composition of the church

As already mentioned above, the Acts record does not include among the converts those won from idolatry, who nevertheless formed a large part of the church at Thessalonica, as it would seem from Paul's letter. But the discrepancy is more apparent than real. The apostle admittedly addresses them as if they were all Gentiles (see i. 9, ii. 14, iv. 1–5), but then the large number of God-fearers mentioned in Acts would come under this category. These, too, would have been formerly idol-worshippers before taking refuge in Judaism and Paul's terms of reference could have been applicable to them, although 1 Thessalonians i. 9 implies that Paul thinks of them as having turned to God from idols as a result of his preaching. In any case, it is unlikely that the church would have been wholly Jewish-Christian, and the reason for the supposed discrepancy may be that the author of Acts at that point in his story is concentrating on Jewish activity and therefore omits the Gentile element, while Paul, concentrating on his call to preach to the Gentiles, groups all the readers under the Gentile category, regarding the Jews as a minority element.

c. The movements of Timothy and Silas

The objections on this score are even less weighty than the previous. Acts xviii. 5 makes clear that these companions of Paul rejoined him at Corinth, but 1 Thessalonians iii. 1 ff. shows Timothy to have been with Paul at Athens. But there is no real difficulty here, for Acts xvii. 16 states that Paul waited for Timothy and Silas at Athens and it may reasonably be supposed that they arrived when Paul was still there. Later, when Paul was at Corinth, they arrived from Macedonia (Acts xviii. 5), which suggests that they had carried out a journey from Athens to Macedonia and back to Corinth which the Acts does not record. If this reconstruction is correct the alleged discrepancy disappears.

THE SECOND EPISTLE

I. AUTHENTICITY

Because this Epistle has been more widely disputed than its counterpart and because the question of its relationship will need discussion, the purpose and date of the Epistle will be left until after these other problems have been settled. This Epistle, in company with 1 Thessalonians, was strongly assailed by the Tübingen school, and the results of their criticism are still apparent in the reserve with which many modern scholars view it. Neil, for instance, claims that most scholars accept it only *faute de mieux*.[1] But it would be truer to say that the arguments against Pauline authorship do not generally commend themselves to modern scholars.[2]

The external evidence is, if anything, rather stronger than for 1 Thessalonians, for it was not only included in the Canon of Marcion and the Muratorian List and was mentioned by Irenaeus by name, but was apparently known to Ignatius, Justin and Polycarp.

Although this evidence enables us with considerable certainty to conclude that the earliest Christians considered this Epistle a genuine work of Paul, yet internal evidence has been supposed by some to make the tradition improbable. There are four main grounds of objection.

a. Eschatology

A change of approach is alleged in the second Epistle as compared with the first in respect of the *parousia*.[3] Here it is less imminent, for certain events must first take place. Some of the earlier critics[4] attempted to heighten the problem by supposing that the 'man of sin' was intended to be identified with Nero Redivivus, which meant that the Epistle could not have been earlier than the last decade or two of the first century, i.e. too late for Pauline authorship. But there has been a change

---

[1] W. Neil, *Thessalonians* (MC), p. xxi.

[2] Among modern scholars the most notable disputant of authenticity is C. Masson, *Les Epîtres aux Thessaloniciens* (1957). He follows the tradition of H. J. Holtzmann (*ZNTW*, 2, 1901, pp. 97–108) and G. Hollmann (*ZNTW*, 5, 1904, pp. 28–38). B. Rigaux (*Les Epîtres aux Thessaloniciens*, 1956, p. 132) cites the following authors who have maintained the authenticity since 1910: J. Weiss, Hadorn, Appel, Feine–Behm, Michaelis, Moffatt, Goodspeed, Lake, Nock, Knox, West and Selwyn. In fact, he can quote no commentator who rejects the Epistle. His work appeared almost simultaneously with C. Masson's and this accounts for his omission to mention the latter's opposition. On theological grounds H. Braun also denies the authenticity (*ZNTW*, 44, 1952–53, pp. 152–156).*

[3] C. Masson (*op. cit.*, pp. 10–11) considers the difference of eschatology the decisive argument. He can see no way of inserting the premonitory signs into 1 Thes. iv. 13 to v. 11. In this he is in direct line with the older German criticism.

[4] Cf. F. H. Kern, *Ueber II Thes. ii.* 1–12 (1839) (cited by Rigaux, *op. cit.*, p. 125 n. 2).

in the twentieth century towards the whole subject of eschatology. As
Neil points out, time sequence does not arise in eschatological thought,[1]
and to attempt to date documents on such grounds must inevitably
lead to a false trail. It must further be borne in mind that 1 Thessalonians
v. 1–11 presupposes some knowledge of eschatological signs on the part
of the readers, which suggests that Paul had given them some oral
instruction in the matter.[2] While the section about the 'man of sin' finds
no parallel in 1 Thessalonians, there is no reason to deny that Paul
could have written it.[3] Earlier attempts to regard it as an independent
apocalypse[4] which was later attached to the Epistle are not now favoured. The work of Bousset on the antichrist legend[5] has shown that
the background of it must be largely found in Jewish apocalyptic
thought and that the man of sin is therefore the Pseudo-Messiah and
not some historical person such as Nero as formerly proposed. Had
the Nero Redivivus myth been in mind in this passage it would at once
date it as post-Pauline. Because of the close similarities between this
passage and Mark xiii it is reasonable to suppose that Paul was acquainted
with Jesus' eschatological teaching.[6] In that case no weighty objection

[1] *Thessalonians* (*MC*, 1950), p. xxii.

[2] Meinertz, *Einleitung*, p. 86 n., compares the two streams of thought in the
Lord's teaching, i.e. no knowledge of the coming and suddenness, with knowledge
of certain intervening signs (cf. Mt. xxiv. 36 ff., Lk. xxi. 34 ff.; and Mt. xxiv.
32 ff., Lk. xxi. 21, 29 ff.). Cf. also Askwith, *op. cit.*, p. 84.

[3] 2 Thes. ii. 5 makes clear that this 'man of sin' teaching is not new to the readers,
for Paul says that he told them of these things while still with them.*

[4] Cf. F. Spitta, *Zur Geschichte u. Lit. des Urchristentums*, I (1893), pp. 109 ff. See
also J. Moffatt, *ILNT*, pp. 81, 82. C. H. Dodd suggests that 2 Thes. i. 7–10 and
ii. 3–10 go back to a Jewish or Jewish Christian apocalypse to which Paul had
added the speculation regarding the imminence of the *parousia: The Coming of
Christ* (1951), *The Apostolic Preaching and its Developments*[2] (1944), pp. 38, 39.

[5] *The Antichrist Legend* (Eng. Tr., A. H. Keane, 1896). The earliest disputant of
the Pauline authorship was J. E. C. Schmidt, *Einleitung in das Neue Testament* (1804),
who based his attack on the discrepancy between 1 Thes. iv. 13–v. 11 and
2 Thes. ii. 1–12. This problem carried no weight for the Tübingen school who denied
the authenticity of both Epistles and whose main stumbling-block was the supposed discrepancy between 2 Thes. ii. 1–12 and 1 Cor. xv and its alleged dependence on the Apocalypse of John (cf. B. Rigaux's admirably concise survey of
critical opinions about 2 Thes. ii. 1–12, *op. cit.*, pp. 124 ff.). This passage has undoubtedly been the focal point of attack in the eyes of advocates of non-authenticity.

[6] G. R. Beasley-Murray (*Jesus and the Future*, 1954, pp. 232, 234) has maintained
that not only 2 Thes. ii but parts of chapter i and 1 Thes. iv and v are paralleled

can be lodged against the language here. A sufficient explanation of the different eschatological emphasis is the need to answer a misunderstanding which had not arisen when 1 Thessalonians was written. The change is not in eschatology but in viewpoint due to changing circumstances.[1]

b. Change of tone

It has been claimed that 2 Thessalonians is more formal and frigid than 1 Thessalonians, which is notable for its warm affection. Whereas in the first Epistle Paul says 'we give thanks' (1 Thes. i. 2), in the second he says 'we are bound to give thanks' (2 Thes. i. 3, ii. 13) and even says 'we command you' (2 Thes. iii. 6, 12). But such changes can hardly be taken too seriously since in any case Paul is having to deal with a different situation and probably wrote in a very different mood. He is warmer towards them in the first Epistle because of the great encouragement news of them had brought him. But he must have been a little perplexed to say the least at the turn of events which prompted the writing of the second Epistle. It is a fallacy to assume that any writer must always write in the same tone, since tone is very much a matter of mood which is in turn easily affected by prevailing circumstances.

c. Readers

In 1 Thessalonians, as we have seen, Gentiles are mainly in mind, but the second Epistle is said to assume a greater knowledge of the Old Testament (cf. i. 6–10, ii. 1–12). But there are no allusions in this Epistle which Gentiles could not have appreciated. The Acts demonstrates the strong Old Testament flavour of primitive Christian preaching, even among Gentiles. Nor can the apocalyptic element be considered unintelligible to Gentiles, since Mark's Gospel includes similar apocalyptic material and is generally reckoned to have been written for Gentiles.

in Mark xiii, which suggests to him that Paul was acquainted with an edition of the eschatological discourse before it was used in the compilation of any gospel. If so the supposed difference of eschatology may be traced to Jesus. Cf. B. Rigaux, *op. cit.*, p. 104.

[1] Even F. C. Baur, *Paul* (Eng. Tr. 1873), p. 488, saw no difficulty in conceiving that a writer might have expressed his thoughts about the *parousia* in two different ways as in 1 and 2 Thessalonians, although he attributed neither to Paul.

d. Similarities

Why, it is asked, should Paul have written two Epistles so close together on the same subject? And why are there such frequent and close similarities in language? Would such a man as Paul have repeated himself in this manner? On the strength of such considerations some writers have therefore concluded that 2 Thessalonians was written by an imitator. Yet, as Neil has rightly pointed out,[1] the assumption here is that it would be a psychological impossibility for a man to have written both Epistles to the same people. But on what basis is psychological impossibility to be judged? If, as we have seen, the probabilities are that the changed situation demanded a similar yet different approach, the objection is nullified.

When the strong similarities are combined with the differences it is in fact more difficult to imagine a writer other than Paul himself. Certainly the similarities are not so striking as to make imitation even a probable solution.[2] What agreements there are are not lengthy, and similarity of wording often occurs in different settings in the two Epistles.[3] These similarities and differences are adequately accounted for by the practical demands of the church at the time.[4]

e. Suggested explanations

Not one of these objections is seen to possess real substance, yet some scholars have considered them of sufficient weight to suggest alternatives to Pauline authorship and these may be listed as follows.*

---

[1] Neil, *Thessalonians (MC)*, p. xxiv. W. Wrede (*Die Echtheit des 2 Thessalonicherbriefes Untersucht*, 1913) shifted the attack from eschatology to the imitator theory, while H. J. Holtzmann was swayed by the same difficulty to place greater stress on the literary dependence of 2 Thessalonians on 1 Thessalonians (*ZNTW*, 11, 1910, pp. 97–108).

[2] Goodspeed (*INT*, p. 21) dismisses the imitation theory on the ground that 2 Thessalonians has too much characteristic Pauline vigour. McGiffert's opinion that a third of 2 Thessalonians is more or less a close reproduction of the first Epistle (*Enc. Bib.*, IV, col. 5044) cannot be sustained, although the striking character of many of the literary resemblances is undeniable. Cf. B. Rigaux, *Les Épîtres aux Thessaloniciens* (1956), pp. 138, 139.

[3] Cf. J. E. Frame, *1 and 2 Thessalonians (ICC*, 1912), p. 49.

[4] It must never be forgotten that the apostle Paul was a missionary pastor, and every good pastor knows the value and indeed the necessity of repetition.

(i) *Pseudonymous authorship.* The theory that 2 Thessalonians is a forgery must be rejected,[1] not only because of the inherent difficulties of the thesis already mentioned, but also for want of a sufficient motive. The writer, moreover, portrays too intimate an acquaintance with the Thessalonian situation (cf. iii. 6–15).

(ii) *Co-authorship.* Since Timothy and Silvanus are linked with Paul in the introduction, it has been suggested that they wrote the second Epistle and that Paul added his own autograph (iii. 17).[2] But since Paul would not have signed anything that he did not assent to, this theory does nothing to remove the supposed difficulties over subject-matter. Further, Timothy and Silvanus are also mentioned in 1 Thessalonians, which led F. C. Burkitt[3] to propose that Silvanus drafted both Epistles and Paul added 1 Thessalonians ii. 18 and 2 Thessalonians iii. 17. But it is difficult to see what problems such a theory solves. It would seem to create more difficulties than Pauline authorship since it would then be necessary to find a reason for such unparalleled procedure on the part of Paul. On the other hand such procedure cannot be ruled out as impossible.

(iii) *The divided-church theory.* A. Harnack[4] suggested that 1 Thessalonians was sent to Gentiles and 2 Thessalonians to Jews. But the evidence for a divided church at Thessalonica is negligible. The greater use of the Old Testament in the second Epistle has been dealt with above, where it was pointed out that this could equally well be designed for Gentile readers. But the most damaging criticism of this theory is that it is inconceivable that Paul the universalist would have fostered such a

---

[1] W. Michaelis, *Einleitung*, p. 231, discusses the improbability from a psychological point of view of a pseudonymous author affixing the statement of iii. 17. G. Milligan, *Expositor*, vi, ix, p. 448, thinks it quite unlikely that a church which possessed one authentic Epistle of Paul would have been prepared to receive a fictitious Epistle also addressed to them.*

[2] F. Spitta, *op. cit.*, pp. 109 ff., maintained that Timothy was the real author. He is answered by W. Lock (*HDB*, iv, p. 748), who rejects the theory because it raises more difficulties than it solves. Cf. also G. Milligan, *1 and 2 Thessalonians* (1908), p. xc; G. G. Findlay, *Expositor*, vi, ii, pp. 251 ff.

[3] *Christian Beginnings* (1924), pp. 129–133.

[4] 'Das Problem des zweiten Thessalonicherbriefs', *Sitzber. d. Berl. Akad. d. Wiss.* (1910), pp. 570–578. Cf. also Lake, *Earlier Epistles*, p. 89. M. Dibelius maintained that 2 Thessalonians was sent to a special group within the church (cf. *A Fresh Approach*, p. 152).

division by separate letters to the rival sections.[1] Furthermore, in
1 Thessalonians ii. 13–16 the Judaean church is actually held up to the
Gentiles as an example, which militates against a separate Jewish fac-
tion. In any case, since the letters have identical superscriptions,[2] Paul
must have taken a considerable risk that the letters might have gone to
the wrong section of the church. Harnack's recourse is to suppose that
some indication of its Jewish destination has dropped out of the second
Epistle, but this only demonstrates the weakness of the theory.[3]

(iv) *The private-public theory.* In order to account for the more formal
tone of 2 Thessalonians Dibelius suggested that this Epistle was designed for public reading. But this is no solution, since in the first
Epistle (v. 27) Paul commands that his letter should be read to all the
brethren, which can only mean that it too was designed for public reading.[4] Commenting on this view, Neil points out that it 'brings the
circle round again after a century of speculation almost to the traditional view. It is so near indeed that it seems hardly worth making
any distinction at all'.[5]

II. THE ORDER OF THE EPISTLES

It has traditionally been assumed and is still widely accepted that
2 Thessalonians followed 1 Thessalonians, but it has been maintained by

[1] There is, moreover, not the slightest hint in 1 Thessalonians that it is not addressed to the whole church (cf. Goguel, *Introduction*, IV, i, p. 334).
[2] If Knox's theory (*Marcion and the New Testament*, pp. 62 ff.) that originally
1 and 2 Thessalonians were combined, and when they were later separated the
superscription of 1 was added to 2, is correct, this argument would not apply. But
see p. 576 n. 2.
[3] Eduard Schweizer ('Die zweite Thessalonicherbrief ein Philipperbrief?' in
ThZ, I, 1945, pp. 90 ff.) attempts to maintain that 2 Thessalonians was originally
a Philippian Epistle, so accounting for Polycarp's reference to Paul's Epistles
(plural) to the readers (i.e. Philippians and 2 Thessalonians). Cf. W. Michaelis'
criticism of this theory (*Einleitung*, p. 231, and *ThZ*, 1945, pp. 282 ff.). It is improbable that a change of place name in the address would occur at a time considerably later than Paul and earlier than Marcion (who knew this Epistle as sent
to the Thessalonians).
[4] M. Dibelius (*A Fresh Approach*, p. 152) suggests that the second Epistle was
intended for a special circle of the church and was written shortly after the first.
E. J. Bicknell, *The First and Second Epistles to the Thessalonians* (1932), p. xxiii,
suggests that the church was no more than a house community, but this gives
insufficient weight to the 'great company' of Acts xvii. 4.
[5] *Thessalonians* (MC), p. xxvi.

some scholars[1] that a reversal of the order solves some of the difficulties. The main reasons in support of this view may be grouped in the following way.

1. The traditional order is attributed not to historical precedence but to size, the longer Epistle naturally coming first. Yet this would not seem a valid conjecture in view of the fact that these Epistles are found in the traditional order in Marcion's Canon, which does not appear to have been dictated by consideration of length.[2]

2. There is nothing in 1 Thessalonians to give rise to a misunderstanding such as is answered in 2 Thessalonians. Yet according to 2 Thessalonians ii. 5 and iii. 10 it was probably Paul's oral instruction which had been misunderstood.

3. The eschatology of 2 Thessalonians is said to be more 'crude and Judaistic' than 1 Thessalonians. The fallacy of any difference in the two Epistles in this respect has already been demonstrated, but quite apart from this fallacy it is not easy to imagine that Paul would have changed his mind about eschatological ideas within the short interval that must have separated the two Epistles.[3]

4. In 1 Thessalonians the trials are said to be over while in 2 Thessalonians they are still ahead. But since 1 Thessalonians was designed partly to encourage, some trials were still expected in the future.

5. In 2 Thessalonians the internal difficulties are spoken of as if they are a new development of which the writer has just heard, whereas in 1

---

[1] Among whom are J. C. West (*JTS*, xv, 1913, pp. 66–74); T. W. Manson (*BJRL*, March 1953, pp. 438 ff.); and F. J. Badcock, *The Pauline Epistles and the Epistle to the Hebrews in their Historical Setting* (1937), pp. 46–52. It was suggested first by Grotius (1640) and was taken up by Baur (1845).*

[2] J. Knox (*Philemon among the Letters of Paul*, 1935, and *Marcion and the New Testament*) and C. L. Mitton (*The Formation of the Pauline Corpus of Letters*, 1955) maintain that in Marcion's Canon both 1 and 2 Corinthians and 1 and 2 Thessalonians were respectively treated as single Epistles and that the original order in which Marcion found the Epistles was, with the exception of Ephesians, in order of length. Even if this is substantially correct it tells us nothing about the relative order of the parts, although as it is hardly likely that the order would have been reversed when they were treated separately it may be reasonably assumed that in the Canon which Marcion took over from the Church 2 followed 1.

[3] F. J. Badcock, *op. cit.*, p. 47, explains the more Jewish character of 2 Thessalonians as due to the more predominantly Jewish character of the church in its earlier stages. 1 Thessalonians, he thinks, was sent later when the church had become more Gentile. J. C. West, *op. cit.*, p. 70, uses the same argument, but appears to overlook the very early Gentile element in the Thessalonian church.

Thessalonians everything is familiar. 1 Thessalonians iv. 10–12, for instance, is said to need 2 Thessalonians iii to be understood. Yet difficulties of the type mentioned in these passages must have been fairly constant in early Christian experience.

6. It is claimed that the words of 1 Thessalonians v. 1 ('you have no need that I write to you concerning times and seasons') would be more relevant if it followed 2 Thessalonians ii. But it would be quite relevant before if they had already been orally instructed.

7. The wording of 1 Thessalonians iv. 9, 13, v. 1, where the subject-matter is introduced with the phrase 'now concerning', is, on the analogy of 1 Corinthians, alleged to indicate matters raised in a previous communication. But the phrase could, of course, equally well be used if Paul had heard of the problems orally from Timothy and Silas.

8. The personal note at the end of 2 Thessalonians in which Paul draws attention to the mark which he affixes to every letter is said to be significant only in a first letter. But if subsequent to sending 1 Thessalonians Paul has heard of spurious letters sent in his name (as 2 Thes. ii. 2 may well suggest) this personal note would be particularly pointed.

9. It has been suggested that Timothy on his visit to Thessalonica would probably have taken a letter and if 2 Thessalonians was written before 1 Thessalonians the former might have been that letter. Not only is this purely conjectural but it seems to be ruled out by the fact that Timothy is mentioned as co-sender not carrier.[1]

It will be seen that none of these reasons is convincing taken separately, nor is the cumulative effect any more so. On the other hand there are certain positive considerations which would seem to favour the traditional order. (1) The problems which are dealt with in 1 Thessalonians seem to have deepened. (2) There appear to be references to a previous letter in 2 Thessalonians (ii. 2, 15; iii. 17),[2] which must refer either to 1 Thessalonians or to a lost Epistle. It is more natural to take the former[3] than

---

[1] F. J. Badcock, *op. cit.*, pp. 46 ff., maintains that Titus took 1 Thessalonians and Timothy 2 Thessalonians. But Timothy is included in the greeting of both. Cf. Feine–Behm, *Einleitung*, pp. 134, 135.

[2] Of these references ii. 2 is not weighty, for the words 'as from us' point to some letter falsely purporting to be Paul's; but the false teachers would perhaps be more likely to attempt a fabrication when a genuine letter had already been received to serve as a pattern.

[3] None of these references is conclusive for a previous genuine letter, for ii. 15, the only one which might imply such a letter with much probability, could per-

the latter view, since there is no hint of such previous correspondence in 1 Thessalonians. (3) It is difficult to see how the warm personal reminiscences in 1 Thessalonians ii. 17–iii. 6 could have followed 2 Thessalonians, which lacks any such references.[1] (4) The words 'as we charged you' (1 Thes. iv. 11) suggest that the tendency towards idleness was reproved in the early period of the church's history (i.e. by oral rebuke), and if so it is more natural to find such a statement in the earlier letter. This latter point is not, however, of much weight since the charging could conceivably have been done by letter (perhaps 2 Thessalonians). But the evidence as a whole is more in favour of the traditional order than the reverse.

III. OCCASION AND PURPOSE

Assuming the correctness of the traditional order we may conclude that 1 Thessalonians was not as effective as Paul had hoped in dealing with the problem of idleness and that fresh misunderstandings had arisen concerning the *parousia*.

It may be that the Thessalonians had received a pseudo-Pauline letter claiming that the day of the Lord was already past (cf. 2 Thes. ii. 2) and such an impression obviously needed to be corrected. This may also be the reason for his personal signature (iii. 17). On the other hand it is not easy to conceive of any Macedonian having the audacity to forge a letter in Paul's name while Paul was still working in the adjoining province.[2] It may be that Paul had merely conjectured such a possibility to account for the Thessalonians' misunderstanding of his teaching. In any case it is indisputable that in some way wrong teaching

haps refer to the present letter (i.e. 2 Thes.). Cf. W. Michaelis, *op. cit.*, pp. 228, 229. C. Masson, who disputes the authenticity of 2 Thessalonians, regards the absence of any reference in 1 Thessalonians to an earlier letter to be inexplicable if the order is reversed (*op. cit.*, p. 11). He also finds difficulty in the passage from one eschatology to another, the same difficulty, in fact, which leads him to reject 2 Thessalonians.

[1] The personal details in i. 7, 8 in which Paul acknowledges the widespread influence of the readers' example have been thought to demand an interval of some duration, which would be more probable if the first Epistle came later (cf. Badcock, *op. cit.*, p. 47). In any case, most scholars admit that an interval of only a few months separated the two Epistles, and this would hardly be sufficient to make much difference. In all probability Paul had himself spread the news.

[2] Cf. Jülicher-Fascher, *Einleitung*[7] (1931), p. 65.

was being associated with Paul's name and he seizes the opportunity in the second Epistle to deny it.[1]

Paul's reason for setting out the signs which must precede the coming of Christ is not to give a literal picture of events but merely to answer the readers' immediate misunderstanding. Since there must first be apostasy and the rise of the man of lawlessness, the day of the Lord cannot already have come and neither was it as imminent as those supposed who had given up work on the strength of it. These latter are strongly reprimanded (iii. 11).

The second Epistle must have been written soon after the first since it almost certainly preceded Paul's next visit to Thessalonica (Acts xx. 1 ff.). During this period Corinth is the only place where Paul is known to have been with Timothy and Silas and it is reasonable to conclude that 2 Thessalonians was written from there. Some scholars have disputed this opinion and have proposed Ephesus as equally suited to the evidence.[2] But there is no mention of Silas at Ephesus in Acts xix, and Timothy is there associated with Erastus.

CONTENTS OF 1 THESSALONIANS

I. GREETING (i. 1)

Silvanus and Timothy are associated with Paul in this greeting.

II. PRAYER OF THANKSGIVING (i. 2–10)

This is a typical form of thanksgiving in which Paul rejoices that the readers had not only themselves received the gospel but had become an example to the Christians of Macedonia and Achaia.

III. PAUL'S MISSION WORK IN THESSALONICA (ii. 1–16)

The apostle next asserts his purity of motive, his independence of any maintenance from them and his strong affection towards them. He appeals to his own exemplary behaviour among them and is thankful

---

[1] C. Spicq, *Les Épîtres Pastorales* (1947), p. 17, points out that the papyri bear testimony to the current practice of letter writers of appending their own conclusion in their own handwriting to their secretary's copy.

[2] Cf. McNeile-Williams, *INT²* (1953), pp. 127, 128.

for their ready acceptance of the Word of God and for their sufferings in its cause at the hands of the Jewish persecutors.

IV. PAUL'S PRESENT RELATIONSHIP TO THE THESSALONIANS (ii. 17–iii. 13)

Paul tells them of his great desire to visit the church and of his rejoicing over them. Then he mentions the mission of Timothy and the good news received from Thessalonica, which leads to a further expression of thankfulness for all the joy they have brought to him. This promotes a prayer for their future growth.

V. PRACTICAL EXHORTATIONS (iv. 1–12)

The apostle next deals with problems of Christian living.

1. He exhorts to moral purity, reminding the believers that God has not called them to uncleanness but to consecration (iv. 1–8).

2. He exhorts them to brotherly love, acknowledging that they have already shown such love but encouraging them to increase it (iv. 9, 10).

3. He exhorts them to honest activity so as to gain the respect of outsiders (iv. 11, 12).

VI. THE PAROUSIA (iv. 13–v. 11)

A problem had arisen over those who had died before the coming of the Lord and those who are grieving are comforted by the sure hope that all Christians, whether living or dead, would share in this event (iv. 13–18). Another problem was the time of the *parousia*, and Paul makes clear that this is unknown. But he uses its suddenness as a spur to sober living in the present (v. 1–11).

VII. FURTHER PRACTICAL EXHORTATIONS (v. 12–22)

These are of a general character embracing social responsibilities (live at peace, admonish the idle, help the weak, etc.) and spiritual obligations (rejoice, pray, give thanks, quench not the Spirit, hold fast the good, etc.).

VIII. CONCLUSION (v. 23–28)

Paul offers another prayer for the readers and exhorts them to pray for him. After a general greeting he closes by ordering them to read the letter to all the brethren.

CONTENTS OF 2 THESSALONIANS

I. GREETING (i. 1, 2)

As in 1 Thessalonians, Silvanus and Timothy are linked with Paul in the greeting.

II. THANKSGIVING (i. 3, 4)

Though apparently rather more formal, this prayer is as full and affectionate as the corresponding thanksgiving in the first Epistle. Paul is even boasting about the readers to other churches.

III. THE JUDGMENT OF GOD (i. 5–10)

Those who at present are afflicting them must expect retribution, but the believer's consolation is in his expectancy of the *parousia*.

IV. PRAYER (i. 11, 12)

After the digression about judgment, Paul reverts to his usual prayer for his converts that they may be worthy of their calling.

V. THE PAROUSIA (ii. 1–12)

There are still problems concerning this and Paul explains certain facts: (1) the day of the Lord has not yet come as some were maintaining; (2) the man of lawlessness must first be revealed; (3) he will be overcome by the Lord Jesus at His coming; (4) but he will before his overthrow deceive and delude many who will be condemned for their unbelief.

VI. FURTHER THANKSGIVING AND PRAYER (ii. 13–17)

By way of contrast Paul rejoices in God's choice of the Thessalonians, and this leads him to exhort them to hold fast to what they have been taught. His prayer is that they may be comforted and established.

VII. EXHORTATIONS (iii. 1–15)

1. As in 1 Thessalonians, Paul requests prayer on his behalf and this leads to an assurance of the faithfulness of God (iii. 1–5).

2. He next deals with problems of discipline, especially the disorderliness resulting from idleness, which is not becoming among Christians (iii. 6-13).

3. A similar disciplinary problem is the case of the man who disobeys Paul's instructions, but who is not to be regarded as an enemy (iii. 14, 15).

VIII. CONCLUSION (iii. 16–18)

This is noteworthy because it contains the apostle's sign-manual to guarantee the authenticity of the letter.

ADDITIONAL NOTES

566. Because of the occurrence of περί in iv. 9, 13, v. 1, 12, C. E. Faw (*JBL*, LXXI, 1952, pp. 217 ff.) suggested that Paul in these chapters may be answering points raised in a letter from the church.

567. [1] Several scholars have contended for a later dating for 1 Thessalonians to allow time for the situation reflected in the Epistle to develop (cf. those listed by W. G. Kümmel, *INT*, 1965, p. 183). W. Schmithals (*ZNTW*, 51, 1960, pp. 230 ff.) argues that the opponents with whom Paul is dealing here, are the same Jewish Gnostic Christian type as resisted in Galatia and Corinth, which leads to a similar dating for these Epistles.

568. In a study of 1 Thessalonians, K.–G. Eckart (*ZTK*, 58, 1961, pp. 30–44) suggests that difficulties arise in the text after ii. 12. He takes ii. 17–iii. 4 as part of a letter of recommendation for Timothy and regards iii. 6–10 as part of a second letter. He thinks iii. 11–13 could belong to either. His division of the Epistle is as follows: i. 1–ii. 12, ii. 17–iii. 4, iii. 11–13 comprises the first letter followed a few weeks later by a second letter consisting of iii. 6–10, iv. 13–v. 11, iv. 9, 10a, v. 23–26, 28. The same problems of compilation met in connection with other partition theories confront this theory, for it is difficult to imagine why anyone would want to join the two letters and add homiletical material. Kümmel (*INT*, p. 185) criticizes Eckart's redactional theory. Cf. also K. Thieme's analysis of the structure, *Festschrift O. Michel* (1963), pp. 450–458.

570. [2] Cf. Kümmel, *INT*, pp. 189 f., for support of authenticity for 2 Thessalonians.

571. [3] As a result of a study of the use of κατέχον in 2 Thes. ii. 6, 7 and a comparison with Qumran literature, O. Betz concludes that 2 Thes. ii does not owe its origin to Qumran, but to Daniel ix and xi (*NTS*, 9, 1963, pp. 276–291). Although he considers the concept to be pre-Pauline, he does not consider that this militates against the authenticity of the letter.

573. Some scholars assume non-authenticity of 2 Thessalonians, as for instance K.–G. Eckart (*ZTK*, 58, 1961, pp. 30–44), who asserts that it cannot be doubted. R. J. Peterson (*JBL*, LXXXVII, 1968, pp. 359 f.), in reviewing C. H. Giblin's book, *The Threat to Faith. An exegetical and theological re-examination of 2 Thess 2* (1967), complains about this author's methodology because Pauline authorship is assumed.

For other writers who support the non-authenticity of 2 Thessalonians, see Kümmel, *INT*, p. 188, where the views of Bultmann, Schoeps, Fuchs, Bornkamm and Beker are mentioned. But Kümmel himself thinks 2 Thessalonians more intelligible if written by Paul (*INT*, p. 189). For the opposite opinion, cf. W. Marxsen, *INT* (1968), pp. 43, 44.

574. [1] A recent hypothesis which suggests that 2 Thessalonians was written in Paul's name has been proposed by P. Day (*ATR*, xlv, 1963, pp. 203–206). He considers that a different approach is found in 2 Thessalonians from what is found in 1 Cor. ix and 1 Thes. iv. 11, 12 on the subject of financial support for the ministry. His idea is that 2 Thessalonians was to prevent a professional clergy. But this theory reads more into 2 Thessalonians than is justified.

576. [1] Kümmel (*INT*, p. 186) rejects the change of order on the grounds that 1 Thes. ii. 17–iii. 10 must be part of the first letter. For a recent advocacy of a change of order in 1 and 2 Thessalonians, cf. R. Gregson (*EvTh*, xxvi, 1966, pp. 76–80) on the grounds of the greater maturity of 1 Thessalonians.

CHAPTER NINETEEN

THE PASTORAL EPISTLES

The Epistles to Timothy and Titus have long been known as the Pastoral Epistles,[1] but this designation is not strictly correct because they cannot be called manuals of pastoral theology. The name, however, is a convenient one to distinguish the group. These Epistles have been more assailed than any of Paul's other letters and it will therefore be necessary to discuss in some detail the question of their authenticity. Before considering the case against the Pauline authorship the testimony of the early Church will be considered in order to show clearly that attacks against the authenticity were unheard of until the modern period.

I. THE AUTHENTICITY OF THE EPISTLES

a. The traditional view

(i) *The internal claims of the Epistles.* In spite of the modern tendency to disregard the greeting in each of the three Epistles, the claim of Pauline authorship must surely be given some weight. To say this is not to preclude all further discussion. But those who deny Pauline authorship must at once accept these Epistles as pseudonymous, and this immediately creates problems of its own in view of the absence of any clear parallel which can be cited in support from early Christian practice. Only two other instances have come down to us of epistles issued pseudonymously in the name of Paul.[2] The Epistle to the Laodiceans is clearly spurious since it has no early Greek attestation and since it did not appear in the Latin church until the fourth century. The so-called Third Epistle to the Corinthians which circulated separately for a time in the Syrian church and was apparently even regarded as Scripture is known to have originated in the *Acts of Paul*, whose spurious pro-

---

[1] First used by D. N. Berdot (1703) and popularized by Paul Anton (1726).

[2] The spurious correspondence between Paul and Seneca (fourth century) is not included because these letters do not possess the New Testament epistolary form. They are certainly not attempts to mould Pauline letters on canonical patterns (cf. M. R. James, *The Apocryphal New Testament*, pp. 480 ff.). For a fuller discussion of epistolary pseudepigraphy, see pp. 671 ff.

duction Tertullian records (*De Baptismo*, 17). This is not impressive evidence for early Christian practice and until more evidence is forthcoming the defenders of Pauline authorship may rightly claim that the statements in the opening part of each Epistle are contributory data in support of authenticity.

(ii) *The external evidence.* This last consideration gains considerable weight in view of the external attestation for the Epistles, which is as strong as that for most of the other Epistles of Paul, with the exception of 1 Corinthians and Romans. There are a number of similarities in language between these Epistles and Clement's Epistle to Corinth and this would appear to be strong evidence in favour of authenticity. But the evidence has been differently interpreted by some who have maintained a second-century origin of the Pastorals, since *ex hypothesi* 1 Clement must have preceded and therefore have been used by the author of the Pastorals (cf. Streeter,[1] Harrison[2]). Others have not considered the similarities close enough to constitute proof of literary dependence either way (cf. Oxford Society of Historical Theology[3]). There are indications that the Epistles were known and used by Polycarp,[4] Justin, Heracleon and others, while by the time of Irenaeus they were definitely regarded as Pauline.[5] Theophilus alludes to their being inspired. This is impressive evidence in support of authenticity,

---

[1] *The Primitive Church* (1929), p. 153.

[2] *The Problem of the Pastoral Epistles* (1921), pp. 177 f. For the reverse opinion, cf. Sir R. Falconer's *Pastoral Epistles* (1937), p. 5.

[3] *The New Testament in the Apostolic Fathers* (1905), pp. 37 ff.

[4] A. E. Barnett, *Paul becomes a Literary Influence* (1941), pp. 182–184, challenges the view that the Pastorals were included in Polycarp's Corpus of Pauline letters, but his reasoning is purely subjective. Having already placed the Pastorals in the period subsequent to Polycarp he accounts for the apparent citations by an appeal to the common use of paranesis. By this means any external evidence may be nullified in the interest of a presupposed theory. There can be no doubt that Polycarp knew and used these Epistles (cf. A. Harnack, *Die Briefsammlung des Apostels Paulus*, 1926, p. 72).*

[5] Cf. J. H. Bernard, *The Pastoral Epistles* (1899), pp. xiv, xv; and J. D. James, *The Genuineness and Authorship of the Pastoral Epistles* (1906), pp. 5–24, for a full discussion of the external evidence. Dibelius, *Die Pastoralbriefe*[3] (1955), p. 2, denies the Polycarp references, but Jeremias, *Die Briefe an Timotheus und Titus* (1953), p. 4, maintains them. It is significant that F. Schleiermacher, who denied the authenticity of 1 Timothy only, maintained that where critical suspicions are established the testimony of the Ancients can hardly be preserved (*Über den Sogenannten ersten Brief des Paulus an den Timotheus*, 1807, pp. 16–19). Cf. also Muratorian Canon.*

but two other considerations are claimed to offset this evidence so completely that it is often stated that uncertainty existed in the early Church over the reception of these Epistles.[1]

The first evidence brought forward against the early reception of these Epistles is Marcion's Canon, which contained only ten Pauline Epistles. The assumption often made from this is that Marcion did not know them and therefore could not include them. But this line of argument would carry considerably more weight if we had no evidence of Marcion's propensity to reject any books which did not support his contentions.[2] His treatment of the Gospels is illuminating, for he rejected Matthew, Mark and John and mutilated Luke on no other grounds, it would appear, than his own preconceived notions.[3] Certainly the Church as a whole did not support him in these contentions and we have no warrant for assuming that it supported his approach to the Pastorals. Tertullian,[4] in fact, expressly states that Marcion rejected them, but in any case we cannot take Marcion's Canon as reflecting the orthodox attitude of his own time towards their reception.[5] It is not difficult to imagine that Marcion would not have been partial to the statement that the 'law is good' (1 Tim. i. 8) since he rejected the Old Testament altogether. Nor would he have taken too kindly to the allusion to 'oppositions of falsely called science' (1 Tim. vi. 20) since he used this very term to describe his own writings. But some scholars are not prepared to accept such an explanation of Marcion's omission of the Epistles on the ground that if he had known

---

[1] As for example by J. N. Sanders, p. 13 in *Studies in Ephesians*, edited by F. L. Cross (1956).

[2] Cf. Tertullian's statement (*Adv. Marc.* v. 1). This does not agree with C. L. Mitton's claim that Marcion received a Canon consisting of only ten Paulines (cf. *The Formation of the Pauline Corpus of Letters*, pp. 38 f.).

[3] Some scholars have disputed that Marcion mutilated Luke because of his strong protestations to the contrary, cf. P. Carrington, *The Primitive Christian Calendar* (1952), p. 46. But why a heretic like Marcion should be given greater credence than Tertullian is mystifying. The secret may lie in the fact that Carrington regards Marcion euphemistically as 'puritanical and evangelical'.

[4] *Adv. Marc.* v. 21. Tertullian is clearly perplexed over Marcion's rejection of the Pastorals and yet his acceptance of Philemon. He can suggest only that Marcion's aim was to carry his editing process even to the number of Paul's Epistles.

[5] It is noteworthy that according to Jerome (preface to his Commentary on the Epistle to Titus) Basilides, like Marcion, rejected these Epistles altogether. While Tatian, although rejecting some of Paul's Epistles, nevertheless defended Titus. Cf. Godet's (*INT*, p. 567) comments on Jerome's statement.

them he could easily have cut out the offending passages as he did in Luke's Gospel.[1] Yet it is difficult to see what use these Epistles in a mutilated state would have been to Marcion had he included them. Since Marcion's evidence is therefore not conclusive for the non-existence of the Epistles or at least the non-acceptance of them in his time, it cannot outweigh the very considerable early attestations in their favour. If we supposed that Marcion was ignorant of the Epistles, their subsequent rapid and undisputed acceptance as the genuine works of Paul would become completely inexplicable.[2]

Another line of evidence which is claimed to support an early uncertainty about the reception of the Pastoral Epistles is the Chester Beatty Papyri from which they are missing. The Codex of the Pauline Epistles (P46), which is generally dated about the middle of the third century, has not been wholly preserved. The end part in which the Pastorals would naturally fall is not extant but many scholars reckon that the original codex when complete could not have contained them, basing their opinion on calculations of how much space the remaining books would take. But quite apart from the fact that we cannot be certain that the scribe did not write smaller in the latter part of the codex when he saw that space was getting limited or else added additional

---

[1] E. J. Goodspeed maintains the earlier contention of F. C. Baur that the Pastorals were in fact designed as anti-Marcionite documents (cf. *INT*, pp. 327–330).

[2] If the use of the Pastorals by Polycarp is allowed, it is inconceivable that his contemporary, Marcion, was entirely ignorant of them, especially in view of Polycarp's contact with the Roman church (while Anicetus was bishop). Although this visit was almost certainly subsequent to Marcion's death it must have been prepared for by earlier correspondence. There is nothing in the manner of Polycarp's citations from the Pastoral Epistles to suggest recently published works. Indeed, it is most difficult to conceive of a disciple of the apostle John (cf. Tertullian, *De praescriptione*, 32 and Jerome *Catal. sacr. eccl.*, 17) readily accepting and using Pauline Epistles which were not authentic and which were not introduced until the rise of Marcionism (c. AD 140). Cf. E. C. Blackman, *Marcion and his Influence* (1948), pp. 52 ff. Goodspeed, *INT* (p. 344), goes as far as to suggest that the supposed use of the Pastoral Epistles in Ignatius and Polycarp must be understood the other way round in view of the historical situation reflected, but this is inconceivable in view of the very widespread use of them as authentic Pauline Epistles, nor is there any intelligible reason why an imitator of Paul would have echoed the language of Ignatius or Polycarp. This quite untenable view is also advocated, although in a slightly modified form, by P. N. Harrison (*Polycarp's Two Epistles to the Philippians*, 1936, pp. 241 ff.). Cf. also A. E. Barnett, *op. cit.* (1941), pp. 182–184. But all these scholars prejudge the evidence by presupposing a date for the Pastorals subsequent to Polycarp's Epistle.

sheets at both beginning and ending to accommodate the additional Epistles,[1] we cannot conclude that the extant remains of the Chester Beatty Papyri are necessarily a true indication of the state of the Canon in Egypt in the third century. The very fact that all that remains comprises some fragments of a codex containing the Gospels and Acts, most of one containing Paul's Epistles and parts of one containing the Apocalypse, is a sufficient indication of the precariousness of this method of argument. It is not the Pastorals alone that would be suspect but all the other books of the New Testament which are not represented in the papyri. Moreover, the early patristic evidence shows widespread use of these Epistles even earlier than the date of these papyri.

The disputants of Pauline authorship cannot therefore appeal to external evidence to show the slightest doubt about the authenticity of these Epistles in the Christian Church from the earliest times. But the defenders of Pauline authorship can not only claim the unquestioned support of antiquity but can point out the not inconsiderable fact that no-one ever questioned it until the early nineteenth century. If the grounds of objection are as overwhelming as they are claimed to be some adequate reason must be given for the extraordinary lack of insight on the part of Christian scholars over so long a period. It is often claimed in mitigation of this situation that it was not until the advent of nineteenth-century criticism that reason was allowed to challenge the sacredness of the canonical *status quo*. But there is no justification for assuming that modern criticism is in any better position than the early Church to pronounce on Pauline authorship. Indeed it is a reasonable assumption that had there been grounds for any doubts they would have made themselves known to some inquisitive minds in the early period when it would have been relatively easy to check up on any uncertain traditions.[2] We conclude therefore that the challengers of Pauline authorship of the Pastoral Epistles virtually take up a position in which they declare that the external evidence cannot be trusted. We turn next to consider the internal objections in detail.

---

[1] Cf. Jeremias, *op. cit.*, p. 4; J. Finegan, *HTR* (1956), p. 93.

[2] The external attestation to the Pastorals should be compared with the New Testament Antilegomena, over which some doubts were at an early period entertained, and which were again called in question by certain Reformation leaders. The complete absence of any positive criticism of the authenticity of these Epistles raises a very serious objection against non-authenticity theories which must be fairly faced by their advocates.

b. The case against Pauline authorship

There are four main divisions under which the objections may be grouped—historical, ecclesiastical, doctrinal and linguistic.

(i) *The historical problem.*[1] All three of the Pastoral Epistles contain historical allusions to the life of Paul and his associates and the following data emerge. (1) Timothy has been left at Ephesus to have charge of the church there, while Paul moves on to Macedonia (1 Tim. i. 3). (2) Similarly at some time Titus has been left in Crete (Tit. i. 5) for the same purpose. In this case the evidence demands that Paul himself had visited Crete. In writing to Titus he requests him to spend the winter with him in Nicopolis (generally assumed to be the city of that name in Epirus). (3) Paul refers to Onesiphorus seeking him out in Rome (2 Tim. i. 16, 17) which suggests that at the time of writing this letter he was in Rome. It is conclusive that he had been there. He is clearly now a prisoner (i. 8, 16, cf. iv. 16). He requests Timothy to bring him his cloak which he has left behind at Troas, informs him of Erastus' residence at Corinth and Trophimus' illness at Miletus in such terms that suggest recent happenings (iv. 13, 20).

From these data it has been concluded that it is impossible to fit these Epistles into the framework of the Acts history. There have been various attempts[2] to do this but most scholars reject these attempts as impossible. We are left therefore with three possibilities.

1. We may regard them as authentic but belonging to a period outside the Acts history, in which case it will be necessary to postulate a second Roman imprisonment with a period of release and extended missionary journeys separating the two. Many scholars reject this solution because there is no hint of it in the Acts and because it has inadequate support in early Christian history. It is therefore regarded as a desperate expedient designed to maintain at all costs the authenticity of the Epistles.[3]

[1] For the corresponding arguments in support of Pauline authorship, see pp. 596 ff.

[2] Cf. e.g. the theory of Vernon Bartlet, *Expositor*, VIII, v (1913), pp. 28–36, 161–167, 256–263, 325–347. 2 Timothy is assigned to the second Roman imprisonment, 1 Timothy to the period immediately subsequent to Paul's Ephesian ministry, and Titus after Paul's visit to Crete on his voyage to Rome. Cf. also F. J. Badcock, *op. cit.*, pp. 115–133.

[3] This has been very forcibly maintained by P. N. Harrison, *The Problem of the Pastoral Epistles* (1921), pp. 102 ff. In his article in *NTS* (May 1956), pp. 250–261, P. N. Harrison describes it as a 'legend'. This approach is widely adopted (cf. J. N. Sauders' remark in *Studies in Ephesians*, p. 12).

2. We may go to the other extreme and pronounce the whole of these Epistles to be the work of some fiction writer who, wishing to impress upon the Church their Pauline origin, invented these historical allusions to create the appearance of verisimilitude much in the way that the authors of other spurious works known from early Christian history have done (e.g. the *Acts of Paul*).[1] This line of criticism was popularized by the Tübingen school of F. C. Baur and was later powerfully advocated by Holtzmann,[2] whose views are in general adhered to by Dibelius.[3] But this view does not commend itself to many scholars who reject the Pauline authorship of the Epistles as a whole.

3. Because of the apparently genuine character of some at least of these historical allusions a third explanation has been postulated. There are, it is suggested, genuine Pauline notes incorporated in the letters, which are nevertheless in bulk the work of a later admirer of Paul. He came into possession of these notes and wished to preserve them in this way for posterity. Far from condemning such a practice we ought to be profoundly grateful for his foresight in preserving these precious Pauline remnants. This, in one of its developed forms, is the theory of Harrison,[4] whose original arrangement of the Pauline notes was in five separate fragments which he claimed could be separately fitted into the Acts history. Subsequently,[5] on embracing Duncan's theory of an Ephesian imprisonment[6] (see pp. 472 ff.), he reduced the number to three, one in Titus (iii. 12–15) and two in 2 Timothy (1) iv. 9–15, 20, 21a and 22b, and (2) i. 16–18, iii. 10, 11, iv. 1, 2a, 5b–8, 16–19, 21b–22a. Of these the one to Titus was written from Macedonia and sent to Corinth just after Paul's severe letter to that church, while the first to Timothy was written a little later when Paul was at Nicopolis (to which he had already summoned Titus) and the second was Paul's swan-song written from Rome at the close of the imprisonment mentioned in Acts (xxviii. 30, 31). There have been many other theories of a similar nature to Harrison's

[1] Cf. for instance, Goodspeed's opinion, *INT*, p. 331.
[2] *Die Pastoralbriefe* (1880). Holtzmann's views were ably criticized by E. Bertrand, *Essai Critique sur l'authenticité des Epîtres Pastorales* (1887).
[3] *Die Pastoralbriefe* (1955, revised by H. Conzelmann). So also Goodspeed, Knox and Barnett.
[4] *The Problem of the Pastoral Epistles* (1921).
[5] In his article on the Pastoral Epistles in the series 'Important Hypotheses Reconsidered', *ET*, LXVII, iii (1955), p. 80.
[6] *St. Paul's Ephesian Ministry* (1929).

but there has been a notable lack of agreement among them, demonstrating the difficulty found by scholars in assessing genuineness.[1]

The 'fragment' or 'genuine-note' theory claims to have advantages over the fictional approach in that it dispenses with the improbability of a fiction writer composing these historical allusions with so accurate a Pauline stamp upon them.[2] On the other hand it claims the advantage over the traditional view in that it dispenses with the postulation of a second Roman imprisonment and confines the history of Paul to the period covered by the Acts.

(ii) *The ecclesiastical problem.*[3] There are references in the Epistles to certain ecclesiastical arrangements which are claimed to be too advanced for the time of Paul, and this line of criticism is based on four main considerations. First, it is maintained that Paul had no interest in organizing the Church. There does not appear to be any uniformity in his churches according to his earlier Epistles but on the contrary there is evidence that he did not favour official organization. In the Corinthian church, where no officials are mentioned, the charismatic ministry is all-important. The passing reference in Philippians i. 1 to bishops and deacons is regarded in a very general sense as contrasted with the rigid use in later periods.[4] The Pastorals are claimed to belong to a later period when each church had its officials and the whole procedure was carefully controlled.

Secondly, it is supposed that the elders reflected in the Pastorals' ecclesiastical set-up were essentially charged with the task of passing on the tradition (Easton calls them tradition-bearers). In view of this it is difficult to see, according to Easton, how Paul could have sanctioned such a system before the tradition was itself fixed. In other

[1] For a concise résumé of the principal fragment theories see Goguel, *Introduction au Nouveau Testament*, IV, ii, p. 500 n. Among the authors he mentions are Hitzig, Weisse, Hausrath, Krenkel, Pfleiderer, McGiffert, Renan, Bacon, Clemen and Moffatt, but no two agree on all the same passsages.

[2] Goodspeed rejects the fragment theory on the ground that the personal touches are no more than would be expected in a work of fiction (*INT*, p. 341).

[3] For the arguments for Pauline authorship, see pp. 599 ff.

[4] Ramsay, 'Historical Commentary on the Epistles to Timothy', *Expositor*, VII (1906), viii, p. 17, takes, on the contrary, the view that Phil. i. 1 supports the view that the Pastorals' type of ecclesiastical set-up existed in Paul's time. See pp. 599 ff.

words the function of these officials is too advanced for the time of Paul.[1]

Thirdly, it is supposed that the situation reflected in the Pastorals would require some time to develop, especially in view of 1 Timothy iii. 6 where Timothy is warned not to appoint a new convert. This suggests an established church and would therefore be much more relevant to a later age than to the time of Paul.[2]

Fourthly, the position of Timothy and Titus themselves is said to approximate to the monarchical episcopate of the early second century. They are to appoint elders, which means that they possess a superior authority. They are generally to exercise jurisdiction in the affairs of the church in a manner which suggests that they are in sole charge. This again, according to disputants of Pauline authorship, favours a later date for the Epistles.[3]

Another objection is that drawn from the heresies reflected in the Pastorals. These are claimed to belong to a time when the Gnostic heresy which reached its climax in the second century was much more developed than it was in the time of Paul. Easton calls it a 'coherent and powerful heresy' which was threatening the existence of the Church.[4] As compared with the Colossian heresy it is said to be more organized and a distinction is drawn between Paul's method of dealing with it and the method adopted in the Pastorals. There he gives the constructive Christian answer to the errors but here he only denounces them and urges Timothy and Titus to have nothing to do with them. Some support may possibly be found for the contention that the Pastorals' heresy shows alignment with second-century Gnosticism in the following data. Both tended to express themselves in rigid asceticism on the one hand and licence on the other; both tended to deny the resurrection of Christ; both showed a speculative approach to the Old Testament. The Gnostic insistence on the need for mediation between God and man, springing from its dualistic philosophy, may also be reflected in the Pastorals' assertion of the sole mediatorship of Christ. These objections which may be answered on other grounds are given lesser importance than formerly by advocates of non-Pauline authorship because of the increasing modern recognition that Gnosticism in its

[1] Cf. B. S. Easton, *The Pastoral Epistles* (1948), p. 226.
[2] M. Dibelius, *Die Pastoralbriefe*[3] (1955), p. 44, considers the requirement impracticable in Paul's lifetime.
[3] Cf. Easton, *op. cit.*, p. 177.   [4] *Op. cit.*, pp. 1, 2.

incipient form must have stretched back into the first century and may have been operative in the time of Paul.[1] Yet there is still a school of thought which considers these Epistles to represent an anti-Marcionite polemic, especially in view of the mention of 'antitheses' in 1 Timothy vi. 20, which was the title of Marcion's book, and the connecting of this with Gnosis in the same passage.[2]

(iii) *The doctrinal problem.*[3] The real problem here is the mixture of what is Pauline and what is claimed not to be. Most scholars admit that there are many traits of Pauline theology, but these are often regarded as mere echoes of Pauline phrases culled from his authentic letters. But the main objection is raised against the absence of characteristic Pauline doctrines and the presence of what may be termed a more stereotyped approach to Christian doctrine. Examples of the former are the great doctrines of the Fatherhood of God, the mystic union of the believer

---

[1] Cf. the discussion on Jewish-Christian heterodoxy in J. Daniélou's *Théologie du Judéo-Christianisme* (1958), pp. 68–98, in which he shows that the later Gnosticism was contributed to by earlier Jewish heterodoxy. In fact he speaks of a Jewish Gnosis. E. F. Scott (*The Pastoral Epistles*, 1936, p. xxix) admitted that early Gnosticism used Jewish ideas although in its more developed state it became strongly anti-Jewish. Oscar Cullmann strongly denies a primitive development from early Judaistic Christianity to a later universalistic Hellenistic Christianity. He maintains on the contrary that both existed in the primitive Church and appeals to the background of the Qumran texts as supporting evidence ('The Significance of the Qumran Texts for Research into the Beginnings of Christianity', *JBL*, 74, 1955, pp. 213–226, reprinted in *The Scrolls and the New Testament*, edited by K. Stendahl, 1958, pp. 18–32).

For the most recent and fullest discussion of Gnosticism cf. R. M. Wilson, *The Gnostic Problem* (1958), who distinguishes three main stages: a pre-Gnostic, a Gnostic proper, and later developments. In the first he places Philo and the Dead Sea Scrolls, in the second the second-century sects, and in the third Manicheism and Mandaism (pp. 97, 98). The heresies of the New Testament literature he classes as Gnosticism in embryonic form. In this respect no distinction can be made between the Colossian heresy and that of the Pastorals. For a discussion of the New Testament heresies as a whole from traces found in Colossians, Ephesians, the Pastorals, 1 John, Rev. i–iii, Jude and 2 Peter, and in Ignatius and the Didache outside the New Testament, cf. Goguel, *The Birth of Christianity* (1953), pp. 393–432.*

[2] Cf. Goodspeed (*INT*, p. 338); W. Bauer, *Rechtgläubigkeit und Ketzerei im ältesten Christentum* (1934), pp. 228 ff; F. D. Gealy, *1 and 2 Timothy and Titus* (IB, 1955), pp. 372 ff.; D. W. Riddle and H. Hutson, *New Testament Life and Literature* (1946), p. 205. See further discussion on p. 618.

[3] For the arguments for Pauline authorship, see pp. 604 ff.

with Christ and the work of the Holy Spirit.[1] These are not in such prominence in the Pastorals as in the earlier Epistles of Paul, and the assumption is therefore made that Paul could not have written these three Epistles without giving expression to such fundamental doctrines. Easton,[2] for instance, considers that the writer's conception of God is remote and that the doctrine of the Spirit meant little to him. Where Pauline doctrines do occur they are sometimes claimed to be un-Pauline as, for instance, the mention of justification by grace in Titus iii. 7. Easton[3] takes this to mean the fruit of baptism which is attained by God's 'power'.

Greater importance is attached to the recurrence in the Pastorals of such terms as 'the faith', 'the deposit', 'and sound teaching', in such a way as to suggest that the tradition of Christian doctrine has now become fixed.[4] There is nothing more to add. Indeed, it has become conventionalized in the form of 'faithful sayings' (of which the Pastorals contain five, but the other Pauline Epistles none) and of Christian hymns epitomizing accepted doctrine (as for instance 1 Tim. iii. 16; Tit. ii. 11–14). But it is denied that the apostle Paul with his amazingly creative mind could ever have descended to such a stereotyped level. This condition of affairs, according to critics of Pauline authorship, fits better the state of the Church at the end of the first century when the transmission of the apostolic doctrine was all-important.

(iv) *The linguistic problem.*[5] The occurrence in the Pastorals of a large number of words unique in the New Testament and a large number of words shared by non-Pauline books of the New Testament but not found elsewhere in Paul has been a major factor for many scholars in rejecting the authenticity of the Epistles.[6] The evidence has been marshalled by Harrison who brings out clearly that the linguistic peculiarities of these Epistles are without parallel in Paul's other writings.[7] This goes not only for the vocabulary but also for the style. Harrison,[8] for instance, collects a group of 112 particles, pronouns and prepositions, which he maintains are a fair indication of style, which occur in the

[1] Cf. Moffatt, *ILNT* (1912), p. 412.   [2] *Op. cit.*, pp. 25, 12.
[3] *Op. cit.*, *ad loc.* Cf. also E. F. Scott, *op. cit.*, *ad loc.*
[4] Cf. Easton, *op. cit.*, p. 203.
[5] For the arguments for Pauline authorship see pp. 607 ff.
[6] 175 Hapaxes (words used nowhere else in the New Testament) and 130 non-Pauline words shared by other New Testament writers.
[7] *The Problem of the Pastorals* (1921).   [8] *Op. cit.*, pp. 36, 37.

other Pauline Epistles but which are absent from the Pastorals. By means of elaborate statistical tables he suggests that the Pastorals do not belong to the same linguistic series as the other Epistles.[1] He concludes on this score that they are not likely to have been written by Paul.

Harrison[2] further uses statistics to suggest that the language of the Pastorals is the language of the second century. He does this by means of a comparison of the vocabulary with that of the apostolic Fathers, apologists and second-century non-Christian writers. He points out that most of the non-Pauline words found in the Pastorals are in fact in use (he claims in common use) in the second century. If his deductions are correct, it would certainly constitute a serious difficulty for those who maintain the Pauline authorship of these Epistles. The validity of these considerations is discussed elsewhere, but it must here be stated that the majority of those who favour the non-Pauline authorship of the Epistles are swayed more by linguistic considerations than by any of the objections mentioned above.[3]

The cumulative effect of these objections is claimed by many scholars to rule out the possibility that Paul was the writer of the Epistles. All the objections are, on the other hand, alleged to be overcome by the theory that a later Paulinist in the early second century produced these Epistles to meet the needs of his own time. This accounts for his re-

[1] P. N. Harrison based his data on a words-per-page method. This had previously been used by W. P. Workman in an attempt to demonstrate that Shakespeare's language showed similar variations to Paul's, *ET*, VII (1896), pp. 418 ff.

[2] *Op. cit.*, pp. 67–86.

[3] Cf., for instance, A. M. Hunter, *Interpreting the New Testament* (1951), p. 64. Many, however, put greater emphasis on the ecclesiastical situation (e.g. E. F. Scott, *Literature of the New Testament*, p. 193). There have been cycles of emphasis in the history of the criticism of the Pastorals. The earlier critics before Baur gave stylistic differences pride of place in their attack on the authenticity, but the Tübingen school switched to historical objections. For a brief historical survey of the period, cf. E. Reuss, *History of the Sacred Scriptures of the New Testament*[5] (Eng. Tr. 1884). Later, through Holtzmann's attack, linguistic considerations again took precedence. A growing suspicion about the usefulness of word-counts may well shift the emphasis in yet another direction. But cf. the article by K. Grayston and G. Herdan, 'The Authorship of the Pastorals in the Light of Statistical Linguistics', *NTS*, 6 (October 1959), pp. 1–15, for the most recent attempt to use statistics in the service of non-Pauline authorship. By means of type-token mathematics these writers conclude that the Pastorals have a very different style from the other Paulines and on the assumption that 'the style is the man' they think it improbable that Paul should change his style to such an extent according to his circumstances.

flecting the ecclesiastical, doctrinal and linguistic atmosphere of his own age, while the incorporation of genuine Pauline notes (if these be admitted) and the frequent use of phrases culled from the other Pauline letters supplies the Pauline atmosphere and accounts for their ready acceptance in the Christian Church as the work of Paul.[1]

c. The case for Pauline authorship

So formidable have the objections appeared to many scholars that there is an aptitude to write off as special pleading or as undue submission to the demands of the Canon any attempt to answer them. Yet a not inconsiderable number of recent scholars have supported authenticity in spite of these objections.[2] The case for Pauline authorship must of necessity be presented largely on the defensive since the onus of proof rests with the challengers. If each objection can be answered in a satisfactory way in agreement with the self-claims of the Epistles to be written by Paul, the authenticity may be regarded as established. Only if in the course of investigations facts come to light which appear conclusive for non-authenticity will the onus of proof pass to the defenders.

(i) *The historical problem.* It has been pointed out that the 'fiction' and 'fragment' theories of these Epistles have arisen because of difficulties many scholars find in accepting the second Roman imprisonment hypothesis. The main ground of this objection is the absence of any allusion to such renewed Pauline activity in the Acts of the Apostles. In other words it is an argument from silence and it implies that only what is included in the Acts record can be considered authentic. But there are many details in Paul's life which the Acts does not record, as the list of Paul's sufferings in 2 Corinthians xi conclusively shows. But can it be maintained that the second imprisonment hypothesis is a legend which owes its origin only to the necessity of finding an historical situation for the Pastoral Epistles when they were once accepted into the Canon? Harrison claims that there is no early external evidence of this tradition of further Pauline activity and when the evidence does

---

[1] Those who, like E. J. Goodspeed, reject the 'genuine-note' theory consider that the pseudonymous production was designed to meet contemporary needs. Goodspeed mentions four of these: lack of efficient Church organization, the menace of the sects, the undermining of the authority of the Old Testament and the misuse of Paul (by Marcion): *INT*, pp. 327–330.

[2] Cf. Wohlenberg, Lock, Meinertz, Thörnell, Schlatter, Spicq, Jeremias, Simpson. See the present writer's commentary on *The Pastoral Epistles* (*TNT*), p. 15.

occur it is an inference with no solid basis.[1] He disclaims Clement of Rome's allusion to the apostle preaching to the boundary of the West as evidence of a release because he interprets this boundary as Rome itself.[2] It may not be conclusive that Clement is referring to Paul's mission to Spain,[3] but the reality of the Spanish mission does not affect the release hypothesis. Paul may easily have changed his mind and returned to the East instead of going to the West as he had originally planned. The scanty patristic evidence of a Spanish visit has been alleged to be no more than deduction from the notices of Paul's intentions in Romans xv. 24, 28.[4] But does this vitiate Paul's further activity in the East? Are we entitled to regard a theory which is demanded by the internal evidence of the Pastorals themselves as legend on the ground that there is no external attestation of such a release? There is no justification for such a conclusion unless there is positive evidence which renders the hypothesis untenable. But there is certainly no evidence to show that Paul did not do any further missionary work, and this must leave the possibility that he did.

But can we proceed from possibility to probability? To answer this question it is necessary to study the grounds on which the apostle was sent to Rome as a prisoner. According to Acts xxvi. 32 Agrippa concluded that Paul might have been set free if he had not appealed to Caesar, and there is no hint that the proconsul Festus disagreed with this judgment. On the contrary Acts xxv. 20 states clearly that Festus was at a loss to know how to deal with Paul's case through lack of understanding of the religious charges laid against him. In his report to the Emperor he could not have been too unfavourable to Paul and

---

[1] *Op. cit.*, pp. 102 ff.

[2] M. Dibelius, *op. cit.*, p. 3, points out that 1 Clement gives no indication of a period of release following an imprisonment. He therefore claims Clement as evidence for a single Roman imprisonment. It should be noted that Clement's statement (v. 5-7) is not intended as a complete record of the closing period of Paul's life, for he is citing Peter and Paul as recent examples of endurance after giving many Old Testament examples of suffering as a result of jealousy. He mentions Peter's many trials and Paul's seven times in bonds but gives no indication at all of their location or chronology.

[3] J. Weiss, *The History of Primitive Christianity* (Eng. Tr. 1937), I, p. 390, argued that there could be no doubt that the author of 1 Clement believed that Paul had carried out his mission to Spain.

[4] Cf. P. N. Harrison, *op. cit.*, p. 108, for a confident assertion that the Muratorian Canon's allusion to Paul's Spanish visit may be traced to the same Romans passage. But Zahn, *INT*, iii, p. 64, considered this notion to be inconceivable.*

unless some further charge were later brought against him it is a fair assumption that the normal course of Roman justice would have resulted in his release. We have already noted (see pp. 528 ff.) that when he wrote Philippians Paul was at least mindful of the possibility of an early release and if this was sent from Rome it would be strong corroborating evidence of the release theory.[1] Another consideration which must be given due weight is the strange abruptness of the end of Acts. Unless Acts was written before the end of the imprisonment which it mentions at its close it is difficult to believe that the author would have concluded his story without mentioning the martyrdom which crowned Paul's labours, if this martyrdom in fact came at the end of the imprisonment.[2] The ending of Acts seems rather to favour than to oppose the theory that Paul's activity is not yet at an end.

If then the second Roman imprisonment theory be admitted as a possibility it remains to suggest the course of events in which Paul was involved. Unfortunately only the most tentative suggestions can be made, owing to the scantiness of the data. The Pastorals tell us that Paul again visited Asia (Troas, 2 Tim. iv. 13, and Miletus, 2 Tim. iv. 20) although it is not necessary to suppose that he visited Ephesus on the strength of 1 Timothy i. 3. But he urged Timothy to stay there when he was *en route* for Macedonia. At some time he paid a visit to Crete, where he left Titus, but his main activity appears to have been in Macedonia and Greece. From the Captivity Epistles we may surmise that

[1] For a discussion of the probabilities of the release theory, cf. A. Schlatter, *The Church in the New Testament Period* (1926, Eng. Tr. 1955), pp. 232–239; F. R. M. Hitchcock, 'The Pastorals and a Second Trial of Paul', *ET*, XLI (1930), pp. 20–23; F. Spitta, *Zur Geschichte und Litteratur des Urchristentum* (1893), i, pp. 106 f.; W. Ramsay, *St. Paul the Traveller and Roman Citizen* (1920), pp. 356 ff.

[2] E. J. Goodspeed, *INT*, p. 189, attempts to offset this argument by suggesting that the author did not mention Paul's death because this would have seemed like comparing his martyrdom with that of Christ. But this suggestion is most unconvincing. For the view that the Acts was written as a defence–brief for Paul's trial at Rome, cf. D. Plooij, *Expositor*, VIII, viii (1914), pp. 511 ff., and VIII, xiii (1917), pp. 108 ff.; G. Duncan, *St. Paul's Ephesian Ministry* (1929), p. 97. See also Michaelis, *Pastoralbriefe und Gefangenschaftsbriefe*, pp. 155–158, for a discussion favourable to the release theory. He makes a special point of the chronology of Paul's life supporting the release hypothesis on the ground that Acts xix. 1–xxviii. 31 represent about nine years dating from AD 53 and this would leave about three years unaccounted for until AD 64, the traditional date of Paul's martyrdom. But not all would agree with this chronology and it is too inconclusive to make the basis of a strong argument. It may, however, be used to corroborate other evidence.

he visited the Lycus valley, no doubt on the same occasion as he urged Timothy to remain at Ephesus, and that he paid his promised visit to Philippi. If the external evidence[1] which suggests that Paul suffered martyrdom in Rome under Nero is correct, he may have been rearrested in the western districts of Macedonia or Epirus (which is mentioned in Titus iii. 12) and taken to Rome.

(ii) *The ecclesiastical problem.* These Epistles contain references to elders, bishops, deacons and widows, and the qualifications which are required of those who hold office are set out in some detail. Most of these qualifications are of a rather obvious moral kind. But are the instructions concerning the appointments to these offices the kind that Paul was likely to give? This question may be answered in the affirmative on the following grounds. There is strong ground for concluding that Paul himself appointed elders in the statement of Acts xiv. 23 that Paul and Barnabas on their return from their first missionary journey appointed elders in every church (i.e. the South Galatian churches). To get over this difficulty B. S. Easton[2] considered the Acts reference to be an anachronism, but this method of dealing with unacceptable evidence does not commend itself. The fact that Paul appointed elders at the very commencement of his missionary labours is strong evidence of his interest in orderly Church government. The comparative absence of reference to the elder-system elsewhere in his Epistles is admittedly rather perplexing, but the church at Philippi, with its bishops and deacons, supports the allusions to the elder-system in the Acts. The further statement that Paul sent for the elders of the Ephesian church when he was passing through Miletus (Acts xx. 17) is indirect evidence that he had sanctioned their appointment if he had not himself appointed them.[3] In the Epistle to the Ephesians, which as we have seen was probably sent to the churches of Ephesus and the Lycus valley, Paul refers to the existence of 'pastors and teachers' in the Church, and these would approximate to the office of elder whose function was both pastoral and didactic.

---

[1] Cf. Zahn, *INT*, iii, p. 63, who cites the *Acts of Peter* which clearly imply a visit by Paul to Spain, sandwiched between two imprisonments. But the first three chapters of the *Acts of Peter* have been thought by some to be an excerpt from the *Acts of Paul* (cf. M. R. James, *The Apocryphal New Testament*, p. 306).

[2] *Op. cit.*, p. 226.

[3] B. S. Easton, *op. cit.*, p. 226, suggests that this also is an anachronism. The approach to the ecclesiastical position in the Pastorals must inevitably be influenced by the view adopted regarding the historicity of Acts.

It is not, therefore, true to say that Paul had no interest in Church organization, although he certainly did not insist on uniformity. If there is some ground for supposing that Paul was an ecclesiastical architect during the course of his missionary labours, it would be foolish to suppose that at the end of his life with the knowledge that he must soon hand over to younger men Paul had shown complete disinterestedness in the way in which his successors were to set about the task. With his vast experience of missionary statesmanship Paul of all men was best qualified to lay down stipulations for the appointment of officers and to give general instructions regarding Church order. He would have been the most shortsighted of men if he had not done so.

The criticism that the elder-system is too advanced for the time of Paul is based on two misconceptions. It assumes that the main function of elders was to transmit the tradition and to a certain extent this must have been true in the later stages of Church development. But this does not rule out the possibility that Paul himself would have seen the need for such authorized transmission. It was of the utmost importance that the teaching of the Church should be entrusted to capable people and for this reason the bishops are to be apt to teach. Only so could the continuity of the doctrine be maintained and it is impossible to believe that the apostle Paul under the guidance of the Spirit of God had no thought for the future. A further misunderstanding arises from the view that by the end of Paul's life he had no conception of a body of doctrine to be passed on. Since he had himself received the early apostolic tradition it is completely unrealistic to suppose that Paul with his creative mind could never have conceived of any form of fixation of doctrine. He must have recognized that no church could hope to survive without some kind of tradition-bearers. The Pastoral Epistles depict an apostle fully alive to this challenge.[1]

But does the situation reflected in the Pastorals suggest a long-established Church, which clearly could not have existed in the time of Paul? It must be borne in mind that the church of Ephesus would have been established about nine or ten years by the time Paul writes to Timothy and the advice not to appoint novices would not be entirely without meaning in such a church. In primitive communities the choice

[1] On this subject, cf. the present writer's *The Pastoral Epistles and the Mind of Paul* (1956), pp. 21 ff., and his commentary, *op. cit.*, pp. 24 ff. Cf. A. Sabatier's opinion that conservation was more urgent than innovation for Paul the apostle (*Paul*, 1903, p. 270).*

of officials is necessarily strictly limited in the opening stages of the work, but in a church of the size of Ephesus, where Paul had himself worked for three years, it must have been an injunction of practical significance that no novice be appointed to office. It is important to notice that this particular request is confined to Ephesus; the position at Crete, which was undoubtedly a more recently established church, was quite different and so Paul omits the mention of novices. This in itself is an indirect confirmation of the historical veracity of the account, which it is difficult to imagine came from the pen of a Paulinist after the end of the century. Presumably when Paul and Barnabas appointed elders in the Galatian churches on their first missionary journey they must have selected 'novices' in the sense of recent converts, for they had no other choice. The same must have applied to the original elders at Ephesus, but the continuation of the practice would not be advisable as Paul recognizes in writing to Timothy. We cannot agree therefore that the Church situation in the Pastorals demands a time long after the life of Paul.

The view that Timothy and Titus represent bishops of the type of Ignatius and his time cannot be sustained.[1] They certainly possessed greater authority than the elders which they were to appoint and the general functions which they are called upon to perform were all exercised by the Ignatian-type bishops, but that does not establish them as belonging to a later age. All that is necessary to account for all the facts is to regard them as apostolic delegates.[2] There is no evidence for the view that Timothy has been appointed the metropolitan of the Ephesian community, nor that Titus was appointed to a similar position in Crete. They are told to perform the kind of function which they had both exercised earlier in Macedonia and Achaia. They are to act essentially as representatives of the apostle to the Gentiles.

There are other reasons why this view must be rejected. The instructions regarding bishops in 1 Timothy and Titus would be strange indeed if monarchical bishops were in existence at the time the Epistles were written. There is no suggestion that one bishop only should be appointed in each church. In Titus i. 5 ff. the word 'bishop' is used interchangeably with 'elder' and since elders are to be appointed in every town there is no question here of monarchical government.

[1] Easton, *op. cit.*, p. 177; F. Gealy, 1 *and* 2 *Timothy and Titus* (IB), 1955, pp. 344 ff.
[2] W. Lock, *The Pastoral Epistles* (1924), p. xix, calls them 'Vicars Apostolic'. Cf. E. F. Scott, *The Pastoral Epistles* (1936), p. xxix.

Moreover, there is no provision for the continuation of the bishop's office as would be expected in a second-century production.

There can be only one conclusion to this examination of the ecclesiastical evidence. It does not take us beyond the time of Paul.[1] But does the same apply to the heresies alluded to in the Epistles? To answer this question it will be necessary first to outline the data which are available from the letters themselves.

1. The main characteristic of the teaching was not so much its falseness as its irrelevance. Paul refers to myths and endless genealogies (1 Tim. i. 3–7), to striving about words and wrangling (1 Tim. vi. 3–5), to godless chatter and 'antitheses' (1 Tim. vi. 20). It seems that the main stock-in-trade of these teachers was empty platitudes which Paul did not even consider it worth while to refute.[2]

2. The teaching had many Jewish characteristics as may be seen from 1 Timothy i. 7, Titus i. 10, 14, iii. 9. The Cretan myths are specifically described as Jewish and it is reasonable to suppose that those at Ephesus were of a similar type. There were also disputes about the law although it is not clear what form these took. The absorbing interest in genealogies gives some indication in view of contemporary Jewish speculations centred mainly around the Pentateuchal genealogies.

3. There were ascetic tendencies which Paul connects with 'doctrines of demons' (1 Tim. iv. 1–5). These tendencies took two forms, celibacy and abstinence from food. Since in this passage in 1 Timothy the future tense is used it may be that these tendencies had not as yet arisen in these churches, but abstinence from food had certainly arisen already at Colossae. It is also possible that the opposite tendency towards licentiousness may be threatening since Paul urges Timothy not to participate in other people's sins but to keep himself pure (1 Tim. v. 22).

4. The only doctrinal error to which Paul definitely refers in these Epistles is the denial of the resurrection hope. Two men, Hymenaeus and Philetus, have swerved from the truth by maintaining that the

[1] Cf. the conclusion of F. B. Clogg, INT[3] (1948), p. 118. Sir W. M. Ramsay maintained that the organization in these Epistles is not advanced beyond that of the church at Philippi (Expositor, VII, viii, p. 17).

[2] F. H. Colson, in an article on 'Myths and Genealogies—A note on the polemic of the Pastoral Epistles', JTS, XIX (1918), pp. 265–271, considers these terms (with 'antitheses') were current in the Greek world of intellectuals and were essentially frivolous. Colson admits, however, the possibility of incipient Gnosticism in the Pastorals' heresy.

resurrection is already past, which meant in effect that they denied the Christian doctrine of resurrection altogether (2 Tim. ii. 17 ff.). A man named Hymenaeus is coupled with an Alexander in 1 Timothy i. 20 as having made shipwreck concerning the faith, but no details are given of the cause. It is at least possible that the same Hymenaeus is being referred to, but we cannot be certain.

It can hardly be maintained that these data point to a 'coherent and powerful heresy'. If anything the allusions suggest just the reverse. Wrangling and chatter are not the usual marks of coherence, nor are idle speculations. The fact that only one matter of doctrinal importance is mentioned, and even that only by way of illustrating godless chatter, does not lead us to suppose that the apostle took these teachers very seriously. His main concern was that Timothy and Titus should not waste time over them. This explains why he does not consider it worth while to answer their contentions as he did the false teaching being propagated at Colossae.[1] Another reason why Paul here denounces instead of refutes is that he is writing to those who were well enough versed in Christian doctrine to do the refuting themselves where necessary. In Colossians Paul is confronting the members of the church who may well have been perplexed over the specious arguments of the false teacher or teachers and who had no-one capable of giving the Christian answer. It is fallacious to compare Paul's references to the heresy in Colossians with those in the Pastorals and then to deny the latter to Paul because he does not treat them in the same way.

Few scholars would now maintain with any certainty that the writer of the Pastorals is combating developed Gnosticism.[2] Yet if the hypothesis of a second-century Paulinist writing in the name of Paul is maintained it follows that some connection with Gnosticism must be traced. It would not be too much to say that the alignment of the Pastorals with second-century Gnosticism might never have

---

[1] Many scholars consider that this change of attitude towards heresy is further proof of non-Pauline authorship. A. McGiffert (A *History of Christianity in the Apostolic Age*, 1897, p. 402) goes so far as to allege that to ascribe the Pastorals' references to the false teachers to Paul is to do him an injustice. Cf. McNeile, *INT*[2] (1953), p. 193. J. Moffatt (*ILNT*, pp. 408 f.), who considered that the writer was dealing vaguely with incipient syncretistic Gnosticism, suggested that the vagueness may be partly due to his desire to avoid anachronisms. But a far more reasonable explanation is that the teaching combated was still at an early and therefore vague stage.

[2] See p. 593 n.1.

occurred had it not been for the need to postulate satisfactory motives for the author when the Pauline origin had once been denied.

(iii) *The doctrinal problem*. Since a good deal of weight is attached to the doctrinal differences between these Epistles and the other Epistles of Paul, this problem must be answered in detail.[1] First, the omission of the great Pauline themes will be considered. This problem may be stated as follows: Could the apostle Paul write three letters such as these without bringing in his characteristic doctrine of the Fatherhood of God or the believer's mystical union with Christ? Many scholars believe that he could not. Easton, as we have previously noted, considered that the conception of God in the Pastorals is one of remoteness. The majestic ascriptions in 1 Timothy i. 17 and vi. 15, 16, where He is described as King of the ages, King of kings, Lord of lords, the only Sovereign, invisible, immortal, contain a mixture of Jewish and Hellenistic terms which admittedly produce an impression of greatness which might suggest unapproachability. But it would not be a fair representation to claim that this sense of the greatness and majesty of God exhausts the writer's conception. If the title 'Father' occurs only in the opening greeting the writer's conviction of the fatherly goodness of God and of His own approach to man is many times reiterated. He is called Saviour, a title which elsewhere in Paul is used only of Christ, which points to His redeeming activity (1 Tim. i. 1, ii. 3, iv. 10; Tit. i. 3, ii. 10, iii. 4). He desires men to be saved and to come to a knowledge of the truth (1 Tim. ii. 4) and His grace has appeared for this purpose (Tit. ii. 11 ff.). His goodness and lovingkindness is described in Titus iii. 4; His providential provision in 1 Timothy vi. 17; His bestowal of gifts upon His servants in 2 Timothy i. 6, 7; His provision of an inspired revelation in 2 Timothy iii. 16; and His gracious commissioning of Paul to preach the gospel (1 Tim. i. 1, 2 Tim. i. 1, Tit. i. 3). These are not signs of remoteness and this objection must be overruled.

The claim that Paul's characteristic doctrine of mystical union with Christ, and particularly his often-repeated phrase 'in Christ', is absent from the Pastorals at least in the usual Pauline sense is not as real an objection as Easton supposed. The phrase is used nine times in the Pastorals, although it is applied in these instances to qualities, whereas

[1] For a fuller discussion, see the writer's *The Pastoral Epistles and the Mind of Paul* (1956), pp. 24 ff.

Paul's usual method is to apply it to persons. But this distinction appears too fine to be substantiated, for qualities 'in Christ' are unintelligible apart from the persons possessing them being 'in Christ'.[1] Moreover, the phrase is used in the earlier Epistles in much the same way as in the Pastorals. Life.in Christ Jesus (as in 2 Tim. i. 1, iii. 12) is paralleled in Romans vi. 11, 23, viii. 2.

The fewness of the references to the Holy Spirit cannot be construed as evidence of the writer's lack of interest in His activity, for otherwise the writer of the Epistle to the Colossians and 2 Thessalonians would be involved in the same charge (both Epistles mention the Spirit once only). All the allusions to the Spirit's activity in the Pastorals would be readily endorsed by Paul and this is a sufficient answer to the objection (cf. 1 Tim. iv. 1; 2 Tim. i. 14; Tit. iii. 5).

No great weight can be attached to the alleged use of Pauline words, such as 'justified' and 'grace', with changed meanings. In Titus iii. 7 there is certainly no exposition of doctrine as is found in the Epistle to the Romans, and yet there is nothing in this statement inconsistent with Paul's earlier exposition. The difficulty would seem to exist more in the mind of the objector than in the mind of Paul.[2]

Of greater importance is the charge that the writer of the Pastorals lives in an age when doctrine has become formalized, when Paul's dynamic conception of 'faith' has become fixed into 'the faith', representing a body of received teaching. When this is linked with other terms such as 'sound teaching' and the 'deposit' it may seem that we have passed out of the apostolic age into an age when conservation is all-important and when Christianity may be thought of as involving acceptance of an official body of doctrine. But Philippians i. 27, Colossians ii. 7 and Ephesians iv. 5 are sufficient evidence that Paul was not

---

[1] The Christology of the Pastorals must be recognized as early. As radical a scholar as H. Windisch has acknowledged this fact and has aligned the Pastorals' Christology with the Thessalonian letters (ZNTW, 1935, pp. 213–238). W. Michaelis, Pastoralbriefe und Gefangenschaftsbriefe (1930), pp. 99, 100, considers the frequency of the phrase 'in Christ' favours the Pauline character of the Pastorals. For an attempt to contrast Paul's use of the phrase with the use in Ephesians, cf. J. A. Allan, 'The "In Christ" Formula in Ephesians', NTS, 5 (October 1958), pp. 54–62. This article contains no reference to the Pastorals' occurrences, although if Allan's method of interpretation were valid it would have some bearing upon them. See pp. 489, 506 for further details.*

[2] On the omission of characteristic doctrines, it should be noted that there is an absence of the 'Church' in Rom. i–xv and of 'faith' in Rom. viii.

unused to speaking of 'the faith' in the same manner in which it is found in the Pastorals.[1] That there is so much concern to maintain 'soundness' of doctrine in these Epistles whereas the term is not found elsewhere in Paul's writings cannot be regarded as unPauline. It is the kind of metaphor which would naturally spring to the mind of one who had been dwelling on the gangrenous effects of the idle chatter of false teachers (2 Tim. ii. 17).

The incorporation of the five 'faithful sayings' and the Christian hymn in 1 Timothy iii. 16 requires some explanation. Can these citations be regarded as later forms developed for catechetical purposes? There can be little doubt that the need for formalized statements of doctrine became evident in the Church at a very early period. There are no intrinsic reasons for denying that such statements in a form easily remembered were in use in the apostolic age, but the real problem is whether Paul would have cited them. This is less problematic since it has been recognized that in all probability Paul cites current statements of doctrine in his other Epistles (e.g. Rom. i. 2–4; Phil. ii. 5 ff. and Col. i. 15 ff.). He appears to be citing a hymn in Ephesians v. 14 and there does not seem any fundamental objection to the view that he is doing so in 1 Timothy iii. 16.[2]

[1] Cf. also the reference in Rom. vi. 17 to the form of doctrine.

[2] If the authenticity of Ephesians is also denied this parallel would of course lose its point. But once admit its genuineness and the Pauline use of hymn citation is no longer improbable. Cf. Lohmeyer, *Der Brief an die Philipper* (1930), p. 91, n. 1, on the Philippian hymn. E. Norden, *Agnostos Theos*, 1913, pp. 250–263, discusses on stylistic grounds two liturgical passages in Pauline writings, Col. i. 12–20 and 1 Tim. iii. 16. Although he accepts the authenticity of Colossians, he groups 1 Tim. iii. 16 with the Roman doxology and assigns them to a date about the time of Marcion. But the fact that Colossians includes such a liturgical form is sufficient indication that this form was not foreign to Paul. Cf. also A. M. Hunter, *Paul and his Predecessors* (1940), pp. 14–40, for a careful discussion of pre-Pauline formulary elements and formulae. M. Goguel, *The Birth of Christianity* (1953), pp. 324 f., finds in 1 Tim. iii. 16 and Tit. ii. 11–14 an echo of Pauline formulae although he thinks the thought behind them is distinctly debased. But this is because he considers the doctrine of these Epistles as conventional and therefore 'deuteropauline'. J. A. T. Robinson has suggested that Paul cites a liturgical formula in 1 Cor. xvi. 20–24 (*JTS*, New Series IV, 1953, pp. 38–41). For a full account of New Testament references to liturgical fragments, cf. F. Cabrol and H. Leclercq, 'Reliquiae liturgicae vetustissimae' in *Monumenta Ecclesiae Liturgica*, vol. XI (1900–1902). See also vol. XII (1913), p. 121, for Pauline hymns. Cf. also J. N. D. Kelly, *Early Christian Creeds* (1950), pp. 1–29, for evidence that Paul had a due regard for teaching authoritatively transmitted.*

(iv) *The linguistic problem.* Since this is the objection which for most critics tips the balance against the Pauline authorship of the Pastorals it is important to see the problem in its right perspective. It must be studied against a background not only of Paul's own usage but also of the literary atmosphere in which he was brought up and which throughout his life he breathed. The occurrence of so many Hapaxes (175) in these three Epistles will certainly constitute a problem if Paul is allowed only a percentage increase in the number of new words he may be expected to use in any new writing. The basis of the objection brought by Harrison is that the Pastorals show a considerably greater number of these Hapaxes per page than any of the other Pauline Epistles, which while showing some variation nevertheless keep within a closely related and gradually ascending series.[1] But numerical calculations cannot with the limited data available from Paul's letters take into account differences of subject-matter, differences of circumstances and differences of addressees, all of which may be responsible for new words.[2] Although there is less reliance than at one time on the

---

[1] W. Michaelis, 'Pastoralbriefe und Wortstatistik', *ZNTW*, xxviii (1929), pp. 70 ff., strongly criticized P. N. Harrison for arranging his graphs in different orders, thus giving a false impression of ascending series.

[2] Several scholars since the publication of Harrison's book in 1921 have made detailed criticisms of his statistical arguments. Cf. Montgomery Hitchcock's two studies, 'Tests for the Pastorals', *JTS*, xxx (1928–1929), pp. 272–279, and 'Philo and the Pastorals', *Hermathena*, lvi (1940), pp. 113–135. Cf. also W. Michaelis, *ZNTW*, xxviii (1929), pp. 69–76, and F. Torm, 'Ueber die Sprache in den Pastoralbriefen' (*ZNTW*, 1918, pp. 225–243). G. Thörnell's *Pastoralbrevens äkhet* (1931) on Paul's literary method in the Pastorals was warmly commended by H. Lietzmann, *ZNTW*, xxxi (1932), p. 90, although he did not accept Thörnell's conclusions for Pauline authenticity. See also P. Gaechter in *ZkT*, 75 (1933), pp. 109 ff., and E. von Dobschütz in *TSK*, civ (1932), pp. 121 ff., for further assessments of Thörnell's arguments. For other arguments against Harrison's methods, cf. the present writer's *The Pastoral Epistles and the Mind of Paul* (1956), pp. 6 ff., and his commentary on *The Pastoral Epistles* (1958), pp. 212–228, and F. J. Badcock, *The Pauline Epistles and the Epistle to the Hebrews in their Historical Setting* (1937), pp. 115–133. B. M. Metzger's article 'A Reconsideration of Certain Arguments against the Pauline Authorship of the Pastoral Epistles', *ET*, lxx, 3 (December 1958), pp. 91–94, criticizes Harrison for failing to take account of the weight of criticism of his position and draws special attention to the opinion of the Cambridge statistician G. U. Yule (*The Statistical Study of Literary Vocabulary*, 1944) who considered that as a basis for statistical study samples of about ten thousand words long are necessary. In this event the Pastoral Epistles cannot supply sufficient data for the statistician. No weight is given to this point, however, in the article by K. Grayston and G. Herdan, *op. cit.*, *NTS*, 6 (October

mere computation of Hapaxes, yet the phenomenon of the Pastoral Hapaxes still exercises a subtle and powerful influence upon many minds, leading them to reject the Pauline authorship.

The contention of Harrison that the author of the Pastorals speaks the language of the second century, based largely on his investigation of the occurrence of the Hapaxes during that period, cannot be maintained for the following reasons. (1) Nearly all the words in question were known in Greek literature by the middle of the first century.[1] (2) Nearly half of them occur in the LXX, with which it may reasonably be supposed Paul was very well acquainted.[2] (3) Many of the Hapaxes occurring in the apostolic Fathers and apologists occur once only in those writings and cannot fairly be claimed as evidence of current usage.[3] (4) The appeal to the writers of the second century, including secular writers, to suggest the literary provenance of the Pastoral Epistles is not valid unless it can be shown that the words could not have been used in the first century, but this cannot be established.[4] The Hapaxes do not, in fact, offer any substantial grounds for maintaining that the author speaks the language of the second century any more than of the first.

There are also a considerable number of words which the Pastorals share with the other New Testament books but which are not found

1959), pp. 1–15. Yet they admit that statistics can do no more than establish differences. In other words, they cannot determine questions of authorship.*

M. Dibelius, although challenging the authenticity, admitted that the statistical[3] method was insufficient for disputing it (*Die Pastoralbriefe* 3, 1955, p. 3). Many of the new words are due to new subject-matter (cf. R. Parry, *The Pastoral Epistles* (1920), pp. cxi–cxxvi) or changed environment (cf. M. Hitchcock, 'Latinity in the Pastorals', *ET*, xxxix (1927–28), pp. 347–352, and E. K. Simpson, *The Pastoral Epistles* (1954), pp. 20, 21) or old age (cf. C. Spicq, *Les Épîtres Pastorales*, EB, 1948, p. cxii; G. Wohlenberg, *Die Pastoralbriefe*[3], 1923, p. 55, makes a comparison with Schiller and Goethe). It is significant that not long after the publication of Harrison's book, Harnack with acute observation commented on the former's extraordinary over-rating of the statistical-lexical method of investigation (*Die Briefsammlung des Apostels Paulus und die anderen vor-constantinisch christlichen Briefsammlungen*, 1926, pp. 74, 75).

[1] Cf. F. R. M. Hitchcock's 'Tests for the Pastorals', *JTS*, xxx (1929), p. 278.

[2] See the detailed lists in the present writer's *The Pastoral Epistles and the Mind of Paul*, pp. 39, 40.

[3] Cf. *The Pastoral Epistles and the Mind of Paul*, pp. 39, 40.

[4] Cf. M. Hitchcock, 'Tests for the Pastorals', *JTS*, xxx (1929), p. 278, and F. J. Badcock, *op. cit.*, pp. 115 ff.; see the writer's *The Pastoral Epistles and the Mind of Paul* (1956), p. 9.

elsewhere in Paul. Harrison applies the same methods to these and suggests that these too support his contention that the Pastorals' language is second century, because of the frequency of their occurrence in second-century writings. But the fact that they occur in other New Testament books shows that they were current also in the first century, and the only real difficulty (if such it is) is to find a reason for Paul's failure to use them elsewhere in his writings. But the difficulty vanishes altogether when once the notion that confines Paul's vocabulary to that used in the ten other Epistles is abandoned. Certainly these non-Pauline words shared with other New Testament writers can contribute nothing to the theory that the Pastorals' language is second century on the ground that the majority of them occur in the ecclesiastical writings of the second century, since the same line of argument would show that all the Pauline Epistles belonged to the same period.[1] The only conclusion to which these considerations can lead is that the language of all the Pauline Epistles including the Pastorals is the current language for the most part of both first and second centuries.

Other linguistic arguments brought by Harrison against the authenticity of the Pastorals are: (1) the noticeable absence from the Pastorals of characteristic Pauline words and characteristic groups of words; and (2) the use of Pauline words with different meanings and the use of different words to express thoughts found in Paul. But the words that Harrison appeals to in section (1) are words frequently used in other parts of the New Testament and indeed in the second-century writers and are not expressions peculiar to the apostle Paul. A reasonable explanation of their absence from the Pastorals is that Paul had no occasion to use them. His subject-matter led him to other words. Little importance can be attached to objection (2) since Paul himself frequently used words with different meanings, in which case any change of expression can hardly be evidence of non-Pauline authorship.[2]

But many writers who are prepared to concede the possibility of changes in Paul's vocabulary are reluctant to do so for Paul's style. The large number of particles, pronouns and prepositions which can be collected from the other Pauline Epistles but are absent from the Pastorals (Harrison[3] collates 112) seems to indicate a different hand.

[1] Cf. the writer's *The Pastoral Epistles and the Mind of Paul*, p. 41 (Appendix D).
[2] These two points are fully discussed in the writer's commentary, *op. cit.*, pp. 221 ff.
[3] *Op. cit.*, pp. 36, 37.

But this evidence is not quite as impressive as it at first seems, as Colossians and 2 Thessalonians have very few of them (less than twenty) and there is considerable variation within the other Pauline Epistles.[1] Harrison not only uses this evidence to support non-Pauline authorship but he compares a similar tendency to dispense with them in the apostolic Fathers from whose writings 21 are missing. But unfortunately for his argument, the Captivity Epistles of Paul lack no less than 59 of the same words, which should indicate on the basis of Harrison's method of deduction an even greater tendency to dispense with them within the other ten Pauline Epistles. Moreover, there are a number of Pauline particles, pronouns and prepositions which are found in the Pastorals and when these are taken into consideration it can be shown that these Epistles are not very different from some of the other Paulines. It may seriously be challenged whether this method of assessing style is a valid one. Harrison mentions also the absence from the Pastorals of many of Paul's characteristic uses of the article and of the particle ὡς, but these again are not uniform throughout his Epistles and it is evident that Paul's style was subject to considerable variation, no doubt owing to his mood of the moment.

d. The case against alternative theories

It is one thing to dispute an accepted position but quite another to provide an alternative solution which is free from the same kind of blemishes which are alleged to vitiate that position. The task of the defenders of Pauline authorship is not ended when the objections raised against it have been answered, however satisfactorily, for confirmatory support for the position adopted here may be found in an exposure of the weaknesses of alternative theories. The 'genuine-note' theory, as the most generally held alternative view, will be considered first and then the fiction theories.

(i) *Problems of compilation.* 1. The first objection arises from the strange procedure adopted by the so-called Paulinist author in the incorporation of the fragments. Why did he put most of the material in 2 Timothy, a short note in Titus and no genuine material at all in 1 Timothy? Since according to Harrison's revised reckoning there were

---

[1] F. Torm, *ZNTW* (1918), pp. 240 ff., points out the subjective character of arguments based on style and maintains the opinion that there are as great differences within the other Pauline Epistles as between these Epistles and the Pastorals

three notes, would it not have seemed the obvious choice to put one in each? But this, of course, further depends on the order in which the Epistles were issued, and there is some difference of opinion on this matter. It has been most widely maintained that 2 Timothy with its greater quantity of Pauline material was issued first and its immediate success prompted the author to produce the other two (so Easton[1]). But would no suspicions have been raised by the time 1 Timothy appeared with its less powerfully authenticated Pauliné stamp? Nor is it easier to account for if 1 Timothy came first, for this would involve the theory that the compiler kept the best genuine notes until the end, or else did not come into possession of them until after the publication of 1 Timothy. But neither of these suggestions is in the least probable.[2]

2. Another difficulty is to understand the reason why the compiler interwove his two genuine notes in 2 Timothy in the way he did. According to P. N. Harrison's theory the first genuine note is incorporated in three parts, the main paragraph (iv. 9-15), the postscript (iv. 20-21a),[3] and the benediction (iv. 22b), while the second note is dispersed into five separated paragraphs (i. 16-18; iii. 10, 11; iv. 1-2a; iv. 5b-8; and iv. 16-19) with a united postscript and benediction (iv. 21b-22a). Together with this interspersed material are four sections of the editor's own composition. But can such a strange intermixture be

---

[1] *Op. cit.*, p. 19. Cf. the present writer's *The Pastoral Epistles and the Mind of Paul*, pp. 30, 31, for a discussion of this view and of the alternative view of M. Dibelius that 1 Timothy and Titus preceded 2 Timothy. Dibelius' view is conditioned by his rejection of the 'genuine-note' theory. E. J. Goodspeed (*INT*, p. 330) regards the three Epistles as forming a corpus and in this way short-circuits the problem of the order of compilation. J. Moffatt (*ILNT*, p. 397) gives a list of scholars considering 2 Timothy to be primary, while M. Goguel, *Introduction au Nouveau Testament*, pp. 502, 503, gives eight reasons in support of this view based mainly on slight differences of doctrinal emphasis.

[2] E. J. Goodspeed's idea that the three Epistles were originally published as a corpus is rather more acceptable than the two alternatives mentioned, but is faced with the difficulty of providing an adequate motive for such a composite compilation (cf. E. J. Goodspeed, *INT*, p. 338).

[3] In his original scheme (*The Problem of the Pastorals*, pp. 118-121) Harrison explained the separation of the postscript from the rest of the letter-fragment by the improbable suggestion that these lines were either on the verso or else distinct from the rest and thus became combined with similar fragments at the end of 2 Timothy. Cf. Michaelis' criticism (*Pastoralbriefe und Gefangenschaftsbriefe*, p. 144); he considers the reconstruction forced and the evidence unfavourable to the editorial process, in fact he can find no grounds on account of which the pseudo-Paul would have chosen such a method of working.

psychologically justified?[1] The whole theory would have been much more credible had the compiler introduced his genuine notes as complete units in 2 Timothy, as he is claimed to have done in Titus, where the genuine note is supposed to be tacked on at the end of the compiler's own material. But his method in 2 Timothy is so completely baffling as to be wellnigh incredible. There is certainly no parallel where genuine notes are mixed in with fictitious personal allusions as must be the case in the fragment theory of 2 Timothy. In the compiler's own sections, Timothy's mother and grandmother are mentioned by name (for what purpose it is not at all clear if the real Timothy was not being addressed), the Asiatics are mentioned generally and Phygellus and Hermogenes in particular, as also the false teachers Hymenaeus and Philetus. Since these allusions are not in the 'genuine' sections, they must have been invented by the Paulinist to create a greater impression of verisimilitude, but why was this necessary if the genuine notes were self-evidently Pauline? And how can we be certain that the compiler did not also compose the 'genuine' notes since he was prone to do this sort of thing?

3. This leads to another problem. How did the genuine notes come to be preserved in the manner in which the theory supposes? There are only two possible alternatives. Either the notes were preserved as complete units or they were not. If the former is held the problem of their disintegrated incorporation becomes all the greater, and if the latter the process of preservation presents an almost insuperable difficulty, for they are not the kind of fragments which anyone would normally want to keep. It is not exactly convincing to postulate a devoted disciple doting over these scrappy remains of the great apostle and conceiving the idea of incorporating them for the benefit of posterity in an encasement of his own work and then attributing the lot to Paul for the sake of the precious fragments.[2]

---

[1] Harrison's own explanation of the editor's method of intercalating the various notes, under his revised plan, is set out in his article 'The Pastoral Epistles and Duncan's Ephesian Theory', *NTS* (May 1956), p. 251.

[2] Cf. G. Salmon, *INT*, pp. 410 ff., A. Plummer, *The Pastoral Epistles* (1888), pp. 9, 10, for acute criticisms of the compilation difficulties of the fiction and genuine-note theories. These difficulties have since their time too often been overlooked. But W. Michaelis lays stress on the methodological difficulties of fragment hypotheses and his criticisms should be carefully noted. He especially draws attention to the problem of the author's purpose in incorporating the notes. If the notes were already known to his readers as authentic the author would not have

But is the 'fiction' theory any more credible in its account of the author's method of compilation? There is generally no very serious attempt to explain the appearance of three Epistles and the most recent advocates of this hypothesis have contented themselves with suggesting an original corpus. But this does not explain the process. It does no more than deduce it from the obvious fact that three Epistles exist. Yet would not one have served the purpose, especially as certain subject-matter is repeated? Surely a single Epistle would have run less risk of detection? Or if, as is sometimes maintained, no one was deceived but rather accepted the Epistles for what they were, i.e. a sincere attempt of some devout Paulinist to give a Pauline approach to current problems, would the churches have regarded so favourably a threefold production as a single production? At best, we are in the realm of conjecture here, but the advocates of the theory cannot produce any parallels for such a fictitious corpus production from the early period, and in the absence of such evidence cannot reasonably claim that the pseudo-Paulinist's activities were in full accord with the literary conventions of his own time. If these Epistles are inventions of a pious author they stand, as a group, unique in early Christian literature.

(ii) *Historical problems.* 1. There is the question of the genuine notes and the Acts. It is said to be one of the great advantages of the fragment theory that it enables us to fit the personalia into the Acts framework by apportioning different parts to different historical settings. Thus in Harrison's revised scheme one note in 2 Timothy belongs to the period of the third missionary journey and the other to the closing weeks of Paul's life.[1] This may at first seem a facile solution, if the presence of notes be admitted at all, but there are difficulties on closer investigation. The main problems surround the first note in 2 Timothy and the note in Titus, both said to have been sent from Nicopolis between Paul's leaving Ephesus and his writing of 2 Corinthians. But this is difficult to sustain for the following reasons. Firstly, it implies that Paul spent the winter in Nicopolis (Tit. iii. 12), but Acts xx. 1–6 sug-

dared to incorporate them with his own material. But if they were not known, of what use would they have been in assisting the readers to accept the authenticity of the Epistles (Michaelis, *Pastoralbriefe und Gefangenschaftsbriefe*, 1930, pp. 134 ff.)?

[1] Michaelis, *Pastoralbriefe und Gefangenschaftsbriefe*, pp. 142–145, has some penetrating historical criticisms of Harrison's original five-note theory and some of his arguments apply also to the revised scheme. Michaelis notes particularly how an Ephesian place of dispatch for the Captivity Epistles affects the historical situation in Harrison's notes.*

gests that he spent the winter months in Greece after having done some missionary work in Macedonia.[1] Secondly, it makes the movements of Titus incomprehensible, for he is summoned to Nicopolis (Tit. iii. 12), sent to Dalmatia (2 Tim. iv. 10) and then returns to Corinth with or before 2 Corinthians in an incredibly short space of time, for all this must have happened between the commencement of the winter and Paul's own arrival in Corinth (which according to Acts xx. 3 must have been early in the winter). Thirdly, if Titus' movements are incomprehensible Timothy's are distinctly contradictory, for although 2 Timothy iv. 21a was written *ex hypothesi* after the note to Titus, Timothy is urged to join Paul before the winter and that after Titus has already left for Dalmatia, which he apparently did not do until winter had already commenced. Fourthly, the movements of Tychicus are in no better position, for according to P. N. Harrison's reconstruction Colossians (which Tychicus is said to have taken while Paul was in prison at the end of his Ephesian imprisonment, on Duncan's hypothesis) preceded Titus iii. 12 and 2 Timothy iv. 12, but if so Tychicus must have dashed round the churches of the Lycus valley to fulfil the mission Paul entrusted to him there, hurried back to Nicopolis or somewhere in the vicinity, only to be sent somewhere, presumably Corinth, to relieve Titus *before* Titus could join Paul (although the reason for this is not at all obvious: Tit. iii. 12) and then to be sent to Ephesus before Paul summoned Timothy (2 Tim. iv. 12), and all this bustling activity must have happened during the summer and early autumn. Enough data have been given to show that in its present form, at least, P. N. Harrison's theory involves many historical contradictions. The problems would certainly be considerably lessened if in accordance with Duncan's[2]

---

[1] Duncan tries to get over this difficulty by making Paul spend part of the winter in Nicopolis and part in Corinth. Michaelis (*op. cit.*, p. 151) criticizes this on the ground that no hint of such movements occurs in 2 Corinthians which, under this scheme, is brought into close proximity with the Titus fragment. It seems much simpler to take Acts xx. 1 ff. at its face value and omit any journey of Paul to Nicopolis. Only by stretching the evidence can the winter of Titus iii. 12–14 be brought into line with Acts xx. 3.

[2] *St. Paul's Ephesian Ministry* (1929), p. 219. In an article in *NTS* (October 1958), pp. 43 ff., Duncan slightly modifies his earlier reconstruction in relation to Titus' movements, but still maintains the theory of two winters. It should be noted, however, that Duncan does not agree with Harrison's two-note theory for 2 Tim. iv, which for him considerably lessens the difficulties. He disputes the reading 'in Rome' in i. 17 and thus by doubtful emendation removes the main reason for Harrison's double-note theory.

hypothesis two winters instead of one separated 1 and 2 Corinthians and a period of some eighteen months elapsed between them, but since this is not the most natural interpretation of the data (see pp. 442 ff.) it cannot be brought as supporting evidence for the fragment theory although it could more easily accommodate it.[1]

2. There is also difficulty over the false teachers. Another criticism of both the 'fragment' and 'fiction' theories, at least in their second-century form, is the difficulty of tying up the allusions to the false teaching in the Pastorals with the second-century Gnosticism. If he is giving to his own age the advice which he conceives Paul would have given, why does the writer not refer to the fundamental dangers of developed Gnosticism? The vagueness of the Pastorals allusions militates against a second-century dating and forces us to suppose that the author has in mind no more than incipient Gnosticism, which would date the Epistles prior to the second century. But in any case, if the author was purporting to give Paul's approach to his own contemporary situation, why did he merely denounce the heresy instead of refuting it if he was already acquainted with Paul's Colossian Epistle? It may be argued that the Paulinist's mind was incapable of refuting the subtle dangers of the heresy, but it is reasonable to suppose he would have done more than call them, rather impatiently, silly myths and stupid controversies and advise his readers to avoid them. We can understand Paul doing this to his trusted associates but it is difficult to believe that a Paulinist would have done so with his avowed intention to express 'Paul's' approach to his Gnostic-threatened churches.

(iii) *Doctrinal difficulties.* The assumption that the writer was so well acquainted with Paul's Epistles that he reproduced a good deal of Pauline phraseology does not adequately account for the strong flavour of Paulinism which is discernible in these Epistles and at the same time explain the absence of some of Paul's major themes. The question needs to be asked whether or not an imitator would have been concerned to reproduce as much as possible the dominant doctrinal characteristics of the apostle? The answer will naturally be affected by the general point of view adopted towards the authenticity problem and will tend to be coloured by subjective considerations. If the author

[1] For an account of the historical difficulties of the fragment theory against the background of an Ephesian origin for the Captivity Epistles, see Michaelis, *Pastoralbriefe und Gefangenschaftsbriefe*, pp. 136 ff. See especially p. 152 for Michaelis' rejection of Duncan's additional year theory.

is assumed to be an imitator it is naturally taken for granted that he either did not understand Paul or that his acquaintance with his Epistles was not close enough to reflect the great Pauline doctrines. Yet the advocates of imitator-theories cannot have it both ways. Either the imitator consciously set out to give a Pauline slant to the present situation or he did not. If he did, he must surely have had more than a nodding acquaintance with the apostle's extant Epistles and must have had more than an ordinary admiration for his personality and teaching. Although it may be argued that imitations always give the impression of secondary thought and that the theology of the Pastorals is inferior to that of Paul's earlier Epistles, yet the fact remains that it is easier to account for Paul himself omitting doctrines fully expressed in earlier letters when he writes to close associates than for a devoted admirer to omit them when imitating those very letters for the benefit of those who had *ex hypothesi* neglected them.[1]

Again, it is significant that if this Paulinist lived in the period of the sub-apostolic Fathers he must have been a giant among them, for the Pastorals' superiority over the writings of these Fathers is generally admitted. Nowhere, in fact, do we find during this period so great a devotedness to Pauline thought, and the difficulty is on the one hand to imagine such a man and on the other to conceive how he managed to persuade his lesser contemporaries to receive his productions almost immediately as Scripture. It is not of course impossible for such a man to have lived during this period and yet be unknown in Christian history. But a theory that requires it is at a greater discount than one that does not.

(iv) *Linguistic difficulties.* There are several passages in the Pastorals where there is no obvious use of Pauline phraseology. The usual explanation, under the fragment theory, that at these points the compiler is simply composing his own material drawn from his own background, means that he must have had frequent lapses during which he forgot his real purpose.[2] Now this is quite conceivable if he were making no very serious attempt to model his own style on that of the apostle and if he had insufficient insight to see any incongruity between his own style and that of the genuine fragments. But the echoing of Pauline vocabulary in the compiler's own sections is strangely distributed.

---

[1] For a further discussion on imitators and imitation, see pp. 681 ff.
[2] Cf. Harrison, *op. cit.*, pp. 90–92.

Harrison[1] himself points out that in 2 Timothy i. 1–15 we have almost the *ipsissima verba* of Paul himself with only the arrangement and slight foreign colour betraying the mind of the Paulinist, whereas in 2 Timothy ii. 15–iii. 6, 1 Timothy v. 1–19, vi. 7–21 and Titus i. 13–ii. 15 the Pauline echoes are particularly sparse. The real question is whether it is more reasonable to suppose that Paul could himself have produced letters showing such linguistic deviations than to postulate an unknown writer attempting to imitate him. The latter alternative at first sight may seem easier because an unknown author's style cannot be verified against any previous works, but it is not for that reason more correct unless it can be shown (1) that Paul could not so have deviated and (2) that an imitator would naturally have done so. But neither of these points has been proved. An imitator can, of course, be conveniently made to act in any way his proposer wishes in order to support his particular hypothesis, but reserve must be exercised before deducing general methods for imitators from particular cases as a comparison of the spurious 3 Corinthians with the spurious Laodicean Epistle shows.

These difficulties in fragment theories apply equally to fiction theories involving conscious imitation of Paul, although any incongruity between the supposed genuine notes and the compiler's own style is avoided. At the same time it is strange that the pseudo-Paul succeeded in producing a few personalia which bore a genuine Pauline stamp, but failed to do so for the main portions of the three letters. It is a real problem for all pseudonymous theories of the Pastoral Epistles to account for the fact that Greek-speaking Christians, some of whom were not oblivious to stylistic differences, seem to have raised no difficulties over the non-Pauline language and style of these Epistles. In the light of this there is strong probability that any modern criticism which stresses these differences may be proceeding from unreal premises.

(v) *Problems of motive.* An important question that must be asked is, Why did the Paulinist produce these writings at all? There appear to be, under the fragment theory, two main explanations. First, he wished to preserve the genuine notes which he had somehow obtained and his purpose in writing was therefore to provide an ingenious historical framework into which they could fit. And secondly, he wished to apply Paul to the crucial questions of his own age, particularly to problems of ecclesiastical arrangements. It is not quite clear in which order

[1] *Op. cit.*, p. 92.

these purposes came, whether he found the notes and these prompted his desire to give a Pauline slant to contemporary problems or whether his study of Paul had convinced him that Paul had something to say in an adapted form to his own age and then by good fortune he stumbled across the 'notes' and saw immediately how invaluable they would be to add veracity to his productions. The difficulty in deciding between these alternatives, and the unconvincing character of both, put the fragment theory at a discount.

The fiction theory is, if anything, faced with less difficulties on this score since it is proposed that some later writer sets out to represent Paul to his own age and the theory is unhampered by the necessity to fit in the fragmentary notes. The most that advocates of this type of theory can suggest is that these Epistles belong to the period subsequent to Marcion and are therefore an orthodox attempt to rescue Paul from being used as a tool for Marcionite doctrine. But this theory is untenable for several reasons. The absence of any clear references to developed Gnosticism has already been mentioned (see pp. 602 ff.) and this cannot be over stressed against the alleged anti-Marcionism of these Epistles. It is quite evident that Marcion and the Pastoral Epistles did not agree, a fact that has already been used as a reason for his rejection of them, but this is a very different thing from maintaining that the Pastoral Epistles combat Marcion. Had they done so and had their motive been recognized among the orthodox Christians there would surely not have been so dangerous a growth of the Marcionite church that Tertullian after a comparatively short time found it necessary to combat Marcion's arguments in detail. The fact is that only 1 Timothy vi. 20 can with any plausibility be appealed to in support of this theory and the rest of the subject-matter has little relevance.[1] A further criticism is the adverse

[1] Riddle (in Riddle and Hutson, *New Testament Life and Literature*, p. 205), who maintains the theory under discussion, sees an anti-Marcionite polemic in the insistence on the unity of God (1 Tim. ii. 5), in the condemnation of certain ascetic practices (1 Tim. iv. 3–5) and in the statement that *all* scripture is inspired and useful (2 Tim. iii. 16). But none of these point specifically to an anti-Marcionite polemic. Paul mentions the unity of God in Rom. iii. 30; similar ascetic practices were prevalent in the first century as well as the second (cf. Paul's dealing with food problems in the Corinthian and Roman Epistles); and the statement on the inspiration of Scripture would be more relevant to a man like Timothy who probably needed a reminder of the profitableness of all Scripture than to Marcion who had, as an *a priori* proposition, rejected the Old Testament altogether. Of course, the statements of these Epistles would be useful in combating Marcionism, but that does not justify this theory. For other supporters of this theory, cf. p. 593 n.2.

judgment of external attestation. The fact that advocates of this theory find it necessary to deny all early traces of the Epistles before Marcion's time and treat most unsatisfactorily the evidence from Polycarp is a measure of the slenderness of its historical veracity. Nor has an adequate explanation been given of the complete absence of any doubts about the genuineness of these Epistles. The authoritative acceptance of them, only forty years after Marcion's Antitheses, by Theophilus of Antioch, who speaks of them as proceeding from the divine Word, and the unquestioned acceptance of them by all subsequent writers is fatal to the anti-Marcionite theory. Moreover, no traces of Marcionite objections to the Pastoral Epistles on the ground of their questionable origin have survived, which demands explanation if these Epistles were produced to combat Marcionism. It is incredible that both orthodox and heretical parties in the second century were so completely deceived about the origin of these Epistles if they were not produced until after AD 140.

Another proposal is that these Epistles were intended to encourage the hard-pressed Church to present Paul as the apostle of sound doctrine and the champion of church custom and order. The personalia would thus be used as a means of conveying sympathy, especially the description in 2 Timothy iv of the solitary, disappointed, needy and book-starved apostle. But this is a further case of making a virtue out of necessity, for the Epistles considered as genuine would serve a similar purpose at a much earlier time and much more effectively, because portraying a real and not fictitious situation. As compared with all these Paulinist theories the traditional acceptance of authenticity supplies a much more reasonable motive.

And finally there is the pseudonymous device. We have refrained from calling the author a 'forger' because many scholars consider this term contains a moral stigma which prejudices the issue.[1] But does the

[1] This approach was not so evident among the earlier and more radical school of critics, who made no attempt to whitewash the pseudo-author. F. C. Baur, *Paul, the Apostle of Jesus Christ* (Eng. Tr. 1876), I, pp. 247–249, II, pp. 98 ff., classed the Pastoral Epistles as 'spurious' (although he did not place the other Pauline Epistles, whose authenticity he disputed, in the same category), while Renan, *Saint Paul*, pp. xxii ff., did not hesitate to use the words 'forger' and 'forgery'. The modern vogue for avoiding such terms (cf. Mitton, *Ephesians*, pp. 25 f.; Masson, *Thessaloniciens*, 1957, p. 13; Chaine, *Les Epîtres Catholiques*, 1939, p. 30) and for criticizing those who use them must be traced either to the exaltation of pseudonymity as a literary art-form (unknown among earlier critics) or else to a

term 'imitator' or 'devout Paulinist' really obviate the moral problem?[1] Can we believe that the author was motivated by the highest intentions of modesty when he attributed these Epistles to Paul, as if it would have been almost an injustice to call his own what was in effect a reproduction of the thought of his master? Although this is the contention of most scholars who reject Pauline authorship it is obviously not without very considerable difficulties. To begin with, not a single comparable parallel from early Christian literary practice can be produced in support, which raises suspicions about its probability.[2] It further supposes that the Christian Church was prepared to condone this so-called modesty and to accept without question these Epistles as the genuine reproduction of Pauline thought, for the exponents of the theory are careful to reject any notion that the Church was deceived about their origin. If the first recipients were not deceived the next generations certainly were, for no hint of their pseudonymous origin has survived. Any theory which requires pseudonymous authorship must, therefore, face the fact that the postulation of pseudonymity is itself hypothetical.

e. Conclusion of the discussion

In spite of the acknowledged differences between the Pastorals and Paul's other Epistles, the traditional view that they are authentic writings of the apostle cannot be said to be impossible, and since there are greater problems attached to the alternative theories it is most reasonable to suppose that the early Church was right in accepting them as such.

   Two other suggestions, which do not attribute authorship to Paul

desire to remove a stumbling-block in the path of all such pseudepigraphic theories. There would appear, however, to be no adequate case for differentiating 'forgery' from 'imitation'. See the discussion of Epistolary Pseudepigraphy, pp. 671 ff.

   [1] In discussing the authenticity of 2 Thessalonians, G. Milligan, *Expositor*, VI, ix, p. 449 n., considered no other word but 'forgery' could so well bring out one man's deliberate use of the name and authority of another in his writing. 2 Thes. iii. 17, 18 excludes the notion of harmless pseudonymous writing. What is true for 2 Thessalonians must be equally true for all proposed New Testament pseudepigrapha. For further comments on the moral issue, cf. pp. 680 f.

   [2] The epistolary form did not readily lend itself to the pseudepigraphist's intentions for it was exposed to greater ease of detection than Gospels, Acts or Apocalypses, particularly when the imitator had a pattern so highly individualistic as that of the apostle Paul.

in the sense that the finished products as they have been preserved are not his work, are worthy of mention. One is that Timothy and Titus themselves edited Pauline material after his death and produced the Epistles in their present form.[1] This is an attempt to attribute the form of the letters to a non-Pauline source in order to obviate the difficulties felt over full Pauline authorship. But it is difficult to believe that either Timothy or Titus would have framed the material in the form of letters addressed to themselves unless the material had already existed in this form. There would seem to be no motive for their doing so. It might perhaps be contended that the peculiarities are attributable to an amanuensis and in this case Timothy and Titus might be considered as good a guess as any.[2] Another suggestion with perhaps greater probability is that Luke was the author since many similarities exist between the language of Luke and the linguistic peculiarities of the Pastorals.[3] There

[1] Cf. A. C. Deane, *St. Paul and His Letters* (1942), pp. 208–220.

[2] J. Jeremias, *Die Pastoralbriefe* (1953), p. 8, suggests Tychicus as author with the co-operation of Timothy, although he acknowledges the form of Paul behind the production. But it is strange no mention is made of Tychicus in 1 Timothy since he was known at Ephesus.

[3] Cf. H. J. Holtzmann, *Die Pastoralbriefe* (1880), pp. 92 ff.; J. D. James, *The Genuineness and Authorship of the Pastoral Epistles* (1906), pp. 154 ff. Robert Scott, *The Pauline Epistles* (1909), pp. 329–371, maintained the Lucan authorship of the Pastorals on the following grounds: (a) similarity of general vocabulary; (b) passages which suggest interdependence with Lucan writings; (c) use of medical terminology; (d) familiarity with the religious ideas of Greece; (e) similar use of favourite words, idioms and other terms. R. Scott allowed the possibility that Paul dictated 2 Timothy to Luke, but favoured the theory that Luke wrote all three Epistles soon after Paul's martyrdom (p. 353). For another editor theory cf. F. J. Badcock, *The Pauline Epistles and the Epistle to the Hebrews in their Historical Setting* (1937), pp. 115–133. J. Moffatt questioned the Lucan hypothesis on the ground that linguistic similarities may be due to a common milieu and he also points out the difficulty of Luke's omission to mention Titus in Acts (*ILNT*, p. 414). O. Roller has suggested that the rigorous conditions of imprisonment would make the use of an amanuensis necessary (*Das Formular der paulinischen Briefe*, 1933, pp. 20, 21); cf. also J. Jeremias, *op. cit.*, pp. 5, 6. But C. Spicq, *Les Epîtres Pastorales* (1947), p. cxix, thinks the rigour of imprisonment should not be overstressed since Ignatius and other martyrs have been able to write letters during rigorous imprisonments. A. Nairne (*The Faith of the New Testament*, 1920, pp. 60, 61) suggested a combination of editor-secretary theory for these Epistles to account for the absence of 'the Pauline mind'. J. A. Eschlimann, 'La Rédaction des Epîtres Pauliniennes', *RB*, LIII (1946), pp. 185 ff., drew a distinction between the use of an amanuensis in dictation (syllable by syllable) and a secretary who was given the main content of the letter to be written. He suggests that Paul could not

is enough evidence not only that amanuenses were frequently given considerable liberty in writing up manuscripts but that Paul himself was in the habit of employing an amanuensis. The major problem is the degree of liberty which a man like Paul would have been prepared to grant. While these editing theories may eliminate some of the lesser objections to Pauline authorship, they do not remove objections based on late dating. The idea of a publication by 'a Pauline school' has appealed to some scholars, but is not without considerable difficulties. It assumes a dramatization of existing material for which no clear parallels exist in the first century of our era.[1] The only form of such a theory which seems at all tenable is that which admits that at least some of the existing material had been addressed to Timothy and Titus and that the editing process was therefore confined to the language and perhaps some of the ideas. But such a theory would be unnecessary if the language and ideas are shown to be not incompatible with authorship by Paul himself.

II. PURPOSE OF THE EPISTLES

If Pauline authorship be accepted the purpose of the three Epistles is self-evident. In 1 Timothy and Titus the apostle means to give his two close associates written instructions about methods of procedure in their respective churches for which they are temporarily responsible. It is most natural to suppose that many of these instructions had been given orally at a recent date and that these Epistles are therefore somewhat confirmatory in character. In the case of Titus, Paul has a specific occasion for writing, to summon his fellow-worker to meet him at Nicopolis. No reason is given for this request. At the same time Titus is to assist Zenas and Apollos on their journey. There are very few data in 1 Timothy to enable a specific occasion to be reconstructed, but Paul expects at some time in the future to visit Timothy at Ephesus (1 Tim. iv. 13), although his statement about this is made in so casual a manner that it can hardly be construed as the major occasion for the letter. It

have written the autograph of 2 Timothy. But W. Michaelis, *Einleitung*, pp. 241–244, after discussing various suggestions for a possible secretary, finds none of those proposed satisfactory and pronounces the secretary hypothesis as not a useful solution to the authenticity question.*

[1] P. Carrington, *The Early Christian Church*, vol. 1 (1957), pp. 260, 261, who inclines to this view, attempts to find a parallel in the traditional form of 'testament' as in the *Testaments of the Twelve Patriarchs*, but he admits the resemblance to be only 'a fleeting one'.

seems probable that the apostle felt the need of giving Timothy not only specific written instructions to guide him in his task of ensuring an orderly organization in the church but also encouragement and even moral challenge to take a firm hand and be unashamed of the gospel.

A quite different situation is found in 2 Timothy, for Paul is now in prison and would appear to be facing the close of his life. He looks back on his accomplished task and looks ahead to his anticipated crown. The Epistle is little concerned with ecclesiastical arrangements but concentrates on Timothy and the task which is being committed to him. The apostle is in a reminiscent mood, and for this reason his concluding Epistle is the most revealing of the three Pastorals. He seems rather uncertain that he will ever see Timothy again although he has summoned him to come as quickly as possible. During the course of the writing he takes the opportunity of warning Timothy again about the false teachers as he had previously done in the first Epistle.

III. DATES OF THE EPISTLES

The chronology of the closing period of Paul's life is too obscure to attach a definite dating to any of these Epistles. Many different estimates of the period between Paul's first arrival in Rome and his execution have been proposed, quite apart from considerable variation in fixing the date of arrival in Rome.[1] Under the second imprisonment theory a longer period is obviously demanded, particularly if the apostle made further journeys in both East and West. In view of the uncertainty the most that can be suggested is that 1 Timothy and Titus belong to a period not long before Paul's death and that 2 Timothy was written when the end was imminent.

According to the various theories of non-Pauline authorship several different later dates have been proposed, ranging mainly from the latter part of the first century to the middle of the second century. The decision rests for the most part on the relationship thought to exist between the Pastorals and second-century Gnosticism, particularly Marcionism.[2] But in considering the problem of authenticity we have

---

[1] See further discussion on pp. 662 ff.

[2] Those maintaining the fragment theory generally tend to date the Epistles earlier than those proposing an entirely fictitious production. E.g. a date about the end of the first century is suggested by J. Moffatt (*ILNT*, p. 416), E. F. Scott (*Literature of the New Testament*, p. 194), M. Goguel (*Introduction au Nouveau Testament*, IV, 2, pp. 476 ff.), whereas such scholars as P. Couchard ('La Première édition de Saint Paul', *Revue de l'Histoire des Religions*, 1926, xxiv, iii, pp. 242 ff.),

given grounds for believing that nothing in the historical situation precludes a date, not only in the first century but also in the lifetime of the apostle.

CONTENTS OF 1 TIMOTHY

I. GREETING (i. 1, 2)

Paul addresses himself to Timothy whom he describes as his true child in the faith.

II. PAUL AND TIMOTHY (i. 3-20)

a. Timothy's task at Ephesus (i. 3-11)

This is particularly concerned with refutation of false teachers who are addicted to irrelevant myths, genealogies and arguments about the law. These counterfeits are contrasted with the glorious gospel entrusted to the apostle.

b. Paul outlines his own experience of the gospel (i. 12-17)

He is overwhelmed with the thought of God's mercy towards him when He transformed him from his old life and appointed him to His service. This leads to a doxology to His praise.

c. Paul issues a charge to Timothy (i. 18-20)

Timothy had a commission similar to Paul's own, for he had been singled out to carry on the spiritual warfare. A sample of the conflict is cited in the case of Hymenaeus and Alexander, who have made shipwreck of their faith.

III. REGULATIONS FOR WORSHIP AND ORDER IN THE CHURCH (ii. 1-iv. 16)

a. The importance and scope of public prayer (ii. 1-8)

Prayer is to be made for all men, even for those in high authority, and

and F. D. Gealy, *1 and 2 Timothy and Titus* (IB), pp. 351 ff., do not hesitate to place these Epistles after the publication of Marcion's Apostolicon (c. AD 140). This later dating is closely allied to the earlier opinion of F. C. Baur, that the Epistles were written after Marcion's *Antitheses.* *

this injunction is given a doctrinal basis in that God, through the ransom of His Son, desires the salvation of all. It was to testify to this that Paul was appointed a preacher.

b. The status and demeanour of Christian women (ii. 9–15)

Paul urges upon women the need for modesty in apparel and submissiveness in attitude and he supports his assertions by an appeal to the story of Adam and Eve. Women must continue in faith, love, holiness and modesty.

c. The qualifications of church officials (iii. 1–13)

The apostle deals first with bishops (iii. 1–7) and gives a list of qualities, mostly moral requirements, which are indispensable. The bishop must not be a recent convert and must be above reproach. Then the requirements for deacons are outlined (iii. 8–13), similar to those for bishops. In both cases the chosen men must have proved themselves in their own homes to be capable of assuming responsibility.

d. The character of the Church (iii. 14–16)

Paul informs Timothy that he hopes to visit him soon. But the purpose of the present Epistle is to give guidance for Timothy's immediate action in the church, which is described here as (1) God's household, (2) a pillar and (3) a bulwark of truth. At this point Paul introduces a hymn expressing the mystery of Christ's incarnation, the universality of its application and the present glory of Christ.

e. Threats to the safety of the Church (iv. 1–16)

Through the Spirit the apostle sees a time of approaching apostasy, which will be marked by deceitful teaching and ascetic practices (iv. 1–5). He proceeds to give detailed instructions to Timothy about the best methods of dealing with false teaching. (1) He must seek the cooperation of the 'brethren'; (2) he must avoid irrelevant speculations; (3) he must cultivate his own religious life so as to be an example in word, conduct and attitude; (4) he must diligently pursue his public ministry; and (5) he must develop what gift he possesses (iv. 6–16). Paul believes that Timothy's example would have a more powerful influence against false teachers than any attempts to combat their silly myths.

IV. DISCIPLINE WITHIN THE CHURCH (v. 1–25)

Various classes of people within the church must be differently treated and Timothy is given some detailed guidance. Different age-groups need to be handled with discrimination (v. 1, 2), while discernment is necessary to determine widows who are really in need (v. 3–8). The enrolment of widows supported as church workers is to be regulated (v. 9, 10), while younger widows are to be dealt with firmly (v. 11–16). Elders must be accorded suitable honour and no indiscriminate charge must be admitted against them without adequate proof (v. 17–20). In dealing with these situations Timothy is to watch his own behaviour, avoiding partiality and hastiness of action, but cultivating purity and a due concern for his health. In choosing personnel Timothy must avoid hastiness of choice which may lead to error because appearances are often deceptive (v. 21–25).

V. MISCELLANEOUS INSTRUCTIONS (vi. 1–19)

a. Concerning slaves and masters (vi. 1, 2)

The apostle does not condemn the yoke of slavery, but urges that Christian slaves should honour unbelieving masters so as not to bring disrespect to the gospel. They should serve believing masters even better because of the bond of Christian love.

b. Concerning false teachers (vi. 3–5)

There follows a trenchant description of the moral depravity of those who do not agree with the teaching of Christ. Such people not only crave for wordy religious controversies but even seize the opportunity to make gain out of them.

c. Concerning the perils of wealth (vi. 6–10)

This arises immediately from the case of religious covetousness. The gain of contented godliness is contrasted with the snares of the mere pursuit of riches, which many have found to be the root of all evils.

d. Concerning the aims of a man of God (vi. 11–16)

Addressed directly to Timothy, these injunctions inculcate the noblest Christian virtues, urge upon him tenacity in Christian warfare and charge him to keep himself unstained and free from reproach. Everything must be viewed in the light of the approaching advent of Christ, the thought of which draws out a magnificent doxology.

e. Concerning wealthy men (vi. 17–19)

Paul returns to the theme of wealth because of the need to give advice to rich Christians. They must not trust in their wealth, but through liberality aim to become rich in good deeds.

VI. CONCLUDING ADMONITION TO TIMOTHY (vi. 20, 21)

Once again Timothy is urged to guard the deposit and to avoid the irrelevances and pretentious knowledge of false teachers. The Epistle closes with a benediction.

CONTENTS OF 2 TIMOTHY

I. GREETING (i. 1, 2)

The wording is almost identical to the greeting of the first Epistle.

II. THANKSGIVING (i. 3–5)

The memory of Timothy produces in Paul an earnest longing to see him again. He rejoices in Timothy's early faith.

III. ENCOURAGEMENT FROM EXPERIENCE (i. 6–14)

a. Timothy's gift (i. 6–10)

He is too timid and needs to be reminded to stir himself up and not be ashamed of witnessing to the Lord, since God had saved and called them both to this holy calling.

b. Paul's testimony (i. 11, 12)

Paul recalls his own appointment as a preacher and asserts that he is not ashamed of the gospel because of his firm confidence in God.

c. Timothy's responsibility (i. 13, 14)

He next lays before Timothy the specific charge to keep to sound teaching and to guard what had been entrusted to him.

IV. PAUL AND HIS ASSOCIATES (i. 15–18)

There had been a general defection from Paul of the Asiatics, of whom Phygellus and Hermogenes are singled out, possibly because they were particularly hostile opponents (i. 15). But the devotion of Onesiphorus is set in strong contrast to these (i. 16–18).

V. DIRECTIONS TO TIMOTHY (ii. 1–26)

a. His main task (ii. 1, 2)

He is to be strong and pursue the task of ensuring the safe transmission of the tradition.

b. Encouragements and exhortations (ii. 3–13)

The apostle uses everyday illustrations from army life, athletics and agriculture to show that service requires self-discipline, and Timothy must therefore be prepared for some hardship (ii. 3–6). Paul's own example of selfless endurance is drawn to his notice and he is reminded of the certainty of ultimately reigning with Christ (ii. 7–13).

c. Advice on the treatment of false teachers (ii. 14–26)

This is expressed in two ways. (1) As positive action (ii. 14, 15). Timothy must show himself as an efficient workman well able to expound the truth. (2) As negative action (ii. 16–19). Paul advises Timothy to shun vain disputings and godless chatter and he cites the case of Hymenaeus and Philetus to illustrate the havoc it causes. Timothy may at the same time rest assured that God's foundation will not be moved by such chatter.

Advice is then given on the teacher's behaviour (ii. 20–26). As there are degrees of honour determined by purity and usefulness, so Timothy is to aim at noble things, to shun senseless controversies and conduct himself with kindly consideration in dealing with his opponents in the hope of effecting in them a change of heart.

VI. THE LAST DAYS (iii. 1–9)

Mention of Timothy's opponents in the last section probably prompted the apostle to turn his attention to the future to foresee a time of moral decadence. He vividly describes the sins which will characterize the men of this period, even under the cloak of religion, and he declares that these corrupted men will be rejected. The apostle thinks of them as already present, for Timothy is urged to avoid them.

VII. FURTHER EXHORTATIONS TO TIMOTHY (iii. 10–17)

Timothy is reminded of the apostle's own teaching and conduct and is specially urged to recall Paul's sufferings at Antioch, Iconium and Lystra (Timothy's home district) in order to give him courage for any future persecutions. He is exhorted to steadfastness and reminded of the indispensable value of the Scriptures for his work as a man of God.

VIII. PAUL'S FAREWELL MESSAGE (iv. 1–18)

a. A final charge (iv. 1–5)

Timothy's main work is to preach the Word. People may not want to listen to the truth, but he must persist in the fulfilment of his evangelistic ministry.

b. Paul's confession of faith (iv. 6–8)

He compares himself to an athlete whose race is nearly over and whose crown of honour is reserved for him by the Lord, whose judgment is righteous.

c. Some personal requests (iv. 9–13)

He hopes that Timothy may have time to reach him soon. He gives him news of his companions and requests Timothy to bring his cloak, books and parchments.

d. A particular warning (iv. 14, 15)

Paul recalls the harm done to him by a certain Alexander and warns Timothy against him.

e. His first defence (iv. 16, 17)

Although all deserted him, the Lord stood by him and granted deliverance.

f. His assurance for the future (iv. 18)

Past deliverances give confidence for future security in the kingdom of heaven.

IX. CONCLUSION (iv. 19–22)

Greetings are sent through Timothy to some of Paul's associates and news given of others. Some previously unmentioned in Paul's Epistles send greetings to Timothy. A benediction closes this valedictory Epistle.

CONTENTS OF TITUS

I. GREETING (i. 1–4)

This is much longer than in the other Pastoral Epistles and amounts to a declaration of the verities with which Paul as a preacher has been entrusted. Titus is described as a genuine child in the common faith.

II. QUALIFICATIONS OF CHURCH OFFICIALS (i. 5–9)

The purpose for which Titus was left in Crete was to appoint elders and to set things in order. Paul therefore gives a list of qualifications required by holders of this office. They must be morally upright and sound in doctrine.

III. FALSE TEACHERS AND THE NEED TO REFUTE THEM (i. 10–16)

The Cretan character is vividly described and one of their own poets is cited in support of their moral decadence and materialism. Paul uses the strongest expressions to describe these people (detestable, corrupt, unfit for anything) and it is no wonder that Titus is urged to rebuke them.

IV. REGULATIONS FOR CHRISTIAN BEHAVIOUR (ii. 1–10)

a. Aged people (ii. 1–3)

The main injunction is to impress on these people seriousness of mind and reverence of behaviour, which were qualities evidently not conspicuous.

b. Younger people (ii. 4–8)

The women are to be domesticated and to love and submit to their husbands, while the men are to be urged to exercise self-control. For this purpose Titus must himself be a model of chaste behaviour and sober speech, so as to give his opponents no ground for censuring him.

c. Slaves (ii. 9, 10)

A submissive attitude to their masters together with honesty and loyalty is enjoined.

V. CHRISTIAN DOCTRINE AND CHRISTIAN LIFE
(ii. 11–iii. 7)

a. The educating power of grace (ii. 11–15)

Coming as it does in the middle of a section giving ethical instruction, this statement of doctrine, which serves as an epitome of the gospel, shows that theology is an indispensable basis for Christian behaviour. It is the grace of God which is the motive behind His redeeming work and it is this which trains men to renounce all unworthy deeds. It is needful for Titus to declare these things.

b. Christians in the community (iii. 1, 2)

Christian behaviour must be marked by loyal citizenship, honest toil and a courteous approach to others.

c. The contrast between paganism and Christianity (iii. 3–7)

(i) Characteristics of paganism (iii. 3). The apostle first describes the characteristics of paganism. The Christian's past life is described as blind slavery to passions, which manifested itself in many vices.

(ii) The power of Christian salvation (iii. 4–7). The appearance of Christ has brought a radical change and has made us heirs of eternal salvation. The contrast with the former condition is striking.

VI. CLOSING ADMONITIONS (iii. 8–11)

a. Cultivate good works (iii. 8)

The Christian's renewed life must express itself in suitable actions, described by Paul as 'good deeds' and distinguished clearly from deeds done to obtain salvation.

b. Avoid false teachings (iii. 9–11)

A further description is given of the futility of these false teachers' speculations, which were leading to disputations. After two admonitions these people must be completely avoided.

VII. CONCLUSION (iii. 12–15)

A personal request is made for Titus to join Paul for the winter and to assist Zenas and Apollos on their journeying. General greetings are exchanged and the letter closes with a benediction.

ADDITIONAL NOTES

585. [4] For a discussion of the relationship between Polycarp and the Pastorals, cf. H. von Campenhausen, 'Polykarp und die Pastoralbriefe', *Sitzungsberichte der Heidelberger Akademie der Wissenschaften, philosophisch-historische Klasse* (1951).

585. [5] The Muratorian Canon links these three letters with Philemon as valuable for ecclesiastical use. They are mentioned after the Epistles sent to churches, but there is no suggestion that they are inferior. It should be noted also that in the *Gospel of Truth*, a Gnostic work, there are no clear references to these Epistles, but this is understandable since the Gnostics generally repudiated them.

593. [1] Cf. further R. M. Wilson's *Gnosis and the New Testament* (1968). In his commentary, C. K. Barrett (*The Pastoral Epistles*, 1963, pp. 12 ff.) accepts that the opponents in the Pastorals are Jewish Gnostic Christians. But Barrett tends to confuse the issue by his use of the word Gnostic. All that can be claimed is that the false teaching shows an early form of what later became organized Gnosticism.

Barrett (*ibid.*, p. 15) interprets the purpose of these letters on the supposition that the false teachers were claiming to be true exponents of Paul, although they were misrepresenting him as the Valentinians did.

597. [4] J. N. D. Kelly (*The Pastoral Epistles*, 1963, p. 10) rejects as 'uncritical' the view that the evidence from both Clement and the Muratorian Canon regarding Paul's visit to Spain is a legendary gloss on Rom. xv. 24, 28. He notes that Clement wrote at most thirty years after Paul's death. Cf. F. F. Bruce, *BJRL*, L (1968), pp. 272 f.

600. [1] On the use of the word *presbyterion* in these Epistles, J. Jeremias (*ZNTW*, 52, 1961, pp. 101–104) contends that 1 Tim. iv. 14 does not support the existence of a third office distinct from that of bishop and deacon (cf. 1 Tim. iii, Phil. i. 1). He sees this as evidence against a late date for the Pastorals.

605. [1] J. A. Allan has followed up his earlier article on the 'In Christ' formula in Ephesians with another on the same formula in the Pastorals (cf. *NTS*, 10, 1963, pp. 115–121). His conclusion is that the usage in these Epistles does not support their Pauline origin. But although Allan has pointed out differences of usage, he has not *proved* by this means that Paul could not himself be responsible for the difference.

606. [2] For a recent study of the faithful sayings, cf. G. W. Knight, *The Faithful Sayings in the Pastoral Letters* (1968). This author considers them to be credal-liturgical expressions.

607 f. [2] Cf. A. Q. Morton and J. McLeman, *Christianity and the Computer* (1964); *idem.*, *Paul, the Man and the Myth* (1966). In these books it is claimed that authorship may be objectively examined by means of statistical experiment. Morton examines several samples of prose from each of a number of ancient authors, basing his comparisons on such criteria as word frequencies and sentence lengths. It is claimed that style is better indicated by words of greatest frequency than by characteristic stylistic expressions on the grounds that it is independent of mood or purpose. Morton chooses such criteria therefore as the frequency of καί and the use of the article. He claims that each author has a certain frequency which shows no significant variations from a statistical point of view and then makes the further deduction that, if significant variations are found, they are indications of another author. The net results of his investigations are that only Galatians, Romans, 1 and 2 Corinthians are genuine (plus Philemon, included on other than statistical grounds). There is no doubt that the conclusion is stated too dogmatically, whatever the merits or otherwise of the method employed. But Morton's statistical methodology has not escaped criticism. Cf. C. Dinwoodie, *SJT*, 18 (1965), pp. 204–218; G. B. Caird, *ET*, lxxvi (1965), p. 176; H. K. McArthur, *ET*, lxxvi (1965), pp. 367–370; J. J. O'Rourke, *JBL*, lxxxvi (1967), pp. 110–112; H. K. McArthur, *NTS*, 15 (1969), pp. 339–349. All are agreed that Morton has based his conclusions on inadequate evidence. Dinwoodie comments, not without reason, that it looks as if the authors came to their conclusions before examining the evidence. McArthur is prepared to grant that Morton's figures show remarkably constant καί frequencies for each author, but he himself examines the same phenomenon in a selection of other Greek authors where the καί variation is considerably greater. It is clear that much more work needs to be done in this field before word frequencies can be used with any confidence. It should, moreover, be noted that most of Paul's letters are too short to provide the minimum length of sample which Morton thought desirable for his examination of Greek prose writers (i.e. 100 sentences). It should be further noted that the method is restricted to a denial of common authorship and cannot establish the reverse. This is partly responsible for the mainly negative results which Morton obtains.

613. [1] C. K. Barrett (*The Pastoral Epistles*, 1963, pp. 10 ff.) is favourable to Harrison's fragment theory, but fails to provide a really satisfactory account of composition. He dismisses any theory which assumes that the compiler possessed a collection of letters, or their disintegrated remains. He thinks we cannot now know the original disposition of these fragments. He contents himself with the view that somehow they came into the author's hands and he made the best sense he could of them. Cf. C. F. D. Moule (*BJRL*, xlvii, 1965, pp. 430–452), who rejects both Harrison's and Barrett's partition theories.

621 f. [3] Secretary hypotheses have won support from J. N. D. Kelly (*The Pastoral Epistles*, 1963, pp. 25 ff.), who maintains that Paul has relied more extensively on his amanuensis for these letters than for any others. But he concludes that they remain essentially his work and enshrine his authentic message. A similar view is held by G. Holtz, *Die Pastoralbriefe* (1965). For a study on the ancient use of secretaries, cf. G. J. Bahr, *CBQ*, 28 (1966), pp. 465–477.

A recent advocate of Luke as the amanuensis to whom Paul allowed greater freedom in the writing of these Epistles is C. F. D. Moule, *BJRL*, xlvii (1965), pp. 430–452. Basing his suggestion on linguistic evidence, he suggests that Luke wrote during Paul's lifetime, partially at his dictation. He accepts the release theory to explain Paul's movements after the end of the Acts' account. E. F. Harrison (*INT*, 1964, p. 342) inclines to favour Luke as amanuensis. Another who pleads for Lucan authorship is A. Strobel (*NTS*, 15, 1969, pp. 191–220) on the basis of language and theology. Cf. also F. F. Bruce's summary (*BJRL*, l, 1968, pp. 265 ff.) of a theory, as yet unpublished, proposed by J. M. Gilchrist, which suggests Luke may have reconstructed later what Paul actually wrote to Timothy and Titus.

A somewhat different variant of the secretary hypothesis is advanced by P. Dornier, *Les Épîtres pastorales* (1969), who regards the Epistles as originally Pauline Epistles which later became adapted by a disciple for the needs of the church.

623 f. [2] As examples of dating among those who reject Pauline authorship, cf. C. K. Barrett (*The Pastoral Epistles*, 1963, p. 18), who cautiously suggests a date between AD 90 and 125, and A. T. Hanson, *The Pastoral Epistles* (*CBC*, 1966), who chooses a date *c.* AD 105. For a date in Polycarp's time, cf. H. von Campenhausen, *Sitzungsberichte der Heidelberger Akademie der Wissenschaften, philosophisch-historische Klasse* (1951), who compares the writings of Polycarp with these Epistles and suggests that Polycarp was the author of the latter.

CHAPTER TWENTY

THE EPISTLE TO PHILEMON

I. OCCASION

It has traditionally been supposed that Philemon was a member of the Colossian church, who had in some way been converted to Christianity through the agency of Paul (cf. verse 19). His slave Onesimus after robbing his master[1] absconded to Rome, where he came into touch with Paul. Through the apostle's influence he became a Christian (cf. verse 10) and proved very useful in ministering to Paul's needs. But the apostle, having persuaded him that his duty was to return, writes this delicate letter appealing to Philemon to reinstate him as a 'brother beloved'. There is no means of knowing how or why Onesimus visited the imprisoned apostle. It has been suggested, not improbably, that Epaphras may have met him either accidentally or through the mediation of some other Christian, and, being pastor of the church to which his master Philemon belonged, took him to Paul to seek his advice.[2] But on this we can only conjecture.

This traditional hypothesis has, however, been challenged by E. J. Goodspeed[3] and J. Knox[4], who have both suggested that Philemon was not the owner of the slave. Though traditionally known as the letter to Philemon, the Epistle is, in fact, addressed to Philemon, Apphia, Archippus and 'the church in your house' (verses 1 and 2). Nothing else is known about Archippus except the reference in Colossians iv. 17, where the Colossians are instructed to tell him to fulfil his ministry. It is suggested by Knox[5] that this 'ministry' is closely connected with the

---

[1] C. F. D. Moule, *Colossians and Philemon* (1957), pp. 34 ff., cites an illuminating papyrus which was a copy of a placard offering rewards for the return of a slave or information regarding his whereabouts. It describes the possessions with which he absconded.*

[2] Cf. Harrison, *ATR*, xxxii (October 1950), p. 272. Cf. P. S. Minear, *The Kingdom and the Power* (1950), p. 102, who suggests that Paul and Onesimus may accidentally have been imprisoned in the same prison.

[3] *New Solutions of New Testament Problems* (1927). In *INT* (1937), pp. 109–124, Goodspeed adheres to the traditional view that Philemon was the owner, but he agrees with Knox in his explanation of Col. iv. 17.

[4] *Philemon among the Letters of Paul* (1935). [5] *Op. cit.*, pp. 25, 26.

letter about Onesimus. His reconstruction may be briefly set out as follows.

1. The real purpose of this Epistle is not merely to plead for the reinstatement of Onesimus; it is to request the owner to make over his slave for the service of God to assist Paul in his work. Verse 15, 'that you might receive him for ever', is understood to mean, 'that you might give a receipt for him for ever'. This is Paul's delicate way of making a big demand on the owner.

2. Since this would be a quasi-legal transaction, the 'church' is also implicated, and is addressed with the intention of encouraging the owner to comply with Paul's request.

3. The owner of the slave was not Philemon, but Archippus, who was also the host of the church mentioned in verse 1.

4. Because Paul did not know Archippus and the matter was rather delicate to address to a complete stranger, one of Paul's own associates, Philemon, whom he calls a 'fellowlabourer', was included in the address. He was perhaps overseer of a group of churches in the Lycus valley, possibly stationed at Laodicea.

5. This Epistle is referred to in Colossians iv. 16 as 'the one from Laodicea',[1] because it passed through that city on its way to Colossae, in the hands of Tychicus and Onesimus.

6. The real destination of Philemon was, however, not Laodicea but Colossae. The Epistle to the Colossians, written and dispatched at the same time, was partially designed to elicit communal support for Paul's request for Onesimus, hence the concluding injunction that Archippus should fulfil his 'ministry' (iv. 17) and the earlier mention of Onesimus (iv. 9).

But ingenious as this theory is it is not without several difficulties.

1. It is strange to find the real addressee mentioned third, which in the case of Paul would be without precedent. Knox[2] cites a fourth- or fifth-century papyrus letter in which a similar procedure is adopted and thinks it is legitimate to claim for Philemon that the real recipient was Archippus. But no ancient writer ever imagined that the latter was the

---

[1] This is a resuscitation of an old theory advocated by C. Wieseler in his *Chronologie des apostolischen Zeitalters* (1848), cited by J. B. Lightfoot, *Colossians* (1900), p. 278. Cf. also Conybeare and Howson, *The Life and Epistles of Paul* (1905), p. 703.

[2] *Op. cit.*, p. 28.

real owner and the most natural understanding of the order of mention is to suppose that the main recipient was named first.[1]

2. The phrase 'the church in your house' in verse 2 is similarly most naturally understood to refer to the house of the one first mentioned, although grammatically it could relate to Archippus. If Philemon's house is meant, it would militate against Knox's suggestion that the latter was overseer of the Lycus valley churches.

3. The 'ministry' which Archippus is to fulfil would seem to imply more than a willingness on his part to relinquish his slave, for it is difficult to conceive of this as a trust 'received' in the Lord. Whenever elsewhere Paul uses the same verb it always denotes what Paul himself or Christians generally have received either by direct revelation or mediated through others. It relates both to Christian ministry and to the content of Christian teaching. There is no close parallel to the use in Colossians iv. 17 suggested by Knox. Nevertheless Paul does sometimes use the word 'ministry' to describe the collection and this might perhaps support Knox's contention that Archippus' ministry involves a financial transaction.[2] But the allusion to Archippus in Colossians iv. 17 would be well accounted for by the supposition that he was deputy to Epaphras in the Colossian church and needed the encouragement of the members to fulfil his task.[3] If this supposition is correct it would also supply an explanation for the mention of this man in the letter to Philemon.

4. Another doubtful assumption on Knox's part is the opinion that Paul did not know the owner of the slave. But the wording of verse 19, 'to say nothing of your owing me even your own self' (RSV), is more intelligently understood if Paul not only knew the owner but had been the means of his conversion. The whole letter is written in too intimate a tone to be a communication to a stranger, and this is particularly borne out by verse 21, 'knowing that you will also do more than I say'.

5. That Paul desired the return of Onesimus may be legitimately inferred from verse 13, but is this the real purpose of the letter? Paul's greatest anxiety does not seem to centre in the owner's willingness to

---

[1] Goodspeed, *INT*, p. 111, notes that this is the usual ancient way, and undoubtedly Paul's way.

[2] Knox points out that Paul in Phm. 13 uses the cognate verb to describe Onesimus' service to Paul in his owner's stead (cf. *op. cit.*, p. 26).

[3] Bishop Lightfoot thinks that the tact and delicacy of Paul's pleading for Onesimus would be nullified if the letter had been intended for publication (*Colossians*, p. 279).

allow Onesimus to stay with Paul but the more serious consideration whether he would be prepared to receive him at all. How else can the words 'receive him as myself' (verse 17) be understood? At the same time there may well have been in Paul's mind the faint hope that the owner would go beyond his explicit request (cf. verse 21) and would release the slave for the work of the gospel.

6. That part of Knox's reconstruction which is most open to question is his identification of this Epistle with that mentioned in Colossians iv. 16. There is little doubt that the apostle is intending an exchange of letters, for Colossians is to be read in the Laodicean church and the Colossian church is to receive and read another from Laodicea. On the face of it, it would be most natural to suppose that as one is an Epistle addressed to a specific church, so also was the other. Knox's theory is hardly covered by the mention of the house-church in Philemon 2, since he himself admits that this church must have been in Colossae and not Laodicea.[1] It is moreover inconceivable that the letters (Colossians and Philemon) arrived at different times, and if Tychicus delivered them both would there have been any need to mention at the end of the Colossian letter that Philemon must also be read? In any case, why should it have been described as the letter from Laodicea? Moreover, if Philemon was really the letter 'from Laodicea', it is strange that in Marcion's list it is included under the name 'Philemon', while what appears to be our Ephesians was named as 'To the Laodiceans'. The latter identification was probably a guess on Marcion's part, but he shows no awareness of any tradition which associated Philemon with the same church.*

It is safe to conclude therefore that the traditional reconstruction is the more probable.

II. AUTHENTICITY

None but the most extreme negative critics have disputed the Pauline authorship of this Epistle.[2] It breathes the great-hearted tenderness of the apostle and its dealing with an intensely difficult situation points to an

[1] Goodspeed, on the other hand, maintains that Philemon's house-church was at Laodicea not Colossae (*INT*, p. 112).

[2] Even F. C. Baur, although denying its authenticity, admitted its noble Christian spirit (*Paul*, p. 476). It was its close connection with Colossians, which was deemed to belong to the second century, that forced the Tübingen school of criticism to reject Philemon. B. Weiss considered this one of Baur's worst blunders (cited by R. J. Knowling, *The Testimony of St. Paul to Christ*, 1905, p. 76)

author of much experience in handling social problems. An exquisite sense of humour, seen in the play on Onesimus' name, relieves the intensity of the plea but undoubtedly strengthens the appeal. We may safely conclude that in this brief Epistle we are listening to the authentic tones of Paul's own pleading.

III. DATE

Its close connection with Colossians makes it virtually certain that the two Epistles belong to the same period and the most probable theory is that Tychicus accompanied by Onesimus took them both to Colossae at the same time (i.e. during the first Roman imprisonment). This view seems to be substantiated by Paul's self-description as 'the aged' (verse 9), which would clearly be more appropriate at the close of his life. Yet the alternative 'ambassador', which many prefer as a more appropriate reading, would give no such indication of dating and no weight can consequently be placed upon this statement. There has been some recent advocacy that this Epistle, in common with Colossians, belongs to the period of the Ephesian ministry,[1] but the same general preference for Rome as the place of dispatch for Colossians holds also for this Epistle.

IV. ONESIMUS

According to Colossians iv. 9 Onesimus was a native of Colossae. It may be surmised that as a result of Paul's plea he was pardoned of any offence he may have committed and that he became a useful member of the Colossian church. Goodspeed and Knox would go further and identify him with the later bishop of Ephesus of the same name whom Ignatius mentions in his Epistle to that church. Knox has pointed out some resemblances between this passage in Ignatius and the language of Philemon, and he regards this as support for his suggestion.[2] There seems to be no positive reason for rejecting the theory that Onesimus

---

[1] Cf. G. S. Duncan (*St. Paul's Ephesian Ministry*, 1929). W. Michaelis, *Einleitung*, pp. 263–265, places Philemon in the same imprisonment period (at Ephesus) as Colossians, Ephesians and even Philippians.

[2] The main passages are Ignatius: *Ad Eph.* ii (cf. Phm. 13) and *Ad Eph.* iii (cf. Phm. 8, 9). What similarities exist are not verbally identical, and hardly warrant the supposition of Knox that Ignatius is purposely using Paul's line of appeal because of its familiarity to Onesimus. Cf. C. L. Mitton's discussion of this evidence in *The Formation of the Pauline Corpus of Letters* (1955), pp. 50 ff. He inclines to favour Knox's theory but admits its speculative character. P. N. Harrison also supports Knox's view (cf. *ATR*, xxxII, 1950, pp. 289–294).*

the slave later became bishop of the Ephesian church, but mere similarity of name cannot of itself confirm the identity. Knox develops still further his speculation about Onesimus by suggesting that as Bishop of Ephesus at the time he was responsible for the collection and publication of the Pauline Corpus. Because of his own intense personal interest in its subject-matter Onesimus ensured that the little letter to Philemon was included. This is not the place to discuss the formation of the Pauline Corpus but there are strong reasons for thinking that a collection existed long before this theory supposes.[1] Yet again there are no positive grounds for denying that Onesimus may have been the original collector of Paul's letters, but there are equally no grounds in support of it. It is no more than a subjective conjecture.

This Epistle brings into vivid focus the whole problem of slavery in the Christian Church. There is no thought of denunciation even in principle. The apostle deals with the situation as it then exists. He takes it for granted that Philemon has a claim of ownership on Onesimus and leaves the position unchallenged. Yet in one significant phrase Paul transforms the character of the master-slave relationship. Onesimus is returning no longer as a slave but as a brother beloved (verse 16). It is clearly incongruous for a Christian master to 'own' a brother in Christ in the contemporary sense of the word, and although the existing order of society could not be immediately changed by Christianity without a political revolution (which was contrary to Christian principles), the Christian master-slave relationship was so transformed from within that it was bound to lead ultimately to the abolition of the system.[2]

---

[1] See pp. 643 ff.

[2] If J. Knox's hypothesis that Paul is really suggesting that the owner should grant his slave his freedom for the sake of the gospel is correct, such an example would have exercised a powerful influence on other slave-owners in Colossae and district. Cf. P. N. Harrison's comments in *ATR*, *op. cit.*, pp. 268–294.

Such a plea as this on behalf of a slave has been paralleled by Pliny the Younger's letter to a friend requesting mercy towards an offending servant of whose penitence he is convinced (cf. J. B. Lightfoot, *Colossians*[3], pp. 316, 317, for the extract). But in this case there is no hint of a possible release. Although this letter expresses Roman nobility at its best, it does not compare in spiritual effectiveness with Paul's plea for Onesimus. For the difference between the Hebrew and Roman systems of slavery, cf. W. O. E. Oesterley, *Philemon*, in *EGT*, IV, pp. 207–209. Cf. also the interesting new fragment on slavery, probably written by Ignatius, published by J. H. Crehan, *Studia Patristica*, I, 1957, edited by K. Aland and F. L. Cross.

H. M. Carson, *The Epistles of Paul to the Colossians and Philemon* (TNT, 1960), pp. 21–24, has a concise note on slavery in which he firmly rejects any suggestion

CONTENTS

I. GREETING (verses 1–3)

As in Colossians, Timothy is linked with Paul in the address, but unlike the Colossian letter this one at once shows the author to be a prisoner. The addressees are Philemon, Apphia, Archippus, and the church in Philemon's house.

II. COMMENDATION OF PHILEMON (verses 4–7)

a. For his faith

Paul's news of Philemon leads him to express his thankfulness to God. He prays that Philemon's example may promote faith in others.

b. For his love

He has been conspicuous for his benevolence towards 'all the saints' and news of this has brought much joy to Paul's heart.

III. APOLOGIA FOR ONESIMUS (verses 8–22)

1. Paul pleads his own condition (verses 8, 9). He is a prisoner and as such has some claim to appeal to Philemon for love's sake.

2. He calls Onesimus his son in the faith, which suggests that he was the means of the latter's conversion (verse 10).

3. In sending back Onesimus Paul contends that he is sending back his own heart. Although previously unprofitable Onesimus has been transformed to become true to his name, which means 'profitable'. Paul would have preferred to keep him but would not do so without Philemon's consent (verses 11–14).

4. Paul suggests that Onesimus' defection may have been overruled so that Philemon might receive a brother beloved instead of a slave (verses 15, 16).

5. Paul now makes a strong plea to Philemon to receive him back and offers to pay any debts which Onesimus has incurred, although he

that the early Christians refrained from attacking this evil system through motives of expediency. Rather by inculcating a sense of responsibility on the part of masters and a sense of self-respect on the part of slaves, Christianity removed the main moral evils of the system.

tactfully implies that Philemon's debt to Paul is even greater. It would greatly refresh his heart to know that Philemon had acceded to his request (verses 17–20).

6. Paul's confidence is so great that he expects Philemon to exceed what he has asked and he makes a further request for a lodging to be prepared for him when he comes (verses 21, 22).

IV. CONCLUSION (verses 23–25)

Greetings are sent, as in Colossians, from Paul's companions, and the usual benediction is added.

ADDITIONAL NOTES

635. [1] On the literary form of this Epistle, cf. U. Wickert (*ZNTW*, 52, 1961, pp. 230–238), who regards it not so much as a private letter, but as an apostolic letter about a personal matter.

638. Knox's theory is opposed by F. F. Bruce, *BJRL*, XLVIII (1965), pp. 81–97. The latter favours a Roman origin for Philemon because of its close connection with Colossians. Bruce cites the view of E. R. Goodenough (*HTR*, 22, 1929, pp. 181 ff.) that a runaway slave might find sanctuary at an altar, perhaps even at the hearth of a private family. If so, the house where Paul was detained in Rome might well have served such a purpose. For a critique of Knox's theory, cf. H. Greeven, *ThLZ*, 79 (1954), cols. 373 ff.

639. [2] The suggestion that Onesimus later became bishop of Ephesus has the cautious support of F. F. Bruce, *op. cit.*, pp. 93, 97.

CHAPTER TWENTY-ONE

THE COLLECTION OF PAUL'S LETTERS

From the early part of the second century of the Christian era there is evidence that the letters of Paul were treasured not merely as isolated communications but as a definite collection of writings, now commonly described as the Pauline Corpus. The history of these writings subsequent to the death of Paul, and the manner in which they came to be formed into such a collection, is obscure through lack of sufficient data. It might be most prudent to leave in obscurity what history has failed to illuminate without attempting any speculative reconstructions were it not for the previous existence of such speculations.[1] Some of these affect not only our approach to early Christian history but our estimation of the Pauline Epistles themselves and in particular of the influence of their author. An investigation into the probable processes of compilation is not therefore out of place in an introductory study of these Epistles.

I. ANCIENT ATTESTATION TO THE PAULINE CORPUS OF LETTERS

Of great significance in our present study is the fact that the earliest Canon of the New Testament writings of which we have any evidence consisted almost exclusively of Pauline writings.[2] Marcion's description of the entire Corpus as the 'Apostolikon' is sufficient indication of the immense prestige which he attached to the apostle Paul, and to a 'collection' of his writings. From Tertullian's comments on Marcion's approach to Paul it is probable that this Corpus was part of a larger Corpus of New Testament writings from which Marcion selected

---

[1] K. and S. Lake, although including a chapter in their *Introduction to the New Testament* on 'The Canonical Collection of the Pauline Epistles', conclude that the collection of the Corpus and its original contents are unknown (p. 100) and this opinion is representative of the cautious attitude of most scholars on this subject.

[2] 2 Pet. iii. 15 f. may be cited here as evidence of a collection of Paul's writings, but widespread differences of opinion regarding the authenticity and date of 2 Peter make this evidence of varying value. If the Epistle is dated before Marcion's time it is a clear indication of the earlier existence of a Pauline Corpus of letters, but it tells us nothing about its composition.

certain writings in support of his own particular brand of teaching.[1] Marcion included only ten Pauline Epistles, excluding the Pastorals.[2] Although many scholars regard this as evidence that the Pastorals were not included in the Pauline Corpus at that time there are strong reasons, based on Tertullian's evidence, for assuming that Marcion's known policy of excision may have been responsible for the omission (see pp. 586 f.). If the recently discovered *Gospel of Truth* from the Nag Hammadi Gnostic library is, as van Unnik thinks, by Valentinus, it may be cited as contemporary evidence from Marcion's time of a New Testament Canon similar to our own. Since both Marcion and Valentinus were in Rome, this would suggest that Marcion selected his Canon from a previously existing although non-formal one. But the evidence is uncertain because not all agree with van Unnik's hypothesis.[3]

By the time of the Muratorian Canon (probably some thirty or forty years later) the thirteen Epistles regarded as belonging to the Corpus were arranged in two groups, church Epistles and private communications. Subsequent to this time the evidence varies between a Corpus of thirteen or fourteen Epistles, according to whether Hebrews was considered to be Pauline or not; but apart from this variation there was no doubt about the content of the Pauline Corpus. In the extant remains of the Chester Beatty Codex of the Epistles the concluding writings are missing and there is some dispute about the original inclusion of the Pastoral Epistles, but this evidence cannot be used as an indication that their canonicity was at that time disputed (see p. 587). In the writings of one Syriac Father, Ephraim, an additional letter to

[1] Cf. P. Batiffol, *RB* (1903), p. 26; C. H. Turner, *JTS*, x (1909), pp. 357 f., J. Moffatt, *ILNT*, p. 60. Since Marcion adapted the Church's Luke to his own requirements, it is most likely that he similarly adapted the Church's Pauline Canon. G. Salmon (*INT*[6], 1892, pp. 358 ff.), on the strength of this argument, maintained that 'the Church's collection of thirteen letters is more ancient than Marcion's collection of only ten'. Cf. Zahn's very full discussion on Marcion's New Testament in *Geschichte des neutestamentlichen Kanons*, I (1888), pp. 585 ff., especially pp. 634 ff.

[2] F. C. Burkitt, *The Gospel History and its Transmission* (1911), pp. 318, 319, wondered whether Marcion may not have been the first collector of Paul's Epistles, but there is no evidence for this tentative suggestion. It is highly improbable that a heretic should have been the first to appreciate the value of the Pauline Corpus especially in view of the speed with which the Ignatian Letters were collected. See Turner's criticism of Burkitt, *op. cit.*, pp. 358 ff.

[3] van Unnik's views are set forth in his essay 'The Gospel of Truth and the New Testament' in *The Jung Codex*, edited by F. L. Cross (1955), pp. 81–129.

the Corinthians was included (3 Corinthians), but this was derived from the spurious *Acts of Paul* and by the time of the Syriac Canon (*c.* AD 400)[1] and the Peshitta it had dropped out of the Pauline Corpus. In the Latin medieval church another, to the Laodiceans, was included, but this was manifestly a forgery on the strength of the reference in Colossians iv. 16.

II. THE PROBLEM OF THE ORIGINAL COLLECTION

Previous to the time of Marcion the evidence is very scrappy. It consists chiefly of isolated citations from the works of the apostolic Fathers. When these are tabulated certain Epistles are found to be cited earlier than others and the real problem centres round the interpretation of these data.[2] There are two possible approaches. Either the evidence may be taken to indicate that the earlier authors cited only the Epistles known to them, in which case their Pauline Corpus was partial, or it may be regarded as an indication of a complete Pauline Corpus from only part of which the authors have cited.

a. *Theories of partial collections*

Because of the diversity among the citations in the apostolic Fathers and of the lack of exact agreement in order between Marcion, the Muratorian Canon, Tertullian and Origen, Kirsopp Lake[3] suggested a gradual process for the formation of the Corpus. Several churches would in the course of time make their own collections which would differ considerably in contents. It is part of Lake's presuppositions that from the first certain churches would value certain Pauline Epistles and would add to their own letter or letters others of which they had heard which were

---

[1] This Canon contains two entries 'Of the Philippians' but this is clearly an erroneous scribal repetition. For the text of this Canon see A. Souter, *The Text and Canon of the New Testament* (1913), p. 226.

[2] Cf. the Oxford Society's *The New Testament in the Apostolic Fathers* (1905), p. 137. A much fuller account is given in A. E. Barnett's *Paul becomes a Literary Influence* (1941). In addition, for Ignatius, see P. N. Harrison's *Polycarp's Two Epistles to the Philippians* (1936), pp. 231 ff., and J. Knox's *Philemon among the Letters of Paul* (1935).

[3] *The Earlier Epistles of Paul* (1927), pp. 356 ff. Cf. B. H. Streeter's *The Four Gospels* (1924), pp. 526 f., *The Primitive Church* (1929), pp. 159 ff., P. N. Harrison, *Polycarp's Two Epistles*, pp. 235 ff. A. Deissmann doubted whether the collection was made all at once, but thought the process was probably begun soon after Paul's death (*Bible Studies*, p. 56).

in the possession of neighbouring churches. After some interval of time comparison of these collections would result in the completed Corpus being accepted by the Christian churches as a whole. The considerable variation in the order in which the Epistles were placed, according to various church Fathers and canonical lists, might appear at first to lend strong support to Lake's opinion. Other scholars have adhered to a similar gradual-collection theory while differing in the detailed reconstruction.[1]

b. Theories of complete collection

Under this heading of theories of complete collection two contrasting hypotheses must be distinguished. First, there is the theory that Paul's letters were highly valued from the first, in which case each individual church would have the urge not only to preserve its own but to obtain copies of others of which it would readily hear through the frequent intercommunication between the Asiatic and European churches. For convenience this type of theory will be called the theory of immediate value, because the *general* value of the Epistles is thought to have been recognized by the original recipients as distinct from their relevance to the specific occasion which prompted them. And secondly, there is the

---

[1] For instance, B. H. Streeter and P. N. Harrison, see previous footnote. This type of theory, while not intrinsically impossible, depends for its basis on negative rather than positive evidence, it being assumed that non-quotation must indicate non-circulation. But this is basically an argument from silence which must be treated with the utmost reserve. If Clement, for example, cites few of Paul's Epistles it is precarious to assert he must have been ignorant of the rest. The case of 2 Corinthians is instructive. J. H. Kennedy (*The Second and Third Epistles to the Corinthians*, 1900, pp. 142–153) discussed at length not only the absence of citation by Clement of 2 Corinthians but the occasions when it would have strengthened his argument to have done so, e.g. where Clement specifically mentions 1 Corinthians when dealing with 'sedition', 2 Corinthians would have been more appropriate. In 1 Clem. v, where Paul is described as an example of endurance, 2 Corinthians xi, which would have supplied admirable illustrations, does not seem to be reflected. Kennedy (pp. 153 ff.) therefore concluded that 2 Corinthians was not published until after Clement's letter (see note on p. 437). But the data on which Kennedy argues could be adequately explained on the simpler expedient that Clement was more impressed by 1 Corinthians than 2 Corinthians, or perhaps better understood it. Cf. also R. H. Strachan, *The Second Epistle to the Corinthians*, pp. xxi, xxii.

G. Zuntz, *The Text of the Pauline Epistles* (1953), pp. 278, 279, suggests that smaller collections may have been made in and around Ephesus and that some editing processes took place at Corinth.

theory of lapsed interest, based on the assumption that for a time subsequent to Paul's death his letters were generally neglected.

(i) *Theories of immediate value.* One of the clearest exponents of this type of theory was A. Harnack[1] who maintained that the letters themselves would strike the recipients with their lasting value and would prompt them to treasure these letters. He drew support for this contention from 2 Corinthians x. 10, where the apostle quotes his opponents' acknowledgment that his letters are 'weighty and powerful'; from 2 Corinthians x. 9, iii. 1, where his skill as a letter-writer is inferred; from 1 Corinthians vii. 17, where Paul implies that he maintains close communication with 'all the churches', presumably by letter; and from 2 Thessalonians ii. 2, iii. 17, where reference appears to be made to the issuing of false letters in Paul's name, which would bear testimony to the great influence of Paul's genuine letters. From this evidence Harnack suggested not only an earlier collection of the Pauline Corpus than Lake assumed, but the deliberate selection of some and rejection of other Pauline Epistles.

It is evident that not all the Epistles that Paul wrote have been preserved. In all probability at least two written to the Corinthians have perished (see pp. 425 f., 437), while certainly the one to the Laodiceans (Col. iv. 16) is lost. Many more of which no hint is given in the canonical writings must have been sent as the apostle daily took upon him 'the care of all the churches' (2 Cor. xi. 28). The problem arises as to the fate of these. If they were excluded as Harnack suggested by definite selection, on what basis was the selection made? His own suggestion was that the determining factor was what was edifying and instructive for the churches generally.[2] Many scholars consider that such arbitrary selection is improbable. Some modification of this theory of immediate value will be given later when the other alternative, which is here called the theory of lapsed interest, has been considered.

(ii) *The theory of lapsed interest.* It was E. J. Goodspeed[3] who strongly

---

[1] *Die Briefsammlung des Apostels Paulus* (1926), pp. 7, 8.

[2] *Op. cit.*, p. 10.

[3] Cf. *New Chapters in New Testament Study*, pp. 22–49; *The Meaning of Ephesians* (1933), pp. 82 ff.; *The Key to Ephesians* (1956), pp. v ff. C. L. Mitton, *The Formation of the Pauline Corpus of Letters* (1955), supports Goodspeed's contentions. Yet they were not propounding a new theory, for Zahn (*INT*, 1909) criticizes a similar view current in his time (Vol. I, p. 161). For other supporters, cf. A. E. Barnett, *op. cit.*, and J. Knox, *Philemon among the Letters of Paul* (1935), both disciples of Goodspeed.

advocated an alternative theory that Paul's influence waned almost completely after his death and was revived only as a result of the publication of the Acts (which he dates some time before AD 90, at least in its original form, which he does not consider necessarily identical with the canonical book). The publication of Acts was therefore the stimulus which prompted the collection of the Pauline letters into a Corpus, and their subsequent publication. This Corpus was therefore prompted by veneration of the apostle and recognition that his true worth could not be appreciated by a single Epistle.[1] The grounds for this theory may be summarized as follows.

1. Firstly there is the absence of use in other New Testament writings until after AD 90. The main basis for this assertion is the lack of any trace of these Epistles in the writings of the Synoptic Gospels or the Acts,[2] and since these are the only writings which Goodspeed dates between Paul's death and AD 90, he considers this to be evidence that Paul was during this period forgotten. The greatest importance is given to the apparent ignorance of Paul's letters on the part of the author of Acts. An author with such admiration for Paul would surely have obtained as many copies of Epistles written by Paul as he could lay his hands upon, it is alleged. The strength of this argument depends on two considerations: the late dating of Acts[3] and the assumption that had Luke been acquainted with Paul's body of letters he must have mentioned his letter-writing activity and must have included echoes of Paul's thought in his own work culled from the collected letters. But the late dating of Acts may reasonably be challenged,[4] while the assigning of other New Testament books, which according to Goodspeed show traces of all Paul's letters, to the same earlier period would seriously weaken his contention.[5]

[1] J. Knox, *The Early Church and the Coming Great Church* (1957), pp. 100 ff., who takes this view, also suggests that the Corpus may have been prompted by a growing experience of unity in the Church. The collected letters are thus viewed as an impressive message to the whole Church. But Knox's view of earlier disunity is exaggerated in an attempt to lend weight to his theory that the second-century catholic church was the earliest united church.

[2] Cf. E. J. Goodspeed's *INT*, pp. 210, 211, *New Chapters* (*op. cit.*), pp. 62, 63.

[3] E. J. Goodspeed produces fifteen reasons for a late date for Acts (*INT*, pp. 191 ff.), but many of these reasons are highly subjective.

[4] Cf. F. F. Bruce's argument for an early date, *The Acts of the Apostles* (1951), pp. 10–14. Also R. B. Rackham, *The Acts of the Apostles* (1901), pp. l–lv.

[5] A. Deissmann, *Light from the Ancient East* (1923), p. 246, suggested that Luke's failure to reflect Paul's Epistles indicates that they were then not widely known.

2. Then there is the sudden increase in their use after AD 90. The evidence of Pauline Epistles used by the writers of Revelation, Hebrews, 1 Clement, 1 Peter, Ignatius, Polycarp and John is appealed to under this claim.[1] Not all of the ten Paulines (Goodspeed excludes the Pastorals from his considerations) are cited in all these works but the evidence seems strong enough to Goodspeed to conclude that at this period the full Corpus was widely known.

3. The search for all available remains is also held to yield evidence in support of this view. Mitton appeals to the dislocations and interpolations in the extant Pauline Epistles in support of the contention that due care had not been taken of the Epistles at an earlier stage.[2] He mentions particularly 2 Corinthians x–xiii, vi. 14–vii. 1, Romans xvi and Philippians iii. 1b–iv. 3 as examples of earlier letters which have been incorporated into other letters. The force of this line of evidence will naturally depend on whether these portions are considered as interpolations or not, but there are strong grounds for disputing that they are (see pp. 430 ff., 425 f., 400 ff., 536 ff.). If, of course, the theory of interpolations could be maintained it would contribute to the view that some of the remains of Paul's letters were in a fragmentary state and were attached by the original collectors to letters which had been preserved intact. But even so the theory of a period of neglect would be no more than an inference from the evidence, which, being itself hypothetical, imparts a particularly inconclusive character to the inference.

4. A further point concerns the emergence of Marcion's Canon. Some scholars consider the Pastorals were issued to offset a tendency for the Pauline Epistles to be appropriated by heretical sects and therefore lost to the orthodox Church.[3] Thus Marcion's Canon, followed by the Pas-

T. W. Manson in a review of Mitton's book (*JTS*, New Series VII, 1956, pp. 286 ff.) found no difficulty in the neglect of Paul either by the Evangelists because of their other subject-matter or by the author of Acts because his main interest was not Paul's theology but Paul's adventures. He further acutely pointed out that a theory of neglect must make clear what is neglected and in this case it could not be the non-existent Corpus and we are therefore left to imagine the coincidence of Pauline neglect in churches stretching from Rome to Galatia.

[1] Cf. E. J. Goodspeed, *INT*, p. 211.

[2] Cf. *op. cit.*, pp. 25 ff. Cf. also S. G. F. Brandon, *op. cit.*, p. 215.

[3] Cf. C. L. Mitton's discussion, *op. cit.*, pp. 38 ff. Cf. also Goodspeed's *New Chapters*, p. 185. A. Harnack, *The Origin of the New Testament* (1925), p. 52, expressed the opinion that the appeal of the Marcionites and Gnostics to the apostle must have made Churchmen nervous. He cited Tertullian as ironically calling Paul '*apostolus hereticorum*'.

torals, has been suggested as evidence of hesitating acceptance of Paul's Epistles[1] on the part of the orthodox Church. But this idea cannot be maintained for it is inconceivable that such hesitation would have been dispelled by the pseudonymous publication of the Pastoral Epistles. It is incredible that Epistles falsely ascribed to Paul could have been immediately accepted in orthodox circles if the orthodoxy of the genuine Epistles was under suspicion.[2]

5. Grounds for this theory are also found in the use of the letter-form convention after AD 90. Since Goodspeed relegates all the New Testament Epistles, except the nine Paulines which he accepts, to a period after AD 90, he is able to attribute the adoption of the letter-form to the influence of the Pauline letter-forms in the recently published Corpus. But the theory that Paul was an isolated innovator in the realm of Christian letter-writing and that for the space of some thirty years no other Christian leader thought to use such a method is highly improbable.[3] Nor is it evident why the published Corpus should have had such extraordinary impact whereas the original individual Epistles had so little effect as to be, on Goodspeed's theory, entirely neglected. The mass of papyrological correspondence which has been discovered in the past half-century is evidence enough of the widespread use of letter-forms in the contemporary world even if the New Testament examples have peculiarities of their own.

6. There is the emergence of sevenfold collections. By grouping the Corinthian Epistles together and similarly the Thessalonian, the Pauline

---

[1] Cf. also W. Bauer's *Rechtgläubigkeit und Ketzerei in ältesten Christentum* (1934), pp. 215 ff. E. J. Goodspeed takes the same view that the Pastorals were written as a group to free the Pauline Collection from suspicion following Marcion's use of it (*Christianity goes to Press*, 1940, p. 60). Cf. also F. D. Gealy, *1 and 2 Timothy and Titus, IB*, pp. 351 ff.

[2] For further discussion of this alleged anti-Marcion motive see pp. 618 f.

[3] A. Deissmann, *Light from the Ancient East* (1923), pp. 233 ff., has no hesitation in regarding the Epistles of Paul as 'non-literary letters'. He cites approvingly U. von Wilamowitz-Moellendorff, 'Die griechische Literatur des Altentums' in *Die Kultur der Gegenwart*[2] (1907), pp. 159 f. He nevertheless regards the other New Testament Epistles (except 2 and 3 John) as in the category of literary Epistles because of the absence of a specific address. E. J. Goodspeed, *New Chapters in New Testament Study*, p. 67, considers that these other Epistles were imitations of Paul's letters, but this could be true, in Deissmann's judgment, only if Paul's letters had become misconceived as literature (*Bible Studies*, 1901, p. 56). Yet the needs of the communities which called forth the production of Paul's letters may have promoted the use of the less personal epistolary type.

Epistles may be said to include seven letters to churches and this is said to be paralleled in the letters to the Asiatic churches in the Apocalypse and the Ignatian group of letters.[1] Because of the unnaturalness of commencing an apocalypse in such a way it is suggested that this has been influenced by a literary convention and the emergence of the Pauline Corpus would be an adequate motive for such a fashion.[2] But the number seven was of such significance to the author of the Apocalypse (occurring nearly fifty times) that it hardly seems necessary to appeal to the publication of a sevenfold Pauline Corpus (if such it was) to account for it. Not more convincing is the supposed parallel between the introductory letter in Revelation i and Ephesians considered as an introductory letter to the Pauline Corpus, for there is a literary unity and purpose behind the first three chapters of the Apocalypse which is entirely lacking from a Pauline collection with Ephesians at its head.[3]

7. The production of Ephesians is brought forward as a further point in favour of the theory. It would not be unfair to say that the need for postulating a satisfactory motive for the pseudonymous production of Ephesians has been the major reason for Goodspeed's hypothesis for the publication of the Corpus. Recognizing that it is not sufficient to deny Pauline authorship without providing an adequate occasion for a Paulinist publication, Goodspeed[4] maintains that Ephes-

[1] It should be noted that the Ignatian Corpus does not furnish an exact parallel, since it contains only six addressed to churches and one to Polycarp. If Polycarp's own letter be included as an introductory note the total would be eight, not seven. Cf. Manson's comments against this sevenfold Corpus theory (*JTS*, New Series VII, 1956, pp. 286 ff.). He makes the following suggestive points in rejecting it. (a) The Muratorian fragment speaks of seven churches not seven letters; (b) the letters of Rev. i–iii never circulated separately and were in fact a unity; (c) Ignatius wrote seven epistles because he had something to say, not because of a hypothetical Pauline Corpus; and (d) if the Pauline Corpus was sevenfold it would become eightfold immediately Ephesians, put out as a genuine letter, was added. These criticisms undoubtedly focus attention on some of the major weaknesses of the theory.

[2] Cf. E. J. Goodspeed, *INT*, pp. 211, 212; C. L. Mitton, *op. cit.*, p. 37.

[3] The Muratorian Canon draws an analogy between John's letters to seven churches and Paul's, but it implies that Paul has followed John. In the case of the Apocalypse the number is clearly symbolic of all. The Canon makes this clear by the statement, 'et Johannes enim in Apocalypsi, licet septem ecclesiis scribat, tamen omnibus dicit' (cited from Bishop Westcott's edition, *On the Canon of the New Testament*[4], 1875, p. 529).

[4] *INT*, pp. 231 ff. Cf. C. L. Mitton, *The Epistle to the Ephesians* (1951), pp. 45–54.

ians is a kind of introductory summary for the entire Corpus (see pp. 512 ff. for further discussion) specially designed for those unacquainted with Pauline thought. This Ephesians-theory is therefore a keystone in Goodspeed's structure. Mitton[1] gives rather guardedly eight reasons supporting this contention and these may be listed as follows.

a. The original collection would probably have been issued in two rolls, and Ephesians and Corinthians (1 and 2) could appropriately have occupied the first roll.[2]

b. The circular character of Ephesians and the omission of any specific destination in its opening verse is in harmony with the theory.

c. The later attachment of the name 'Ephesians' to the Epistle would be adequately explained if the publication was made from Ephesus.

d. The use of a sevenfold corpus in the Apocalypse, as mentioned above, with its introductory letter is thought to have been influenced by the Pauline Corpus with Ephesians at its head.

e. The Ignatian Letters with the introductory epistle of Polycarp follow the same pattern.

f. Ignatius shows acquaintance with 1 Corinthians and Ephesians but there is doubt about the rest (although Goodspeed maintained that he knew all but 2 Corinthians and 2 Thessalonians[3]). The suggested explanation is that Ignatius had not long been acquainted with the published Corpus and those that headed the Corpus gained most attention, particularly the first roll if the hypothesis stated in (a) above is correct.

g. The address in 1 Corinthians, not only to the Corinthians them-

---

[1] *The Formation of the Pauline Corpus of Letters*, pp. 66–74.

[2] While Corinthians and Ephesians *could* have occupied the first roll, there is more reason to suppose that Galatians shared this position with Corinthians as in the Canons of both Marcion and Tertullian. For a criticism of the Goodspeed-Knox hypothesis for the order of the Epistles, cf. C. H. Buck, *JBL* (1949), 68, pp. 351–357. Jack Finegan (*HTR*, 1956, pp. 85–103), on the basis of stichometry, explains the various orders of the Pauline letters and considers it probable that length was in every case the determining factor, the varying positions being caused by varying methods of computing *stichoi*. He thinks it possible that the original collection was contained in a codex and that no evidence can be brought in support of the two-roll theory. For Knox's reply, cf. *HTR*, 50 (1957), pp. 311–314.

[3] Cited without reference in C. L. Mitton's *op. cit.*, p. 70. It is most damaging to this theory that both Clement of Rome and Ignatius are so deeply impressed by Ephesians that it is inconceivable that it was published only a few years previously.

selves but also to those 'that call upon the name of the Lord Jesus Christ in every place' (which is suggested to be an editor's addition), would fit the theory that 1 Corinthians stood at the head of the Corpus preceded only by Ephesians as a covering letter.

h. The strange order in which the Muratorian fragment places the Epistles could be explained if the scribe reversed the order in the two scrolls mentioned above, thus placing Corinthians before Ephesians and then adding the other Epistles ending with Romans. But Knox,[1] who suggests this, himself admits its fanciful character.

The speculative and inconclusive character of these eight reasons will be immediately apparent and the question arises whether a more satisfactory theory for the collection of the Pauline Corpus cannot be suggested.

(iii) *A theory of an early personal collection.* In those hypotheses so far considered we have found examples of early church collections and of later church collections, while Goodspeed's own theory proposes that the work of publication was probably in the hands of the author of Ephesians. Knox[2] and Mitton[3] both warmly recommend the suggestion that Onesimus was the collector, although they admit its speculative character. But might not a more probable theory be that the collector was one of Paul's personal associates who conceived the usefulness of such a collection very soon after Paul's death?

This hypothesis would avoid the obvious weaknesses of the Good-speed hypothesis, particularly the assumption of the wholesale neglect of Paul after his death. That a period of neglect should follow the in-credible missionary activities of the indefatigable apostle, to be itself followed by a period of extraordinary literary influence, is a cycle difficult to conceive. Since all the major churches in the world at that time had either been founded by Paul or had had living contacts with him it is impossible to postulate a complete neglect of him so soon. A gradual lack of grasp of his importance and a waning of his influence would be nearer the regions of probability.[4] He may have been criti-cized and some of his statements may have seemed hard to understand, but the neglect theory, based as it is on hypothetical dating of other

[1] Cf. *Marcion and the New Testament*, p. 71.
[2] Cf. *Philemon among the Letters of Paul* (1935). See the discussion of this in the introduction to Philemon, pp. 639 f.
[3] Cf. *op. cit.*, pp. 50 ff.
[4] Cf. H. A. A. Kennedy, *The Theology of the Epistles* (1919), pp. 9 ff.

New Testament books, does less than justice to the apostle as we know him from his letters and the Acts.[1]

There are certain data, in fact, which would seem to support the opposite contention that Paul's memory would have been cherished after his death. The evidence is admittedly somewhat inferential but is worth pondering.

1. The principle of exchanging letters which the apostle himself encouraged (Col. iv. 16) would have impressed itself upon his close associates.[2] It is not improbable that Paul instructed them to extend this principle. But in any case they would themselves have readily recognized the value of exchange.

2. The apostle encouraged the public reading of letters (1 Thes. v. 27). This may of course be restricted to the original delivery of 1 Thessalonians but it is clear that all his Epistles addressed to churches were intended to be publicly read.[3] This may well have whetted the appetite for more.

3. The fact that some of Paul's letters were undoubtedly lost may be otherwise interpreted than by postulating a lack of care. They may have been of such a character that they could supply no edification for any except the immediate recipients and for this reason were never repeated or treasured. None would be able to discern better than Paul's personal friends between the particular and general character of his writings.

4. The general address of 1 Corinthians must have been intended for wider distribution than the specific address to the Corinthian church. There is no textual evidence in support of the theory that these general words were added later when the Corpus was formed,[4] and until such evidence is forthcoming they must be given their full weight. This is not to suggest that Paul had any other churches specifically in mind when writing the Epistle for it is clearly addressed to the particular problems of the Corinthian church. But it is at least possible that Paul recognized that his enunciation of principles would have relevance to a wider audience.[5]

---

[1] As the Ignatian letters were requested by the Philippian church soon after the martyr had passed on his way through the city (Polycarp, *Ad Phil.* xiii. 2) it is inconceivable that Paul's correspondence was treated with any less respect.

[2] Cf. Th. Zahn, *INT*, I, pp. 161 f.

[3] Cf. G. Milligan, *The New Testament Documents* (1913), p. 211.

[4] Cf. C. L. Mitton, *op. cit.*, p. 72.

[5] G. Salmon (*INT*, p. 359) cites the evidence of Eusebius (iv. 23) that in Dionysius' lifetime his letters had already passed into general circulation.

5. The probability that other Epistles of Paul had the character of circular letters (Romans and Ephesians) adds further weight to the suggestion that he himself envisaged the sharing of his matured reflections among groups of churches.

6. The earliest apostolic Fathers show great respect for the apostle and refer to him in such a way as to suggest that their respect for him was generally recognized. Clement (v. 5-7) calls him 'the greatest example of endurance'. Did he learn this from the Acts history or was it common knowledge? Since he recounts details which are not included in the Acts he must have culled part at least of his data from elsewhere. He speaks, for instance, of Paul's seven imprisonments and of his being a herald in the West. It is not impossible that Clement knew Paul during his Roman imprisonment some thirty years earlier.[1] Similarly Ignatius has great respect for the apostle (cf. Rom. iv. 3, Eph. xii. 2), calling him 'sanctified' and 'right blessed' and praying that he might be found in his footsteps. Such high regard for Paul on the part of both Ignatius and his readers is more probable if Paul's Epistles had been loved and cherished for a considerable time than if they had been published no more than twenty years previously. Ignatius assumes his readers will acknowledge unquestionably Paul's spiritual authority over them.

7. An early date for Acts would account for the absence from that book of any allusion to the Pauline Corpus, and would therefore allow for the possibility of publication of the Epistles in the period immediately following Paul's death.

In the light of these considerations the following tentative suggestions may be examined. In the period after Paul's death conditions would have been most favourable for a stimulation rather than a diminution of interest in his writings. Tychicus had recently been on a mission to the Lycus valley with Colossians, Philemon and Ephesians (assuming the Roman origin of these). He had since been to Ephesus (2 Tim. iv. 12) where Timothy had also been for a time in residence. Titus, another of Timothy's companions, had gone to Dalmatia (2

---

[1] Clement assumes, in writing to the Corinthians (xliv. 3 ff.), that some of those still holding office were originally appointed by the apostles, and this would suggest a continuity of witness especially to the particular apostle whose labours had resulted in the establishment of the Corinthian church. In section xlvii of the same epistle, the author not only reveals his own acquaintance with Paul's letter (i.e. 1 Corinthians) but assumes that his readers are equally acquainted with it.

Tim. iv. 10) and since he had previously been in Crete he may well have had contact with the churches of Achaia and Macedonia *en route*. His close relations with the Corinthian church are in any case well known. Timothy had himself been in close touch with the Philippian and Thessalonian churches and had in all probability maintained this link. Had he gone to Rome on Paul's summons (2 Tim. iv. 9, 21) he would have had an opportunity to obtain a copy if need be of the Epistle sent there. Moreover, Timothy's home town was one of the South Galatian towns and as in all probability Paul's letter to the Galatians was sent to the churches in that region he would have had access to that Epistle.

On hearing of Paul's death, Timothy, who was generally regarded as Paul's successor in maintaining the links between the Pauline churches, may have recognized the need for generally bolstering his own authority by means of a Pauline collection of writings. He may have been prompted to this by Paul's own words addressed to him in 2 Timothy ii. 2 where he is urged to commit to faithful men 'the things that you have heard of me'. How better could this be done than by collecting up the Pauline letters and depositing them with the various churches? This would well suit Paul's own notion of his teaching as a 'deposit'. Further, Timothy was told to collect the 'parchments' for Paul and although we can only conjecture what these were, is it quite out of the question that they were copies in note form of some of the apostle's communications? If such a suggestion does not commend itself it is at least suggestive that Timothy probably retained the parchments after Paul's death and possession of them may have stimulated the desire to make a fuller collection of Paul's writings.

A publication of the Pauline letters by Timothy would have been invaluable for welding together the Pauline churches after the apostle's death. It would also account for the supposed literary connections of these Epistles with Hebrews and the Epistles of John, James and Peter. It is much more probable under this hypothesis that the difficulties of Pauline thought caused a decline of influence rather than that lack of immediate interest caused the letters to be neglected for a time. The latter theory ignores the large number of people who owed much to the apostle and who must still have been alive during this 'neglect' period. Would these have allowed his memory to fade? Would they not have treasured his literary remains since his letter-writing propensities were so widely known? It might be objected that the original recipients of Galatians or 2 Corinthians would not have been too keen about preserving them, but this difficulty would be obviated if Timothy were the collector, particularly if he knew that the letters had effected the desired change. This would enhance their general spiritual value.

Since Timothy and his associates were in touch with all the churches to which Paul addressed Epistles it is reasonable to suppose that they took an active part in the collection. This would also account for the inclusion of the Pastoral Epistles. In this way the influence of the great apostle was preserved for posterity.[1]

[1] In his article on 'The Epistolary Form in the New Testament', *ET*, LXIII (1951–52), pp. 296 ff., R. L. Archer argues for an early personal collection but from a rather different angle from that suggested above. He approaches it from the dispatching end rather than the receiving end and proposes that Paul kept copies or partial copies of all his letters. The impetus for their subsequent publication he finds in Seneca's thesis that a worthy collection of letters should set forth a philosophy and this he suggests was the Christians' response. The inclusion of letters of an essentially personal character (like Philemon) which was deprecated by Seneca in his opposition to Cicero's writings, would nevertheless have been favoured in his time by those belonging to the school of Cicero who were gaining increasing influence. Archer therefore thinks that Seneca's eccentricity and Roman admiration for Cicero's style may have given us nearly half the New Testament. But it is difficult to believe that Paul or the Christian Church were influenced by either Seneca's opinions or Cicero's practice. The choice of literary forms was dictated by the needs of communities or individuals and the preservation of these forms was prompted by their general interest and spiritual power. At the same time Archer has done well to point out the contemporary Roman literary atmosphere as part of the background against which the Pauline Corpus came into being. Cf. L. Mowry, *JBL*, LXIII (1944), pp. 73–86 for a discussion of the early circulation of Paul's letters.

PAUL AND HIS SOURCES

Source criticism has mainly confined itself to the problems of the Gospels and the Acts and very little attention has been paid to the source criticism of the Pauline Epistles. This is undoubtedly because the Epistles cannot be dissected into clear-cut literary sources as the Synoptic Gospels have been. Nevertheless a wrong approach to these Epistles has often resulted from a failure to recognize Paul's debt to his predecessors. He has too often been treated as an isolated phenomenon entirely responsible for his own theological outlook, which has then been regarded either as an alien imposition upon the simpler teaching of Jesus, or as a powerful by-product of Christianity which had little effective impression upon Paul's contemporaries. But all presentations of Paul which drive a wedge between him and primitive Christianity are falsely based, for there is considerable evidence to show that he inherited a great deal not only of primitive teaching but also of primitive teaching forms.

I. THE PRIMITIVE KERYGMA

In his study of the apostolic preaching, Dodd[1] made a distinction between *kerygma* (preaching) and *didachē* (teaching), and cited evidence from parts of the Acts and of the Pauline Epistles of a primitive pre-Pauline *kerygma*. The passages from the Epistles point to a primitive substratum on which the major Pauline doctrines were based. The most important passage is 1 Corinthians xv. 1–7 where the apostle clearly states that he preaches what had been delivered to him. This central tradition concerned the death and resurrection of Christ. The same emphasis is found in Romans i. 4, viii. 34. The connection between Christ's death and our sins also found an element in the earliest preaching tradition (cf. 1 Cor. xv. 3; Gal. i. 3, 4). Dodd finds two other aspects of primitive preaching, eschatology (Rom. ii. 16; 1 Thes. i. 10) and the work of the Holy Spirit in the believer (Gal. iv. 6).[2]

---

[1] *The Apostolic Preaching and its Developments* (1936).
[2] See also H. A. A. Kennedy, *The Theology of the Epistles* (1919), pp. 97–118.

A. M. Hunter[1] calls attention to other evidence of pre-Pauline formulae and *kerygma* in Romans x. 8, 9, the confession that Jesus is Lord in Romans iv. 24, 25, the belief in the resurrection of Jesus and in His death for sins and the recurrent connection between faith, hope and love in Romans v. 1–5; 1 Corinthians xiii; Galatians v. 5, 6; Ephesians iv. 2–5; Colossians i. 4, 5; 1 Thessalonians i. 3, v. 8. Hunter[2] finds pre-Pauline formulary material not only in 1 Corinthians xv. 3 ff. but also in 1 Corinthians xi. 23–25 (the institution of the Supper).[3] He speaks of these passages, together with 2 Thessalonians ii. 15, as examples of guarded tradition.

II. PRIMITIVE CATECHISMS

The suggestion that Paul and other New Testament writers made use of existing catechetical forms was suggested by Archbishop Carrington,[4] who drew attention to two main features emerging from the passages which he had previously studied. In 1 Thessalonains iv he suggested that there were traces of a Christian 'holiness code' based on the holiness code in Leviticus xvii–xx. This suggestion was followed up by E. G. Selwyn.[5] Both these writers connect this primitive Christian catechism with baptism. The main features of the teaching given to new converts were as follows: abstinence from walking as the Gentiles walk, avoidance of certain sins, recognition of the call to holiness through the Spirit and exhortations to brotherly love. Selwyn notes close parallels with similar material in 1 Peter and suggests that the influence of Silvanus, who is associated with the writing of that Epistle and of the Thessalonian correspondence, accounts for these connections. If this is so it shows the influence of existing catechetical formulae on Paul as well as upon other New Testament writers.

The other part of Carrington's thesis is that a remarkable sequence of four phrases occurs in much the same order in Colossians, Ephesians, 1 Peter and James. He describes this sequence by the Latin words *Deponente* (put off), *Subiecti* (be subject), *Vigilate* (watch) and *Resistite* (resist). All four parallel passages are introduced by some reference to

[1] *Paul and his Predecessors* (1940), pp. 25–40. For faith, hope and love as a primitive Christian triad, cf. Hunter, *ET* (June 1938), pp. 428, 429.
[2] *Op. cit.*, pp. 14–24.
[3] So also J. Jeremias, *The Eucharistic Words of Jesus* (1955), pp. 106 ff.
[4] *The Primitive Christian Catechism* (1940), pp. 12 ff.
[5] *The First Epistle of St. Peter* (1947), pp. 369 ff.

the new creation or the new birth and three of them contain references to what Carrington calls 'catechumen virtues' connected with the worship of God, and three of them close with an exhortation to stand (*State*).[1] He regards this as suggestive evidence of an early Christian baptismal *torah* drawn up on the basis of Jewish catechetical tradition.

Selwyn develops and modifies this thesis, illustrating it more widely from other New Testament evidence. He admits that not all his conclusions have equal probability,[2] but thinks it is undeniable that catechetical and liturgical sources underlie most of the New Testament Epistles. This much seems highly probable and throws some light on Paul's approach to current teaching forms and lessens the weight of objections against formalized statements such as are found in the Pastoral Epistles. If Paul is influenced by early catechetical forms, the presence in his writings of certain 'faithful sayings' becomes more explicable. If Selwyn is correct in his suggestion that Silvanus may have edited or helped to produce a baptismal formula, it cannot be ruled out of court that Paul may have done the same.

III. EARLY CHRISTIAN HYMNS

Attention has already been drawn in this Introduction to suggestions that there are hymns in some of Paul's Epistles. Hunter includes in his evidence for Paul's debt to his predecessors the passage in Philippians ii. 6–11. He rejects the idea that it is original because it interrupts the flow of paranesis, contains instances of non-Pauline diction and lacks characteristic Pauline ideas (see pp. 539 f. for a discussion of this hymn). With this passage Hunter links Ephesians v. 14 which he regards as a citation of a baptismal hymn with its rhythmical phraseology and its cult-style invocational appeal. The evidence seems stronger for this latter than for the former since in Philippians Paul gives no indication that he is citing the words of another.[3] Yet the possibility that he is cannot be altogether dismissed. The same may be said of Colossians i.

---

[1] Cf. Carrington, *op. cit.*, pp. 42, 43 for a convenient table showing the parallels.

[2] *Op. cit.*, p. 459.

[3] Unless E. Lohmeyer be correct in his unusual view that in the phrase ἐν χριστῷ (Phil. ii. 5) the preposition is 'a sort of citation formula' ('Eine Art von Zitationsformel', *Kyrios Jesus*, 1928, p. 13) corresponding to the Hebrew b̊ (cf. *Aboth* iii. 7: 'it is written in David'; Rom. xi. 2; Heb. iv. 7). But the absence of any verb indicating quotation in Phil. ii. 5 makes the suggestion improbable.

PAUL AND HIS SOURCES 661

15–17 which many scholars have regarded as pre-Pauline.[1] Some have traced this to Hellenistic Jewish formulae[2] or have even derived it from a Gnostic hymn,[3] yet neither of these ideas is in the least probable. If the hymn is not Pauline then it must have been derived from the earlier tradition that Paul had received.

Whether these hymns are admitted as pre-Pauline or not they draw attention to an important factor all too often overlooked. The apostle recognized the value of rhythmic expressions of Christian truth and would not have regarded these, as some scholars have tended to do, as steps away from the nobler heights of creative thinking towards a stereotyped formality. But hymns are more easily remembered than abstract statements of truth (e.g. 1 Cor. xiii). The Philippian and Colossian hymns with their high Christology present their truths in forms of not easily forgotten beauty.

Mention must also be made of the rhythmic passages in the Pastoral Epistles which may well be current formulae of Christian doctrine. 1 Timothy iii. 16 is a particularly striking example which, both in its form and content, wears the appearance of a much used liturgical formula. Compare also 2 Timothy ii. 11–13 and Titus iii. 4–7.

[1] Cf. F. F. Bruce, *Colossians*, p. 192, and especially C. Masson, *L'Epître aux Colossiens (CNT)*, 1950, *ad loc.* See additional note to p. 551 (on p. 562).

[2] Norden, *Agnostos Theos*, pp. 252 ff.; M. Dibelius, *Die Kolosserbrief (LHB)*, pp. 10 f.

[3] E. Käsemann, in *Neutestamentliche Studien für R. Bultmann* (1949), pp. 133 ff.

THE CHRONOLOGY OF THE LIFE OF PAUL

Throughout this Introduction little attention has been paid to precise dating of the letters owing to lack of sufficient data to establish an indisputable chronology of Paul's life. It has been sufficient to indicate the relative historical order as far as can be definitely ascertained, although even here many differences of opinion exist. Yet the reticence to fix precise dates does not mean that studies in Pauline chronology are regarded as unimportant. It is rather due to the complexity of the problems and the wide variation of views regarding their probable solutions that they have been omitted from the previous studies. But some account of the issues involved may not be out of place if only to demonstrate the impossibility of arriving at any fixed conclusions.*

I. THE MAIN CHRONOLOGICAL DATA

a. The Gallio inscription

The most certain point of departure in the quest for a chronological scheme is the inscription at Delphi already mentioned in connection with the date of the Thessalonian letters (see p. 566). This gives the date of a letter from Claudius to the people of Delphi during the time of Gallio's proconsulate, and enables the commencement of the latter's year of office to be fixed as either midsummer AD 51 or 52. There are supporters for both alternatives. Michaelis[1] prefers the former date on the ground that it is hardly possible to accommodate the necessary communications between Gallio and Claudius within the period June 1st to August 1st, AD 52 (the latest date possible for the letter mentioned in the inscription). But others see no difficulty here and incline to the later date.[2]

b. The recall of Felix

The dating of this event which coincides with the end of Paul's Caesarean imprisonment is less easy to fix with precision. Josephus and Tacitus

[1] *Einleitung*, p. 152. So also Leon Morris, *1 and 2 Thessalonians* (*TNT*), p. 15.

[2] Cf. Feine-Behm, *Einleitung*, p. 126; Wikenhauser, *New Testament Introduction*, p. 361.

both supply data for the commencement of Felix' years of office but unfortunately do not quite agree. Josephus[1] regards Cumanus as sole procurator of Judaea, but Tacitus[2] speaks of Felix as holding joint office with him. When both were brought before Quadratus, the legate of Syria, in AD 52 because of troubles between the Galilaeans and Samaritans, Felix was let off (because his brother was a favourite of the Emperor) and Cumanus condemned. It was supposed by C. H. Turner[3] that Felix had been subordinate until AD 52, when his own procurator-ship began.[4]

The termination of the period depends on the interpretation of the evidence from Eusebius, who dates Festus' arrival in Nero's second year (i.e. between September AD 56 and September AD 57). If this is correct it would supply another fixed date for Pauline chronology. But it is not certain how reliable Eusebius' statement is[5] and many scholars[6] have preferred a later date for the commencement of Festus' procurator-ship, i.e. AD 60 (this was in fact the older assumption). There is evidence from Tacitus[7] that Pallas, brother of Felix, was retired from public office in AD 55, but it is impossible to suppose that the trial of Felix took place earlier than this and it must, therefore, be assumed that even after his retirement Pallas was still sufficiently influential to secure a favour-able judgment on behalf of his brother. According to Tacitus,[8] Pallas was poisoned in AD 62, the year in which Poppaea married Nero, as a result of which the Jews had a more favourable hearing. Turner[9] therefore thinks that the acquittal of Felix must have happened some time before this and suggests the years AD 57, 58 and 59 as most favour-able. Of these years AD 58 is the most generally accepted by those who disagree with the older dating of AD 60.

---

[1] *Antiquities*, XX. vi. 1–3, viii. 9.

[2] *Annals*, XII. 54.

[3] Article on 'Chronology of the New Testament', *HDB*, I, pp. 417 f.

[4] This agrees with Eusebius' *Chronicles* (Jerome's version), which states that Felix arrived as procurator in Claudius' eleventh year, if the years are calculated in the Eastern fashion from September to September (cf. Turner's discussion, *op. cit.*, p. 418).*

[5] Cf. B. W. Bacon, 'A Criticism of the New Chronology of Paul', *Expositor*, v, vii (1898), pp. 123–136.

[6] E.g. J. B. Lightfoot, *Biblical Essays*, 1893; Feine-Behm, *Einleitung*[11] (1956), p. 126; Wikenhauser, *New Testament Introduction* (1958), p. 361.

[7] *Annals*, XIII. 14, 15.   [8] *Annals*, XIV. 65.

[9] *HDB*, I, p. 419.

c. The edict of Claudius

This edict, referred to in Acts xviii. 2, is reported by Suetonius,[1] but unfortunately he gives no date. The earliest evidence for a precise dating is found in the statement of the fifth-century historian Orosius[2] that the edict was issued in the ninth year of Claudius, i.e. AD 49–50. This he claimed to have received from Josephus, but there is no mention of it in Josephus' extant works.

d. The days of unleavened bread at Philippi

According to Acts xx. 6 Paul was in Philippi during the days of unleavened bread, after which he left for Troas hoping to arrive in Jerusalem by Pentecost (Acts xx. 16). By calculating from the number of days mentioned in Acts xx. 6, 7 Ramsay[3] maintained that Paul and his party left Philippi on a Friday and since Paul was in a hurry to reach Jerusalem he thought he must have left on the day following the completion of the feast of unleavened bread. This would place the slaying of the Passover that year on a Thursday, which according to Ramsay was true for AD 57. But O. Gerhardt[4] came to a different conclusion and considered the evidence of Acts points to a Passover on Tuesday, which on astronomical evidence occurred in AD 58.[5] Yet again from the same data Michaelis[6] suggests AD 56, during which year the Passover fell on a Sunday or Monday (as Gerhardt agrees) by allowing an interval before the departure from Philippi on the Wednesday. The different constructions which can be put on the same evidence demonstrate its inconclusive character. In any case, it is not absolutely certain whether the Jews always fixed the Passover when they actually saw the new moon, and if not, astronomical calculations would have no value.

e. Paul's martyrdom

The tradition that both Peter and Paul suffered martyrdom under Nero was the firm belief of the Church Fathers. It is particularly based on the early evidence of 1 Clement v, vi which certainly suggests that these apostles suffered at the same time as a great multitude was tortured (which can hardly refer to any other happening than the Neronian

---

[1] *Claudius*, 25. [2] *Hist.* VII. vi. 15 (cited in *HDB*, I, p. 417).

[3] *Expositor*, v, i (1896), pp. 336 ff.

[4] *Neue kirchliche Zeitschrift*, 33 (1922), pp. 89 ff.

[5] Michaelis, *Einleitung*, p. 154, cites Zahn as supporting a similar dating of the Passover.

[6] *Op. cit.*, p. 154.

persecutions). Although it tells us nothing about the actual date of Paul's death, it is generally supposed that this took place early in the period of persecution (i.e. AD 64). But some scholars[1] have followed Eusebius in placing the martyrdom of Paul towards the end of Nero's reign (AD 68), thus dissociating his death from the fierce persecution which followed the great fire, for which the Christians were made scapegoats (i.e. AD 64). Yet Turner[2] challenges the reliability of Eusebius' evidence on this occasion, especially as this writer appears to assign the whole persecution to the same year. Many who have inclined to this later dating have done so because it allows more time for Paul's additional activities subsequent to his release from his Roman imprisonment.[3] But the earlier dating is more generally preferred, and would not in itself exclude further activity provided an early date for the arrival at Rome can be reasonably maintained.

II. SUBSIDIARY DATA

Among the other historical dates which may contribute towards a chronology of Paul's life are the following.

1. Aretas (cf. 2 Cor. xi. 32) was not in possession of Damascus until AD 34 at the earliest and possibly not before the accession of Caligula in AD 37.[4] This means that Paul's first journey to Jerusalem cannot be before this date (cf. Gal. i. 17, 18).

2. It is generally agreed that Herod Agrippa's death took place in AD 44, which means that Paul's first missionary journey must be subsequent to this date.

3. After Herod's death the famine relief contributions were taken up to Jerusalem and as there is evidence from Josephus that famine conditions existed during the period of the proconsulship of Alexander AD 46-48), this mission of Barnabas and Saul (Acts xi. 29, 30) must therefore fall within that period.[5]

4. Turner[6] suggested that external evidence supported the view that

[1] E.g. J. B. Lightfoot, *Biblical Essays* (1893). Moffatt, *ILNT*, pp. 62, 63, surveys twenty-two chronological schemes of Paul's life and eight of these, including Zahn, Ramsay, G. G. Findlay and Farrar, prefer AD 67 or 68.
[2] *Op. cit.*, p. 420.
[3] This naturally has no influence with those who deny the authenticity of the Pastorals.
[4] Cf. Turner, *op. cit.*, p. 416 and G. Ogg, 'A New Chronology of Saint Paul's Life', *ET*, XLIV (1953), p. 123.
[5] Cf. Turner, *op. cit.*, pp. 416, 417. Josephus, *Antiquities*, XX. v. 2.   [6] *Op. cit.*, p. 417.

Sergius Paulus was not proconsul of Cyprus during the years AD 51–52, although there is no positive evidence for a precise dating of his tenure of office. But the evidence available would certainly require a date for the first missionary journey before AD 51.

5. The marriage of Felix to Drusilla could not have taken place until AD 53 and Paul's first appearance before them must therefore have been after that date.[1]

It will be seen from the above evidence that little external support of a conclusive kind can be found for a fixed scheme of chronology. The introductory studies in the various Epistles have shown similar lack of data in all but a few cases. Little more can be done than to establish a relative chronology, but this must be regarded as tentative in view of wide differences of opinion over many of the Epistles, e.g. Galatians and the Captivity Epistles. The following historical framework is somewhat general but will furnish some guide to the data already given.

Conversion of Paul	35	(32)	
Famine Visit to Jerusalem	46		
Commencement of first missionary journey	47		
Apostolic Council	49		(Galatians?)
Paul at Corinth (second missionary journey)	50–51	(52)	Thessalonians (The Captivity Epistles?) Corinthians, (Galatians?) Romans
Culmination of the third missionary journey in arrest at Jerusalem	56	(58)	
End of imprisonment at Caesarea	58	(60)	
Arrival at Rome	59	(61)	
End of first imprisonment at Rome	61	(63)	(The Captivity Epistles?)
(Further missionary activity)			} The Pastoral Epistles
End of second imprisonment and martyrdom at Rome	64	(67)	

[1] Cf. Josephus, *Antiquities*, XX. vii. 1, 2 for an account of Drusilla's desertion of her former husband.

It will be seen that the main differences in the various chronological schemes affect the latter half of these entries. The dates in brackets representing the latest proposed vary from one to three years from the other dates mentioned. This scheme with its variations may, therefore, serve as a useful working basis for a chronology of Paul's life.[1]

III. A NEW CHRONOLOGY

It is not surprising that attempts have been made to explore new territories in Pauline chronology and one recent attempt to do this requires special mention. John Knox[2] has proposed the following scheme.

Conversion	37
First Jerusalem visit (after three years)	40
Evangelistic activity (Syria, Cilicia, Galatia, Macedonia, Greece, Asia)	40–51
Second Jerusalem visit (after fourteen years)	51
Collection scheme and evangelistic activity	51–52
Final Jerusalem visit and arrest	53

The basis of this radical revision of Pauline chronology is a disinclination to favour the evidence of Acts and therefore a total reliance on data from the Pauline Epistles. In other words attempts to harmonize the Epistles with Acts are completely rejected. Because of this no importance is attached to the Gallio incident as recorded in Acts and the Delphic inscription consequently becomes irrelevant in Knox's scheme.

Another criticism of this reconstruction is that Knox places the events of the second missionary journey before the Council of Jerusalem, which is most improbable, unless again Luke's historical sequence is to be completely disregarded. Knox's explanation that Luke has antedated

---

[1] The unbracketed dates approximate to the schemes of Turner, *op. cit.*, p. 424, and Michaelis, *Einleitung*, p. 153. The bracketed dates approximate to Lightfoot's scheme (cf. also Feine-Behm *op. cit.*, pp. 125 ff.), but many other schemes prefer intermediate dates (cf. Moffatt's useful table of comparison, *ILNT*, pp. 62, 63).

[2] *Chapters in a Life of Paul* (1954) and earlier in his article 'The Pauline Chronology', *JBL*, LVIII (1939), pp. 15–29.*

the Council in order to dispose of this troublesome matter at the outset of the Gentile mission is not convincing, as Ogg[1] has pointed out, for it is inexplicable why he did not then place it before the first missionary journey.

Knox's starting-point is also questionable for it assumes too long a period after the Crucifixion before Paul's conversion, but it is necessitated by his view that Paul was a product of Christian communities outside Palestine. This necessarily affects his dating of the Apostolic Council. But it is much more probable that the conversion occurred about AD 35, i.e. fourteen years before AD 49, for this fits in well with the evidence of the Gallio inscription and maintains the historicity of the Acts account. It will be observed that in Knox's proposals as indeed in the scheme previously outlined the fourteen years of Galatians ii. 1 must be regarded as inclusive of the three years of Galatians i. 18, but it should be noted that not all scholars are agreed on this point.[2] If the period between Paul's conversion and the Council was seventeen years this would require an earlier date for the conversion[3] in view of the Gallio inscription making a later date for the Council impossible.

Another criticism of Knox's theory is the inadequate time allowed between the Council and Paul's arrest at Jerusalem for all the activities of the third missionary journey. Moreover, the date of the arrest is governed by the less probable date for the commencement of Festus' procuratorship (i.e. AD 55).[4] Quite apart from the summary manner in which he disposes of the Acts data, Knox's scheme cannot be said to

[1] *ET,* LXIV (1953), p. 123.

[2] It is instructive to note that no fewer than seventeen of the twenty-two schemes cited by Moffatt, *op. cit.*, 62, 63, regard the period as seventeen years and not fourteen years. Opinions of expositors differ regarding the interpretation of ἔπειτα in Gal. ii. 1. It may be taken to express the interval between his conversion and the visit to Jerusalem about to be mentioned, or the interval which has elapsed since his last visit to the apostles. The context seems slightly more favourable to the latter view (cf. Burton, *Galatians*, 1921, p. 68) and this has clearly weighed heavily with many scholars.

[3] The date of Paul's conversion must be related to the date of the Crucifixion which is variously fixed between the limits AD 29–33. G. Ogg, *The Chronology of the Public Ministry of Jesus* (1940), pp. 244 ff., maintains the latest date, which means that Paul's conversion cannot possibly be fixed before AD 35 at the earliest. If Ogg is right a period of seventeen years can hardly be fitted in between the conversion of Paul and the Council of Jerusalem.

[4] Among earlier scholars Holtzmann, Harnack and McGiffert all dated Paul's arrest as Knox does in AD 53 (see Moffatt's table, *op. cit.*, 62, 63).

offer an acceptable reconstruction. It is certainly no improvement on the more traditional systems. His claim that it spreads Paul's missionary activity more evenly over his Christian life is no justification for the theory unless the traditional unevenness can be shown to be unlikely, but all that is clear from the Acts and the Epistles is that we know less about the earlier period than the later. A simple explanation of this fact is that Luke was more acquainted with the later period, which in any case had far wider implications for the history of Christianity.

However unsatisfactory the present state of our knowledge about the chronology of Paul's life is considered to be, the solution is not likely to be found along the lines that Knox has suggested if any credence at all is to be given to the sequence of events in Acts. It was the Tübingen school in the nineteenth century which first took up this approach and the number of speculative reconstructions which resulted should be a warning against any further attempt to construct a scheme without reference to Acts.

ADDITIONAL NOTES

662. Cf. W. G. Kümmel's discussion (*INT*, 1965, p. 274). G. Ogg, *The Chronology of the Life of St. Paul* (1968), has a thorough examination of all the chronological problems affecting Paul's life. His chronological outline differs slightly from that given on p. 666. He dates the Jerusalem Conference AD 48, but he places the arrest of Paul in Jerusalem in AD 59 and his arrival in Rome in AD 62. Paul's martyrdom is dated in AD 64. Ogg rejects the genuineness of the Pastoral Epistles and therefore is not obliged to find room for further activity in the east, nor for a visit to Spain. Kümmel (*INT*, p. 180) cites AD 31/32 as the date of Paul's conversion, three years earlier than Ogg's dating.

663. [4] Kümmel (*INT*, p. 179) discounts the usefulness of the Festus dating for Pauline chronology.

667. [2] M. G. Suggs ('Concerning the Date of Paul's Macedonian Ministry', *Nov. Test.*, 4, 1960, pp. 60–68) supports the chronological theory of J. Knox. Cf. J. C. Hurd's essay in *Christian History and Interpretation* (1967), pp. 225–248, in which he stresses the need to consider Paul's theology as well as his biographical notices in any assessment of chronology.

In a study of Paul's so-called Silent Years, R. E. Osborne (*JBL*, LXXXIV, 1965, pp. 59–65) suggests that there are various indications of activity during this period. Paul refers to being in the regions of Syria and Cilicia (Gal. i. 22). Osborne thinks he may then have established the churches in Galatia. Some of the various hardships suffered by Paul (2 Cor. xi. 23 ff.) must have happened before his return to Tarsus. This writer also places a visit to Crete (Tit. i. 5) and to Nicopolis (Tit. iii. 12) during the same period. He considers this latter suggestion more probable than the release theory. But see the discussion on pp. 596 ff.

For Kümmel's chronological scheme for the events from Paul's conversion to his arrival at Jerusalem at the end of the second journey, cf. *INT*, p. 180.

EPISTOLARY PSEUDEPIGRAPHY

I. THE PROBLEM

In discussions on the authenticity of canonical Epistles which contain within them clear indications of authorship, the practice of pseudepigraphy (i.e. the publication of documents under assumed names) unavoidably comes under consideration. It merits careful investigation as it must form a part of any theory which denies traditional authorship. In the foregoing discussions on the Pauline Epistles it has been noted that some scholars still regard certain Epistles as pseudepigrapha, namely Colossians, Ephesians, 2 Thessalonians and the Pastoral Epistles, although not all with the same degree of confidence. Frequently in justification of this type of theory it is claimed that pseudonymity was a widespread literary device in the ancient world and it is assumed without much careful investigation that the Christian Church would quite naturally adopt the same practice. But is this a true assumption? To answer such a question it is necessary to consider what evidence is available that would throw light on the practice.

There was certainly a great quantity of pseudepigraphic literature in Graeco-Roman, Jewish and Christian environments. Not only has much of this literature been preserved, but numerous notices of other literature since lost occur in ancient writers. A comprehensive survey would be beyond the scope of this book and our attention will therefore need to be confined to the field of epistolary pseudepigraphy. While this form cannot be regarded entirely in isolation from the general run of pseudepigraphic literature, it is clearly of greater importance than the other forms in the criticism of New Testament Epistles.

Professor Frederic Torm[1] in his suggestive study on the psychology of pseudepigraphy shows that in the early examples of this type of literature in the Greek world two motives are discernible, the art of deceptive imitation and the desire to satisfy curiosity in the personal lives of celebrated men. In this latter case the authors attempted to describe not what the great men had said but what the commonplace

---

[1] *Die Psychologie der Pseudonymität im Hinblick auf die Literatur des Urchristentums* (1932).

people thought they would have said.[1] While these motives led to the widespread production of forged epistles in the Greek secular world, the number of pseudepigraphic letters in Jewish and Christian religious literature is surprisingly scant. No doubt in the Christian world it was more difficult to escape detection when the pseudepigrapha were in letter form than when they took the shape of gospels, acts and apocalypses. Most of the Jewish pseudepigrapha belonged to the sphere of apocalyptic and are not therefore in epistolary form.

II. JEWISH EXAMPLES

It is particularly significant that among the mass of Jewish apocryphal and pseudepigraphic writings only two make any pretence to use the epistolary form, the *Epistle of Jeremy* and the *Letter of Aristeas*, and neither of these is in the strict sense a true epistle. The former is more a homily and the latter an apologetic narrative. These writings must be set against the background of the evident tolerance of the Jewish approach to pseudepigrapha in general. The reason for this recourse to pseudepigraphy, according to Charles,[2] was the fixation of the law and the cessation of prophetic utterances. No new prophets could gain a hearing and so any budding reformer who wished to propagate his views found it easier to do so under the assumed name of an acknowledged hero of the past. The *Epistle of Jeremy* is an example of this. The author wished to exhort his contemporaries against idol-worship and did so by means of a letter to an imaginary group of people in Babylon in the time of the prophet Jeremiah. Not only the title but the opening statement leave the reader in no doubt that the author is putting out his message under cover of Jeremiah's name. The use of his name would at once commend it for he was highly regarded among the Jews and, in fact, gave his name to other forms of pseudepigraphic literature as is clear from the remains of the Qumran Library.

Naturally the readiness of Jewish authors to resort to this mode of expression in their apocalyptic productions[3] would have predisposed

---

[1] *Op. cit.*, p. 12. Torm cites here the opinion of J. P. Mahaffy, *The Silver Age of the Greek World* (1906), p. 441. Cf. also M. Dibelius, *A Fresh Approach*, pp. 140, 141.

[2] *The Apocrypha and Pseudepigrapha in English* (1913), vol. II, p. 1.

[3] Cf. L. H. Brockington, 'The Problem of Pseudonymity', *JTS* (New Series IV, 1953), pp. 15–22, who claims to find five lines of development in the Jewish practice of pseudonymity, the fifth stage being apocalyptic. Yet epistolary pseudonymity finds no place in this scheme of development. Brockington does

their contemporaries to try out other pseudonymous forms but the astonishing reluctance in the use of pseudepigraphic epistolary literature calls for some explanation. It would seem most probable that the absence of any ancient canonical precedent played a not inconsiderable part in this reluctance, but the greater ease of detection must have acted as the main deterrent. A new form of literature would need to be based on the authoritative writings and this was more easily achieved by apocalyptic forms than epistolary. Indeed, it is rather remarkable that any false epistles gained currency. In the case of the *Epistle of Jeremy* it was no doubt regarded rather as an addition to the canonical book than as an imitation. It is not without significance that in the Vulgate it appears as chapter six of *The Book of the Prophet Baruch*. Yet on the most generally favoured dating it was not produced until some four or five hundred years after the time of Jeremiah. Nevertheless it is fairly easy to find a motive for the production. It seems to be a reaction against Jeremiah's insistence that the exiles should settle in Babylon without warning them about the dangers of the Babylonian idolatry. This letter therefore purports to be another letter from the same prophet supplementary to the canonical book and containing a biting indictment of idolatry.[1] It was issued under Jeremiah's name because it was intended to supply a supposed deficiency in the canonical treatment of Babylonian idolatry. Unfortunately there is no evidence which helps us to ascertain in what spirit the original production was received. Did the recipients take it to be a long-lost letter of the real Jeremiah or did they receive it as a newly-produced but none the less sincere pseudepigraphon which attempted to express what Jeremiah would have said had he lived in their day and had he been acquainted with the true nature of Babylonian worship? In the absence of any positive evidence it might at first seem arbitrary to pronounce a judgment in favour of either of these alternatives. Yet the former is without doubt the more intelligible, for if the latter were true it would leave unanswered the real motive for the pseudepigraphic device. If pseudonymity was the only means by which the author could gain his desired ends it is a necessary

not deal with the omission since he concentrates on the Old Testament where no such cases occur.

[1] Cf. R. H. Pfeiffer, *History of New Testament Times with an Introduction to the Apocrypha* (1949), pp. 426–432, for a concise description of the contents and purpose of this epistle. Cf. C. J. Ball in Charles' *The Apocrypha and Pseudepigrapha in English* (1913), vol. I; and E. Schürer, *A History of the Jewish People in the Time of Jesus Christ* (n.d.), II, vol. III, p. 195.

corollary that the recipients must be unaware of the device, for otherwise he might just as well issue it in his own name.

The other Jewish example, the *Letter of Aristeas*, has a distinctly Hellenistic bias. In fact, it purports to be written by a Gentile although it aims at the glorification of Jewish culture, religion and literature (especially the LXX version of the Scriptures). It is generally assumed to belong to the period *c.* 100 BC and represents a Jewish apologetic designed for a Gentile environment (i.e. Alexandria). A peculiarity about the book is the obscurity which surrounds its author, who although described as being present at the inception of the LXX translation is otherwise unknown. This factor marks the work as different from the productions of apocalyptic writers, who generally ascribed their works to well-known and therefore authoritative heroes of the past (e.g. Enoch, Moses, Jeremiah, Baruch). The nature and purpose of this letter did not lend itself to this procedure for it demanded the attestation of one assumed to have been a witness of the production of this historic and authoritative version.

The letter-form seems to have been dictated by its apologetic purpose. It is an attempt to place the production in an historic setting much earlier than the author's own time. But the epistolary form merges into narrative and lacks the usual personal introduction. Nevertheless the addressee, the author's brother Philocrates, is kept in mind through the letter, while the author contrives to describe the events as much as possible as an eye-witness. That the legend related in this letter not only exercised considerable influence on Rabbinic, Hellenistic, Jewish and Christian writers, but that it also in the course of its history acquired many accretions and elaborations, may be some indication of its original reception. It is not impossible that some core of historical truth may lie behind the legend, but Aristeas' account contains some obvious historical blunders which give away its pseudepigraphic origin.[1] Since its aim is to recommend the Greek Scriptures to those who were apparently underestimating or ignoring them, or even entirely ignorant of them, it is easy to see that these historical improbabilities would not have been evident to the original readers. The letter would have had little point if the original readers had not assumed that

---

[1] Cf. H. G. Meecham, *The Oldest Version of the Bible* 1932), pp. 133 ff.; P. Wendland, *Der Brief des Aristeas* in *Die Pseudepigraphen zum Alten Testament* (edited by E. Kautzsch) (1900), pp. 1 ff.; H. T. Andrews, in Charles' *Pseudepigrapha* (1913), pp. 83-122; R. H. Pfeiffer, *History of New Testament Times* (1949), pp. 224 ff.

the writer was in reality closely connected with the production of the LXX in the time of Ptolemy II Philadelphus of Egypt (285–245 BC). But this means that 'Aristeas' must have been a pseudonym used to create the impression of greater antiquity for the letter and to hide the author's true identity. This type of production contains more differences than similarities when compared with the alleged Pauline pseudepigrapha in the New Testament, for it was not modelled on any known authoritative writing, nor was it associated with the name of an authoritative teacher. The sole similarity is its aim to provide earlier attestation for contemporary requirements. The same tendency may be traced as the main motive of much later pseudepigraphic literature and may be considered as one of the most characteristic features of this type of literature.

III. CHRISTIAN NON-CANONICAL EXAMPLES

The scantiness of Jewish examples finds a parallel in the New Testament Apocrypha, which bears further testimony to the general unsuitability of this type of pseudepigraphic literature for apologetic or didactic purposes. There are only six noteworthy examples—some letters of Christ and Abgarus, a letter of Lentulus, epistles of Paul to the Laodiceans and to the Corinthians, some correspondence between Paul and Seneca and an epistle of the apostles.[1] The legendary and fictitious character of the first two and the last two is at once evident from their contents, while none but the correspondence between Paul and Seneca had any impact on the Christian Church. Moreover, none of these is in a true epistolary form. The literary device lies very close to the surface. Yet the epistles to the Laodiceans and to the Corinthians are quite different in this respect for they are both modelled on the pattern of Paul's New Testament letters and are both specifically ascribed to him in phrases identical with those from authentic Pauline letters.

The inclusion in the *Acts of Paul* of the Corinthian epistle (sometimes known as 3 Corinthians), together with one addressed to Paul from the Corinthians, allows a relatively precise reconstruction of its origin. The self-confessed inventor of this spurious book of Acts incorporated this

---

[1] These six are the only epistles or epistolary correspondences which M. R. James includes in his *Apocryphal New Testament* (1924) although he mentions others, e.g. the *Letter of Christ* concerning Sunday and the *Epistle of Titus*. Both of these James describes as dull, a description which would not be inappropriate for the majority of Christian apocryphal books.

pseudonymous epistolary material to add verisimilitude to his production and to give what he conceived to be Paul's answer to contemporary errors. The whole work was composed out of love of Paul according to Tertullian's account.[1] Yet the later separate circulation of the letter to the Corinthians (as 3 Corinthians) under Paul's name actually gained temporary canonicity in the Eastern Syriac-speaking church and this in spite of the fact that the pseudonymous author, a presbyter of the province of Asia, was not only condemned for his practice but was also deprived of his office. There is no reason to suppose that this high regard for the epistle in the Eastern church in the fourth century was either widespread or long-lived.[2] It was rejected before the production of the Peshitta (the authorized Syriac version) early in the fifth century. Nor are there any grounds for supposing that during the period of its temporary inclusion in the Syriac Canon it was recognized as a pseudonymous work. The natural inference from the evidence is that its canonicity depended on its genuine apostolicity and that when Rabbula, Bishop of Edessa, worked on the revision of the old Syriac texts he also worked on a canon which recognized the spuriousness of 3 Corinthians.[3]

The remaining epistolary example, that to the Laodiceans, is even more striking for its extraordinary period of canonicity in the medieval Church. Its origin is not certain. It is doubtful whether it is to be equated with the mention of forged epistles in the Muratorian Canon, where the statement is made, 'There is current also one to the Laodiceans and another to the Alexandrians forged in favour of Marcion's heresy'. The extant epistle to the Laodiceans does not, however, fit the case for it does nothing to forward Marcion's heresy.[4] It is no more than what

---

[1] *De Baptismo,* 17.

[2] Ephraim commented upon it, but it is absent from the Syriac Canon of about AD 400 (cf. Souter, *The Text and Canon of the New Testament* (1913), p. 226.

[3] Souter, *op. cit.,* pp. 184 f., maintains that the tradition of the Assyrian church came from Rome with Tatian as its probable intermediary. There is a striking similarity between the order in Marcion's Canon and the Syriac Canon (and Ephraim's). 3 Corinthians, omitted from the other two, is placed after 2 Corinthians in Ephraim's order. Clearly Ephraim regarded it as a genuine epistle of Paul. The *Acts of Paul,* as a whole, had a much wider circulation, for Clement of Alexandria, Origen, Hippolytus and 'Ambrosiaster', representing both East and West, knew and used the work, although none of them seems to have treated it as canonical.

[4] M. R. James, *op. cit.,* p. 478, concedes that the word 'forged' may possibly be singular and refer to the Alexandrian epistle only.

M. R. James called 'a feebly constructed cento of Pauline phrases',[1] based mainly on Philippians. There seems to be a perfectly reasonable explanation of the motive for its production in the desire to produce a letter answerable to Colossians iv. 16. It springs from a particular regard for the apostle Paul that excludes as unthinkable that any of the inspired apostle's productions could be lost. Unlike so much of the early pseudepigraphic literature it is aimed neither at the glorification of an ancient apostle nor the propagation of heretical notions.

IV. DISPUTED NEW TESTAMENT EXAMPLES

It is against this sketchy background that the problem of possible pseudepigrapha in the New Testament must be approached. The absence of any close contemporary epistolary parallels must put the investigator on his guard against a too facile admittance of the practice in New Testament criticism. If it be admitted at all it must be regarded rather as contrary to general contemporary religious tendencies than as a fully-accepted literary convention. It is not enough to cite the widespread secular use of the device without producing evidence to show why Christian writers should conform to non-Christian and in fact non-religious patterns in their approach to the highly significant matter of their own religious writings. It may of course with some reason be argued that the religious letter was a form peculiarly adapted to and developed by the needs of the Christian Church, but could the same apply to pseudepigraphic letters? As has been shown the evidence for this latter development is practically non-existent.

No mention has so far been made of the evidence of the New Testament itself. It may justly be maintained that if the evidence is conclusive for the pseudonymous authorship of any New Testament Epistle that in itself would stand irrespective of contemporary supporting evidence. This is virtually the position adopted by many scholars over 2 Peter and having accepted pseudonymity in this case it is then used to substantiate the claim that pseudepigraphy was a common Christian practice. The fallacy of this approach is seen when so prolific an advocate of New Testament pseudepigraphy as Goodspeed[2] can claim that the sheer quantity of examples lessens the problem. In this way the vital missing link is apt to be forgotten. Whatever hypotheses modern criticism postulates which involve ascriptions of pseudonymity, those ascriptions convey with them a problem which is absent from con-

[1] *Op. cit.*, p. 479.   [2] *New Chapters in New Testament Study* (1937), p. 172.

clusions which are independent of pseudonymous origins. In other words, pseudonymous hypotheses are at a discount when compared with authentic works and require for that reason the most convincing grounds for their substantiation. Our foregoing considerations of the Pauline literature and its problems have demonstrated that in none of the alleged pseudepigrapha is the evidence anywhere near convincing or conclusive. Scholars who think it is in one or more of the disputed Epistles are forced to adopt a pseudo-Pauline authorship which succeeded in getting the epistle through the mesh of early Christian suspicion and facilitated its emergence without challenge in an incredibly short time to take its place among the genuine Epistles. While this procedure was not impossible the difficulties inherent in such hypotheses are all too seldom appreciated.[1]

So far only the external evidence has been studied to ascertain whether epistolary pseudepigraphy was an accepted religious literary convention, but certain other comments are necessary to put the whole subject into its right perspective. Torm has drawn attention to the importance of psychological considerations in each individual case. No general rule can be pronounced which is valid in all cases. The problem is whether the religious consciousness of the writer is consistent with the use of the pseudonymous device. Torm[2] considers that the mental life behind the writers of the forged letters of Greece and Rome held no profoundness and their resort to this method presents therefore no difficulty. The problem is obviously greater for religious pseudonymity than for secular. Men of deep religious convictions whose productions display a deep spiritual appreciation present the greatest problem of all if their works are pronounced to be pseudonymous. Yet the existence among the Jews of so many pseudepigraphic apocalypses, in some at least of which there are not lacking some passages of elevated thought, requires some explanation. It can only be that the religious interest of the author took so firm a hold upon him that he

---

[1] In an article on 'Pseudonymity in the New Testament', *Theology*, vol. LVIII (February 1955), pp. 51 ff., J. C. Fenton, while naming twelve possible pseudepigrapha in the New Testament, nevertheless recognizes and discusses the problem. But he approaches it from the point of view that pseudonymous writing was an accepted literary form in the ancient world and from Jewish practice was continued in the Christian Church. He is dealing with the subject quite generally, but among his twelve proposed pseudepigrapha, eight are epistles. He makes no distinction between the various classes of pseudepigraphic literature.

[2] *Op. cit.*, p. 12.

was prepared to resort to a questionable means to attain his commendable purpose. But religious history does not substantiate the principle that the end justifies the means. It is rather the reverse, for where this principle has been widely applied, as for instance in the Middle Ages, it has resulted in spiritual deterioration.

In the literary question under review everything depends on whether the pseudonymous means was in fact regarded by the author's contemporaries as questionable. What little evidence there is in the early Christian period on this matter points to the conclusion that it was. The condemnation of the Asian presbyter already mentioned who admitted the production of the *Acts of Paul* shows clearly enough that where the pseudonymous device was recognized it was not merely not tolerated but emphatically condemned. It will not do to suggest that the presbyter was really condemned for the heresy contained in the book and not for its literary form, for Tertullian makes no mention of this. From his report it seems evident that the writer of such a work was not considered fit to hold office in a Christian church, despite the fact that he claimed to have done it from the highest motive, for love of Paul. Similarly there is the evidence of the Muratorian Canon quoted above in which letters forged in the name of Paul are not only mentioned but specifically rejected and compared to genuine Epistles as gall is compared with honey. Admittedly in this case the productions supported the Marcionite heresy and may have been rejected on that score, yet the fact that they are specifically described as forged (*finctae*) is not without considerable significance.[1]

From about the same period comes the evidence of Serapion of Antioch (*c*. 190), recorded by Eusebius. In writing to the church at Rhossus in Cilicia where he had discovered the *Gospel of Peter* in use, he said, 'we receive both Peter and the other Apostles as Christ; but as experienced men we reject the writings falsely inscribed with their names, since we know that we did not receive such from our fathers.'[2] Nevertheless Serapion allowed it to be read at first until it was clear to him that it was attached to the heresy which Marcianus held.[3] This

---

[1] If the word should be singular and the Alexandrian epistle alone is intended, the argument would still stand.

[2] Cited in Westcott's *On the Canon of the New Testament*[4] (1875), p. 386.

[3] In his article 'On the Moral Character of Pseudonymous Books', *Expositor*, IV, iv, p. 101, J. S. Candlish takes the evidence of Serapion to indicate that the fact that a book bore a fictitious name was not sufficient to condemn it, so long as

evidence seems at first perplexing, for on the one hand the fictitious character of the book was fully recognized and the book consequently rejected, and on the other hand, its use was permitted so long as it was not thought to teach error. There is clearly a distinction between authoritative writings and those merely permitted to be used, as there is also between apostolic and fictitious. Serapion does not appear to recognize any intermediate position. In fact none of the evidence so far educed makes room for the notion of a pious Paulinist using pseudonymity as an accepted literary device. It may have been an accepted convention in pagan circles, but it seems to have been far from accepted in the second-century Church, and must have been even less acceptable in the first century.

The only conclusion to which the evidence would seem to point is that if pseudepigrapha must on the basis of criticism be admitted within the New Testament Canon, they must have been received without their recipients being aware of their true character. If this is a valid conclusion the charge of deliberate deception can scarcely be avoided. Yet such deception is difficult to reconcile with the high spiritual quality of the New Testament writings concerned. In these matters, however, generalities may become meaningless and it is therefore necessary to study each proposed pseudepigraphon to discover whether it is psychologically probable that the contents were produced by one who has knowingly resorted to a practice which was frowned upon by the leaders of the Church.

Once dispose of the fiction of an accepted literary convention which Christian authors would have used without question and the investigator who feels the need to posit pseudonymity must justify his action by a thorough psychological examination of the mental consciousness of the author. Many investigators of the Epistle to the Ephesians who have recognized differences from Paul's other letters have nevertheless refrained from concluding for pseudonymity on the ground that the

it was harmless. Yet it is evident that the fictitious character of the work is to be recognized by the readers, who are assumed to be orthodox Christians. It seems that Serapion was not well informed about this pseudepigraphic work at first, although he himself rejected it on the grounds of its false name. He probably did not wish to interfere with the reading customs of the church unnecessarily for he says, 'If this is the only thing which seems to create petty jealousies among you, let it be read' (Westcott, *op. cit.*, p. 386). N.B. M. R. James, *op. cit.*, p. 14, has 'scruples' for 'petty jealousies' (μικροψυχίαν), which more clearly supports the above interpretation of the evidence.

nobility of thought in this Epistle ill befits the mental approach of an imitator of Paul. Moreover, would the alleged Paulinist have had no twinge of conscience when he exhorted his readers to speak the truth (Eph. iv. 15, 25) and to be girt about with truth (Eph. vi. 14)? There are no similar statements in Colossians, but the even stronger negative exhortation to the readers not to lie to one another (Col. iii. 9) expresses a similar sentiment. In 2 Thessalonians, in the very passage which has been the main cause of dispute, there is a sharp distinction between truth and delusion (ii. 10–12). It is difficult to imagine a pseudonymous author writing such a passage without sensing its incongruity with his own literary delusion. Nor is it different in the Pastoral Epistles for 'the truth' figures so largely as to be in the minds of some an un-Pauline element. Pseudepigraphic hypotheses must assume that the author's notion of the truth contained nothing inconsistent with a literary method which he must have known would deceive many if not all his readers. It cannot be maintained that 'truth' is here used for the formal contents of the gospel and would therefore not apply to literary conventions, for we have seen reason to doubt whether the method proposed was ever such an accepted literary convention. It should further be noted that in every one of these disputed Pauline Epistles there is mention of deceit and deceivers. Of the two pseudo-Pauline Epistles mentioned from the New Testament Apocrypha, 3 Corinthians contains no mention of truth or deception, while the Epistle to the Laodiceans twice mentions 'the truth of the gospel' (4, 5) but this is no more than a reproduction of Galatians ii. 14 in common with the author's policy merely to repeat genuine Pauline phrases. There is no evidence in this latter epistle of independent thought and no evidence therefore of the author's own mental consciousness.

V. IMITATION AND ITS DETECTION

Some attention must be given to another aspect of pseudonymity. What steps would an imitator take to avoid detection? Is it ever a valid argument that peculiarities must be Pauline because an imitator would have avoided anything un-Pauline? While this line of argument must clearly be used with reserve, it must be allowed that an imitator would make some attempt to avoid as much as possible dissimilarities with his model. Yet this supposition is challenged by many scholars. Mitton, for example, comments, 'With such good friends an imitator need never fear detection. Any slip or inconsistency, any instance of his own personality peeping through into his work, is only further proof that his work is genuine, because no imitator would be foolish enough to make such a slip or to include in his work any kind of discrepancy. Such an argument is surely a somewhat desperate expedient. It may even be asked whether those who resort to it do not thereby reveal a consciousness of some weakness in the position they seek to maintain.'[1]

Now if this criticism is valid, the converse must also be true. A genuine author must always live in fear lest his work should be regarded as an imitation and not the real thing, for if he deviates in the least from his former style or uses words which he has not used before or allows more of his personality to peep through than hitherto his work cannot be genuine. But such a state of affairs would be intolerable. The vital difference between the genuine Paul and an imitator of his is that no author ever considers what impression a different style will have upon critical recipients, whereas in the nature of the case an imitator cannot fail to give some attention to this. If he is making a sincere attempt to reproduce Paul a tension between his own personality and that of Paul immediately arises, and he will do his best to see that his own personality does not protrude. It is reasonable to suppose that as far as possible non-Pauline traits would be avoided.

Moreover, if this assumption is a 'desperate expedient', literary criticism would be brought to a standstill, for an imitator would be given a completely free hand while a genuine author would be hamstrung within the limits of his previous works. It introduces a distinction which is not only unreal but psychologically completely unjustified. By its use any work may be pronounced pseudonymous on the grounds of the slightest inconsistency, as nineteenth-century rational criticism abundantly shows. A more realistic approach is to assume that an author's own claims are valid unless they are psychologically improbable.

An interesting light is thrown on this problem by the evidence of the two spurious works mentioned above, the so-called 3 Corinthians and the Epistle to the Laodiceans. It is neither internal inconsistency nor the personality of the imitator peeping through that has led to the confident judgment that they are spurious. It is, on the contrary, the sheer weight of external evidence. It is highly significant that of these two works that which adheres most faithfully to Pauline phraseology

---

[1] *Ephesians*, pp. 28, 29.

enjoyed the greater popularity. In other words, the imitator who kept the closer to his model was the more successful.

This brief study of epistolary pseudepigraphy in its bearing on the Pauline Epistles leaves us with the impression that psychological difficulties lie in the path of theories of pseudonymous authorship and advocates of them must come to grips with these problems in presenting their case.

ADDITIONAL NOTE

For further literature on pseudonymity, cf. A. Meyer, 'Religiöse Pseud-epigraphie als ethisch-psychologisches Problem', *ZNTW*, 35 (1936), pp. 262 ff.; J. A. Sint, *Pseudonymität im Altertum* (1960); K. Aland, 'The Problem of Anonymity and Pseudonymity in Christian Literature of the First Two Centuries', *JTS*, n.s., xii (1961), pp. 39 ff.; and my article, 'The Development of the Idea of Canonical Pseudepigrapha in N. T. Criticism', *Vox Evangelica* (1962). The latter two articles are reproduced in SPCK Collections 4, *The Authorship and Integrity of the New Testament* (1965). Aland argues that many early works, which were originally anonymous, later became pseudonymous. Because of their close connection one cannot be considered apart from the other. But Aland makes a dubious assumption when he explains that a writer who was conscious of writing according to the Spirit chose anonymity, for this would imply the further assumption that a writer who gave his name requires some explanation. This means that, in Aland's view, anonymity and pseudonymity in early Christian times were the normal procedure.

But such a reversal of what would normally be expected is insupportable. It cannot account for the Pauline Epistles. Those that Aland considers genuine are undoubtedly manifestations of the work of the Spirit and yet Paul appends his name. Moreover, those which he regards as non-authentic cannot readily be treated as originally anonymous. Indeed, Aland's theory breaks down over the Pauline Epistles. Moreover, Aland appeals to the *Didache* as the key to the transition from anonymity to pseudonymity, because it claims to be the teaching through the twelve apostles. In his opinion, the writer knew himself to be charismatic and was acknowledged as such. Aland's choice of illustration is strange, because the vague reference to the apostles is mentioned in a quite different way from an author who writes a letter in another's name. If the *Didache* is the best example of the emergence of pseudepigraphy in Christian writings it would be necessary to ask why the movement towards personal authorship went any further. Why, for instance, were the Pastorals attributed to Paul? Was this because it was seen to be a more effective method than the vaguer *Didache*? And why, if the *Didache* was *ex hypothesi* recognized as a work of the Spirit, was it not received into the Canon?

The fact is that Aland is supposing that pseudonymity was 'the logical conclusion of the presupposition that the Spirit himself was the author' (*op. cit.*, p. 8). But this still does not explain why pseudonymity was necessary. If the Spirit was

NEW TESTAMENT INTRODUCTION

so obviously the author, what would be gained by attaching the name of any or all of the apostles? Aland's thesis not only leaves the major question unanswered but also confuses the work of the Spirit. Since Paul's Epistles are the most personal in the New Testament and yet contain much evidence of his awareness of the activity of the Spirit, it is difficult to suppose, as Aland does, that a named author would arouse more suspicion than an anonymous or pseudonymous writing.

CHAPTER TWENTY-TWO

THE EPISTLE TO THE HEBREWS

This Epistle raises several problems, for not only is it anonymous, but its destination and purpose are both obscure. The importance of careful examination of all these problems, even if no dogmatic conclusions can be reached, cannot be exaggerated since they affect both the approach to the Epistle as a whole and the understanding of the argument. Moreover, its modern relevance clearly depends on a right appreciation of its original setting.

I. AUTHORSHIP

a. External evidence

A review of the early history of this Epistle at once places in its true perspective the discussion on authorship, for it becomes immediately evident that there was no firm tradition on this matter in the earliest period.

There are remarkable parallels between this Epistle and the Epistle sent by Clement of Rome to the Corinthians (cf. Heb. xi. 7 and *1 Clement*, ix. 4 and xii. 1; Heb. i. 3f. and *1 Clement*, xxxvi. 1f.) which make it certain that Clement was in possession of the Epistle. Suggestions that trace both to a common source[1] or suppose that the author of Hebrews was acquainted with *1 Clement* cannot seriously be maintained.

The sequence of thoughts which are parallel to the Epistle, especially in *1 Clement*, xxxvi, supports the contention that Clement had the Epistle before him, although he uses some freedom in his citations. This latter fact does not detract from the authority which for Clement was clearly invested in the Epistle, for he uses the same freedom in citations from other New Testament Epistles.[2] Yet he gives no hint of authorship.[3]

---

[1] A. Nairne mentioned the idea, but admitted it to be in the realm of fancy, that both authors were influenced by the Roman liturgy (*The Epistle to the Hebrews*, 1917, p. xxxix). He thought that Clement had read the Epistle.

[2] It has been suggested that Clement assumes that the Corinthians would know of Hebrews and regard it as authoritative. (Cf. K. Endemann, *NkZ*, 21, 1910, p. 103.)

[3] This by itself would not be decisive since he cites Pauline letters without indication of Pauline origin (except in the case of 1 Cor.). (Cf. B. F. Westcott, *On the Canon of the New Testament*,[4] 1875, p. 50.)

There is little other positive evidence about the Epistle until the end of the second century.[1] It was excluded from Marcion's Canon, but the Epistle would certainly not have appealed to him with his aversion to the idea of any continuity between the Old Testament and Christianity, which forms so integral a part of the thought-structure of the Epistle. It is further omitted from the Muratorian Canon, although this may be due to the corrupt state of the text of that Canon. In any case it was definitely not included in the Pauline Epistles, for these are restricted to seven churches. At the end of the century, however, more specific references are made to it, but these at once reveal a divergent tradition. In the East the Epistle was probably regarded as Pauline, at least from the time of Pantaenus. Clement of Alexandria, who described the Epistle as Paul's (Eusebius, *HE*, vi. 14), derived this opinion from 'the blessed presbyter', who is generally supposed to be his predecessor at Alexandria, Pantaenus. Origen was equally certain that the thoughts were Pauline, but he could not imagine the style to be his. His own supposition was that one of the pupils of the apostle wrote down from memory what he had heard. For this reason he not only did not quarrel with any church which regarded it as Paul's but even himself cited it similarly. Yet he added his famous caution, 'But who wrote the Epistle God only knows certainly.' At the same time he mentions that some held 'Clement, who became bishop of Rome', and others Luke, to be the author.[2]

Subsequent to Origen, the Eastern Church generally did not doubt the canonicity of the Epistle and indeed assumed its Pauline authorship. In the Chester Beatty papyrus (P46), the Epistle appears among the Pauline Epistles, being placed after Romans,[3] and this represents the position not later than the mid-third century. In the majority of early Greek manuscripts it is placed after 2 Thessalonians and before the personal letters of Paul.[4]

In the West the only early evidence of views on authorship comes

[1] Van Unnik, *The Jung Codex* (ed. F. L. Cross, 1955), pp. 115ff., finds traces in the *Gospel of Truth*. Cf. the further study of S. Giversen, *Studia Theologica*, XIII, fasc. II (1959), pp. 87–96, who finds parallels but many differences.

[2] Origen obviously regarded the idea of Pauline authorship as of some antiquity, for he mentions that the tradition was handed down by 'men of old' (Eusebius, *HE*, vi. 25, 11–14).

[3] Cf. F. G. Kenyon, *The Chester Beatty Biblical Papyri* (1936), fasc. III, p. viii. Cf. also his *The Story of the Bible* (1936), p. 116.

[4] Cf. Feine-Behm, *Einleitung in das Neue Testament*[11] (1956), p. 221.*

from Tertullian who attributed it to Barnabas in the only place where he mentioned it.[1] This isolated use of the Epistle suggests that it did not possess the same authority as the Epistles of Paul which were extensively cited by the same writer.[2] As already mentioned, the Muratorian Canon omits it, but this cannot be cited as evidence for its definite rejection from the Roman Canon. Eusebius,[3] who follows the general eastern tradition in including this Epistle among the Pauline Epistles, mentions that in his time the Roman Church disputed the Pauline authorship and that on the grounds of this some others were rejecting the Epistle. It was similarly omitted from the later African Canon, while Cyprian never mentions it. This reflects the prevailing approach of the West towards this Epistle until the time of Hilary, Jerome and Augustine.[4] These writers show the impact of eastern ideas on the western churches, but it is significant that, although Hilary regarded the Epistle as canonical, he does not specifically cite it as Paul's.[5] The other writers are similarly witnesses to a compromise affecting the Western Church, for neither seems convinced of Pauline authorship and yet both cite it as Paul's. It was their willingness to do this that finally settled the matter in the West and secured for Pauline authorship an unchallenged position until the Reformation, when Erasmus, Luther and Calvin all questioned it.[6] For Luther this involved its relegation to the end of the Bible with other books considered by him to be of lesser value. His own theory was that Apollos wrote it. Later Grotius returned to the earlier theory of Lucan authorship, while subsequent investigators have devoted themselves to pressing the claims of a wide variety of possibilities.

[1] De pudicitia, 20. Cf. Westcott, op. cit., p. 367. J. V. Bartlet (Exp., VI, v, 1902, p. 423) maintained that Tertullian was magnifying Hebrews at the expense of Hermas (the reverse procedure from what he imagined is found in the Muratorian Canon).

[2] T. Zahn cites some evidence which suggests that both Hippolytus and Irenaeus might have known and quoted Hebrews, although not regarding it as Pauline (Introduction to the New Testament, Eng. Tr. 1909, II, pp. 295, 310).

[3] HE, iii. 3.

[4] There is something to be said for the view that early Western opinion, in its rejection of Pauline authorship, was more consistent than the Eastern Church with its vacillations over Pauline authorship (cf. K. Endemann, NkZ, 21, 1910, pp. 102ff.).

[5] Cf. A. Souter, The Text and Canon of New Testament (1913), p. 190. Hilary uses the introductory formula, maxime cum Scriptum sit.

[6] Cf. Ibid., pp. 198ff.

The divergent early views and the later speculations do not suggest that discussion of various theories is likely to be very profitable, but the process is worth while if only to illustrate many facets of the author's background, which are necessarily brought to the fore in such discussions.

b. Various suggestions

Investigations will commence with those names which commanded some ancient respect and the most notable of these is clearly Paul. (i) *Paul*. Most modern writers find more difficulty in imagining how this Epistle was ever attributed to Paul[1] than in disposing of the theory. The grounds for dispute may be set out as follows:

1. Its anonymity would not conform to Paul's style, although this fact did not deter nineteenth-century[2] supporters of Pauline authorship, who regarded it rather as confirmatory than damaging, since an apostle to the Gentiles could hardly have addressed an Epistle to the Hebrews without incurring the resentment of the readers. But this attaches too much weight to the title. Clement of Alexandria, who expresses a similar opinion, cites with some approval the view of Pantaenus that the absence of Paul's name was occasioned by respect for the Lord, whom he presumably regarded as the Apostle to the Hebrews, and by the fact that Paul regarded this Epistle as a work of supererogation. But these explanations are clearly unconvincing in helping to remove what is an obvious difficulty for the acceptance of Pauline authorship. Moreover, nowhere in the Epistle does the author lay claim to any apostolic authority, which would certainly be strange for Paul.

2. But difference of style is even more apparent and would seem to make the theory of Pauline authorship inconceivable. The language, as Origen noted, is more Greek, with its more polished periods, its more designed argumentation and its absence of the usual Pauline abruptness, digressions and even disorderliness.[3] Where breaks in the

---

[1] Cf. F. D. V. Narborough, *The Epistle to the Hebrews* (1930), p. 9.

[2] Cf. Bishop C. Wordsworth, *St. Paul's Epistles* (1872), p. 370. For the most recent advocacy of Pauline authorship, cf. W. Leonard, *The Authorship of the Epistle to the Hebrews* (1939). H. C. Thiessen (*INT*,[4] 1956, p. 301) considers that rejection of Pauline authorship is not absolutely certain.*

[3] Feine-Behm (*op. cit.*, p. 222) maintain that this Epistle is one of the best Greek writings in the New Testament and most scholars would agree with this judgment.*

argument occur, the writer always picks up the threads in a deliberate, almost leisurely, manner, in strong contrast to Paul's habit of losing his line of argument altogether.[1] This clear difference cannot be mitigated by the difference of form, assuming this Epistle to be more an oration than an Epistle in the sense of Paul's letters. The most that could be supposed is that a member of the Pauline circle wrote down such an oration as he had heard Paul preach it, but, if so, much of the oratorical effects must be due to the reporter rather than to the orator.[2]

3. An even more damaging objection is the absence of the characteristic Pauline spiritual experience.[3] There is no suggestion of the author being dominated by a spiritual crisis comparable to the Damascus experience and there is consequently an absence of that tension so characteristic of Paul. It need not, of course, be supposed that similar background experiences must be brought into every writing of an author, but in spite of some personal allusions this author does not project himself into his writing as Paul habitually does.

4. There are undoubtedly theological differences between this Epistle and the Epistles of Paul, in spite of the many similarities (for these latter see pp. 722f.). Whereas Paul makes much of the resurrection, our author concentrates on the exaltation. Whereas Paul calls special attention to the redemptive aspect of the work of Christ, this Epistle deals more with His cleansing, sanctifying and perfecting work. This Epistle also makes more of the idea of the new covenant, but lacks the familiar Pauline tension between flesh and spirit and the believer's mystic union with Christ. A rather different approach to the law is also suggested, since our author appears to regard it as an instrument for the attainment of man's highest end and never, as Paul does, as a possible scene of conflict. Most significant of all, there is no mention in Paul of the High-Priesthood of Christ, which forms the central theme of this Epistle.[4]

While full weight must be given to these differences in discussing

[1] F. W. Farrar (*The Epistle to the Hebrews*, 1888, p. xxxviii) well said of this writer, 'He has less of burning passion and more of conscious literary control.'

[2] See the discussion on the literary form on pp. 724ff.

[3] E. F. Scott (*The Literature of the New Testament*, 1932, p. 198) went so far as to suggest that the author does not even seem to be acquainted with Paul's teaching.

[4] Cf. Feine-Behm (*op. cit.*, pp. 222, 223) for a statement on these differences. In connection with Christ's High-Priesthood, it should be noted that certain hints suggest that Paul at times thought along these lines, as did Peter and John (cf. O. Moe's discussion in *ThI Z*, 72, 1947, cols. 335–338).*

the problem of authorship, it should be noted that differences from Paul do not amount to disagreements with Paul (see discussion on Paulinism on pp. 722f.). Nor must it be supposed that these doctrinal differences necessarily exclude Pauline authorship. Yet if they do not *require* its rejection, it must be admitted that they appear to suggest it. Some allowance must be made for the different reader-circle that would be involved if Paul were author (but see objection 1 above). It may not be a fair comparison to set writings directed to Gentiles over against a writing which appears to have been sent to Jews (see later discussion pp. 698ff.). There is no certain knowledge, moreover, as to how Paul would have dealt with the high-priest theme had he applied himself to it. Too much emphasis should not, perhaps, be laid upon these doctrinal differences. After all, that acute scholar, Origen of Alexandria, recognized here the thoughts of Paul.

5. The different historical position of the author is generally considered to be conclusive against Pauline authorship. In ii. 3 it is evident that the author had received his Christian instruction directly from those who had heard the Lord,[1] whereas Paul was particularly insistent that he was brought into salvation by a supernatural revelation (cf. Gal. i. 12). On occasions Paul identified himself with the experience of his readers rather than allowing his own to predominate, but it is questionable whether he would ever have set himself so definitely in contrast to those who had personally heard Jesus Christ in the flesh.

There seems little doubt from these considerations and from the uncertainty of early Christian attestation that Paul was not the author of this Epistle. This is not to deny the possibility, but rather to confirm the improbability. But if not Paul, who was the author?

(ii) *Barnabas.* This suggestion deserves second place in our considerations because it is the only other one which has early ecclesiastical support. In fact it may possibly be the oldest attested since Tertullian does not attribute it to Barnabas as if it were his own conjecture and it is reasonable to suppose that it was current at a still earlier period.[2]

---

[1] Cf. F. D. V. Narborough (*op. cit.*, p. 10) who argues that the author had been converted in the ordinary course of evangelization.

[2] J. Moffatt (*ILNT*,[2] 1912, p. 437) suggested that Tertullian may be reflecting a Roman tradition. But A. Harnack (*Das Neue Testament um das Jahr* 200, 1889, pp. 79ff.) thought there was no reason to suppose that any churches with whom Tertullian was in touch regarded Hebrews as by Barnabas. A. Nairne (*The Epistle of Priesthood,*[2] 1915, pp. 3, 4) thought the idea was a guess on the part of simple Christians.

Tertullian supports Barnabas

Yet, because the evidence is restricted to Africa, it cannot be claimed that this suggestion commanded much general consent. But Westcott suggested[1] that the Epistle may have been mentioned in the Claromontanus List under the name of Barnabas, since stichometry (i.e. measurement by number of lines) appears to lend support to that conjecture, and if so, this second witness would extend the area of attestation. Moreover, two other witnesses to the same idea are the fourth-century *Tractatus de Libris* and the comment of Philastrius (fourth-century bishop of Brescia).[2] But all these would still restrict it to the Western Church.

The strongest basis for this claim is the certainty that Barnabas as a Levite would have been intimately acquainted with the temple ritual. Nevertheless this detail must not be overstressed since the author's main obsession seems to be the biblical cultus rather than contemporary ritual procedure. At the same time there is nothing in the Epistle to condemn the suggestion, even if there is similarly nothing to commend it. It may be added that the description of him as a son of consolation (Acts iv. 36) and the author's description of his work as 'a word of consolation' (Heb. xiii. 22) furnishes an ingenious parallel, which would support the general suitability of Barnabas as the possible author.[3] Barnabas might well have been capable of such a literary production, but the data for determining that he did produce it are practically non-existent.

Because of the generally assumed Hellenism of the Epistle it is an important question whether or not a man whose known connections were with Jerusalem and Cyprus would have sufficiently imbibed the Greek outlook to produce an Epistle with Alexandrian colouring. Apart from the fact that the Alexandrian background has probably been over-stressed (see later discussion), it is not improbable that some Hellenistic speculation of the Philonic type had penetrated into Cyprus.[4]

[1] *The Epistle to the Hebrews* (1889), pp. xxviii, xxix. The number of *stichoi* (lines) cited would not fit the *Epistle of Barnabas*, but would suit the Epistle to the Hebrews.

[2] Cf. J. V. Bartlet, *Exp.*, VI, v (1902), p. 426.

[3] K. Endemann, *NkZ*, 21 (1910), pp. 121, 122, pointed out in addition the sevenfold use of παρακαλειν—παράκλησις.

[4] Among those who have favoured Barnabas as author may be mentioned Salmon, Bartlet, Wickham, Riggenbach, Bornhäuser and Badcock; E. C. Wickham (*The Epistle to the Hebrews*, 1910, p. xii) maintained that the Epistle

But two considerations are not very favourable to this theory. If Barnabas had been the author, would he have described his own introduction to the gospel in the terms of ii. 3? And if it had been known that he was the author, is the rise of the Pauline tradition capable of any explanation? It might be contended in answer to the latter that Barnabas' name alone was not sufficiently authoritative to command canonical acceptance for the Epistle, as is evident in the case of the spurious Epistle which circulated under his name, but it is not conceivable that the substitution of Paul's name for that of Barnabas could have secured canonicity if any other tradition were already established or at least in some circulation.[1] In connection with the first consideration, it is not absolutely certain that ii. 3 would necessarily exclude Barnabas, unless, of course, it is interpreted as indicating a second generation situation. The early Acts narrative does not give any concrete data about the way that Barnabas became a Christian, although it is difficult to believe that he had never personally heard the Lord if he were a resident in Jerusalem.[2] Moreover, Barnabas, as an early member of the Jerusalem church, was presumably in sympathy with the general approach of those first Jewish Christians.[3] But the approach in this Epistle is very different, with its broader Hellenistic outlook.[4]

The comparison of this Epistle with the so-called *Epistle of Barnabas* proves conclusively that the same writer could not have written both Epistles, although there are some common features. Both deal with the Old Testament and both appear to write against a background of

suits Barnabas' character as a Hellenist by birthplace, but a Hebrew by race. K. Endemann (*op. cit.*, pp. 102–126) went so far as to claim that Barnabas alone fitted all the evidence. H. Strathmann (*Der Brief an die Hebräer*,[6] 1953, p. 71) is favourable, but admits its conjectural character.

[1] Cf. McNeile-Williams, *INT*[2] (1953), p. 237. It is not an altogether convincing suggestion of Renan's that it was Barnabas' lot to be lost in the greater glory of the apostle Paul, although J. V. Bartlet (*op. cit.*, p. 427) favoured this idea.

[2] Tertullian (*De Pudicitia*, 20) says of Barnabas, *qui ab apostolis didicit*, which would agree with ii. 3, but on the other hand it was probably no more than a deduction from the Epistle itself.

[3] J. V. Bartlet (*op. cit.*, p. 420) regarded ii. 3 simply as an instance in which the author identifies himself with his readers and which does not require the author to have received his Christian teaching secondhand. In fact, Bartlet maintained that all the New Testament evidence shows that Barnabas was a man of considerable influence in Jerusalem, which, he thought, strongly suggested that he was a personal hearer of the Lord (pp. 411ff.).

[4] Cf. Feine-Behm, *op. cit.*, p. 230.*

Alexandrian rather than Judaistic ideas. Both mention levitical institutions and both contain teaching about the temple (or tabernacle). But there the resemblances end.[1] The *Epistle of Barnabas* is greatly inferior in spiritual grasp, in historical appreciation and in breadth of understanding of the problems with which it deals. It is sufficient to remark that if Barnabas were the genuine author of this *Epistle of Barnabas*, he could not possibly be regarded as author of the Epistle to the Hebrews. But the former *Epistle*, which is strictly anonymous, appears to have been spuriously attributed to the illustrious name of Paul's companion.[2] When compared with the Epistle to the Hebrews it can only be said that the ascription of the latter to Barnabas has much more to commend it than is the case with the former, but beyond that we cannot go.

(iii) *Luke*. There were some in Origen's day who attributed the Epistle to Luke, while Clement of Alexandria regarded him as translator from Paul's Hebrew original and this notion of Luke's connection with the Epistle has found supporters among modern critics.[3] The main prop for the theory is the literary affinities of this Epistle with the Lucan writings.[4] In addition to verbal and stylistic similarities, there are some features which have been supposed to connect the Epistle closely with Acts and especially with Stephen's speech. F. D. V. Narborough brings out the following similarities: both contain reviews of Hebrew history; both stress the call of Abraham and mention Abraham's non-possession of the land; both describe the tabernacle as divinely ordered; and in both the tradition that the law was mediated by angels finds a place.[5]

[1] Cf. B. F. Westcott's comparison, *op. cit.*, pp. lxxx–lxxxiv.

[2] Cf. K. Lake, *The Apostolic Fathers* (1912), I, p. 337.

[3] J. Moffatt gives a list of authors who have supported this contention (*ILNT*, p. 435). A compromise suggestion was made by F. J. Badcock in his book *The Pauline Epistles and the Epistle to the Hebrews in their historical setting* (1937), p. 198. He considered that the voice was Barnabas', but the hand was Luke's. He also thought that Philip might have had something to do with it, thus accounting for similarities with Stephen's speech. All these were, of course, acquainted with Timothy.

[4] The arguments were clearly brought out by A. R. Eager, *Exp.*, VI, x (1904), pp. 74–80, 110–123. Cf. also Moffatt, *op. cit.*, pp. 435, 436. Cf. the article by C. P. M. Jones, 'The Epistle to the Hebrews and the Lucan Writings', in *Studies in the Gospels* (ed. D. E. Nineham, 1957), pp. 113–143.

[5] *Op. cit.*, p. 11. W. Manson (*The Epistle to the Hebrews*, 1951, p. 36) mentioned in addition the distinctive call to 'go out'; the idea of the 'living Word'; the incidental allusion to Joshua; and the heavenward direction of the eyes.

The force of these comparisons naturally depends on the theory that Stephen's speech was composed by Luke, but if Luke is reproducing an independent genuine tradition the comparisons have less weight. It may well be that the author was acquainted with Luke's writings and was greatly influenced by them in ideas and phraseology,[1] but this is a mere conjecture and there is little more that can be said in support of Lucan authorship. Moffatt wisely concluded that all that can fairly be postulated is community of atmosphere.[2] But even this would be questionable if the essentially Jewish background of the Epistle be admitted.[3]

(iv) *Clement.* The remarkable parallels which exist between the Epistle and Clement's epistle, as already mentioned, no doubt led to the early notion of common authorship,[4] or at least to the theory of Clement as translator.[5] But Westcott[6] has sufficiently demonstrated that the differences outweigh the similarities. Clement's language and style, method of citation, range of thought and insight are all removed from those of the author of Hebrews. There is in Clement an absence of that creative contribution to Christian theology which is so evident a feature of the canonical Epistle. The parallels and similarities are well accounted for by Clement's acquaintance with this Epistle.

(v) *Silvanus.* The most that can be said in support of this suggestion[7] is that Silvanus was a member of the Pauline circle and was associated with the writing of 1 Peter. The latter consideration is thought to have some relevance because of certain literary resemblances between 1 Peter and Hebrews. There is no disputing these similarities, but the mere fact of verbal similarities cannot establish identity of authorship without

[1] Cf. Westcott, *op. cit.*, p. lxxvi.
[2] *ILNT*, p. 437. W. H. Simcox (*Exp.*, III, viii, 1888) drew attention to the verbal and theological similarities between Hebrews, the Pastoral Epistles and the Lucan writings, but suggested three different writers all belonging to the same circle.
[3] Cf. Feine-Behm, *op. cit.*, p. 229.
[4] Cf. Eusebius, *HE*, iii. 38. This view was revived by Erasmus and has been held by various more recent scholars (cf. Moffatt, *op. cit.*, p. 438, for details). K and S. Lake (*INT*, 1938, p. 158) mention the theory favourably, but do not commit themselves to it.
[5] As, for instance, by Jerome (cf. Eusebius, *HE*, iii. 37).
[6] *Op. cit.*, p. lxxvii.
[7] Cf. F. Godet, *Exp.*, III, vii (1888), pp. 264, 265. It had previously been maintained by Mynster (1825) and Boehme (1825) (mentioned by Wohlenberg, *NkZ*, 24, 1913, p. 760).

other corroborating evidence.[1] It must remain, therefore, an unsupported hypothesis, especially in view of the uncertainty of the precise part played by Silvanus in the production of 1 Peter. Moreover, the differences outweigh the similarities, for there is no evidence in 1 Peter of a similar method of citation and Alexandrian background of thought. It must be remembered that Silvanus was a Jerusalem Jew.[2]

(vi) *Apollos*. Ever since Luther[3] embraced the idea of Apollos as author of the Epistle, this conjecture has won adherents,[4] particularly among those who emphasize the Alexandrian background. The main arguments in support are:

1. Apollos' close acquaintance with Paul, thus accounting for Pauline influences.

2. His connection with Alexandria, which would account for the Alexandrian colouring.

3. His knowledge of the Scriptures, which would explain the biblical content of the argument and the use of the LXX version.

4. His eloquence, which well suits the oratorical form of the Epistle.[5]

5. His contacts with Timothy.

6. His considerable influence in various churches.

---

[1] G. Wohlenberg (*NkZ*, 24, 1913, pp. 742–762) examined these similarities very thoroughly and argued that common authorship better explained the relationship than use of Hebrews by the author of 1 Peter, or a common milieu theory (as von Soden proposed).

[2] Recently T. Hewitt (*The Epistle to the Hebrews*, TNT, 1960, pp. 26–32) has favoured Silvanus, following Selwyn's claims for such a close relationship between this Epistle and 1 Peter, which goes beyond common sources, traditions or circumstances. Since Selwyn regarded Silvanus as the real author of 1 Peter, it is, therefore, proposed that he also wrote Hebrews. Four lines of evidence are said to support this.

    1. Silas was known at Rome (1 Pet. v. 13) and at Jerusalem.

    2. Timothy and Silas were well known to each other.

    3. Silas, when attached to the Jerusalem church, would be well acquainted with the temple cultus.

    4. The writers of both 1 Peter and Hebrews were steeped in the LXX.

But too little is known about Silas to be certain.

[3] Moffatt does not regard Luther as the originator of the idea (cf. *ILNT*, p. 438).

[4] Among recent advocates are T. W. Manson, Ketter, Howard, Spicq and Lo Bue. It was also favoured by Zahn, *INT*, II, p. 356, hesitatingly.*

[5] See Moffatt, *The Epistle to the Hebrews* (ICC, 1924), pp. lviff., for a discussion of the author's rhetorical tendencies. Cf. also Narborough, *op. cit.*, p. 15.

Luther: 15:46

Heb.
6:46 6:1
10:26, 2:3
12:17

There is no doubt that this hypothesis is a happy one in many respects and there are no data which can be brought against it.[1] Yet the absence of any early tradition in support is a serious difficulty, especially as it might have been expected that the Alexandrian church would have preserved such a fact, if fact it was. Moreover, Acts xviii. 24ff. tells nothing about Apollos' Philonic education. Neither is there any knowledge of literary activity on his part.[2] The most that can be said is that this is a plausible conjecture, but even if established it would add little or nothing to our understanding of the historical situation of the letter apart from making a Roman destination (see later discussion) less probable.[3] Nevertheless there is something to be said for the view that if some famous unknown did not write the Epistle, Apollos fits the requirements as well as any.

(vii) *Philip*. It was Sir William M. Ramsay[4] who maintained a Caesarean origin for this Epistle and postulated that Philip the deacon sent it to Jerusalem to commend Paulinism to the Jewish Christians there. Since it was sent, in Ramsay's opinion, after Philip had conversed with Paul, this would well account for the Pauline influences in the writing. But why should Philip have couched his approach in so Hellenistic a form if this were his purpose? And why was the Pauline influence not considerably greater than it is?

(viii) *Priscilla*. Harnack[5] proposed that Priscilla, with the assistance of her husband, might have written the letter, and he supported his contention by appealing to the enigma of anonymity. The name of a woman as author would have been so prejudicial to its acceptance that it would be omitted for reasons of prudence. That this pair were illustrious teachers is indicated by their ability to instruct such a man as

---

[1] This was strongly maintained by F. W. Farrar, *The Epistle to the Hebrews* (1888), p. lviii.

[2] A rather fanciful theory was proposed by E. H. Plumptre (*Exp.*, I, i, 1875, pp. 329–348, 409–435) that Apollos was not only author of this Epistle, but, before his enlightenment by Aquila and Priscilla, author of the Book of Wisdom also.

[3] T. W. Manson has avoided this difficulty by postulating a Colossian destination (see p. 710).

[4] *Exp.*, v, ix (1909) pp. 407–422; *Luke the Physician and other studies* (1908), pp. 301–308.

[5] *ZNTW*, I (1900), pp. 16–41. This idea was favourably regarded by J. Rendel Harris in the appendix of his *Side Lights on New Testament Research* (1908).

Apollos. The writer, like these two, had close associations with Timothy and had come under the influence of Paul. Another point made by Harnack was that Paul seems now to be dead and had in his last letter specially mentioned both Timothy and Aquila and Priscilla, and this will fit the circumstances of the Epistle. Moreover, since the author is so closely identified with his readers and hopes to return to them, this would be intelligible if the group were the church in Aquila and Priscilla's house. Moreover, in the list of heroes in Hebrews xi, certain women are mentioned and this is supposed to indicate a woman's interest. But those mentioned are not particularly prominent and one of the most renowned of early women heroes,[1] Deborah, is omitted altogether. The use of the plural in xiii. 18[2] cannot seriously be claimed as support for joint authorship, since xiii. 19 is emphatically in the singular, as also xi. 32 and xiii. 22, 23.[3] In further support of this view can be cited the pilgrim approach (xi. 13–16); the reference to nautical terms (iii. 6, 14, vi. 19, xiii. 9); the interest in the tabernacle, since Aquila and Priscilla were tent-makers; and the interest in childhood (v. 12, xi. 23, xii. 7) and parenthood (vii. 3, xi. 23).[4]

There are no reasons for supposing that the Epistle shows such signs of femininity as would warrant this hypothesis, especially in view of Paul's own declared opinion against women teachers (1 Cor. xiv. 34f.). It can hardly be supposed that Priscilla with her close connections with the apostle would have proceeded so contrary to his policy.[5] It is true that she assisted her husband in instructing Apollos in the Christian truth, but this was a private action. It need not indicate, as Harnack supposed,[6] that Priscilla, who is mentioned first in Acts xviii. 26, must have been of high intelligence to instruct the educated Apollos, for the way of God was understood not by intellectual but by spiritual intelligence.

---

[1] Harnack (*op. cit.*, pp. 40, 41, n. 6) placed little weight on this.

[2] The plural in v. 11 appears to be an epistolary usage.

[3] Harnack supposed one author, who is at times joined by another in exhortations (*op. cit.*, p. 37).

[4] Cf. F. B. Clogg, *INT*[3] (1948), pp. 138, 139.

[5] F. D. V. Narborough also points out that the authoritative tone of the Epistle does not accord with the idea of feminine authorship, in view of other New Testament teaching (*op. cit.*, p. 12). Cf. also the criticisms of C. C. Torrey, *JBL*, xxx (1911), pp. 142ff.

[6] *Op. cit.*, p. 36.

c. Conclusion

In the light of the preceding discussions,[1] an open verdict is clearly the safest course and in this the opinion of Origen can hardly be improved upon. It may not appeal to the mind to admit that a thinker of so profound a type should remain anonymous and yet, as A. Nairne pointed out, the precision of a name would not much illuminate the background.[2] Of greater importance is the situation which the Epistle was intended to answer.

II. THE READERS

In discussing the addressees, it is necessary to examine the title, 'To the Hebrews', since this in modern times has often been summarily dismissed, because it did not belong to the original text and because the earliest definite attestation for it is early third century.[3] Thus E. F.

---

[1] No mention has been made in these discussions of the proposal of A. M. Dubarle, *RB*, XLVIII (1939), pp. 506–529, that Jude was the author. He finds similarities in vocabulary, syntax, stylistic processes, mentality and culture between Hebrews and the Epistle of Jude. But similarities of this kind may be accounted for by the common background of Jewish Christianity.

[2] *The Epistle to the Hebrews* (1917), p. lvii. Moffatt, (*ILNT*, p. 442), Michaelis (*Einleitung in das Neue Testament*,[3] 1961, p. 272), Michel (*Der Brief an die Hebräer*,[11] 1960, p. 11), Meinertz (*Einleitung*,[5] 1950, pp. 144, 145), Dibelius (*A Fresh Approach to the New Testament and Early Christian Literature*, 1937, p. 197) and W. Neil (*The Epistle to the Hebrews*, 1955, pp. 14ff.) all decline to propose any definite name. A. S. Peake (*Hebrews*, n.d., p. 10) suggestively inferred that since the writer knew the community so well (see next section), he was probably one of their leaders, who was for a time separated from them. E. J. Goodspeed's idea that Hebrews may have been originally pseudonymous, rather than anonymous (*INT*, 1939, p. 257), may at once be dismissed, for had the letter originally borne an ascription to Paul, it is impossible to envisage any situation in which it would lose its ascription and still continue to be regarded with some favour. There are no parallels to this kind of thing among the pseudepigrapha.*

[3] It is so described by Tertullian and was probably the traditional title before his time (*De Pudicitia*, 20). Pantaenus seems to have known it under this title also (Zahn, *INT*, II, p. 294). Zahn considered that the very brief title was added for ease of reference when Hebrews was bound with various other letters (*ibid.*, p. 295). But this could only have happened to the original autograph and must, therefore, have occurred at a very early date. It is an interesting conjecture, but no more. H. Thyen (*Der Stil der jüdisch-hellenistischen Homilie*, 1955, p. 16) thinks that the title was attached on the incorporation of the Epistle into the Pauline Epistles.

THE EPISTLE TO THE HEBREWS

Scott describes it as a guess,[1] while F. D. V. Narborough regards it as suspiciously vague.[2] Yet while admitting that the title may not be authentic,[3] we ought not to dismiss it too lightly since there is no evidence that the Epistle bore any other address.[4] It expressed at least the common belief at an early period concerning the destination.[5]

Yet 'the Hebrews' would not naturally describe a local group since it is a national title and, in order to define the readers more closely, it is necessary to take careful account of the internal evidence.

a. Internal evidence in support of a particular community

There are several indications which dispose of any idea of a general address and lead to the definite conclusion that a specific local community was in mind.

(i) *It has a definite history.* The author mentions 'former days' (x. 32) and persecutions which have been endured (x. 32, xii. 4). The description of these trials is sufficiently detailed to require the assumption of definite knowledge by the author of the readers' past circumstances. He speaks of their public exposure to abuse, of their sympathy with others so treated, of their joyful resignation to the plundering of their property in the cause of Christ (x. 33, 34) and of their generosity in ministering to other Christians (vi. 10). He knows the circumstances under which they became Christians (ii. 3), and he knows their present state of mind (cf. v. 11ff., vi. 9f.). Their attitude towards their leaders is evidently needing correction (xiii. 17).

(ii) *It has definite links with the writer.* In addition to the evidence just adduced, it is clear that he knows them personally and hopes soon to revisit them (xiii. 19, 23). He urges prayer on his behalf (xiii. 18) and mentions the release of Timothy as an item of news in which they would be personally interested, especially as the writer hopes to have Timothy with him on the visit.

[1] *The Literature of the New Testament*, p. 200.
[2] *Op. cit.*, p. 20.
[3] F. Godet (*Exp.*, iii, vii, 1888, p. 242) was disposed to regard the superscription as the author's own, because of the way the Epistle begins.
[4] The evidence is well collated by B. F. Westcott, *The Epistle to the Hebrews*, pp. xxviiff. Cf. G. Hoennicke's suggestion that the absence of an address may be due to persecution circumstances, or may be due to later intentional omission. *NkZ*, 29 (1918), p. 350.
[5] In spite of Moffatt's opinion that at the time of the affixing of the title, the circumstances of its origin had been lost sight of (*ILNT*, p. 432).

(iii) *It was a section of a larger community*. Not only does the Epistle narrow down the addressees to a local community, but implies that only part of that group is mainly in mind. The statement in v. 12 that the readers ought by now to be teachers contains the implication that they are capable of a teaching ministry, and this could hardly apply in general to the rank and file members of the church. At the same time they are not the most prominent members of the community, since in that case they would not be urged to submit to their leaders.[1] Moreover, the readers appear to form a homogeneous group, which is more likely in a small community than in a larger.[2] So there is much to support the contention that they were a small house-community, which had broken away from and was at least acting independently of the main group of Christians to which they were attached. This may well be why they are urged not to forsake the general Christian assembly (x. 25), i.e. in favour of their own house-group. Such groups are known to have existed, for Paul mentions no less than three in Rome (Rom. xvi. 5, 14, 15) and there may have been many more, not only at Rome but in all large cities.[3]

All that has so far been established does not indicate the nationality of the readers, for which the general argument of the Epistle is the only source of information available and this will next be discussed. The further question of the locality cannot be dealt with until the nationality question has been settled. There are three main possibilities: Jewish Christians, Gentile Christians or Christians irrespective of race.

b. Internal evidence in support of a Jewish Christian destination

The most obvious support for this view is the wide appeal made to the Old Testament and the author's assumption that his readers will be acquainted with the details of the levitical cultus. Furthermore, the whole argument of the Epistle would have obvious relevance to Jewish Christians, with its stress on the necessity for Messiah's sufferings, the reasons for the supersession of the levitical priesthood, the notion of a spiritual instead of a material sanctuary and the fulfilment of the pro-

---

[1] N.B. that in xiii. 24 they are urged not only to greet their own leaders, but also all Christians generally, which suggests that they had separatist tendencies.

[2] So A. Harnack, *op. cit.*, p. 21.

[3] A. Nairne (*The Epistle of Priesthood*,[2] 1915, p. 10) declined to see in the readers a house-church with a general membership, but preferred rather to think of some scholarly men who were accustomed to meet as a group.

mise of a new covenant in Christ.[1] There is a significant, although almost incidental, reference in ii. 16 to the descendants of Abraham which would make a direct appeal to Jewish Christians. Moreover, the author's argument proceeds in a manner which would well fit the background of Jewish readers with its references to Moses, Joshua and the Aaronic order.[2]

Against this has been placed the language of the Epistle, which is claimed to be a more literary and polished Greek than could be expected from a Jewish writer.[3] Yet this in itself does not rule out a Jewish Christian destination since all the Jews of the Dispersion used Greek and there is no need to suppose that the language and style of the author represent the language and style of the readers. Similarly the citations from the LXX instead of the Hebrew Old Testament admittedly disfavour a Palestinian destination, but do not altogether exclude Jewish Christian readers. Again, it has been maintained that the Epistle deals with biblical ritual, not with Judaism, as might be expected if Jewish Christians were specifically in mind.

These objections and others[4] have been used to support the theory of a Gentile destination, which will next be discussed.

c. Evidence claimed to support a Gentile destination

Some scholars have strongly argued for Gentile readers on the grounds that there is nothing in the Epistle which demands a Jewish destination. The traditional view is said to have arisen under the influence of the

---

[1] Cf. E. C. Wickham (op. cit., p. xvi) for an elucidation of these points.

[2] Riggenbach strongly argued that many of the statements of the Epistle would be unintelligible unless addressed to those who were born Jews (e.g. ix. 15, xiii. 13). The appeal to the fleshly weakness of Jesus, His sufferings and His transference to another world would cause offence only to Jews (Der Brief an die Hebräer, 1913, pp. xxiii–xxv). V. Burch (The Epistle to the Hebrews, 1936, pp. 1ff.) brought further arguments in support of a Jewish destination by maintaining that the author has been influenced by the synagogue lectionaries and by the Maccabean story, both in his choice of themes and in the structure of his Epistle. If Burch's thesis is admitted, a Gentile destination would be impossible to imagine. But J. Héring (L'Epître aux Hébreux, 1954, p. 129) criticizes Burch on the grounds that many passages from the Jewish liturgies, to which Burch appeals, are not used in this Epistle.

[3] Cf. E. F. Scott, op. cit., p. 200.

[4] K. Endemann (NkZ, 21, 1910, p. 122) pointed to the explanation of Hebrew words in Heb. vii. 2 and to the details in ix. 1–10 as evidence that the Epistle was not intended for Hebrews.

702 NEW TESTAMENT INTRODUCTION

title, which is regarded as erroneous.[1] Gentiles as well as Jews would be acquainted with the Old Testament when they became Christians, as the LXX was regarded as authoritative Scripture by all Gentile churches. The idea of Gentiles inheriting much from Israel's past history is further supported by the New Testament conception of Christians as the New Israel. The argument of the Epistle, although difficult, was not more difficult for Gentiles than the Epistle to the Romans.[2] There is, moreover, no mention of the Jewish-Gentile controversy, which is usually taken to indicate a time when the controversy was settled,[3] or else to point to a community which was not troubled by it. But this omission of the controversy would, on the whole, favour Jewish Christians rather than Gentiles, since it was for the latter that the controversy was acute. It has also been maintained that the stress on the humanity and fleshly weakness of Jesus would well offset any Docetic-like claims,[4] in which a distinction was made between the heavenly Christ and the human Jesus.

The fact that the writer does not mention the temple must not be pressed too far, but it would certainly be more strange for Jewish than for Gentile readers, assuming for the present argument that the temple in Jerusalem is still standing. Yet the writer goes back to first principles as the basis of his argument and this is better demonstrated from the tabernacle. This factor is, therefore, neutral, for arguments based on the Pentateuch would have relevance for both Jews and Gentiles. The further argument that iii. 12 (falling away from the living God) would be appropriate only for Gentiles must be given little weight, since the Epistle presents all apostasy as an abandonment of the living God.[5] Some stress has been laid on the mention of 'dead works' (vi. 1, ix. 14) as inapplicable to Jews, as well as the elementary principles listed in vi. 1ff.[6] But it is doubtful whether there is evidence enough to conclude with E. F. Scott[7] that the writer did not understand Judaism, because its central feature was law and not sacrificial ritual. That may very well be true, but all that can safely be deduced from the Epistle is that the

[1] So J. Moffatt, *ILNT*, p. 432; E. F. Scott, *op. cit.*; R. H. Strachan, *The Historic Jesus in the New Testament* (1931), p. 90; F. D. V. Narborough, *op. cit.*, pp. 20ff. A more recent advocate of a Gentile destination is G. Vos, *The Teaching of the Epistle to the Hebrews* (1956), pp. 14ff.

[2] Cf. Feine-Behm, *op. cit.*, p. 227.*

[3] Cf. McNeile-Williams, *INT*, p. 231.   [4] Cf. Feine-Behm, *loc. cit.*

[5] Cf. M. Dods, *The Epistle to the Hebrews* (*EGT*, 1910), p. 232.

[6] Cf. G. Vos, *op. cit.*, pp. 14-18.   [7] *Op. cit.*, p. 200.

author deals not with Judaism but with the Old Testament, a fact which provides no determining evidence in the discussion of destination.[1]

d. Evidence for a mixed community of readers

Since none of the evidence so far educed compels a Jewish Christian destination and none leads to any positive conclusion regarding a wholly Gentile destination, a compromise has been suggested.[2] Neither Jews nor Gentiles are in mind, but Christians generally, who had become discouraged and needed challenging to renewed effort. But Westcott[3] rejected the notion of a mixed community on the grounds that the letter betrays no such mixture, nor does it touch on points of heathen controversy.

It is clear that no dogmatic conclusion can be reached on the grounds of internal evidence, yet a definite balance in favour of a Jewish Christian destination must be admitted, if any credence at all is to be attached to the traditional title.[4] The problem of the readers is, on the other hand, so intimately connected with the problem of the purpose that any decision must await the result of investigations on this matter. That type of reader which best accounts for the method of argument and general aim of the Epistle will naturally carry most weight.[5]

III. PURPOSE

There is almost as much difference of opinion about the writer's aims as about his own identity and that of his readers. This problem is nevertheless of greater importance, since it affects the interpretation of the Epistle. The writer describes his writing as 'a word of consolation' (xiii. 22) and full attention must be given to this before proposing other

[1] After reviewing the evidence for destination, A. Wikenhauser (*New Testament Introduction*, 1958, p. 465) maintains that the balance of evidence is against a Jewish Christian destination.

[2] Cf. E. F. Scott, *op. cit.*, pp. 200, 201; also Feine-Behm, *loc. cit.*

[3] *The Epistle to the Hebrews*, p. xxxvi.

[4] A. B. Davidson (*The Epistle to the Hebrews*, n.d., p. 9) was so sure of a Jewish destination that he said of the title, 'Anyone reading the Epistle now would stamp it with the same title, apart from all tradition respecting its origin or destination.'

[5] The suggestion has even been made that the readers are not Christians at all, but Jews as yet undecided about Christianity. Cf. P. Stather Hunt, *Primitive Gospel Sources* (1951), p. 291 and F. C. Synge, *Hebrews and the Scriptures* (1959), pp. 44ff., who take πρός to mean 'against' and not 'to' the Hebrews.

aims. That there are many hortatory passages scattered throughout the Epistle cannot be denied. These would well conform to the idea of 'consolation', although some (especially chapters vi and x) contain serious warnings. But the problem is to find the purpose of the doctrinal sections. These cannot be so easily fitted into the 'consolation' theme. Perhaps the author wished to remind his readers of his essentially pasortal and practical purpose and, if so, the carefully worked out passages on the theme of Christ as High Priest must be interpreted in the light of xiii. 22 and not vice versa.[1] That is to say, the writer's arguments are not to be regarded as a theological treatise or an intellectual exercise, but as a burning issue of vital practical importance. But what was this issue? There have been various suggestions which will now be outlined.

a. To warn Jewish Christians against apostasy to Judaism

This is the most widely held view and is supported by the assumption that chapters vi and x suggest that the readers are tempted to apostatize. Since the argument of the Epistle is designed to show Christ's superiority over the old order, it is further assumed that the apostasy in question must involve a return to Judaism. In xiii. 13 the readers are exhorted to make a clear break and to come outside 'the camp', which may reasonably be interpreted as the camp of Israel. The challenge of the hour for Jewish Christians is to sever connections with their ancient faith, since Christianity is of a different and higher order.[2]

The main problem of these Christians was dissatisfaction, not with

---

[1] Th. Haering ('Gedankengang und Grundgedanken des Hebräerbriefs', *ZNTW*, 18, 1917–18, pp. 145–164) drew attention to the close relationship between the statements regarding the faith and the admonitions as part of the basic sequence of thought in the Epistle, similar to the framework of ancient admonition discourses. Some have considered the possibility that Hebrews was designed for catechetical purposes, which would agree with the writer's description in xiii. 22 (cf. G. Schille's article, 'Die Basis des Hebräerbriefes', *ZNTW*, 47, 1957, pp. 270–280).

E. Käsemann (*Das wandernde Gottesvolk, Eine Untersuchung zum Hebräerbrief*, 1939, pp. 10, 11) suggested that the 'word of encouragement' was to Christians whose hope was wavering in the same way as that of the wandering Israelites. Cf. V. Burch (*op. cit.*, pp. 113ff.) for a similar idea, but without the Gnostic background which Käsemann brings in. Cf. also G. Bornkamm (*Studien zu Antike und Urchristentum*, 1959, pp. 188–203), who regards the High Priest theme as an interpretation of the Church's baptismal confession of Christ as Son of God.

[2] Cf. A. Nairne, *The Epistle to the Hebrews*, p. lxxiv.

true Christianity but with Christianity as it was as yet imperfectly understood by them. It was little more than a reformed Judaism, which in the end was not regarded as in the ancient camp of Israel, for their compatriots would ostracize them for their professed Christian connections. Nor was it in the new 'camp' of the Church. The hankering after the old must have been very real, for the new camp had no prestige comparable to that which Judaism derived from Moses, and the danger of apostasy was correspondingly great.[1] In place of the grandeur of the ritual of the old order was substituted a spiritual conception centred entirely in a Person and no longer in a splendid temple. It must have caused much perplexity in the minds of the recently converted Jews. Now, if this be a true picture of the situation, the writer would aim to show the incomparable superiority of Christianity in fulfilment of all the glories of the old order and by this means would encourage the readers to resist any temptation to return to Judaism. Such an apostasy he describes in very severe terms, but there is no hint that any had as yet fallen a prey to this temptation. In spite of the fact that some modern scholars[2] have disputed the traditional interpretation, it does at least account for the main drift of the argument and, in this respect, has much to commend it.

At the same time the apostasy in vi. 1ff. need not be a turning back to Judaism, since no indication is given there of its nature. This applies also to the statement in x. 29. The fact is, the identification of the apostasy with an act of deliberate turning away from Christianity to Judaism is an inference drawn from the author's preoccupation with the levitical cultus. But the inference may, nonetheless, be a true one.

Some difference of opinion exists among the advocates of this theory as to the more precise identification of the Jewish Christians in mind. The idea that the Epistle was a general circular[3] cannot be seriously entertained in view of the evidence already cited that a definite community was in mind. This hypothesis involves some editorial processes for which there seems to be no warrant within the Epistle itself. More

---

[1] Cf. C. Spicq, *L'Epître aux Hébreux* (1952), pp. 221, 222; M. Dods, *The Epistle to the Hebrews* (*EGT*, 1910), pp. 237ff.

[2] Notably J. Moffatt and E. F. Scott.

[3] Cf. M. Dibelius, 'Der himmlische Kultus nach dem Hebräerbrief', *ThBl*, 21 (1942), pp. 1–11. In his book *A fresh approach to the New Testament and early Christian Literature* (1936), p. 196, Dibelius regarded the letter as a written speech with a conventional letter conclusion. He disputed that the Epistle related to a specific occasion.

to the point is the theory that a house-community of Jewish Christian intellectuals is being addressed. A. Nairne thought of these people as a group of the author's friends, who, like himself, had received an Alexandrian education.[1] They would be Hellenistic Jews by birth and training who had embraced Christianity, but were finding it hard to give up Judaism.

An alternative view is that the small community consisted of converted Jerusalem priests.[2] It is stated in Acts vi. 7 that a great many priests were obedient to the faith as a result of the preaching of Stephen, and it is an attractive hypothesis that some of these had formed into a separate group and were strongly tempted to return to their former dignity in connection with the temple ritual. With their Jewish experience and ability they ought by now to be teachers (v. 12), but their Christianity was as yet elementary and immature (vi. 1, 2). It may be objected against this hypothesis that no other New Testament evidence supports the idea of an exclusively priestly community, but the smallness of the number involved in this case may well be the reason for the absence of corroborative evidence. This must remain a conjecture, although a conjecture which deserves careful consideration.

Another modification of this view which might be a possible solution is the hypothesis that the readers were formerly connected with a Jewish movement akin to the Qumran sect known to us from the Dead Sea Scrolls and were weighing the advantages of their former allegiance against their new faith. The severance of the Covenanters from the Jerusalem temple and the repudiation of the current sacrificial system might lend some support to this idea. These Covenanters were diligent students of the Old Testament Scriptures and endeavoured to interpret them in the light of contemporary events.[3] Might it not be that the author of this Epistle is giving a Christian interpretation of the Old Testament to rectify false methods of exegesis and to show that the hope of the future lies, not in the restoration of the old covenant as the sectaries believed, but in the establishment of a new covenant in

---

[1] Op. cit., p. lxxii.

[2] So K. Bornhäuser, Empfänger und Verfasser des Hebräerbriefes (1932); M. E. Clarkson, ATR, xxix (1947), pp. 89–95; and C. Sandegren, EQ, xxvii (Oct. 1955), pp. 221–224. C. Spicq speaks favourably of the theory and connects the community with Jerusalem (op. cit., pp. 226–231). Sandegren suggests that the original address may have been 'To Priests' instead of 'To Hebrews', since the two words are similar in Greek uncial writing.*

[3] Cf. F. F. Bruce, Biblical Exegesis in the Qumran Texts (1960), pp. 7ff.

which all the ritual of the old is seen to be fulfilled in Christ? The greatest tragedy would be to forsake the new for the old, an action which would amount to re-crucifying the Son of God. Another common element is the priestly emphasis in both the Qumran Community[1] and in the argument of the Epistle to the Hebrews, while a further interesting feature is the continuance of 'instruction about ablutions' (Heb. vi. 2, RSV), which finds a parallel in the constant lustrations of the Covenanters.[2] The esoteric doctrines of the sect might also be alluded to in Hebrews xiii. 9, especially the idea of cultic foods.

Yet the evidence for such an hypothesis is not strong and must remain no more than a conjecture. The existence of such a Jewish Christian group converted from the Essenes is not otherwise attested, although it is not impossible that such a group existed. The main problem would seem to be the absence of any positive treatment of the ancient law, which loomed large in Qumran thought.

b. To challenge restricted Jewish Christians to embrace the world mission

This is the most recent proposal, ably advocated by William Manson.[3] While admitting that the readers were Jewish Christian, he was not satisfied that the threatened danger was apostasy from Christianity to Judaism. To him it was a failure to embrace the world-mission purpose of God. The readers shared the restricted approach of the Jerusalem church and were content to regard Christianity as little more than a sect of Judaism. It may be that they were anxious to retain the advantage of sheltering under a *religio licita*, which was only available so long as they were classed as Jews. According to Manson, the writer's absorbing interest in the Old Testament ritual was to reassure these Christians, who were missing the cultus of Judaism, that the universal truths of Christianity were of far greater consequence. He further claimed that the antecedents of the Epistle are to be sought in the speech of Stephen where a similar approach to the cultus is found.[4] Although

[1] Cf. J. T. Milik, *Ten Years of Discovery in the Wilderness of Judaea* (1959), pp. 99ff.

[2] *Ibid.*, p. 101.

[3] *The Epistle to the Hebrews* (1951). His theory is taken up by W. Neil, *The Epistle to the Hebrews* (*TC*, 1955).

[4] Details are stated above, pp. 693f. in the section on the theory of Lucan authorship of this Epistle.

not all would agree that the writer's view of history coincides with Stephen's,[1] yet there seems little doubt that his universalism finds an echo in Stephen's declaration that the Most High dwells not in houses made with hands.

While there is much insight in this hypothesis, it is difficult to imagine that such strong words concerning apostasy could apply to a failure to appreciate the world mission of Christianity. The terminology of vi. 6 and x. 29 seems to imply a definite act of apostasy against Christ Himself, and, while a denial of universalism would certainly be a denial of Christ's expressed purpose to redeem men of all nations, it is open to question whether such an attitude constitutes re-crucifying Christ and exposing Him to contempt. These terms point rather to a positive renunciation of Christianity.

c. To announce the absolute character of Christianity to mainly Gentile Christians

Christian believers, surrounded as they were by many other faiths, would require an assurance of the greatness and superiority of Christianity over all other religions. They would want to know that it presented a method of worship which was not one of many, but was unique because none other taught the perfect way of worship.[2] The writer would, therefore, appeal to the Old Testament in order to prove the glory of Christianity and for this reason would not specifically deal with Judaism. The author's knowledge of the latter is not first hand. It is book-knowledge or even, in E. F. Scott's opinion, no true knowledge at all.[3] In order to account for the great emphasis on the cultus, Moffatt suggested that the Gentile Christians were perhaps affected by speculative or theoretical Judaism.[4]

But the most damaging criticism of this hypothesis is the absence of any references to pagan rites or mysteries or to tables and cups of demons,[5] as, for instance, are suggested by Paul's treatment of the Corinthian situation. Nor can a case be made out for regarding this

---

[1] E.g. J. P. Alexander (*A Priest for Ever*, 1937, p. 17) finds Paul nearer to Stephen than the author of Hebrews.

[2] Advocated by J. Moffatt, *ILNT*, pp. 444ff.; *The Epistle to the Hebrews* (*ICC*), pp. xxivff.; and R. H. Strachan, *op. cit.*, pp. 74ff.

[3] Cf. *op. cit.*, p. 200, where he maintains that the author misunderstood what Judaism meant.

[4] *Op. cit.*, p. 445.   [5] Cf. the criticisms by W. Manson, *op. cit.*, p. 22.

Epistle as a Christian Gnosis,[1] for there are no traces of Gnostic tendencies. On the other hand, due weight must be given to the fact that the author betrays no consciousness of any distinction between Jewish and Gentile Christianity and this *may* be evidence that Gentiles were included in the author's purpose. At the same time it is difficult to believe that the detailed and elaborate argument based on levitical ritual would have convinced Gentile Christians of the absolute character of Christianity. Only those who were already convinced of the greatness of Judaism would see the point of the author's attempts to show the supreme worth of Christianity by means of its superiority to Judaism. This line of argument might have had relevance to former proselytes, but hardly to those who had had no former connection with the Jewish cultus.[2]

d. To counteract an early type of heresy

This suggestion has been maintained in two forms:

1. As an answer to a sect of Jewish Gnostics,[3] or
2. An answer to the specific Colossian heresy.[4]

The two suggestions are clearly closely allied, especially if the Jewish character of the Colossian heresy is maintained. Under the hypothesis that Gnosticism is being combated, the threatened apostasy is understood as a forsaking of Christianity in preference for an incipient Gnosticism, which not only maintained the mediation of angels and thus depreciated the unique mediatorial work of Christ, but also tended towards asceticism on the one hand and immorality on the other. This theory would account for the prominence of 'angels' in the argument at the commencement of the Epistle, for the mention of strange teachings and salvation by meats (xiii. 9) and for the reference to meats and

---

[1] Cf. E. F. Scott, *The Epistle to the Hebrews* (1922), p. 41.

[2] A. C. Purdy, in his article, 'The purpose of the Epistle to the Hebrews in the Light of Recent Studies in Judaism', *Amicitiae Corolla* (ed. H. G. Wood, 1953), pp. 253–264, partially sides with Moffatt in rejecting the idea of an apostasy to Judaism. But he also rejects the notion that speculative Judaism is in mind and considers that the problems behind Hebrews were normative to first-century Judaism.

[3] F. D. V. Narborough, *op. cit.*, pp. 20–27.

[4] T. W. Manson, 'The Problem of the Epistle to the Hebrews', *BJRL*, xxxii (1949), pp. 1–17.

washings in ix. 10. The uncompromising rigorism of the author is
claimed to be more intelligible when seen against such a background.
Deliberate wrongdoing of the kind which some Jewish Gnosticism
allowed could obtain no forgiveness (vi. 4–8, x. 26–31). Immorality
is, in fact, specifically mentioned in xii. 16.

This Jewish Gnostic theory has been further modified in T. W.
Manson's attempt to set the argument of the Epistle against the background of the Colossian heresy. He suggested that chapters i–iv answered the doctrine of intermediaries as reflected in Colossians ii. 18,
and chapters v–x the ritual tendencies which also formed part of the
same heresy (cf. Col. ii. 14ff.). His theory is that Apollos sent the Epistle
to the Colossian church before Paul wrote his own Epistle, which was
not, in fact, produced until after he had seen and read the former. But
the theory seems to demand that Apollos wrote only to the Jewish
section of the Colossian false teachers, since the Epistle to the Hebrews
completely ignores the other element in the Colossian heresy, i.e. the
Gnostic philosophy. This is an interesting suggestion, however, and
may be linked with the suggestion mentioned earlier that Jewish
Christians influenced by the Qumran type of Judaism may have been
in mind. It is not impossible that this type of heresy was more widely
diffused than is generally recognized and, therefore, the need to locate
the heresy in Colossae is not immediately apparent, nor, in fact, is the
need to postulate Apollos as author.[1]

What all of these theories of the author's purpose make abundantly
clear is that the readers needed to be warned against turning away from
Christianity, but it is impossible to be quite certain by what they were
tempted. The positive knowledge that the author aims to show the
all-sufficiency and supremacy of Christ over other agencies and His
complete fulfilment of the Jewish ritual system enables an intelligent
interpretation of the argument,[2] even if a more precise understanding
of the readers' circumstances would throw added light upon certain
obscurities in the statements made.

[1] McNeile-Williams criticize Manson's view on the ground that Clement of
Rome acknowledged the Epistle as authoritative and yet it was known as non-
Pauline. They find it difficult to see how Clement came to possess a copy with
such an unchallenged status twenty or thirty years later (INT, p. 238).
[2] A recent writer, A. Wikgren ('Patterns of Perfection in the Epistle to the
Hebrews', NTS, 6, 1960, pp. 159–167), suggests that the author is presenting a kind
of philosophy of history through symbolic patterns of perfection.

IV. DESTINATION

It may seem futile to pin down to any definite locality a community of whose circumstances so little definite information can be gathered, and it will not be surprising that several suggestions have been made. The following brief review of them will once again focus attention on the extraordinary complexity of the attempt to reconstruct the historical situation.

a. Palestine

Many have maintained a Jerusalem or Palestinian destination, but most of these have done so in the belief that Jewish Christians, who were tempted to apostatize to Judaism, are in mind.[1] One of the most important considerations is the existence or otherwise of the temple, a problem which also influences the dating. Westcott[2] found no difficulty in the author's use of 'tabernacle' for 'temple' and maintained that the Jerusalem temple was still standing and that the readers must have lived in its vicinity.[3] He supported this from patristic evidence that 'Hebrews' was used as a description for the Jerusalem church, but this will carry no weight for those who regard the title as no more than an early guess. There is the further evidence that a crisis is imminent (i. 2, iii. 13, x. 25, xii. 27) and this might be understood as the approaching siege of Jerusalem. The former sufferings which the readers endured (x. 32, xii. 4) would be accounted for by the known persecuting zeal of the Jerusalem Jews against the early Christians (Acts *passim*). Other corroborating evidence which might seem to support the Jerusalem destination[4] is the absence of the Gentile-Jewish controversy, which would not have affected an all-Jewish church, and the fact that no church ever laid claim to this Epistle, which is readily understandable after Jerusalem was destroyed. Another factor which has predisposed some scholars to prefer a Jerusalem destination has been their accept-

[1] F. Delitzsch (*Commentary on the Epistle to the Hebrews*, 1868, p. 20) maintained that the title must indicate Palestinians, since in Palestine alone was a distinction made between Hellenists and Hebrews. But the Epistle contains no such contrast.*

[2] *The Epistle to the Hebrews*, p. xl.

[3] G. A. Barton (*JBL*, LVII, 1938, pp. 199, 200) argues that in every case where the author mentions the performance of parts of the ritual he uses the present tense. This, he thinks, is intentional and points to the continuity of the temple ritual with the old tabernacle ritual.

[4] Cf. G. Salmon, *INT*[6] (1892), pp. 427ff.

ance of Barnabas as the author. But, apart from the fact that the author problem is indecisive, very little is known about the movements of Barnabas to be certain of his continued connection with the Jerusalem church, although this is quite probable.[1]

Several objections have been lodged against this hypothesis, the most damaging of which appears to be the improbability of any author addressing a Jerusalem group in the terms of ii. 3[2]; the difficulty of the Hellenistic approach if Jerusalem Jews are in mind (unless, of course, a small Hellenistic section of the predominantly Hebrew church is visualized); the apparent discrepancy between the generosity of the community to which the Epistle is addressed (vi. 10, x. 34, xiii. 16; cf. also xiii. 2, 5) and the poverty of the Jerusalem church[3]; the seeming inappropriateness of v. 12 as a reference to Jerusalem Hebrew Christians, and the use of the LXX. Moreover, the description of the leaders in xiii. 7 would seem strange if the Jerusalem leaders were in mind.[4] It is further thought that the situation in x. 32ff. supposes *one* previous persecution which would not fit the Jerusalem church in Acts,[5] while if xii. 4 means that the church had as yet suffered no martyrdoms, this would not be true of Jerusalem. Most of these objections would, however, be removed if the destination were more generally Palestine, or some adjoining district where the Greek language was dominant, but where the Jewish Christians still maintained close contact with the Jerusalem church.

b. Rome

The majority of modern scholars favour Rome as the destination mainly on the strength of the following evidence.

---

[1] There is little ground for the opinion of G. Edmundson (*The Church in Rome in the first century*, 1913, pp. 80–82) that Barnabas was for a time in Rome. The evidence cited was the Clementine Recognitions, which Edmundson thought might here have preserved a genuine tradition.

[2] Cf. Moffatt, *ILNT*, p. 446. If the whole of the Jerusalem church was in mind, ii. 3 would be inconceivable, but if a small group only was in view, it is not entirely impossible that none of them had heard the Lord personally. (Cf. A. Nairne, *The Epistle of Priesthood*, 1915, p. 20.)

[3] Peake (*op. cit.*, p. 23) discounted this argument on the ground that poverty would not exclude kindness to fellow Christians, and it must be admitted that none of the references mentioned above absolutely demands the idea of material generosity. At the same time xiii. 5 would have little relevance to poverty-stricken people.

[4] Cf. Feine-Behm, *op. cit.*, p. 226.*   [5] *Ibid., loc. cit.*

1. The fact that it was at Rome that the Epistle was first known, as early in fact as the first century, for it must have been authoritative some time before Clement of Rome cites it in AD 95 in his Corinthian Epistle.

2. The concluding salutation in xiii. 24 (οἱ ἀπὸ τῆς Ἰταλίας) seems more naturally understood of Italians who are away from Italy and are sending greetings home, than of Italians sending greetings to some other non-Italian destination.[1] Yet the phrase is ambiguous and cannot sustain too much weight.[2]

3. Timothy, who is mentioned in xiii. 24, was known to the Roman Christians (cf. Col. i. 1, Phm. 1).

4. The description of the leaders in xiii. 7, 17, 24 is similar to that in 1 Clem. i. 3 (ἡγούμενοι; cf. 1 Clem. xxi. 6 and Hermas, Vis. ii. 2, 6, iii. 9, 7, where προηγούμενοι is used).[3]

5. The allusions to the generosity of the readers in vi. 10ff., x. 32ff., would agree with the known history of the Roman church from other sources.[4]

6. The reference to meats in xiii. 9 suggests a tendency which is similar to that seen in Romans xiv.[5]

7. The spoliation of goods referred to in x. 32 could be explained either by Claudius' edict (AD 49) or by Nero's persecution, both of which affected the Roman Christians (assuming that other Jewish

---

[1] 'They of Italy' would in that case need to describe the whole Italian church, but this is improbable. Michaelis (op. cit., p. 270) points out a parallel in the reference to Asiatic churches in 1 Cor. xvi. 19.

F. J. Badcock (The Pauline Epistles and the Epistle to the Hebrews in their historical setting, 1937, p. 192) maintained a third alternative, i.e. Italians on the way home from Jerusalem sending greetings to a Hellenistic group in Jerusalem from Caesarea.

[2] McNeile-Williams prefer the former meaning (INT, p. 233), but Narborough feels similarly about the alternative (op. cit., p. 27). F. Lo Bue (JBL, lxxv, 1956, pp. 52–57) suggested that 'they of Italy' were Aquila and Priscilla, which is not entirely improbable. Michel (op. cit., p. 368) admits an ambiguity, but understands the phrase to point to an Italian colony outside the Italian peninsula.

[3] A. Harnack (ZNTW, 1, 1900, p. 21) made the further comparison of Heb. xiii. 7 with 1 Clem. v. The latter describes Peter and Paul as examples and Harnack thought that these apostles were the 'leaders' referred to in Hebrews. But this rather vague description of them is most unlikely.

[4] So Feine-Behm, op. cit., p. 228. A. Harnack (op. cit., p. 20) refers to the letter of Dionysius of Corinth in this connection.

[5] Cf. Davidson, op. cit., p. 16.

Christians, like Aquila, would be caught up in a general expulsion of Jews).

But on the other hand, ii. 3 is difficult if Rome was in mind, for there could have been few who had been evangelized by eye-witnesses, especially accompanied by signs and miracles, unless the community in question consisted of those who had infiltrated to Rome in the course of commerce or trade. The difficulty is not insuperable, and in view of the external evidence this destination has much to commend it. Owing to the scarcity of extant data about the circulation of the New Testament writings in the sub-apostolic period during the latter part of the first century, it is not possible to put too much stress on Clement's knowledge of the Epistle. He appears to be acquainted with 1 Corinthians and Ephesians and probably many other of Paul's Epistles which were not sent to Rome. That Christian writings were being exchanged at this period is, therefore, indisputable and it is impossible to dogmatize about the circulation of the Epistle to the Hebrews. A period of twenty to thirty years (if Hebrews is dated early) would be ample for the Epistle to reach Rome if it was elsewhere regarded as authoritative. It is further difficult to pin down the particular troubles, which are reflected in x. 32f., to any specific event in Rome. The Neronian persecutions would appear to be much too severe, unless the group addressed in this Epistle was unobtrusive enough to escape the worst of the onslaught. Moreover, these troubles were in 'former days', which suggests some interval, and this would only be possible if the Epistle were dated much later (see discussion on the date). Perhaps a more weighty objection is the different type of Judaism which seems to be reflected in the Epistle to the Hebrews as compared with that in the Epistle to the Romans, the latter showing little evidence of the Hellenism which seems to influence the former. But again the solution may be found in the restricted number to whom the Hebrews was probably sent. If addressed to the whole church at Rome, the absence of any reference to Gentiles in the Epistle would also be inconceivable, but the difficulty would be less acute for a smaller house-group.[1] All that can safely be claimed, however, is that we know that it *was* used in Rome in the first century, but insufficient literature is preserved from other

---

[1] E. Nestlé (*ET*, x, 1899, p. 422) pointed out that the title, 'To the Hebrews', would not be surprising for Rome, since inscriptions record a synagogue there known simply as Ἑβραίων.

districts to enable us to pronounce more confidently on any alternative theory.

c. Other suggestions

The Alexandrian colouring has suggested an Alexandrian destination, but this seems dubious because the church at Alexandria not only laid no claim to it, but the early Alexandrian Fathers assumed it was addressed to the Hebrew people of Palestine by Paul. Furthermore, Alexandrian ideas were so widely diffused that almost any place in the Hellenistic world would be equally suitable on this score. T. W. Manson's idea of Colossae has already been discussed (p. 710), while Asia Minor has been represented by an Ephesian destination (F. W. Farrar),[1] or Galatian destination (A. M. Dubarle),[2] and more vaguely by an Asiatic Centre (Perdelwitz).[3] F. Rendall ventured to propose Syria (perhaps Antioch), but without any special considerations which would not equally well apply to other proposed Jewish Christian destinations.[4] V. Burch,[5] however, on the basis of the Maccabean background which he claims for the Epistle, concludes more confidently for Antioch as its destination because this was the 'Shrine of the Maccabees'. But his arguments here are too tortuous to admit of certainty.

The claims of Corinth have recently been advocated,[6] but this suggestion is not likely to receive wide support because of the difficulty of ii. 3. Still others have proposed Cyprus on the supposition that Barnabas was the author,[7] while A. Klostermann[8] proposed that the title was a scribal error for 'to the Bereans'.

[1] *Op. cit.*, p. xxxiv, largely on the grounds that Apollos, whom he thought was author, and Timothy were connected with it.

[2] *RB*, XLVIII (1939), pp. 506–529.

[3] *ZNTW*, 11 (1910), pp. 105–110. Cf. also A. B. Davidson's still vaguer, 'Some community of the Dispersion in the East' (*op. cit.*, p. 18).

[4] *The Epistle to the Hebrews* (1883), pp. xvii, xviii. His main argument was based on the title, which, he thought, must indicate Hebrew-speaking Jewish Christians, but this is a rather more restricted usage than is necessary.

[5] *Op. cit.*, pp. 137ff.

[6] F. Lo Bue, *op. cit.*, pp. 52–57. It was earlier suggested by H. Appel, *Der Hebräerbrief ein Schreiben des Apollos an Judenchristen der Korinthischen Gemeinde* (1918), cited by Feine-Behm, *op. cit.*, p. 227.*

[7] Cf. Riggenbach, *op. cit.*, pp. xlv, xlvi; A. Snell, *New and Living Way: An Explanation of the Epistle to the Hebrews* (1959), p. 18.

[8] *Zur Theorie der biblischen Weissagung und zur Charakteristik des Hebräerbriefes* 1889), p. 55, cited by O. Michel, *op. cit.*, p. 12.

V. DATE

The difficulty of settling the precise circumstances of the readers and the identity of the author naturally affects the dating. But the *terminus ad quem* is certainly fixed by Clement's epistle, which is generally dated at AD 95.[1] The *terminus a quo* is determined by the answer to the problem of the relationship of the Epistle to the fall of Jerusalem (AD 70). Was the temple still standing? The only information we have is the use of present tenses in references to the ritual (cf. vii. 8, ix. 6f., 9, 13, xiii. 10), but these need not mean that the temple ritual is still continued, since Clement also used present tenses to describe similar ritual (*1 Clem.* xli).[2] In these cases the present tenses describe what Moses had established and are a natural literary device. Of greater weight would seem to be the absence of any indication in the Epistle of the catastrophe for, if it had already happened, it would have been a conclusive argument for the cessation of the old cultus.[3] For this reason many scholars date the Epistle before AD 70, either in the early part of the decade or when the trials of the siege had become imminent.[4] These considerations will naturally have little weight for those who deny that the author has any interest in the temple, but is wholly absorbed with the tabernacle.

Quite apart from this, however, there are certain other indications which support a date before the fall of the city. The tone of the Epistle and the call to 'come out' would have particular point if the doom of the city was imminent, especially in view of the warning of Jesus in Mark xiii. 14f. E. C. Wickham[5] argues that the appeal to the heroes of

---

[1] Cf. E. T. Merrill (*Essays in Early Christian History*, 1924, pp. 217ff.) who denies authorship by a bishop named Clement and dates it *c.* AD 140. But this dating is not usually followed.

[2] Wickham (*op. cit.*, p. xviii) draws a distinction between Clement's use and that of the author of Hebrews, for it makes no difference to his argument whether the ritual was discontinued or not. But the present is found also in Josephus, Justin and the Talmud. (Cf. Farrar, *op. cit.*, p. xxxv.)

[3] Cf. T. W. Manson (*BJRL*, XXXII, 1949, pp. 1–17), who maintained a date prior to Paul's letter to Colossae, considered that the use of the Melchizedek high-priesthood argument rather than an appeal to the destruction of the temple makes it most probable that the temple still stands.

[4] Cf. G. A. Barton, *JBL*, LVII (1938), pp. 205–207. A. Nairne (*The Epistle of Priesthood*, p. 22) suggested that the clash of the Jews with Rome imposed a claim to loyalty on the part of the readers, who had only imperfectly understood Christianity.

[5] *Op. cit.*, p. xix.

the past in chapter xi becomes more significant if there still existed the possibility of their return to the faith of their fathers in the form of the historic ritual. The reference to Timothy, which supports the view that the Epistle was written by a member of the Pauline circle, is perhaps more intelligible if placed as near as possible to Paul's time, but this cannot be pressed since the later history of Timothy is unknown. The ecclesiastical situation appears to be primitive, for no church officials are mentioned by name, but only 'leaders' generally (xiii. 7, 17).

Time must be allowed for the 'former days' during which the readers had been persecuted. If this former persecution was Nero's, that would at once date the Epistle later than the fall of Jerusalem. But destination enters into this discussion, for if Palestinians are in mind the Neronic persecutions would have no relevance. In fact it seems almost unnecessary to assign the persecution mentioned to any specified historic occasion, for Jewish Christians must have been constantly under fire from Jewish enemies of the gospel (cf. Acts). Even if Jewish Christians at Rome are in mind, it is not impossible that a certain amount of ill-treatment and confiscation took place in the execution of Claudius' edict for the expulsion of Jews from the Imperial City (cf. Acts xviii. 2), and this would undoubtedly have involved Christian Jews (compare the case of Aquila).[1] If Hebrews x. 32ff. refers to this, an interval of some fifteen years separated the two persecutions and this would allow and, in fact, require a date previous to AD 64. But it seems a fair inference from chapter xiii that Paul is no longer alive, in which case the Epistle must not be dated long before AD 64.

Advocates for a later date base their contentions on the imminence of the persecution subsequent to Nero's, i.e. Domitian's,[2] and on the later development of the thought. Thus sometime in the decade

---

[1] It is significant that the references to persecution in Heb. x are comparatively mild. Moffatt suggested that they may amount to no more than mob violence (*ILNT*, p. 453).

[2] D. W. Riddle (*JBL*, XLIII, 1924, pp. 329–348), on the grounds of a comparison between Hebrews and *1 Clement*, concluded that the former could only recently have been received by the author of the latter and must, therefore, belong to the same period. But his assumption here is without foundation. Cf. also Goodspeed's view that *1 Clement* was written in response to Heb. v. 12, the latter Epistle having only recently been produced subsequent to Paul's letter-collection (*INT*, pp. 258, 259); cf. also his article in *JBL*, XXX (1911), pp. 157–160. H. Windisch (*Der Hebräerbrief*,[2] 1931, p. 126) claimed that at least ten years must separate Hebrews and *1 Clement*, but, if so, it might as well be thirty years.*

AD 80–90[1] is chosen by those for whom this line of evidence carries any weight. Unfavourable to this hypothesis is the statement that the readers have not yet 'resisted unto blood', which would not fit Nero's persecution unless the small group addressed had been treated less severely than most. The alleged use of some of Paul's Epistles is also claimed to support this later date, since time would be required for the circulation of these Epistles.[2] Yet literary affinities are unreliable in settling questions of date, unless they indicate literary dependence so certainly that some chronological arrangement of the writings is possible. Those who maintain an earlier date place little emphasis on Paul's literary influence on the author, for the fact that he belonged to the Pauline circle is sufficient explanation of many parallels with Pauline thought and phraseology. Another argument for a later date is based on the supposition that ii. 3 implies second generation Christianity, but no weight can be attached to this since the statement may perfectly well be understood of the original members of the community.[3]

In view of all the data available, it would seem reasonable to regard this Epistle as having been sent either just before the fall of Jerusalem, if Jerusalem was the destination, or just before the Neronic persecutions if it was sent to Rome.*

VI. BACKGROUND

Interest in the theological affinities of the Epistle was only aroused when Pauline authorship became widely disputed. Until then it was treated as part of the Pauline Corpus and integrated into the Pauline theology. But in recent times there have been several different attempts to reorientate the Epistle and to put it in its rightful place in the development of Christianity. The first strong reaction was towards Philonism and a strongly Hellenistic interpretation of the Epistle, but there have

---

[1] Cf. E. F. Scott, *The Literature of the New Testament*, p. 199; Feine-Behm, *op. cit.*, p. 231. Feine-Behm reject the view of M. S. Enslin, who arbitrarily dates it about AD 110. McNeile-Williams narrow the date down to *c.* AD 80–85 (*INT*, p. 235) and Michaelis to soon after AD 80 (*op. cit.*, p. 273).

[2] H. von Soden (*JPTh*, 10, 1884, p. 493) argued for a period of time subsequent to the end of Paul's Jewish-Gentile conflict.

[3] Cf. A. S. Peake, *op. cit.*, p. 9. A. Harnack (*ZNTW*, 1, 1900, p. 29) agreed that 'second generation Christians' must be understood genealogically, not chronologically.

been other attempts to define more closely the author's relationship to the primitive tradition, to Paulinism and to Johannine thought.

a. Philonism

The movement which treated the Epistle as a Philonic interpretation of Christianity reached its peak at the end of the nineteenth century in the complete denial of any Paulinism. Ménégoz,[1] for instance, denied the possibility of any conciliation between the point of view of Paul and that of Hebrews, and refuted any idea of the author's dependence on Paul's Epistles.

That there are certain similarities between the two authors no-one would deny. In both there is a tendency towards allegory, a reverence for the text of the LXX, similar formulae of citation, a readiness to attach importance even to the silence of Scripture (cf. Heb. vii. 3), the appeal to Melchizedek as a type,[2] a similar interpretation of the apparent in the light of the real and many significant words and phrases common to both.[3] A few other features might be mentioned, such as the attaching of meaning to individual names (vii. 2), the contrast between the earthly and the heavenly (cf. ix. 23f., viii. 1ff.), the created and the uncreated (ix. 11), the past and the future (ii. 5, ix. 1ff., xiii. 14), the transitory and the abiding (vii. 3, 24, x. 34, xii. 27, xiii. 14).[4] There may be here, as in Alexandrian Judaism, a trace of the background of the Platonic theory of ideas,[5] but antitheses were not the sole property of the philosophers and were, in fact, inherent in the transference from Judaism to Christianity. Yet inferences drawn from these data have given rise to different opinions. There is at the present time less inclination to conclude that the author shows a direct dependence on Philo's works,[6] since literary similarities cannot prove conscious use by one author of another's work. They may, however, indicate a similar

---

[1] *La Théologie de l'Epître aux Hébreux* (1894), pp. 249, 250.

[2] Until Philo, the Melchizedek theme seems to have held little interest among the Jews. (Cf. the study of G. Wuttke, *Melchisedech, der Priesterkönig von Salem,* 1927, Beihefte *ZNTW*).*

[3] Cf. C. Spicq, *L'Epître aux Hébreux*, pp. 39–91, for a thorough examination of these Philonic connections.*

[4] Cf. Feine-Behm, *op. cit.*, p. 223.*

[5] J. Héring (*op. cit.*, p. 10) maintains that the author's thoughts are nearer Platonic than a biblical framework, although he admits a difference in outlook.

[6] Cf. W. Manson, *op. cit.*, p. 184.

background, and may further suggest in the case of Hebrews that the author had been educated under Philonic influence.[1] Caution is nevertheless needed in drawing even this inference since religious phraseology and ideas cannot be regarded as the property of one man, and, even if language and style show some close affinities with Philo's writings, there are marked differences in the author's methods and outlook. As compared with the allegorization of Philo, which is integral to his whole approach to Old Testament exegesis, the writer to the Hebrews does not strictly allegorize, although he comes near to it in dealing with Melchizedek.[2] The long section on the levitical cultus proceeds on the assumption that Christ brings out its full implications in His own fulfilment of it, and in this respect the writer is much closer to primitive tradition than to Philo. This leads up to another fundamental difference. Philo does not treat the Old Testament history as history, but as a framework for his philosophical ideas. But for the writer to the Hebrews the history is treated literally, as the catalogue in chapter xi shows. The force of his argument would be considerably weakened if he were assumed to have Philo's view of history. E. F. Scott[3] has pointed out another difference in that Philo dispenses with ceremonial in favour of inward communion, whereas the author of this Epistle still thinks of worship in terms of sacrifice. In other words, his approach is more thoroughly biblical. He does not, as Philo, bring certain philosophical presuppositions to his understanding of the Old Testament, but approaches it with the sole key that Christ has fulfilled the old order. If this appears to have any affinities with Philo's theory of ideas, it is little more than superficial, for the early Christians generally regarded the Christian fulfilment as essentially 'better' than the old. Although all had not reached the same complete appreciation of it as the author of this Epistle, there is nothing imported into this approach from Hellenism, which could not have been a development from the primitive Christian tradition. At the same time the author's Hellenistic background would have equipped him thoroughly to express in an adequate form what was, in fact, inherent in the tradition.[4]

[1] C. Spicq agrees with Ménégoz that the author is a Philonist converted to Christianity (op. cit., p. 198).

[2] V. Burch (op. cit., 1936, p. 84) vigorously disputes any dependence of the author on Philo for his Melchizedekian theme.

[3] The Epistle to the Hebrews, p. 56.

[4] Cf. C. K. Barrett in The Background of the New Testament and its Eschatology (ed. W. D. Davies and D. Daube, 1956), pp. 363–393, for a similar view.

But although many scholars[1] would still maintain in general an Alexandrian exegetical approach, there are indications of a movement away from this position towards a greater stress on the eschatological outlook of the writer and this will be considered under our next heading.

b. Primitive tradition

A parallel, yet later, reaction against treating the Epistle as Paulinist is the attempt to trace its origin in the primitive tradition. This movement is of the utmost importance in establishing the modern relevance of the Epistle, for it implies that the author is no mere antiquarian divorced from the main current of Christian development. Details have already been given of the remarkable similarities between Hebrews and Stephen's speech[2] and, on the basis of this, the Epistle has been interpreted. The author shows a close acquaintance with the facts of Jesus' earthly life and this has been supposed to provide evidence of acquaintance with the Synoptic Gospels. It is not certain that dependence can be established, but it is significant that the author reflects in his argument three allusions to the Synoptic tradition: the temptation of Christ, the cleansing of the temple and the rent veil.[3] Yet there is little about priesthood in the earliest traditions of primitive preaching, as preserved for us in the Acts, and as this forms so central a part of the author's argument, it must be considered a development, though a perfectly natural one, from that primitive tradition.[4]

W. Manson has pointed out that the author shares the predominant eschatological approach which Jewish Christianity inherited from Judaism.[5] The 'two-age' theology can be traced behind the doctrine of the Epistle, with the implication that the 'age to come' has already come.[6] R. H. Strachan,[7] while maintaining that the author's views are

---

[1] E.g. R. H. Strachan, *op. cit.*, p. 78; F. D. V. Narborough, *op. cit.*, pp. 20ff. E. Käsemann (*op. cit.*, pp. 52–116) makes much of the Gnostic background of the Epistle, but few other scholars give much weight to this aspect of the author's Greek background (cf. Käsemann's review of Michel's commentary, *ThLZ*, 75, 1950, cols. 427–430).

[2] See pp. 693f.   [3] Cf. C. Spicq, *op. cit.*, pp. 99–109.*

[4] Cf. L. O. Bristol, 'Primitive Christian Preaching and the Epistle to the Hebrews', *JBL*, LXVIII (1949), pp. 89–97. See also V. Taylor, *The Atonement in New Testament teaching*[2] (1945), pp. 111ff. and R. V. G. Tasker, *The Gospel in the Epistle to the Hebrews* (1950).

[5] *Op. cit.*, pp. 184f.   [6] Cf. C. K. Barrett, *op. cit.*, p. 391.   [7] *Op. cit.*, p. 79.

based on the Platonic doctrine of the two worlds, nevertheless agreed that his mind is still governed by the Jewish apocalyptic view of history.

c. Paulinism

In spite of the swing away from Pauline influences in the interpretation of the Epistle, the problem of the relation of the Epistle to Pauline doctrine remains. In general, those inclined to stress either of the preceding influences tend to deny or else reduce to a minimum the impact of Paul upon the author.[1] Yet there are many parallels which cannot be lightly passed over, and which imply a much closer liaison in thought between the two writers than is often imagined.

H. Windisch[2] has listed a number of similarities between Paul and this Epistle, of which the following are the most striking:

> A similar doctrine of Christ, His previous glory and part in creation (Heb. i. 2, 3, 6: 1 Cor. viii. 6; 2 Cor. iv. 4; Col. i. 15–17).
>
> His self-humbling (Heb. ii. 14–17: Rom. viii. 3; Gal. iv. 4; Phil. ii. 7).
>
> His obedience (Heb. v. 8: Rom. v. 19; Phil. ii. 8).
>
> His self-offering for us (Heb. ix. 28: 1 Cor. v. 7; Eph. v. 2).
>
> A similar view of the new covenant (Heb. viii. 6: 2 Cor. iii. 9ff.).
>
> A similar view of Abraham's faith as an example (Heb. xi. 11, 12, 17–19: Rom. iv. 17–20).
>
> A similar view of the distribution of gifts by the Spirit (Heb. ii. 4: 1 Cor. xii. 11).
>
> An appeal to the same Old Testament passages (e.g. Ps. viii in Heb. ii. 6–9 and 1 Cor. xv. 27; Deut. xxxii. 35 in Heb. x. 30 and Rom. xii. 19; Hab. ii. 4 in Heb. x. 38, Rom. i. 17 and Gal. iii. 11).
>
> A similar use of the athletic metaphor of the Christian life (Heb. xii. 1: 1 Cor. ix. 24).

---

[1] Cf. Ménégoz, op. cit., p. 184, in contrast to Philonism, and E. F. Scott, op. cit., pp. 49ff. The latter admits it to be perplexing that the author, although having some contacts with the Pauline circle (e.g. Timothy), was so unaffected by Paul's work—an evidence, he thinks, that Paul's influence in his own age was not as wide as is often supposed.

[2] Op. cit., pp. 128, 129.

It can hardly be maintained, therefore, that the author shares no affinities with the apostle Paul. Indeed, Windisch himself considered this must indicate either a Pauline disciple or else a writer who, in common ·with Paul, had reproduced similar elements in the tradition.[1]

At the same time differences in approach have already been noted (see p. 689), and many scholars have drawn a strong antithesis between the two writers. If the writer of Hebrews is dealing with Judaism he deals with it in a different way from Paul,[2] although, as already noted, he deals with biblical data rather than Judaism. His approach to the law is different, for he never appears to wrestle with the law after Paul's manner,[3] although it must be recognized that Paul never disputed the validity of the law. The real question is whether there are any fundamental positions which the author assumes to which Paul would have taken strong exception and the answer must surely be in the negative. If it may reasonably be maintained that Paul would have said them in a different way, it may not be deduced that he would not have consented to the expression of them. Our conclusion must be that, while showing independence, the writer of this Epistle is as much in line with Paulinism as with the primitive tradition.

d. Johannine thought

Not much attention has been paid to affinities with the Johannine literature, but it has generally been supposed that this Epistle represents a position midway between the Pauline and the Johannine theology.[4] C. Spicq[5] cites many parallels and concludes that the author was dependent on the Johannine catechesis, which was later crystallized into the Gospel and Epistles. The result of these different lines of investigation is really to demonstrate the remarkable affinity of this Epistle with all phases of early Christian development. It may necessitate a revision of much modern theory about that development, for criticism has tended to think too rigidly of straight-line development in terms of sequence, as if this Epistle must be fitted into a scheme dominated by chronology. A truer appreciation of the facts would seem to require

[1] It is significant that Windisch, although he paid full attention to the Philonic background, nevertheless considered the author of this Epistle to be nearer to Paul than is any other New Testament writer (cf. A. Nairne, *The Epistle to the Hebrews*, p. lxiii, for an appraisal of Windisch's approach).

[2] Cf. R. H. Strachan, *op. cit.*, p. 87; E. F. Scott, *op. cit.*, pp. 93ff.

[3] Cf. J. P. Alexander, *op. cit.*, p. 58.   [4] Cf. R. H. Strachan, *op. cit.*, p. 103.

[5] *Op. cit.*, pp. 109-138.

a theory of co-lateral development in which Pauline thought, the theology of Hebrews and the catechesis of John could all find a place contemporaneously.

e. The Old Testament

In the course of the previous discussions many references have been made to the author's use of the Old Testament and it goes almost without saying that this formed a dominant characteristic of his background. He cites the LXX version and for the most part adheres to it more closely than does the apostle Paul. His citations from it are introduced by formulae which indicate great reverence for the sacred text and a belief in its divine origin. He treats it both literally and symbolically.[1] The whole Epistle is a classic example of an authoritative answer to the question, How are Christians to regard the Old Testament revelation? The emphasis on the cultus may well have been given because, in the author's own mind, this was the most difficult material to which to ascribe a contemporary Christian relevance, and the author's skilful interpretation of the fulfilment of the Old Testament in Christ must have been of immense value to many who had either to rethink their approach (as the Jews) or to grapple with unfamiliar Scripture (as the Gentiles). If it were for no other reason but this, the inclusion of this Epistle in the Christian Canon would be amply justified.

VII. LITERARY FORM

The possession of a conclusion without an introductory greeting and without address raises a problem as to the form of the letter. Its conclusion and its personal allusions to the readers mark it out as a letter, whereas its style, method of argument and various incidental indications (e.g. 'time would fail me to tell', xi. 32) point rather to a sermon. Theories which have postulated a lost introduction, whether accidental or intentional, are quite unconvincing in view of the absence of any textual evidence.[2] Similarly, attempts to regard chapter xiii, or parts of it, as a postscript added to a homily are also faced with lack of

---

[1] Cf. R. Rendall, *EQ*, xxvii (1955), pp. 214–220, for the author's method in using Old Testament quotations and J. van der Ploeg, *RB*, LIV (1947), pp. 187–228. F. C. Synge (*op. cit.*, pp. 53, 54) disputes that the Old Testament context had any significance for the author of this Epistle, but this is probably an exaggeration. *

[2] Cf. Moffatt, *ILNT*, pp. 428, 429, for details. Cf. also Feine-Behm, *op. cit.*, p. 225.

textual support. Nevertheless, the form of the Epistle presents certain problems.

A. Deissmann regarded the Epistle as the first example of Christian art-literature,[1] but this must not be pressed in view of the definite historic situation which the Epistle was clearly designed to meet. It does not read like 'a mere literary exercise'.[2] In the same way the historical situation disposes of the circular view of its origin.[3]

Yet its oratorical character almost demands that it was originally a spoken sermon, or at least was prepared for delivery to some community.[4] Was it a sermon prepared by the author but read to the community by another?[5] Or was it first a delivered sermon which the hearers and especially the leaders urged the preacher to preserve in permanent form?[6] In the former case some epistolary conclusion must have been added to give personal greetings from the absent writer to the congregation he hopes soon to visit, and in the latter case the preacher would have added the greetings as a kind of covering letter at the time of supplying the church with the written copy. But the problem is not easy to solve.[7] There is no doubt that the writer has his readers in mind

[1] *The New Testament in the light of modern research* (1929), p. 51.

[2] To quote W. Manson, *op. cit.*, p. 5. O. Roller (*Das Formular der paulinischen Briefe*, 1933, pp. 213ff.) has shown that during the first century AD a form of letter was prevalent that did not belong to the general category of Greek letters, although written in Greek. The formulae used in these were oriental rather than Greek. It may be that this Epistle was never intended to conform to the normal Greek literary practice, hence the omission of the normal introduction.

[3] As M. Dibelius maintained, *ThBl* (1942), pp. 1–11.

[4] Many writers have advanced this view. Cf. P. Wendland, *Die urchristlichen Literaturformen* (LHB, 1912), pp. 306–309; E. Burggaller, *ZNTW*, 9 (1908), pp. 110–113; R. Perdelwitz, *ZNTW*, 11 (1910), pp. 59–78; H. Windisch, *op. cit.*, p. 122; Moffatt, *ILNT*, p. 428; E. F. Scott (see footnote [5]); G. Salmon (see footnote [6]). A. B. Bruce (*The Epistle to the Hebrews*, 1899, p. 10) maintained that this Epistle is too long and abstruse to be a sermon, but he thought that parts (e.g. chapter xi) might have been. P. Carrington, *The Primitive Christian Calendar* (1952), pp. 43, 44, has made the interesting suggestion that the Epistle may have been a *megillah* ('roll') for the Day of Atonement.

[5] E. F. Scott, *The Literature of the New Testament*, p. 199.

[6] G. Salmon, *INT*, p. 429. In his view it was a sermon of Barnabas' preached at Jerusalem.

[7] A. Nairne rejected the sermon theory and was inclined to regard the title as a playful subtlety meaning, 'To those who are Hebrews indeed' (*The Epistle to the Hebrews*, p. lxxiii). C. Spicq (*op. cit.*, p. 21) regarded the Epistle as an apologetic tractate. But cf. W. Nauck, article 'Zum Aufbau des Hebräerbriefes' in *Judentum Urchristentum Kirche* (Festschrift für Joachim Jeremias, ed. W. Eltester, 1960), pp. 199–206.*

throughout his composition because he punctuates his doctrinal argument with direct moral exhortations to them.

A comparison with 1 John is instructive as a parallel case in which no author's name is stated, nor any addressees defined. This would seem to support the contention that Hebrews had no other introduction than that which it now possesses, yet it has been objected that the parallel is not close since in 1 John i. 4 the writing makes clear that the author is purposing to *write* to the readers, whereas Hebrews contains no reference to writing until xiii. 22.[1] But if the author urges the readers to 'bear with' his 'word of exhortation', 'for I have written to you briefly' (RSV), it is most natural to suppose that the whole was originally composed as a letter.

Assuming, however, that it was originally a homily, the question of the purpose and extent of the epistolary conclusion at once arises. Some have treated xiii. 22–25 as a later addition on the strength of which, because of its Pauline flavour, the whole Epistle was included in the Pauline canon.[2] Others have regarded the addition as a fictitious device of the author, especially framed to give the impression of Pauline origin.[3] The former of these alternatives is excluded by the common outlook, purpose and style to be found in both i–xii and xiii.[4] The latter is most improbable since no author wishing to suggest

[1] Cf. Moffatt, *ILNT*, p. 429.

[2] Feine-Behm (*op. cit.*, p. 224) cite Overbeck, *Zur Geschichte des Kanons* (1880), for this view.*

[3] Cf. P. Wendland, *loc. cit.* W. Wrede (*Das literarische Rätsel des Hebräerbriefe*, 1906, pp. 1–5) gives a useful survey of theories of a similar nature. He mentions the view of Berger, de Wette, Overbeck, Weizsäcker and Perdelwitz, who all regarded xiii. 22–25 (or 18–25) as an addition to the homily. Wrede himself thought that the writer changed his mind. His first intention was a homily. Then he began to turn it into an Epistle in chapter xiii, and finally decided to give it a Pauline flavour in verses 22–25. In the latter portion he was influenced by Phm. 22 and Phil. ii. 19–24 (cf. *ibid.*, pp. 39–43). C. C. Torrey (*JBL*, xxx, 1911, pp. 137–156) has a similar theory, but extends the additions to include xiii. 1–7, 16–19.

[4] This is strongly maintained by C. Spicq in his article 'L'authenticité du chapitre xiii de l'Epître aux Hébreux' in *Coniectanea Neotestamentica XI in honorem Antonii Fridrichsen* (1947), pp. 226–236. Spicq finds in Heb. xiii four major themes from the body of the Epistle; the elimination of Mosaism which obliged Christians to break with the levitical cultus; the analogy between our Lord and the levitical sacrifices; life on earth as a pilgrimage; and perseverance in the faith assured by a docile attitude towards the leaders. The first three may be admitted, but there is no basis for the fourth in either part. Spicq adds many other parallels affecting style and articulation. For a linguistic comparison between i–xii and xiii, cf. C. R.

Pauline origin would have been foolish enough to neglect the use of an introductory formula in chapter i announcing authorship. A third view is that the concluding three verses were added by Paul to an Epistle written by one of his associates.[1] The description, 'our brother Timothy' and the word 'grace' in the greetings are claimed to support this.[2] But it is strange that Paul gives no hint of his identity and three verses are, after all, a very narrow basis on which to form an estimate of authorship.

Yet another and highly improbable view is that Hebrews xiii is part of the 'severe letter' of Paul to Corinth.[3] Some similarities may suggestively be found, but the processes by which such an ending came to be attached to an anonymous letter like Hebrews are too baffling to be readily credible.

VIII. LITERARY AFFINITIES

Because so much stress is placed on literary affinities some attention must be paid to those affecting this Epistle, although considerable reserve is necessary before making any deduc ons from these data. Of the Pauline Epistles the parallels with Romans are most marked, but other less striking parallels are found in 1 and 2 Corinthians, Colossians and Philippians.[4] There are similarly parallels with 1 Peter and many of these are common only to Hebrews and 1 Peter in the New Testament.[5] Again the Lucan writings furnish many parallels, although these are mostly in vocabulary.[6] Attention has already been drawn to Johannine parallels (see pp. 723f.), but in this case it is the underlying catechesis and not the written Gospel which is in mind.

In the case of the Pauline Epistles, 1 Peter and the Lucan writings, various inferences regarding authorship have been made, based on the

Williams (*JBL*, xxx, 1911, pp. 129–136) who considered one author wrote both parts. Cf. also H. Strathmann, *Der Brief an die Hebräer* (1953), p. 68.*

[1] Cf. F. J. Badcock, *op. cit.*, pp. 199, 200, for this view. As he maintained in any case a composite authorship (Barnabas/Luke), an appended postscript by Paul presented no difficulty to him.

[2] G. A. Simcox made a comparison between Heb. xiii. 20, 21 and 2 Tim. iv. 5–8 and concluded that both passages were Pauline (*ET*, x, 1899, pp. 430ff.).

[3] Cf. E. D. Jones, *ET*, xlvi (1935), pp. 562–567.

[4] Cf. F. D. V. Narborough, *op. cit.*, p. 16, for details. E. J. Goodspeed (*INT*, p. 256) and A. E. Barnett (*Paul becomes a Literary Influence*, 1941, pp. 69–88) maintain that Hebrews reflects all of Paul's Epistles, except 2 Thessalonians and Philemon.

[5] Cf. Moffatt, *ILNT*, p. 440; Narborough, *op. cit.*, p. 12.

[6] Cf. Moffatt, *op. cit.*, p. 436. See comments on pp. 693f.

NEW TESTAMENT INTRODUCTION

supposition that strong literary parallels point to identity of authorship. Yet none of these inferences has very widely commended itself. Alternatively, theories of literary dependence have been proposed. The author's use of some or all of the above-mentioned writings may at least be considered a possibility, but beyond that we cannot go. It is notably difficult to establish the direction in which literary dependence took place and this inevitably leads to difference of opinion. For instance, if 1 Peter is Petrine, it probably preceded Hebrews,[1] but if it is not apostolic (see pp. 774ff.) and Hebrews is dated early, Hebrews must have preceded 1 Peter. If both are late, who can determine the direction of dependence? It is probably better to leave out any appeal to literary parallels altogether, until some more objective method of determining dependence can be devised.

IX. ITS MODERN RELEVANCE

If the Epistle has been relatively neglected, it is because the argument seems obscure to those unfamiliar with the Old Testament background. Old Testament criticism has had its repercussions on the influence of this Epistle for, so long as much of the Old Testament remains under suspicion, the relevance of this Epistle cannot possibly be appreciated. Yet it gives to our contemporary age the same message as it gave to its original readers, an assurance of the superiority and finality of Christ and a clear insight into the Christian interpretation of Old Testament history and forms of worship. It is no wonder that the language of this Epistle has become the language of devotion, moulding the expression of praise and petition, for it meets the fundamental need of man; it speaks of a way of approach and a method of worship which is superior to all others, and which is unaffected by the march of time.

CONTENTS

I. THE SUPERIORITY OF CHRISTIANITY (i. 1–x. 18)

This is contrasted with several different methods of approach and culminates in the doctrinal exposition of Christ as the eternal High Priest.

[1] F. J. Badcock (op. cit., pp. 191, 192) maintained the reverse in view of the originality of the Epistle to the Hebrews, and he thought that Peter might easily have become acquainted with it through Mark or Silvanus.

a. Superiority to the old revelation (i. 1–3)

The divine character of the prophetical messages is at once admitted but the vital difference in Christianity is in the glorious Person who has become God's medium. This opening statement sets the tone for the whole Epistle, for Christ is introduced both in His royal dignity and in His fulfilled Priesthood.

b. Superiority to angels (i. 4–ii. 18)

This contrast derives particular force from the belief that angels were messengers of the old revelation and Christ is seen to be greater than both the revelation itself and also its messengers. The writer in the course of this explanation digresses to exhort the readers to heed this great revelation declared through Christ (ii. 1–4). In view of this superiority to angels, some explanation is required of Christ's humiliation and this next occupies the writer's thoughts leading him to explain why the incarnation was not only necessary but fitting (see verse 10). In becoming man, like His brethren, He was qualified to perform His high-priestly work (verse 17) and this is another incidental indication of the main exposition to follow. His seeming inferiority to angels was therefore only temporary and was an essential part of His redeeming activity.

c. Superiority to Moses (iii. 1–19)

It was equally important to settle the relationship of Christ to Moses and the writer makes clear that Moses was only the representative of the house of Israel in the rôle of a servant whereas Christ, as Son, held a superior office. The readers are identified with the house and thus Christ's authority over them is emphasized (verses 1–6).

The greatness of Moses could not prevent many of the Israelites from losing their inheritance and this fact is used by the writer to exhort the readers to hold fast (iii. 7–19). As in the preceding sections the Old Testament is used to support the argument and the word 'today' from Psalm xcv is interpreted of the present day of grace.

d. Superiority to Joshua (iv. 1–13)

The mention of 'rest' from Psalm xcv recalls to the writer's mind the parallel between the rest offered to Israelites and that available for Christians. Even if some Israelites lost their inheritance, others did enter the promised land under Joshua (see verse 8, RSV), but the inheritance did not amount to 'rest'. *That* still remained and is identified by the writer as the rest given to believers. In pondering this theme of rest he thinks of God resting after creation and implies that the Christian's rest is of the same quality (verses 1–10). Because of this some resolve is required if the inheritance is not to be lost, and the seriousness of this warning is brought home by the living character of God's word (verses 11–13).

e. The superior Priesthood of Christ (iv. 14–vii. 28)

1. The writer has now reached the point of discussing more fully what he has adumbrated already in ii. 17ff., that Christ is a High Priest of superior qualifications to any other. He fulfils the two fundamental requirements of sympathy and divine appointment (iv. 14–v. 10). In order to demonstrate the first the writer alludes to Christ's agony in the garden, and to prove the second he draws from two Old Testament testimonia, in one of which he introduces the order of Melchizedek to which he declares that Christ was designated. This latter theme is of such importance that the author intends to develop it, but at this stage he skilfully introduces a searching challenge (v. 11–vi. 20).

2. The next section is an interlude in the doctrinal argument containing warnings and encouragements. The writer becomes suddenly conscious of the difficulty of his exposition (verse 11) and remembering the dullness of the readers he takes the opportunity of challenging them to strive for greater maturity (verse 14). It was time they grew up and left behind the elementary doctrines (vi. 1–3). The alternative to advancement is going back and the thought of apostasy strikes the writer so forcefully that he issues a solemn warning as to its consequences (vi. 4–8). He is not meaning to suggest that his readers have actually turned back, however, for he commends them for their love and then encourages them to press on to inherit the promises (vi. 9–12). The thought of promises reminds him of Abraham and his experience of God's immutable word as a guarantee of great security, like a good anchorage. But Christians have a further Guarantor in the person of their High Priest, who belongs to the order of Melchizedek (vi. 13–20).

3. The expression 'after the order of Melchisedec' clearly needs explaining, so the writer appeals to the Genesis story (Gn. xiv) to bring out certain features in Christ's Priesthood which he intends to demon-

strate as being superior to Aaron's. Melchizedek's names are suggestive (peace and righteousness), as is also the strange way in which he appears and disappears from the story (illustrative of Christ's eternal existence), and his evident superiority to Abraham and thus to the later levitical order (vii. 1-10). But this type of argument must be brought into concrete relationship to the levitical priesthood and the first difficulty is that Christ belonged to a different tribe from what the law prescribed for the priesthood (vii. 11-14). Yet the law cannot be considered perfect and the qualification of the superior High Priest is not therefore genealogical but spiritual (indestructible life; verse 16). This makes possible the High-Priesthood of Christ, which is seen to be superior in its solemn divine attestation, its permanence and the sinlessness and perfection of the Holder (vii. 15-28).

f. The superiority of the priestly work of Christ (viii. 1–x. 18)

The real crux of the argument is now reached. A high priest must have functions; what then are Christ's? He obviously cannot minister on earth, so He is shown to have a superior sanctuary, heaven itself (viii. 1-6). Moreover, the covenant under which Christ ministers is a new covenant foreshadowed by Jeremiah, which makes the old obsolete (viii. 7-13). This leads the writer to describe some of the ritual of this obsolete covenant in order to bring out more clearly the greater glory of the new. The new order of sacrifice needs no continuous repetition. Whereas the Aaronic high priest entered once a year, Christ not only entered once for all but entered a heavenly and not an earthly sanctuary. He took no animal blood, but offered His own through the Spirit. This demonstrates the superiority of Christian atonement (ix. 1-14) and leads to a further development in the argument, since Christ becomes Mediator of the new covenant through His death (ix. 15).

But the death of an eternal High Priest seems paradoxical and is explained by analogy with a legal testament, which becomes valid only on the death of the testator (ix. 16-22). The uniqueness of the sacrifice of Christ is then reiterated in order to emphasize its timelessness and its effectiveness for the removal of sin (ix. 23-28). The whole argument for the superiority of Christ's atonement is now summed up in contrast to the levitical system (x. 1-18) and the completeness of His act is particularly demonstrated by His enthronement in heaven (x. 12), the same conception as that with which the discussion began (i. 3).

II. EXHORTATIONS BASED ON THE PRECEDING ARGUMENTS (x. 19–xiii. 17)

a. The superior method of approach should be used (x. 19–25)

All that is necessary is faith in this High Priest and this will affect our approach, not only to ourselves but to others. Mutual encouragement is so valuable that assemblies of Christians should not be neglected.

b. The dangers of apostasy must be noted (x. 26–31)

The possibility of those who have understood the privileges of the Christian way spurning the truth they know causes the writer to issue another warning similar to that of chapter vi.

c. Yet memory of past days is cause for encouragement (x. 32–39)

The writer recalls their former steadfastness and does not wish them to think he is censuring them too severely, but emphasizes their need to hold on to their confidence.

d. Examples of historic endurance are cited to illustrate the triumph of faith (xi. 1–40)

The need for endurance stated in the last chapter leads to the introduction of illustrations. Faith in this case is not used in the same way as in Paul for it describes here an attitude of trust with a strong element of hope and fortitude. Most attention is paid to the patriarchs, but the whole history of the past could furnish examples.

e. But the greatest example of all is Jesus Christ (xii. 1–11)

If the readers are at present suffering they should look at Jesus Christ in His endurance upon the cross and should remember that discipline is necessary for God's sons.

f. Moral inconsistencies must be avoided (xii. 12–17)

There is need for resolution in pursuing the right path and certain specific injunctions are given for the avoidance of bitterness and immorality. Esau's example is cited as a warning.

g. The superiority of the new covenant is again maintained (xii. 18–29)

Its great glory, its great Mediator and its great stability are all mentioned, together with another exhortation to take advantage of this new way of worship, remembering the awesomeness of God.

h. Practical results must follow from these considerations (xiii. 1–17)

There are exhortations affecting social life (1–3), private life (4–6) and religious life (7–9, 17) interspersed with a concluding doctrinal section explaining the Christians' new altar (10–16).

III. CONCLUSION (xiii. 18–25)

The author requests prayer on his behalf, especially that he might the sooner be able to return to the readers, and follows this with a moving benediction, which passes into a doxology. A final appeal to the readers, a reference to Timothy, greetings from some Italian Christians and a brief benediction then close the Epistle.

ADDITIONAL NOTES

686. [4] Cf. W. G. Kümmel, *INT* (1965), p. 275. C. P. Anderson (*HTR*, 59, 1966, pp. 429–438) argues that Hebrews was attached to a Pauline Epistle before the Corpus was collected. On the position of Hebrews in the Canon, cf. W. H. P. Hatch, *HTR*, 29 (1936), pp. 133 ff.

688. [2] Most modern Roman Catholic scholars do not take the position of Leonard in supporting Pauline authorship, but they do support some Pauline connection. The author is regarded as a disciple of Paul. E. Grässer, 'Der Hebräerbrief 1938–63' (*TR*, 30, 1964, pp. 128–236), in his very full survey of literature cites the following who hold this opinion: Wikenhauser, Benoit, Kuss, Spicq, Cambier, Schierse, Rigaux.

688. [3] Cf. Kümmel, *INT*, p. 277.

689. [4] Cf. Kümmel, *ibid.*

692. [4] Cf. Kümmel, *INT*, p. 282.

695. [4] H. Montefiore, *The Epistle to the Hebrews* (1965), pp. 9 ff., is favourable to the theory of Apollos as author. It fits in with his particular idea of its connection with the Corinthian church. See additional note on 718 below. Cf. also J. H. Davies, *A Letter to the Hebrews* (1967).

698. [2] F. F. Bruce, *Commentary on the Epistle to the Hebrews* (1964), pp. xxxv ff., is content to suggest a hellenistic Jewish Christian as author. He thinks he belonged to a similar kind of milieu as Stephen which had connections with a sect like Qumran. On this latter point, compare his article, *NTS*, 9 (1962), pp. 217–232 (see additional note on 706 [2] below).

702. [2] Cf. Kümmel, *INT*, p. 280.

706. [2] There have been several studies centring on the subject of Hebrews and Qumran which have shown similarities of thought. Cf. J. Daniélou, *Qumran und* *der Ursprung des Christentums* (1958), pp. 148 ff.; C. Spicq, 'L'Épître aux Hébreux, Apollos, Jean-Baptiste, les Hellénistes et Qumran' in *Revue de Qumran*, I (1958-59), pp. 365 ff.; H. Braun, *TR*, 30 (1964), pp. 1-38; Y. Yadin, 'The Dead Sea Scrolls and the Epistle to the Hebrews' in *Scripta Hierosolymitana*, 4 (1958), pp. 36-53. A fuller treatment is to be found in H. Kosmala's *Hebräer-Essener-Christen* (1959), who advances the theory that the Hebrews were former members of the Qumran community who, although Messianically orientated, had not come to see in Jesus the fulfilment of their Messianic hopes. F. F. Bruce, in the article referred to in the additional note on 698 [2], carefully studies the points of contact on the following themes: angels, biblical exegesis, prophet-priest-King, purification, the house of the Lord, sacrifice, earthly copies of heavenly realities, saints and martyrs. His conclusion is that the writer was a Hellenist, not a Qumranite.

Two recent articles have compared the Melchisedek teaching in Qumran and Hebrews. Cf. M. de Jonge and A. S. van der Woude (*NTS*, 12, 1966, pp. 301-326), who consider that the conception in Hebrews (an angel inferior to the Son of God) differs strongly from that of Qumran (Messianic high priest). J. A. Fitzmeyer (*JBL*, LXXXVI, 1967, pp. 25-41) suggests, however, that the prominence of the Melchisedek theme in Qumran may account for its appearance in Hebrews.

711. [1] A. Ehrhardt, *The Framework of the New Testament Stories* (1964), p. 109, considers Hebrews to be a message of consolation from Christians at Rome to those in Palestine.

712. [4] Cf. Kümmel, *INT*, p. 281.

715. [6] H. Montefiore (*op. cit.*) advances the theory of a Corinthian destination for Hebrews. This is supported by J. M. Ford, *CBQ*, 28 (1966), pp. 402-416.

717. [2] W. Marxsen (*INT*, 1968, pp. 221 f.) considers Hebrews could not have been written much before Clement's letter.

718. H. Montefiore (*op. cit.*) proposes a much earlier date than usual (AD 52-54), based on his view of Corinth as its destination. He thinks it belongs to the same period as I Corinthians, and was published just prior to it.

719. [2] On the Melchisedek theme, see additional note on 706 [2] above.

719. [3] For the relationship between Hebrews and Philo, cf. S. G. Sowers, *The Hermeneutics of Philo and Hebrews* (1965), who considers that both authors belonged to the same Alexandrian Jewish school. Cf. also R. Williamson, *A Critical Re-examination of the Relationship between Philo and the Epistle to the Hebrews* (1967); *idem.*, *SJT*, 16 (1963), pp. 415-424. Williamson does not consider that the author was much influenced by Platonism.

719. [4] Cf. Kümmel, *INT*, p. 277.

721. [3] E. Grässer (*ZNTW*, 56, 1965, pp. 63-91) submits that in Hebrews the history of Jesus is transmitted only as part of the *kerygma*. He notes that more interest is shown here in the historical Jesus than in the writings of Paul or John. The same author, in his *Der Glaube im Hebräerbrief* (1965), considers the background to be 'gnostic' pre-Christian philosophies. For a criticism of this position, cf. O. Michel, *ThLZ*, 91 (1966), cols. 35 f.; C. F. D. Moule, *JTS*, n.s., XVII (1966), pp. 147–150; A. Vanhoye, *Biblica*, 47 (1966), pp. 139–141. For a more sympathetic appraisal, cf. D. B. Bronson, *JBL*, LXXXIV (1965), pp. 458 f.

724. [1] On the text used by the author in his many citations, G. Howard (*Nov. Test.*, 10, 1968, pp. 208–216) claims that these are not consistently from LXX. Some show partial dependence on Hebrew. Cf. F. Schröger, *Der Verfasser des Hebräer-brief als Schriftausleger* (1968) for a study of Old Testament citations.

725. [7] There have been many studies which have concentrated attention on the composition of this Epistle, some finding here a combination of two or more parts (for a bibliography, cf. E. Grässer, 'Der Hebräerbrief 1938–1963', *TR*, 30, 1964, pp. 160 ff.). A. Vanhoye, *La Structure littéraire de l'Épître aux Hébreux* (1963), finds what he calls a concentric symmetry in Hebrews, made up as follows: eschatology, ecclesiology, offering, ecclesiology, eschatology. Cf. also his article in *Studia Evangelica*, II (1964), pp. 493–501.

726. [2] For a comment on Heb. xiii. 22–25, cf. J. D. Legg, *EQ*, XL (1968), pp. 220–223. He considers that this was written by Paul, but that the rest of the Epistle was the work of Timothy.

726 f. [4] The importance of Hebrews xiii for an understanding of the Epistle is brought out by F. V. Filson, *'Yesterday': A Study of Hebrews in the Light of ch. 13* (1967), who sees the Epistle as an exhortation, particularly directed towards those attached to their Jewish heritage.

Dgr. categorizes the literary style thus

not → 1 Jewish

but → 2 Greek < Athens / Alexandrian {ornate / embelishment}

The name Jesus occurs 13 Times ,(1)to Joshua

CHAPTER TWENTY-THREE

THE EPISTLE OF JAMES

This is the first of the Catholic or general Epistles, so called because
they lack indications of a specific address. It is consequently more difficult in these cases to reconstruct the historical situation to which they
belong, which in itself opens the way for a variety of conjectures. Yet
a careful criticism is not left without some indication of their circumstances of origin and the effort involved in ascertaining these will be
repaid by the greater clarity with which the books will be understood.
With the exception of 1 Peter and 1 John the Catholic Epistles have
played only a minor part in moulding the thought of the Christian
Church and have been largely overshadowed by their more illustrious
companion Epistles in the New Testament, notably by the Epistles of
Paul. If this is true in the modern Church, it will be no great surprise
to find that a similar phenomenon occurred in the ancient Church.
This must be borne in mind when surveying the external evidence.

The Epistle of James has suffered much through misunderstandings,
the most notable example of which was Martin Luther's oft-quoted
description of it as an Epistle of straw. The course of nineteenth-
century criticism dealt a further blow against the Epistle and has left in
its wake a general inclination to regard James as a product of an inferior
Christian outlook in contrast to the strong meat of Pauline theology.
Yet while attention to the differences is invaluable for demonstrating
the wide variety of early Christian religious experiences, the Epistle of
James can be rightly understood only within the context of the whole
New Testament Scriptures. Its contribution is very different from that
of Paul's letters and yet it was a true instinct that led the Church to
include it in its Canon, for it represents an age of transition, without
knowledge of which our appreciation of early Christian history would
be the poorer and our grasp of ethical Christianity incomplete.

I. AUTHORSHIP

a. The external evidence for the Epistle

The earliest Christian writer to mention this Epistle as the work of
James was Origen, who also clearly recognized the Epistle as Scripture.

In one of his citations Origen has been thought to imply some doubt,[1] but since on numerous occasions he cites it as Scripture without hesitation,[2] it is highly questionable whether he himself felt any reserve over accepting it. It is to be noted that there is no mention of it in the Muratorian Canon (which also makes no mention of Hebrews and the Petrine Epistles), but this may be due to the obviously corrupt state of the text of that Canon and little weight may, therefore, be attached to it as an evidence of exclusion from the Canon of the Roman Church. Yet it may be significant that the African Canon also omits this Epistle.

The evidence of Eusebius is interesting, for, although he classes it among the disputed books (*Antilegomena*), he cites it as if it were genuine.[3] He mentions that the Epistle of James was said to be by the Lord's brother, but that some regarded it as 'spurious'.[4] All that may certainly be deduced from this is that not all Christians of Eusebius' acquaintance regarded it as authentic. His own practice would seem to reveal his personal approach to the Epistle, but it is just possible that in citing it as James', he is merely following conventional procedure,[5] for he says, 'But nevertheless we know that these have been publicly used with the rest in most churches.' What hesitancy there was at this time may well be accounted for by uncertainty over the identification of 'James'.[6] Jerome similarly voices some uncertainty over it and in one place regards it as published by another in the name of James, the Lord's brother,[7] and yet he also cites from it as from Scripture. Another evidence unfavourable to the authenticity of James is its omission from the early Syriac Canon.[8]

The problem is to know what inferences to draw from this evidence. There are two possibilities. It may either be supposed that the doubts

[1] In his commentary on the Gospel of John, he mentions James with the formula, ὡς ἐν τῇ φερομένῃ Ἰακώβου ἐπιστολῇ ἀνέγνωμεν (on Jn. xix. 6).

[2] Cf. *Ad Rom.* iv. 1 and *Hom. in Lev.* ii. 4. Cf. also *Hom. in Josh.* vii. 1.

[3] J. B. Mayor (Epistle of James,[3] 1913, p. xlix) cites *Eccl. Theol.* ii. 25, iii. 2; *Comm. in Psalm*, p. 648 Montf. (as Scripture) and p. 247 (as by the holy apostle).

[4] Eusebius, *HE*, ii. 23.

[5] Cf. W. O. E. Oesterley, *The General Epistle of James* (*EGT*, 1910), p. 387.

[6] Cf. R. V. G. Tasker, *The General Epistle of James* (1956), p. 19.

[7] In *De Vir. Ill.* ii: 'Jacobus qui appellatur frater Domini . . . unam tantum scripsit epistolam . . . quae et ipsa ab alio quodam sub nomine ejus edita asseritur.' (Cf. Westcott, *On the Canon of the New Testament*,[4] 1875, p. 448.)

[8] It formed a part of the Peshitta but was not included in the statement in the Doctrine of the Addai (cf. Souter, *The Text and Canon of the New Testament*, 1913, pp. 225f.) nor in the Syriac Canonical list dated about AD 400 (*ibid.*, p. 226).

regarding the Epistle are evidence of non-apostolic authorship, in which case the other evidence on this disputed question will be viewed with a disposition against the authenticity of the Epistle. Or else some explanation of the phenomenon may be sought and, if an adequate answer can be given, not only will the internal evidence be more favourably considered, but there will also be a greater inclination to include the traces of the Epistle found before AD 200. These traces have been fully examined by J. B. Mayor,[1] who claimed to find quotations or allusions in Clement of Rome, Pseudo-Clement (*2 Clement*), the *Didache, Barnabas*, the *Testaments of the XII Patriarchs*, Ignatius, Polycarp, *Hermas* and some of the later second-century Fathers. Even if Mayor's evidence were admitted in detail, this list would need to be adjusted, since few scholars would now date the *Testaments* in the Christian era. But Mayor's allusions have not commended themselves generally.[2] At the same time, it is probable that much more weight should be given to some, at least, of this evidence than is the usual practice. Especially does this seem true of Clement and *Hermas*. Yet those who on other grounds conclude for a second-century date for James are bound by that very fact to find some other explanation for the similarities. Some resort to the theory of a common *milieu* to which James and the other writers are indebted,[3] while others reverse the dependence and maintain that 'James' was acquainted with Clement and *Hermas*.[4]

The real crux lies in the treatment of this second-century evidence.

[1] *Op. cit.*, pp. li–lxiii. Cf. also G. Kittel, *ZNTW*, 43 (1950–51), pp. 55–112 for a more recent full examination.

[2] Oesterley (*op. cit.*, p. 386) does not deny the possibility of indebtedness, but considers the similarities are not sufficient to prove it. But many writers, such as J. H. Ropes (*A critical and exegetical commentary on the Epistle of St. James, ICC*, 1916, pp. 43ff.), neglect this line of evidence altogether. See also E. C. Blackman, *The Epistle of James* (1957), p. 31, and K. Aland, *ThLZ*, 69 (1944), col. 102.

[3] Cf. J. Moffatt, *ILNT*, p. 467; K. Aland, *loc. cit.*; O. J. F. Seitz (*JBL*, LXIII, 1944, pp. 131–140; LXVI, 1947, pp. 211–219) explained the connection between James, *1* and *2 Clement* and *Hermas* by the common use of an apocryphal work (probably the same source which is behind 1 Cor. ii. 9).

[4] Moffatt cites Pfleiderer for this view. More recently F. W. Young (*JBL*, LXVII, 1948, pp. 339–345) has suggested that in the similar treatment of the Rahab story in James and *1 Clement* it seems probable that James is the borrower. But even if literary dependence could be established, it could equally well be the other way round. G. H. Rendall's opinion that Clement is a 'born quoter, with little originative gift' (*The Epistle of James and Judaistic Christianity*, 1927, p. 102) is much to the point here. Cf. also R. J. Knowling, *The Epistle of St. James* (1904), pp. xlix–li.

Before citing his detailed lists of indirect parallels, J. B. Mayor makes the following comment on the direct evidence for the authenticity of the Epistle (i.e. in more or less formal catalogues) and on the difference in approach between the East and West, the latter being much more tardy in its recognition than the former. 'The difference is easily explained from the fact that the Epistle was probably written at Jerusalem and addressed to the Jews of the East Dispersion; it did not profess to be written by an apostle or to be addressed to Gentile churches and it seemed to contradict the teaching of the great apostle to the Gentiles.'[1] Among others who have maintained the authenticity of the Epistle, the opinion of two may be noted on this point. R. J. Knowling[2] considered that the circumstances of writing presuppose a Jewish Christian reader-circle which would partly explain the obscurity which surrounded the letter in its earlier history, together with the fact that it does not claim apostolic authority. R. V. G. Tasker[3] has drawn attention to the lesser interest in the reproduction of the general Epistles as compared with the specific church Epistles, because the latter were indisputably apostolic. On the whole it is not altogether surprising that this brief Epistle of James was not much quoted in the earliest period, for it did not possess such wide appeal as the more dynamic Epistles of Paul. It is the kind of letter which could easily be neglected as, in fact, the treatment of it in the modern Church abundantly shows and, once neglected, a fertile soil was provided for future doubts, especially at a time when spurious productions were being attributed to apostolic names.

b. The traditional view of authorship

After this brief survey of external attestation it is possible to examine the internal data for the traditional view of authorship with an open

---

[1] *Op. cit.*, p. li.

[2] *Op. cit.*, p. liii. In a similar vein H. F. D. Sparks (*The Formation of the New Testament*, 1952, p. 129) writes, 'The fact that the Epistle is a Jewish-Christian document, whoever wrote it, may have been in itself sufficient to discredit it in the eyes of Gentile Christians; while its essentially practical attitude would inevitably make it seem of little consequence to those whose main interests were theological. Accordingly, its neglect by the early Church is by no means an insuperable barrier to accepting the Lord's brother as the author.'

[3] *Op. cit.*, p. 19. A. Carr (*The General Epistle of St. James*, CGT, 1896, p. ix) regarded the absence of citation as capable of satisfactory explanation on the grounds of the letter's freedom from controversial subjects and its address to a group (i.e. Jewish Christians) which soon lost its specific identity.

mind. There is no conclusive evidence for the late appearance of the Epistle and possibly even some evidence for its early influence.

(i) *The author's self-identification.* The writer introduces himself quite simply as 'James, a servant of God and of the Lord Jesus Christ', but his very simplicity has turned out to be ambiguous; for James is a common name and the accompanying description is not sufficiently distinctive to assist the identification. Any man called James who was engaged in Christian work would fit the description, except for the obvious authority which the writer assumes. Moreover, the Epistle itself does nothing to alleviate this ambiguity. Nevertheless, assuming for the present that this opening address is authentic, there are only two New Testament people known as James who could with much credence come into the picture and even these can be fairly easily narrowed down to one. James, the son of Zebedee, of the apostolic band, has found many supporters in the course of Church history, but he would be ruled out almost certainly by the fact that he was killed by Herod in AD 44 and it is reasonably certain that the Epistle was written later than that. However, there is now general agreement that the opening greeting is intended to point to James, the Lord's brother, who became leader of the church at Jerusalem. The simplicity of the description is in support of this, for it is evident that a well-known James must have been intended, and as far as the biblical record is concerned, the Lord's brother is the only James who appears to have played a sufficiently prominent part in early Christian history.

Thus far there is general agreement, but at this point opinions diverge, for there have been various theories based on the assumption that the James mentioned in the opening greeting was not the true author of the Epistle. Some theories assume that the name is no more than a pseudonym attached to the letter to add a note of authority, while others regard the salutation as a later interpolation and, therefore, as no part of the original writer's design. These alternative theories will be dealt with below,[1] but for the present the not unreasonable assumption will be made that the writer intended to indicate that he really was James, the Lord's brother.[2] To discover whether this is a true assumption, it is necessary to examine carefully the other evidences which support it.

[1] See pp. 753ff.
[2] K. Baltzer and H. Köster (*ZNTW*, 46, 1955, pp. 141f.) suggest, on the basis of a reference in Hegesippus, that James was called Obadiah, that 'the servant' clause in Jas. i. 1 may have some connection with Ob. i. 1 (LXX).

(ii) *The author's Jewish background*. That the author's mind has drawn much from the Old Testament can hardly be denied. Admittedly the direct quotations number only five (cf. i. 11, ii. 8, 11, 23, iv. 6), three from the Pentateuch, one from Isaiah and one from Proverbs. Yet the indirect allusions are innumerable (cf., e.g., i. 10, ii. 21, 23, 25, iii. 9, iv. 6, v. 2, 11, 17, 18).[1] When the writer requires illustrations for prayer and patience he turns to Old Testament characters. His approach to ethical problems and his denunciations and warnings find striking parallels in the Old Testament prophetical books. He appears as a kind of Christian prophet.

There are many other less obvious indications of a Jewish mind. There are traces of Hebrew idioms behind the Greek forms of language; there are instances of the well-known Hebrew love of assonance; there are expressions which are reminiscent of Hebrew fullness of speech; and there are instances of the Hebrew prophetic style.[2] To cite this as evidence of Jewish background is not to prejudge the further question of the Epistle's original language (see discussion below, p. 766). It merely shows that the author's mind was fully at home with Jewish methods of thought and expression.

The description of the addressees in terms of the Jewish Diaspora is a further corroboration of the view that the author was a Jew, whatever be the meaning of James' expression, which is further discussed in the section dealing with destination. Certain other terms such as 'Lord of Sabaoth' (v. 4) would come much more naturally to a Jew than to a Greek. Moreover, the author refers to Jewish formulae when writing about oaths, stresses the Jewish law (ii. 9-11, iv. 11, 12) and mentions the major constituent of the Jewish creed, i.e. the unity of God (ii. 19).*

From this evidence, it seems conclusive that the author was a Jew, and that there is no reason to suppose that James, the Lord's brother,

---

[1] Mayor (*op. cit.*, pp. lxix ff.) finds parallels from the following books: Genesis, Exodus, Leviticus, Numbers, Deuteronomy, Joshua, 1 Kings, Job, Psalms, Proverbs, Ecclesiastes, Isaiah, Jeremiah, Ezekiel, Daniel and seven minor prophets. In addition there are parallels with the Wisdom literature. Some scholars have maintained the author's literary dependence on these latter books (particularly Wisdom and Ecclesiasticus). Cf. A. Plummer, *St. James* (*Exp. Bib.*, 1891), p. 74 and R. J. Knowling, *op. cit.*, pp. xv, xvi. It must, however, be recognized that James' spiritual standpoint is much superior to that of the authors of these Wisdom books. Cf. G. Salmon (*INT*, p. 465) and J. H. Ropes (*op. cit.*, pp. 18, 19) against James' close knowledge of these books.

[2] For details of all these characteristics, see Oesterley, *op. cit.*, pp. 393-397.

must be excluded. But the following considerations are more positively in support of the traditional theory of authorship.

(iii) *Similarities between James and the Acts.* That there are some parallels
between this Epistle and the speech and letter attributed to James in the
Acts is indisputable. These deserve mention in detail because of their
significance. Χαίρειν ('greeting') is used both in James i. 1 and in the
letter recorded in Acts xv. 23 and elsewhere only in Acts xxiii. 26.
'The honourable name by which you are called' (Jas. ii. 7) reminds us
of Acts xv. 17. The exhortation to the 'brethren' (ἀδελφοί) to hear is
found in both James ii. 5 and Acts xv. 13. Parallels are found in the
case of isolated words such as:

> ἐπισκέπτεσθε (Jas. i. 27; Acts xv. 14)
> ἐπιστρέφειν (Jas. v. 19, 20; Acts xv. 19)
> τηρεῖν (or διατηρεῖν) ἑαυτόν (Jas. i. 27; Acts xv. 29)
> ἀγαπητός (Jas. i. 16, 19, ii. 5; Acts xv. 25).

These parallels are remarkable in that they all occur within so short a
passage attributed to James in Acts and because they are of such a
character that they cannot be explained by the common accidents of
speech.[1]

Yet these data cannot at once be claimed as conclusive evidence of a
common mind behind the respective passages, since all scholars would
not admit the verbal correctness of the Acts speeches, and if what is
preserved in Acts xv is composed in the author's own words (i.e. Luke's)
it could not support our present argument. To discuss the Acts speeches
at this point is not possible, but even on the supposition that Luke is not
giving the *ipsissima verba* of James, it still remains remarkable that he
has happened to preserve these parallels. It is, of course, a possible
explanation that the author of Acts has reproduced echoes from James,
which would necessitate the theory that he attempted to conform his
speeches and letters to the style of known models, but the parallels are
of too incidental a kind to make this at all likely. It is no more probable

---

[1] Tasker (*op. cit.*, p. 26) is cautious against placing too much weight on these
resemblances, because resemblances between James' speech and other New
Testament books could be cited where similarity of authorship is not in question.
But if, on other grounds, similarity of authorship may be presupposed, as for
instance in tradition, the resemblances would naturally possess more weight. On
the other hand, not all scholars admit the force of the parallels at all (e.g. McNeile-
Williams, *INT*, p. 209, explain them away).

*in fact this may corroborate that the author of Acts
believed James to be the author of this Epistle if it
predated Acts.*

that the author of James (assuming now a later writer) included in his pseudonymous Epistle echoes from the letter of James in Acts, for this was generally contrary to pseudepigraphic procedure. It may reasonably be maintained, therefore, that this evidence from Acts, while not conclusive, is yet corroborative of the traditional view of authorship.

(iv) *Similarities with the teaching of Jesus.* Again the parallels are of such a character that the more notable of them deserve special mention, particularly as there are more parallels in this Epistle than in any other New Testament book to the teaching of our Lord in the Gospels. The following passages are compared with the Sermon on the Mount:

i. 2. Joy in the midst of trials (cf. Mt. v: 10–12).
i. 4. Exhortation to perfection (cf. Mt. v. 48).
i. 5. Asking for good gifts (cf. Mt. vii. 7ff.).
i. 20. Against anger (cf. Mt. v. 22).
i. 22. Hearers and doers of the Word (cf. Mt. vii. 24ff.).
ii. 10. The whole law to be kept (cf. Mt. v. 19).
ii. 13. Blessings of mercifulness (cf. Mt. v. 7).
iii. 18. Blessings of peacemakers (cf. Mt. v. 9).
iv. 4. Friendship of the world as enmity against God (cf. Mt. vi. 24).
iv. 10. Blessing of the humble (cf. Mt. v. 5).
iv. 11, 12. Against judging others (cf. Mt. vii. 1–5).
v. 2ff. Moth and rust spoiling riches (cf. Mt. vi. 19).
v. 10. The prophets as examples (cf. Mt. v. 12).
v. 12. Against oaths (cf. Mt. v. 33–37).

In these instances the common ideas are obvious enough, but it is noticeable that nowhere does James cite the words of the Lord. There is no proof, therefore, of dependence on the Gospel of Matthew.[1] The parallels suggest rather that James is reproducing reminiscences of oral teaching which he had previously heard.[2]

[1] M. H. Shepherd (*JBL*, lxxv, 1956, pp. 40–51) disagrees with this judgment. He finds eight main discourses in James, all of which show parallels with, although no citations from, Matthew. He concludes that the author (a second-century writer) knew Matthew probably through hearing it read in church.

[2] Cf. Feine-Behm, *op. cit.*, p. 239; G. Kittel, *ZNTW*, 41 (1942), pp. 91ff. Owing to the omission of the chief motives which produced the Synoptic Gospels, Ropes (*op. cit.*, p. 39) maintained that James in religious ideas is nearer to the collectors of the sayings of Jesus than to the Gospel authors themselves. But his distinction is somewhat arbitrary. E. Lohse (*ZNTW*, 47, 1956, pp. 1–22) disagrees with Kittel and maintains that the method of making allusions to the Lord's words is similar

In addition to these parallels there are others from different parts of our Lord's teaching, such as the following:

i. 6. Exercise of faith without doubting (cf. Mt. xxi. 21).

ii. 8. Love to one's neighbour as a great commandment (cf. Mt. xxii. 39).

iii. 1. On the desire to be called teacher (cf. Mt. xxiii. 8–12).

iii. 2f. On the dangers of hasty speech (cf. Mt. xii. 36, 37).

v. 9. The Divine Judge at the doors (cf. Mt. xxiv. 33).

It will be noted that all the parallels so far quoted are from Matthew's Gospel, and this fact must be given due weight in discussions on the relationship between the two books, but some of these parallels are found also in Mark and still others might be cited from Luke.[1] The cumulative effect of this evidence must be in favour of the presumption that the author was in close touch with the teaching of Jesus.[2] It should, moreover, be observed that these parallels are not produced in any mechanical way, but with a real understanding of the point of view from which our Lord proclaimed His teaching.[3] This means that they are more than merely linguistic similarities, which would in themselves prove inconclusive.

to that found in the *Didache* and is no evidence, therefore, for an early dating (similarly K. Aland, *op. cit.*, cols. 103, 104). But it certainly does not exclude an early dating.

[1] K. Aland (*op. cit.*, cols. 99, 100) maintains that James is indebted to Lk. iv. 25f. for his reference to the three and a half years of rainlessness in Elijah's time, but he uses this as an argument for a late date. But who is to say that James did not hear our Lord speak these words? After all, they are set in the synagogue of Nazareth. B. H. Streeter (*The Primitive Church*, 1929, p. 193) suggested that James in his Sermon on the Mount allusions is nearer Luke than Matthew, and probably used the same recension of Q as did Luke.

[2] The view of O. Cone ('James (Epistle)', *Enc. Bib.*, 1914, col. 2322) that the evangelic tradition had made only an indistinct impression upon the writer's mind is clearly refuted by the facts. McNeile-Williams (*INT*, p. 208) minimize the closeness of the connections even with the Sermon on the Mount and suggest dependence on some variant oral tradition.

[3] Knowling has an illuminative comment on this fact. He writes of the Sermon on the Mount, 'In the Sermon and in the Epistle, the meaning of the old Law is deepened and spiritualised and the principle of love is emphasised as its fulfilment; in each, righteousness is set forth as the doing of the Divine Will in contrast to the saying, "Lord, Lord!"; . . . in each, God is the Father, Who gives liberally every good and perfect gift, the God Who answers prayer, Who delivers us from evil. Who would have men merciful as their Father is merciful; in each, Jesus is Lord and Judge . . .' (*op. cit.*, pp. xxi, xxii).

(v) *Agreements with the New Testament account of James.* Our first introduction to James, the Lord's brother, is as an unbeliever in the claims of Jesus (cf. Mk. iii. 21; Jn. vii. 5). But it was not a hostile unbelief. He probably had great respect for Jesus, but could not agree with His methods and as yet had no understanding of the significance of His mission.[1] It was the resurrection which caused the change, for not only do we find that the Lord's brethren were mentioned among the disciples (Acts i. 14), but that James was specially singled out for a resurrection appearance (1 Cor. xv. 7). Probably James told Paul about it when they met (Gal. i. 19). It is significant that Paul, in referring to him, implies that James was numbered among the apostles; in fact he names him among the three pillars of the Jerusalem church.

When he presided at the all-important Jerusalem Council, there is no doubt that he held a commanding position in the local church, taking precedence even over Peter. Yet, at the same time, no specific office is ascribed to him and it is probably an anachronism to call him bishop of Jerusalem. Nonetheless the authority with which he addressed the church on that occasion (Acts xv. 13ff.) is in full agreement with the tone of authority which the author of the Epistle assumes in his salutation.[2] The same is true of the account of Paul's final visit to Jerusalem, when James alone is mentioned by name among the elders of the church. Moreover, Paul accedes to James' request (or was it a command?) to observe a Jewish vow.

These incidents point to an important characteristic about James, which became elaborated in Christian tradition.[3] He was still devoted to the law and zealous for the continuance of Jewish ritual requirements. His outlook was correspondingly limited. The full freedom of the gospel had not yet reached him. He lived in an age of transition.[4] It is

---

[1] See Mayor, *op. cit.*, pp. xlv, xlvi.

[2] T. Henshaw (*New Testament Literature in the Light of Modern Scholarship*, 1952, p. 359) denies that the author writes with authority, for he claims that he says nothing for which he could not find warrant in previous authorities.

[3] For the evidence from tradition, cf. Tasker, *op. cit.*, pp. 27, 28.

[4] Cf. G. H. Rendall, *op. cit.*, pp. 110ff. for a concise account of James' position. G. Kittel (*ZNTW*, 30, 1931, pp. 145–157) considered that James was not a fanatical Jew and that he disagreed with the ritualistic Jewish Christian party. He was a moderate, as the account of the Apostolic Council shows and was not, therefore, a zealous opponent of Paul. (Cf. also *ZNTW*, 43, 1950–51, pp. 109–112.) But K. Aland (*op. cit.*, cols. 101–102) disagreed with this opinion on the strength of Acts xxi and the early Christian tradition.

not surprising, therefore, to find him the author of an Epistle in which many of the cardinal Christian doctrines are not mentioned (see later discussion on this). Nor is it surprising to find him addressing himself in a general manner to Jewish Christians.

(vi) *The conditions within the community.* The problem of the circumstances of the readers will be discussed later, but one aspect of it needs to be mentioned here. The community appears to belong to the period before the fall of Jerusalem. The oppressors are wealthy landowners, who, after the siege of Jerusalem, virtually ceased to exist in Judaea, to which district the Epistle is generally thought to have been sent. It was evidently a pressing social evil for the wealthy to extort from the poor and to live luxuriously on the proceeds, a condition of affairs which is well attested in the period leading up to the siege. Certainly the position described in James v. 1–6 would well fit this period[1] and, if so, would be in harmony with the hypothesis that the author was James, the Lord's brother.

Arguments along these lines are bound to be mainly negative, but they can demonstrate that no social conditions are implied in the Epistle which belong to a period later than the life of James, and thus indirectly they may lend support to the traditional authorship. Not all have agreed on the interpretation of these conditions and their objections will be considered below. But there is nothing anachronistic in assigning this Epistle to an early date. In fact, in addition to the social surroundings of the community, the internal conditions of quarrelsomeness among the Christians may well point to an early stage in the history of the community before much maturity had been reached.[2]

Two other considerations point in the direction of an early Jewish origin. The rather abrupt reference to 'wars and fightings' (iv. 1) would have been highly relevant to the explosive conditions of internecine strife in the period just before the siege of Jerusalem. And again the thoroughly Jewish background of the letter is evidenced by the absence of any allusion to masters and slaves and by the omission of any denun-

---

[1] Rendall (*op. cit.*, p. 32) remarked, 'As a mark of time it should be noted that these economic conditions, the day of large land-holders preying upon a burdened peasantry, came to an end with the Jewish War, and point decisively to an earlier date.'

[2] Ropes (*op. cit.*, p. 41), who rejects the traditional view, nevertheless recognizes that the conditions of life indicated in the Epistle need not imply a long lapse since the formation of the churches.

ciation of idolatry, both of which would have been inappropriate in
an epistle attributed to such a devoted Jewish Christian as James.[1]

c. Arguments against the traditional view

In spite of the strong tradition, which appears to have early roots, and
the many indications from internal data which support the tradition
that James, the Lord's brother, was the author, there is a strong body
of opinion which rejects this view. The grounds of these objections
will now be considered.

(i) *The Greek is too good for a Galilaean peasant.* The style of Greek is
generally good and cultured and this fact has been regarded as conclusive against the traditional view. Thus Dibelius makes the categorical statement, 'The style is frequently cultured, the Greek vocabulary
large, the entire diction not that of a man whose real language was
Aramaic.'[2] While admitting the good quality of the Greek, which has
been pronounced by competent authorities to be among the best in
the New Testament,[3] some modifications are necessary. Oesterley[4] has
drawn attention to some indications of a Hebrew background to the
language, while Ropes[5] admitted that the language was Koiné with a
biblical tinge. Rendall[6] went so far as to maintain with some cogency
that the author's hand 'is not that of a skilled or practised writer, with
easy command of his resources or his pen'.

With these modifications regarding the Greek style, the fact still
remains that it is paradoxical that one of the most Jewish letters in the
New Testament should have been written by an author apparently so
much at home in the Greek language, and some sympathy must be felt
for the objection that a Galilaean could not have acquired such facility,

---

[1] Cf. on this point, Knowling, *op. cit.*, pp. xii, xiii.

[2] *A Fresh Approach to the New Testament and Early Christian Literature* (1937),
pp. 229, 230.

[3] Cf. J. H. Moulton and W. F. Howard, *A Grammar of New Testament Greek*, II
(1929), p. 27.

[4] *Op. cit.*, pp. 393–397. Cf. also A. Wikenhauser, *New Testament Introduction*,
p. 483.

[5] *Op. cit.*, pp. 24f. A. Wifstrand (*Studia Theologica*, II, 1948, pp. 170–182) considers the language to be that of the hellenized synagogue.

[6] *Op. cit.*, p. 34. In his chapter on 'Form, Style and Composition', Rendall
maintained that these indications are fully in keeping with what we know of
James.

since his native tongue was Aramaic.[1] Yet this appears to be largely an *a priori* argument. It clearly can neither be proved nor disproved that James, a Galilaean, was incapable of writing this Epistle. It has been maintained that there was nothing to induce James to learn Greek since all his dealings appear to have been with Jewish Christians.[2] But this opinion takes insufficient account of the known bilingual character of Galilee.[3] There were many Greek towns in that district, and because of this it must surely be assumed that it was in the power of any Galilaean to gain a knowledge of Greek.[4] If *a priori* arguments are to be used, it would be more reasonable to assume that James was bilingual than the reverse.

Yet the problem still remains whether a peasant could have acquired sufficient education to write the type of Greek found in the Epistle, even supposing him to have been bilingual from early years.[5] Rendall answered emphatically in the affirmative, maintaining that the Jewish people were the most literary of all the Mediterranean nations and citing the LXX as evidence of the Jewish adoption of Hellenism.[6] Oesterley[7] on the other hand admitted the possibility of such learning, but denied the probability. The question cannot be decided conclusively on *a priori* suppositions. But one consideration would appear to tip the balance in favour of James being bilingual, and that is his position as leader of the Jerusalem church. Constant travellers to and from Jerusalem would bring him in touch with people from various parts[8]

[1] McNeile-Williams (*INT*, p. 205) put it too strongly when they say, 'Anyone who knew the early conditions knew that St. James could not have written the Epistle in its Greek shape and yet it gradually acquired "apostolic" repute.' This assumes that those responsible for its 'apostolic' status must have been entirely ignorant of the early conditions, in spite of the fact that most of them were Greek speaking.

[2] So Oesterley, *op. cit.*, p. 400.

[3] Moffatt (*ILNT*, p. 474) cites J. Hadley, *Essays Philological and Critical* (1873), pp. 403f., as the best statement of the case known to him. Cf. also Zahn, *INT*, 1 (1909), pp. 34–72; J. H. Moulton, *A Grammar of New Testament Greek*, 1 (1908), pp. 6ff.; and more recently S. Liebermann, *Hellenism in Jewish Palestine* (1950), pp. 100ff.

[4] J. B. Mayor, *op. cit.*, p. ccxxxvi. A. T. Cadoux's comparison with Burns' mastery of English is not an exact parallel, but is, at least, suggestive (*The Thought of S. James*, 1944, p. 37).

[5] Cf. E. Lohse, *ZNTW*, 47 (1956), pp. 19, 20.

[6] *Op. cit.*, p. 39.*   [7] *Op. cit.*, p. 399.

[8] Cf. R. V. G. Tasker, *op. cit.*, p. 29; A. Ross, *The Epistles of James and John* (1954), p. 19.

and the majority of them would undoubtedly be Greek speaking. It may even be argued with some cogency that opportunities for public speaking and debate would develop in him some mastery of the rhetorical style such as vivid illustrations and rhetorical questions.[1] Again there is a reasonable possibility that James may have employed a Greek amanuensis.[2] On the whole, it would seem that not much importance should be attached to the objections based on language and it is significant that most weight is now placed on other considerations.[3]

(ii) *The author does not claim to be the Lord's brother.* It has been maintained that James would surely have described himself in this way in order to add to the authority with which the Epistle would go out to Jewish Christians.[4] But this type of argument is not as valid as at first appears. For the apostle Paul recognized that knowledge of Jesus Christ in the flesh was no longer important (2 Cor. v. 16) and the same consideration would lead the Lord's kinsmen to refrain from claiming any advantages due to family ties with Him. Oesterley[5] imagined that this argument was weakened by the mention in John xix. 25–27 of our Lord's concern for His mother, but the parallel is not obvious. Our Lord's reference to His mother was due to compassion, but a very different motive would have operated if James had mentioned his relationship. His reference to himself as a 'servant' is far more becoming.

(iii) *The author makes no reference to the great events of our Lord's life.* Particularly surprising is the omission of any reference to the death or resurrection of Jesus.[6] Since James is specially mentioned by Paul as a witness of the risen Christ (1 Cor. xv. 7), it might reasonably be expected

[1] Cf. Tasker, *loc. cit.*

[2] G. Kittel (*ZNTW*, 43, 1950–51, p. 79) suggested that James wrote through a Hellenistic Jewish Christian belonging to the primitive Church, possibly from the Stephen circle.*

[3] E. C. Blackman (*op. cit.*, p. 26) mentions the excellence of the Greek as a difficulty, but does not discuss. J. H. Ropes (*op. cit.*) laid no weight upon it. But M. Dibelius (*Der Brief des Jakobus*,[10] 1958, pp. 15f.) regarded the Greek as a conclusive objection to an author brought up as a Jew in Palestine.

[4] So Oesterley (*op. cit.*, p. 397), who argues that, for the Dispersion Jews, the more authoritative the author the more effective the letter.

[5] *Ibid.*

[6] On the absence of reference to Christ's death, cf. Ropes, *op. cit.*, p. 33; and on the resurrection, Oesterley, *op. cit.*, p. 398. McNeile-Williams (*INT*, pp. 203, 204) find this a particular difficulty, for they note the absence of the 'personal spell' of Jesus upon the author.

that this event would have made so deep an impression on his mind that he could not have written an epistle of this kind without reference to it. The relevance of this argument must at once be admitted, but there are certain considerations which considerably lessen its weight. In the epistle ascribed to James in Acts xv, there is no reference to any theological tenet, but that letter was sent for a more restricted purpose than this and the parallel is, therefore, somewhat loose. At the same time it is easy to assume that in every Christian communication the great Christian doctrines must appear, without examining sufficiently the basis for this assumption. The author, in this case, obviously assumes his readers' cognizance with these doctrines, otherwise he would have made a point of mentioning them.[1] But the real problem is whether an early Christian writer like James would ever have made such an assumption when writing a general circular.

To explain this phenomenon, reference must be made to the purpose of the letter, which may fairly simply be described as ethical and not doctrinal. It may of course be maintained that for the Christian Church doctrine and practical exhortation are inseparable, but it must be remembered that this view of the matter is drawn mostly from Paul. It is not absolutely certain that all moral exhortations were invariably backed by theological considerations, although it is unquestionable that the dynamic for behaviour proceeded from the Christian's experience of Christ. A fair conclusion of this matter would be that, although it might have been expected that James would have mentioned the death and resurrection of Jesus in his ethical Epistle, it cannot be said to be entirely incomprehensible for him not to have done so.

(iv) *The conception of the law in this Epistle is said to differ from what might be expected from James.* It has been maintained that James' conception of law may be summarized as moral law, whereas from Acts and Galatians we are led to expect that the law for him would involve ritual as well as moral requirements.[2] There is a curious silence regarding the burning question of circumcision with which James was so deeply involved. Yet this will be an embarrassment only if the Epistle is dated during the intensity of the conflict. If the Epistle is dated before the Apos-

---

[1] Unless, of course, he was ignorant of them, but this is highly improbable.

[2] Cf. Blackman, *op. cit.*, pp. 25f. O. Cone ('James (Epistle)', *Enc. Bib.*, 1914, col. 2322) thought that it was very improbable that a writer to Jewish Christians would so entirely ignore the Mosaic law and ritual, but his argument is not self-evident if James' purpose was wholly ethical.

tolic Council (see discussion below), it is not surprising that circumcision is not mentioned, for until then it seems to have been taken for granted.[1] The picture of James drawn from Acts and Galatians is naturally influenced by the conflict over Hellenistic Christianity, but it must be remembered that in both sources James is represented as a leader of conciliatory action and by no means as a bigot for Jewish ritualistic demands. That James' position was misrepresented in tradition is not surprising since Peter's clash with Paul seems to have been occasioned by 'certain men from James' (Gal. ii. 12), and it is not altogether improbable that these men were more zealous for legal observances than their leader. Even in the account of Paul's meeting with James in Acts xxi. 18ff., James suggests the vow, not on the grounds of strong personal conviction, but because of avoiding offence among the many thousands of Jews who had become Christians. It was a matter of expediency.

In view of this it should occasion no surprise that James does not raise the matter in an epistle which is almost wholly ethical. Moreover, the approach of James to the moral law is closely linked to the teaching of Jesus on the same theme. It is precisely the type of ethical instruction to be expected from a Jewish Christian about the mid-first century, especially from a man so closely acquainted with the moral teaching of Jesus as James must have been.[2]

(v) *The author's relation to other New Testament books is said to be unfavourable to James, the Lord's brother.* There are parallels between this Epistle and some of Paul's Epistles (1 Corinthians, Galatians, Romans)[3] and 1 Peter. Only those who maintain literary dependence on the part of the author of this Epistle find difficulty here over the authorship, mainly on the grounds of dating, on the assumption that James must be considerably later than the Epistles he is citing, particularly if the Pauline Corpus

[1] K. Aland (*op. cit.*, p. 100) considers that the absence of ritualism from a Jewish Christian before the mid-first century is unthinkable. But the omission of allusions to it need not mean that James has dispensed with it entirely.

[2] Cf. Feine-Behm, *op. cit.*, p. 244. It is interesting to note that earlier critics of authenticity often based their late dating of James on the mistaken grounds that it presents Christianity as a *nova lex* (cf. Knowling's criticisms, *op. cit.*, p. lxii).

[3] Cf. J. Moffatt, *ILNT*, p. 466; W. Sanday and A. C. Headlam, *The Epistle to the Romans* (1895), p. lxxviii. J. B. Mayor (*op. cit.*, p. lxxxix) also adds some parallels with 1 Thessalonians, 2 Corinthians, Philippians, Colossians, Ephesians, and the Pastorals.

of letters is already in existence. In the case of Paul, the most notable parallel is the faith versus works debate and much will clearly depend on whether Paul corrects James (or a misunderstanding of him) or vice versa. Many notable names may be cited in support of both these possibilities, for the whole subject has been very thoroughly discussed.[1] It is both impossible and unnecessary to repeat the main points of the discussion, but, on the whole, probability favours rather more the view that Paul is acquainted with a perversion of the kind of teaching proposed by James than that James is safeguarding against a perversion of Paul. If this view is correct, any objection to James' authorship would at once be removed, but since the alternative is not impossible, it needs to be considered whether such a viewpoint must exclude the possibility of James' authorship.

There are no sure grounds for supposing that James could not have known Paul's teaching on faith as the sole means of salvation, nor even that he could not have been acquainted with the Epistle to the Romans. The data available do not allow any such conclusion to be reached. The same may be said of allusions to other Pauline Epistles, although, if James' dependence on these could be established, it would support a later date for James and make authorship by the Lord's brother more difficult.

In short, the arguments based on literary dependence are really arguments which are assumed to prove a late date and would support the assignment of the Epistle to the sub-apostolic period. A case in point is the alleged dependence of James on 1 Peter, which, if established, would make an early date for James difficult to maintain on the basis of the authenticity of 1 Peter. But it would naturally be impossible for those who hold to the non-apostolic authorship of Peter to maintain the apostolic authorship of James. The dependence of James on 1 Peter is by no means certain, but there are undoubtedly several parallels as the following will show:

James i. 1; 1 Peter i. 1	James iii. 13; 1 Peter iii. 2, 4
James i. 2f.; 1 Peter i. 6f.	James iv. 1; 1 Peter ii. 11
James i. 12; 1 Peter v. 4	James iv. 6f.; 1 Peter v. 5f.
James i. 18; 1 Peter i. 23	James iv. 10; 1 Peter v. 6.
James i. 21; 1 Peter ii. 1f.	

---

[1] For details of some representative treatments, see p. 765 n.1.

But although the majority of scholars favour the priority of 1 Peter,[1] some, such as J. B. Mayor,[2] argue strongly for the reverse, while yet others, such as J. H. Ropes,[3] prefer to appeal to a common spiritual atmosphere.

It is better not to depend on arguments based on literary use of other Epistles in cases where the evidence leaves room for wide variations of opinion, and little real weight can, therefore, be put on the objection under consideration.[4] The same may be said regarding parallels with *Clement* and *Hermas*, but in these cases probability is certainly more on the side of the priority of James than vice versa, as has already been seen.[5] The theory that James is based almost wholly on secondary material is highly questionable[6] and even if it be held that James echoes other New Testament books, the most that could be supposed with certainty is that the author possessed a mind receptive of common Christian ideas. It would help very little in deciding the question of authorship.

(vi) *The external evidence is said to raise suspicions against the tradition.* This objection has been left until last, although it is invariably the jumping-off ground for criticism of the tradition. But it has already been discussed and some plausible explanations of the tardy reception of the Epistle suggested (see p. 739). Because of this, the argument cannot be considered conclusive either way, like so many of the other details, although it would naturally carry weight if the cumulative effect of other evidence should be felt to point towards non-authenticity.

d. Alternative theories regarding the origin of the Epistle

Some account must now be given of the ideas advanced by those who dispute the traditional ascription of the Epistle. There are six different theories which come to our notice.

(i) *That the Epistle is pseudonymous.* It has been proposed that the ascription to James is a literary device used by the original writer, who

---

[1] Cf. Moffatt, *ILNT*, p. 338; McNeile-Williams, *INT*, p. 211.

[2] *Op. cit.*, pp. xcviii f. Cf. R. J. Knowling (*op. cit.*, p. xlvi) and F. Spitta (*Der Jakobbrief*, in *Zur Geschichte und Literatur des Urchristentums*, II, 1896, pp. 183–202), who even suggested that 1 Peter has used James as a model.

[3] *Op. cit.*, p. 22. Many scholars, not surprisingly, admit uncertainty about the relationship.

[4] Mayor (*op. cit.*, p. xciii) suggested that Heb. xi was written with the Epistle of James in mind, and if this view is correct it would support an early date.

[5] See p. 738.   [6] As T. Henshaw, *op. cit.*, pp. 352ff., appears to hold.

was an unknown teacher of the sub-apostolic age. In support of this the widespread practice of using pseudonymous ascriptions in the early Christian period is usually appealed to, or else the unknown writer is supposed to have had the same relation to James as had the author of Mark's Gospel to Peter.[1] The former alternative is defective because of the lack of any close epistolary parallels,[2] while the latter may be questioned as an inaccurate analogy. Mark's connection with Peter is well attested and his position as 'interpreter' unquestionable, but even so his work was not issued under Peter's pseudonym, nor was it ever later ascribed to him. The most damaging criticism of this kind of theory lies in the simplicity of the description of the author and in the lack of an adequate motive. Had the real author wished to indicate beyond dispute that he was interpreting or recording the actual teaching of James, the Lord's brother, why did he leave the title so ambiguous? Ropes[3] attempted an answer by supposing that during the first and second centuries a letter in the name of James would seem to the Christian public to be claiming the authority of the great James, and no further identity would, therefore, be needed. But it was not the usual practice of pseudonymous writers to play down their heroes—rather the reverse.[4]

The absence of motive for a pseudonymous production such as James is a strong argument against it. If the letter is merely a moralizing tract, why did it need James' authority and why should he be chosen?[5]

[1] So McNeile-Williams, *INT*, p. 205: 'If he was the "interpreter" of St. James it is easy to understand how the latter's name was adopted by the writer.'

[2] See pp. 671 ff. Cf. also the present writer's article on the general dilemma confronting hypotheses of pseudonymity in *Vox Evangelica*, 1 (ed. R. P. Martin, 1962).

[3] *Op. cit.*, p. 51.

[4] Rendall (*op. cit.*, p. 106) argued against the pseudonymous theory on the grounds that no-one would have issued an epistle under James' name unless he was already known as a letter-writer. Knowling (*op. cit.*, p. xxiv) cites a spurious epistle which commenced, 'James, bishop of Jerusalem'. J. Marty (*L'Epître de Jacques*, 1935, p. 249), who upheld the pseudonymity theory, explained the absence of any other identification allusions by appealing to the paraenetic nature of the contents (as in the *Epistle of Barnabas*).

[5] A. T. Cadoux rightly mentioned that James' name would not have retained interest among Gentiles for long and this must constitute a difficulty for any pseudonymity theory (*op. cit.*, p. 38). The best that H. von Soden could suggest was that the author may have known and venerated James, the Lord's brother, or perhaps the orthodox had to reclaim James from the Ebionite appeal to his authority (*JPTh*, 10, 1884, p. 192).

And if James intends to oppose Paul, why is there no greater stress on his authority?

(ii) *That the Epistle was an anonymous production later attributed to James.* To avoid the difficulties of an intentional pseudonymity, some scholars have proposed that the attribution to James belongs to a later stage in the history of the Epistle.[1] While this theory is more conceivable than the theory of pure pseudonymity, it avoids few of the difficulties of the latter, and creates new difficulties of its own. It now becomes necessary to account for the ascription. The best that can be done is to imagine that certain Christians thought the anonymous tract was of such value that the Church ought to class it among its apostolic books and the only way possible was to attach to it an apostolic name. But this whole theory is highly artificial, for it is difficult to believe that the churches generally would have been prepared to receive a work merely because it bore a name which could be apostolic. In the period when spurious apostolic works began to be prolific, particularly in support of Gnostic ideas, the vigilance of the Church was much too intense to allow such a work as James to slip through its net. The mere fact that doubts were expressed over James in the third century is evidence enough that many were very guarded about the books to be authorized.

(iii) *That the Epistle was by some other 'James'.* This is closely akin to the last, but rather more plausible. James was a common name and it might well have happened that some later James wrote the Epistle and that he was subsequently mistaken for James of Jerusalem. This theory was mooted by Erasmus[2] and has been maintained by many since.[3] But the absence of any early evidence for it seems distinctly unfavourable to it. An unknown writer, whose name was James, would surely have realized that his readers would confuse him with the well-known James and, unless he intended such confusion, would have given more specific description of his own identity. This type of theory does not carry with it much conviction.

---

[1] For instance A. C. McGiffert, *A History of Christianity in the Apostolic Age* (1897), p. 585. He thought the form of ascription was influenced by Jude. L. E. Elliott-Binns (*Galilean Christianity*, 1956, pp. 47ff.) maintains this type of theory although claiming a very early date for the Epistle. He thinks that the ascription was added in Jewish Christian and Ebionite quarters to exalt James at Peter's expense.

[2] Cited by Moffatt, *ILNT*, p. 472.

[3] A modern treatment of this view may be found in D. W. Riddle and H. H. Hutson's *New Testament Life and Literature* (1946), pp. 198ff.

(iv) *That the Epistle was originally a Jewish document.* Because of the strong Jewish background of the Epistle, it has been maintained by F. Spitta[1] and L. Massebieau[2] that the major part of the letter is pre-Christian. A later author has Christianized this material by the addition of the name of Christ in i. 1 and ii. 1. But this theory may be criticized on the following grounds:

1. It is incredible that the Christianizing process would have been confined to such meagre modifications and, in any case, the text in both these instances does not lead us to suppose an interpolation.[3]

2. It is a forcing of the evidence to maintain, as Spitta does, that it is more reasonable to find the antecedents of James' teaching in Jewish moral teaching than in the Sermon on the Mount. As Mayor[4] has cogently pointed out, in most of Spitta's parallels the Jewish material shows far less resemblance to James than the Christian material, but the reverse would be necessary if Spitta's theory were right.

3. The Epistle is not marked by distinctively Jewish teaching. In other words it does not require a non-Christian Jew as its author. A Jewish Christian could quite well have written it and there is, therefore, no evidence to support the theory of pre-Christian origin.

4. The whole Epistle breathes a Christian spirit, in spite of the absence of specific Christian doctrine. Had Spitta given more attention to this, he would not have conceived an interpolator who was content with two brief insertions.

Many scholars who have not shared Spitta's viewpoint have nevertheless been indebted to him for drawing attention to the Jewish background of James' thought.

(v) *That the Epistle was patterned on the twelve patriarchs.* This is the theory proposed by Arnold Meyer.[5] The idea is that an earlier author had produced an allegory on Jacob's farewell address to his twelve sons

---

[1] *Op. cit.,* pp. 1ff.

[2] 'L'Epître de Jacques, est-elle l'oeuvre d'un Chrétien?' in *RHR* (1895), pp. 249–283. *N.B.* More recently M. E. Boismard (*RB,* LXIV, 1957, p. 176n.) writes rather favourably of a Jewish origin. He maintains that in this letter Κύριος always refers to God, not Christ.

[3] Cf. Ropes, *op. cit.,* p. 32; and Tasker, *op. cit.,* p. 34.   [4] *Op. cit.,* pp. clxxv ff.

[5] *Das Rätsel des Jakobusbriefes* (1930). Cf. also W. K. Lowther Clarke's comparison of James with the *Testament of the XII Patriarchs, Concise Bible Commentary* (1952), pp. 914, 915. H. Thyen (*Der Stil der jüdisch-hellenistischen Homilie,* 1955 pp. 14–16), who favours Meyer's view, supposes that a Jew has summarized a synagogue homily on the theme of Jacob's address to his sons.

and that this has been adapted for Christian purposes. The ascription to James is traced to 'Jacob', who addresses the twelve tribes. The moral teaching of the Epistle is then connected with the various patriarchs. One or two examples will illustrate. The theme of joy (i. 2) is connected with Isaac, patience (i. 3, 4) with Rebecca, the passage on hearing (i. 19–24) with Simeon. These connections of thought are not only generally far from obvious, but in most cases so extremely subtle that the point of them would never be conceived by any but devotees of the allegorical method.

Ingenious as the theory is, its very ingenuity is its greatest barrier. As Tasker[1] aptly remarks, 'At least we might have expected that the author would have given his readers some clue as to what he was really doing; and how strange it is that Christendom should have had to wait so long for the key to the understanding of his purpose!' There are far easier ways to account for the ascription to James than this connection with Jacob, and it would be wiser to leave allegory alone when attempting to discover the origin of the Epistle, unless there is some indisputable indication that it was intended so to be understood. But such certain hints are lacking.[2] Moreover, it would be strange indeed to discover allusions to Job and Elijah in a testament of Jacob, although such anachronistic lapses are not entirely unknown in Jewish pseudepigrapha.[3] But it is not to be expected in such a writing as this Epistle, which does not look ahead as all the Jewish apocalypses did.

(vi) *That the Epistle incorporates some genuine material.* An attempt to mediate between the traditional view and the various alternatives so far outlined is found in the idea that an editor has worked over, adapted and added to an original core of genuine material. The genuine core may have been either written or oral, and perhaps consisted of some homily (or homilies) of James, the Lord's brother, which had made an impression upon the editor's mind.[4]

[1] *Op. cit.*, p. 36.

[2] Blackman (*op. cit.*, p. 29), who does not find Meyer's theory convincing, nevertheless considers it a merit that it attempts to indicate a unity in James. But it is hardly a merit if the unity proposed is an artificial one.

[3] Marty (*op. cit.*, p. 255 n.) cites as a parallel the *Testament of Adam* in which David and Judas Maccabaeus are mentioned.

[4] Cf. Rendall (*op. cit.*, p. 33) for one presentation of this type of theory, although it should be noted that he does not fully commit himself on the question of whether James himself or a reporter penned the Epistle.

W. Bieder (*ThZ*, v, 1949, p. 94 n. 2) inclines to a similar view. A more thorough-

This type of theory has many advantages over the previously mentioned proposals, for it can account both for the somewhat disjointed character of the contents and for the tradition connecting the Epistle with James, the Lord's brother. But it cannot adequately account for the adaptation of the material into a letter-form. It is, of course, conceivable that someone recognized the general value of James' homilies and was prompted, therefore, to edit them into a kind of circular under the name of James who, after all, was the true author of the material used. But a thing is not true because it is conceivable, but because the evidence requires it, and this can hardly be said in this case. If the editor was working under the supervision of James himself, this would amount almost to the traditional view. But if he is editing some time later than James' lifetime[1] the problem of motive becomes acute, for why a later editor should suddenly have conceived such a publication plan when the great majority of the intended readers must have known that James was already dead is difficult to see, and it is even more difficult to understand how the letter came to be received. If some real connection with James would have been generally recognized, why the need for this theory at all, since it would possess no advantage over the traditional view? It would furnish no better explanation for the tardiness of recognition among the Church's orthodox writers.

e. Conclusion

It would seem preferable to incline to the traditional view on the principle that the tradition has a right to stand until proved wrong. Although some of the arguments for alternative views are strong, yet none of these views has any better claim to credibility than the tradition. In these circumstances the authorship of James, the Lord's brother, must still be considered more probable than any rival.*

II. THE ADDRESSEES

During the course of the discussion on authorship, many other questions have been partially answered, and this is one of them. Not only

going editorial theory is advanced by Oesterley, *op. cit.*, p. 405. Cf. also C. M. Edsman (*ZNTW*, 38, 1939, pp. 11–44), who suggested that the author has taken over and combined disparate material, much of it of a Hellenistic provenance (he cites parallels from the Hermetic literature and Clement and Origen of Alexandria). But a Jewish basis is much more probable (cf. L. E. Elliott-Binns, *NTS*, 3, 1957, pp. 148–161, on the background of Jas. i. 18).

[1] So Oesterley, *op. cit.* His tentative suggestion was that a genuine text of James was enlarged by a process of comments upon it.

does the Epistle presuppose an author with a Jewish background, but also readers with the same background. Yet on this latter point some considerable caution must be exercised, for wide differences of opinion exist. There are several possibilities: that the readers were unconverted Jews, or else Christian Jews, or else Hellenists, or else Christians generally, both Jew and Gentile. The most probable of these can be decided only from a discussion of the address of the letter and the circumstances of the readers.

a. The meaning of Diaspora in i. 1

At first sight 'the twelve tribes in the dispersion' (RSV) would seem to point fairly conclusively to Jews. Such an interpretation would be in full accord with the technical Jewish use of the term to describe those of their number living outside Palestine. In this case the addressees would be Jewish Christians scattered throughout the Empire. This interpretation would, of course, fit in well with authorship by James of Jerusalem, and is, in fact, the traditional interpretation.

Yet since in 1 Peter it is necessary to attach a spiritual and not a literal meaning to 'dispersion' (see discussion on pp. 794f.), is it not reasonable to suppose a similar interpretation here? The idea of the Christian Church as the new Israel would make a strong appeal to the early Christians and would arise naturally out of the conviction that the Christian teaching was a continuation of the Old Testament.[1] Moreover it has been pointed out that the twelve tribal divisions of Israel had long since disappeared and must, therefore, be understood metaphorically.[2] But caution must enter here in view of Acts xxvi. 7 and Matthew xix. 28, where the twelve tribes would seem to describe the Jewish people. The difficulty is to decide whether James and 1 Peter both mean the same thing by the word 'dispersion'. While it would be more natural to suppose that they do, it need not necessarily follow, for, unlike James, 1 Peter makes no mention of the twelve tribes. That the idea of a Christian Diaspora was current seems undeniable, but that James thought of it in this sense is not beyond challenge. What other factors, therefore, may be deduced to settle the matter?

---

[1] J. H. Ropes (op. cit., p. 40) interpreted the word as a reference to the dispersion of Christians generally. So also Moffatt, ILNT, p. 464; Marty, op. cit., ad loc. J. Schneider (Die Kirchenbriefe, NTD, 1961, pp. 3, 4) understands the addressees as Jewish Christians outside Palestine who came under James' jurisdiction.

[2] Cf. E. F. Scott, The Literature of the New Testament (1932), p. 211.

b. The circumstances of the readers

The regular meeting-place of the addressees is styled a 'synagogue' (ii. 2) and this at once suggests Jewish Christian groups.[1] The view that Jews and not Christians are being addressed has already been discussed and dismissed, but it is difficult to avoid the impression that the Christians have a Jewish background. James mentions nothing about Christ as Messiah, but this seems to be assumed. Nor does he mention circumcision, which, as already pointed out, would be understandable if the readers were Jewish and the letter was sent before the Council of Jerusalem. Even if sent later, the omission of any reference to circumcision would certainly favour a Jewish, rather than a mixed Jewish-Gentile, group of Christians, unless, of course, the Epistle were dated so late that the controversy was by then forgotten.

It would seem from this Epistle that the believers were mainly poor. The allusions to the rich are more intelligible if these were unbelievers who were on the fringe of the church and were taking advantage of their wealth and influence to intimidate the poor Christians.[2] At the same time rich men must at times have attended the Christian synagogues, otherwise the discussion in chapter ii would not be relevant.

Little is said about church organization, but two allusions are significant. Elders are referred to in v. 14, 15, although in connection with faith healing, not church rule. There also appears to have been a group of people known as teachers (cf. iii. 1), whose duties may have overlapped, but were distinct from, those of the elders. Nevertheless the reference may have nothing to do with a teacher's office, but may merely allude to the process of teaching.

The Christians were people of weak faith, who needed strong exhortations to more consistent Christian living, which accounts for the ethical content of the Epistle. It cannot be denied that the general outlook of the believers was immature, as must often have happened in the primitive period both among Jews and Gentiles. This theory of Jewish Christian immaturity is supported by the apparent zealousness for the law coupled with a failure to practise it (cf. i. 22ff., ii. 8ff.). They had in fact brought into the church many of the failings of Judaism.

---

[1] H. von Soden (*JPTh*, 10, 1884, p. 179) maintained that this word was widespread in the Greek world for gatherings. But the Jewish sense is more natural.

[2] Mayor (*op. cit.*, p. cxvi) considered that oppression by the rich is more intelligible for a Jewish community than a Gentile.

To sum up, it seems better to regard the letter as addressed to Jewish Christians, but the alternative view that Christians generally may be in mind has much to be said for it.[1] (See the discussion on the destination of 1 Peter, pp. 792ff.)

III. DATE

It is obvious that decisions about the authorship will affect opinions about the date. The alternatives are easily stated. If the Epistle was by James, the Lord's brother, it must have been before AD 62,[2] the most likely date for his martyrdom, whereas if some other author wrote it, the only certain fact is that it must have been produced after an interval of some years from James' death. But within each of these alternatives there is room for difference of opinion. Advocates of the traditional authorship may be subdivided into two groups in respect of dating: those who prefer a date before AD 50[3] and those who date it towards the end of James' life.[4] Those who take any other view of authorship vary between late first century and late second century, the majority preferring a date about AD 125. With such wide variation in the results of different investigations, it must be expected that the processes by which these results are attained will in themselves prove somewhat inconclusive. The main evidence appealed to in discussions of dating is as follows:

a. The absence of reference to the fall of Jerusalem

This is naturally a pivotal point in any chronology affecting Jewish people. It has been maintained[5] that any author writing after the event must have made some allusion to it, but this may be questioned on the ground that Christians were not as deeply affected by it as were

---

[1] Von Soden (loc. cit.) argued that none of the references which appear to indicate Jews can be considered conclusive, since similar evidence would result in the readers of Paul's letters to the Galatians, Corinthians and Romans being declared Jewish.

[2] According to Josephus (Antiquities, xx. 9. 1), although Hegesippus less probably has AD 68 (cf. Eusebius, HE, ii. 23. 18).

[3] Recently by G. Kittel, ZNTW, 41 (1942), following Zahn and Schlatter; H. C. Thiessen, INT, p. 278 (AD 45–48); and A. Ross, op. cit., p. 20. Earlier by J. B. Mayor, op. cit., pp. cxxi ff.; and J. V. Bartlet, The Apostolic Age (1907), pp. 203ff.

[4] The majority of those accepting authorship by the Lord's brother.

[5] So J. B. Mayor, op. cit., p. cxxii.

non-Christian Jews. Nevertheless a Christian Jewish writer (and particularly a Palestinian writer) could hardly have remained entirely unaffected.

In further support of this contention, it may be said that the social conditions reflected in the Epistle distinctly favour a date prior to the siege, after which landowning Palestinian Jews virtually ceased to exist.[1] If the addressees were farther afield this factor would not be so relevant, but even then some reference to the siege might be expected if Jews were being addressed.

b. The absence of reference to the Jewish-Gentile controversy

The author either intentionally ignores this or else is unaware of it and both are inconceivable after it had become a burning issue. This consideration not only favours a date before the fall of Jerusalem, but before the rise of the controversy (i.e. before AD 50). This is admittedly an argument from silence[2] and a perfectly natural explanation might be possible if more data were available. If, for instance, some community were addressed that was exclusively Jewish Christian, the Gentile problem would not yet have arisen. Nevertheless, such a circumstance could hardly be postponed long after the Jerusalem Council.

c. The primitive character of church order

This has already been mentioned above (see p. 760) and it is necessary here to do no more than draw attention to the fact that this favours an early dating. It would support a date within James' lifetime better than a later period.

d. The Jewish tone of the letter

This again has already been discussed. It was used as an argument for an early date by J. B. Mayor,[3] who maintained that it pointed to the earliest possible date after Pentecost. It would certainly be more natural in an early letter and to this extent may be cited in support of a date before AD 50, although it need not exclude a date in the seventh decade.

e. The state of the Christians

The addressees do not appear to be very recent converts. Indeed the condition of the Christians has been thought to point to a date much

---

[1] Cf. Rendall, op. cit., p. 32.　　[2] Cf. Tasker, op. cit., p. 31.　　[3] Op. cit., pp. cxxiv f.

later than James' lifetime, because the Church has been invaded to such an extent by worldliness.[1] There is, however, bound to be a large subjective element entering into any assessment of this kind of evidence. It has not been unknown for churches to develop the kind of errors to which James alludes after a very brief history and this consideration can really lead us nowhere in determining chronological questions.[2] Moreover, as pointed out already (see pp. 760f.), the social conditions within the community favour an early rather than a late date.

f. Exposure of Christians to persecution

This may at first sight exclude the earliest date mentioned and may, in fact, seem to point to a second-century date (i.e. during Trajan's persecution). But the allusions in the Epistle do not require anything different from the persecution which followed Stephen's death, and the conditions which prompted that Jewish hostility must often have been repeated. Clearly this is another factor that can help little in fixing the date.

g. The relation to other New Testament letters

Here again differences of opinion over the order of priority of James, Paul's Epistles and 1 Peter in particular almost entirely cancel out literary affinities as useful data in fixing the period of publication. If James is used by Paul and Peter, an early date is clearly demanded, but if James is the user, an early date is almost as certainly excluded.[3] In fact it could be argued that time would be needed for copies of Paul's Epistles and 1 Peter to reach James. In cases like this any decisions are almost bound to be influenced by prior considerations and can contribute very little on their own merit. It can safely be said that nothing in the parallels with other New Testament books excludes the possibility of a date within James' lifetime, although the evidence might be used in theories of later dating.

h. The relation to the Apostolic Fathers

Some resemblances between James and 1 Clement may be cited as throwing light on dating. The latter appears to cite the former,[4] but

---

[1] Cf. E. F. Scott, op. cit., p. 211.

[2] Mayor (op. cit., p. cxxviii) used as a parallel the fact that faults seem to have existed in most of the primitive churches.

[3] Cf. McNeile-Williams, INT, p. 211.   [4] So Rendall, op. cit., p. 102.

many scholars who date James in Hadrian's reign naturally cannot agree to this order of dependence.[1] Presuppositions again influence decisions and the same may be said of the relation of James to the *Shepherd of Hermas*, although the majority of scholars would agree that James is prior to *Hermas*.[2] It is significant, therefore, that *Hermas* may well be citing James, in which case this would be evidence for the circulation of James in the early second century and for its origin long before *Hermas*. It supplies a further indication of a first-century date.[3]

i. Conclusion

The general drift of these considerations is more in the direction of an early date than a later one and this accords with what has already been said on the subject of authorship. But it is less easy to decide between AD 50 and AD 62 as to the most likely early date. The former has much to be said for it and is probably to be preferred.

IV. PURPOSE

Since there is so little evidence about the precise circumstances of the readers, it is not easy to arrive at any definite conclusion regarding the purpose. One thing, however, is clear. The Epistle is essentially practical and would appear to be designed to correct certain known tendencies in behaviour. Such problems as the true attitude to wealth, the control of the tongue, the approach to oaths, Christian prayer and other practical themes are discussed. They appear to come out of the author's own pastoral experience.*

But what light does the faith versus works passage (Jas. ii) throw on the author's purpose? This has already been touched upon above (p. 752) and the suggestion made that Paul in his approach to the matter is counteracting a misunderstanding of James and, if this is correct, it must be clearly understood that James is exposing the fallacy of a dead orthodoxy, i.e. a piety in which profession produces no results. If, on the other hand, James is subsequent to Paul, various other

---

[1] Cf. McNeile-Williams, *op. cit.*, p. 212. Cf. also F. W. Young, *JBL*, LXVII (1948), pp. 339–345.

[2] Cf. Moffatt's discussion, *ILNT*, p. 467. Dibelius (*A Fresh Approach to the New Testament and Early Christian Literature*, 1937, pp. 226f.) classes James in the same literary *genre* as Hermas. Cf. also Knowling, *op. cit.*, pp. 1ff.

[3] A very full survey of the relation of James to the Apostolic Fathers will be found in the article of G. Kittel, *ZNTW*, 43 (1950–51), pp. 55–112.

considerations enter into his purpose. Either James writes to counteract a misunderstanding of Paul on the part of some Christians or else he writes independently of Paul and happens to touch upon a matter of burning importance with which Paul had also had to deal.[1] The former encounters difficulties, since James' treatment would not adequately clarify Paul's own teaching. There is, for instance, no reference to the 'works of the law', which would be of special interest to any Jewish Christians affected by Paul's teaching. The second view is possible and should not lightly be dismissed, but some sort of acquaintance of one with the other's teaching would almost be expected, particularly since both Galatians and Acts point to the association of the two men.

Another theory which has recently come to the fore is that James has an anti-Gnostic purpose, the advocates of which theory obviously prefer a second-century date. The main representative of this view is H. J. Schoeps,[2] who finds certain Gnostic catchwords taken up by the author. But the improbability of so late a date has already been shown, while the 'catchwords' might have been culled by the Gnostics from James' letter.

V. LITERARY FORM AND STYLE

J. H. Ropes made much of the similarity of James to the form of the Greek diatribe, the form used by popular moralists. Characteristics of this style, which he claimed to find in this Epistle, are truncated dialogue with an imaginary interlocutor, the question and answer method, the use of certain set formulae, frequent imperatives, rhetorical questions, apostrophes and many other literary devices to add vividness.[3]

---

[1] On the faith versus works controversy, cf. the following works: for the priority of James to Paul, Mayor, *op. cit.*, pp. lxxxix–xcviii; Rendall, *op. cit.*, pp. 71–83; Carr, *op. cit.*, p. xxxvii; for the view that James corrects a misunderstanding of Paul, P. Feine, *Theologie des Neuen Testaments*[7] (1936), pp. 407f.; G. Kittel, *ZNTW*, 41 (1942), pp. 94ff.; Dibelius, *op. cit.*, pp. 227, 228; against this view, cf. Knowling, *op. cit.*, p. xliv; for the use by both of a common stock of language, cf. Knowling, *op. cit.*, p. xlvi. J. Tielemann (*NkZ*, 44, 1933, pp. 256–270) maintained with much probability that had James written to different readers he might have approximated more closely to Paul.

[2] *Theologie und Geschichte des Judenchristentums* (1949), Excursus I on 'Die Stellung des Jakobusbriefes', pp. 343–349. Cf. also C. M. Edsman, *ZNTW*, 38 (1939), pp. 11–44.*

[3] Ropes, *op. cit.*, pp. 12ff. Blackman (*op. cit.*, pp. 23, 24) assumes that the influence of diatribe is now generally admitted.

That certain rhetorical devices are used cannot be gainsaid, but it is another matter to classify the work on this score alone with the Greek diatribe. Indeed, the strong Jewish background, which has already been noted, would exclude the probability of Ropes' view.[1]

The question has been raised whether this Epistle was originally written in Aramaic and was later translated into Greek. It was F. C. Burkitt[2] who strongly advocated this view, but in order to maintain it he had to regard the Greek text as a free translation, in view of its freedom from Aramaisms. The theory was an attempt to provide a *via media* between the traditional view and the alternatives. The language difficulty in the traditional view of authorship is overcome, but the theory puts rather more onus than one would expect on the translator and for that reason has not commended itself. The same is true of W. L. Knox's[3] basic Aramaic document, plus oral reminiscences, plus Hellenistic cultural influences. The editor must have been a man of genius to weld all this together into a unity, which never gives the impression of translation-Greek in any of its parts.

It is worth observing the poetical element in this Epistle, for this may provide an offset to the theory of overmuch Greek influence. Certain features typical of Hebrew poetic style (such as parallelism) are found in the Epistle,[4] and it may be supposed that such poetic forms had made a deep impression on the author long before he wrote his Epistle. It is significant that this same feature is apparent in our Lord's teaching, and it is an interesting conjecture that a love for Hebrew poetic forms may have been particularly encouraged in that Nazareth home.

Some notice must also be taken of the way this letter fits into current New Testament forms of teaching. It is widely held that the early Church made use of contemporary ethical codes for its moral teaching. This is not impossible provided ample allowance is made for Christian interpretation. No doubt some patterns of moral instruction were developed for catechetical purposes and it is highly probable that traces

[1] Rendall (*op. cit.*, p. 33) maintained that Ropes pressed his evidence too far Cf. also A. Wifstrand (*Studia Theologica*, II, 1948, pp. 177, 178), who calls Ropes' view 'a grotesque overstatement'. He finds many instances of what he calls 'spontaneous semiticisms', which are quite foreign to the diatribe.

[2] *Christian Beginnings* (1924), pp. 65–70.

[3] *JTS*, XLVI (1945), pp. 10–17. Knox treats the Epistle as a 'collection of Genizah fragments from the church of Pella or even of Jerusalem'.

[4] Cf. A. Carr, *op. cit.*, pp. xli–xlv.

of these have survived in the New Testament writings. What marks James off from the rest is that its ethical teaching occupies the whole Epistle and is not, as in other cases, linked with doctrinal passages. It may well be that some of the types of ethical material which formed an important aspect of catechesis have here been more fully preserved. In other words James is writing as he was in the habit of teaching.[1]

Closely akin to this idea of ethical catechetical patterns is the further idea that traces of a primitive baptismal liturgy may be found. This has been particularly worked out by M. E. Boismard[2] in a comparison between James and 1 Peter, in which he claims to find evidence that both are influenced by earlier, baptismal, stereotyped forms, including hymns.[3] More will be said about this kind of hypothesis in dealing with 1 Peter, but the matter is not easy to assess owing to the lack of data about early liturgies. There is a tendency to read back later practices into the primitive period, and special caution is needed to ensure that this does not happen in this case.

CONTENTS

An analysis of this Epistle is difficult because of the lack of any clearly defined thread of thought running through it. The following scheme merely describes the sections in the order in which they occur.

a. Greeting (i. 1)
James introduces himself and very generally defines his readers.

b. Trials and how to meet them (i. 2–4)
Trials are to be faced joyfully, for they will then have a stabilizing effect on character.

---

[1] Cf. Blackman, *op. cit.*, pp. 13–23. P. Carrington (*The Primitive Christian Catechism*, 1940) and E. G. Selwyn (*The First Epistle of Peter*, 1947, pp. 365–466) have developed the idea of patterns of ethical instruction.

[2] 'Une liturgie baptismale dans la prima Petri: II. Son influence sur l'épître de Jacques', *RB*, LXIV (1957), pp. 161–183. Cf. also J. Cantinat in Robert-Feuillet, *Introduction à la Bible* (1959), II, p. 563.

[3] E.g. Boismard cites Jas. i. 12 as a fragment of such a hymn; also Jas. iv. 6–10, where there is a fairly close parallel to 1 Pet. v. 5–9.

c. Wisdom and how to obtain it (i. 5–8)

James assumes that all true wisdom comes from God and can be received in response to faith. Doubt can lead only to instability.

d. Wealth and how to regard it (i. 9–11)

Its transitory character is insisted upon and therefore it becomes irrelevant for the Christian. Rich and poor arrive at a common level.

e. Temptation and trial distinguished (i. 12–15)

Trials are used of God to develop endurance and lead to reward. But temptation springs not from God but from a man's own evil desires.

f. Good gifts (i. 16–18)

Not only does God send trials, but all perfect gifts. The basic gift of life is provided by His unchangeable will.

g. Hearing and doing (i. 19–27)

When the word is heard and received all that is opposed to God's righteousness must be put away. Hearers of the word are warned of the dangers of not doing and a special explanation is given of the difference between vain and pure religion.

h. Against partiality (ii. 1–13)

The theme of rich and poor recurs, although now it is the Christian attitude towards them that is emphasized. God has chosen the poor to be rich in faith, whereas so often it is the rich who are the oppressors. The royal law of love is in any case opposed to partiality, and those who do not fulfil this law fail in respect of the whole law.

i. Against a barren faith (ii. 14–26)

In this well-known passage James exposes the fallacy of an inoperative orthodoxy. He illustrates from both Abraham and Rahab that the faith which is commended is that which is linked with works. On the other hand, James is not decrying the need for faith, for he assumes this as a basis. He will show his faith in fact by his works.

j. Qualities required in teachers (iii. 1–18)

(i) *Control of speech* (iii. 1–12). A teacher has a great responsibility and should not rush into the task without contemplating the dangers of uncontrolled speech. The tongue is liable to become the most undisciplined member of the body, with the result that the whole is affected. By means of various illustrations James shows the deadly danger of untamed speech and the extraordinary inconsistency with which the same lips can utter blessings and cursings.

(ii) *True wisdom* (iii. 13–18). There is a distinct contrast between a wisdom which results in jealousy and bitterness and that which produces good fruits and which is from above. Those who have the latter are truly the wise and understanding.

k. *Dangers* (iv. 1–17)

(i) *Human passions* (iv. 1–10). One of the worst manifestations of false wisdom is the unloosing of passion, seen in the outbreak of strife and the tendency to compromise with the world. The antidote is humiliation and submission to God who will exalt those who are truly repentant.

(ii) *Evil speaking* (iv. 11, 12). James attacks the general human failing of being critical of others and points out that those who do this are being critical of the law.

(iii) *Rash confidence* (iv. 13–17). The folly of planning apart from the will of God is vividly described and its tendency to arrogance noted.

l. *Warnings to wealthy oppressors* (v. 1–6)

James thinks next of those who put all their confidence in riches and who use their wealth as an opportunity to oppress those less fortunate. Such men are denounced in language which recalls the Old Testament prophets.

m. *Encouragements to the oppressed* (v. 7–11)

The quality most needed is patience, and this is enjoined by reference to the Lord's coming. The farmer awaiting the harvest illustrates the quality, while the prophets and the patriarch Job show how to be patient in the midst of suffering. But its real basis is the compassion of the Lord.

n. *Against oaths* (v. 12)

The Christian's word should be so unequivocal that oaths become redundant.

o. The power of prayer (v. 13–18)

If a Christian is sick, prayer is enjoined upon the elders of the Church, and the power of such a method is illustrated by appeal to the fervent prayer of Elijah when he prayed for rain.

p. Help for the backslider (v. 19, 20)

A special commendation and reward is promised to those who help others to turn back from the errors of their ways.

ADDITIONAL NOTES

741. On the Palestinian background, cf. D. Y. Hadidian, *ET*, LXIII (1951–52), pp. 227 f.

748. [6] R. H. Fuller (*INT*, 1966, p. 154) locates James 'in Hellenistic Jewish Christianity and in the sub-apostolic age'. He thinks that James antedated the publication of the Pauline Corpus.

749. [2] On the problem of the Greek style of this Epistle, cf. A. F. J. Klijn (*INT*, 1967, p. 150), who considers that the letter was sent to a destination outside Palestine, which accounts for its Greek style. But cf. R. H. Gundry (*JBL*, LXXXIII, 1964, pp. 404–408) for recent support for the use of Greek in Palestine.

758. The traditional view of authorship is accepted by C. L. Mitton, *The Epistle of James* (1966); A. F. J. Klijn, *INT*, pp. 149–151. But against, cf. B. Reicke, *The Epistles of James, Peter and Jude* (1964).

764. *The purpose.* Among the various suggestions which have been made the following may be noted. C. E. B. Cranfield (*SJT*, 18, 1965, pp. 182–193) sees in James a proclamation of the gospel, for those who may be unable to distinguish the inconsistencies between this proclamation and their own practice. According to F. Mussner, *Der Jacobusbrief* (1964), James wrote from Jerusalem for the Diaspora, and according to Mitton for Jewish-Christian visitors to Jerusalem, who would therefore take back with them some record of James' teaching.

The theology. Cf. K.-G. Eckart (*ThLZ*, 89, 1964, cols. 521–526), who contends from the evidence of James' language that his theology is based on early Christian tradition. On the theological background of James, cf. G. Baumann, *ThZ*, XVIII (1962), pp. 401 ff.; W. Marxsen, *Der 'Frühkatholizismus' im NT* (1958), pp. 22 ff.; E. Lohse, *ZNTW*, 48 (1957), pp. 1 ff.

765. [2] For further studies on the relationship between James and Paul, cf. W. Schmithals' *Paul and James* (1965). (See comment on this in additional note on p. 391.) Cf. J. Jeremias, *ET*, LXVI (1954–55), pp. 38 ff.; G. Eichholz, *Glaube und Werk bei Paulus und Jakobus* (1961). The view of H. J. Schoeps, mentioned on p. 765 had an earlier advocate in H. Schammberger, *Die Einheitlichkeit des Jk. im antignostischen Kampf* (1936). Cf. also W. G. Kümmel's discussion, *INT* (1965), p. 286.

CHAPTER TWENTY-FOUR

THE FIRST EPISTLE OF PETER

I. THE EPISTLE IN THE ANCIENT CHURCH

No discussion of the value of this Epistle for today can proceed without first establishing its position in the ancient Church. It is against such a background that examination of the problem of authorship must be made, and this in turn affects the dating of the Epistle and the historical situation that it was originally intended to meet.

So strong is the evidence for the use of this Epistle in the early Church that C. Bigg[1] regarded it as proved and maintained that it was considered to be canonical as early as this word had a meaning. There are clear parallels in Clement of Rome's *Epistle to the Corinthians*[2] which would appear to indicate his knowledge and use of this Epistle. Some scholars do not admit the certainty of Clement's borrowing, but J. W. C. Wand[3] has no doubt about it and uses this fact as a basis for his discussions on the date of the Epistle. The traces in Ignatius, *Barnabas* and *Hermas* are more open to dispute, but Polycarp's definite citations from the Epistle can hardly be challenged. Yet he does not cite it as Peter's nor does he mention Peter in his epistle, and this has been taken to infer that he knew it only as an anonymous work, since in the case of Paul's Epistles he twice names the apostle in citations. But it was not Polycarp's normal habit to name his authorities when quoting, and it must therefore be assumed that when he did so there was some special reason. Nor is the reason far to seek, for Paul, unlike Peter, had in fact written to the same church to which Polycarp now addresses his letter and this fact is used as a basis for special appeal. As F. H. Chase[4] has pointed out, the citations from 1 Peter are of a general hortatory type, whereas in the Pauline citations epigrammatic, axiomatic statements are introduced. This may be accounted for by the probability that Polycarp echoes 1 Peter from memory, but in some cases cites Paul's words from manu-

---

[1] *The Epistles of St. Peter and St. Jude* (1901), p. 15.

[2] Cf. Bigg's list of citations, *op. cit.*, p. 8. The authors of *The New Testament in the Apostolic Fathers* (1905), p. 137, however, consider these parallels as not worthy of serious attention.

[3] *The General Epistles of St. Peter and St. Jude* (1934), p. 9.   [4] *HDB*, III, p. 781.

scripts in his possession. Whether this conjecture is probable or not does not, however, alter the fact that Polycarp's omission to cite this Epistle as Peter's is no evidence that he knew it only without its opening address,[1] for it is inconceivable that subsequent to Polycarp's time an epistle already so widely revered and used would have 'acquired' a Petrine authority which it did not previously possess.[2]

By the time of Irenaeus it was often quoted as Petrine. Tertullian and Clement of Alexandria have examples of the same procedure. Others who during the same period witness to the authority of the Epistle are Theophilus of Antioch, the author of the *Letter of the Churches of Vienne and Lugdunum* (Lyons) and the writer to Diognetus.[3] From this evidence it may justly be concluded that the attestation for this Epistle is as strong as for the majority of the New Testament writings. Yet one gap remains to be filled. The Muratorian Fragment omits reference to both Epistles of Peter, and some scholars have supposed that this could only mean that the church of Rome towards the close of the second century did not regard the Epistles as canonical. But at this point the text of the fragment is open to doubt and Westcott's conjecture that we have here a chasm is probably correct.[4] At least the

---

[1] As A. Harnack maintained, *Die Chronologie der altchristlichen Literatur* (1897), I, p. 463. Cf. also his *1 Clemensbrief*, p. 57n. Wand (*op. cit.*, p. 11) points out the fallacy of Harnack's argument, since *1 Clement* cites the opening greeting of 1 Peter (Introduction to *Ad Cor.*).

[2] There are possibly echoes in the Valentinian *Gospel of Truth*; cf. W. C. van Unnik, *The Jung Codex* (ed. F. L. Cross, 1955), pp. 115ff. It is just possible that Papias knew the Epistle under the name of Peter, but the evidence cannot be regarded as conclusive (cf. F. H. Chase, *HDB*, III, p. 780). Eusebius expressly states that Papias quoted the former Epistle of John and that of Peter (*HE*, iii. 39. 17), and if he is here reflecting a true tradition there is no question that 1 Peter was named as Peter's at a much earlier period than Irenaeus. In view of the fact that no evidence exists to the contrary, it seems reasonable to regard this as authentic tradition.

[3] For details of these witnesses, cf. C. Bigg, *op. cit.*, p. 11.

[4] *On the Canon of the New Testament*[4] (1875), pp. 216, 217. Zahn's conjecture that the reference to the *Apocalypse of Peter* should be omitted and a reference be inserted indicating acceptance of both Epistles of Peter (*Geschichte des neutestamentlichen Kanons*, I, 1888, pp. 315f.), was strongly criticized by Harnack (*Das Neue Testament um das Jahr 200*, 1889, p. 84) on the grounds that no other evidence exists in the West for 2 Peter being named at this period. But neither Zahn's emendation nor Harnack's criticism is relevant here, since no importance can be attached to an emended text in the history of the Canon, while the omission of any earlier citation of 2 Peter in the West contributes nothing to the evidence for 1 Peter.

clearly corrupted state of the text makes any certain inferences from omissions precarious, and this evidence, or rather lack of it, can hardly offset the widespread authority which the Epistle enjoyed as the foregoing data have proved. Although it may not have been used as freely in the West as in the East, there is no evidence that it was ever disputed.

In spite of the fact that this attestation seems conclusive enough for the authenticity of this Epistle, B. H. Streeter[1] challenged it on the grounds that, if the Epistle was written by Peter in Rome, it would be expected that the Latin churches would most quote it, but this type of argument is fallacious, since it was not sent to the West but to the East.

Our conclusion must be that this Epistle not only exerted a wide influence on early Christian writings, but that it also possessed for them apostolic authority. This makes clear that the primitive Church, as far back as any evidence exists, regarded it as a genuine Epistle of Peter, and thus any discussion of objections to Petrine authorship must sufficiently take account of this fact.

II. AUTHORSHIP

The very great weight of patristic evidence in favour of Petrine authorship and the absence of any dissentient voice raises so strong a presupposition in favour of the correctness of the claims of the Epistle to be Peter's own work that it is surprising that this has been questioned. Yet because some scholars either have wholly rejected the genuineness of the opening address or else have proposed various theories to get over the difficulties which are thought to be involved in the traditional view, it will be necessary to examine these difficulties. The main objections will first be given and then the possible answers to these objections from the point of view of Petrine authorship.[2] Finally, certain

---

[1] *The Primitive Church* (1929), p. 119.

[2] In common with many other parts of the New Testament, 1 Peter came under the fire of criticism in the early nineteenth century mainly on the grounds of its relationship to the Pauline Epistles. (For details, cf. A. F. Walls' Introduction to A. M. Stibbs' *The First Epistle General of Peter*, TNT, 1959, p. 18.) But many other grounds of objection have been raised by such critics as Holtzmann, Jülicher, von Soden, Streeter, Goodspeed, E. F. Scott and F. W. Beare. At the same time the traditional position has been maintained by a steady stream of scholars among whom have been such notable names as Chase, Salmon, Hort, Zahn, Bigg, Selwyn, Michaelis, McNeile-Williams. For this reason it is surprising to find Beare asserting so confidently that the case against the attribution to Peter is

considerations will be mentioned about the difficulties of alternative
theories.

a. The objections to apostolic authorship

(i) *Linguistic and stylistic objections.* That the writer was thoroughly at
home in the Greek language is admitted by all. The Epistle has a fairly
polished style which has been influenced by the Greek of the LXX with
which he is intimately acquainted, as is evident not only from his direct
citations but also from the many instances where his language is
moulded by Old Testament forms. This very fact has proved to some
scholars to be a stumbling-block to the acceptance of Petrine authorship. It is suggested that the writer's acquaintance with the LXX is a
literary knowledge and not the kind of knowledge that a practising
Jew would possess, for he shows no evidence of his religious inheritance such as Paul so clearly shows.[1] The writer's vocabulary is extensive and varied and his command of Greek syntactical usages not
inconsiderable.[2] Indeed, his Greek is smoother than that of Paul, who
was highly trained in comparison with Peter. And herein lies the main
difficulty.

Can such facility in the Greek language be imagined in a Galilaean
fisherman, whose native tongue was Aramaic and whose educational
background would not dispose towards linguistic ability? F. W.
Beare[3] feels the difficulty so keenly that he answers emphatically in the
negative. The incidental description of Peter in Acts iv. 13 as 'illiterate'
ἀγράμματος is claimed to add weight to this objection, although it
should be noted that the more probable meaning of this word in the
context is 'not formally trained'.[4] In fact, in the traditional allusions to
Peter, he is depicted as needing an interpreter when addressing people
whose mother tongue was Greek. The tradition may, of course, be

overwhelming (*The First Epistle of Peter,*[2] 1958, p. 29). This overstatement is
justly criticized by J. W. C. Wand ('The Lessons of First Peter', *Interpretation,* IX,
1955, pp. 387–399).

[1] Cf. F. W. Beare, *op. cit.,* p. 27.

[2] Cf. F. H. Chase, *HDB,* III, p. 782, for details. Cf. also J. H. Moulton and W. F.
Howard, *A Grammar of New Testament Greek* (1929), II, p. 26; R. Knopf, *Die
Briefe Petri und Judä*[7] (1912), p. 16, that only Luke and the author of the Epistle to
the Hebrews compares with this author's feeling for Greek style. There are a
number of *Hapaxes* in this Epistle.

[3] *Op. cit.,* pp. 28f.

[4] Cf. A. F. Walls, *op. cit.,* p. 24 n. 3.

wrong, but it is strong enough to raise doubts about Peter's facility in the Greek tongue.[1]

(ii) *Historical objections.* A major crux in the attack on Petrine author-ship is the historical situation presupposed in the Epistle. The author is writing to persecuted Christians (cf. 1 Pet. i. 6, ii. 12, 15, iv. 12, 14–16, v. 8, 9), and particularly mentions reproach suffered for the name of Christ. It is therefore supposed that Christianity has now become a crime in itself, as distinct from the mere social nuisance which it was considered to be at an earlier time. This cannot, it is claimed, be out-breaks of mob violence, but official organized opposition to Christi-anity. Yet although the Neronian persecutions were directed against Christians in Rome there is no evidence that such persecution spread to the provinces to which this letter is addressed (i.e. Pontus, Galatia, Cappadocia, Asia and Bithynia). But if the Neronian persecution is ruled out, the Epistle must be dated during either the Domitianic or Trajanic persecutions and in either case this would dispose of apostolic authorship, since Peter, according to tradition, was martyred in the time of Nero.[2]

Moreover, parallels between the situation described in Pliny's correspondence with the Emperor Trajan and that suggested by this Epistle lead some scholars to conclude that the same occasion is in mind.[3]

[1] Cf. R. Knopf, *op. cit.*, p. 17.

[2] Cf. O. Cullmann, *Peter: Disciple, Apostle, and Martyr*, 1953, pp. 89–152, for the evidence of Peter's martyrdom. W. M. Ramsay's view that Peter lived on until near the end of Vespasian's reign (*The Church in the Roman Empire*, 1893, pp. 209f.) has gained no support (but cf. P. Gardner-Smith's article 'I Peter' in *Encyclopaedia Britannica*[14]).

[3] E.g. H. J. Holtzmann, *Lehrbuch der historisch-kritischen Einleitung in das Neue Testament*[2] (1886), p. 494; F. W. Beare, *op. cit.*, pp. 13ff. Cf. J. W. C. Wand (*op. cit.*, p. 15) for details of these parallels. He admits that they are 'powerfully attrac-tive'. No doubt the enquiry of Pliny as to whether the name or the crimes associa-ted with the name was to be the subject of punishment strongly disposes the minds of some scholars to accept a dating of the Epistle in Trajan's reign, as also the fact that Pliny was Governor of one of the very provinces to which 1 Peter was addressed. The most recent advocates of a Trajanic date are J. Knox, 'Pliny and 1 Peter: A note on 1 Pet. iv. 14–16 and iii. 15', *JBL*, LXXII (1953), pp. 187–189, and F. W. Beare, *op. cit.*, pp. 9–19. Knox maintains that 1 Peter was written to urge Christians to refuse to be condemned on any other charge than their pro-fession of Christianity. He thinks they were being condemned for 'inflexible obstinacy' and hence needed to be exhorted to make their defence with gentleness and reverence (1 Pet. iii. 15). But any refusal to recant, in whatever spirit, would surely have been regarded as 'inflexible obstinacy'!

Some form of this theory is held by many[1] who dispute the unity of the Epistle and who draw attention to the different approach towards persecutions after iv. 12 (but see the discussion on the Unity, pp. 797ff.).

Another objection which may be mentioned here is the want of any known connection of Peter with any of the Asian churches among which the Epistle was designed to be circulated. Furthermore, these Gentile districts would more naturally come under the supervision of the apostle Paul, in which case it is thought to be strange to find Peter addressing them after Paul's death, since his ministry was concerned with the circumcision.

A different kind of historical objection is that raised by B. H. Streeter[2] over the use of such a term as 'fellow-elder' (v. 1) by an apostle, and the author's claim to be an eyewitness of the sufferings of Christ which, he thought, could not have been written by Peter, who was not present during the whole period of the passion. Moreover, it is maintained that an apostolic author such as Peter would have reflected in his writing far more reminiscences of his personal contacts with Jesus,[3] and of his knowledge of the sayings of his Master. But this objection cannot be regarded as serious since the presence of such reminiscences in the case of 2 Peter is regarded by some as an objection against apostolic authorship,[4] and there is no sure canon of criticism which can pronounce on the validity of either.

(iii) *Doctrinal objections.* Opponents of Petrine authorship place much emphasis on the affinities in thought between this Epistle and the Pauline letters.[5] It is maintained that the author has borrowed from

---

[1] For example, R. Perdelwitz, *Die Mysterienreligionen und das Problem des ersten Petrusbriefes* (1911); B. H. Streeter, *The Primitive Church*, pp. 122ff.; H. Windisch-H. Preisker, *Die katholischen Briefe*[3] (1951), pp. 76, 77, 159. W. Nauck (*ZNTW*, 46, 1955, pp. 68–80) rejects any distinction between hypothetical and real persecutions because both are essential to the whole picture.

[2] *Op. cit.*, pp. 120, 121.

[3] Cf. F. H. Chase, *HDB*, III, p. 787, for details. R. Knopf (*op. cit.*, p. 15) makes much of this objection, particularly because of the tradition that Peter was behind Mark's Gospel, as a result of which it might be expected that some evidence of Peter's discipleship with the Lord would be included in an epistle under his name.

[4] Cf. Bigg, *op. cit.*, p. 232.

[5] Cf. E. F. Scott (*The Literature of the New Testament*, p. 220), who goes so far as to maintain that the writer must have studied several of Paul's Epistles. Similarly, F. W. Beare (*op. cit.*, p. 25) writes of the author as 'a man who is steeped in the Pauline letters'.

some of these, particularly Romans and Ephesians.[1] But even apart from literary connections the author's theological background is so much akin to Paul's that he has been regarded as a member of the school of Paul.[2] Yet how could this have happened to Peter? Some scholars[3] feel that this is too much to ask of the elder apostle, who had never had any close connections with Paul, and who had in fact ranged himself against him.[4]

A corollary to the alleged borrowing from Paul's Epistles is the supposed want of any originality in this Epistle. In other words it is considered that there is nothing characteristically unPauline in it.[5] Even the absence of reference to the question of the law has been regarded as a difficulty in a letter written by the leader of Jewish Christianity.[6] In other words, this difference from Paulinism is rather evidence of Pauline influence than the reverse. Such an objection depends for its weight on the assumption that no apostle of Peter's stamp could have lacked originality. Indeed it assumes that all apostles must have been creative. A different objection of an almost opposite kind is the alleged maturity of the author's thought and its kinship with the Old Roman Creed,[7] in particular the doctrine of the descent into Hades.

When all these objections are cumulatively considered, they will appeal to different minds with different force, but the fact that they have seemed to some scholars sufficiently conclusive against Petrine

[1] Quite apart from the problem of Peter borrowing from Paul, the parallels with Ephesians have been used as further evidence for a late date for 1 Peter by those who already reject the Pauline authorship of Ephesians (cf. C. L. Mitton, *The Epistle to the Ephesians*, 1951). In his first edition (pp. 9, 10) Beare could assert that since most scholars now regard Ephesians as a second generation work, 1 Peter must be even later. But Beare is here exaggerating the support for the late dating of Ephesians. For the parallels with Romans, cf. W. Sanday and A. C. Headlam, *The Epistle to the Romans* (*ICC*, 1895), pp. lxxiv ff.; but note Wand's strictures about accepting all these as evidence of literary dependence (*op. cit.*, p. 19). Cf. the further remarks on Literary Affinities on pp. 803ff.

[2] Cf. M. Dibelius, *A Fresh Approach to the New Testament and Early Christian Literature* (1936), p. 188.

[3] Cf. F. W. Beare, *op. cit.*, p. 25.

[4] Cf. E. F. Scott, *op. cit.*, p. 220; R. Knopf, *op. cit.*, p. 18.

[5] Cf. A. Jülicher-E. Fascher, *Einleitung*[7] (1931), pp. 193ff. F. W. Beare (*op. cit.*, p. 25) slightly modifies this position by admitting that the writer has a mind of his own, but 'has formed himself on Paul's writings'.

[6] Cf. Knopf, *op. cit.*, p. 17.

[7] Mentioned by McNeile-Williams, *INT*, p. 223.

authorship is reason enough for carefully examining their validity. In considering this, it is as well to recognize that those swayed by these objections generally pay no heed to the external evidence, although they have at times been caused no small embarrassment when they have attempted to explain it.

b. An examination of the objections to apostolic authorship

(i) *Linguistic and stylistic objections.* It is a difficult matter to decide whether any man could or could not attain to fluency in a language other than his own, when so little is known about the personal capacities of the man in question. More stress may have been given to Peter's former occupation of fishing than is really justified, for at the most conservative dating of this Epistle an interval of more than thirty years separated Peter the writer from Peter the fisherman, and who can measure what facility he might have achieved over so long a period? Even if Aramaic had been his native tongue, he lived in a bilingual area[1] and would not only have used Greek of a colloquial kind before his Christian ministry, but would regularly have used it in his conversations with Hellenistic Jews, even at Jerusalem or Antioch.[2] Moulton and Howard,[3] in fact, suggest that Peter's Greek may have been better than his Aramaic.[4]

The widespread use of the LXX version by a Palestinian Jew is not extraordinary when he is addressing himself to Gentile areas, for the Greek version of the Scriptures was the Bible of the Gentile Churches, and Peter could hardly have been unacquainted with it when working among Hellenistic Jews.[5]

But do the words of Papias about Peter's interpreter being Mark really support the contention that Peter's Greek was so poor that he needed the services of an interpreter? Clearly the words are intended to authenticate Mark's Gospel, and it is straining the language to suppose that Papias meant to imply Peter's linguistic inability.

We must conclude, therefore, that it cannot be asserted that Peter *could* not have written this Epistle on the grounds of language and style.

[1] See discussion on pp. 747ff. in connection with the Epistle of James.
[2] Cf. Moulton and Howard, *op. cit.*, p. 26.   [3] *Ibid., loc. cit.*
[4] Knopf (*op. cit.*, pp. 16, 17) admitted that a Galilaean might know Greek sufficiently well to make himself intelligible, but thought that there is a great difference between this and the Greek of 1 Peter. Similarly, Beare, *op. cit.*, p. 28.
[5] Cf. A. F. Walls (*op. cit.*, p. 25), who mentions that in James' speech in Acts a point is reinforced by a citation from the LXX.

At most we may note its extraordinary character, and at least we may
maintain that no conclusive barrier to apostolic authorship exists on
this score. Yet in order to meet the difficulty felt by many scholars, an
alternative view has been postulated suggesting that an amanuensis,
Silvanus, has either himself been responsible for the stylistic characteristics, or was in fact the author of the Epistle, writing under Peter's
direction.[1]

We are left in no doubt that Peter employed Silvanus as his scribe
or secretary, for he tells us so in v. 12. But did this amount to co-authorship, and if it did not, what degree of latitude did Peter allow Silvanus
in expressing his thoughts? It is well known that ancient secretaries
were at times allowed considerable freedom in writing down their
master's ideas. Indeed, in certain cases the secretary would be given
only the barest outline of the contents and would then produce the
letter in conformity with the outline.[2] The master would, of course,
check over the finished product and it would be assumed that the
contents were authenticated by him. Although the language would be
that of the amanuensis the fundamental ideas would be those of the
master.

In the case of 1 Peter, Silvanus would well fill the bill, for if he is to
be identified with the Silas of Acts[3] he was well acquainted with Paul
and was, in fact, associated with him in the address of both the Thessalonian letters. Some have suggested co-authorship with Paul in the
production of these letters, and if this is a valid deduction it is not
improbable that a similar combination with Peter resnlted in the
production of 1 Peter. Selwyn[4] has strongly argued for this probability

---

[1] This assumes that 1 Pet. v. 12 means that Silvanus was Peter's scribe and not
merely the bearer of the Epistle.

[2] Cf. the instructive discussion of J. A. Eschlimann, 'La Rédaction des Epîtres
Pauliniennes', *RB*, LIII (1946), pp. 185ff.

[3] Most scholars incline to this identification although no conclusive proof is
available. Cf. the detailed study of L. Radermacher, *ZNTW*, 25 (1926), pp.
287–299; cf. also Bigg, *op. cit.*, pp. 83ff.

[4] Cf. *The First Epistle of St. Peter*, Essay II, pp. 365–466. On the other hand,
Beare (*op. cit.*, pp. 188ff.) has equally strongly criticized this hypothesis of a common author behind Thessalonians and 1 Peter on the grounds of dissimilarity of
style between the different writings and the existence of difference of tone. This
view was shared by W. L. Knox in his criticism of Selwyn's position (*Theology*,
XLIX, 1946, pp. 342–344). Cf. also B. Rigaux (*Les Epîtres aux Thessaloniciens*, *EB*,
1956, pp. 105–111), who appealed to parallels between Thessalonians and the
'Manual of Discipline' of the Dead Sea Community.

on the grounds of close connection of thought and language between I Peter, the Thessalonian Epistles and the Apostolic Decree in Acts xv, of which Silas was one of the bearers. But similarities of thought are capable of various explanations and the employment of expressions in common use by different authors may be as reasonable an explanation as common authorship (or co-authorship). Nevertheless, where a name is known to have been associated with different groups of writings similarity may be not insignificant. The Silvanus hypothesis cannot, therefore, be ruled out, and forms a reasonable alternative for those whose main objection to Petrine authorship is linguistic.

Certain criticisms of this amanuensis-hypothesis should not go unnoticed. It is strongly rejected by F. W. Beare,[1] who calls it 'a device of desperation'. To him the teaching of the Epistle, with its lack of stress on the work of the Spirit, is proof enough against the theory of early authorship.[2] But one's estimate of any hypothesis is partly conditioned by presuppositions, and those for whom the other difficulties loom large will not be disposed to dispense with the linguistic problem on such a basis as an amanuensis theory.[3] Another problem is the absence of any salutation from Silvanus, which would be strange indeed if he were the secretary or part-composer (cf. Rom. xvi. 22 where Tertius the scribe sends his own greetings). This suggests that Silvanus played a far less important part than the amanuensis hypothesis implies. Not only so, but v. 12 would stand as a rather obnoxious piece of self-commendation, unless in fact Peter himself added this conclusion. It is further difficult to imagine that the direct appeal of v. 1ff. could have been the indirect work of a secretary. The personal authority is so real that it would be necessary to maintain that for this part of the letter the apostle had dictated. It is also significant that the statement in v. 12 which mentions Silvanus may indicate either the bearer or the

---

[1] *Op. cit.*, p. 183. In the appendix of his second edition, Beare gives a careful criticism of Selwyn's arguments (*op. cit.*, pp. 188ff.). Against Beare's comment, cf. P. Carrington, 'St. Peter's Epistle', in *The Joy of Study* (ed. S. E. Johnson, 1951), p. 58.

[2] *Ibid.*, p. 28. Cf. A. F. Walls (*op. cit.*, p. 29) for a sufficient answer to Beare's contention.

[3] F. W. Beare regards the mention of Silvanus in v. 12 as no more than a part of the machinery of pseudonymity (*op. cit.*, p. 29). But pseudonymous writers did not usually introduce such specific additions as this, which might be the means of betraying their disguise, at least in epistolary impersonations. There is no extant example of it in pseudepigraphical Christian literature.

secretary and some doubt exists therefore about the method of composition.[1]

Another criticism is based on the fact that Silvanus was a Jerusalem Christian and would not, therefore, be equipped with Greek as our author clearly was.[2] But there were certainly some Greek-speaking Jews in Jerusalem, and there is no basis for excluding Silvanus from their number. Indeed, he may have been chosen for this reason as a delegate to convey the letter of James to Greek-speaking churches of Antioch, Syria and Cilicia (Acts xv. 33ff.).

To sum up, the amanuensis theory has nothing to disprove it, but neither has it evidence enough to be conclusive about its correctness. If Peter had the help of Silvanus it would seem improbable, by reason of the whole tone of the letter, that the author allowed too much freedom to his secretary. At least the finished article was given out very definitely as Peter's personal message, invested with his own special authority.[3]

(ii) *Historical objections.* The question of the identification of the persecution reflected in this Epistle is crucial to this problem of authorship, as has already been pointed out. But a prior problem is scantiness of adequate data about early persecutions. Much of the weight of objection from an historical point of view has been based on the assumption of general provincial persecution directed against Christians in the reign of Domitian. But this assumption has met with recent suspicion, for there are very few data in support. It is known that Flavius Clemens and Domitilla his wife were persecuted in Rome with one or two others, but there is no more than a strong presumption that this limited persecution was on account of their Christian profession and no evidence at all for any widespread persecution affecting the prov-

---

[1] Cf. the detailed discussion of F. H. Chase (*HDB*, III, p. 790), who cites other instances where the Greek διά introduces the bearer and not the amanuensis of a letter. But P. Carrington (*op. cit.*, pp. 57, 58) argues (in opposition to Beare) that the expression signifies the producer of the Epistle on the analogy of the *Epistle of the Church at Smyrna* (relating Polycarp's death) as written 'through Marcianus' (διά) who must have been the composer since a separate amanuensis is mentioned.

[2] Cf. Beare, *op. cit.*, pp. 189f.

[3] W. Bornemann ('Der erste Petrusbrief—eine Taufrede des Sylvanus?' *ZNTW*, 19, 1919–20, pp. 157f.) accounted for Silvanus' connection with the Epistle by supposing that 1 Peter was really a baptismal address delivered by Silvanus (cf. also L. Radermacher, *op. cit.*, pp. 287–299). But this does not explain why it was then adapted into a letter in Peter's name.

inces named.[1] This makes it impossible to relate our Epistle with any certainty to this period.

But assuming some official persecution was either active or imminent in these provinces of Asia Minor, is it still possible that the situation under Trajan may be reflected? The parallels are not as striking as has often been claimed. The name 'Christian' may by that time, and in fact for some time previously, have acquired a technical connotation, but that does not immediately identify 1 Peter iv. 14 (being reproached for the name of Christ) with this situation, for all Christian suffering from the commencement of the Church was regarded as 'in the name'. Indeed it was prepared for by our Lord Himself.[2] But it should further be remembered that Pliny was requesting an imperial judgment which involved a clarification of the whole position of Christians. Neither Pliny's enquiries nor Trajan's reply suggest that procedure against Christians was a new departure.[3] Moreover, there is no suggestion that the kind of problem confronting Pliny was worldwide, and yet 1 Peter v. 9 shows that the kind of suffering that the Christians were called upon to endure was liable to befall Christians anywhere. Moreover, there is a further difference between Pliny and 1 Peter, for in the former a state of affairs is reflected which is a continuation of a past policy, whereas in the latter a fiery trial seems to be regarded as a new experience (1 Pet. iv. 12). To sum up, there is little to commend this identification and it cannot be said to be demanded by the evidence.[4]

But does the Neronian persecution fare any better? It is true that no evidence exists that provincial districts were affected, although Tertullian[5] makes a statement about an *institutum Neronianum* making Christians outlaws, but no trace of this edict remains. Yet Christians were certainly made scapegoats in Rome, and the savage nature of

---

[1] Cf. J. W. C. Wand's clear discussion of this point (*op. cit.*, p. 16). He cites without disapproval E. T. Merrill's opinion that Domitian did not persecute Christians at all (in his *Essays in Early Christian History*, 1924, pp. 148ff.). If the Apocalypse is dated during Domitian's reign this would, of course, supply supporting evidence of hostile and general persecution in part, at least, of the provinces connected with the Epistle. See pp. 172f. for more detailed discussion of the Domitianic persecutions.

[2] Cf. Mk. xiii. 13; Lk. xxi. 12.

[3] For a well-reasoned appraisal of the historic situation behind Pliny's correspondence, cf. J. W. C. Wand, *op. cit.*, pp. 15f.; A. F. Walls, *op. cit.*, pp. 54ff.

[4] A. M. Hunter (Introduction and Exegesis to *The First Epistle of Peter*, IB, 1957, p. 79) justifiably calls it 'very rash'.

[5] *Ad Nationes*, vii.

Nero's treatment of them must have been widely known throughout the provinces, where great apprehension must have arisen among the Christians. Peter may well have imagined an extension of the attack and wished to warn the Asian Christians of what was in store for them. There is nothing in the references to persecution in this Epistle which rules out this hypothesis.

One other question remains. Are the references to suffering in the Epistle sufficiently clear to show that official persecution was in mind? In the first part of the Epistle the sufferings are of a general kind (i. 6, 7, iii. 13–17), but in the latter part a fiercer opposition seems to be envisaged (iv. 12ff.). Yet there is much to be said for the view that the kind of sufferings are not martyrdoms but reproaches due to the fact that Christians were considered odious in the eyes of their neighbours. The *apologia* (iii. 15) which they must be prepared to give when necessary is equally well explained by the need for a general Christian testimony as by the need for legal defence. In fact there is little distinctive about the 'persecutions' in 1 Peter which would not apply to the opposition that Christians had to endure from the inception of the Church.[1] What Peter is concerned about is to prevent Christians from suffering for wrongdoing, but he implies that all other kinds of suffering were designed by God for their welfare. Suffering as a Christian is contrasted with suffering as a murderer, thief, evil-doer or busybody (1 Pet. iv. 15, 16), and although the parallelism would appear to demand legal penalties in both cases,[2] yet all that need be implied is some action on the part of magistrates, as for instance happened in the case of Paul's troubles with Silas at Philippi. The fiery trial ($\pi\acute{u}\rho\omega\sigma\iota\varsigma$) of iv. 12 may indicate some form of persecution by incendiarism, in which case the Neronian persecutions would furnish a striking parallel, or it may be used metaphorically of any trial which has the refining effect of fire.

Although it may be impossible to reach any indisputable conclusion,

---

[1] C. F. D. Moule ('The Nature and Purpose of 1 Peter', *NTS*, 3, 1957, pp. 7ff.) maintains that there are parallels with other New Testament passages on the subject of persecution and concludes that this shows how much can be explained 'by postulating harrying by local opponents, sometimes leading to imprisonment by local authorities or even (as in the case of Stephen) death'. The same position was cogently maintained by E. G. Selwyn in his article 'The Persecutions in 1 Peter' in *Studiorum Novi Testamenti Societas Bulletin* (1950), pp. 39–50. Cf. also his article in *ET*, LIX (1948), pp. 256–259, in which he considered the persecution situation to be no different from that reflected in the Pauline Epistles and Acts.

[2] So Wand, *op. cit., ad loc.*

it may be maintained with confidence that nothing in these references to persecution excludes the possibility that the self-claims of the Epistle to be Petrine are genuine.

The problem of Peter writing to districts under Paul's supervision is not a serious one, for if Paul were now dead (as is most generally supposed) there would be no question of a clash of territories.[1] It would not be unnatural, in fact, for the surviving senior apostle to send a message of encouragement to Gentile churches if the apostle to the Gentiles was no longer alive. But it is certainly not established that this Epistle was, in fact, directed to Pauline churches. Of the provinces mentioned, Paul worked, as far as we know, only in Galatia and Asia, and even in the northern districts of these he had in all probability not worked.[2] No doubt these areas had been evangelized by converts of Paul, but had probably not known him personally. This may account for the absence of any reference to him, although there is no particular reason why such a reference should have been included in any case.[3] If the tradition of Peter's residence in Rome is correct,[4] too much emphasis must not be laid upon the present enlargement of Peter's commission as a minister to the circumcision, or the history of the period will be too unnaturally departmentalized.

That Peter would not describe himself as a fellow-elder and would not have claimed to be a witness of Christ's sufferings (v. 1) is by no means as self-evident as Streeter supposed. Quite apart from the fact that the term 'elder' seems to have been used as late as the time of Papias[5] as a description of apostles, and therefore could not have been regarded in the primitive Church as an inferior title, the context almost demands such a description for the exhortation of the elders to have its fullest effect. It is, as H. Windisch[6] pointed out, an expression of modesty on the writer's part. It is even more an evidence of his sympathy with his readers.[7] That Peter had not witnessed all of Christ's sufferings

[1] E. H. Plumptre (*The General Epistles of St. Peter and St. Jude*, 1879, pp. 60ff.) got over the difficulty here by supposing that the Epistle was addressed to Jews who came under Peter's jurisdiction.

[2] Cf. McNeile-Williams, *INT*, pp. 214, 215, for the probable route which the bearer traversed in his delivery of the letter. There is little doubt that the order of mention of the provinces indicates the sequence of visits.*

[3] Cf. J. Moffatt, *ILNT*, pp. 339, 340.   [4] Cf. O. Cullmann, *op. cit.*, pp. 70–152.

[5] See the comments on Papias' statement on pp. 886ff.

[6] *Die katholischen Briefe*, *ad loc.*

[7] Cf. Selwyn, *The First Epistle of St. Peter*, *ad loc.*

would certainly not prevent him from calling himself a witness, and Streeter's objection on this score must be rejected as unworthy of further consideration.

(iii) *Doctrinal objections.* There has been such widespread assumption that Peter's Epistle is but an echo of Paulinism that it is refreshing to find an increasing tendency to mark the individual contribution of Peter in the field of New Testament theology. J. W. C. Wand[1] has pointed out both the absence of such Pauline doctrines as justification, law, the new Adam, and the flesh, and the presence of highly characteristic methods in Peter's own presentation, such as his copious use of Old Testament citations and moral codes, his church-consciousness, historic consciousness and Christ-consciousness. Peter's teaching cannot be systematized into a theological school of thought, but there is enough distinctiveness about it to differentiate it from Paul's approach. The most notable contribution is the doctrine of Christ's descent into Hades, which in its focus upon the resurrection of Christ stands in direct relationship to Peter's emphasis on the resurrection in the early Acts speeches. As an eyewitness of the risen Christ Peter would never forget the profound impression which that stupendous event made upon his mind, and the doctrine of the descent,[2] however obscure it is to modern minds, would surely be more natural as a part of primitive reflection upon the significance of the resurrection than as a later development, or as a peculiar fancy of a pseudonymous author.

At the same time, no serious student of Paul and Peter would deny that there is much common ground between them, which cannot wholly be explained by their common Christian background. Some Pauline influence on Peter's mind is generally supposed to be required by the content of the Epistle, but this would be damaging to Petrine authorship only if two presuppositions can be established. First, it must be shown that the New Testament presentation of Peter makes it

[1] *Op. cit.*, pp. 17ff. For a similar challenge to the theory of Paulinism, cf. Selwyn's article, *ET*, LIX (1948), pp. 256–259. He makes a strong point of the underlying common teaching of the Church.

[2] There have been several special discussions of this passage in recent years, particularly by Bo Reicke in his exhaustive monograph, *The Disobedient Spirits and Christian Baptism* (Acta Seminarii Neotestamentica Upsaliensis, ed. A. Fridrichsen, XII, 1946). Cf. C. E. B. Cranfield, *ET*, LXIX (1958), pp. 369–372; R. Bultmann, in *Coniectanea Neotestamentica XI in honorem Antonii Fridrichsen* (1947), pp. 1–14; J. Jeremias, *ZNTW*, 42(1949), pp. 194–201; and S. E. Johnson, *JBL*, LXXIX (1960), pp. 48–51.

psychologically inconceivable that he was susceptible to outside influence, particularly from so powerful a personality as Paul. But the data available do not depict Peter as a man of fertile ideas, but as a man of action. Paul's successful resistance to Peter's weak compromise at Antioch is sufficient indication of the direction in which mental influences were likely to flow. Indeed, traces of other New Testament literature such as James and Hebrews are further evidence of the receptive character of this author's mind, and such receptivity is not incompatible with the sympathetic character of Peter.[1] Secondly, it must be shown that Peter and Paul represent divergent tendencies which are unlikely to have permitted close liaison between them. But this is a view of history which is a legacy from the Tübingen school of criticism, with no basis in the New Testament. That both made their own contribution to Christian thought and that Paul's was the greater must be acknowledged, but there is such singular lack of any real divergence between their writings that it is fortuitous either to charge Peter with lack of originality or to regard the Epistle as an attempted reconciliation between opposing parties. The plain facts are that both represent vital aspects of early Christianity.[2]

c. Alternative theories

Before a full appraisal of the problem of authorship can be made, it is essential to examine the probabilities of the alternative views of authorship and these will now be listed and their difficulties noted.

(i) *A pseudonymous letter.* This is the most obvious alternative to Petrine authorship and the earliest critics of the traditional view automatically assumed it. Although the notion of the Tübingen school that the letter was a later celebration of the union between rival Pauline and Petrine parties, thus accounting for the Pauline elements under a Petrine pseudonym, has now been completely abandoned,[3] the idea of an intentional pseudonymous letter has been retained, harnessed to other less questionable motives. H. von Soden[4] suggested that Silvanus issued

---

[1] Cf. Zahn, *INT*, II, p. 176.

[2] Selwyn, in his article on the Eschatology of 1 Peter in *The Background of the New Testament and its Eschatology* (ed. Davies and Daube, 1956), pp. 394–401, shows the background to be essentially Jewish, a further reminder of a primitive origin.*

[3] Cf. A. Harnack, *Die Chronologie der altchristlichen Literatur*, I, p. 456.

[4] *Die Briefe des Petrus, Jakobus, Judas* (1891), p. 117.

the letter in the name of Peter who was renowned as a martyr (1 Pet. v. 1 is understood in this sense), in order to encourage Christians who were suffering in the Domitianic persecutions. But this theory may at once be dismissed, for the sudden appearance of a letter from one so long dead would raise immediate suspicions.[1] Moreover, it would be unintelligible why Silvanus did not then publish the Epistle in his own name.[2] A. Jülicher[3] proposed as author an unknown Roman teacher, whose knowledge of Paul eminently fitted him for the task, but who chose Peter's name to invest his work with the authority of the apostle who had suffered beside Paul in Rome, but this is little more conceivable.

It has been more recently supposed that the main difficulties in this older conception of pseudonymity may be removed by the assumption that the pseudonym is not an intentional device to deceive, but merely an acknowledged literary practice. Thus F. W. Beare[4] argues that the readers would well recognize the pseudonym as a harmless device. They would even accept it as evidence that the author was more concerned about his message than about his own authority. Such a notion of pseudonymity as an accepted literary device has commended itself to many modern scholars because it appears to remove any moral stigma from the older hypothesis of wholehearted pseudonymity. For this reason the description of such a process as 'forgery' is ruled out as unfair and misleading. But to maintain this type of hypothesis at all it is clearly necessary to draw a definite distinction between ancient and modern literary practice, a distinction which in itself is open to criticism.

Basic to this suggestion is the assumption that the author had no intention to deceive. He may be represented, in fact, as a man who, through motives of modesty, uses the convention of pseudonymity to encourage much-harassed Christians in his own time. It would be further necessary to assume that the readers would readily recognize the device and presumably be prepared to overlook any incongruities such as those mentioned above. The readers would in that case even

[1] McNeile-Williams (*INT*, p. 219) rightly point out that to use Peter's name and yet refer to his martyrdom would be too great a blunder for any writer to commit. E. F. Scott (*op. cit.*, p. 221) rejected the idea of a deliberate forgery for much the same reason, although he disputed Petrine authorship.

[2] Cf. R. Knopf's criticisms, *op. cit.*, p. 18. F. W. Beare (*op. cit.*, p. 29) dismisses the theory with hardly a comment.

[3] *Einleitung*, pp. 199, 200.   [4] *Op. cit., loc. cit.*

applaud the author's selfless industry. But the crux of the theory is whether pseudonymity of this type was ever an accepted literary convention. Appeal to the mass of early Christian pseudepigrapha can only mislead unless there is careful differentiation of literary types. F. Torm[1] has demonstrated that early Christian epistolary pseudepigrapha were so rare that this cannot possibly be regarded as a conventional form, and, if it was not, the main basis of this type of theory collapses.

Thus when F. W. Beare[2] declares that there 'can be no possible doubt that Peter is a pseudonym', the grounds of his confidence may be challenged. In any case, his own attempt to explain the use of the pseudonym is most unsatisfactory, for he considers it to be a kind of dramatic re-creation of the personality of the pseudonym, comparable with the monologues of Browning. But are we to suppose that an author, under the stresses of an impending and serious persecution, composed a letter with such attention to a purely literary technique? The idea is surely incredible. It will not do to dismiss the whole problem, as Beare does,[3] by merely stating that the question of authorship was unimportant and that it was the teaching that mattered, for it is obvious that the teaching had to be authenticated by an authorized teacher. Clearly, to maintain a theory of literary pseudonymity as distinct from deceptive pseudonymity, it is necessary to provide more adequate parallels and more suitable motives than Beare has been able to do. The difficulty here is the general difficulty of all hypotheses of early Christian epistolary pseudonymity.

F. Torm[4] in his penetrating examination of pseudonymous methods and motives maintains that it is impossible to make out an intelligible case for the use of pseudonymity in 1 Peter. The fact that the author's purpose is encouragement means that personal relations between readers and writer would play a much more important part than apostolic authority. Why did not the author, if not Peter, publish his encouragements in his own name? There seems to be no satisfactory answer to this question. The Epistle deals with no heresy which might have required apostolic authority to refute it. Moreover, the mention of Silvanus and Mark cannot be regarded as part of the pseudepigraphical machinery, for a pseudo-Peter would surely avoid associating

---

[1] *Die Psychologie der Pseudonymität im Hinblick auf die Literatur des Urchristentums* (1932). Cf. the appendix on Epistolary Pseudepigraphy, pp. 671–684 above.
[2] *Op. cit.*, p. 25.   [3] *Op. cit.*, p. 29.
[4] *Op. cit.*, pp. 41–44.

so closely with Peter those who, according to the Acts and the Pauline Epistles, were associates of Paul. Nor would a pseudo-Peter make Peter echo the influence of Paul.

(ii) *An anonymous letter later attributed to Peter.* Conscious of the unsatisfactory character of theories of intentional pseudepigraphy which had been proposed, and yet persuaded that the Epistle possessed non-Petrine characteristics, Harnack[1] proposed a compromise. The opening and closing sentences (i. 1ff. and v. 12ff.) were, in his view, appended later, thus freeing the main body of the letter from any attachment to Peter's name and enabling him to propose that a Roman teacher familiar with Paul's letters felt free to address areas through which Paul had travelled in his mission work. A similar idea was maintained by B. H. Streeter,[2] who nevertheless divided the main material into (1) a bishop's homily to newly baptized converts (i. 3–iv. 11) and (2) a bishop's pastoral letter, addressed to neighbouring churches.[3] Neither Harnack nor Streeter could produce manuscript evidence in support of the spuriousness of the beginning and ending which entirely depends on subjective considerations. Streeter's suggestion that Aristion was the bishop and author of the main part does nothing to enhance his theory. A. C. McGiffert's[4] opinion that the attachment of Peter's name was no more than a scribal guess is no more probable.

Theories of anonymous circulation are generally proposed only as an offset to the difficulties of pseudonymous authorship.[5] But the problem is merely moved a stage farther to pseudonymous attribution. That an epistle circulated without the author's name presents no difficulty in view of the Epistle to the Hebrews,[6] but that it should later undergo scribal additions of the type conjectured raises serious problems.

In the absence of positive manuscript evidence any theories of inter-

---

[1] *Die Chronologie der altchristlichen Literatur*, i, pp. 457ff.*

[2] *The Primitive Church*, pp. 123ff.; cf. W. Bornemann (*ZNTW*, 19, 1919–20, pp. 143–165) who regards i. 3–v. 11 as a baptismal address by Silvanus.

[3] See pp. 797ff. for discussion on partition theories.

[4] *A History of Christianity in the Apostolic Age* (1897), pp. 593ff. His own guess was that Barnabas was the author.

[5] Cf. K. and S. Lake, *INT* (1938), pp. 165ff.

[6] Harnack's citing of Ephesians, *Barnabas* and *II Clement* as not wholly dissimilar is inconsequential whatever view is taken of the author problem in these cases, since in none of them is an address and closing salutation 'added' to give precision to the author's name (cf. Chase's criticism, *HDB*, iii, p. 787).

polation are highly suspicious, for two reasons. (1) It is difficult to conceive how an epistle originally circulating as anonymous could ever acquire an apostolic name, a specific address and concluding greetings without raising the least suspicion among any churches ir the area purporting to be addressed. (2) Resort to interpolation theories is so thoroughly subjective that it is altogether too facile a means of removing difficulties. In the nature of the case theories which deal with the text as it stands are more credible than those which depend on speculative scribal additions for which no evidence exists.

Both the variety and dubious character of those alternative views are in themselves favourable to apostolic authorship, since disputants must not only produce good reasons for rejecting the traditional position, but must themselves produce an alternative explanation of all the facts which is more satisfactory than the rejected hypothesis. When so careful a critic as E. F. Scott[1] fairly acknowledged that the attribution of the Epistle to Peter must have been due to a misunderstanding no longer discoverable, this gives the measure of perplexity experienced by advocates of non-Petrine authorship.

d. Conclusion of the discussion on authorship

The result of this survey of various theories leaves us in no doubt that the traditional view which accepts the claims of the Epistle to be apostolic is more reasonable than any alternative hypothesis. We may see here a true reflection of the apostle's experience of Jesus Christ and his lasting contribution to the doctrine of the Christian Church. If there is not the depth of the mind of Paul, there is a warm affection which is unmistakable and a deep sympathy with those whom he seeks to help.

Indirect support for this view of the Epistle may be found in various echoes of Jesus' teaching,[2] some faint traces of events in which Peter played a part which are recorded in the Gospels (as e.g. the possible allusion in v. 5 to the girding incident in Jn. xiii. 4f., and the reference to shepherding the flock in 1 Pet. v. 2ff., and Jn. xxi. 15–17). There are also parallels with the Acts speeches[3] attributed to Peter which are not without significance.

---

[1] *Op. cit.*, p. 221.

[2] Cf. the list of references in Chase's article (*HDB*, III, pp. 787, 788).*

[3] For details see the section on literary affinities on pp. 803ff. Cf. also Wand's discussion, *op. cit.*, pp. 26–28.

III. PURPOSE

Assuming that Peter is writing as he says he is to the 'dispersion scattered throughout Pontus, Galatia, Cappadocia, Asia and Bithynia' (1 Pet. i. 1, RSV), we may ascertain the purpose of the Epistle with a fair degree of precision. It is clearly designed for a specific group of Christians although scattered over a wide area. The keynote of the letter is hope and Peter wishes to exhort these Christians to live in accordance with the hope they have received through Christ. He gives practical guidance to assist in their human relationships and particularly exhorts them to endure suffering in a joyful manner for Christ's sake. His main purpose is, therefore, hortatory, but not infrequently he introduces theological considerations which press home the ethical injunctions. In particular he presents the work of Christ as a stimulus for the Christian endurance of suffering, while at the same time drawing out more fundamental aspects of its meaning.[1] In this way he shows the indissoluble link between doctrine and practice.[2] This is possibly what he means when he states his own purpose in v. 12 as being to exhort and testify 'that this is the true grace of God'. Some difference of opinion exists over the precise meaning of the latter phrase, but it seems best to regard it as referring to the message of the gospel which the author is claiming to have written or, under the Silvanus hypothesis,[3] to have caused to be written.

Different explanations of the purpose are suggested by those who

---

[1] This emphasis on the work of Christ has led some scholars to see in this Epistle a homily designed for the Feast of Redemption (cf. Selwyn, *The First Epistle of St. Peter*, pp. 62ff.). Connected with this feast was the baptismal ceremony, and this would lend support to the hypothesis that this Epistle is based on a baptismal homily. Its applicability for such a Christian festival is undoubted, but this is very different from claiming that the author intended it for this purpose. The historic occasion appears to be too specific for that.

[2] That the author of 1 Peter in ii. 11, 12 is drawing out the close connection between Christian behaviour and preaching has been suggestively brought out by W. Brandt in his article in *Manet in Alternum, Eine Festschrift für O. Schmitz* (ed. W. Foerster, 1953), pp. 10–25. He concludes that Christian behaviour continues the challenge of the Word. Cf. also W. C. van Unnik's discussion on good works (*NTS*, 1, 1954–55, pp. 92–110; *NTS*, 2, 1956, pp. 198–202).

[3] J. W. C. Wand (*op. cit.*, pp. 29–30) conjectures that these words are added to authenticate Silvanus' teaching which Peter is claiming to be his own, and in view of the fact that some may have disputed it he also commends Silvanus himself as a faithful brother.

maintain a pseudonymous authorship and a later date. E. J. Goodspeed[1] holds that this epistle, like *1 Clement*, was called forth by the exhortation in Hebrews v. 12 that the readers (whom he identifies with the Roman Church) should become teachers. He also maintains that this Epistle aims to undo the harm done by the book of Revelation in its attitude towards the State.[2] But it is incredible that any who needed 'milk' (first principles) should be able so rapidly to reach the maturity and spiritual inspiration required to produce 1 Peter. Moreover, that Epistle is not primarily didactic but practical, while its brief and restrained advice on State relationships would be incredible as a counteraction to the Apocalypse. The whole idea may be dismissed as pure speculation without any basis in fact.[3]

Those who dispute the unity of 1 Peter naturally place a still different construction on the purpose. This will become clear when the various theories involving liturgical materials are examined below (see pp. 798f.). But a typical hypothesis is that of F. W. Beare,[4] who regards the letter proper as confined to iv. 12–v. 11, in which the author sends an urgent message to those already in the throes of a fiery persecution and therefore in need of encouragement. To strengthen that message Beare believes that parts of a baptismal discourse were incorporated. Reasons will later be given for considering this hypothesis to be improbable.

IV. DESTINATION

Although this Epistle possesses the character of a circular letter, it differs from the other general Epistles of the New Testament in specifying the area in which the readers are confined. But there are certain problems attached even to this.

1. Are the districts which are mentioned to be taken politically or geographically? If the former, the area would be considerably greater than the latter, for the ethnic area of Galatia was but a part of the provincial district. Yet it seems most probable that only the northern part was intended, in which case the letter was directed to those parts north

---

[1] *INT*, pp. 267ff. It is far-fetched to see in 1 Pet. v. 12 (the word 'exhort') an echo of Heb. xiii. 22 (*ibid.*, p. 271).

[2] Other parallels which Goodspeed finds are the Asiatic address of both writings and the offsetting of Petrine authorship against Johannine (*ibid.*, *loc. cit.*).

[3] It is quite unconvincing for Goodspeed (*op. cit.*, p. 280) to claim that such a theory fully explains both the pseudonymity and the address (i.e. churches other than Rome).

[4] *Op. cit.*, pp. 7, 8.

of the Taurus mountains. This conclusion is supported by the fact that Pontus and Bithynia, which formed one administrative Roman province, are yet not only mentioned separately, but one comes first and the other last.

2. Was any of this area within the sphere of Paul's influence? This has already been discussed (see p. 784) and the suggestion made that Paul did not in fact work in those areas, except Asia. The correctness of this depends on what view is taken of the North or South theory for the destination of Galatians. But the statement in Acts xvi. 6, 7 that Paul was forbidden by the Spirit to preach either in Asia or in Bithynia on his second journey would suggest that Luke is explaining the absence of any personal evangelistic activity by Paul in that district.

3. Why are the districts mentioned in the order in which they stand in i. 1? There have been four different explanations. First, those who regard the words as an interpolation see only an entire lack of order, for which the unintelligence of the scribe is held to be responsible.[1] Secondly, others who follow the pseudonymous interpretation and date the Epistle in the reign of Trajan connect the mention of Pontus first and Bithynia last with the governorship of Pliny over the joint province.[2] Thirdly, the hazardous guess that the order was dictated by rhythmical considerations is not likely to commend itself.[3] Fourthly, a more generally accepted explanation is that the order represents the itinerary of the bearer of the letter, who may well have landed at a port of Pontus, visited the churches in the districts named in that order and then returned to Bithynia.[4] Of these explanations there is no doubt that the last is the most reasonable, in spite of F. W. Beare's[5] objection that such a route could not be planned in an area of intense persecution. If the persecution has not yet reached the stage of intensity, this objection would be invalid.

Having established the destination, our next enquiry concerns the character of the readers, and this enquiry will be approached from two

[1] B. H. Streeter thought the address was added when Pliny began to persecute the Christians, but the occasion, even if correct, does not explain the strange nature of the addition, especially the splitting of Pliny's official province (cf. *The Primitive Church*, p. 126).

[2] Cf. Beare, *op. cit.*, pp. 23f.

[3] Cf. W. L. Knox, *Theology*, XLIX (1946), p. 344.

[4] Cf. F. J. A. Hort, *The First Epistle of Peter* (1898), p. 15; Moffatt, *ILNT*, p. 327.

[5] *Op. cit.*, pp. 22f.

angles, social and racial. The district was generally economically prosperous although there was a wide disparity between the landowners and merchants on the one hand and the working classes on the other.[1] The churches were mainly drawn from the latter group, if any significance may be attached to the fact that slaves but not masters are mentioned in the injunctions for social behaviour (ii. 18–25). Yet much is said about the duties of citizenship (ii. 11–17) which would apply mainly to free men (see especially verse 16), and our conclusion must be that these churches, like most in the primitive period, were mixed in respect of the social status of their members.[2]

As to their racial group there have been three proposals: Jewish, Gentile or Jewish-Gentile.

1. The theory that Jewish Christian readers are addressed is as old as Origen but has not gained much recent support.[3] B. Weiss,[4] made much of the wide use of the LXX in citations and the unintelligible character of the argument for those unfamiliar with its Old Testament background. Added to this is the strangely Jewish flavour of the address—'elect strangers of the Diaspora', all three terms of which have Jewish connotations. But this line of argument proceeds on the assumption that what is true of the writer must be true of the readers. The Jewish background of the writer can hardly be denied, but this tells us nothing about the background of the readers.[5] At the same time caution must be exercised before concluding that Gentile readers would not have been sufficiently acquainted with the LXX. The use of 'diaspora' may be equally well interpreted as symbolical of the Christian Church conceived as the New Israel, a thought many times echoed in the New Testament. But the most damaging criticism of the theory of Jewish addressees is the manner in which the writer appeals to the readers' previously 'vain way of life' (i. 18), mentions their 'former lusts in ignorance' (i. 14), speaks of them having done what the Gentiles do (iv. 3, 4, then follows a list of Gentile vices), and reminds them that they were once a 'no-people' but were called out of darkness (ii. 9, 10). It is difficult to see

[1] Cf. Selwyn, *op. cit.,* pp. 48, 49.
[2] Cf. Wand, *op. cit.,* pp. 31, 32.
[3] Its most enthusiastic modern supporter has been D. Völter, *Der I Petrusbrief— seine Entstehung und Stellung in der Geschichte des Urchristentums* (1906). But his arguments gained little support. Yet cf. R. Leconte, *Les épîtres catholiques* (1953), p. 65.
[4] *A Manual of Introduction to the New Testament* (1887), II, pp. 137ff.
[5] Cf. Selwyn, *op. cit.,* p. 43.

how these words could apply to any but Gentiles.[1] Moreover, there is no evidence of the existence of all-Jewish Christian churches in the provinces named in the address, and it would in any case be difficult to conceive in provinces such as Asia and Galatia which had, at least in part, come under Paul's influence.[2]

2. In the light of these considerations it would seem certain that Gentile Christians were mainly in mind, and this is supported by the fact that the areas addressed were predominantly Gentile. Yet in these same areas there were strong Jewish communities and the most probable solution is therefore the third.

3. That these churches were mixed[3] is highly probable from what we know of the primitive communities generally. Many of the Jews of the Dispersion were only loosely attached to Judaism, and would have formed, with the Gentile proselytes, a ready audience for the first evangelistic impact of the Christian missions. Of the origin of these churches nothing is known. As already pointed out, they lay mainly beyond the area evangelized by the apostle Paul, but two suggestions are, at least, probable. If Silvanus were known to them he may have been responsible for the establishing of at least some of these churches. The church at Ephesus, while Paul was ministering there, evangelized the province of Asia (Acts xix. 10), and the mission might well have continued beyond the borders of the province. It has been suggested that Peter had worked in this district, although the use of the third person in i. 12 would seem to exclude this suggestion. A more probable idea is that the nucleus of the churches in this district consisted of those who were converted on the day of Pentecost.[4]

V. DATE

In the course of the preceding discussions the problems of the persecution during which this letter was sent received careful attention and

---

[1] In reply to these criticisms, Leconte (*op. cit.*, pp. 65f.) maintains that i. 18 could refer to the futility of antiquated Jewish ritual, that similarly i. 14 could mean Jewish pre-Christian passions and that iv. 3, 4 refers only to Gentile behaviour as a pattern and does not necessarily identify the readers as Gentiles. Moreover, he thinks that iii. 20, 21, i. 17 and ii. 9 are all more applicable to Jewish Christians. While these arguments cannot be lightly dismissed the alternative interpretation of these references as addressed mainly to Gentile readers would seem more natural.

[2] R. Knopf (*op. cit.*, pp. 2ff.) made a strong point of this in criticizing Weiss.

[3] As Selwyn (*op. cit.*, p. 44) concluded.   [4] Cf. Moffatt, *ILNT*, p. 327 n.

since the answer to this problem determines the dating there is little more to be said. The three main proposals are: (1) in Trajan's reign (*c.* AD 111); (2) in Domitian's reign (AD 90–100); (3) in Nero's reign (*c.* AD 62–64). We have seen what little justification there is for preferring either of the first two and nothing prevents the third from being the most probable. Whether it was before or after the death of Paul is difficult to decide with certainty. There has in fact been some difference of opinion whether Peter was martyred before Paul, but the most generally accepted opinion is the reverse. Yet the dating of 1 Peter does not hinge upon any decision regarding this. There are a few internal considerations which favour the Neronian date mentioned above. Selwyn[1] pointed out that the doctrine and ecclesiastical organization are fairly early and would suit a date not much after AD 60. He also maintains, on a literal interpretation of the writer's own description of his readers as 'elect sojourners', that some crisis must recently have occurred to cause the scattering of the Christians. This he thinks was the martyrdom of James, the Lord's brother, at the hands of the Jews, thus making the breach between Christianity and Judaism public and decisive, with Christians unable to shelter under the legality of the Jewish faith. Selwyn even suggested that Paul's death may have been caused by James' martyrdom, since Nero's Jewishly-inclined mistress Poppaea may well have heard from Jewish sources of the way in which the Jerusalem Jews had treated the Christian leader, which would be tantamount to an official Jewish denunciation of Christianity.

Another indication of probable dating is the teaching of 1 Peter with regard to the State (1 Pet. ii. 13–17). The approach is so conciliatory that it would better fit the period up to AD 64 than a later period. It seems difficult to imagine any writer urging submission to the infamous Nero after the commencement of his notorious blood-bath of AD 64. Yet it must be remembered that the civil administration of the provinces would not immediately be affected by the personal caprice of the emperor, and in any case it would have been folly for Christians to have shown any open evidence of sedition, since suspicion enough had already been stirred up against them by Nero's action. It is impossible to fix the date with any exactness, but the period immediately preceding or during the Neronian persecutions would appear to be the most probable.

[1] *Op. cit.*, pp. 56ff.

VI. UNITY

Because of the doxology at iv. 11 and the different emphasis on the persecutions in the subsequent section, it has been proposed by various scholars that the Epistle as it now stands does not represent an original unity. The following are the various attempts to explain this break and the general method of composition.[1]

a. A combination of a baptismal sermon and a general address

This view was maintained by B. H. Streeter[2] who placed an interval of two or three years between the two parts to account for the greater severity of persecution and who suggested that an editor, at a considerably later time, joined the two parts to form an epistle, adding the opening address and closing salutations. Although the homiletical form of the Epistle is fairly plain, it is no more than might be expected from a man whose vocation was preaching and not writing. Such a man could hardly fail to dress up his thoughts in homiletical forms. Yet it is not impossible that the Epistle may embody an address, or even more than one address, given orally before being recorded. If there was need for exhortations and encouragements of this kind to be written, there was equal need for them to be spoken. But Streeter's partition theory is improbable on several grounds. (1) The second part (iv. 12–v. 7) does not strike the reader as a separate entity,[3] for its themes echo what is contained in the first part and follow quite naturally from it. (2) The appearance of a doxology in the body of the Epistle, which Streeter supposed marked the end of the first part, is not peculiar to 1 Peter.[4] In Paul's letters particularly there are doxologies that are included before the finale (e.g. Gal. i. 5; Rom. xi. 36; Eph. iii. 21; 1 Tim. i. 17). A readier explanation is the writer's natural outburst of praise when contemplating the purpose of all Christian service. It is certainly by no means evident that a doxology must mean the conclusion of the writer's train of thought. (3) The theory involves a clumsy process on the part of the compiler of the Epistle. The advantages of joining the two parts and turning them into a pseudonymous letter

[1] For a useful survey of the most recent theories, cf. the article by R. P. Martin on the composition of 1 Peter in *Vox Evangelica*, 1 (ed. R. P. Martin, 1962).

[2] *The Primitive Church*, pp. 123ff.*   [3] Cf. J. W. C. Wand, *op. cit.*, p. 2.

[4] Cf. B. F. Westcott's note on the apostolic doxologies, *The Epistle to the Hebrews*[2] (1892), pp. 464, 465.

with closing greetings, which raise a number of difficulties, are altogether too obscure. Such procedure can claim no parallels and must be classified as an unsupported speculation.

b. *An original liturgy adapted to a literary form*

One presentation of this hypothesis is that of H. Preisker,[1] who considers that the first section is a liturgy for a baptismal service minus the rubrics (with the baptismal rite taking place between i. 21 and i. 22).[2] At iv. 12 the service is designed for the whole congregation, which explains why the present tense is used in connection with the persecutions, since these would affect established Christians but not novices. But if this were a true account of the origin of its contents, the liturgy must have been considerably adapted to make it suitable for an epistolary form. The many instances of 'now' in the Epistle need not be regarded as evidence of a liturgy in process (as Preisker assumes), but rather the realization on the part of the Christians of the importance of the present in their eschatological outlook.[3] The supposed references to baptism in this Epistle are certainly not strong (the only explicit reference is iii. 21) and the figurative expressions (such as are found in i. 23 and ii. 2) are more naturally explained of spiritual regeneration without reference to any external rite, particularly as the rebirth is specifically effected through the word[4] without reference to water.

Another form of this theory is the paschal hypothesis of F. L. Cross.[5] The key to this approach is the connection between the 'suffering' (πάσχω) so prominent in 1 Peter and the *pascha* (or Easter) festival.[6] Cross appeals to the similarity between the Pascal Baptismal Eucharist and the themes of this Epistle: baptism, Passover, passion, resurrection,

---

[1] In the third edition of H. Windisch's *Die katholischen Briefe* (1951), pp. 156ff.

[2] Preisker's idea of a baptismal act at this juncture was strongly criticized by F. Hauck in his review of Preisker's revision of Windisch's Commentary (*ThLZ*, 77, 1952, pp. 34, 35) on the grounds that the perfect tense in verse 22 refers to sanctification attested in Christian living.

[3] Cf. E. G. Selwyn, in *The Background of the New Testament and its Eschatology* (ed. W. D. Davies and D. Daube, 1956), pp. 394f. This point is well criticized by C. F. D. Moule, *NTS*, 3 (1957), pp. 1ff.

[4] This λόγος cannot be the baptismal formula as Preisker would maintain (cf. Moule, *op. cit.*, p. 6; Beare, *op. cit.*, p. 86).

[5] *1 Peter: a Pascal Liturgy* (1954).

[6] This comparison between πάσχω and *pascha* is open to strong objection on lexical grounds. Cf. W. C. van Unnik's criticisms (*ET*, LXVIII, 1956, pp 79–83).

moral duties. His main source is the *Apostolic Tradition* of Hippolytus, but not all scholars will agree on the inferences he draws from this source.[1] As A. F. Walls has pointed out, even if a correspondence is established, it should be possible to make sense of the Epistle without calling on such parallels. After all, the material is preserved for us in the form of an Epistle which is certainly not unintelligible apart from a liturgical explanation.[2] It is more likely, in fact, that the liturgy was moulded by the previously existing Epistle.[3]

c. A double letter which was later combined

A suggestion by C. F. D. Moule[4] that two letters (i. 1–iv. 1 plus conclusion, and i. 1–ii. 10, iv. 12–v. 14) were written by Peter at the same time and were united in the process of transmission, suffers the handicap of most partition theories in lacking all vestige of textual support, although it has in its favour the maintenance of the common authorship of the two parts.[5] Moreover, if, as Moule suggests, each letter was addressed to different parts where different conditions of persecution obtained, it is all the more difficult to imagine how they came to be united in the form in which we now have them. Such a combination by a copyist or editor would be rather unusual and requires some satisfactory explanation, not only of the compiler's purpose but also of his method. The whole theory has an artificial ring about it, which raises suspicions whether any ancient editor would ever have combined the two letters in this way. At the same time it cannot be pronounced impossible. Yet the crucial question is whether it is really necessary.

[1] Cf. A. F. Walls' criticism, *op. cit.*, pp. 61, 62.

[2] T. C. G. Thornton, in his article '1 Peter, a Paschal Liturgy?', *JTS*, New Series, XII, i (1961), pp. 14–26, complains that Cross uses the word 'liturgy' too vaguely and suggests that on the same basis liturgy could be found in most New Testament books.

[3] M. E. Boismard has carried the liturgical explanation which he favours for 1 Peter into other parts of the New Testament (e.g. Titus, 1 John, Colossians, James) in his attempt to demonstrate the influences of liturgies on Christian writings (cf. his articles in *RB*, LXIII, 1956, pp. 182–208; *RB*, LXIV, 1957, pp. 161–183; and his monograph *Quatre Hymnes Baptismales dans la Première Epître de Pierre*, 1961).*

[4] *Op. cit.*, pp. 6ff.

[5] But W. Bieder (*Grund und Kraft der Mission nach dem ersten Petrusbrief, Theologische Studien*, 29, 1950), who similarly maintains two writings (i. 3–iv. 11, iv. 12–v. 11), regards both as post-apostolic.

d. A letter, with a postscript for a particular church

Somewhat akin to the foregoing is the view[1] that the concluding part may be regarded as a postscript designed for particular communities which were subjected to severe persecution and therefore needed special encouragement. This is a more likely explanation than the foregoing because it preserves the essential unity of the Epistle as it stands and is in harmony with the internal indication that it was sent to a specific group of churches. But it hardly seems to be demanded by the evidence. In v. 1 the author addresses 'the elders among you' and the advice given would be applicable to elders of any church. In fact, it is not easy to see what parts of iv. 12–v. 11 would not have been generally relevant.

e. A circular type of letter in its present form

None of the evidence set out by exponents of the preceding theories demands the surrender of the essential unity of the Epistle, and it remains, therefore, the most reasonable approach to assume that the whole was directed to all the churches in the areas mentioned, and that the writer may have intended to finish at iv. 11, but further developments prompted him to add the additional material before attaching the concluding salutations. Or else in the concluding part he may be giving a brief practical summary of points already mentioned theoretically.[2] A theory of this kind has the advantage of not requiring the postulating of any partition and assumes quite naturally that the double doxology merely indicates two stages in the process of composition. It is a safe principle that if the Epistle can be adequately interpreted as a unity, it should be.[3]

f. Interpolation theories

The subject of the unity of the Epistle cannot be left without mention of the attempts to find interpolations in the present text. Among earlier scholars who advocated such theories were A. Harnack,[4] whose theory

---

[1] Cf. J. H. A. Hart, *EGT*, v, pp. 29, 30.

[2] Cf. T. C. G. Thornton (*op. cit.*, p. 26), who considers that no theory is satisfactory which accounts for the first part without giving a satisfactory explanation of how and why the latter part was added.

[3] Many recent scholars have been anxious to maintain the unity; cf. F. V. Filson, *Interpretation*, ix (1955), pp. 400–412; W. Nauck, *ZNTW*, 46 (1955), pp. 68–80. C. E. B. Cranfield (*The First Epistle of Peter*, 1950, p. 18), although considering i. 3–iv. 11 as originally a sermon, still maintains the unity of the Epistle.

[4] *TU*, II, ii (1884), pp. 106–109.

of later additions in i. 1, 2 and v. 12–14 has already been mentioned; W. Soltau,[1] who made the discovery of a whole series of interpolations, which transformed an early tract into a Petrine Epistle; and in a similar vein, but differing considerably in detail, D. Völter.[2] These theories have commanded little support, for they appeal only to ultra-critical minds. A more recent tendency in the same direction is found in Bultmann's[3] treatment of the passage iii. 18–22, where he separates verses 19–21 for no other reason than that this section spoils his own interpretation of the passage as a hymn. Generally speaking there is far less inclination than formerly to resort to such drastic methods and little serious attention need therefore be given to such theories.

VII. PLACE OF WRITING

The author has given greetings from the church at 'Babylon' (v. 13) and it may reasonably be assumed that it is from 'Babylon' that he writes. But what does he mean by Babylon? Is it literal or is it a cryptogram? That Peter was in Mesopotamian Babylon[4] when he wrote this letter is most unlikely for several reasons. (1) Peter is nowhere else associated with this region; (2) the Eastern Church did not until a late period claim any association with Peter in its Church origins; (3) the area itself was very sparsely populated, especially in the period subsequent to the migration in AD 41[5] and the resultant massacre of large numbers of Jews at Seleucia; (4) early tradition centred the activities of Peter in the West

---

[1] TSK, 78 (1905), pp. 302–315; 79 (1906), pp. 456–460. W. Soltau considered that the original Epistle consisted only of i. 3–22a, i. 23–ii. 4, ii. 6–11, ii. 13–iii. 18, iv. 1–4, iv. 7–19, v. 6–11, which was later worked over by two different hands. C. Clemen (TSK, 1905, pp. 619–628) strongly criticized this theory, particularly because of the improbability of a final editor affixing so vague an address to a letter form, since this, according to Deissmann, was rare.

[2] Op. cit. Cf. also idem, ZNTW, 9 (1908), pp. 74–77. For details of all three of these theories, see Moffatt, ILNT, pp. 342–344.

[3] In his article 'Bekenntnis-und Liedfragmente im ersten Petrusbrief', in Coniectanea Neotestamentica XI in honorem Antonii Fridrichsen (1947), pp. 1–14. This method of criticism is dismissed with little consideration by J. Jeremias, ZNTW, 42 (1949), pp. 194–201. Cf. also C. E. B. Cranfield, ET, LXIX (1958), pp. 369–372.

[4] This opinion was maintained by Calvin in an attempt to dissociate the name of Peter with Rome, in opposition to Roman Catholic claims. Cf. H. Alford, Greek Testament[4] (1871), IV, pp. 127, 128. H. C. Thiessen (INT[4], 1956, p. 285) is a recent upholder of this view.

[5] Cf. Josephus, Antiquities, xviii. 9. 8.

and not the East; (5) Mark almost certainly found a sphere of activity in the West, but nothing is known of him working in the East.

Another suggestion which may be dismissed with little consideration is that an Egyptian Babylon is meant.[1] But the Alexandrian church laid no claim to it and this Babylon was so small a district that it seems highly improbable that Peter made his headquarters there without such a fact leaving any trace in early tradition. Yet another idea is that the Epistle originated in the region of Antioch. Boismard[2] maintains this view on doctrinal grounds (the descent into hell idea, he thinks, was connected with that district) and historical grounds (the believers were first called Christians there).[3]

But the majority of scholars favour Rome as the place of writing taking 'Babylon' as symbolic, in the same sense as in the Apocalypse.[4] The Roman martyrdom of Peter is fairly well attested,[5] and if this is genuine tradition it seems highly improbable that in the immediate past Peter had been residing in Babylon.[6] But the problem arises why Peter resorted to symbolic expression. There is little indication in the context that any figurative meaning was intended, although the meta-

[1] Michaelis (*Einleitung*, p. 287) cites de Zwaan as a recent advocate of the view that a military colony named Babylon in the Nile delta is meant. Cf. also G. T. Manley, *EQ*, XVI (1944). This colony is mentioned by Strabo, xvii. 30 and Josephus, *Antiquities*, ii. 15. 1.

[2] *RB*, LXIV (1957), p. 181 n. 2. Beare (*op. cit.*, p. 204) disputes this because of the absence of trace in Ignatius and because of the links with *1 Clement*. Yet Beare noted that the *Apostolic Tradition*, with which 1 Peter shows some similarities (cf. F. L. Cross, *op. cit.*, pp. 12ff.), may point to a Syrian background (*op. cit.*, p. 204).

[3] Knopf (*op. cit.*, p. 25) having disputed Petrine authorship saw no more reason to regard the Babylon (= Rome) reference in v. 13 as authentic than the author's name in i. 1. As he maintained an Asiatic destination, he considered an Asiatic place of origin was therefore most probable. Beare (*op. cit.*, pp. 31, 202ff.) first favoured the same district as the addressees, but later changed to Rome.

[4] For a clear discussion of the whole matter, cf. O. Cullmann, *Peter: Disciple, Apostle, and Martyr* (1953), pp. 82–86. Cullmann thinks that Rome is most probable, but does not entirely exclude the possibility of an alternative.

[5] Cf. Cullmann's detailed discussion, *op. cit.*, pp. 89–152. He places most reliance on a statement of Gaius, a text of Tertullian against Callistus and the declaration of Porphyrius. For a briefer statement, cf. J. Lowe, *Saint Peter* (1956), pp. 23–45. Cf. also J. Munck (*Petrus und Paulus in der Offenbarung Johannis*, 1950, pp. 30ff.), who finds a reference to the martyrdom of both Peter and Paul at Rome in Rev. xi.

[6] E. Lohse (*ZNTW*, 45, 1954, pp. 83–85) maintains a Roman place of origin particularly on the grounds of affinities of language with *1 Clement*, which he sets out in detail. But it is not clear why this should demonstrate the place of despatch.

phorical use of 'diaspora' in i. 1 may give an indication of the author's bent of mind. It is probable that the cryptogram was used as a security measure.[1] At the time of writing, Rome was the centre of vicious action against Christianity and avoidance of any mention of the Roman church would be a wise move if the letter fell into official hands. The writer evidently assumed that the readers would have understood the symbolism.[2]

As a further proposition, some have seen in the reference to 'she in Babylon' a woman rather than a church, and linking this passage with 1 Corinthians ix. 5, have ventured on the conjecture that Peter's wife is intended.[3] But this is a strange description for his wife, and although it may be contended that an abstraction like 'the church in Babylon' is an unnatural partner for 'my son Mark' in the greetings of v. 13, yet the abstraction represents a specific group of people. There is nothing unnatural in this combination, and, in fact, 'the church and Mark' seems more probable than 'my wife and Mark'.[4]

VIII. LITERARY AFFINITIES

That there is behind this Epistle clear evidence of the author's Old Testament background will be disputed by few, in spite of Perdelwitz's[5] attempt to prove that the background is to be found in the mystery religions. Not only does 1 Peter cite the Old Testament several times, but the allusions are in many instances drawn from it (cf. for instance, the lamb (i. 19), the whole passage ii. 4–10, the parallels with Is. liii in ii. 21ff., Sarah (iii. 6) and Noah (iii. 20)).

Recently, in conjunction with liturgical theories for the Epistle, stress has been laid upon the use of the Exodus typology and of Psalm xxxiv. The former is used by Boismard[6] in support of his baptismal homily hypothesis and by Cross,[7] who finds several traces of it in 1

---

[1] Cf. Selwyn, *The First Epistle of St. Peter*, p. 243.

[2] C. F. D. Moule (*NTS*, 3, 1957, pp. 8, 9) disputes the security grounds because of the plain exhortation to loyalty in ii. 13–17. He regards the motive as homiletic, Babylon being used as symbolic of the Christian's exile in the world. It should be noted here that the metaphorical use of 'Babylon' is found in contemporary Jewish pseudepigraphical literature and in the Church Fathers (see Cullmann, *op. cit.*, p. 84, for details).

[3] Cf. C. Bigg, *op. cit.*, p. 197; and H. Alford, *op. cit.*, p. 387.

[4] Cf. Moffatt, *ILNT*, p. 328.

[5] *Die Mysterienreligionen und das Problem des ersten Petrusbriefes* (1911).

[6] Cf. *RB*, LXIII (1957), pp. 182ff.　　　　[7] *Op. cit.*, pp. 24f.

Peter i and ii, in support of his Paschal Vigil theory. But it is open to criticism on two grounds. (1) It is strange, if the Exodus motif was so dominant, that the flood allusion has been used rather than the wilderness allusion to illustrate baptism[1]; and (2) some allusions to Exodus are not surprising in an epistle which presents the Christian believers as the New Israel, and need not point to any liturgical use of the Old Testament.

The same may be said of Bornemann's theory[2] that the whole Epistle is a homily based on Psalm xxxiv, though here again a liturgical theorist such as Boismard[3] thinks that the Psalm formed part of the liturgical ceremony. It is better to regard this Psalm,[4] with its theme of God's protection of the loyal sufferer, as part of the author's own background, which would be clearly relevant to his present theme.

Several connections of thought have been found between this Epistle and other New Testament writings and the most important of these are Romans, Ephesians, Hebrews, James and the Acts. Sanday and Headlam[5] cite eight passages from Romans showing close affinities with this Epistle, although Wand[6] reduces their significance by accounting for the resemblances, either as showing common Old Testament influence or common lists of duties, or as evidence of the semi-liturgical character of the material. Yet some dependence of 1 Peter upon Romans is generally admitted. In the case of Ephesians C. L. Mitton[7] claims to have established sufficient parallels to conclude that the author of 1 Peter has used Ephesians. But because he regards Ephesians as non-Pauline he is obliged to regard 1 Peter as non-Petrine. The parallels may be admitted and the question of dependence granted, but if there are strong grounds for assuming the early dating of 1 Peter this should indicate an early and therefore Pauline origin for Ephesians.[8] On the other hand, literary

[1] Cf. Moule's criticisms, NTS, 3 (1957), pp. 4, 5.
[2] ZNTW, 19 (1919–20), pp. 143ff.
[3] Cf. RB, LXIV, pp. 180ff. Moule (op. cit., loc. cit.) disputes this on the ground that there is no evidence that Ps. xxxiv was ever connected with the Passover.
[4] Jeremias (ZNTW, 42, 1949, pp. 199, 200) finds evidence of the influence of Ps. xvi. 8–11 on the author's Descensus doctrine.
[5] The Epistle to the Romans (ICC, 1895), pp. lxxiv ff.*
[6] Op. cit., p. 19.
[7] Cf. The Epistle to the Ephesians (1951), pp. 176–197; and his article 'The Relationship between 1 Peter and Ephesians', JTS, New Series, 1 (1950), pp. 67ff.
[8] C. L. Mitton (op. cit., p. 196) admits this result must follow if 1 Peter is ascribed to Peter. One of the reasons that Beare brings forward for the refusal of Petrine

dependence is not certain. In fact, it is impossible to *prove* such a theory
in this case, for the similarities may be due to oral influences. If Peter
had heard Paul discourse at Rome it may account for a similar sequence
of ideas.[1] But since most scholars[2] incline towards literary dependence
theories rather than oral influence theories, it remains to remark that it
would not be altogether surprising if Peter at Rome had been acquainted with both Romans and Ephesians, since these bear the form
of circulars and a copy of Ephesians might easily have been accessible
at Rome.[3]

In the case of Hebrews there are certain similarities of phrases which
have suggested to some that one author may have used the other's work,
but the resemblances are not close enough to be certain of literary
dependence and again a common milieu may be the reason for the
similarities.[4] It is interesting to note, nevertheless, that both letters have
a similar purpose of encouragement and both have a similar doctrinal
emphasis in setting forth an objective and future hope, in connecting
the sufferings of Christ with future glory and in their focus on the
atoning work of Christ.[5]

There is little room to dispute the literary parallels between this
Epistle and the Epistle of James.[6] Yet there is again difference of opinion

authorship to this Epistle is the Deutero-Pauline character of Ephesians, which he
regards as established (*op. cit.*, 1958, pp. 195f.). But in this he underestimates
the weight of opinion in favour of the Pauline authorship of Ephesians (see pp.
479 ff.). It will be recognized that Ephesians and 1 Peter stand or fall together in
this type of criticism.

[1] Selwyn (*op. cit.*, pp. 363–466) in a very thorough investigation traces most of
the similarities to common material and if he is correct this would considerably
lessen literary dependence. Cf. his article in *ET*, LIX (1948), pp. 256–259, in which
he also challenges the theory of Paulinism. Others who take a similar line are
E. Lohse, *ZNTW*, 45 (1954), pp. 73–83; and P. Carrington, 'Saint Peter's Epistle'
in *The Joy of Study* (ed. S. E. Johnson) (1951), pp. 57–63.

[2] Among the most recent writers to do so are J. Coutts, *NTS*, 3 (1957), pp.
115–127, in comparing 1 Pet. i. 3–12 and Eph. i. 3–14, Mitton (see p. 804 n. 7)
and Beare, *op. cit.*, pp. 193ff.

[3] Cf. Zahn, *INT*, II, p. 177.

[4] Cf. Moffatt's *ILNT*, p. 440, for a concise list of similar phrases and expressions.

[5] Cf. J. H. B. Masterman, *The First Epistle of Peter* (1912), pp. 36ff.; J. W. C.
Wand, *op. cit.*, pp. 25, 26. Selwyn thought the author of Hebrews had either read
1 Peter or was in touch with someone who knew the author of 1 Peter (*op. cit.*,
pp. 462, 463).

[6] Cf. the concise list in Wand, *op. cit.*, p. 25; Bigg, *op. cit.*, p. 23. Cf. also
Boismard, *RB*, LXIII (1957), pp. 161–183.

as to the direction in which the dependence lies. It is more generally considered that Peter used James than the reverse,[1] and there is no intrinsic reason why he should not have echoed the language of his fellow 'pillar' apostle, in view of what has already been noted of his sympathetic and impressionable character.

More suggestive are the parallels between the Acts speeches of Peter and this Epistle. In the speech at Pentecost, compare Acts ii. 16ff. and 1 Peter i. 10 for the idea of fulfilment of Old Testament prophecy; Acts ii. 17 and 1 Peter i. 20 for the idea of Christ's manifestation in the last days; Acts ii. 23 and 1 Peter i. 20 for the fore-ordination by God of the death of Jesus; Acts ii. 24ff. and 1 Peter iii. 19 for the triumph over Hades; and Acts ii. 32–36 and 1 Peter i. 21 for the connection between the resurrection and exaltation of Christ. Similar comparisons may be made between the speeches in Solomon's porch (iii. 12–26) and in Cornelius' house (x. 34–43).[2] But what conclusions may fairly be drawn from these data? The answer will naturally depend upon the degree of veracity which is attached to the Acts speeches and to the *ipsissima verba* of the Epistle as authentically Petrine. Although these similarities may not be considered conclusive, yet they could be regarded as confirmatory, if at least the substance of the Acts speeches is traced to a Petrine source and there seems no strong reason for denying this.[3] These similarities are what we should expect in common material attributed to the apostle Peter. J. W. C. Wand[4] has, however, pointed out that in the Epistle there is a development of the ideas in the Acts speeches, but this development is of such a character that it is explicable as a maturing of thought in one mind.

IX. SOURCES

The question arises to what extent this Epistle is indebted to traditional Christian materials and it was one of Selwyn's[5] great contributions to the study of the Epistle to make a detailed investigation along these lines. He suggested three main sources: a liturgical source, a persecution

---

[1] Bigg, however, maintains that James used 1 Peter (*loc. cit.*).

[2] Cf. Wand's list, *op. cit.*, p. 27; A. F. Walls, *op. cit.*, pp. 35, 36.

[3] Cf. F. F. Bruce, *The Speeches in Acts* (1944), and *The Acts of the Apostles* (Greek text, 1951), pp. 18ff. Cf. also Selwyn (*op. cit.*, pp. 33–36), who regarded the connection as historical rather than literary, the mind of Peter being the common ground between them.

[4] *Op. cit.*, p. 28.   [5] *Op. cit.*, Essay II, pp. 365–466.

fragment and catechetical material. In his suggestions about the latter material he has been supported by P. Carrington's studies in the primitive Christian catechism.[1] It is not at all improbable that some of the ideas in this Epistle, especially in the sphere of moral exhortations, followed closely the patterns of early Christian instruction. The existence of Christian moral codes after the form of pagan equivalents and even influenced by their content, although with a Christian interpretation, may well be possible during the apostolic period. There must have been an interchange of language and ideas between the apostolic writings and the primitive catechesis which was so largely inspired by the apostolic oral teaching. But to what extent the catechesis can be disentangled from the writings and what precise value it would be if this could be achieved with any certainty is an open question. Selwyn's arguments, in fact, have not gone unchallenged, particularly by Beare,[2] who prefers to regard the Pauline Epistles as the main source of the material that Selwyn regarded as traditional. But since he uses this as an argument for the late dating of 1 Peter his estimate of the data on this issue is somewhat influenced by his presuppositions.[3]

Some reference must be made to theories that hymn fragments lie buried in 1 Peter, advocated mainly by Bultmann[4] and Boismard.[5] The former suggests three examples, iii. 18–20, i. 20 and ii. 21–24, but in each of these he claims that the fragments are mixed up with credal forms and need disentangling. But Bultmann's resort to textual emendations undermines confidence in his critical analysis. Boismard's presentation is rather less open to objection on these grounds. He finds four hymns—the first in 1 Peter i. 3–5, the second in i. 20, iii. 18, 22, iv. 6, the third in ii. 22–25, the fourth in v. 5–9. But he has to do some manip-

---

[1] *The Primitive Christian Catechism* (1940).   [2] *Op. cit.*, pp. 193ff.

[3] Two recent German writers have argued in the direction of Selwyn's position. E. Lohse (*ZNTW*, 45, 1954, pp. 68, 69) finds dependence on common paraenetic material rather than upon Paul's Epistles. He believes that moral instruction followed naturally from the kerygmatic (preaching) material, as 1 Pet. ii. 21–25 strikingly illustrates. W. Nauck (*ZNTW*, 46, 1955, pp. 68–80) finds similar patterns in 1 Peter on the theme of joy through suffering and compares this with the occurrence of the same theme in other New Testament books and even in the *Apocalypse of Baruch* and other Jewish apocrypha and pseudepigrapha. But see Beare's criticism that Nauck subordinates the data to an overriding theory (*op. cit.*, p. 194).

[4] *Op. cit.*, pp. 1–14.

[5] Particularly in his *Quatre Hymnes Baptismales dans la première Epître de Pierre* (1961).

ulating of his material to arrive at his rhythmic forms.[1] The theory cannot be examined here, but it may be noted as characteristic of an increasing tendency to discover hymn fragments within the New Testament writings.

One other source, although more of background than of literary dependence, has been proposed. Perdelwitz,[2] in maintaining that the form of the Epistle has been strongly influenced by the mystery religions, cited many pagan parallels to Christian baptism and the Christian mysteries. This type of theory has gained very little support. The evidences deduced are almost entirely questionable inferences, such as the idea that the allusion to the blood of Christ in i. 2ff. finds analogy in the bath of bull's blood, by which rebirth was attained in the cults of Cybele and Mithras. But the allusion is so plainly to the Old Testament sacrifices that to appeal to a revolting pagan ritual as its background is not only entirely unnecessary, but robs the words of 1 Peter of their deepest significance.[3] This whole hypothesis of the author's heathen background may be dismissed as unfounded.[4]

CONTENTS

I. GREETINGS (i. 1, 2)

Peter introduces himself as an apostle and addresses the believers in various provinces. He reminds them of their election, sanctification and redemption.

II. THE NATURE OF CHRISTIAN SALVATION (i. 3–ii. 10)

The apostle next draws attention both to the privileges and to the responsibilities of Christian salvation.

a. The blessings of the gospel (i. 3–9)

Believers are born into a new way of life and become heirs of a heavenly inheritance (verses 3, 4). But future hope is linked with present security

---

[1] For instance, in his fourth hymn, Boismard admits that what has been preserved is rather a paraphrase than the form of the hymn itself (op. cit., p. 14).

[2] Op. cit.   [3] Cf. the criticisms of A. F. Walls, op. cit., pp. 37–39.

[4] Beare (op. cit., pp. 16ff., 27) is partially influenced by this theory.

in spite of trials and afflictions (5, 6). These have only a refining effect on true faith and they can, in fact, lead to inexpressible joy because faith has been fortified by love to Christ (7–9).

b. These blessings were foreseen (i. 10–12)

Christian salvation has a long history, for the prophets were granted insight through the Spirit into the sufferings and glories of Christ. The same Spirit has made it known to the readers, who have therefore become more privileged even than angels.

c. The heirs of these blessings must change their manner of life (i. 13–16)

The gospel involves transformation in thought and behaviour. The mind must be alert to make use of the grace provided (13) and the conduct must be conformed to God's holiness (14–16).

d. The basis of the believer's confidence must not be forgotten (i. 17–21)

The Christian, like the Israelite, must never forget the deliverance already obtained in the past and the cost of that redemptive act. Indeed his present faith has as its basis a divine purpose which reaches back to a period before the beginning of the world. In Christ the believer may have absolute confidence for present and future. The resurrection is the guarantee of this.

e. The heirs have present responsibilities (i. 22–ii. 3)

Purified souls have an obligation to love the brethren and this thought is supported by an appeal to the power of the Word of God in regeneration. Since the believers are regarded as new-born babes they have an ethical obligation to reject all that is opposed to love (see ii. 1) and to foster the development of a genuine spiritual appetite.

f. The heirs form a spiritual community (ii. 4–10)

The apostle thinks of the Christian Church as the new Israel and describes it in terms of the old. His mind goes to the temple and he thinks of Christians as living stones. And because this spiritual edifice consists of living people, he identifies them as a living priesthood (4, 5). But the thought of living stones leads his mind to dwell on Christ, the Chief Corner-stone. There have been two different reactions to Him: some have stumbled through disobedience, others have inherited wonderful privileges (6–10).

III. CHRISTIAN RELATIONSHIPS (ii. 11–iii. 12)

So far the apostle has dealt mainly with doctrine, but now he comes to practical issues affecting Christian life in the present world.

a. In the pagan world (ii. 11, 12)

Christians are aliens in a pagan environment, but their conduct may be the means of leading others to glorify God.

b. In the State (ii. 13–17)

Any government official, from the emperor downwards, who maintains just government, must be obeyed, for Christians are not intended to be anarchists. The problems of dishonest or illegal government are not discussed.

c. In the household (ii. 18–iii. 7)

Two different problems arose in domestic life and the apostle deals with both.

    1. Slaves must respect masters, whatever their character might be (ii. 18). There should be no resentment even of wrong punishment, in view of the supreme example of Christ, whose punishment was not for His own sins but for ours (ii. 19–25).

    2. Wives and husbands have specific Christian responsibilities (iii. 1–7). Wives with unbelieving husbands may win them by Christian example. Their approach to adornment should be modest and their relation to their husbands submissive. The husbands are more briefly exhorted, but are reminded to honour their wives as joint heirs.

d. In the Church (iii. 8–12)

The most pressing need is for Christian unity, which involves humility and a readiness to develop brotherly love. Retaliation must be excluded by blessing, a principle which is illustrated from Psalm xxxiv.

IV. CHRISTIAN SUFFERING AND SERVICE (iii. 13–iv. 19)

This is clearly a subject of great importance for the readers and the apostle discusses it in some detail.

a. The blessings of suffering wrongfully (iii. 13–17)

This at once constitutes a paradox, but several important principles are enunciated in support of it. 1. No-one can harm the righteous.

2. Fear of man must be replaced by reverence for Christ. 3. When defence is made before man it must be accompanied by a true Christian deportment. Whatever then happens will never destroy the believer's joy. 4. The Christian's conscience must be kept clear.

b. The powerful example of Christ (iii. 18–22)

Undeserved suffering is not alien to Christianity for Christ Himself suffered unjustly, but this has borne rich fruit in that He has been able to bring a people to God. The apostle then brings in a somewhat obscure reference to Christ's preaching to imprisoned spirits, which reminds him of God's patience in the time of the flood. This latter thought leads the apostle to think of baptism and to connect it with a Christian's cleanness of conscience. This forms somewhat of a digression but the apostle returns again to his theme of Christ's example.

c. Suffering in the flesh (iv. 1–6)

There is a marked contrast between suffering in the flesh and indulging in the flesh. Christ's example should lead to the ready acceptance of the former when God wills it and the firm rejection of the latter. Those who indulge in human passions must be prepared to render an account to the divine Judge.

d. The urgent need for holy living (iv. 7–11)

The thought of approaching judgment leads the apostle to urge certain practical principles of behaviour. Soberness, love, hospitality, liberality, the gift of speech, and service are all inculcated as means whereby God may be glorified.

e. Encouragements in special suffering (iv. 12–19)

A fiery ordeal is anticipated and the readers must be prepared. One encouragement is the thought of sharing Christ's glory as well as His sufferings. Another is the obvious contrast between a Christian and a common criminal in the reason for his suffering. If reproached for the name of Christ, the Christian must glorify God. The thought of judgment re-occurs, but this time relative to Christians (the household of God). The thing to do is to entrust one's soul to God.

V. CHRISTIAN DISCIPLINE (v. 1–11)

This is seen from two points of view, one in reference to corporate discipline and the other to personal discipline.

a. Corporate discipline (v. 1–6)

Elders have special responsibilities to tend the flock, but they must watch the spirit in which they do it. Younger men must submit to elders, and both groups must develop the grace of humility, which is the only befitting attitude before God.

b. Personal discipline (v. 7–11)

The believer must transfer his anxieties to God and develop a constant watchfulness particularly for the devices of his enemy the devil. This leads to another echo of the suffering-theme, but only for the purpose of reassuring the sufferers about the glories in store in the future. A doxology makes a fitting conclusion to this section.

VI. CONCLUSION (v. 12–14)

The apostle concludes with a reference to his helper Silvanus, to the church at 'Babylon' and to Mark, followed by a brief benediction.

ADDITIONAL NOTES

784. [2] The problem of the provinces named in 1 Pet. i. 1 would completely vanish if the reference to the 'exiles' is interpreted metaphorically of the true people of God, scattered as exiles on earth (cf. W. G. Kümmel, *INT*, 1965, p. 294).

786. [2] R. H. Fuller (*INT*, 1966, p. 158), who disputes apostolic authorship, thinks that 1 Peter 'reflects the later rejudaization of Paulinism'.

789. [1] W. Marxsen (*INT*, 1968, p. 236) regards 1 Peter as a 'manifesto', for which the authority of Peter was claimed at a later date.

790. [2] R. H. Gundry, 'Verba Christi in 1 Peter' (*NTS*, 13, 1967, pp. 336–350), analyses many instances of parallels between the words and ideas in 1 Peter and in the Gospels' sayings of Jesus. He claims that most of these occur in contexts where Peter himself is prominent, which leads him to claim that this supports the genuineness of 1 Peter and of the Gospel traditions. But E. Best (*NTS*, 16, 1970, pp. 95–113) takes a different view. He suggests that the parallels are found in two blocks in Luke (vi and xii) and in some isolated sayings elsewhere (Mt. v. 16; Mk. x. 45). From this he concludes that the Lucan passages were known to the author of 1 Peter, but not the Gospel. His reasoning is based on the absence from 1 Peter of what he calls 'many other usable logia' in the rest of Luke. But this is a precarious method of reasoning. See also C. Spicq (*StTh*, 20, 1966, pp. 37–61) for another study of the Gospel parallels.

797. [2] G. Baumann (*Nov.Test.*, 4, 1960, pp. 253–260) suggests as a result of studying parallels between Matthew's beatitudes and 1 Peter that the same baptismal theology lies behind both.

799. [3] A. R. C. Leaney (*NTS*, 10, 1963, pp. 133–139) examines the connection between 1 Peter and the Jewish Haggada for the Passover service known as *Sedev*, and the evidence is claimed to support the view that 1 Peter was modelled on a Passover service.

804. [5] W. G. Kümmel (*INT*, p. 297) thinks the dependence of 1 Peter on Romans is improbable, because the parallels can be explained by the catechetical tradition (so Selwyn). He nevertheless admits that the author of 1 Peter stands in the succession of Pauline theology and cannot reconcile this with a Peter who could be withstood by Paul at Antioch (Gal. ii. 11 ff.).

CHAPTER TWENTY-FIVE

THE SECOND EPISTLE OF PETER

This is the most problematical of all the New Testament Epistles because of early doubts regarding its authenticity and because internal evidence is considered by many to substantiate those doubts. In short, the majority of scholars reject it as a genuine work of the apostle Peter, in spite of its own claims, and regard it as a later pseudepigraphon.[1] To obtain a true appraisal of all the evidence, the external attestation will first be considered in order to see the problem in its historical setting, then a review of the internal claims and internal difficulties will be considered, and finally a brief examination of alternative theories of authorship will be made.

I. THE EPISTLE IN THE ANCIENT CHURCH

There are various ways of approaching early evidence of canonicity or non-canonicity of New Testament writings.

1. We can take the earliest known quotation from a book and conclude that the book was not canonical until a period just prior to the date of citation.

2. We may give citations a relative value and enquire whether the authors whose works are extant and who wrote prior to the date of the first citation had any cause in their writing to cite the New Testament book in question, on the assumption that no Christian writer was obliged to cite all parts of the New Testament in his possession which he regarded as Scripture.

3. We can place most emphasis on evidence of rejection in part, at least, of the early Church.

Of all these approaches the first is clearly most likely to lead us astray in view of the paucity of evidence before the last quarter of the second century. This first approach needs balancing with the second and yet

[1] In many commentaries and works of introduction this is assumed without much discussion as if it has almost become an established fact. Cf. K. and S. Lake, *INT* (1938), pp. 167, 168; W. Michaelis, *Einleitung*, pp. 289, 290; H.Windisch-H. Preisker, *Die katholischen Briefe*, p. 83; C. E. B. Cranfield, *I and II Peter and Jude* (*TC*, 1960); J. Moffatt, *The General Epistles* (*MC*, 1928).

this is much more difficult to establish and is consequently generally neglected. The third approach, although seldom used, is not without considerable significance in determining the positive as opposed to the negative attitude of the contemporary Church. It has special point in the case of 2 Peter, where early doubts nowhere took the form of definite rejection. An attempt must, nevertheless, be made to ascertain the probable reason for the doubts.

It will be convenient to regard Origen as the pivotal Christian Father in this discussion, because reviews[1] of the evidence so often commence with the statement that the Epistle was not certainly known until his time and the authenticity becomes immediately suspect, especially as he also mentions doubts held by some about it. He uses the Epistle at least six times in citations and shows little hesitation in regarding it as canonical. Some uncertainty about the validity of this evidence has been expressed because the citations all occur in those works preserved only in Rufinus' Latin translation and it is not always certain that Rufinus can be relied upon.[2] At the same time there seems to be no reason why he should erroneously attribute to Origen citations from a New Testament Epistle such as 2 Peter. Some suggestion of doubt on Origen's part might be inferred from Eusebius' statement[3] that he held Peter to have left one acknowledged Epistle and 'perhaps also a second, for it is disputed'. But Origen mentions no explanation for the doubts which were apparently current among some Christians, neither does he give any indication of the extent or location of these doubts. It is a fair assumption, therefore, that Origen saw no reason to treat these doubts as serious, and this would seem to imply that in his time the Epistle was widely regarded as canonical.[4]

Before Origen's time, the evidence is somewhat inconclusive. His predecessor, Clement of Alexandria, is said by Eusebius[5] to have commented on all the Catholic Epistles in his *Hypotyposes*. If so, he must have regarded this Epistle as on the same footing as the others, as he probably did the *Epistle of Barnabas* and the *Apocalypse of Peter*. There are some

[1] Cf. J. W. C. Wand, *The General Epistles of St. Peter and St. Jude* (1934), pp. 140, 141.

[2] Cf. F. H. Chase, *HDB*, III, p. 803.   [3] *HE*, vi. 25.

[4] Origen (*Hom. in Josh.* vii. 1) speaks of Peter sounding aloud with the two trumpets of his Epistles, which M. R. James thinks is characteristic of his manner and, therefore, genuine (*The Second Epistle General of St. Peter and the General Epistle of St. Jude*, 1912, p. xix).

[5] *HE*, vi. 14.

similarities of language between 2 Peter and Clement's extant works, but these are not sufficiently clear to be regarded with certainty as citations.[1] The same may be said of Theophilus of Antioch, Aristides, Polycarp and Justin Martyr.[2]

There are one or two faint allusions in Irenaeus' writings, of which the most notable is the statement that the day of the Lord is as a thousand years,[3] but he does not attribute this to Peter. It is possible that Psalm xc. 4 was his source. But the widespread influence of Chiliasm, which held that the world would last six thousand years corresponding to the six days of creation, presupposes an origin of apostolic authority. There are one or two striking resemblances between our Epistle and the *Letter of the Churches of Lyons and Vienne*, which seem to demand the supposition that the author was acquainted with 2 Peter. Some have claimed to find traces of the Epistle in the writings of Ignatius, Hermas and Clement of Rome, but these again are too insubstantial to lead to any conclusion in favour of dependence.[4] One passage in the so-called *2 Clement* looks very much like an echo of 2 Peter, since both speak of the destruction of the earth by fire, but it is not a citation (cf. *2 Clement*, xvi. 3 and 2 Peter iii. 10).[5] Similar references to Noah in *1 Clement*, vii. 6 and 2 Peter ii. 5 may also be noted. Moreover, van Unnik has recently suggested that it may be referred to in the *Gospel of Truth*,[6] probably published in the early part of the second century.

An important consideration is the witness of the Muratorian Canon, which omits reference to the Epistle. If it could be concluded with certainty from this that the Epistle was unknown at that time in the West, it would be demonstrated that an early date for the Epistle is highly improbable. Yet, since the Muratorian Canon omits reference to 1 Peter and since its present text is almost certainly incomplete, no

---

[1] Cf. Bigg, *The Epistles of St. Peter and St. Jude* (ICC, 1901), pp. 202, 203 for details.

[2] Cf. *idem, op. cit.*, pp. 204, 205; Wand, *op. cit.*, pp. 141f. But James (*op. cit.*, p. xviii) considers the first two as probable.

[3] *Adv. Haer.*, v. 28. 3; cf. also v. 23. 2.

[4] Cf. Bigg, *op. cit.*, pp. 209, 210 for details. Much greater weight would be given to these allusions if on other grounds an early date proved probable. Cf. R. A. Falconer (*Exp.*, VI, vi, 1902, p. 225), who also includes a reference in the *Epistle of Barnabas*, xv.

[5] In the same passage, *2 Clement* refers to the imminence of the day of judgment, whereas 2 Peter mentions the day of the Lord.

[6] *The Jung Codex* (ed. F. L. Cross, 1955), p. 116. The allusions are to 2 Pet. i. 17, ii. 2.

such construction can be put on its omitting to mention 2 Peter.[1] T. Zahn[2] made an ingenious attempt to emend the text of the Canon to include a reference to both Epistles of Peter in place of the *Apocalypse of Peter*. But even if the emendation is possible it could hardly be used with any confidence in support of 2 Peter. Yet it should be noted that, unlike its reference to the Epistles to the Alexandrians and Laodiceans, the Canon does not pronounce either of the Petrine Epistles as spurious, and its evidence must, therefore, be regarded as purely negative. The argument from silence must, as always, be used with the greatest reserve.

So far no mention has been made of writers subsequent to Origen. The most important of these is Eusebius, who placed this Epistle among the *Antilegomena*. He makes it clear that the majority accepted the Epistle as authentic, together with James and Jude, but he himself had doubts about it. In fact he mentions two grounds for his doubts: first, writers whom he respected did not regard it as canonical, and secondly, it was not quoted by 'the ancient presbyters'. Under the latter objection Eusebius may have meant 'by name'.[3] In any case Eusebius' comments are important as giving the earliest record of the reasons for the doubts, but they would have more significance if Eusebius had said who the other writers were whose opinions he respected. As it is, we are obliged to conclude that Eusebius and certain others were doubtful about the Epistle, although the majority regarded it as canonical. Even Eusebius, however, did not class it within his 'spurious' classification, in which category he placed the *Apocalypse of Peter*.[4]

Although Cyprian does not himself cite 2 Peter, his contemporary Firmillian of Caesarea in correspondence with him[5] makes a clear reference to his Epistle and it is highly improbable that Cyprian would have been ignorant of the allusion. At a slightly earlier period Hippolytus several times makes use of the words of this Epistle, which means that in Origen's time it must have been known and used in the West as well as in the East. The evidence from Jerome is important because, although he unreservedly accepted the Epistle with the other Catholic Epistles,

---

[1] Bigg (*op. cit.*, p. 204) thinks that some words in the Canon attached to Acts may allude to 2 Pet. i. 14.

[2] See p. 772 n. 4.

[3] Cf. Bigg, *op. cit.*, pp. 200, 201. Eusebius (*HE*, iii. 3. 1) says of 2 Peter that 'We have received it as not canonical' (οὐκ ἐνδιάθηκον).

[4] Cf. B. F. Westcott, *On the Canon of the New Testament*, p. 415.

[5] Cyprian, *Epp.*, lxxv. 6, cited by Bigg, *op. cit.*, p. 203.

he notes that doubts existed over its authenticity, based on the differences of style. He himself explains this supposed difficulty by suggesting
that Peter used two different amanuenses for his two Epistles.[1] Subsequent to Jerome's time no further doubts were expressed (although the
Syriac-speaking Church did not receive the Epistle until sometime
later, i.e. between the Peshitta (AD 411) and the Philoxenian Version
(AD 506)).

This external evidence has been given in some detail because of the
important influence it has had on the entire problem of 2 Peter. As
compared with other New Testament books, the early positive evidence
in support of its authenticity is the most sparse, while the expression of
doubts in the third and fourth centuries must be given full weight. Yet
where the majority accept a given book, the minority opinion must be
viewed with proportionate reserve. At the same time it must be admitted that the external evidence is not strongly favourable in the case
of this Epistle. A mitigating factor, which has all too often been overlooked, is the influence of the pseudo-Petrine literature upon Church
opinion. If Gnostic groups had used Peter's name to drive home their
own particular tenets, this fact would cause the orthodox Church to
take particular care not to use any spurious Petrine Epistles. Some of the
more nervous probably regarded 2 Peter suspiciously for this reason,
but the fact that it ultimately gained acceptance in spite of the pseudo-
Petrine literature is an evidence more favourable to its authenticity
than against it, unless the orthodox Church Fathers had by this time
become wholly undiscerning, which is not, however, borne out by the
firm rejection of other works attributed to Peter.

In the foregoing discussion no account has been taken of the evidence
of either the *Apocalypse of Peter* or the Epistle of Jude. The latter Epistle
is a clear case of literary borrowing, but the majority of scholars regard
2 Peter as the borrower. Some attention must later be given to this
question, but for our present purpose it should be noted that certain,
not inconsiderable, arguments have been advanced for the alternative
theory. If this alternative could be substantiated Jude would become
the earliest external witness to 2 Peter[2] and would considerably change
the complexion of the external evidence as a whole.[3]

---

[1] Cf. *Epistle to Hedibia*, 120; *Quaest.* xi, cited by Bigg, *op. cit.*, p. 199.

[2] This was strongly maintained by R. A. Falconer in his essay dealing with the
external attestation (*Exp.*, VI, vi, 1902, pp. 218ff.).

[3] See later discussion on this, pp. 922ff.

The relation of the Epistle to the *Apocalypse of Peter*[1] is of a different kind, although in this case also the direction of dependence has been variously understood. Some scholars have confidently affirmed that 2 Peter borrowed from the *Apocalypse* and others as confidently have maintained the reverse (see discussion on pp. 858ff.). Harnack[2] made much of the fact that earlier attestation existed for the *Apocalypse* than for 2 Peter. Certainly Clement of Alexandria had a high regard for the *Apocalypse*, commenting on it and perhaps even treating it as Scripture.[3] But the other evidence brought forward by Harnack is mostly later and of questionable value for the discussion. It is much more probable that the author of the *Apocalypse* takes his cue from 2 Peter and, if this is so, the former book will constitute valuable evidence for the circulation of the latter in the first half of the second century. Such evidence would not, of course, rule out the possibility that 2 Peter was a non-authentic work, but the nearer the attestation is traced back towards the first century, the greater is the presumption against this.[4]

It would seem a fair conclusion to this survey of external evidence to submit that there is no evidence from any part of the early Church that this Epistle was ever rejected as spurious, in spite of the hesitancy which existed over its reception. In view of this we may proceed to the considerations arising from the Epistle itself without prejudice, although we shall bear constantly in mind the doubts of the early Church,[5]

[1] For an English translation of this Apocalypse, see M. R. James, *The Apocryphal New Testament* (1924), pp. 505–521.

[2] Cf. his *Das Neue Testament um das Jahr 200* (1889), pp. 83f., in answer to Zahn's *Geschichte des neutestamentlichen Kanons*. Harnack cited Methodius, Porphyrius (who attacked it), an Asian bishop (who defended it) and the fifth-century Palestinian Christians, who read it during the Lenten season. He also thought that both the Clementine letters and Hippolytus show traces of the book (cf. *ThLZ*, 1884, p. xiv). It should be noted, however, that doubts are expressed about it in the Muratorian Canon.

[3] Although this was maintained by Harnack, it was disputed by Westcott, *op. cit.*, p. 352.

[4] If any credence could be given to F. W. Farrar's opinion that Josephus had read 2 Peter (*Exp.*, II, iii, 1882, pp. 401–423; III, viii, 1888, pp. 58–69), this would constitute very early attestation. But the idea seems rather improbable (see further discussion on p. 858).

[5] In view of the great emphasis often placed on the adverse external evidence for 2 Peter, it would be valuable to cite the conclusions of two scholars who did not accept authenticity, but nevertheless were cautious about the external attestation. F. H. Chase (*op. cit.*, p. 807), after his very full examination, admits that lack of early evidence does not *prove* its spuriousness, but nevertheless creates a presump-

of the Reformers[1] and of modern criticism regarding its authenticity.[2]

II. AUTHORSHIP

a. The Epistle's own claims

There can be no doubt that the author intends his readers to understand that he is the apostle Peter. He calls himself somewhat strikingly Symeon (or Simon) Peter, a servant and an apostle of Jesus Christ (i. 1). He states that the Lord showed him the approach of his own death (i. 14). He claims to have been an eyewitness of the transfiguration (i. 16–18) and records the heavenly voice which he had himself heard on the 'holy mount'. He mentions a previous Epistle which he had written to the same people (iii. 1) and refers to the apostle Paul in terms of intimacy as 'our beloved brother Paul' (iii. 15), although he admits with refreshing candour that Paul's letters contain many difficult statements.

Such evidence certainly leaves us with the impression that the author is the apostle Peter. But the veracity of all these statements has not only been called in question, but other internal evidence has been brought forward, which is alleged to make the self-claims of the Epistle untenable and these objections will need to be carefully considered. Before doing so it should be fully recognized, as E. F. Scott[3] has pointed out, that we have no choice but to regard 2 Peter as either genuine or

tion against its genuineness and throws the burden of proof on the internal evidence. J. B. Mayor (*The Epistle of St. Jude and the Second Epistle of St. Peter*, 1907, p. cxxiv) concludes by suggesting that 'if we had nothing else to go upon in deciding the question of the authenticity of 2 Peter except external evidence, we should be inclined to think that we had in these quotations ground for considering that Eusebius was justified in his statement that our Epistle πολλοῖς χρήσιμος φανεῖσα μετὰ τῶν ἄλλων ἐσπουδάσθη γραφῶν.'

[1] Erasmus regarded 2 Peter as either spurious or written by Silvanus on Peter's direction. Luther found reason for doubt in 2 Pet. ii. 9, 15, but still thought it credible that it may be an Epistle of the apostle. Calvin inclined to regard it as a letter written by a disciple at Peter's direction (see Zahn, *INT*, II, p. 283, for details).

[2] Modern critical doubts can be traced back to Grotius who dated the Epistle in Trajan's time, but it was not until J. S. Semler's (*Paraphrasis ep. Petri II et Judas*, 1784) time that the Epistle was characterized as a forgery. Later J. G. Eichhorn (*Historische-kritische Einleitung in das Neue Testament*, III, 1814, pp. 624–656) rejected it, chiefly because of its dependence on Jude, and his opinion dominated much later critical enquiry.

[3] *The Literature of the New Testament* (1932), p. 227.

as a later work deliberately composed in his name. In other words, if its genuineness is found to be untenable, the only alternative is to regard it as spurious, in the sense of being a forgery.[1]

b. The case against Petrine authorship

(i) *The personal allusions.* The claims of the Epistle itself are discounted by the majority of scholars on the grounds that these personal allusions are no more than a literary device to give the appearance of authenticity to a pseudonymous production. Support for this process is found in the mass of pseudepigraphic literature, Jewish and Christian, which flourished before and during the early period of Church history, in which some attempt was made to give verisimilitude to the pseudonym. In most of them the literary device is obvious enough and so it is assumed that the author of 2 Peter, in spite of his efforts to identify himself with the apostle Peter, has really betrayed his hand.

1. The addition of the Jewish name 'Simon' to the Greek name 'Peter' in the superscription (i. 1) looks like a conscious attempt to identify the Peter of the Epistle with the Peter of the Gospels and Acts, where alone the double name is found.[2] But in all the Gospels, 'Peter' is more common than the compound.[3] The usage in 2 Peter is, therefore, unexpected, especially in view of the absence of 'Simon' from the salutation of 1 Peter. If the alternative reading 'Symeon' is accepted, the form of the name might be claimed as a further indication of the author's interest in archaic forms.[4]

2. The reference to the Lord's prediction of Peter's death as imminent in i. 14 is generally supposed to be an allusion to John xxi. 18f.[5] If this is a case of literary dependence, it clearly rules out the apostolic author-

---

[1] Not all scholars, however, agree that these are the only alternatives. J. W. C. Wand regards the Epistle as pseudepigraphic, but declines to call it 'a deliberate and unabashed forgery' (*op. cit.*, p. 144) and many modern scholars would share his reluctance. See further comments on p. 845.

[2] 'Simon Peter', apart from the few instances where 'Simon surnamed Peter' occurs, is found only in Mt. xvi. 16; Lk. v. 8, and in many of the references to Peter in John's Gospel (16 times).

[3] Cf. the note on this combination in C. Bigg, *op. cit.*, p. 89.

[4] Cf. J. W. C. Wand (*op. cit.*, p. 146), 'Simeon is used of Peter only in Acts xv. 14 and its use here may be an intentional archaism.' But Wand is not too sure about this.

[5] Cf. Feine-Behm, *op. cit.*, p. 254; T. Henshaw, *op. cit.*, p. 394; F. H. Chase, *op. cit.*, p. 809. J. Moffatt (*ILNT*, p. 366) definitely claims that this is a method used by the author to add *vraisemblance* to his writing.

ship of 2 Peter, because of the late dating of John. Moreover, how did the apostle know that his end was to be so soon? This is considered to be an attempt to indicate that the letter was written just before the apostle's death.[1]

3. The statement in i. 15 looks like a promise of the publication of literary work after Peter's departure. This is often supposed to refer to the production of Mark's Gospel,[2] and it is, therefore, a self-conscious attempt on the author's part to identify his work by means of the apostolic 'source' of that Gospel.

4. The references to the transfiguration narrative (i. 16ff.) are considered to be forced. Undoubtedly one of the greatest privileges which Peter enjoyed was to witness the transfiguration of Christ, but it is maintained that the incident is introduced into 2 Peter merely to add verisimilitude to the narrative,[3] as much as to say that this Peter is the Peter who witnessed Christ's glory and heard the heavenly voice. Moreover, the description of the mount as 'holy' is generally thought to indicate a time when sacred places were revered, which is most unlikely in apostolic times.

(ii) *Historical problems.* There are many problems of an historical kind which are cited as adverse to apostolic authorship. The main problems may be grouped as follows:

1. The reference to Paul and his letters (iii. 15). Several indications are claimed to be found here of a period subsequent to the apostles. A corpus of Pauline Epistles is known. Indeed, 'all his letters' may well suggest a time when the complete corpus is known.[4] Further, these letters are placed on an equality with 'the other scriptures', which would seem to indicate a time well after the apostolic age. Quite apart

---

[1] Cf. E. Käsemann's idea that 2 Peter was intended to be a last testament of Peter, *ZTK*, 49 (1952), p. 280 (reproduced in his *Exegetische Versuche und Besinnungen*, 1960, p. 142).

[2] Cf. J. B. Mayor's discussion, *op. cit.*, pp. cxlii ff.

[3] Cf. Chase, *HDB*, III, pp. 809, 810. Chase did not consider that in themselves the references to Peter's approaching death and to the transfiguration are unnatural, but that when considered against the background of the omission of the passion, resurrection and ascension, they become a serious ground for questioning the authenticity.

[4] Cf. Wand, *op. cit.*, p. 143. This fact weighs heavily with A. E. Barnett, *The Second Epistle of Peter (IB)*, 1957, p. 164. Cf. also Moffatt (*ILNT*, pp. 363, 364) who calls this 'an anachronism which forms an indubitable water-mark of the second century'.*

from this, a difficulty is felt over Peter's admission of his inability to understand Paul's writings.

2. Another problem is the reference to the 'second letter' in iii. 1. If 2 Peter is pseudepigraphic, it is highly probable that this reference has been included to claim a definite connection with 1 Peter,[1] a process not unknown among pseudepigraphists. That there are difficulties in this assumption will be demonstrated later, but it should be noted for the present that the datum does not necessarily require this interpretation.

3. It is also thought that the occasion reflected in the Epistle is too late for Peter's time. It is often confidently affirmed that the situation envisaged in the Epistle belongs to the second century, particularly to the period of intense Gnostic activity.[2] If this affirmation is correct, there can be no question of apostolic authorship and the Epistle must be firmly dated in the sub-apostolic period. But rather less confidence is now being put in the identification of early Gnostic movements and the evidence, as will be seen later,[3] is not sufficient to declare that 2 Peter's false teachers were, in fact, second-century Gnostics. Nevertheless, if other evidence pointed to a later origin, the connections with Gnostic thought might be corroborative evidence.[4] A further consideration is the mixture of past and future tenses, which is thought to suggest an author who first assumes a prophetic rôle and then lapses into a description of his own contemporary scene.[5]

4. The statement in iii. 4 suggests that the first generation of Christians is now past. 'Since the fathers fell asleep' would seem to suggest a second or third generation dating, which would put the Epistle well outside the apostolic period.[6] This, of course, assumes that the 'fathers' are the first generation of Christians, including the apostles, but this interpretation is by no means certain and too much weight should not

---

[1] Cf. Moffatt, op. cit., p. 365.

[2] Cf. Wand, op. cit., p. 144: 'It probably belongs to the Egypt of the first quarter of the second century, and was written to circumvent the Christian Gnosticism that was soon developed into a specific system by Basilides.'

[3] Cf. R. M. Wilson, The Gnostic Problem (1958). Cf. the discussion of the Colossian heresy, pp. 546 ff.

[4] Cf. Feine-Behm, op. cit., p. 256.*

[5] Cf. F. H. Chase, op. cit., p. 811.

[6] So writers of such widely differing viewpoints as Barnett, op. cit., loc. cit.; Michaelis, op. cit., p. 290; Cantinat, op. cit., p. 597. Indeed, most disputants of non-Petrine authorship make much of this.

be placed upon it. At the same time, it is undoubtedly possible to interpret the evidence as supporting a late date.

5. The reference to 'your apostles' in iii. 2 (RSV) is considered strange for an apostolic author. This statement is thought to be too cold and general coming from the apostle Peter. Moreover, the combination of prophets and apostles is characteristic of second-century writers when referring to Scripture (e.g. Muratorian Canon and Irenaeus).[1]

(iii) *Literary problems.* The remarkably close parallels between this Epistle and that of Jude cannot be left out of the authorship problem of this Epistle. If, as is generally supposed, 2 Peter is the borrower from Jude, the date of 2 Peter would then be directly governed by the date of Jude. The latter date is not usually fixed as early as Peter's lifetime and, therefore, it follows that 2 Peter cannot be by Peter.[2] The difficulty here is the appeal to two factors over which there has been, and still is, some difference of opinion. It is not absolutely conclusive, in spite of an overwhelming majority verdict in favour, that 2 Peter actually borrowed from Jude,[3] neither is it certain that Jude must be dated later than Peter's lifetime. But those who are convinced that these can be asserted without fear of contradiction are quite entitled to point out the difficulty. At the same time the bare use of Jude does not in itself exclude Petrine authorship, as some scholars who have maintained authenticity together with Jude's priority have recognized.[4]

Not only is there literary connection between these two Epistles, but also between 2 Peter and the Pauline Epistles and 2 Peter and 1 Peter. Unlike 1 Peter, which seems to show definite links with some of Paul's Epistles (see pp. 804f.), this Epistle is far less clearly influenced by Paul's thought. Nevertheless, the author is clearly acquainted with a

---

[1] For details, cf. Chase, *op. cit.*, p. 811. He regarded this reference as an elaboration of the simple phrase in Jude 17 by a post-apostolic author using phraseology current in his own days.

[2] Cf. J. W. C. Wand, *op. cit.*, p. 142; F. H. Chase, *op. cit.*, p. 814, who did not support the priority of 2 Peter to Jude, but nevertheless did not consider it impossible that Peter should cite Jude. The latter Epistle, he thought, may not be later than Peter's lifetime.*

[3] See the discussion of this on pp. 919 ff. Spitta, Zahn and Bigg were staunch supporters of the priority of 2 Peter.

[4] Cf. most recently E. M. B. Green, *2 Peter Reconsidered* (1961), pp. 10, 11. But cf. H. F. D. Sparks (*The Formation of the New Testament*, 1952, p. 136) who considers that 2 Peter's use of Jude is decisive against Petrine authorship. The same view was expressed by Knopf, *Die Briefe Petri und Judä* (1912), p. 253.*

number of Pauline Epistles, including one sent to the same readers as his own Epistle (iii. 15). There have been many suggestions regarding the identity of this letter,[1] but it is impossible to come to any conclusion. It was probably an epistle now lost. The main difficulty is in the apparent overlap of apostolic provinces. If Paul had previously written to them, why does Peter now address them? It could be that Paul was dead and Peter is, therefore, taking a pastoral interest in some of the former's churches. This difficulty has already cropped up in connection with 1 Peter (see p. 784), where it was seen that very little weight can be attached to it.

The relationship between 1 and 2 Peter is variously interpreted according to whether the former is regarded as authentic or not. If not, then the decision regarding 2 Peter must follow suit.[2] But if 1 Peter is by Peter, this supplies a standard of comparison, which is of vital importance. In other words, the question must be posed whether the author of 1 Peter could have written 2 Peter, and the verdict given by the majority is in the negative.[3] Those who regard the author of 2 Peter as definitely borrowing ideas from 1 Peter, but putting them in a different way, consider this a strong argument against the authenticity of 2 Peter. The linguistic and doctrinal problems arising from a comparison between the two Epistles will be considered under the next two heads. Moreover, the literary question of their different use of the Old Testament needs noting. The first Epistle is certainly more full of obvious citations and allusions, whereas the second has no formal quotations and fewer allusions. It is felt, therefore, that we are here dealing with different minds. Chase,[4] for instance, refers to the

[1] Of the various suggestions which have been made, the most notable is the Epistle to the Romans (cf. Mayor, op. cit., pp. cxxxvii, 164, 165). Mayor cites the following other suggestions which have been proposed—Ephesians (sometimes with Galatians and Colossians), 1 Corinthians, Hebrews, Thessalonians. Zahn considered that the Epistle is now lost (INT, II, p. 199).

[2] This follows from the fact that no scholar unconvinced of the authenticity of 1 Peter would ever be convinced of any arguments for 2 Peter. Moreover, if 2 Pet. iii. 1 refers to 1 Peter, it must clearly come later (cf. R. Knopf, op. cit., p. 250).

[3] Wand's statement of the case may be cited as representative. Referring to the author he says, 'But if he is St. Peter, it is certainly not the Peter that we know: it is not the bluff fisherman of Galilee, nor the Spirit-possessed preacher of Acts, nor the courageous theologian of the first Epistle. The two Epistles indeed show a contrast at nearly every point' (op. cit., p. 143).

[4] Op. cit., p. 813.

writer of 1 Peter as 'instinctively and apparently unconsciously' falling into Old Testament language, but this is less obvious in 2 Peter.

(iv) *Stylistic problems*. It has been seen that as early as the time of Jerome the stylistic differences between 1 and 2 Peter were noted and an attempt was made to explain them by referring both Epistles to different amanu-enses. Those modern scholars who regard 1 Peter as having been written by Silvanus make any stylistic comparisons with 2 Peter irrelevant. But the Greek of 2 Peter is more stilted than that of 1 Peter. Chase[1] charac-terized the vocabulary of the writer as 'ambitious' and yet considered its extraordinary list of repetitions as stamping it as 'poor and inade-quate'. The style shows a great dearth of connecting particles and an aptitude for cumbrous sentences. Nevertheless, after carefully setting out this evidence, Chase admitted that there is nothing which absolutely disproves Petrine authorship, although he thought it was hard to recon-cile such authorship with the literary character of the Epistle.[2] On the other hand, if the view that the Greek of 2 Peter is an artificial literary language learnt from books is correct, and if it is as far removed from everyday language as is often supposed,[3] the difficulty in attributing it to Peter would clearly be considerable.

(v) *Doctrinal problems*. Much emphasis has been placed on the irrecon-cilability of the doctrine of 1 and 2 Peter. It is pointed out that many of the major themes in 1 Peter do not occur at all in 2 Peter (e.g. the cross, resurrection, ascension, baptism, prayer).[4] The great emphasis in 2 Peter is rather on the *parousia*. Käsemann[5] goes so far as to discover an in-ferior view of Christ (who is no longer regarded as a redeemer);

---

[1] *Ibid.*, p. 809. R. H. Strachan (*The Second Epistle General of Peter, EGT*, 1910, pp. 110–112) criticized Chase's statements as too sweeping, although he agreed with him in rejecting Petrine authorship.

[2] Mayor is equally cautious in pressing the linguistic argument, *op. cit.*, pp. lxviii ff.

[3] Cf. J. H. Moulton and W. F. Howard's confident assertion to this effect (*A Grammar of New Testament Greek*, II, 1929, pp. 5, 6).

[4] Chase (*op. cit.*, p. 812) considered that the omission of the resurrection was the crucial point.

[5] *ZTK*, 49 (1952), pp. 272–296. In Käsemann's view, three passages presuppose a post-apostolic situation (iii. 2, ii. 21, and i. 12) and hence he thinks an apostolic mask had to be worn to show the connection between the author's own message and apostolic times. W. Michaelis (*op. cit.*, p. 290) disputes Käsemann's opinion that the eschatology is the central theme of the Epistle, but he is impressed by the argument that the eschatology is far removed from apostolic times.*

an eschatology not orientated to Christ; and an inadequate ethical outlook in which the major evil is imprisonment in a material existence.
Although not everyone who disputes the authenticity of the Epistle
would go all the way with Käsemann, most would agree that the two
Epistles differ in outlook. Indeed, many would consider that the
change in approach to the *parousia* presupposes a considerable delay
after the publication of 1 Peter.[1] It will be necessary to examine this
kind of argument more carefully when putting the case for Petrine
authorship, but in order to appreciate its true weight, it should be noted
that much of the evidence brought forward in support is due to
subjective assessments which naturally appeal differently to different
minds

Another factor which may be mentioned here is the Hellenistic
background. Certain expressions seem to suggest acquaintance with
Greek modes of thought and this is considered highly improbable for a
Galilaean fisherman. The idea of ἀρετή (moral excellence) applied to
God, of virtue combined with faith, of knowledge, of sharing the
divine nature and the term 'eyewitnesses' (ἐπόπται), which was used in
the mystery religions, are the major examples of such Greek expressions.[2] If the use of these terms is indicative of the impact of Hellenistic
ideas on the author's mind, it may certainly be difficult to maintain
Petrine authorship, especially because in 1 Peter they are not so frequent.

When all these considerations are taken together they build up so
great an impression of non-authenticity that many scholars do not even
discuss the possibility that the tradition of apostolic authorship might
after all be correct. But the impartial critic must also examine carefully
the foundations for the non-authenticity theory and present in the best
possible light the evidence which many able scholars have produced in

[1] Cf. J. Cantinat, in Robert-Feuillet's *Introduction à la Bible*, II, p. 597.

[2] Cf. Feine-Behm, *op. cit.*, pp. 255, 256. Cf. also H. Windisch's note for further
examples, *op. cit.*, p. 85. Of ἐπόπται, Chase remarked that 'it is not one which we
should have expected St. Peter to use'. Indeed he called it 'artificial'. But the corresponding verb ἐποπτεύω is used twice in 1 Peter (ii. 12, iii. 2) and nowhere else
in the New Testament. A. Deissmann (*Bible Studies*, 1901, pp. 360ff.) has drawn
attention to many verbal parallels between 2 Peter and an inscription containing
a decree of the inhabitants of Stratonicea in Caria in honour of Zeus Panhemerios
and Hekate, the most striking of which is the parallel use of the expression τῆς
θείας δυνάμεως. Deissmann suggested that the similarities show that the author of
2 Peter has 'simply availed himself of the familiar forms and formulae of religious
emotion' (p. 362). There is, of course, no reason why Peter himself might not have
done this.*

support of Petrine authorship. It will, therefore, be our next task to examine the arguments stated above and then to produce any positive arguments for apostolic authorship.

c. The case for Petrine authorship

(i) *The personal allusions.* In spite of the widespread custom of appealing to contemporary pseudepigraphic practice in support of the view that the personal allusions are merely literary devices, considerable caution is necessary before this kind of argument can be allowed any weight. It must at once be recognized that there are no close parallels to 2 Peter, if this Epistle is pseudepigraphic. The normal procedure was to adopt a fairly consistent first person style, particularly in narrative sections. This style was not specially adapted for Epistles, and this is probably the reason for the paucity of examples of pseudepigrapha in this form. It is much easier to account for the development of pseudonymous Acts and Apocalypses (as those attributed to Peter), although even these appear to be later developments than 2 Peter (see pp. 858ff. on the relationship of 2 Peter to the *Apocalypse*). Comparative study of pseudepigraphy cannot, of course, lead to a conclusive rejection of a pseudepigraphic origin for 2 Peter, because 2 Peter may be in a class of its own, but it does lead to the demand that evidences for pseudepigraphic origin should be conclusive. It is against this background that the following examination will be conducted.

1. It must at once seem strange that the author uses the double name Simon Peter, when the name Simon does not appear in 1 Peter, which was presumably used as a model, if 2 Peter is pseudepigraphic. The difficulty is even greater if the form 'Symeon' is the correct reading, for neither in the Apostolic Fathers nor in the Christian pseudepigraphic literature is it used. Indeed, it occurs elsewhere only in Acts xv. 14 and is obviously a primitive form. M. R. James,[1] who disputed the authenticity of 2 Peter, admitted that this was one of the few features which made for the genuineness of the Epistle. We should certainly expect that an imitator of 1 Peter would have kept closer to his model in the salutation, since in iii. 1 he is going to imply that his present letter is in the same sequence as the first. It is not possible in this case to treat the variation as an unconscious lapse on the part of the author, for he would hardly have begun his work with a lapse and, in any case, would not have lapsed into a primitive Hebrew form no longer in use in his own

---

[1] *The Second Epistle of St. Peter and the General Epistle of St. Jude* (1912), p. 9.

day. The only alternative is to assume that the use of the name Simeon was a deliberate device to give a greater impression of authenticity. In that case it would be necessary to suppose that the author had been studying the book of Acts or else that the form had independently survived orally in the author's own circles. On the whole, the author's name presents much greater difficulty for the pseudepigraphic writer than for Peter himself, who, in any case, would enjoy greater liberty in varying the form. If Zahn is right in holding that the recipients were Jewish Christians, it might be possible to explain the Hebrew form of the name on the grounds that for such readers this would be more appropriate. But Zahn's hypothesis is generally disputed (see discussion below).

2. There is undoubtedly a connection between 2 Peter i. 14 and the saying in John xxi. 18f., but there is no need to explain this by literary dependence. If Peter himself wrote 2 Peter and heard with his own ears the Lord's prediction, there would be nothing extraordinary in the connection. The main problem is how Peter would have known that the event was so imminent. The situation would be modified if the word ταχινή meant not 'soon', as it is generally rendered, but 'swift', which is the meaning it must sustain in ii. 1 of this Epistle. There is a strong presumption that it means the same in both places. The emphasis would not then be on the imminence, but on the manner of Peter's death. But in any case, if a pseudepigraphist was making an indirect allusion to John xxi. 18,[1] where Peter is told that some violent death awaited him when he was old, there would be less point in the ταχινή to indicate imminence. It did not require much foresight for an old man to suggest that his end was not far away. Moreover, a pseudepigraphist writing this would not appear to add anything to the information contained in the canonical sources, in spite of writing after the event. This may, of course, be a tribute to the pseudepigraphist's skill, but it could equally well be a witness to the veracity of Peter's own statement.

3. The meaning of 2 Peter i. 15 is problematic. The statement reads, 'And I will see to it that after my departure you may be able at any time to recall these things' (RSV). But to suppose that this refers to Mark's

[1] It is just possible that it is not Jn. xxi. 18 which is in mind but some other special revelation from the Lord, similar to those which Paul seems to have had (cf. Acts xx. 23, 25, 38, xxi. 11). H. Windisch cites other similar cases from extra-canonical sources, *op. cit.*, p. 88. F. Spitta (*Der zweite Brief des Petrus und der Brief das Judas*, 1885, pp. 88f.) denies any connection with Jn. xxi.

Gospel is precarious for there is no evidence to support it. 'These things' are presumably things already mentioned in verse 12, which points back to the doctrinal statements of the preceding verses.[1] Evidently the anticipated document was to be doctrinal in character and it is difficult to see how this was fulfilled in Mark's Gospel. It is better to suppose that this projected letter was either never written or has since been lost. It can hardly be regarded as an evidence of a pseudepigraphist's hand, in spite of Käsemann's suggestion that this allusion was included to give 2 Peter the character of a testament of Peter.[2] Yet there is a great difference between this Epistle and Jewish apocalyptic books in testamentary form, which all share the pattern of a discourse addressed to the immediate descendants, but which is really destined for future generations. This latter type of literature proceeded from a review of the past to a prophecy of the future. While both these elements may be found in 2 Peter, the Epistle can be clearly understood without recourse to the testamentary hypothesis, which could certainly not be said of the farewell discourses of Jewish apocalyptic.

4. But are the references to the transfiguration narrative natural for the apostle Peter? There is no denying that the pseudepigraphists were in the habit of making passing allusions to known events in the lives of their assumed authors, in order to create the historical setting necessary for their literary productions. But there is no parallel to Peter's allusion to the transfiguration, for the prophetic section does not require such a setting to make it intelligible. Indeed, it is difficult to see why a pseudepigraphist would have chosen this particular incident, especially as it does not, like the death and resurrection of Jesus, play a prominent part in early Christian preaching.[3] The only justification for the choice would be the possibility of using it as an introduction to an esoteric revelation in the same way as the book of Enoch uses Enoch's journey through the heavens. But the author of 2 Peter does not claim to be making any new revelation on the basis of his hero's experiences on the mount of transfiguration. He appeals to it almost incidentally as a verification of the

[1] Cf. Zahn, *INT*, II, p. 201.

[2] J. Munck compares 2 Peter with other farewell discourses, especially in Jewish apocalyptic, in his article on 'Discours d'adieu dans le Nouveau Testament et dans la littérature biblique', in *Aux Sources de la Tradition Chrétienne* (1950), pp. 155–170.

[3] The same difficulty does not arise if Peter himself were author, because his choice of the incident may have been influenced by the desire to cite the occasion when the greatest glory was seen.

prophetic word he intends to impart. But this is a perfectly natural procedure and does not in itself demand a pseudepigraphic author. Peter
himself could just as naturally have referred to his own remarkable
experience, as he does in 1 Peter v. 1.

Moreover, the form of this transfiguration account differs from the
Synoptic accounts in certain details, and this demands an explanation. Is
this easier to account for on the authenticity hypothesis than the pseudepigraphic? It would, at first sight, seem strange that any writer, introducing an allusion to an historical incident, would have varied the
account. There is no mention of Moses and Elijah; the Synoptic 'hear
him' is omitted; an emphatic ἐγώ is added; the order of words is
changed; and the words ὃν εὐδόκησα are only partially paralleled in
Matthew and not at all in Mark and Luke. Such variations suggest an
independent tradition,[1] and as far as they go favour a Petrine authorship
rather than the alternative. It is, of course, possible to suppose that 2
Peter is reproducing an account from oral tradition, but it is much more
natural to assume that this account is a genuine eyewitness account.
It is significant that there is a complete absence of embellishments, such
as are often found in the apocryphal books, and in fact can be illustrated
in relation to the transfiguration from the fragment attached to the
Apocalypse of Peter.

The idea of the 'holy mount' (τὸ ὄρος τὸ ἅγιον) need not be as late
a development as some scholars suppose,[2] for the central feature is not
the veneration of a locality, but the appreciation of the sanctity of an
impressive occasion in which the writer himself shared. The real issue is
whether a pseudepigraphist would have singled out this particular
mountain for special veneration. There does not appear to be any compelling reason why he should have done so. If he merely sensed that
Peter would have regarded the mount as holy because of the theo-
phany, the description might just as well reflect the real reactions of the
apostle. As a genuine eyewitness account, it is highly credible; as a
pseudepigraphic touch, it would have been a device of rare insight,
which for that very reason makes it less probable.

It will be seen from these considerations so far that there is little
tangible evidence for non-authenticity from the personal allusions.

---

[1] Cf. E. M. B. Green, *op. cit.*, p. 27.

[2] The same description of the mount as holy is found in the *Apocalypse of Peter*,
but since the author of this work has clearly used 2 Peter (see discussion on pp. 858ff.)
this cannot be cited as independent evidence in support.

There is, in fact, nothing here which requires us to treat the Epistle as pseudepigraphic.

(ii) *Historical problems.* 1. Many scholars who might be prepared to admit that the preceding evidences are not conclusive but corroborative, consider that the allusion to Paul tips the scales against Petrine authorship. But here again caution is needed. It must at once be noted that Peter's words need not imply the existence of an authorized corpus of Paul's letters. The 'all' in iii. 16 need mean no more than all those known to Peter at the time of writing.[1] There is no suggestion that even these were known to the readers. Indeed, the writer is informing them of the difficulties in understanding these letters and it can hardly be supposed that they would have been unaware of this had they been acquainted with them. On the other hand, the Epistles in question have had sufficient circulation for the false teachers to twist them from their true interpretation.

Of much greater difficulty for the authenticity of the Epistle is the apparent classification of Paul's Epistles with the 'other scriptures'. Now this again is a matter of interpretation. It is possible to contend that γραφαί does not mean 'scriptures' but writings in general.[2] The meaning would then be that these false teachers show no sort of respect for any religious writings and that this attitude was extended to Paul's writings. Such an interpretation is supported by the fact that in i. 21 Old Testament prophecy is clearly regarded as bearing the mark of divine inspiration, whereas the reference to Paul lacks such a distinctive claim. He writes 'according to wisdom', but it is nonetheless a wisdom given to him (iii. 15). Moreover the writer appears to be classing his own writing on the same level as Paul's, which would point to a time before the accepted veneration of Paul's writings (unless, of course,

[1] If *all* of Paul's Epistles were now collected it is extraordinary that an author who indicates his respect for them shows such comparatively little reflection of their thought in his Epistle. Indeed there is much greater evidence of their influence in 1 Peter, a fact which may be explained by the greater amount of similar material common to those Epistles and 1 Peter. The major theme of 2 Peter does not provide such close parallels. This seems a better solution than that of R. A. Falconer (*Exp.*, VI, vi, 1902, pp. 468, 469), who maintained that 2 Peter was published earlier than 1 Peter, at a time when Paul's letters were less well known.

[2] This was Zahn's view, *INT*, II, p. 277. Cf. also Spitta (*op. cit.*, p. 294), who interpreted it of other writings of Paul's associates. Falconer (*op. cit.*, p. 469) took the same view.

a pseudepigraphist is doing this to secure authority for his own writing
—but see the discussion below, pp. 846f.).

But the usual New Testament interpretation of γραφαί is 'Scriptures' (i.e. Old Testament) and it must be considered as more likely
that that is its meaning here. Is it possible to conceive of Paul's writings
being placed so early on a par with the Old Testament? It is not easy to
answer this question with any certainty. Many scholars[1] would answer
categorically in the negative on the grounds that allowances must be
made for a considerable delay before such veneration of Paul's writings
was reached. Indeed, some[2] would maintain that a period of
neglect followed Paul's death and that interest was revived only after the
publication of Acts, but this hypothesis is open to serious criticism.[3]
When all has been said there is practically no evidence at all to show
precisely when Paul's letters first began to be used alongside the Old
Testament.

There is no denying that Paul himself considered his own writings
to be invested with a special authority and, moreover, that he expected
his readers generally to recognize this fact (cf. 2 Thes. iii. 14; 1 Cor. ii.
16, vii. 17, xiv. 37–39). We may either interpret this as the overbearing
attitude of an autocrat or else as evidence of the apostle's consciousness
of writing under the direct inspiration of God. But if the latter alternative
is correct and if it were recognized by the churches generally,
there would be less surprise that during the apostolic age writings of
apostolic men were treated with equal respect to that accorded to the
Old Testament. There can be no doubt that in both 1 and 2 Peter the
prophetical and apostolic teaching is placed on a level (cf. 1 Pet. iv. 11,
i. 10, 11).[4] That this was characteristic of the primitive period seems to
be borne out by the readiness with which the sub-apostolic age treated
the apostolic writings with such respect. Admittedly, the Apostolic
Fathers do not as explicitly place Paul on the same level of inspiration
as the Old Testament, but it may be claimed that this is implicit in their
approach. If by AD 140 Marcion could be sufficiently daring to exalt
his *Apostolicon* to the complete detriment of the Old Testament, at

[1] To cite one of the most recent among these, A. E. Barnett, *The Second Epistle
of Peter* (IB, 1957), p. 204. Cf. also Chase, *op. cit.*, p. 810.
[2] Cf. E. J. Goodspeed, *New Chapters in New Testament Study* (1937), pp. 22–49;
The Key to Ephesians (1956), pp. v ff.
[3] For a full discussion of this hypothesis, see pp. 643ff.
[4] Cf. E. M. B. Green's discussion of this, *op. cit.*, pp. 30ff.

some time previously the orthodox Christian Church must virtually have treated them as equal. Marcion was not introducing a *volte-face*, but pushing the natural development to an extreme limit in the interests of dogmatic considerations. Similar developments are found in the growth of second-century pseudepigraphic apostolic literature, which must presuppose an existing body of *authoritative* apostolic literature. To place 2 Peter in the vanguard of this movement may at first seem a reasonable hypothesis, but it does not explain why this writer is so much in advance of his contemporaries in his regard for Paul's writings. Is it not more reasonable to suggest that in the apostolic period Peter may have recognized the value of Paul's Epistles even more fully than the later sub-apostolic Fathers? These latter do not speak of Paul as 'our beloved brother', but in more exalted ways as, 'the blessed and glorious Paul' (Polycarp, *Ad Phil.* iii); 'the blessed Paul' (*1 Clement*, xlvii. 1; Polycarp, *Ad Phil.* xi); 'the sanctified Paul . . . right blessed' (Ignatius, *Ad Eph.* xii. 2). The description in 2 Peter would be almost over-familiar for a pseudepigraphist, although it would be wholly in character with what we should expect of the warm-hearted apostle portrayed in the Synoptic Gospels.[1] This is either a genuine appreciation on the part of Peter himself or skilful representation by his imitator. The former alternative is rather easier to conceive than the latter.

Another consideration arises here. Would a pseudepigraphist have adopted the view that Peter did not understand Paul's writings? It is strange, at least, that he has such an idea of Peter's ability in view of the fact that he considers it worthwhile to attribute the whole Epistle to Peter. The history of Jewish and early Christian pseudepigraphy shows a marked tendency towards the enhancement of heroes and there is no parallel case in which the putative author is made to detract from his own reputation. Rather than pointing to a later origin, this self-candour of Peter's is a factor in favour of authenticity. It is surely not very surprising that Peter, or any of the other original apostles for that matter, found Paul difficult. Has anyone ever found him easy?

2. In evaluating the reference to the 'second letter' in 2 Peter iii. 1, the first problem to settle is whether or not this is a reference to 1

---

[1] Mayor (*op. cit.*, p. 166) candidly admits, 'There are many difficulties in the way of accepting the genuineness of this Epistle; but the manner in which St. Paul is spoken of seems to me just what we should have expected from his brother apostle.'

Peter. It is generally taken for granted and probability seems strongly to support this contention. Since there is a clear reference to an earlier letter and since 1 Peter already is known to us, it is a natural assumption that the two letters are to be identified. Both Spitta[1] and Zahn[2] rejected this assumption because they held that, whereas 1 Peter was addressed to Gentiles, 2 Peter was addressed to Jewish Christians. Few, however, have followed them in this (see further comments on readers below, pp. 848f.). In addition they both maintained that in 1 Peter the author does not seem to have preached personally to these people, whereas in 2 Peter he has (cf. 1 Pet. i. 12; 2 Pet. i. 16). This distinction may be right, but is not absolutely demanded by the evidence. Bigg[3] maintained that 'nothing more need be meant than that the recipients knew perfectly well what the teaching of the apostles was'. A much more weighty consideration is that 1 Peter does not fit the context of 2 Peter iii. 1, which clearly implies that the former Epistle is like the present in being a reminder about predictions of coming false teachers.[4] There is much to be said for the view that the former Epistle of 2 Peter iii. 1 is not 1 Peter, but a lost epistle.[5] On this assumption the reference could not be regarded as a literary device, for it would have no point unless the previous letter were well known. On the other hand, 2 Peter iii. 1 does not absolutely demand that both Epistles should say the same thing and it may be possible to make 1 Peter fill the bill by appealing to the frequent allusions to prophetic words within that Epistle. Since there is room for difference of opinion on the matter, it can hardly be claimed that here is a clear indication of pseudonymity, although it might be corroborative evidence if pseudonymity were otherwise established. There is, in any case, nothing unnatural about the reference if both Epistles are Petrine.

3. The next problem to discuss is the occasion reflected in the Epistle. It is a legacy from the criticism of F. C. Baur and his school that a tendency exists for all references to false teachers in the New Testament in some ways to be connected up with second-century Gnosticism. In spite of greater modern reluctance to make this unqualified assumption, the idea dies hard that no heresy showing the

---

[1] *Op. cit.*, pp. 486ff.   [2] *INT*, ii, p. 208.
[3] *Op. cit.*, p. 289.   [4] Cf. Zahn, *op. cit.*, ii, pp. 195ff.
[5] This may be maintained quite apart from the theory that 1 and 2 Peter were addressed to different racial groups. R. A. Falconer (*op. cit.*, pp. 47f., 117f., 218f.) suggested that 2 Peter was a circular to the church throughout Samaria.

slightest parallels with Gnosticism could possibly have appeared before the end of the first century. The facts are that all the data that can be collected from 2 Peter (and Jude) are insufficient to identify the movement with any known second-century system. Rather do they suggest a general mental and moral atmosphere which would have been conducive for the development of systematic Gnosticism. Indeed, it may with good reason be claimed that a second-century pseudepigraphist, writing during the period of developed Gnosticism, would have given more specific evidence of the period to which he belonged and the sect that he was combating.[1] This was done, for instance, by the author of the spurious *3 Corinthians* and might be expected here. The fact that the author gives no such allusions is a point in favour of a first-century date and is rather more in support of authenticity than the reverse. (But see the further discussion on these false teachers, pp. 853ff.)

4. The objection based on iii. 4, regarded as a reference to a former generation, is rather more weighty, although it is subject to different interpretations. Everything depends on the meaning in this context of οἱ πατέρες (the fathers). Most commentators assume that these are first generation Christians who have now died. The meaning of the verse would then be that questions have arisen over the veracity of the *parousia*, because ever since the first generation of Christians died everything has continued in the created order, just as they always have done previously. This interpretation would make good sense, but would clearly imply some interval since the first generation and this would at once exclude Petrine authorship. But is it correct? Nowhere else in the New Testament nor in the Apostolic Fathers is πατέρες used of Christian 'patriarchs' and the more natural interpretation would be to take it as denoting the Jewish patriarchs,[2] in which case the statement

---

[1] Cf. E. M. B. Green's comments on this, *op. cit.*, p. 26.

[2] Mayor (*op. cit.*, pp. 148f.) discusses this view but rejects it, first because the word πατέρες is sometimes used of the pre-Mosaic patriarchs, sometimes of Moses and his contemporaries, sometimes of the prophets; and secondly because no-one, in view of the rise of the Christian Church, could say that all things continue as they were. But the predominant New Testament use of the word, used absolutely, is of the ancient patriarchs and there is nothing against that interpretation in 2 Peter. With reference to Mayor's second point, the context clearly shows that the scoffers would go back not merely to apostolic times but to creation itself and their thought would relate to the winding up of the created order. For this reason Peter points out that the same God whose word brought it into being will finally bring it to consummation. This is surely what is meant by 'the day of the Lord' (2 Pet. iii. 10).

would amount to a rather exaggerated declaration of the changeless-
ness of things. This would certainly give a reasonable connection with
the allusion to the creation account and later to the flood.

Either interpretation is possible, but if this is the report of a second-
century pseudepigraphist it needs to be explained how he could have
thought that Peter would be able to look back on the first generation of
Christians from some even earlier age.[1] We should need to assume that
he gave himself away through a foolish slip in historical detail, a not
uncommon failing among pseudepigraphists. But the explanation is not
very substantial since the statement in 2 Peter iii. 4 is put into the mouths
of the scoffers and would on this hypothesis presumably reflect current
opinions. But questions regarding the *parousia* would be much more
natural in the apostolic age than later. The Apostolic Fathers do not
betray such concern over the delay in the *parousia*.[2]

5. Zahn's[3] interpretation of the reference to 'your apostles' was to
restrict it to those who had actually worked among the readers and he
saw no difficulty in the writer including himself. The point of the
ὑμῶν is that of contrast with the false teachers who in no sense belong
to the readers. The combination of prophets and apostles is, of course,
found in Ephesians ii. 20, and is no certain evidence of a second-
century provenance.[4]

(iii) *Literary problems.* Assuming for our present purpose that Jude is
prior to 2 Peter (but see the discussion on this on pp. 919ff.), the problem
arises whether the apostle Peter could or would have cited the lesser-
known Jude. It has been suggested that no apostle would ever have

[1] If the reference is to Christian 'fathers', it is, of course, possible that some of
these would certainly have died before Peter (so Spitta and Zahn maintained). In
this case the reference would constitute no difficulty for Petrine authorship,
although it would be difficult in a pseudepigraphic writing, for the writer would
hardly have worked out such a subtle possibility. On the other hand the article
would not naturally denote a few.

[2] A very similar statement about the continuity of things in relation to the Lord's
coming is, it is true, found both in *1 Clement*, xxiii. 3f. and *2 Clement*, xi. 2f., but
the latter looks like a borrowing from the former since the same vine illustration
is used (unless both borrowed from a lost apocalypse of Eldad and Modad; cf.
K. Lake, *The Apostolic Fathers*, 1912, I, p. 51). *1 Clement* cites it as γραφή and *2
Clement* as a 'prophetic word', and both are, therefore, referring to questionings
which must have arisen much earlier.

[3] *INT*, II, pp. 204, 205. Cf. the same kind of thing in 1 Pet. i. 12.

[4] On this, cf. pp. 504 f.

made such extensive use of a non-apostolic source,[1] but this supposition is fallacious, for it has already been seen from 1 Peter that Peter was the kind of man who was influenced by other writings. But the position in 2 Peter is admittedly of a different character in that it seems to involve the author in an expansion of an existing tract without acknowledgment. If Jude is prior to 2 Peter, therefore, it must be regarded as unexpected that such use is made of it and this would weigh the evidence rather against than for authenticity. At the same time it is equally, if not more, unexpected for a pseudepigraphist to adopt such a borrowing procedure. Indeed, it is quite unparalleled among the Jewish and early Christian pseudepigrapha. The question arises why so much of Jude needed to be incorporated. About the only reasonable suggestion on the late-date theory is to suppose that Jude's tract had failed because of its lack of an impressive name and so the same truths with considerable additions were attributed to Peter.[2] But did no-one have any suspicions about this process? It would have been less open to question had the author made his borrowing from Jude less obvious.

Yet perhaps not too much emphasis should in any case be placed on this feature since there is no mention of difficulty over borrowing in any of the comments of Church Fathers concerning the retarded reception of this Epistle. If 2 Peter is prior, the difficulty would vanish altogether as far as that Epistle is concerned and it would then be necessary only to explain why Jude published an extract of a major part of 2 Peter under his own name. In that case, it would seem that Jude is writing when the situation predicted in 2 Peter has already been fulfilled and his Epistle would then be intended to remind the readers of this fact (cf. Jude 17).

Nothing need be added to what has already been said on the literary connections between this Epistle and Paul's Epistles, but the relation-

---

[1] E. H. Plumptre (*The General Epistles of St. Peter and St. Jude*, 1879, p. 80) made the suggestion that Peter was sent Jude's letter, realized the seriousness of the dangers mentioned and wrote a letter about it to the recipients of 1 Peter, for whom his name would carry more weight than Jude's.

[2] M. Dibelius (*A Fresh Approach to the New Testament and Early Christian Literature*, p. 209) makes an ingenious attempt to explain 2 Peter's wide use of Jude. Because he believes that Jude 17, 18 prompted the production of 2 Peter, he supposes that the author of 2 Peter desired to make clear that his Epistle was the source of Jude and, therefore, incorporated nearly the whole of it. But this extraordinary procedure finds no parallel and looks too much like an artificial expedient to support a theory.*

ship between 1 and 2 Peter is more significant. Several similarities between the Epistles exist, but not all scholars are agreed as to the reason for these. If Peter were author of both, there would be a ready explanation. If he were author of 1 Peter but not 2 Peter, direct imitation would need to be postulated, although this is difficult in view of the differences. If both were pseudepigraphic, it would be the first Christian instance of the development of a group of writings attributed to a famous name.

The difference in the use of the Old Testament in the two Epistles should not be exaggerated. While the variation in formal quotation must be admitted, it is a remarkable fact that where 2 Peter approaches the nearest to direct quotations, these are made from Psalms, Proverbs and Isaiah, all of which are formally cited in 1 Peter. Indeed Proverbs and Isaiah are particular favourites of both authors.[1] This kind of subtle agreement suggests the subconscious approaches of one mind rather than a deliberate imitation. It is difficult to regard it as purely accidental. Two other factors may be mentioned by way of corroboration. The similar appeal to the history of Noah is suggestive, although this could conceivably have been due to imitation. The estimate of the Old Testament in both authors is remarkably similar, for the statement in 2 Peter i. 20, 21 regarding the inspiration of Scripture prophecy through the agency of the Spirit of God is fully consonant with the obviously high regard for the prophetic Scriptures in the first Epistle (cf. 1 Pet. i. 10–12).

(iv) *Stylistic problems.* It is notoriously difficult to devise any certain criteria for the examination of style and this is particularly true where comparison is made between two short Epistles. The area of comparison is so restricted that the results may well be misleading. Moreover, subjective impressions are likely to receive greater stress than is justified. At the same time, no-one can deny that the stylistic differences between the Epistles are real enough. Mayor[2] pointed out that the vocabulary common to the two Epistles numbers 100 words, whereas the differences total 599. Variations of subject-matter would naturally account for many of the differences and it is not easy to decide what significance is to be attached to the rest. Both Epistles have a number of words found nowhere else in the New Testament (59 in 1 Peter, 56 in 2 Peter)[3] and among these there are in both certain words of particular

[1] Cf. R. A. Falconer, *Exp.*, VI, vi (1902), p. 51.　　　[2] *Op. cit.*, p. lxxiv.
[3] Cited from Mayor's totals, *op. cit.*, pp. lxxii, lxxiv.

picturesqueness. On the whole these word totals have little importance in view of the small quantities of literature from which they are taken. But the grammatical words are rather a different matter. The fewer particles in 2 Peter than 1 Peter point to a different style, which may indicate a different hand. It may be possible to account for some of this variation by reference to the different mood of each writing. 1 Peter is more calmly deliberative than 2 Peter, which seems to have been produced in a state of strong feeling.

The aptness for repetitions found in 2 Peter has been noted and it is certainly marked.[1] But, although it is rather more noticeable in 2 Peter than in 1 Peter, there are many instances of it in the latter.[2] At times the author of 2 Peter falls into metrical cadences and this has been found a difficulty, but prose writers at times use poetic forms and this need occasion no great surprise.[3]

If the linguistic characteristics are considered too divergent to postulate common authorship between 1 and 2 Peter, the difficulties would, of course, be considerably lessened, if not obviated, by the amanuensis hypothesis for one Epistle. If Peter, for instance, were author of 1 Peter, with the assistance of Silvanus as amanuensis, and author and scribe of 2 Peter, it would be possible to account for these stylistic differences and similarities.[4] Or, if Jerome's hypothesis is preferred, both Epistles might be attributed to different amanuenses. This may be regarded by some as a desperate expedient to avoid a difficulty, but so widespread was the use of amanuenses in the ancient world that it ought not to be dismissed from consideration, at least as a possibility. There is now no means of telling what liberty of expression would be granted by Peter to any amanuensis whom he may have employed. It is in the realm of conjecture to declare that an apostle would or would not have done this or that.[5]

---

[1] Cf. Bigg, *op. cit.*, pp. 225, 226.   [2] Bigg, *op. cit.*, pp. 226, 227, gives a list
[3] Cf. *Ibid.*, pp. 227, 228.
[4] This is Zahn's solution, but was criticized by Chase (*op. cit.*, p. 813) on the grounds that it involves giving up the real Petrine authorship of 1 Peter in order to defend the authenticity of 2 Peter.
[5] It has been suggested that Peter may have written the letter in Aramaic, which was later translated into Greek (cf. G. Wohlenberg, *Der erste und der zweite Petrusbriefe und der Judasbrief*, Zahn xv,[3] 1923, p. xxxvi). But Moulton and Howard (*A Grammar of New Testament Greek*, II, 1929, pp. 27, 28) can find very few traces of any Semitisms in the language. Yet cf. J. Chaine (*Les Epîtres catholiques*, 1939, p. 18) for a list of Hebraisms in both Epistles. E. G. Selwyn (*The*

(v) *Doctrinal problems.* Much New Testament criticism is dominated by an over-analytical approach and this is particularly true in doctrinal comparisons. It is a fallacious assumption that any author of two works must give equal attention in both to the same themes, or must always approach any one theme in a similar way. The fact that 2 Peter deals more fully with the *parousia* theme than 1 Peter constitutes no difficulty for those who consider this difference to be due to difference of purpose. But is this sufficient to explain the important omissions of Petrine themes from 2 Peter? Could the author of 1 Peter have written an Epistle without mentioning the cross or resurrection of Christ? This is an important question which cannot be lightly dismissed. Whereas in 1 Peter there are specific references to the atoning work of Christ (e.g. i. 18, ii. 21ff.), there are less specific allusions in 2 Peter. Frequently Christ is called Saviour (σωτήρ).[1] Through Him men are purged from sin (i. 9). It is the Master who has 'bought' believers (ii. 1), and this cannot refer to anything other than a redemptive act in Christ. Apart from the implicit background of the cross, these allusions in 2 Peter would be unintelligible.

The resurrection and ascension of Christ appear to be replaced by the transfiguration, and this is certainly unexpected. But the author's purpose is to authenticate his own personal knowledge of the glory of Christ, which appears to have been more illuminated on the mount of transfiguration than during the resurrection appearances.[2] In the latter

Christian Prophets and the Prophetic Apocalypse, 1900, p. 157) argued with some plausibility that Luke may have been instructed by Peter to write this Epistle. He based his suggestion on parallels with Luke-Acts.

[1] It is not enough explanation for Käsemann to refer to this title and to that of Lord (κύριος) as stereotyped predicates of Christ (*op. cit.*, p. 285). To call a thing stereotyped at once labels it as secondary, but the use of the titles, whether separately or combined, in this Epistle need not be so explained. The combination is not found precisely in this form elsewhere in the New Testament, but the combination of the two ideas is certainly primitive. It should be noted that 'our Lord Jesus Christ', which is used six times in 2 Peter, is found several times in Paul's letters and cannot be designated 'stereotyped'. Indeed, a sure witness to the fact that the language here does not belong to the period of formal titles is the absence of such forms from the earlier Apostolic Fathers. 'Our Lord Jesus Christ' occurs six times in *1 Clement*, once in Ignatius and five times in Polycarp, but not once in combination with 'Saviour'. 'Jesus Christ our Saviour' occurs only in the greeting in Polycarp's letter.

[2] The writer is not here dealing with a denial of the resurrection as far as we know from the context. It was a question of the fullest possible authentication of his witness to Christ's glorious nature. (Cf. R. A. Falconer, *op. cit.*, pp. 463, 464.)

the full majesty was veiled. But does the emphasis in 2 Peter betray a degenerate Christology? A fair assessment of the evidence would not support such a contention. The titles applied to Christ are 'Saviour', 'Lord' and 'Master'. He is central in the whole thinking of the believer (cf. ii. 20, i. 2, 8). To Him is ascribed eternal glory (iii. 18). Käsemann is dominated by the thought of non-Christian religious notions in the text, but these do not proceed naturally from the Epistle itself. It should be noted that the great emphasis on the Lordship of Christ in this Epistle presupposes the resurrection and ascension, since without these the doctrine could not have developed.[1]

Turning to the eschatology of the Epistle, we must enquire whether Käsemann is justified in regarding this as sub-Christian. The hope of the *parousia* with its practical outcome in providing a motive for holy living is fully in accord with the eschatology of the rest of the New Testament (2 Pet. iii. 1ff.; cf. 1 Jn. ii. 28, iii. 3).[2] If anything, the eschatology is more primitive than in some parts of the New Testament and this is a point in its favour.[3] The description of the ἔσχατον ('end'), although dramatic with its accompanying destruction of the heavens and earth by fire,[4] is seen to be extraordinarily restrained when compared, for instance, with the *Apocalypse of Peter*. An important factor for the dating of the Epistle is the absence of the second-century Chiliastic interpretation of Psalm xc. 4, in spite of the fact that this

---

[1] H. Alford (*The Greek Testament*,[4] IV, 1871, p. 155) maintained that the Lordship of Christ is most prominent here because of the purpose to warn and caution against rebellion.

[2] This is acknowledged even by some who deny the authenticity of the Epistle. H. F. D. Sparks, for instance, sees in the answer of 2 Peter to the eschatological problem 'fundamentally no more than a second-century reaffirmation of the central hope of the primitive gospel' (*op. cit.*, p. 137).

[3] This is well brought out by E. M. B. Green (*op. cit.*, pp. 18f.). He finds in 2 Peter the paradoxical tension betweeen realized and unrealized eschatology, which was so typical in the apostolic period.

[4] This idea of the destruction of the world by fire (ἐκπύρωσις) had its origins perhaps in Persian thought, but occurs nowhere else in the Bible. In Stoic thought it was linked with ἀποκατάστασις and it may be significant that this latter word occurs in a Petrine speech in Acts iii. 21. It is found in the Dead Sea Scrolls and in the fourth Sibylline Oracles (lines 172–177). It was nevertheless regarded with suspicion by Irenaeus (*Adv. Haer.* i. 7. 1) and Origen (*Contra Celsum*, iv. 11. 79), a fact which no doubt contributed to the hesitations over 2 Peter. But the Christian belief must have been founded on an authoritative document, i.e. in all probability Peter 2.

passage is quoted in 2 Peter iii. 8.[1] A second-century pseudepigraphist would have done well to avoid this possible pitfall.

The different terms used in 1 Peter and 2 Peter to describe the Lord's coming have often been noted (ἀποκάλυψις and its cognate verb in 1 Peter and παρουσία, ἡμέρα κυρίου, ἡμέρα κρίσεως in 2 Peter), but little weight may be put upon this. Paul in 1 Corinthians and 2 Thessalonians uses both ἀποκάλυψις and παρουσία, and there is no reason why Peter should not have used both words on different occasions.

As to the ethics of 2 Peter, there are exhortations in the Epistle which show the ethical appeal to be based on doctrine (cf. i. 8f., where fruitfulness is particularly stressed; iii. 11ff., where Christian behaviour is geared to the eschatological hope). There is emphasis on stability, restraint of passion, righteousness, purity. A variety of moral virtues is enumerated (i. 5ff.). But is the impetus mainly self-effort? Käsemann[2] and many others believe that it is. Moreover, the work of the Holy Spirit is mentioned only once (i. 21) and then in relation to the inspiration of Scripture. The reason for this may lie in the particular tendencies of the readers. It is evident that the false teachers, at least, do not put much self-effort into their 'Christian' behaviour, and the writer is clearly fearful lest their lax approach should infect the Christian believers to whom he is writing. This would explain the stronger emphasis on individual zeal than is found in 1 Peter. The absence of any close connection between ethics and the doctrine of the Spirit does not mean that the writer did not recognize such a connection, but rather that he saw no need to emphasize it (cf. Paul's approach in Colossians where the Spirit is mentioned once only, Col. i. 8).

On the whole it cannot be said that there are any substantial differences in doctrine when this Epistle is compared with other New Testament books. Although there are omissions, there are no contradictions. There are no features which are of such a character that they could not belong to the apostolic age. The doctrinal considerations are, in fact, rather more favourable to a primitive than to a later origin for the Epistle.

[1] J. Moffatt (*ILNT*, p. 362 n.) objected that Chiliasm was not universal in the second century, neither was Ps. xc. 4 its starting-point, as Rev. xx. 4f. shows. But the latter reference cannot be cited as evidence for second-century Chiliasm, while Chiliastic tendencies are found in as widely differing writers as Barnabas (xv. 4), Justin (*Dial.* 81) and Irenaeus (*Adv. Haer.* v. 28. 3, 23. 2).

[2] For a concise and clear discussion of the position of Käsemann, cf. E. M. B. Green, *op. cit.*, pp. 19, 20.

NEW TESTAMENT INTRODUCTION

Little comment is needed on the Hellenistic terms used in this Epistle, for it is impossible to say what degree of impact on an author's mind environment might be expected to have. It will obviously differ with different minds. The main problem over 2 Peter is whether the apostle Peter, with his Jewish fisherman's background, could reasonably be expected to be acquainted with these expressions. None of the terms is of a type which could not have formed part of the vocabulary of a bilingual Galilaean. The difficulty arises only when it is assumed that in 2 Peter they are used in a developed sense as in Greek philosophy or the mystery cults. In that case a fisherman would have to be ruled out. But the bandying about of some such terms as 'knowledge' (γνῶσις) or 'virtue' (ἀρετή) need not suppose acquaintance with current philosophical discussions, any more than it does today. This is the kind of evidence which is most convincing to those who have already concluded on other grounds that 2 Peter cannot have been produced in the first century AD.

So far the approach to Petrine authorship has been mainly negative in the course of examining the arguments brought against it. But there are a few considerations of a more positive character.

(vi) *Additional considerations.* 1. Similarities with the Petrine speeches in Acts will first be considered. No great weight can be attached to these similarities since they are merely verbal and their significance will naturally depend on the degree of credibility assigned to the Acts speeches. At most they can be corroborative. For instance, the words 'obtained' (i. 1; cf. Acts i. 17), 'godliness' (i. 6; cf. Acts iii. 12), 'day of the Lord' (iii. 10; cf. Acts ii. 20) and 'punished' (ii. 9; cf. Acts iv. 21) all occur in both books. The incidental character of these parallels could be a point in their favour, since a pseudepigraphist might be expected either to have included more obvious parallels or else to have ignored the Acts source altogether. They might be regarded as echoes of one man's vocabulary, but the argument obviously cannot be pressed.

2. There are certain indirect personal reminiscences, which might support Petrine authorship. Words are used (σκηνή, 'tabernacle' and ἔξοδος, 'departure') which are found together in Luke's transfiguration narrative. They are used in a different context in 2 Peter, but this in itself would support the suggestion that they had made a deep impression on Peter's mind and are subconsciously brought into play as Peter muses about the transfiguration (i. 17f.). It may be a subtle psychologi-

cal support that these two words are used *before* the transfiguration account is included, but at a point in the Epistle where the writer's mind is moving rapidly towards its inclusion.

3. The superiority of 2 Peter over the Petrine spurious books is another point in its favour. A comparison of its spiritual quality with the spiritual tone of the *Gospel of Peter*, the *Preaching of Peter*, the *Acts of Peter* and the *Apocalypse of Peter* cannot fail to impress even the most casual reader with the immeasurable superiority of the canonical book. This is in itself no conclusive evidence of the authenticity of 2 Peter, for if this Epistle is pseudepigraphic it could conceivably follow that this pseudepigraphist excelled himself, while the others did not. But the problem goes deeper than this, for spiritual quality is not a matter of skill, but of inspiration. In spite of all the doubts regarding the Epistle, the discernment of the Christian Church decided in its favour because the quality of its message suggested its authenticity. It was the same discernment which confidently rejected the spurious Petrine literature.

d. Conclusion

The summing up of the case for and against authenticity is not easy, because there are strong arguments on both sides. The external evidence, at least, indicates a certain lack of confidence in the book, although the cause is not specifically stated. At the same time the internal evidence poses many problems, not all of which can be answered with equal certainty, but none of which can be said categorically to exclude Petrine authorship. The dilemma is intensified by the difficulties confronting alternative views of authorship. If, in deference to the repeated demands of many modern scholars, the word 'forgery' is omitted from the discussion,[1] we are left as our only alternative to suppose that a well-intentioned author ascribed it to the apostle Peter, presumably in order to claim his authority for what was said, but nevertheless supposing that no-one would have been deceived by it. The latter supposition is difficult to substantiate, but even if it be taken as possible, the writer must have paid minute attention to the process of introducing allusions to give an air of authenticity. If the whole process was a contemporary literary convention, it is difficult to see

[1] There was less hesitancy about this at the beginning of this century as is evident from E. A. Abbott's monograph, *Contrast; or a prophet and a forger* (1903), in which he calls the author of 2 Peter not only a forger, but a pilferer, a false prophet, vulgar and dishonest.

why the personal authentication marks were used at all. The fact is that the general tendency among pseudepigraphists was to avoid rather than include supporting allusions to their main heroes. It was enough to allow them to introduce themselves by means of some ancient name.

In addition to this there are difficulties in finding a suitable occasion which might have prompted such a pseudonymous Epistle. It is a fair principle to suppose that pseudonymity would be resorted to only if genuine authorship would fail to achieve its purpose. In this case it would require a situation in which only apostolic authority would suffice. In most of the acknowledged Christian pseudepigrapha, a sufficient motive is found in the desire to propagate views which would not otherwise be acceptable. Thus the device was used widely among heretical sects. But in orthodox circles the need would be less pressing, for the whole basis of their tradition was apostolic and any literary works whose doctrine was wholly in harmony with that tradition would not need to be ascribed rather artificially to an apostolic author. The writer of 2 Peter says nothing which the apostolic writers of the other books of the New Testament would not have endorsed. There is no hint of esoteric doctrine or practice. What was the point, then, of ascribing it to Peter? Since the false teachers were showing no respect for Paul (2 Pet. ii. 16), would they have shown any more for Peter? If it be maintained that these teachers were using Peter's name against Paul and that this obliged the orthodox Church to answer them in Peter's name, would they not be using the very method they would condemn in their opponents? The fact is that no advocate of a pseudonymous origin for 2 Peter has been able to give a wholly satisfactory account of the motive behind it,[1] and

---

[1] Examples of recent attempts to do this may be cited. A. E. Barnett (*op. cit.*, p. 165) is content to call 2 Peter, 'a plea for loyalty to the tenets of primitive Christianity', and to claim that the pseudonym would symbolize original and authoritative Christianity. P. Carrington ('Saint Peter's Epistle', in *The Joy of Study*, ed. S. E. Johnson, 1951, p. 61) says, 'In 2 Peter the stage is carefully set so as to re-create in the imagination of the reader a bygone age; for a work of fiction is obliged to produce a complete illusion'. The Catholic writer Cantinat in Robert-Feuillet's *Introduction à la Bible*, II, p. 599, accounts for the pseudonym as being the means used to cover with the authority of his chief the teaching of one of Peter's disciples who was endeavouring to reproduce the essential message of the apostle. K. H. Schelkle (*Die Petrusbriefe, der Judasbrief*, 1961, p. 181) adopts a similar view. Dibelius (*op. cit.*, p. 208) finds the fundamental motive for writing in the author's desire to provide the literary reference for the prophecy referred to in Jude 17, 18. Thus Jude would ostensibly appear to be citing 2 Pet. iii. 3. But it is difficult to

this must be taken into consideration in reaching a verdict on the matter.

The choice seems to lie between two fairly well defined alternatives. Either the Epistle is genuinely Petrine (with or without the use of an amanuensis), in which case the main problem is the delay in its reception. Or it is pseudepigraphic, in which case the main difficulties are lack of an adequate motive and the problem of its ultimate acceptance.[1]

Both obviously present some difficulties, but of the two the former is easier to explain. If 2 Peter was sent to a restricted destination (see discussion below) it is not difficult to imagine that many churches may not have received it in the earlier history of the Canon.[2] When it did begin to circulate it may well have been received with some suspicion, particularly if by this time some spurious Petrine books were beginning to circulate. That it ultimately became accepted universally must have been due to the recognition not merely of its claim to apostolic authorship, but also of its apostolic content.[3] Under the latter hypothesis it would be necessary to assume that its lack of early attestation and the existence of suspicions were because its pseudepigraphic

believe that Jude 17, 18 would lead anyone to compose an epistle in the name of Peter. If 2 Peter were not in our possession, it would be more natural to take Jude's ἔλεγον as indicating oral teaching. Käsemann (*op. cit.*, pp. 279, 280) sees the need for the pseudonym in the author's intention to authenticate the orthodox teaching in face of the Gnostic challenge. For this purpose, he thinks, an apostolic name was necessary. A. Schlatter (*Die Briefe des Petrus, Judas, Jakobus, der Brief an die Hebräer*, 1950, p. 89) suggests vaguely that Peter was chosen as he was chief apostle.

[1] A third alternative has often been advocated and has recently been maintained by the Catholic writers J. Chaine (*op. cit.*, p. 31) and R. Leconte (*Les Epîtres catholiques*, 1953, p. 96) who, while denying Petrine authorship, yet consider that the author was a disciple of Peter. But this still strictly comes under the category of pseudepigraphy; indeed Chaine admits this.

[2] The poor state of the text may provide some indication of limited early circulation, especially if A. Vansittart is right that for some time it existed in a single copy only (*Journal of Philology*, III, 1871, pp. 357ff.).

[3] Something of the perplexity arising from the apostolic content is seen in the opinion of E. G. Homrighausen (Exposition, *The Second Epistle of Peter*, IB, XII, 1957, p. 166) who, while maintaining its pseudonymous origin, nevertheless admitted that it 'breathes Christ and awaits his consummation' and, furthermore, he asserted that 'what we have is Petrine in character and spirit'. One wonders if the early Christians were as cautious and yet conflicting in their assessment as this modern writer.

origin was known, and that its later acceptance was due to the fact that this origin was forgotten and the Epistle mistakenly supposed to be genuine. While there is nothing intrinsically impossible about this reconstruction, it requires greater credibility than the authenticity hypothesis. The dilemma for pseudepigraphic hypotheses is caused by the fact that attestation for the book would be expected very soon after its origin on the assumption that some would at once assume from its ascription that it was genuine. This evidently happened in the case of the *Apocalypse of Peter* which is attested in the Muratorian Fragment, but never commanded any further acceptance except in Egypt. But in spite of Harnack's arguments for placing 2 Peter in the late second century, few modern advocates of pseudepigraphic origin place it so late. At a period when the orthodox were on the alert to test the validity of all literary productions, it is difficult to see how an earlier pseudepigraphic production would have gained currency after a considerable interval of time, especially against marked suspicions.

III. THE READERS

The Epistle is vaguely addressed 'to those who have obtained a faith of equal standing with ours in the righteousness of our God and Saviour Jesus Christ' (RSV). This very general destination contrasts strikingly with the specific provinces mentioned in 1 Peter. But does this mean that the author has no particular community in view, but is addressing a kind of circular to Christians everywhere? At first sight, his opening words would certainly give that impression, but this must be tested by the contents of the subsequent subject-matter and by the various historical allusions.

The first necessity is to determine whether 1 and 2 Peter were sent to the same readers. Those who interpret 2 Peter iii. 1 as a reference to 1 Peter have an immediate answer. The second Epistle is meant to be addressed primarily to the readers of the first, who may, therefore, be specifically localized. But under this interpretation it would be necessary to suppose that the more general address was used because of the more general applicability of the message to Christians of all areas. Yet there are difficulties in this view, for the author appears to be thinking of particular people known to him personally. In i. 16 he refers to the time 'when we made known to you the power and coming of our Lord Jesus Christ' (RSV), which clearly presupposes a period of previous mission work among the readers. He also sees the particular threat from false teachers who evidently are already active (cf. ii. 10f.) and will gain admittance to the church secretly (ii. 1). He may, of course, be speaking generally here,[1] but his words become more intelligible if he has definite people in mind.

On the basis of i. 16, Zahn[2] considered that the author had been associated with the other eyewitnesses of the transfiguration in mission work among the readers and these would, therefore, be particularly described as 'your apostles' (iii. 2). But the plural in i. 16 need not absolutely refer to more than one and may be here no more than a stylistic avoidance of the singular. Nevertheless, since in the immediately preceding verses the singular is used, the change to the plural probably has some significance in including other eyewitnesses beside the writer. This helps us in ascertaining the readers only if we assume with Zahn[3] that the people concerned must be Jewish Christians, largely on the grounds of a distinction between 'your apostles' and other apostles, and of the absence of specific reference to Gentile readers. Zahn suggested the destination as Palestine and the adjoining regions, but few others have been convinced that the readers are more Jewish than Gentile. The reverse seems rather to be true since the author is clearly apprehensive lest his readers will be affected by the practices of the false teachers, which are much more closely allied to Gentile vices than Jewish. The truth probably lies between the two extremes, and the people in mind may well have been a Jewish-Gentile community or communities. In this connection it should be recalled that nowhere in 2 Peter is the Old Testament certainly cited, although there are many allusions to its examples and echoes of its language. Evidently Peter assumes his readers' acquaintance with it, even more so than in 1 Peter, where it is several times cited, but where there are fewer passing allusions. This might perhaps support Zahn's contention, but the absence of specific appeal to scriptural authority is difficult to conceive if the readers were Jewish Christians.

In the absence of sufficient data there is no option but to leave the location of the readers as an open question, but in this case it makes no vital difference to the interpretation of the Epistle.

[1] Moffatt (*ILNT*, p. 368) even regards i. 12f. and iii. 1f. as 'literary drapery', and thus argues that 'there is an entire absence of any personal relation between the writer and the church or churches'.

[2] *INT*, II, pp. 204f.   [3] *Ibid.*, pp. 206ff.

IV. OCCASION AND DATE

Some reference has already been made to both occasion and date when discussing authenticity, and it will be necessary, therefore, only to gather together the different suggestions which have been made.

a. On the assumption that 2 Peter is genuine

As indicated in the discussion on the readers, Peter has apparently worked among these people and is now addressing exhortations to them which he would have delivered orally had he been present among them. He clearly realizes his own work is nearly finished for he alludes to his own passing and this no doubt provides the impetus for the present letter. Yet this Epistle has about it such an air of urgency that it must be supposed that some definite threat of an infiltration of false teachers had suddenly arisen which necessitated its despatch. But since the future tense is mainly used, it must further be supposed that this Epistle is intended to have a preventative effect. The author wishes to strengthen these Christians in faith and practice so that they will be in a position to resist the ungodliness of these threatening false teachers. In this respect the occasion of 2 Peter differs from that of Jude, where the author is obliged to deal with a situation which has already arisen.

The date of the Epistle under this assumption would be towards the end of Peter's life, i.e. before AD 68. It seems most probable that 2 Peter was written not long after 1 Peter, i.e. at a time when Peter was old enough to realize that his passing could not be far away.[1]

b. On the assumption that 2 Peter is pseudepigraphic

Once get away from the apostolic period and both occasion and date become very difficult to specify. In fact, a variety of dates from late first century to late second century have been proposed. There are few fixed points, since no Gnostic sect can be identified with the false teachers. But a *terminus ad quem* is certainly fixed at AD 150 in view of the use made of the Epistle by the author of the *Apocalypse of Peter*,

---

[1] Two other features which support a date just before AD 70 are the absence of references to the fall of Jerusalem and the fact that Paul seems to be dead, since Peter writes to people to whom Paul had previously written (so Kühl, cited by Chase, *HDB*, III, p. 798). The second argument is stronger than the first. F. W. Lewis (*Exp.*, v, x, 1899, pp. 319, 320) argued that it was inconceivable that Mark or Silas left Paul during his lifetime to join Peter.

which must have been issued shortly after this date. Those who date 2 Peter later are obliged to regard that Epistle as the borrower, but the evidence is strongly against this.[1]

The most generally proposed occasion is the rise of Gnosticism and the consequent need to combat it in the name of the leading apostle Peter. Because no definite Gnostic movement is in mind, there is a greater readiness to date the Epistle during the first quarter of the second century before the more organized Gnostic movements developed. But the false teaching reflected in the Epistle is of such a character that a first-century date would suit equally well and there is no strong reason for postulating a second-century date, even if pseudepigraphy is admitted. In the end the predominating factor has been the external attestation. The later the Epistle can be placed the less difficulty is thought to be found in the neglect of it until the third century. Some advocates[2] of non-apostolic authorship date the Epistle about AD 80 on the assumption that it cannot be too far distant from that period if it was written by a personal disciple of the apostle.

V. THE INTEGRITY OF THE EPISTLE

This Epistle has not escaped the attentions of source-critical advocates and various partition theories have been proposed. These may briefly be summarized as follows:

1. Some theories are based on the view that interpolations have been made from Jude. It was first proposed by L. Bertholdt[3] that 2 Peter ii was a later interpolation based on Jude. A similar view was expressed by E. Kühl,[4] who added iii. 1, 2 as well, while W. F. Gess[5] extended the interpolation to encompass i. 20b to iii. 3a, and J. V. Bartlet[6] modified it to ii. 1–iii. 7.

---

[1] See discussion on pp. 858ff. Among those who affix a late date may be cited A. Harnack, *Das Neue Testament um das Jahr 200* (1899), pp. 81ff.; M. Dibelius, *op. cit.*, p. 209; R. Knopf, *op. cit.*, p. 257; and E. J. Goodspeed, *INT*, p. 349; *A History of Christian Literature* (1942), pp. 52–54. The latter's dating of the *Apocalypse* is AD 125–150 and of 2 Peter AD 140–160. J. Moffatt, *ILNT*, pp. 367, 368, is more cautious.

[2] So Leconte, *op. cit.*, p. 96, and J. Chaine, *op. cit.*, pp. 33, 34.

[3] In his *Historischkritische Einleitung in sämmtliche kanonische und apokryphische Schriften des alten und neuen Testaments* (1812–19), pp. 3157ff.

[4] *Die Briefe Petri und Judä* [6] (1897), supported by W. Weiffenbach, *ThLZ*, 23 (1898), cols. 364ff.

[5] *Das apostolische Zeugniss von Christi Person II*, II (1879), pp. 412ff.

[6] *The Apostolic Age* (1907), pp. 518–521.

2. Other theories are based on combinations of different sources. As early as H. Grotius,[1] questioning arose over the integrity of the Epistle, for that Dutch scholar regarded 2 Peter iii as originally a letter distinct from chapters i and ii. There is some superficial support for this in the form of the opening of chapter iii, provided the first letter is regarded as a reference to the earlier part of our present Epistle (i.e. chapters i and ii). A similar theory has quite recently been proposed by M. McNamara,[2] who restricts the former letter to chapter i and thinks chapter ii is probably another independent letter. This writer interprets i. 15 to mean that the author intends to write further letters and this interpretation has prompted him to find these in parts of 2 Peter. An even more complicated theory was proposed by E. I. Robson,[3] who claimed to discover the following: a moral fragment (i. 5b–11); a personal statement and narrative (i. 12–18); a prophetic discourse (i. 20b–ii. 19); and an apocalyptic fragment (iii. 3b–13). These, he thought, were of apostolic origin or bore an apostolic imprimatur.[4]

Now all these theories are vitiated by the continuity of style throughout all parts of the Epistle.[5] The same peculiarities, such as frequent repetitions, are constant throughout. Admittedly the peculiar words are more concentrated in chapter ii than in the rest of the letter, but this is mainly due to the special subject-matter and can certainly not be regarded as evidence of an interpolation. In fact, there are no evidences of any sutures which would naturally suggest the patching together of different sources. There is, moreover, no textual evidence in support of such theories. The false teachers in both chapters ii and iii appear to be the same people. The doctrinal approach in the separate parts is uniform.[6] In short, the Epistle wears the appearance of a unity and may be quite intelligibly interpreted under this supposition. There is, therefore, no compelling reason to consider interpolation theories as at all necessary, and since the various hypotheses differ widely in detail, it is reasonable

---

[1] *Adnotationes in Actus Apostolorum et in Epistolas Catholicas* (1641).

[2] 'The Unity of Second Peter: A Reconsideration', *Scripture*, XII, 17 (1960), pp. 13–19.

[3] *Studies in the Second Epistle of Peter* (1915).

[4] In this way he endeavoured to save something of the authenticity of the Epistle.*

[5] McNamara (*loc. cit.*) recognized this difficulty and was forced to suppose that his three letters were either the work of the same author or had the same redactor.

[6] Cf. Feine-Behm, *op. cit.*, p. 255.

to suppose that they proceed more from the imagination of their originators than from the demands of the facts.

No more convincing are any theories of scribal displacements, such as that proposed by P. Ladeuze,[1] who rearranged the Epistle so that iii. 1-16 stood after ii. 3a. The idea was to smooth out the awkwardness of the sequence of tenses in chapter ii and the apparent digression in the same chapter. But Moffatt[2] has well criticized this type of theory on the grounds that the process required by such a copyist's error seems too elaborate and is anyway unnecessary as an explanation of the interchange of present and future tenses. If it happened at all, it must have happened to the archetype of all extant manuscripts, leaving no trace of the 'original' behind. This kind of theory must be dismissed as highly improbable.

VI. THE FALSE TEACHERS

Unlike the parallel Epistle of Jude, 2 Peter does not at once plunge into a discussion of the false teachers. It introduces the subject gradually, and although the main data occur in chapter ii there are some indications in chapter i which are significant. For instance, the writer contrasts the authentic truth with 'cleverly devised myths' (i. 16), which suggests the speculative and even imaginative character of the teaching. He then maintains that Scripture prophecy is not by private interpretation, which further suggests that he had in mind people who were interpreting the Scriptures in this way (i. 20, 21). This same thought is still uppermost in his mind in iii. 16 and was evidently a particular characteristic of these teachers. It is noteworthy in this respect that the author does not merely denounce their tendency to twist the Scriptures, but prepares for this in a positive way by asserting his own view of inspiration.

There is no break between i. 21 and ii. 1, for Peter now contrasts the outlook and actions of the false teachers with the true interpretations of which he has just spoken. Their teachings are 'destructive heresies', of which the worst example is their denial of the Master who bought them. It is noteworthy that the last phrase (τὸν ἀγοράσαντα αὐτοὺς) does not occur in the parallel passage in Jude, and it is possible that these particular false teachers made a special point of denying the redemptive work of Christ. It would also appear that their doctrine of God was defective for they 'deliberately ignore this fact, that by the word of God heavens existed long ago' (iii. 5, RSV). What their doctrine of

[1] RB, X (1905), pp. 543-552.   [2] ILNT, pp. 370, 371.

creation was is not stated, but they apparently did not ascribe to God His rightful power.

The details in chapter ii are almost wholly concerned with practical errors and most of the points mentioned are those which also occur in Jude (for a fuller description of these characteristics, see pp. 912ff.). Licentiousness and exploitation are the first two details mentioned (ii. 2, 3), and these are followed by descriptions of ancient judgments on similar excesses, particular stress being laid on Lot's reactions to his licentious environment, presumably as a special example for the believers in the face of their approaching threat. There is a promise of deliverance for the godly at the same time as certain judgment for those who indulge their passions (ii. 9, 10). The description of the behaviour of these people is vivid: revelling in dissipation, carousing, adulterous, slaves of corruption. Moral looseness could hardly be more clearly delineated and this must be reckoned as a major factor in the way of life which these people were threatening to introduce. Indeed, their behaviour is not only condemned in itself, but its enticing effects are also strongly denounced (ii. 18f.). These immoral practices were, moreover, not done in the dark as if the doers were ashamed, but openly in broad daylight (ii. 13). Another characteristic is insubordination to authority (ii. 10ff.), which could only lead to anarchy.

A special feature of 2 Peter's false teachers, as distinct from Jude's, is a denial of the *parousia* and a consequent mockery of those who looked forward to it (iii. 3ff.). 2 Peter iii is largely devoted to maintaining, not only the reality of the *parousia*, but the consummation of the present world order and the establishment of the new. The teachers were clearly advocating an approach strongly opposed to primitive eschatology and we may detect a large element of rationalism.

Bearing in mind these characteristics, to what extent do they approximate to any of the Gnostic movements? Certainly most of the features are found in Gnosticism, but care must be taken to ensure that tendencies are not confused with fully developed systems. The Gnostics' approach to Scripture would be well described by 2 Peter iii. 16, for they objected to proofs from Scripture on the grounds that the living voice was more authoritative.[1] By the living voice they meant their own secret traditions, which led them to deny the validity of the orthodox apostolic writings and to substitute their own. But the 'twisting'

---

[1] Irenaeus frequently charges the Gnostics with dishonesty in the treatment of Scripture (cf. *Adv. Haer.* i. 3. 6, 8. 1, 9. 1).

of apostolic writings and in particular those of Paul did not need to wait until developed Gnosticism.[1] Rather was it a cause than an effect. The derogation of existing apostolic sources was a necessary prelude to the substitution of pseudo-apostolic writings to bolster up contrary opinions. The state in 2 Peter appears very primitive. Teaching which challenged their licentious behaviour (which Paul's Epistles constantly do) was a ready target for mishandling and this must have occurred during the genesis of these movements.

The emphasis on γνῶσις in this Epistle may at once suggest a counter-balance to the claim to superior knowledge in all Gnostic systems, but in 2 Peter γνῶσις is only one of a number of virtues and in the list given in i. 5, 6, it is not stressed out of proportion to the rest, as we should expect if the writer were controverting any Gnostic system. The mere occurrence of the idea is not sufficient to provide any certain connecting link.[2]

As to the remaining data, there is little to assist in any identification. Extreme licentiousness was not unknown in second-century Gnosticism, particularly among the Carpocratians (see comment on Jude, p. 914). But licentious behaviour was so general in the pagan world that it is precarious to use this as a point of contact with Carpocratianism. This is the kind of threat that one would expect to occur as soon as Christianity challenged its pagan environment. Indeed it was found in the Corinthian church in Paul's day and in the Asiatic churches reflected in Revelation ii, iii. There are in fact many points of contact between the false teachers in 2 Peter, the libertines of Corinth and the Nicolaitans of Asia.[3]

---

[1] Chase (op. cit., p. 811) objected that there is no trace in apostolic times of false teachers supporting their views by a dishonest interpretation of Scripture. True, but our total knowledge of them is slight, and such practice is certainly not impossible.

[2] Some support may possibly be found in that the earliest sects who claimed the name 'Gnostic' were noted for their active advocacy of immoral living (Iren., Adv. Haer., i. 25. 6; Hippolytus, Haer. v. 6). This would, of course, fit in well with the description in 2 Peter of the active propagandists for immorality. But it is impossible to affix a commencing date to this tendency. E. Käsemann (ZTK, 49, 1952, p. 272) strongly maintains a Gnostic situation, but he comes to the subject already convinced that 2 Peter is a second-century document.

[3] E. M. B. Green (op. cit., p. 26) gives the following suggestive parallels with the Corinthian situation:

2 Pet. ii. 19;	1 Cor. vi. 12, 13.	2 Pet. ii. 1;	1 Cor. xi. 18ff.
2 Pet. ii. 1;	1 Cor. vi. 18–20.	2 Pet. iii. 4;	1 Cor. xv. 12.
2 Pet. ii. 10;	1 Cor. viii.	2 Pet. iii. 3;	1 Cor. xv. 32.
2 Pet. ii. 13;	1 Cor. xi. 21.		

Some of these similarities are closer than others, but there is sufficient proximity

The approach to the *parousia* does not fit any known system of Gnosticism. Too great an interval had passed for interest to be maintained in an imminent coming, but the form of the scoffers' question (iii. 4) suggests a time when belief in the near return was still very much alive. This feature certainly fits a first-century date better than a second.

In concluding this discussion it should be noted that these threatened trouble-makers are called 'false prophets' (ψευδοπροφῆται) and 'false teachers' (ψευδοδιδάσκαλοι), both of which terms would seem to emphasize false doctrine rather than behaviour and yet the Epistle is mainly about the latter. The total details given are not sufficient to allow any more precision than to speak of a general antinomian tendency.

VII. RELATION TO I PETER

It is important to bear in mind the precise literary relationship between these letters and this can be done quite independently of any particular decision regarding authorship, although it clearly has some bearing upon that subject. The similarities between them go far beyond the common ascription to Peter. Both contain a group of remarkable and vivid words which occur only in their respective Epistles in the New Testament. There are, moreover, a few striking words and ideas common to both, e.g. the word ἀρετή in both is ascribed to God (2 Pet. i. 3; I Pet. ii. 9), ἐπιχορηγήσατε in 2 Peter i. 5 compares with χορησεῖ in I Peter iv. 11, and there are many other verbal comparisons of the same kind.[1] On stylistic points of comparison, the most notable is a similar use of the article. Both use nouns frequently without articles and both use phrases introduced by articles.[2] The dissimilarities of language and

to claim that the tendencies seen at Corinth would very rapidly develop into the errors found in the 2 Peter teachers. (Cf. also W. M. Ramsay's comparison of 2 Pet. ii. iff. with I Cor. x.; *Exp.*, VI, iii, 1901, pp. 106ff.)

[1] Cf. the following:
   The salutations (2 Pet. i. 2; I Pet. i. 2).
   Brotherly affection (2 Pet. i. 7; I Pet. i. 22, iii. 8).
   The testimony of the prophets (2 Pet. i. 19, 20; I Pet. i. 10–12).
   The reference to Noah (2 Pet. ii. 5, iii. 6; I Pet. iii. 20).
   'Without spot or blemish' (2 Pet. iii. 14; I Pet. i. 19).
   The reference to the consummation of all things (2 Pet. iii. 10; I Pet. iv. 7).
   The reference to freedom (2 Pet. ii. 19; I Pet. ii. 16).
For a detailed discussion of similarities and differences, cf. Mayor, *op. cit.*, pp. lxviii–cxiv.
[2] Cf. Mayor, *op. cit.*, pp. lxxix–lxxx, for details.

style have already been mentioned in discussing authorship (see pp. 825f.). Mayor's[1] conclusion is worth quoting, 'There can be no doubt, I think, that the style of 1 Peter is on the whole clearer and simpler than that of 2 Peter, but there is not that chasm between them which some would try to make out.' In addition to these differences in vocabulary and style, Chase[2] brings four other differences—the use of the Old Testament; the reminiscences of the Lord's teaching; the use of Paul's Epistles; and doctrinal differences. All of these have already been considered and reasons have been given for them.

The whole question of the relation between these Epistles has been brought into sharp relief by G. H. Boobyer's attempt to show how the author of 2 Peter has used 1 Peter.[3] He suggests that 2 Peter iii. 1 was written with 1 Peter i. 10–12 in mind and, on the strength of this, suspects further allusions to the first Epistle. He then compares 2 Peter i with 1 Peter i, and having concluded for the dependence of the former on the latter, he thinks dependence must have continued beyond the salutation. Although he admits differences, he thinks 2 Peter i. 3–11 was written under the influence of 1 Peter i. 3–9. Similarly he compares 1 Peter i. 10–12 with 2 Peter i. 12–21 and claims to find an allusion to 1 Peter v. 1 in the introduction to the transfiguration account. 2 Peter i. 14 is particularly examined from this point of view and Boobyer thinks that a combination of the 1 Peter allusion and a knowledge of the Synoptic narrative of the transfiguration (probably Matthew or Mark) accounts for it.

Now Boobyer has examined this evidence from the point of view that the author of 2 Peter has made a *literary* use of 1 Peter, for he does not regard the former as Petrine. His justification for maintaining a literary dependence is based on his acceptance of 2 Peter's literary use of Jude. But his evidence here would equally well support the contention that the same author wrote both 1 and 2 Peter, for in that case we should expect the kind of parallels to which he refers. It may not be possible to dispute *literary* dependence, but neither is it possible, on the kind of evidence cited by Boobyer, to *exclude* common authorship. When, for instance, in considering 2 Peter i. 12–13, Boobyer says,

[1] *Op. cit.*, p. civ. This caution is in marked contrast to Moffatt's approach (*ILNT*, p. 364).
[2] *Op. cit.*, pp. 812, 813.
[3] 'The Indebtedness of 2 Peter to 1 Peter' in *New Testament Essays: Studies in Memory of T. W. Manson* (ed. A. J. B. Higgins, 1959), pp. 34–53.

'Much in this section, in fact, could be an outflow from 1 Peter i. 10–12', this could equally well have happened in the mind of one man through association of ideas, as in two minds with one drawing from another. There is no critical principle which can enable an indisputable choice to be made between these two alternatives, but it is a fair conclusion that the kind of relationship which is found between the two Epistles does not prohibit the tradition of Petrine authorship from being maintained.

VIII. OTHER LITERARY CONNECTIONS

In 1882, Ezra Abbott[1] maintained that both 2 Peter and Jude were dependent on Josephus, particularly on two passages of his *Antiquities*.[2] This was based on a number of parallel words in both groups of writings, the assumption being that one was dependent on the other and, since Josephus shows no acquaintance elsewhere with the New Testament, the only solution is to suppose that the writers of 2 Peter and Jude were acquainted with Josephus' works. But the argument is fallacious on several grounds. Most of the words cited were in common use and are found in other writers (e.g. in Philo).[3] Moreover, the contexts bear no relationship to each other and it is impossible to establish literary dependence unless they do.[4] Further, if a pseudepigraphic writer, wishing to produce a Petrine Epistle, consulted Josephus, his method of ensuring verisimilitude is puzzling in the extreme. Farrar[5] argued that Josephus was dependent on 2 Peter, but this seems highly unlikely. If the writer of 2 Peter was a Jew, as he was if the Epistle is authentic, some similarities between him and Josephus might not be so surprising. The evidence in any case is quite insufficient to establish any literary connection.

As this line of argument has now fallen into disuse, so is there less readiness than formerly to maintain the dependence of 2 Peter on the *Apocalypse of Peter*. Both contain references to the transfiguration[6] and

---

[1] *Exp.*, II, iii (1882), pp. 49–63.

[2] Paragraph 4 of the Preface and iv. 8. 2. The relevant passages are quoted in full in Mayor (*op. cit.*, pp. cxxviii f.), who admits marked resemblances of language.

[3] Cf. Zahn, *INT*, II, p. 291 n. 14. Salmon cites from Dr. Gwynn similar evidence for 1 Peter (*INT*, p. 506).

[4] Cf. G. Salmon (*op. cit.*, p. 499) whose criticisms of both Abbott and Farrar are very lucid.

[5] *Exp.*, III, viii (1888), pp. 58–69.

[6] In *The Apocryphal New Testament* (1924), p. 507, M. R. James regards this incident as part of the *Gospel of Peter* and not the *Apocalypse*, and if this is correct, the above statement would need modification.

both describe certain eschatological features, but apart from the additional fact that both are ascribed to Peter, there is not a great deal to be said. Verbal coincidences are slight. In the list cited by M. R. James,[1] only two extend to more than one word, although common ideas are stronger. There is a reference to false prophets who shall teach perverse doctrines (cf. 2 Pet. ii. 1), although the *Apocalypse* does not emphasize, as 2 Peter does, any particular Christological error.

In the *Apocalypse* the main attention is upon the continuous torments of the lost, which is most naturally understood as an imaginative reconstruction from 2 Peter's hint of the condemnation and destruction of the false teachers (note especially the reference to the continuity of these in 2 Pet. ii. 3). Other incidental verbal parallels are all more easily explained on the assumption of the priority of 2 Peter than vice versa, and this conclusion must have an important bearing on the date and authenticity of 2 Peter. The two works, while touching superficially on similar themes, differ widely in the spiritual grasp of their respective authors and there are few who would regard the *Apocalypse* as in anywhere near the same spiritual class as 2 Peter. From this point of view alone, it is hardly conceivable that the superior work was prompted by the inferior, for imitations have a greater tendency to deteriorate than to improve.[2] Bigg's[3] opinion that 2 Peter i. 15 prompted the whole prolific family of pseudo-Petrine literature is highly probable.

The main problem about 2 Peter and the *Apocalypse of Peter*, if this conclusion is correct, is the apparently later reception of the former as compared with the latter. Perhaps the greater obscurity of 2 Peter during the second century may be because the nature of its subject-matter did not have the same popular appeal as the *Apocalypse*, which promised retribution (or rather retaliation) to those under whom the Christians

---

[1] *The Second Epistle general of St. Peter, and the general Epistle of St. Jude* (1912), p. xxvii. Cf. also Chase's clear comparison of parallel texts, *op. cit.*, pp. 814, 815.

[2] For those maintaining that 2 Peter was basic to the *Apocalypse*, cf. F. Spitta, 'Die Petrusapokalypse und der zweite Petrusbrief', *ZNTW*, 12 (1911), pp. 237–242; Bigg, *op. cit.*, pp. 207–209; J. Chaine, *op. cit.*, pp. 3, 4; Mayor, *op. cit.*, p. cxxxiii; Zahn, *INT*, II, p. 273. This is a formidable list, yet in spite of it many have maintained the contrary opinion (N.B. especially A. Harnack, *op. cit.*, pp. 81ff.; F. C. Porter, *The Message of the Apocalyptic Writers*, 1905, p. 355; and Moffatt, *ILNT*, p. 367). For the alternative view that both books proceeded from the same circle of thought, cf. F. H. Chase, *HDB*, III, p. 816; M. R. James, *op. cit.*, p. xxviii; McNeile-Williams, *INT*, p. 247. W. Sanday (*Inspiration*, 1893, p. 347) posited the same author for both books.

[3] *Op. cit.*, p. 215. Cf. also Wand, *op. cit.*, p. 140.

were suffering. Its period of appeal was, however, short and in this it contrasts strikingly with 2 Peter.

IX. THE MODERN MESSAGE

It is relevant to enquire into the contemporary usefulness of this Epistle in view of the widespread denial of its authenticity. It has largely been neglected, in common with the companion Epistle of Jude. But, although it deals with a local situation, it is not without a positive contribution for any age. Some scholars would restrict its value to its historical contribution to our knowledge of Antinomianism and early Christian eschatology.[1] But while this must be acknowledged, its primary value is religious. It contains passages of spiritual illumination which have been, and will undoubtedly continue to be, a means of strength and challenge to Christians in all ages.[2] The first chapter is particularly notable in this respect. But even the description of false teachers is not without salutary warning for an age in which moral standards are declining, while the sombre description of the approaching consummation of the age is lightened by the assurance of the Lord's forbearance. In spite of its apocalyptic ring, the dissolution of the elements by fire sounds strikingly relevant in an age of multi-megaton atomic bombs. The consequent exhortation to self-examination in 2 Peter iii. 11 could not be more relevant than for today, and we may be grateful indeed that this precious letter has been preserved for us in spite of all the questionings regarding it.

CONTENTS

I. GREETING (i. 1, 2)

The writer introduces himself in this Epistle as Simon Peter and addresses those who share the same faith as he possesses.

II. TRUE KNOWLEDGE (i. 3–21)

a. *The quest for a higher nature* (i. 3, 4)

Every Christian has access to a divine power which enables him to live

---

[1] Cf. T. Henshaw, *op. cit.*, p. 396.

[2] E. F. Scott (*op. cit.*, p. 229), who rejects its authenticity, admits the real religious value of some impressive passages which it contains.

a godly life. His attitude towards the present world must be to escape from its corruption through receiving a share of the divine nature. This is real knowledge.

b. The progressive character of Christian virtues (i. 5–11)

This Christian knowledge is many-sided and contains aspects far removed from mere intellectual apprehension although it includes this. The apostle gives a list of virtues which should be striven for, reaching a climax in love (verses 5–7). This is the way to become fruitful in the knowledge of Christ, and those who are diligent in this direction will have an abundant entrance into God's kingdom.

c. The apostolic attestation of Christian knowledge (i. 12–21)

1. The author expresses his intentions to remind the readers of these things, not only while he still lives, but also after he has died, through his writings (verses 12–15).

2. The content of the Christian message is contrasted with mythology, for the author has had first-hand acquaintance with a real event, the transfiguration, which testified to the glory of Christ (verses 16–18).

3. On the basis of this an exhortation is addressed to the readers to pay attention to the prophetic word to which the apostle and his fellow eyewitnesses bear testimony. A warning is added about the private interpretation of prophetic Scriptures, because these are inspired by the Spirit of God (verses 19–21).

III. FALSE KNOWLEDGE (ii. 1–22)

By way of contrast attention is now focused upon advocates of false knowledge who will trouble the Church.

a. What may be expected from the false prophets (ii. 1–3)

Their coming will be secretive. They will deny the Master. They will lead others into immoral practices. They will exploit others in their greed by deceptive methods. But their destruction is certain.

b. What they may expect from God (ii. 4–10)

Examples of God's judgment are quoted from earlier history to illustrate the fate of these enemies of the truth. The fate of the fallen angels, the ante-diluvian world, and Sodom and Gomorrah shows the certainty of judgment against sin, but also the assurance of divine mercy towards the godly by the examples of Noah and Lot.

c. A description of ungodly people (ii. 11–22)

The apostle now describes people he has already observed and draws attention to their arrogance, their irrational outlook, their immoral conduct, their bad effect on others, their greed and their deceptive promises. Some of these people have already known something of Christ, but their return to their former ways is deplored in strong terms. It would have been better for them not to have known the truth at all.

IV. THE PRESENT CHALLENGE (iii. 1–18)

In this closing portion of the Epistle, the apostle turns to present problems and exhortations.

a. A reminder (iii. 1, 2)

The present letter, like the former one which the readers have received, has for its purpose to remind them of the apostolic prediction about scoffers to come. Since it is witnessed by the prophetic word and the Lord's own teaching, the rise of these scoffers should not take them unawares.

b. An explanation (iii. 3–10)

There are some who are turning the delay in the Lord's return into an occasion for scoffing. But they ignore that creation itself is the work of God, who in His own time will bring it to consummation. As God acted in judgment by water in the time of the flood, so He will act in judgment by fire at the day of judgment. The delay in the coming should therefore be interpreted as an act of mercy, and not as an evidence of God's indifference to His promises. In any case, the timing of the final act is unknown, but will surely come.

c. An exhortation (iii. 11–18)

In view of approaching judgment what sort of persons ought the Christians to be? The apostle mentions three things: holiness, godliness, expectancy. The life must conform to the hope of a new creation where righteousness dwells. There must be a zeal for purity, and tranquillity. Paul's letters mention the Lord's forbearance and this should be an encouragement, although some have twisted his meaning. The Epistle ends with a warning to the readers against being carried away by error, and an earnest plea to them to grow in the grace and knowledge of Christ.

ADDITIONAL NOTES

822. [4] A. F. J. Klijn (*INT*, 1967, p. 162) considers the reference to the Pauline Corpus in 2 Pet. iii. 15, 16 to be an indication of a date at the end of the first century. He also thinks the eschatology points to the same period. But both factors *could* have obtained at an earlier date.

823. [4] Kümmel (*INT*, 1965, p. 304) considers the opponents to bear the essential characteristics of second-century Gnosticism.

824. [2] Kümmel (*INT*, p. 303) states categorically, 'Since Jude belongs in the postapostolic period, Peter cannot have written II Peter.' Cf. also W. Marxsen, *INT* (1968), pp. 241 ff.

824. [4] For a further presentation of E. M. B. Green's defence of the authenticity of 2 Peter, cf. his *The Second Epistle General of Peter and the General Epistle of Jude* (*TNT*, 1968).

826. [5] C. H. Talbert (*VC*, 20, 1966, pp. 137–145) discusses the delay of the *parousia* in relation to 2 Peter. This delay was appealed to by heretics to justify their realized spiritualized eschatology. Talbert follows Käsemann's view that these heretics were Gnostics.

827. [2] Cf. Kümmel, *INT*, pp. 303 f.

838. [2] B. Reicke, *The Epistles of James, Peter and Jude* (1964), dates this Epistle in the 90s, a view shared by C. Spicq, *Les Épîtres de Saint Pierre* (1966). Spicq regards this Epistle as a *testimentum Petri*.

852. [4] For the view that 2 Pet. iii. 1–13 is composite, cf. D. von Allmen (*RThPh*, 99, 1966, pp. 255–274), who suggests that the Epistle is combating an extreme Hellenization of the gospel.

CHAPTER TWENTY-SIX

THE JOHANNINE EPISTLES

THE FIRST EPISTLE

This Epistle has always been loved and meditated upon in the Christian Church and with good reason. It combines profound thoughts with simplicity of expression. It is both practical and reflective. It gives insight into early Christian conditions in such a manner as to provide principles of thought and action which are applicable in any age. Yet nevertheless the Epistle poses many critical problems and attempts must be made to settle these if a full appreciation of its message is to be attained.

I. AUTHORSHIP

In one sense the authorship is not the most important issue, for the exegesis of the letter is not greatly affected by our conclusions regarding authorship. Yet it becomes more personal if an individual name can with any confidence be attached to it. And this is particularly so when tradition has anything to contribute on this question.

a. External evidence

The earliest clear allusion to the content of this Epistle is to be found in Polycarp.[1] Probably Papias may also be cited in support.[2] Some have found coincidences of language in Justin, Barnabas, Hermas and even Clement of Rome, but since these might possibly be explained as the common milieu of Christian thought, it is better to appeal to the more certain evidence. Irenaeus cited the Epistle as by the Lord's disciple John, the writer of the Fourth Gospel.[3] Both Clement of Alexandria[4] and Tertullian[5] similarly cite it as John's. The Muratorian Fragment is somewhat confused on the Johannine Epistles, although it cites 1 John

---

[1] *Ad Phil.* vii, cf. 1 Jn. iv. 2. A. E. Brooke, *The Johannine Epistles (ICC,* 1912), p. liii, adds 1 Jn. iii. 8, ii. 18, ii. 22 and 2 Jn. 7, as partial parallels.

[2] Cf. Eusebius, *HE,* iii. 39. 3, 17 (a reference here to John's former Epistle—ἀπὸ τῆς Ἰωαννοῦ προτέρας ἐπιστολῆς).

[3] *De Haer.* iii. 16. 5, 8.

[4] *Strom.* ii. 15. 66, iii. 4. 32, iii. 5. 42, 44, iv. 16. 100.

[5] *Adv. Marc.* v. 16; *Adv. Prax.* xxviii; *Adv. Gnost.* xii.

evidently as authoritative.[1] Origen frequently cites the Epistle and refers to it as by John. Dionysius, Origen's pupil, regarded the Epistle as written by the author of the Gospel, but distinguished its style from that of the Apocalypse, which he consequently attributed to a different author.

This evidence[2] is sufficient to show that from very early times the Epistle was not only treated as Scripture but was assumed to be Johannine, in spite of the fact that no specific claim to this effect is made by the writer himself. This strong tradition cannot easily be set aside, especially as no alternative theory of authorship was suggested in the early Church, as it was, for instance, in respect of the Apocalypse. It is against this strong traditional background of Johannine authorship that the internal evidence must now be examined to ascertain whether or not the ancient Church was uncritical in its assumptions.

b. Internal evidence

(i) *The writer's own claims.* This Epistle and the Epistle to the Hebrews are the only New Testament Epistles in which no author's name is given, but in 1 John, unlike Hebrews, the introduction is clearly intended to tell us something about the author. He is writing about what he (or rather 'we') had heard, seen, looked upon and touched (1 Jn. i. 1). In no more vivid way could the writer indicate that he was an eyewitness.[3] When he says further that 'the life was manifested, and we saw it', he draws attention at once to the times when he companied with Christ. Yet not all scholars would so interpret the first person plural. If this is no more than an epistolary device by which the author is associating his message with that of the original eyewitnesses,[4] or is using the first person plural generally of all believers (as in iv. 7–19), it would

---

[1] See further discussion of this evidence in reference to 2 John (p. 885).

[2] For a fuller statement and examination of it, cf. A. E. Brooke, *op. cit.*, pp. lii–lxii.

[3] Cf. Feine-Behm (*op. cit.*, p. 261), who appeal to the same phenomenon in Jn. i. 14.*

[4] C. H. Dodd (*The Johannine Epistles*, 1946, pp. 2, 3) suggests that the neuter pronouns must refer to the contents of the announcement and not to Christ. To him the 'we' is generalizing for all believers (cf. p. 12). H. Conzelmann, in his article 'Was von Anfang war', in *Neutestamentliche Studien für Rudolf Bultmann* (ed. W. Eltester, 1954), pp. 194–201, maintains that the author of the Epistle has imitated the Gospel in 1 Jn. i. 1–4 and has feigned (*fingiert*) the rôle of the Evangelist. But see Michaelis' criticisms of this view, *Einleitung*, Ergänzungsheft zur 3, Auflage, p. 38.

no longer be evidence for the author's own claims. But is such an interpretation defensible? When the author says in iv. 13, 'By this we know that we abide in him' (RSV), the plural clearly stands for general Christian experience, but the actions described in i. 1–5 do not appear to be of this general character. 'What we have seen with our own eyes' loses its point unless it is specific. What the writer is concerned to claim at the outset is that his proclamation is based on his own personal experience and the experience of those closely associated with him. Admittedly the 'we' soon broadens out, and the statement in iv. 14 in which the words 'we have seen' (τεθεάμεθα) also occur could be understood generally, but it is much more natural to understand the words as referring to actual eyewitnesses.[1] It would bring no authentication of his message if the author were referring only to the fact of the incarnation which all Christians generally had 'seen'. This is, in fact, an unwarranted weakening of the author's language, and we can confidently proceed on the assumption that he intended his readers to understand that he was one of the original eyewitnesses of the life of Jesus.

This is important in dealing with authorship, for obviously if this indication is taken at its face value and is not regarded as a literary device to create the impression of authenticity, it narrows the field of possible authors. It is clearly in complete harmony with the traditional ascription to John, the apostle.

(ii) *The general impression of the Epistle.* Quite apart from this specific eyewitness claim, the Epistle contains an unmistakable air of authority. The much repeated address to 'little children' (τεκνία) could have been written only by someone of considerable authority to those who would at once acknowledge his right to address them in this manner—a veritable father in God. He clearly expects not only to be heard, but to be obeyed (cf. iv. 6, as well as the whole impression of the Epistle). He writes in categorical, almost dogmatic, terms. There is no disputing the truth of what he says. He condemns error in no uncertain terms (cf. ii. 18ff., iv. 1ff.), and leaves no opportunity for compromise. His letter at once creates the impression that here is a man who knows beyond question where he stands and expects all other Christians to conform to the same standard, because he knows it to be true. The author, in short, stands out as a man of considerable spiritual stature.

His use of τεκνία to describe his readers would also seem to suggest

---

[1] As A. E. Brooke, *op. cit.*, p. 121, does.

an elderly man who could use more familiar terms without fear of being misunderstood, and this again is in full agreement with the traditional picture of the venerable apostle John during his later years of ministry in Ephesus. There is, moreover, a style of language, with its somewhat restricted powers of expression, its limited vocabulary and its lack of literary polish, which is not surprising in an ageing man to whom maturity of thought was much more important than elegance of expression.

(iii) *The relationship to Johannine thought.* The connection of this Epistle with the Fourth Gospel deserves a section of its own and is dealt with below, but some comments upon it are necessary here since the problem of authorship cannot be discussed apart from it. It will be shown that similarities of thought and even expression are so striking that it is a fair assumption, disputed by only a minority of critics, that the author of this Epistle was the author of the Fourth Gospel. This at once raises many problems which cannot here be fully discussed. It is the prevailing opinion that John the apostle did not write the Gospel and those who have come to that conclusion must naturally exclude him from the authorship of the Epistle. But there is a danger here of arguing in a circle. It is better to examine the relationship of Gospel and Epistle in the light of what has already been discussed from external and internal evidence. If the tradition is correct which attributed the Epistle to the apostle John, is there anything in its relationship with the Gospel which is out of keeping with this?

Since the same traditions which ascribed the Epistle to John ascribed also the Gospel, it is not surprising to find such strong marks of similarity between the two works, in thought, style, expression, ideas and imagery. There are undoubtedly some differences, mainly in emphasis and subject-matter, but these are explicable by the difference in purpose, occasion and form of the two works.

It may, therefore, be said that what is known as 'Johannine thought' pervades the Epistle, as would be expected if John the apostle were the author. But this does not demonstrate his authorship *per se*, since the same would be true if some other writer wrote both Gospel and Epistle. Some of the alternative theories of authorship must next be considered.

(iv) *Various proposals regarding authorship.* 1. The apostle John has the support, as has been shown, of tradition, and is in harmony with the self-claims of the Epistle. Many able scholars[1] have sided with the tradition in the absence of any conclusive arguments to the contrary and this seems the most reasonable approach. But many others, probably the majority, reject this view. There is no doubt that this is largely due to the trends of criticism on the Fourth Gospel, but there are signs that conclusions on the authorship of the latter book may not be as final against apostolic authorship as many have supposed.[2]

2. The most popular alternative theory, that a second John, known as John the Elder, was the author of this Epistle, gains strong support from the fact that 2 and 3 John, which may reasonably be regarded as being written by the same author (see discussion on p. 895), both introduce their author as 'the elder'. The theory has also claimed support from Papias' reference to John the Elder,[3] a much discussed passage which does not, however, leave it indisputable that John the Elder was ever a personality distinct from the apostle John.[4] This theory really involves attributing the writings to an unknown in all but the vaguest name, and while there is nothing intrinsically impossible about this (as the anonymous Epistle to the Hebrews shows), it is extremely difficult on this hypothesis to account for the unchallenged tradition of the Church in favour of apostolic authorship. It is admitted by most students of the New Testament Canon that this Epistle gained acceptance on the ground of its supposed apostolic origin, but were the Church Fathers likely to become confused about two Johns? And if John the Elder were author of 1 John, why did he not introduce himself more clearly (even the Elder of 2 and 3 John is nameless)? An anonymous epistle from him is more difficult to conceive than from John the apostle, since all would admit the authority of the latter without further description and 1 John clearly implies that the readers will recognize the writer's personal authority. Yet it has been argued in the reverse direction that an apostle writing to combat false teaching (see

---

[1] Cf. W. Michaelis, *Einleitung*, pp. 293, 294. Cf. also B. F. Westcott, *The Epistles of John* (1892), pp. xxx, xxxi; G. Findlay, *Fellowship in the Life Eternal* (1909), pp. 47ff.

[2] Cf. J. A. T. Robinson's article in *The Gospels Reconsidered* (1960), pp. 154–166. The whole question is fully discussed on pp. 241 ff. above.

[3] D. Smith (*The Epistle of John, EGT*, v, 1910, pp. 161, 162) suggested that since Papias echoed 3 Jn. 12, which shows that he was acquainted with John's self-description as Elder, he may have used the same title for this reason.

[4] A. E. Brooke (*op. cit.*, p. lxii), who attributes the Epistles to John the Elder, admits that no satisfactory solution exists regarding his personality.

below) would surely weight his exhortations by appeal to his apostolic office. But the fact remains that the early Church recognized his apostolic claims.

On the whole the Elder theory, although it appears to have many plausible aspects, raises more difficulties than the traditional view.

3. A third theory is that the author was a disciple of the Evangelist. Those who deny identity of authorship with the Gospel are obliged to hold this even more remote theory if they regard John the Elder as the author of the Gospel. Thus C. H. Dodd agrees with the commonly held view regarding the Gospel, and speaks simply of the Presbyter in connection with the Epistle. He is content to leave him without a name, although he thinks the author has left 'a recognizable self-portrait in his three epistles'.[1]

Much the same kind of theory is maintained by M. Dibelius who also distinguishes between the writer of the Gospel and the writer of 1 John. The former he calls 'the unknown evangelist', while the latter is 'a less original person and essentially of a type common in the Church'.[2] But this reduces the Epistle itself to the commonplace in a manner contrary to the testimony of most Christians of both ancient and modern times. If the author of this Epistle was a 'common type' the early Church must have been well supplied with spiritual geniuses whose literary productions were, oddly enough, not sufficiently appreciated to have been preserved. Such an approach to the author problem is too far-fetched to command general consent and provides no solution to the question why this particular letter should ever have been preserved.[3]

In spite of all assertions to the contrary, it must be admitted that these alternative theories do not provide as adequate an explanation of the high regard in which this Epistle was held as the traditional testimony.

II. OCCASION AND BACKGROUND

It is impossible to grasp the purpose of this Epistle until something has been said about the background of thought to which it belonged.

---

[1] Op. cit., p. lxxi.

[2] A Fresh Approach to the New Testament and Early Christian Literature (1937), p. 211.

[3] J. Moffatt (ILNT, pp. 592, 593), although disinclined to hold to identity of authorship for Gospel and Epistle, is nevertheless very cautious in suggesting an alternative. The best he can do is to maintain that the two authors belonged to the same circle, the writer of 1 John having 'an individuality and purpose of his own'. Cf. also H. Windisch-H. Preisker, Die katholischen Briefe[3] (1951), p. 110.

Although the data from the Epistle itself are very slight, there are just enough indications of false teaching being combated to enable a general comparison to be made with the earliest of the Gnostic tendencies, particularly with Docetism. This evidence is as follows: ii. 22, 'who is the liar but he who denies that Jesus is the Christ? This is the antichrist, he who denies the Father and the Son' (RSV); and iv. 3, 'and every spirit which does not confess Jesus is not of God. This is the spirit of antichrist, of which you heard that it was coming, and now it is in the world already' (RSV).

The main feature in the form of heresy being contested was, therefore, a denial of the incarnation. This was true of all Gnostics (using the term in its broadest sense of those who sought salvation by illumination). The idea of an incarnate deity was unintelligible and, therefore, rejected. Docetism evolved a means of getting over the intellectual difficulty by making a distinction between the human Jesus and the heavenly Christ, the latter only appearing to take a human form.[1] The incarnation was not, therefore, a reality. This solution, which made a wide appeal, had the added advantage, so it was thought, of avoiding the anomaly of Christ sharing in such an inherently evil thing as matter As these Gnostics believed that all matter was evil there was nothing for it but to deny that Christ had contact with flesh. The dangerous character of this heresy is at once apparent, for it was an attempt to preserve Christ's deity at the expense of His humanity, and all in the interests of a higher intellectualism. But the question arises whether developed Docetism is really in view in this Epistle. That similar tendencies are in mind seems highly probable, but John gives no indication of any apparent or phantasmal body, and this suggests that the form of heresy being forged out was no more than an adumbration of the type attested by Ignatius.[2]

It is, at least, certain that these false teachers came within the general category of Gnosticism,[3] although that term needs further definition in

[1] Cf. G. G. Findlay's discussion of this, op. cit., pp. 218ff. Jülicher-Fascher, Einleitung, pp. 227f., maintained that John was combating Docetism.

[2] Ad Trall. x; Ad Smyrna, ii, iii; Ad Ephes. vii. J. Cantinat, in Robert-Feuillet's Introduction à la Bible, II, p. 699, rightly points out that the heretics in this Epistle, unlike the Docetists, did not regard Jesus as either Messiah or Son of God. Yet there is clearly some connection of thought between the two outlooks, if not identity.

[3] We may at once reject the view that Judaizers or Jews are in view (cf. G. Bardy, RB, xxx, 1921, p. 349), for these false teachers had themselves withdrawn from the Christian community, and it is highly improbable that they would then

view of the wider understanding of it obtained from the recent discovery of the Nag Hammadi library. If we restrict the term Gnosticism to those developed second-century systems of thought which absorbed within their pagan background certain Christian ideas, and by this means threatened the orthodox Church, our Epistle would seem to belong to a stage somewhat before these developed Christian Gnostic systems, although there were many straws to indicate the direction of the mental winds which were surrounding the Church.

One of the movements which may lie behind this Epistle was that of Cerinthus. Whatever truth there may be in Polycarp's story of the apostle John's encounter with Cerinthus at the baths of Ephesus, from which the apostle is said to have fled when Cerinthus entered lest judgment should fall upon him, it is not improbable that Cerinthus was spreading his doctrines when John resided in Ephesus. His doctrine of the unknown Father could perhaps be combated in ii. 23f.; and v. 6, the linking of water and blood in reference to Christ's coming, could reflect Cerinthus' denial of the necessity of the cross in the messianic work of salvation and his emphasis on Christ's baptism.[1] The teaching of this heretic had a decidedly Jewish flavour about it, but there is nothing to lead us to suppose that the readers generally were Jewish Christians. The concluding verse (v. 21), which warns against idolatry, would seem to rule this out. But there may well have been Jewish Christian Gnostics who were troubling the Church.[2]

In addition to wrong doctrine, the false teachers were also guilty of wrong practice. They had an inadequate sense of sin (i.e. an antinomian approach) which John shows to be fallacious. The constant emphasis on mutual love was no doubt to offset the pride engendered in the initiates of Gnostic-like systems.[3]

According to iv. 1, it would appear that the false prophets had

attempt to influence the Christians from outside if their purpose was a Judaizing of Christianity. For a full study of these false teachers, cf. A. Wurm, *Die Irrlehrer im ersten Johannesbrief* (1933).

[1] For a full discussion, see A. E. Brooke (*op. cit.*, p. xlv), who concludes that although other forms of false teaching are alluded to in 1 John, the main teaching attacked is that of Cerinthus. Feine-Behm (*op. cit.*, pp. 260, 261) are much more uncertain about such an identification, although they point out the similar features.*

[2] H. Windisch (*op. cit.*, p. 127) points out that the language of the Epistle suggests a group of antichrists not simply a single individual.

[3] Cf. J. Moffatt, *ILNT*, p. 586. H. Windisch (*loc. cit.*) is sceptical about this because it is nowhere in the Epistle applied to Gnostic haughtiness

belonged to the Christian community, but had now gone out into the world (κόσμος seems to be used of the non-Christian sphere). In this case the probability is that they are still harassing the believers from an outside position, possibly by appealing to the intellectual attractions of their systems. Such a state of affairs was regarded as serious by the apostle and provides the immediate occasion for the Epistle. Christians generally must be informed of this insidious error.

III. PURPOSE

In an atmosphere of rising interest in a merging of Christianity with the higher forms of paganism to the detriment of the former, there was, therefore, a pressing need for the presentation of adequate Christian antidotes to combat the danger. It was a critical period for the Church, and the apostle recognizes this. He will write a letter, somewhat in the form of a tract (see section below on literary form), to warn and instruct the believers in his own district about the seriousness of the peril. But his approach is to be wholly positive. He will present a wholesome picture of true Christian life, and only incidentally denounce the error. He believes that truth is the best answer to false teaching, although he makes perfectly plain what his own estimate of that teaching is. He refers to these prophets as antichrists (ii. 18) because they possess the spirit of *the* Antichrist (ii. 18, 22, iv. 3).

Fortunately the author has stated his own purpose in such terms as to leave in no doubt his immediate intention. In i. 3f., he writes, 'That which we have seen and heard declare we unto you also, that ye also may have fellowship with us . . . and these things we write, that our joy may be fulfilled (i.e. completed)' (RV). In v. 13 he is even more specific, 'These things have I written unto you, that ye may know that ye have eternal life, even unto you that believe on the name of the Son of God' (RV). A comparison of this latter statement with John xx. 31 shows a close connection in the purpose for which both writings were written, that is, to instruct in true knowledge those who already believe. And the knowledge to be imparted is a fellowship and a possession ('eternal life').

Quite apart from the false teachers, therefore, the author has an edificatory purpose.[1] Christians need to be challenged about the dis-

---

[1] A. E. Brooke (*op. cit.*, p. xxx) wisely remarks of the writer, 'He is a pastor first, an orthodox theologian only afterwards.' Several scholars have stressed the writer's purpose of presenting a true Christian Gnosis in opposition to the Gnosis of the false teachers; cf. R. Rothe, *Der erste Johannis Brief praktisch erklärt* (1878), p. 4.

tinctive features of their faith, especially the necessity for the exercise of love. Nowhere else in the New Testament is the combination of faith and love so clearly brought out, and it seems probable that this is emphasized because the behaviour of the readers leaves much to be desired. The writer needs to exhort them not to love the world (ii. 15ff.) in terms which suggest a condition of worldliness among them, while the warning against idolatry in v. 21 gives an illuminating insight into their spiritual condition.

According to C. H. Dodd,[1] the writer has in mind people who are unworthily using such phrases as: 'we are born of God', 'we are in the light', 'we have no sin', 'we dwell in God', 'we know God'. He uses the same phrases himself, but puts them into their true Christian context, a procedure which can be illustrated from Paul's occasional use of the language of current Greek philosophy or pagan mysticism (e.g. 'wisdom', 'knowledge', 'fullness'). In other words, this Epistle expresses the true Christian method of conveying the message by the sublimated use of current catchwords. There is something to be said for this interpretation, although it must be borne in mind that some, at least, of the catchwords had originated from Christian sources. Such ideas as sin, light, rebirth and knowledge may have a wrong connotation in Gnostic circles, but for the Christian they belong to the essence of the message he has to proclaim.[2]

IV. FORM AND DESTINATION

This Epistle does not conform to the general characteristics of contemporary letters. It has no introductory material, no author's greeting, no thanksgiving and no concluding salutations. It mentions no-one's name throughout. It reads more like a homily than an epistle. It is not difficult to imagine a Christian congregation listening to its delivery with its frequent personal exhortations.[3] It is only occasionally that words occur which remind us that this is not an address but a letter (e.g. ii. 1, 26).

[1] *Op. cit.*, p. xix.
[2] There is no support for the view of D. W. Riddle (*JR*, 13, 1933, p. 65) that the unique feature of these Epistles is that belief is now mediated by an institutional ecclesiasticism. Only a strained exegesis can make 1 Jn. i. 1, 2 refer to sacramental ordinances.
[3] Among those who regard the Epistle as a homily are E. Lohmeyer, *ZNTW*, 27 (1928), pp. 256–261; C. H. Dodd, *op. cit.*, p. 21; and J. Moffatt, *ILNT*, pp. 583, 584, who calls it a 'tract or manifesto which is thrown into a vague epistolary form' and further identifies it as a catholic homily.*

Several scholars have classed this Epistle as a general tractate or a diatribe in letter form.[1] But there are difficulties in this view because a definite historical situation lies behind the letter. When the false teachers are mentioned, the readers themselves are referred to by way of contrast in a manner which suggests the writer's acquaintance with them personally (cf. ii. 21, iv. 4). The circle of readers is, therefore, fairly limited, and is confined to those with Christian experience (i. 3, ii. 1, 20, 27). The addressees are many times called 'children' and many times addressed as 'beloved', which indicates a personal relationship between readers and writer which would be lacking in a general tractate.[2]

The suggestion has been made by R. Bultmann[3] that the original Epistle ended at v. 13 and that verses 14–21 were added later by an ecclesiastical editor. But this idea is not likely to commend itself, not only because far less confidence is now being placed in editorial theories, but also because the style and characteristic ideas of the concluding portion do not differ from the former part.[4]

The most satisfactory explanation is that 1 John was written to a group of people, possibly in more than one Asiatic community, with whom the author was personally acquainted and who were threatened with the same infiltration of false teaching. The supposition of Augus-

[1] Cf. M. Dibelius, op. cit., pp. 209ff.; A. Deissmann, Light from the Ancient East[2] (1927), p. 244; H. Windisch, op. cit., p. 136. M. Meinertz (Einleitung, p. 277), who regards this Epistle as a covering letter for the Gospel, considers that the absence of a literary beginning and conclusion can be explained only on the assumption that the readers knew the author to be an outstanding apostolic personality. On the contrary Moffatt considered that this type of hypothesis was 'suggested by the early juxtaposition of the two writings in the canon rather than by any internal evidence' (op. cit., p. 594).

[2] Cf. Feine-Behm, op. cit., p. 259.*

[3] 'Die kirchliche Redaktion des 1 Joh.', in In memoriam Ernst Lohmeyer (ed. W. Schmauch, 1951), pp. 189–201.

[4] R. Bultmann bases his argument on a comparison of verses 14–21 with the appendix to John's Gospel (chapter xxi), which he also regards as a later addition. Thus he considers 1 Jn. v. 13 to be a conclusion like Jn. xx. 31. Moreover, he maintains that this passage does not fit the rhythm of the preceding sections, where ethical paraenesis alternates with Christological instruction, nor does he consider the content of the passage to be in keeping with the preceding point of view.

W. Nauck (Die Tradition und der Charakter des ersten Johannesbriefes, 1957, pp. 133f.) criticizes Bultmann's position. He cannot conceive how a later editor could be so skilful as to compose an appendix showing the same literary characteristics as the earlier part (Nauck cites similar rhythm patterns).

tine that the churches of Parthia are in mind has no foundation and probably arose from a corruption of the text.[1]

A further question affecting the unity of the Epistle is the use or non-use by the author of a previously existing document, which has been worked over and in the process has been modified. Again it is Bultmann[2] who has been the most zealous exponent of this theory. His main contention is that i. 5b–10 is stylistically different from ii. 1f., and that the latter passage is the author's own commentary upon and modification of the former. There is, therefore, a distinction between the authors of the two parts. Moreover, Bultmann considers the earlier part to belong to a particular type of literary production (a Revelation-discourse). Various other German scholars[3] have produced modifications of Bultmann's theory, but this type of hypothesis which rests on source-differentiation has very slender support and can certainly not point to difference of authorship. W. Nauck[4] has recognized this, for although admitting the author's use of an earlier document, he maintains that the author had himself prepared it for an earlier occasion (perhaps a previous letter, ii. 12–14). 1 John is so obviously a unity as it now stands that all attempts to disentangle possible sources must inevitably be highly speculative and can hardly hope to achieve any general agreement. At the same time the group of scholars who have worked on this Epistle have done well to draw attention to its literary characteristics, particularly its rhythmic qualities. This may well be partly due to the

[1] Cf. Michaelis, *op. cit.*, pp. 291, 292; Westcott, *op. cit.*, p. xxxii.*

[2] 'Analyse des ersten Johannesbriefe', *Festgabe für A. Jülicher* (1927), pp. 138–158; and more recently in his article (see note 3 above). But it was E. von Dobschütz (*ZNTW*, 8, 1907, pp. 1ff.) who really started this line of enquiry by making an examination of iii. 1–10. Cf. E. Haenchen's comprehensive survey of recent literature on the Johannine Epistles, *TR*, n.f., 26 (1960), pp. 1–43, especially pp. 30ff.

[3] H. W. Beyer, *ThLZ*, 54 (1929), pp. 606–617; H. Windisch–H. Preisker, *op. cit.*, pp. 168–171; H. Braun, *ZTK*, 48 (1951), pp. 262–292. Windisch, in his edition, had adopted a modified editor-hypothesis, in which he envisaged that 1 John had been issued in two editions, thus accounting for the apparent contradictions between the various parts (*op. cit.*, p. 136). But Preisker, in his appendix to Windisch's Commentary (*op. cit.*, pp. 168–171), advances a theory of two earlier documents which the final author (or editor) used. This hypothesis is based on supposed differences of eschatology within the Epistle itself. For one of these documents, Preisker follows the theory of E. von Dobschütz, Windisch and Bultmann and for the other proposes the following passages: ii. 28, iii. 2, 13, 14, 19, 20, 21, iv. 17, v. 18, 19 (pp. 170, 171).

[4] *Op. cit.*, especially pp. 122–127. Cf. also O. A. Piper, *JBL*, LXVI (1947), p. 450.

catechetical method employed in teaching important Christian truth after the pattern of Jewish teaching.[1] This would certainly help to explain such phenomena as the constant repetitions and the antithetical parallels.[2] These and similar devices would ensure the retention of the teaching and we may well suppose that our author, particularly if he were the apostle John, would, after long years of this method of teaching, have developed such a style in letter writing.[3]

V. RELATION TO THE FOURTH GOSPEL

Because of the particular importance of this subject for both authorship and date, some brief indication will be given of the nature of the two views which are held: (1) that the points of contact are so strong as to be accounted for only on the theory of common authorship; or (2) that the differences are so great that common authorship must be excluded. Were it not that the latter has such an able advocate as C. H. Dodd,[4] it would almost have been unnecessary to discuss the matter, since the majority of scholars have not favoured it. Only the briefest summary can be given here of either view, but the following comments will enable some assessment of the position to be made.

[1] Cf. the discussion of F. Büchsel (*ZNTW*, 28, 1929, pp. 235–241), who found various forms of antithesis in the Epistle and by comparison with similar cases in the Mishnah concluded this style to be of Hebraic origin. He is critical of Bultmann's contention of an opposition between i. 5b–10 and ii. 1f. Piper (*op. cit.*, pp. 437ff.) finds various expressions which point to a common faith, expressed in credal statements, axioms, prophecies, commandments and eschatological rules. Some of Piper's details may be challenged, but there can be no doubt that the author's background reflects early catechetical usage.

[2] W. Nauck (*op. cit.*, pp. 15ff.) cites many examples of this phenomenon from various parts of the Epistle.*

[3] E. Lohmeyer (*op. cit.*, pp. 225–263) attempted to find in this Epistle a sevenfold structural form. But there is an artificial ring about all such theories. The Epistle does not strike the reader as an elaborately worked out homiletical exercise. At the same time it is just possible that the author may have had such a predisposition for the number seven that this number coloured his literary arrangement. Lohmeyer maintained that the same phenomenon is found in John's Gospel and in the Apocalypse. He also suggested that it may have been a current form, since it occurs in the Apocalypses of Ezra and Baruch (*op. cit.*, pp. 261–263). As contrasted with Bultmann, Lohmeyer traced the different styles within the structure to the personality of the author and to his religious outlook (*op. cit.*, p. 260).*

[4] *Op. cit., idem, BJRL*, XXI (1937), pp. 129–156. Another advocate of note was H. J. Holtzmann, 'Das Problem des 1 Johannesbrief in seinem Verhältniss zum Evangel', *JPTh*, 7 (1881), pp. 690–712, 8 (1882), pp. 316–343.*

a. Similarities

Certain similarities are at once apparent even on a casual reading of the two books. The same use in both of such abstract ideas as 'light', 'life', and 'love', the same occurrence of 'eternal life' as the believer's possession, and the same description of Christ as Logos, at once come to mind.[1] But this first impression is strongly reinforced when detailed comparisons of language are made. As in the Gospel, so in the Epistle there are frequent repetitions almost to the point of monotony, while both works are noted for the simplicity of constructions used; both contain Hebraistic antithetical parallelisms and both contain characteristic phrases such as 'to have sin', 'to do the truth', 'to abide', 'to overcome the world', 'the spirit of truth'. Similar antitheses occur, such as light and darkness, truth and error, God and the world, love and hate, the children of God and the children of the devil. Some of the more notable extended parallels in language are found in the following comparisons.[2]

1 John i. 2, 3; John iii. 11	1 John iii. 16; John x. 15
1 John i. 4; John xvi. 24	1 John iii. 22; John viii. 29
1 John ii. 11; John xii. 35	1 John iii. 23; John xiii. 34
1 John ii. 14; John v. 38	1 John iv. 6; John viii. 47
1 John iii. 5; John viii. 46	1 John iv. 16; John vi. 69
1 John iii. 8; John viii. 14	1 John v. 9; John v. 32
1 John iii. 13; John xv. 18	1 John v. 20; John xvii. 3.
1 John iii. 14; John v. 24	

These parallels are enough to show either that one author produced both works or else that the author of one was intimately acquainted with the other work and has echoed its language in his own. Both books belong to the same background of thought, with their emphasis on the importance of the incarnation, on the new birth as the method of entering upon the spiritual benefits of Christ's work, and on the overthrow of the devil, who is conceived as exercising a powerful influence on the present world order. The traditional view that both works proceeded from one mind would appear to be well based, and yet cer-

[1] As early a critic as Dionysius of Alexandria pointed out these and other ideas in which the Gospel and Epistle agree together (see Eusebius, *HE*, vii. 25. 18–21).

[2] Cf. B. F. Westcott (*op. cit.*, pp. xli–xliii) for these parallels set out conveniently in the Greek text, or more fully in Holtzmann, *JPTh*, 7 (1881), pp. 691–699.

tain differences have been pointed out which require careful consideration.

b. Differences

It will be useful, as a basis for discussion, to give a brief summary of the grounds on which C. H. Dodd[1] has disputed this traditional opinion.

(i) *Stylistic differences.* The language of the Epistle is not reckoned to be of the same intensity as that of the Gospel, although Dodd admits this kind of impression is apt to be subjective. He therefore demonstrates the impression by means of linguistic data, such as the fewer number of compound verbs in the Epistle and the greater absence of particles and conjunctions. Moreover, the language of the Epistle is said to approximate more to that of Hellenistic philosophy and to have no examples of Semitisms in contrast to the Gospel. Certain expressions (about forty in number) occur in the Epistle and not in the Gospel and the same is true in the reverse direction, many of them being characteristic of the Gospel.[2]

(ii) *Religious background.* Whereas the Old Testament background is indisputable in the case of the Gospel, where many direct citations are made and where the author shows close acquaintance with Jewish ideas, in the Epistle there is only one definite reference to the Old Testament (iii. 12). On the contrary, according to Dodd, the Hellenistic element is more dominant (e.g. 'God is Light', seed and unction conferring supernatural knowledge, 'God is love'). He concludes, 'the Epistle is not only less Hebraic and Jewish; it is also more free in its adoption of Hellenistic modes of thought and expression'.[3]

(iii) *Theological differences.* C. H. Dodd[4] notes three theological differences which he considers to be of particular significance. (1) The eschatology is more primitive than in the Gospel, i.e. there is an absence of that reinterpretation which has come to be known as realized eschatology; (2) the interpretation of the death of Christ is claimed to be more primitive, which is particularly seen in the author's use of 'ex-

---

[1] *The Johannine Epistles,* p. xlviii.

[2] Holtzmann had earlier cited a list of fifty peculiarities in the Epistle. These are conveniently listed in A. E. Brooke, *op. cit.,* pp. xiii ff.

[3] *Op. cit.,* p. liii.

[4] *Ibid.,* pp. liii, liv. Dodd drops the earlier argument against the Epistle based on confusion between the action of God and of Christ. Brooke has effectively dealt with this (*op. cit.,* pp. xvi and xvii).

piation' (ii. 2, iv. 10); and (3) the doctrine of the Spirit is confined to popular belief and is not as elevated as in the Gospel (hence the new birth can be spoken of without mentioning the Spirit's activity in the process as in Jn. iii. 5–8). Differences on such important themes of Christian theology as these, according to Dodd's view, point to a widely different outlook from that shown by the writer of the Fourth Gospel.

It should be noted that in spite of his emphasis on these differences Dodd maintains a close connection between the two authors, i.e. that the writer of the Epistle was a disciple of the Evangelist. But are his objections to unity of authorship really valid?

The linguistic objections have been well answered by W. G. Wilson,[1] who has produced statistical evidence to show that more variations of 'grammatical' words occur in the acknowledged Pauline letters than Dodd has claimed to exist between 1 John and the Gospel. He also questions some of the Aramaisms, which Dodd finds in the Gospel but not in 1 John. Arguments from vocabulary are precarious, for as Wilson again shows, similar and even greater variations occur within the Pauline letters. It is impossible by this method to pronounce with any confidence that the two works could not proceed from one author, particularly in view of the disparity in length and variation in purpose.

As for the difference in religious background, this must not be overstressed without due regard to the different purpose of the two writings. The Epistle has always in mind the background of Gnostic ideas and it is to be expected that the writing would be more flavoured by Hellenistic than by Hebraic modes of expression. Old Testament citations may have had little interest for the readers of the Epistle, who were evidently influenced by current Hellenistic ideas, and the absence of them may well tell us more about these readers than about the author unless we are to suppose that the early Christian writers were indifferent to the type of language which would most achieve their purpose. We may perhaps assume that authors would make some adjustment in different writings to suit the background of the readers. Nevertheless, in the case of these two works it may not be quite as easy to explain if both were designed, as is often supposed, for the same audience (see below). Yet it should not be overlooked that of the direct Old Testa-

---

[1] 'An examination of the Linguistic Evidence adduced against the Unity of Authorship of the First Epistle of John and the Fourth Gospel', *JTS*, XLIX (1948), pp. 147ff. Cf. also the criticisms of W. F. Howard, *JTS*, XLVIII (1947), pp. 12–25.*

ment citations in the Gospel, all but a few are attributed to various speakers in the course of the narrative. Only a few appear to be introduced by the writer himself for apologetic purposes (cf. ii. 17, xii. 38, 40, xix. 24, 36). It is not so striking, therefore, that in the Epistle, with its completely different motive, the apologetic or even didactic use of the Old Testament is lacking. There may, of course, be greater approximation in the Epistle to Hellenistic thought, but not all would agree with Dodd over his derivations, as when, for instance, he makes 'God is light' and 'God is love' to be of Hellenistic origin. It is equally possible to construe them as Christian developments from a Hebrew background, due to our Lord's teaching that He is the Light of the world and the supreme example of love. To appeal to the Hermetic literature to explain this usage, as Dodd does,[1] is to appeal to later notions to account for earlier, for there is no certain evidence that the Hermetic literature reflects the thought-background of Hellenistic mysticism at this period. We may treat with some reserve, therefore, the claims to an exclusively Hellenistic background to this Epistle.

The theological differences are equally inconclusive as the following considerations show.

1. The force of the argument from eschatology depends almost entirely on acceptance of Dodd's own interpretation of the eschatology of the Fourth Gospel, but there are strong grounds for rejecting his contention that the primitive eschatology is lacking (cf., e.g., Jn. v. 25–29).[2] Admittedly, the word Antichrist does not appear in the Gospel and occurs three times in the Epistle (1 Jn. ii. 18, 22, iv. 3), but this indicates not difference of eschatology but difference in the expression of it (cf. the Johannine expression, 'prince of this world', Jn. xii. 31, xiv. 30, xvi. 11, which serves a similar purpose).[3]

2. Is there any fundamental difference in the interpretation of the

[1] Op. cit., pp. 108–110.

[2] The idea of the ἔσχατον in Jn. vi. 39, 40, xii. 48 is not so very different from its use in 1 Jn. ii. 18. It is difficult to maintain difference of authorship on such grounds.

[3] A. E. Brooke (op. cit., p. xviii) points out that the Epistle presents what he calls 'the spiritualizing of the conception of Antichrist as fulfilled in many forms of anti-Christian teaching'.

O. A. Piper, in his article, '1 John and the Didache of the Primitive Church', IBL, LXVI (1947), pp. 444, 445, draws a distinction between ἀντίχριστος and ψευδόχριστος (Mk. xiii. 22; Mt. xxiv. 24) and considers the former to be a development from the latter, yet the change is terminological and not theological.

death of Christ? That there are some different ideas is undeniable,[1] but this tremendous event was too great to be confined within narrow limits and it is a tortuous kind of argument to relegate the 'expiatory' (or more accurately the 'propitiatory') explanation to the primitive apostolic preaching and then to maintain that the Fourth Gospel approach is more developed. Dodd gives far too little attention to the sacrificial language of the Gospel, and, therefore, gives a one-sided picture of the work of Christ in terms of exaltation and triumph.[2]

c. The problem of priority

Another problem which is of importance for the dating of this Epistle is the question of its priority or otherwise to the Fourth Gospel. Such questions are difficult to establish on literary grounds, for so much depends on subjective impressions, but the main arguments for the priority of each book will be tabulated, if only to give some indication of the highly inconclusive character of the evidence. The following details are taken mainly from Brooke, who has a full discussion on this question.

The arguments for the priority of the Epistle are:

1. The introductory passage (i. 1–4) is said to present a less developed Logos doctrine than that of the Johannine prologue.

2. The reference to Christ as Paraclete (ii. 1) has been claimed to prepare for the use of the same term for the Holy Spirit in the Gospel.

3. The eschatology of the Epistle is supposed to be more primitive (see discussion above).

4. The conception of the work of Christ in the Epistle in reference to propitiation approximates nearer to Paul's ideas and is, therefore, supposed to be earlier than the Gospel.

5. The passage John xix. 34f. is thought by some to be a misunderstanding of 1 John v. 6.

6. It is supposed that the Greek of the Gospel is better than that of the Epistle—a highly subjective judgment.[3]

---

[1] Although the word ἱλασμός does not occur in the Gospel, the idea lying behind it is not absent (cf. i. 29, xi. 51ff., xii. 24, xv. 39).

[2] B. F. Westcott (op. cit., p. xlv) considered the propitiation doctrine in the Epistle to be a development from the discourse of Jn. vi. 51, 56f.

[3] A glance at these will suffice to show that they almost all depend on a particular interpretation of the relevant passages, but, as Brooke (op. cit., pp. xix ff.) has shown, these are capable of entirely satisfactory alternatives which make them quite inconclusive as evidence for priority. For instance, the description of 'the

7. Attestation for the Epistle is claimed to be earlier than that for the Gospel.

Not more conclusive are the arguments for the priority of the Gospel, which consist of the following considerations.

1. Several passages in the Epistle, which are parallel in thought to statements in the Gospel, are said to be more intelligible if the Gospel was already known to the readers.[1] While it may readily be agreed that the Gospel throws light upon the language of the Epistle, this concession need not be proof of the priority in publication of the former, since the readers may well have been acquainted with its content orally long before this time.

2. Some indications have been found within the Epistle of direct references to the Gospel. Thus i. 3, 5, which mentions a proclamation that God is light is accordingly thought to refer to the Gospel, where this theme is prominent. Similarly ii. 14 (the aorist ἔγραψα ὑμῖν three times repeated) is supposed by some to refer to an earlier writing, which is then rather precariously identified as the Gospel.[2] But neither of these references is at all conclusive, for the former could well be understood and appreciated by the readers apart from the Gospel, whereas in the latter case, the thrice repeated ἔγραψα is immediately preceded by a thrice repeated γράφω, and the context in each case gives no justification for supposing that the three aorists were any more retrospective than the presents, quite apart from the fact that what the writer says he has written bears no relation to the contents of the Gospel.

Logos of life' would appear more intelligible if the readers knew the content of Jn. i, even if not the written record of it. Christ as Paraclete is alluded to in John by the reference to 'another' Paraclete. The eschatology has already been dealt with, as also the conception of Christ's death. Argument 5 is ruled out if the incident related in Jn. xix. 34 (the 'water and blood' passage) was an actual occurrence, while argument 6 need not be taken seriously. The concluding argument is based on a fact not altogether surprising, since the briefer and simpler Epistle may have been more popular and therefore more cited.

T. Henshaw (op. cit., pp. 379, 380) maintains that both books may have been written by a bi-lingual person whose native language was Aramaic, but who habitually spoke Greek. He then claims that the Gospel is written in more idiomatic Greek than the Epistle. But if this were so, we should expect more Aramaic flavouring in the Epistle than in the Gospel, which is not, however, supported by the facts.

[1] For a detailed comparison of these in the Greek text, cf. Brooke, op. cit., p. xxiii. Holtzmann, JPTh, 7 (1881), pp. 691–699, made the same point.

[2] Cf. Meinertz, Einleitung, p. 275.

In view of these considerations it is difficult to be certain about the question of priority, although the balance seems rather more in favour of the priority of the Gospel.[1] The theory that 1 John was a kind of covering letter for the Gospel[2] is improbable, for there appears to be no adequate *raison d'être* for such a letter. The introduction makes it clear that the readers of the Epistle are not unacquainted with the Christian message and its purpose cannot, therefore, be evangelistic. Its dealing with a specific situation would seem to account better for its origin (see under Purpose above).

VI. RELATION TO THE TEACHING OF PAUL

This problem assumed greater proportions at an earlier age than it does today, for an antithesis between Paul and the original apostles, which was assumed as the basis of Baur's reconstruction of early Christian history, is no longer reckoned to be valid by the majority of scholars.[3] That there is no essential antithesis, although many differences of emphasis, between Pauline and Johannine teaching has been amply demonstrated and the whole movement of modern biblical theology is away from divisive theories. For a careful summary of coincidences of doctrine between this Epistle and the Pauline Epistles, reference may be made to A. Plummer's chapter on this subject.[4]

VII. DATE

There is little specific material to which to appeal in affixing a date. The letter belongs to a period when Gnosticism is certainly on the horizon, although not as yet fully developed. A date towards the end of the first century would well suit this circumstance. Again, the close connection with the Fourth Gospel, whatever decision is reached regarding priority, requires a date during the same period as the publication of the Gospel and, as this is generally dated about AD 90–95, it is usual to suppose that the Epistle followed it at a slightly later date.[5]

[1] W. Michaelis (*op. cit.*, p. 294) favours the reverse conclusion, supposing that 1 John was issued before the appearance of chapters i–xx of John's Gospel.

[2] Cf. Meinertz, *op. cit.*, p. 277. This view was earlier maintained by J. H. A. Ebrard, *Biblical Commentary on the Epistles of St. John* (1860), pp. 14–34.

[3] It still finds some echoes in such writers as S. G. F. Brandon, *The Fall of Jerusalem and the Christian Church*[2] (1957).

[4] *The Epistles of St. John* (1886), pp. lxii–lxvi.

[5] E. F. Scott (*The Literature of New Testament*, pp. 260, 261) dates both books rather later, at the beginning of the second century. Some writers, such as T.

This dating rests on the assumption of common authorship for the Gospel and Epistle, but if this is denied, other grounds for dating must necessarily be brought into play. Thus Dodd[1] tentatively dates all three Johannine Epistles between AD 96 and 110, but his reasoning is far from conclusive. The upper limit is fixed by Ignatius' letters, which Dodd admits represent a rather later situation. The earlier date he fixes by the cessation of the Domitian persecutions (i.e. on the accession of Nerva in AD 96), since the Epistles reflect tension but not persecution. But this state could equally well have obtained before Domitian's persecutions commenced.[2]

THE SECOND EPISTLE

This letter, like 3 John, is so brief that it could have been contained on a single papyrus sheet. Yet both letters have been preserved for their importance for the Christian Church. No-one would suppose that their influence on Christian thought has been great, but they nevertheless make a contribution to our knowledge of contemporary affairs, even if it is no more than a glimpse that is given. In spite of their brevity they both raise problems for criticism, some of which are not easy to answer with any confidence.

I. AUTHORSHIP

Although these two Epistles are known as Epistles of John, they do not in their text give their author's name and it is consequently necessary to investigate the history of their attribution to John. It is in the light of this that the internal evidence must be viewed.

a. External evidence

That the attestation for 2 John is not as strong as for 1 John must at once be admitted. Yet the brevity of the letter and the lesser likelihood

---

Henshaw (*op. cit.*, pp. 378f.), place some interval between the two books in order to account for the differences. Henshaw, in fact, suggests a date about AD 80 for the Epistles and AD 100 for the Gospel, if both are by one author.

[1] *Op. cit.*, pp. lxviii, lxix. H. J. Holtzmann (*JPTh*, 8, 1882, pp. 316–342), who maintained dissimilar authorship, suggested that a fairly developed form of Gnosticism was in view, which therefore required a later date.

[2] Always assuming that the Domitian persecutions were as widespread as is generally supposed (see pp. 952f.).

of its being quoted by Christian authors must be given full weight in
assessing the evidence (the same applies to 3 John).[1] It is possible that
Polycarp[2] contains an allusion to 2 John 7, but since 1 John iv. 2, 3
furnishes a better parallel, no weight can be placed on this. The evidence from Irenaeus[3] is more certain, for it is clear that he not only
knew 2 John, but assumed it to be by the apostle John.

The Muratorian Fragment is ambiguous in its witness to the Johannine Epistles, since it specifies only two, while in the earlier part of the
list dealing with John's Gospel a quotation is made from 1 John i. 1f.
The evidence has been variously interpreted, but all agree that if two
Epistles only were known, they must have been 1 and 2 John (but see
discussion under 3 John).[4]

Clement of Alexandria knew of more than one Johannine Epistle,[5]
and in a Latin fragment of one of his works[6] refers to the second
Epistle, although in this fragment it is erroneously said to be written to
virgins, a mistake which may possibly have originated with the
translator. Origen cites neither 2 nor 3 John, although he knew of
their existence. He mentions that all do not admit their genuineness.[7]
Another Alexandrian, Dionysius,[8] mentions the second and third
Epistles as circulating as works of John, and the implication is that he
accepted them as such, in spite of the fact that the title 'Elder' is used.
Eusebius placed this Epistle (with 3 John) among the disputed books,[9]
while even in the time of Jerome some were ascribing 2 and 3 John to
a different author (John the Elder) from 1 John.[10] But after his time, the
Epistles were both received without question, except in the Syriac
Church, where the earliest evidence for their canonical authority is at

[1] C. H. Dodd (*The Johannine Epistles*, 1946, p. xvi) writes of 2 and 3 John, 'It
should however be borne in mind that both are extremely short and contain very
little material for quotation.'
[2] *Ad. Phil.* vii. 1.   [3] *Adv. Haer.* iii. 16. 3, 8.
[4] P. Katz (*JTS*, New Series, VIII, 1957, pp. 273, 274) considers it improbable
that 2 and 3 John would be separated and suggests an emendation to this Canon
to make it mean 'two in addition to the Catholic (epistle, i.e. 1 John)'. Cf. the view
of E. C. Selwyn (*The Christian Prophets and the Prophetic Apocalypse*, 1900, pp.
140–142) that at that time 2 and 3 John formed one Epistle. This avoids any
emendation.
[5] *Strom.* ii. 15. 66.
[6] Latin *adumbrationes*: cf. also Eusebius, *HE*, vi. 14. 1, for a statement suggesting
that Clement commented on all the Catholic Epistles.
[7] *In Joann.* v. 3 (Eusebius, *HE*, vi. 25).
[8] Eusebius, *HE*, vii. 25.   [9] *Ibid.*, iii. 25. 3.   [10] *De Vir. Ill.* xi. 18.

the beginning of the sixth century, although they had no doubt been used as Scripture for some time before this.[1]

It has already been pointed out that absence of citation may be accounted for by the character of the letters, but does this equally account for the doubts which were expressed regarding them among later writers? It is significant that the earlier writers appear to have less hesitation about apostolic authorship than the later,[2] which is the reverse of what would be expected if the doubts were based on accurate tradition. It is just possible that the ascription to John the Elder caused more confusion at a later date because of the belief in some circles in a John the Elder distinct from John the apostle. Once these Epistles were attributed to a non-apostolic presbyter, their canonical status would have been more difficult to establish.[3] But the evidence for John the Elder is very restricted and of dubious value and this explanation must be received with reserve. On the whole, there are no conclusive external reasons for denying the authenticity of these Epistles.

b. Internal evidence

(i) *The Epistle's own claims.* The author describes himself as 'the Elder' (2 Jn. 1) and it is clearly necessary to discuss the significance of this title. The Greek word πρεσβύτερος primarily indicates seniority. It may mean no more than 'the old man' and be an affectionate title used of and by the venerable author. This interpretation need not suppose it to be a rather familiar nickname, as sometimes happens in modern usage,[4] but merely a descriptive title indicative of both the age and authority of the author. Evidence is not wanting that supports this idea of seniority, particularly in relation to apostolic authority, for

---

[1] Since they are not in the Peshitta, it must be assumed that they were added to the Syriac Canon later than AD 411.

[2] A. Plummer (*op. cit.*, p. lxx) pointed out that the nearer the witnesses are to the apostle John, the more favourable they are to his authorship. In fact, they express no alternative view.

[3] The interesting form of the Cheltenham (or Mommsenian) Canon (*c.* AD 360), which gives an African Canon of about the same date as Athanasius' list (*c.* AD 367) in which all three Johannine Epistles were included in the Canon, witnesses to lingering doubts. Although this African Canon includes '*Epistulae Iohannis* III', the words '*una sola*' appearing on the next line indicate a preference for the first Epistle only.

[4] C. H. Dodd (*op. cit.*, p. 155) seems to assume this and therefore rules out this explanation of the term.

Papias' well-known reference to John the Elder includes within it references to a number of the apostles apparently under the same title.[1] Quite apart from the dispute whether Papias intended to make a distinction between John the apostle and John the Elder, it would seem that he saw no incongruity in calling apostles 'elders' and it would, therefore, be wrong to conclude *ipso facto* that the Elder of 2 and 3 John could not be John the apostle.[2] At the same time, the question must be faced why the author, if he were John the apostle, calls himself simply 'the Elder', particularly as in 2 John there is a matter over which some authority must be exercised. Yet it is surely intelligible that the aged apostle, in writing more intimate letters, would prefer the more affectionate and less formal title than the more official one, particularly as by this time he was no doubt the last surviving of the original apostles.[3]

Although there is no strong reason to question the possibility that 'the Elder' means the apostle John, as it has generally been interpreted in the tradition of the Church, some serious consideration must be given to the alternative view that another writer known as John the Elder was the real author and that he was later confused with the apostle. This view is certainly possible, but it stands on shaky foundations unless it can be demonstrated with reasonable certainty that such a person as John the Elder really existed. But Papias is the real key to this problem and he has expressed himself in a manner which falls short of lucidity. Since Eusebius tells us that Papias was 'a man of very mean intellectual power', it is not surprising that his powers of expression were limited. At all events it is highly probable that Papias

[1] 'And again, if any one came who had been a follower of the Elders, I used to enquire about the sayings of the Elders—what was said by Andrew, or by Peter, or by Philip, or by Thomas or James, or by John or Matthew, or any other of the Lord's disciples, and what Aristion and the Elder John, the disciples of the Lord, say. For I did not think that I could get so much profit from the contents of books as from the utterances of a living and abiding voice' (Eusebius, *HE*, iii. 39. 4).

[2] Many scholars do not agree that Papias calls the apostles 'elders', but claim that he distinguishes between them (cf. C. K. Barrett, *The Gospel according to St. John*, 1956, pp. 89ff.).

[3] R. H. Charles (*Commentary on the Revelation of St. John*, 1920, I, p. xliii n. 1) rejected this view because in 3 John 'he would naturally have availed himself of his power as an apostle to suppress Diotrephes and others who disowned his jurisdiction and authority, which they could not have done had he been an apostle.' But Charles seems to overlook that 3 John was addressed to an individual well known to John, who certainly did not need to be impressed by apostolic authority.

never meant to distinguish between John the apostle and a John the Elder, for both appear to be called Elders and both are described as disciples of the Lord.[1] This method of differentiating between two men who shared the same name is quite unintelligible. Moreover, Aristion is mentioned with the elder John, but is given no title and the only fair inference is that John was marked out from Aristion. If the title of Elder was meant to indicate the apostle, this is fully intelligible, but if not it must be supposed that Aristion was not even of sufficient importance to hold any office, although described as a disciple of the Lord.[2]

A few later writers assumed that Papias meant to indicate two Johns, and this fact has often been supposed to show that this is the correct interpretation. The most important of these is Eusebius, who appealed to Papias' Elder John as an alternative to an apostolic author for the Apocalypse. Jerome assigned 2 and 3 John to the Elder John and 1 John to the apostle. The evidence of Dionysius is inconclusive, for although he mentions two tombs of John in Ephesus, he does not suggest John the Elder as the probable writer of the Apocalypse, although he denied it to the apostle John. This evidence is not strong and is further considerably weakened by reference to Irenaeus, who knew Papias' work well and also knew much about Ephesus, but makes no mention of John the Elder. He refers to a presbyter, but not by name, describing him rather as 'a disciple of the Apostles', which at once distinguishes him from Papias' Elder John. This presbyter, in fact, was Irenaeus' own teacher and was not improbably Polycarp. Such evidence suggests that 'Elder' was much used during the sub-apostolic age, but it is not evidence for the existence of an Elder John.

Is there then a possibility that 2 and 3 John were written by an un-

[1] Moffatt's opinion (*ILNT*, p. 600) that Papias' statement contains an implicit distinction between οἱ πρεσβύτεροι and οἱ τοῦ Κυρίου μαθηταί is not borne out by the more obvious interpretation of the Greek. Cf. C. K. Barrett's discussion along the same lines (*op. cit.*, pp. 88–92). T. Zahn (*INT*, II, p. 452), who strongly maintained that Papias referred to only one John, pointed out that Eusebius' interpretation of Papias' evidence was self-contradictory. He rejected the view of Haussleiter (*Theologisches Literaturblatt*, 1896, cols. 465–468) that ἢ τί Ἰωάννης was an interpolation of Papias' text. Moffatt comments quite characteristically on both Zahn's and Haussleiter's opinions, 'John the presbyter is not to be emended out of existence in the interests of John the apostle' (*op. cit.*, p. 601).

[2] It should be noted that Papias' statement refers to ὁ πρεσβύτερος Ἰωάννης not Ἰωάννης ὁ πρεσβύτερος which would be more natural if intended to distinguish him from Ἰωάννης ὁ ἀπόστολος.

named Elder, who later became confused with the apostle John? There are difficulties with this view. It is difficult, for instance, to see how or why such an attribution would be made unless the close similarity of these Epistles with 1 John and the Gospel should be appealed to. But if so it must be supposed that the unknown Elder had either consciously imitated John's style to give the impression of Johannine authorship, which is highly improbable since in that case he would have chosen a different title from 'the Elder',[1] or, if the similarities with the other Johannine writings were accidental, he must have been so close a student of John that subsequent Church Fathers were unable to distinguish his own writings from the master's and this can hardly have happened accidentally. The case for considering the Elder as a simple description of the aged apostle seems much more intelligible than either of these alternatives.

(ii) *Relationship to other Johannine writings.* In the last paragraph reference was made to the similarity of 2 John to 1 John and the Fourth Gospel and this requires further comment. A. E. Brooke[2] has set out the evidence very fully in his commentary and it is necessary here to give only a general indication of the position. There are many phrases in both 2 and 3 John which are either identical with phrases in 1 John or appear to be reminiscent of these.[3] Moreover, the two smaller Epistles become more intelligible on a number of points if a knowledge of the First Epistle is presupposed.[4] Brooke's own conclusion is as follows: 'We are compelled to choose between common authorship and conscious imitation. And the freedom with which the same and similar tools are handled points clearly to the former as the more probable alternative.'[5]

What bearing has this conclusion on the question of authorship? If common authorship with 1 John is assumed it will be seen that the solution of this question is inseparably bound up with the origin of the Fourth Gospel, since all these writings share so many common characteristics (see discussion of authorship of 1 John on pp. 864 ff.). The

---

[1] C. H. Dodd (*op. cit.,* p. lxv) regards deliberate imitation as less likely than unconscious habits of speech as an explanation of the similarities.

[2] *Op. cit.,* pp. lxxiv ff.

[3] C. H. Dodd (*op. cit.,* p. lxiv) even goes so far as to assert that a large part of 2 John is a sort of résumé of 1 John.*

[4] A. E. Brooke (*op. cit.,* p. lxxv) mentions especially 2 Jn. 9 and 3 Jn. 11 (cf. respectively 1 Jn. ii. 23 and 1 Jn. iv. 20, iii. 6).   [5] *Ibid., loc. cit.*

fact is that common authorship with 1 John and the Gospel is the assumption which best explains all the similarities, although there are unquestionably certain differences. These latter can be explained generally by the changed circumstances and purposes of the second and third letters as compared with the other writings.[1]

(iii) *Summary of views on authorship.* To sum up, the following comments may be made:

1. Authorship by the apostle John, which has such strong external support, is seen to be a quite reasonable deduction from the internal evidence.

2. Authorship by the Elder John, proposed by most of those disputing apostolic authorship either of the Epistles or the Gospel, has far less ancient attestation but far more modern opinion behind it. It would have greater weight if the Elder John (i.e. as distinct from the apostle) were known with certainty to have existed.

3. Authorship by an unknown Elder has even less ancient testimony and cannot be considered as probable.

The conclusion reached is that John, the Son of Zebedee, was the author of all three Epistles.

II. DESTINATION

The writer of 2 John addresses his letter to the Elect Lady, but little did he realize the problems he was creating for later critics in using so enigmatic an address. The fact is that his words (ἐκλεκτῇ κυρίᾳ) have been construed in five different ways: 'the Elect Lady', 'an Elect Lady', 'Electa the Lady', 'the elect Kyria', 'Electa Kyria'. Of these, however, the last three can almost certainly be eliminated, for there is no parallel use of Electa[2] as a lady's name, while Kyria is used only very rarely in this sense. The combination of two such rare uses would be incredible,

---

[1] Earlier writers who have emphasized differences are Pfleiderer, Jülicher, Schwartz. Cf. A. E. Brooke (*loc. cit.*, pp. lxxv f.) for a criticism of their main positions. Some scholars, such as W. Bousset (*Die Offenbarung*, 1906, pp. 43f.) and J. Moffatt (*ILNT*, pp. 480ff.) differentiated 1 John from 2 and 3 John and then identified the author of the latter with the John of the Apocalypse (John the Elder). Cf. also E. C. Selwyn, *op. cit.*, pp. 133ff.; and J. H. A. Ebrard, *op. cit.*, pp. 359ff. But this position is contested by R. H. Charles, *op. cit.*, I, pp. xli ff., and H. Windisch, *op. cit.*, pp. 143, 144.

[2] Verse 13, where the same word is used to describe the lady's sister, is sufficient to dismiss this possibility, for it would be incredible for two sisters both to bear the same name and a name which was nowhere else attested.

while even if either could be used separately the accompanying description (i.e. 'elect' or 'lady') would normally require the article (as in Γαΐω τῷ ἀγαπητῷ in 3 Jn. 1). 'The elect Kyria' is just possible on the analogy of Rufus, the elect, in Romans xvi. 13, although even here the article is used. Of the other two possibilities, that which inserts the article is probably to be preferred since the address is evidently intended to be specific.

But who was the Elect Lady? To this two quite different answers have been given. Either she was an individual acquaintance of the writer, or else she was a community under his general supervision. There have been advocates for both alternatives although the majority of scholars prefer the latter. In favour of the former it may be said that:

1. This is the most obvious understanding of the words, and it is a fair canon of criticism that if the literal meaning makes sense recourse should not be made to a metaphorical treatment.

2. The reference to the lady's children is quite intelligible if these were by now grown-up.

3. The greeting from the lady's nephews in verse 13 is also quite possible if taken literally.[1] According to this interpretation, the writer is addressing a lady of some standing, warning her of certain dangers and preparing the way for his coming visit.

Yet there are strong arguments for the alternative view.

1. The lady is not only beloved by the writer but by all who know the truth, which could mean that 'she' was known universally by Christians.[2] This would be more intelligible if used of a community than of an individual.

2. Neither she herself nor any of her children or nephews is mentioned by name, which detracts from the personal character of the letter (this is in strong contrast to 3 John).

3. The subject-matter is probably more suitable for a community

---

[1] J. Rendel Harris (Exp., VI, iii, 1901, pp. 194–203) suggested that Κυρία should be understood as an affectionate and not a formal term (i.e. as equivalent to 'my dear lady'). It therefore supports an individual destination. But his evidence has been criticized by G. G. Findlay, op. cit., pp. 24ff., and A. E. Brooke, op. cit., pp. lxxx, lxxxi. W. M. Ramsay (Exp., VI, iii, 1901, pp. 354–356) pointed out that Κύριος and Κυρία were colourless terms.

[2] The 'all' need not here be understood in a general sense as Dom J. Chapman supposed in concluding that some important church such as Antioch or Rome must be in mind (JTS, V, 1904, pp. 357ff., 517ff.). It can quite naturally be understood of all the Christians within the author's own district.

than an individual, with its warnings against false teachers, although this might have been equally necessary for a prominent private person in the habit of entertaining visitors freely.

4. The predominance of the second person plural rather than the singular suggests a composite understanding of the addressee (cf. verses 8, 10, 12).

5. 'The new commandment' of the Lord, referred to in verse 5, has more point if applied to a community rather than to the narrower limits of a family circle.

6. The personification of the Church in a feminine form is in harmony with other New Testament usage, for not only does Paul develop the idea of the Church as the Bride of Christ (Eph. v. 29f.; 2 Cor. xi. 2ff.), but Peter uses a feminine expression to describe the Church 'in Babylon' (1 Pet. v. 13—although the usage here may be occasioned only by the feminine form of ἐκκλησία, which is omitted but inferred).

7. The greeting in verse 13 is more natural if sent from one church to another than from a group of people to their aunt by means of a third party.

When these arguments for the collective interpretation are considered carefully, it cannot be said that they are conclusive, and they do not specifically exclude the possibility of the alternative view. For instance, a Christian who was particularly generous in hospitality may well have been known throughout a wide circle of churches and the 'all' of verse 1 need not be regarded too rigidly of every single Christian. What the writer seems to mean is that all true Christians who knew the lady loved and respected her as he himself did. The anonymous character of the personal allusions are as perplexing for either view, while the subject-matter is not irrelevant for an individual household, neither is the collective plural of verses 8, 10, 12 if the exhortations are directed both to the lady and her children. The salutation from nephews and nieces to their aunt via the writer may be regarded as perfectly natural, in view of what often happens in correspondence, when relatives may say, 'Give them our greetings when you write'.

It is difficult to decide, and sympathy must be felt for Bishop Westcott's[1] conclusion that the problem of the address is insoluble. This would undoubtedly be the safest course to adopt, but if some preference is desired, it would seem rather better to adopt the more literal meaning

---

[1] *Op. cit.*, p. 224

because this would help to account for the reluctance of some of the early Christians to use the Epistle. A private letter written to a lady would not seem of sufficient importance to receive canonical status. On the other hand some ancient commentators not only regarded the Epistle as addressed to a church, but to the universal Church,[1] a notion untenable in view of the mention of the sister in verse 13. Attempts to identify a particular church have not been highly successful. Findlay[2] suggested Pergamum on the grounds that the church there was troubled by false teachers, probably of the same type as mentioned in this Epistle. Chapman,[3] far less probably, suggested Rome. The fact is that nobody knows, although somewhere in Asia is highly probable.

III. OCCASION AND PURPOSE

Certain data may be culled from the Epistle to indicate the setting. There can be no doubt that the false teachers mentioned in verse 7 are the same as those referred to in 1 John (see discussion on pp. 869 ff.). This means that they were Docetists whose doctrine was seriously threatening the church. The false teachers were itinerating among the churches and were taking advantage of the hospitality of Christian people. There was need for these people to be put on their guard against these danger-ous teachers. The advice to have nothing to do with these men may at first sight appear harsh and ungracious, but it must be remembered that the teaching which was denying the true humanity of Christ was, in fact, undermining the foundations of the Christian faith and strong action was necessary. Hospitality was an indispensable requisite for the spread of propaganda and the refusal of it would be an effective deter-rent, whether the content of the propaganda were true or false. The New Testament makes it clear that it was the Church's responsibility to offer hospitality to the messengers of truth, which meant that it was an equal responsibility to use discernment in refusing hospitality to the opponents of truth (cf. also the *Didache*, xi). To do otherwise was actively to participate in the spreading of error.

It would seem, therefore, that John is desiring to forewarn his readers against the infiltration of this error and his primary purpose in writing

[1] E.g. Clement (cited by A. E. Brooke, *op. cit.*, p. 169).

[2] *Op. cit.*, pp. 30ff.

[3] *Op. cit.*, *loc. cit.*, based on a comparison with 1 Pet. v. 13. But cf. J. V. Bartlet (*JTS*, VI, 1905, pp. 204ff.), who disagreed with Chapman and tentatively suggested Thyatira.

is to put them on their guard and to stress in no uncertain tones the serious character of the false teaching. He makes quite clear that the doctrine is not the doctrine of Christ and that these people are not of God (verse 9). They are, in fact, opposed to Christ (symbolized in one expression, ὁ ἀντίχριστος). The readers are challenged to self-examination, lest they should lose what they have gained.

Many scholars have linked the occasion of 2 John with that of 3 John. Findlay,[1] for example, considered that 2 John was the letter referred to in 3 John 9 and that both are complementary in respect of hospitality, since 3 John deals with the refusal of Diotrephes to do what he should have done, i.e. offer hospitality to the emissaries of the truth. This interpretation necessitates treating κυρία as a reference to the same church of which Gaius (3 Jn. 1) was a member, the idea being that Gaius was incurring the displeasure of Diotrephes by keeping an open house for John's representatives, whom Diotrephes had banned. This interpretation is certainly possible, but in the absence of any allusion in 3 John to the false teaching of 2 John, it is better to keep them apart. The more recent and somewhat revolutionary view of Käsemann on these Epistles will be discussed when dealing with 3 John, although his interpretation of 3 John affects the purpose of 2 John. (See pp. 897 f.)

IV. DATE

If internal evidence alone be relied on as an indication of date, there is little data available. Since the false teaching links this Epistle so closely to 1 John, it must be supposed that it was issued about the same time, probably soon afterwards.[2] If any credence can be given to the view[3] that the ἔγραψα of 1 John ii. 26 refers to our 2 John, the reverse order would obtain, but the identification is doubtful since ἔγραψα can be understood to refer to 1 John, in conformity with frequent literary custom.

THE THIRD EPISTLE

So close is the connection between this Epistle and the last that much of what has already been said sheds light on the problem of this Epistle. The problem of authorship will practically resolve itself into a discussion of the relationship between the two letters.

[1] *Op. cit.*, p. 8. C. H. Dodd (*op. cit.*, p. 161) describes this suggestion as 'not very probable'.

[2] See discussion on the date of 1 John, pp. 883 f.

[3] Cf. H. H. Wendt, *ZNTW*, 21 (1922), pp. 144–146.

I. AUTHORSHIP

As in 2 John the writer introduces himself as 'the Elder', and so the decision reached with respect to 2 John should apply here. Little further discussion is needed except to elucidate one or two particular features of 3 John which differ from 2 John. First, the external attestation is not quite so strong for this Epistle. It is not certain that any evidence for it can be cited before the third century, if the Muratorian Canon is thought to refer to two Johannine Epistles only. But the absence of early attestation is not very surprising in view of the character of its contents.[1]

Next to be noted are its similarities to 2 John and also its differences. In both Epistles much stress is laid on the 'truth', although in 3 John it is not so clearly opposed to error. A similar context of erroneous teaching may nevertheless be assumed. Both speak of hospitality, although in 2 John it is forbidden for the false teachers and in 3 John it is commended for the true. In both the writer rejoices over others who walk in the truth: the elect lady's children (2 Jn. 4) and Gaius (3 Jn. 3). In both she author intimates, in almost identical words, his intention to visit the recipients (cf. 2 Jn. 12 and 3 Jn. 14), and in both he intimates that he had much to write but would rather not write (cf. 'paper and ink' in 2 Jn. 12 with 'pen and ink' in 3 Jn. 13). The conclusion seems inescapable that the same writer is at work in both letters. This is further confirmed by the differences. The more specific occasion of 3 John accounts naturally for the diversity in subject-matter and for the closer conformity of this Epistle to the form of a genuine private letter. There would, in fact, be less grounds for disputing 3 John than 2 John on the basis of literary form.[2]

II. DESTINATION

3 John has one advantage over 2 John in that the recipient is named. Who the 'beloved Gaius' was, however, is anyone's guess. It is highly unlikely, with so common a name, that he is to be identified with any other Gaius mentioned in the New Testament. He is clearly well known to the author, who warmly commends him not only for his consistent Christian life, but also for generous hospitality. Whether he held any office in any church is not known, nor is it certain that he belonged to

[1] C. H. Dodd (*op. cit.*, pp. lxiii, lxiv) points out that it is so unimportant that it is difficult to suggest why anyone should have fabricated it.

[2] C. H. Dodd (*op. cit.*, p. lxv) discusses the possibility that 3 John is genuine and 2 John is an imitation based on 1 and 3 John, but considers that such a theory is not completely plausible.

the same church as Diotrephes,[1] whose high-handed behaviour forms the main subject of the letter.

It is not possible to be any more specific than this,[2] but as it has already been shown that this Epistle is closely related both to 1 John and 2 John, and as these Epistles are fairly reasonably assigned to an Asian destination, it may be supposed that Gaius' church was one of the circuit of Asiatic churches under the general supervision of the apostle John.

III. OCCASION AND PURPOSE

It is possible to be rather more certain here. John has apparently sent out some itinerant representatives, who have returned and reported to him their experiences (verse 3). They speak highly of Gaius who entertained the strangers (verses 3, 5), who were probably acting for the apostle because, due to old age, he was no longer able to move among his churches. But one man, Diotrephes, has not been prepared to receive these brethren and has even banned the members of his church who were prepared to do so. In addition Diotrephes had been making none too complimentary remarks about the apostle himself ('prating against me with evil words', verse 10, RSV). From the manner in which Diotrephes has exerted authority, it is reasonable to suppose that he occupied the position of leader of this church, although he may even have assumed this position himself. At least, he did not acknowledge John's authority (verse 9), and there appears to exist something of a personal feud between them.

Thus the apostle writes to Gaius to acquaint him with the present position. There are two possibilities here. If Gaius belongs to the same church, it would seem that the apostle wrote two letters: one to the church, which he feels certain will not be received because of Diotrephes' personal antipathy towards him and the other to the only faithful member of the same church whose loyalty he could trust.[3] But it is

---

[1] J. V. Bartlet (*op. cit.*, p. 213) assumes that both were elders, but disputes that Diotrephes held any authoritative office above his fellow presbyters.

[2] G. G. Findlay (*op. cit.*, pp. 36f.) makes the conjecture that Gaius belonged to the church of Pergamum on the grounds of his identification of the elect lady of 2 John with this church and some rather precarious evidence from the Apostolic Constitutions to the effect that the apostle John appointed Gaius of Derbe as bishop of Pergamum (although Findlay does not regard the bishop as Paul's companion of Acts xx. 4).

[3] This is G. G. Findlay's theory, *op. cit.*, p. 38. Cf. also A. E. Brooke, *op. cit.*, pp. lxxxi ff.

possible that Gaius belonged to a neighbouring church and was being forewarned about the high-handed activity of Diotrephes. The former alternative appears to be slightly more probable.

If we assume the correctness of this interpretation of the occasion, the writer must be commending Gaius for his stand against Diotrephes and assuring him that he will deal with him as soon as he visits the church. But the position of Demetrius must also be taken into account. John holds him in great regard (verse 12) and appears to be commending him to Gaius. The Epistle, therefore, partakes of the character of a letter of commendation for Demetrius. Some have supposed him to have been a member, if not even the leader, of the band of itinerant missionaries. But this seems ruled out because Gaius has already received these and so would not need the apostle's commendation—unless, of course, even Gaius had not sufficiently respected him, which seems quite out of character with what we know of him from the opening portion of the Epistle. The most natural assumption is that Demetrius has no connection with John's representatives whom Diotrephes has already rejected, but that because of his commission from John it is anticipated that Diotrephes will treat him similarly. John therefore commends him to Gaius' private hospitality rather than to the church. He was in all probability the bearer of the letter.

Some reference must be made to the somewhat revolutionary interpretation of the evidence given by Käsemann.[1] He is not the only scholar who has seen in Diotrephes an early example of monarchical episcopacy, mainly on the ground of his power to excommunicate (as Käsemann understands verse 10). But he has gone further and deduced that the Elder has acted against the authority of the monarchical Diotrephes (understanding 'elder' in its second-century official sense). The assumption is that it is the Elder who is undisciplined and who has organized his own Gentile mission contrary to the authority of Diotrephes. The Elder writes, therefore, to justify his actions and to re-establish himself before the church from which he has been excommunicated (so Käsemann infers from verse 10).

This theory, which defends the reputation of Diotrephes and defames the writer of the letter into 'a simple presbyter of the third Christian

---

[1] E. Käsemann, ZTK, 48 (1951), pp. 292–311 (reproduced in his Exegetische Versuche und Besinnungen, 1960, pp. 168–187). But cf. G. Bornkamm's examination of and disagreement with this theory, in his article 'πρεσβύτερος', Kittel's Theologisches Wörterbuch, VI, p. 671.

generation',[1] must be rejected on several grounds. The tone of author-ity within the letter and also the specific mention of authority is sufficient to show that the Elder is more than a simple late presbyter. Moreover, verse 10 is not naturally to be understood of excommuni-cation, but of refusal to grant hospitality.[2] The writer does not write as a pleading excommunicant, for verse 10 does not suggest that he expects any difficulty in gaining a hearing when he comes to the church. Indeed, the terms in which he refers to his approaching visit suggest an authoritative visit (cf. 1 Cor. iv. 19). An even more serious difficulty for Käsemann's view is the Johannine colouring of the letter, which he explains as a working in of traces of Johannine theology. But the skill required to do this vitiates the whole theory, for it is highly improbable that a simple presbyter would have been capable of giving such a presentation of Johannine flavouring that the original purpose of the letter became entirely forgotten. As Michaelis rightly points out, this theory does nothing to lead to a better understanding of the Johannine literature as a whole.[3]

Nothing has so far been said about the doctrinal views of Diotrephes, because the Epistle supplies no data on this matter. Yet W. Bauer[4] considered him to be a heretical leader ('Ketzer-haupt'). There might be something to be said for identifying this man with the same heresy which is condemned in 2 John, but if so it is strange that nothing is said about Diotrephes' heretical views. Gnostic tendencies might well have fostered such an exhibition of pride as is seen in his love of the pre-eminence (verse 9), but Gnostics were not the only ones addicted to arrogance and it is not necessary to appeal to heretical views to account for a failing which is all too often the accompaniment of orthodoxy.

IV. DATE

There is nothing further to add to the comments on 2 John, for this Epistle must have been written about the same time as that. Those who maintain that the two Epistles are complementary suggest that they were written and sent on the same occasion; but, even if this supposi-

[1] Op. cit., p. 311.

[2] Cf. W. Michaelis' careful criticism of Käsemann on this point (op. cit., p. 299).

[3] Op. cit., p. 300. E. Haenchen (TR, n.f., 26, 1960, pp. 267–291) gives a useful summary of different explanations of the occasion of 2 and 3 John, and includes a careful criticism of Käsemann's views.

[4] Rechtgläubigkeit und Ketzerei im ältesten Christentum (1934), p. 97. Käsemann (op. cit., p. 298) rejects this view, and most other scholars would agree with him.

tion is rejected, it is quite clear that no great time interval separated them. Naturally if 2 John is the earlier letter referred to in 3 John 9[1] the sequence of publication would be established, but since this is unlikely, there is no clear indication whether 3 John preceded or followed 2 John. In all probability this Epistle and 2 John were the latest Johannine writings and the latest of all the New Testament literature, but some would concede this position to the Fourth Gospel.[2]

CONTENTS OF 1 JOHN

I. THE MESSAGE AUTHENTICATED (i. 1–4)

In place of the usual salutation and specific address, the writer claims first-hand knowledge of the living message which he intends to impart. He gives some indication of the content of that message; that is, the fellowship which Christians enjoy both among themselves and with God. The writing is intended to deepen that fellowship.

II. THE PRINCIPLES OF FELLOWSHIP EXPLAINED (i. 5–ii. 29)

a. The necessity for purity (i. 5–ii. 2)

Against the background of God as light, it is impossible to have fellowship with Him unless we are equally pure and this can be achieved only by the sacrificial act of Jesus Christ, who has thus become the believer's constant Advocate. There is, however, a demand for the believer to walk continually in the light.

b. The manifestations of the life of fellowship (ii. 3–17)

1. There must be obedience to God's commandments. It is not sufficient to claim to do so by words, without supporting it by

---

[1] A view maintained by T. Zahn, *INT*, III, p. 378; G. G. Findlay, *op. cit.*, p. 8. M. Dibelius (*op. cit.*, p. 212) thought that it may have been 2 John. On the other hand B. F. Westcott (*op. cit.*, p. 240) emphatically regarded the letter as lost and most scholars have inclined to this view. It is very improbable that 1 John is meant because 3 John is obviously intended for a much smaller reader circle, and the letter in 3 Jn. 9 would seem to have been concerned with a specific situation (cf. W. Michaelis, *op. cit.*, p. 301).

[2] So W. Michaelis, *op. cit.*, pp. 294, 301.

deeds. The believer's walk is a sure test of his fellowship with God (ii. 3–6).

2. A new commandment requires the exercise of love. Light and love go together as do darkness and hate. Only those who show love are truly walking in the light (ii. 7–11).

3. The life of fellowship is applicable for all age-groups. Children, young men, and fathers are all in turn addressed and the possibility of victory over evil is assumed, on the basis of their knowledge of God (ii. 12–14).

4. The fellowship means a rejection of worldliness. The apostle thinks of the world in the sense of a harmful environment which must never be the object of the believer's affection (ii. 15–17).

c. Threats to those in the fellowship (ii. 18–29)

Already many antichrists have come and the apostle foresees a time when all opposition will be focused upon one impersonation of evil. Those who have dissociated themselves from the believers clearly do not belong to them. Antichrists are first contrasted with God's anointed ones and then defined as those who deny both God and Christ (ii. 18–22). But believers are in a very different position as heirs of eternal life, for they have the inner anointing of God and need no other teacher (ii. 23–27). Believers are, therefore, exhorted to abide in Christ so as to be unashamed at His coming. Their righteous deeds are evidence of their regeneration (ii. 28, 29).

III. THE CHILDREN OF GOD (iii. 1–24)

1. First the privileges of believers are set forth and the chief of these is the assurance that they will bear Christ's likeness (iii. 1–3).

2. Next, sin is regarded as lawlessness. But again believers have nothing to fear if they abide in Him. Their lives will be without sin, in the sense of an habitual attitude of mind. They are God's children in contrast to the devil's and as such they must act rightly and love the brethren (iii. 4–10).

3. Love to one another is illustrated by its antithesis. The case of Cain is cited in contrast to Abel. In contrast to hate, which is likened to murder, love is essentially sacrificial. Christ's own self-offering is in fact cited as a pattern for ours. Again the fallacy of profession without deeds is emphasized (iii. 11–18).

4. The believer should enjoy confidence before God. This he may

do if his own heart does not condemn him. Where self-condemnation exists God will deal with it, but the believers' responsibility is again defined as love to one another (iii. 19–24).

IV. THE SPIRIT OF TRUTH (iv. 1–6)

Because of the prevalence of error, there need to be sure tests of truth. One of the tests is the attitude towards Christ. A real grasp of the fact of the incarnation is essential. Any who deny this are regarded as being possessed by the spirit of Antichrist who dominates the world, but the Christian believers are assured that they will overcome error.

V. MORE ON THE THEME OF LOVE (iv. 7–21)

a. The powerful effect of God's love (iv. 7–12)

Since God is love, the believer's love to God must reflect the same love. Its supreme example is seen in the sending of Christ to be a propitiation for our sins. But this high concept of love is the pattern for Christians' love for one another.

b. The perfecting of God's love in us (iv. 13–21)

We have received (1) the Spirit and (2) the testimony that God sent His Son to be our Saviour. Our duty is to confess Christ and in this way we shall experience more of God's love until it becomes perfected. When it is perfected it will cast out fear and give confidence for the judgment day. Again mere profession is strongly condemned and brotherly love is made a test for the reality of our love to God.

VI. SECRETS OF A VICTORIOUS FAITH (v. 1–5)

The first requirement mentioned is obedience to God's commandments, which has already been mentioned before. But now the character of Christian commandments is explained as not burdensome. Obedience to God is not, therefore, onerous. Moreover, duty when linked with faith leads to victory. The world is a defeated foe for the believer in Christ.

VII. GOD'S WITNESS TO THE GOSPEL (v. 6–12)

As the Epistle began with the authentication of the message, so it closes with the same theme. A threefold witness to Christ is mentioned, the Spirit, the water and the blood, the latter two probably referring to the baptism and sacrificial death of Christ. This testimony is greater than human testimony, and anyone who does not believe it makes God a liar.

VIII. SPIRITUAL CONFIDENCE (v. 13–20)

There are a number of affirmations in this concluding passage which reflect a strong confidence in God.

1. The writer's purpose is that his readers should know that they have eternal life (v. 13).

2. We know that God hears and answers our prayers and we should pray for those who are not already past hope (v. 14–17).

3. We know the regenerate soul does not make a habit of sinning for God preserves him (v. 18).

4. We know we belong to God (v. 19).

5. We know the purpose of the incarnation (v. 20).

IX. WARNING AGAINST IDOLS (v. 21)

CONTENTS OF 2 JOHN

I. GREETING (verses 1–3)

It is noticeable that the word 'truth' occurs three times in this greeting and this may be said to be the keynote of the Epistle. The triple benediction is grounded in truth and love.

II. WALKING IN THE TRUTH (verses 4–6)

The combination of truth and love is again found in this section, and the latter is mentioned as in the first Epistle as not a new commandment.

III. ERRONEOUS TEACHERS (verses 7–11)

1. The nature of their error is stated as a denial of the incarnation.

2. The rise of this error should lead to self-examination.

3. The exponents of the error should not be offered hospitality.

IV. CONCLUSION (verses 12, 13)

The writer mentions future plans and sends greetings.

CONTENTS OF 3 JOHN

I. GREETING (verse 1)

Gaius is named as the recipient.

II. COMMENDATION OF GAIUS (verses 2–8)

The writer not only loves the man, but prays for him and rejoices over him, for he is a follower of the truth. He gives him instructions about giving hospitality to the brethren and even to strangers.

III. CRITICISM OF DIOTREPHES (verses 9, 10)

This man is ambitious and arrogant and has acted in a high-handed manner which does not meet with the writer's approval.

IV. COMMENDATION OF DEMETRIUS (verses 11, 12)

He is highly spoken of both by the visiting brethren and by the writer himself.

V. CONCLUSION (verses 13–15)

Reference to future plans and the formal greetings bring the letter to a close.

ADDITIONAL NOTES

865. [3] For a careful discussion of the indications of an eyewitness, cf. J. R. W. Stott, *The Epistles of John* (TNT, 1964), pp. 26 ff.

871. [1] Cf. W. G. Kümmel (*INT*, 1965, p. 310), who maintains that 1 John shows no trace of the special doctrine of Cerinthus. He prefers to speak more generally of a developed form of Gnosticism.

873. [3] A recent writer, J. C. O'Neill, has analysed 1 John into a series of twelve poetic Jewish admonitions which have been modified to express a Christian point of view: *The Puzzle of 1 John* (1966).

874. [2] An ingenious explanation of the structure of 1 John has been made by P. J. Thompson (*Studia Evangelica*, II, 1964, pp. 487–492), who compares it with. Ps. 119.

875. [1] Cf. J. A. T. Robinson (*NTS*, 7, 1960, pp. 56 ff.) for the view that the readers were Diaspora Jews.

876. [2] Cf. Kümmel's criticisms of theories which involve the revision of an original *Vorlage* (*INT*, pp. 308 f.).

876. [3] K. Weiss (*ZNTW*, 58, 1967, pp. 247–255) examines the various uses in 1 John of the first person style. He interprets the first person plural in i. 1 ff. as timeless and identifies it with Christian tradition. Only in conditional sentences is 'we' personal, while the form 'this we know' reflects a distinction between genuine and non-genuine experience. Yet Weiss maintains the unity of the Epistle.

876. [4] For other more recent supporters of the view that John and 1 John are not from the same hand, mention may be made of E. Haenchen (see p. 875 n.2), and R. Bultmann, *Die drei Johannesbriefe*[7] (1967). But Kümmel (*INT*, p. 324) and Klijn (*INT*, p. 168) take the opposite view. Cf. also E. D. Freed (*ZNTW*, 55, 1964, pp. 156–197), who compares Jn. i–xx with the Johannine Epistles and thinks the variations of thought are insufficient to suggest different sources.

879. [1] For another writer who does not find stylistic criteria favourable to the view that John and 1 John stem from different authors, cf. A. P. Salom, *JBL*, LXXIV (1955), pp. 96 ff.

889. [3] In a study of the concept of 'truth' in the Johannine writings, R. Bergmeier (*ZNTW*, 57, 1966, pp. 93–100 suggests that the idea in 2 and 3 John differs from that in the Gospel and 1 John.

CHAPTER TWENTY-SEVEN

THE EPISTLE OF JUDE

I. CANONICITY

Not only in early times, but also increasingly in our own day doubt has been expressed regarding the authenticity of this Epistle. It is therefore necessary to give careful attention to the external evidence. There are traces of Jude in the letter of Clement of Rome, the *Shepherd of Hermas,* Polycarp, *Barnabas,*[1] and perhaps the *Didache,*[2] although it is impossible to say whether the slight allusions found in these writings are due to literary acquaintance. Polycarp's allusions are perhaps the most certain, while at a later time Athenagoras definitely knew the Epistle.[3] The Muratorian Canon mentions the Epistle of Jude together with two Epistles of John as being received, but the form of the statement may suggest that some had doubted their authenticity.[4] They are mentioned rather strangely after the spurious Marcionite works as in definite contrast to these.[5] Tertullian knew Jude and mentioned his use of Enoch.[6] Clement of Alexandria commented upon it in his *Hypotyposes,*[7] while Origen did not appear to question the authenticity himself, although he mentioned the doubts of others.[8] Later, at Alexandria, Didymus[9] found it necessary to defend Jude against its disputants (on the ground of its citing apocryphal books). Eusebius, at Caesarea, was less certain about its authenticity and classed it among the disputed books.[10] As in the case of other disputed books, Jude was not received into the Syriac Canon until a late date due, no doubt, to the extremely cautious approach of the Eastern Church.

[1] For the evidence, cf. C. Bigg, *St. Peter and St. Jude* (*ICC,* 1901), pp. 307, 308.
[2] Cf. *Didache,* ii. 7 and Jude 22f.; *Didache,* iii. 6 and Jude 8–10.
[3] Bigg (*op. cit.,* p. 307) considers that there is a 'clear reference to Jude'.
[4] Cf. Bigg, *op. cit.,* p. 14.
[5] After commenting on these 'fel enim cum melle misceri non congruit', the Fragment proceeds, 'Epistula sane Iudae et superscripti Johannis duas in Catholica habentur'.
[6] *De cultu fem.* i. 3.　　　　　[7] Cf. Eusebius, *HE,* vi. 14.
[8] Cf. Bigg, *op. cit.,* p. 306, for the evidence.　　[9] Cf. Bigg, *op. cit.,* p. 305.
[10] *HE,* iii. 25. 3. But in ii. 23. 25 he seems to imply that Jude with James should be classed as *notha* (spurious) because of lack of citation by name among the ancients.

Enough has been said to show that the Epistle had considerable use at an early period, and the later doubts which occurred must not be allowed to obscure this fact. The attestation for it is particularly strong and questionings appear to have arisen mainly because of the author's use of apocryphal books.

II. AUTHORSHIP

The writer introduces himself as 'Jude, the servant of Jesus Christ and brother of James' (verse 1). The first question that arises is the identification of this Jude. It was a common name and there would have been no need to identify him with any other Jude mentioned in the New Testament, were it not for the special phrase which shows his relationship to James. There can be no doubt that the author intended his readers to think of this James as James of Jerusalem, the Lord's brother.[1] This would have been a very natural assumption since James of Jerusalem was well known. It is also natural to suppose that the lesser-known Jude wished to commend himself on the strength of his brother's wider reputation. As seen in the discussion on James (p. 749) the other description ('a servant of Jesus Christ'), which prefers the idea of service to any claim of flesh-relationship to the Lord, need occasion no surprise. If we assume this identification is correct, we may suppose that Jude, as some of the other brothers of the Lord, engaged in itinerant preaching (1 Cor. ix. 5). It may well be, therefore, that the people whom Jude has in mind in this letter are those among whom he has been itinerating. So far the evidence for authorship seems fairly definite, but some objections have been raised to this identification.

1. The letter is supposed by some to be too late to make it possible that Jude, the Lord's brother, was author. The evidence of Hegesippus, recorded by Eusebius,[2] of Jude's grandsons being brought before Domitian is sometimes used to support a second-century origin for the Epistle.[3] It is cited as conclusive evidence that Jude could not have survived long enough to write this Epistle. But this line of argument is faulty. As J. B. Mayor[4] shows, it is at least probable that Jude, if still alive, was in his seventies at the commencement of Domitian's reign

---

[1] Cf. Mk. vi. 3 where a Jude is mentioned among the brethren of the Lord.
[2] *HE*, iii. 19.
[3] Cf. J. Moffatt, *ILNT*, p. 356.
[4] *The Epistle of St. Jude and the Second Epistle of St. Peter* (1907), p. cxlviii.

(i.e. AD 81),[1] and there is no ground, therefore, for disputing that this Jude could have been author, provided the Epistle was not written later than the ninth decade of the first century. But many scholars believe that it was.

2. The effect of dating on authorship can be considered only against a full discussion of the occasion of the Epistle (see discussion on pp. 909 ff.). But, anticipating the result of that discussion, we may dispute all the grounds on which a late dating is based. At most, the arguments cited (the description of the heretics and their connection with Gnosticism, the references to apostles as of an earlier generation and the fact that the faith is now well established) are capable of an interpretation which dates them well before the turn of the century and it is precarious, therefore, to pre-judge the question of authorship on this basis alone.[2]

3. Some have disputed the reading of verse 1, claiming that ἀδελφός is an interpolation and regarding the author as an unknown Jude who was *son* of an unknown James.[3] But this solution is not only unsupported by any textual evidence, but is altogether improbable.[4] For it would never have gained any general circulation unless it had been assumed that the James was the well-known Jerusalem leader of that name.[5] If that had been intended it would come under intentional pseudonymity, which seems highly unlikely when so obscure a name as Jude has been used. Moreover, this would be quite out of character in a pseudepigraphon, since in such writings one of the major factors was attribution to an already well-known name.[6]

---

[1] Bigg (*op. cit.*, p. 318) regards Jude as older than our Lord and thinks he could not have written much after AD 65. R. Knopf, *Die Briefe Petri und Judä* (1912), p. 207, similarly argues that by AD 70 Jude must have been an old man.

[2] As do E. F. Scott (*The Literature of the New Testament*, p. 226) and J. Moffatt (*op. cit.*, pp. 355, 356).

[3] So E. F. Scott, *op. cit.*, p. 225; T. Henshaw, *op. cit.*, p. 389. A. Harnack, *Die Chronologie der altchristlichen Literatur bis Eusebius* (1897), pp. 465ff., supposed the interpolation to extend to the whole phrase ἀδελφός δὲ 'Ιακώβου, added later to increase the authority of the writing.

[4] Cf. W. Michaelis, *Einleitung*, p. 303.

[5] It was Hegesippus who first referred to Jude as the brother of the Lord, as far as records go (cf. Bigg, *op. cit.*, p. 317).

[6] A pseudonymity theory for Jude is particularly difficult. Jülicher–Fascher (*Einleitung*, p. 216) are hard pushed to explain the choice of name and can do no better than suggest that the writer belonged to a group where James was revered, but was satisfied with a lesser member of the family for his pseudonym. R. Knopf (*op. cit.*, p. 207) makes no attempt to explain, but recognizing the difficulty of the omission of the title of honour (the Lord's brother) weakly suggests that for the author Christ, the heavenly Lord, had no brothers.*

4. Another idea which has been circulated is that the Jude was Jude the apostle, called Judas of James in Luke vi. 16; Acts i. 13.[1] It is supposed that 'Ιούδας 'Ιακώβου means Jude the brother of James rather than the son of James, but the latter rendering is the most probable. Moreover, our author not only does not claim to be an apostle, but seems to regard the apostles as apart from himself (verses 17, 18), although this statement does not conclusively exclude an apostolic author.[2]

5. Yet another hypothesis is that of Grotius[3] who identified this Jude with a second-century bishop of Jerusalem, who bore that name. This necessitated treating the words, 'brother of James', as equivalent to an episcopal title at Jerusalem. But there are no parallels to support this view.

There seems, therefore, no reason to suppose that this Jude was other than the Lord's brother.[4] In fact, although kinship with Christ was not stressed as a qualification of importance in the New Testament era,[5] Christians would undoubtedly treat the Lord's brethren with respect, and this would account, not only for the authority with which Jude writes, but also for the wide regard which the Epistle gained in the Christian Church.

III. DATE

The fact that the suggestions of scholars regarding the date of writing vary between AD 60 and 140 is a sufficient reminder that much of the so-called evidence on this subject amounts to little more than guesses.

---

[1] Bigg (*op. cit.*, p. 319) cites Keil as holding this view.

[2] There is even less to be said for E. C. Selwyn's idea that the Jude intended was the Judas Barsabbas who accompanied Silas as a messenger carrying the letter from the Jerusalem church (Acts xv. 22) (*The Christian Prophets and the Prophetic Apocalypse*, p. 148).

[3] Cf. Moffatt, *ILNT*, p. 357 n. Streeter, *The Primitive Church* (1929), pp. 178–180, considered Jude to be third bishop of Jerusalem on the slender evidence of a passage in the *Apostolic Constitutions.**

[4] Some, as in the case of James, have professed to find a difficulty in the character of the Greek, which is claimed to be too good for a Galilaean. But see the remarks on James, pp. 747 ff. Cantinat, in Robert-Feuillet's *Introduction*, II, p. 607, suggests that some Jewish Hellenist assisted in the writing of the Greek.

[5] Clement of Alexandria thought that Christians may have been in the habit of calling Jude 'the Lord's brother' and that Jude purposely called himself '*servant* of Jesus Christ and *brother* of James' to correct this usage (see Bigg's discussion of this, *op. cit.*, p. 318).

As it would not be profitable to discuss all the propositions, three main periods will be considered—the apostolic age, the latter part of the first century and the first part of the second century.

a. Evidence for an early date

This dating depends very largely on the decision reached regarding authorship. If Jude, the Lord's brother, was the author, the dating must naturally be confined to the reasonable limits of his life. Unfortunately we cannot be sure whether Jude was younger or older than our Lord, although the former is more probable. If the latter, he would be a son of a former marriage, but there is no evidence which clearly suggests the correctness of this view.[1] Assuming then that Jude was born in the early part of the Christian era, it would seem necessary to suppose that the Epistle could not have been later than about AD 70. But such an early dating has been rejected by many scholars for the reasons given below.[2]

b. Evidence against an early date

It is claimed that verse 3 relates to a time when Christianity was established sufficiently to have an orthodox body of doctrine ('our common salvation').[3] On the basis of this assumption it is supposed that the author could not have belonged to the first generation of Christians.[4] But this deduction is fallacious, for the expression 'common salvation' does not belong any more clearly to a late date than to an earlier. From the first there was a 'common' basis of belief among all Christians, although no doubt the contents of this common salvation became clearer as time went on. The exhortation to contend for the faith once for all delivered to the saints (verse 3) is equally indefinite regarding its timing. It may imply such development that 'faith' is now equivalent to a fixed body of doctrine, and orthodoxy is to be gauged by this standard. But the evidence does not demand a long time interval. If the apostle Paul could speak of a specific standard of teaching to which the Roman Christians had already been committed before

[1] This view is maintained by Bigg, *op. cit.*, p. 318.
[2] F. H. Chase (art., 'Jude, Epistle of', *HDB*, II, p. 804) suggested a date late in the apostolic age, particularly because he found echoes of the language of Colossians and Ephesians.
[3] Cf. E. F. Scott, *op. cit.*, p. 226.
[4] Cf. T. Henshaw, *op. cit.*, p. 389; J. Moffatt, *ILNT*, p. 357

he wrote to them (Rom. vi. 17), there is no need to relate this allusion in Jude to a much later period.[1] Our knowledge of the development of early Christian doctrine is after all far too limited to conclude with any confidence the precise date when Christians had a formal basis of faith. It would be strange indeed if the apostles themselves had never conceived the need for defining the common faith.[2]

The next consideration is the reference to the apostles in verse 17 ('But you must remember, beloved, the predictions of the apostles of our Lord Jesus Christ'—RSV). Does this mean that the apostolic age is past? This would certainly be a very natural interpretation and would imply some interval during which there has been a tendency to forget the apostolic teaching.[3] But it should be remembered that Jude is referring to apostolic predictions of scoffers who would arise in the Church, and the fulfilment of such predictions does not necessarily require a long period. It would seem, of course, that the readers were in possession of the apostolic writings to which this statement refers and this would require one of two alternatives: either the apostolic writings have by now been widely distributed, which would require an interval of time, or else some specific prediction is intended, which would suggest that an earlier epistle was sent by an apostle to the same people.[4] Zahn, who maintained that 2 Peter preceded Jude, strongly contended that Jude is here referring to that Epistle. This raises the whole question of the relation between the two Epistles (see discussion below, pp. 919 ff.), but few scholars have followed Zahn's opinion in this. 2 Peter iii. 3 would certainly furnish a very suitable antecedent to this reference. But the apostles are referred to in the plural and it is therefore somewhat difficult to confine the reference to one particular writing.

Leaving aside for the moment Zahn's interpretation, it is, of course,

[1] Cf. J. B. Mayor (op. cit., pp. 61f.) for a full discussion of Paul's approach in its bearing on the present passage.
[2] The word 'common' (κοινή) has been understood somewhat differently as pointing to a time when the opposition between Jewish and Gentile Christianity had passed (cf. Feine-Behm, op. cit., p. 253). This is possible, but is probably too restricted an interpretation. If true, however, it could not require a date later than Ephesians, where the middle wall of partition is already demolished.
[3] Cf. E. F. Scott, op. cit., p. 226.
[4] A third possibility would be to suppose that the readers had actually heard the apostles speak (cf. J. W. C. Wand, op. cit., p. 190). But some literary reference seems more probable.

true that more than one of the apostles forecast the rise of scoffers and trouble-makers and it seems, therefore, to have been a general expectation in the Church. At the same time Jude appears to be making a specific quotation and evidently has in mind one particular statement which he regarded as fully representative of the whole group. To cite Peter in this way would be most natural and so far supports Zahn's view. It is difficult, at least, to make any late dating depend on an interpretation of this verse.[1]

Another problem is the identification of the false teachers who have crept in unawares (verses 4f.). Many scholars have confidently pronounced these to be Gnostics and have, therefore, relegated the Epistle to the second century.[2] The connection of these teachers with Gnosticism is more fully discussed below (p. 914), but in view of the caution with which many scholars are now pronouncing on the limits of Gnosticism, and in view of the need for a clearer distinction between developed Gnosticism and incipient Gnosticism, it is unsafe to base calculations of date on such evidence.

It is further maintained that the description of the false teachers bears a close resemblance to passages in the Pastoral Epistles. If these latter are dated late, this line of argument would require a still later date for Jude.[3] But since there are good reasons for assigning an early date to the Pastorals,[4] these descriptions in Jude constitute no difficulty. Once again evidence of this kind is so governed by other considerations that different minds form different estimates of it. Clearly it can form no certain basis for dating.

To conclude, it is not possible to be very precise on the matter of dating. The most specific evidence is drawn from the probable life-

[1] J. W. C. Wand (*op. cit.*, p. 188) rightly points out that there is no need to suppose that all the apostles were now dead.

[2] So E. F. Scott (*loc. cit.*) confidently asserts, 'The type of Gnosticism attacked in the Epistle is one which came into existence considerably after Apostolic times.' But no evidence is produced in support. Moffatt (*ILNT*, pp. 353ff.), after surveying the evidence, is more cautious and agrees with Harnack in describing the teaching as 'the incipient phases of some local, possibly syncretistic, development of libertinism upon Gnostic lines'. But such a tendency is almost impossible to date with any certainty.

[3] J. Moffatt (*op. cit.*, p. 355) suggested that Jude 17 referred to 2 Tim. iii. 1f. and 1 Tim. iv. 1ff. T. Henshaw (*op. cit.*) finds similarities not only with the Pastorals but also with Ignatius' writings.

[4] Cf. the present writer's *The Pastoral Epistles* (*TNT*, 1957), pp. 16 ff., and see pp. 584 ff. above.

span of Jude, if he were the Lord's brother. Bigg[1] thought this fixed a limit of about AD 65, because he accepted the theory that Jude was older than our Lord. But others,[2] who regard him as younger, find it possible to extend the period to AD 80. It is difficult to be more precise than to suppose a date somewhere between AD 65 and 80. Advocates of the theory that Jude combats developed Gnosticism naturally date the Epistle well into the second century,[3] but many who do not identify Jude as the Lord's brother are more cautious and date the Epistle at the turn of the century.[4] Once accept an unknown author and anyone's guess becomes as valid as another's.

IV. THE FALSE TEACHERS

This short Epistle contains a number of details regarding the trouble-makers, which enable a picture to be drawn of them, but which are insufficient to ensure a close alignment with other known heresies. These facts will first be set out under the two categories of doctrine and practice, and then the implications will be discussed.

Under the heading of doctrine there is not a great deal of evidence, but what there is is highly significant. In verse 4, Jude says that these teachers are denying the one Master and Lord, Jesus Christ, and in this they are in line with such heresies as were influencing the Colossian church. Since the majority of heresies introduce errors regarding the person of Christ, this feature alone offers little assistance in tracing the origin or connections of these false teachers. It could even be that Jude means that their licentiousness is in fact denying Christ, without thinking of any doctrinal error, but the two things usually go together.

Lying behind their immoral practices was a fundamental misconception of the Christian doctrine of grace. They were essentially libertines who disregarded the restraints of God's grace (verse 4) and considered that immoral indulgence was perfectly legitimate. Another

---

[1] Cf. op. cit., p. 315. R. Leconte (Les épîtres catholiques, 1953, p. 49) dates the Epistle rather less specifically as during the last years of the apostolic age.

[2] E.g. J. B. Mayor, op. cit., p. cxlv. T. Zahn (INT, II, p. 255) prefers c. AD 75.

[3] J. Moffatt (op. cit., p. 357) cites many older scholars who maintained this view (i.e. dates ranging from AD 130 to 160), but the external evidence for attestation makes such a theory impossible. E. J. Goodspeed (INT, p. 347) dates it about AD 125.

[4] So H. Windisch-H. Preisker, Der katholischen Briefe, p. 48; W. Michaelis, op. cit., p. 303.

feature which touches upon doctrinal error is their preference for their own dreamings (verse 8) rather than for God's revelation. These dreamings may be ecstasies during which they claimed to receive messages from God, but the whole method was fundamentally opposed to God's method of making Himself known, for it involved some definite defiling of the flesh (verse 8). From verse 19 it would be a fair inference that their doctrine of the Holy Spirit was sadly wrong, in fact entirely absent. It has been suggested that these people were making themselves out to be spiritual in conformity with the well-known Gnostic description of higher initiates, and in all probability Jude is making it clear that, from a Christian point of view, they are devoid of the Spirit. One concluding feature is their doctrine of angels, to which there appears to be a reference in verse 8, where Jude mentions their insolence towards the glorious ones (δόξαι). But all that can be inferred from this is that they were critical of the orthodox doctrine of angels.

Their moral culpability is much more plainly illustrated. Indeed, it seems to have been of such a character that Jude is deeply shocked by it. The people are acting worse than irrational animals (verse 10, RSV). They are licentiously indulging in unnatural lust (verses 4, 7, 16, 18). Their passions apparently rule them. They have consequently become defiled (verses 8, 23). Not only so, they are also discontented, arrogant, avaricious (verse 16). In some way, they were using their very errors to further their own financial gains.

So much for their characteristics.[1] It remains to enquire what the historical circumstances of these people were. From verse 4 it would seem that these teachers were, at least outwardly, members of the church. They were affecting it from within in spite of the fact that their whole approach was opposed to true Christianity. Had they been allowed to continue they would have destroyed the church, which no doubt accounts for Jude's severity. The next question is whether these teachers were Jews or Gentiles, but this is easily answered since none of their characteristics is prominent, if found at all, in Jewish Christianity. Because the author cites Jewish pseudepigrapha it cannot at once be inferred that all his readers are Jewish, although it may well suggest that he himself is. A further matter that should be noted is the

---

[1] T. Zahn (*INT*, II, pp. 242ff.) has a very full discussion on these false teachers, including some valuable comments on exegetical details. Cf. also H. Werdermann, *Die Irrlehrer des Judas- und 2 Petrusbriefes* (1913).

fact that Jude represents these men as being a direct fulfilment of an earlier prophecy (verses 17, 18) and as having been already designated for condemnation (verse 4). Whatever these statements may specifically refer to, it is quite certain that Jude feels that the Christians should not have been taken unawares. Moreover, it should also be noted that the mention of Cain and Balaam may give some indication of the connection of these teachers with other heretical movements, especially as the latter is mentioned in Revelation ii. 14 in connection with both false teaching and immorality in the church of Pergamum. Balaam appears to have been an all-inclusive symbol of heretical doctrine and practice.[1]

Some have seen in these allusions definite connections with certain second-century Gnostic sects. Pfleiderer[2] argued that Jude was combating the Carpocratians, a mid-second-century sect noted for their immoral practices, particularly their advocacy of promiscuous sexual indulgence. Clement of Alexandria[3] noted the close connection between Jude's false teachers and this sect, but regarded Jude's references as prophetic. Undoubtedly the description in Jude would fit any heresy in which immoral practices played a major part, but this similarity alone is not sufficient to identify Jude's references with any particular sect. The same goes for attempts to connect them up with the Ophites, of which a branch was called 'Cainites'. These people appear to have reversed good and evil and it is not surprising that their behaviour conformed to immoral patterns. But these sects, as far as our knowledge of them goes, belong to a date too late for our Epistle and we are obliged, therefore, to suppose that in the first century there were adumbrations of the moral degeneracy which was to reach its climax in these later sects.

As with the other heretical movements or tendencies which are reflected in the New Testament, so with Jude's false teachers, we must regard them as embryonic forms of later developments. They appear to present us with a kind of cross-section of movements which were inevitable as soon as Christianity had made a deep enough impact on the world of pagan thought and behaviour out of which it grew. As far as Jude is concerned, he saw at once that this subversive move-

---

[1] Cf. J. B. Mayor, *op. cit.*, p. clxxvi.

[2] Mentioned by J. W. C. Wand, *op. cit.*, p. 211, from his *Urchristentum*, pp. 835ff.

[3] *Strom.* iii. 2. 6–10. Cf. also Irenaeus (*Adv. Haer.* i. 25. 1), who mentions that the adherents of Simon Magus and the Carpocratians scoffed at angels.

ment was highly dangerous and that the only possible treatment for it was downright condemnation.

It will be noted that many of the characteristics of the movement in Jude are found equally strongly in 2 Peter, but a few striking differences may be seen. The author of 2 Peter is less drastic in his approach towards those whom he combats and it may well be that the error has less of a grip.[1] In 2 Peter the special targets for attack are the newly converted (2 Pet. ii. 18, 19), but this is less clear in Jude. Moreover, Jude says nothing about these teachers' wrong handling of the Scriptures, which is prominent in 2 Peter iii. 15, 16, nor does he mention erroneous teaching about the *parousia* (cf. 2 Pet. iii. 1ff.). Both writers, however, in dealing with the heretics make much of the judgments of God, especially illustrating their theme from the Old Testament, although Jude omits to mention the flood, which receives special attention in 2 Peter iii. Whereas the two Epistles deal with very closely related situations, the differences should put us on our guard against too readily identifying them.

V. PURPOSE

When Jude began to write, his purpose was to produce a treatise on the 'common salvation' for the edification of his readers (verse 3). Since he speaks of his eagerness (σπουδή) to do this, it is abundantly clear that a far more pressing need arose before which the original purpose had to be dropped. This former purpose must not, however, be entirely lost sight of in considering the circumstances of the readers. Jude evidently recognized their need of some constructive teaching about the Christian faith before he was faced with the problem of the insidious false teachers.

The nature of the error, described in the last section, presented an immediate challenge to Jude who devoted almost the entire Epistle to an all-out denunciation of the false teachers. At the close (verses 17ff.) he suddenly seems to realize the need for being positive in his approach to his readers, and gives a series of exhortations which were clearly intended to offset the evil effects of the false teachers. Indeed, even these exhortations finish with a direct challenge to them to rescue any who are not yet in the grip of the evil, like brands snatched from the fire

---

[1] J. W. C. Wand (*op. cit.*, p. 209) interprets the change differently, maintaining that by the time of 2 Peter the error has gained such a grip that Jude's forthright approach would be less effective.

(verse 23). There is little theological content in the letter, for the purpose was essentially practical. Jude does not give any reasoned refutation of the tenets held by the false teachers, as Paul did when dealing with the Colossian heresy. Their moral lapses were too blatantly obvious to need such refutation. They deserved only unconditional denunciation. Yet it should be pointed out that Jude regarded his own Epistle as an exhortation (verse 3, παρακαλῶν) exactly as did the writers of Hebrews and 1 Peter (Heb. xiii. 22; 1 Pet. v. 12). His main purpose was to warn rather than to condemn.

VI. DESTINATION

The address is so vaguely expressed that it gives no indication whatever of the locality of the readers. Those who are 'called', 'beloved' and 'kept' (verse 2, RSV) might be Christians anywhere and the question immediately arises whether Jude intended his letter to be a general circular.[1] This seems to be excluded by his apparent acquaintance with certain specific people whom he knows to have crept into the church by guile and whose behaviour is so vividly portrayed that it suggests first-hand acquaintance with the false teachers too. It can hardly be doubted that Jude has in mind a concrete situation, however much he may have supposed that the Church generally needed the same message.

Because of the use of Jewish Apocrypha, it has been maintained by some that the destination must be placed in a Jewish setting.[2] But this evidence points more to the author than to the readers and any attempt to fix the region (as, for instance, in Syria) must be regarded as purely speculative. Nevertheless, certain data point to a district within the region of Palestine. The probability is that verses 17, 18 mean that these readers had heard at least some of the apostles and that they had some acquaintance with Paul. On the strength of these considerations Wand[3] suggests Antioch and this seems as good a suggestion as any. Some scholars[4] have maintained a Gentile destination because of the improbability of a Greek epistle being sent to Jewish readers, but this would only apply to Palestine. The syncretistic heresy combated might suggest Gentile rather than Jewish Christian readers, but there is insufficient information about this period to decide. If Wand's suggestion is

[1] T. Henshaw (op. cit., p. 390) understands it in this way.
[2] Cf. M. Meinertz, Einleitung[5] (1950), p. 258.
[3] Op. cit., p. 194.   [4] Cf. R. Knopf, op. cit., p. 203.

valid both Jews and Gentiles would, of course, be involved and this theory is probably correct.

VII. USE OF APOCRYPHAL BOOKS

This brief Epistle is alone among the New Testament books in citing a Jewish apocryphal work, the book of Enoch. It also appears to make references to another pseudepigraphon, the *Assumption of Moses*,[1] although no text has been preserved which contains the account of the dispute between the archangel Michael and the devil over the body of Moses (verse 9).

When in verse 14 Jude refers to Enoch, the seventh from Adam, as prophesying and then cites words which are preserved in 1 Enoch i. 9 almost *verbatim*, there can be very little doubt that he was making a direct citation from the apocryphal book, which he assumes his readers will be not only familiar with, but will also highly respect. Some have supposed that Jude regards Enoch as Scripture, but the word προφητεύω is used on only one occasion in the New Testament for a citation from the Old Testament.[2] Nevertheless, if it cannot be demonstrated that Jude regards Enoch as Scripture, he clearly holds it in high esteem and considers it legitimate to cite it in support of his argument. This has been regarded by many, ancients as well as moderns, as a difficulty. How can a writer who cites an apocryphal book be inspired? Tertullian[3] gets over the difficulty by maintaining the authenticity of Enoch, but in this he is unsupported by any others. Jerome[4] gives expression to a quite different point of view when he mentions that the doubts which had arisen about the Epistle were due to its using an apocryphal book in an authoritative way. This latter approach was much more widespread. Some modern exegetes, wishing to preserve the integrity of Jude, but imagining that this would be impaired if the Enoch citation were admitted, deny the latter and claim that oral tradition had preserved a true saying of Enoch and that Jude is citing the tradition, not the book.[5] But under this theory the book must have included the oral

---

[1] This book is named in several canonical lists. It is quoted by Clement of Alexandria and Origen and was mentioned by Didymus. (Cf. R. H. Charles, *The Assumption of Moses*, 1897, pp. 107–110, for the Greek fragments.)

[2] Cf. Mt. xv. 7 (Mk. vii. 6) which uses it to introduce a citation from Is. xxix. 13. The cognate noun, προφήτης, could even be used for a heathen poet (Tit. i. 12).

[3] *Idol.* xv; *Apol.* xxii.   [4] *De Vir. Ill.* iv.

[5] Cf. the view of J. Stafford Wright, *EQ*, xix (1947), p. 102. Most of the older conservative commentators took the same view (cf. H. Alford, *The Greek Testament*,[4] 1871, IV, p. 198, who mentions this as possible).

tradition in a form almost directly in agreement with that cited by Jude. Yet since the book of Enoch, at least in its major parts, was written long before the Epistle of Jude, this theory is highly improbable. It could hardly have arisen apart from a desire to shield Jude from doing what was considered impossible for an inspired writer.

But is it possible to maintain Jude's dependence on Enoch and still leave in no question his inspiration, or his right to a place in the Canon? The difficulties are not insuperable if Jude is not citing Enoch as Scripture, and there is no conclusive evidence that he is. He seems rather to be recognizing that what Enoch had said has turned out to be a true prophecy in view of the ungodly conduct of these false teachers. On the other hand, when Jude specifically calls Enoch 'the seventh from Adam', this would appear to indicate that he regarded the book as a true work of the ancient Enoch, in which case he would certainly have regarded the book as a part of Scripture. But against this it must be noted that in the book of Enoch itself Enoch is twice mentioned as being in the seventh generation from Adam, a description obviously added for identification purposes.[1] Whatever the answer to this problem, it is clear that Jude regards the words he cites as invested with some authority, although this need give no indication of what he thought of the rest of the book. This may be indicated by the claim that he echoes its language in other parts of his Epistle. F. H. Chase,[2] for instance, sets out parallels with words and phrases from fourteen other verses in Jude, and if these can be maintained it would be evidence enough of the dominating influence of the book of Enoch on the author's mind. But many of the parallels are very slight and have weight only on the prior assumption that Jude definitely used the book as a basis.

The use of the *Assumption of Moses* is of interest as adding further evidence of Jude's regard for non-canonical accounts. It is unfortunate that in this case the original text has been lost and there is no means of verifying the extent of Jude's indebtedness. But since Clement, Origen and Didymus all assume that Jude used such a book, it is quite possible that he quoted it. He may, on the other hand, be citing a traditional story, which was the basis of the apocryphal book. The evidence is

[1] In Enoch lx. 8 (from the Book of Noah), xxxvii. 1ff.; cf. also the symbolic significance of the number seven in xciii ('I was born the seventh in the first week').

[2] *HDB*, iii, pp. 801, 802.

insufficient to be certain. But in any case the allusion tells us nothing about Jude's view of Jewish pseudepigrapha generally, but only of his acceptance of the validity of the particular incident to which he alludes.

To conclude this comment, it should be noted that the mere citation of non-canonical books cannot be construed as a point unfavourable to the canonicity of the Epistle. Paul refers to a rabbinical midrash in 1 Corinthians x. 4, a heathen poet in his speech at Athens (Acts xvii. 28), and names the magicians who withstood Pharoah as Jannes and Jambres (2 Tim. iii. 8), evidently drawn from some non-canonical source, but his Epistles are not for that reason regarded as of inferior value as inspired literature.

VIII. RELATION TO 2 PETER

In order to deal adequately with the relationship between Jude and 2 Peter, it would be necessary to set out in detail the parallel texts and to indicate the verbal agreements. Such an examination would not only fall outside the scope of our present purpose, but would be unnecessary since it has already been thoroughly carried out.[1] All that is possible here is to give some indication of the nature of the relationship and of the various theories that have been proposed to account for it.

a. Its nature

That the relationship is very close is clear from the most casual comparison of the Epistles. Most of 2 Peter ii is paralleled in Jude. There are also parallels in the other two chapters.[2] The common material deals almost wholly with the false teachers and only incidentally touches on other subject-matter. 2 Peter contains more positive Christian teaching, while Jude concentrates on denunciations. That the two groups of false teachers were closely allied is undeniable, but it has already been shown (see pp. 912 ff. above) that they were not absolutely identical. The problem at once arises, therefore, how it came about that both Epistles use such similar descriptions of these people[3] and the natural conclusion is that one has used the other. This has given rise to two different theories of dependence, of which the view that Jude is the basis of 2 Peter is much more widely held than the reverse. But there is

---

[1] This is most clearly done in Mayor's Commentary where the parallel Greek texts are set out side by side.

[2] The main parallels are between Jude 4–18 and 2 Pet. ii. 1–18 and iii. 1–3.

[3] The similarities often stretch to the parallel use of unusual words, striking metaphors and similar Old Testament illustrations.

a third possibility—that both have used the same source, incorporating the materials into their Epistles in different ways. These three possibilities will be considered in turn.

b. The hypothesis that Jude is prior

1. Since Jude is briefer than 2 Peter, it is considered more probable that this was the source rather than the borrower. There would be an obvious point in an enlargement of an earlier work where the additions would enable the author to append his own special features. But the opposite is less easy to imagine, especially when the briefer Epistle appears merely to extract a portion of the longer and append little more than a salutation and a doxology. There seems to be no adequate reason for the publication of the shorter Epistle at all if 2 Peter already exists, and still less so under so obscure a name as Jude. This argument is undoubtedly a strong one for the priority of Jude.

2. A comparison between the manner in which both approach the problem of the false teachers would also seem to confirm the priority of Jude. His treatment gives the appearance of greater spontaneity. He goes right into the subject without the long introduction that 2 Peter thinks necessary. Moreover, he refers to the trouble-makers as if he has already had first-hand acquaintance with them, whereas in 2 Peter the tenses of the verbs vary between the future and the present.[1] This argument is not as strong as the first, but deserves consideration.

3. Jude is harsher than 2 Peter, which suggests that the latter recognized the need to tone down the model. However, while it may seem easier to explain the change in this way, the reverse relationship is not absolutely excluded. It is at least conceivable that Jude considered that 2 Peter's rather softer approach needed more strength in it when applied to his own particular reader-constituency. There is no certain criterion for deciding whether harshness must always be prior. Common experience knows only too well that both harshness and softness can at times claim priority.

4. Supposing Jude to be prior, it is possible to suggest in some cases of minor changes the reason for the modification in 2 Peter. One example will suffice. In 2 Peter ii. 17 and Jude 12, 13 occur the combination of waterless 'clouds' carried by winds and the reference to outer darkness. In 2 Peter the darkness is reserved for those likened to clouds and mists but in Jude it is reserved for those likened to

---

[1] See further comment on these tenses on pp. 923 f.

wandering stars. Whereas the former, according to most commentators, is inappropriate, the latter exactly fits. It may well be explained as 2 Peter's telescoping of Jude's metaphors, causing the reference to the meteors to be omitted, but if Jude is using 2 Peter it would have to be supposed that he noticed the inappropriate metaphor and adjusted it in his own production, a less likely (though nevertheless not impossible) procedure.[1] Such occurrences could be multiplied.

5. A far less probable line of argument is that which sees in some of 2 Peter's allusions indirect echoes of hints contained in Jude. Thus the number seven is mentioned in both Jude 14 and 2 Peter ii. 5 (see RSV),[2] but the totally different contexts make any argument based on this seem fanciful (cf. also the 'building up' metaphor found in 2 Peter i. 5–7 and Jude 20, but again the connection is extremely slight).

6. Jude's use of apocryphal books and the absence of any direct citation from them in 2 Peter is thought to be an almost conclusive argument that Jude is prior and that 2 Peter has intentionally excised these references because of their unorthodox character. The example which is generally cited in support is 2 Peter ii. 11 and its parallel in Jude 9. Jude refers to the archangel Michael, but 2 Peter only vaguely to 'angels' and, according to Wand,[3] 'blurs the point of the railing at dignities'. Similarly 2 Peter's reference to 'great swelling words' (ii. 18) is thought to be an 'unnecessary expansion' (Wand) of Jude 16, culled probably from the same apocryphal book. But this method of argument is not conclusive, for Jude might have cited some specific example known to him to illustrate 2 Peter's reference to angels. Nevertheless, there is something to be said for the argument that apart from Jude the reference in 2 Peter ii. 11 is barely intelligible. It is significant that 2 Peter contains no reference to the book of Enoch,[4] which Jude

[1] R. A. Falconer (*Exp.*, VI, vi, pp. 220, 221) argues with some force that Peter would hardly have emptied Jude's powerful metaphor of its picturesqueness had he been echoing it.

[2] J. B. Mayor (*op. cit.*, p. 192) finds a symbolic contrast between Noah as the eighth (in 2 Peter) and Enoch as the seventh (in Jude), but such a method of exegesis is by no means obvious or convincing.

[3] *Op. cit.*, p. 133.

[4] In spite of the efforts of some scholars to emend the text of 1 Pet. iii. 19 to include a reference to Enoch. Cf. J. Rendel Harris, *Exp.*, VI, v (1902), pp. 317–320; but against, cf. C. Clemen, *Exp.*, VI, vi, pp. 318ff. More recently, E. J. Goodspeed, *JBL*, LXXIII (1954), pp. 91, 92, maintains the emendation, against B. M. Metzger, *Theology To-day* (1946), p. 562.

formally cites. It may be possible to consider this as prudent on his part since Enoch was not regarded as Scripture, but it could equally well be explained by the author's ignorance of the book, or at least lack of interest in it.

7. A comparison of the theology of both Epistles led Mayor[1] to conclude for the priority of Jude. In references to God, for instance, certain periphrases which have a Hellenistic flavour are found in 2 Peter but not in Jude (cf. 2 Pet. i. 3, 4). While differences of emphasis may be noted in relation to the teaching on grace, apostasy, punishment, the possibility of repentance, and eschatology, yet it is difficult to use such data as indications of the priority of one Epistle.

8. Linguistically the Greek of Jude is less awkward than the Greek of 2 Peter.[2] Chase[3] argues that the use of parallel words and phrases in Jude is more natural than in 2 Peter, and this is considered an argument in support of Jude's priority. In other words it is considered more likely that the more polished language has been obscured by a writer less at home in Greek than that a more obscure style has been polished up by another writer. But this contention is open to challenge. Indeed, the opposite is generally assumed to be an argument for the priority of Mark over Matthew in examinations of the Synoptic problem. It is difficult, therefore, to attach much weight to such evidence.

c. *The hypothesis that 2 Peter is prior*

The three main advocates of this view are Spitta, Zahn and Bigg, but in more recent times their opinion has been very largely discounted. All three, contrary to most of the adherents of the view discussed above, maintained the Petrine authorship of 2 Peter and were, therefore, rather more disposed to consider it prior to Jude. The main reasons for this view are as follows:

1. It is first of all maintained that Jude makes reference to 2 Peter. This is based on a particular interpretation of Jude 4 and 17. The former verse mentions condemnation which had already been designated (οἱ πάλαι προγεγραμμένοι). This is understood to refer to an earlier

[1] *Op. cit.*, pp. xvi ff.
[2] Moulton and Howard, *A Grammar of New Testament Greek*, ii (1929), pp. 27f., contrast Jude, who was quite at home in Hellenistic idiom (citing the opinion of Mayor), and the author of 2 Peter, whose Greek is an artificial dialect learnt from books.
[3] *HDB*, ii, p. 803.

writing,[1] which may then be identified with 2 Peter, since that Epistle does in fact refer to condemnation on precisely the kind of people mentioned in Jude. Moreover, in Jude 17 the readers are exhorted to remember the apostles' predictions, and words are there cited which occur almost *verbatim* in 2 Peter iii. 3. Zahn maintained that in view of this evidence 'by the ordinary canons of criticism we should conclude that Jude knew and prized 2 Peter as an apostolic writing and made it the basis of parts of his letter'.[2] But this view has been criticized on the grounds first that πάλαι in Jude 4 means 'of old' and not 'lately', in which case the reference is to the book of Enoch (as in verses 14, 15) and not to 2 Peter[3]; and secondly that if a genuine 2 Peter were being referred to in Jude 17, why was not Peter mentioned by name? And why is the statement attributed to the apostles as a group?[4] And further, why is it introduced with the word ἔλεγον, which suggests habitual oral teaching? None of these objections is strong enough to overthrow the *possibility* that Jude refers to 2 Peter, although whether he is actually doing so is a different matter. The interpretation of πάλαι is impossible to decide with confidence, while Jude might conceivably have had a reason for grouping the apostles together. The context of verse 17 shows the statement against the background of 'loud-mouthed boasters' and the apostolic witness is evidently intended to be a conclusive contrast to this kind of thing. This type of plural is so frequently used in the New Testament that it seems to have been employed here quite generally, almost with an adjectival significance. It is obvious that *all* the apostles had not given expression to this precise statement, but all had endorsed it. In fact in 2 Peter iii. 3 the readers are exhorted to recall the predictions of the prophets and the commandment of the Lord through the apostles. Jude 17 looks like a combination of both statements.

2. The use of the future tense in 2 Peter and the present tense in Jude with reference to the false teachers is also thought to point to the priority of 2 Peter. What 2 Peter foresaw, Jude has now experienced. This would be a strong argument if 2 Peter had consistently used the

---

[1] So T. Zahn, *INT*, II, pp. 250f., 265.

[2] Cf. Zahn, *loc. cit.* The same contention was made by Spitta, *Der Zweite Brief des Petrus und der Brief des Judas* (1885), pp. 145, 146.

[3] Cf. Wand, *op. cit.*, p. 198; Mayor, *op. cit.*, pp. 24, 25. The latter stresses the fourfold occurrence of ἀσεβεῖς and its cognates in Jude 14, 15.

[4] Cf. F. H. Chase, *op. cit.*, p. 802.

future in preference to the present (but cf. ii. 10, 17, 18, iii. 5 where the present is used). The generally held interpretation of the usage in 2 Peter is that the author assumes a prophetic rôle to add verisimilitude to his message, but he could not sustain it.[1] But a better explanation of the mixture of tenses is the supposition that the beginnings of the movement are already visible, but that further developments are anticipated in the future. In that case the tenses of Jude would be more intelligible if subsequent to 2 Peter.[2]

3. It is claimed to be inexplicable why an 'apostolic' writer (i.e. Peter, or an admirer of Peter, if 2 Peter is not genuine) should take over so much of the writing of an obscure man like Jude, whereas it is highly intelligible why the lesser man should be influenced by the greater.[3] This is another kind of argument whose value is difficult to assess, for there is no reason why Peter himself should not have borrowed from others (indeed he appears to have been influenced by Paul, see pp. 785f.). Nevertheless, if both Epistles are genuine, it may be said that we should expect the writing of Peter to be basic to Jude rather than vice versa. But the argument should not be allowed too much weight especially on the strength of Jude's obscurity, for as a brother of the Lord he may have been well known to a fairly wide circle of Christians.[4]

4. None of the above arguments is conclusive for the priority of 2 Peter, although each could support it. In the final analysis, priority can be decided only on minute comparisons of style, but even here the criteria are almost wholly subjective. To take the reference to railing at dignitaries as an example (Jude 8; cf. 2 Pet. ii. 10), whereas Wand[5] considers 2 Peter blurs Jude's point (as mentioned above), Bigg[6] considers Jude has 'altered and spoiled St. Peter's point and quite destroyed the parallel'. Obviously both approach the data having already made up their minds in which direction the dependence lies and both have reasonable arguments in support. A full-scale stylistic comparison between the two Epistles would not lead to any more certain criteria. Does this then mean that the examination of the whole question must

---

[1] Cf. Wand, op. cit., p. 132.

[2] Another possibility is to suppose that Peter knew of the activity of the false teachers through Jude's Epistle and writes to warn a different reader-circle of the approaching threat, an intelligible suggestion in favour of Jude's priority.

[3] Mayor (op. cit., p. xxiii), who admits that probability would favour this latter alternative, is not prepared to press it because of such well-known borrowers as Milton and Handel, who drew from the works of lesser men.

[4] Cf. Wand, op. cit., p. 132.   [5] Ibid., p. 133.   [6] Op. cit., p. 217.

end in deadlock? Some have proposed a *via media*, which must next be considered.

d. The hypothesis that both used a common source

It is a tempting solution of the difficulty to suggest that both writers are drawing from an existing tract and that this accounts for their similarities. Such a solution has not found many advocates because it is asumed that the similarities are too close to be accounted for in this way and because the situation in both Epistles seems too concrete. Zahn[1] further objected to this idea because it would involve Jude in making references to a lost epistle (i.e. in Jude 17), which was also used by 2 Peter, and this seemed to him a less acceptable solution than to regard the earlier epistle as 2 Peter itself.

The whole idea was worked out particularly by E. I. Robson,[2] who considered that several independent tracts of this nature were circulat- ing (see discussion on the unity of 2 Peter, pp. 851ff.) and that both writers have incorporated one of these in their writings, with editorial adapta- tions. It is certainly possible that some general writing, dealing with moral perverters and their condemnation, may well have been circu- lating, and there is nothing intrinsically unlikely in the idea that both Peter and Jude may have drawn from it. But Jude is more difficult in this respect than 2 Peter, since he seems to refer back to earlier *apostolic* teaching, and if the tract postulated were an apostolic tract, it seems incredible that it needed to be incorporated into two other writings to ensure its preservation. Moreover, did Jude take it over as it stood, add- ing only salutation and doxology? If so, what was the point of it? There seems no satisfactory answer.

e. Conclusion

The problem, like so many other purely literary problems of New Testament criticism, must be left unresolved. It does not affect the authenticity problem of either letter.[3] But before assuming that no definite solution can be found, there are one or two considerations which ought to be given more weight than they are generally ascribed.

[1] *INT*, II, p. 266.   [2] *Studies in the Second Epistle of St. Peter* (1915).
[3] Some scholars have maintained the authenticity of 2 Peter, while at the same time admitting the priority of Jude (cf. E. M. B. Green, *2 Peter Reconsidered*, 1961, p. 11). Zahn (*op. cit.*, p. 285) cites Hug, Wiesinger, Weiss and Maier among earlier scholars who adopted this position.

The first is to decide which hypothesis furnishes the more reasonable occasion for the production of both letters. If Peter wrote 2 Peter for a certain constituency and shares the contents of his letter with Jude, suggesting that the latter use the passages about the false teachers in a letter to be sent to his own constituency, where the trouble-makers were not only threatening but were actively operative, all the phenomena would be accounted for. This is Bigg's[1] solution and appears to be, at least, a reasonable probability. The other alternative, if both are genuine, is to suppose that Jude took the initiative and sent his production in a similar way to Peter. But if one or both of these letters were pseudonymous, the wholesale borrowing is less easy to explain. It was not the normal practice of pseudepigraphists to incorporate other material in this way, however indebted the authors were to earlier works, and no very satisfactory reason has yet been given for such a procedure in this case. An admirer of Peter, who published a letter in his master's name, but incorporated into it almost the whole of Jude, looks more like a figment of imagination than a real person, for it is difficult to conceive why he kept closer to Jude than to 1 Peter. If, on the other hand, a pseudo-Jude extracted portions of a pseudo-Petrine Epistle in order to publish the extract under the name of a less auspicious pseudonym, his mysterious purpose becomes all the more obscure.

One concluding comment is necessary. The unity of 2 Peter (see pp. 851 ff.) means that if Peter used Jude he adapted it to fit in with his own style, so that no grammatical seam joining his 'source' to his own additions is now visible.[2] He has, therefore, incorporated his source into his own mind. And this phenomenon would obviously be easier to conceive in the reverse direction, where less 'seaming' was necessary. The vocabulary too tells rather more in favour of 2 Peter's priority, for Jude uses many words not used by Peter and this is readily intelligible if a new mind is brought to bear on Peter's material.[3] Yet the

---

[1] Op. cit., p. 316. If, as Bigg suggests, Peter sent his letter to Jude because he was alarmed at the spread of the errors, this may account for Jude's change of purpose (verse 3).

[2] Cf. Bigg's careful study of the grammar (op. cit., pp. 224, 310).

[3] It is often overlooked that although the parallels between these Epistles stretch to a wide range of subject-matter, yet verbal agreements are not impressive. If statistics are any guide, the following data may supply some indication. Out of the parallel passages comprising 2 Peter i. 2, 12, ii. 1–4, 6, 10–12, 15–18, iii. 2, 3 and Jude 2, 4–13, 17, 18, the former contain 297 words and the latter 256 words, but they share only 78 in common. This means that if 2 Peter is the borrower he has

Epistles are too short to lead to certainty. The verdict must remain open.

IX. LITERARY CHARACTER

Jude's language is influenced by his familiarity with the Old Testament. Chase[1] even suggested that the writer was steeped in the LXX, but Bigg[2] disagreed with this judgment. Certainly Jude's mind is full of Old Testament allusions although he does not directly cite from it. It is a fair assumption that he was well acquainted with its text, since it served as the Scriptures of the early Church. His style has a vividness and vigour which well expresses his intense abhorrence of the immorality he has observed. At times it has a poetical ring (cf. verses 12, 13). Yet the Epistle is not the work of a literary artist, but of a passionate Christian prophet. Chase[3] has pointed out that the Greek lacks the ruggedness of broken sentences (as in Paul), the power of epigram (as in James) and oratorical persuasiveness (as in Hebrews). The writer's vocabulary is stronger than his power to connect up his separate statements. Chase concludes that 'the writer's Greek is a strong and weighty weapon over which, however, he has not a ready command'. A special feature is the love of threes,[4] which, with the carefully constructed doxology, points to an orderly mind.[5] In the way he ends his Epistle with a doxology Jude shows kinship with Paul in his Roman letter. These two letters are, in fact, the only two with this form of elaborate ending in the New Testament.

changed 70% of Jude's language and added more of his own. Whereas if Jude borrowed from 2 Peter, the percentage of alteration is slightly higher, combined with a reduction in quantity. Clearly there can be no question of direct copying or of editorial adaptation. It is also significant that out of twelve parallel sections, Jude's text is verbally longer than 2 Peter's on five occasions, showing that neither author can be considered more concise than the other. The passages showing the greatest verbal agreement are 2 Pet iii. 2, 3 and Jude 17, 18 (16 words), the very passages which Zahn maintained prove that Jude was citing 2 Peter. Perhaps at this point the author relied on his 'copy' rather than his memory. The only other passages where extended verbal agreement is found are 2 Pet. ii. 12 and Jude 10, 12a (14 words), the only passages incidentally where the order of the two Epistles slightly diverges (Jude 11 corresponds to 2 Pet. ii. 15, 16).

[1] *HDB*, II, p. 800.   [2] *Op. cit.*, p. 311.   [3] *Ibid.*, p. 801.
[4] Cf. Moffatt's discussion (*ILNT*, p. 347) and Mayor's much fuller treatment (*op. cit.*, p. lvi).
[5] Chase (*loc. cit.*) suggests that Jude may be echoing words which had been repeated so often for liturgical purposes that they had acquired a set form, a not impossible idea.

It is not certain that the author was acquainted with Paul's writings, although some scholars[1] have confidently asserted this. Literary dependence is difficult to establish on the basis of isolated phrases, which after all might be no more than language common among Christians. At any rate no certain conclusion can be reached over this.

X. THE VALUE OF THE EPISTLE

Perhaps more than any other New Testament book, the Epistle of Jude is assumed to have little or no permanent value and is, therefore, virtually excluded from the practical, as distinct from the formal, canon of the many sections of the Church. E. F. Scott[2] can find little permanent religious value except in the concluding doxology. Henshaw[3] takes up a similar position, but attaches to it a value for historical purposes. But to deny a permanent spiritual value to the letter is to miss its main message, which is relevant to any period of history. Indeed, Jude illustrates his theme of divine judgment on evil practices by quoting examples from the past. If the examples Jude cites for his own day (Israelites, Sodom and Gomorrah, Cain, Balaam, Korah) had relevance then, his whole Epistle must have relevance now, unless the nature of divine justice and the character of human lasciviousness and kindred evils has changed. As long as men need stern rebukes for their practices, the Epistle of Jude will remain relevant. Its neglect reflects more the superficiality of the generation that neglects it than the irrelevance of its burning message.

CONTENTS

I. GREETING (verses 1, 2)

Jude addresses those who are called, beloved and kept.

II. THE REASON FOR WRITING (verses 3, 4)

He intended to write a doctrinal treatise, but changed his mind because

---

[1] Chase (*op. cit.*, p. 802) finds verbal parallels in 1 Thes. i. 4, 2 Thes. ii. 13, Rom. i. 7, 1 Cor. i. 2 with the salutation; Col. ii. 7 with verse 20; and Rom. xvi. 25ff., Eph. i. 4, iii. 20, Col. i. 22, 1 Thes. v. 23, 2 Thes. iii. 3, 1 Cor. i. 8 with the doxology. Wand (*op. cit.*, p. 192), who relates the doxology to a stereotyped liturgical form, concludes that the parallels 'are worthless as proofs of literary dependence'.

[2] *Op. cit.*, p. 226.   [3] *Op. cit.*, pp. 391f.

the faith of the believers was being undermined by ungodly persons, who were immoral and were denying Christ.

III. REMINDERS FROM THE PAST (verses 5–7)

Three examples of divine judgment are next cited to illustrate the certainty of retribution against wrongdoers: the unbelieving Israelites; the fallen angels; and the people of Sodom and Gomorrah.

IV. THE UNGODLY PERSONS (verses 8–19)

1. Their insubordination to authority is in contrast to the restraint of the archangel Michael in his dispute with the devil over Moses' body. They act in fact like irrational animals (verses 8–10).

2. Their greed for gain is paralleled from the stories of Cain, Balaam and Korah (verse 11).

3. Their unseemly behaviour is vividly described by a series of striking metaphors (verses 12, 13).

4. Their activities were predicted in the book of Enoch, and the character of their ungodliness is particularly seen in their manner of speech. They are at once malcontents and flatterers, concerned only with their own interests (verses 14–16).

5. Their rise was predicted by the apostles and their unspiritual character should at once be recognized (verses 17–19).

V. EXHORTATION TO THE BELIEVERS (verses 20–23)

Jude has said enough about the ungodly people and now turns to more positive instruction. Believers are (1) to build themselves up in the faith; (2) to pray in the Spirit; (3) to keep in God's love; (4) to await God's mercy; (5) to help waverers; (6) to snatch some out of danger; (7) to be merciful; and (8) to hate defilement. There are few passages where so much exhortation is given so concisely.

VI. DOXOLOGY (verses 24, 25)

The Epistle concludes with praise to the God who is able to keep His people and who will at length present them faultless before His glorious presence.

ADDITIONAL NOTES

907. [6] Kümmel (*INT*, 1965, p. 301) favours a pseudonymous theory for Jude and infers that this is supported if the reference to James goes back to a pseudonymous James. But this reasoning seems faulty, for no pseudonymous writer who wanted to create the impression that this letter was written by Jude would have mentioned another epistle known to be pseudonymous. If it be argued that he did not know that James was pseudonymous, it would have provided neither motive nor pattern for his own pseudonymous production. There are no parallels to such procedure in the extant New Testament pseudepigrapha.

908. [3] In addition to those mentioned, who identify Jude with the second-century bishop of Jerusalem, cf. G. Klein, *Die zwölf Apostel* (1961), p. 100.

CHAPTER TWENTY-EIGHT

THE BOOK OF REVELATION

I. THE BOOK IN THE ANCIENT CHURCH

Among many Christians this book is almost entirely neglected, largely due to its apparent obscurities and remoteness from current methods of thought and expression.[1] But such neglect did not characterize the earliest history of the book. Not all were equally certain about its right to be included in the Canon, although even here the major doubts do not belong to the earliest period. There is no doubt that the majority valued the book.[2]

In many ways this early recognition is not surprising in view of the fact that it was originally addressed, and presumably sent, to seven Asiatic churches, which would ensure an initial circulation over a considerable area. Moreover, its message possessed such a general application that it would readily spread its influence beyond the boundaries of Asia.

In all probability it was known during the period of the Apostolic Fathers, although not all scholars are prepared to admit that the seeming parallels are proof of acquaintance with the book. The *Shepherd of Hermas* several times refers to the coming great tribulation (*Vis.* ii. 2, 5, 7, iii. 6) which in all probability is an echo of Revelation ii. 10, vii. 14, while i. 1, 3 may be compared with Revelation xvii. 3 (the Spirit carrying the prophet into a wilderness). But quite apart from these parallels there are many common images in the two writers which are most naturally explained if Hermas knew our Apocalypse; for example, the representation of the Church as a woman, the enemy as a Beast, the description of fiery locusts proceeding from the mouths of beasts, the idea of the apostles being part of a spiritual building, and the description

[1] There has been no neglect of the book in scholastic circles, as a glance at the special bibliography will show. E. Lohmeyer's articles in *TR*, n.f., 6 (1934). pp. 269-314; *TR*, n.f., 7 (1935), pp. 28-62, review a great many books and articles between 1920 and 1934, and the volume of such studies has not since diminished.

[2] For a thorough examination of the external evidence, cf. N. B. Stonehouse, *The Apocalypse in the Ancient Church* (1929).

of the faithful in white garments with crowns on their heads.[1] Yet it is just possible that both books are drawing from the same milieu of thought and that dependence of one upon the other is not the only explanation.[2] It is perhaps surprising that a work so largely eschatological as the *Shepherd* should not contain more definite parallels, but no strong argument can be made to depend on absence of such reminiscence.

The parallels from *Barnabas* and Ignatius are less convincing. *Barnabas* vii. 9, xxi. 3 may be compared with Revelation i. 7, 13, xxii. 10f. respectively, but the parallels are not sufficient to establish dependence. In Ignatius the most notable parallels are *Ad Eph.* xv. 3 (cf. Rev. xxi. 3), *Ad Philad.* vi. 1 (cf. Rev. iii. 12), but these are not only very slight, but appear to have nothing to do with each other, apart from incidental verbal parallels. Clearly this kind of evidence cannot be pressed.

In the period subsequent to the Apostolic Fathers[3] the position was very different, for there is clear attestation of circulation over a wide area. Justin[4] knew the book and attributed it to the apostle John and considerable weight must be attached to this witness.[5] Melito, who was bishop of Sardis (one of the seven churches addressed), apparently wrote a treatise on the Apocalypse of John (according to Eusebius, *HE*, iv. 26). In the Syrian church it was equally well known and respected, for Theophilus of Antioch cites it.[6] When Irenaeus wrote his book against heresies, he explicitly cited the Apocalypse generally as by 'John, a disciple of the Lord', whom he clearly meant to identify with the apostle [7].

[1] *Vis.* ii. 4, Rev. xii. 1ff.; *Vis.* ix. 6–10, Rev. xiii; *Vis.* iv. 1, 6, Rev. ix. 3; *Vis.* iii. 5, 1, Rev. xxi. 14; *Vis.* viii. 2. 1, 3, Rev. vi. 11. Cf. also ii. 10, iii. 11.

[2] Cf. I. T. Beckwith, *The Apocalypse of John* (1919), p. 337. H. B. Swete (*The Apocalypse of St. John*, 1907, pp. cvi, cvii) does not even mention these parallels with *Hermas*, but R. H. Charles, *A Critical and Exegetical Commentary on the Revelation of St. John* (1920), I, p. xcvii n. 2, considers they may rightly be appealed to.

[3] Whether Papias knew the book or not is uncertain. According to Andreas, Papias not only knew it, but witnessed to its credibility (cf. Charles, *op. cit.*, I, p. xcviii for details), but Eusebius gives no supporting evidence for this (*HE*, iii. 39).

[4] *Dial.* 81. Cf. also *Apol.* i. 28 for a clear allusion to Rev. xii. 9, xx. 2.

[5] As this is mentioned by Eusebius (*HE*, iv. 18), who did not himself accept apostolic authorship, its reliability cannot be questioned. It is particularly important, as Justin for a time lived in Ephesus.

[6] Cf. Eusebius, *HE*, iv. 24.

[7] Cf. *Adv. Haer.* iv. 14. 2, 17. 6, 18. 6, 21. 3; v. 28. 2, 34. 2, where he cites as 'John in the Apocalypse', and iv. 20. 11, v. 26. 1 as 'John the disciple of the Lord'. In iii. 1. 1 he uses this description and then adds by way of further identification that he leaned on Jesus' breast, and published the Gospel while residing in Ephesus.

Since he also mentioned ancient copies of the book, it is clear that he knew of its circulation at a much earlier time.[1] It is further significant that the *Letter of the Churches of Vienne and Lyons* cites the Apocalypse in one place as Scripture.[2] The Muratorian Canon shows that no doubts existed over the Apocalypse in the Roman church towards the end of the second century.[3]

Tertullian cited the book frequently and regarded it as by the apostle John.[4] Similarly Clement of Alexandria accepted the apostolic authorship and cited the book as Scripture.[5] The same goes for Origen.[6] There is no need to cite further evidence in support, for there are few books in the New Testament with stronger early attestation. But mention must be made of the beginnings of doubts regarding the book.

Marcion rejected it, but this occasions no surprise in view of his exclusive Pauline preferences. A vigorous attack was made on the book by the Alogi, a group of people so nicknamed by Epiphanius[7] because they rejected John's Logos doctrine. These people not only rejected both Gospel and Apocalypse, but attributed the latter to Cerinthus,[8] as did Gaius of Rome.[9] But this attack was not treated seriously by other Western Christians, for subsequent to this no other Western writer seems to have doubted the book, except Jerome, but even he showed vacillation about his own position.[10]

It was in the East that more sustained criticism was brought to bear upon the book, particularly in the comments of Dionysius, although he still regarded the book as inspired.[11] His main attack was against apostolic authorship, which he questioned on the basis of a comparison with the

---

[1] Cf. Eusebius, *HE*, v. 8.

[2] Cf. Eusebius, *HE*, v. 1. 58, where the formula ἵνα ἡ γραφή πληρωθῇ is used.

[3] 'Johannes enim in apocalypsi, licet septem ecclesiis scribat, tamen omnibus dicit.' Some consider that the *Apocalypse of Peter* was accorded similar status, but the most natural interpretation of the text does not support this, since the further words occur, 'Apocalypsin etiam Johannis et Petri tantum recipimus, quam quidam ex nostris legi in ecclesia nolunt'. At the same time it is evident that some treated them as of equal standing, at least for reading purposes in the church.

[4] *Adv. Marcion.* iii. 14.   [5] *Paed.* ii. 119; *Quis dives*, 42; *Strom.* vi. 106, 107.

[6] *In Johann.* v. 3; cf. Eusebius, *HE*, vi. 25. 9.   [7] *Haer.* li. 3.   [8] *Ibid.*, li. 33.

[9] According to Eusebius, *HE*, iii. 28. 1, 2. Westcott (*On the Canon of the New Testament*, p. 275, n. 2) disputes that Gaius meant the Apocalypse, but rather books written in imitation of it.

[10] Cf. Charles, *op. cit.*, p. cii, for details.

[11] Cf. Eusebius, *HE*, vii. 25. He mentioned that some before his time disputed that the work was John's or that it was a revelation.

Gospel of John, and concluded that both could not have been written by the same author. Most of his arguments have been taken up and developed by modern scholars and will be considered when we deal with the problem of authorship. Eusebius,[1] who records this criticism of Dionysius, is himself inclined to follow it, although it is worth noting that he appears to be uncertain whether to place it among the undisputed books (ὁμολογούμενα) or the spurious books (νόθα). There was doubt about the book at the Council of Laodicea (c. AD 360), for it was not included among the canonical books, while in the Eastern Church it was at first omitted, for the Peshitta Version (early fifth century) does not include it, although the later Philoxenian Version (early sixth century) does. Even so, doubts lingered on in the Syrian church.[2]

It is against this background of early Christian testimony that the internal problems connected with authorship must now be considered.

II. AUTHORSHIP

Although the author calls himself only 'John', it was traditionally assumed that this John was the apostle and consequently it will be most convenient to set out first the various considerations for this opinion, next to consider arguments against it and finally to survey the various alternative suggestions.

a. The case for apostolic authorship

(i) *External testimony.* Much of this evidence has already been given in the previous survey, but it will be as well to summarize here those witnesses who testified not only to the use of the book, but also to its authorship. In the second and early third centuries, the following writers clearly witness to their belief in apostolic authorship: Justin,[3] Irenaeus, Clement, Origen, Tertullian and Hippolytus. Indeed they

---

[1] *HE*, iii. 24. 18, 25. 4.

[2] Junilius mentioned doubts about it (c. AD 551). Much later Bar Hebraeus (died AD 1208) regarded it as by Cerinthus or some other John. In the Armenian church it was not until the twelfth century that the book was regarded as canonical. See Charles, *op. cit.*, I, p. cii, for details.

[3] Some have questioned the reliability of this evidence for *apostolic* authorship because Justin only twice out of forty-seven occurrences of the name John calls him 'the apostle', while on sixteen occasions he is described as 'disciple'. Cf. J. E. Carpenter, *The Johannine Writings* (1927), p. 41. But the descriptions are not mutually exclusive.*

assume it without discussion. So strong is this evidence that it is difficult to believe that they all made a mistake in confusing the John of the Apocalypse with John the apostle. The usual treatment of this evidence by those who deny apostolic authorship is to suppose that these early Fathers were unaware of the true origin of the book and, therefore, guessed that the John must have been the well-known son of Zebedee. This has frequently been based on the theory of two Ephesian Johns, who could quite easily be mixed up, or else on the theory that the only John of Ephesus was the Elder who was later mistaken for the apostle. If all this evidence is due to a mistake it would be an extraordinarily widespread case of mistaken identity. It must be conceded that taken as a whole it points very strongly to the probability that the John of the Apocalypse was, in fact, John the apostle.

But the advocates of apostolic authorship must take account of the later questionings, particularly on the part of Dionysius, whose views had so great an influence on Eastern opinion. Since this Alexandrian, with his critical turn of mind, rejected apostolic authorship, his testimony must certainly be set against the earlier witnesses already mentioned. Now Dionysius came to his conclusion on the basis of a comparison with the Gospel of John in which he considered, first the character of the writer, then his thought and style, and finally the linguistic differences between the two writings.

Under the first point, he particularly emphasized the fact that the writer of the Apocalypse mentions his own name, whereas the writer of the Gospel does not. It was while commenting on this that Dionysius mentioned other possible identifications of John—John Mark or a second John in Asia, the latter on the basis of hearsay about two tombs said to be John's at Ephesus. Under the second point, Dionysius, while admitting marks of agreement, nevertheless claimed that the Apocalypse presents a different range of thought from the Gospel, omitting as it does such frequent mention of 'life', 'light', 'truth', 'grace' and 'love'. The concluding objection was based on the claim that the Gospel and Epistle are in correct Greek, whereas the Greek of the Apocalypse is inaccurate. Such a careful and scholarly weighing of the evidence cannot be lightly dismissed, especially as all the grounds to which Dionysius appealed are still the mainstays of the opponents of apostolic authorship. The criticisms will be dealt with later, but it is necessary here to assess their historical weight. Are they to be regarded as more important than the unquestioning pronouncements of earlier Christian writers, in view of the fact that they proceed from an obviously serious and able critic?

Three comments may be made about Dionysius' criticisms.

1. They are not based on ancient testimony, but on subjective judgment. They, therefore, derive no value from the fact that a third-century Christian made them, having, indeed, no more value than a twentieth-century critic's assessment of the differences.

2. Dionysius' statements about the Greek tend to be misleading, for he seems to have overlooked the Semitic flavouring behind the Greek of the Gospel, and his opinion on the inaccuracies of the Apocalypse does not stand up to modern critical judgment, which generally admits that the grammatical deviations are not due to ignorance (see discussion below).

3. Dionysius' alternative suggestion does not inspire confidence, for his 'second John' has remarkably flimsy testimony to his existence. It is strange that such a scholar as Dionysius should give credence to a traveller's tale about the two tombs of John in Ephesus without entertaining the possibility that the rival tomb may be due to some local opportunist, after the pattern of the extraordinary multiplication of relics in subsequent history. In any case, Dionysius' inference that there may have been two Johns is an interpretation of the tale which seems to have been drawn out by his critical dilemma. If John the apostle was not the writer there must have been two Johns at Ephesus and the tale could, therefore, be made to do service in support. In this Dionysius foreshadowed, as a man born before his due time, those modern schools of criticism which have peopled early Christian history with a whole army of unknown writers, whose works attained as great a prominence as their authors obtained obscurity.

(ii) *Evidence from the book itself.* Although the book does not claim to be written by John the apostle and gives no incidental allusions in support of this claim (for these factors as a basis of criticism, see below pp. 942f.) yet there are internal considerations which are difficult to explain unless the author were the apostle John. The first is that he is clearly known by the name John to the seven Asiatic churches and is fully acquainted with the history of each church. He is, moreover, a man of considerable authority, who can expect the churches to receive what he has written as a revelation from God. But this leads to another consideration. His book, although belonging to the genre of apocalypse, nevertheless differs from the Jewish patterns in that it is not ascribed to an honoured ancient name (such as Enoch, Ezra or Baruch). This apocalyptist prophesies in his own name, a departure from tradition which could have arisen only through the conviction that the spirit of prophecy had once again become active and that there was no need for pseudonymous devices.[1] But such a bold departure from precedent demands an author of such stature that all would naturally acknowledge his leadership. This kind of departure is favourable to apostolic authorship, although this argument is not conclusive. The *Apocalypse of Peter* might be cited as an early example of a pseudonymous apocalypse, but there are vital differences between the two situations, as well as a glaring disparity between their contents. The *Apocalypse of Peter* is a poor imitation of the canonical book and seems to have arisen in competition with it. It will not do, therefore, to cite this book in support of the contention that the Apocalypse of John is pseudepigraphic.

The strong impression given in John's Apocalypse of the author's own personality, although perfectly in harmony with apostolic authorship, may, of course, be equally applicable to some such unknown John as John the Elder or John the Prophet (see discussion below). But one feature which seems more in accord with apostolic authorship is the writer's own consciousness of inspiration.[2] In Revelation xxii. 9 the writer is included by the angel among 'your brethren the prophets'. In x. 10 he symbolically eats a scroll received from the hand of an angel and is then commanded to prophesy. In i. 1, 11, 19 he claims to be writing down a divine revelation as he has seen it. In xxii. 6-8 an angel assures him that what he has heard is trustworthy and that the God of the spirits of the prophets has sent His angel to make known what is soon to take place, thus suggesting that the writer was in a direct line of succession with the older prophets. The conclusion of the book, xxii. 18ff., is itself sufficient to show the writer's own awareness of the importance of his own writing. Grim penalties are promised for those who add to or detract from the words of the book. Whereas something

---

[1] Cf. F. C. Burkitt, *Jewish and Christian Apocalypses* (1914), p. 6. 'The Christian Apocalypse of John . . . breathes a new Spirit' (i.e. as compared with the Jewish apocalypses).

[2] C. C. Torrey (*The Apocalypse of John*, 1958, pp. 79f.) goes as far as to say that in calling his book a 'prophecy', the writer was, in fact, making a specific claim for his work to be included in the Jewish Scriptures. This theory rests on Torrey's assumption that at the time of its production no differentiation was made between Jews and Jewish Christians, and that the writer conceives of the Church as made up exclusively of Jews (cf. Rev. vii. 3-8, xxi. 12).

of this kind of thing can be illustrated from pseudepigraphic writings, in which similar statements are made in order to increase the validity of the book, yet in this case there is no attempt to bolster the writer's own authority—the authority is that of Christ Himself.

A fair conclusion from the book's own claims would be to maintain that the evidence is quite inconclusive, but that there does not appear to be anything which makes apostolic authorship impossible[1] (some minor objections and difficulties will be considered below).

(iii) *Comparisons with the Synoptic description of John.* If the apostle John were the author it would be a relevant enquiry to ascertain whether the representation of him which the Apocalypse gives accords with the Synoptic picture. There are, in fact, some remarkable parallels. John and James are called 'Boanerges', 'sons of thunder', and the Apocalypse certainly contains its share of stormy descriptions. These were the two who wanted the Lord to call down fire from heaven upon Samaritan villages, indicative of their own fiery temperament and their aptitude to give vent to righteous anger. Something of this temperament appears in the apocalyptic writer, as is seen in his description of the hostile Jews (ii. 9, iii. 9), of the Beast and all whom he represents, of Rome in the image of the harlot, of the plagues and judgments which will be the expression of the righteous wrath of God. The picture of John, found in the Fourth Gospel, is noticeably presented in a softer light and this will be considered under our next heading. But this concurrence with the Synoptic tradition, as Swete[2] pointed out, 'may well lead us to hesitate before we definitely reject the attribution of the Apocalypse to the Apostle John'.

(iv) *Relationship with other Johannine books.* It is possible here to give only a brief indication of the similarities of thought which have led most scholars to admit a close connection between our book, the Gospel of John and 1, 2 and 3 John, and have convinced many of common authorship. The whole subject is complicated by the problems surrounding the authorship of the other Johannine books, particularly the Gospel. Since the latter problem cannot be discussed here and since the present argument naturally depends on whether apostolic authorship can be maintained for the Gospel, the evidence will have to be presented

---

[1] E. Stauffer (*Theology of the New Testament*, 1955, pp. 40, 41) strongly maintains that this book, together with the Gospel and Epistles, is the work of the apostle John.

[2] *Op. cit.*, p. clxxxii.

for the moment on the assumption that the traditional ascription is correct. If common authorship can be established, it will at least mean that the problem of the authorship of this book cannot be settled apart from the other literature, although, of course, the arguments adduced may suggest different things to different minds.

The similarities are mainly seen in common ideas and common theology, but they also reach to terminology. Both books use the word 'Logos' of Christ, an expression used nowhere in the New Testament apart from the Johannine literature (Jn. i. 1; Rev. xix. 13). Here, as also in the other writings, Christ is described as a Lamb, although a different Greek word is used (ἀρνίον in Revelation, ἀμνός in the Gospel). In both Gospel and Apocalypse, figures of speech involving waters, springs, etc., are used (cf. Jn. iv. 10f., 14, vii. 38; Rev. vii. 17, xxi. 6, xxii. 17). In both the figure of the Shepherd is used of Christ (Jn. x. 1ff., cf. xxi. 16f.; Rev. vii. 17). Both contain the suggestion that a temple is no longer needed for the worship of God (Jn. iv. 21; Rev. xxi. 22) and both contain a symbolical allusion to manna (Jn. vi. 31f.; Rev. ii. 17). A notable similarity is the common variation in the citation from the Old Testament found in John xix. 37 and Revelation i. 7, where Zechariah xii. 10 is cited in a form differing from the LXX.

There is a noticeable love of antithesis in both books. The contrasts between light and darkness, truth and falsehood, the power of God and the power of this world, which are so frequently reiterated in the Gospel, lie behind the whole conception of the Apocalypse. Moreover, several technical terms which are characteristic of the Gospel recur in the Apocalypse, such as ἀληθινός, μαρτυρία, νικᾶν and such a phrase as τηρεῖν τὰς ἐντολάς.

These similarities are, at least, sufficiently striking to point to a common milieu of thought if not to common authorship.[1] They will need, of course, to be set over against the various differences which will be considered later, but our present purpose is to demonstrate what internal support might be found for the remarkably strong early tradition. Before proceeding with this, there is one more line of argument of a rather more subtle kind. It is brought out by Austin Farrer, in his contention that behind all the Johannine literature there is an

[1] In his recent book on *Zeit und Geschichte in der Offenbarung des Johannes* (1952), p. 56, M. Rissi asserts that the style and thought peculiarities of the Apocalypse in reference to the end time are very strongly reminiscent of John's Gospel and the Johannine Epistles and this opinion would seem to be justified.

underlying identity of rhythm.[1] Comparing the Gospel and Apocalypse, he finds the same kinds of pattern and thinks this is not the sort of thing that can be invented.[2] This kind of argument is very difficult to assess and its value will clearly depend on the validity of the images which Austin Farrer extracts, but one factor which is undeniably common between the two writings is the symbolical use of the number seven. The Apocalypse is constructed on this pattern and so is the Fourth Gospel (cf. for instance its seven 'signs', its seven-day opening of the Lord's ministry, its seven-day account of the passion story). This characteristic would not be so significant were it not confined in the New Testament to the Johannine writings.[3] While it is not conclusive for common authorship, since it might represent a literary device of a certain school of thought, yet it would certainly seem to point in that direction.

b | The case against apostolic authorship

In spite of the strong tradition and the internal support just considered, many scholars reject apostolic authorship either with or without a rejection of common authorship with the Gospel. The grounds of both positions will be considered together.

(i) *Linguistic differences.* As already mentioned,[4] as early as Dionysius (third century AD) the strange Greek of this book constituted a difficulty. The irregularities are undeniable. The writer seems on the surface to be unacquainted with the elementary laws of concord. He places nominatives in opposition to other cases, irregularly uses participles, constructs broken sentences, adds unnecessary pronouns, mixes up genders, numbers and cases and introduces several unusual constructions.[5] That the grammatical usages of this book differ from those of the Gospel would seem to be demonstrated beyond doubt. But the real problem is whether one mind could adopt these different usages. Many scholars

---

[1] *A Rebirth of Images* (1949), pp. 25ff. Farrer considers that the author was not an apostle but an apostolic man (p. 23).

[2] *Ibid.*, p. 25.

[3] Cf. Lohmeyer's elaborate sevenfold theory for 1 John. See p. 876 n. 3 for details.

[4] See p. 935.

[5] For exhaustive examples, cf. R. H. Charles' section on The Grammar of the Apocalypse, *op. cit.*, I, pp. cxvii–clix. Swete (*op. cit.*, pp. cxxii f.) gives more concise examples. ἀπὸ ὁ ὢν (i. 4) obviously transcends normal grammatical accord.

are strongly biased towards dissimilar authorship on this ground alone.[1] But various explanations of the difference have been offered.

(1.) Westcott[2] maintained an early date for the Apocalypse and supposed that an interval of some twenty years would suffice for John to improve his Greek sufficiently to write the better Greek of the Gospel. But this solution is inadequate, for quite apart from the doubtfulness of the early dating (see discussion on pp. 958ff.), the Greek of the Apocalypse is not simply an inaccurate form of Greek such as a learner writes before he has mastered the laws of the language, but a mixture of correct and incorrect forms which appear to be due to choice,[3] not to accident, carelessness or ignorance. It would probably be going too far to speak of 'the grammar of ungrammar' as Archbishop Benson[4] did, although there is no doubt that the author had his own very definite reasons for using unusual grammatical constructions. Thus the theory of an improvement period would appear to break down.

(2.) Zahn[5] had a different explanation. The apocalyptic language was influenced profoundly by Old Testament models, especially as the book claims to be a prophecy. This at once distinguishes it from the Gospel. The same author, writing now in a prophetic and now in a didactic style, would naturally use different language. Moreover, Zahn suggested that since prophecy was given in an ecstatic state, the form as well as the content was received and the writer, therefore, had less freedom in polishing up the finished product. There may be truth in this suggestion, but its force will depend upon the degree to which the author is assumed to have had a genuine ecstatic experience.[6]

[1] E.g. R. H. Charles, loc. cit.

[2] The Gospel according to St. John (1887), p. lxxxvi.

[3] Thus Charles (op. cit., p. clii) concludes that most of the abnormalities 'are not instances of mere licence nor yet mere blunders, as they have been most wrongly described, but are constructions deliberately chosen by our author'. Charles thought that a good number of them were due to reproduction of Hebrew idioms.

[4] E. W. Benson, The Apocalypse (1900), pp. 131ff.

[5] INT, III, pp. 432f. W. Hendriksen, More than Conquerors (Tyndale Press edition, 1962), pp. 12f., and J. B. Phillips, The Book of Revelation (1957), p. xiii, make similar suggestions.

[6] Some writers, who take the view that the apocalyptist selected and arranged his material in order to produce a drama of visions, suggest that the style might unconsciously have been adopted to fit in with a supposed prophetic or ecstatic experience (cf. Beckwith, op. cit., p. 355).

(3.) Yet another possibility is the use of amanuenses. There is no certain information about this in the case of either the Gospel or the Apocalypse and the explanation must be regarded as purely suppositional. But it could perhaps have happened that someone better acquainted with Greek was responsible for the final form of the Gospel, while the Apocalypse is the author's own work.[1] This would seem more reasonable than vice versa,[2] and might indeed account for the greater preponderance of Hebraisms in the Apocalypse as compared with the Gospel (see further discussion below). Such an hypothesis would account for both the similarities and the differences, since one dominant personality would be behind the two writings. It should be noted, incidentally, that in spite of linguistic and grammatical differences the Apocalypse has a closer affinity to the Greek of the other Johannine books than to any other New Testament books.

(ii) *Internal indications of non-apostolic authorship.* (1.) The most obvious objection which has been brought is the absence of any apostolic claims. Thus Charles[3] was suspicious of apostolic authorship on the grounds that John claims to be a prophet and not an apostle. This objection is based on the assumption that no apostle could write without claiming his apostolic authority. But this is a misconception. Certainly Paul had to assert his apostleship in most of his letters, but that was because he was not one of the twelve and there were people who never allowed him to forget this. But the case would be different with John. He would not need to claim his office among those who never disputed it.[4] It was not on the strength of his apostolic commission, but on the strength of his prophetic inspiration that he gave out his revelation.

(2.) This non-apostolic claim is further thought to be buttressed by the absence of any allusions to incidents in the Gospels in which John had a part, and by the fact that he does not claim to have known Christ

---

[1] Beckwith (*op. cit.*, p. 356), who regards this suggestion as plausible, cites the cases of Josephus and Paul. If the Apocalypse was written on Patmos, the use of an amanuensis would be improbable for that book.

[2] W. Michaelis (*op. cit.*, p. 307) strongly criticizes the view of P. Gaechter, who advocated in several studies in the Roman Catholic *Theological Studies*, VIII (1947), IX (1948), X (1949), that an amanuensis was used for the Apocalypse. If the theory were correct the secretary must have been extremely incompetent.

[3] *Op. cit.*, p. xliii.

[4] Cf. F. J. A. Hort, *The Apocalypse of John, I–III* (1908), pp. xxxvi f. It is true that Peter makes clear his apostolic identity in 1 Pet. i. 1, but this is the sole example transmitted to us.

in the flesh.[1] But this kind of argument must be discounted, for it cuts both ways. Had the author brought in numerous personal reminiscences, as the author of the *Apocalypse of Peter* does, he would just as certainly have been charged with overdoing his identification, as this author is now charged with underdoing it. Clearly such a method of argument is too subjective. In any case there are few appropriate places in a book dealing with the glorified Christ for the inclusion of references to His human life.[2]

3. More objective but no more conclusive is the argument based on the references to apostles in Revelation xviii. 20, xxi. 14, which are regarded as retrospective to a period now past.[3] Dealing first with xviii. 20, it should be noted that this argument would exclude the author from the prophets also, but he expressly claims to be among their number (see p. 942 above), and in view of this little weight can be attached to it. In xxi. 14, where the twelve apostolic names are inscribed on the foundation stones of the New Jerusalem, it is supposed that this number could not include the writer. A similar argument is made for the non-apostolic authorship of Ephesians on the basis of Ephesians ii. 20, iii. 5.[4] In any case, if an apostolic author has a message to impart which mentions the apostolate, is he to emend the message out of motives of modesty or append a note indicating his own inclusion in the number?[5] Such a statement could surely be made by an apostolic author without any trace of presumption.

(iii) *Non-Johannine elements.* Many scholars, in spite of admitting that strong similarities exist between the Apocalypse and the other Johannine literature, yet maintain that the differences far outweigh the similarities. The linguistic problem has already been discussed. It remains, however, to consider the theological and other differences.

1. The doctrine of God is said to be mainly concerned with His creatorship and majesty, whereas in the Gospel and First Epistle the

[1] So Charles, *op. cit.*, p. xliii. T. S. Kepler (*The Book of Revelation*, 1957, p. 17) argues from this that the author was not an eyewitness.
[2] Cf. Beckwith, *op. cit.*, p. 351.
[3] Cf. Charles, *loc. cit.*
[4] See pp. 504 ff.
[5] Zahn (*INT*, III, p. 430) cites as a parallel the statement in Lk. xxii. 30 (= Mt. xix. 28) in which our Lord speaks of the apostles occupying twelve thrones, but which could have been reported only by the apostolic hearers themselves. Cf. also F. J. A. Hort, *The Apocalypse of St. John, I–III* (1908), p. xxxvi.

emphasis is on God's love.[1] This is true but the two are not mutually exclusive. The justice of God which is so powerfully stressed in the Apocalypse is but the complement of the love of God so strongly presented in the Gospel. The wrath of God is seen in opposition not so much to individuals as to the principles of evil behind them. God is doing battle with the personification of wickedness. He can do no other than hate that wickedness and pour forth His judgment upon it. If it were not so vividly expressed in the Apocalypse it would have to be deduced from His character as holy love. But in any case it is not absent from other parts of the New Testament where the love of God is also stressed (cf. Rom. ii. 4–9; Mt. xxii. 7, 12f., xxiv. 28, 30, xxv. 12; Jn. iii. 36, ix. 39; 1 Pet. iv. 17f.).

(2.) The Christology of the Apocalypse and the Gospel may at first seem to be different, since Christ is portrayed in the Apocalypse as the all-conquering Messiah who rules nations with a rod of iron, whereas in the Gospel He is the Revealer and Renewer. But again there is no contradiction, for in a book whose theme is mainly judgment, this is just the kind of picture one would expect. At the same time, the Christ of the Apocalypse is Redeemer of His people as Lamb of God (i. 5, v. 9, vii. 14, xii. 11, xiv. 4) and as the Fount of Life for those who thirst (xxi. 6, xxii. 17). It has already been pointed out that the Logos conception occurs in both books, but some scholars find a difference of usage.[2] It is true that in the Gospel the idea is absolute whereas in the Apocalypse the descriptive τοῦ θεοῦ is added, but no serious objection can be based on such a difference.

(3.) The doctrine of the Spirit similarly shows no essential difference in spite of the fact that in Revelation i. 4 mention is made of the seven spirits. Admittedly this does not occur in the Gospel, but it is not alien to the Paraclete concept, if the symbolism is understood as depicting perfection.[3] The spirit addresses the messages to the churches (ii, iii), speaks from heaven (xiv. 13) and issues the concluding invitation (xxii.

[1] Cf. Moffatt, *ILNT*, p. 502.

[2] So Lohmeyer, *Die Offenbarung des Johannes*[2] (1953), pp. 202, 203. Cf. also Moffatt, *loc. cit.*

[3] R. H. Charles (*op. cit.*, I, p. cxiv) considered the conception to be 'grotesque' and therefore assigned it to an editor. But his reason for doing so is purely arbitrary. When the same phrase occurs in iii. 1 it becomes a 'redactional addition' instead of a 'manifest interpolation' (p. 78). Cf. the same phrase in iv. 5, v. 6. It may have arisen, as Swete suggests (*op. cit.*, p. 6), because the Spirit is described as operating in seven churches.

17). It cannot be maintained that the writer of the Gospel could not have expressed the Spirit's activity in this form, although it is perhaps surprising that no mention is made of His regenerating activity. But again the different emphasis in the book might explain this.

4. Eschatology is another doctrine on which differences have been noted, since the Gospel is more interested in the present age than the future. Much of this difficulty has been occasioned by the assumption that the author of the Gospel has a wholly spiritual view of the *parousia* contrasted with the Synoptic view, which is more in harmony with the Apocalypse. The modern notion of realized eschatology for the Gospel[1] tends to obscure the traditional eschatology which also occurs in the Gospel (e.g. v. 25ff. and the references to the 'last hour'), although without the traditional imagery found in the Synoptists. Since the Apocalypse has an eschatological theme it is not surprising that a different emphasis is found, but only a one-sided interpretation of the Johannine eschatology could definitely exclude the possibility that Gospel and Apocalypse were both written by the same author.

(iv) *Historical difficulties.* In recent years much discussion has surrounded the problem of the date of the apostle's death. There is evidence for two conflicting traditions. The strongest tradition maintained that John lived to a ripe old age at Ephesus, while a challenging tradition considered that he was martyred at the same time as James. Support for an early death, however, is none too reliable. Nevertheless, since many scholars prefer this tradition to the other, which is disposed of as a mistake on the part of Irenaeus, it naturally cannot be left out of any discussion on the authorship of the Apocalypse. If the apostle died at the same time as James, he is at once ruled out as author of either Gospel or Apocalypse, no matter how strong other evidence against this might be. If, on the other hand, as even the alternative tradition allows, he died as a martyr, although not at the same time as James, the apostolic authorship is not at once excluded since no time limit is set. Yet it may be said that the tradition of an early death is by no means so certain as to override the strong tradition to the contrary.[2]

The whole matter is, of course, bound up with the further problem of the two Johns at Ephesus (see pp. 935f.), for if it be decided that

---

[1] Cf. C. H. Dodd, *The Apostolic Preaching and its Developments*[2] (1944), pp. 65ff.

[2] W. Bousset (*Die Offenbarung Johannis,*[2] 1906, pp. 35, 36) considered that the evidence for John's early death was so strong that he did not discuss apostolic authorship, but concluded for John the Elder.

there was only one and that he was not the apostle, the exile on Patmos must *ipso facto* be some other John. On the other hand, if there were two Johns at Ephesus, the tradition of the apostle's early death must clearly be wrong.

A further difficulty has been raised against apostolic authorship on the grounds that if the apostle were still alive towards the close of the first century he would have been too old to produce such literature and especially the Apocalypse with its virile imaginativeness.[1] Advocates of an early date for the Apocalypse naturally find less difficulty here.[2] But the difficulty would remain for the Gospel if written by the same author. The criticism is not without point, but requires considerable caution since we cannot be certain of John's age when he was first called to be an apostle, neither do we know at what age his mental capacities would be incapable of producing literature. If an 'uninspired' George Bernard Shaw could continue writing until well into his nineties, who can restrict the capabilities of an 'inspired' apostle?

To sum up the discussion on apostolic authorship, it is not easy, indeed not possible, to come to any definite conclusion. Whether we are biased one way or the other will depend very largely on the weight given to the early tradition, and the convincing character of any alternative. The various other suggestions will, therefore, next be listed in order to set the whole evidence in its true light. Suffice it to say that no evidence makes the traditional apostolic ascription impossible.

c. Alternative theories

(1) *John the Elder.* Papias' statement regarding the 'two' Johns has been discussed elsewhere (p. 887 n. 1) and the opinion expressed that it is far from conclusive that a John the Elder ever lived. But since many scholars are inclined to put faith in his existence, it is well to consider what implications this has for the identification of the author of the Apocalypse. Advocates of the theory that John the Elder wrote the Apocalypse appeal at once to Dionysius' statement about a second John at Ephesus. It is to be observed that Dionysius does not cite Papias for this, but a traveller's report (φασίν), and his suggestion about a second John is no more than tentative ('Άλλον δέ τινα οἶμαι τῶν 'Ασία γενομένων). Nevertheless supposing his conjecture was correct, does this solve the problem? Presumably Dionysius ascribed the Gospel to one John and the Apocalypse to the other. But modern scholars ascribe the Gospel and

---

[1] Cf. Hort, *op. cit.*, p. xl.   [2] Cf. A. Farrer, *op. cit.*, p. 23.

Epistles to the Elder, in which case the only possibilities are to ascribe the Apocalypse to the apostle, if identity of authorship is denied, or to the Elder, if identity is accepted or to a third John if apostolic as well as identical authorship is rejected.[1]

Leaving aside the problem of the Gospel, which cannot be discussed here, we must decide whether it is conceivable that John the Elder could have been author of this book. At first sight there seems nothing against it, but, since our knowledge of the shadowy Elder is nil, this is not surprising. The main problem it raises concerns the consciousness of the author. If he used his own name 'John' he must have assumed that all his readers would at once have known who he was. But he must also have known that, if the apostle was also resident at Ephesus, many would confuse the two and the writer would then be culpable for not making his own identity clearer. It is difficult to see how confusion of the two could have become so widespread, and indeed unchallenged, so soon after its publication. The Elder theory seems tenable only on the supposition that John the apostle had never lived at Ephesus, and that from the early second century the whole Church mistakenly assumed that he had.

(ii) *John the prophet.* Charles[2] was obliged to invent this third John because he had attributed the other Johannine books to the Elder. Since we know no more, if as much, about John the Prophet than we do about John the Elder it is difficult to assess this proposition. It really says no more than what the book itself claims, i.e. that the author was called John and that he prophesied. This is really a confession of defeat. And yet does any closer identification really matter? Different minds will have different answers, but this is not quite in the same category as an anonymous book like the Epistle to the Hebrews. The undefined 'John' would naturally be mistaken for the apostle, but would the churches of Asia really be able to distinguish between John the Prophet and John the Elder? Was the Asiatic church overrun with brilliant Christians by the name of John, who would only need to announce their name for the Christians to know which was meant? The position must have been very complicated and seems hardly credible.

In similar vein, with similar difficulties, is the postulation of an 'uni-

[1] Bousset (*op. cit.*, p. 49) regarded the Elder as being the author of the Apocalypse and 2 and 3 John and the witness behind the Fourth Gospel.
[2] *Op. cit.*, p. xliii.

dentified John',[1] or an inspired apostolic man,[2] for in either case he must have intended to gain acceptance under an apostolic name (even if he shared the same name) or else have achieved this end without intending it.

(iii) *An intentional pseudonym.* The improbability of this view has already been mentioned, and it is included here only for the sake of completeness.[3] A writer could never have palmed off his work as apostolic after the assumed writer was known to be dead without some attempt to explain why the book had not appeared before, (a device common among pseudepigraphists.) This procedure certainly happened at a later date, but was always detected and was never granted the authority given to this book. Undoubtedly pseudonymity here raises far more problems than it solves.[4]

(iv) *John Mark.* There would be no need to mention this proposition had it not been referred to by Dionysius,[5] although he does not seem to have been impressed by it. Indeed, he rejected it on historical grounds because Mark did not accompany Paul to Asia. But on linguistic grounds it has nothing to commend it, while Mark gives no indication in his Gospel of possessing the prophetical qualities of the author of the Apocalypse.[6]

d. Conclusion

To extract a conclusive or even satisfactory result from all this mass of conjecture seems impossible. The most certain line of evidence is the early tradition and there would seem to be some excuse for taking refuge in this for want of a better alternative. At least, if this is the true solution it at once explains the rise of the tradition, which none of the

---

[1] Cf. e.g. T. Henshaw, *op. cit.*, p. 417.*

[2] So A. Farrer, *op. cit.*, p. 23.

[3] The earlier disputants of apostolic authorship resorted to this theory. Beckwith (*op. cit.*, p. 345) cites Semler, Volkmar, Scholtau and more recently Weizsäcker, Wernle, Bacon.

[4] Practically all modern scholars reject this solution. Cf. R. H. Charles, *op. cit.*, II, pp. 43ff.; F. Torm, *Die Psychologie der Pseudonymität im Hinblick auf die Literatur des Urchristentiums* (1932), p. 29.

[5] It has been held in modern times by Hitzig and in part by Spitta (cf. Zahn, *INT*, III, p. 434, n. 2).

[6] Cf. the criticisms of Zahn, *op. cit.*, III, pp. 428, 429, and Swete, *op. cit.*, p. clxxvi.*

others satisfactorily does.[1] But many prefer to leave the authorship an open question.[2]

III. DATE

An examination of the problem of the date of this writing raises many problems which are by no means easy to solve, and several different hypotheses have been proposed in an effort to provide a satisfactory solution. Although the main purpose of the book may be considered apart from the question of date, this question is not unimportant in the quest to ascertain the precise historical background, nor is it entirely irrelevant for arriving at a satisfactory interpretation of the book. The most widely held view is that this Apocalypse was written during the reign of Domitian, more precisely towards the end of that reign, i.e. AD 90–95, and reasons for this dating will first be given. After this alternative theories will be considered.

a. Arguments in favour of a Domitianic date

(i) *Emperor worship.* Even a casual reading of the Apocalypse is sufficient to impress the reader that the background is one of conflict between the ruling powers and the Christian Church (see further discussion on p. 962). The great representative of the opposing party, the Roman Empire, is personified in the figure of a Beast, who is evidently meant to represent the reigning emperor. The main focus of attention wherever this Beast is mentioned is his demand for universal worship (cf. xiii. 4, 15f., xiv. 9–11, xv. 2, xvi. 2, xix. 20, xx. 4) and his insistence that all should bear his 'mark'. These references can be interpreted only by reference to the imperial cult. But does this in itself help us to place the background of the Apocalypse in its right place in the development of this cult? This is clearly an important question in relation to the date, for if it points to a fairly well defined period it will greatly assist in answering other problems.

That the idea of emperor worship arose even before the rise of Christianity cannot be disputed. Julius Caesar claimed divine honours

---

[1] A. Schlatter (*Die Briefe und die Offenbarung des Johannes*, 1950, p. 127), who accepted apostolic authorship for all the Johannine writings, pointed out that no other apostle has given so complete a presentation—faith in the Gospel, love in the Epistles, hope in the Apocalypse. The same idea was emphasized much earlier by C. E. Luthardt, *Die Lehre von den Letzten Dingen*[2] (1870), p. 167.

[2] Cf. Boismard in Robert-Feuillet's *Introduction à la Bible*, II, p. 741.

and, although Augustus was not so forward in encouraging this, there were temples in his and Rome's honour in some of the provinces. Caligula made a demand for the universal worship of his statue, although whether any effort was made to enforce this is very dubious. No evidence of it has survived, but the order for Caligula's statue to be placed in the temple of Jerusalem is some indication of his own mad schemes in this direction. What would have happened had he lived to insist on the carrying out of his project cannot be foreseen. But at this period in the development of the cult there is nothing to correspond with the situation reflected in the Apocalypse. It is the period from Nero to Domitian which saw the rapid development of emperor worship into an official policy of imperial politics. Not all the intervening emperors took their divine honours seriously. Vespasian was an example of this, but Domitian determined not only to treat it seriously, but to enforce it. What is not certain is the method he adopted to deal with any who were disinclined to offer him homage. No knowledge of any rescript or edict has survived from the first century which enforced emperor worship. The earliest official pronouncement belongs to the reign of Trajan.

If there are lacking official records of the enforcement of emperor worship, there is ample evidence to show that the attitude of the State in this matter was bound sooner or later to clash with the Christian Church, and this much is abundantly clear from the Apocalypse. The issue has become a challenge between homage to Christ and homage to Caesar. But does this represent a development which could not have been reached before the time of Domitian? Many scholars[1] believe that it does, although there are some who have maintained that the book contains no details which could not have obtained during the time of Nero (see discussion below).

Before passing on to the closely linked problem of the persecution background, it is well to recognize that, although the emperor worship presupposed in the Apocalypse would well suit the later period of Domitian's reign, there is no conclusive evidence that it could not

---

[1] So Charles, *op. cit.*, p. xciv. 'There is no evidence of any kind to prove that the conflict between Christianity and the imperial cult had reached the pitch of antagonism that is presupposed in the Apocalypse of John before the closing years of Domitian's reign.' Cf. similarly, Moffatt, *ILNT*, p. 504; I. T. Beckwith, *op. cit.*, p. 201; H. B. Swete, *op. cit.*, pp. civ, cv, all of whom consider the evidence to be quite conclusive on this point.

have occurred earlier. In other words the evidence based on emperor worship would not of itself be enough to close the discussion on the date.

(ii) *Persecutions.* Of greater importance is the identification of the persecution which has either just commenced or is immediately impending, for the book itself furnishes more data for deciding this problem. It is well to cite these data first and then to discuss their significance against the known historical background of imperial persecutions.

(1.) The writer himself appears to have been in exile on the island of Patmos, because of his Christian profession (i. 9). But it is not quite certain that he is still there.[1] And in any case there is no definite reference to an imperial action which resulted in this exile. It might quite easily have been a local proconsular decision.

. (2.) In the church at Pergamum a Christian named Antipas had been killed, presumably some time previous to the writing of the letter addressed to that church (ii. 13). This would appear to be an isolated instance of persecution, for there is no hint of a general outbreak in this district.

(3.) The church at Smyrna is warned of imminent imprisonments (ii. 10), which suggests a rather more widespread and organized threat. There is a possibility of the death penalty, for the Christians are urged to be faithful unto death.[2]

(4.) Some have already suffered martyrdom according to vi. 9, for the writer sees their souls under the altar and wants to know how long they must wait to be avenged. But the description here is notably general, embracing 'those who had been slain for the Word of God and for the witness they had borne', which is wide enough to include the Old Testament martyrs as well as Christian martyrs. All that can certainly be deduced from this is that at some previous time certain people had been martyred for the sake of their testimony. It tells us nothing about how many were involved, nor how widespread was the persecution, nor indeed whether these martyrs belonged to the same district as the readers. In all probability they did not. The statement may, in fact, be a reference to those who were victims of Nero's infamous outrage against the Christians in Rome, which would not

---

[1] Cf. Michaelis, *op. cit.*, p. 317.

[2] Michaelis (*loc. cit.*) supposes that the instigators here are Jews and not the imperial officials.

greatly assist us in arriving at a date for the Apocalypse, apart from its requiring a date subsequent to that event.

(5.) In the message to the church in Philadelphia there is a reference to 'the hour of trial which is coming on the whole world, to try those who dwell upon the earth' (iii. 10), which would certainly seem to refer to more than local actions against the Christians. Here we seem to be in the presence of a threat which could only come from the emperor himself, with power of enforcement through the whole world. At the same time this world-wide 'trial' may be intended in an eschatological sense of the troublous time expected immediately before the *parousia*,[1] in view of the statement of iii. 11. The trial has apparently not yet begun.[2]

(6.) In certain passages regarding the great harlot (i.e. Rome) there are statements about her being drunk with the blood of the saints (xvii. 6, xviii. 24, xix. 2; cf. also xvi. 6, xx. 4), which suggests a period of widespread persecution, although since these references occur in visions it is not possible to be certain that such persecutions had actually begun. On the other hand fierce persecution was obviously to be anticipated in the not too distant future.

The next question which arises is whether this persecution situation fits best into the Domitianic period. The majority of scholars would answer in the affirmative. But whatever the final decision on this matter may be, the evidence is not as conclusive as many suppose. As pointed out in discussing 1 Peter (pp. 781 f.), data about the Domitianic persecutions tend to be elusive. This emperor put to death his relative Flavius Clemens and banished his wife on a charge of sacrilege (ἀθεότης),[3] which strongly suggests that it was on the basis of their Christianity, since the wife, Domitilla, is known from inscriptions to have been a Christian. In addition to this, Clement of Rome contains a vague reference to 'sudden and repeated misfortunes and calamities',[4] which had recently befallen the church in Rome. Since Clement's Epistle is generally thought to belong to the time of Domitian this

---

[1] Cf. Swete, *op. cit.*, p. 56.

[2] Michaelis (*op. cit.*, p. 316) considers that the references in the letters to the churches do not reflect a position in which the State is definitely the persecutor, and a Domitianic date is, therefore, too late. Charles (*op. cit.*, p. xciv) agreed with this type of approach, but considered that these references are to material earlier than the main book and that they have been re-edited.

[3] According to Dio Cassius, *Hist. Rom.* lxvii. 14.

[4] *Clement 1*, i (K. Lake's translation, *The Apostolic Fathers*, 1912, p. 9).

could refer to the outbreak of persecution. But the identification is by
no means certain for there are few data in the letter to enable the date
to be fixed without dispute. Several later Christian writers speak of a
Domitianic persecution of Christians, as for instance Eusebius[1] and
Sulpicius Severus.[2] Two writers, Tertullian[3] and Hegesippus (according to Eusebius[4]) mention that Domitian stopped the persecution.
One writer only, Orosius, who tends to make extravagant statements
in other respects, mentions widespread persecutions.[5] It would seem a
fair conclusion from this evidence that Domitian persecuted some
Roman Christians, but that no definite evidence of any persecution
outside Rome is forthcoming. But this does not necessarily mean that
it did not happen, and if on other grounds the Apocalypse must be
dated during this period, the evidence of the book itself would be
sufficient to show that persecution had in fact spread to Asia. The
strength of the Caesar-cult in Asia and the fact that a new Caesar-
temple was erected in Ephesus during Domitian's reign[6] would make
some persecution there in his time highly probable.[7]

(iii) *The background of the Nero myth*. Many scholars assume that behind
Revelation xiii and xvii lies the widely believed myth that Nero would
return to Rome and, since this form of the myth did not develop until
after about AD 80, it is supposed that the book must have been issued
after this. According to Charles[8] the development shows a modification of the earlier form of the myth, in which it was thought that Nero
was not really dead but had escaped to the East (a belief which by this
time had had to be abandoned) and this idea was combined with current theories about Belial and Antichrist. But does the Apocalypse itself really demand this? The Beast with the mortal wound which has
now been healed (xiii. 3) may be illustrated by the current Nero myth,
but in its later forms that myth involved Nero returning at the head
of a Parthian army to recapture his lost throne,[9] with the consequent
destruction of Rome. Yet there is no reference to Parthians, either in
chapter xiii or xvii. The Beast represents the embodiment of evil, a

---

[1] *HE*, iii. 18. 4.   [2] *Chronicle*, ii. 31.   [3] *Apology*, v.   [4] *HE*, iii. 20.

[5] Cf. Hort, *op. cit.*, p. xxiv, for the quotation.

[6] Cf. Feine-Behm, *op. cit.*, p. 286.*

[7] Moffatt (*ILNT*, p. 504), who adhered to the Domitianic date, admitted
the paucity of evidence for a general Asiatic persecution, but suggested that the
few drops of rain (i.e. the few cases of hardship and persecution) warned of an
approaching storm.*

[8] *Op. cit.*, I, p. xcvi.   [9] *Ibid.*, II, p. 81.

conception quite comprehensible without recourse to a Nero myth, which, according to Tacitus, had become a 'joke' (*ludibrium*) by Domitian's time.[1] Moreover, since the Apocalypse represents the Beast as returning from the dead, this could only refer to Nero after a period when the idea that he had not really died had ceased to be believed because too great an interval had elapsed since his supposed disappearance.[2] If then an allusion to the Nero myth is still maintained as underlying the language of Revelation xiii and xvii, it must be regarded as extremely inconclusive for a Domitianic date. The most that can be said is that it may possibly point to this.[3] But if, on the other hand, the Nero-myth background is denied, the allusions to the returning 'king' will furnish no information for purposes of dating.[4]

(iv) *The condition of the Asiatic churches.* Here we are on firmer ground, for the letters to the seven churches (chapters ii and iii) supply certain positive indications of internal conditions. In some of the churches there has been a marked deterioration (e.g. Ephesus, Sardis, Laodicea). It is significant that this has happened in the two churches known to be Pauline and it is thought, therefore, to indicate a considerable interval since the foundation of the Church.[5] All the letters, in fact, give the impression that the churches have a history behind them. But it is difficult to assess the length of time needed for deterioration to set in. All depends on the spiritual standard of the original church. That all the apostolic churches were not equal in this respect is abundantly clear from the Pauline Epistles themselves. Spiritual decline and heretical ideas take little time to develop in fertile soil, and some caution is necessary before concluding for a later date on these grounds.[6]

But Charles' argument[7] regarding the church of Smyrna would seem

---

[1] *Hist.* i. 2; cf. C. C. Torrey, *op. cit.*, p. 73.

[2] Cf. Zahn, *INT*, III, p. 444. Cf. also C. Clemen, *ZNTW*, 2 (1901), pp. 109f., 11 (1910), pp. 204f.

[3] Swete comments, 'The legend has been used by St. John to represent the revival of Nero's persecuting policy by Domitian "portio Neronis de crudelitate"' (*Tert. Apol.* v) (*op. cit.*, pp. 163, 164).

[4] It is significant that Augustine was the first Christian writer to speak of Nero returning from the dead (*Civ. Dei*, xx. 19. 3), but does not connect this with the Apocalypse.

[5] A. Ramsay (*The Revelation and the Johannine Epistles*, 1910, p. 5) considered the omission of any mention of Paul in the Ephesian letter to require an interval of a full generation.

[6] Feine-Behm, *op. cit.*, p. 287, are very cautious on this point.*

[7] *Op. cit.*, I, p. xciv; followed also by Moffatt, *ILNT*, p. 507.

to have considerable weight, for he maintains that this church did not exist until after AD 60–64. His evidence for this is drawn from a statement in Polycarp's letter to the Philippians,[1] in which he implies that the Smyrnaeans[2] had not known the Lord when Paul wrote to the Philippians. From this Charles concludes that the letter to this church could hardly have been written earlier than AD 75. But Torrey[3] challenges this interpretation of Polycarp's statement, maintaining that what Polycarp means is that Paul boasted about the Philippians among the earliest established churches of Asia and Europe, but that this could not have included Smyrna. In other words, Smyrna had not such a long history as Philippi. But that does not require a post-Pauline date, although it might suggest it.

Another factor which might be more conclusive is the reference to the Nicolaitans, who have been active both in the church at Ephesus (ii. 6) and in the church at Pergamum (ii. 15). They are introduced in such a way as to suggest an established and well-known sect which needed only to be referred to by name. Although mention is made of such a sect by Irenaeus, Hippolytus, Tertullian, Clement of Alexandria and others, little is known of its tenets or of its origin. In the time of Irenaeus its adherents were supposed to have been followers of Nicolaus, mentioned in Acts vi. 5, who was assumed to have turned heretical. If this tradition is correct (and the fact that it is most unusual for any Christian mentioned in the New Testament to be later associated in tradition with heresy suggests that it may be true), the formation of the sect must have been in the early period. Yet it is still impossible to say how soon it affected the church at Ephesus. Perhaps Paul saw the danger threatening at the time of his address to the Ephesian elders (Acts xx. 29, 30).

In spite of the fact that each of the grounds which has been examined from the internal conditions of the churches could be disputed as a pointer to a Domitianic date, it must be admitted that a date towards the close of the century would allow more time for the conditions to develop. The Lord's strong revulsion at the state of the Laodicean

---

[1] *Ad Phil.* xi. 3. 'But I have neither perceived nor heard any such thing among you, among whom the blessed Paul laboured, who are praised in the beginning of his Epistle. For concerning you he boasts in all the churches who then alone had known the Lord, for we had not yet known him' (Lake, *op. cit.*, p. 297).

[2] Polycarp was bishop of Smyrna, and the 'we' presumably means his church.

[3] *Op. cit.*, pp. 78f.

church would certainly become more intelligible after a considerable interval.

(v) *Arguments deduced from the relationship of the Apocalypse to other New Testament writings.* It is probable that our author used the Gospel of Matthew and perhaps also the Gospel of Luke.[1] If the widely held dating of these books is correct (i.e. AD 80–85), the Apocalypse would need to be dated subsequent to this, which would support a Domitianic date. But since this dating of the Gospels is conjectural and may very well be wrong it would be precarious to base any argument upon it. Moreover, the parallels may be drawn from oral tradition or even first-hand acquaintance where the teaching of our Lord is paralleled.

(vi) *The traditional dating of the book.* Undoubtedly a strong argument in favour of a Domitianic date is the fact that the earliest and the weightiest external witnesses attest it. Irenaeus[2] is quite specific that the Apocalypse 'was seen no such long time ago, but almost in our own generation, at the end of the reign of Domitian'. Since Irenaeus' own

---

[1] Charles (*op. cit.*, I, p. lxxxiii) gives a detailed list of parallels, the most notable of which are as follows. Parallels with Matthew: Rev. i. 3, Mt. xxvi. 18; Rev. i. 7, Mt. xxiv. 30; Rev. i. 16, Mt. xvii. 2; Rev. iii. 2, xvi. 15, Mt. xxiv. 42, 43; Rev. iii. 5, Mt. x. 32 (Lk. xii. 8); Rev. vi. 4, Mt. x. 34; Rev. vi. 12, 13, Mt. xxiv. 29 (cf. also Mk. xiii. 24, 25, Lk. xxi. 25); Rev. xi. 15, Mt. iv. 8; Rev. xiii. 11, Mt. vii. 15; Rev. xvii. 15, Mt. xx. 16, xxii. 14; Rev. xix. 7, Mt. v. 12; Rev. xxi. 10, cf. Mt. iv. 8. The Lucan parallels are less numerous but the following are worth noting: Rev. i. 3, Lk. xi. 28; Rev. v. 5, Lk. vii. 13, viii. 52; Rev. vi. 10, Lk. xviii. 7, 8; Rev. vi. 15, 16, Lk. xxiii. 30; Rev. vi. 17, Lk. xxi. 36; Rev. xi. 3, 6, Lk. iv. 25; Rev. xii. 9, Lk. x. 18; Rev. xiv. 4, Lk. ix. 57; Rev. xviii. 24, Lk. xi. 50. Many of these parallels are no more than verbal echoes and may not indicate literary dependence. They may do no more than indicate the author's acquaintance with the oral tradition.

E. F. Scott (*The Book of Revelation*,[4] 1941, p. 30) maintained that the author was so familiar with the apocalyptic section of the Synoptic Gospels that he used it as a framework for his own prophecy. Scott suggested that he found it in Mark's Gospel. But this supposition is dubious, although it would not be surprising if our Lord's apocalyptic teaching had deeply influenced the author's mind. But there is no evidence that he *consciously* modelled his own book on it.

J. Oman (*The Book of Revelation*, 1923, p. 29) raised the question whether John would have possessed any MSS of other New Testament books in exile and thought that any parallels with other books would more likely be due to memory than to literary dependence.*

[2] *Adv. Haer.* v. 30. 3. F. H. Chase (*JTS*, VIII, 1906, pp. 431–435) disputed that Irenaeus was referring to the Apocalypse. He argued that it was John and not his writing that 'was seen'.

connection with Asia Minor and acquaintance with Polycarp in his youth would give him a good opportunity to receive reliable opinion on this matter, this evidence must be treated seriously. Yet it is, of course, possible that Irenaeus made a mistake.[1] Later tradition mostly supports Irenaeus' testimony,[2] although there is some evidence for the time of Nero[3] and even one witness for the time of Claudius,[4] but this was no doubt an error for Nero Claudius. The testimony of this external evidence is so strong that even Hort,[5] an advocate for a Neronian date, concluded, 'If external evidence alone could decide, there would be a clear preponderance for Domitian.' On the principle that a strong tradition must be allowed to stand unless internal evidence makes it impossible, which is certainly not true in this case, the Domitianic dating must have the decision in its favour.[6] But some brief indication of the arguments for an earlier date must be given in order to stress the need for caution against being too dogmatic.[7]

---

[1] Hort (op. cit., p. xxxii), who preferred a Neronian date for the Apocalypse, thought that Irenaeus' statement may have been a mere guess.

[2] For details, cf. Swete, op. cit., p. xcix; or Charles, op. cit., I, p. xciii.

[3] So the Syriac Apocalypse and the apocryphal Acts of John.

[4] Epiphanius, Haer. li. 12. 233 (probably based on Hippolytus).   [5] Op. cit., p. xx.

[6] An attempt to reconcile the tradition with an early date was made by H. B. Workman, Persecution in the Early Church (1906), p. 46 n. 3. He suggested that the letters were sent separately in Nero's time, but the entire work was not published until Domitian's reign. He also held to composite sources (p. 358).

[7] No reference has been made to arguments for a late date based on three minor points: (a) the reference to the 'Lord's day' (i. 10); (b) the apparent liturgical purpose of the book (cf. i. 3); and (c) the supposition that the angels of the churches represent monarchical bishops. The third point is definitely open to challenge, while the other two indicate nothing regarding dating. How early the first day of the week was called the Lord's Day we do not know, neither do we know enough about early Christian liturgical practice to place i. 3 in its true perspective (if indeed it is to be understood liturgically!). Cf. the comments of Michaelis, op. cit., p. 317; and Feine-Behm, op. cit., pp. 287, 288.

Another incidental corroboration of a Domitianic date is suggested by the reference in Rev. vi. 6 being understood as an allusion to Domitian's edict in AD 92 for the regulation of crops (cf. Moffatt, ILNT, p. 507, and Exp., VII, vi, 1908, pp. 359–369). Torrey (op. cit., p. 79) rejects this theory, originally proposed by Reinach in 1901, while Michaelis (loc. cit.) calls it 'quite uncertain' (ganz unsicher).

It has not been thought necessary in the discussions on date to comment on the critical analytical views of such scholars as Völter, who maintained a date as late as AD 140 for the addition of chapters i–iii, which, he considered, combated Cerinthianism (Das Problem der Apocalypse, 1893, pp. 375ff.). But see p. 967 for a review of compilation theories.

b. Arguments in favour of a Neronian date

(i) *The identification of the sixth king of Rev. xvii. 10.* In view of the mention of the seven hills in verse 9 there can be little doubt that the primary reference[1] in verse 10 is to the sequence of Roman emperors. Since five have fallen, the sixth must be the reigning emperor. Now the identification will depend on whether calculations commence with Julius Caesar or Augustus. The latter is the more natural since he was the first to be proclaimed emperor, and he would have had particular significance, in view of the fact that it was during his reign that the Christian Church commenced. In this case, Nero was the fifth emperor and it may be supposed, therefore, that the Apocalypse belongs to the time of his death and the period immediately following. There is some doubt about the sixth, but advocates of the earliest date would suppose that he was Galba.[2] It may at least be said in favour of this method of calculation that it avoids the necessity for ignoring altogether the three minor claimants for the throne in the year following Nero's death, viz. Galba, Otho and Vitellius, in order to make the sixth king Vespasian. But it may reasonably be objected that these three emperors would have no importance for the provincials, who would naturally enumerate only the settled heads.[3] At the same time, if John is actually writing before the collapse of Galba, the position would be different, but the fatal objection is that the eighth king cannot be identified with Vitellius, who reigned for only a very short time. Some advocates of the Domitianic date, on the other hand, make the sixth king to be Vespasian and the eighth Domitian, but this is difficult because the eighth is said to be one of the seven returned to reign. The only solution is to regard Domitian as a kind of reincarnation of Nero, because he continued the persecuting policy of his predecessor. But even then the vision comes in the reign of the sixth king and not the eighth. Perhaps the seer received his vision earlier than he published it,[4] or perhaps we have here a

---

[1] This is not to exclude the possibility that it may have a secondary futuristic reference in common with Hebrew prophetical method.

[2] This is strongly argued by C. C. Torrey (*op. cit.*, pp. 58ff.) who dates the book in AD 68 just after the Neronian persecutions and the emperor's death.

[3] So Moffatt, *ILNT*, p. 506. Hort (*op. cit.*, pp. xxviii, xxix) considered the year of anarchy should be treated as an interval on the strength of Suetonius' comment (*Vesp.* i) (cf. also Lohmeyer, *op. cit.*, p. 143).*

[4] W. Sanday (*JTS*, VIII, 1907, pp. 489 ff.) thought that what had been written at one time had been adapted to another, hence the confusion.

genuine prophecy. This latter supposition, which is in full harmony with the book's own claims to be a revelation, would necessarily date the book before Domitian, in the early years of Vespasian (see below). Or even more probably, perhaps, the numbers of the kings should be regarded symbolically.[1]

(ii) *The identification of the number 666* (Rev. xiii. 18). Many attempts were made to interpret this symbol in ancient times, but not until recent times[2] has it ever been calculated on the basis of the Hebrew transcription of the name Nero(n) Caesar, which in Hebrew enumeration makes a total of 666. But there are some insuperable difficulties here. Irenaeus[3] discusses the identification, but assumes without question that the calculation must be done in Greek, although he comes to no satisfactory conclusion.[4] It is true that a textual variant arose in early times which read 616,[5] which might possibly refer to Gaius Caesar (the mad Caligula) or else Nero Caesar (i.e. without the Hebrew letter 'n'— a distinct advantage). But the variant reading witnesses to early perplexity over this number. Another reason for rejecting the above-mentioned hypothesis is the fact that the author would hardly expect his Asiatic readers to understand a Hebrew cipher, unless, of course, Torrey's view that the book was originally written in Aramaic be accepted.[6] It seems better to suppose that the key was well enough known to the original readers, but that it soon became lost in the sub-

[1] So Lohmeyer (*op. cit.*, p. 143), who treated the number as typical of apocalyptic tradition. Lohmeyer maintained that the 'eighth' is symbolical for a superhuman form and considered that the 'five' bear an apocalyptical unity. Even if Lohmeyer's comparisons with Mandaean parallels are open to challenge as a basis for interpretation, yet his rejection of the literal historical method of interpretation is worthy of careful consideration (cf. *ibid.*, pp. 145–147 for his excursus on this). Cf. also M. Kiddle, *The Revelation of St. John* (1940), pp. 349–351.

[2] According to Zahn (*INT*, III, p. 447 n. 4) it was Fritzsche (1831) who first proposed this identification.

[3] *Adv. Haer.* v. 28–30.

[4] It should be noted, however, that the idea of enumeration in Hebrew and the significance of numbers attached to ancient personalities was familiar to Jewish exegetes. It was valuable in maintaining the validity of the Law as, for instance, when Moses married an Ethiopian, it was discovered that her name totalled 736, which was also the total for the phrase 'fair of appearance'. The offending alien was thus conveniently explained away (cf. Carpenter, *op. cit.*, p. 137).

[5] This alternative reading is mentioned by Irenaeus and was known by the Donatist Tyconius (see Zahn, *op. cit.*, p. 448, for details).

[6] Cf. his comment on this cipher, *op. cit.*, p. 60.

sequent history of the book.[1] It is hardly a safe guide in chronological discussions.[2]

(iii) *Supposed references to the pre-siege conditions in Jerusalem.* In xi. 1ff., there is a description of the measuring of the city of Jerusalem, with special reference to the temple. Does this refer to a time, therefore, when the temple is still standing? It might well be so, but this would date it before AD 70. Against this it should be noted that there is no need to interpret this description literally of the temple of Herod, although its form is no doubt suggested by that temple.[3] Moreover, Clement of Rome also refers to the temple in the present tense and no-one would suppose because of this that his writing must be dated before AD 70. Yet there is point in Torrey's contention that the absence of any reference to the siege of Jerusalem is difficult to imagine in a Jewish book after AD 70. The only problem is to be sure that we are dealing with a Jewish book. But if we are, this argument must be allowed some weight. Nevertheless, some who acknowledge a pre-siege date for chapter xi resort to a theory of sources to explain it away from any considerations of date.[4]

This evidence as a whole, while suggestive, cannot be regarded as at all conclusive, and indeed, in view of the strong external evidence for a later date, must be regarded as doubtful. It would be strange, if the book really was produced at the end of Nero's reign, that so strong a tradition arose associating it with Domitian's.

---

[1] In a recent article E. Stauffer makes the plausible suggestion that the number should be calculated in Greek from the official title of the reigning emperor. He believes that emperor to be Domitian, but suggests the calculation should be made from the abbreviation of the full title Αυτοκρατωρ Καισαρ Δομετιανος Σεβαστος Γερμανικος (i.e. Α. ΚΑΙ. DOMET. ΣΕΒ. ΓΕ, which totals 666). Abbreviations were usual on coins, but this form is uncommon and would have been chosen for greater security (see article '666' in *Coniectanea Neotestamentica*, XI, 1947, pp. 237–241). But other suggestions have been made which appear to be equally plausible (cf. W. Hadorn's argument for Trajan according to his surname ULPIOS, which in Greek totals 666; *ZNTW*, 19, 1920, pp. 11–29).

[2] It has been more generally recognized that a safer procedure is first to fix the date and then to decipher the number. There are more indications of the former than the latter.

[3] Cf. Swete, *op. cit.*, *ad loc.* Cf. A. Feuillet (*NTS*, 4, 1958, pp. 183–200), who calls the temple reference a pure symbol.

[4] Cf. Beckwith, *op. cit.*, p. 208; Charles, *op. cit.*, I, p. xciv.

c. Arguments for a Vespasianic date

A dating during the period AD 70–80 has been favoured by some,[1] largely owing to the identification of the sixth king with Vespasian, which then allows any time during the full period of his reign as possible for the production of the book. But there are some fatal objections. Vespasian did not take seriously the idea of kingly divinity and as far as is known was not a persecutor of the Church. Moreover, the period of his reign was marked by comparative calm and would not well fit the tumultuous background of the Apocalypse. Charles[2] has maintained that the background of the letters to the churches belongs to Vespasian's reign, but that the writer has re-edited them in Domitian's. Editorial theories[3] of this sort vitiate the argument which depends upon them, for whatever does not agree with the point of view maintained is too easily got rid of by editorial ingenuity or stupidity. If this method must be rejected, the fact remains that the text of xvii. 10 would seem most naturally to point to Vespasian as the reigning emperor and it is not satisfactory to resort as Charles[4] does to relegating xvii. 10, 11 to earlier sources. It would be much more reasonable in view of the impasse which seems to follow all historical attempts to interpret this statement, to regard it symbolically,[5] and so leave it out of calculations of date.[6]

IV. PURPOSE

Assuming that the first three chapters form an integral part of the book (see the discussion on Unity, pp. 967ff. below), we may at once say that it was designed for a specific group of people with specific needs. The main portion of the book (chapter iv onwards) appears to be prepared on a much broader canvas, but nevertheless the more local purpose is not lost sight of, as xxii. 16 shows. Evidently the writer originally intended his message to be read aloud in the churches to

[1] Moffatt (*ILNT*, p. 503) cites B. Weiss, Düsterdieck, Bartlet, C. A. Scott as maintaining this opinion.

[2] *Op. cit., loc. cit.*

[3] M. E. Boismard seems to favour some such theory (cf. his comment in Robert-Feuillet's *Introduction*, II, p. 742).

[4] *Op. cit.*, I, p. xcvi.   [5] Cf. Michaelis' discussion, *op. cit.*, pp. 316, 317.

[6] A. Feuillet (*NTS*, 4, 1958, pp. 183ff.) considers that the book was published in Domitian's reign but issued as if in Vespasian's, a process which he calls 'antedatation' and supports from Jewish apocalyptic usage.

whom it was addressed (i. 3), in which case it may well be described as a circular letter.[1]

The letters to the seven churches reveal much about the internal conditions of these churches, which helps us to fix with some accuracy the writer's purpose. As a true prophet he must record the challenges he has received from the Lord of the Church and must pass them on as he has been commanded (i. 11). The Lord has some things to commend but also many things to condemn. There is a manifest tendency towards spiritual deterioration. Some churches are being subjected to the pressure of immoral environments. Some are affected by false teachers. In most of the churches there is need for the call to repent, while in at least one church, Laodicea, material prosperity has resulted in spiritual decline to such a degree that it has caused revulsion to the Church's Lord. Yet, in spite of the words of criticism, for most of the churches the dominating theme of the letters is encouragement. Whoever is prepared to listen is invited to do so, as the formula at the end of each letter shows. Moreover each message ends with a promise. A remarkably practical note is thus struck at the very beginning.

Beyond the need to challenge the churches is the problem of the increasing opposition between the Church and State. But all this was to be viewed against the background of the end time and this leads John to contemplate in the Spirit the consummation of the ages. He paints in vivid colours the various judgments which are to fall upon those whose activity is motivated by the spirit of Antichrist. Throughout the book there are hints at coming triumph, but it is not until towards the end that the final overthrow of the Beast and of Babylon (the Roman Empire) and even of Satan himself is portrayed. This belief in the ultimate triumph of Christianity over all opposing forces brought a remarkable optimism at a time when the Roman Empire was increasing its power and when the Christian Church in proportion was pitifully small. The whole book is, therefore, a message of hope particularly adapted to those who are passing through, or who know they may soon be called to pass through, fierce temptation.

But it may well be intended to forewarn those who were indifferent to the coming threats and who would not be prepared for the storm when it broke. They needed to be told the true nature of the imperial

[1] By the end of the book the writer almost seems to anticipate that the book will have a wider public (xxii. 18) and that it will be of vital importance to ensure its integrity. Cf. Swete, *op. cit.*, p. xcviii.

power, particularly when the titular head of the empire demanded divine worship. No-one who had heard this book read could be in any doubt about the issues involved and any compromise was out of the question.

Because it portrays the triumph of right over wrong and all is brought into subjection to God, Charles[1] called the book 'the Divine Statute Book of International Law', and there is aptness in the description. In an age of political intrigues this book succoured the conviction that all true government proceeds from God and is upheld by God. Its basis is the certainty of the ultimate triumph of divine justice.*

V. DESTINATION

It is not difficult to decide on the immediate destination of the book, for it was obviously intended for the churches of Asia mentioned in chapters ii and iii. It is not, however, addressed to all the Christian churches of the province, for there were certainly Christians at Troas (Acts xx. 7ff.), Hierapolis and Colossae (cf. Col. ii. 1, iv. 13, 16) in the first century and almost certainly at Tralles and Magnesia, since Ignatius addressed letters to them in the early second century. What then was the principle that John used in his choice of churches? It was definitely not their civic importance, although the first three are in order of civic dignity, for the inclusion of such small towns as Thyatira and Philadelphia to the exclusion of much larger towns sufficiently disposes of this.

W. M. Ramsay[2] supposed that the choice of churches was governed by the great circular road which linked them all and which, therefore, provided a convenient network for the distribution of the letters throughout the whole province. The order of mention would then represent the route which the messenger took in delivering the book. There is much to be said for this suggestion. But it must not be lost sight of that John is recording his messages as direct communications from the Lord of the Church and it may, therefore, be supposed that these were the churches which were especially under his care and for which he had been particularly burdened before the Lord. It has been suggested that the itinerary is an imaginary one, since the letters are addressed to the 'angels' of the churches[3] and not to the churches

---

[1] *Op. cit.*, I, p. ciii.   [2] *The Letters to the Seven Churches of Asia* (1904), p. 183.
[3] Elsewhere in the book the word 'angel' is always used of spiritual beings and it is reasonable to suppose that 'guardian angels' are here meant in accordance with current belief. But it is strange to find the guardian angels so strongly condemned for the misdeeds of their churches (cf. Swete, *op. cit.*, pp. 21, 22).

themselves, and this in such a book would not be altogether surprising. Yet the messages are so definitely linked to the historical circumstances that it is impossible to suppose that John did not intend each church to take special note of its own message.[1] Indeed, as Ramsay has clearly shown, each message not only suits the needs of the churches but also reflects the geographical background.

It would seem, therefore, that in the book as a whole the writer thinks primarily of the immediate needs of his Asiatic churches, but that he foresees that the message of Christian triumph over the adverse forces of evil would have a much wider relevance. It is difficult not to feel that he envisaged the distribution of the book to a wide Christian public beyond the seven churches named. The early attestation for the book shows, at least, that such wide distribution actually occurred.

VI. SOURCES

In common with every other book in the New Testament, the Apocalypse has been subjected to the source-critic's analysis and it will be necessary to give a brief indication of the results.

The most obvious source of ideas and mental images is the Old Testament. The author has drawn most from the books of Daniel,[2] Ezekiel[3] and, to a lesser degree, Zechariah, which have supplied the forms to express new apocalyptic revelations. But his mind was also saturated with other parts of the Old Testament, particularly Isaiah (whose words are reflected more than any other), Jeremiah, Joel and Exodus (in the parallels with the plagues). Indeed so basic is the Old

[1] Oman (*The Book of Revelation*, 1923, p. 28) suggested that John on Patmos knew that he would be unable to communicate with the outside world and therefore addressed the message to the 'guardian angels', who he believed would be able to communicate with the churches.

[2] Most notable are the reminiscences of the persecuting Antiochus Epiphanes (Dn. vii; cf. Rev. xiii. 1ff., xvii. 12, xx. 4) and the figure of the Son of man coming in judgment (Dn. vii. 7–13, 22; cf. Rev. xiv. 14, xx. 4, 12).

[3] Cf. such common ideas as the initial throne-vision (Ezk. ix; Rev. iv. 1–11); the scroll written on both sides (Ezk. ii. 9; Rev. v. 1), and the eating of a scroll (Ezk. iii. 3; Rev. x. 10); the four products of the fourth seal (Ezk. xiv. 21; Rev. vi. 8); the marked foreheads (Ezk. ix. 4; Rev. vii. 3); coals of fire thrown from heaven to earth (Ezk. x. 2; Rev. viii. 5); an assembly of birds as a symbol of judgment (Ezk. xxxix. 17f.; Rev. xix. 17f.); Gog and Magog (Ezk. xxxviii–xxxix; Rev. xx. 7–10); the messianic Jerusalem (Ezk. xl–xlvii; Rev. xxi). For a concise table showing how Ezekiel dominates the structure of the Apocalypse, cf. P. Carrington, *The Meaning of the Revelation* (1931), pp. 64, 65.*

Testament to the writer's mental concepts that out of 404 verses in the entire book there are only 126 which contain no allusion to it.[1] Yet it should be noted that nowhere does the writer quote from the Old Testament, and even where his language echoes the Old Testament he rarely uses the *ipsissima verba*.[2] There is no conscious attempt to construct a mosaic from Old Testament materials. Rather has the language of the Old Testament so moulded the author's thought that he cannot write without reflecting it. As Swete[3] remarked, it is as though his 'words and thoughts arrange themselves in his visions like the changing patterns of a kaleidoscope, without conscious effort on his own part'. It is important to recognize this fact, for it means that the book is more than a dramatic compilation; it is an experience under the control of the Holy Spirit (i. 10).

Many scholars have considered the Jewish apocalypses to be a more certain source for the author than the Old Testament, but it is because this notion must be rejected that the Old Testament background has been considered first. The apocalyptic form which our book possesses may certainly be paralleled from the Jewish pseudepigrapha. Apocalypses were in vogue and were generally written in the name of some such ancient worthy as Enoch, Abraham, Ezra or Baruch, who was made to predict the history of the Jewish people from his (the assumed author's) time up to the real author's time, and to include in the same vein an extension of the history into the future. The idea was to use the past history to give confidence in the future predictions. While the style used has many similarities with the Apocalypse of John in that imagery is used to symbolize events, yet there are some vital differences which suggest that, although the writer was acquainted with the Jewish works, he is independent of them and cannot be considered as a continuation of them.[4] To begin with, he does not use a pseudonym, but writes in his own name. Secondly, he does not focus attention on past history, but concentrates on the present and future. Thirdly, he is more in alignment with the Old Testament prophets in the denunciation of evil and in the moral exhortations to nobler living. And finally,

---

[1] From the list of citations in Westcott and Hort's text. See Swete, *op. cit.*, pp. cxxxix ff., for a selected list of the most important examples; or Charles, *op. cit.*, I, pp. lxviii ff., for a more exhaustive list.*   [2] Cf. Swete, *op. cit.*, p. liii.

[3] *Loc. cit.* Lohmeyer speaks suggestively of the Old Testament as the Seer's 'Atmosphäre' (*op. cit.*, p. 196).*

[4] Cf. the article by G. E. Ladd, 'The Revelation and Jewish Apocalyptic', *EQ*, XXIX (1957), pp. 94–100, for a discussion of the differences.*

the spiritual grasp of the writer is far removed from the pedestrian and often gloomy approach of the apocalyptists. It is no wonder that the books of the latter were never even considered for canonical status, while the work of the former, in spite of its many obscurities, was recognized from earliest days as having the stamp of inspiration upon it. Nevertheless, this is not to say that John does not reflect any of the apocalyptical writings. Charles[1] has listed eighteen passages where he thinks there is dependence, or at least parallel thoughts. The force of the evidence will appeal differently to different minds, but in the present writer's judgment, there is little to conclude for the dependence of the Apocalypse on these Jewish pseudepigrapha. Almost all the passages are from 1 Enoch, and for the author's acquaintance with this book there is certainly something to be said, but the others are more doubtful.[2] To give two examples of the influence that Jewish apocalyptic is supposed to have exerted, in iv. 6 the description of the cherubim, according to Charles,[3] owes more to such literature than to Ezekiel, to which it is also clearly indebted. Moreover, in vi. 11 the idea that the world would end when the number of the martyrs is complete is paralleled almost exactly in 1 Enoch xlvii. 3, 4.[4]

The sources so far referred to are those which affected the author's background of thought. Some comment must now be made on the theory that our author has used literary sources which he has incorporated in his own work. Charles,[5] for instance, found such sources behind vii. 1–8, xi. 1–13, xii, xiii, xvii, xviii and perhaps xv. 5–8, of which some are reckoned to be Greek and some Hebrew. But Charles' grounds were wholly subjective and for that reason must be regarded with caution. At the same time he did not, as did many earlier interpreters, infer from the use of sources the disunity of the book (see discussion below). Yet if the author is presenting what he claims to be a direct revelation from God in the prophetic manner, it is impossible to think of him editing literary sources as carefully as Charles' theory supposes. This type of critical analysis can carry no

---

[1] Op. cit., I, pp. lxxxii f.

[2] Charles (loc. cit.) includes the Testaments of the XII Patriarchs, the Assumption of Moses, the Psalms of Solomon and 2 Enoch. Lohmeyer (op. cit., p. 196) admits the parallels but thinks they point to tradition, not necessarily to books.

[3] Op. cit., I, pp. 117ff.

[4] Other parallels mentioned by Charles (op. cit., I, pp. 178f.) are 4 Ezra iv. 35, which appears to have been indebted to our apocalypse here, and 2 Baruch xxx. 2 similarly.   [5] Op. cit., p. lxii.*

conviction among those who treat the visions of the Apocalypse as genuinely ecstatic.

VII. UNITY

Because some scholars have supposed that the book contains incongruities and adjacent passages which are unrelated to each other, various theories have been proposed which involve compilation from one or more sources, which have later been edited. It is possible here to give only the briefest indication of these theories, which were mainly in vogue at the turn of the century and are now largely discounted. For the sake of clarity they will be classified under three main types.

a. Compilation theories

There have been several hypotheses which suppose that an editor (or editors) has taken over some independent sources and welded them into a unity.[1] Some (Weyland, Holtzmann, de Faye) supposed the combination of two Jewish sources, while others (Schmidt and Spitta) maintained three sources, either all Jewish or a mixture of Jewish and Christian, which were later adapted and modified by an editor. Other forms of this type of theory were the two-source theory, in which one was Jewish and one Christian (J. Weiss) or both were Christian Hebrew sources (Bruston). A more complicated theory (propounded by Völter) supposed that the basic apocalypse was written by Mark, who added an appendix (AD 68), and then a revision was made by Cerinthus in Vespasian's time and a later revision in Domitian's time. Two considerations are sufficient to dispose of this type of theory. First of all, the impression of unity which the Apocalypse gives, both in form and content, would have to be attributed to the skill of the compiler, which is most difficult to concede. Secondly, the linguistic peculiarities in the Greek, which have already been mentioned, run throughout all parts of the book and must therefore be attributed to the author and not to an editor.

b. Revision theories

This type of theory assumes one basic source which has been worked over. E. Vischer's[2] is the most notable form of this hypothesis, for he

[1] Details of these theories may conveniently be found in Beckwith, *op. cit.*, pp. 224ff.; Moffatt, *ILNT*, pp. 489ff.; Bousset, *op. cit.*, pp. 108ff.

[2] 'Die Offenbarung Johannes eine jüdische Apokalypse in christlicher Bearbeitung', *TU*, II, iii (1886). Others who have advanced similar theories are Harnack, Martineau, S. Davidson and von Soden (cf. Moffatt, *ILNT*, p. 490, for details).

postulated that the original was a Jewish apocalypse and that an editor has adapted this for Christian purposes. He accounted for the impression of unity by supposing that the editor, who appended the Christian additions, was also the translator of the Jewish work. But the whole theory was based on the insecure supposition that there were irreconcilable elements (Jewish versus Christian), which were due more to the proposer's faulty exegesis than to the real facts of the case. Moreover, the final editor must have been wholly blind to these supposed contradictions. Such differences as are found (e.g. in the presentation of Messiah) are certainly not evidence of different authorship, but of changes of emphasis within one mind.[1]

c. Incorporation theories

Many scholars, who are convinced of the unity of the book, but who at the same time consider sources to have been used, have proposed an original apocalypse in which are incorporated various fragments of Jewish apocalyptic writing. This was first suggested by C. von Weizsäcker[2] and has been followed with many variations in the precise delineation of the incorporated material.[3] The contention in this kind of theory is that when these portions are extracted a basic unity of plan is revealed. But would any author encrust his own original pattern with the accretions of several other fragments? It is difficult if not impossible to believe that he would.[4]

---

[1] W. H. Simcox (*The Revelation of St. John the Divine*, CGT, 1893, pp. 215-234) gave a very balanced criticism of Vischer's theory, but was not convinced by it because of the unity of style throughout. M. G. Glazebrook (*The Apocalypse of St. John*, 1923, p. 16) accounted for some of the inconsistencies by assuming that the book records the author's experiences over some twenty years and by assuming that the disorder of the xx-xxii section was due to an abrupt cessation of the work before final revision could be made. This is, at least, a more probable revision theory than Vischer's, but assumes some stupidity on the part of the final editor.

[2] In his *Das apostolische Zeitalter der christlichen Kirche*[3] (1902), pp. 486ff.

[3] Others who have maintained similar theories are Sabatier, Schön, Pfleiderer, Bousset, Jülicher, McGiffert, C. A. Scott, Charles, Moffatt (cf. *ILNT*, p. 490).

[4] Charles gets over this by importing into his account of the origin of the work an unintelligent editor, who was a disciple of the author. But he is confident of the unity of the book, on the grounds of the basic similarity of grammar in all its various parts. He uses this also as a criterion for his reconstruction (cf. Charles, *Lectures on the Apocalypse*, Schweich Lectures, 1922, pp. 11ff.).

d. The traditional theory

This denies that any sources have been incorporated and supposes that the author is directly responsible for all the material in the book. This has the great advantage of accounting most adequately for the unity and of dispensing with any arbitrary methods of distinguishing sources.[1] It accounts for the alleged differences in the different parts of the book as due to normal variations in literary productions of an apocalyptic kind, although it does not deny that the author's mind has been influenced by the thought-forms of earlier material.[2]

VIII. STRUCTURE

So many and so varied have been the theories of the plan of this book that it is quite impossible in a work of this kind to give an adequate account of them. What will be attempted, therefore, is to give a brief survey of the main types of theories and to give sufficient indication of where the student interested in further enquiries may find the detailed analyses.

The majority of interpreters of this book assume that the action is not intended to be continuously described, but rather that successive groups of visions each portray similar events in different ways. By this means the recurring allusions to the approaching end of the age become intelligible. Yet under this general category, which may be termed theories of recapitulation, there have been numerous different theories of the structure of the book. On the other hand some theories are based on the assumption that the visions are in a continuous sequence throughout. These different theories may roughly be summarized as follows.

a. The patchwork theory

In this type of theory, which regards the book as a compilation but not necessarily by a mere editorial process, it is useless to look for a development of thought, for the author has been too deeply influenced by his sources to weld them into a closely-knit whole. Moffatt's[3] plan for the

---

[1] Moffatt (ILNT, p. 491) admitted that most of the above theories are handicapped by what he called 'Overprecision and arbitrary canons of literary criticism'.

[2] Advocates of this theory do not, of course, maintain that the book contains no obscurities, but rather that the obscurities are not necessarily due to the use of different materials or of derangements.*

[3] ILNT, pp. 485-488.

book illustrates this, for he postulated what he called 'intermezzos' to form the sutures between the various visions (e.g. vii. 1–17, x. 1–xi. 14, xiv. 1–20). Yet the whole has certainly the appearance of a unity which the author himself has impressed upon the material. Moffatt referred to 'the kaleidoscope of visions' in the book and this well sums up his view of its structure.[1]

b. The poetic theory

Kiddle[2] rejects the idea of treating the book according to any strict chronological scheme and in this respect his theory is somewhat akin to the preceding. But he considers that John has so mastered his material that it is useless to regard the work as a compilation. The author himself is not a calculating and careful arranger of vision-materials, but a visionary prophet and poet. To expect a logically worked out plan is, therefore, irrelevant. The poet aims to build up an impression and is not at all concerned about repeating himself, or arranging his material in a design which would pass the mechanical demands of many literary critics. Thus the recurring themes are all part of the total impression of the inevitability of coming judgment, each repetition of the theme adding some new colouring to the whole picture. There is much to be said for this kind of approach, for it avoids the forced attempts to reduce the book to a clearly defined plan of development.[3]

c. The symbolism theory

Closely allied to the last is the interpretation of the author's design by reference to the symbolism underlying the book. This type of theory has had many advocates, but has been given a new impetus recently through the work of Austin Farrer.[4] This writer traces three

[1] Carpenter (op. cit., p. 28) refers to separate sketches rather than to a coherent order between the scenes. M. E. Boismard (RB, LVI, 1949, pp. 507–539) has a similar theory, for he finds two sets of visions, one in Nero's time and one in Vespasian's or early in Domitian's time. The two were later combined and the letters added. At the same time Boismard does not regard it as necessary to dispense with unity of authorship. See also Robert-Feuillet's Introduction, pp. 122ff., for Boismard's doublet theory.*

[2] Op. cit., pp. xxviiff.

[3] This idea of a poetic purpose is in line with the poetic form which many scholars have noted (e.g. Lohmeyer, op. cit., pp. 185f.; Charles, op. cit., pp. 41ff.; N. W. Lund, Chiasmus in the New Testament, 1942, pp. 321–411).*

[4] A Rebirth of Images (1949).

successive symbolical threads in this book which furnish the key to the interpretation of the whole—the number seven, the Jewish liturgy, and astrology (the signs of the zodiac).[1] It need occasion no surprise that Farrer manages to fit all the complexities of the Apocalypse into his scheme, for the pursuer of symbols can see them wherever he chooses.[2] There is bound to be much manipulation with the plain meaning of the words and it is difficult to imagine what the original readers of the Apocalypse would have made out of Farrer's inter-pretations. He anticipates this objection[3] and maintains that they 'would understand what they would understand, and that would be as much as they had time to digest', which nicely side-tracks the difficulty. If this theory does not appeal to less symbolical minds, Farrer has made some provocative suggestions which may at least in some measure illustrate the subconscious images in the author's mind, even though they hardly seem convincing as an explanation of the main structure of the book. An author who had a burning message to proclaim may be expected to put it in a form more readily understood than this theory supposes.

d. The drama theory

Even more recently an American, J. W. Bowman,[4] has proposed that the book should be regarded in its entirety as a drama designed after the pattern of contemporary dramatic productions. Hence it consists of a prologue, a seven-act play and an epilogue. Between each of the acts are passages which serve to introduce the following act, in a way comparable to the stage-props of contemporary drama. In this scheme Bowman regards chapters i. 5–iii as Act I of the drama and considers that only i. 1–4 and xxii. 21 have been appended to give the work the appearance of a letter. He argues that since the number seven figures so largely in the book, it is reasonable to suppose that it provides the key to its structure (compare the next theory considered). The so-called 'stage props' (e.g. i. 9–20, iv. 1–v. 14, viii. 2–6, xi. 19, xv. 1, 8, xvi. 1, xvii. 1, 2, xx. 4–6) are paralleled by the habit of dramatists in intro-

---

[1] Farrer was not the first to connect the twelve houses of Israel with the signs of the zodiac (cf. C. E. Douglas, *JTS*, xxxvii, 1936, pp. 49–56, who nevertheless thought that John was using ancient traditions).

[2] Cf. T. W. Manson's criticism in *JTS*, L (1949), pp. 206–208.

[3] *Op. cit.*, p. 21.

[4] 'The Revelation to John: Its Dramatic Structure and Message', in *Interpretation*, IX (1955), pp. 436–453.

ducing gods to give information necessary for the audience. On the other hand, Bowman suggests that in these sections John is thinking more of the imagery of the temple than of the theatre.[1] There might be something to be said for this as far as the author's own conception of it is concerned, but the stage-prop idea must surely have been far from his mind.

e. The sevenfold design theory

It is, of course, clear that the number seven held a particular fascination for the author and all scholars would acknowledge this. But few have carried this to such lengths as Loenertz and Lohmeyer, who have both maintained that the number is the key to the whole structure of the book. The former[2] recognizes a distinct break at iii. 22 and consequently treats the book in two main visions, which together comprise seven groups of seven. The latter[3] goes even farther and finds seven-structures in strophes and sometimes in the divisions of strophes, much as he does in the First Epistle of John. The theory is worked out very ingeniously, but the impression is inescapable that if Lohmeyer is right the author of this book has developed his literary technique to such a degree that he must have concentrated more on the form than on the content. Yet a reading of the book does not give one the idea of a literary artist so much as of a prophet whose burning messages would transcend mere literary devices. At the same time, Lohmeyer has drawn attention to an important aspect of the relation of this book to the other Johannine literature in that all this literature contains similar sevenfold patterns.[4]

f. Transposition theories

All the preceding theories have assumed that some of the series of visions recapitulate on the previous series, but there have been attempts to treat the visions as strictly consecutive. It is significant that two lead-

---

[1] In a suggestive article on the influence of the Greek drama on the Apocalypse of John, R. R. Brewer maintained the opposite view, even finding the counterpart of the altar in the Dionysian altar before the throne in Greek theatres (*ATR*, XVIII, 1936, pp. 74–92).

[2] *The Apocalypse of St. John* (Eng. tr. by H. J. Carpenter, 1947).

[3] *Op. cit.*, pp. 185f.

[4] Archbishop Benson held a theory between this and the preceding, for he considered the book was like the relating of a drama, yet was not a drama. He made much of the seven choric songs which divided the action into seven parts (*op. cit.*, pp. 37ff.).

ing exponents of this view, Charles and Oman, have both achieved their end by means of textual rearrangements. Charles[1] considered that the concluding editor was not only stupid but morally culpable. Many interpolations were introduced (e.g. i. 8, viii. 7–12, xiv. 3e–4ab, xiv. 15–17, xxii. 18b–19). Charles arranged the visions in three continuous series, and to get over the difficulty of the repetitions, some of these visions are described as 'proleptic' (e.g. vii. 9–17, x.1–xi. 13, xiv). Whatever the merits of Charles' reconstruction, its considerable demerit is that continuity of plan is achieved only at the expense of quite arbitrary excisions or adjustments, a subjective procedure which cannot commend itself as being in accordance with the principles of scientific criticism.

Oman[2] differs from Charles in that he conceives of the derangements as being accidental and not intentional and he endeavours to produce an explanation of the present state of the text. Oman still, however, postulates some editorial additions,[3] which became necessary when the editor had arranged the sheets (although incorrectly) in the order which seemed right to him. The striking thing about this theory is the claim that the book naturally falls into sections of almost equal length in the Greek text, calculating on thirty-three lines for each papyrus sheet. The resultant rearrangement is considerable.[4] Moreover, some of the editorial glosses are not obvious and appear to be assumed more to make the text fit the theory than because of internal probability. In addition Oman admits that two sections are of different length and must be treated as exceptions. It would seem easier to imagine a writer carefully constructing a sevenfold structure with numerous sevenfold substructures than to conceive an author laboriously fitting his

[1] Commentary on the Revelation of St. John, I, pp. 1ff.

[2] J. Oman, The Book of Revelation (1923).

[3] In a second book, The Text of Revelation. A Revised Theory (1928), Oman considers these additions to be doublets, which the first editor repeated from his author.

[4] Oman's revised order is as follows: i. 9–iii. 22, xxii. 10–12, x. 1–11, xi. 1–13, xii. 1–14, xii. 14–xiii. 11, xiii. 11–18, xiv. 6–12, xv. 5, 6, xvi. 2–16, viii. 6–11 (+ other insertions from viii), xix. 11–15, xiv. 19, 20, xix. 16–21, xvi. 17–xvii. 9, xvii. 9–xviii. 6, xviii. 6–19, xviii. 19–xix. 9, i. 7, iv. 1–v. 2, v. 2–vi. 1, vi. 2–17, vii. 1–17, viii. 1–5, xvi. 4–7, viii. 6–13, ix. 1–7, ix. 7–21, xi. 14–19, xiv. 1–5, 13, 14, xiv. 14–19, xv. 1, 6–xvi. 1, xv. 2–4, xxi. 9–24, xxi. 24–xxii. 5, 6, 8, 9, xvi. 15, xxii. 14–17, 20 (+ insertions from xix. 10), i. 3–6, xx. 1–10, xx. 11–xxi. 1, 3–8, xxii. 18, 19, 21. McNeile-Williams (INT, p. 259), while admitting that this revised text reads more smoothly, yet rightly point out that it involves even greater manipulations than his original theory.

sections so accurately to his papyrus sheets. In any case, Oman maintains that some of the original sheets contained passages which are now
found in various parts of the Apocalypse, and it is impossible to see how
they came to be so distributed. A misplacement of whole sheets is
intelligible, but a redistribution of fragments of any one sheet is surely
highly improbable.[1]

g. The liturgical pattern theory

The presence of many liturgical features, particularly the numerous
hymns, has recently led to the theory that behind the structure of this
book is to be found a primitive form of the Paschal Vigil. The main
exponent of this view is M. H. Shepherd,[2] who has suggested that the
Seer has adopted the liturgy as a general framework for his book. Thus
he holds that i–iii represent the Scrutinies, iv–vi the Vigil, vii the
Initiation, viii–xix the Synaxis and xix–xxii the Eucharist. Several
interesting parallels occur, but these cannot prove that the structure of
the book is indebted to the liturgical pattern, for the evidence for the
latter is not sufficiently early for us to be certain of its primitive form.
This is a difficulty which confronts all liturgical theories for New
Testament books. Yet it is not impossible that some of the hymns may
have been in common use and that the writer's mind was well stocked
with them. One feature of this particular theory which is commendable
is its assumption not only of the unity of the book, but also of its
consecutive and logical sequence.

IX. THE PERMANENT MESSAGE

The history of the interpretation of the book does not concern us here,
except in so far as it throws light upon its permanent message. The
Historicist school of interpretation which regards the book as in some
measure a prophetic forecast of future history down to the consummation of time can have no possible doubt about its continual value.
This view, which was popular during the Reformation because of the
identification of the power of the Roman Church with Antichrist, is
capable of great flexibility and adjustments, as the history of the interpretation of the enigmatic number 666 abundantly shows. But alongside
this school of thought has been the Contemporary Historical school
which has denied all future reference and confined the purpose of the

---

[1] Cf. Carpenter's criticisms (*op. cit.*, pp. 187, 188).

[2] *The Paschal Liturgy and the Apocalypse* (1960), pp. 75–97; cf. also E. Lohse, *Die
Offenbarung des Johannes* (1960), pp. 48ff.*

Apocalypse to the immediate circumstances of the author's own day. As a consequence there was no point in attempting a full-scale exegesis of its riddles, because the key, which was well known to its original readers, has now been irretrievably lost. The logical outcome of such an interpretation is that the book might as well be discarded. It has no message for our modern age. Another school of interpretation is the Futurist which sees the main portion of the book as a description of events which are to take place immediately before the Parousia. Coupled with this interpretation is the idea that chapters i–iii contain successive predictions of the successive periods of Church history. But such an interpretation is possible only at the expense of sound exegetical principles. It is better to conclude that in line with the Hebrew prophets, there are both immediate and distant points of view in this book, and that its relevance is thus both historical and eschatological.

The Literary Critical method of dealing with the book, which concentrates attention on sources and grammatical form, has done very little to re-establish interest in this book in spite of its claims to have solved much of its enigmatic symbolism. Although this method has thrown light upon many obscurities, it must in the end be recognized that the abiding value of the book rests not on its sources nor on its form, but on its message.

But the problem is to discover some means of expressing this message in a form relevant for every age. This has led to the Symbolic school of interpretation which uses the imagery to illustrate spiritual truths irrespective of the original historical context, a school of thought which has had its advocates in all periods of Church history. Yet its divorce from historical background inevitably makes it more subjective, although it has not been without its real spiritual values. A surer exegesis will want rather to draw out the permanent spiritual values against the historical background. The book will then still claim its place in the Canon, because it enunciates principles which are always applicable. These principles may briefly be summarized as follows.

1. The first principle is that faith triumphs over might. This is the most obvious conviction which must strike every reader of the book. All the gathering power of antagonistic forces, whether personified in Rome (= Babylon), the Beast or Antichrist, which seem at the time of writing to be irresistible, are laid low at the end. Their evil designs and malicious persecutions may be vividly described in the body of the book, but the confidence in their final overthrow, which is glimpsed

now and then, reaches its climax when mighty Rome is reduced to dust and irrevocable judgment is carried out against Antichrist and the Beast. In the end it is the Lamb who is victorious, and this conviction has brought immeasurable comfort in all ages to those who have seemed so helpless in a time of crisis and persecution.

2. The second principle is the inevitability of judgment. Although closely linked with the first principle, this should be separated from it because of the frequency with which it has been overlooked, particularly in our modern age. The idea that sin and evil in all its manifestations in a materialistic age is doomed to final judgment is not palatable for our easy-going society. But the idea of judgment is integral to Christianity. It was emphasized by our Lord and by all the apostles. If John's imagery sometimes appears to be crude and even horrific, and if his spirit seems to be vindictive it must not be forgotten that judgment is a fearful theme for a poet's pen. He was attempting to describe the indescribable, and if he used current apocalyptic terms to assist him, his fundamental message of judgment must not be allowed to elude us because our modern literary tastes find the apocalyptic forms abhorrent. Judgment is an idea which no amount of sophistication will ever make attractive and John has grasped that more fully than his modern denigrators.

3. The third principle is that the Christian approach presents the true philosophy of history. John looks at the present in the light of the future, as well as in terms of the past. If it be objected that the future is unknown and his method is, therefore, invalidated, it must be recognized that the Christian view of history assumes an onward movement to a final satisfactory consummation. Without this confidence there seems no ground for anything but pessimism and this was never truer than in a nuclear age. This book with its powerful assurance that there are ultimate values which far outstrip the claims of pure materialism has a particular relevance for today.

The book is, therefore, a book of encouragement and exhortation. To those who combat the great forces of evil with apparently little success, the book brings particular inspiration. And to those who are inclined in any age to forsake their faith because the odds against them seem to be too great, the book issues a powerful challenge to endurance.[1]

[1] Cf. H. H. Wernecke, *The Book of Revelation Speaks to us* (1954), pp. 32, 33, who is a lucid exponent of the symbolic method of interpretation. Cf. also A. Burnet, *The Lord reigneth* (1946).*

CONTENTS

I. THE PREFACE (i. 1–3)

John calls his book both a revelation from God and a prophecy which is to be read aloud.

II. THE SEVEN LETTERS (i. 4–iii. 22)

a. The introduction (i. 4–20)

The writer sends a general greeting to the seven Asiatic churches. This is followed by an introductory vision in which he is commanded to write what he sees for these churches, and by a majestic vision of Christ in the midst of the churches.

b. The letters to the churches (ii. 1–iii. 22)

Each message is intended to meet a specific internal condition and each ends with a promise to those who are victorious.

1. Ephesus is a church with a fine past, but a loveless present (ii. 1–7).
2. Smyrna is subjected to special attack from Satan, and Christians who are faithful in the midst of it are promised a reward (ii. 8–11).
3. Pergamum is another church placed in a satanic environment, and some, who have been drawn away towards false teaching, are called on to repent (ii. 12–17).
4. Thyatira is affected by immorality, but those who have not been deceived are urged to hold on to what they possess (ii. 18–29).
5. Sardis is described as a dead church, with a few only who have not become soiled by their environment. The advice to these people is to wake up (iii. 1–6).
6. Philadelphia receives warm commendation for its past loyalty and is promised special protection in the coming world-wide trial (iii. 7–13).
7. Laodicea is condemned for compromise, but is still given the opportunity to repent (iii. 14–22).

III. VISIONS INTRODUCING THE PROPHECY (iv. 1–v. 14)

a. The vision of God (iv. 1–11)

The writer records vividly a scene in heaven which is dominated by the throne of God and the worship which is offered to Him.

b. The vision of Christ (v. 1–14)

The scene is still in heaven but now the focus is on the Lamb, who is alone worthy to open the seven-sealed scroll which He holds in His hand. Again the worship is described, and several groups join in the responses.

IV. THE SEVEN SEALS (vi. 1–viii. 1)

a. The first six seals opened (vi. 1–17)

After each of the first four is broken, a rider on a horse appears, representing conquest, war, famine and death. On the opening of the fifth seal, the cry of the martyrs is heard and they are told to wait a little longer. Immediately afterwards, terrible calamities come into focus as the sixth seal is broken; this is the Lamb manifesting His wrath.

b. The sealing of God's people (vii. 1–17)

In contrast to this awful scene of wrath is the moving description of the sealing of God's people, represented by twelve thousand from each tribe. Following this ceremony is another vision of the Lamb being worshipped. A conversation between one of the elders and the writer results in an explanation of the great multitude of worshippers.

c. The seventh seal (viii. 1)

This leads to the revelation of the seven trumpets, but only after half an hour of silence.

V. THE SEVEN TRUMPETS (viii. 2–xiii. 18)

a. The trumpeters introduced (viii. 2–5)

The scene is in heaven as the seven trumpeters prepare to blow their trumpets. They wait for an eighth to fling a censer down to earth, which results in violent disturbances in the natural order, a clear hint at what is to be expected when the trumpets are blown.

b. The first four trumpets (viii. 6–12)

Hail and fire, volcanic eruption, a poisonous star and a darkening of the sun, moon and stars follow the blasts on these trumpets.

c. *The eagle's warning* (viii. 13)

An eagle's expression of woe from mid-heaven heightens the expectation for the next three trumpets.

d. *The fifth and sixth trumpets* (ix. 1–21)

The former of these shows a glimpse into a bottomless pit, which is presided over by Apollyon (the Destroyer). It is a place of torture (ix. 1–12). The latter shows four angels whose mission is destruction, and again the description is one of dreadful power to hurt; yet in spite of it those unaffected refuse to repent (ix. 13–21).

e. *The little book eaten* (x. 1–xi. 2)

In the midst of a thunderstorm, John sees an angel with a scroll and hears him announce the seventh trumpet-blast at which God's mystery is about to be completed. John is commanded to eat the scroll, following which he is told to prophesy and to measure the temple.

f. *The two heavenly witnesses* (xi. 3–13)

Still the trumpet-blast must wait until two witnesses have prophesied for three and a half years. But they are opposed by the Beast from the pit, are killed but rise again and return to heaven.

g. *The seventh trumpet* (xi. 14–xii. 17)

Before the woe is announced a vision is seen depicting once again worship in heaven, but the emphasis is now on God's wrath. To the accompaniment of thunderstorm and earthquake the scene changes and there appears a pregnant woman who is molested by the appearance of a dragon (xii. 1–4). A child is born but is at once taken to heaven and this is the signal for a war between Michael and his angelic hosts and the dragon (xii. 5–9). Victory is proclaimed in heaven, but the dragon resolves to attack the woman and her children who witness to Jesus (xii. 10–17).

h. *The Beasts* (xiii. 1–18)

The character of the opposition is now more clearly described. A Beast emerges from the sea having a terrifying appearance and yet is the object of worship (xiii. 1–4). It is blasphemous in its speech and tyrannical in its power (xiii. 5–10). Another Beast emerges from the earth, who has particular power to deceive by miraculous actions and who compels all to receive his mark, the mysterious 666 (xiii. 11–18).

VI. VISIONS OF THE WORSHIPPERS OF THE LAMB (xiv. 1–20)

a. The purity of the martyrs (xiv. 1–5)

In contrast to the last description, the scene now shows those marked with the Lamb's mark and their song of adoration is heard.

b. The angels' announcement (xiv. 6–11)

Three angels announce the dawn of the judgment hour, the doom of Babylon, and the condemnation of the worshippers of the Beast.

c. The martyrs commended (xiv. 12, 13)

Blessing and rest await those who die in the Lord.

d. The harvest of wrath (xiv. 14–20)

In two visions the Son of man and an angel, both with sickles, reap the earth (xiv. 14–20).

VII. THE SEVEN BOWLS (xv. 1–xviii. 24)

a. Introductory scenes (xv. 1–8)

Three successive scenes prepare the way for the pouring out of the bowls. Seven angels are seen holding the last plagues (xv. 1); those who have gained victory are seen praising God (xv. 2–4); and the angels come forth from the heavenly temple holding the seven bowls of God's wrath (xv. 5–8).

b. The bowls of wrath (xvi. 1–21)

In quick succession these are poured out at the command of a voice in the temple. The first produces ulcers, the second pollution of the sea, the third pollutes rivers and springs to look like blood, the fourth produces scorching heat, the fifth darkness and anguish, the sixth the drying up of the Euphrates and the appearances of frog-like fiends and the seventh the dramatic announcement of the end as 'Babylon' falls to the accompaniment of terrible upheavals in the natural world.

c. An explanation (xvii. 1–xviii. 24)

'Babylon' is first described and her great sins enumerated (xvii. 1–6). This harlot is then more precisely identified with the imperial city

(Rome) (xvii. 7–18). In spite of the dominion it exercises the Lamb will overcome it. Then follows a description of the fall of 'Babylon' (xviii. 1–3), a comment from heaven upon it (xviii. 4–8), lamentation on earth over it (xviii. 9–20) and a parabolic illustration of the finality of its destruction in the casting of a great stone into the sea (xviii. 21–24).

VIII. FURTHER VISIONS OF WORSHIP (xix. 1–10)

a. Hymns of praise in heaven (xix. 1–8)

First is heard a hymn to God for His avenging of His martyred servants and then follows the marriage hymn of the Lamb.

b. John is also commanded to worship God (xix. 9, 10)

IX. VISIONS OF THE LAMB'S JUDGMENT (xix. 11–xx. 15)

a. The appearance of the King of kings (xix. 11–16)

In the description of the 'word of God' there are echoes from the introductory vision in chapter i. But now He comes forth in wrath.

b. The destruction of the Beast, the false prophet and their followers (xix. 17–21)

The resultant carnage is vividly described as God's feast for the birds of heaven.

c. Satan bound for a thousand years (xx. 1–3)

d. The reign of Christ (xx. 4–6)

This is described as the first resurrection.

e. The final destruction of Satan (xx. 7–10)

His fate is to endure ceaseless torture.

f. The last judgment (xx. 11–15)

The present natural world disappears and the second resurrection takes place as death and Hades are cast into the destroying fire.

X. VISIONS OF THE NEW ORDER (xxi. 1–xxii. 5)

a. A new creation (xxi. 1–8)

This takes the place of the old order and is dominated by the descent of the New Jerusalem. It is a place without death or evil.

b. The splendours of the new Jerusalem (xxi. 9–xxii. 5)

Its twelve gateways, its measurements (also in multiples of twelve), its jewelled foundation stones, its glory and purity, its Tree of Life with its twelve fruits, and its ceaseless light, are all described.

XI. CONCLUDING EXHORTATIONS (xxii. 6–21)

a. An angelic endorsement (xxii. 6, 7)

b. John's own exhortation (xxii. 8)

c. Christ's message (xxii. 9–16)

There is an echo here of the introduction to the book. The whole is clearly designed for the churches there addressed.

d. The Spirit and the Church's invitation (xxii. 17)

e. A concluding warning (xxii. 18–21)

A severe penalty is threatened for all who tamper with the book, which then closes with a brief prayer and benediction.

ADDITIONAL NOTES

934. [3] Another second-century testimony to apostolic authorship is mentioned by A. Helmbold (*NTS*, 8, 1961, pp. 77–79), who cites the evidence of the *Apocryphon of John* which identifies its author as 'John the brother of James, these who are the sons of Zebedee'. As the MS includes a citation from Rev. i. 19, the writer is in all probability purporting to be the same person as the author of the canonical book. Since the *Apocryphon* may be dated *c.* AD 150, this provides an early witness for apostolic authorship.

948. [1] Cf. T. F. Glasson, *The Revelation of John* (1965), for the view that an unidentified John wrote the Apocalypse.

948. [6] The proposal that the John of Patmos was John Mark was supported by J. N. Sanders, *NTS*, 9 (1962), pp. 75–85. The identifying of this John with John the apostle, in his view, began as a heretical opinion.

953. [6] Cf. W. G. Kümmel (*INT*, 1965, p. 327), who cites R. Schütz, *Die Offenbarung des Johannes und Kaiser Domitian* (1933), pp. 18 ff.

953. [7] L. W. Barnard (*NTS*, 10, 1963, pp. 251–260) rejects the view that there was no persecution under Domitian, as propounded by R. L. P. Milburn (*CQR*, 139, 1945, pp. 154–164) and L. E. Elliott-Binns, *The Beginnings of Western Christendom* (1948), p. 102. Cf. also B. Newman's discussion of the Domitian hypothesis, which he regards as a fallacy (*NTS*, 10, 1963, pp. 133–139). He places much emphasis on the witness of Irenaeus, but points out that Irenaeus does not connect the Apocalypse with persecution.

954. [6] Kümmel (*INT*, p. 329) is less cautious than Feine-Behm over claiming that the Asiatic churches of Smyrna and Laodicea require many years after AD 60 to reach the state reflected in the letters sent to them. He thinks probability favours a date *c.* AD 90–95.

956. [1] Cf. L. A. Vos, *The Synoptic Traditions in the Apocalypse* (1965), who finds no proof that the author of the Apocalypse knew of the Synoptic Gospels, but concludes that the earlier traditions were by now stable.

958. [3] Another method of calculating the kings in Rev. xvii. 10 is put forward by A. Strobel (*NTS*, 10, 1964, pp. 443–445). He suggests that the commencing date should be the death of Christ, which would make Domitian the sixth king 'who now is'. He claims that the Epistle of Barnabas follows the same method. If this theory is correct, it would remove Rev. xvii. 10 from support of the Neronian date. But cf. L. Brun (*ZNTW*, 26, 1927, pp. 28 ff.) for a calculation from the time of Caligula which still makes Domitian the sixth king.

963. For the view that vengeance is not the dominating theme in the Revelation, cf. G. B. Caird, *The Revelation of St. John the Divine* (1966), who considers the dominating note to be love, and W. Klassen (*CBQ*, 28, 1966, pp. 300–311), who thinks it to be the series of blessings.

964. [3] For the relationship between Revelation and Ezekiel, cf. A. Vanhoye, *Biblica*, 43 (1962), pp. 436–476.

965. [1] On the text forms between the Old Testament citations, cf. L. P. Trudinger, *JTS*, n.s., xvii (1966), pp. 82–88.

965. [3] In his commentary, *The Revelation of St. John the Divine* (1964), A. Farrer regards the book as a re-reading of the Old Testament, as a result of the revelation through Christ. He treats the book essentially as a meditation (see pp. 23 ff).

965. [4] The claim that Revelation is an apocalyptic book has come under criticism from J. Kallas (*JBL*, LXXXVI, 1967, pp. 69–80) on the grounds that the apocalyptists saw suffering as the work of opposing forces, a view which he claims was shared by Jesus, Paul and Luke. The Apocalypse on the other hand sets out a realized eschatology. But this view is rejected by B. W. Jones (*JBL*, LXXXVII, 1968, pp. 325–327), who thinks that a more important distinction is the absence of pseudonymity in the Revelation. Cf. A. Feuillet, *L'Apocalypse, État de la question* (1963), who tends to minimize apocalyptic parallels.

966. [5] Cf. G. B. Caird (*ET*, LXXIV, 1962, pp. 103–105) for a discussion of the sources of symbolism underlying the book. He finds traces of Babylonian and Canaanite myths.

969. [2] Cf. M. Rissi (*Interpretation*, 22, 1968, pp. 3–17) for a view of the basic unity of the book.

970. [1] For a theory of the Apocalypse as a continual series of events, cf. S. Giet, *L'Apocalypse et l'histoire* (1957). For a twofold structure, cf. M. Hopkins (*CBQ*, 27, 1965, pp. 42–47), who sees iv–xi as relating to Christianity's triumph over Judaism and xii–xx as an apocalyptic assurance of victory over Rome. Cf. the earlier view of G. Bornkamm (*ZNTW*, 36, 1937, pp. 132 ff.) that vi–viii. 1 was an overture, viii.2–xiv.12 sets out the theme of preparation and xv–xxii. 6 the final events. This avoids a theory of recapitulation in the book.

970. [3] For a somewhat similar view, cf. L. Morris (*Revelation*, TNT, 1969, pp. 21 ff.), who regards the author as 'an artist in words'.

974. [2] Others have seen liturgical elements in Revelation, particularly hymnic forms, cf. O. Cullmann, *Early Christian Worship* (1953); S. Läuchli, *ThZ*, xvi (1960), pp. 359 ff.; G. Delling, *Nov.Test.*, 3 (1959), pp. 107 ff.; J. J. O'Rourke, *CBQ*, 30 (1968), pp. 399–409; L. Thompson, *JR*, 49 (1969), pp. 330 ff. Cf. Kümmel (*INT*, p. 326), who is not favourable to the view that liturgy has influenced the structure.

976. [1] Some have seen theological problems in the book. Cf. Kümmel's discussion on this (*INT*, pp. 331–333). For a survey of commentaries on the book of Revelation, cf. G. R. Beasley-Murray, *Theol.*, LXVI (1963), pp. 52–56.

GENERAL BIBLIOGRAPHY

Abbott, E. A., *Contrast: or a prophet and a forger*, 1903.
Abbott, E. A., *Corrections of Mark*, 1901.
Abbott, E. A., *Johannine Grammar*, 1906.
Abbott, E. A., *Johannine Vocabulary*, 1905.
Abbott, E. A., Peabody, A. P. and Lightfoot, J. B., *The Fourth Gospel*, 1892.
Abbott, T. K., *The Epistles to the Ephesians and the Colossians (ICC)*, 1899.
Abrahams, I., *Studies in Pharisaism and the Gospels*, I, 1917.
Adcock, Sir F., *Thucydides and his History*, 1963.
Adeney, W. F., *Philippians (PC)*, 1928.
Adeney, W. F., *St. Luke (CB)*,[2] 1922.
Adeney, W. F., *1 and 2 Thessalonians and Galatians (CB)*, 1903.
Aland, K., Eltester, W. and Klostermann, E., editors, *Studia Evangelica*, 1959.
Albertz, M., *Die Botschaft des Neuen Testament*, I, 1947, II, 1952.
Albertz, M., *Die synoptischen Streitgespräche*, 1921.
Albright, W. F., *The Archaeology of Palestine*, 1949.
Alexander, J. A., *A Commentary on the Gospel of Mark*, r.p. 1960.
Alexander, J. P., *A priest for ever*, 1937.
Alexander, N., *The Epistles of John (TC)*, 1962.
Alexander, W., *The Epistles of John (Exp. Bib.)*, 1901.
Alford, H., *The Greek Testament*, Vol. I,[6] 1868, Vol. IV,[5] 1871.
Allan, J. A., *Ephesians (TC)*, 1959.
Allan, J. A., *Galatians (TC)*, 1951.
Allen, W. C., *The Gospel according to St. Mark*, 1915.
Allen, W. C., *The Gospel according to St. Matthew (ICC)*, 1907.
Allen, W. C. and Grensted, L. W., *Introduction to the Books of the New Testament*, 1918.
Allo, E. B., *L'Apocalypse de Saint Jean (EB)*,[3] 1933.
Allo, E. B., *Saint Paul, Première Épître aux Corinthiens (EB)*, 1935.
Allo, E. B., *Saint Paul, Seconde Épître aux Corinthiens (EB)*, 1937.
Althaus, P., *Der Brief an die Römer (NTD)*,[10] 1966.
Althaus, P., *Das sogenannte Kerygma und der historische Jesus*, 1958.
Anderson, H., *Jesus and Christian Origins*, 1964.
Andrews, H. T., *1 and 2 Thessalonians (PC)*, 1928.
Appel, H., *Der Hebräerbrief ein Schreiben des Apollos an Judenchristen der Korinthischen Gemeinde*, 1918.
Archer, G. L., *The Epistle to the Hebrews: A study manual*, 1957.
Argyle, A. W., *The Gospel according to Matthew (CBC)*, 1963.
Arndt, W. F., *The Gospel according to St. Luke*, 1956.

Arndt, W. F. and Gingrich, F. W., *A Greek-English Lexicon of the New Testament*, 1957.

Askwith, E. H., *The Epistle to the Galatians, an essay on its Destination and Date*, 1899.

Askwith, E. H., *The Historical Value of the Fourth Gospel*, 1910.

Askwith, E. H., *An Introduction to the Thessalonian Epistles*, 1902.

Ayles, H. H. B., *Destination, Date and Authorship of the Epistle to the Hebrews*, 1899.

Bacon, B. W., *The Fourth Gospel in Research and Debate*,[2] 1918.

Bacon, B. W., *The Gospel of Mark: its Composition and Date*, 1925.

Bacon, B. W., *The Gospel of the Hellenists*, 1933.

Bacon, B. W., *Introduction to the New Testament*, 1900.

Bacon, B. W., *Is Mark a Roman Gospel?*, 1919.

Bacon, B. W., *Studies in Matthew*, 1930.

Badcock, F. J., *The Pauline Epistles and the Epistle to the Hebrews in their Historical Setting*, 1937.

Bailey, J. A., *The Traditions common to the Gospels of Luke and John*, 1963.

Bailey, J. W., *1 and 2 Thessalonians (IB)*, 1955.

Baillie, D. M., *God was in Christ*,[2] 1955.

Baldensperger, W., *Die Prolog des vierten Evangeliums*, 1898.

Balmforth, H., *The Gospel according to St. Luke (Clar B)*, 1930.

Barclay, W., *The First Three Gospels*, 1966.

Barclay, W., *Galatians and Ephesians (DSB)*,[2] 1958.

Barclay, W., *Hebrews (DSB)*, 1957.

Barclay, W., *The Letters to the Corinthians (DSB)*,[2] 1956.

Barclay, W., *Letters to the Seven Churches*, 1957.

Barclay, W., *The Mind of St. Paul*, 1959.

Barclay, W., *Romans (DSB)*,[2] 1957.

Barker, G. W., Lane, W. L. and Michaels, J. R., *The New Testament Speaks*, 1969.

Barnett, A. E., *Paul becomes a Literary Influence*, 1941.

Barnett, A. E. and Homrighausen, E. G., *The Epistle of Jude (IB)*, 1957.

Barnett, A. E. and Homrighausen, E. G., *The Second Epistle of Peter (IB)*, 1957.

Barr, A., *A Diagram of Synoptic Relationships*, 1938.

Barrett, C. K., *The Epistle to the Romans (BC)*, 1958.

Barrett, C. K., *The First Epistle to the Corinthians (BC)*, 1968.

Barrett, C. K., *The Gospel according to St. John*, 1956.

Barrett, C. K., *The Holy Spirit and the Gospel Tradition*, 1947.

Barrett, C. K., *Luke the Historian in Recent Study*, 1961.

Barrett, C. K., *The Pastoral Epistles (N Clar B)*, 1963.

Barth, K., *The Epistle to the Romans* (Eng. Tr. by E. C. Hoskyns), 1933.

Barth, K., *Erklärung des Philipperbriefs*,[4] 1953.

Bartlet, J. V., *The Acts (CB)*, 1901.

Bartlet, J. V., *The Apostolic Age*, 1907.

Bartlet, J. V., *St. Mark (CB)*, 1922.

Bartsch, H. W., editor, *Kerygma und Mythos*, 1948–55.

Bate, H. N., *A Guide to the Epistles of St. Paul*,[2] 1933.

Bauer, B., *Kritik der paulinischen Briefe*, 1850–52.

Bauer, W., *Das Johannesevangelium (LHB)*,[2] 1925.

Bauer, W., *Die katholischen Briefe des Neuen Testaments*, 1910.

Bauer, W., *Rechtgläubigkeit und Ketzerei in ältesten Christentum*, 1934.

Baur, F. C., *Paul, the Apostle of Jesus Christ*, 1873.

Bea, A., *The Study of the Synoptic Gospels. New Approaches and Outlooks*, 1965.

Beare, F. W., *The Earliest Records of Jesus*, 1962.

Beare, F. W., *The Epistle to the Colossians (IB)*, 1953.

Beare, F. W., *The Epistle to the Ephesians (IB)*, 1953.

Beare, F. W., *The Epistle to the Philippians (BC)*, 1959.

Beare, F. W., *The First Epistle of Peter*,[2] 1958.

Beare, F. W., *St. Paul and his Letters*, 1962.

Beasley-Murray, G. R., *A Commentary on Mark Thirteen*, 1957.

Beasley-Murray, G. R., *Jesus and the Future*, 1954.

Beasley-Murray, G. R., *Preaching the Gospel from the Gospels*, 1956.

Becker, H., *Die Reden des Johannesevangeliums und der Stil der gnostischen Offenbarungsreden*, 1956.

Becker, U., *Jesus und die Ehebrecherin. Untersuchungen zur Text- und Überlieferungsgeschichte von Jn 7: 53–8: 11*, 1963.

Beckwith, I. T., *The Apocalypse of John: Studies in Introduction*, 1919.

Beet, J. A., *St. Paul's Epistles to the Corinthians*,[7] 1902.

Beet, J. A., *St. Paul's Epistles to the Ephesians, Philippians, Colossians and to Philemon*, 1890.

Beet, J. A., *St. Paul's Epistle to the Galatians*,[3] 1887.

Beet, J. A., *St. Paul's Epistle to the Romans*,[10] 1902.

Behler, G.-M., *Les Paroles d'adieux du Seigneur*, 1960.

Behm, J., *Die Offenbarung des Johannes (NTD)*,[6] 1953.

Bennett, W. H., *The General Epistles (CB)*, n.d.

Benoit, P., *St. Matthieu (Sainte Bible)*,[3] 1961.

Benson, E. W., *The Apocalypse: structure and principles of interpretation*, 1900.

Bernard, J. H., *The Gospel according to St. John (ICC)*, 1928.

Bernard, J. H., *The Pastoral Epistles (CGT)*, 1899.

Bernard, J. H., *The Second Epistle to the Corinthians (EGT)*, 1910.

Bertholdt, L., *Historischkritische Einleitung in sämmtliche kanonische und apokryphische Schriften des alten und neuen Testaments*, 1812–19.

Bertrand, E., *Essai critique sur l'authenticité des Épîtres Pastorales*, 1887.

Best, E., *The Letter of Paul to the Romans* (CBC), 1967.

Best, E., *One Body in Christ*, 1955.

Best, E., *The Temptation and the Passion*, 1965.

Betz, O., Hengel, M. and Schmidt, P., editors, *Abraham unser Vater* (*Festschrift O. Michel*), 1963.

Beyer, H. W., *Die Apostelgeschichte* (NTD),[9] 1959.

Beyer, H. W., *Der Brief an die Galater* (edited by P. Althaus) (NTD),[9] 1962.

Bicknell, E. J., *The First and Second Epistles to the Thessalonians* (WC), 1932.

Bieder, W., '*Grund und Kraft der Mission nach dem ersten Petrusbrief*', *Theologische Studien*, 29, 1950.

Bieder, W., *Kolosserbrief*, 1943.

Bigg, C., *The Epistles of St. Peter and St. Jude* (ICC), 1901.

Bisseker, H., *The Pastoral Epistles* (PC), 1928.

Black, M., *An Aramaic Approach to the Gospels and Acts*,[3] 1968.

Black, M., *The Scrolls and Christian Origins*, 1961.

Blackman, E. C., *The Epistle of James* (TC), 1957.

Blackman, E. C., *Marcion and his Influence*, 1948.

Blaiklock, E. M., *The Acts of the Apostles* (TNT), 1959.

Blaiklock, E. M., *The Christian in Pagan Society*,[2] 1956.

Blair, E. P., *Jesus in the Gospel of Matthew*, 1960.

Blass, F., *Philology of the Gospels*, 1898.

Blenkin, G. W., *The First Epistle General of Peter* (CGT), 1914.

Blunt, A. W. F., *The Acts of the Apostles* (Clar B), 1923.

Blunt, A. W. F., *The Epistle of Paul to the Galatians* (Clar B), 1925.

Blunt, A. W. F., *The Gospel according to St. Mark* (Clar B), 1929.

Boismard, M. E., *L'Apocalypse* (*Sainte Bible*), 1950.

Boismard, M. E., *Quatre Hymnes Baptismales dans la première Épître de Pierre*, 1961.

Boman, T., *Hebrew Thought compared with Greek*, 1960.

Bonnard, P., *L'Épître aux Galatiens* (CNT), 1952.

Bonnard, P., *L'Épître aux Philippiens* (CNT), 1950.

Bonnard, P., *L'Évangile selon Saint Matthieu* (CNT), 1963.

Bonsirven, J., *L'Apocalypse de Saint Jean* (*Verbum Salutis*), 1951.

Boobyer, G. H., *St. Mark and the Transfiguration Story*, 1942.

Boor, W. de, *Der Brief des Paulus an die Römer*, 1962.

Bornhäuser, K., *Empfänger und Verfasser des Hebräerbriefes*, 1932.

Bornhäuser, K., *Das Johannesevangelium eine Missionsschrift für Israel*, 1928.

Bornhäuser, K., *Studien zum Sondergut des Lukas*, 1934.

Bornhäuser, K., *Studien zur Apostelgeschichte*, 1934.

Bornkamm, G., *Das Ende des Gesetzes*,[2] 1958.

Bornkamm, G., *Jesus of Nazareth*, 1960 (Eng. Tr. from German edition, 1956).

Bornkamm, G., *Studien zu Antike und Urchristentum*, band 28, 1959.

Bornkamm, G., Barth, G. and Held, H. J., *Tradition and Interpretation in Matthew*, 1963 (Eng. Tr. from German edition, 1960).

Bousset, W., *The Antichrist Legend* (Eng. Tr. by A. H. Keane), 1896.

Bousset, W., *Kyrios Christos*,[3] 1926.

Bousset, W., *Die Offenbarung Johannis (KEK)*,[2] 1906.

Bowman, J., *The Gospel of Mark. The New Christian Jewish Passover Haggada*, 1965.

Bowman, J. W., *The Drama of the Book of Revelation*, 1955.

Bowman, J. W., *Hebrews, James, I and II Peter*, 1962.

Box, G. H., *St. Matthew (CB)*, 1922.

Braaten, C. E. and Harrisville, R. A., *The Historical Jesus and the Kerygmatic Christ*, 1964.

Brandon, S. G. F., *The Fall of Jerusalem and the Christian Church*,[2] 1957.

Brandon, S. G. F., *Jesus and the Zealots. A Study of the Political Factor in Primitive Christianity*, 1967.

Branscombe, B. H., *The Gospel of Mark (MC)*, 1937.

Braun, F.-M., *Jean le Théologien et son Évangile dans l'Église ancienne (EB)*, 1959.

Braun, F.-M., *Jean le Théologien. Les grandes traditions d'Israël et l'accord des Écritures selon le Quatrième Évangile (EB)*, 1964.

Braun, H., *Qumran and the New Testament*, 1966.

Briggs, C. A., *The Messiah of the Gospels*, 1895.

Bring, R., *Pauli Brev till Galaterna*, 1958 (Eng. Tr. by E. Wahlstrom, *Commentary on Galatians*, 1961).

Brooke, A. E., *The Johannine Epistles (ICC)*, 1912.

Brown, D., *The Structure of the Apocalypse*, 1891.

Brown, R. E., *The Gospel according to John i–xii*, 1966.

Browning, W. R. F., *The Gospel according to St. Luke (TC)*, 1960.

Bruce, A. B., *The Epistle to the Hebrews*, 1899.

Bruce, A. B., *The Synoptic Gospels (EGT)*, 1907.

Bruce, F. F., *The Acts of the Apostles* (Greek text),[2] 1952.

Bruce, F. F., *Biblical Exegesis in the Qumran Texts*, 1960.

Bruce, F. F., *Commentary on the Book of Acts (NLC)*, 1954.

Bruce, F. F., *Commentary on the Epistle to the Hebrews (NLC)*, 1964.

Bruce, F. F., *The Epistle of Paul to the Romans (TNT)*, 1963.

Bruce, F. F., *The Epistle to the Colossians (NLC)*, 1958.

Bruce, F. F., *The Epistle to the Ephesians*, 1962.

Bruce, F. F., *The Speeches in the Acts of the Apostles*, 1944.

Bruce, F. F., *The Spreading Flame*, 1958.

Bruce, F. F., editor, *Promise and Fulfilment (Essays presented to S. H. Hooke)*, 1963.

Brunner, E., *Der Römerbrief*, 1948 (Eng. Tr. 1959).

Büchsel, F., *Die Johannesbriefe*, 1933.

Buckler, W. H. and Calder, W. M., editors, *Anatolian Studies presented to Sir William Ramsay*, 1923.

Bultmann, R., *Die drei Johannesbriefe (KEK)*,[7] 1967.

Bultmann, R., *Das Evangelium des Johannes (KEK)*,[13] 1953.

Bultmann, R., *The History of the Synoptic Tradition* (Eng. Tr. by J. Marsh from the 3rd German edition, 1958),[2] 1968.

Bultmann, R., *Primitive Christianity in its Contemporary Setting*, 1956.

Bultmann, R., *Theology of the New Testament* (Eng. Tr.), I, 1952, II, 1955.

Bultmann, R. and Kundsin, K., *Form Criticism* (Eng. Tr. by F. C. Grant),[2] 1962.

Bultmann, R. and Soden, H. von, editors, *Festgabe für A. Jülicher*, 1927.

Bundy, W. E., *Jesus and the First Three Gospels*, 1955.

Burch, V., *The Epistle to the Hebrews, its sources and message*, 1936.

Burch, V., *The Structure and Message of St. John's Gospel*, 1928.

Burgon, J. W., *The Last Twelve Verses of the Gospel according to St. Mark vindicated against recent objectors and established*, 1871.

Burkill, T. A., *The Injunctions to Silence in Mark's Gospel*, 1956.

Burkill, T. A., *Mysterious Revelation: An examination of the Philosophy of Mark's Gospel*, 1963.

Burkill, T. A., *The notion of miracle with special reference to St. Mark's Gospel*, 1959.

Burkitt, F. C., *Christian Beginnings*, 1924.

Burkitt, F. C., *The Earliest Sources for the Life of Jesus*,[2] 1922.

Burkitt, F. C., *The Gospel History and its Transmission*,[3] 1911.

Burkitt, F. C., *Jewish and Christian Apocalypses*, 1914.

Burnet, A. W., *The Lord Reigneth*, 1946.

Burney, C. F., *The Aramaic Origin of the Fourth Gospel*, 1922.

Burney, C. F., *The Poetry of our Lord*, 1925.

Burrows, M., *The Dead Sea Scrolls*, 1955.

Burton, E. D. and Goodspeed, E. J., *A Harmony of the Synoptic Gospels in Greek*, 1922.

Burton, E. de W., *The Epistle to the Galatians (ICC)*, 1921.

Burton, H., *The Gospel according to St. Luke (Exp. Bib.)*, 1909.

Bussmann, W., *Synoptische Studien*, I, 1925, II, 1929, III, 1931.

Butler, B. C., *The Originality of Matthew*, 1951.

Cabrol, F. and Leclercq, H., *Monumenta Ecclesiae Liturgica*, Vol. XI, 1900–02, Vol. XII, 1913.

Cadbury, H. J., *The Book of Acts in History*, 1955.

Cadbury, H. J., *The Making of Luke-Acts*,[2] 1958.

Cadbury, H. J., *The Style and Literary Method of Luke (HTS)*, 1919, 1920.

Cadoux, A. T., *The Sources of the Second Gospel*, 1935.

Cadoux, A. T., *The Thought of St. James*, 1944.

Caird, G. B., *The Revelation of St. John the Divine* (BC), 1966.
Caird, G. B., *Saint Luke* (Pel C), 1963.
Campenhausen, H. von, *Kirchliches Amt und geistliche Vollmacht*, 1953.
Candlish, R. S., *The First Epistle of John*, 1866.
Carpenter, J. E., *The Johannine Writings*, 1927.
Carpenter, S. C., *Christianity according to St. Luke*, 1919.
Carr, A., *The General Epistle of St. James* (CGT), 1896.
Carrington, P., *According to Mark*, 1960.
Carrington, P., *The Meaning of Revelation*, 1931.
Carrington, P., *The Primitive Christian Calendar*, 1952.
Carrington, P., *The Primitive Christian Catechism*, 1940.
Carson, H. M., *The Epistles of Paul to the Colossians and Philemon* (TNT), 1960.
Carter, C. W. and Earle, R., *The Acts of the Apostles*, 1959.
Cave, S., *The Gospel of Paul*, 1928.
Cerfaux, L., *Le Christ dans la Théologie de S. Paul*, 1954.
Cerfaux, L., *Littérature et Théologie Pauliniennes*, 1960.
Cerfaux, L., *Receuil Lucien Cerfaux*, 1954.
Cerfaux, L. and Dupont, J., *Les Acts des Apôtres*,[2] 1958.
Chadwick, G. A., *The Gospel according to St. Mark* (Exp. Bib.),[6] 1896.
Chaine, J., *Les épîtres catholiques* (EB),[2] 1939.
Chapman, J., *Matthew, Mark and Luke*, 1937.
Charles, R. H., *Commentary on the Revelation of St. John* (ICC), 2 vols., 1920.
Charles, R. H., *Lectures on the Apocalypse* (Schweich Lectures), 1922.
Charles, R. H., *Studies in the Apocalypse*, 1913.
Charles, R. H., editor, *The Apocrypha and Pseudepigrapha in English*, 1913.
Charnwood, Lord, *According to St. John*, 1925.
Chase, F. H., *The Credibility of the Book of the Acts of the Apostles*, 1902.
Clark, A. C., *The Acts of the Apostles*, 1933.
Clark, A. C., *The Primitive Text of the Gospels and the Acts*, 1914.
Clogg, F. B., *An Introduction to the New Testament*,[3] 1948.
Cole, R. A., *The Epistle of Paul to the Galatians* (TNT), 1965.
Cole, R. A., *The Gospel according to St. Mark* (TNT), 1961.
Colwell, E. C., *The Greek of the Fourth Gospel*, 1931.
Conybeare, W. J. and Howson, J. S., *The Life and Epistles of St. Paul*, 1905.
Conzelmann, H., *Die Apostelgeschichte* (LHB), 1963.
Conzelmann, H., *Der Brief an die Epheser, an die Kolosser* (NTD),[9] 1962.
Conzelmann, H., *The Theology of St. Luke* (Eng. Tr.), 1960.
Correll, A., *Consummatum Est*, 1958.
Cottam, T., *The Fourth Gospel Rearranged*, 1952.
Cox, G. E. P., *The Gospel according to St. Matthew* (TC), 1952.
Cox, S., *The private letters of St. Paul and St. John*, 1867.
Craig, C. T., *The First Epistle to the Corinthians* (IB), 1953.

Cranfield, C. E. B., *The First Epistle of Peter*, 1950.

Cranfield, C. E. B., *The Gospel according to St. Mark* (*CGT*, n.s.), 1959.

Cranfield, C. E. B., *I and II Peter and Jude* (*TC*), 1960.

Creed, J. M., *The Gospel according to St. Luke*, 1930.

Cross, F. L., *I Peter: A Paschal Liturgy*, 1954.

Cross, F. L., editor, *The Jung Codex*, 1955.

Cross, F. L., editor, *Studia Evangelica*, II, 1964.

Cross, F. L., editor, *Studies in Ephesians*, 1956.

Cross, F. L., editor, *Studies in the Fourth Gospel*, 1957.

Cross, F. M., *The Ancient Library of Qumran and Modern Biblical Studies*,[2] 1961.

Crum, J. M. C., *The Original Jerusalem Gospel*, 1927.

Crum, J. M. C., *St. Mark's Gospel*, 1936.

Cullmann, O., *Christ and Time*, 1951.

Cullmann, O., *Christology of the New Testament*,[2] 1963.

Cullmann, O., *Early Christian Worship* (Eng. Tr.), 1953.

Cullmann, O., *Le Nouveau Testament*, 1966 (Eng. Tr. *The New Testament*, 1968).

Cullmann, O., *Peter: Disciple, Apostle, and Martyr*,[2] 1962.

Curtis, W. A., *Jesus Christ the Teacher*, 1943.

Dahl, N. A., *Kerygma and Dogma*, 1955.

Dale, R. W., *The Epistle of James and other Discourses*, 1895.

Dalman, G., *The Words of Jesus*, 1902.

Daniélou, J., *Qumran und der Ursprung des Christentums*, 1958.

Daniélou, J., *Théologie du Judéo-Christianisme*, 1958.

Daube, D., *The New Testament and Rabbinic Judaism*, 1955.

Davey, J. E., *The Jesus of St. John*, 1958.

Davidson, A. B., *The Epistle to the Hebrews*, n.d.

Davies, J. G., *He ascended into Heaven*, 1958.

Davies, J. H., *A Letter to the Hebrews* (*CBC*), 1967.

Davies, W. D., *Christian Origins and Judaism*, 1962.

Davies, W. D., *Invitation to the New Testament. A guide to its main witnesses*, 1966.

Davies, W. D., *Paul and Rabbinic Judaism*, 1948.

Davies, W. D., *The Setting of the Sermon on the Mount*, 1964.

Davies, W. D. and Daube, D., editors, *The Background of the New Testament and its Eschatology*, 1956.

Dean, J. T., *St. Paul and Corinth*, 1947.

Deane, A. C., *St. Paul and his Letters*, 1942.

Deissmann, A., *Bible Studies*, 1901.

Deissmann, A., *Light from the Ancient East*,[3] 1927.

Diessmann, A., *The New Testament in the Light of Modern Research*, 1929.

Deissmann, A., *St. Paul* (Eng. Tr.),[2] 1926.

Deissmann, A., 'Zur ephesinischen Gefangenschaft des Apostels Paulus', in Anatolian Studies presented to Sir William Ramsay (edited W. H. Buckler and W. M. Calder), 1923.

Delafosse, H., Le Quatrième Évangile, 1925.

Delff, H., Die Geschichte des Rabbi Jesus von Nazareth, 1889.

Delitzsch, F., Commentary on the Epistle to the Hebrews, 1868 (German edition, 1857).

Denney, J., St. Paul's Epistle to the Romans (EGT), 1900.

Dibelius, M., An die Thessalonicher I and II, an die Philipper (LHB),[3] 1937.

Dibelius, M., A Fresh Approach to the New Testament and Early Christian Literature, 1936.

Dibelius, M., From Tradition to Gospel (Eng. Tr.),[2] 1934.

Dibelius, M., Gospel Criticism und Christology, 1935.

Dibelius, M., Jungfrauensohn und Krippenkind, 1932.

Dibelius, M., Die Kolosser-, Epheser- und Philemonbriefe (LHB),[2] 1927.

Dibelius, M., Die Pastoralbriefe (edited by H. Conzelmann) (LHB),[3] 1955.

Dibelius, M., Studies in the Acts of the Apostles (Eng. Tr.), 1956.

Dibelius, M. and Greeven, H., Der Brief des Jakobus (KEK),[10] 1958.

Dibelius, M. and Kümmel, W. G., St. Paul,[3] 1964.

Dinkler, E., editor, Zeit und Geschichte (Dankesgabe für R. Bultmann), 1964.

Dobschütz, E. von, Die Briefe an die Thessalonicher (KEK),[7] 1919.

Dobschütz, E. von, Christian Life in the Primitive Church (Eng. Tr.), 1904.

Dodd, C. H., According to the Scriptures, 1952.

Dodd, C. H., The Apostolic Preaching and its Developments,[2] 1944.

Dodd, C. H., The Authority of the Bible, 1938.

Dodd, C. H., The Bible and the Greeks, 1935.

Dodd, C. H., The Coming of Christ, 1951.

Dodd, C. H., Ephesians, Colossians and Philemon (AB), 1929.

Dodd, C. H., The Epistle of Paul to the Romans (MC), 1932.

Dodd, C. H., Historical Tradition in the Fourth Gospel, 1963.

Dodd, C. H., History and the Gospel, 1938.

Dodd, C. H., The Interpretation of the Fourth Gospel, 1953.

Dodd, C. H., The Johannine Epistles (MC), 1946.

Dodd, C. H., The Meaning of Paul for to-day, 1920.

Dodd, C. H., More New Testament Studies, 1968.

Dodd, C. H., New Testament Studies, 1953.

Dods, M., The Epistle to the Hebrews (EGT), 1910.

Dods, M., The Gospel according to St. John (Exp. Bib.),[2] 1894.

Dods, M., The Gospel of St. John (EGT), 1907.

Doeve, J. W., Jewish Hermeneutics in the Synoptic Gospels and Acts, 1954.

Dornier, P., Les Épîtres pastorales, 1969.

Douglas, C. E., The Mystery of the Kingdom, 1915.

Dow, J., *Galatians* (*AB*), 1929.

Drummond, J., *An Inquiry into the Character and Authorship of the Fourth Gospel*, 1903.

Du Bose, W. P., *The Gospel according to St. Paul*, 1907.

Du Bose, W. P., *High Priesthood and Sacrifice*, 1908.

Duncan, G. S., *The Epistle of Paul to the Galatians* (*MC*), 1934.

Duncan, G. S., *Jesus, Son of Man*, 1948.

Duncan, G. S., *St. Paul's Ephesian Ministry*, 1929.

Dupont, J., *Études sur les Actes des Apôtres*, 1967.

Dupont, J., *Les Sources du Livre des Actes*, 1960.

Dupont-Sommer, A., *The Essene Writings from Qumran*, 1961.

Eadie, J., *Commentary on Colossians*, 1856.

Eadie, J., *Commentary on Ephesians*,[3] 1883.

Earle, R., *The Gospel according to Mark*, 1957.

Easton, B. S., *Early Christianity: the Purpose of Acts and other papers* (edited by F. C. Grant), 1954.

Easton, B. S., *The Gospel according to St Luke*, 1926.

Easton, B. S., *The Gospel before the Gospels*, 1928.

Easton, B. S., *The Pastoral Epistles*, 1948.

Easton, B. S. and Poteat, G., *The Epistle of James* (*IB*), 1957.

Ebeling, G., *The Nature of Faith* (Eng. Tr.), 1961.

Ebrard, J. H. A., *Biblical Commentary on the Epistles of St. John*, 1860.

Ebrard, J. H. A., *The Epistle to the Hebrews*, 1853.

Edmundson, G., *The Church in Rome in the First Century*, 1913.

Edwards, D., *The Virgin Birth in History and Faith*, 1941.

Edwards, H. E., *The disciple who wrote these things*, 1953.

Edwards, R. A., *The Gospel according to St. John*, 1954.

Edwards, T. C., *A Commentary on the First Epistle to the Corinthians*, 1897.

Edwards, T. C., *The Epistle to the Hebrews* (*Exp. Bib.*), 1888.

Ehrhardt, A., *The Framework of the New Testament Stories*, 1964.

Eichholz, G., *Glaube und Werk bei Paulus und Jakobus*, 1961.

Eichholz, G., *Jakobus und Paulus: ein Beitrag zum Problem des Kanons*, 1953.

Eichhorn, J. G., *Historische-kritische Einleitung in das Neue Testament*, 1814.

Eisler, R., *The Enigma of the Fourth Gospel*, 1938.

Ellicott, C. J., *The Pastoral Epistles of St. Paul*,[5] 1883.

Ellicott, C. J., *St. Paul's Epistles to the Philippians, Colossians and Philemon*,[5] 1888.

Ellicott, C. J., *St. Paul's Epistles to the Thessalonians*,[4] 1880.

Ellicott, C. J., *St. Paul's Epistle to the Ephesians*,[5] 1884.

Ellicott, C. J., *St. Paul's Epistle to the Galatians*,[4] 1867.

Ellicott, C. J., *St. Paul's First Epistle to the Corinthians, with Commentary*, 1887.

Elliott-Binns, L. E., *The Beginnings of Western Christendom*, 1948.

Elliott-Binns, L. E., *Galilean Christianity*, 1956.

Ellis, E. E., *The Gospel of Luke* (CB, n.s.), 1966.

Ellis, E. E., *Paul's Use of the Old Testament*, 1957.

Eltester, W., editor, *Judentum, Urchristentum, Kirche* (*Festschrift für Joachim Jeremias*), 1960.

Eltester, W., editor, *Neutestamentliche Studien für Rudolf Bultmann*, 1954.

Emmet, C. W., *St. Paul's Epistle to the Galatians*, 1912.

Erbes, K., *Die Offenbarung Johannis. Kritisch untersucht*, 1891.

Evans, C. F., *The Beginning of the Gospel*, 1968.

Evans, E., *The Epistles of Paul the Apostle to the Corinthians* (Clar B), 1930.

Fairweather, W., *The Background of the Epistles*, 1935.

Falconer, Sir R., *The Pastoral Epistles*, 1937.

Farmer, W. R., *Synopticon*, 1969.

Farmer, W. R., *The Synoptic Problem. A Critical Analysis*, 1964.

Farmer, W. R., Moule, C. F. D. and Niebuhr, R. R., editors, *Christian History and Interpretation*, 1967.

Farrar, F. W., *The Epistle to the Hebrews* (CGT), 1888.

Farrer, A., *The Glass of Vision*, 1948.

Farrer, A., *A Rebirth of Images*, 1949.

Farrer, A., *The Revelation of St. John the Divine*, 1964.

Farrer, A., *St. Matthew and St. Mark*, 1954.

Farrer, A., *A Study in St. Mark*, 1951.

Fascher, E., *Die formgeschichtliche Methode*, 1924.

Feine, P., *Theologie des Neuen Testaments*, 1936.

Feine, P. and Behm, J., *Einleitung in das Neue Testament*,[11] 1956.

Feine, P., Behm, J. and Kümmel, W. G., *Einleitung in das Neue Testament*,[12] 1963 (Eng. Tr. by A. J. Mattill, Jnr, *Introduction to the New Testament*, 1965).

Fenton, J. C., *Saint Matthew* (Pel C), 1963.

Feret, H. M., *A Christian Vision of History*, 1958.

Feuillet, A., *L'Apocalypse. État de la question*, 1963.

Filson, F. V., *The Gospel according to St. John*, 1963.

Filson, F. V., *The Gospel according to St. Matthew* (BC), 1960.

Filson, F. V., *The New Testament against its Environment*, 1950.

Filson, F. V., *A New Testament History. The Story of the Emerging Church*, 1964.

Filson, F. V., *The Second Epistle to the Corinthians* (IB), 1953.

Filson, F. V., *Three Crucial Decades: Studies in the Book of Acts*, 1963.

Filson, F. V., 'Yesterday': A Study of Hebrews in the Light of Ch. 13, 1967.

Findlay, G. G., *The Apostle Paul: a Sketch of the Development of his Doctrine*, 1891.

Findlay, G. G., *The Epistles of Paul the Apostle*, 1892.

Findlay, G. G., *The Epistles to the Thessalonians* (CGT), 1904.

Findlay, G. G., *Fellowship in the Life Eternal*, 1909.

Findlay, G. G., *Romans* (PC), 1928.

Findlay, G. G., *St. Paul's First Epistle to the Corinthians* (EGT), 1901.

Findlay, J. A., *The Acts of the Apostles*,[4] 1952.

Findlay, J. A., *The First Gospel and the Book of Testimonies*, 1933.

Findlay, J. A., *Jesus in the First Gospel*, 1925.

Flender, H., *St. Luke: Theologian of Redemptive History* (Eng. Tr.), 1967.

Flew, R. N., *Jesus and His Church*, 1956.

Foerster, W., editor, *Manet in Aeternum* (*Eine Festschrift für O. Schmitz*), 1953.

Foulkes, F., *The Epistle of Paul to the Ephesians* (TNT), 1963.

Frame, J. E., *The Epistles to the Thessalonians* (ICC), 1912.

Freed, E. D., *Old Testament Quotations in the Gospel of John*, 1965.

Friedrich, G., *Der Brief an die Philipper, Der Brief an Philemon* (NTD),[9] 1962.

Frost, B., *Ephesians-Colossians. A dogmatic and devotional commentary*, 1946.

Frost, B., *To the Hebrews*, 1947.

Fuchs, E., *Studies of the Historical Jesus* (Eng. Tr. by A. Scobie), 1964.

Fuller, D. P., *Easter Faith and History*, 1965.

Fuller, R. H., *A Critical Introduction to the New Testament*, 1966.

Fuller, R. H., *The New Testament in Current Study*, 1962.

Furneaux, W. M., *The Acts of the Apostles: A Commentary for English readers*, 1912.

Gaechter, P., *Das Matthäus-Evangelium. Ein Kommentar*, 1964.

Gardiner, E. A., *The Later Pauline Epistles*, 1936.

Gardner, H., *The Limits of Literary Criticism*, 1956.

Gardner-Smith, P., *The Christ of the Gospels*, 1938.

Gardner-Smith, P., *St. John and the Synoptic Gospels*, 1938.

Gardner-Smith, P., editor, *The Roads Converge*, 1963.

Gärtner, B., *The Areopagus Speech and Natural Revelation* (Eng. Tr. from *Acta Seminarii Neotestamentici Upsaliensis*, XXI), 1950.

Gärtner, B., *John 6 and the Jewish Passover*, 1959.

Gärtner, B., *The Temple and the Community in Qumran and the New Testament*, 1965.

Garvie, A. E., *The Beloved Disciple*, 1922.

Garvie, A. E., *Romans* (CB), 1901.

Garvie, A. E., *Studies of Paul and his Gospel*, 1911.

Gaugusch, L., *Der Lehrgehalt der Jakobusepistel: eine exegetisch Studie*, 1914.

Gealy, F. D., *1 and 2 Timothy and Titus* (IB), 1955.

Gebhardt, H., *The Doctrine of the Apocalypse and its Relation to the Doctrine of the Gospel and Epistles of John*, 1878.

Geldenhuys, J. N., *Commentary on the Gospel of Luke* (NLC), 1950.

Georgi, D., *Die Gegner des Paulus im 2 Korintherbrief*, 1964.

Gerhardsson, B., *Memory and Manuscript*, 1961.

Gerhardsson, B., *Tradition and Transmission in Early Christianity*, 1964.

Giblin, C. H., *The Threat to Faith. An exegetical and theological re-examination of 2 Thess 2*, 1967.

Gibson, J. M., *The Gospel according to St. Matthew (Exp. Bib.)*, 1890.

Gieseler, J. K. L., *Historisch-kritischer Versuch über die Entstehung und die frühesten Schicksale der schriftlichen Evangelien*, 1818.

Giet, S., *L'Apocalypse et l'Histoire*, 1957.

Gifford, E. H., *The Epistle to the Romans*, 1886.

Gilmour, S. M., *The Gospel according to St. Luke (IB)*, 1952.

Glasson, T. F., *Moses in the Fourth Gospel*, 1963.

Glasson, T. F., *The Revelation of John (CBC)*, 1965.

Glazebrook, M. G., *The Apocalypse of St. John*, 1923.

Glover, T. R., *Paul of Tarsus*,[2] 1925.

Gnilka, J., *Der Philipperbrief*, 1968.

Godet, F., *Commentary on St. Paul's Epistle to the Romans* (Eng. Tr.), 1888–89.

Godet, F., *Commentary on St. Paul's First Epistle to the Corinthians* (Eng. Tr.), 1893.

Godet, F., *Introduction to the New Testament: The Collection of the Four Gospels and the Gospel of St. Matthew*, 1899.

Godet, F., *Introduction to the New Testament: I. St. Paul's Epistles* (Eng. Tr.), 1899.

Godet, F., *Studies on the Epistles* (Eng. Tr.), 1903.

Goguel, M., *Introduction au Nouveau Testament*, III, 1922, IV, 1925.

Goguel, M., *La Naissance du Christianisme*, 1946 (Eng. Tr. *The Birth of Christianity*, 1953).

Gomme, A. W., *A Historical Commentary on Thucydides*, 1945.

Goodspeed, E. J., *Christianity goes to press*, 1940.

Goodspeed, E. J., *A History of Christian Literature*, 1942.

Goodspeed, E. J., *Introduction to the New Testament*, 1937.

Goodspeed, E. J., *Key to Ephesians*, 1956.

Goodspeed, E. J., *Matthew, Apostle and Evangelist*, 1959.

Goodspeed, E. J., *The Meaning of Ephesians*, 1933.

Goodspeed, E. J., *New Chapters in New Testament Study*, 1937.

Goodspeed, E. J., *New Solutions to New Testament Problems*, 1927.

Goppelt, L., *Die apostolische und nachapostolische Zeit*, 1962.

Gore, C., *The Epistles of St. John*, 1920.

Gould, E. P., *The Gospel according to St. Mark (ICC)*, 1896.

Goulder, M. D., *Type and History in Acts*, 1964.

Grafe, E., *Die Stellung und Bedeutung des Jakobusbriefes in der Entwicklung des Urchristentums*, 1904.

Grant, F. C., *The Earliest Gospel*, 1943.

Grant, F. C., *The Epistle to the Hebrews in the King James' Version with introduction and critical notes*, 1956.

Grant, F. C., *The Gospel according to St. Mark (IB)*, 1951.

Grant, F. C., *The Gospels, their origin and growth*, 1957.

Grant, F. C., *Roman Hellenism and the New Testament*, 1962.

Grant, P. W., *The Revelation of John*, 1889.

Grant, R. M., *The Earliest Lives of Jesus*, 1961.

Grant, R. M., *A Historical Introduction to the New Testament*, 1963.

Grässer, E., *Der Glaube im Hebräerbrief*, 1965.

Grayston, K., *The Epistles to the Galatians and Philippians (EC)*, 1958.

Grayston, K., *The Letters of Paul to the Philippians and to the Thessalonians (CBC)*, 1967.

Green, E. M. B., *2 Peter Reconsidered*, 1961.

Green, E. M. B., *The Second Epistle General of Peter and the General Epistle of Jude (TNT)*, 1968.

Green, F. W., *The Gospel according to St. Matthew (Clar B)*, 1936.

Griesbach, J. J., *Commentatio qua Marci evangelium totum e Matthaei et Lucae commentariis decerptum esse demonstratur*, 1789.

Grill, J., *Untersuchungen über die Entstehung des vierten Evangeliums*, I, 1902, II, 1923.

Grobel, K., *Formgeschichte und synoptische Quellenanalyse*, 1937.

Grosch, H., *Die Echtheit des zweiten Briefes Petri*,[2] 1914.

Grosheide, F. W., *The First Epistle to the Corinthians (NLC)*, 1954.

Grundmann, W., *Das Evangelium nach Lukas*,[2] 1961.

Grundmann, W., *Das Evangelium nach Matthäus*, 1968.

Guilding, A., *The Fourth Gospel and Jewish Worship*, 1960.

Gundry, R. H., *The Use of the Old Testament in St. Matthew's Gospel, with special reference to the Messianic hope*, 1967.

Gunkel, H., *Schöpfung und Chaos in Urzeit und Endzeit* (on Genesis i and Revelation xii), 1895.

Guthrie, D., *The Epistle to the Hebrews in Recent Thought*, 1956.

Guthrie, D., *Galatians (CB, n.s.)*, 1969.

Guthrie, D., *The Pastoral Epistles (TNT)*, 1957.

Guthrie, D., *The Pastoral Epistles and the Mind of Paul*, 1956.

Guy, H. A., *The Acts of the Apostles*, 1953.

Guy, H. A., *The Origin of the Gospel of Mark*, 1954.

Hackett, H. B., *A Commentary on the Original Text of the Acts of the Apostles*, 1877.

Hadley, J., *Essays Philological and Critical*, 1873.

Hadorn, W., *Die Offenbarung des Johannes*, 1928.

Haenchen, E., *Die Apostelgeschichte neu übersetzt und erklärt (KEK)*,[13] 1961.

Haenchen, E., *Der Weg Jesus: eine Erklärung des Markus Evangeliums und der kanonischen Parallelen*, 1966.

Halliday, W. R., *The Pagan Background of Early Christianity*, 1925.

Hanson, A. T., *The Pastoral Epistles (CBC)*, 1966.

Hanson, A. T., *Studies in the Pastoral Epistles*, 1968.

Hanson, A. T., editor, *Vindications*, 1966.

Hanson, R. P. C., *The Acts in the Revised Standard Version (N Clar B)*, 1967.

Hanson, R. P. C., *2 Corinthians (TC)*, 1954.

Hanson, S., *The Unity of the Church in the New Testament: Colossians and Ephesians*, 1946.

Hare, D. A. R., *The Theme of Jewish Persecution of Christians in the Gospel according to St. Matthew*, 1967.

Harnack, A., *The Acts of the Apostles* (Eng. Tr.), 1908.

Harnack, A., *Die Briefsammlung des Apostels Paulus*, 1926.

Harnack, A., *Die Chronologie der altchristlichen Literatur bis Eusebius*, 1897.

Harnack, A., *The Date of Acts and the Synoptic Gospels* (Eng. Tr.), 1911.

Harnack, A., *Luke the Physician* (Eng. Tr.), 1907.

Harnack, A., *Das Neue Testament um das Jahr 200*, 1889.

Harnack, A., *The Origin of the New Testament* (Eng. Tr.), 1925.

Harnack, A., *The Sayings of Jesus* (Eng. Tr.), 1908.

Harnack, A., *What is Christianity?* (Eng. Tr.), 1901.

Harris, J. R., *The Origin of the Prologue of St. John's Gospel*, 1917.

Harris, J. R., *Side Lights on New Testament Research*, 1908.

Harris, J. R., *Testimonies*, I, 1916.

Harrison, E. F., *Introduction to the New Testament*, 1964.

Harrison, P. N., *Paulines and Pastorals*, 1964.

Harrison, P. N., *Polycarp's Two Epistles to the Philippians*, 1936.

Harrison, P. N., *The Problem of the Pastorals*, 1921.

Harrisville, R. A., *The Miracle of Mark: A Study in the Gospel*, 1967.

Hart, J. H. A., *The First Epistle General of Peter (EGT)*, 1910.

Hartingsveld, L. van, *Die Eschatologie des Johannesevangeliums*, 1962.

Hartmann, L., *Prophecy Interpreted. The Formation of Some Jewish Apocalyptic Texts and of the Eschatological Discourse Mark 13 par.* (Eng. Tr. by N. Tomkinson and J. Gray), 1966.

Hastings, A., *Prophet and Witness in Jerusalem. A Study of the Teaching of St. Luke*, 1958.

Hauck, F., *Die Kirchenbriefe (NTD)*,[8] 1957.

Hauck, Fr., *Der Brief des Jakobus*, 1926.

Haupt, E., *The First Epistle of St. John. A Contribution to Biblical Theology* (Eng. Tr. by W. B. Pope,) 1879.

Hawkins, Sir J. C., *Horae Synopticae*,[2] 1909.

Headlam, A. C., *The Fourth Gospel as History*, 1948.

Headlam, A. C., *The Life and Teaching of Jesus the Christ*, 1923.

Heard, R., *An Introduction to the New Testament*, 1950.

Heathcote, A. W., *An Introduction to the Letters of Paul*, 1963.

Hebert, G., *The Christ of Faith and the Jesus of History*, 1962.

Heinzelmann, G., *Der Brief an die Philipper (NTD)*,[7] 1955.

Henderson, I., *Myth in the New Testament*, 1952.

Hendriksen, W., *Exposition of the Gospel according to John*, 1953.

Hendriksen, W., *More Than Conquerors* (Tyndale Press edition), 1962.

Hengstenberg, E. W., *The Revelation of John* (Eng. Tr. by P. Fairbairn), 1851.

Henry, C., editor, *Jesus of Nazareth: Saviour and Lord*, 1966.

Henshaw, T., *The Foundation of the Christian Church*, 1946.

Henshaw, T., *New Testament Literature in the Light of Modern Scholarship*, 1952.

Herder, G., *Von der Regel der Zustimmung unserer Evangelien*, 1797.

Héring, J., *L'Épître aux Hébreux (CNT)*, 1954.

Héring, J., *La première Épître de St. Paul aux Corinthiens (CNT)*, 1948 (Eng. Tr. by A. W. Heathcote and P. J. Allcock, *The First Epistle of Saint Paul to the Corinthians*, 1962).

Héring, J., *La seconde Épître de St. Paul aux Corinthiens (CNT)*, 1958.

Heuschen, J., editor, *La Formation des Évangiles*, 1957.

Hewitt, T., *The Epistle to the Hebrews (TNT)*, 1960.

Higgins, A. J. B., *The Historicity of the Fourth Gospel*, 1960.

Higgins, A. J. B., *Jesus and the Son of Man*, 1964.

Higgins, A. J. B., *The Lord's Supper in the New Testament*, 1952.

Higgins, A. J. B., *The Reliability of the Gospels*, 1952.

Higgins, A. J. B., editor, *New Testament Essays: Studies in Memory of T. W. Manson*, 1959.

Hirsch, E., *Frühgeschichte des Evangeliums*,[2] 1951.

Hirsch, E., *Studien zum vierten Evangelium*, 1936.

Hitchcock, F. R. M., *A Study of Romans xvi*, 1936.

Hoare, F. R., *The Original Order and Chapters of St. John's Gospel*, 1944.

Hobart, W. K., *The Medical Language of St. Luke*, 1882.

Hodge, C., *A Commentary on the Epistle to the Romans*,[2] 1875.

Hodge, C., *A Commentary on the First Epistle to the Corinthians*,[3] 1863.

Hodge, C., *A Commentary on the Second Epistle to the Corinthians*,[6] 1959.

Holland, H. S., *The Fourth Gospel*, 1923.

Holtz, G., *Die Pastoralbriefe*, 1965.

Holtzmann, H. J., *Einleitung in das Neue Testament*, 1885.

Holtzmann, H. J., *Kritik der Epheser- und Kolosserbriefe*, 1872.

Holtzmann, H. J., *Die Offenbarung des Johannes*, 1908.

Holtzmann, H. J., *Die Pastoralbriefe*, 1880.

Holtzmann, H. J., *Die Synoptischen Evangelien*, 1863.

Holwerda, D. E., *The Holy Spirit and Eschatology in the Gospel of John. A Critique of Rudolph Bultmann's Present Eschatology*, 1959.

Hooke, S. H., *Alpha and Omega*, 1961.

Hooker, M. D., *Jesus and the Servant*, 1958.

Hooker, M. D., *The Son of Man in Mark*, 1967.

Hopwood, P. G. S., *The Religious Experience of the Primitive Church*, 1936.

Hort, A. F., *The Gospel according to St. Mark* (Greek text), 1914.

Hort, F. J. A., *The Apocalypse of John, i–iii*, 1908.

Hort, F. J. A., *The Christian Ecclesia*, 1897.

Hort, F. J. A., *The Epistle of St. James* (part), 1909.

Hort, F. J. A., *The First Epistle of St. Peter (i. 1–ii. 17)*, 1898.

Hort, F. J. A., *Judaistic Christianity*, 1894.

Hort, F. J. A., *Prolegomena to St. Paul's Epistles to the Romans and Ephesians*, 1895.

Horton, R. F., *The Pastoral Epistles (CB)*, 1901.

Hoskier, H. C., *Concerning the text of the Apocalypse*, 1929.

Hoskyns, Sir E. C. and Davey, F. N., *The Fourth Gospel*,[2] 1947.

Hoskyns, Sir E. C. and Davey, F. N., *The Riddle of the New Testament*,[3] 1947.

Howard, W. F., *Christianity according to St. John*, 1943.

Howard, W. F., *1 and 2 Corinthians (AB)*, 1929.

Howard, W. F., *The Fourth Gospel in Recent Criticism* (edited by C. K. Barrett),[2] 1955.

Howard, W. F., *The Gospel according to St. John (IB)*, 1952.

Huby, J. and Benoit, P., *St. Marc (Sainte Bible)*,[3] 1961.

Huck, A. and Lietzmann, H., *Synopsis of the First Three Gospels* (edited by F. L. Cross),[9] 1949.

Hudson, J. T., *The Epistle to the Hebrews*, 1937.

Hudson, J. T., *The Pauline Epistles, their Meaning and Message*, 1959.

Hugedé, N., *Commentaire de l'Épître aux Colossiens*, 1968.

Hugedé, N., *Saint Paul et la culture grecque*, 1966.

Hughes, P. E., *Paul's Second Epistle to the Corinthians (NLC)*, 1962.

Hughes, P. E., *Scripture and Myth*, 1956.

Hummel, R., *Die Auseinandersetzung zwischen Kirche und Judentum im Matthäusevangelium*, 1963.

Hunt, B. P. W. S., *Primitive Gospel Sources*, 1951.

Hunt, B. P. W. S., *Some Johannine Problems*, 1958.

Hunter, A. M., *According to John*, 1968.

Hunter, A. M., *The Epistle to the Romans (TC)*, 1955.

Hunter, A. M., *The Gospel according to St. John (CBC)*, 1965.

Hunter, A. M., *The Gospel according to St. Mark (TC)*, 1949.

Hunter, A. M., *Interpreting Paul's Gospel*, 1954.

Hunter, A. M., *Interpreting the New Testament 1900–1950*, 1951.

Hunter, A. M., *Introducing New Testament Theology*, 1957.

Hunter, A. M., *Introducing the New Testament*,[2] 1957.

Hunter, A. M., *Paul and his Predecessors*,[2] 1961.

Hunter, A. M. and Homrighausen, E. G., *The First Epistle of Peter (IB)*, 1957.

Hurd, J. C., *A Bibliography of New Testament Bibliographies*, 1966.

Hurd, J. C., *The Origin of 1 Corinthians*, 1965.

Huther, J. E., *Petrus und Judas Briefe (KEK)*, 1877.

Hyatt, J. P., editor, *The Bible and Modern Scholarship*, 1965.

Jackson, F. J. F., *The Acts of the Apostles (MC)*, 1931.

Jackson, F. J. F., *The Life of St. Paul*, 1927.

Jackson, F. J. F., *Peter: Prince of Apostles*, 1927.

Jackson, F. J. F. and Lake, K., editors, *The Beginnings of Christianity*, 1920–33.

Jacquier, E., *Les Actes des Apôtres (EB)*,[2] 1926.

Jacquier, E., *Le Nouveau Testament dans l'Église Chrétienne*, 1911.

James, J. D., *The Genuineness and Authorship of the Pastoral Epistles*, 1906.

James, M. R., *The Apocryphal New Testament*, 1924.

James, M. R., *The Second Epistle general of St. Peter and the general Epistle of St. Jude (CGT)*, 1912.

Jameson, H. G., *The Origin of the Synoptic Gospels*, 1922.

Jaubert, A., *La Date de la Cène*, 1957 (Eng. Tr. *The Date of the Last Supper*, 1965).

Jelf, W. E., *A Commentary on the First Epistle of St. John*, 1877.

Jeremias, J., *Die Briefe an Timotheus und Titus (NTD)*,[8] 1963.

Jeremias, J., *The Eucharistic Words of Jesus* (Eng. Tr.), 1955.

Jeremias, J., *Jesus' Promise to the Nations* (Eng. Tr.), 1958.

Jeremias, J., *The Parables of Jesus* (Eng. Tr.),[2] 1963.   •

Jeremias, J., *Unknown Sayings of Jesus* (Eng .Tr.),[2] 1964.

Jeremias, J., *Die Wiederentdeckung von Bethesda*, 1949.

Johnson, M. D., *The Purpose of the Biblical Genealogies*, 1969.

Johnson, S. E., *The Gospel according to St. Mark (BC)*, 1960.

Johnson, S. E., *The Gospel according to St. Matthew (IB)*, 1951.

Johnson, S. E., editor, *The Joy of Study*, 1951.

Johnston, C. N., *The Seven Churches of Asia*, 1916.

Johnston, G., *Ephesians, Philippians, Colossians and Philemon (CB, n.s.)*, 1967.

Jones, M., *The Epistle of St. Paul to the Colossians*, 1923.

Jones, M., *The Epistle to the Philippians (WC)*, 1912.

Jones, M., *The New Testament in the Twentieth Century*, 1924.

Jones, M., *St. Paul the Orator*, 1910.

Jülicher, A., *Introduction to the New Testament* (Eng. Tr. from the 3rd German edition), 1904.

Jülicher, A. and Fascher, E., *Einleitung in das Neue Testament*,[7] 1931.

Kahler, M., *The so-called Historical Jesus and the Historic Biblical Christ* (Eng. Tr.), 1964.

Käsemann, E., *Essays on New Testament Themes*, 1964.

Käsemann, E., *Exegetische Versüche und Besinnungen*, I, 1960.

Käsemann, E., *Jesu letzter Wille nach Johannes 17*, 1966 (Eng. Tr. *The Testament of Jesus*, 1968).

Käsemann, E., *Verkündigung und Forschungen*, 1950–51.

Käsemann, E., *Das wandernde Gottesvolk, Eine Untersuchung zum Hebräerbrief*, 1939.

Kautzsch, E., editor, *Die Apokryphen und Pseudepigraphen des Alten Testaments*, 1900.

Keck, L. E. and Martyn, J. L., editors, *Studies in Luke–Acts*, 1966.

Kehl, N., *Der Christushymnus im Kolosserbrief*, 1967.

Kelly, J. N. D., *A Commentary on the Pastoral Epistles (BC)*, 1963.

Kelly, J. N. D., *Early Christian Creeds*, 1950.

Kelly, J. N. D., *The Epistles of Peter and Jude (BC)*, 1969.

Kennedy, H. A. A., *The Epistle to the Philippians (EGT)*, 1903.

Kennedy, H. A. A., *St. Paul and the Mystery Religions*, 1913.

Kennedy, H. A. A., *St. Paul's Conception of the Last Things*, 1904.

Kennedy, H. A. A., *The Theology of the Epistles*, 1919.

Kennedy, J. H., *The Second and Third Epistles of St. Paul to the Corinthians*, 1900.

Kenyon, Sir F., *The Bible and Modern Scholarship*, 1948.

Kenyon, Sir F., *The Chester Beatty Biblical Papyri*, 1936.

Kenyon, Sir F., *The Story of the Bible*, 1936.

Kenyon, Sir F., *The Text of the Greek Bible*,[2] 1949.

Kepler, T. S., *The Book of Revelation*, 1957.

Ketter, P., *Hebräerbrief, Jakobusbrief, Petrusbrief, Judasbrief (Herder's Bibelkommentar)*, 1950.

Kiddle, M., *The Revelation of St. John (MC)*, 1940.

Kilpatrick, G. D., *The Origins of the Gospel according to St. Matthew*, 1946.

Kirby, J. C., *Ephesians, Baptism and Pentecost. An Inquiry into the Structure and Purpose of the Epistle to the Ephesians*, 1968.

Kirk, K. E., *The Epistle to the Romans (Clar B)*, 1937.

Kittel, G., *Die Probleme des palästinnischen Spätjudentums und das Urchristentum*, 1926.

Klassen, W. and Snyder, G. F., editors, *Current Issues in New Testament Interpretation*, 1962.

Klein, G., *Die zwölf Apostel*, 1961.

Klijn, A. F. J., *An Introduction to the New Testament*, 1967.

Klostermann, A., *Zur Theorie der biblischen Weissagung und zur Charakteristik des Hebräerbriefes*, 1889.

Klostermann, E., *Das Lukasevangelium (LHB)*,[4] 1950.

Klostermann, E., *Das Markusevangelium* (LHB),[4] 1950.
Klostermann, E., *Das Matthäusevangelium* (LHB),[2] 1927.
Knight, G. W., *The Faithful Sayings in the Pastoral Letters*, 1968.
Knopf, R., *Die Apostelgeschichte*, 1906.
Knopf, R., *Die Briefe Petri und Judä* (KEK),[7] 1912.
Knowling, R. J., *The Acts of the Apostles* (EGT), 1900.
Knowling, R. J., *The Epistle of St. James* (WC), 1904.
Knowling, R. J., *The Testimony of St. Paul to Christ*, 1903.
Knowling, R. J., *The Witness of the Epistles*, 1892.
Knox, J., *Chapters in a Life of Paul*, 1954.
Knox, J., *The Church and the Reality of Christ*, 1964.
Knox, J., *The Death of Christ: The Cross in New Testament History*, 1959.
Knox, J., *The Early Church and the Coming Great Church*, 1957.
Knox, J., *The Epistle to the Romans* (IB), 1954.
Knox, J., *Marcion and the New Testament*, 1942.
Knox, J., *Philemon among the Letters of Paul*, 1935.
Knox, R. A., *A New Testament Commentary for English Readers*, Vols. II, III, 1954–56.
Knox, W. L., *The Acts of the Apostles*, 1948.
Knox, W. L., *St. Paul and the Church of Jerusalem*, 1925.
Knox, W. L., *St. Paul and the Church of the Gentiles*, 1939.
Knox, W. L., *Some Hellenistic Elements in Primitive Christianity* (Schweich Lectures), 1944.
Knox, W. L., *Sources of the Synoptic Gospels*, I, 1953, II, 1957.
Koch, K., *Was ist Formgeschichte?*, 1964 (Eng. Tr. *The Growth of the Biblical Tradition*, 1969).
Kosmala, H., *Hebräer-Essener-Christen*, 1959.
Köster, H., *Synoptische Überlieferung bei den apostolischen Vätern*, 1957.
Kragerud, A., *Der Lieblingsjünger im Joh.*, 1959.
Krenkel, M., *Josephus und Lucas*, 1894.
Kühl, E., *Die Briefe Petri und Judä* (KEK), 1897.
Kümmel, W. G., *Introduction to the New Testament* (see under Feine, P., Behm, J. and Kümmel, W. G.)
Kümmel, W. G., *Das Neue Testament*, 1958.
Kundsin, K., *Topologische Überlieferungsstücke im Joh.*, 1925.

Ladd, G. E., *The New Testament and Criticism*, 1967.
Lagrange, M.-J., *L'Évangile de Jésus-Christ* (EB), 1954.
Lagrange, M.-J., *Évangile selon St. Jean* (EB),[5] 1936.
Lagrange, M.-J., *Évangile selon St. Luc* (EB),[8] 1948.
Lagrange, M.-J., *Évangile selon St. Marc* (EB),[4] 1929.
Lagrange, M.-J., *Évangile selon St. Matthieu* (EB),[7] 1948.

Lagrange, M.-J., *Saint Paul, Épître aux Galates (EB)*,² 1950.

Lagrange, M.-J., *Saint Paul, Épître aux Romains (EB)*, 1916.

Lake, K., *The Apostolic Fathers (The Loeb Classical Library)*, 1912.

Lake, K., *The Earlier Epistles of Paul*, 1927.

Lake, K., *Paul, his Heritage and Legacy*, 1934.

Lake, K. and S., *An Introduction to the New Testament*, 1938.

Lambrecht, J., *Die Redaktion des Markus-Apokalypse*, 1967.

Lamont, D., *Studies in the Johannine Writings*, 1956.

Larson, M. A., *The Essene Heritage, or The Teacher of the Scrolls and the Gospel Christ*, 1967.

Laurentin, R., *Structure et Théologie de Luc, I–II (EB)*, 1957.

Law, R., *The Tests of life: a study of the First Epistle of St. John*, 1909.

Leaney, A. R. C., *The Epistles to Timothy, Titus and Philemon (TC)*, 1960.

Leaney, A. R. C., *The Gospel according to St. Luke (BC)*, 1958.

Leaney, A. R. C., *The Letters of Peter and Jude (CBC)*, 1967.

Leconte, R., *Les épîtres catholiques (Sainte Bible)*,² 1961.

Lee, E. K., *The Religious Thought of St. John*, 1950.

Lee, E. K., *A Study in Romans*, 1962.

Leenhardt, F. J., *L'Épître aux Romains (CNT)*, 1957.

Leighton, R., *A Practical Commentary upon the First Epistle of St. Peter*, 1831.

Lenski, R. C. H., *The Interpretation of John's Revelation*, 1935.

Leonard, W., *The Authorship of the Epistle to the Hebrews*, 1939.

Léon-Dufour, X., *Concordance of the Synoptic Gospels in seven colours*, 1956.

Lessing, G. E., *Neue Hypothese über die Evangelisten als bloss menschliche Geschichtsschreiber*, 1778.

Lewis, F. W., *Disarrangements in the Fourth Gospel*, 1910.

Lewis, G., *The Johannine Epistles (EC)*, 1961.

Lias, J. J., *The First Epistle of St. John, with expository and homiletical treatment*, 1887.

Liebermann, S., *Hellenism in Jewish Palestine*, 1950.

Lietzmann, H., *The Beginnings of the Christian Church*, 1937.

Lietzmann, H., *Der Brief des Apostels Paulus an die Galater (LHB)*,³ 1932.

Lietzmann, H., *Der Brief des Apostels Paulus an die Römer (LHB)*,⁴ 1933.

Lietzmann, H., *Die Briefe des Apostels Paulus an die Korinther (LHB)*,⁴ 1933.

Lietzmann, H., *Die drei ältesten Martyrologien (Kleine Texte, 2)*, 1911.

Lightfoot, J. B., *Biblical Essays*, 1893.

Lightfoot, J. B., *Notes on the Epistles of St. Paul*, 1895.

Lightfoot, J. B., *St. Paul's Epistles to the Colossians and Philemon*, 1879.

Lightfoot, J. B., *St. Paul's Epistle to the Galatians*, 1890.

Lightfoot, J. B., *St. Paul's Epistle to the Philippians*, 1878.

Lightfoot, R. H., *The Gospel Message of St. Mark*, 1950.

Lightfoot, R. H., *History and Interpretation in the Gospels*, 1935.

Lightfoot, R. H., *Locality and Doctrine in the Gospels*, 1938.
Lightfoot, R. H., *St. John's Gospel: a Commentary*, 1956.
Lindars, B., *New Testament Apologetic*, 1961.
Lindsey, R. L., *A Hebrew Translation of the Gospel of Mark*, 1969.
Lock, W., *The Epistle to the Ephesians* (*WC*), 1929.
Lock, W., *The Pastoral Epistles* (*ICC*), 1924.
Loenertz, R. J., *The Apocalypse of St. John* (Eng. Tr. by H. J. Carpenter), 1947.
Loewenich, W. von, *Das Johannesverständnis im zweiten Jahrhundert* (Beiheft *ZNTW*, 13), 1932.
Loewenich, W. von, *Paul: His Life and Work* (Eng. Tr.), 1960.
Lohmeyer, E., *Der Brief an die Philipper* (*KEK*) (edited by W. Schmauch),[11] 1956.
Lohmeyer, E., *Galiläa und Jerusalem*, 1936.
Lohmeyer, E., *Der Kolosser- und der Philemonbrief* (*KEK*),[11] 1957.
Lohmeyer, E. and Bornkamm, G., *Die Offenbarung des Johannes* (*LHB*),[2] 1953.
Lohmeyer, E. and Sass, G., *Das Evangelium des Markus* (*KEK*),[12] 1953.
Lohmeyer, E. and Schmauch, W., *Das Evangelium des Matthäus* (*KEK*), 1956.
Lohse, E., *Die Briefe an die Kolosser und an Philemon* (*KEK*),[14] 1968.
Lohse, E., *Mark's Witness to Jesus Christ*, 1955.
Lohse, E., *Die Offenbarung des Johannes* (*NTD*),[8] 1960.
Loisy, A., *Les Actes des Apôtres*,[2] 1925.
Loisy, A., *L'Apocalypse de Jean*, 1923.
Loisy, A., *Évangile selon Luc*, 1924.
Loisy, A., *Les Évangiles synoptiques*, 1907–08.
Loisy, A., *Le Quatrième Évangile, deuxième édition refondue: Les Épîtres dites de Jean*, 1921.
Longenecker, R. N., *Paul, Apostle of Liberty*, 1964.
Lowe, J., *Saint Peter*, 1956.
Lowstuter, W. J., *1 and 2 Timothy and Titus* (*AB*), 1929.
Lowther Clarke, W. K., *Concise Bible Commentary*, 1952.
Luce, H. K., *St. Luke* (*CGT*), 1949.
Lumby, J. R., *The Acts of the Apostles* (*CGT*), 1899.
Lund, N. W., *Chiasmus in the New Testament: A Study in Form-geschichte*, 1942.
Lütgert, W., *Amt und Geist im Kampf*, 1911.
Lütgert, W., *Gesetz und Geist*, 1919.
Luthardt, C. E., *Die Lehre von den letzten Dingen*,[2] 1870.
Lüthi, W., *Die Apostelgeschichte ausgelegt für die Gemeinde*, 1958.

Macgregor, G. H. C., *The Gospel of John* (*MC*), 1928.
Macgregor, G. H. C. and Ferris, T. P., *The Acts of the Apostles* (*IB*), 1954.
Macgregor, G. H. C. and Morton, A. Q., *The Structure of Luke and Acts*, 1964.

Macgregor, G. H. C. and Morton, A. Q., *The Structure of the Fourth Gospel*, 1961.

Macgregor, G. H. C. and Purdy, A. C., *Jew and Greek: Tutors unto Christ*,[2] 1959.

Machen, J. G., *The Origin of Paul's Religion*, 1921.

Mackintosh, R., *Galatians* (PC), 1928.

Maier, F., *Der Judasbrief*, 1904.

Major, H. D. A., Manson, T. W. and Wright, C. T., *The Mission and Message of Jesus*, 1937.

Malateste, E., *St. John's Gospel 1920–65*, 1967.

Manson, T. W., *The Beginnings of the Gospel*, 1950.

Manson, T. W., *On Paul and John*, 1963.

Manson, T. W., *The Sayings of Jesus*, 1949.

Manson, T. W., *Studies in the Gospels and Epistles*, 1962.

Manson, T. W., *The Teaching of Jesus*,[2] 1935.

Manson, W., *The Epistle to the Hebrews* (Baird Lectures), 1951.

Manson, W., *The Gospel of Luke* (MC), 1930.

Manson, W., *Jesus the Messiah*, 1943.

Marlé, R., *R. Bultmann et l'interprétation du N.T.*, 1956.

Marsh, J., *The Gospel of St. John* (Pel C), 1968.

Marshall, L. H., *Formgeschichte and its limitations*, 1942.

Martin, G. C., *Ephesians, Colossians, Philemon and Philippians* (CB), 1902.

Martin, H., *The Seven Letters. Christ's Message to His Church*, 1957.

Martin, R. P., *Carmen Christi: Philippians ii. 5–11 in Recent Interpretation and in the Setting of Early Christian Worship*, 1967.

Martin, R. P., *An Early Christian Confession: Philippians ii. 5–11 in Recent Interpretation*, 1960.

Martin, R. P., *The Epistle of Paul to the Philippians* (TNT), 1959.

Martin, R. P., editor, *Vox Evangelica*, I, 1962, II, 1963.

Martindale, C. C., *St. John and the Apocalypse*,[2] 1958.

Marty, J., *L'Épître de Jacques* (Étude Critique), 1935.

Martyn, J. L., *History and Theology in the Fourth Gospel*, 1968.

Marxsen, W., *Einleitung in das Neue Testament*, 1963 (Eng. Tr. *Introduction to the New Testament*, 1968).

Marxsen, W., *Der Evangelist Markus*,[2] 1959 (Eng. Tr. *Mark the Evangelist*, 1969).

Marxsen, W., *Der 'Frühkatholizismus' im NT*, 1958.

Massaux, E., *Influence de l'Évangile de St. Matthieu sur la littérature chrétienne avant St. Irenée*, 1950.

Massie, J., *Corinthians* (CB), 1902.

Masson, Ch., *L'Épître aux Colossiens* (CNT), 1950.

Masson, Ch., *L'Épître aux Ephésiens* (CNT), 1952.

Masson, Ch., *Les Épîtres aux Thessaloniciens, à Philemon* (CNT), 1957.

Masterman, J. H. B., *The First Epistle of St. Peter*, 1912.

Mattill, A. J., Jnr and Mattill, M. B., *A Classified Bibliography of Literature on the Acts of the Apostles*, 1966.

Maurer, C., *Ignatius von Antiochen und das Johannesevangelium*, 1949.

Maycock, E. A., *A letter of wise counsel: studies in the first epistle of Peter*, 1957.

Mayor, J. B., *The Epistle of St. James*,³ 1913.

Mayor, J. B., *The Epistle of St. Jude and the Second Epistle of St. Peter*, 1907.

Mayor, J. B., *Further Studies in the Epistle of St. James*, 1913.

Mayor, J. B., *The General Epistle of Jude (EGT)*, 1910.

McArthur, H. K., editor, *In Search of the Historical Jesus*, 1969.

McClymont, J. A., *St. John (CB)*,² 1922.

McCown, C. C., *1 and 2 Thessalonians (AB)*, 1929.

McDowell, E. A., *The Meaning and Message of the Book of Revelation*, 1951.

McGiffert, A. C., *A History of Christianity in the Apostolic Age*, 1897.

McNeile, A. H., *The Gospel according to St. Matthew*, 1915.

McNeile, A. H., *St. Paul: His Life, Letters and Christian Doctrine*, 1932.

McNeile, A. H. and Williams, C. S. C., *Introduction to the New Testament*,² 1953.

Meecham, H. G., *The Oldest Version of the Bible*, 1932.

Meeks, W. A., *The Prophet-King. Moses Traditions in the Johannine Christology*, 1967.

Meinertz, M., *Einleitung in das Neue Testament*,⁵ 1950.

Meinertz, M., *Der Jakobusbrief und sein Verfasser in Schrift und Ueberlieferung*, 1905.

Meinertz, M., *Die Pastoralbriefe des heiligen Paulus*,⁴ 1931.

Ménégoz, E., *La Théologie de l'Épître aux Hébreux*, 1894.

Menoud, P. H., *L'Évangile de Jean d'après les recherches récents*,² 1947.

Menzies, A., *The Earliest Gospel*, 1901.

Menzies, A., *The Second Epistle of the Apostle Paul to the Corinthians*, 1912.

Merrill, T., *Essays in Early Christian History*, 1924.

Metzger, B. M., *Index to Periodical Literature on Christ and the Gospels*, 1966.

Metzger, B. M., *Index to Periodical Literature on the Apostle Paul*, 1960.

Metzger, B. M., *The New Testament: its background, growth and content*, 1965.

Meye, R. P., *Jesus and the Twelve: Discipleship and Revelation in Mark's Gospel*, 1968.

Meyer, A., *Das Rätsel des Jakobusbriefes*, 1930.

Meyer, E., *Ursprung und Anfänge des Christentums*, 1921–23.

Meyer, H. H., *Über die Pastoralbriefe*, 1913.

Michael, J. H., *The Epistle of Paul to the Philippians (MC)*, 1928.

Michaelis, W., *Der Brief des Paulus an die Philipper*, 1935.

Michaelis, W., *Die Datierung des Philipperbriefes*, 1933.

Michaelis, W., *Einleitung in das Neue Testament*,³ (with *Ergänzungsheft*) 1961.

Michaelis, W., *Die Gefangenschaft des Paulus in Ephesus und das Itinerar des Timotheus*, 1925.

Michaelis, W., *Pastoralbriefe und Gefangenschaftsbriefe*, 1930.

Michaelis, W., *Die Sakramente im Joh.*, 1946.

Michel, O., *Der Brief an die Hebräer (KEK)*,[12] 1966.

Michel, O., *Der Brief an die Römer (KEK)*,[10] 1955.

Miegge, G., *Gospel and Myth in the Thought of Rudolph Bultmann*, 1960.

Milik, J. T., *Ten Years of Discovery in the Wilderness of Judaea*, 1959.

Milligan, G., *New Testament Documents*, 1913.

Milligan, G., *St. Paul's Epistles to the Thessalonians*, 1908.

Milligan, G., *The Theology of the Epistle to the Hebrews*, 1899.

Milligan, W., *The Book of Revelation (Exp. Bib.)*, 1898.

Milligan, W., *Discussions on the Apocalypse*, 1893.

Milligan, W., *The Revelation of St. John* (Baird Lectures), 1887.

Minear, P. S., *The Kingdom and the Power*, 1950.

Mitton, C. L., *Commentary on the General Epistle of James*, 1966.

Mitton, C. L., *The Epistle to the Ephesians*, 1951.

Mitton, C. L., *The Formation of the Pauline Corpus of Letters*, 1955.

Mitton, C. L., *The Gospel according to St. Mark (EC)*, 1957.

Moffatt, J., *The Epistle to the Hebrews (ICC)*, 1924.

Moffatt, J., *The First and Second Epistles to the Thessalonians (EGT)*, 1910.

Moffatt, J., *The First Epistle of Paul to the Corinthians (MC)*, 1938.

Moffatt, J., *The General Epistles (MC)*, 1928.

Moffatt, J., *Introduction to the Literature of the New Testament*,[3] 1918.

Moffatt, J., *The Revelation of St. John the Divine (EGT)*, 1910.

Mollat, D., *St. Jean (Sainte Bible)*,[3] 1961.

Montefiore, C. G., *Rabbinic Literature and Gospel Teachings*, 1930.

Montefiore, C. G., *The Synoptic Gospels*,[2] 1927, r.p. 1968.

Montefiore, H., *The Epistle to the Hebrews (BC)*, 1965.

Montefiore, H. and Turner, H. E. W., *Thomas and the Evangelists*, 1962.

Morgan, W., *The Religion and Theology of Paul*, 1917.

Morgenthaler, R., *Die lukanische Geschichtsschreibung als Zeugnis*, 1949.

Morgenthaler, R., *Statistik des neutestamentlichen Wortschatzes*, 1958.

Morris, L., *The Dead Sea Scrolls and John's Gospel*, 1960.

Morris, L., *The Epistles of Paul to the Thessalonians (TNT)*, 1956.

Morris, L., *The Epistles to the Thessalonians (NLC)*, 1959.

Morris, L., *The First Epistle of Paul to the Corinthians (TNT)*, 1958.

Morris, L., *The New Testament and the Jewish Lectionaries*, 1964.

Morris, L., *The Revelation of St. John (TNT)*, 1969.

Morris, L., *Studies in the Fourth Gospel*, 1969.

Morrison, C. D., *The Powers that Be*, 1960.

Morton, A. Q. and McLeman, J., *Christianity and the Computer*, 1964.

Morton, A. Q. and McLeman, J., *Paul, the Man and the Myth*, 1966.

Moule, C. F. D., *The Birth of the New Testament*, 1962.

Moule, C. F. D., *The Epistles to the Colossians and Philemon* (CGT, n.s.), 1957.

Moule, C. F. D., *The Gospel according to Mark* (CBC), 1965.

Moule, C. F. D., *The Phenomenon of the New Testament*, 1967.

Moule, H. C. G., *The Epistle to the Philippians* (CGT), 1897.

Moulton, H. K., *Colossians, Philemon and Ephesians* (EC), 1963.

Moulton, J. H., *A Grammar of New Testament Greek*, I, 1908.

Moulton, J. H. and Howard, W. F., *A Grammar of New Testament Greek*, II, 1929.

Mounce, R. H., *The Essential Nature of New Testament Preaching*, 1960.

Mowinckel, S., *He that Cometh*, 1956.

Muller, J. J., *The Epistles to the Philippians and to Philemon* (NLC), 1955.

Munck, J., *The Acts of the Apostles* (revised by W. F. Albright and C. S. Mann), 1967.

Munck, J., *Christ and Israel: An Introduction to Romans 9–11*, 1967.

Munck, J., *Paul and the Salvation of Mankind*, 1959.

Munck, J., *Petrus und Paulus in der Offenbarung Johannis*, 1950.

Murphy-O'Connor, J., editor, *Paul and Qumran*, 1968.

Murray, J., *The Epistle to the Romans* (NLC), I, 1960, II, 1965.

Murray, J. O. F., *The Epistle to the Ephesians* (CGT), 1914.

Mussner, F., *The Historical Jesus in the Gospel of St. John*, 1967.

Mussner, F., *Der Jacobusbrief*, 1964.

Nairne, A., *The Epistle of Priesthood*,[2] 1915.

Nairne, A., *The Epistle to the Hebrews* (CGT), 1917.

Nairne, A., *The Faith of the New Testament*, 1920.

Narborough, F. D. V., *The Epistle to the Hebrews* (Clar B), 1930.

Nauck, W., *Die Tradition und der Charakter des ersten Johannesbriefes* (*Wissenschaftliche Untersuchungen zum N.T.*), 1957.

Neil, W., *The Epistles of Paul to the Thessalonians* (MC), 1950.

Neil, W., *The Epistles to the Thessalonians* (TC), 1957.

Neil, W., *The Epistle to the Hebrews* (TC), 1955.

Neil, W., *The Letter of Paul to the Galatians* (CBC), 1967.

Neill, S., *The Interpretation of the New Testament*, 1964.

Nepper-Christensen, P., *Das Matthäusevangelium—ein judenchristliches Evangelium?*, 1958.

Neufeld, V. H., *The Earliest Christian Confession*, 1963.

Nicklin, T., *Gospel Gleanings*, 1950.

Nineham, D. E., *Saint Mark* (Pel C), 1963.

Nineham, D. E., editor, *The Church's Use of the Bible*, 1963.

Nineham, D. E., editor, *Studies in the Gospels*, 1955.

Noack, B., *Zur johanneischen Tradition*, 1954.

Nock, A. D., *St. Paul*, 1938.

Norden, E., *Agnostos Theos*, 1913.

Nunn, H. P. V., *The Authorship of the Fourth Gospel*, 1952.

Nunn, H. P. V., *The Fourth Gospel*, 1946.

Nunn, H. P. V., *The Son of Zebedee*, 1927.

Nygren, A., *Commentary on Romans*, 1952.

Odeberg, H., *The Fourth Gospel interpreted in its Relation to Contemporaneous Religious Currents*, 1929.

Oepke, A., *Die Briefe an die Thessalonicher (NTD)*,[9] 1962.

Oepke, A., *Der Galaterbrief*, 1937.

Oesterley, W. O. E., *The Epistle to Philemon (EGT)*, 1910.

Oesterley, W. O. E., *The General Epistle of James (EGT)*, 1910.

Ogg, G., *The Chronology of the Life of Paul*, 1968.

Ogg, G., *The Chronology of the Public Ministry of Jesus*, 1940.

Olivier, A., *L'Apocalypse et ses enseignements*, 1955.

Oman, J., *The Book of Revelation*, 1923.

Oman, J., *The Text of Revelation. A revised theory*, 1928.

O'Neill, J. C., *The Puzzle of 1 John*, 1966.

O'Neill, J. C., *The Theology of Acts in its Historical Setting*, 1961.

Oostendorp, D. W., *Another Jesus: A Gospel of Jewish Christian Superiority in II Corinthians*, 1967.

Osty, E., *St. Luc (Sainte Bible)*,[3] 1961.

Oxford Society, *The New Testament in the Apostolic Fathers*, 1905.

Packer, J. W., *The Acts of the Apostles (CBC)*, 1966.

Paley, W., *Horae Paulinae*, 1790.

Palmer, F., *The drama of the Apocalypse in relation to the literary and political circumstances of its time*, 1903.

Parker, P., *The Gospel before Mark*, 1953.

Parry, R. St.J., *A discussion of the General Epistle of James*, 1903.

Parry, R. St.J., *The Epistle to the Romans (CGT)*, 1912.

Parry, R. St.J., *The First Epistle to the Corinthians (CGT)*, 1916.

Parry, R. St.J., *The Pastoral Epistles*, 1920.

Patten, C. S., *Sources of the Synoptic Gospels*, 1915.

Patzer, H., *Das Problem der Geschichtsschreibung des Thukydides und die thukydideische Frage*, 1937.

Peake, A. S., *A Critical Introduction to the New Testament*, 1909.

Peake, A. S., *The Epistle to the Colossians (EGT)*, 1903.

Peake, A. S., *Hebrews (CB)*, n.d.

Peake, A. S., *The Pauline Epistles and 1 Corinthians (PC)*, 1928.

Peake, A. S., *The Revelation of John*, 1920.

Percy, E., *Die Botschaft Jesu*, 1953.

Percy, E., *Die Probleme der Kolosser- und Epheserbriefe*, 1946. r.p. 1964.

Percy, E., *Untersuchungen über den Ursprung der johanneischen Theologie*, 1939.

Perdelwitz, R., *Die Mysterienreligionen und das Problem des ersten Petrusbriefes*, 1911.

Pfeiffer, R. H., *History of New Testament Times, with an Introduction to the Apocrypha*, 1949.

Philippi, F., *Das Buch Henoch, sein Zeitalter und sein Verhältniss zum Judasbriefe*, 1868.

Phillips, J. B., *The Book of Revelation* (translation), 1957.

Phillips, J. B., *Letters to Young Churches*, 1947.

Pieters, A., *Studies in the Revelation of St. John*, 1954.

Plooij, D., *Studies in the Testimony Book*, 1932.

Plummer, A., *Commentary on St. Luke* (ICC), 1896.

Plummer, A., *The Epistles of St. John* (CGT), 1886.

Plummer, A., *The Gospel according to St. John* (CGT), 1900.

Plummer, A., *The Pastoral Epistles* (Exp. Bib.), 1888.

Plummer, A., *St. James and St. Jude* (Exp. Bib.), 1891.

Plummer, A., *The Second Epistle to the Corinthians* (CGT), 1903.

Plummer, A., *The Second Epistle to the Corinthians* (ICC), 1915.

Plumptre, E. H., *The General Epistle of St. James* (CBS), 1878.

Plumptre, E. H., *The General Epistles of St. Peter and St. Jude* (CBS), 1879.

Pokorny, P., *Der Epheserbrief und die Gnosis*, 1965.

Porter, F. C., *The Messages of the Apocalyptical Writers*, 1905.

Prat, F., *Théologie de Saint Paul*, 1949.

Preston, R. and Hanson, A. T., *The Revelation of Saint John the Divine* (TC), 1957.

Preuschen, E., *Die Apostelgeschichte* (LHB), 1912.

Price, J. L., *Interpreting the New Testament*, 1961.

Prümm, K., *Diakonia Pneumatos. Der zweite Korintherbrief als Zugang zur apostolischen Botschaft*, 3 vols., 1960–67.

Quasten, J., *Patrology*, I, 1950.

Quispel, G., *Gnosis als Weltreligion*, 1951.

Rackham, R. B., *The Acts of the Apostles* (WC),[14] 1951, r.p. 1964.

Radford, L. B., *The Epistle to the Colossians and the Epistle to Philemon* (WC), 1931.

Ragg, L., *St. Luke* (WC), 1922.

Ramsay, A., *The Revelation and the Johannine Epistles*, 1910.

Ramsay, Sir W. M., *The Bearing of Recent Discoveries on the Trustworthiness of the New Testament*, 1915.

Ramsay, Sir W. M., *The Church in the Roman Empire*,[6] 1900.

Ramsay, Sir W. M., *The First Christian Century*, 1911.

Ramsay, Sir W. M., *A Historical Commentary on St. Paul's Epistle to the Galatians*, 1899.

Ramsay, Sir W. M., *A Historical Commentary on the Epistles to Timothy* (Expositor, VII, 7, 8, 8; VIII, 1), 1909–11.

Ramsay, Sir W. M., *The Letters to the Seven Churches of Asia*, 1904.

Ramsay, Sir W. M., *Luke the Physician and other studies*, 1908.

Ramsay, Sir W. M., *St. Paul the Traveller and Roman Citizen*, 1920.

Ramsay, Sir W. M., *Was Christ born at Bethlehem?*, 1898.

Raney, W. H., *The Relation of the Fourth Gospel to the Christian Cultus*, 1933.

Rawlinson, A. E. J., *The Epistles to the Ephesians, Colossians and Philemon* (PC), 1928.

Rawlinson, A. E. J., *The Gospel according to St. Mark* (WC),[7] 1949.

Redlich, B., *St. Paul and his Companions*, 1913.

Redlich, E. B., *Form Criticism*, 1939.

Redlich, E. B., *An Introduction to the Fourth Gospel*, 1939.

Redlich, E. B., *The Student's Introduction to the Synoptic Gospels*, 1936.

Rehkopf, F., *Die lukanische Sonderquelle*, 1959.

Reicke, B., *The Epistles of James, Peter and Jude*, 1964.

Reicke, B., *Glaube und Leben der Urgemeinde* (AbThANT), 1957.

Reicke, B., *The Gospel of Luke*, 1964.

Reicke, B., editor, *Coniectanea Neotestamentica XI in honorem Antonii Fridrichsen*, 1947.

Reitzenstein, R., *Die hellenistischen Mysterienreligionen*, 1927.

Reitzenstein, R., *Das iranische Erlösungsmysterium*, 1921.

Renan, E., *Les Évangiles*, 1877.

Renan, E., *Saint Paul*, 1869 (Eng. Tr. *The History of the Origins of Christianity*, Bk. III: *Saint Paul*, n.d.).

Renan, E., *Vie de Jésus*, 1863.

Rendall, F., *The Epistle to the Galatians* (EGT), 1903.

Rendall, F., *The Epistle to the Hebrews*, 1883.

Rendall, G. H., *The Epistle of James and Judaistic Christianity*, 1927.

Rendall, G. H., *The Epistles of St. Paul to the Corinthians*, 1909.

Rendtorff, H., *Der Brief an die Epheser, an die Kolosser, Der Brief an Philemon* (NTD),[7] 1955.

Rendtorff, H., *Getrostes Wandern*, in *Die urchristlichen Botschaft* (editor, O. Schmitz),[7] 1951.

Rengstorf, K. H., *Das Evangelium nach Lukas* (NTD),[8] 1958.

Reumann, J., *Jesus in the Church's Gospels*, 1969.

Reuss, E., *History of the Sacred Scriptures of the New Testament*, 1884.

Réville, J., *Le quatrième Évangile, son Origine et sa Valeur historique*, 1901.

Rhys, H., *The Epistle to the Romans*, 1961.

Richardson, A., *The Gospel according to St. John (TC)*, 1959.

Richardson, A., *The Gospels in the Making*, 1938.

Richardson, A., *The Miracle-stories of the Gospels*, 1941.

Ridderbos, H. N., *The Epistle to the Galatians (NLC)*, 1954.

Ridderbos, H. N., *Paul and Jesus*, 1958.

Riddle, D. W. and Hutson, H. H., *New Testament Life and Literature*, 1946.

Rigaux, B., *Les Épîtres aux Thessaloniciens (EB)*, 1956.

Rigaux, B., *Saint Paul et ses Lettres*, 1962.

Rigaux, B., *Témoignage de l'Évangile de Marc*, 1965 (Eng. Tr. *The Testimony of St. Mark*, 1966).

Rigaux, B., *Témoignage de l'Évangile de Matthieu*, 1967.

Riggenbach, E., *Der Brief an die Hebräer (Zahn's Kommentar)*, 1913.

Rissi, M., *Zeit und Geschichte in der Offenbarung des Johannes*, 1952.

Rist, M. and Hough, L. H., *The Revelation of St. John the Divine (IB)*, 1957.

Ristow, H. and Matthiae, K., editors, *Der historische Jesus und der kerygmatische Christus*, 1962.

Robert, A. and Feuillet, A., *Introduction à la Bible*, II, *Nouveau Testament*, 1959 (Eng. Tr. by P. W. Skehan et al., *Introduction to the New Testament*, 1965).

Robert, J. W., *Commentary on the General Epistle of James*, 1963.

Roberts, C. H., *An Unpublished Fragment of the Fourth Gospel*, 1935.

Robertson, A. and Plummer, A., *The First Epistle to the Corinthians (ICC)*, 1911.

Robertson, A. T., *Studies in the Epistle of James* (edited by H. F. Peacock),[2] 1959 (original edition, 1915).

Robertson, J. A., *The Epistle to the Philippians (AB)*, 1929.

Robinson, J. A., *St. Paul's Epistle to the Ephesians*,[2] 1904.

Robinson, J. A. T., 'The New Look on the Fourth Gospel', in *The Gospels Reconsidered*, 1960.

Robinson, J. M., *A New Quest of the Historical Jesus*, 1959.

Robinson, J. M., *The Problem of History in Mark*, 1957.

Robinson, T. H., *The Epistle to the Hebrews (MC)*, 1933.

Robinson, T. H., *The Gospel of Matthew (MC)*, 1928.

Robinson, T. H., *St. Mark's Life of Jesus*, 1922.

Robinson, W. C., Jnr, *Der Weg des Herrn*, 1964.

Robson, E. I., *Studies in the Second Epistle of St. Peter*, 1915.

Rohde, J., *Rediscovering the Teaching of the Evangelists* (Eng. Tr.), 1968.

Roller, O., *Das Formular der paulinischen Briefe*, 1933.

Roller, O., *Münzen, Geld und Vermögensverhältnisse in den Evangelien*, 1929.

Ropes, J. H., *The Apostolic Age in the Light of Modern Criticism*, 1906.

Ropes, J. H., *A critical and exegetical commentary on the Epistle of James (ICC)*, 1916.

Ropes, J. H., *The Singular Problem of the Epistle to the Galatians*, 1929.

Ropes, J. H., *The Synoptic Gospels*, 1934, r.p., 1960.

Ross, A., *The Epistles of James and John (NLC)*, 1954.

Rothe, R., *Der erste Johannis Brief praktische erklärt*, 1878.

Round, D., *The Date of St. Paul's Epistle to the Galatians*, 1906.

Rowley, H. H., *The Relevance of Apocalyptic*, 1944.

Ruckstuhl, E., *The Chronology of the Last Days of Jesus*, 1965.

Ruckstuhl, E., *Die literarische Einheit des Johannesevangeliums*, 1951.

Rushbrooke, W., *Synopticon*, 1880.

Russell, D., *Preaching the Apocalypse*, 1935.

Sabatier, A., *Paul* (Eng. Tr.), 1903.

Sahlin, H., *Der Messias und das Gottesvolk*, 1945.

Sahlin, H., *Studien zum dritten Kapitel des Lukasevangeliums*, 1949.

Sahlin, H., *Zur Typologie des Johannesevangeliums*, 1950.

Salmon, G., *Introduction to the New Testament*,[6] 1892.

Salmond, S. D. F., *The Epistle to the Ephesians (EGT)*, 1903.

Sanday, W., *The Criticism of the Fourth Gospel*, 1905.

Sanday, W., *Inspiration*, 1893.

Sanday, W. and Headlam, A. C., *The Epistle to the Romans (ICC)*, 1895.

Sanday, W., editor, *Oxford Studies in the Synoptic Problem*, 1911.

Sanders, E. P., *The Tendencies of the Synoptic Tradition*, 1969.

Sanders, J. N., *The Foundations of the Christian Faith*, 1950.

Sanders, J. N., *The Fourth Gospel in the Early Church*, 1943.

Sanders, J. N. and Mastin, B. A., *The Gospel according to St. John*, 1969.

Schammberger, H., *Die Einheitlichkeit des Jakobusbriefes in antignostischen Kampf*, 1936.

Schelkle, K. H., *Die Petrusbriefe, der Judasbrief*, 1961.

Schlatter, A., *Das Alte Testament in der johanneischen Apokalypse*, 1912.

Schlatter, A., *Der Brief des Jakobus ausgelegt*, 1932.

Schlatter, A., *Die Briefe des Petrus, Judas, Jakobus, der Brief an die Hebräer*, 1950.

Schlatter, A., *Die Briefe und die Offenbarung des Johannes*, 1950.

Schlatter, A., *The Church in the New Testament Period* (Eng. Tr.), 1955.

Schlatter, A., *Der Evangelist Johannes*, 1930.

Schlatter, A., *Das Evangelium des Lukas*, 1931.

Schlatter, A., *Die Kirche des Matthäus*, 1929.

Schlatter, A., *Petrus und Paulus nach dem I Petrusbrief*, 1937.

Schleiermacher, F., *A critical Essay on the Gospel of St. Luke* (Eng. Tr.), 1825.

Schleiermacher, F., *Über den sogennanten ersten Brief des Paulus an den Timotheus*, 1807.

Schlier, H., *Der Brief an die Epheser*,[5] 1965.

Schlier, H., *Der Galaterbrief (KEK)*,[12] 1962.

Schmauch, W., editor, *Lohmeyer Gedenkenschrift*, 1951.

Schmid, J., *Zeit und Ort der paulinischen Gefangenschaftsbriefe*, 1931.

Schmidt, J. E. C., *Einleitung in das Neue Testament*, 1804.

Schmidt, K. L., *Der Rahmen der Geschichte Jesu*, 1919.

Schmithals, W., *Die Gnosis in Korinth. Eine Untersuchung zu den Korintherbriefen*, 1956.

Schmithals, W., *Paulus und Jakobus*, 1963 (Eng. Tr. *Paul and James*, 1965).

Schnackenburg, R., *Die Johannesbriefe*,[2] 1963.

Schnackenburg, R., *Das Johannesevangelium*, I, 1965 (Eng. Tr. by K. Smyth, *The Gospel according to St. John*, 1968).

Schneckenberger, M., *Ueber den Zweck der Apostelgeschichte*, 1841.

Schneemelcher, W., editor, *Das Problem der Sprache in Theologie und Kirche*, 1959.

Schneider, J., *Die Kirchenbriefe (NTD)*,[9] 1961.

Schneider, J., *The Letter to the Hebrews*, 1957.

Schniewind, J., *Das Evangelium nach Markus (NTD)*,[8] 1958.

Schniewind, J., *Das Evangelium nach Matthäus (NTD)*,[9] 1960.

Schniewind, J., *Die Parallelperikopen bei Lukas und Johannes*, 1914.

Schoeps, H. J., *Paulus. Die Theologie des Apostels im Lichte der Jüdischen Religionsgeschichte*, 1959 (Eng. Tr. by H. Knight, *Paul*, 1961).

Schoeps, H. J., *Theologie und Geschichte des Judenchristentums*, 1949.

Schonfield, H. J., *Saints against Caesar: the rise and reactions of the first Christian Community*, 1948.

Schreiber, J., *Theologie des Vertrauens: Eine redaktionsgeschichte Untersuchung des Markusevangeliums*, 1967.

Schröger, F., *Der Verfasser des Hebräerbrief als Schriftausleger*, 1968.

Schubert, P., *Form and Function of the Pauline Thanksgivings*, 1939.

Schulz, S., *Komposition und Herkunft der johanneischen Reden*, 1960.

Schulz, S., *Untersuchungen zur Menschensohnchristologie*, 1957.

Schumacher, R., *Die beiden letzten Kapitel des Römerbriefs*, 1929.

Schürer, E., *A History of the Jewish People in the Time of Jesus Christ* (Eng. Tr. from 2nd German edition), 1886–90.

Schürmann, H., *Quellenkritische Untersuchungen des lukanischen Abendmahlsberichtes*, 1953–57.

Schütz, R., *Die Offenbarung des Johannes und Kaiser Domitian*, 1933.

Schweitzer, A., *The Mysticism of Paul the Apostle*, 1931.

Schweitzer, A., *Paul and his Interpreters*, 1912.

Schweizer, E., *Church Order in the New Testament* (Eng. Tr.), 1961.

Schweizer, E., *Ego Eimi*, 1939.

Schweizer, E., *Der erste Petrusbrief (Prophezei:Schweizerisches Bibelwerk für die Gemeinde)*,[2] 1949.

Schweizer, E., *Das Evangelium nach Markus (NTD)*,[11] 1967.

Scott, C. A. A., *The Book of Revelation*, 1905.
Scott, C. A. A., *Christianity according to St. Paul*, 1927.
Scott, C. A. A., *The Epistle to the Romans (AB)*, 1929.
Scott, C. A. A., *Footnotes to St. Paul*, 1935.
Scott, C. A. A., *Revelation (CB)*, n.d.
Scott, C. A. A., *St. Paul, the Man and the Teacher*, 1936.
Scott, C. A. A., *The Second Epistle to the Corinthians (PC)*, 1928.
Scott, E. F., *The Book of Revelation*,[4] 1941.
Scott, E. F., *The Epistles of Paul to the Colossians, to Philemon and to the Ephesians (MC)*, 1930.
Scott, E. F., *The Epistle to the Hebrews*, 1922.
Scott, E. F., *The Epistle to the Philippians (IB)*, 1955.
Scott, E. F., *The Fourth Gospel, its Purpose and Theology*,[2] 1908.
Scott, E. F., *The Literature of the New Testament*, 1932.
Scott, E. F., *The Pastoral Epistles (MC)*, 1936.
Scott, E. F., *Paul's Epistle to the Romans*, 1947.
Scott, E. F., *Varieties of New Testament Religion*, 1946.
Scott, R., *The Pauline Epistles*, 1909.
Scrivener, F. H. A., *A Plain Introduction to the Criticism of the New Testament* (edited by E. Millar),[4] 1894.
Scroggie, W. G., *A Guide to the Gospels*, 1948.
Selby, D. J., *Towards an Understanding of St. Paul*, 1962.
Selwyn, E. C., *The Christian Prophets, and the Prophetic Apocalypse*, 1900.
Selwyn, E. G., *The First Epistle of St. Peter*, 1946.
Shaw, R. D., *The Pauline Epistles*, 1924.
Shepherd, M. H., *The Paschal Liturgy and the Apocalypse*, 1960.
Sherwin-White, A. N., *Roman Society and Roman Law in the New Testament*, 1963.
Sidebottom, E. M., *The Christ of the Fourth Gospel*, 1961.
Sidebottom, E. M., *James, Jude and 2 Peter (CB, n.s.)*, 1967.
Simcox, W. H., *The Revelation of St. John the Divine (CGT)*, 1893.
Simon, M., *St. Stephen and the Hellenists in the Primitive Church*, 1958.
Simon, W. G. H., *1 Corinthians (TC)*, 1959.
Simons, E., *Hat der dritte Evangelist den kanonischen Matthäus benutzt?*, 1880.
Simpson, E. K., *The Epistle to the Ephesians (NLC)*, 1958.
Simpson, E. K., *The Pastoral Epistles*, 1954.
Sint, J. A., *Pseudonymität im Altertum*, 1960.
Sjöberg, E., *Der verborgene Menschensohn in den Evangelien*, 1955.
Smith, B. T. D., *St. Matthew (CGT)*, 1927.
Smith, D., *The Epistles of John (EGT)*, 1910.
Smith, D., *The Life and Letters of St. Paul*, 1919.
Smith, D. M., Jnr, *The Composition and Order of the Fourth Gospel. Bultmann's Literary Theory*, 1965.

Smith, H. M., *The Epistle of James*, 1914.

Snell, A., *New and Living Way. An Explanation of the Epistle to the Hebrews*, 1959.

Soden, H. von, *Der Brief an die Hebräer*, 1899.

Soden, H. von, *Die Briefe des Petrus, Jakobus, Judas*, 1891.

Solages, B. de, *A Greek Synopsis of the Gospels*, 1959.

Souter, A., *The Text and Canon of the New Testament*,[2] 1954.

Sowers, S. G., *The Hermeneutics of Philo and Hebrews*, 1965.

Sparks, H. F. D., *The Formation of the New Testament*, 1952.

Sparks, H. F. D., *A Synopsis of the Gospels*, 1964.

Spicq, C., *L'Épître aux Hébreux* (EB), 1952.

Spicq, C., *Les Épîtres de Saint Pierre* (EB), 1966.

Spicq, C., *Les Épîtres Pastorales* (EB), 1948.

Spitta, F., *Die Apostelgeschichte, ihre Quellen und deren geschichtlicher Wert*, 1891.

Spitta, F., *Der Jakobbrief*, in *Zur Geschichte und Literatur des Urchristentums*, II, 1896.

Spitta, F., *Die Offenbarung des Johannes*, 1889.

Spitta, F., *Zur Geschichte und Literatur des Urchristentums*, 1893.

Spitta, F., *Der zweite Brief des Petrus und der Brief des Judas*, 1885.

Spivey, R. A. and Smith, D. M., Jnr, *Anatomy of the New Testament. A Guide to its Structures and Meaning*, 1969.

Spörri, T., *Der Gemeindegedanke im ersten Petrusbriefe* (Neutest. Forschungen, II. 2), 1925.

Stacey, W. D., *The Pauline View of Man*, 1956.

Stagg, F., *The Book of Acts. The Early Struggle for an unhindered Gospel*, 1955.

Stamm, R. T., *The Epistle to the Galatians* (IB), 1953.

Stanton, V. H., *The Gospels as Historical Documents*, 1923.

Stauffer, E., *Festschrift, Donum Gratulatorium*, 1962.

Stauffer, E., *Jesus and His Story*, 1960.

Stauffer, E., *Theology of the New Testament* (Eng. Tr.), 1955.

Steinmann, A., *Die Apostelgeschichte übersetzt und erklärt*,[4] 1934.

Stendahl, K., *The School of St. Matthew and its use of the Old Testament*,[2] 1968.

Stendahl, K., editor, *The Scrolls and the New Testament*, 1958.

Stevenson, J., editor, *A New Eusebius*, 1957.

Stewart, J. S., *A Man in Christ*, 1935.

Stibbs, A. M. and Walls, A. F., *The First Epistle General of Peter* (TNT), 1959.

Still, J. I., *St. Paul on Trial*, 1923.

Stokes, G. T., *The Book of the Acts of the Apostles* (Exp. Bib.),[4] 1894.

Stonehouse, N. B., *The Apocalypse in the Ancient Church*, 1929.

Stonehouse, N. B., *Origins of the Synoptic Gospels*, 1963.

Stonehouse, N. B., *Paul before the Areopagus and other New Testament Studies*, 1957.

Stonehouse, N. B., *The Witness of Luke to Christ*, 1951.

Stonehouse, N. B., *The Witness of Matthew and Mark to Christ*, 1944.

Stott, J. R. W., *The Epistles of John* (*TNT*), 1964.

Strachan, R. H., *The Fourth Evangelist, Dramatist or Historian?*, 1925.

Strachan R. H., *The Fourth Gospel*,[3] 1941.

Strachan, R. H., *The Historic Jesus in the New Testament*, 1931.

Strachan, R. H., *The Second Epistle General of Peter* (*EGT*), 1910.

Strachan, R. H., *The Second Epistle of Paul to the Corinthians* (*MC*), 1935.

Strack, H. L. and Billerbeck, P., *Kommentar zum Neue Testament aus Talmud und Midrasch*, 1922–61.

Strathmann, H., *Der Brief an die Hebräer* (*NTD*),[8] 1963.

Strathmann, H., *Das Evangelium nach Johannes* (*NTD*),[8] 1955.

Strauss, D., *Life of Jesus*, 1835.

Strecker, G., *Der Weg der Gerechtigkeit*,[2] 1966.

Streeter, B. H., *The Four Gospels*, 1924.

Streeter, B. H., *The Primitive Church*, 1929.

Sutcliffe, E. F., *A Two Year Public Ministry*, 1938.

Swete, H. B., *The Apocalypse of St. John*,[2] 1907.

Swete, H. B., *The Gospel according to St. Mark*,[3] 1927.

Synge, F. C., *The Epistle to the Ephesians*, 1941.

Synge, F. C., *Hebrews and the Scriptures*, 1959.

Synge, F. C., *Philippians and Colossians* (*TC*), 1951.

Tasker, R. V. G., *The General Epistle of James* (*TNT*), 1956.

Tasker, R. V. G., *The Gospel according to St. John* (*TNT*), 1960.

Tasker, R. V. G., *The Gospel according to St. Matthew* (*TNT*), 1961.

Tasker, R. V. G., *The Gospel in the Epistle to the Hebrews*, 1950.

Tasker, R. V. G., *The Nature and Purpose of the Gospels*, 1944.

Tasker, R. V. G., *The Second Epistle of Paul to the Corinthians* (*TNT*), 1958.

Taylor, R. O. P., *The Groundwork of the Gospels*, 1946.

Taylor, V., *The Atonement in New Testament Teaching*, 1945.

Taylor, V., *Behind the Third Gospel*, 1926.

Taylor, V., *The Epistle to the Romans* (*EC*), 1955.

Taylor, V., *Formation of the Gospel Tradition*, 1935.

Taylor, V., *The Gospel according to St. Mark*, 1953.

Taylor, V., *The Gospels*,[5] 1945.

Taylor, V., *The Life and Ministry of Jesus*, 1954.

Taylor, V., *The Person of Christ in New Testament Teaching*, 1958.

Temple, W., *Readings in St. John's Gospel*, 1943.

Tenney, M. C., *The Gospel of John* (*NLC*),[2] 1954.

Tenney, M. C., *New Testament Survey*,[2] 1961.

Tenney, M. C., *New Testament Times*, 1967.

Theron, D. J., *Evidence of Tradition*, 1957.

Thiessen, H. C., *Introduction to the New Testament*,[4] 1956.

Thomas, W. H. G., *Let us go on: The Secret of Christian Progress in the Epistle to the Hebrews*, 1923.

Thomson, G. H. P., *The Letters of Paul to the Ephesians, to the Colossians, and to Philemon* (CBC), 1967.

Thrall, M., *The First and Second Letters of Paul to the Corinthians* (CBC), 1965.

Thyen, H., *Der Stil der jüdisch-hellenischen Homilie*, 1955.

Tilesse, G. M. de, *Le Secret Messianique dans l'Évangile de Marc*, 1968.

Tinsley, E. J., *The Gospel according to St. Luke* (CBC), 1965.

Tödt, H. E., *Der Menschensohn in der synoptischen Überlieferung*, 1959.

Torm, F., *Die Psychologie der Pseudonymität im Hinblick auf die Literatur des Urchristentums*, 1932.

Torrance, T. F., *The Apocalypse To-day*, 1959.

Torrey, C. C., *The Apocalypse of John*, 1958.

Torrey, C. C., *Documents of the Primitive Church*, 1941.

Torrey, C. C., *The Four Gospels: A New Translation*, 1933.

Toynbee, J. and Perkins, J. W., *The Shrine of St. Peter*, 1958.

Trilling, W., *Das wahre Israel*, 1959.

Trocmé, E., *La Formation de l'Évangile selon Marc*, 1963.

Trocmé, E., *Le 'Livre des Acts' et l'Histoire*, 1957.

Turner, C. H., *The Gospel according to St. Mark*, 1928.

Turner, C. H., *Studies in Early Church History*, 1912.

Turner, G. A. and Mantey, J. R., *The Gospel according to John*, 1964.

Turner, H. E. W., *Historicity and the Gospels*, 1963.

Turner, H. E. W., *Jesus, Master and Lord*,[2] 1954.

Unnik, W. C. van, *The New Testament*, 1964.

Unnik, W. C. van, *Tarsus or Jerusalem, The City of Paul's Youth* (Eng. Tr. by G. Ogg), 1962.

Unnik, W. C. van and Sevenster, G., editors, *Studia Paulina*, 1953.

Unnik, W. C. van, editor, *Neotestamentica et Patristica*, 1962.

Usteri, J. M., *Commentar über den ersten Petrusbriefe*, 1887.

Vaganay, L., *Le Problème synoptique*, 1954.

Vanhoye, A., *La Structure littéraire de l'Épître aux Hébreux*, 1963.

Vaughan, C. J., *The Epistle to the Hebrews*, 1890.

Vaughan, C. J., *Lectures on the Revelation*, 1882.

Vaughan, C. J., *St. Paul's Epistle to the Romans*,[7] 1890.

Vincent, M. R., *The Epistles to the Philippians and Philemon* (ICC), 1897.

Völter, D., *Der I Petrusbrief—seine Entstehung und Stellung in der Geschichte des Urchristentums*, 1906.

Völter, D., *Die Offenbarung Johannes keine ursprünglich jüdische Apokalypse*, 1886.

Völter, D., *Das Problem der Apokalypse*, 1893.

Vos, G., *The Teaching of the Epistle to the Hebrews*, 1956.

Vos, L. A., *The Synoptic Traditions in the Apocalypse*, 1965.

Vouaux, L., *Les Actes de Paul et ses letters apocryphes*, 1913.

Wand, J. W. C., *The General Epistles of St. Peter and St. Jude (WC)*, 1934.

Ward, A. M., *The Gospel according to St. Matthew (EC)*, 1961.

Watkins, C. H., *St. Paul's Fight for Galatia*, 1913.

Watkins, H. W., *Modern Criticism considered in its relation to the Fourth Gospel*, 1890.

Way, A. S., *Letters of St. Paul and Hebrews*, 1921.

Wegenast, K., *Das Verständnis der Tradition bei Paulus und in den Deuteropaulinen*, 1962.

Weiss, B., *Die Johannes-Apokalypse*, 1882.

Weiss, B., *Die katholische Briefe (KEK)*,[6] 1900.

Weiss, B., *Lukasevangelium (KEK)*,[9] 1901.

Weiss, B., *Manual Introduction to the New Testament* (Eng. Tr.), I, 1887, II, 1888.

Weiss, B. and J., *Die Pastoralbriefe (KEK)*,[7] 1907.

Weiss, J., *Das älteste Evangelium*, 1903.

Weiss, J., *Der ersten Korintherbrief (KEK)*, 1910.

Weiss, J., *The History of Primitive Christianity* (Eng. Tr.), 1937.

Weiss, J., *Paul and Jesus*, 1909.

Weizsäcker, C. von, *Das apostolische Zeitalter der christlichen Kirche*, 1886.

Welch, A. C., *Visions of the End: A Study of Daniel and Revelation*,[2] 1958.

Wellhausen, J., *Einleitung in die drei ersten Evangelien*,[2] 1911.

Wellhausen, J., *Das Evangelium Marci*, 1903.

Wellhausen, J., *Das Evangelium Matthaei*, 1904.

Wendland, H. D., *Die Briefe an die Korinther (NTD)*,[7] 1956.

Wendland, P., *Die hellenisch-römische Kultur in ihren Beziehungen zu Judentum und Christentum (LHB)*, 1907.

Wendland, P., *Die urchristlichen Literaturformen (LHB)*, 1912.

Wendling, E., *Ur-Markus*, 1905.

Wendt, H. H., *Die Apostelgeschichte*,[8] 1899.

Wendt, H. H., *Die Johannesbriefe und das johanneische Christentum*, 1925.

Werdermann, H., *Die Irrlehrer des Judas- und 2 Petrusbriefes*, 1913.

Wernecke, H. W., *The Book of Revelation Speaks to us*, 1954.

Werner, M., *Der Einfluss paulinischer Theologie im Mk-Ev* (Beiheft ZNTW, I), 1923.

Westcott, B. F., *The Epistles of John*, 1892, r.p. (with addition by F. F. Bruce) 1966.

Westcott, B. F., *The Epistle to the Hebrews*, 1889.

Westcott, B. F., *The Gospel according to St. John*, 1887.

Westcott, B. F., *An Introduction to the Study of the Gospels*,[7] 1888.

Westcott, B. F., *On the Canon of the New Testament*,[4] 1875.

Wetzel, G., *Die synoptischen Evangelien*, 1883.

White, N. J. D., *The First and Second Epistles to Timothy and the Epistle to Titus* (*EGT*), 1910.

Wickham, E. C., *The Epistle to the Hebrews* (*WC*), 1910.

Wikenhauser, A., *Die Apostelgeschichte und ihr Geschichtswert*, 1921.

Wikenhauser, A., *New Testament Introduction* (Eng. Tr. of 2nd German edition), 1958.

Wikenhauser, A., *Der Sinn der Apokalypse des hl. Johannes*, 1931.

Wikenhauser, A., *Synoptische Studien für A. Wikenhauser*, 1935.

Wilckens, U., *Die Missionsreden der Apostelgeschichte*,[2] 1963.

Wilckens, U., *Weisheit und Torheit*, 1959.

Wilcox, M., *The Semitisms of Acts*, 1965.

Wilder, A. N. and Hoon, P. W., *The First, Second and Third Epistles of John* (*IB*), 1957.

Wiles, M. F., *The Spiritual Gospel*, 1960.

Wilkens, W., *Die Entstehungsgeschichte des vierten Evangeliums*, 1958.

Williams, A. L., *The Epistles to the Colossians and Philemon* (*CGT*), 1907.

Williams, A. L., *The Epistle to the Galatians* (*CGT*), 1910.

Williams, A. L., *The Hebrew Christian Messiah*, 1916.

Williams, C. S. C., *The Acts of the Apostles* (*BC*), 1957.

Williams, R. R., *The Acts of the Apostles* (*TC*), 1953.

Williams, R. R., *The Letters of John and James* (*CBC*), 1965.

Williamson, R., *A Critical Re-examination of the Relationship between Philo and the Epistle to the Hebrews*, 1967.

Williamson, R., *The Epistle to the Hebrews* (*EC*), 1965.

Wilson, R. McL., *Gnosis and the New Testament*, 1968.

Wilson, R. McL., *The Gnostic Problem*, 1958.

Windisch, H., *Der Hebräerbrief* (*LHB*),[2] 1931.

Windisch, H., *Johannes und die Synoptiker*, 1926.

Windisch, H., *Der zweite Korintherbrief* (*KEK*), 1924.

Windisch, H. and Preisker, H., *Die katholischen Briefe* (*LHB*),[3] 1951.

Wohlenberg, G., *Der erste und der zweite Petrusbriefe und der Judasbrief* (*Zahn's Kommentar*),[3] 1923.

Wohlenberg, G., *Die Pastoralbriefe*,[3] 1923.

Wolf, C. A., *Ein exegetischen und practischen Commentar zu den drei Briefen St. Johannes*, 1881.

Wood, C. T., *The Life, Letters and Religion of St. Paul*, 1925.

Wood, H. G., *Jesus in the Twentieth Century*, 1960.

Wood, H. G., editor, *Amicitiae Corolla*, 1933.

Woolf, B. L., *The Background and Beginnings of the Gospel Story*, 1935.

Wordsworth, C., *St. Paul's Epistles*, 1872.

Workman, H. B., *Persecution in the Early Church*, 1906.

Wrede, W., *Die Echtheit des 2 Thessalonicherbriefes untersucht*, 1913.

Wrede, W., *Das literarische Rätsel des Hebräerbriefes*, 1906.

Wrede, W., *Das Messiasgeheimnis in den Evangelien*, 1901, r.p. 1963.

Wrede, W., *Paulus*, 1907.

Wright, A., *The Composition of the Four Gospels*, 1890.

Wright, A., *St. Luke in Greek*, 1900.

Wright, A., *Some New Testament Problems*, 1898.

Wright, A., *Synopsis of the Gospels in Greek*, 1896.

Wright, G. E. and Fuller, R. H., *The Book of the Acts of God*, 1957.

Wurm, A., *Die Irrlehrer im ersten Johannesbrief*, 1933.

Wuttke, G., *Melchisedech, der Priesterkönig von Salem* (Beihefte *ZNTW*), 1927.

Yule, G. U., *The Statistical Study of Literary Vocabulary*, 1944.

Zahn, T., *Die Apostelgeschichte*, 1919–21.

Zahn, T., *Geschichte des neutestamentlichen Kanons*, I, 1888, II, 1890.

Zahn, T., *Introduction to the New Testament* (Eng. Tr.), 1909.

Zahn, T., *Die Offenbarung des Johannes* (*Zahn's Kommentar*), 1924–26.

Zahn, T., *Die Urausgabe der Apostelgeschichte des Lukas*, 1916.

Zahrnt, H., *The Historical Jesus* (Eng. Tr.), 1963.

Zimmermann, K., *Der Apostel Paulus. Ein Lebensbild*, 1962.

Zuntz, G., *The Text of the Epistles*, 1953.

In the following lists commentators and writers of special studies on individual books are mentioned by name and date only. The full title of their writings may be obtained by reference to the General Bibliography.

MATTHEW

Commentators: Allen (*ICC*) 1907, Argyle (*CBC*) 1963, Benoit (*Sainte Bible*)[3] 1961, Bonnard (*CNT*) 1963, Box (*CB*) 1922, Bruce (*EGT*) 1907, Cox (*TC*) 1952, Fenton (*Pel C*) 1963, Filson (*BC*) 1960, Gaechter 1964, Gibson (*Exp. Bib.*) 1890, Green (*Clar B*) 1936, Grundmann 1968, Johnson (*IB*) 1951, Klostermann (*LHB*)[2] 1927, Lagrange (*EB*)[7] 1948, Lohmeyer-Schmauch (*KEK*) 1956, McNeile 1915, Robinson (*MC*) 1928, Schlatter 1929, Schniewind (*NTD*)[9] 1960, Smith (*CGT*) 1927, Tasker (*TNT*) 1961, Ward (*EC*) 1961, Wellhausen 1904.

Authors of Special Studies: Bacon 1930, Blair 1960, Bornkamm, Barth and Held 1963, Butler 1951, Farrer 1954, Findlay 1925, 1933, Goodspeed 1959, Gundry 1967, Hare 1967, Hummel 1963, Kilpatrick 1946, Massaux 1950, Nepper-Christensen 1958, Rigaux 1967, Stendahl[2] 1968, Strecker[2] 1966, Trilling 1959.

MARK

Commentators: Alexander r.p. 1960, Allen 1915, Bartlet (*CB*) 1922, Blunt (*Clar B*) 1929, Branscombe (*MC*) 1937, Bruce (*EGT*) 1907, Carrington 1960, Chadwick (*Exp. Bib.*)[6] 1896, Cole (*TNT*) 1961, Cranfield (*CGT*, n.s.) 1959, Crum 1936, Earle 1957, Gould (*ICC*) 1896, Grant 1943, (*IB*) 1951, Hort 1914, Huby and Benoit (*Sainte Bible*)[3] 1961, Hunter (*TC*) 1949, Johnson (*BC*) 1960, Klostermann (*LHB*)[4] 1950, Lagrange (*EB*)[4] 1929, Lightfoot 1950, Lohmeyer-Sass (*KEK*)[12] 1953, Marxsen[2] 1959, Mitton (*EC*) 1957, Moule (*CBC*) 1965, Nineham (*Pel C*) 1963, Rawlinson (*WC*)[7] 1949, Schniewind (*NTD*)[8] 1958, Schweizer (*NTD*)[11] 1967, Swete[3] 1927, Taylor 1953, Turner 1928, Weiss 1903, Wellhausen 1903.

Authors of Special Studies: Abbott 1901, Bacon 1919, 1925, Beasley-Murray 1957, Best 1965, Boobyer 1942, Bowman 1965, Burgon 1871, Burkill 1956, 1959, 1963, Cadoux 1935, Farrer 1951, 1954, Guy 1954, Haenchen 1966, Harrisville 1967, Hartmann 1966, Hooker 1967, Lambrecht 1967, Lindsey 1969, Lohse 1955, Menzies 1901, Meye 1968, Rigaux 1966, Robinson, J. M. 1957, Robinson, T. H. 1922, Schreiber 1967, Tilesse 1968, Trocmé 1963, Wendling 1905, Werner 1923, Wrede 1901.

LUKE

Commentators: Adeney (*CB*)[2] 1922, Arndt 1956, Balmforth (*Clar B*) 1930, Browning (*TC*) 1960, Bruce (*EGT*) 1907, Burton (*Exp. Bib.*) 1909, Caird

(*Pel C*) 1963, Creed 1930, Easton 1926, Ellis (*CB*, n.s.) 1966, Geldenhuys (*NLC*) 1951, Gilmour (*IB*) 1952, Grundmann[2] 1961, Klostermann (*LHB*)[4] 1950, Lagrange (*EB*)[8] 1948, Leaney (*BC*) 1958, Loisy 1924, Luce (*CGT*) 1949, Manson (*MC*) 1930, Osty (*Sainte Bible*)[3] 1961, Plummer (*ICC*) 1896, Ragg (*WC*) 1922, Reicke 1964, Rengstorf (*NTD*)[8] 1958, Schlatter 1931, Tinsley (*CBC*) 1965, Weiss (*KEK*)[9] 1901, Wright 1900.

Authors of Special Studies: Barrett 1961, Bornhäuser 1934, Cadbury (*HTS*) 1919, 1920,[2] 1958, Carpenter 1919, Conzelmann 1960, Flender 1967, Harnack 1907, Hastings 1958, Hobart 1882, Keck and Martyn 1966, Krenkel 1894, Laurentin (*EB*) 1957, Macgregor and Morton 1964, Morgenthaler 1949, Ramsay 1908, Rehkopf 1959, Sahlin 1949, Schleiermacher 1825, Schürmann 1953–57, Stonehouse 1951, Taylor 1926.

JOHN

Commentators: Barrett 1956, Bauer (*LHB*)[2] 1925, Bernard (*ICC*) 1928, Brown 1966, Bultmann (*KEK*)[13] 1953, Charnwood 1925, Dods (*Exp. Bib.*)[2] 1894, (*EGT*) 1907, Filson 1963, Hendriksen 1953, Holland 1923, Hoskyns and Davey[2] 1947, Howard (*IB*) 1952, Hunter (*CBC*) 1965, Lagrange (*EB*)[5] 1936, Lightfoot 1956, Loisy 1921, Macgregor (*MC*) 1928, Marsh (*Pel C*) 1968, McClymont (*CB*)[2] 1922, Mollat (*Sainte Bible*)[3] 1961, Plummer (*CGT*) 1900, Richardson (*TC*) 1959, Sanders and Mastin 1969, Schlatter 1930, Schnackenburg 1968, Strachan[3] 1941, Strathmann (*NTD*)[8] 1955, Tasker (*TNT*) 1960, Tenney (*NLC*)[2] 1954, Turner and Manty 1964, Westcott 1887.

Authors of Special Studies: Abbott 1905, 1906, Askwith 1910, Bacon[2] 1918, 1933, Baldensperger 1898, Becker 1956, 1963, Bornhäuser 1928, Braun (*EB*) 1959, 1964, Burch 1928, Burney 1922, Colwell 1931, Correll 1958, Cottam 1952, Cross, ed. 1957, Davey 1958, Dodd 1953, 1963, Drummond 1903, Edwards, H. E. 1953, Edwards, R. A. 1954, Eisler 1938, Freed 1965, Gärtner 1959, Garvie 1922, Glasson 1963, Grill 1902, 1923, Guilding 1960, Harris 1917, Hartingsveld 1962, Headlam 1948, Higgins 1960, Hirsch 1936, Hoare 1944, Holwerda 1959, Howard 1943, 1955, Hunt 1958, Hunter 1968, Käsemann 1968, Kragerud 1959, Kundsin 1925, Lamont 1956, Lee 1950, Lewis 1910, Loewenich 1932, Macgregor and Morton 1961, Malateste 1967, Manson 1963, Martyn 1968, Maurer 1949, Meeks 1967, Menoud 1947, Michaelis 1946, Morris 1960, 1969, Mussner 1967, Noack 1954, Nunn 1927, 1946, 1952, Odeberg 1929, Percy 1939, Raney 1933, Redlich 1939, Réville 1901, Roberts 1935, Ruckstuhl 1951, Sahlin 1950, Sanday 1905, Sanders 1943, Schulz 1960, Schweizer 1939, Scott[2] 1908, Sidebottom 1961, Smith 1965, Strachan 1925, Temple 1943, Watkins 1890, Wiles 1960, Wilkens 1958.

ACTS

Commentators: Bartlet (*CB*) 1901, Beyer (*NTD*)[9] 1959, Blaiklock (*TNT*) 1959,

Blunt (*Clar B*) 1923, Bruce[2] 1952, (*NLC*) 1954, Carter and Earle 1959, Cerfaux and Dupont[2] 1958, Conzelmann (*LHB*) 1963, Findlay[4] 1952, Furneaux 1912, Guy 1953, Hackett 1877, Haenchen (*KEK*)[13] 1961, Hanson (*N Clar B*) 1967, Harnack 1908, Jackson (*MC*) 1931, Jacquier (*EB*)[2] 1926, Knopf 1906, Knowling (*EGT*) 1900, Knox 1948, Loisy[2] 1925, Lumby (*CGT*) 1899, Lüthi 1958, Macgregor and Ferris (*IB*) 1954, Munck 1967, Packer (*CBC*) 1966, Preuschen (*LHB*) 1912, Rackham (*WC*)[14] r.p. 1964, Reicke 1957, Steinmann[4] 1934, Stokes (*Exp. Bib.*)[4] 1894, Wendt[8] 1899, Williams, C. S. C. (*BC*) 1957, Williams, R. R. (*TC*) 1953, Zahn 1919–21.

Authors of Special Studies: Bornhäuser 1934, Bruce 1944, Cadbury 1955,[2] 1958, Chase 1902, Clark 1933, Dibelius 1956, Dupont 1960, 1967, Easton 1954, Filson 1963, Gärtner 1955, Goulder 1964, Jackson and Lake 1920–33, Keck and Martyn 1966, Macgregor and Morton 1964, Mattill and Mattill 1966, Norden 1913, O'Neill 1961, Schneckenberger 1841, Simon 1958, Spitta 1891, Stagg 1955, Trocmé 1957, Wikenhauser 1921, Wilckens[2] 1963, Wilcox 1965, Zahn 1916.

GENERAL WORKS ON THE GOSPELS AND ACTS

Aland, Eltester and Klostermann, ed. 1959, Albertz 1947, 1952, Bailey 1963, Bartsch 1948–55, Beasley-Murray 1954, Black 1961,[3] 1968, Bornkamm 1960, Burkitt[3] 1911,[2] 1922, 1924, Clark 1914, Doeve 1954, Gardner-Smith 1938, Gerhardsson 1961, Gieseler 1818, Grant, F. C. 1957, Grant, R. M. 1961, Harnack 1908, 1911, Headlam 1923, Herder 1797, Higgins 1952, Hirsch[2] 1951, Lessing 1778, Lightfoot 1935, 1938, Macgregor and Morton 1964, Meyer 1921–23, Nicklin 1950, Nineham, ed. 1955, Percy 1953, Renan 1877, Richardson 1938, 1941, Schniewind 1914, Stanton 1923, Stauffer 1960, Streeter 1924, Sutcliffe 1938, Tasker 1944, Taylor, R. O. P. 1946, Taylor, V.[5] 1945, 1954, Torrey 1933, Turner[2] 1954, 1963, Westcott[7] 1888, Windisch 1926, Wood 1960, Woolf 1935, Wright 1890.

SYNOPTIC GOSPELS

Abrahams 1917, Albertz 1921, Barclay 1966, Barr 1938, Bea 1965, Beare 1962, Bultmann[2] 1968, Bundy 1955, Bussmann 1925–31, Chapman 1937, Crum 1927, Farmer 1964, Griesbach 1789, Hawkins[2] 1909, Hunt 1951, Jameson 1922, Jeremias[2] 1963, Knox 1953, 1957, Köster 1957, Léon-Dufour 1956, Loisy 1907–08, Major, Manson and Wright 1937, Manson[2] 1935, 1949, 1962, Montefiore 1930,[2] r.p. 1968, Parker 1953, Patten 1915, Plooij 1932, Redlich 1936, Ropes 1934, Sanday, ed. 1911, Sanders 1969, Simons 1880, Solages 1959, Sparks 1964, Stonehouse 1944, 1963, Vaganay 1954, Wellhausen[2] 1911, Wetzel 1883.

FORM CRITICISM

Althaus 1958, Anderson 1964, Braaten and Harrisville 1964, Bultmann and

Kundsin[2] 1962, Dahl 1955, Dibelius[2] 1934, 1935, Easton 1928, Ebeling 1961, Fascher 1924, Fuchs 1964, Grobel 1937, Hanson, ed. 1966, Hebert 1962, Henderson 1952, Henry, ed. 1966, Hughes 1956, Kahler 1964, Koch 1969, Marlé 1956, Marshall 1942, McArthur, ed. 1969, Miegge 1960, Redlich 1939, Ristow and Matthiae, ed. 1962, Robinson 1959, Rohde 1968, Schmidt 1919, Taylor 1935, Zahrnt 1963.

ROMANS

Commentators: Althaus (*NTD*)[10] 1966, Barclay (*DSB*)[2] 1957, Barrett (*BC*) 1958, Barth 1933, Beet [10] 1902, Best (*CBC*) 1967, Bruce (*TNT*) 1963, Brunner 1959, de Boor 1962, Denney (*EGT*) 1900, Dodd (*MC*) 1932, Findlay (*PC*) 1928, Garvie (*CB*) 1901, Gifford 1886, Godet 1888–89, Hodge[2] 1875, Hunter (*TC*) 1955, Kirk (*Clar B*) 1937, Knox (*IB*) 1954, Lagrange (*EB*) 1916, Leenhardt (*CNT*) 1957, Lietzmann (*LHB*)[4] 1933, Michel (*KEK*)[10] 1955, Murray (*NLC*) 1960, 1965, Nygren 1952, Parry (*CGT*) 1912, Rhys 1961, Sanday and Headlam (*ICC*) 1895, Scott, C. A. A. (*AB*) 1929, Scott, E. F. 1947, Taylor (*EC*) 1955, Vaughan[7] 1890.
Authors of Special Studies: Hitchcock 1936, Hort 1895, Lee 1962, Munck 1967, Schumacher 1929.

1 AND 2 CORINTHIANS

Commentators: (An asterisk indicates 1 Cor., two asterisks 2 Cor., and the absence of either 1 and 2 Corinthians).
Allo* (*EB*) 1935, Allo** (*EB*) 1937, Barclay (*DSB*)[2] 1956, Barrett* (*BC*) 1968, Beet[7] 1902, Bernard** (*EGT*) 1910, Craig* (*IB*) 1953, Edwards* 1897, Ellicott* 1887, Evans (*Clar B*) 1930, Filson** (*IB*) 1953, Findlay* (*EGT*) 1901, Godet* 1893, Grosheide* (*NLC*) 1954, Hanson** (*TC*) 1954, Héring* (*CNT*) 1948, Héring** (*CNT*) 1958, Hodge*[3] 1863, Hodge**[6] 1959, Howard (*AB*) 1929, Hughes** (*NLC*) 1962, Lietzmann (*LHB*)[4] 1933, Massie (*CB*) 1902, Menzies** 1912, Moffatt* (*MC*) 1938, Morris* (*TNT*) 1958, Parry* (*CGT*) 1916, Peake* (*PC*) 1928, Plummer** (*CGT*) 1903, (*ICC*) 1915, Prümm** 1960–1967, Rendall 1909, Robertson and Plummer* (*ICC*) 1911, Scott** (*PC*) 1928, Simon* (*TC*) 1959, Strachan** (*MC*) 1935, Tasker** (*TNT*) 1958, Thrall (*CBC*) 1965, Weiss* (*KEK*) 1910, Wendland (*NTD*)[7] 1956, Windisch** (*KEK*) 1924.
Authors of Special Studies: Dean 1947, Georgi** 1964, Hurd* 1965, Kennedy 1900, Oostendorp** 1967, Schmithals 1956.

GALATIANS

Commentators: Adeney (*CB*) 1903, Allan (*TC*) 1951, Barclay (*DSB*)[2] 1958, Beet[3] 1887, Beyer (*NTD*)[9] 1962, Blunt (*Clar B*) 1925, Bonnard (*CNT*) 1952, Bring 1961, Burton (*ICC*) 1921, Cole (*TNT*) 1965, Dow (*AB*) 1929, Duncan

(*MC*) 1934, Ellicott[4] 1867, Emmet 1912, Grayston (*EC*) 1958, Guthrie (*CB*, n.s.) 1969, Lagrange (*EB*)[2] 1950, Lietzmann (*LHB*)[3] 1932, Lightfoot 1890, Mackintosh (*PC*) 1928, Neil (*CBC*) 1967, Oepke 1937, Ramsay 1899, Rendall (*EGT*) 1903, Ridderbos (*NLC*) 1954, Schlier (*KEK*)[12] 1962, Stamm (*IB*) 1953, Williams (*CGT*) 1910.

Authors of Special Studies: Askwith 1899, Ropes 1929, Round 1906, Watkins 1913.

EPHESIANS

Commentators: Abbott (*ICC*) 1899, Allan (*TC*) 1959, Barclay (*DSB*)[2] 1958, Beare (*IB*) 1953, Beet 1890, Bruce 1962, Conzelmann (*NTD*)[9] 1962, Dibelius (*LHB*)[2] 1927, Dodd (*AB*) 1929, Eadie[3] 1883, Ellicott[5] 1884, Foulkes (*TNT*) 1963, Frost 1946, Johnston (*CB*, n.s.) 1967, Lock (*WC*) 1929, Martin (*CB*) 1902, Masson (*CNT*) 1952, Moulton (*EC*) 1963, Murray (*CGT*) 1914, Rawlinson (*PC*) 1928, Rendtorff (*NTD*)[7] 1955, Robinson[2] 1904, Salmond (*EGT*) 1903, Schlier[5] 1965, Scott (*MC*) 1930, Simpson (*NLC*) 1958, Synge 1941, Thomson (*CBC*) 1967.

Authors of Special Studies: Cross, ed. 1956, Goodspeed 1933 and 1956, Holtzmann 1872, Hort 1895, Kirby 1968, Mitton 1951, Percy 1946, Pokorny 1965.

PHILIPPIANS

Commentators: Adeney (*PC*) 1928, Barth[4] 1953, Beare (*BC*) 1959, Beet 1890, Bonnard (*CNT*) 1950, Dibelius (*LHB*)[3] 1937, Ellicott[5] 1888, Friedrich (*NTD*)[9] 1962, Gnilka 1968, Grayston (*EC*) 1958, (*CBC*) 1967, Heinzelmann (*NTD*)[7] 1955, Johnston (*CB*, n.s.) 1967, Jones (*WC*) 1912, Kennedy (*EGT*) 1903, Lightfoot 1878, Lohmeyer (*KEK*)[11] 1956, Martin, G. C. (*CB*) 1902, Martin, R. P. (*TNT*) 1959, Michael (*MC*) 1928, Michaelis 1935, Moule (*CGT*) 1897, Muller (*NLC*) 1955, Robertson (*AB*) 1929, Scott (*IB*) 1955, Synge (*TC*) 1951, Vincent (*ICC*) 1897.

Authors of Special Studies: Martin 1960, 1967, Michaelis 1925, 1930, 1933.

COLOSSIANS

Commentators: Abbott (*ICC*) 1899, Beare (*IB*) 1953, Beet 1890, Bieder 1943, Bruce (*NLC*) 1958, Carson (*TNT*) 1960, Conzelmann (*NTD*)[9] 1962, Dibelius (*LHB*)[2] 1927, Dodd (*AB*) 1929, Eadie 1856, Ellicott[5] 1888, Frost 1946, Hugedé 1968, Johnston (*CB*, n.s.) 1967, Jones 1923, Lightfoot 1879, Lohmeyer (*KEK*)[11] 1957, Lohse (*KEK*)[14] 1968, Martin (*CB*) 1902, Masson (*CNT*) 1950, Moule (*CGT*, n.s.) 1957, Moulton (*EC*) 1963, Peake (*EGT*) 1903, Radford (*WC*) 1931, Rawlinson (*PC*) 1928, Rendtorff (*NTD*)[7] 1955, Scott (*MC*) 1930, Synge (*TC*) 1951, Thomson (*CBC*) 1967, Williams (*CGT*) 1907.

Authors of Special Studies: Holtzmann 1872, Kehl 1967, Percy 1946.

THESSALONIANS

Commentators: Adeney (*CB*) 1903, Andrews (*PC*) 1928, Bailey (*IB*) 1955, Bicknell (*WC*) 1932, Dibelius (*LHB*)[3] 1937, Dobschütz (*KEK*)[7] 1919, Ellicott[4] 1880, Findlay (*CGT*) 1904, Frame (*ICC*) 1912, Grayston (*CBC*) 1967, Masson (*CNT*) 1957, McCown (*AB*) 1929, Milligan 1908, Moffatt (*EGT*) 1910, Morris (*TNT*) 1956, (*NLC*) 1959, Neil (*MC*) 1950, (*TC*) 1957, Oepke (*NTD*)[9] 1962, Rigaux (*EB*) 1956.
Authors of Special Studies: Askwith 1902, Giblin 1967, Wrede 1913.

THE PASTORALS

Commentators: Barrett (*N Clar B*) 1963, Bernard (*CGT*) 1899, Bisseker (*PC*) 1928, Dibelius (*LHB*)[3] 1955, Dornier 1969, Easton 1948, Ellicott[5] 1883, Falconer 1937, Gealy (*IB*) 1955, Guthrie (*TNT*) 1957, Hanson (*CBC*) 1966, Holtz 1965, Holtzmann 1880, Horton (*CB*) 1901, Jeremias (*NTD*)[8] 1963, Kelly (*BC*) 1963, Leaney (*TC*) 1960, Lock (*ICC*) 1924, Lowstuter (*AB*) 1929, Meinertz[4] 1931, Parry 1920, Plummer (*Exp. Bib.*) 1888, Ramsay (*Expositor*) 1909–11, Scott (*MC*) 1936, Simpson 1954, Spicq (*EB*) 1948, Weiss (*KEK*)[7] 1907, White (*EGT*) 1910, Wohlenberg[3] 1923.
Authors of Special Studies: Bertrand 1887, Guthrie 1956, Hanson 1968, Harrison 1921, 1964, James 1906, Knight 1968, Meyer 1913, Michaelis 1930, Schleiermacher (*1 Tim.*) 1807.

PHILEMON

Commentators: Beet 1890, Carson (*TNT*) 1960, Dibelius (*LHB*)[2] 1927, Dodd (*AB*) 1929, Ellicott[5] 1888, Friedrich (*NTD*)[9] 1962, Johnston (*CB*, n.s.) 1967, Leaney (*TC*) 1960, Lightfoot 1879, Lohmeyer (*KEK*)[11] 1957, Lohse (*KEK*)[14] 1968, Martin (*CB*) 1902, Masson (*CNT*) 1957, Moule (*CGT*, n.s.) 1957, Moulton (*EC*) 1963, Muller (*NLC*) 1955, Oesterley (*EGT*) 1910, Radford (*WC*) 1931, Rawlinson (*PC*) 1928, Rendtorff (*NTD*)[7] 1955, Scott (*MC*) 1930, Thomson (*CBC*) 1967, Vincent (*ICC*) 1897, Williams (*CGT*) 1907.
Author of Special Studies: Knox 1935.

THE LIFE AND THOUGHT OF PAUL

Barclay 1959, Barnett 1941, Baur 1873, Beare 1962, Cave 1928, Cerfaux 1954, 1960, Davies 1948, Deane 1942, Deissmann[2] 1926, Dibelius and Kümmel[3] 1964, Dodd 1920, Du Bose 1907, Eichholz 1961, Ellis 1957, Findlay 1891, Garvie 1911, Glover[2] 1925, Heathcote 1963, Hugedé 1966, Hunter 1954,[2] 1961, Jackson 1927, Jones 1910, Kennedy 1904, 1913, 1919, Knowling 1903, Knox, J. 1954, Knox, W. L. 1925, 1939, Lake 1934, von Loewenich 1960, Longenecker 1964, Machen 1921, McNeile 1932, Mitton 1955, Morgan 1917, Morton and McLeman 1966, Munck 1959, Murphy-O'Connor, ed. 1968, Nock 1938, Ogg

1968, Paley 1790, Prat 1949, Ramsay 1920, Redlich 1913, Renan 1869, Ridderbos 1958, Rigaux 1962, Roller 1933, Sabatier 1903, Schmid 1931, Schmithals 1965, Schoeps 1961, Schubert 1939, Schweitzer 1912, 1931, Scott 1927, 1935, 1936, Selby 1962, Stacey 1956, Still 1923, van Unnik 1962, Way 1921, Wegenast 1962, Weiss 1909, Wood 1925, Wordsworth 1872, Wrede 1907, Zimmermann 1962.

HEBREWS

Commentators: Alexander 1937, Archer 1957, Barclay (*DSB*) 1957, Bowman 1962, Bruce, A. B. 1899, Bruce, F. F. (*NLC*) 1964, Davidson n.d., Davies (*CBC*) 1967, Delitzsch 1868, Dods (*EGT*) 1910, Du Bose 1907, Ebrard 1853, Edwards (*Exp. Bib.*) 1888, Farrar (*CGT*) 1888, Frost 1947, Grant 1956, Héring (*CNT*) 1954, Hewitt (*TNT*) 1960, Hudson 1937, Ketter 1950, Manson 1951, Michel (*KEK*)[12] 1966, Moffatt (*ICC*) 1924, Montefiore (*BC*) 1965, Nairne[2] 1915, (*CGT*) 1917, Narborough (*Clar B*) 1930, Neil (*TC*) 1955, Peake (*CB*) n.d., Rendall 1883, Riggenbach 1913, Robinson (*MC*) 1933, Schlatter 1950, Schneider 1957, Scott 1922, Snell 1959, Soden 1899, Spicq (*EB*) 1952, Strathmann (*NTD*)[8] 1963, Thomas 1923, Vaughan 1890, Vos 1956, Westcott 1889, Wickham (*WC*) 1910, Williamson (*EC*) 1965, Windisch (*LHB*)[2] 1931.
Authors of Special Studies: Ayles 1899, Bornhäuser 1932, Burch 1936, Filson 1967, Grässer 1965, Guthrie 1956, Käsemann 1939, Klostermann 1889, Leonard 1939, Ménégoz 1894, Milligan 1899, Schröger 1968, Sowers 1965, Synge 1959, Tasker 1950, Vanhoye 1963, Williamson 1967.

JAMES

Commentators: Bennett (*CB*) n.d., Blackman (*TC*) 1957, Bowman 1962, Carr (*CGT*) 1896, Chaine (*EB*)[2] 1939, Dale 1895, Dibelius-Greeven (*KEK*)[10] 1958, Easton and Poteat (*IB*) 1957, Gaugusch 1914, Hauck 1926, (*NTD*)[8] 1957, Hort 1909, Ketter 1950, Knowling (*WC*) 1904, Leconte 1953, Mayor[3] 1913, Mitton 1966, Moffatt (*MC*) 1928, Mussner 1964, Oesterley (*EGT*) 1910, Plummer (*Exp. Bib.*) 1891, Plumptre (*CBS*) 1878, Reicke 1964, Robert 1963, Robertson-Peacock[2] 1959, Ropes (*ICC*) 1916, Ross (*NLC*) 1954, Schlatter 1932, 1950, Schneider (*NTD*)[9] 1961, Sidebottom (*CB*, n.s.) 1967, Smith 1914, Soden 1891, Spitta 1896, Tasker (*TNT*) 1956, Williams (*CBC*) 1965, Windisch-Preisker (*LHB*)[3] 1951.
Authors of Special Studies: Cadoux 1944, Eichholz 1953, Grafe 1904, Marty 1935, Mayor 1913, Meinertz 1905, Meyer 1930, Parry 1903, Rendall 1927, Schammberger 1936.

1 AND 2 PETER

Commentators (An asterisk indicates 1 Peter, two asterisks 2 Peter, and the absence of either 1 and 2 Peter).

Barnett and Homrighausen★★ (*IB*) 1957, Beare★[2] 1958, Bennett (*CB*) n.d., Bigg (*ICC*) 1901, Blenkin★ (*CGT*) 1914, Bowman 1962, Chaine (*EB*)[2] 1939, Cranfield★ 1950, Cranfield (*TC*) 1960, Green★★ (*TNT*)1968, Hart★ (*EGT*) 1910, Hauck (*NTD*)[8] 1957, Hort★ 1898, Hunter and Homrighausen★ (*IB*) 1957, Huther (*KEK*) 1877, James★★ (*CGT*) 1912, Kelly (*BC*) 1969, Knopf (*KEK*)[7] 1912, Kühl (*KEK*) 1897, Leaney (*CBC*) 1967, Leconte (*Sainte Bible*)[2] 1961, Leighton★ 1831, Masterman★ 1912, Maycock★ 1957, Mayor★★ 1907, Moffatt (*MC*) 1928, Plumptre (*CBS*) 1879, Reicke 1964, Rendtorff★[7] 1951, Schelkle 1961, Schlatter 1950, Schneider (*NTD*)[9] 1961, Schweizer★[2] 1949, Selwyn★ 1946, Sidebottom★★ (*CB*, n.s.) 1967, Soden 1891, Spicq (*EB*) 1966, Spitta★★ 1885, Spörri★ 1925, Stibbs-Walls★ (*TNT*) 1959, Strachan★★ (*EGT*) 1910, Usteri★ 1887, Wand (*WC*) 1934, Windisch-Preisker (*LHB*)[3] 1951, Wohlenberg[3] 1923.

Authors of Special Studies: Abbott★★ 1903, Boismard★ 1961, Cross★ 1954, Green★★ 1961, Grosch★★[2] 1914, Perdelwitz★ 1911, Robson★★ 1915, Völter★ 1906, Werdemann★★ 1913.

THE JOHANNINE EPISTLES

Commentators: Alexander, N. (*TC*) 1962, Alexander, W. (*Exp. Bib.*) 1901, Brooke (*ICC*) 1912, Büchsel 1933, Bultmann (*KEK*)[7] 1967, Candlish 1866, Cox 1867, Dodd (*MC*) 1946, Ebrard 1860, Findlay 1909, Gore 1920, Haupt 1879, Jelf 1877, Law 1909, Lewis (*EC*) 1961, Lias 1887, Plummer (*CGT*) 1886, Ramsay 1910, Ross (*NLC*) 1954, Rothe 1878, Schlatter 1950, Schnackenburg[2] 1963, Smith (*EGT*) 1910, Stott (*TNT*) 1964, Westcott 1892, r.p. 1966, Wilder and Hoon (*IB*) 1957, Williams (*CBC*) 1965, Windisch-Preisker (*LHB*)[3] 1951, Wolf 1881.

Authors of Special Studies: Lütgert 1911, Nauck 1957, O'Neill 1966, Wendt 1925, Wurm 1933.

JUDE

Commentators: As for 2 Peter, except Strachan, for whom substitute Mayor (*EGT*) 1910; add Plummer (*Exp. Bib.*) 1891.
Authors of Special Studies: Maier 1904, Philippi 1868, Werdermann 1913.

REVELATION

Commentators: Allo (*EB*)[3] 1933, Barclay 1957, Behm (*NTD*)[6] 1953, Boismard 1950, Bonsirven 1951, Bousset (*KEK*)[2] 1906, Bowman 1955, Caird (*BC*) 1966, Carpenter 1927, Carrington 1931, Charles (*ICC*) 1920, Douglas 1915, Farrer 1964, Feret 1958, Glasson (*CBC*) 1965, Glazebrook 1923, Grant 1889, Hadorn 1928, Hendriksen 1962, Hengstenberg 1851, Holtzmann 1908, Hort 1908, Johnston 1916, Kepler 1957, Kiddle (*MC*) 1940, Lenski 1935, Loenertz 1947, Lohmeyer-Bornkamm (*LHB*)[2] 1953, Lohse (*NTD*)[8] 1960, Loisy 1923, Martin

1957, Martindale[2] 1958, McDowell 1951, Milligan (*Baird Lectures*) 1887, (*Exp. Bib.*) 1898, Moffatt (*EGT*) 1910, Morris (*TNT*) 1969, Olivier 1955, Peake 1920, Pieters 1954, Preston and Hanson (*TC*) 1957, Ramsay, A. 1910, Ramsay, W. M. 1904, Rist and Hough (*IB*) 1957, Russell 1935, Schlatter 1950, Scott, C. A. A. 1905, (*CB*) n.d., Scott, E. F.[4] 1941, Simcox (*CGT*) 1893, Spitta 1889, Swete[2] 1907, Torrance 1959, Vaughan 1882, Weiss 1882, Welch[2] 1958, Wernecke 1954, Wikenhauser 1931, Zahn 1924–26.

Authors of Special Studies: Beckwith 1919, Benson 1900, Brown 1891, Charles 1913, (*Schweich Lectures*) 1922, Erbes 1891, Farrer 1949, Feuillet 1963, Gebhardt 1878, Giet 1957, Gunkel 1895, Hoskier 1929, Lund 1942, Luthardt[2] 1870, Milligan 1893, Munck 1950, Oman 1923, 1928, Palmer 1903, Porter 1905, Rissi 1952, Rowley 1944, Schlatter 1912, Schonfield 1948, Schütz 1933, Selwyn 1900, Shepherd 1960, Stonehouse 1929, Torrey 1958, Völter 1886, 1893, Vos 1965.

WORKS OF INTRODUCTION

An asterisk indicates works which deal only with Paul's Epistles. Others are on the whole New Testament.

Allen and Grensted 1918, Bacon 1900, Badcock* 1937, Bate*[2] 1933, Bauer* 1850–52, Clogg[3] 1948, Conybeare and Howson* 1905, Cullmann 1966, (Eng. Tr.) 1968, Davies 1966, Dibelius 1936, Eichhorn 1814, Fairweather* 1935, Feine-Behm[11] 1956, Feine-Behm-Kümmel[12] 1963, (Eng. Tr.) 1965, Findlay* 1892, Fuller 1966, Godet 1899, *1899, *1903, Goguel 1922–25, Goodspeed 1937, Grant 1963, Harnack 1925,* 1926, Harrison 1964, Heard 1950, Henshaw 1952, Holtzmann 1885, Hoskyns and Davey[3] 1947, Hudson* 1959, Hunter 1951,[2] 1957, Jacquier 1911, Jones 1924, Jülicher-Fascher[7] 1931, Klijn 1967, Kümmel (Eng. Tr.) 1965, Lake, K.* 1927, Lake, K. and S. 1938, Lightfoot* 1895, Marxsen 1963, (Eng. Tr.) 1968, McNeile-Williams[2] 1953, Meinertz[5] 1950, Metzger 1965, Michaelis[3] 1961, Milligan 1913, Moffatt[3] 1918, Neill 1964, Peake 1909, Price 1961, Reuss 1884, Riddle and Hutson 1946, Robert and Feuillet 1965, Salmon[6] 1892, Schmidt 1804, Scott, E. F. 1932, Scott, R.* 1909, Shaw* 1924, Smith* 1919, Sparks 1952, Tenney[2] 1961, Thiessen[4] 1956, van Unnik 1964, Weiss 1887–88, Wikenhauser 1958, Zahn 1909.

AUTHOR INDEX

SUBJECT INDEX

Abraham, 238, 693

ACTS

Authorship: *see* Luke

Characteristics: relation to other N.T. books, 336; view of history, 336 f.; portrait of primitive communities, 337; record of primitive theology, 337 f.; focus on Peter and Paul, 338 f.

Christology, 338, 384

Date: arguments for a date before AD 64, 340 ff., 382; arguments for a date AD 70–85, 345 f.; arguments for a second-century date, 347 f., 382

Historicity: Luke's political knowledge, 354 f.; relationship with Paul's Epistles, 355 ff.; the speeches in Acts, 359 ff.

Language, 378 f.

Purpose: a narrative of history, 349; a spiritual gospel, 350; an apology, 350 ff., 382 f.; a defence brief, 352 f., 383, 598; a theological document, 353 f., 383

Sources: factors affecting them, 363 ff.; various types of theory: personal information, 368 ff.; combination of written and oral sources, 370 f.; combination of duplicate sources, 371 ff.; combination of complementary sources, 373; Antiochene source, 373 f.; itinerary theory, 374 ff.; fiction theory, 376; theories of successive redactions, 376 f.

Speeches, 359 ff., 385, 742 f., 806, 844

Text, 377 f.

Acts of John, 263

Acts of Paul, 251, 473, 475, 488, 584, 590, 599, 645, 675, 679

Acts of Peter, 599, 845

Acts of Titus, 473, 475

Address of the Ephesian Epistle, 508 ff.

African Canon, 687, 737, 886

Agrippa II, 75

Alexandrian background of Hebrews, 691, 695, 715, 719 ff.

Alogi, 230, 270, 933

Amanuensis hypotheses: 1 Peter, 779 ff.; 2 Peter, 840; Revelation, 942

Ancient historiography, 360, 384 f.

Angel worship, 548 f., 562

Anonymity, 683, 688, 696, 755, 789 f.

Antichrist, 872, 880, 953

Anti-Gnosticism, 765

Anti-Marcionite Prologues, 61, 73, 96, 99, 103, 129, 260

Antinomianism, 401, 860

Antitheses in Johannine literature, 939

Aphraates, 261 f.

Aphrodite, a heathen goddess, 421

Apocalypse of Peter, 815, 817, 818, 819, 828, 831, 842, 845, 848, 850, 858 ff., 933, 937, 943

Apocalyptic language, 830, 941, 965 f.

Apocryphon of John, 982

Apollos, 687, 695 f., 710, 715

Apologetics, 16, 26

Apologia: Romans, 399; Thessalonians, 565; 1 Peter, 783

Apophthegms, 195, 207

Apostasy, 704 ff., 707, 708, 709

Apostolic Tradition, 802

Aquila, 696 f., 714, 717

Aramaic, Aramaisms, 38 f., 46 f., 50, 75, 80 f., 123 f., 134, 172, 318, 370 f., 378 f., 748, 766, 879, 882

Archippus, 546, 554, 635 ff.

Areopagitica, 107, 362, 384

Aristion, 76, 267, 888

Assumption of Moses, 917 ff.

Athens, 421, 565, 569

Augustine, 129, 335, 687

Babylon, 801, 803

Barnabas, 455, 461 ff., 690 ff., 712, 715, 864

Barnabas, Epistle of, 269, 692 f., 738, 771, 815, 816, 843, 864, 905, 932, 983

Basilides, Basilideans, 110, 480, 586, 823

'Beloved disciple', 245 ff., 331

Berea, 565

Bernice, 75

Bishops, 522, 591 f., 599 ff., 632

Caesarean imprisonment, 526 f.

Caesar's household, 527, 534 f.

Caligula, 73, 950, 959

Canonicity, 17 ff., 229 f.

Captivity Epistles, 472 ff.

Carpocratians, 855, 914

Carthaginian Calendar, 261

Catechesis, 16, 28, 126, 224, 231, 234 f., 287, 659, 807

Cerinthus, Cerinthianism, 270, 550, 551, 871, 903, 933, 934

Chester Beatty papyri, 405, 412, 587 f., 644, 686

Duration of the ministry of Jesus, 294

Ebionites, 82, 755
Editorial influences, 436
Editorship in criticism, 226 ff.
Egerton Papyrus (2), 270, 283
Eldad and Modad, 837
Elders, 459, 463, 522 f., 591 f., 599 ff., 632, 760, 776, 784
'Elect Lady' of 2 John, 890 ff.
'Elements' in the Colossian heresy, 548
Emperor worship, 949
Enoch, 548, 830, 905, 917 f., 921, 966
Epaphras, 100, 545 f., 556
Epaphroditus, 522, 524 f., 528 ff., 539, 542 f.
Ephesian imprisonment, 472 ff., 531, 543; internal evidence, 472 ff., 478; external evidence, 473, 475 f.; difficulty of Acts silence, 476; Duncan's explanation, 477 f.
EPHESIANS
  Address of the Epistle, 520
  Arguments against and for authenticity: linguistic and stylistic, 482 f., 491 f.; literary, 483 ff., 492 ff. (relation to Colossians, 483 f., 492 ff.; different use of words, 484 f., 495 f.; conflation, 485, 496; dependence on 'genuine' Pauline Epistles, 485 f., 496 ff.; relation to non-Pauline N.T. books, 486, 500 f.; literary form, 487, 501; author's self-protestations, 487, 501 f.); historical, 487 f., 502 f.; doctrinal, 488 ff., 503 f.; conclusion of discussion, 507 f.
  Authorship, traditional view: self-claims, 479 f.; external attestation, 480; Pauline structure, 480; language and literary affinities, 481; theological affinities, 481, 520; historical data, 481 f.
  Christology, 489, 505 f.
  Date, 515 f.
  Destination: introduction, 508 ff.; Laodicea, 510; a circular letter, 510 f.; Paul's spiritual testament, 511 f.; an introduction to the Pauline Corpus, 512 ff.; a philosophy of religion for the whole Christian world, 514; a general safeguard, 514
  Liturgical theory for Ephesians, 521
  Purpose, 515
Epiphanius, 270, 933
Erastus, 396, 424, 523, 532
Eschatology, 281, 332, 398, 567, 570 f., 578 f., 860, 880 f., 945
Essenes, Essenism, 278, 297, 320, 448, 549, 550, 707

Eusebius, 76, 103, 114, 155, 258, 262, 266, 268, 270, 273, 331, 654, 663, 665, 686 f., 737, 815, 817, 864, 885, 887 f., 905 f., 932, 933 f.
Evangelistic purpose of Mark, 57 f.
Exclusivism in the Colossian heresy, 548
Existential philosophy, 193 f.
Exodus typology: in John's Gospel, 312; in 1 Peter, 803 f.
External evidence for the Gospels, 17 ff.; Matthew, 33 ff.; Mark, 69 ff.; Luke-Acts, 99 ff.; John, 258, 266, 283 f.; Ephesians, 480; Colossians, 554; 1 Thessalonians, 567; 2 Thessalonians, 570; Pastorals, 585 ff.; Hebrews, 685 ff.; James, 736 ff.; 1 Peter, 771 f.; 2 Peter, 814 ff.; 1 John, 864 f.; 2/3 John, 884 ff.; Jude, 905; Revelation, 931 f.
External testimony, a right approach to this, 220 ff.

Faith versus works controversy, 764 f.
Fall of Jerusalem: see Jerusalem, Fall of
False teaching, 615, 853 ff., 870 ff., 912 ff., 955 f.
Felix, recall of, 662 f.
Festus, 597, 663
Flavius Clemens, 781, 952
Forgery, 821
Formal doctrinal expression in the Pastorals, 594, 605 f.
Form criticism: general criticisms, 208 ff.; limits, 210 f.; reasons for its rise, 188 ff.
Form criticism, types of theory: missionary preaching theory, 191 f.; Christian imagination theory, 193 ff.; theory of purely literary analysis, 206; theories of limited value, 207 f.; theories of theological composition, 214 ff.
Form criticism, value of, 211 ff.
Form-historical method, 131
Formless stories, 207
Four source theory, 131 ff.
Fragment theory for the Gospels, 123 f.

Gaius, 396, 895 ff.
Gaius of Rome, 270, 933
GALATIANS
  Authenticity, 468
  Date: according to North Galatian theory, 457 f., 471; according to South Galatian theory, 458; Jerusalem visits, 458 ff.
  Destination: North Galatian theory, 450 ff. (general use of term, 450; Luke's usage, 450 f.); South Galatian theory, 452 ff. (testimony of Acts, 452 f.;

The following table shows the correspondence between page numbers in the present volume and the three former volumes (shown in brackets). 13 (I.11), 21 (19), 53 (49), 90 (84), 121 (114), 188 (178), 199 (183), 206 (186), 220 (195), 237 (212), 328 (300), 336 (303), 386 (II.15), 393 (21), 421 (46), 425 (48), 450 (72), 472 (92), 479 (99), 522 (140), 545 (161), 564 (179), 584 (198), 635 (247), 671 (282), 685 (III.11), 736 (60), 771 (95), 814 (137), 864 (186), 905 (226), 931 (251).